CALENDAR

April

LAWNS *Sow seed and protect with cotton. Mow established lawns with blades at medium height. Apply a fertiliser followed a fortnight later by a selective weedkiller.*

SHRUBS *Transplant evergreen trees and shrubs. Layer magnolias, hamamelis,* Hydrangea paniculata *and* Chimonanthus praecox. *Prune lavender, santolina and* Forsythia suspensa.

ROSES *Apply a mulch. Weedkiller can be used to keep down weeds.*

RHODODENDRONS *Remove faded flowers. Mulch with peat or garden compost.*

PERENNIALS *Support with pea sticks or canes.*

CHRYSANTHEMUMS *Harden off cuttings.*

DAHLIAS *Plant tubers. Take cuttings of tubers started into growth in March.*

CARNATIONS AND PINKS *Feed border plants with general fertiliser. Support floppy types.*

ANNUALS *Complete sowing of hardy and half-hardy annuals. Move seedlings pricked off from previous sowings to a cold frame. Watch out for aphids.*

BULBS *Continue to plant gladioli and acidantheras. Dead-head early bulbs.*

LILIES *Stake tall lilies as flower buds form.*

ROCK PLANTS *Divide spring-flowering gentians and saxifrages after flowering.*

WATER PLANTS *Plant water lilies and other plants. Overgrown lilies can be lifted and divided. Prick off seedlings of bog primulas.*

HEATHERS *Lightly shear winter heathers.*

HOUSE PLANTS *Increase watering and give regular feeds. Pot on plants that are root bound; divide if suitable.*

FRUIT *Feed with Nitro-chalk or sulphate of ammonia. Protect trees in flower from late frosts with netting. Begin spraying as needed, but not during blossoming.*

May

LAWNS *Mow at least once a week. Apply weedkiller if necessary. Feed poorly growing grass with sulphate of ammonia at ½ oz. per square yard; water copiously afterwards. Spike badly drained areas.*

SHRUBS *Prune early-flowering shrubs such as* Kerria japonica *and* Prunus triloba.

ROSES *Spray roses against pests and diseases, and apply a general rose fertiliser.*

PERENNIALS *Support tall perennials. Weed borders regularly. Pinch out the growing tips of michaelmas daisies, golden rod, heleniums and other vigorous plants to form bushy, self-supporting plants.*

CHRYSANTHEMUMS *Plant outdoor-flowering plants early in the month. Stop the plants about the middle of the month.*

DAHLIAS *Plant out young dahlias from cuttings after danger of frost is over.*

ANNUALS *Plant out half-hardy annuals after risk of frost has passed. Sow biennials – Canterbury bells, foxgloves, sweet williams and wallflowers.*

BULBS *To make room for bedding plants, lift bulbs that have finished flowering and heel them into spare ground.*

IRISES, ROCK PLANTS, HEATHERS *Remove faded flowers from irises, spring-flowering rock plants such as gentians and saxifrages, and winter-flowering heathers. Top-dress heathers with peat.*

HOUSE PLANTS *Water more freely; give weekly liquid feed to older plants.*

FRUIT *Feed figs with liquid manure, and mulch. Start de-shooting fan peaches and nectarines, and thin when fruits are the size of marbles. Water well in dry spells. Put straw round strawberry plants.*

June

LAWNS *Mow at least once a week.*

SHRUBS *Take leaf-bud cuttings of clematis, and softwood cuttings of fuchsia, cotoneaster, hypericum and deutzia early in the month. Serpentine layer young shoots of clematis at the end of the month.*

HEDGES *Trim privet and* Lonicera nitida.

ROSES *Disbud hybrid tea roses grown for large blooms. Remove suckers. Spray against greenfly and diseases.*

RHODODENDRONS *Remove faded flowers.*

PERENNIALS *Cut down early-flowering perennials to 3 in. from the ground.*

CHRYSANTHEMUMS *Complete stopping of outdoor-flowering plants.*

DAHLIAS *Pinch out tips of leading shoots. Water, mulch and spray against pests.*

ANNUALS *Support tall-growing annuals. Prick off seedlings of biennials.*

BULBS *Divide daffodils and narcissi when the leaves start to yellow. In mild areas, plant De Caen anemones for autumn.*

LILIES *In humid weather, spray with Bordeaux mixture to prevent lily disease.*

IRISES *Tall bearded irises may need supporting. After flowering, cut back stems.*

HOUSE PLANTS *Water and feed regularly. Syringe several times a week. During hot spells, stand hardy plants, such as ivy, fatsia, cissus and* Saxifraga stolonifera, *outside in shade; spray from overhead once a day.*

FRUIT *Cover with netting against birds. Begin thinning apples, pears, gooseberries and plums. Pinch out side-shoots on figs. Summer prune red currants and gooseberries. Peg down strawberry runners.*

Turn to inside back cover for July–December

READER'S DIGEST

New Illustrated Guide to Gardening

READER'S DIGEST

New Illustrated Guide to Gardening

How to plant and care for flowers, shrubs, fruit and vegetables

BASED ON THE 'READER'S DIGEST ILLUSTRATED GUIDE TO GARDENING'

PUBLISHED BY THE READER'S DIGEST ASSOCIATION LIMITED
LONDON NEW YORK MONTREAL SYDNEY CAPE TOWN

READER'S DIGEST
NEW ILLUSTRATED GUIDE
TO GARDENING
was edited and designed by
The Reader's Digest Association
Limited, London

Printed in Great Britain

CONSULTANT EDITOR

Roy Hay, MBE, VMH

TECHNICAL ADVISER

Kenneth A. Beckett

Major contributors

John R. McBain Allan, BSc (Hort.), NDH
R. S. Aylett
Harry Baker, NDH
Ann Bonar, BSc (Hort.)
Audrey V. Brooks, BSc, MIBiol.
P. R. Chapman, ARPS
Keith M. Harris, BSc, DAS (Cantab), DTA (Trin.)
H. Raymond Jeffs
Reginald Kaye
F. P. Knight, VMH, FLS
Roy Lancaster, FLS
M. E. Leeburn
David McClintock
F. R. McQuown, MA, FLS
Margaret J. Martin, MSc, ARIC
R. H. Menage
John Negus, Dip. Hort. (Wisley)
Frances Perry, MBE, FLS, VMH
Brigadier C. E. Lucas Phillips, OBE, MC
Ray Procter, AHRHS
David Pycraft
Peter Russell, Dip. Hort. (Wisley)
David Sander
Peter J. Seabrook, NDH
James F. Smith
Michael Upward
Tony Venison
Patrick Walker

Artists

Norman Barber
David Baxter
Leonora Box
Helen Cowcher
Terence Dalley, ARCA
Jackson Day Designs
Brian Delf
Ian Garrard
Tony Graham, LSIA
Roy Grubb
Vana Haggerty
Nicolas Hall
Gary Hincks
David Hutter
Richard Jacobs
Gillian Kenny
Sarah Kensington
Patricia Ann Lenander
Richard Lewington
Constance Marshall
Sean Milne
Thea Nockels
Charles Pickard
Charles Raymond
John Rignall
John Roberts
Anne Savage
Kathleen Smith, MSIA
Les Smith
Joyce Tuhill
John Western
Michael J. Woods
Elsie Wrigley

Photographers

Michael Boys
Peter Coats
Valerie Finnis
Oluf Nissen
Reference:
Maria Bartha
R. J. Corbin
Roger Elson
Michael Warren

The publishers wish to thank the staffs of the Royal Horticultural Society's Garden, The Royal National Rose Society and Merrist Wood Agricultural College for their help in demonstrating many of the techniques illustrated in this book.

Contents

GOOD GARDENING STEP BY STEP 9
CREATING A GARDEN 11
ANNUALS AND BIENNIALS 25
BULBS AND CORMS 35
CACTI 43
CARNATIONS AND PINKS 51
CHRYSANTHEMUMS 60
DAHLIAS 71
FERNS 78
FRUIT 82
GREENHOUSE GARDENING 137
HEATHERS 160
HOUSE PLANTS 164
IRISES 178
LAWNS 184
LILIES 192
ORCHIDS 198
PERENNIALS 204
RHODODENDRONS AND AZALEAS 216
ROCK PLANTS 220
ROSES 224
SHRUBS AND CLIMBERS 241
TREES 281
VEGETABLES 284
WATER PLANTS 324
GUIDE TO PLANTS AND FLOWERS 329
GUIDE TO SHRUBS AND TREES 360
PLANT DISORDERS 377
UNDERSTANDING THE SOIL 401
INDEX 406

Good gardening step by step

Advice that will help you to fill your garden with colour for months on end, and to grow fruit, vegetables and herbs for daily use in the kitchen

This book is intended for the practical gardener who wants instant advice on how to grow trees, shrubs, flowering plants, fruit and vegetables; and how to succeed with plants in the house and under glass outside. All this information is given in alphabetical order for easy reference, with practical, step-by-step illustrations of the techniques involved.

A guide to plant names Plants can be found in this book under the names most commonly used by gardeners, seed merchants and nurserymen. Hawthorn, for example, is listed under its traditional name and this is followed by hawthorn's botanical name, *Crataegus*. The flowering nutmeg, however, is listed under its botanical name, *Leycesteria*, because that is how it is named in most catalogues.

Plants are classified botanically by genus, species and variety. The first name is the genus (plural, genera) – for example *Crataegus*. Each genus is made up of a number of species – for example, *Crataegus oxyacantha*, *C. pubescens*, and *C. monogyna*. When a species varies from its true type, the result is known as a variety. The variety name is then added to the other two. If the variety occurred naturally in the wild, the plant's full name is printed in italics – *Crataegus pubescens stipulacea*. If the variety was bred in a garden or arose as a mutant (sport) and is maintained only in cultivation it is known as a cultivated variety or cultivar. The cultivar name is printed in roman type inside single quotation marks – *Crataegus oxyacantha* 'Paul's Scarlet'.

Another term commonly encountered by gardeners is *hybrid*. A hybrid plant occurs when two species of the same genus are interbred. The new plant is given a name preceded by a multiplication sign. *Crataegus* × *lavellei* is a hybrid between *C. crus-galli* and *C. pubescens stipulacea*. Hybrids can also occur between plants of different genera, in which case the name of the new hybrid genus is preceded by a multiplication sign: × *Cupressocyparis* is a hybrid between *Cupressus* and *Chamaecyparis*.

Some highly popular plants with numerous cultivars or hybrids are divided into groups which are given grex (or group) names. One example is *Hydrangea macrophylla* which is divided into Hortensia and Lacecap groups. So the cultivar 'Altona' has the full name *Hydrangea macrophylla* Hortensia 'Altona'.

Creating a garden

Learn the lesson of nature when you design a garden that will be pleasing to the eye and easy to maintain. Make the most of your walls and fences to grow attractive climbing plants and plan for all-the-year colour

The secret of successful garden design is to follow the lessons of nature, and plan the design in flowing curves rather than in geometric patterns.

Most gardens are box-shaped, following the lines of the boundaries. A rectangular lawn is surrounded by straight borders, and the viewer's eye is carried to the back fence and to the corners.

This layout emphasises the boundaries of the garden rather than the garden itself. And regardless of how thoroughly the fences may be covered with climbers, they are still among the most dominant features.

But the borders do not have to follow the straight lines of the boundaries; the lawn does not have to be a square or a rectangle in the centre of the garden.

In nature, lines are rarely straight. The folds of a hill, the long arc of a beach, the meandering of a river, are all examples of how curves occur under natural conditions. A sweeping curve of this type has a vigour that carries the eye along it. By designing the lawn in a strong sweeping line, the eye is led around the garden rather than to its boundaries.

The vegetable and fruit garden, together with compost heap, incinerator and shed, should where possible be screened from the ornamental garden.

Screening can be by an evergreen hedge, a row of trees, a rose pergola or even a temporary screen of sweet peas, gladioli or dahlias. However, any screen should follow and complement the lawn shape.

A small garden may be designed with only a single lawn curve running from one corner near the house to the diagonally opposite corner, leaving the other two sides straight. Even this reduces the box effect, and at the same time creates a border which broadens behind the curve to hide the compost heap and the incinerator.

Before setting out to re-plan a garden, take stock of all the existing features, both good and bad, inside the garden and beyond its boundaries.

Where a tree in a neighbouring garden provides an attractive feature, there is no point in obscuring it with trees or high shrubs of your own. They would either detract from the neighbouring tree or compete with it. Try to plan a recess in the border to focus the view towards it. However, where an ugly view appears on the skyline, such as a factory chimney in the distance or a house wall close by, try to plan a peak in the border for trees or high shrubs.

Draw your design to scale on paper, and plot in the essential features – lawn, border, fruit area, and so on. Transfer the design to the garden by using wooden pegs at 3–4 ft intervals to mark the main lines.

Do not attempt to complete a design and planting scheme in one season. First establish the basic design of the lawn curves and the resulting borders.

Final touches – a rock garden, a dividing hedge, a dry-stone wall, a rose pergola or a small pool – can be added later. Borders can always be made wider or narrower. Sheds can be taken down and rebuilt in more suitable positions. Terraces can be rebuilt or reshaped.

Making the most of fences and walls

Climbing roses are particularly suitable for walls facing west and north-west, where they are well watered by rain-bearing winds. They produce a mass of blooms and provide an attractive means of covering a high boundary wall. They can be supported on galvanised wires stretched horizontally between vine eyes fixed to the wall. The first wire should be 3 ft from the ground, followed by others 9–12 in. apart, and 1–2 in. away from the wall

Fences and walls are often neglected or left as dull demarcation lines rather than being used as a background for trees, shrubs and tall perennials.

With a very few exceptions, traditional wooden fences are not attractive on their own, and while they serve as useful boundaries they are better disguised from view. Where space and money allow, a fence can be hidden by a shrub border or golden and blue-green conifers; these will eventually obscure the fence and at the same time give wind protection.

In small gardens, where such a border may be too overpowering, a fence can be covered with climbing and rambling plants. Some form of support is necessary for all climbers except ivy, climbing hydrangea and Virginia creeper, which are self-clinging.

The cheapest support can be made by stretching galvanised wire horizontally between vine eyes fixed into the fence. Place the first wire about 3 ft from the ground, and repeat every 9–12 in. up to the top of the fence. Other types of support are wooden trellis painted with wood preservative, panels of plastic-coated steel mesh, and all-plastic mesh.

Fix all supports 1–2 in. away from the wall. Twining plants, such as honeysuckle, will then weave in and out. Others, like clematis, will cling by twisting their leaf stalks around the supports. Stems of roses may be pushed in and out of mesh as they grow, but they may be difficult to remove later.

Tall boundary walls make excellent backgrounds for climbing and twining plants. As for fences, supports are necessary for all but the few self-clinging climbers.

Before buying plants, note which way the wall or fence faces.

Evergreen ivies, the rampant Russian vine (*Polygonum baldschuanicum*), the climbing hydrangea, pyracanthas and Virginia creeper will all thrive against a fence or wall facing towards any point of the compass.

Walls facing south or south-west give great scope for growing shrubs and other plants that are not fully hardy in the open.

Almost any shrub and climber can be grown against a south-facing wall, but it is particularly suitable for passion flower (passiflora), ornamental and grape vines, *Campsis radicans*, the evergreen ceanothus and other wall shrubs that need warmth.

South-facing walls are also excellent for espalier and fan-trained fruit trees, such as apple, pear, peach, nectarine and fig. However, they need a bed at least 2 ft wide at the foot of the wall, and it is advisable to avoid planting deep-rooting perennials in front. Annuals and bulbs are more suitable. Access is also necessary for pruning the fruit trees each year.

Walls facing west and north-west are ideal for a great many plants, particularly hydrangeas and camellias, roses, clematis and honeysuckle. As most rain comes from the west, borders against west and north-west-facing walls are especially suited for plants that need moist soil and a humid atmosphere, such as abutilon and desfontainea.

North-facing walls can be covered with clematis, honeysuckle, ivies, ornamental vines (vitis) and hydrangeas, and with shrubby plants such as pyracantha, viburnum, forsythia, winter jasmine and camellia.

East-facing walls may be treated like north walls, but neither clematis nor honeysuckle will thrive there.

In town gardens, the wall area often exceeds that of the garden itself. House walls are perfect for covering with vigorous climbers, according to aspect. The wistaria is one of the most successful climbers on any high wall, except one facing north or north-east. Dark gardens totally enclosed by high walls can be lightened by painting the shadiest one white. The other walls might be painted in shades of olive-green or terracotta.

On front walls avoid anything that will swamp windows, clutter up gutters or creep under roof tiles. Roses, chaenomeles, choisya, mahonia, wall-trained magnolia and camellia and, if the soil is lime-free, rhododendrons are better choices.

Low retaining walls between areas at different levels lend themselves to imaginative plantings at the top and the base. Pinks, campanulas, sedums, saxifrages and aubrietas are among the finest plants for the top of low, sunny walls, with alyssum and ivy-leaved pelargoniums trailing down the side. Primulas, ramondas and some of the anemones and irises are best in cool shade. For the base of the wall, annuals and spring-flowering bulbs are ideal for both a sunny and lightly shaded position.

If the retaining wall is long or runs at angles, the outline, both at the top and below, can be softened with low-growing shrubs, such as *Potentilla fruticosa*, genista, hypericum, iberis, helianthemum, *Cotoneaster horizontalis* and creeping juniper.

Drystone walls are used as dividers in large gardens or for flanking a long row of steps. Most rock-garden plants are perfect for a drystone wall. The top can be turned into a flowering carpet of dianthus, phlox, saxifrage, sedum, sempervivum and many other rock plants. Trailing plants, such as androsace, gypsophila, helianthemum and thyme, can be set into the sides of the wall, and low-growing, flowering shrubs and dwarf conifers can be used for focal points at intervals along it.

This wall of Cotswold stone is planted with hybrid tea roses and French marigolds. At the near end is a sprawling Cotoneaster conspicuus *and at the far end a golden-flowered* Potentilla fruticosa

Decorating paths and steps

The straight lines of this old flagstone path are softened with spreading perennials and shrubs. On the left is a clump of white-flowered London pride (Saxifraga × urbicum) *nestling below a group of deep pink paeonies. On the right, more paeonies show above the dark green of a tall clump of lavender* (Lavandula spica). *Just before the step at the end of the path is a low-growing conifer, with a pink climbing rose draped over the stone wall above*

Most gardens have steps of some kind. They may be no more than a single slab from house to terrace or from terrace to lawn, but more often they consist of a flight. Many gardens which slope naturally, either towards or away from the house, have raised terraces, sometimes with balustrades from which steps lead down into the garden proper. A sloping garden may also be landscaped into several large or small beds at different levels; the elevations are retained by low walls, interconnected with steps.

While steps are seldom sufficiently attractive to form a feature on their own, they can add character to any garden when decorated with plants that harmonise with the general planting scheme.

Choose the kind of plants that will soften the outline of the edges, and not obscure the steps altogether. Prostrate plants should trail along the outer edges of steps, not across them. A small, shallow flight of steps decorated with hummock-forming clumps of perennials or shrubs is more attractive than one with tall conifers placed like sentinels. Colour is a major consideration: the mellowness of natural stone steps is best complemented by muted shades of green, silver-grey and pale yellow; a strong colour scheme, on the other hand, diverts attention from the starkness of dull concrete steps.

In a wide, shallow flight of steps, many of the cushion-forming plants recommended for paved gardens (p. 17) can be grown in cracks at the foot of risers. *Campanula portenschlagiana*, alpine dianthus, the pink *Erigeron mucronatum* and *Phlox subulata* are all suitable for this purpose.

In most cases, however, it is preferable to plant at the sides of the steps, allowing at planting time for the eventual spread. Trailing alyssum and aubrieta, gypsophila, pelargonium, geranium and thymus will drape themselves from the upper steps. Along the sides of the lower steps can be grown mat-forming *Iberis sempervirens* and other candytufts, dryas and pink or red *Polygonum affine* and *P. vaccinifolium*.

Where space permits, low-growing shrubs give a mature appearance: lavender, genista, helianthemum, the grey-leaved *Santolina incana* and silvery senecio are suitable for planting at the sides of steps. Heathers and prostrate conifers in blue and gold are invaluable for all-year colour.

Many suburban gardens have a surplus of paths, cutting the plot into several small rectangular or square beds. In the back garden a path may be necessary to give access to tool shed, compost bin and greenhouse but, wherever possible, it should follow the contours of the lawn and never run straight down or across the centre.

A path of brick or crazy paving, or stepping-stones in the lawn, can be an invitation to meander round the garden. The solid grey concrete path is too often an eyesore. It is no easy task to break up and dispose of a concrete path, but it is possible to disguise it to some extent. Where an existing path runs down the centre of the garden, a curved lawn can make the path less obvious. Continue the fluid curved lines on either side of the path, or alter the axis of the lawn to 45 degrees across the path.

Cushion and mat-forming rock plants can be grown in small pockets to decorate brick and paving-slab paths. The same type of plants, as well as low-growing shrubs, may be planted along the edges of concrete paths to soften the stark lines.

Front-garden paths from the road to the house are generally straight and uniformly embellished with a narrow, floral border at either side. A more welcoming entrance can be made by doing away with one of the borders and widening the path. Where the path reaches the house, it can be swung into a bold curve embracing the width of the porch. One bed, perhaps with roses, along the path is ample for the average front garden, and the kerb of the path can be disguised with low edging plants.

The outline of grey concrete steps is successfully hidden by a planting of Bergenia cordifolia *and artemisia on the right, with* Stachys lanata *across the top of the steps. At the top is a flowering Hortensia hydrangea and a clump of hostas. On the left, a variegated form of Lacecap hydrangea grows beside a* Helleborus lividus corsicus, *and across the side of the steps are yellow-green* Alchemilla mollis *and* Cotoneaster dammeri

Terraces and paved gardens

An atmosphere of quiet seclusion is heightened by plants in muted colours. The rounded steps are decorated, on the left, with Cotoneaster horizontalis, Elaeagnus pungens, *a white floribunda rose in bud, and* Helleborus corsicus. *On the right there are pots of lilies against a background of Virginia creeper. The urns on the balustrade are planted with pink petunias and silver-grey senecios. In the centre of the terrace, an ornamental container spills over with trailing pelargoniums, and to the rear is a tub of agapanthus. In the paving are aubrieta, chamomile and alyssum*

One of the aims of garden planning is to associate the garden with the house so that one complete unit is created. The garden, viewed through a window, should be a natural extension of the house. The eye should sweep freely across an open lawn to the perimeters, to the prospect of hidden surprises behind curves, or be drawn to an apparently distant focal point.

The uniting link between house and garden is the terrace, usually leading from the living-room into the garden.

The shape and size of the terrace are usually determined by the garden area and by aspect. Where a new terrace is being built, it should ideally harmonise in shape with the garden. A garden design based on curved lines should be repeated in a rounded terrace, and a formal rectilinear garden outline should be echoed by a square or rectangular terrace.

Existing terraces can be made to conform to a curved garden design by hiding sharp corners with low-growing shrubs, or by adding to the front a curved strip of contrasting stone material as a standing area for containers.

Rounded terraces can be straightened out to some extent by means of additional stones of different material and colour, or by planting slender pyramidal trees at either end of the terrace.

A sunny or lightly shaded terrace will be used as a living and entertaining area in summer. It must, therefore, be large enough to accommodate garden furniture, such as tables and chairs, and to give easy access to both house and garden.

Even where the rear of the house faces north or east, and a sunny sitting-out area is better sited somewhere else in the garden, a terrace against the house still provides a natural link between house and garden. It pushes the garden away from the immediate house walls, creating a feeling of space and opening vistas.

Older houses are often raised well above the garden area, and an existing terrace may be an elevated platform shut off from the garden by a low stone balustrade. Here, ornate containers are perfectly at home, and formal urns placed along the balustrade, or pots containing trailing plants, enhance the mellowed brickwork.

The outline of the steps leading from the terrace to the garden can be softened with containers or with plantings of low, graceful shrubs on either side (p. 14). The bed at the foot of a balustrade can be treated as for a retaining wall and planted with shrubs, perennials, annuals and bulbs.

Most modern houses are built with the ground floor raised only a few inches above ground level. The terrace is on the same level as the garden, and steps are therefore unnecessary.

On any type of terrace, leave small planting pockets between the stonework for cushion-forming plants, such as artemisia, armeria, dianthus, thyme and small-leaved mint or even the tiny rock rose (helianthemum). Reserve these planting pockets for those parts of the terrace that are not used for furniture or frequent walking.

Small beds can be made at the rear of the terrace next to the house wall. Climbers – for example, roses intermingled with clematis – can then be trained up the wall and above the windows. This is not feasible on walls with large picture windows; these are better embellished with a slender pillar rose or a camellia on either side.

Dark corners near doors or on the shady side of the terrace are ideal for shade-loving perennials such as hosta, primula and lily-of-the-valley, and for shrubs like mahonia and skimmia.

In very small gardens, the paved terrace may cover the entire area. If a high wall surrounds the garden it can be decoratively covered with climbers growing in tubs. Shrubs and other flowering plants can be grown in more tubs, window-boxes, troughs and hanging baskets.

Where space allows, a small, low pool, set off-centre, makes an attractive feature, planted with one or two water lilies.

An old plum tree on the left gives dappled shade to this large open terrace which merges easily with the curved lawn. In the foreground is a large bed of mixed Impatiens holstii, *which flower profusely from late spring until autumn. The low plant container holds a dwarf* Juniperus communis '*Compressa*' *underplanted with miniature sedums. The curved shrub border which begins behind a clump of pink hydrangeas is stocked in the first peak with a massed display of roses, all in shades of red and pink. The group includes modern shrub, climbing, floribunda and hybrid teas*

Plant containers and hanging baskets

There are so many different plant containers – from heavily ornate to starkly plain – that one can always be found that is suitable for any site in the garden. Containers are chiefly thought of as additions to terraces, but they can be used to brighten any odd corner of the garden. They extend a welcome at the front door, and a large tub will hide a drain cover. Both pots and hanging baskets can break up the vertical plane of a blank house wall, and a window-box can be a year-round delight.

The huge old-fashioned stone urns, often on pedestals, and heavily decorated with floral or geometric designs and scalloped sides and lips, are fast becoming collectors' items, but attractive replicas are made in heavy-duty polystyrene. They are easier to shift around, inexpensive and generally long-lasting. Wooden tubs, made from oak beer barrels sawn in half, can still be found at a price. It is worthwhile treating them with a wood-preservative before planting, and painting the metal bands with a rust-proofing liquid. Wooden window-boxes, too, should be treated with wood-preservative before being painted. Do not use creosote; it can harm plants.

A tub of Senecio (Cineraria) maritima *and santolina forms a permanent silver-grey display. A trailing thyme adds colour in summer, and in winter the green stems emphasise the silver*

Small and large plant containers are also made from pre-cast concrete. They are more difficult to move than plastic containers, but last longer.

Whatever the type of container, it must have adequate drainage holes in the base, which should be covered with a porous material, such as broken clay pots, pebbles or vermiculite. As space is confined, good soil is another necessity; John Innes No. 2 potting compost is the most suitable. Lime-hating plants, such as rhododendrons, azaleas, pieris, camellias and some heathers, must be grown in a lime-free soil, such as John Innes acid compost, or a limeless peat compost.

Containers dry out quickly, and frequent watering is essential. For additional plant vigour, give a regular liquid feed every two weeks. Remove the top 2–3 in. of soil every spring and replace with fresh compost. Check the brackets of window-boxes to make sure they are firmly anchored.

Hanging baskets should be lined with damp moss or with black plastic sheeting. John Innes No. 2 or a soil-less compost is suitable and the plants should be inserted at intervals from the base up, not planted at the top only. Pierce holes in plastic sheeting to take the plants' roots. In dry weather, a hanging basket needs a thorough soaking at least once a day.

Window-boxes, 6–8 in. deep, are suitable for growing a large variety of plants. In spring they can come alive with bulbs planted the previous autumn: snowdrops and crocuses, dwarf daffodils, narcissi and low-growing tulips, hyacinths, scillas and dwarf irises.

Many summer bedding plants grow perfectly in window-boxes, but avoid tall-growing kinds which spoil the proportions of the box. A charming effect can be created by mixing trailing plants, like pelargoniums, lobelias and dwarf nasturtiums, with petunias, marigolds, *Begonia semperflorens*, tuberous begonias and salvias. Do not overlook dwarf shrubs and conifers which add form and permanency to a box: potentillas, fuchsias, hebes and dwarf conifers, such as the upright types of juniperus.

In winter, dwarf conifers, especially the golden and blue forms, are excellent in window-boxes. They can be grown with winter-flowering heathers, variegated ivy and the attractive little bulb *Cyclamen coum*, which flowers quite happily in shade in early winter.

A spring window-box of Tulipa kaufmanniana *and forget-me-nots will be replanted with bright annuals for summer. A variegated* Vinca minor *gives an evergreen foreground*

Stone, concrete and plastic containers can be filled with the same plants as window-boxes, and for very large and deep containers the choice is even wider. Keep a correct balance by planting tall plants with low-growing and trailing ones. The evergreen foliage of variegated ivy and *Vinca minor* makes a good foil for the bright colours of pelargoniums, sweet williams, calendulas, calceolarias and heliotropes.

Many house plants are also effective with summer bedding plants. The arching leaves of chlorophytum complement agapanthus; a cordyline, set at the rear of a low container with bedding plants, adds both height and form; the flaming colours of coleus mix happily with the silver-grey of *Senecio (Cineraria) maritima* and helichrysum.

Large tubs make ideal containers for lilies,

hydrangeas and fuchsias, both in sun and light shade. Bay trees, trained as standards, are still favourites as sentinels at front doors; but for a less formal effect plant winter jasmine or *Forsythia intermedia*. Roses, clematis, azaleas, camellias and *Acer palmatum* are also good tub plants. For deeper shade, plant tubs with pieris, mahonias, hostas, bergenias, *Brunnera macrophylla* and *Helleborus orientalis*.

Hanging baskets are viewed from below and should consist mainly of trailing plants,

A hanging basket in a shady site (left) can be planted with colourful mixed nasturtiums, while good plants for a basket in sun or light shade (right) are trailing fuchsias and lobelias

such as nasturtiums, tradescantias, fuchsias, *Lysimachia nummularia*, petunias, pelargoniums, lobelias, begonias and zebrinas.

Most cushion-forming alpines will make charming hummocks between stones in paved areas. They can be grown on a terrace together with plants in containers. The following alpines will thrive and spread over many years, provided they are grown in sun: dianthus, sedum, campanula, armeria, *Phlox subulata*, thymus, sempervivum, saxifraga, *Erinus alpinus*, acaena and the shrubby helianthemum. Dwarf forms of juniperus and *Thuja occidentalis* are also excellent for pockets among paving stones; low forms of *Picea abies* give attractive colour and texture where they have room to spread.

This huge terracotta urn is almost hidden by trailing green and variegated ivy and blue lobelia. The pink-and-red colour scheme is composed of ivy-leaved and zonal pelargoniums; a bright green hebe is not yet in flower. Alyssum, chamomile, lobelia and thyme are planted in the paving

Creating focal points with plants and ornaments

This small stone statue at the end of a pergola serves three purposes. It makes a perfect focal point, seen as it is at the end of a path and through a series of stone and wooden arches. It adds a classical charm to the shady, dark green background of rhododendrons. And at the same time it distracts the eye from the tool shed and neighbouring garage. The pergola is covered with roses and wistaria, and underplanted with regal lilies and white petunias

One way to give a greater visual interest to a garden is to create focal points with particularly striking plants, or with carefully placed garden statues.

A focal point is often used to stress a particular feature of the garden, such as a sweeping curve in the lawn or a sunny corner. But it can also divert the attention away from an unattractive view; for instance, an outstanding shrub, a small statue or a sundial will arrest the eye before it moves on to an ugly skyline. Garden furniture, small rock gardens or a pool can also be used. Be sure that any focal point is placed so that it blends into the garden design and does not look like an afterthought. Do not place it in the middle of a lawn where it would clutter up the open centre. Instead, keep it to the edge of the lawn or put it in a planting peak or some other wide part of the border.

A focal point in a corner is useful to attract the viewer's attention along the diagonal axis of a lawn in a short, wide garden. In the front garden, an attractive tree might be planted by the front gate where it is visible from the living-room window.

Never create two focal points that are both visible from a main viewpoint, such as the kitchen window or the terrace. They will only divide the viewer's attention and cancel each other out.

The choice of plants suitable for focal points varies according to the size of the garden. In a large area an excellent focal point could be a tall conifer. Dawn redwoods (metasequoia), swamp cypresses (taxodium), cedars and cypresses are ideal for the large garden. Columnar blue or golden Lawson cypresses, slim golden thujas and grey-leaved junipers are more suitable for smaller gardens. If possible, plant conifers where they will be lit by the sun from behind in winter.

The focal point can be made even stronger by planting a different coloured plant in front; for example, a golden elaeagnus or a red-stemmed *Cornus alba*. The tall, cream-white plumes of cortaderia (pampas grass) are excellent against a background of dark conifers, or in an isolated lawn group, to create a focal point of their own.

Ornamental cherries – weeping, fastigiate or spreading – are among the finest trees for any type of garden, planted where they catch the spring and autumn sunlight. Liquidambar, flowering crab apple, nyssa, mountain ash and *Rhus typhina* are glorious where autumn sun enhances their vivid leaf colours and fruits.

As lawn focal points, few plants surpass the low, purple forms of Japanese maples or a

The giant cardiocrinum makes a spectacular focal point for a lightly shaded site at the edge of a lawn. As the flowers fade in late summer, the seed capsules remain, turning from pale green to yellow

group of mixed golden and green heathers accented by a low conifer like *Picea glauca* 'Albertiana Conica'.

Some of the maples and many of the birches are outstanding focal trees in winter when the sun can illuminate their attractive, peeling bark. Modern shrub and species roses, magnolias, *Paeonia suffruticosa* and the evergreen camellias are other good choices for focal planting.

Some tall-growing herbaceous perennials, such as *Crambe cordifolia*, kniphofia (red-hot poker), *Rodgersia podophylla* and the large and stately lily-like cardiocrinum are also suitable as focal points. Variegated forms of the tall, graceful grass miscanthus (or eulalia), planted in bold clumps, are ideal for placing around the lawn edges.

Wooden arches covered with honeysuckle, or with climbing roses and clematis, give an atmosphere of quiet retreat to a garden seat sheltering behind a deep curve or in a sunny corner. A series of arbours, forming a pergola, should lead to some point, such as a statue, a variegated shrub, a clump of perennials or a fountain, rather than end abruptly in the boundary wall.

Water is always fascinating, whether it is a running stream or a still pool. In a small garden, a stream with a waterfall over rocks may be ruled out for practical reasons, and a large deep pool may be out of proportion with the garden. But a small pool, set off-centre in a lawn or hidden behind a deep curve in the border, can make a charming and restful feature. Ideally, it should conform in size and outline to the overall garden design: an oval pool in a curved design, and a rectangular one in a garden of straight lines. The pool is best sited in full sun and away from overhanging trees.

Choose deep-water plants for the middle of the pool, and set marginal plants, such as water irises, day lilies, ferns and hostas, along the edges.

Where space does not permit a pool, a miniature water garden can still be accommodated. A tub painted with a waterproofing compound will hold a single water lily. It can be sunk in a border or left standing free. On an even smaller scale are shallow, concrete saucers. They are too small for plants or fish, but they will mirror surrounding plants in the water. Coloured pebbles laid over the base of the saucer give a more attractive effect.

In a very small garden, a formal pool can serve as the centre of attraction, especially where the entire garden is paved and most plants are grown in containers. A softly playing fountain can be incorporated in the pool, but it should be placed so that the water will not splash and damage the leaves of water lilies.

Genuine stone statuary is in short supply; but good reproductions are now becoming available. Any pieces of statuary, such as nymphs, urns on pedestals, animals, busts and ornate stone cornices, can be used for garden decoration and focal points, provided they blend into the garden picture. A statue placed at the end of a path, in a shady corner or where a pergola terminates, appears to serve a purpose; in a recess it draws the eye. It could also be placed close to a coniferous boundary hedge where it will break up the long, dark expanse.

Sundials are no longer required to fulfil their original purpose of telling the time, yet

A sundial makes a good focal point at the edge of a lawn, in a position of full sun; trailing plants can be planted to cover the base. Herb gardens, which need full sun, are also ideal beneath sundials

they still exert constant fascination. In gardens, they make fine focal points at the edge of a lawn or in a curve in full sun. The base of the plinth can be covered with low plants, such as shrubby hebes, potentillas and variegated ivy, splashed with trailing pelargoniums.

A secluded but sunny recess is ideal for a bird bath. It will bring new life and added interest to the garden at any time of year. But remember to change the water for the birds once every day, and to break any ice that forms in winter.

Adding colour to shaded sites

The dappled shade thrown by the smoke tree (Cotinus coggygria), *with its purple-red autumn colours, is intensified by a wooden arch densely covered with dark green ivy. In the centre of the grove stands a perennial euphorbia whose bright green, near succulent leaves remain attractive long after the yellow flowers in May and June have faded. Below the euphorbia, a prostrate* Juniperus horizontalis *sprawls near clumps of ornamental, variegated mint, alongside which are grey-green leaved garden pinks. Variegated ivies drape themselves over a low stone wall in the background*

Gloomy areas of the garden appear to be more of a problem than they really are. In fact, a shady site has definite advantages, for many plants require at least partial shade for healthy growth. Shade is usually created by either trees or walls. Tree shade may be dappled or dense, depending on the tree. Shade caused by walls is not so heavy, as light comes from the sky above and even if there is no direct sun a certain amount of reflected light is almost sure to reach the site at some time of the day.

When choosing plants for a shady area, keep in mind the soil and the amount of moisture it receives and contains. Many shade-loving plants require moist conditions – seldom found beneath large trees or hedges with shallow roots, which quickly absorb all available moisture. Narrow borders at the foot of high walls and fences may be sheltered from rain and will need frequent watering.

For vigorous growth, the soil should be fertile; poor soils can be enriched by working in plenty of well-rotted garden compost or leaf-mould before planting. All shaded soils benefit from an annual, deep mulch applied in spring.

Dappled, dry shade beneath deciduous trees and shrubs is a favourite habitat for many spring and autumn-flowering bulbs, including colchicums, cyclamens, eranthis, erythroniums and snowdrops.

The lily-of-the-valley thrives in both light and dense shade, and many lilies are happiest in the light woodland conditions found in a shrub border, particularly if the soil is slightly acid.

Many colourful herbaceous perennials grow best in light, dry shade. Blue colours are provided by *Campanula portenschlagiana*, brunnera, ajuga, *Campanula persicifolia* and *Tradescantia virginiana*. For reds, choose between *Pulmonaria saccarata*, *Saxifraga umbrosa* and red varieties of the true geraniums. Yellow colours and whites can be provided by lysimachias, lamiums and the elegant polygonatums known as Solomon's seal.

In dappled, moist shade the choice of herbaceous perennials is just as wide. The great majority of ferns, many of them evergreen, give fine ground-cover. Colour can be added by planting candelabra primulas, dicentras, monardas and mertensias among the ferns.

Other perennials that grow well in moist, shady positions are astilbes, hostas, liatris, aconitum, hemerocallis, the white trinity flower (*Trillium grandiflorum*) and the golden trollius (the globe flower).

Many shrubs also thrive in dappled shade and in fertile soil kept reasonably moist. In dry shade, they need extra watering during the growing season.

Deciduous shrubs for these sites include fothergillas, with white flowers and brilliant autumn leaves, and hypericums which carry a profusion of yellow flowers. The evergreen camellias, mahonias and *Skimmia japonica*, aucuba and fatshedera are at their most outstanding in shady sites. Rhododendrons and pieris also prefer the shade of trees, but need acid soil.

The evergreen vincas, with their star-shaped blue flowers, make excellent ground-cover in shady sites.

Plants for north-facing borders A north-facing border can provide ideal growing conditions for many plants, as long as the site is well sheltered from strong winds, has sufficient light and is not overshadowed by tall trees.

All the shrubs that have been recommended for tree shade can be grown together with cotoneaster, choisya, fuchsia, *Garrya elliptica*, hydrangea, kerria, philadelphus, ribes and symphoricarpos.

Many of the finest perennials are at home in a north-facing border. These include bergenias and brunneras, the Japanese anemones and the graceful aquilegias, all the campanulas, paeonies and phlox, golden rod and the autumn-flowering sedums. Any space remaining will accommodate annuals, such as pansies, antirrhinums, nasturtiums and clarkias.

Angles between buildings and boundary fences can create the gloomiest corners in the garden. For spring colour, plant lily-of-the-valley and hellebores. Summer-flowering perennials that will grow in deep shade include campanula, polygonatum and *Viola cornuta*. *Hypericum calycinum*, mahonia, skimmia and vinca will thrive here too, in association with green-leaved ivy.

One of the best plants for heavy shade is the perennial euphorbia, which brings gleaming colour to a dark site with its yellow-green flowers throughout the summer. And ferns such as dryopteris and gymnocarpium will provide brightness with their delicate display of fresh green, feathery fronds.

Clumps of Japanese anemones bring late-summer colour to a shaded north-facing border. The dainty pink-and-white flowers stand up well to autumn rains and winds

Less work, more enjoyment

A garden for relaxation rather than toil has been created here around a rough rye-grass lawn, showing obvious signs that children play on it. Even the daisies have not been weeded out, but are allowed to flourish in the short grass. The mower easily follows the smoothly curved lawn line, and the wide surrounding borders are planted mainly with weed-suppressing clumps of pale green dryopteris ferns, providing contrast with the bold foliage of the hostas in the foreground

The sensible gardener plans his garden in such a way that there is a sound proportion of enjoyment to work. Too many ambitious schemes, such as complicated topiary clipping of hedges and diversions of energy on trimming lawn edges round awkwardly shaped beds, can make gardening a year-round chore instead of a pleasant relaxation.

Time can be saved by planning a border of herbaceous perennials that are self-supporting in all but exposed gardens. In sunny or lightly shaded borders, such easily grown plants as achilleas, centaureas, doronicums, echinops, heleniums, kniphofias, lupins, michaelmas daisies, phlox, sedums and veronicas can be grown without any support.

Weeds can also be smothered with ground-cover plants which form an attractive green carpet, and sometimes one that flowers.

Ground-cover plants include acaena, aubrieta, dwarf dianthus, dryas, sedum and thymus; in shady borders some of the best ground-cover plants are convallaria, *Geranium endressii*, lamium, pulmonaria, *Vinca major* and *V. minor*.

In shrub borders, green and variegated ivy is ideal for ground-cover, and the evergreen foliage makes an effective background for small spring-flowering bulbs, such as cyclamen and crocus.

A mixed border of herbaceous perennials and shrubs is less time-consuming than a completely herbaceous one, and a shrub border is the easiest of all. By careful selection of shrubs for all seasons, a shrub border can remain attractive throughout the year. It needs little attention apart from occasional pruning, and weeds can be suppressed with ground-cover plants.

As well as the perennial ground-cover plants already mentioned, there are many suitable carpeting shrubs, such as hypericum, heaths and heathers (*Erica carnea* and calluna), mahonia, potentilla and low conifers.

Astilbes, bergenias, calthas, dicentras, hostas, hemerocallis and trollius are good choices for shady, slightly moist borders.

Annuals & biennials

A garden can be quickly filled with colour using annuals and biennials. They flower longer than many other plants and are ideal for filling gaps in a border

Almost any patch of soil can be transformed into a blaze of colour in two or three months with annual flowers grown from seed.

Annuals are plants that grow, flower, produce seed and die in one growing season. Some provide a longer-lasting flower display than many other types of plants, and are invaluable for starting a new garden from scratch. They can also be used to provide bright patches of colour among shrubs or perennials.

Annuals are easy to grow and are available in a wide range of colours and heights, from tiny dwarfs to climbers which will rapidly cover fences with a vivid show of blooms.

Similar plants to annuals are the biennials, which grow one year, flower the next and are then discarded. Probably the plant most commonly grown as a biennial is the popular wallflower that flowers in spring. In fact, wallflowers are short-lived perennials, but after their second year they flower poorly.

Annuals are classified on the seed packets as either hardy or half-hardy. Hardy annuals are those that will stand up to cold spring weather, and can be sown outdoors where they are intended to flower. Mostly, they do not require a particularly rich soil in which to grow.

Examples of hardy annuals are clarkias, eschscholzias, godetias, larkspurs, and Virginian stocks.

Half-hardy annuals will not start into growth in cold conditions, and so the seeds and seedlings need protection in spring.

To obtain the longest possible flowering season they should be sown under glass early in the year, and planted out when they are well developed – after the weather and soil have warmed up.

A number of half-hardy annuals can be sown in the open, provided you wait until late May or early June and choose a sheltered position. However, the flowering season will be much shorter.

The hardiness of some plants may vary according to the part of the country where they are grown. A plant that is hardy in the south-west of Britain may not be hardy in the north-east where the temperatures can be much lower.

A greenhouse is not essential for growing half-hardy annuals. A cold frame, cloches, or even a sunny window indoors can be used to germinate the seeds. The instructions

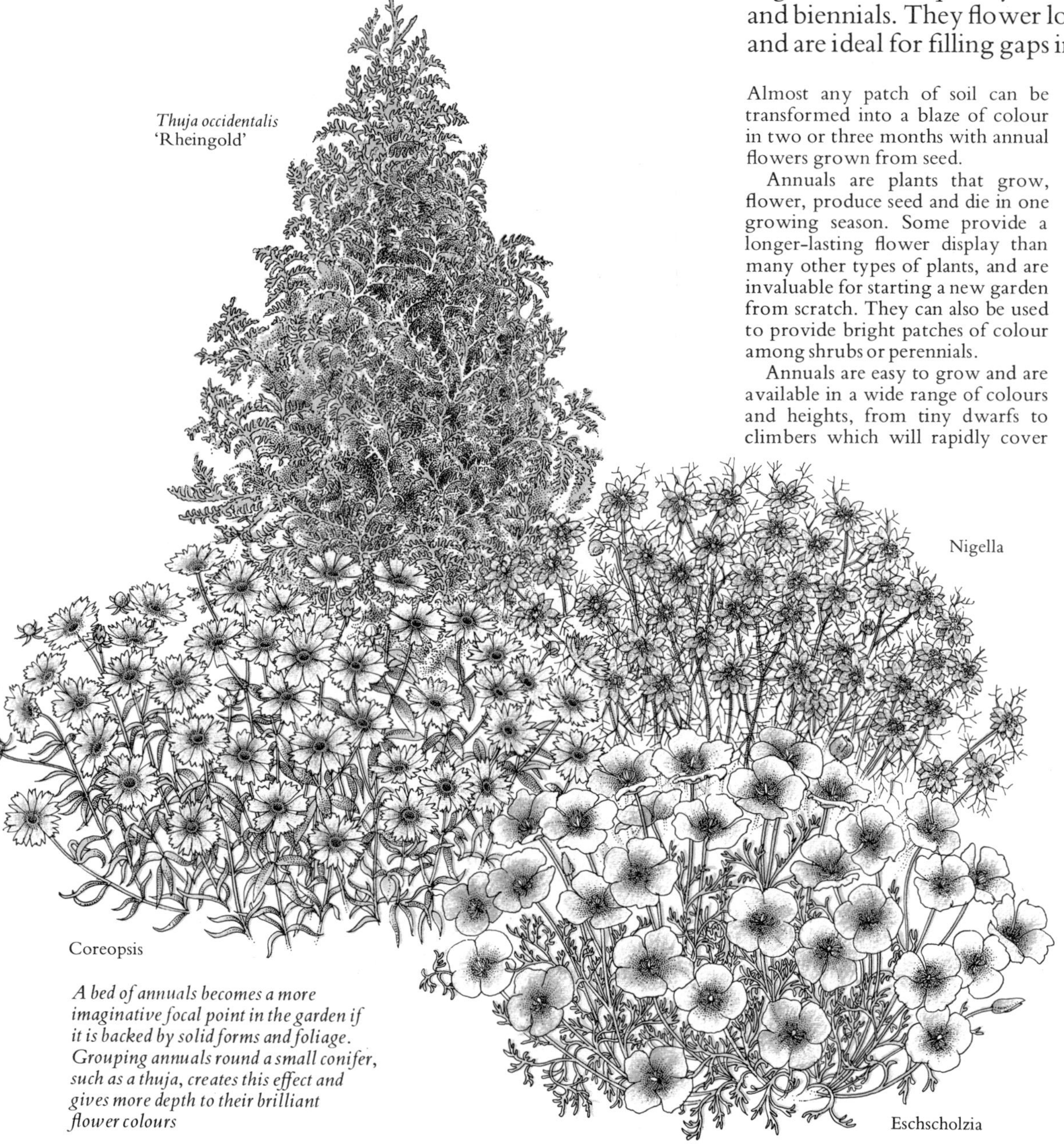

A bed of annuals becomes a more imaginative focal point in the garden if it is backed by solid forms and foliage. Grouping annuals round a small conifer, such as a thuja, creates this effect and gives more depth to their brilliant flower colours

in the catalogue or on the seed packet will indicate what degree of heat is required for germination.

Petunias, *Salvia splendens*, ageratums, African and French marigolds, nemesias and zinnias are some of the most popular half-hardy annuals.

Biennials, which may be said to bridge the gap between annuals and perennials, include sweet williams, brompton stocks, Canterbury bells and wallflowers. They are usually sown in the late spring or early summer, transplanted to nursery beds, planted out in the autumn and allowed to bloom the following year. To enable them to build up their strength, they must be well established in their winter quarters before the frosts set in.

Many annuals and biennials have been cottage-garden favourites for centuries. Stocks, sunflowers, snapdragons, larkspurs, candytufts and many others are mentioned in books which are more than 300 years old.

Over the years seedsmen have improved them, and vastly enlarged the horizons open to the amateur gardener.

One of the most exciting advances in recent years has been the development of the F1 and F2 hybrids, the result of careful selecting and inbreeding from two different parent lines of plant to get purity of desirable characteristics, and finally cross-pollinating them to combine the best characteristics of each.

It requires several generations of this kind of breeding to produce plants of the desired quality, and consequently some gardeners may be deterred by the relatively high price of the seed, especially as further seeds produced in the garden do not run true to type and will produce plants that will deteriorate from year to year.

But the first generation of flowers, grown from F1 hybrid seed, will show such outstanding improvements on the less-expensive types that they are well worth trying.

F2 hybrids are an attempt to improve quality without the very high cost of the F1 method. In some cases – as, for example, with pansies – it has worked. Generally, the F2 hybrids are an improvement on conventional seed, though not so spectacular as the F1.

Apart from their uses for bedding and in borders, annuals can be grown for various special reasons.

People interested in flower arranging, or in having a touch of summer around the house in winter, can grow 'everlasting' flowers, such as helichrysums, limoniums (statice), molucellas and helipterums, as well as ornamental grasses. Both flowers and grasses are ideal for drying and displaying indoors.

Annual climbers such as morning glory and some nasturtiums add the dimension of height that is so attractive in a well-planned garden.

To grow in window-boxes, tubs and hanging baskets, there are a great many suitable hardy and half-hardy annual and biennial plants, including ageratums, calendulas, petunias, wallflowers and also trailing lobelias.

For the labour-saving 'wild' patch at the bottom of the garden there are annuals such as nasturtiums, Californian poppies, forget-me-nots, nemophilas and pot marigolds, that will seed themselves year after year, producing an annual flush of colour for next to no effort.

And there are easy-to-grow plants such as mignonettes, nicotianas, stocks, wallflowers and violas, that are prized because of their scent, and others such as alyssums, clarkias and nigellas, which are attractive to pollinating insects, such as butterflies and bees.

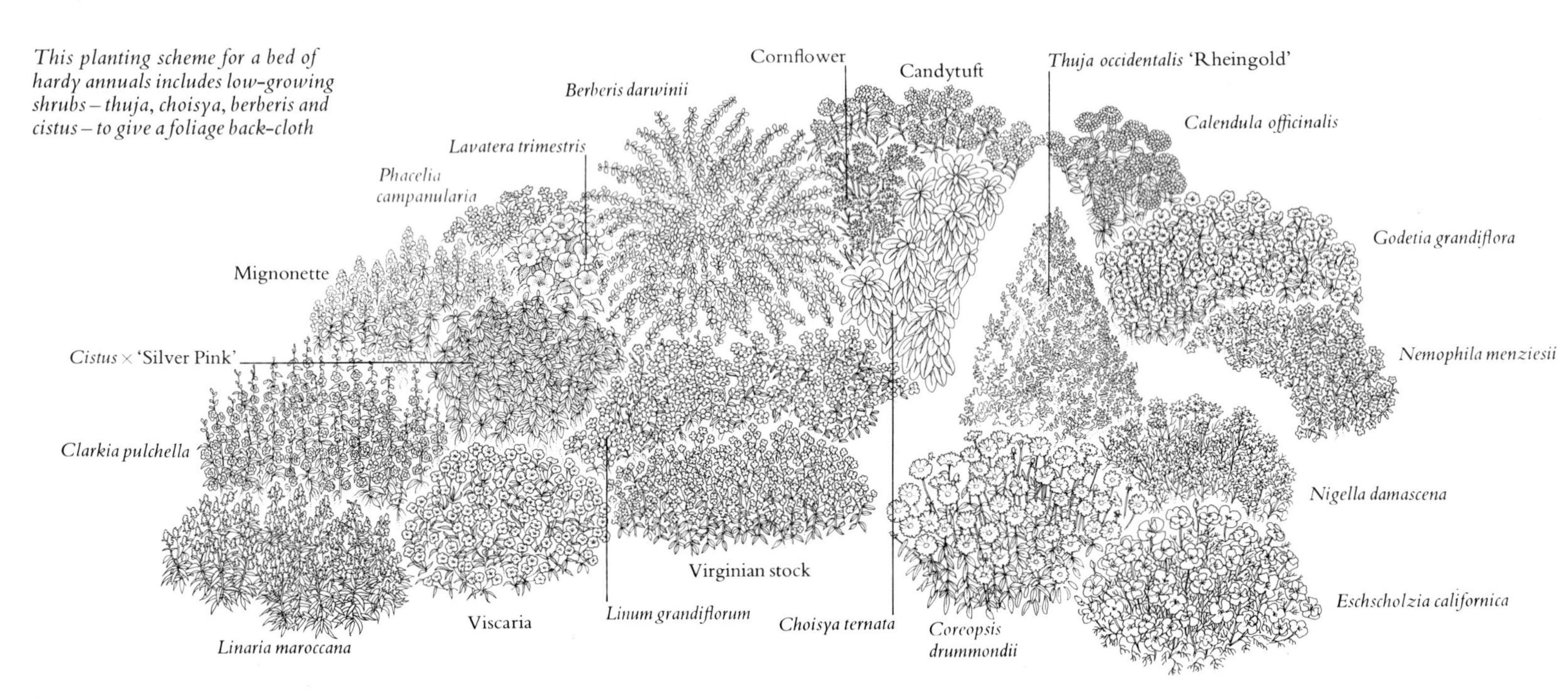

This planting scheme for a bed of hardy annuals includes low-growing shrubs – thuja, choisya, berberis and cistus – to give a foliage back-cloth

How to make a success with hardy annuals

Clearing the site and preparing the soil

As soon as annuals begin to fade – between late September and the middle of October – pull each plant from the soil.

If a plant resists, loosen the soil with a fork.

When all the old plants have been removed, apply a 1–2 in. layer of peat, manure or garden compost to the surface of the soil. This enables light, dry soil to retain moisture, helps to break up heavy soils and adds nutrients to the soil.

Turn over the soil and compost together with a fork. Leave it lumpy, as a better soil surface is produced if winter frosts are allowed to penetrate deeply and break it down naturally.

It is easier to turn over moist soil, so if the ground is hard, water it thoroughly the day before. If the soil is too sticky after rain, leave it for a few days before digging.

In spring, as soon as the soil is dry enough, loosen up the top 6–8 in. (9–12 in. if it was a severe winter) with a fork. When forking over the soil look out for leatherjackets (leathery, slate-grey larvae, rather like legless caterpillars) and wireworms (segmented yellow-brown, worm-like creatures). Both pests feed on the roots of plants. If you see either, sprinkle on some bromophos or HCH powder. One treatment should be enough to eradicate these pests.

Just before sowing, add some general fertiliser, such as Growmore or John Innes base, to the soil. Scatter the fertiliser evenly over the soil at the rate of two handfuls to the square yard. Then rake it lightly into the top 1 in. of soil.

Finally, rake over the soil to obtain a fine tilth – a light, crumbly, easily worked surface.

Fork in manure or garden compost in the autumn, leaving the soil lumpy for frost to get in

How and when to sow the seed

Before sowing annuals in a border or plot, it is best to prepare a plan well in advance – so that flowers can be grouped according to their colour and height.

Put the tallest varieties at the back of the border – or the centre if it is surrounded by lawn – and the lowest at the front.

It is better to buy seed than harvest your own, as this is likely to be of uncertain quality. If ordering by post, order as soon as possible to ensure that you get what you want. Most seed firms issue their catalogues in November.

Hardy-annual seeds can be sown from March to May to flower during the summer, and the hardiest varieties in early September to flower the following spring and early summer.

If the soil is dry, water it thoroughly the day before sowing. With heavy soil, first lightly fork into the top 3–4 in. a bucket of fine sedge peat to the square yard, to prevent the soil from caking.

With a swan-neck hoe, mark out the sowing areas, working from the plan.

Within each sowing area, seeds may be either sown in grooves or drills, or scattered over the whole area and then raked into the soil. The advantages of sowing in drills are that it is easier to hoe weeds between seedlings in regular lines than between those growing haphazardly; and that all the seeds are sown at an even depth.

Make shallow drills with a hoe or the edge of a rake, $\frac{1}{4}$–$\frac{1}{2}$ in. deep. Sow thinly to avoid too much thinning later.

Sowing will be made even easier if the sowing areas are marked out with sand. This provides a permanent mark if you are interrupted by rain when sowing.

The distance between drills will be determined by the size of the plants. In general, drills for tall, narrow plants should be spaced half the height of the plant apart; drills for dwarf, bushy plants the full height of the plant apart. The height the plant may be expected to reach will be given on the seed packet.

After sowing seeds in drills, cover them by running the point of the swan-neck hoe along each ridge created when the drill was made.

Alternatively, lightly draw a rake along the length of the drill.

Then firm the soil with the flat side of the hoe or rake, or walk lightly down the drill.

If sowing by the broadcast method, carefully rake in the seeds so that they are just buried.

In dry weather water all seeds with a sprinkler or fine-rose watering can two days after sowing, and again a week later. Wet the soil thoroughly to make sure the moisture penetrates deeply.

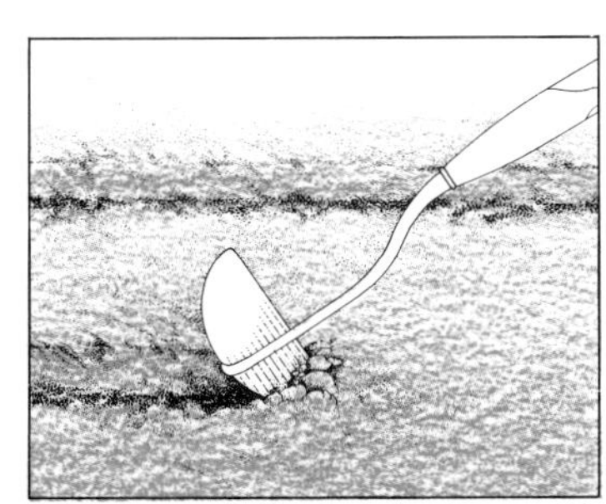

1 *Mark out drills, $\frac{1}{4}$–$\frac{1}{2}$ in. deep, with one side of a swan-neck hoe*

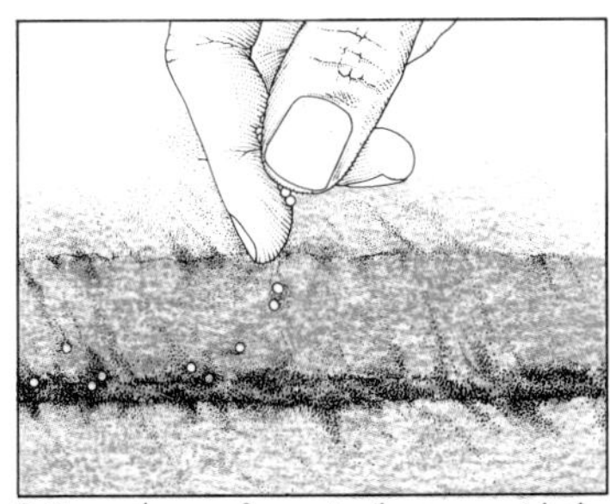

2 *Sow the seed sparingly to avoid the need for too much thinning later*

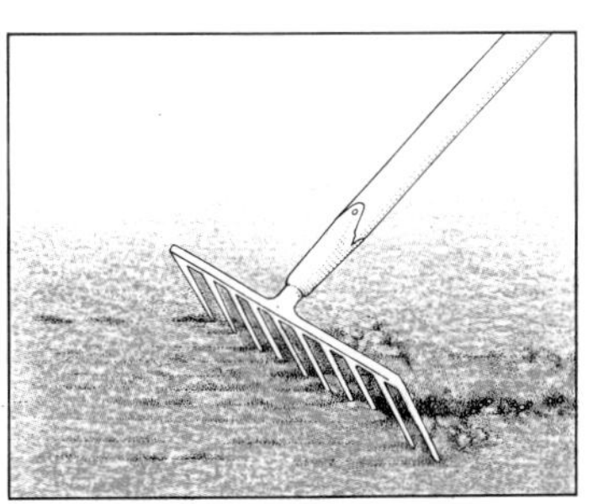

3 *Thinly cover the seed by drawing a rake lightly along the drill*

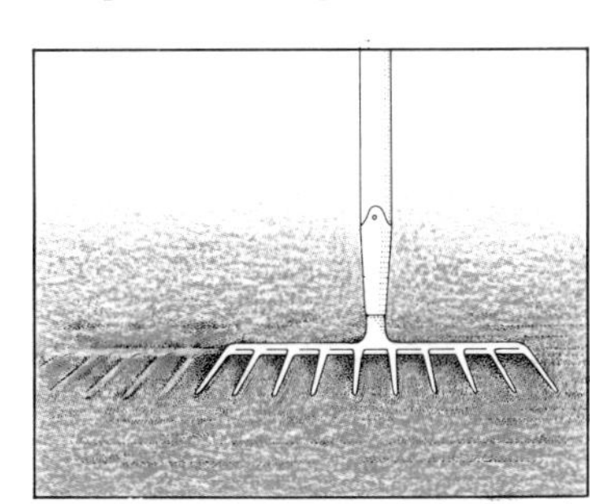

4 *Firm the soil gently with the flat side of the rake. Water in dry weather*

Seeds packaged for convenience

As well as being sold loose in packets, seeds are now available in two forms – pelleted seed and tape seed – that provide ease and accuracy of sowing.

Each pelleted seed is coated with a decomposable material, usually clay. This increases its size and makes it easier to handle. With precise spacing possible, there is no need for thinning. Many seeds are now pelleted, including small ones like alyssum and antirrhinums.

Tape seed consists of a line of evenly spaced seeds held between two ½ in. wide strips of decomposable paper or plastic material. The strip can be unwound and cut up as required. The tape is laid in a ½ in. furrow, anchored with very small lumps of earth to maintain the accurate spacing, and covered with another ½ in. of soil.

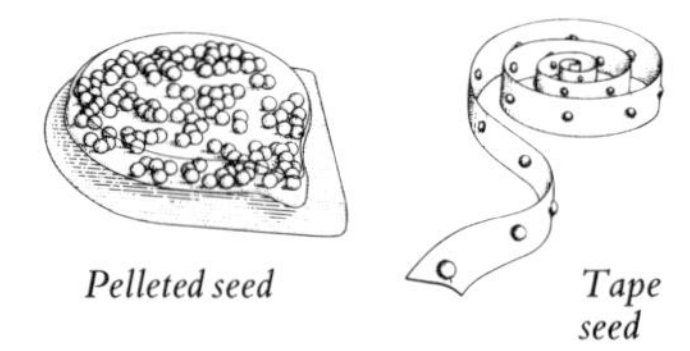

Pelleted seed *Tape seed*

Protecting seedlings from birds and cats

Many birds eat seedlings. The best method of protecting young plants against them is to insert low stakes around the perimeter of the bed, tie black thread to one of them and loop it criss-cross over the bed. Alternatively, green netting can be spread over the bed.

If cats or dogs are a nuisance, keep them away by sprinkling a proprietary animal repellent over the bed.

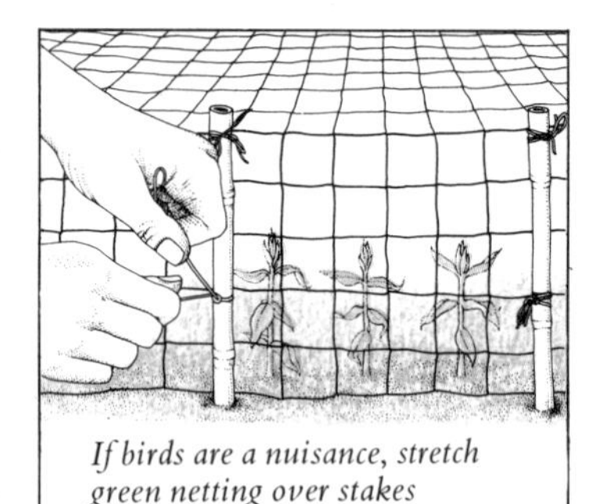

If birds are a nuisance, stretch green netting over stakes

The best way to stake tall flowers

Some annuals that grow over 2 ft tall need to be supported. After the final thinning, insert pea sticks at intervals of about 12 in. around each group of seedlings. Also insert two or three more sticks in the centre of the group.

The pea sticks should be about two-thirds the ultimate height of the plants. When the plants are in full summer growth, the supports will be hidden.

Alternative methods of supporting are with plastic plant stakes or – less satisfactory – with hazel sticks or canes and green twine.

Some tall annuals need support. Insert pea sticks around each group of seedlings

Spacing and thinning out seedlings

When the seedlings have about two or three true leaves (as opposed to the minute round or oval seed leaves that appear after germination has taken place), they should be thinned out. At this stage the roots are undeveloped and the removal of unwanted seedlings will cause little disturbance to adjacent plants. The best time to do this is when the soil is moist, so that they come out easily. It is often an advantage to soak the seed bed the day before, and to ease up the seedlings with a fork before pulling them up.

Lift each unwanted seedling with one hand. At the same time, with the other hand, press a finger on the soil each side of the seedling to avoid disturbing the roots of the other seedlings that are being retained to develop into mature plants.

For the correct distances between thinned-out seedlings, consult the seed packet. A good general guide is to thin spring-sown seedlings once (4–6 in. apart); autumn-sown seedlings twice (2–3 in. apart in autumn, 6–9 in. apart in spring). Try to keep the strongest seedlings, if possible pulling up the puny ones.

Discard the removed seedlings, unless there is a bare space in the garden that you are able to transplant them to. Discarded plants should not be left lying on the ground, as they will attract pests. Put them on the compost heap.

As the plants grow, avoid any check in growth by ensuring that the soil never dries out.

To thin seedlings, pull out each unwanted seedling with one hand while pressing down the soil on each side with the fingers of the other hand

Dead-heading to encourage further flowering

Faded or damaged blooms should be removed throughout the flowering season. If the dead blooms are left, the plant's energy goes into producing seed rather than more flowers. This dead-heading will increase the vigour of the plant, and encourage further flowering. Snap off the bloom between finger and thumb with a twisting motion.

If you want to save some seed for the next season (although this will probably be inferior to commercial seed), allow one or two blooms to wither on each plant. Then harvest the seed when ripe.

With finger and thumb, snap off flowers with a twisting motion as soon as they fade, to encourage more blooms and to increase the vigour of the plant

Raising your own half-hardy annuals from seeds

Sowing indoors or in the greenhouse

Sow seeds of half-hardy annuals from February to early April.

Petunias, asters, schizanthus and nemesias are some of the more familiar examples of these popular garden flowers.

If you are sowing in pots or seed trays that have been used before, first disinfect them by scrubbing them in a solution of household bleach, then rinsing.

Fill some 3 in. pots or a seed tray with moist John Innes or proprietary seed compost.

Firm the mixture down to $\frac{1}{2}$ in. from the top of the container, using the base of another pot or a flat piece of wood.

Sow the seeds on top of the compost by opening up the packet and making a semi-funnel of it; hold this above the compost and tap it on a fingernail on the other hand. Space the seeds evenly.

Cover large seeds with a $\frac{1}{4}$ in. layer of sieved compost (a coarse flour sieve is ideal). Small seeds need just covering. Very fine seeds, such as begonia, need no covering.

Water the compost by standing the tray in water halfway up its sides. Remove the tray when the compost is thoroughly wet.

Label the containers, cover them with glass or polythene and put them in a heated frame or propagator at a temperature of 12–18°C (54–64°F).

Alternatively, place a plastic bag over each container and secure it with a rubber band, or fold it underneath. This provides the moist atmosphere needed for germination. Put the pots or trays in a warm, shady place, such as an airing cupboard or a warm, north-facing window-sill.

If moisture forms on the inside of the bag, lift it and flick it with a finger. Do this every day, or the seedlings may rot.

From five days to three weeks after sowing, growth will appear above the surface of the compost. With most seedlings, this will be in the form of a pair of small round or oval seed leaves.

The cover should now be removed and the pot moved to a position giving more light, either indoors or in the greenhouse.

As soon as the first true leaf appears from between the seed leaves, the seedlings are ready to be pricked out into trays.

1 *Fill a tray or 3 in. pot with moist seed compost and firm it down*

2 *Sprinkle the seeds on the surface of the compost, spacing them evenly*

3 *Cover the seeds with $\frac{1}{4}$ in. of sifted compost. Fine seeds need no covering*

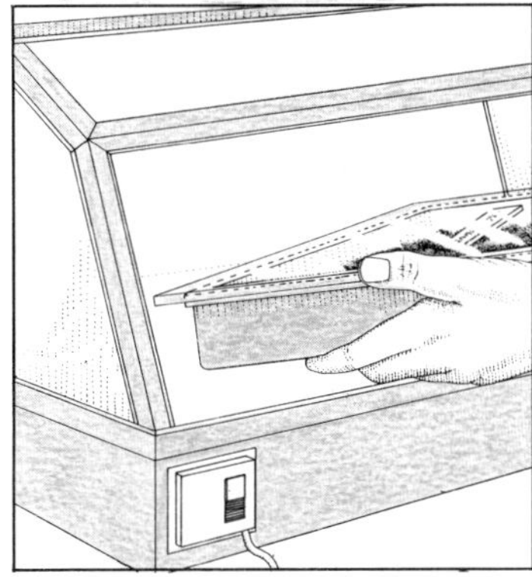

4 *Water the compost and place the tray or pot in a propagator*

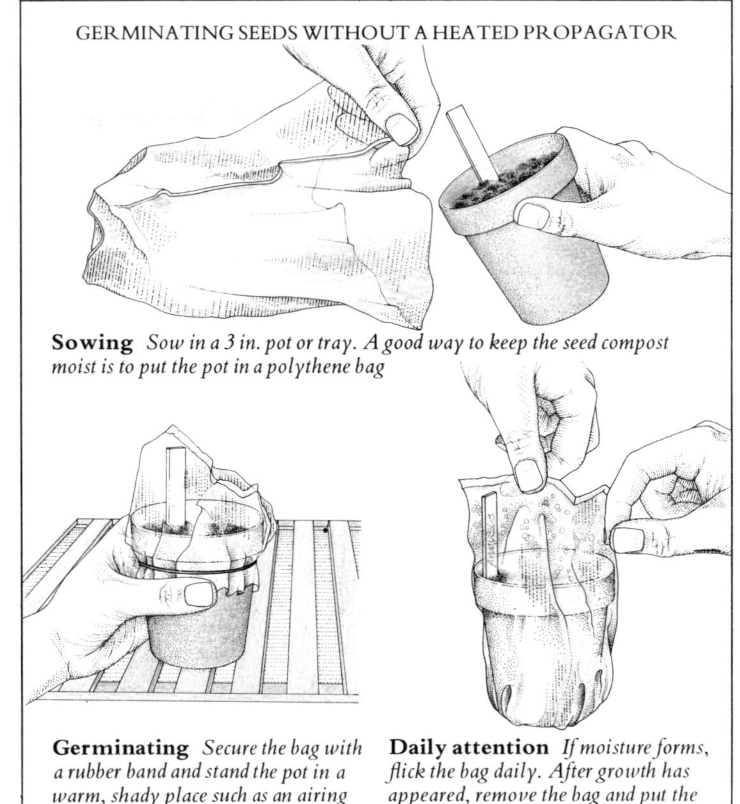

GERMINATING SEEDS WITHOUT A HEATED PROPAGATOR

Sowing *Sow in a 3 in. pot or tray. A good way to keep the seed compost moist is to put the pot in a polythene bag*

Germinating *Secure the bag with a rubber band and stand the pot in a warm, shady place such as an airing cupboard or north-facing window-sill*

Daily attention *If moisture forms, flick the bag daily. After growth has appeared, remove the bag and put the pot in a lighter position*

Pricking out the seedlings without damaging them

Fill a seed tray with moist potting compost and firm it in. Use John Innes No. 1 or a peat-based compost.

Before planting the seedlings in the tray, make all the planting holes with a dibber or pencil, to ensure even spacing. The holes should be 1–1½ in. apart each way. A standard seed tray (about 13 × 8 in.) will take 40–90 seedlings.

Carefully lever a clump of seedlings, with their compost, from their container with a plant label.

Hold each seedling by a seed leaf – never the stem, which can be easily damaged. Using a dibber or pencil, tease it away from the others. With tiny seedlings, such as begonias, cut a V-shaped notch in the end of the label, and lift each seedling by sliding the notch under the leaves.

Try to keep the root system of each seedling intact. Then lower it into its planting hole.

With the dibber or pencil, firm in the compost around the seedling. Do not damage the roots or stem, but firm sufficiently for the seedling not to yield if gently tugged.

Label the tray and water the compost, using a fine-rosed can.

Place the tray in a cold frame or greenhouse, or on a window-ledge indoors, away from direct sunlight.

Two or three days later, move containers on a window-ledge into direct sunlight, those in a greenhouse or cold frame into a sunlit position lightly shaded by green polythene or hessian on the roof.

Avoid full shade – this produces spindly plants. Keep the compost moist, but do not soak it.

BEWARE OF DAMPING OFF

Damping-off disease turns the base of the seedling brown and kills it. The disease is encouraged by planting seedlings too closely and by over-watering. Remove dead seedlings and treat the others with liquid Cheshunt compound or captan powder. Next time allow more space

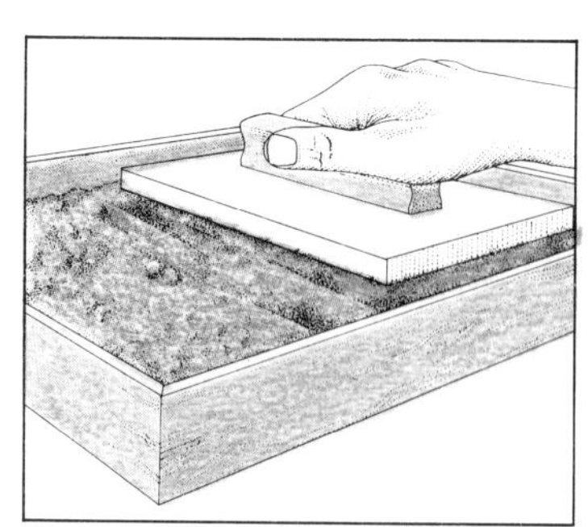

1 *Fill a seed tray with moist potting compost and firm it*

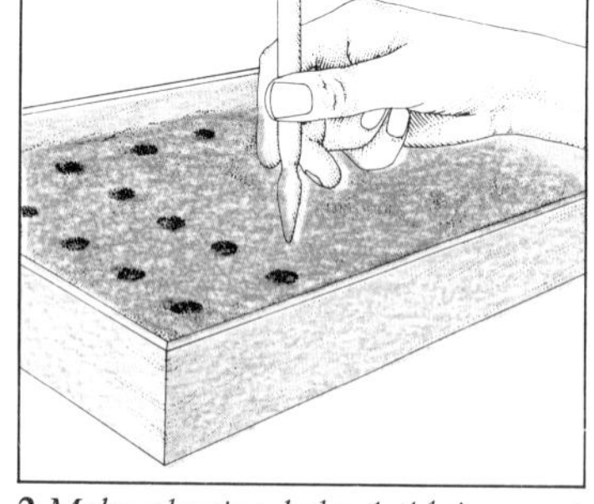

2 *Make planting holes 1–1½ in. apart with a dibber or pencil*

3 *Lever up a clump of seedlings with a plant label*

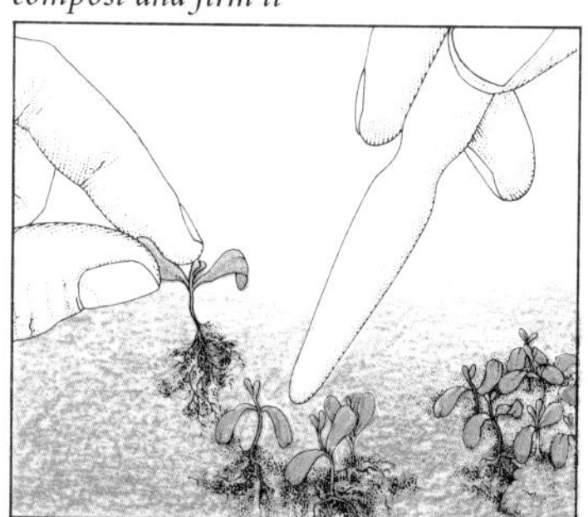

4 *Hold a seedling by a seed leaf and tease it gently away from the others*

5 *Plant each seedling in the compost and firm it with the dibber*

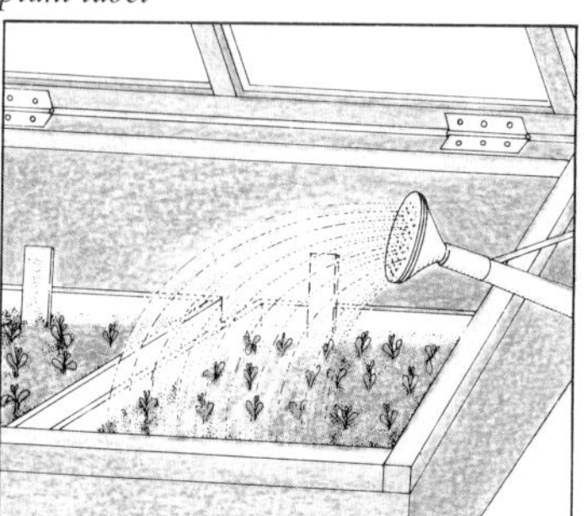

6 *Water the seedlings with a fine-rose can, and put them in a cold frame*

Hardening off the young seedlings

When the young plants are well established and making sturdy growth – from four to eight weeks after pricking out – start hardening them off. Transfer seedlings from a greenhouse or window-ledge to an unshaded cold frame, cloches or a polythene tunnel.

For the first few days, open the frame or cloches, or raise the sides of the tunnel *slightly* during the day. Gradually increase this ventilation until by mid-May at the earliest (the end of May in northern England and in frosty areas) the frame or cloches are completely open. Delay opening fully if the weather is cold, wet or windy.

Keep frames, cloches or tunnels closed at night until all danger of frost has passed.

Speeding up the hardening-off process can result in stunted growth and/or a red or purple discoloration of the entire seedling. If this happens, return the seedlings to the conditions they were growing in before hardening off. Wait until normal green growth has returned, then harden them off gradually in the correct way.

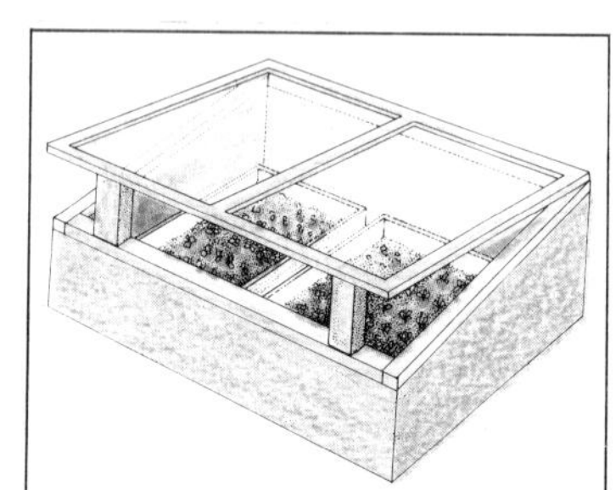

For the first few days, open the frame slightly for a few hours a day. Gradually increase the ventilation until, by mid-May at the earliest, the frame is completely open

Planting out and aftercare in the flower bed

Once hardened off, the young annuals should be planted out between the third week in May and the second week in June. Plant when the soil is moist. During a dry period it may be necessary to water the soil thoroughly the day before.

Prepare the site in the same way as for hardy annuals (p. 27).

Bang one end of the seed tray on the ground to open up a gap between the other end and the compost.

Place a trowel or the fingers of both hands underneath the compost, and gently break away the first row of plants.

Separate each plant individually with a label or trowel, ensuring that there is a good root system.

The correct spacing between plants will depend on the species. A good general rule is to space plants half their eventual height apart, except for plants of spreading habit, which are spaced full height apart. Dig a planting hole with a trowel, wide and deep enough to accommodate the plant's root system.

Insert the plant so that the base of its stem is level with the surface of the soil. Fill the hole and firm in the plant with your fingers.

Immediately after planting, encourage any plant that is not normally bushy to produce several stems and blooms, by pinching out its growing tip.

If you buy half-hardy annuals ready for planting out, ensure that they have no flowers on them. The early flowering will have been the result of mineral and water deficiencies. Consequently they will be of poor quality.

Watering is unnecessary, except during prolonged dry periods.

For staking and dead-heading and protection against birds and cats, see page 28.

1 *Bang one end of the box on the ground to loosen the compost*

2 *Break away the first row of plants with your fingers or a trowel*

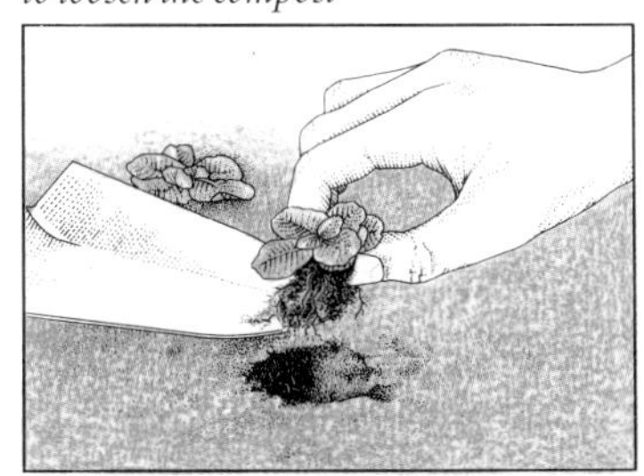

3 *Dig a hole with a trowel and plant each seedling with a good root ball*

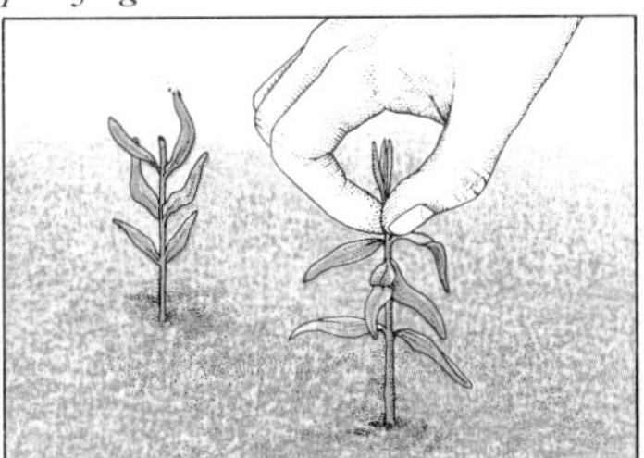

4 *Encourage more stems on any plant not normally bushy by pinching out the tip*

What can go wrong with annuals and biennials

Aphids and starvation are two of the most common problems. If your plants show symptoms not described here, turn to the full-colour identification chart of pests and diseases starting on page 377. Chemicals recommended in the third column below can be looked up on page 398 for a list of commercial preparations.

Symptoms	Cause	Cure
Young stems stunted or distorted, flowers not developing properly; covered with small, sticky green or black insects	Aphids (blackfly and greenfly)	Spray with derris, malathion, dimethoate, formothion or pirimicarb
Leaves finely mottled, with a generally silvery appearance, especially during hot, dry weather	Thrips	Spray or dust with malathion, HCH, nicotine or derris
Shoots and leaves stunted and crippled, leaves sometimes with small ragged holes – particularly on the younger ones. Flower buds deformed or fail to develop	Capsid bugs	Spray with HCH, malathion, nicotine or diazinon
Whole plant rather thin and small, the leaves sometimes yellowish; possibly only an early flush of small flowers	Starvation	Apply a liquid fertiliser at weekly intervals and if possible mulch with decayed manure or compost. In addition, and for early and rapid results, spray with a foliar feed. Regularly remove faded flowers
Seedlings, particularly those thickly sown in pots, pans or boxes under glass, rot at ground level and topple over	Damping-off disease	Water with captan or Cheshunt compound. The best approach is to avoid this disease by using a sterilised seed compost, sowing thinly, not over-watering, and using a captan seed dressing
Plant stunted, with small or malformed leaves showing yellow mottling or veins. Flowers poor, or may fail to develop	Virus disease	Destroy plants, preferably by burning, as soon as symptoms are noticed
Irregular, ragged holes eaten in leaves and petals	Earwigs	Spray or dust with HCH; or trap earwigs in flower pots stuffed with straw
Young shoots spun together with fine threads, the growing point within eaten out by a small, greenish caterpillar	Tortrix caterpillars	Spray with HCH, derris or trichlorphon, or pick off infested shoots by hand
Leaves and young shoots covered with a fine whitish or greyish powder, accompanied by stunting or slight crippling of the plant	Mildew	Spray with benomyl, thiophanate-methyl or sulphur

Two ways to grow sweet peas

How and when to sow the seed

Sweet peas are among the most attractive, sweet-smelling and prolific-flowering annuals. A single plant can produce nearly 50 flower spikes.

The plants do best in good soil in an open, sunny position.

Seed can be sown in October, in a cold greenhouse or cold frame (or out of doors in warm, sheltered areas), in order to produce flowers in late spring and summer.

Alternatively, sow the seed in a propagator heated to 16°C (61°F) in January or February, or in a cold frame or cloche from February to April, or outdoors in the flowering position in March or April.

Most sweet-pea seeds have hard coats, so soak them in water overnight. Seeds that are still hard can be nicked with a knife or file.

Germination is improved by treating the seeds with a captan seed dressing before sowing. Sow the seeds $\frac{1}{2}$ in. deep, in pots or trays of seed compost.

After germination, grow the seedlings on in cool conditions.

Seedlings in a heated propagator should be put into cold frames as soon as the second true leaf shows. Those in a cold greenhouse or frame should be well ventilated and the house or frame completely opened on sunny days from March onwards.

Plant out autumn-sown plants in March or April and later-sown plants in early May. They can now be grown in one of two ways – the bush or the cordon method.

Growing natural plants by the bush method

The bush method allows natural, unrestricted growth, with support if necessary.

The soil needs to be in good condition for unrestricted plants. Prepare it in the way described for hardy annuals (p. 27).

Dig a hole for each plant with a trowel, wide enough for the roots to be spread out. Plant firmly. After planting, water in.

Plant the young sweet peas 6 in. apart, either in a row or in groups of two or three, with 8 or 9 in. between the groups.

Place small twigs by each plant to keep it off the ground, or support it against a short cane with twine or a metal ring. This keeps the plant away from slugs and worms, and starts it climbing before the main supports are inserted in the ground.

Three to six weeks after planting, put in the main supports. For those varieties over 3 ft tall, insert 5–6 ft high canes or pea sticks, or provide plastic netting to that height. Support dwarf forms with 3 ft high pea sticks.

Watering is necessary only during dry spells.

Once good growth has started, apply a liquid feed every 10–12 days. Irregular feeding can lead to the flower buds dropping off.

In May, mulch the plants with a 1–2 in. deep layer of well-rotted manure or garden compost to conserve moisture during the summer, but ensure that the mulch is kept away from the stems.

If you do not use the flowers for cutting, remove them as soon as they fade – if seeds are allowed to set, further flowering is restricted.

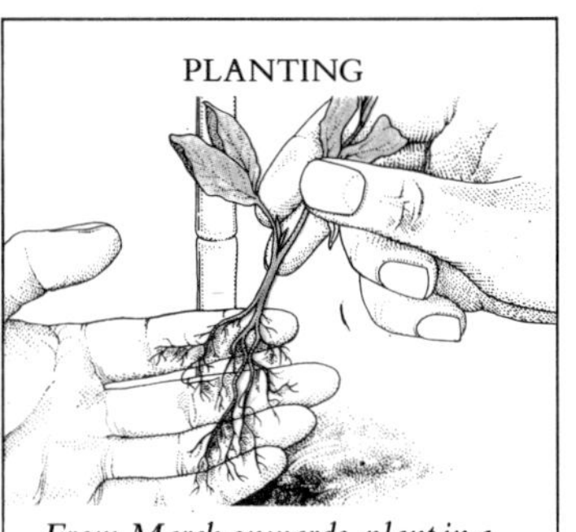

From March onwards, plant in a hole with the roots spread out

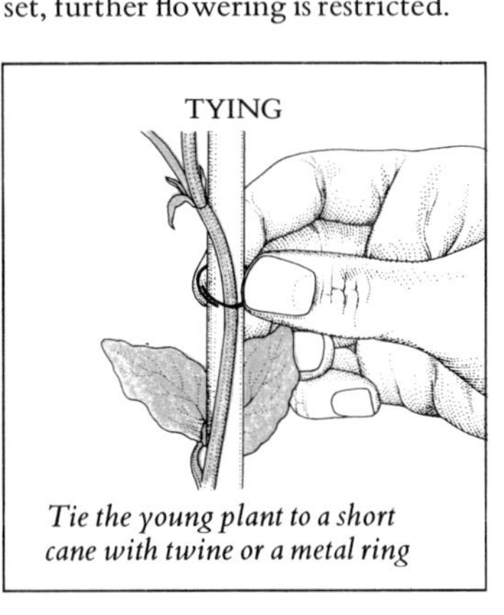
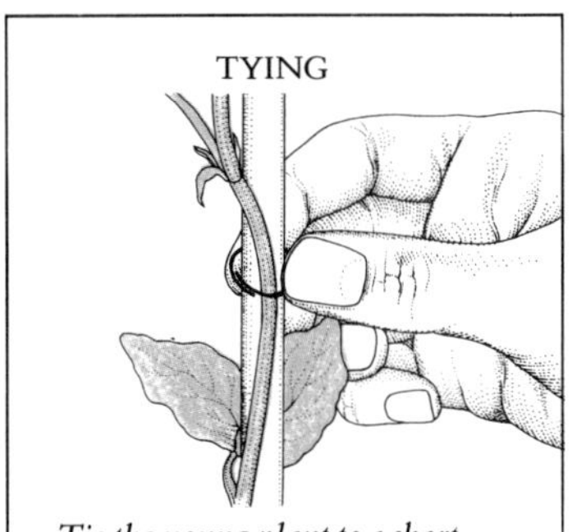

Tie the young plant to a short cane with twine or a metal ring

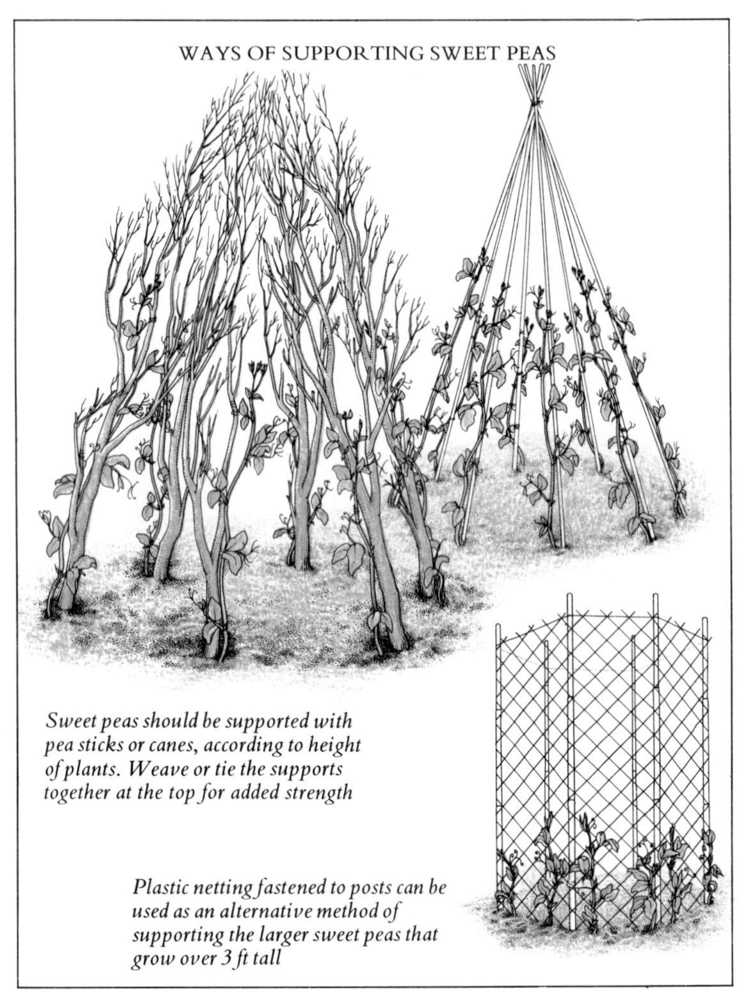

Sweet peas should be supported with pea sticks or canes, according to height of plants. Weave or tie the supports together at the top for added strength

Plastic netting fastened to posts can be used as an alternative method of supporting the larger sweet peas that grow over 3 ft tall

Growing exhibition blooms by the cordon method

The cordon method involves a more elaborate system of supporting the plants. It sacrifices quantity to give exhibition-type blooms or large flowers for cutting.

Plants can be raised by any of the methods already mentioned, but for the best results seeds should be sown in autumn in individual pots and planted out in spring.

Basal shoots, which carry the best flowers, should be encouraged by pinching out the growing tip of the main shoot when it has two well-formed leaves.

In autumn, double dig the soil (p. 405), mixing well-rotted manure or garden compost into the bottom spit, and three or four handfuls of sterilised bonemeal, or half that amount of superphosphate, to the square yard, into the top spit.

In February, as soon as the soil is fit to work, fork in a proprietary sweet pea fertiliser at the recommended rate.

To support the plants, first insert a stout post, standing 6–7 ft above the ground, at both ends of each row. Space the rows about $4\frac{1}{2}$ ft apart. Attach a 15 in. long cross-piece to each post at the top and stretch two parallel wires, 12 in. apart, between them. At 8 in. intervals along the wires, and on alternate sides, insert a cane and tie it to the wire.

In March or April, plant autumn-sown sweet peas, one beside each cane. Do not bunch the roots, and water well after planting. Tie the shoots of the sweet peas loosely to the canes.

When the plants are about 9 in. tall, select the strongest shoot on each and carefully remove the others, making sure you do not damage the main stem.

At this stage, and from now on, remove the tendrils from each pair of leaflets.

As the plants now lack their natural method of clinging to a support, they must be tied to the cane – but only lightly, to allow the stem to swell as it grows.

In addition, all side-shoots must be nipped out when young.

Once good growth has started, apply a liquid feed every 10–12 days.

In May, mulch the plants with a 1–2 in. deep layer of well-rotted manure or garden compost, but keep it away from the stems.

Remove any flowering stems that bear less than four buds, as soon as the buds appear. As stems bearing four or more buds appear, leave them to develop.

Flowers should be cut when the lowest bloom on each flowering stem shows full colour. Cut with a knife or scissors to avoid tearing the main stem. If flowers are not cut, remove them as soon as they fade.

Bud-drop can be even more troublesome with cordon sweet peas than bush plants. To combat this, fine sprinkling from overhead is beneficial, together with regular watering in dry weather.

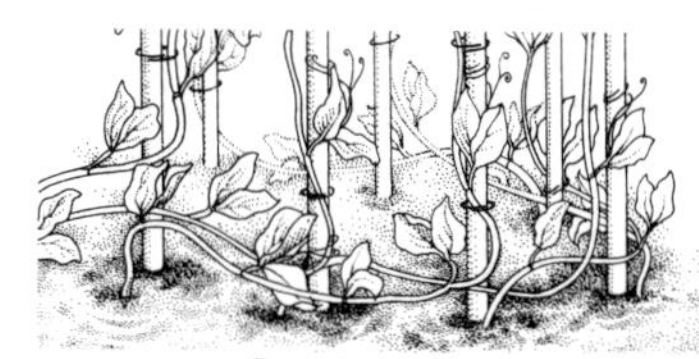

Layering cordons

When the cordons reach the top of their canes, about July, they must be layered (this is not the layering used in propagation). Untie the plants and lay them carefully on the ground, along the line of canes, to their full length. Then take the end of each plant gently up the nearest cane for about 12 in. and fasten it. Fasten the end of the next plant to the next cane, and so on. Take plants near the end of the row round the end post, and fasten to canes on the other side.

Flowers will continue to be produced on the new growth.

HOW TO SUPPORT CORDONS

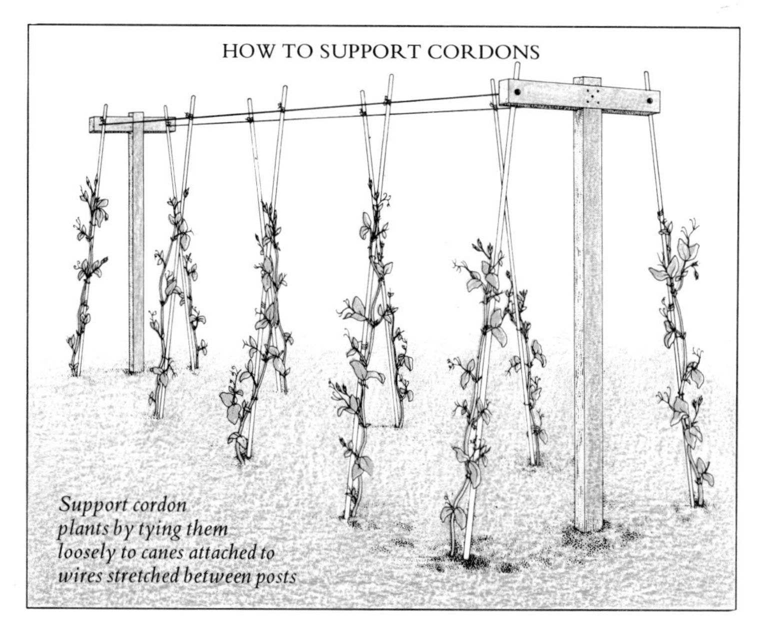

Support cordon plants by tying them loosely to canes attached to wires stretched between posts

REMOVING UNNECESSARY GROWTH

1 *When plants are 9 in. high, remove the weakest shoots carefully*

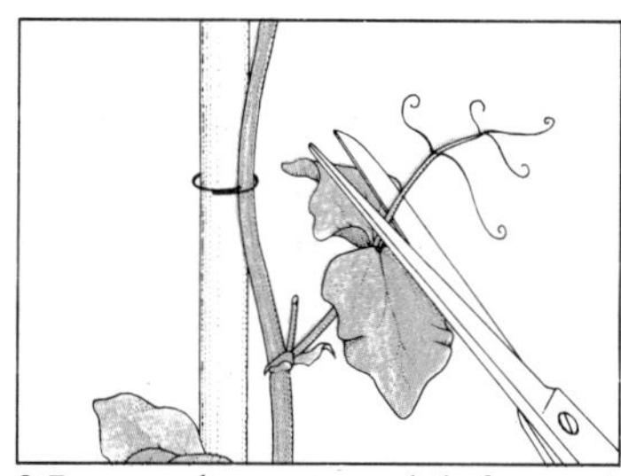

2 *Remove the young tendrils from each pair of leaflets*

3 *Tie each main shoot to a cane and pinch off all young side-shoots*

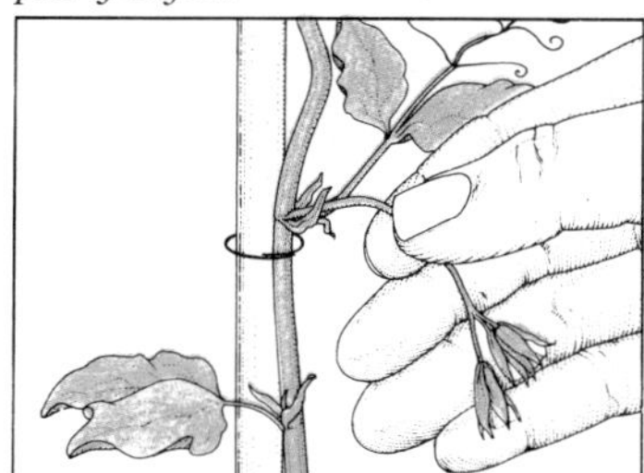

4 *As soon as buds appear, remove any stems bearing less than four buds*

How to grow biennials

Biennials are plants that complete their life-cycle in two growing seasons. They produce leaves and sometimes stems during the first year, but do not flower until the next year.

Generally included among biennials are some plants that are actually perennials, but are usually grown as biennials. This is because after producing vigorous growth and plenty of blooms in their second year, they deteriorate to such an extent that it is not worth retaining them. Examples of this type of plant are Brompton stocks, polyanthus, sweet williams, forget-me-nots and wallflowers.

Sow seeds between May and July. Prepare a bed in a sunny or lightly shaded position. The soil should be fertile but not too rich, otherwise weak plants will result.

Draw drills and sow seeds as for hardy annuals (p. 27). Do not sow thickly, or spindly plants will result. If the weather is dry, water in the seeds with a sprinkler or a watering can fitted with a rose.

Life-cycle of the wallflower *One of the most widely grown biennials, the wallflower blooms in spring at the same time as many bulbs. The life of the wallflower starts almost a year earlier, when the seeds are sown*

When the seedlings are 2–4 in. high, lift them carefully and transplant them to another sunny or lightly shaded nursery bed.

If the weather is dry when you are transplanting, water the plants thoroughly.

If it is more convenient, plants can be raised in a cold greenhouse or cold frame and then pricked out into seed trays or beds, as for half-hardy annuals (p. 29). Sow between May and July and take care not to allow the temperature to rise above about 20°C (68°F).

It is essential for biennials to be planted out in their flowering positions by mid-October, otherwise they may not have a chance to establish themselves before the onset of severe weather. This includes those that have been raised in a greenhouse or frame.

Before planting, clear the planting-out bed, dig over the soil and work in a light dressing of well-rotted manure or garden compost, together with 4 oz. (4 rounded tablespoons) of sterilised bonemeal or 2 oz. of superphosphate.

Lift the biennials from their first quarters, easing them out with a fork, with as many roots attached as possible. If the soil is very dry, water it first to ease lifting and lessen damage to the roots.

After lifting the plants, put them into their permanent positions as soon as possible, before their roots can dry out. Firm in the plants and water them.

In cold areas, plants put out in exposed positions will need winter protection. Lay light evergreen branches around them.

To replace plants lost through winter cold, it is wise to retain a few plants in the first bed. In spring they can then be used to fill in any gaps caused by plants dying.

Although biennials are usually transplanted, they can be thinned in their sowing positions and allowed to grow on and flower.

Treat the plants in summer as for hardy annuals (p. 28).

1 *Between May and July, sow the seeds thinly – to avoid spindly plants*

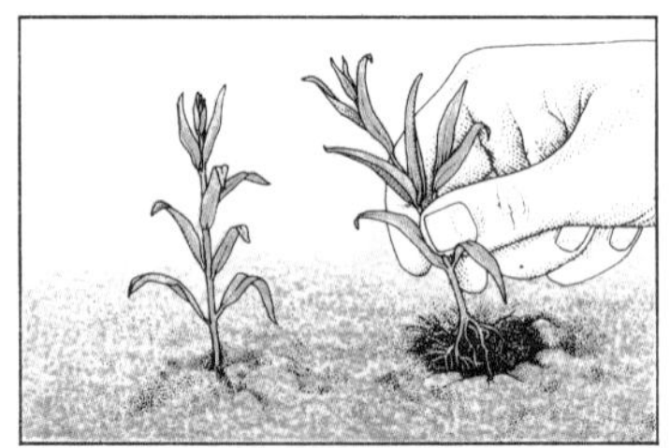

2 *Six weeks later, when plants are 2–4 in. high, transplant to a new bed*

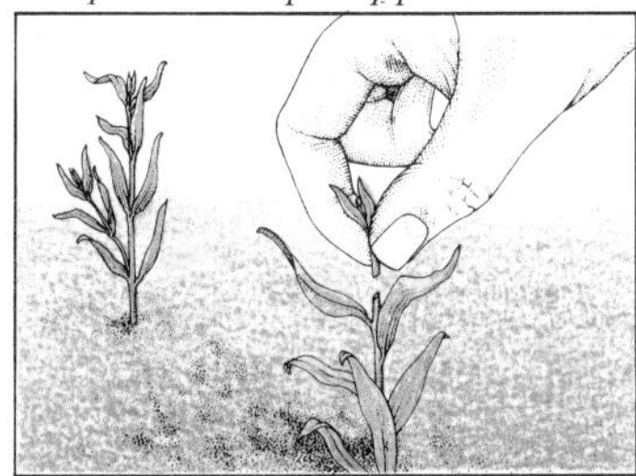

3 *A few weeks later, pinch out the tip of each plant to make it bushy*

4 *By mid-October at the latest, plant in final positions, perhaps with bulbs*

Annuals and biennials for cut flowers

A special flower bed can be set aside for growing annuals and biennials to provide a succession of cut flowers. If it is kept some distance from the house it will not spoil the appearance of the garden with its regimental lines of plants.

Sow the seeds in rows, allowing enough space between seeds to give the plants plenty of room for development, and to make it easy to hoe between them.

Sow four rows, then leave a space before sowing another four, and so on. The spaces will serve as paths from which to pick the flowers without trampling on them.

In a small garden, where there is no room for special beds, plants can be thinned of their blooms instead of being stripped entirely.

The best times of day for cutting flowers are early morning and evening when the sun is not too hot. Water the plants thoroughly the day before cutting and, when cutting, take a container of water with you and place the blooms in it.

Try always to cut strong, well-fed plants – these will have succulent stems that will draw up water well.

Cut the base of each stem at an angle to produce a larger surface for absorbing water. Strip the leaves from that part of the stem that will be in water, or they will soon make it stagnant.

Place the flowers up to their necks in deep containers of water in a cool place for 8–12 hours so that they can take up water before being handled and put in a warm room.

Examples of annuals and biennials that will last well in water after cutting are: antirrhinum, aster, calendula, candytuft, carnation, clarkia, cosmos, dahlia, digitalis, gaillardia, godetia, gypsophila, helichrysum, larkspur, mignonette, nigella, stock, sunflower, sweet pea, verbena and zinnia.

Gladiolus 'Picardy' (Large flowered)

Bulbs & corms

From the first January snowdrop to the last autumn nerine, bulbs and corms provide a wealth of colour throughout the year and most need little attention

The wide range of hardy bulbs and corms available from nurserymen and garden supply centres is one of the greatest assets for easy gardening. Once planted, they will happily look after themselves for years, with the minimum of attention.

While the large majority of herbaceous perennials, annuals and bedding plants flower only during the summer months, the outdoor flowering season for bulbs extends from January right through to December. As the changing seasons of the year unfold, bulbs herald each new phase – from the first winter snowdrop to the last autumn nerine or crocus.

Another advantage of bulb growing is the ease with which these plants adapt themselves to their habitats. They grow well in most soils, seldom need mulching, feeding or staking, and for the most part thrive equally well in light shade and full sun. In every garden, however small, there is room for bulbs. The spring-flowering bulbs in particular flourish in a large number of settings. They can be naturalised in great swathes in lawns and wild gardens. Clumps of bulbs brighten the beds and borders before they reawaken after the dormant season. They nestle in vivid patches beneath trees and shrubs, and fill the odd corners of rock gardens and paved areas. They will grow in tubs, pots, window-boxes and even hanging baskets. In winter, they fill the home with fragrance and colour. Flowers of most bulbs last surprisingly well when they are cut, and are ideal for flower arrangements.

The finest displays are best prepared if some sort of planning is undertaken. It is worth while roughing out planting plans on paper.

Before planning, however, it is a good idea to study schemes in other gardens, both public and private. Also, do not hesitate to experiment. Although mistakes may occur at first, through experience you will gradually learn which are the best forms of grouping, which colours and flowers associate well with one another and which clash, or where a splash of contrasting colour is needed, and so on.

Most specialist bulb growers offer both species and hybrid plants. The species are true replicas of bulbs growing in the wild. Hybrid plants are obtained by cross-breeding, through pollination, of two species or varieties within the same genus. When a satisfactory strain is obtained, it must be reproduced by division of the bulblets from the parent bulb. Popular hybrids are cheaper than species and have larger, more vivid-coloured, blooms. They are often sold by weight, especially narcissi. Occasionally, new hybrid strains are introduced and offered for sale at extremely high prices; it takes 20–25 years to develop a new hybrid and then produce enough bulbs to make it economic.

While many new narcissi have been raised in the British Isles, the Dutch bulb breeders are mainly responsible for the development of the tulip and hyacinth hybrids.

Although some bulbs may be expensive to buy, most will reproduce themselves steadily each year without any special attention.

Bulbs and corms fall into four main categories: winter and early-spring flowering, spring flowering, summer flowering and autumn flowering.

First flowers of the year The well-known snowdrop (galanthus) is the first to make its appearance each year, raising its drooping white bell flowers above the ground in January. Shortly afterwards come the blue, star-shaped *Chionodoxa luciliae*, the early crocuses, cyclamens and scillas.

Another forerunner of spring is the small winter aconite (*Eranthis hyemalis*), with its bright golden flowers above a ruffled collar of green leaves.

All of these plants associate well with one another, planted in groups beneath deciduous trees and in the rock garden. For an indoor display, these winter-flowering bulbs can also be grown in pots and taken indoors just as the flowers begin to show colour. After flowering, plant them out in the garden.

Heralds of spring March, April and May are the months when the spring-flowering bulbs appear. First come the crocuses, the green-tipped shoots pushing through earth and grass to reveal their goblet-shaped blooms of yellow, lavender, white, mauve and violet; some are striped or heavily marked with a contrasting colour, and in bright sunshine they all open flat, revealing the deep golden anthers.

The large narcissus group flowers from February to April. Many catalogues list the trumpet-shaped types by their common name of daffodil, and those with short cup flowers as narcissi, although botanically they all belong to the narcissus genus. Many of them are sweetly scented, and they can be left undisturbed for years in beds and borders, or naturalised in grass, while the smaller types make an effective display in rock gardens.

Other heralds of spring are the hyacinths and muscaris, the early tulips and the spring snowflake (*Leucojum vernum*), with flowers like rounded snowdrops, the white petals tipped with pale green or yellow.

Crocuses and narcissi look best naturalised in grass or planted in bold groups beneath trees. Other spring-flowering bulbs are more effective in formal planting schemes, where they mix well with wallflowers and polyanthus. Muscaris and large-flowered crocuses can also be grown in hanging baskets, where they show to great advantage when combined with spring-flowering heathers.

Hyacinths are ideal for planting in window-boxes, so that the heavy scent of the dense flower spikes can be fully appreciated. For outdoor planting, it is advisable to use the smaller-sized bulbs – about 5 in. (12–13 cm.) in circumference – in preference to the larger bulbs for indoor flowering. The flower spikes are somewhat smaller, but they withstand wind and rain better. The small species, such as *H. amethystinus* and *H. azureus*, are ideal for a rock garden or the front of a border.

The first species tulips, perfect in rock gardens and raised beds, appear in March, while the larger hybrids flower through April and May. The Darwin tulips are probably the most popular, with their strong stems, each of which carries the typical cup-shaped flower. They are majestic when grown in groups in formal bedding schemes. These bulbs may also be grown in rows for cutting. The flowers last over a longer period than the late-blooming parrot tulips which flower in May.

Vivid summer displays The onset of early summer is marked by the appearance of erythroniums, the elegant fritillarias, the bright blue scillas and the anemones. Being small in stature, they are ideally suited for the front of borders or for growing in troughs.

Ranunculus, ixias and sparaxis come next, in warm sunny borders, where they slowly give way to the ornamental onions (allium) and the species gladioli.

High summer brings the stately gladiolus hybrids, the arching sprays of crocosmias and the fragrant acidantheras. All of these are equally at home in herbaceous borders or among shrubs. For cut flowers, a row or two of gladioli can be grown in the vegetable garden.

Many small bulbs, such as Iris reticulata, Anemone blanda, Narcissus triandrus albus *and muscaris (grape hyacinth) are ideal plants for the rock garden. They can also be used to fill the front of a border, or be grown in tubs and window-boxes*

Every colour of the spectrum is represented in gladiolus hybrids. The trumpet-shaped flowers, in massed array along the strong stems, open from the lower part of the stem upwards. The hybrids range through the large flowered, the butterfly, the miniature and the primulinus groups. Their brilliant display lasts well into September.

Colour in autumn and winter In September the dainty autumn crocuses (colchicum) and *Crocus speciosus* take over from the gladiolus hybrids. Like the spring-flowering crocuses, these are best grown in bold groups beneath deciduous trees and in pockets in the rock garden or, in the case of colchicums, naturalised in grass, in clumps or drifts where they make an attractive splash of colour and may be left undisturbed for many years.

Autumn also brings *Amaryllis belladonna* with massive trumpet-shaped, pink or white flowers. Then there are nerines, proudly carrying their bright pink and red flowers on tall leafless stems, and sternbergias with their bright yellow, crocus-shaped flowers which bloom from September to November.

As the year closes, bulbs of hyacinths, daffodils and tulips, potted in September for indoor-flowering, brighten the dark months. And outdoors, *Cyclamen coum* planted in small clusters under the bare trees, open their fine pink and white flowers in late December, harbingers of another spring.

The most-loved flowers from bulbs and corms

Narcissus 'Caravelle' (Trumpet daffodil)

Narcissus 'Merlin' (Small-cupped narcissus)

Crocus vernus 'Remembrance'

Daffodils and narcissi

No garden is complete without clumps of golden-yellow, trumpet-shaped daffodils, dancing in the spring breezes.

Daffodils were known to man in ancient times – sculptures of them have been found in Egyptian tombs, and narcissi are referred to in the works of Homer and Socrates.

The daffodil is one of the best bulbs for naturalising in the garden, as it grows well under trees, in corners of lawns and on grassy banks.

Most garden varieties of daffodil are raised from the wild narcissus. There are now more than 8000 varieties of narcissus, grouped into a number of divisions according to flower shape and colour.

The flower consists of a central trumpet or cup, surrounded by six petals. Daffodils have trumpets that are as long, or longer than the surrounding petals.

The trumpet is frilled or flared at the outer edge, and the six overlapping petals are usually pointed at the tips. Colours vary: in some, such as the old favourite 'King Alfred', both trumpet and petals are clear yellow; others have petals of a deeper or paler shade than the trumpets. Bi-colour daffodils have yellow trumpets and white petals, and a third group has both white trumpets and white petals.

The word narcissus is popularly used to mean varieties with a short central trumpet, no larger than a shallow cup. However, between the daffodils and the short-cupped narcissi come varieties with various-sized cups. With these there is a great variation in colour – the cups and petals range from white through cream and yellow to pink, red and orange; they are sometimes the same colour, and sometimes contrasting.

Dissimilar to both daffodils and short-cupped narcissi are the double-flowered varieties, in which the cups are indistinguishable from the petals. They are white, cream, pale yellow or orange.

Triandrus and cyclamineus narcissi have pendent, bell-shaped trumpets and backswept petals. Tazetta narcissi carry several blooms on each stem. And poeticus narcissi have frilled coloured centres and conspicuous white petals that do not overlap each other.

Jonquils are outstanding for their sweet fragrance. Each stem bears a small cluster of flowers with shallow cream, yellow or orange cups and rounded or pointed petals in contrasting colours.

See list of narcissi in the Guide beginning on page 329.

Crocuses

Massed crocuses make a brilliant show of colour in early spring, when there are few other plants in flower in the garden.

The yellow, blue or purple blooms open before the daffodils, and – as with daffodils – look best growing in grass or in groups among shrubs.

Most crocuses grown today are hybrids or named varieties. But some species are also obtainable, such as *Crocus ancyrensis* (also called 'Golden Bunch') which produces up to 20 small flowers from each corm.

As well as the spring-flowering crocuses there are others that flower in autumn and winter. They all grow from small, flattish corms. The winter and spring crocuses produce their stemless globular flowers at the same time as the grass-like leaves. The autumn-flowering type develops leaves after the flowers.

The crocus flower, 3–5 in. high, is composed of six petals which in the hybrids and named varieties are rounded, and in the species, pointed. In bright sun, the petals open out flat, revealing the conspicuous golden or orange anthers.

Winter-flowering crocuses, which appear outdoors from February and onwards, have been developed from *C. chrysanthus* and other species. The flowers are 3 in. high and range in colour through shades of yellow, blue and purple. Many are marked with contrasting stripes, or have markings at the base of the petals; the inner colour frequently differs from the outside.

The large-flowered crocuses which bloom in March are Dutch varieties of *C. vernus*. They are the largest of the crocuses. The flowers measure 5 in., and are white, blue, lilac, red-purple and golden-yellow, sometimes striped with different colours.

Autumn-flowering crocuses appear from September to November. The flowers, which are 4–5 in. high, are pure white, lavender or violet-blue. They are similar to the larger-flowered autumn crocus (*Colchicum autumnale*), which bears pinkish or lilac-coloured flowers.

Gladioli

The name gladiolus comes from the Latin meaning a sword, which describes the shape of the leaves; but it is the superb flowers which make the plants so attractive.

The colours vary from pale yellow to bright scarlet, providing a brilliant summer display and long-lasting cut flowers.

The individual florets, on a long thick stem, all face in the same direction and are set on either side of the stem. The flower spike may measure up to 2 ft and consists of from 16 to 26 trumpet-shaped florets, composed of six petals; the lower three, known as the falls, are slightly reflexed. The flowers are sometimes all the same colour, but more often bi-coloured or tri-coloured, with conspicuous markings in the throat of each floret.

Gladioli are half-hardy corms and are listed in four different groups, according to the size and shape of the flowers. The large-flowered hybrids, more suitable for garden display than floral decoration, produce 2 ft long flower spikes, and the triangular, overlapping florets are 4–6 in. wide.

Primulinus gladioli have more slender flower spikes, 15 in. long, with separate, 2–3 in. wide florets, arranged in a zigzag pattern. They differ from the typical gladiolus flower in that usually the upper petal is hooded and folded over the anthers and stigma.

The miniature gladioli also have the upper petal slightly hooded, but the flowers are smaller (1½–2 in.) than the primulinus gladioli. The florets, which often have frilled or ruffled petals, are set closely on 15 in. long spikes.

Butterfly gladioli are similar to the large-flowered varieties in petal and floret arrangement, but the spikes are shorter (up to 18 in.), the edges of the petals are often frilled and ruffled, and the individual florets are about 3 in. wide. They have the most distinctive throat markings.

Hyacinths

In the drab days of winter, the scented blooms of hyacinths bring colour and cheer into normally flowerless rooms.

Although hyacinths are widely used for indoor flowering, they are also ideal as outdoor plants and for window-boxes and tubs.

Some growers produce heat-treated bulbs which, if planted in autumn, will flower indoors at Christmas, instead of from January onwards. The technique of forcing bulbs into early flower is illustrated on page 41.

Most hyacinths are derived from a single species, *Hyacinthus orientalis*, and most of the modern varieties have the characteristic large, single-spike flowers. They are known as Dutch hyacinths.

Large bulbs with large flower heads are ideal for the home, but outdoors, smaller bulbs with smaller stalks and flower heads withstand the rain and severe weather better.

The strongly scented flowers are available in white, cream, yellow, salmon, pink, red, light and dark blue and purple.

The Roman hyacinths (*H. orientalis albulus*) differ in having a smaller flower spike to each bulb. There are very large bulbs with 9–12 flower spikes, called 'Multiflora'. The individual flowers, in shades of white, pink and blue, are more loosely set on the spike than the Dutch hyacinth. Best grown indoors, they flower from January to March; treated bulbs will bloom at Christmas.

Snowdrops

The snowdrop is one of the earliest heralds of spring, as the pearl-like green buds push up through the snow in January and February. In very cold weather the buds stay closed, and will not open until they feel the warmth of the sun.

Snowdrops (galanthus) should not be confused with snowflakes (leucojums) which flower later in spring or in summer. Snowdrops have three long petals and three short ones. The six petals of snowflakes are all the same size, and two or more flowers are carried on each stem to the snowdrop's one.

Snowdrops can be planted in groups in a herbaceous or mixed border, in a corner of the lawn or in rough grass under trees.

The bulbs dry out quickly if left in the open, so it is best to replant them as soon as possible after flowering. If you buy dry bulbs get them into the ground as soon as possible. They may not flower well the first year, as they take time to become established, but once recovered they flower well and need little attention. They grow best in a heavy moist soil, with some shade.

Although they are rarely seen indoors, snowdrops can be grown in pots in the same way as crocuses or hyacinths. Keep them comparatively cool. A cold frame is best until the flower buds are visible, then they may be brought into a cool greenhouse or room preferably not above 10°C(50°F).

Tulips

More than 300 years ago the tulip was brought from Turkey to Holland, and from there to the rest of Europe. In the intervening centuries, Dutch bulb growers have bred, cross-bred and altered the original varieties to such an extent that it has become necessary to divide them into groups according to their different characteristics.

Tulips, like other bulbs, produce a wealth of colour with little attention. Only pests, diseases or flooding will prevent them flowering the first year after planting.

The tulip grows from a pointed and thin-skinned bulb which produces a single erect flower stem. One or two large, lance-shaped leaves appear near ground level, and two or three smaller ones higher up on the stem. The flower is goblet-shaped with six petals.

According to grouping, the tulip flower varies from a short goblet to large and rounded (Darwin tulips), through double, paeony-like or pointed, lily-shaped blooms. Others are angular in outline or they open flat into star-shaped blooms (Kaufmanniana tulips) or into twisted and fringed flowers (parrot tulips).

A variety that was more popular in Victorian days than now is the Rembrandt tulip. It is similar in shape to the Darwin, but the contrasting colours are fused or 'broken'.

Tulips are available in many colours – white, red, pink, orange, violet, mauve and purple. Some are self-coloured, but many of them have two colours.

Species tulips, available from specialist bulb growers and ideal for rock gardens, are exquisite, with short, sturdy stems and goblet-shaped flowers of exceptionally brilliant self or bi-colours.

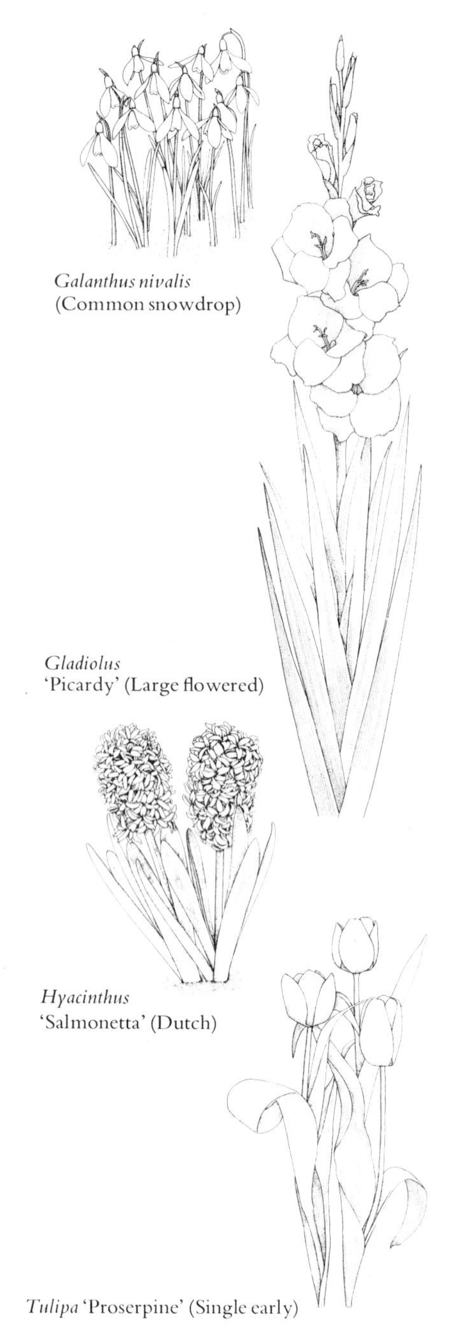

Galanthus nivalis (Common snowdrop)

Gladiolus 'Picardy' (Large flowered)

Hyacinthus 'Salmonetta' (Dutch)

Tulipa 'Proserpine' (Single early)

How to plant bulbs and corms

Choosing sites and preparing the ground

Given a reasonable, well-drained soil and protection from strong winds, most bulbs will thrive in any part of the garden. They can be grown in beds, borders, rock gardens and tubs, and some of the small ones, such as snowdrops, winter aconites and crocuses, can be planted underneath shrubs and trees.

Others, especially daffodils and crocuses, naturalise themselves happily in grass, where they can be left undisturbed for years.

Most bulbs prefer a sunny position, but a few – cyclamens, endymions, erythroniums, snowdrops and winter aconites – all do well in shaded sites. Some bulbs, including acidantheras, amaryllis, nerines and sparaxis, are sensitive to cold weather and are best grown at the foot of a south-facing wall where they get maximum sun, and protection from wind. If planting spring-flowering bulbs in grass, bear in mind that not until the leaves have turned yellow can the grass around them be mown. So plant them on a site which will not be in the foreground of the view from the house.

Plant spring-flowering bulbs from September to November, and summer-flowering in March – or April/May for the less-hardy types. Plant autumn-flowering bulbs during July and August.

Whatever the time of year, the planting site must first be carefully prepared. Dig the ground over and remove all weeds and stones.

Mix peat or well-rotted garden compost into the soil (a 2 gallon bucket to the square yard), and leave it to settle for a few days before planting. Fertilisers are usually unnecessary, but on poor soils mix in either sulphate of potash, or John Innes base fertiliser at 3 oz. (about 3 tablespoons) to the square yard.

Bulbs in rock gardens and paved areas

Any low-growing bulbs, whether spring, summer or autumn flowering, establish themselves easily in rock gardens, and in small spaces between paving stones.

Remove any covering of gravel or granite chippings from the site and dig out holes twice as deep as the bulbs with a trowel. Plant the bulbs singly, or in small groups of three or four.

After planting, level the soil with the trowel, replace the gravel and label the site.

Good bulbs to provide welcome colour in the rock garden early in the year include: snowdrops (*Galanthus*), winter crocuses (*Crocus chrysanthus*), *Chionodoxa luciliae*, hardy cyclamens (*Cyclamen coum*), aconites (*Eranthis*), dwarf narcissi and *Scilla bifolia* and *S. tubergeniana*.

After the spring bulbs there are dwarf alliums and gladioli to give summer colour. These can be followed by sternbergias and autumn crocuses, including many species that bloom throughout winter.

Small bulbs look particularly attractive growing through such mat-forming plants as thyme and acaena. The bright green foliage provides a striking background to the flowering bulbs.

Where the mat-forming plant is firmly rooted in, slightly loosen it with a hand fork and then plant the bulbs with a blunt dibber.

If the plant has only a central root, as with *Gypsophila repens*, roll the matted stems to one side and plant the bulbs with a narrow trowel.

Some bulbous plants, particularly snowdrops, are best transplanted while still growing. After flowering, these should be planted at the same depth or slightly deeper and kept moist until the leaves start to turn yellow.

Planting bulbs in groups for formal display

Before planting a formal display, lay the bulbs over the area, spacing them at regular intervals. The distance between each bulb should be equivalent to the eventual spread of the plant. Begin planting from the centre of the site. With a trowel, dig holes about twice as deep as the bulbs. Insert each bulb, point or bud uppermost, and give it a twist so that the base is firmly in contact with the soil. Cover the bulb with the excavated soil and plant the others in the same way.

When the whole area has been planted, set a label in the centre for identification and mark the perimeter of the area in some way, so that other plants will not later be planted there in error.

If new herbaceous perennials or bedding plants are being put out at the same time – as, for instance, when wallflowers are being grown with mid-season tulips – plant them in their positions before setting the bulbs between them.

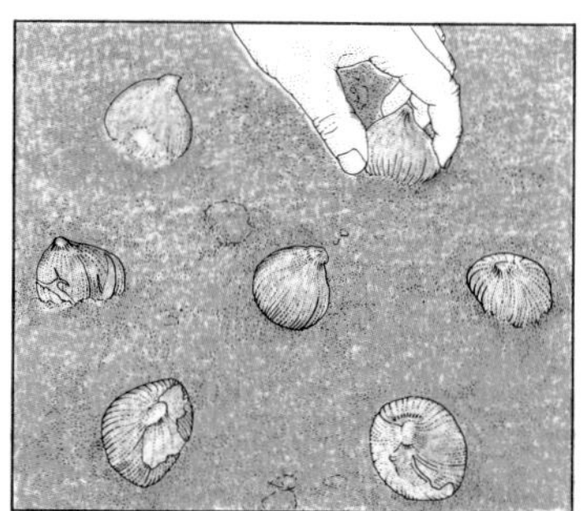

1 *Lay the bulbs over the chosen area, spacing them at regular intervals*

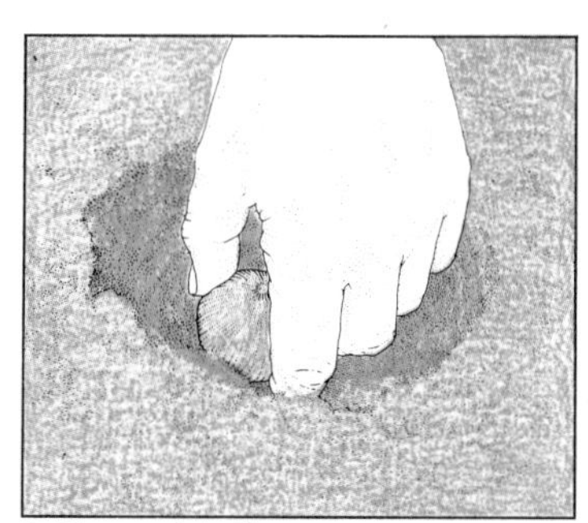

2 *Place each bulb, point uppermost, into a planting hole twice its depth*

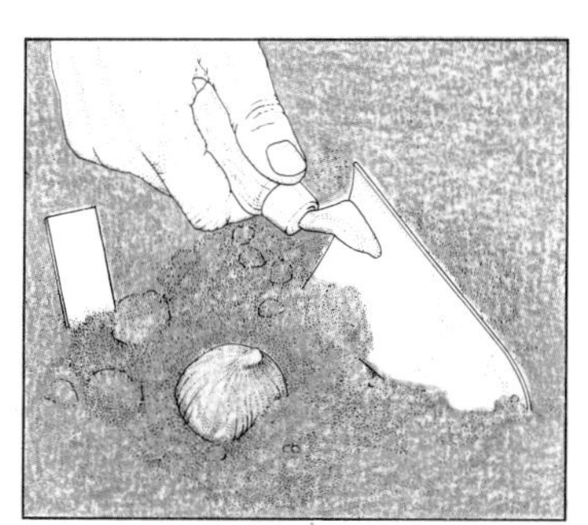

3 *Cover the bulbs with soil removed from the planting holes. Label the area*

Growing bulbs for cut flowers

When picking flowers for indoor decoration, it is advisable to cut only a few blooms from each clump so as not to exhaust the bulbs.

Where space allows, however, a piece of ground can be set aside for growing rows of narcissi, tulips and gladioli.

Prepare the soil in the normal way, and plant the bulbs slightly closer than the eventual spread of the plant. Allow $1\frac{1}{2}$–2 ft between the rows.

When cutting bulb flowers, take as few leaves as possible. Cut the flowers in the early morning or late evening, using sharp scissors or a sharp knife. Then place them in water in a cool place for several hours, to allow them to soak up plenty of water, which will prolong their life when they are placed in the warmth of a living-room.

Lifting, drying and storing bulbs and corms

Bulbs are lifted from the ground for three main reasons: to make room for other plants; because they are not hardy enough to spend the winter outdoors; or because they are congested.

Spring-flowering bulbs such as hyacinths, narcissi and tulips should ideally be left until the foliage has died down. This is seldom possible if the space is needed for summer plants, and the bulbs must therefore be dug up and transferred to a spare piece of ground to complete their growing season.

Insert a garden fork in the ground, well clear of the plants and deep enough to come right underneath the clump. Carefully ease up the bulbs, complete with soil, leaves and stems. Crumble away the soil round the bulbs without rubbing off the skins. Discard any bulb that is pulpy or shows signs of rotting. Now move the bulbs to a spare bed in a sunny or lightly shaded part of the garden.

Dig a trench, about 12 in. deep, 12 in. wide, and long enough to take all the lifted bulbs. Lay a piece of fine wire or plastic netting at the bottom of the trench and place the bulbs on it at a slight angle. They can be set almost touching each other, but at least half the stems and leaves must be clear of the top of the trench. Leave the wire netting to protrude above the trench a little at both ends.

Fill in the trench with soil, and water thoroughly during dry spells. When the leaves and stems have shrivelled, the bulbs can be taken up for storing. Just pull the wire netting at the ends and the bulbs are lifted out. If only a few bulbs are lifted before they have finished growing, it is easier to lay them in deep trays of damp peat. The rows can overlap each other, but the leaves should be clear of the peat. Cover the bulbs with more peat, and place the trays in a lightly shaded place to complete the drying out. Keep the peat moist.

When the leaves have withered completely, remove the bulbs from the trench or trays; pull off the dead leaves, roots and old shrivelled skins. The bulblets attached to the mother bulb can be used for propagation; otherwise discard them. Place the cleaned bulbs, uncovered, in single layers in shallow boxes and store them in a cool, dry place until replanting in autumn.

In the mildest districts, gladioli may be left undisturbed in the ground throughout the year, but elsewhere the corms should be lifted when the leaves begin to turn brown in October. Lift them with a garden fork. Cut off the top stems and leaves about 1 in. above the corm. Place the corms, uncovered, in trays in a cool, airy shed, until they are dry, after seven to ten days.

Break away the old shrivelled corms and separate the small cormlets, which can be used for increasing the stock.

Remove the tough outer skins from the large corms and examine them carefully; burn any that show signs of lesions or rotting. Dust the remaining corms with HCH to control thrips, and with quintozene to prevent dry rot and scab.

Store the corms in trays, in a cool but frost-free place, until spring. Acidantheras, ixias and sparaxis should also be lifted in October and dried and stored in exactly the same way as gladioli.

Overgrown clumps of hardy bulbs can be lifted any time between July and September, split up and replanted at once. Congested clumps of snowdrops should be divided after flowering in March.

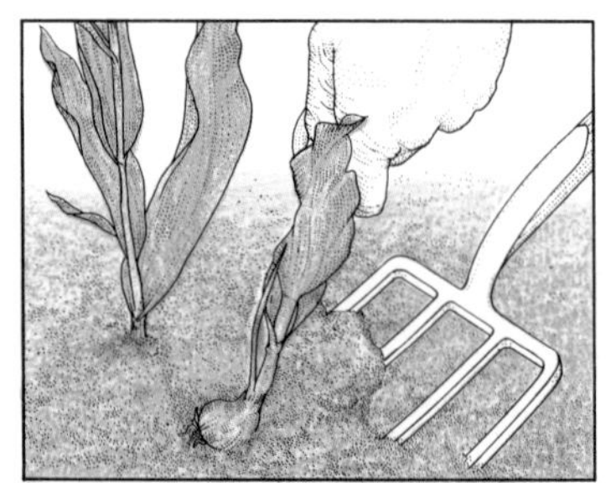

1 *After the flowers fade, lift the bulbs with a fork and remove the soil*

2 *Lay the bulbs in deep trays of damp peat or, with large numbers, set them on fine wire or plastic netting at the base of a trench, then fill with soil*

3 *When the leaves and stems have all shrivelled, lift the bulbs*

4 *Before storing, first pull off the dead leaves from each bulb*

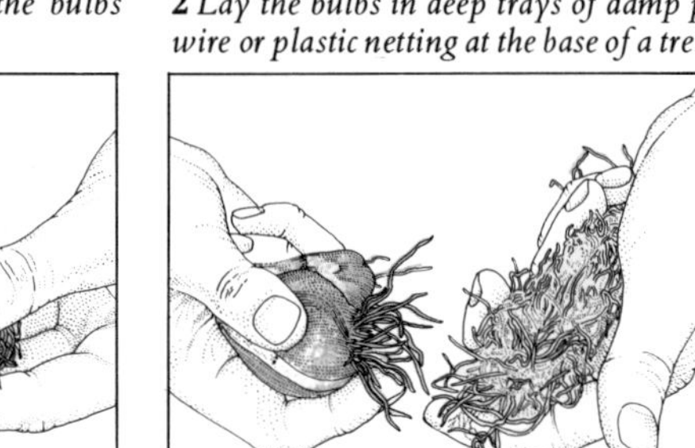

5 *Then remove the dead roots and peel away the dead, papery skins*

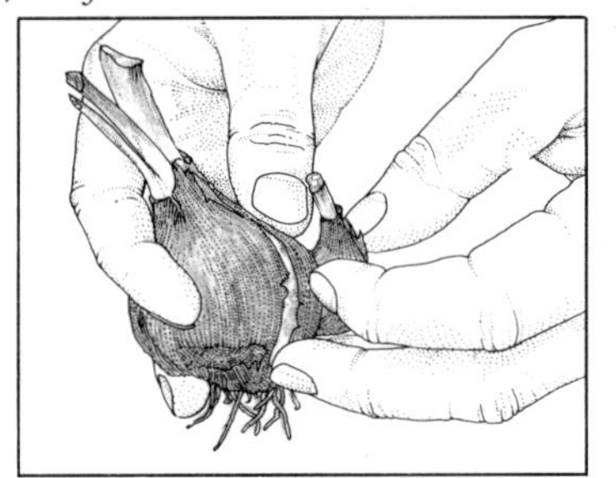

6 *Detach any small bulbs, which can be used to grow new bulbs*

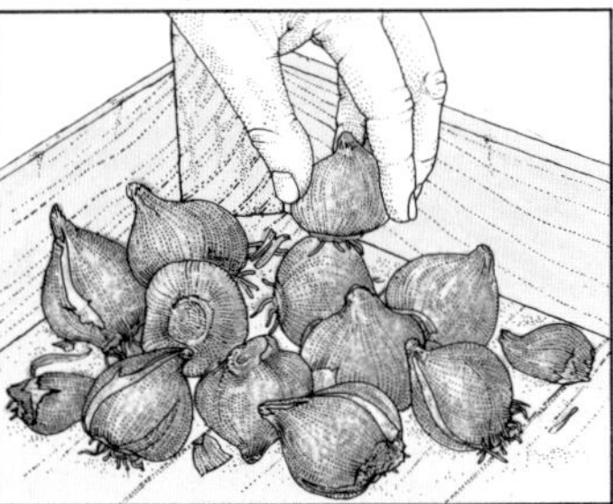

7 *Put the bulbs in boxes and store in a dry, cool place until planting time*

How to grow bulbs for indoor flowering

Many of the hardy bulbs that bloom in the open during spring can be made to flower indoors weeks earlier, by potting them up in late summer, allowing time in cool conditions for root growth and then forcing flowers to grow by placing them in gentle heat.

The most popular spring-flowering bulbs for indoor flowering are hyacinths, crocuses, narcissi and daffodils, snowdrops, scillas, dwarf irises and tulips. Growers subject a proportion of some species – notably hyacinths, daffodils and tulips – to varying periods of heat and cold, which induces very early flowering, around Christmas.

Bulb catalogues usually indicate those varieties that respond best to indoor flowering. Of the narcissi, 'Paper White' and 'Soleil d'Or' are particularly suitable. Good daffodils for forcing are 'Golden Harvest' and 'King Alfred'. For forced tulips, use early single or early double-flowered varieties. Large-flowered Dutch hyacinths are available in a wide range of colours. The crocuses recommended for forcing are the *C. chrysanthus* varieties, such as 'Blue Pearl', and the large-flowered *C. vernus* varieties, such as 'Little Dorrit'.

The best compost to use is John Innes No. 2 potting compost, or a proprietary soil-less compost. A special bulb fibre, cleaner to use than compost, is also available but, as it contains no fertiliser, the bulbs will receive no nourishment to store away. They may be planted in the garden after flowering, but may take two years to flower again.

Bulbs can be planted singly in 4–5 in. pots, but look more effective close together in bulb containers or bowls.

Potting up bulbs for forcing

Bulbs should be potted up for forcing in late August or September. Bought or stored bulbs sometimes have old roots attached. Trim these off with scissors, as close to the base as possible.

If the container has no drainage holes, place a few small lumps of charcoal over the base. These absorb surplus water and any gases created by decomposing material in the compost, and so prevent the compost becoming too acid. This is unnecessary with bulb fibre, which already contains charcoal. If the container has drainage holes, cover them with stones or bits of old pot.

Put a layer of moist compost over the charcoal or stones (bulb fibre must be thoroughly moist). The depth depends on the size of container and bulbs: small bulbs, such as crocuses and tulips, should be covered by the compost, while the necks of the larger hyacinth and daffodil bulbs should just show above the compost level.

Press the bulbs on to the compost so that their bases are in firm contact with it. Plant the bulbs so that they are touching, and pack compost around them so they are held firm when the roots start to grow. Level off the compost about ½ in. below the top of the container.

POTTING BULBS IN LATE SUMMER

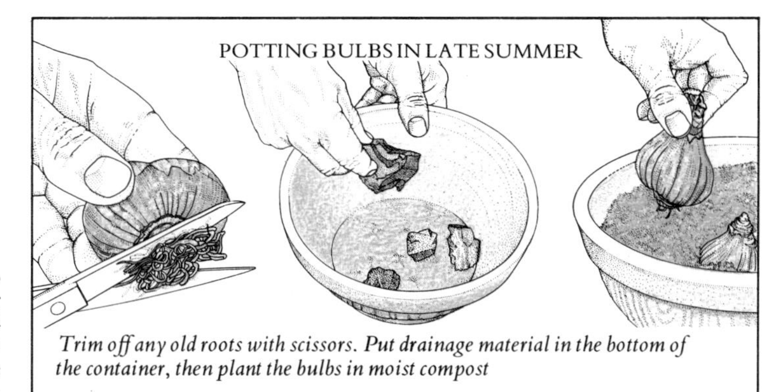

Trim off any old roots with scissors. Put drainage material in the bottom of the container, then plant the bulbs in moist compost

HOW TO OBTAIN A MASSED DISPLAY OF DAFFODILS

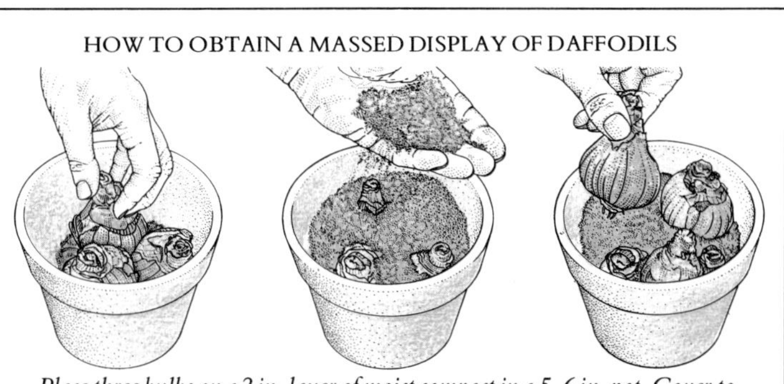

Place three bulbs on a 2 in. layer of moist compost in a 5–6 in. pot. Cover to the necks, then set three more bulbs between them and repeat

Storing spring-flowering bulbs after potting

Spring-flowering bulbs are hardy and need a prolonged period of low temperature and darkness after potting to allow them to develop.

Spread moist peat over the bottom of a large tub or box and place the planted containers on it. Fill in with more moist peat until the containers are covered by 2–3 in. Enclose the container with black polythene. Another method is to place pots or bowls on the ground and cover them with peat; or bury the potted bulbs 6 in. below soil level.

Where only one or two containers have been planted, a simple alternative is to put each in a black polythene bag and tie it at the top. Ensure that the bag is full of air, so that shoots do not rub against it.

Keep the containers outdoors in a shaded place or indoors in a cool, dark place at a maximum of 10°C (50°F) for eight to ten weeks.

The containers should occasionally be examined to check that the compost has not dried out.

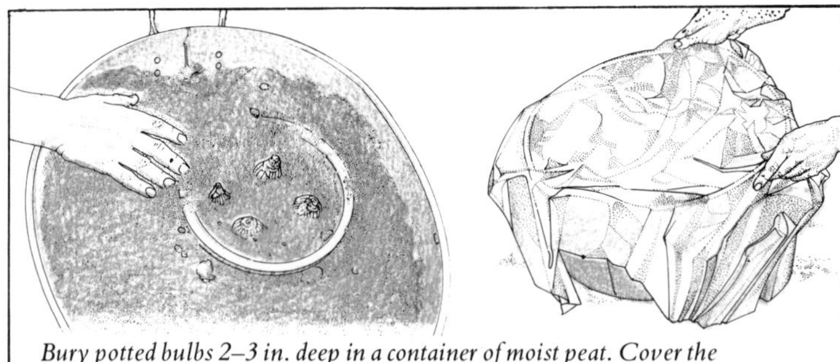

Bury potted bulbs 2–3 in. deep in a container of moist peat. Cover the container with black polythene and put it in a cool, shaded place

Bringing bulb containers indoors for forcing

After eight to ten weeks of storage, when bulbs have produced 1–2 in. high shoots, remove them from their cool beds to a shaded position indoors or in a cool greenhouse with a temperature of 10–16°C (50–61°F). Prepared hyacinths and tulips should be brought inside four to six weeks before flowering, and prepared daffodils six to eight weeks. So, any bulbs for Christmas should be brought in by mid-November.

Gentle forcing for early flowers can begin when the shoots are about 4–5 in. high and the flower buds are visible. Move one bowl at a time into a temperature of 18°C (64°F) to ensure a succession of flowers. Do not move the bowls into higher temperatures until the flowers have started to open.

Keep the compost moist at all times, but avoid over-watering.

The aftercare of forced bulbs

When the flowers have died, cut off the dead heads and plant the bulbs in the garden.

Alternatively, if the bulbs have been grown in compost, water them until the leaves have withered and died down. Then stop watering, to dry off the bulbs. When the compost is thoroughly dry, empty out the contents of the containers. Remove any dried compost, dead roots and dead skin from the bulbs, then store them in boxes in a dry, airy shed until the autumn.

Bulbs that have been grown in compost will often flower outdoors during the first year after planting out, but bulbs that have been grown in bulb fibre may need more time to recover.

Prepared bulbs for Christmas flowering will probably take about two years to flower again.

Growing crocuses and snowdrops in special pots

Special clay pots can be bought for growing small bulbs, such as crocuses and snowdrops, in several layers. The pots have holes round the sides, and the bulbs are planted so that the flowers will grow out through the holes.

Fill one of these pots to half its depth with moist compost or bulb fibre, and plant the bulbs in the compost with their necks showing through the holes. Add more compost and set more bulbs in position. On the top layer, point the necks of the bulbs through the opening.

Like other bulb containers, crocus bowls should be kept in a cool, dark place, preferably outdoors, until the shoots are 1–2 in. high.

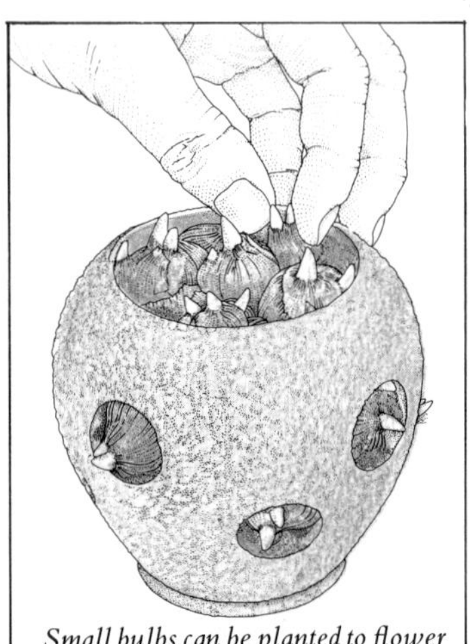

Small bulbs can be planted to flower through holes in pots

Growing hyacinths in glass jars

Hyacinths are ideally suited to growing in water. Most gardening shops sell hyacinth jars with constricted necks for this purpose.

Fill a jar with water to ½ in. from the neck and put in a small lump of charcoal to keep the water fresh. Place a hyacinth bulb in the opening of the jar, root end down.

Put each jar in a cool, dark place until the roots growing into the water are about 4 in. long and leaves are showing. Then move the jars to a warmer and lighter place. Top up the jars with water as the level falls.

At the end of the flowering season, discard the bulbs, which will have used up all their stored nourishment and will be of no further use.

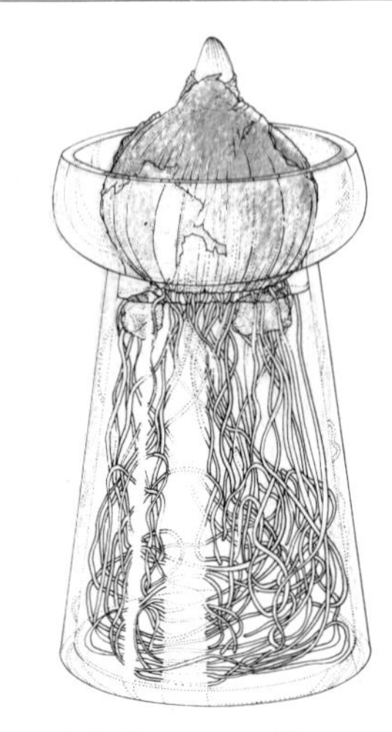

Hyacinth bulbs grow well in water, in special jars with constricted necks

Cacti

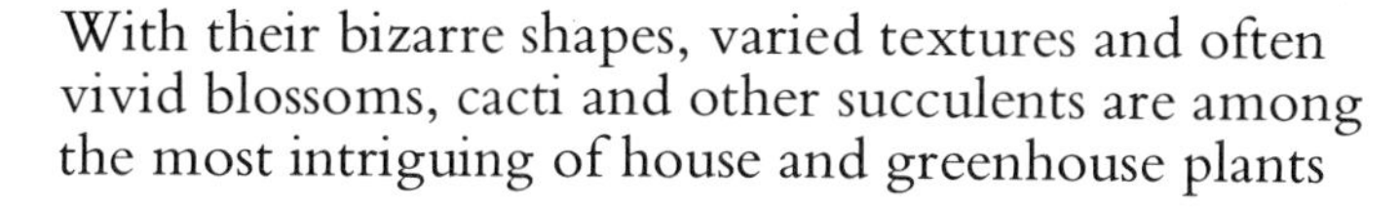

With their bizarre shapes, varied textures and often vivid blossoms, cacti and other succulents are among the most intriguing of house and greenhouse plants

Plants that store water in their tissues during rainy seasons, and draw on it in periods of drought, are called succulents. There are two main types: those that store the water in their leaves and those that store it in their stems.

Cacti, the largest single family of succulents, are the best known examples of the stem type, and the various shapes into which their stems have developed hold a great fascination for gardeners.

Many people who do not have a garden find this no bar to collecting cacti as a hobby for, although a greenhouse is ideal, there are plenty of varieties that will flourish in a warm conservatory or on sunny window-sills, where their bizarre shapes give an original touch to any indoor display of pot plants.

Some of the most spectacular types which might have impressed travellers abroad need the long, hot summers that are rare in the British Isles. But there are many other cacti which will do well in our cooler climate.

It is not always easy to differentiate cacti from other stem succulents, – they are sometimes very similar

in form. The one reliable distinguishing feature is the areoles that cacti always bear. These are small, cushion-like structures on the stems, from which spines and flowers are produced.

Cacti are thought of as plants from parched areas, but they rarely grow in areas where the rainfall is less than 10 in. a year – although some have survived in areas where only 3–4 in. has been recorded.

Cacti also need mineral salts to survive, and although deserts are normally considered to be barren land, the soil is in fact often rich in minerals that originate in weathered rocks.

Desert cacti often receive their year's supply of water in the course of a very short rainy season, during which they grow and flower. Many need a cool, dry winter rest period. The reason that few can survive outdoors in a British winter is not just the cold, but the combination of cold and wet soil conditions.

The desert cacti vary greatly in form. They may grow as columns over 40 ft high, or as tiny spheres less than 1 in. in diameter. Their stems are usually covered in either wax or hairs, which reduce water loss from evaporation.

Recognising a cactus *Most cacti store water in their stems and have areoles (inset, left) which carry spines and flowers. Most other succulents (right) store water in their leaves*

The stems of some other succulents are 'mealy' – covered with a substance which looks like small, powdery porridge oats. This is another method by which cacti reduce water evaporation.

Cacti are usually green, as they contain chlorophyll and carry out photosynthesis, a process normally performed by leaves. Their root systems are extensive, some near the surface to catch dew, others deep delving to pick up ground water low down.

Many desert cacti have spines, which act as a defence against animals trying to eat them.

Cacti also occur in wet forests in Central and South America, where they grow with their roots in the debris that collects in the crotches of trees. Usually these cacti, which include the popular Christmas cactus and the Easter cactus, have flattened, leaf-like stems.

Contrary to the popular belief that they flower only every seven years, most cacti bloom regularly, if they are given the right conditions – although the very large cacti will not flower in a greenhouse that does not allow them to achieve their full size.

The typical flowers are trumpet-shaped, and they vary in size from $\frac{3}{8}$ in. to 6 in. across. Usually they open only in warm sunshine, but there are some whose flowers are seen only at night. If there is prolonged cloud, the flower buds may not develop at all.

In general, cactus flowers are more showy than those of other succulents. The blooms come in many colours, except pure blue, though there are many shades of mauve and violet. Most nocturnal-flowering types are white, and often carry a sweet, lily-like scent. This attracts night-flying moths, which pollinate the flowers. Most cactus flowers last only for a day or two. Some nocturnal-flowering plants have an even shorter period of glory. They wait until about midnight before opening, and then fade before morning.

Seed pods sometimes appear if the flowers have been pollinated successfully. They are often brightly coloured, as in the case of the mammillarias, many of which will produce them without artificial pollination methods being employed. The pods are mostly various shades of red and are long-lasting.

Seed pods may take a long time to form. A whole year may elapse after pollination has taken place, so that one year's flowers and the previous year's pods sometimes appear on the same cactus.

Nearly all 1700 species of cactus are native to Mexico, western and southern USA and South America.

Some succulents that are not true cacti, however, are native to Britain. These are the stonecrops, or sedums, that grow on rocks, walls, steep banks or cliffs, where the soil may be very shallow and soon dries, even though heavy rain may have fallen.

Species that can be found in this country are *Sedum acre*, *S. album*, *S. anglicum*, *S. reflexum*, *S. roseum* and *S. telephium*.

The pennywort, *Umbilicus rupestris*, is fairly common in the western parts of the British Isles and is easily recognised by its round, dimpled, shiny leaves about the size of an old penny piece and, in summer, its drooping green-white flowers, carried on a stem up to 15 in. long.

Native British succulents *The most common succulents native to the British Isles are the stonecrops, or sedums (left), found on rocks, banks and cliffs. The pennywort (right) is also fairly common in western parts of the British Isles, where it grows in stony places, particularly drystone walls*

How to grow healthy cacti

The care of cacti in the house

Nearly all cacti originated in deserts, and so enjoy bright sunlight.

To grow the widest range, a heated greenhouse with a minimum winter temperature of 5°C (41°F) is necessary. But many cacti can be grown as house plants in a south or west-facing window, provided they are put outdoors in a sunny place during the summer.

A few cacti originated in tropical rain forests and require shady growing conditions. If plants are to be kept indoors permanently, these forest cacti, such as epiphyllums, rhipsalidopsis and schlumbergeras, are good choices. Keep them in a position beside an east or north-facing window.

It is better to use tap water than rain water when watering cacti. Rain water can contain bacteria and fungi that might harm the plants.

Central heating causes problems for desert cacti, which need a cold, dry winter rest in order to flower well. In winter they should be kept in an unheated room, where the temperature remains between 5°C (41°F) and 10°C (50°F). Otherwise the high temperature, and the need consequently for watering to prevent the plants from shrivelling, may cause them to grow in the wrong season. It is better to keep them in a dry cold frame in winter than in a centrally heated room.

Do not shut them between the curtains and the window on winter nights, as they may be damaged by a pocket of cold air.

Mis-shapen growth *Lack of light has distorted this flat-stemmed opuntia. Rotate plants receiving light from a window, to ensure even growth*

What can go wrong with cacti

Apart from the troubles pinpointed in the table, cacti are susceptible to several common greenhouse pests, such as ants, scale insects, thrips and woodlice. Spray these pests with a systemic insecticide as soon as they appear.

Root mealy bugs, which cause discoloration, are less common, but discourage them by watering compost with a malathion solution.

Symptoms	Cause	Cure
Corky, pale brown patches	Old damage by mealy bugs or red spiders; erratic watering	No remedy, though healthy tops can be severed and rooted as cuttings
Distinct rings of growth, getting progressively smaller towards the top of the plant	Too little water plus starvation	Repot or feed during the growing season. Water correctly
Wrinkling and softening; little or no growth	Too little water; root rot	Water correctly
Fluffy patches of whitish, waxy wool	Mealy bugs	Spray with malathion or wipe over with methylated spirit
Thin, pale, sappy growth	Too shaded; too much heat at the wrong time of year (usually in winter)	Keep in a sunny site and follow a correct heating regime
Base becomes soft and wet, followed by the collapse of whole or part of plant	Basal stem rot	No cure, but firm, green tip may be severed and rooted
Yellowish or brownish mottling	Red spider mites	Spray with malathion, formothion, dimethoate or derris

Growing cacti out of doors

The tougher, larger cacti can be used to make an exotic display in the open garden, while they are getting their summer sun. But first take cuttings (see p. 47) to maintain your stock if they become too big to return indoors, or become straggly.

Add extra grit to a south-facing garden bed to ensure good drainage. Then put the plants into the bed.

The large opuntias make good background plants. *Opuntia robusta* and *O. tuna* become tree-like and grow 2–3 ft high. Avoid delicate species such as *O. microdasys*.

The columnar cereus also make good background plants.

Smaller plants, such as the 3–6 in. echeverias or sempervivums, can be planted between the larger plants.

Outdoor cactus gardens blend well with yuccas, herbaceous perennials that come from the same desert areas.

Cactus gardens should be regarded as summer gardens only, and the plants discarded or returned to the greenhouse in autumn. In mild areas, however, they may overwinter successfully.

Succulents with a decorative covering of 'meal' on their leaves need to be given protection from the rain if put out of doors.

The sturdier cacti and other succulents can be planted out of doors in a well-drained site facing south, to provide an exotic summer display

When plants need repotting

Cacti need to be repotted when the mineral salts in their compost have been absorbed by the plant, or washed away by the water or, in the case of vigorous, young specimens, when the roots have filled the pot. Inspect the roots of new plants after you have bought them.

Ideally, repotting is carried out in the spring, but it can be done at any time of the year. It provides an opportunity to check the roots for pests, especially root mealy bugs.

Disinfect new pots to prevent them spreading pests or disease.

A moist, well-drained compost is essential. Use equal parts of John Innes No. 2 compost and a coarse sand, or a soil-less potting compost.

Tap the pot against a work bench to loosen the soil ball. If tapping fails, push a pencil through the central hole in the base of the pot.

Remove the plant, using a folded newspaper to protect your hands from spiny plants.

Take care to disturb the roots as little as possible. Old caked soil should be taken from the base of the plant and loose soil shaken off.

Take a pot one size larger than the old one and, if it is a clay pot, put a crock over the central hole.

Hold the plant in the centre of the pot and pour in new compost, ensuring it does not rise above the old soil mark on the stem. Spread the compost round the plant with a spoon.

Tap the pot on the working surface to settle the compost down. Withhold water for a few days to prevent rotting of damaged roots.

Large plants seldom need repotting, but the top layer of compost should occasionally be renewed.

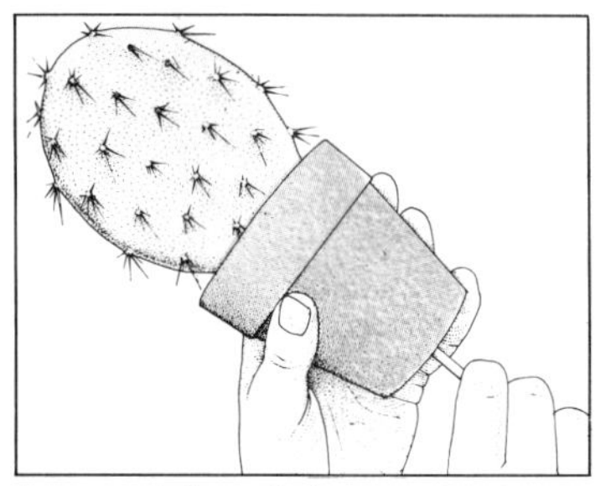

1 *A pencil through the central hole will loosen plants*

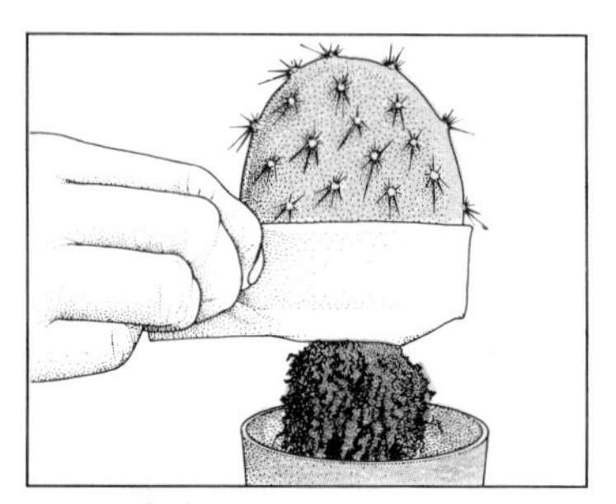

2 *Use a folded newspaper to protect your hands against spines*

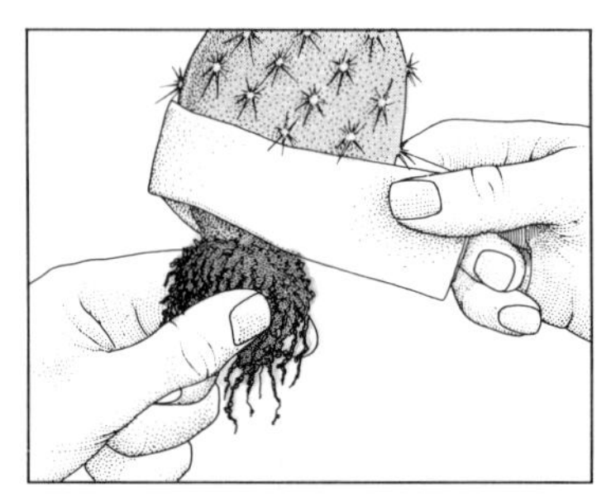

3 *Remove old soil from the base of the plant and shake off loose soil*

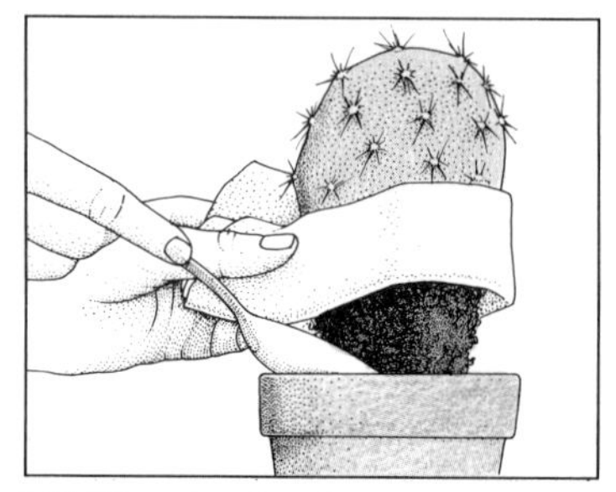

4 *Holding the plant in position, spread new compost round it with a spoon*

When to water and how to feed

Cacti should always be watered in the growing period whenever the soil looks dry. When dormant they need no water at all, or just enough to prevent the soil drying out completely. However, if kept in a living-room, more water should be given. Exceptions are the forest cacti, such as epiphyllums, which should not be allowed to dry out completely and should be kept damp in winter. But over-watering can rot the roots of all cacti.

Every fortnight during the flowering period, give plants a liquid feed with tomato fertiliser, at the same strength as for tomatoes.

WATERING

Stand pots in water until the surface of the compost is damp

FEEDING

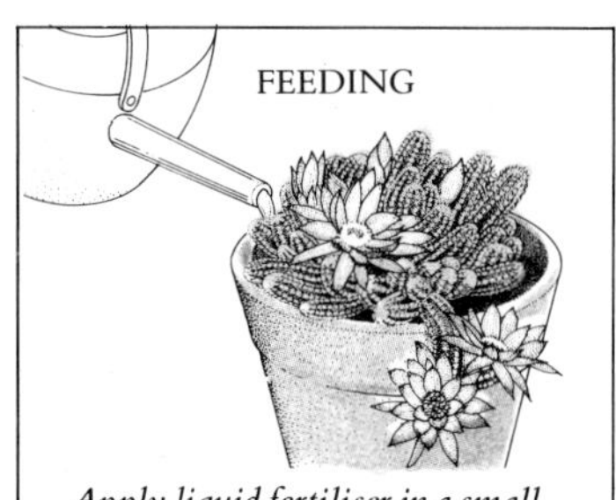

Apply liquid fertiliser in a small can to prevent splashing

WATERING STONE PLANTS

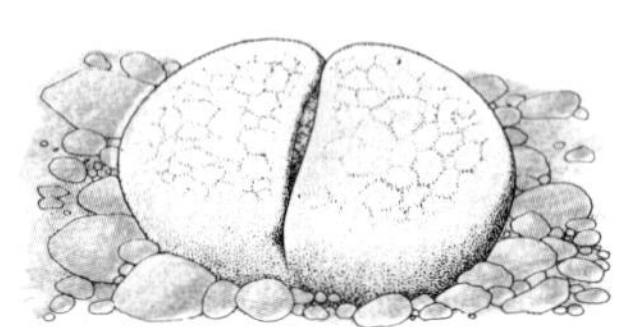

1 *Lithops and conophytums, the stone plants, should not be watered after late autumn*

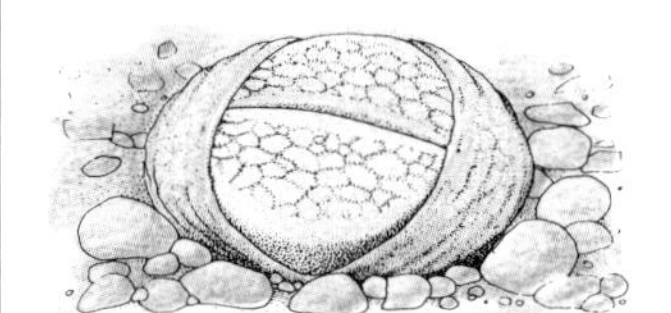

2 *In spring the new plant emerges, but water only when the old leaves have become dry*

The need to keep cacti clean

To prevent plants with shiny stems or pads becoming dusty in the house, wipe them occasionally with a damp sponge. This helps them to breathe and absorb sunlight.

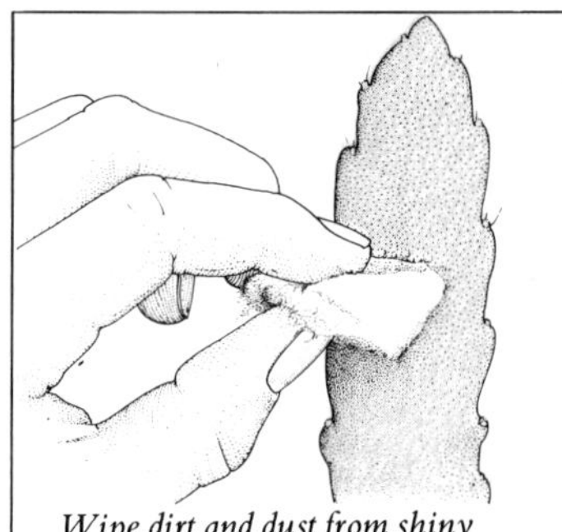

Wipe dirt and dust from shiny plants, especially in industrial areas

Growing new plants from cuttings

Taking cuttings is the simplest and most generally used method of propagating cacti and succulents.

A piece of the stem is cut off with a sharp knife or a razor blade and is rooted in compost.

If the plant is of a type that has individual leaves, a leaf can easily be removed and made to root.

Some plants produce offsets, or smaller versions of the parent plant, which need only to be cut away and potted in compost. Some of these offsets are already equipped with their own roots.

A succulent, such as *Kalanchoe tubiflora*, grows plantlets on leaf-ends, which fall and root readily.

No harm is done to the parent plant by taking cuttings, and it will continue growing normally.

Apart from pereskia cuttings, which should be potted up as soon as they are taken, cuttings of cacti must be left to dry until the cut surface has formed a callus. The time taken ranges from one or two days for the small wound of opuntias, to five days or a week for the large-stemmed cerei.

The drying-off period is essential to avoid rotting – the main danger to these cuttings. For the same reason, cactus cuttings should not be covered with propagating covers or polythene to aid rooting.

May and June, the period of maximum growth, is the best time to take cuttings, but they can be taken at other times if necessary: for example, when plants drop their leaves or make leggy growth their tops can be removed and treated as cuttings.

The time taken for cuttings to root varies from one plant to another, but it is indicated by signs of new growth.

Cuttings should never be taken out of the compost before growth has appeared on them, as this disturbance can cause damage to the embryo roots of the young plant.

How to take stem cuttings of cacti

To take a stem cutting, remove a horizontal section of stem – whether globular, columnar, strap-like or segmented – by cutting the stem straight across.

Use a sharp knife or a razor blade, except for tough-stemmed plants such as epiphyllums, which will require cutting with secateurs.

Slender-stemmed columnar cacti yield enough material for several cuttings from one stem. Make sure that you know which is the top and which the bottom of each section. Their growth will be distorted if they are put into the compost the wrong way up.

With opuntias, each cutting should normally be one complete segment or more, cut off at the joints. With small-jointed cacti, such as Christmas cactus, each cutting should consist of two or three segments.

Put all cuttings in a warm, dry place for about three days, to allow a callus to form on the wound.

Once calluses have formed, fill a $2\frac{1}{2}$ in. pot to within $\frac{1}{2}$ in. of the top with moist, sandy compost, such as equal parts of John Innes No. 2 potting compost and coarse sand or grit. Insert the cuttings into the compost, just deep enough to keep them in an upright position.

Keep the compost just moist. Over-watering can rot cuttings.

Stem cuttings should root after one to three weeks. The time varies according to the genus.

They should then be potted individually into pots containing the same sort of compost as before. The pots should be large enough to hold the plant's root system comfortably.

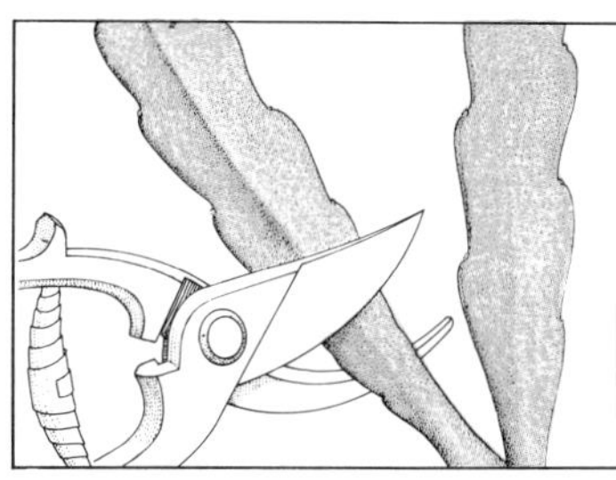

1 *Slice through the stem with secateurs or a sharp knife*

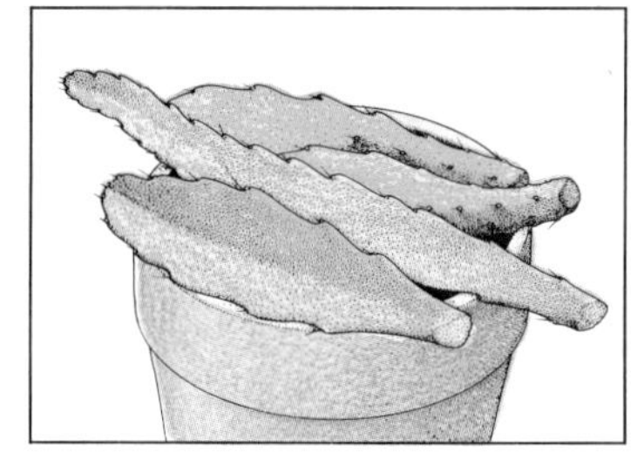

2 *Put cuttings in a warm, dry place until a callus forms*

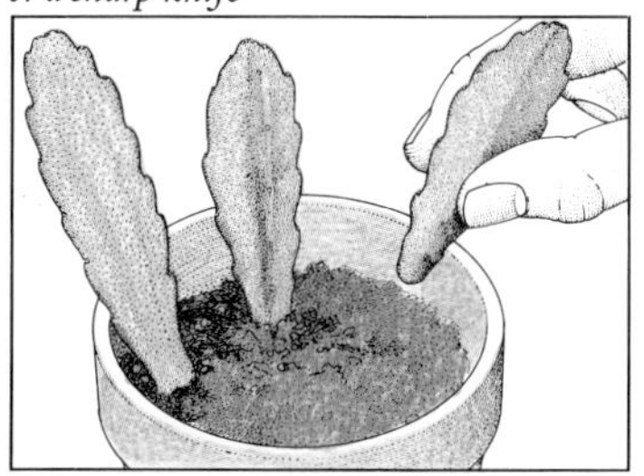

3 *Insert cuttings into compost, just deep enough to keep them upright*

4 *When cuttings show signs of growth, remove and pot them on*

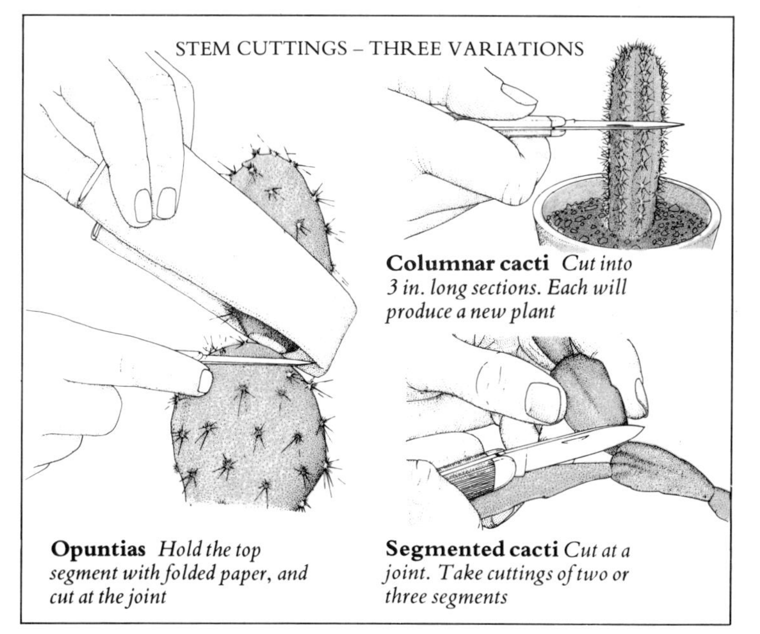

STEM CUTTINGS – THREE VARIATIONS

Columnar cacti *Cut into 3 in. long sections. Each will produce a new plant*

Opuntias *Hold the top segment with folded paper, and cut at the joint*

Segmented cacti *Cut at a joint. Take cuttings of two or three segments*

Taking cuttings from leafy plants

Many succulent plants, such as echeverias, sedums, crassulas and haworthias, can be reproduced from single leaves. Pull the leaves from the plant with your fingers or tweezers and allow them to dry for a day or two.

Then insert them in a moist, sandy compost, just deep enough to ensure they stay upright. If inserted too deep, they will rot.

Small cylindrical or globular leaf cuttings may be simply laid flat on the surface, and if kept moist they will root.

Cuttings of both types will usually root in about a fortnight.

Rooting is then followed by the appearance of a small leaf cluster. This will grow rapidly to form a rosette of branching leaves.

At this stage, the cutting is potted on into a 2–2½ in. pot, containing equal parts of John Innes No. 2 compost and coarse sand. Do not remove the parent leaf until it has withered.

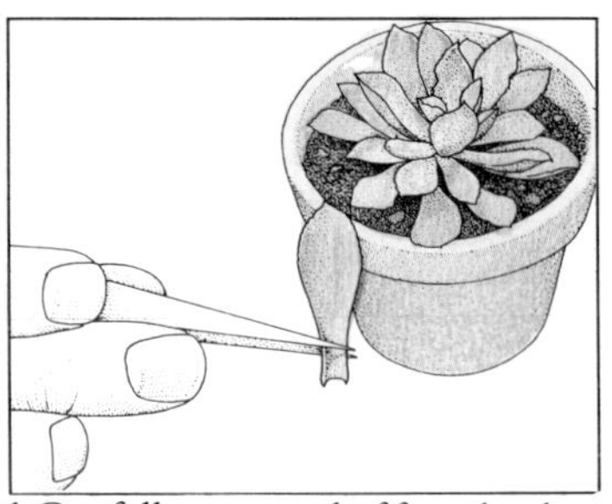

1 *Carefully remove a leaf from the plant with fingers or tweezers*

2 *Do not push in the leaf too deeply – just enough to hold it up*

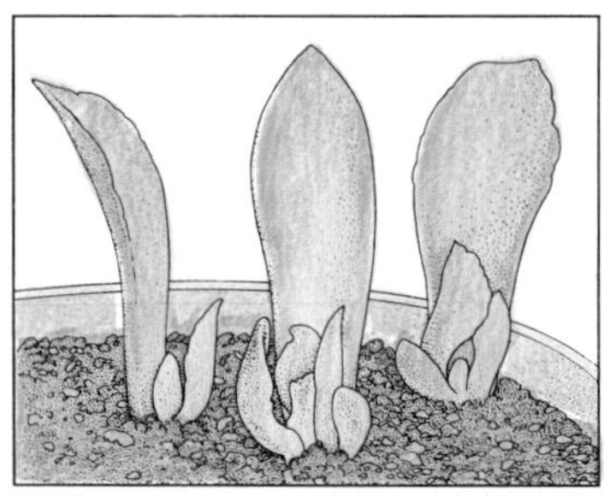

3 *The appearance of shoots beside the leaf shows the cutting has taken*

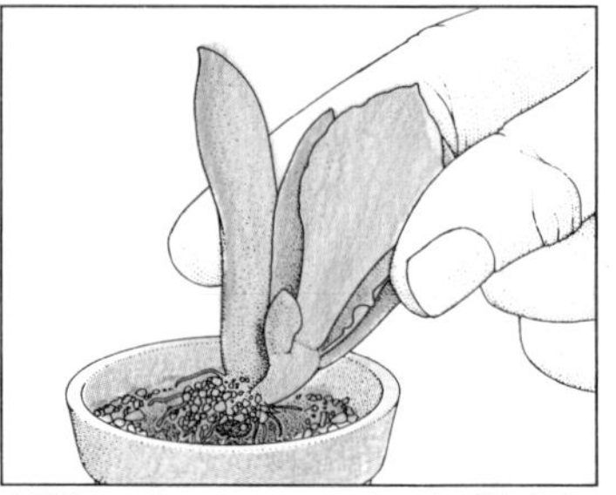

4 *When the rosette reaches leaf height, the cutting is ready for potting on*

Propagating cacti from offsets and offshoots

Some cacti and other succulents produce young plantlets which appear round the base and are miniature versions of the parent plants. These offsets usually come from below ground level, or from low lateral shoots on the plant.

Certain cacti, such as some echinopsis and rebutia, produce offsets which have their own root systems. They can be detached and potted up as separate, young plants. These offsets should not be detached from the parent until the roots have developed.

Other offsets have no roots. They can be cut away, dried off, pressed slightly into moist, sandy compost and treated as cuttings.

Sometimes confused with offsets are offshoots – lateral branches sent out by the stumps of plants after cuttings have been taken from them. Offshoots can be treated as cuttings. While the stump continues to grow new offshoots it can be kept, but once it stops it should be discarded.

OFFSETS AND OFFSHOOTS

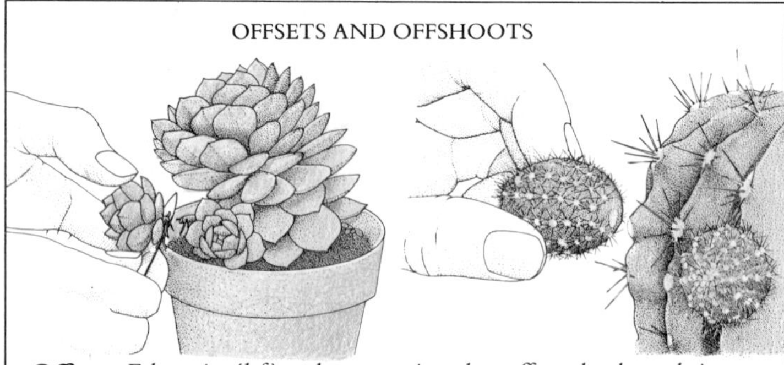

Offsets *Echeverias (left) and some cacti produce offsets that have their own roots, and these can be potted up. Echinopsis offsets (right) appear on the lower part of the stem, not round the base of the plant*

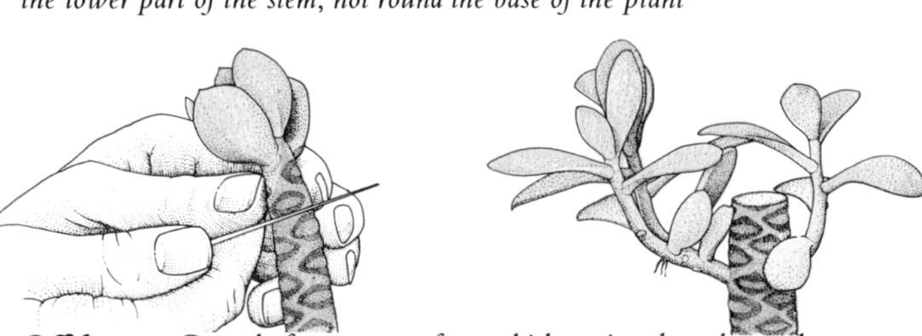

Offshoots *Growths from a stump from which cuttings have been taken are known as offshoots. They also make good cuttings*

Propagating 'stone' plants by division

Succulents that resemble clusters of stones can be divided.

Loosen the soil around the base of one of the plantlets and tear it away from its neighbour, making sure a small piece of stem comes with it.

If no tissue is torn, the plantlet can be potted immediately.

If tissue is torn, dry the plant off for a few days, and then insert it in compost in the normal way.

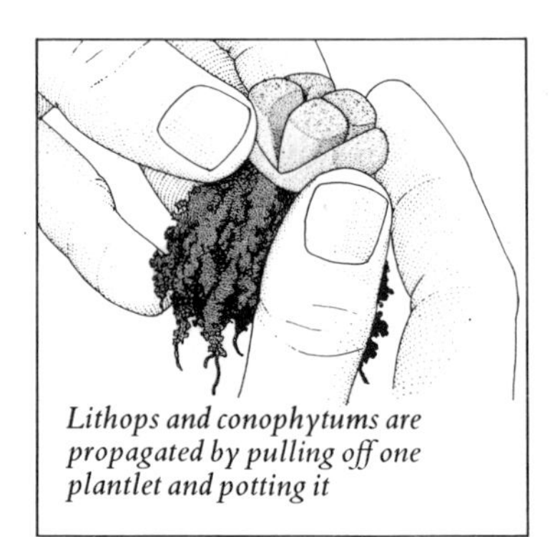

Lithops and conophytums are propagated by pulling off one plantlet and potting it

Growing cacti from seed

Producing your own cactus seed

While seedsmen provide packets of cactus seed, you may wish to grow several specimens of an unusual plant in your collection.

Cacti produce male and female flowers on the same plant, while euphorbias produce flowers of one sex only on each plant. Male flowers can always be identified by the tiny yellow pollen grains they bear.

Those plants that are either entirely male or female cannot produce seed unless flowers of the opposite sex, on another plant of the same species, are open at the same time. So it is best to pollinate both types manually. Dab the male flowers with a fine brush to pick up the pollen, and then brush the pollen on to the female flowers. With plants that have both male and female flowers, it is safest to pollinate from another plant of the same species.

With most species, seed pods begin to appear about a week after fertilisation. The pods grow in size and gradually change colour as they become more ripe.

With the euphorbias, a covering of nylon or fine-mesh wire needs to be placed over the plants at this stage, as the seed pods burst open with explosive force, dispersing the seed.

With most other plants, remove the ripe pods with forceps and put them in a dry, warm place so that they can dry out.

Put the seeds on blotting paper to dry. In a centrally heated room this may take only one day.

When dry, the seeds separate easily and are ready to be sown immediately; or they can be stored in labelled envelopes until you are ready to sow them.

HOW TO POLLINATE EUPHORBIAS

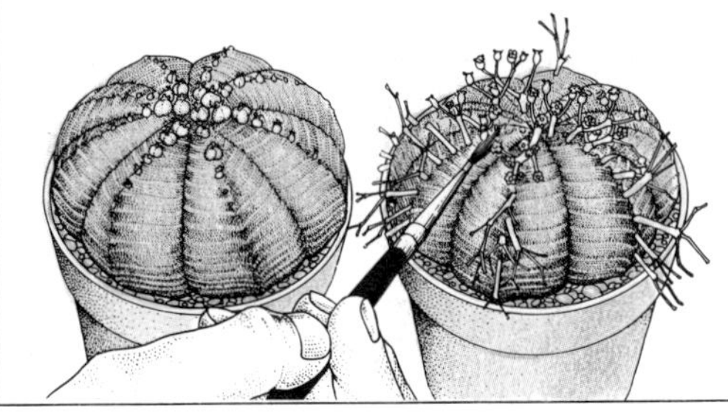

The best way of pollinating euphorbias is to dab the male flowers with a fine brush to pick up the tiny yellow pollen, and then dust it on to the female flowers

HOW TO COLLECT SEED

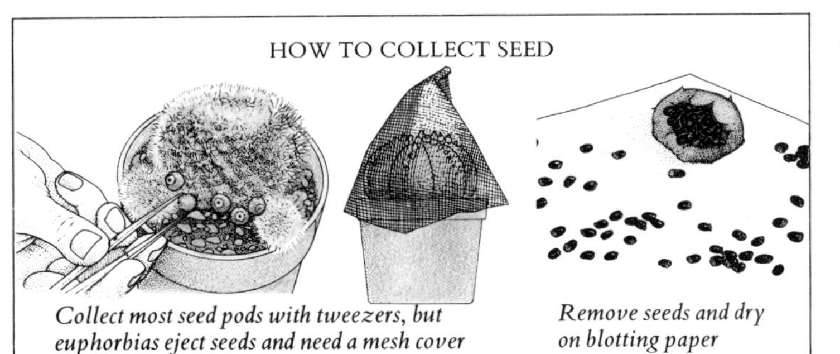

Collect most seed pods with tweezers, but euphorbias eject seeds and need a mesh cover

Remove seeds and dry on blotting paper

Sowing seeds and potting the plants

Thoroughly wash a 3 in. or 4 in. pot or seed pan, and put a layer of gravel in the bottom. Fill the pot with seed compost – either John Innes or a peat-based variety. Sift some more compost over the surface.

Sow the seeds. Do not cover them with compost.

Put the pot in water until the compost is moist.

Place the pot in a plastic bag, or cover it with a piece of glass to prevent drying out. Cacti need a temperature of 21–27°C (70–81°F) for germination.

The seedlings will develop spines in a few days to a month. Now remove the cover.

When the seedlings are $\frac{1}{8}$–$\frac{1}{4}$ in. in diameter, transplant them into a seed tray containing potting compost, such as John Innes No. 2.

When they have grown to $1\frac{1}{2}$–2 in. across, pot them individually into 2–$2\frac{1}{2}$ in. pots.

1 *Sift the top layer of compost, to provide a good rooting medium*

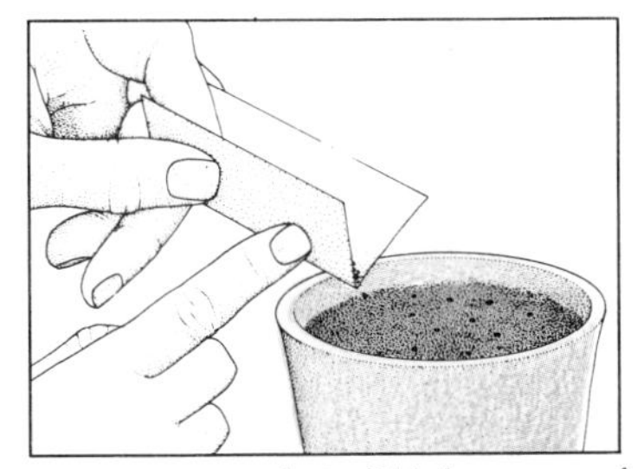

2 *Place tiny seeds in folded paper, and tap it to spread them evenly*

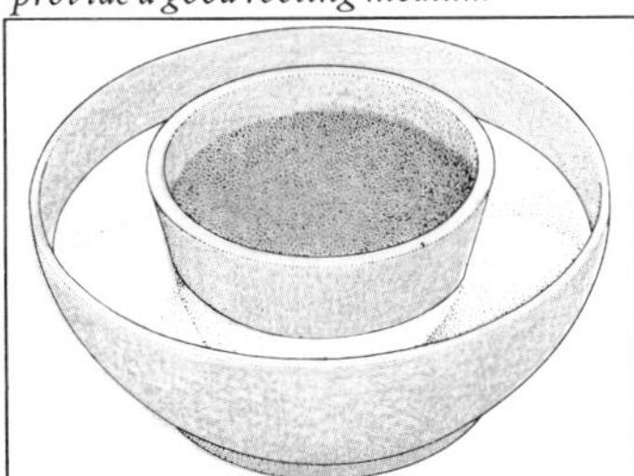

3 *Put the pot in water, and leave it until the compost surface is damp*

4 *When the spines begin to grow, the seedlings are ready for a seed tray*

5 *When transplanting, take care to disturb the roots as little as possible*

6 *When young plants are $1\frac{1}{2}$–2 in. across, move them into 2–$2\frac{1}{2}$ in. pots*

Propagating cacti by grafting

Although it is possible to graft other succulent plants as well as cacti, this is difficult and not often undertaken. In any case, most succulents are propagated more easily by cuttings. All grafted succulents you are likely to see, therefore, are cacti.

Grafting consists of bringing together the upper part of one plant, called the scion, and the rootstock of another, called the stock, so that they form one plant.

It is usually carried out on plants which are difficult to grow on their own root systems, on plants that contain no chlorophyll and have been artificially kept alive, or on those that cannot easily be grown from seed, offsets or cuttings.

Usually there is no significant difference between grafted cacti and those grown naturally, especially if the rootstock is concealed. But sometimes the union of two species accelerates growth in a way that is not typical of the species.

Though many amateur growers shrink from grafting because it appears such drastic treatment, it is a fairly simple process. It is best done sometime between May and August, in a dry atmosphere with a temperature of 19–21°C (66–70°F). Any strong-growing cactus can be used as rootstock, but it must bear some relation to the size of the cactus to be grafted.

Usually, the aim is to make the graft as unobtrusive as possible, and this can be done by hiding the neck of the rootstock with pebbles.

But grafting can also be used to produce an unusual shape, as when a trailing cactus on a columnar one gives a 'weeping' plant.

WHY CACTI ARE GRAFTED

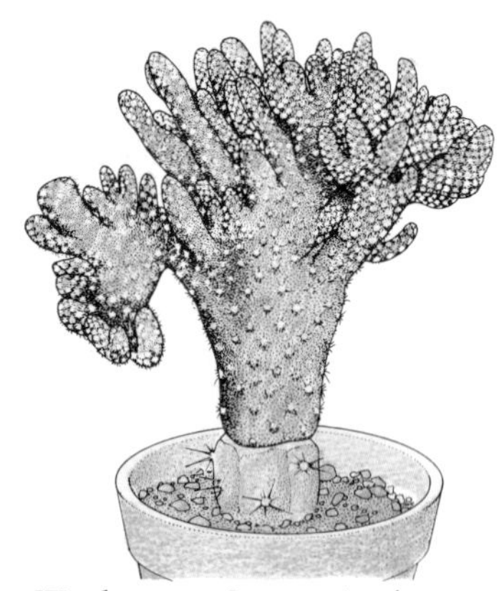

Weak roots *Some cacti such as* Opuntia claveroides *have weak roots and need a stronger rootstock*

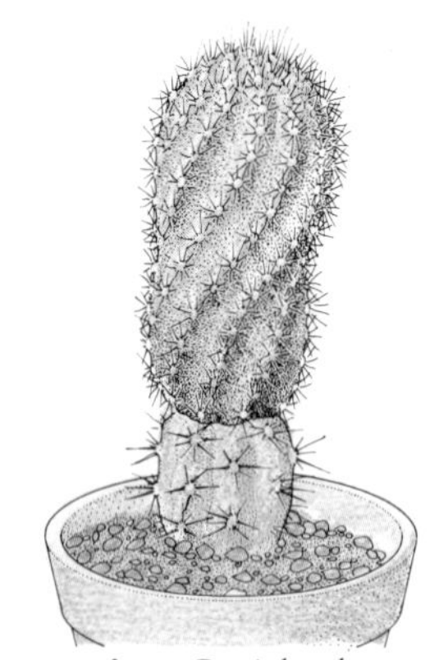

Propagation *Cacti that do not easily grow from seed, cuttings or offsets are increased by grafting*

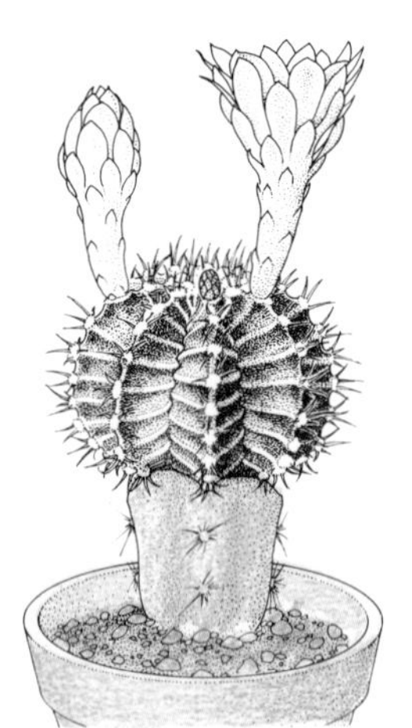

No chlorophyll *Coloured types such as the gymnocalycium 'Black Cap' need a green rootstock*

Cactus species suitable as rootstocks

Cacti which provide the rootstock for grafting should be easy to grow and propagate. The most usual stock for grafting is trichocereus, a columnar cactus which can be grown easily from seed. Most species of it are suitable, but species with smaller spines such as *Trichocereus spachianus* are easier to use.

One-year-old trichocereus seedlings can be used for grafting small scions. The cut tops can be rooted and grown on to take larger scions.

The softer-stemmed echinocereus species also make useful stock, especially for sickly, rather dried scions. Suitable species are *Echinocereus dubius*, *E. enneacanthus* and *E. pentalophus*. They branch freely and root easily, and so can be freely propagated by stem cuttings. Pads of *Opuntia robusta*, about 1–2 in. high, also make good rootstock.

Echinopsis species such as *Echinopsis eyriesii* and its hybrids are sometimes useful, as they form offsets prolifically. Mostly globular, they root easily and quickly, and can be used for grafting when about $\frac{3}{4}$–1 in. across. A section is cut from the top to correspond to the diameter of the scion, and the graft is made in the usual way.

How to graft a columnar cactus

A vigorous, well-rooted rootstock, about the same size as the plant to be grafted (the scion), is essential. Trichocereus is the most common rootstock.

Cut off the top of the rootstock with a sharp, clean razor blade. The top section can be dried and rooted for future use (see p. 47).

Chamfer the edges of the stock with a razor blade, to remove any spines and prevent the surface becoming concave.

Cut the plant to be grafted in a similar manner. Both surfaces to be joined must be level and smooth.

Press the scion on the freshly cut stock with a rotary motion, which will remove air bubbles. Try to match up the central bundle of tissues, which carries sap around the plant. This is in the form of a ring, which varies in diameter from 1 in. in the larger plants to $\frac{1}{4}$–$\frac{1}{2}$ in. in the smaller.

Place rubber bands round the top of the scion and the base of the pot. A piece of cottonwool can be placed on top of the scion to prevent the rubber bands bruising it.

The grafted plant should be placed in a warm, shady part of the greenhouse or house and watered.

After one or two weeks, the scion should be attached to the rootstock. The rubber bands can then be carefully removed.

If the graft has not taken, the two parts will separate at a touch.

If more than one offspring is required from the original scion, sever it once it shows signs of growth, leaving about $\frac{1}{2}$ in. of scion on the rootstock.

Graft the severed portion on to another rootstock.

Offsets will form around the $\frac{1}{2}$ in. of scion remaining on the first rootstock. When they are about $\frac{1}{2}$ in. in diameter, remove them and root them, or re-graft.

Carnations & pinks

The scent and beauty of carnations place them among the noblest flowers. Buttonhole types need a greenhouse, but border carnations and the smaller pinks grow outdoors

Carnations are among the most elegant of flowers, having reached a perfection of bloom matched by few other plants. Their variety of colour adds beauty to any garden, and they are excellent as cut flowers. Until half a century ago carnations were the hallmark of the well-dressed man.

Since Classical times carnations have been grown for the beauty of their flowers and for their scent.

The Greeks described them as long ago as 300 BC, and in *The Winter's Tale* Shakespeare wrote: 'The fairest flowers o' the season are our carnations.'

Legend has it that William the Conqueror introduced the carnation to Britain. This story lacks verification, but it is a fact that the species *Dianthus caryophyllus*, which is the main ancestor of the carnation, does grow wild in Normandy.

The word carnation appears to be derived from the Latin *corona*, meaning a chaplet or garland, from the ancient practice of using the flowers to make the garlands that were worn during Roman festivals.

Carnations belong to the genus dianthus along with pinks and sweet williams.

They are divided into two types: border (or outdoor) carnations, and perpetual-flowering (or greenhouse) carnations.

Border carnations were popular in English gardens in the 16th century, but it was not until the late 19th century that the perpetual-flowering variety began to be developed by horticulturists in the United States.

Border carnations are quite hardy and flower outdoors during July in the South, and during August in the North. They flower once each year.

The blooms are heavy and large, and some grow up to 3½ in. across. They are borne on stout stems which must be carefully staked.

The flowers differ from perpetual carnations in that the petals are not serrated on the edge, but are smooth and flat.

Colour classifications of border carnations are extensive, but the main ones are known as selfs, fancies, cloves and picotees.

Selfs have flowers of one decided colour. There are varieties in almost every colour except blue.

Fancies have a single-colour background with stripes or bars in a contrasting colour.

Cloves are not confined to any particular colour, but are distinguished by their scent which resembles the aromatic spice – hence their name. Cloves were once used for flavouring wine and beer, which gave carnations their old name of 'Sops-in-Wine'.

Picotees were the show flowers of a century ago. They have ground colours of white or yellow and a regular margin of rose, scarlet, crimson or purple on the edge of every petal. There is no colour on the white or yellow ground.

The perpetual-flowering carnation – the kind generally seen in florists' shops – is a greenhouse perennial. It produces flowers for cutting throughout the year, and does not need very high temperatures to flower in winter. The blooms are double with serrated petals, and often fragrant.

In the 1920's the well-dressed man would hardly venture out without a carnation in his buttonhole. The fashion faded, for no other reason than that West End tailors reduced the size of buttonholes, so that they would no longer take a large flower, or they eliminated them altogether.

'Pink Sim' (Perpetual-flowering carnation)

It is not easy to define a pink. In French and German, the word for pinks means 'little carnations', but enthusiasts in England and Scotland look on this as an unfair description. They say, quite rightly, that a pink is light and dainty with the flower carried on a slender stem.

But although it may have almost perfect form, it never has the solid sculptured form of the carnation.

The old-fashioned pink, derived from *Dianthus plumarius*, is not widely grown now as it has fewer flowers than modern pinks. In the first year the plant has only one central stem, with side growths producing flowers a year later.

Modern pinks grow faster and produce many more blooms, mainly during June and July, and again in September and October.

They originated when the late Montagu Allwood deliberately crossed an old-fashioned pink with a perpetual-flowering carnation to produce a plant with a longer flowering period.

His experiment succeeded, resulting in the hybrid plants known as *D.* × *allwoodii*, from which modern pinks are derived.

They must be propagated more often than old-fashioned pinks – normally every two or three years.

There is one marking which is only found in pinks, namely the laced pink.

In this type the dark zone (or eye) at the base of each petal is extended in a band round the petal near the edge. The remainder of the petal – the ground colour – is white, creamy-white or pink. The whole flower thus has a dark centre with a surround of concentric dark rings.

Carnations and pinks are known for their tolerance to alkaline soils, but they also grow well in a wide range of other soils provided they are not too acid.

These plants are also remarkably tolerant to chemical pollution and are hardly affected by the salt spray in seaside gardens.

However, poor drainage, heavy shade or the drip from trees are usually fatal to them.

The amount of artificial heat they will stand varies.

Pinks will stand very little at all; they are definitely outdoor plants.

Border carnations are also outdoor plants, but some exhibition varieties need controlled watering, so exhibitors often grow them in unheated greenhouses with plenty of ventilation.

When ordering, it is sensible to specify outdoor varieties if these are required.

The perpetual-flowering carnation is a greenhouse plant in Britain, but the greenhouse must be well ventilated and it is unwise to allow the winter night temperature to exceed 10°C (50°F).

It is not easy to give a reliable list of varieties of carnations and pinks. The main reason is that varieties deteriorate quite suddenly and unpredictably, or sometimes a variety is superseded by a better one, in which case the old variety rapidly disappears from the catalogues of the nurserymen.

Sometimes, as in the case of the old-fashioned pink 'Mrs Sinkins', a variety deteriorates but is retained in the catalogue because of enormous demand.

However, if a good specialist nurseryman says he no longer stocks a particular variety, but offers another in its place, it is usually safe to take it.

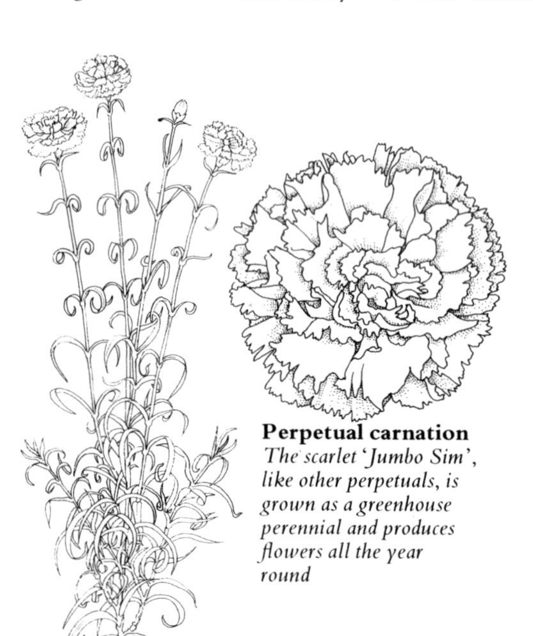

Perpetual carnation *The scarlet 'Jumbo Sim', like other perpetuals, is grown as a greenhouse perennial and produces flowers all the year round*

Old-fashioned pink *'Emil Paré' and other old-fashioned pinks are no longer widely grown, as they flower in June only*

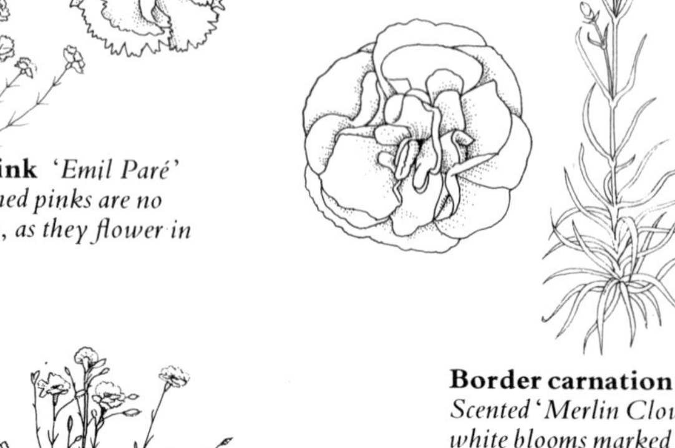

Border carnation *Scented 'Merlin Clove' has white blooms marked with crimson. As with other border carnations, it flowers only once each year*

Modern pink *'Doris', a scented variety, has salmon flowers. All modern pinks flower in June and July and again in autumn*

Border carnations for the open garden

Choosing the site and planting

Border carnations are hardy perennials grown in the open border to flower during July in the South and August in the North.

Select a site in the garden that is open and not overshadowed. The bed should be well dug and manured in late summer, and a light dressing of lime applied if this has not been done for a year or two. If the soil is known to be alkaline, do not add lime. Carnations and pinks do well in neutral and alkaline soil, but will tolerate slightly acid conditions. Bonfire and wood ashes have a beneficial effect on carnations and pinks, and should be added before planting at a rate of about four handfuls to the square yard.

New stock can be planted in either autumn or spring. The advantage of autumn planting is that the roots can get a good grip before the cold weather arrives (provided planting is done before the end of October) and so make a good start towards full growth in early spring. There may, however, be winter losses. Spring planting, as long as it is done before mid-April, is quite satisfactory. Even early May is all right when spring is late.

Using a trowel, dig holes about 15 in. apart to give the plants room to bloom for two seasons, but if they are to remain in the ground for longer, increase the distance to 18 in. Though it is possible to leave them in the border for three or even four years, it is better to propagate after two years (p. 55). In a restricted area, 9 in. is the minimum spacing.

Dust the holes with HCH powder as a precaution against wireworms and leatherjackets. Bury the roots, but not the stem – only about $\frac{1}{4}$ in. should be covered, with the lower leaves clear of the ground. Firm the soil round the plant.

Keep the plant upright by tying it to a short cane. Metal ring ties of the type used for sweet peas are ideal. Finally, water lightly.

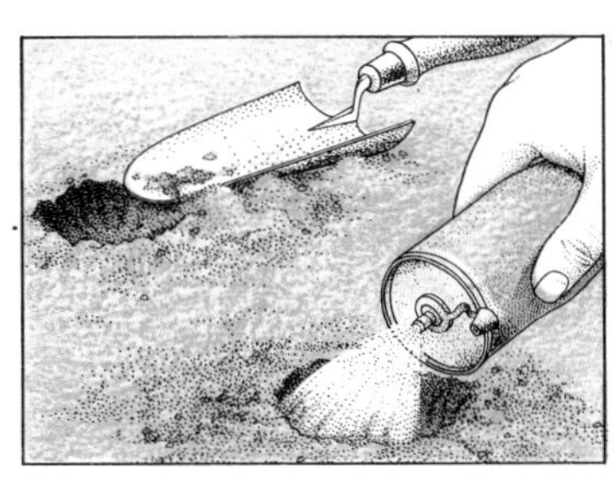

1 *Dust the planting hole with HCH powder against wireworms and grubs*

2 *Do not plant too deeply; only $\frac{1}{4}$ in. of stem should be covered*

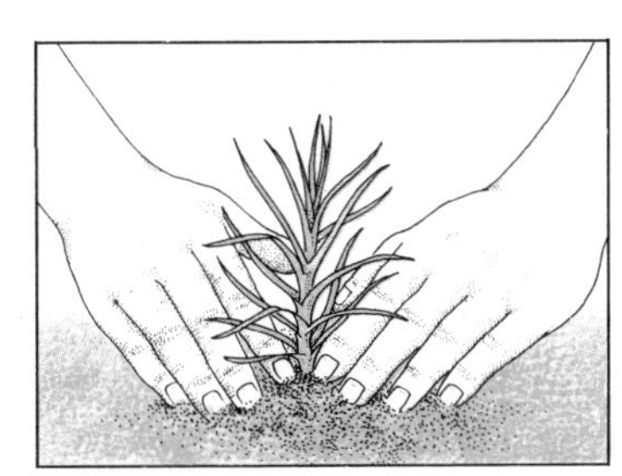

3 *Firm in the plant by hand, keeping the lower leaves clear of the soil*

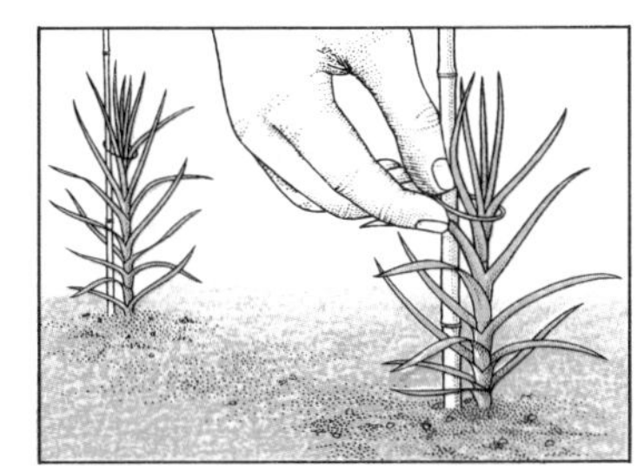

4 *Attach the plant to a short cane, using metal rings if possible. Lightly water*

Caring for young plants in winter and spring

If the planting is done in autumn, check the sticks and ring ties during winter to make sure they are secure, otherwise the plants may be broken or snapped in high winds.

To prevent birds attacking the young stems, tie thin black cotton tightly between canes or stakes, about 6 in. above the ground. Do not use strong thread or nylon, as it may injure the birds.

Watch out for rust disease among border carnations in late autumn. This appears as raised chocolate-brown spots on the leaves. Remove infected leaves and burn them. Spray plants with maneb, thiram or zineb at 10–14 day intervals.

In spring, break up the surface crust of the soil. Carnations are shallow rooted, so this treatment should be no more than a $\frac{1}{2}$ in. scratching of the surface with a hoe or cultivator. Remove weeds by hand when they are small.

Do not add mulches of bulky organic matter, because of the risk of stem rot. Inorganic materials, such as limestone chippings, can be used as mulches to keep down weeds, and do not harm the plants. However, border carnations will tolerate dry conditions.

If for any reason the bed was not properly manured before planting, two or three applications of a general-purpose fertiliser may be given at intervals of six weeks or so during the growing season.

If no wood or bonfire ashes were put on, add sulphate of potash to the first application of fertiliser at 1 oz. (1 tablespoon) to the square yard. This will help produce blooms of better quality.

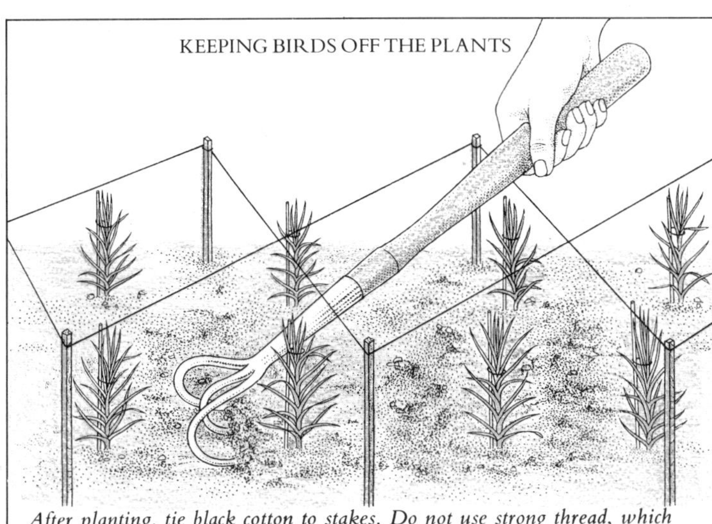

KEEPING BIRDS OFF THE PLANTS

After planting, tie black cotton to stakes. Do not use strong thread, which may injure the birds. In spring, break up the soil around the plants

Watering, supporting and disbudding

The plants withstand dry conditions well, and watering is not usually necessary except in very dry weather. Then the roots should be given a thorough soaking – up to 5 gallons to the square yard. Light watering may do more harm than good.

In its first year, a border carnation grows one flowering stem, 2–2½ ft high, with several flowers growing on side stems. In the second year there are several flowering stems.

To support the heavy flowers, insert a 3 ft cane for each flowering stem and tie the main stem to it with string, raffia or wire ring ties. The side stems can be supported by larger loops of string.

A crown bud forms in June at the top of the stem, and usually provides the best and largest bloom. Side-shoots grow from the stem, each one carrying a bud, or buds. Some of these shoots must be removed to ensure good-quality blooms.

When the buds are about the size of a pea, pinch out all the side-shoots and buds below the crown bud, for a distance of 3 in.

On the side-shoots that remain, leave only terminal buds; carefully pinch off any others.

Supporting the blooms *Tie the stem with raffia, string or wire ring ties to a 3 ft cane*

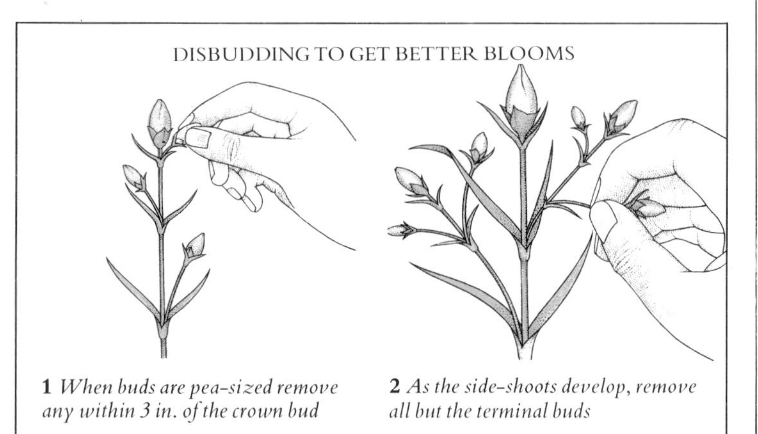

1 *When buds are pea-sized remove any within 3 in. of the crown bud*

2 *As the side-shoots develop, remove all but the terminal buds*

Cutting the flowers for indoor decoration

Cut border carnations when the blooms are half open. Water the plants well the day before and do the cutting in the early morning or late evening, when the stems are full of moisture.

Do not snap off the stems, but use small scissors or secateurs. The blooms will last longer if they are stood up to their necks in water for 12 hours before arranging.

Put the container in a cool draught-free place. Keep water off the blooms as it will mark them.

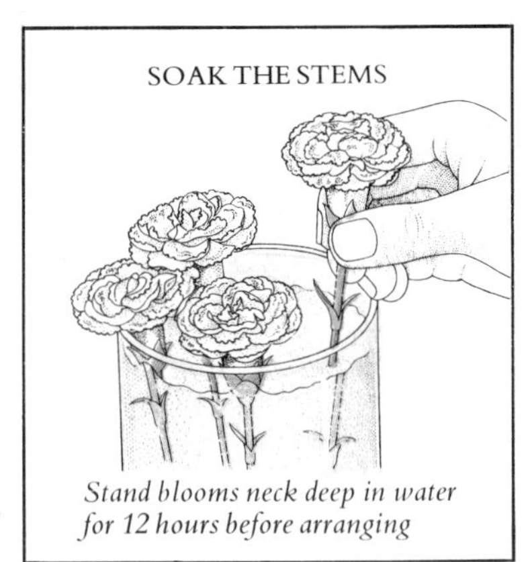

Stand blooms neck deep in water for 12 hours before arranging

What can go wrong with carnations and pinks

This chart describes the most common problems likely to occur in the growing of carnations and pinks. If your plants show symptoms not described here, use the chart of pests and diseases on page 377. For chemical trade names, see page 398.

Symptoms	Cause	Cure
Leaves mottled and yellowing, sometimes shrivelling and covered with a fine webbing	Red spider mites	Spray with malathion or dimethoate
Young leaves and shoots reduced in vigour, often malformed and sticky	Aphids	Spray with derris or malathion
Bleached spots on petals	Thrips	Spray with HCH or malathion
Leaves develop small blisters and later the growing tips yellow and die	Carnation fly	Spray with dimethoate or malathion
Leaves or petals eaten and spun together with webbing (small active caterpillar hidden in spun leaves)	Carnation tortrix moth	Spray with malathion or dimethoate
Calyx (the green covering which protects the flower in bud) splits lengthways, allowing the petals to spread and form a shapeless bloom	Split calyx	The exact cause is not known. Important factors seem to be overfeeding and lack of lime. Avoid too much nitrogenous manure or fertiliser, and apply a dressing of lime annually to maintain the pH around 7
Seedlings collapse	Damping off caused by overcrowding, plus high temperature and humidity	Attacks may be checked by watering with captan or zineb

Producing new plants by layering

The easiest method of increasing border carnations is by layering in July or August, after the plants have finished flowering.

Select vigorous side-shoots (young ones which have not borne flowers), and strip off some of the lower leaves by pulling them downwards. Leave four or five fully developed pairs of leaves at the tip of each shoot.

To counteract any stiffness in the stem, bruise it between joints with either a thumbnail or pliers.

Insert the point of a sharp pen-knife below the lowest joint that still has leaves attached. Cut down through the next joint and, turning the blade, make a downward and outward cut to form a tongue on the stem. Open out the cut carefully. Make a shallow hole and fill it with planting mixture (equal parts of soil, sand and peat). Press the cut into the soil and push a layering pin over the cut, so that it is held about 1 in. below the soil. Pins can be bought, or made from wire, in the shape of a hairpin with 3 in. legs.

Pack the soil in round the cut with the fingers, and add a little more planting mixture to level the surface. The layered plant should be kept watered for the next six weeks.

After six weeks, lift the layering pin slightly, and pull gently on the layered plant. It will hold firm if it has rooted; an unrooted plant will be loose. If it is loose, leave it for another fortnight and then discard it if it has not rooted.

When the layer has rooted, cut it off at the layering pin on the side nearest to the parent plant.

After two weeks lift the layered cuttings, keeping the root systems intact. Place them in their flowering positions in the border, following the method for siting and planting given on page 53. If the bed is not ready, they can be potted into $3\frac{1}{2}$ in. pots of peat and coarse sand.

1 *After the plant has flowered, select a vigorous side-shoot and strip off some of the lower leaves by pulling them downwards, leaving four or five pairs of leaves at the tip*

2 *Bruise the stem between the joints, with a thumbnail or pliers*

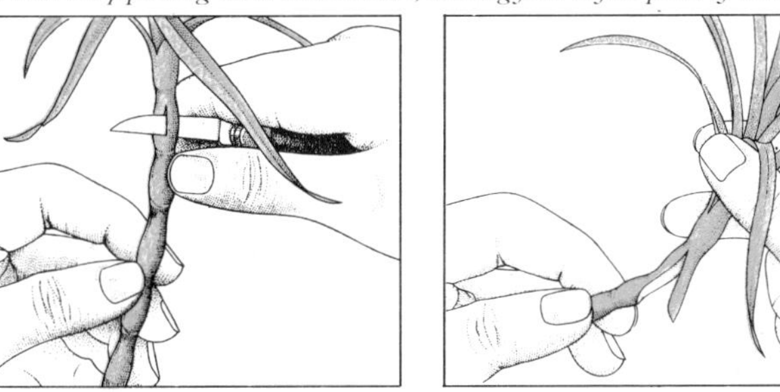

3 *Insert knife tip below the lowest leafed joint and cut through next joint*

4 *Open the cut carefully, ready to push the layer into the soil*

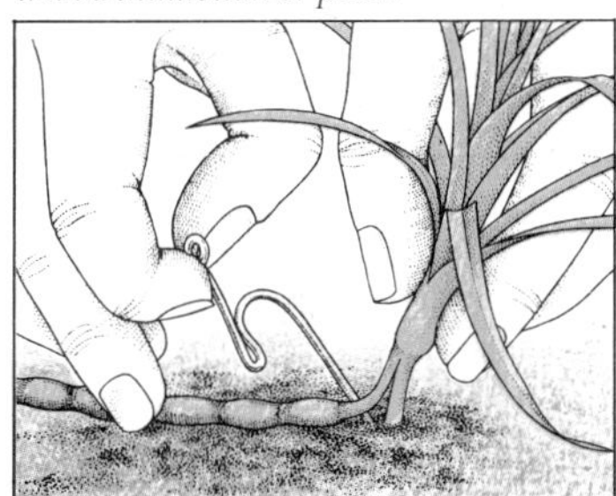

5 *Fill a hole with a soil-sand-peat mixture, and push the cut into it*

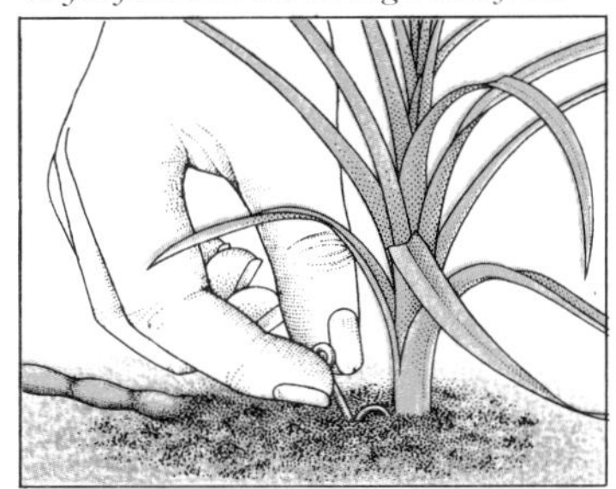

6 *Push a layering pin over the cut until it is 1 in. below the surface*

7 *After six weeks pull the plant gently to see if it has rooted*

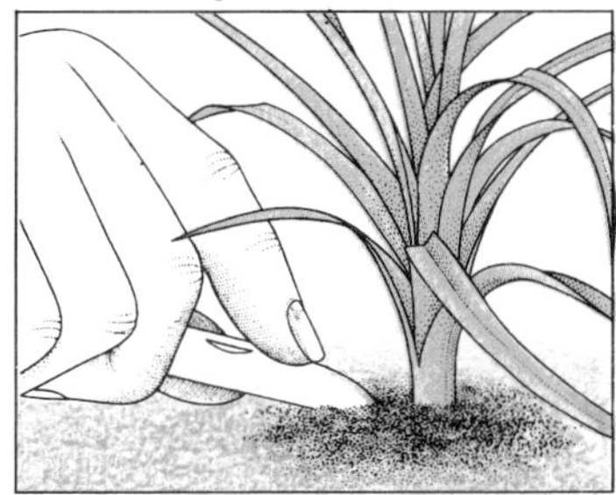

8 *When it has rooted, cut it off on the plant side of the pin*

Modern pinks: how to grow and increase them

Modern pinks are a cross between old-fashioned pinks and perpetual (or greenhouse) carnations.

They are now more commonly grown than the old-fashioned pinks, as they produce many more flowers which are larger and more regular in shape. Some have an even stronger scent than the old pinks.

Most modern pinks need to be propagated every two years, as they lose their vitality and form if left longer. However, some strong-growing varieties can be left for three years. (A specialist nursery is the best source of advice on which are the strong-growing types.)

Planting young pinks in early spring

The preparation of the soil for planting pinks is the same as for border carnations. However, pinks are more tolerant and will often thrive in poor, shallow soil where border carnations would grow poorly.

They can be planted in autumn or during mild spells in winter, but make sure that leaves and other garden debris do not collect around the base of the plants. Stem rot might result.

As pinks flower a month earlier than border carnations – between June and July – they cannot be planted quite so late. So if you buy new plants, get them in the ground before the end of March. And water them thoroughly during dry spells.

Small-growing varieties which will stay in the bed for two years should be planted at 8 in. intervals. Stronger-growing kinds which will be retained for only two years are planted 12 in. apart, and strong-growing varieties that are to remain for three years are planted 12–18 in. apart. Do not bury the stem or allow the lower leaves to touch the soil, though make sure the roots are bedded in firmly.

Plant firmly, but avoid burying the stem too deep as this may cause it to rot

Stopping the plants to make bushy growth

The young plants are stopped in their first season to encourage breaks, or side-shoots, and to create strong, bushy growth.

The plant should have produced nine or ten fully developed pairs of leaves before it is stopped. It may reach this stage in the autumn, but any plants that have not developed enough by mid-September should not be stopped until spring. The new side growths would be damaged by the cold weather. Plants bought from a nursery in the spring may already have been stopped – look to see if the growing tip has been pinched out.

Stopping is best done in the early morning in damp weather when the stems are full of moisture and so break more easily.

Select the sixth, seventh or eighth joint from the base, and hold it between finger and thumb. With the other hand, hold above the joint and bend the stem sharply down.

Usually it will snap out cleanly, but if it does not, bend the stem to the other side at right angles. If this fails, do not pull at it; cut it cleanly as close above the joint as possible. (Do not merely pinch out the growing tip – this will result in only one or two breaks near the top.)

The side-shoots will now develop from the leaf joints. Stopping the shoots delays flowering in modern pinks, but it is essential to build up good side growths before flowers are produced.

Modern pinks need be stopped only in their first year. Do not stop them during the second or third flowering season.

Old plants seldom need stopping, as they will usually make good side-shoots. If they do not produce such growths, remove one-third of the flower stems. After flowering, remove old flower stems completely, and thoroughly water the plants, using a watering can with a fine rose.

Apply a high-potash fertiliser to encourage the plants to flower again in the same season. Some modern pinks may continue flowering up to Christmas in mild weather.

After this time, however, remove all bud-bearing stems, as they will produce poor blooms in early spring and retard summer flowering.

1 *Wait until the plant has developed nine or ten pairs of fully grown leaves*

2 *Take the sixth or seventh joint from the base and bend the stem sharply*

3 *If the stem does not snap cleanly, cut it. Breaks now grow from the joints*

4 *The result is a bushy, shrub-like plant with a succession of flowers*

Producing new plants from cuttings

Pinks can be propagated by layering in the same way as border carnations, but the method is not so easy owing to the smaller size of the stems.

Cuttings are therefore the main method of increasing the stock. The season for propagating begins when the main flowering has finished, and goes on until about the third week in August.

Select shoots that are growing strongly but have not begun to lengthen for flowering. (The same shoots could also be used for layering.) If the shoots are too short they will probably be dormant, and may remain dormant as cuttings.

Long shoots – with the distance between the joints lengthening – will produce leggy plants.

The cuttings should have plenty of sap in them when taken, so, unless there has been rain, water the plants well the day before the cuttings are to be taken. Cut off the selected shoots with a sharp knife close to the main stem.

Strip off the lower leaves from each shoot by pulling them downwards. Leave three or four pairs of fully developed leaves below the top of the cutting.

Place the cutting on a piece of cardboard or some other soft surface. Using a sharp knife or single-edged razor blade, cut just below the topmost joint that has been stripped of its pair of leaves.

Put crocks or gravel in the bottom of a $3\frac{1}{2}$ in. pot or, better still, use a perforated zinc drainage filter, the dome side up. Filters are sold by nurseries. They do not clog, and will prevent larger worms entering the bottom of the pot when it is in a cold frame. Fill the pot loosely with John Innes No. 1 potting compost to within $1\frac{1}{2}$ in. of the rim and then top up with a mixture of equal parts peat and coarse sand. Water this with a fine-rosed can. No firming is needed.

Push the cuttings into the compost, so that the base of the lowest leaves is not covered.

The cuttings will not be planted firmly, so tilt them inwards slightly to allow them to support each other and not fall out when watered.

Put 9–12 cuttings in a pot, depending on their size, and water with a fine-rosed can to settle the planting mixture round them. Label each pot of cuttings with the name of the variety and date of planting.

After taking cuttings from one plant, dip the knife blade in methylated spirit and place it in a hot flame (a small spirit lamp or gas lighter will do) before moving on to the next plant. This will sterilise the blade and prevent any diseased plant infecting other cuttings.

The parent plant should now be discarded, unless it is young enough to have another flowering season – no more than two years old. If it is proposed to keep the parent plant, do not take so many cuttings that its appearance is spoilt.

Place the cuttings in a cold frame, in a polythene bag or in a cold propagating case where they get full light but no direct sunlight. If necessary, paint some form of greenhouse shading on the glass.

Syringe with water round the inside of the frame in warm weather to keep the atmosphere humid.

After four or five days, lift the frame cover a fraction of an inch. Do not let the air in the frame become too dry until after the cuttings have rooted.

Rooting takes place after 18–30 days, and is indicated by the cuttings growing upright, the leaves spreading out, and growth developing at the tips. Take the glass off the frame gradually during the course of a week or so to allow the young plants to harden.

After two or three weeks, they can be planted out where they are to flower. For a few weeks after planting, water them in dry weather.

1 *Select a strong shoot which has not grown longer than the others. Cut off close to the main stem and strip the lower leaves, leaving three or four pairs of fully grown leaves*

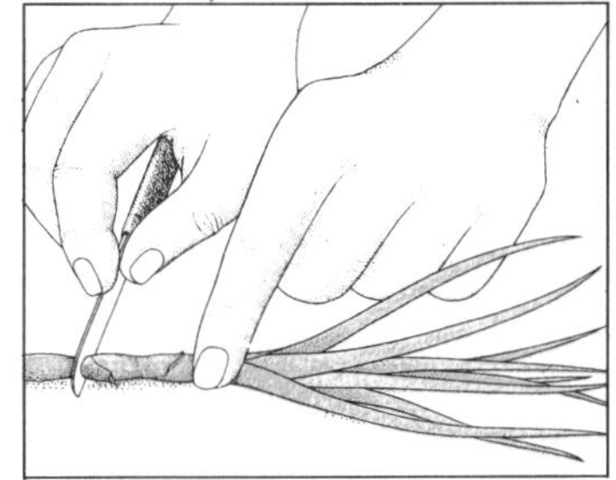

2 *Sever just below the topmost joint that has been stripped of its leaves*

3 *Push the cuttings into a mixture of peat and sand on John Innes No. 1*

4 *A $3\frac{1}{2}$ in. pot will take 9–12 cuttings, all leaning inwards for support. Water the pots and put in a cold frame. Rooting takes place after 18–30 days*

Old-fashioned pinks

The older type of pink, such as the famous variety 'Mrs Sinkins', grows like a border carnation, and produces one central stem in the first year bearing the flowers, and side growths flowering a year later.

Old-fashioned pinks must never be stopped.

Taller or weak-stemmed varieties may need supporting with short pea sticks. To maintain vigorous compact plants, remove the flowering stems completely as soon as the last flower has faded.

Many of the old pinks began to lose their vigour about 40 years ago, and have now been largely replaced by modern pinks.

Old-fashioned pinks should be propagated by cuttings, as described under modern pinks, or by layers as with border carnations. They can be left for four or five years before propagation is necessary – in which case, they should be planted initially about 12 in. apart.

Although taking cuttings is the best method of propagation, two methods that still give fairly good results with old-fashioned pinks are to take pipings or slips. A piping is made by pulling out the top of a shoot without using a knife.

The problem is that the break usually occurs in a soft part of the stem, and above instead of below a joint. Both factors tend to retard rooting of pipings.

Slips are complete side-shoots detached from the main stem by a downward pull, and may or may not be trimmed before being put in the rooting medium.

The disadvantages are that the main stem of the plant is damaged, the base of the cutting is hard, and therefore roots slowly, and the joints are so close together that the bases of several leaves may be buried, which can cause rotting.

Named varieties must be raised from cuttings, pipings, slips or layers. Interesting results can also be obtained by saving your own seed. Growing pinks from seed is a cheap and easy way of obtaining large numbers of plants, the best of which can be propagated later.

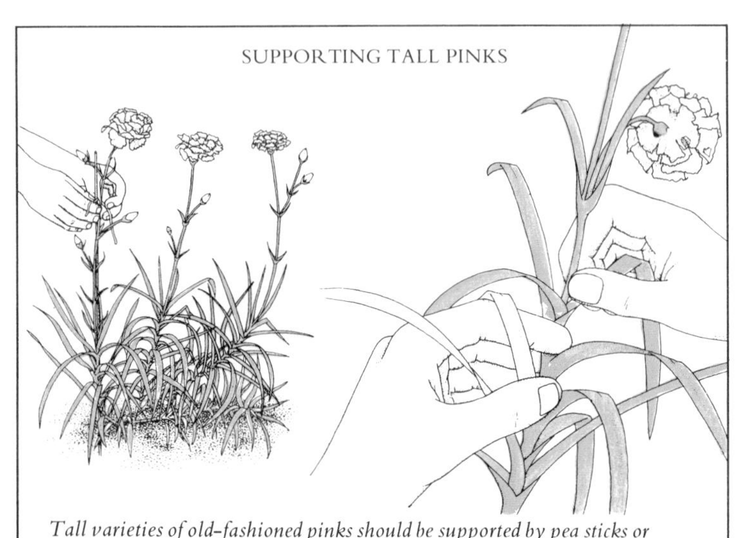

SUPPORTING TALL PINKS

Tall varieties of old-fashioned pinks should be supported by pea sticks or canes. Blooms should be removed as soon as they fade

Perpetual carnations under glass

The perpetual-flowering carnation is a greenhouse plant in Britain. Although it will survive low temperatures, it does better under glass.

The easiest method of culture is in pots in a heated greenhouse, so that blooms can be produced throughout the year. Commercial growers use beds instead of pots, although this system is more prone to the spread of soil-borne diseases. The perpetual carnation tends to branch, and produces a flower at the end of each branch. The plant should be stopped to encourage breaks, and usually a second stopping is made.

Propagation is from cuttings taken from flowering plants. Perpetuals should be propagated every three or four years.

Potting nursery plants in late spring

For the beginner, the best size of plant to work from comes in a 3–3½ in. pot, and will be delivered in April or May by the nursery. This plant will have been stopped once, the main stem having been broken at the seventh joint from the base.

When the plants arrive, they will need to be repotted into 4 in. pots with John Innes No. 2 compost.

To remove the plant from its old pot, place a hand across the pot, with the stem between the first and second fingers. Turn the pot upside-down and tap the base.

Put the root ball into the 4 in. pot and fill round it with more compost. Firm this with the fingers, leaving ½ in. between the surface and the top of the pot for watering.

Keep the base of the lowest leaves out of the soil. Leave the newly potted plant in a shady part of the greenhouse for two or three days. After three days it should be watered, and stood in full light. When the roots are well through the soil ball – after about three weeks – transfer the plant to a 6 in. pot or, if it is a strong-growing variety that will flower for three years, use an 8 in. pot and insert a 5 ft cane for support later.

Throughout the life of the plants – except for two or three days after potting – the atmosphere should never be allowed to become close or muggy. A minimum temperature of 7°C (45°F) should be maintained.

1 *Nurseries provide plants in 3–3½ in. pots in April/May after first stopping*

2 *When the plants arrive, repot into 4 in. pots, using John Innes No. 2*

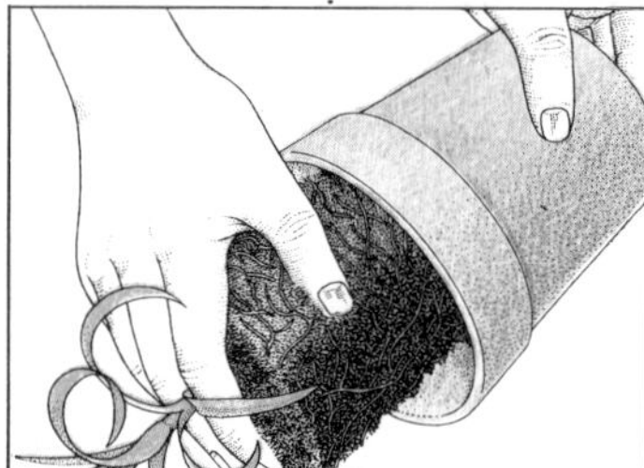

3 *Check root growth after three weeks; if necessary move to a 6 in. pot*

Stopping the plants to get more blooms

If you have grown the plants from cuttings they will require a first stopping. The time for this is in March or April, when they are about 8–10 in. tall. (This will have been done on plants obtained from a nursery.)

Wait until about nine fully developed pairs of leaves have formed, then select a joint on the stem about six or seven pairs of leaves up from the base. Hold the joint between finger and thumb and, with the other hand, bend the stem above sharply left and right. It should snap off easily. If not, cut it with a clean, sharp knife just above the joint.

After this first stopping, five to seven side-shoots will appear. Some of the side-shoots will require stopping when they are about 7 in. long. This is known as second stopping.

Choose the joint nearest the top which has a clear area of stem between it and the next joint above. Break off the shoots above this, leaving about six fully formed pairs of leaves. Pulling a bunch of leaves from the tip is useless – the shoot will grow again from the top in a weakened condition.

Side-shoots that have not had a second stopping will flower in summer. Stopped shoots will produce side-shoots that flower later. A second stopping up to the middle of June will produce autumn flowers; a stopping from then until the middle of July will produce winter flowers; and an August stopping will give early spring flowers.

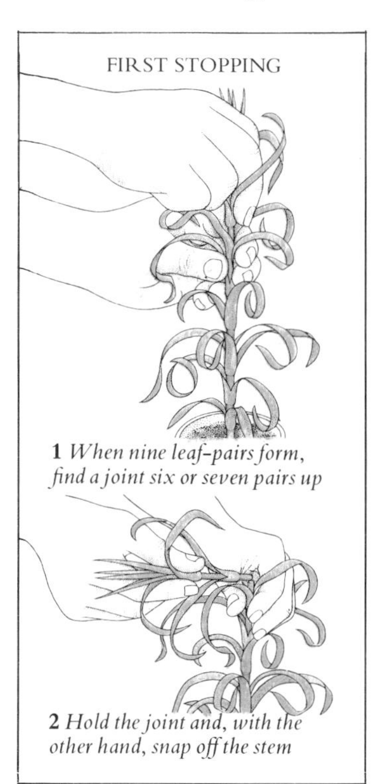

FIRST STOPPING

1 *When nine leaf-pairs form, find a joint six or seven pairs up*

2 *Hold the joint and, with the other hand, snap off the stem*

SECOND STOPPING

When side-shoots are 7 in. long, snap off the ends

Encouraging a good bloom on each side-shoot

To encourage one good bloom on each side-shoot, perpetual carnations should be disbudded. With finger and thumb, break off all the flower buds and their stems except the top, or crown, bud. This should be done when the buds are the size of a pea.

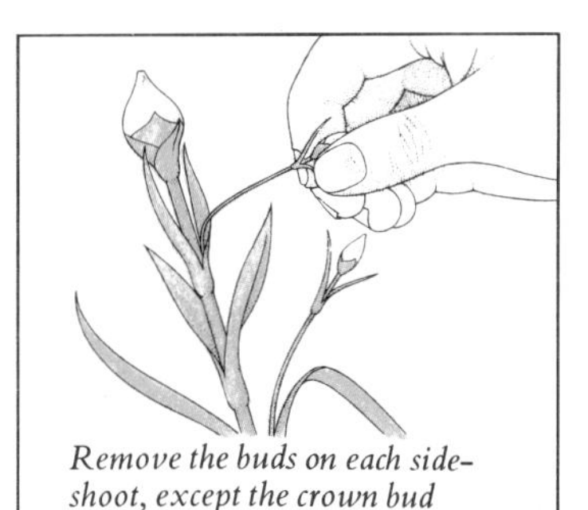

Remove the buds on each side-shoot, except the crown bud

When the flowers begin to appear

When the flower buds begin to show colour, make sure they do not get wet when watering.

At this time, provide some form of shading in the greenhouse if the weather is hot. Use a blind or butter-muslin curtains, or paint a shading compound on the outside of the glass. This will not be washed off by rain, if applied on a dry day, but is easy to remove with a long-handled brush and bucket of water.

Blooms should be cut in the early morning when the stems are filled with moisture. Make the cut low down on the flower stem, and cut at a slant, which will help the flowers take up more water.

Leave the cut flowers for 24 hours in a container of water, with the blooms just above the surface. They will then last longer.

What can go wrong with perpetuals

This chart describes the most common problems that are likely to occur in the growing of perpetuals. If your plants show symptoms not described here, turn to the chart of pests and diseases on page 377. For chemical trade names, see page 398.

Symptoms	Cause	Cure
Leaves mottled and yellowing, sometimes shrivelling and covered with a fine webbing	Red spider mites	Spray with malathion or dimethoate
Young leaves and shoots reduced in vigour, often malformed and sticky to the touch	Aphids	Spray with derris or malathion
Bleached spots on petals	Thrips	Spray with HCH or malathion
Leaves and young stems yellow and wilt and finally die	Wilt	Cut out infected stems. If the whole plant is infected, lift and burn. As a preventative, replace stock with young plants every third year, and if grown in a greenhouse border replace the soil every three years
Leaves of greenhouse plants have small brown pustules which erupt when mature. Plants are weakened and the foliage looks unsightly	Rust	There is no totally successful chemical cure, but thiram gives some control. Rust is rarely a problem if the greenhouse is well ventilated

Chrysanthemums

The chrysanthemum, the 'Golden Flower of the East', was first grown in China in 500 BC. It is now one of the most popular plants in British gardens

The chrysanthemum is the second most popular flower in Britain, ranking next after the rose. It first became popular in this country about 100 years ago.

Chrysanthemums can be grown in rock gardens or mixed borders, in pots, in window-boxes or in a greenhouse. They are ideal as cut flowers in the home and for exhibition showing.

There are three groups in the chrysanthemum genus – annuals, herbaceous perennials and the more specialised perennials, often known as florists' chrysanthemums.

Annuals, which produce single flowers with beautiful rings and zones of colour (such as *Chrysanthemum carinatum*), are all grown from seed.

Among the hardy perennials are *C. maximum*, the white flower known as the Shasta, King Edward or moon daisy. The most common varieties are 'Esther Read' and 'Everest'. Pyrethrums are also perennial chrysanthemums, with coloured daisy-like flowers, popular for cutting. Pyrethrums are usually listed separately in nurserymen's catalogues.

Korean hybrids are half-hardy perennials with single and semi-double flowers, usually grown as dwarf bushes about 2 ft tall. They are normally lifted for winter, but they can survive in the ground if the weather is not too severe.

Florists' chrysanthemums are grown for more elaborate decoration, either in the garden or for exhibition. Their growth is controlled by pinching out growing tips and buds.

Varieties which flower in the open before October are known as 'early flowering'. Those that bloom after the frosts have begun are called 'late flowering', and must be moved under glass in the autumn.

Chrysanthemum flowers are classified according to their form.

Incurved Close, upward-curving florets in the form of a globe.

Reflexed The florets curve downwards from a central tuft. There is also a less curved form called medium reflexed.

Intermediate Loosely incurving or semi-reflexing.

The incurved, reflexed and intermediate varieties are further divided into large-flowered and medium-flowered types, according to size. Mediums can grow to about 6 in. in diameter, large blooms 8–10 in.

Pompons and semi-pompons Small, spherical or half-spherical blooms about $\frac{3}{4}$ in. in diameter.

Single Blooms with five or less rows of ray florets round a central disc or daisy eye.

Anemone centred Similar to the single chrysanthemums, but the central disc consists of tubular florets forming a raised cushion.

Spidery Blooms with thin, long, quilled and rolled petals.

As well as the normal method of controlling the form of chrysanthemums by pinching out growing tips, the large florists' chrysanthemums can be grown as sprays. They are allowed to grow naturally, apart from having the main stem pinched out once. Clusters of small flowers then form on branched stems, 3–4 ft high. Most exhibition varieties give good sprays.

Charms These are bushy plants covered with masses of star-like flowers. They are grown in pots to flower from the end of October in the greenhouse, after being kept outdoors through the summer.

Cascades The flowers are often similar to charms, though the form of the plant is different. They are usually placed on a high shelf so that the long stems can be trained downwards to give a cascade effect.

Growing chrysanthemums in the open garden

Enriching the soil with manure and fertiliser

Chrysanthemums grown for cut flowers or for exhibition need rich soil, so prepare the ground thoroughly. If a special bed can be set apart, it is easier to manage adequate ground preparation and carry out necessary seasonal jobs. As a guide, a plot 12 ft by 10 ft will accommodate about 40 plants for exhibition or 60 for cut flowers.

Choose a site which is well drained, as chrysanthemums dislike being waterlogged. The site should also be sunny and sheltered from the wind. Dig the plot over in autumn so that frost and winter weather will break down the soil. Incorporate a 2 gallon bucket of well-rotted manure or garden compost together with a handful of coarse, sterilised hoof and horn meal to the square yard.

In April spread a dressing of general chrysanthemum fertiliser (one handful to the square yard) and fork it in about 3 in. deep.

Preparing young plants from a nursery

Plants delivered from a nursery usually arrive in March or early April, though if they come before early May they will be all right.

Generally they are individually wrapped in polythene to prevent loss of moisture, but if they seem dry stand them in jars of water overnight to allow them to recover. Plant the chrysanthemums in boxes, about 3 in. deep, 10 in. wide and 16 in. long (tomato trays from the greengrocer are excellent) or else in 3–3½ in. pots. Boxes do not dry out so quickly. Half fill the boxes with John Innes No. 1 potting compost and place the plants on this.

Do not put more than 12 plants to one tray. Gently spread out all the roots, fill the tray with more compost and, after firming the plants slightly with the fingers, water them with a very fine-rosed spray. Label the plants.

If pots are used, put a small crock in the bottom of the pot, half fill the pot with John Innes No. 1 compost and place the plant in it. Gently spread out the roots and fill the pot with compost to within ½ in. of the top. Lightly firm with the fingers and water with a fine-rosed spray. Label the plants.

If you have a greenhouse, keep the boxed or potted plants on the floor. On warm sunny days spray the surrounding area with water to give a humid atmosphere. After a few days, when the plants have become established, move them on to the staging, but shade them on sunny days, otherwise they will flag. As soon as possible move the plants to a cold frame, since cooler conditions are much better for them.

If no greenhouse is available, newly arrived plants can be put straight into a cold frame after boxing or potting.

Whether the plants are straight from the nursery or have spent some days in the greenhouse, the treatment in the frame is the same.

First keep the frame light closed for a few days, spraying the plants lightly with water in very warm weather and shading them from bright sun.

After about a week the frame light can be lifted a little and gradually opened more each day to a gap of about 6 in. Keep the plants just moist – do not over-water. Sprinkle slug pellets inside the frame and on the surface of the potting compost, and also spray with a systemic insecticide.

After a week the frame light can be gradually opened wider still until it is fully open by about early May. Replace it only when frost threatens. If the plants do become frosted, the danger lies not so much in the freezing, but in a quick thaw. Spray the plants lightly with cold water and shade from the early-morning sun. This allows them to thaw slowly.

At this stage, birds may attack the plants and nip out the growing tips. To prevent them landing on the frame, push some canes into the ground round the outside edge and tie thin black cotton at a height that will deter the birds. Use only thin tacking cotton which will break easily if they fly into it. Nylon or other strong thread may injure the birds. If the plants have to be kept longer in the frames because of the risk of late frosts, water them with a weak liquid fertiliser.

1 *If newly delivered plants are dry, stand them in water overnight*

2 *Half fill 3 in. deep trays with potting compost. Spread out the plant's roots, then fill the tray with more compost. Alternatively, plant in 3–3½ in. pots*

3 *Put the plants in a closed cold frame and spray in warm weather*

4 *Sprinkle slug pellets inside cold frame and spray with insecticide*

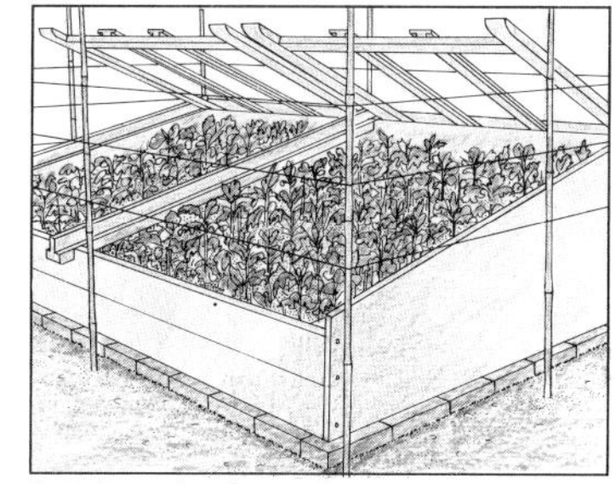

5 *When the frame has been opened, tie cotton around it to repel birds*

Planting out in early summer

Early May is generally soon enough for planting out chrysanthemums. Insert 4 ft canes at each planting position. The best scheme is to plant in double rows with 15 in. between plants and rows. With a trowel make a hole as near to the cane as possible and just a little larger than the root ball of the plant. Mix a sprinkling of fish manure into the bottom of the hole, carefully remove the plant from the box and place it in the hole. Firm it in with the fingers, leaving a small depression around the stem to collect any rain. Tie the plants loosely to canes with raffia or garden string. Sprinkle slug pellets around the base of each plant and fix labels to the canes or in the ground. Once again, avoid over-watering. Do not water them for several days after planting.

Birds will still be a menace, so immediately after planting, wind cotton, running from cane to cane, at the level of the growing tips and lower down. If your garden is not protected from wind, fix a strip of hessian on the exposed side of the plants to act as a windbreak. This can be removed after about a fortnight.

Finally, spray with an insecticide, such as malathion.

1 *Tie each plant loosely to the cane with raffia or garden string*

2 *Label each cane and sprinkle slug pellets around the base of the plants*

Feeding, watering and spraying

In wet weather, sprinkle chrysanthemum fertiliser around each plant every ten days from the end of June until the buds are secured (see overleaf). Then stop all feeding. If the weather is dry, use a liquid feed while watering the plants.

Water plants thoroughly once a week in dry weather.

Spray the plants once a week with an insecticide, alternating with malathion and HCH.

To prevent mildew, spray with Bordeaux mixture or dinocap once every three weeks, after the plants have been moved to their final beds.

FEEDING THE PLANTS

Sprinkle fertiliser every ten days; use liquid feed in dry spells

What can go wrong with chrysanthemums

This chart describes the most common problems that are likely to occur in the growing of chrysanthemums. If your plants show symptoms that are not described here, turn to the full-colour chart of pests and diseases starting on page 377. Trade names for the chemicals are given on page 398.

Symptoms	Cause	Cure
Sinuous whitish lines in the leaf tissue	Leaf miners	Remove mined leaves. Spray with HCH
Distorted flower buds and flowers, leaves crippled or with small holes	Capsid bugs	Spray with HCH, malathion, diazinon or nicotine. Keep down weeds
Leaves and petals eaten	Caterpillars or earwigs	Spray with malathion, HCH or derris
Young shoots eaten off, especially on stools	If slime trails are present, probably slugs. If no slime trails, probably caterpillars	Spread slug pellets around plants, or spray as recommended above against caterpillars
Stunted or crippled stems and leaves	Aphids	Apply derris, malathion or HCH
Whitish powder over leaves and shoots, which may also be malformed	Mildew	Spray with Bordeaux mixture or dinocap
Brown spots under leaves, severe infestations of which can cause yellowing and premature death of foliage	Rust disease	Apply menazon, thiram or zineb
Leaves and shoots regularly wilting during warm sunny weather (pot plants in particular)	Lack of sufficient water; probably also a result of being pot bound	Check dampness of soil at least once a day and pot on if necessary. If wilting continues, the cause is probably verticillium wilt or root rot, so destroy the plants
Thin stems, small pale leaves and flowers	Starvation	Feed or pot on
Flowers on greenhouse plants fail to develop properly and brown off prematurely, particularly in the centre	Grey mould	Remove damaged flowers and maintain a more airy atmosphere by ventilating freely on warm days. Spray with captan or thiram
Leaves with a pale or brownish flecking, growth less vigorous and flower buds checked in growth	Red spider mites	Spray with malathion, dimethoate or derris, or introduce predators into the greenhouse (p. 398)
Leaves, particularly the lower ones, show dark patches beneath, then turn yellow and brown all over and hang limply against the stem. Plants are checked in growth and flowers may be malformed, or small and poor in quality	Leaf and bud eelworms	No easy cure; plants are best destroyed. The cure is to plunge the stools when they are dormant into warm water at 43°C (109°F) for 30 minutes. The water must not fluctuate by more than a few degrees from 43°C. Plant in fresh soil

'Stopping' the plants to get bigger blooms

If a chrysanthemum is allowed to grow naturally, it will develop into a bush-like plant, giving a mass of small flowers.

To obtain good blooms for cutting, garden decoration, or for exhibition, the plant must be restricted or 'stopped'. Stopping also brings the flowering season forward, since many varieties, if left to grow naturally, would bloom too late and be spoilt by autumn frosts.

To stop the plant, pinch out the growing tip of the main stem just above the first pair of fully developed leaves. With most varieties, do this in late May or early June.

Branches will appear or 'break' from the main stem at the leaf axils – the points where the leaves grow from the main stem. It is on these 'breaks' that the flowers will develop. As the breaks grow, pinch out all those that are not required, one at a time, over a few days, until only the number needed remain – six to eight breaks for cut flowers and two or three for exhibition.

Select those breaks which are neither excessively weak nor excessively thick. This will result in shoots of equal thickness and length.

During June and July, the remaining breaks will themselves form side-shoots from their leaf axils. Remove these when they are about 1 in. long and easy to handle, without damaging the rest of the plant.

On some early-flowering varieties, the first stopping does not give the required number of breaks. In this case, make two stoppings, one in late April and one in early June. (Check the chrysanthemum chart for stopping times, p. 69.)

NATURAL GROWTH AND STOPPING

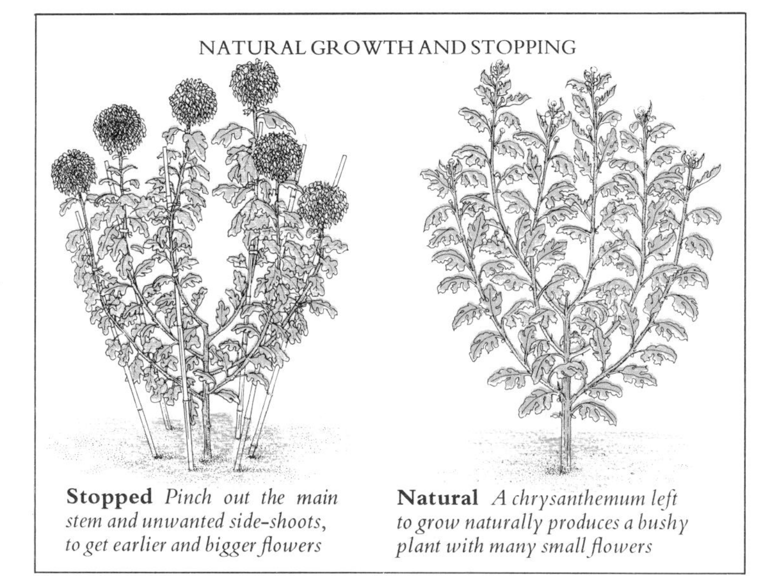

Stopped *Pinch out the main stem and unwanted side-shoots, to get earlier and bigger flowers*

Natural *A chrysanthemum left to grow naturally produces a bushy plant with many small flowers*

1 *In late May, pinch out the main stem above the first pair of full leaves*

2 *New shoots, or 'breaks', will appear from the leaf axils on the main stem*

3 *Pinch out the unwanted breaks over several days, leaving six or eight*

4 *In June and July, remove side-shoots that grow on the remaining breaks*

Securing the main bud on each side branch

By late July or early August a flower bud, known as the crown bud, forms at the tip of each break. This is usually surrounded by a cluster of smaller buds or shoots. To avoid a cluster of small and inferior blooms, the main or crown bud must be 'secured'.

To secure the crown bud, pinch off the side buds and their shoots, one at a time over several days, as with stopping the breaks. If you wish to delay flowering of the crown bud (when the blooms are required for a specific date such as an exhibition or a birthday), these shoots can be allowed to grow up to 2 in. and then be removed.

Do not let them grow any longer or they will starve the crown bud. The time from securing the bud until the bloom is ready varies from six to nine weeks.

An alternative, known as 'running on', is to pinch out the crown bud and allow one of the surrounding shoots to grow on. This will delay flowering up to a fortnight, but with the second method the final bloom will be smaller.

1 *By late July a group of buds form at the top of each break*

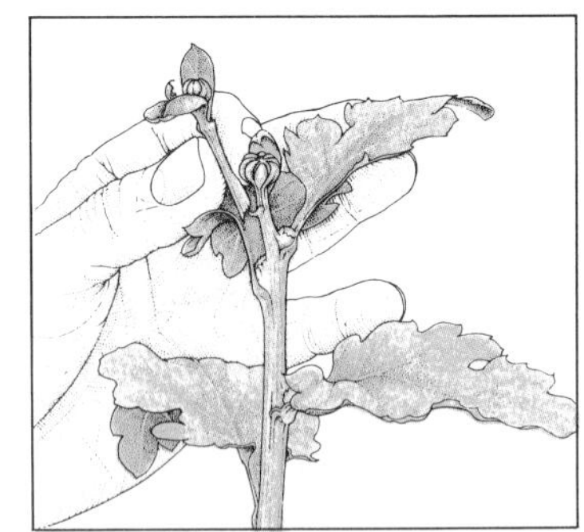

2 *Pinch out the side buds to produce a bigger bloom on the crown bud*

Preventing damage to the blooms

Most gardeners may be content to gather chrysanthemums for indoor decoration, or even leave them to add colour to the garden, with no extra care. But for perfect blooms, such as for exhibition, they must be protected against heavy rain or hail, as well as industrial 'fall-out' from any nearby factories.

One method of protection is to construct an open-sided framework with a sloping roof about 6 ft 3 in. at its highest point and 5 ft 6 in. at its lowest. Over this, covers made of heavy-grade polythene can be firmly secured on lath supports. This protects the blooms, and at the same time allows them to be displayed.

Place the covers over the plants when the buds first begin to show colour, around mid-August. Do not cover earlier, otherwise the blooms will develop long, weak stems.

An alternative method is 'bagging', putting greaseproof paper bags over the blooms. The size of the bag depends on the size of the final bloom – 10 in. wide is usually adequate. Bag the flowers when the first hint of colour appears on the top of the bud. Spray with insecticide before covering the blooms. Use two bags, one inside the other, the outer one having a series of holes punched in it about 3 in. from the opening. This will allow any rain that soaks through to drain away without penetrating the inner one. Write the date on the outer bag.

Tuck in the two corners to make the inner bag more spherical and inflate it. This gives it shape so that it will fit round the growing bloom. Now place the bag over the bud, gather it in about 3 in. down the stem, and tie it firmly with wire tape or wet raffia.

Press the top of the bag down slightly to provide a protective cushion of air round the developing bloom. Finally, fasten a loose tie around plants standing next to each other to prevent the bags knocking into each other and damaging the blooms.

It will take about six to nine weeks for the blooms to develop fully – a corner can be torn off a bag to examine a bloom but always twist the corner to seal the bag after checking.

TWO WAYS OF PROTECTING PLANTS

Frame *Open-sided framework of wood and polythene prevents heavy rain, hail and industrial pollution spoiling the blooms*

Bagging *Putting the blooms inside two greaseproof bags also prevents damage to the blooms by heavy rain and wind*

Cutting the blooms for indoor display

The day before the blooms are to be cut, give the plants a good watering. If possible, cut them the following morning, while the stems still contain a lot of moisture.

Cut the stem about 2 ft below the bloom with secateurs.

Strip the leaves from the bottom of the stem to a point midway along it and then bruise the bottom 3–4 in. with a hammer. This will help to preserve the blooms. Put the flowers immediately into a deep container of water.

Leave them for 24 hours in a cool, shady place.

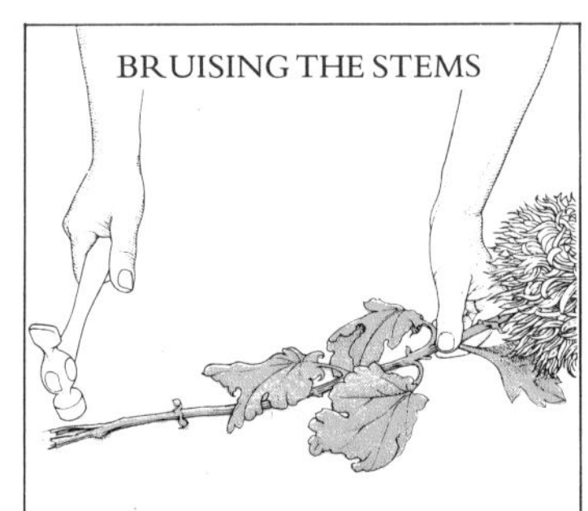

BRUISING THE STEMS

Bruise the base of the stem to make cut blooms last longer

Sprays and October varieties

Growing sprays for garden or indoor decoration

If your aim is simply to obtain plenty of good flowers without bothering too much about their size, the stopping and timing instructions can largely be ignored. Most early-flowering types will give perfectly good results if the growing tips are pinched out once, when the plants are 8–9 in. high. Nothing more needs to be done, other than staking.

Instead of having one or two large blooms on each stem, the plants will grow into bushes carrying clusters of smaller flowers. These sprays can be used for floral art.

Varieties good for this are listed by nurseries as 'Sprays'.

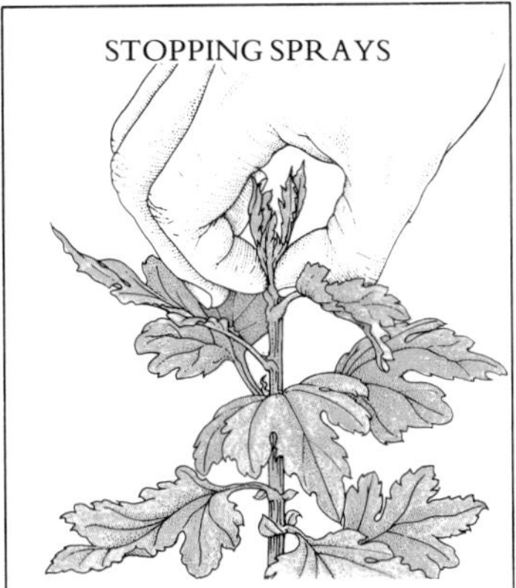

When plants are 8–9 in. high, pinch out above the first full leaves

October-flowering plants in the greenhouse

Chrysanthemums sold as October-flowering varieties are mainly late versions of the early-flowering kinds, and should be grown in a greenhouse. They can be grown in the open in warm parts of the country, but must be moved into a greenhouse if there is a risk of frost in October.

In May, plant October-flowering varieties in open ground and stop and disbud the plants in the same way as early-flowering types. In September, carefully remove them from their beds.

Cut the ties and take away the cane. Insert a fork well under the roots, and lift each plant with as much soil on the roots as possible.

Put the plants in the greenhouse border, or in tubs or large boxes. Replace the canes and ties.

Give the plants as much room as possible in the greenhouse. The more light and air they can receive, the better they will grow.

Ventilate freely in mild weather. Only frost protection is required. Heat will weaken the plants.

1 *Loosen the soil with a fork, then push the fork under the stool and lift*

2 *Put the plants in the greenhouse border, or in tubs or boxes*

New plants from cuttings

Lifting the stools for winter and starting new growth

Most modern chrysanthemums are fairly hardy, but they dislike excessive damp, which damages the blooms, or frost, which damages the plants. The stools (base of the plants) must therefore be lifted and stored under cover so that new plants can be grown from them.

A partial rest after flowering seems to benefit the stools. Leave the plants until late September and then cut the stems down to 9 in.

To lift the stools, loosen the soil around the roots with a fork, then insert the fork well below the roots on one side of the plant and lift.

Using sharp secateurs, take away all new basal growth as this will be of little use for propagation. It is not necessary to remove all the soil, but take away the top layer. Place the stools in boxes (tomato trays are ideal) labelling each variety and keeping them separate.

Fill any gaps and cover the stools with either John Innes No. 1 compost or a mixture of equal parts peat and sand with a little fertiliser added. Pack the compost around the stools.

Lightly water the trays to settle the new compost around the roots. Place the boxes in a cold frame. Close the lights only if frost is forecast. Otherwise the staging of a cold greenhouse is adequate. The stools should have plenty of light, and though resistant to light frost they must not be exposed to wet conditions. They will need no more watering until about late December. Dust with HCH powder and put slug pellets on the soil.

In early January, move the stools from the cold frame to the greenhouse staging, and water them. A greenhouse temperature of 7°C (45°F) will encourage new growth.

1 *Cut down the main stems to 9 in. in late September or early October*

2 *Loosen the soil with a fork, push the fork below the roots and lift*

3 *Cut off all new basal growth at ground level with secateurs*

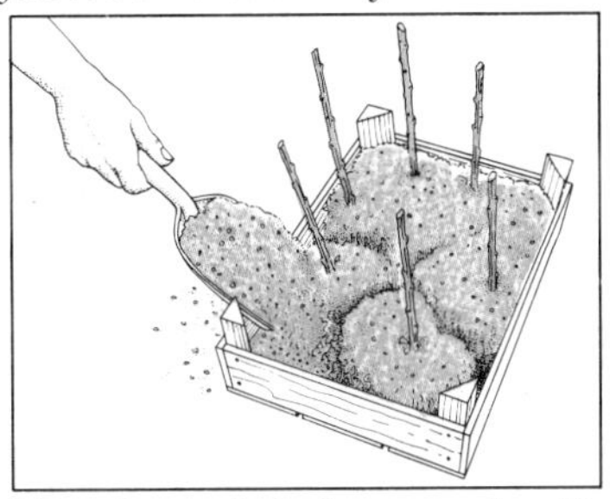

4 *Put the stools in boxes, pack with compost, and store in a cold frame*

Raising the cuttings under glass

If a heated propagator is available, the best time to take cuttings is from late February to the middle of March. With only an unheated frame, cuttings can still be taken, but since a later start must be made – late March or early April – earlier-flowering varieties should be used. Later ones would not produce blooms before the first frosts, so young plants must be bought from a nursery.

Fill 3 in. deep seed trays with moistened John Innes No. 1 compost and sprinkle a layer of fine sand on top of the compost. Firm the surface slightly with a flat piece of wood. If seed trays are not available use 3 in. pots, placing four cuttings in each pot.

Remove one of the new basal growths from the stools – ideally it should be about $2\frac{1}{2}$–3 in. long, but a cutting from a longer growth will also work. In the absence of basal growth, use cuttings from the main stem. This should be a last resort, as they tend to bud prematurely.

Using sharp scissors or a razor blade, remove the lower leaves carefully from the cutting, ensuring that no skin is stripped from the stem; this makes the cutting vulnerable to the fungus disease known as 'damping off'.

Use a razor blade to make a straight cut across the stem immediately below one of the nodes (leaf joints) from which the leaves have been removed. The prepared cutting should now be about $1\frac{1}{2}$–2 in. long.

Immerse the cutting completely in a jar of weak insecticide, and then dip the bottom $\frac{1}{4}$ in. of wet stem into hormone rooting powder.

Although the use of a hormone rooting powder results in 99 per cent successful rooting, it is not essential. Chrysanthemum cuttings root easily without a rooting powder.

Using a thick piece of wire (about $\frac{1}{8}$ in.) or similar implement, make holes about 1 in. deep and insert the cuttings, spaced $1\frac{1}{2}$–2 in. apart. Gently firm the compost round the stems with the fingers, then settle the cuttings in by watering them with a fine-rosed spray.

An alternative method of planting, which is quick and simple, is to hold the cutting between finger and thumb, dip it into the hormone powder, then gently push it into the compost to a depth of about 1 in.

No firming of the compost is necessary since the watering will wash the sand into any spaces between the cuttings and the compost, although in a light peaty soil it is an advantage to press the soil lightly with the fingers.

With good cuttings that are about $\frac{1}{8}$ in. thick, and a little practice, few will snap and time is saved.

Label the box of cuttings with the varieties and their date of planting and place it in a propagator supplied with gentle bottom heat, or back in the cold frame if the cuttings have been taken in late March or early April. Do not water again until the compost has dried out, though a light spraying with clean water on warm days will prevent the cuttings from drooping.

Rooting takes place in about ten days in a propagator, and after four to five weeks in an unheated cold frame. This is shown by the much healthier appearance of the leaves.

When rooting has taken place, the cuttings are ready – after a watering – to be lifted and moved into pots or deeper boxes.

Now treat the young plants in the same way as newly arrived plants from a nursery (p. 61).

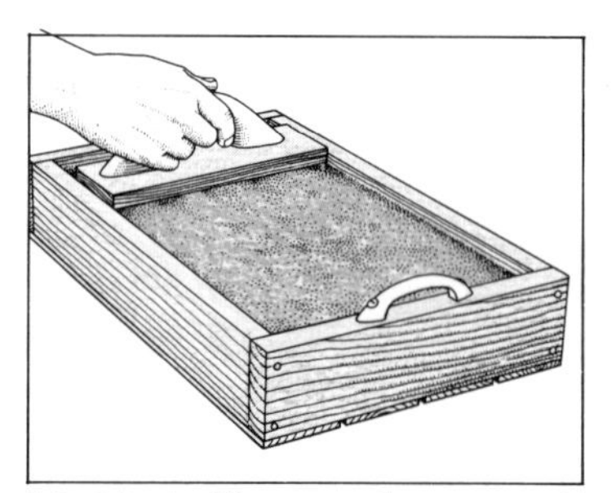

1 *In March, fill a tray with compost, add a little sand, then firm down*

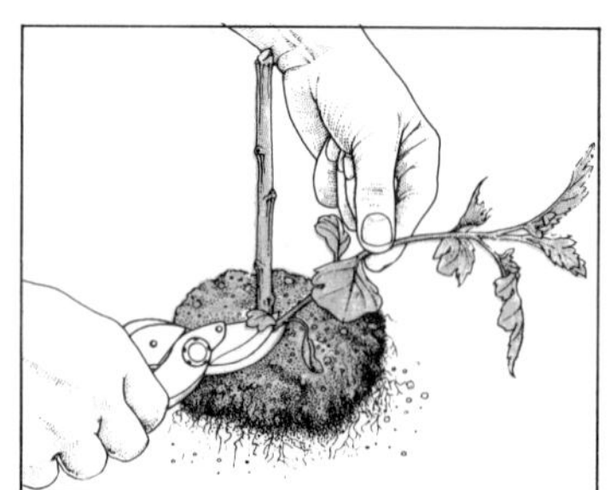

2 *Remove one of the new $2\frac{1}{2}$–3 in. basal growths from the stool*

3 *Nip off the lower leaves carefully, without stripping skin from the stem*

4 *Cut the stem below a leaf joint with a razor blade*

5 *Make 1 in. deep holes about $1\frac{1}{2}$–2 in. apart, and insert the cuttings*

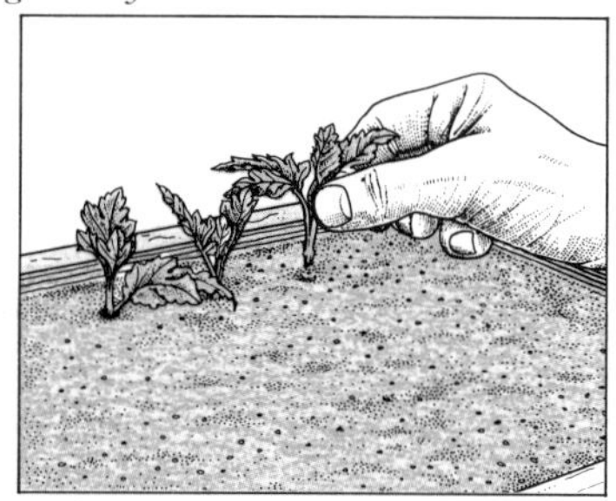

6 *Alternatively, just push the cuttings gently into unfirmed compost*

7 *Place the tray in a propagator with bottom heat, or in a cold frame*

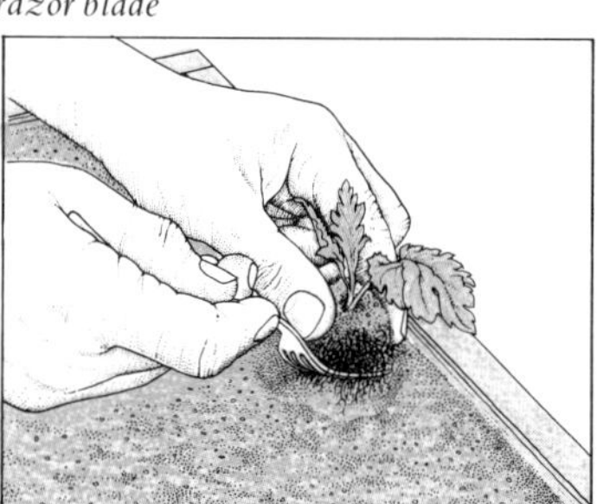

8 *After rooting, lift the cuttings and treat them as nursery plants*

Late chrysanthemums in the greenhouse

Moving young plants into larger pots

The treatment of greenhouse chrysanthemums – usually known as 'late-flowering' types – is the same as for garden varieties until the nursery plants have been set in boxes or in 3–3½ in. pots in a frame or greenhouse. Do not overcrowd the boxes. Nine plants to a box 16 in. by 10 in. and 3 in. deep is the maximum.

When pots are used, the plants will need an intermediate move from the 3–3½ in. pots into 5 in. or 6 in., depending on the vigour of each plant (some plants will produce stronger and thicker growth). From mid-March look at each plant's root system once a week.

To do this, hold the plant with its stem between forefinger and second finger, invert the pot and tap the bottom. The soil ball will drop out. If roots are breaking through and around the compost, the plant is ready for repotting. Select a 5 in. or 6 in. pot, and half fill it with John Innes No. 2. This slightly richer mixture is needed as the plants will develop quickly.

Place the ball of roots centrally in the prepared pot and fill up around it with John Innes No. 2. Make the compost moderately firm.

The new compost should just cover the root ball and still leave ½ in. space for watering.

Insert a short cane and fasten the plant loosely to it. Water carefully with a can fitted with a rose.

Final potting Towards the end of May, the young plants – whether raised in pots or boxes – must have their final potting. Use moist John Innes No. 3 potting compost and pots that are not too big for the roots.

As a general guide, incurves, reflexed and intermediates need 8½ in. pots and medium singles 7½–8½ in.

Use the same potting procedure as described above, making sure the compost is moderately firm. Insert a 4 ft cane and loosely tie the plant in two places.

Stand the plants outside in a sheltered, shaded place.

After final potting, water is seldom needed for at least three days. Spray the foliage on warm days to prevent the plants flagging.

1 *With the stem between forefinger and second finger, tap out the plant*

2 *Put some compost in a larger pot, put in the plant, and add more compost*

Stopping the plants to get bigger blooms

For the general principles of stopping see page 63.

Most late-flowering chrysanthemums require slightly different treatment – in some cases a second stopping, which produces better blooms with some varieties. Two stoppings may also be required if blooming is to be delayed.

The method is the same as for first stopping. Pinch out the side-shoots resulting from the first stopping so that breaks are encouraged to form on these shoots. These second breaks will produce terminal buds which are known as second crown buds as distinct from those formed after the first stopping, which are known as first crown buds.

Incurved The best blooms are obtained on second crown buds resulting from a stopping in March or April, followed by another in June.

Reflexed and intermediate Many of these give November blooms on a natural break from cuttings taken at the end of February. If a natural break has not been made by mid-June, then the plant should be stopped immediately.

Christmas flowering for certain late-flowering varieties requires two stoppings, in April and late July.

Anemone-centred Two stoppings are needed – one at the beginning of April and the other in mid-June.

Singles The best flowers appear from second crown buds from stoppings in mid-April and June. Restrict each plant to nine blooms.

1 *Second stopping means pinching out shoots produced from the first stopping*

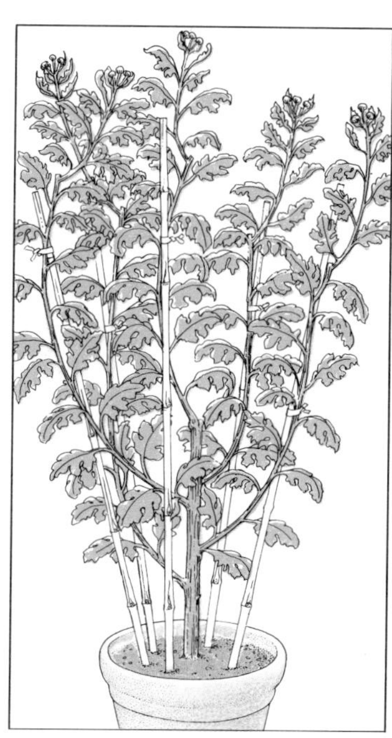

2 *New breaks now produce terminal buds known as second crown buds*

A summer standing ground in full sun

After plants have been in their final pots for three weeks, move them to a prepared standing ground in full sun outdoors until the autumn.

The standing ground should be a position as open as possible. Stand the pots on tiles, bricks or a concrete path, to keep out worms. The plants need good support, so drive firm posts, piping or fencing standards into the ground at either end of the row of pots. Fasten two straining wires between them at about 2 ft and 5 ft above the ground.

Firmly tie the supporting canes to the straining wires with garden string. This will prevent the pots being blown over.

When watering the potted chrysanthemums, each plant requires separate attention. They must not be allowed to dry out, though over-watering can do a lot of harm. Make a daily inspection; a general guide is to water every other day from the end of June onwards, except when it rains heavily.

Feed the plants regularly. For large blooms sprinkle a teaspoon of chrysanthemum fertiliser on the surface once a week; it will dissolve when the plants are watered. Combined with this, apply a general liquid fertiliser once a week.

However, a simple and adequate programme for those not aiming at prize-quality blooms, is to give the plants three feeds of solid chrysanthemum fertiliser during summer.

Apply a dessertspoon to each plant at the beginning of July, another in August, and finally before housing the plants in September.

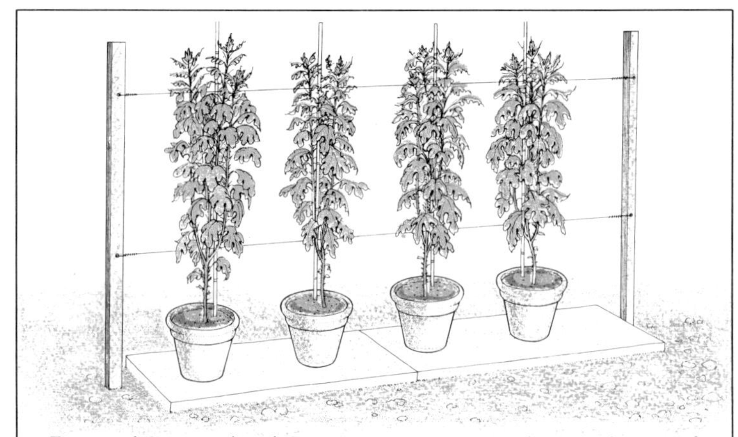

From mid-June until mid-September stand the pots on tiles or bricks outside the greenhouse. Put posts at each end of the row, and fasten straining wires between them at 2 ft and 5 ft from the ground. Tie the plant canes to the wires to prevent the pots being blown over

Returning plants to the greenhouse

When the buds just begin to show colour – about mid-September – take the plants into the greenhouse.

Tilt each pot, supporting it with three bricks, and spray the foliage with a mixture of fungicide and insecticide. Stand the pot upright to drain.

For the first ten days after housing, leave the ventilators open to allow the plants to become acclimatised. As the weather becomes cooler reduce the ventilation, but use a fan to keep the air moving. Avoid high temperatures, especially during bright sunny days. Shade the glass if necessary with butter-muslin.

At night, maintain a steady heat of about 10–13°C (50–55°F). This will allow the blooms to develop properly and prevent moisture forming on them. Do not feed the plants once they have been housed.

SPRAYING THE FOLIAGE

Before returning the pot to the greenhouse, tilt it against three bricks, and spray both sides of the leaves with a mixture of fungicide and insecticide

Storing pots over winter and taking cuttings

Once the blooms have been cut, reduce the heating to about 4°C (39°F). To produce cuttings for next year, treat the plants exactly as with outdoor varieties (p. 65), except that before storing, basal growths should be cut down only as far as the last pair of leaves above the soil. This allows shoots to develop from the leaf axils, which can be used if there are no fresh basal growths.

During December or January, water the plants and increase the temperature to 7–10°C (45–50°F). This will provide material for cuttings a little earlier than the outdoor varieties – some time between late December and early February – according to the variety. Cuttings are taken and propagated in the same way as for the outdoor plants.

Sometimes basal growth can be stimulated by removing the plants from their pots, washing off the old soil, and planting them in fresh compost in 6 in. pots.

GROWING NEW PLANTS

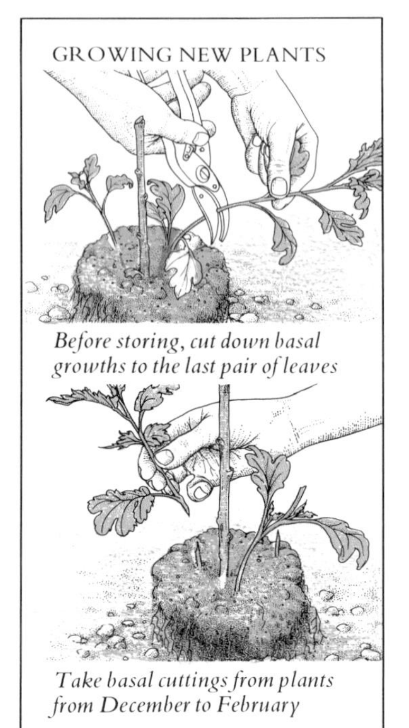

Before storing, cut down basal growths to the last pair of leaves

Take basal cuttings from plants from December to February

Chrysanthemums for garden and greenhouse

Because of the many varieties being introduced each year, any list of chrysanthemums will eventually be out of date. However, this list gives a guide to varieties which will form the basis of a good collection lasting for several years.

The height of plants has been omitted, as it can vary according to which part of the country they are grown, the height above sea level, position of growing site, how early the plant's life is started and the cultural methods of the grower.

The heights of varieties listed in nurserymen's catalogues will give a rough guide, but most catalogues underestimate the height to which the plants will finally grow. Add 12–18 in. to the height given. This is particularly important with greenhouse chrysanthemums which can grow to 5–6 ft. A few varieties may grow even taller.

Early varieties for growing outdoors

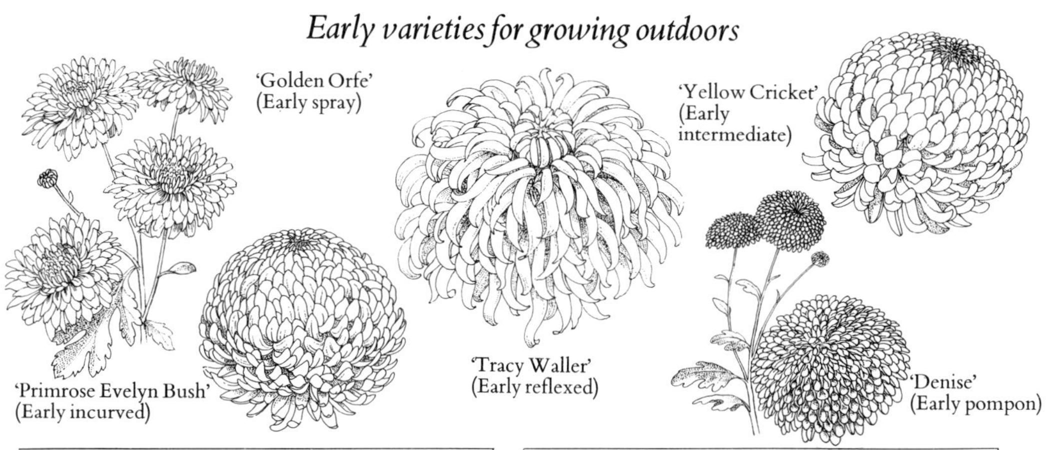

REFLEXED

Name	Colour	Date of cuttings	Stopping dates
Large flowered			
'Alpine Snow'	White	Mid-Feb.	Early May
'Cecily Starmer'	Pink	Mid-Feb.	Mid-May
'Cherry Tracy Waller'	Red	Mid-Feb.	Mid-May
'Grace Riley'	Bronze	Mid-Feb.	Mid-May
'Salmon Tracy Waller'	Salmon	Mid-Feb.	Mid-May
'Smart Fella'	Yellow	Early Feb.	Early May
'Tracy Waller'	Pink	Mid-Feb.	Mid-May
Medium flowered			
'Alice Jones'	Light bronze	Mid-Feb.	Mid-May
'Bronze Eve Gray'	Bronze	Mid-Feb.	Mid-May
'Early Red Cloak'	Red	Early Feb.	Mid-May
'Eve Gray'	Pink	Mid-Feb.	Mid-May
'Karen Rowe'	Pink	Late Feb.	Early June
'Mexico'	Red	End Feb.	Early June
'Munich'	Purple	Late Feb.	Mid-May
'Value'	Bronze	Early Jan.	Mid-April
Medium reflexed			
'Bellair'	Purple	Late Feb.	Early June
'Breitner'	Pink	Late Feb.	Early June
'Corbei'	White	Late Feb.	Early June
'Mendip'	Red	Late Feb.	Early June
'Pinksmoor'	Pink	Late Feb.	Early June
'Stardust'	Yellow	Late Feb.	Early June
'Yvonne Arnaud'	Pink	Late Feb.	Early June

INTERMEDIATES

Name	Colour	Date of cuttings	Stopping dates
Large flowered			
'Arctic Glow'	White	Late Feb.	Mid-May
'Crown of Gold'	Yellow	Late Feb.	Early June
'Evelyn Bush'	White	Early Feb.	Late May
'Gladys Sharpe'	Yellow	End Jan.	Early May
'Keystone'	Purple	Mid-Feb.	Mid-May
Medium flowered			
'Bill Else'	Yellow	Late Feb.	Early June
'Cricket'	White	End Feb.	Early June
'Lynn'	White	Mid-Feb.	Late May
'Primrose Cricket'	Pale yellow	End Feb.	Early June
'Tibshelf Gem'	Yellow	Mid-Feb.	Early June
'Yellow Cricket'	Yellow	End Feb.	Early June

INCURVED

Name	Colour	Date of cuttings	Stopping dates
Large flowered			
'Ermine'	White	Late Feb.	Mid-May
'Pat Amos'	White	Mid-Feb.	Mid-May
'Primrose Evelyn Bush'	Pale yellow	Early Feb.	Late May
'Yellow Pat Amos'	Yellow	Mid-Feb.	Mid-May
Medium flowered			
'Iris Riley'	Pink	Late Feb.	Early June
'Nancy Matthews'	White	Late Feb.	Mid-June

POMPONS

Name	Colour	Date of cuttings	Stopping dates
'Andy Pandy'	Yellow	Mid-Feb.	Pinch out the growing tip when plants are 9 in. tall. No further stopping is required
'Bright Eye'	Yellow	Mid-Feb.	
'Bronze Fairie'	Bronze	Mid-Feb.	
'Cameo'	White	Mid-Feb.	
'Denise'	Yellow	Mid-Feb.	
'Fairie'	Pink	Mid-Feb.	
'Salmon Fairie'	Salmon	Mid-Feb.	

SPRAYS

Name	Colour	Date of cuttings	Stopping dates
'Adeline'	White	Mid-Feb.	Late May
'Gerrie Hoek'	Pink	Mid-Feb.	Late May
'Golden Orfe'	Yellow	Mid-Feb.	Late May
'Lilian Hoek'	Bronze	Mid-Feb.	Late May
'Madeline'	Pink	Mid-Feb.	Late May
'Pennine Cream'	Pale yellow	Mid-Feb.	Late May
'Pennine Pink'	Pink	Mid-Feb.	Late May
'Pennine Shell'	Salmon	Mid-Feb.	Late May
'Piccolo'	Pale yellow	Mid-Feb.	Late May
'Red Lilian Hoek'	Red	Mid-Feb.	Late May
'Yellow Lilian Hoek'	Yellow	Mid-Feb.	Late May

After the initial stopping no further restriction is required. Most of the other early-flowering varieties will also give good sprays if they are not disbudded after the initial stopping.

Late varieties for the greenhouse

'Audrey Shoesmith' (Late incurved)

'Stargazer' (Late single)

'Joy Hughes' (Late reflexed)

'Red Balcombe Perfection' (Late intermediate)

REFLEXED

Name	Colour	Date of cuttings	Stopping dates
Large flowered			
'Bridal Gown'	White	Early Jan.	Mid-June
'Elizabeth Woolman'	Pink	Early Feb.	Mid-June
'Jim Draycott'	White	Mid-Feb.	Mid-June
'Mary Selvey'	Claret	Early Feb.	Early June
'Walkers Jewel'	Pale pink	Early Feb.	Mid-June
Medium flowered			
'Beechview Flame'	Red	Mid-Feb.	Mid-June
'Capri'	Purple	Early Feb.	Early June
'Deep Pink Joy Hughes'	Pink	Mid-Jan.	Early June
'Golden Princess Anne'	Yellow	Late Feb.	Late June
'Icelander'	White	Mid-Feb.	Mid-June
'Joy Hughes'	Pink	Mid-Jan.	Early June
'Princess Anne'	Pink	Late Feb.	Late June
'Regency'	Purple	Early Feb.	Mid-June
'Shirley Garnet'	Red	Early Feb.	Early June
'Stuart Shoesmith'	Light bronze	End Feb.	Mid-June

INTERMEDIATES

Name	Colour	Date of cuttings	Stopping dates
Large flowered			
'Balcombe Perfection'	Bronze	Early Jan.	Early May
'Beacon'	Red	Mid-Jan.	Mid-April and early June
'Daily Mirror'	Purple	Mid-Jan.	Mid-April and mid-June
'Golden Balcombe Perfection'	Yellow	Early Jan.	Early May
'Goldfoil'	Yellow	Mid-Jan.	End May
'Lagoon'	Pink	Early Feb.	Mid-June
'Red Balcombe Perfection'	Red	Early Jan.	Early May
Medium flowered			
'Brenda Till'	Pale yellow	Early Feb.	Early June
'Lilian Shoesmith'	Light bronze	Mid-Feb.	Early June
'New Era'	Purple	Early Feb.	Mid-June

INCURVED

Name	Colour	Date of cuttings	Stopping dates
Large flowered			
'Audrey Shoesmith'	Pink	Late Dec.	Mid-April and June
'Eva Randall'	Bronze	Mid-Feb.	Mid-June
'Mavis Shoesmith'	Pink	Mid-Feb.	Early June
'Polar Gem'	White	Mid-Jan.	Mid-April and early June
'Primrose Polar Gem'	Pale yellow	Mid-Jan.	Mid-April and early June
'Red Shirley Model'	Red	Mid-Jan.	Mid-May
'Shirley Model'	Pink	Mid-Jan.	Mid-May
'Yellow Marvel'	Yellow	Mid-Jan.	Mid-April and mid-June
Medium flowered			
'Brett Williams'	Yellow	Early Feb.	Mid-May
'Dorothy Foley'	Pink	Early Feb.	Mid-June
'Lovely Shirley'	Pink	Mid-Jan.	Mid-May
'Minstrel Boy'	Bronze	Mid-Feb.	Late June
'Ron Shoesmith'	White	Early Feb.	Early June
'Waterloo'	Bronze	Early Feb.	Early June

LATE SINGLES

Name	Colour	Date of cuttings	Stopping dates
Medium flowered			
'Jinx'	White	Mid-Jan.	Mid-April and mid-June
'Lilian Jackson'	Pink	Mid-Jan.	Mid-April and mid-June
'Nancy Sherwood'	Yellow	Mid-Jan.	Mid-April and mid-June
'Stargazer'	Yellow	Mid-Jan.	Mid-April and mid-June

OTHER TYPES

Late Anemones, Pompons, Spidery and Sprays

There are not many varieties offered by nurserymen in these sections; all those that are listed in their catalogues without exception give very good results.

'Gladys M. Reynolds'
(Giant cactus)

Dahlias

The brightness of the flowers, their complex shapes, and the rich foliage of the dahlia, add an exotic touch of colour to the garden in the late summer months

The dahlia comes originally from Mexico. It was known to the Aztecs and recorded by European adventurers to the country in the late 16th century. Eventually, the Spanish introduced it to Europe in the 18th century. But the plant was then very different from the modern dahlia.

The original species, *Dahlia imperialis*, had single lilac flowers and grew to between 6 ft and 18 ft high. Smaller species were also discovered, including *D. coccinea*, which had single red flowers. From two or more of these small, single-flowered species, modern plants developed, with large, complex blooms.

The plant was called dahlia in honour of Dr Andreas Dahl, an eminent Swedish botanist.

The dahlia is basically a subtropical plant needing rich soil, constant watering and regular feeding. It has tuberous roots, hollow stems and usually rich green leaves.

The richness of colour in the leaves makes a striking background for the exotic colours and shapes of the blooms.

The flowers grow in a large selection of colours and petal formations, and are ideal for garden display, exhibition and indoor decoration.

Dahlias bloom from late July, through August and September, until autumn frosts occur.

There are two groups of dahlias: bedding dahlias, grown annually from seed, and tuberous, which although suitable for mixed borders are best grown on their own.

Tuberous dahlias are further classified into groups according to the form of their flowers. The most popular groups are the decoratives, cactus, ball and pompon. Other groups grown include collerettes, single flowered, anemone flowered and paeony flowered.

Decoratives have a formal shape and fully double flowers with no central disc. The florets are broad and rounded at the ends, and are usually slightly twisted.

Cactus dahlias have fully double flowers, but they have narrow, pointed florets which are rolled back (or quilled) for more than half their length. Semi-cactus dahlias are similar to cactus, except that the florets are broader and quilled for half their length or less.

Decoratives, cactus and semi-cactus can be grouped according to the size of their blooms. These are, giant (over 10 in. diameter), large (8–10 in.), medium (6–8 in.), small (4–6 in.) and miniature (under 4 in.).

Ball dahlias are another popular group. The flowers are rounded like a ball, though sometimes flattened on top. The florets are blunt or rounded at the tip, and are arranged spirally. Each one is rolled for more than half its length.

There are two divisions of ball dahlias: small, with flowers 4–6 in. in diameter, and miniatures with flowers less than 4 in. in diameter.

The flowers of pompons are similar to ball dahlias, but are much smaller (less than 2 in.) and more globular. The florets are rolled for the whole of their length.

Collerettes have flowers with yellow centres made up of stamens and a single row of florets round the edge. An inner collar of smaller florets surrounds the stamens, lying between them and the petals – hence the name collerette.

Single-flowered dahlias have blooms consisting of a single outer ring of florets, which may overlap, and a central disc of stamens. The flowers are up to 4 in. in size.

Anemone-flowered dahlias are the same size, but they have double flowers with flat, outer florets surrounding a densely packed group of shorter florets, often of contrasting colours.

Paeony-flowered dahlias may also grow to 4 in. in diameter. Each flower consists of two or more rings of flat ray florets and a central disc.

The other dahlia group – bedding dahlias – includes those plants not exceeding 2 ft in height. They are sub-divided according to the form of their blooms, but most of them are either single or decorative types, and most are small flowered.

Leaf colour can vary widely with different types of dahlias. The range spreads from deep bronze or greenish-red through to emerald-green. Variegated foliage is unusual, except occasionally in young plants. The colour usually reverts to normal as the plants mature.

Leaf texture and form can differ also. Some leaves are softer than others, but they do not last well when cut. Those with a tough, leathery skin are better for display.

Leaf forms can range from the very rounded types, as with decorative types of dahlias, to many-lobed, finely cut shapes, some of which may be almost fern-like in appearance.

Named dahlia varieties are propagated by taking stem cuttings from the tuber crowns, but others, such as the Coltness hybrids, can be grown from seed. The flowers are then normally of mixed colours.

Dahlias are best grown in a bed on their own, where there is plenty of light. They should not be in the shade of buildings or overhanging trees. They can, however, be used in the herbaceous border: yellow, scarlet and bronze varieties contrast well with michaelmas daisies.

In a shrub border facing south-east, south or south-west, which will get plenty of sun, a group of dahlias will give a splash of colour against the autumn foliage.

Planting distances depend on the height of the plant. Tall-growing dahlias (4–5 ft) should be about 2–3 ft apart, medium types (3–4 ft) about 2 ft apart and the bedding types 15 in. apart.

Plant bedding varieties in groups of five or seven along the edge of the border or in an exclusive bed, either all one variety or mixed.

Decoratives, cactus, semi-cactus, collerettes, ball and pompon should be planted singly, or in groups of three of one variety.

If mixing types in a dahlia bed, the best display is made by planting in groups of three in a triangle.

It is essential to be able to reach each plant for tying, disbudding, fertilising and weeding, so leave a path between groups of plants or through the rows.

At the end of the season there is usually no urgency to clear the bed and lift the tubers if the dahlias have been grown for garden display. They can be left in the ground until autumn frosts blacken the leaves.

With exhibition plants, however, there is little point in leaving them in the ground after the tubers have ripened. A spell of cold, wet weather may encourage fungi and bacteria to become active, and valuable plants may be destroyed.

As soon as the tubers are fully ripe, lift them. Ripeness is evident when the plant becomes weaker, blooms are poorly coloured and tend to become daisy-eyed, and bud production is much slower.

Do not lift the tubers before they are ripe, as they must absorb sufficient nourishment to carry them through winter and to help them produce strong, new growth in the following season.

Anemone flowered *Flat, outer florets surround packed shorter florets*

Single flowered *One ring of florets encircles a central disc of stamens*

Paeony flowered *Two or more rings of flat florets surround a central disc*

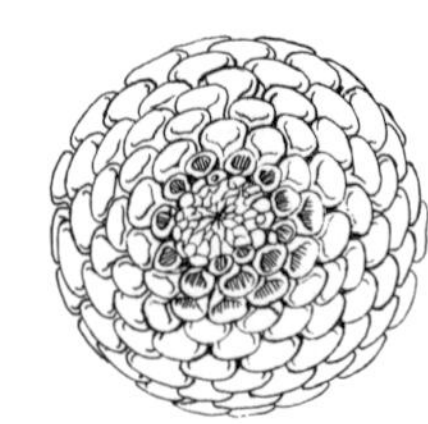

Ball *The spherical flowers have blunt, quilled florets, set in a spiral pattern*

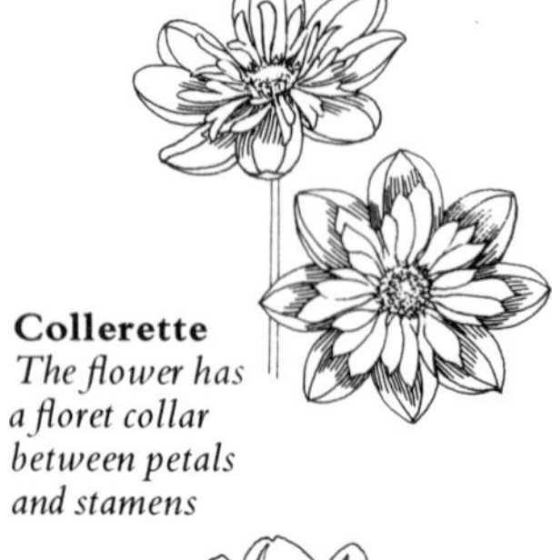

Collerette *The flower has a floret collar between petals and stamens*

Cactus *The double flower has narrow, pointed florets quilled for more than half their length*

Semi-cactus *Similar to cactus, but florets broader and quilled for less than half their length*

Pompon *The flower is spherical, but smaller than a ball type. Florets are fully quilled*

Decorative *The double flower has no central disc. Florets are broad, usually with blunt ends*

Where, when and how to plant dahlias

Heavy manuring: the recipe for good blooms

Dahlias will thrive in any soil that is neither too acid nor too alkaline. A good medium loamy soil which is slightly acid is ideal.

Dahlias are gross feeders, so in autumn dig a heavy dressing of farmyard manure, compost or other organic material into the soil. Add a dressing of 4 heaped tablespoons of sterilised bonemeal to each square yard. Leave the surface rough, so that frost and winter weather break it down thoroughly.

Position dahlias in a warm, sunny site where they will get plenty of air. Provided the plot is not completely overshadowed by trees or high buildings, a certain amount of afternoon shade is useful.

If there is any doubt about the food available in the soil, a proprietary dahlia fertiliser can be applied after the first flower buds have appeared.

How to plant and space the tubers

Plant tubers around mid-April, as soon as the ground is workable. Tall-growing dahlias (4–5 ft) should be about 2–3 ft apart, medium types (3–4 ft) at 2 ft, while bedding types should be spaced every 15 in.

New growth on dahlias arises not from the tuberous roots but from the crown, which is the base of the old stem. Make sure that one or more tubers are attached to a piece of old stem with an eye.

Insert 1 in. square stakes in the bed where the tubers are to be planted. The stakes should be shorter than the eventual height of the plants.

Dig a 6 in. deep hole in front of the stake, so that the eye (or bud point) on the base of the old stem can be planted against the stake.

Half fill the hole with planting mixture, made up of a bucket of peat to 4 oz. (4 tablespoons) of organic fertiliser rich in nitrogen, such as fish manure. Place the tuber on this so that the crown is about 2 in. beneath the soil surface.

Cover the tuber with more soil mixed with planting mixture and, if there are several tuberous roots on the stem, make sure the soil fills all the spaces between them, to keep out slugs.

After filling the hole completely, firm the soil with the fingers. Do not water. Label the stake.

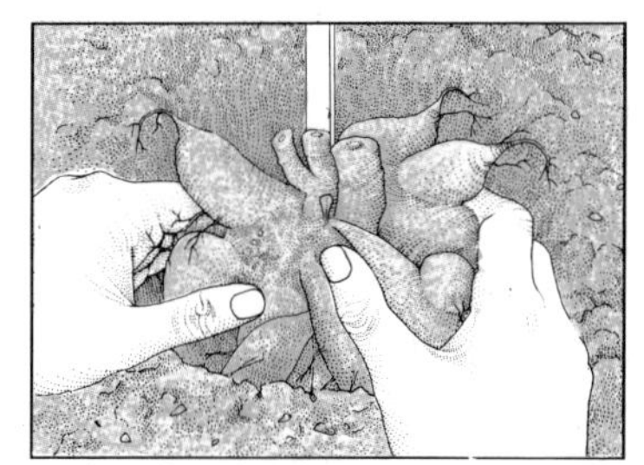

1 *Place the tubers horizontally in a 6 in. hole, the stem close to a stake*

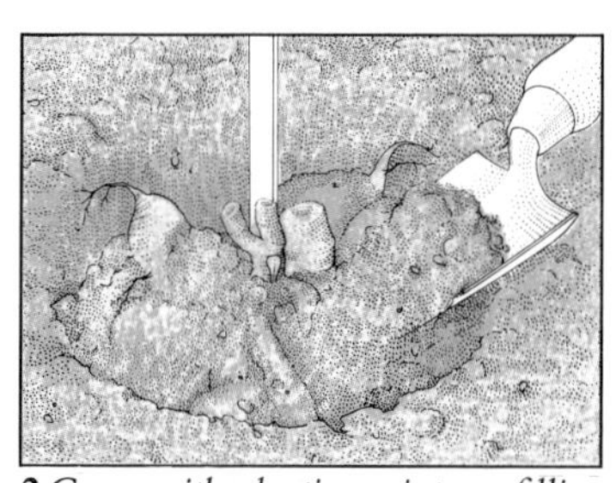

2 *Cover with planting mixture, filling the spaces between the tubers*

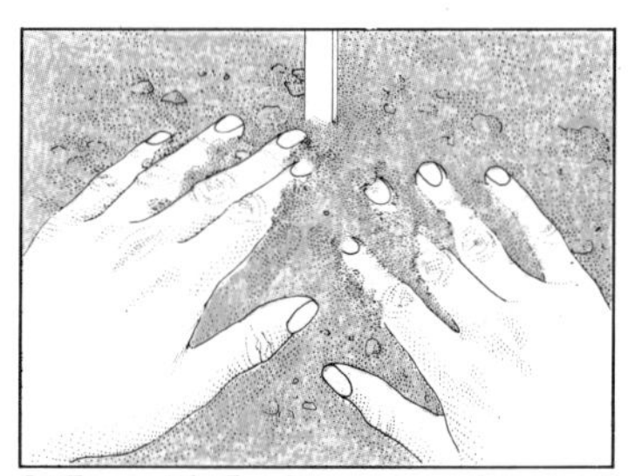

3 *Firm with the fingers, and then label the stake. Do not water*

Planting out young pot-grown plants

Young dahlia plants can be bought from nurseries, already growing in pots. Plant them out in late May or early June, when there is no risk of frost. Insert stakes in the bed as described under planting tubers.

Prepare a planting mixture of a bucket of peat to 4 oz. (4 tablespoons) of organic fertiliser rich in nitrogen, such as fish manure.

Water the dahlias at the time of planting out and, if the weather is dry, again within two days.

Using a trowel, dig a hole next to the stake and large enough to take the root ball (about 6 in. deep). Put a couple of handfuls of planting mixture in the hole.

Remove the plant from the pot with its soil ball intact. If the roots circle round the outside of the soil ball, do not tease them out as this can cause damage.

Place the root ball in the hole and fill the space round it with the planting mixture. Firm gently with the fingers.

Top up the space above the root ball with more planting mixture, but leave a saucer-shaped depression about 2 in. deep round the stem. This will help to collect moisture and give the young plant a good start.

If the soil is very heavy and retentive, do not make a depression, as stagnant water round the neck of the dahlia can be harmful.

When the plant starts to make new growth, the depression can be filled by raking in a little of the surrounding soil and levelling the plot.

1 *Water the potted dahlias about an hour before planting*

2 *After digging a 6 in. hole beside the stake, remove plant from the pot*

3 *Put the root ball in the hole, and fill in around it with planting mixture*

4 *Top up the hole, leaving a depression around the stem to collect moisture*

Caring for dahlias throughout the year

Water thoroughly as the buds develop

When potted plants or tubers are first planted out, they must not be over-watered as this may injure them. It does the roots no harm to search for moisture. But, when dahlias approach their flowering season, they need a lot of moisture if they are to give the best results. In dry spells the plants should be watered freely.

Use an automatic sprinkler, which throws up a fine spray high enough for the water to fall vertically on the plants. This will ensure that the whole area around the dahlias receives a thorough soaking.

When watering with a can, give about 3 gallons of water to each plant when they are spaced at 2–3 ft intervals. Use less when they are closer together.

In hot, sunny weather, water the plants every five days or so on heavy soils. On lighter soils, where the water drains away quickly, water the plants more frequently – about every three days.

Use a sprinkler, so that a fine spray falls on the plants

Mulching to keep down the weeds

When the plant is about 12 in. high, put a 1 in. layer of clean dry straw, peat, grass mowings or old farmyard manure round the base, but not against the stem. This mulch will help to keep down weeds and conserve moisture.

Do not mulch too early in the season. The first or second week of July is usually early enough. The ground should be moist when the mulch is applied – and should be well soaked immediately afterwards.

If mulching with grass clippings, do not use grass from a lawn that has been recently treated with a selective weedkiller.

If weeds appear, remove them by hoeing, which will also keep the soil open. Do not disturb more than the top inch of soil.

In July, mulch with peat or grass mowings. Water the mulch

Remove weeds by hoeing, but do not hoe more than 1 in. deep

Supporting dahlias as they grow

Dahlias need support to prevent wind damage.

Two or three weeks after planting tie the dahlia, looping string around its stake about 4–8 in. above the ground, and then taking the string round the stem in a figure-of-eight. Tie the knot against the stake.

As the plant grows, make further ties higher up the stem. Check that the lower ties have not become too tight round the main stem.

To prevent damage to the side growths, insert thin canes firmly in the ground – say three in a triangular pattern round the main stake and about 9 in. from it – sloping outwards. Loop soft string round these to retain the side growths.

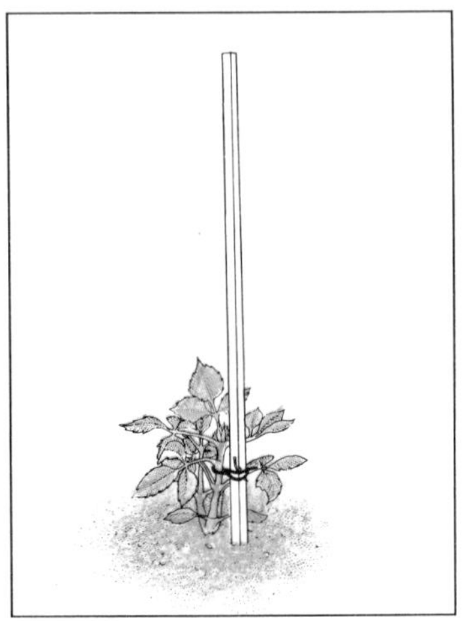
1 *Two or three weeks after planting, tie the plants to stakes with string*

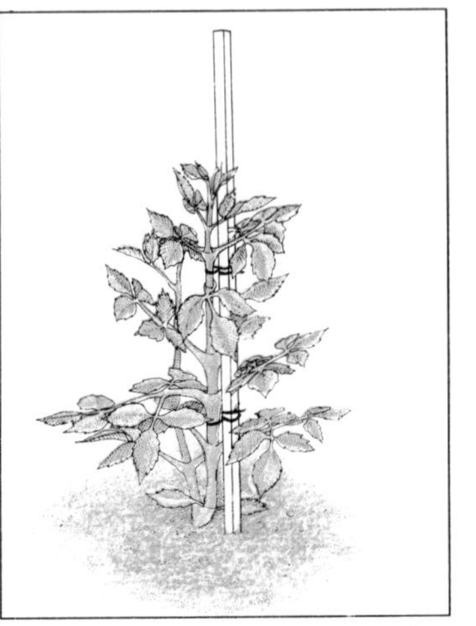
2 *As the plants grow, add more ties. Check lower ties are not too tight*

3 *Support side-shoots with string looped round a triangle of stakes*

Pinching out – or 'stopping' – for more blooms

Most larger-flowered dahlias send up strong centre growths, but make little side growth until the centre shoots develop flower buds.

Therefore the plant is 'stopped' or pinched out.

Two or three weeks after planting, pinch out the growing point of the stem. This is usually late May or early June for tuber-grown plants, mid to late June for pot-grown ones.

A fortnight later, half a dozen or so new growing points will be seen developing in the leaf axils. These are lighter than the older leaves. Remove the uppermost pair of shoots, to promote vigorous growth in the lower side-shoots.

These side-shoots will each produce a terminal bud, with 'wing' buds just below it. For large blooms, pinch off the wing buds when they are big enough to be removed without injuring the terminal bud.

To promote longer-stemmed side-shoots and encourage growth in the upper part of the dahlia, cut off leaves that grow from the main stem a few inches from the ground.

1 *Two or three weeks after planting, pinch out the growing point*

2 *A fortnight later, remove the top pair of side-shoots in the leaf axils*

3 *For large blooms, pinch off the wing buds a few weeks later*

4 *Cut off the lower leaves growing within a few inches of the ground*

What can go wrong with dahlias

If your plants show symptoms that are not described here, turn to the full-colour identification chart of pests and diseases on page 377.

For a comprehensive selection of trade names of recommended chemicals turn to page 398.

Symptoms	Cause	Cure
Young shoots, particularly shoots bearing flower buds, become stunted or somewhat malformed and covered with small, sticky black or green insects	Aphids	Spray with malathion, pirimicarb, or a systemic insecticide. An early-season spraying, to prevent attack, is advisable
Flower buds and opening flowers are deformed; leaves develop irregular holes and a ragged or malformed appearance	Capsid bugs	Spray with malathion, HCH or nicotine
Petals eaten, leaving a ragged appearance	Earwigs	Spray with trichlorphon. Alternatively, invert a 3 in. pot on a stake after loosely packing it with straw. Shake out the pot daily over a bowl of hot water
Leaves and shoots of young plants eaten away. Silvery slime trails sometimes apparent	Slugs or snails	Apply a slug killer, either liquid or pellets
Leaves develop yellow or brown rings or spots and may be distorted. Plants are stunted, with small blooms	Virus	No chemical cure. Remove and burn plants immediately to prevent spreading
Plants appear smaller than usual with thin stems and rather small yellowish leaves	Starvation	Dahlias are gross feeders and to do well need a moist fertile soil; apply a dressing of rotted compost or manure and feed with a general fertiliser
In autumn, leaves and young shoots blacken, wilt and die	Frost	Remove frosted foliage and lift tubers, placing in a frost-free place for the winter

An extra feed for healthy growth

Soil that has been prepared will not need much additional food during the growing season. Mulching with well-decayed farmyard manure will help growth if the soil is light, or if first-class show blooms are to be cultivated by the keen gardener.

An additional feed can be given after the second pinching out. Scatter a handful of a proprietary dahlia fertiliser round the base of the plant. Do not allow it to come into contact with any of the leaves, as they will scorch very easily.

Alternatively, use any general fertiliser that contains equal proportions of nitrogen, phosphate and potash. Avoid high-nitrogen feeds at this time of the year, as they will encourage leaf growth and lower the storage quality of the tubers for the winter.

Water well after feeding with a solid fertiliser to make sure that it reaches down to the plant's roots.

Normal feeding should stop at the end of August, but a top-dressing of superphosphate and sulphate of potash (in equal parts by weight) can be given in mid-August or very early September. This will help the plant to produce healthy tubers for winter storing.

Cutting flowers for indoor display

The best time to cut dahlia blooms is in the evening or early morning, when the air is cool and the stems are full of moisture.

Cut the stems with a sharp knife, rather than scissors or secateurs which might bruise the stems and reduce their ability to take up water. Make the cut at an angle of 45 degrees.

The length of stem should be in proportion to the size of the flower. Giant blooms will probably need stems about 2 ft long; smaller blooms proportionately shorter.

It is best to carry a jug of warm water with you when cutting the blooms. Plunge them into this warm water, carry to the house and transfer to a bucket of cold water up to the top of the stems. Then cut another inch off the stems while they are under water.

Leave the blooms for a few hours in a cool place before displaying them.

Use a sharp knife to prevent bruising. Cut with long stems, and then plunge the stems up to the blooms in cold water

Storing tubers to survive the winter

At the end of the growing season dahlias should be lifted and stored during the winter in a frost-free place. The following spring they can be used to produce cuttings, or they can be replanted directly into the ground to flower again.

In some mild parts of the country, where the soil is sandy and the water table low, the tubers can be left in the ground over winter, but there is always the danger that in a particularly severe winter they will be killed. The damage to the tubers is caused by a combination of cold and damp.

Immediately after the first frosts in autumn have blackened the foliage, cut the stems back to about 6 in. above the ground. The roots can be left in the ground for two or three weeks if the frosts come early; but they should be lifted immediately if hit by a November frost.

With a fork, loosen the soil around the tubers without damaging them, and lift them by pressing back on the fork handle. Using a blunt-ended stick, carefully remove surplus soil from between the tubers. Take care not to break off the old stems. Tie labels to the stumps of the stems for easy recognition in the following spring.

Place the tubers upside-down in an airy, dry place for about a fortnight, to allow the moisture to drain out of the stems. If it collects there it will cause the necks to rot, and although the tubers may not be damaged, the area of new growth will be lost. The tubers must be completely dry before they are stored for the winter.

Dust the tubers with flowers of sulphur to prevent fungus attack.

Store the tubers in a cool frost-free place away from draughts.

A simple method is to place 6 in. of dry leaves or peat in the bottom of a 2 ft deep cold frame. Space out the tubers on the leaves, keeping them 9 in. from the sides of the frame. Cover them with another layer of dry leaves or peat, at least 12 in. deep.

Finally, cover them with a piece of felt or similar material to absorb condensation. The felt will insulate the roots against heavy frosts. Replace the frame top.

Alternatively, store the tubers in trays of dry sand or peat beneath the staging in a cool greenhouse, or in a dry cellar or cupboard. Never store them in a warm cupboard – they will shrivel rapidly.

Where only a small number of tubers is to be stored, netting or sealing the roots are quite adequate methods to use.

For netting, first wrap the roots in straw. Place them inside garden netting drawn tightly into a hammock shape. Hang this from the roof of a shed or greenhouse until the spring. Or the tubers can be sealed in an old trunk lined with expanded polystyrene sheeting (sold in rolls for insulating walls).

Alternatively, seal them by placing the roots in a heavy grade, black polythene bag without any additional packing material, and seal the bag tightly with wire. This method will prevent the roots from dehydrating; however, there is a danger of them sweating and rotting. Keep the tubers in a shed, or underneath the stairs indoors. In spring, new shoots will have developed on the crowns of the tubers.

It is advisable to inspect the tubers every few weeks, to check for disease or shrivelling. Diseased portions can be cut off, and the wounds dusted with flowers of sulphur. Place shrivelled tubers in a bucket of water overnight to plump them up. Dry thoroughly before returning them to storage.

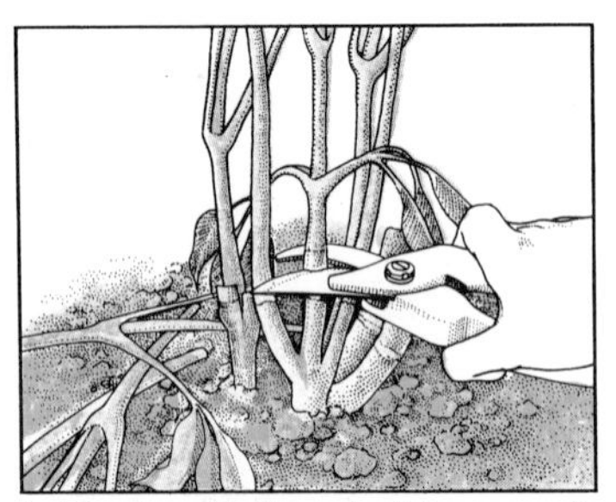

1 *After frost blackens the foliage, cut the stems back to about 6 in. long*

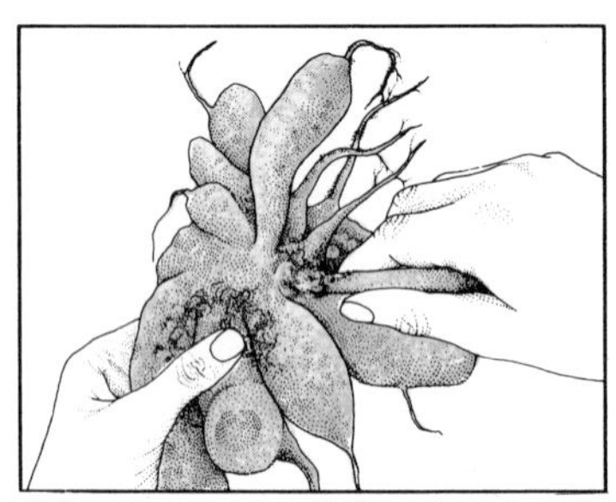

2 *Remove loose soil from between the tubers with a blunt stick*

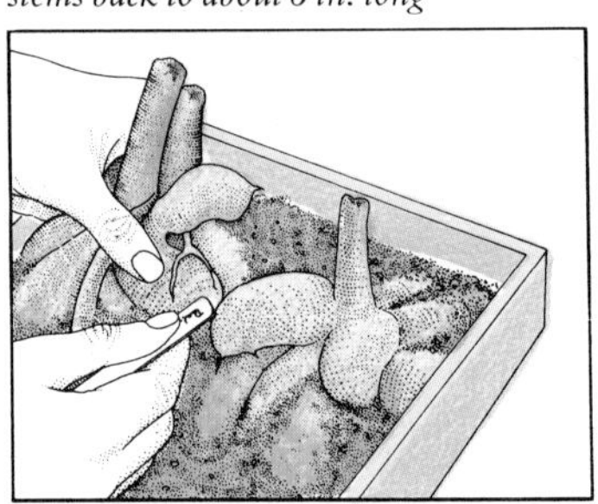

3 *Place the tubers on a 6 in. layer of peat or dry leaves in a deep box*

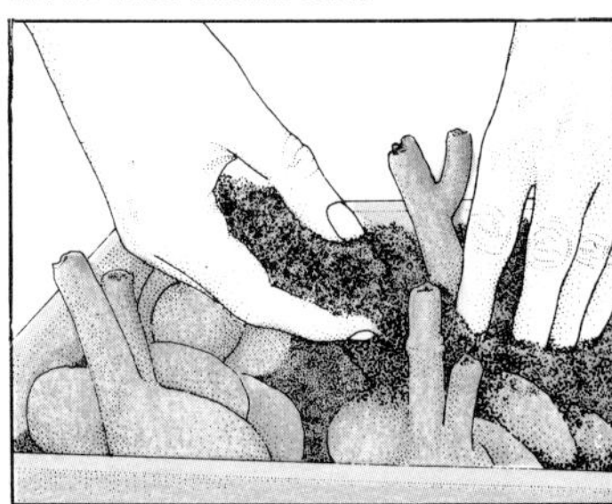

4 *Cover the tubers with another layer of peat or dry leaves, at least 12 in. deep*

How to grow new dahlias from existing stock

Taking cuttings for the greatest number of plants

New dahlia plants can be raised from cuttings or by division of the tubers. Most bedding types can be grown from seed, but this method is not usually successful with the tall, large-flowered varieties; seed produces few plants which even approach the form and colour of the parent plant. Cuttings and division of tubers will produce plants exactly like the parent variety.

In late February or early March, take the old tubers out of store, clean away any old soil and cut out any diseased parts. Dust the wounds with flowers of sulphur.

Place the tubers in a suitable container, such as a tomato box or a kipper box, on a layer of light soil, peat or potting compost. Cover them with the same material to just below the crowns.

Water moderately so that the tubers are kept moist.

Put the box in a greenhouse, heated to 16–18°C (61–64°F).

In two or three weeks, when the shoots are 3–4 in. long, cut them off a little above their bases with a sharp knife or razor blade. Do not cut out a portion of the crown, as this will prevent new shoots forming which can be used to make further cuttings for more new plants.

Sometimes, the first shoots produced are found to be hollow when removed. These are very difficult to root and it is best to throw them away. Subsidiary buds will develop, and these secondary growths are usually of normal size and more suitable for propagation as cuttings.

Trim the shoots back to just below the lowest leaf joint. Remove the lowest pair of leaves, taking great care not to injure the young buds in the leaf axils.

Fill a 3 in. pot with equal parts of peat and sand. Cover the top of pot with $\frac{1}{4}$ in. of fine sand before making holes about 1 in. deep round the edge. Put four cuttings in each pot.

Dip the base of each cutting in water and then into hormone rooting powder. Place the cuttings in the holes and firm the compost up to the cuttings. Water them, label the pot and mark the date.

Place the cuttings in an unheated propagating case in the greenhouse, and keep them moderately moist. Avoid excessive moisture and condensation – which can cause damping off – by allowing a little ventilation, especially at night. Shade them from direct sunlight.

When the cuttings have rooted, after two or three weeks – indicated by new leaves starting to grow – pot them singly into 3 in. pots. Use either John Innes No. 1 compost or a proprietary peat-based compost at this stage.

If peat pots are used, the plants can be planted out in their final positions without disturbing the roots at all.

After potting, shade the plants for two days. Keep them in a well-ventilated greenhouse until the end of April, then move them to a cold frame for hardening off. The frame light need not be closed unless there is likelihood of a frost. Plant out in late May or early June (p. 73).

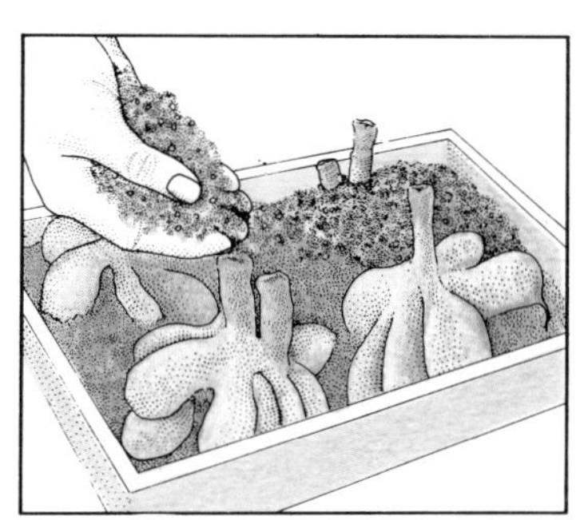

1 *In February or March, put the tubers in damp peat or compost*

2 *When the shoots are 3–4 in. long, cut above the base with a sharp knife*

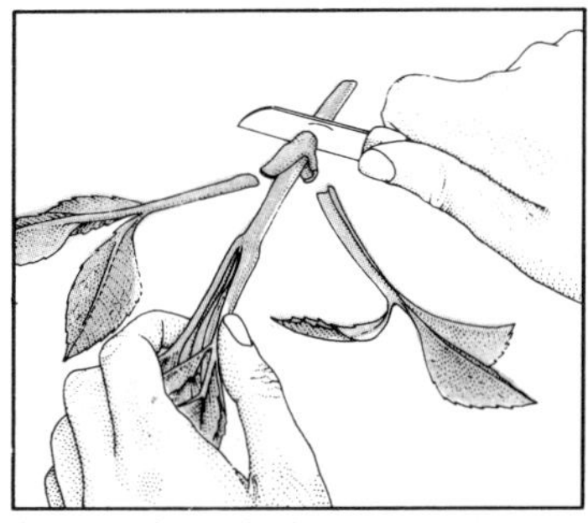

3 *Trim shoots back to just below the lowest leaf joint with a sharp knife*

4 *Wet base of cutting and dip in rooting powder. Put in prepared holes in pots*

5 *Place the pots in an unheated propagating case in a greenhouse*

6 *After two or three weeks, pot the cuttings singly in 3 in. pots*

7 *Keep in a well-ventilated greenhouse, shading the plants for two days*

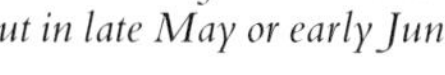

8 *Move to a cold frame in late April; plant out in late May or early June*

Ferns of different types can bring the beauty of natural woodland to a shady and otherwise uninteresting corner of the garden. The taller ferns are arranged as a background, under the shade of the tree. Smaller ferns have been planted among the rough stones in the foreground

Ferns

In places where the sun rarely shines, ferns create delicate patterns of green. And they mix well with other shade-loving plants, such as primroses and snowdrops

Ferns, with their arching fronds and cool green colours, are ideal for parts of the garden where there is little sun. They can transform a difficult corner, where few other plants will thrive, into a tranquil oasis of gentle foliage.

They are among the most ancient plants on earth, first appearing over 400 million years ago, long before any plants bore flowers.

There are about 10,000 species of ferns growing throughout the world. The majority come from warmer countries and cannot be grown in British gardens. About 50 species are found growing naturally in Britain – mainly in western parts where the higher humidity ensures the moisture needed for fertilisation.

A fascinating property of hardy ferns is their ability to produce offspring with widely varying shapes of fronds. In Victorian and Edwardian times the collection of unusual forms became a major gardening craze, until 2000 varieties were known. During the two world wars many were lost, but in recent years interest in ferns has revived.

A real enthusiast will use ferns alone in a shady border, mixing species of different sizes, shapes of frond and shades of green.

However, some flowering plants, including primroses, will thrive in similar conditions to ferns and mix well with them.

Acanthus mollis contrasts well with the male fern (*Dryopteris filix-mas*). Bleeding heart (*Dicentra spectabilis*) will mix in with the larger hartstongue ferns (*Asplenium scolopendrium*). Hellebores also associate well, but they dislike top-dressings of acid peat. Beech leaf-mould, which is alkaline, is preferable as a mulch.

Some of the finest foliage plants to associate with fern fronds are hostas, with their variegated leaves in blue or gold, or striped with green and white.

Ferns look best when growing far enough apart to prevent the fronds from intermingling. The spaces between the plants, or at the front of the border, can be filled with low-growing ground-cover plants such as bergenias, or lilies-of-the-valley, in particular the variety 'Fortin's Giant'. Lily-of-the-valley is very invasive, however, and should be fenced in with slates, tiles, or a rigid plastic shield, sunk into the ground, to keep the roots within reasonable bounds.

Epimediums also make good edging plants in a fern border, and dwarf daffodils, snowdrops, chionodoxas, eranthis and scillas scattered through the border will combine with the ferns to create a natural woodland effect.

Daffodils should be used only with large ferns, which will cover their untidy leaves when the flowers have finished. Tall woodland lilies look very elegant, rising above the arching fronds, when planted amongst a group of ferns.

Ferns need not be restricted to a shady corner. Some grow well in dappled shade beneath trees, and their serrated fronds make a strong contrast with the smooth bark on the trunks of slender varieties.

Many ferns are evergreen and are invaluable for brightening up the garden in winter. The shield ferns (polystichum), hartstongue ferns (*Asplenium scolopendrium*) and the polypodies (polypodium) are particularly delightful, especially when their fronds are edged with hoar frost.

In the rock garden, too, the evergreen spleenworts remain bright when most other plants become jaded and past their best.

Planting hardy ferns

Ferns will grow in all soils except heavy, badly drained ones. They need a position shaded from midday sun and protected from gales.

The right sort of shade is provided by the north side of a house or fence, which protects the plants from prolonged sunlight but leaves them open to the sky.

Shade cast by trees is also ideal for ferns, provided they are not directly under the branches where rain water will drip on them. There are exceptions, however, and some ferns thrive in dense shade and dripping water – the hard fern (*Blechnum spicant*), most dryopteris, the oak fern (*Gymnocarpium dryopteris*), the beech fern (*Thelypteris phegopteris*) and the soft shield fern (*Polystichum setiferum*).

The best time for planting ferns is autumn or spring.

If ferns are delivered some time before they can be planted, do not allow the roots to dry out.

During moist weather, dig over the planting bed to a depth of 12 in. and break up the soil.

Sprinkle sterilised bonemeal over the surface at the rate of a good handful to every square yard. Add a 1 in. layer of leaf-mould or garden compost on top of the bonemeal, and then fork it all in.

For cultivation purposes, ferns can be divided into three types: crown-forming ferns, ferns with rhizomatous roots, and spleenworts.

A crown-forming fern is one whose fronds emerge from a stout root in the form of a shuttlecock, or crown. Examples are the male fern (*Dryopteris filix-mas*) and lady fern (*Athyrium filix-femina*).

When planting this type, first snap off or cut away any old woody frond bases. This enables new roots to emerge more quickly.

Dig a planting hole to the depth of the fern's root system, place the fern in the hole and fill with soil so that the crown is flush with the surface – not below.

Firm the plant in with the feet.

Rhizomatous-rooted ferns usually throw up fronds along the rhizome without forming a crown.

When planting them, make a shallow depression in the soil with a fork. Place the rhizome in the depression, fill in with soil, and firm down with the fingers.

Spleenworts are a group of ferns that grow best horizontally. They are ideal for rock gardens or drystone walls.

To plant, first lift a stone away from the wall or rock garden. Place the fern on its side in the hole and cover its roots generously with leaf-mould. Then replace the stone.

PREPARING THE SOIL BEFORE PLANTING

1 *Dig the soil in autumn or spring, and sprinkle on bonemeal*

2 *Add a 1 in. layer of leaf-mould, and fork it into the soil*

THE THREE PLANTING TECHNIQUES

Crown-forming ferns *Remove old frond bases and plant with the crown flush with the surface. Examples are the male fern and lady fern*

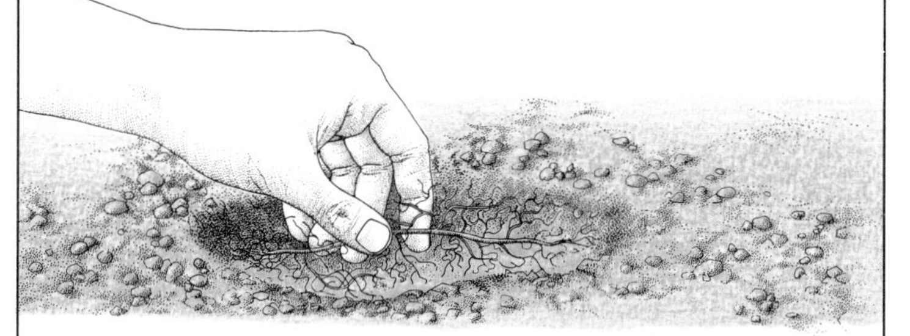

Rhizomatous ferns *Lay the rhizome in a shallow hole, cover with soil and firm with the fingers. Examples include oak ferns and polypodies*

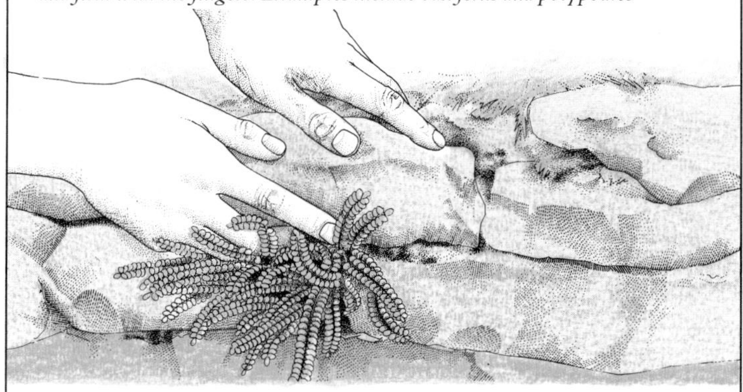

Spleenworts *Ideal for rock gardens or drystone walls. Remove a stone, plant the fern on its side with leaf-mould, and replace the stone*

Keeping ferns healthy

Watering, feeding and general care

Once they are established, ferns need watering only if the soil dries out during very hot periods.

After planting, cover the entire surface around the ferns with a 1 in. deep mulch of garden compost, leaf-mould or peat. This will help to conserve moisture during dry spells.

Repeat this mulch each autumn and again in spring. Also in spring, scatter sterilised bonemeal around the plants at the rate of a good handful to the square yard before spreading the mulch on the bed.

Weed ferns by hand, as forking or hoeing can damage the root system which in established ferns is near the surface of the soil.

Each spring, remove dead fronds with a knife or secateurs, as near to the crown as possible. This will encourage new shoots to form.

MULCHING

Mulch ferns in spring and autumn with leaf-mould or peat. In spring apply bonemeal before the mulch

What can go wrong with ferns

If your plants show symptoms that are not described here, turn to the full-colour identification chart, which lists pests, diseases and other plant troubles, on page 377.

Look up chemicals on page 398 for lists of trade names.

Symptoms	Cause	Cure
Fronds collapsing or wilting badly during warm or dry spells	Vine weevil larvae (grubs), which eat through the roots	Sprinkle HCH powder on the ground around the plant, or water thoroughly with malathion solution
Leaves eaten off, particularly while young and unrolled	Slugs or snails	Sprinkle slug pellets around the plants, preferably while young foliage is emerging, if slugs are known to be troublesome
Young fronds eaten around the edges	Woodlice	Apply carbaryl powder to the soil close to the fern crowns (not on leaves)
Blackish-brown streaks or narrow blotches across the fronds, severe attacks causing death of fronds	Eelworms	No effective cure; badly infected plants should be lifted and burnt
Sticky patches, sometimes covered with a sooty mould. Fronds may be distorted	Aphids or capsid bugs	Spray with malathion or formothion

How to increase your ferns

Division – the easiest method of propagation

The easiest way to propagate crown-forming ferns, such as male ferns and lady ferns, is by division of the crowns in March.

Dig up a clump of ferns carefully with a fork and cut off the fronds.

With a small clump, it may be possible to pull the crowns apart with the hands.

If the clump is very large, use two garden forks. Push them back to back into the centre of the clump, ensuring that the prongs do not enter the crowns.

Gently push the handles together and pull them apart until the clump is broken into two. It may sometimes be best to make the final division with a sharp knife, to cause the minimum damage.

Sub-divide the two new clumps by the same method, to produce several new plants, each with its own root system.

Plant these as described for crown-forming ferns on page 79.

Rhizomatous ferns can also be propagated by division.

In March, dig up a clump of ferns and cut off the fronds.

With a sharp knife, cut the rhizome into sections, each with at least one growing point – the point from which new shoots are emerging.

Plant these out as described for rhizomatous-rooted ferns on page 79. Each will form a new fern.

HOW TO DIVIDE FERNS

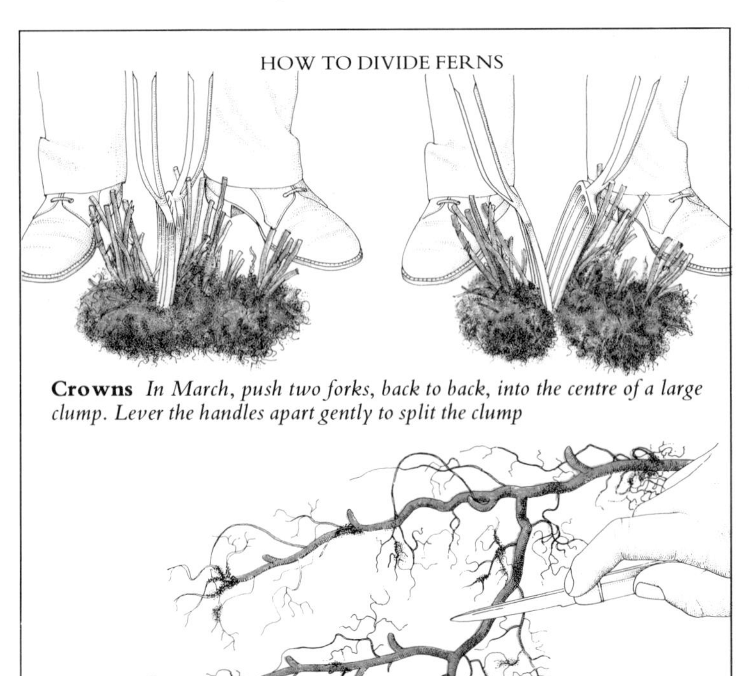

Crowns *In March, push two forks, back to back, into the centre of a large clump. Lever the handles apart gently to split the clump*

Rhizomes *In March, lift the fern and cut the rhizome in pieces, each with at least one growing point. Each piece will grow into a new fern*

Growing hartstongue ferns from frond bases

Hartstongue ferns can be grown from the bases of existing fronds, as dividing them is a slow means of propagation.

This job should be done during the spring or summer months, ideally in April or May.

Dig up a fern and wash the soil from the roots.

Break the rootstock in half, to get at the frond bases.

With a sharp knife remove a frond base. Cut cleanly and as close to the rootstock as possible. Cut off as many frond bases as required.

From each frond base cut off the remains of the old frond at one end.

Then cut off the old roots from the other end.

Place a $\frac{1}{2}$ in. deep layer of peat at the bottom of a seed tray. Then add $\frac{1}{2}$ in. of sterilised coarse sand (sterilise the sand by putting it in a fine-mesh sieve and pouring boiling water over it).

Lay the frond bases on the sand. A $6 \times 8\frac{1}{2}$ in. seed tray will take about 50–60 bases.

Place a plastic propagating top (or plastic bag on a sterilised bamboo frame) over the tray and put it in a shady place. No ventilation is needed.

The following spring, young plants should have grown from the bases. Pot them individually in $2\frac{1}{2}$ in. pots of John Innes No. 2 potting compost.

As they develop, pot them on into the next-size pot until a strong root system has been established. Then plant them into the garden in spring or autumn.

1 *In spring, break the rootstock in half to get at the frond bases*

2 *Cut away each of the frond bases, as close to the rootstock as possible*

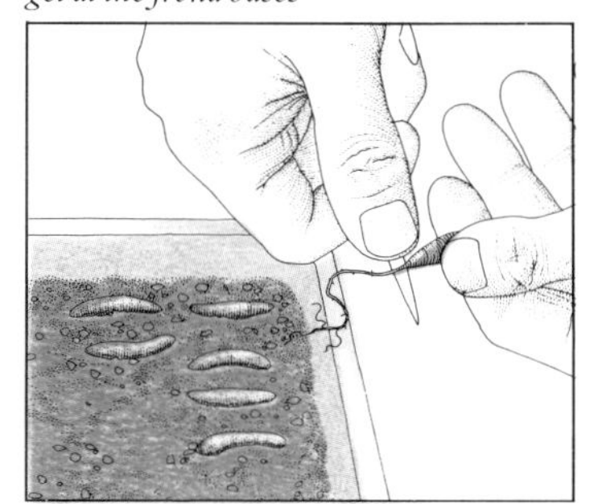

3 *Trim the bases, lay them on sand and cover with a propagating top*

4 *A year later the young ferns are ready for planting in pots*

Growing soft shield ferns from bulbils

Some varieties of the soft shield fern produce brown, knob-like bulbils along the midrib of each frond in late summer.

To grow new plants, first detach some fronds from the fern.

Place a $\frac{1}{2}$ in. deep layer of peat at the bottom of a seed tray. Then add a $\frac{1}{2}$ in. layer of sterilised coarse sand (this can be sterilised by putting sand in a fine-mesh sieve and pouring boiling water over it).

Place the fronds flat on the sand, with the bulbils uppermost, and fasten them in place with a bent piece of galvanised wire.

Place a plastic propagating top (or plastic bag supported by a sterilised bamboo frame) over the tray and put it in a shady place. No ventilation is needed.

The following spring, young plants should be growing from the bulbils on each frond.

When these are large enough to handle, carefully remove the old fronds from the tray, taking care not to tear the root systems of the new ferns as you lift them.

Detach the new plants from the old fronds, and pot them individually in $2\frac{1}{2}$ in. pots of John Innes No. 2 compost.

As they develop, pot them on into the next-size pot until a strong root system has been established. Then plant them in the garden.

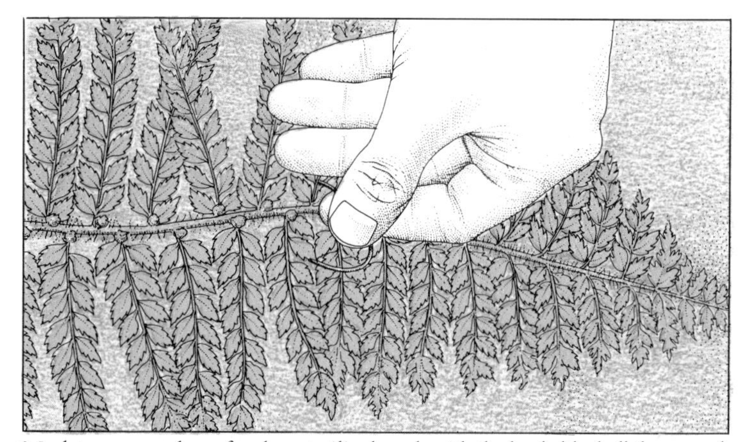

1 *In late summer, lay a frond on sterilised sand, with the knob-like bulbils upward. Fasten with a loop of wire and put a propagating cover on the tray*

2 *By the following spring, young ferns should be growing from the bulbils*

3 *Remove the old frond and put the new plants in individual $2\frac{1}{2}$ in. pots*

Fruit for all seasons

Even a small garden has room for fruit – not only bushes and canes, but also trees in restricted form, trained against a wall or fence or grown in a small, open space

Most fruits fall into two main types – soft and tree fruits. Among the soft fruits are blackberries, blueberries, blackcurrants, gooseberries, loganberries, raspberries, red and white currants and strawberries. Tree fruits include apples, figs, cherries, peaches, pears and plums. A few fruits, such as grapes, melons and rhubarb, do not belong in either category.

Soft fruits

These are grown in the form of either bushes or canes, except for strawberries, which occur as low-growing bedding plants. Bushes have permanent spreading branches that start either at ground level or just above – on a short 'leg'. They generally grow about 4 ft high, with a breadth equal to their height.

Blackcurrants, blueberries, red and white currants and gooseberries are grown as bushes. Gooseberries and red and white currants can also be grown in restricted form as cordons – with one, two or three branching stems.

Canes are slender shrubs with stems starting at ground level, or just below. They need to be trained to a post or wires, and are cut away every year after fruiting and replaced by new growth. Blackberries, loganberries and raspberries grow as canes.

Tree fruits

These are grown in several different forms, the most suitable for the average garden being bush, cordon, espalier, fan and dwarf pyramid. Two other forms were once widely planted in gardens – standard and half-standard. However, these take up so much room that they are generally suitable only for orchards.

Bush trees are traditionally the most popular form for apples and pears, and are grafted on a dwarfing or semi-dwarfing rootstock. They have a 24–27 in. high stem, and at this height branches radiate to form the head of the tree. Dwarf bushes average 8–10 ft in height and spread, bushes 10–12 ft.

Cordons are one of the best forms for a small garden. They have a single stem with no major spreading branches. They take up very little space, are easy to manage, and have a high yield for their size. However, they involve a high initial cost, as 6–12 cordons are needed to give an adequate supply for a family.

Cordons have to be supported on wires; they can be grown upright, but are usually trained at an angle of 45 degrees to enable a longer main stem to be grown. The average length is 10–12 ft, the oblique height 7 ft. A variation is the U-shaped double cordon, usually grown upright. Apples and pears are most suitable for training as cordons.

Espaliers have a single central stem with pairs of opposite horizontal branches supported along wires. They need careful pruning and training. This form is best suited to apple and pear trees. The average height is 8 ft, and the average spread 10–15 ft.

Fan-shaped trees have branches trained on supporting wires to form a fan shape; they are usually grown against a wall. All the trees dealt with in this section can be trained as fans. They are decorative, but take a lot of wall space and need careful pruning. The average height is 10 ft, and the average spread 15–20 ft.

Dwarf pyramids have a central stem with branches that begin about 15 in. from the ground and get progressively shorter towards the top. This form is best suited to apples and pears, but there is a modified form for plums. The average height is 7–10 ft, the average spread 3–6 ft.

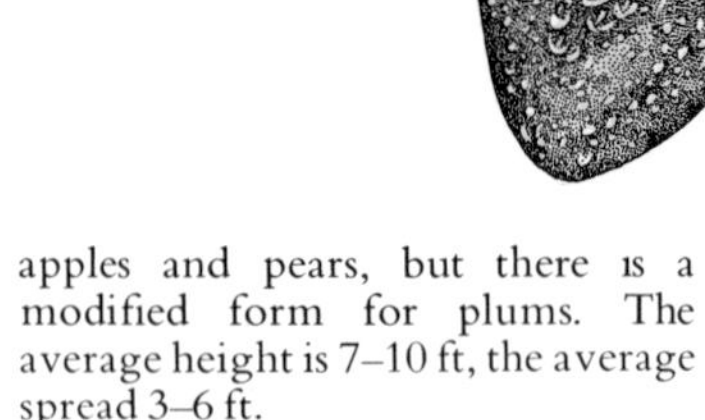

Standards and half-standards are the same shape as a bush, but larger. Standards have 6 ft stems, and an average height and spread of 20–30 ft; half-standards have 4 ft stems, and an average height and spread of 15–20 ft. Prune them in the same way as bush trees.

Pollination

Flowers will not develop into fruit unless fertilised. Pollen is usually transferred by wind and insects.

Most fruit trees have both male and female organs in the same flower, but not all are self-fertile (fertilised by their own pollen). Some need to be grown with another variety of a similar kind, that flowers at the same time, so that cross-pollination can take place.

Before ordering trees, find out their pollinating needs from the list of varieties in the appropriate section for the type of fruit. Soft fruits, except for blueberries, can be fertilised by their own pollen.

Pruning

Fruit pruning is carried out in two main stages – training the young tree or bush to the shape required, then regular pruning once the framework has been established.

For fruit trees, the basic training is generally the same as that given for apples. After that, the system varies. As one of the main aims is to regulate the crop and improve the quality of the fruit, pruning depends on the habit of growth of the tree.

Apples, sweet cherries and pears

bear fruit mostly on wood that is two years old or more. The aim is, therefore, to maintain a balance between old and new wood.

Blackberries, blackcurrants, blueberries, figs, loganberries, peaches, raspberries (summer-fruiting) and sour cherries bear fruit mostly on one-year-old wood. Autumn-fruiting raspberries and grapes bear fruit on current season's wood. With all these, the aim is to replace shoots that have already fruited.

Plums, red currants, gooseberries and damsons, fruit on one-year-old and older wood. The aim is to produce plenty of new wood.

Melons are annuals, so the whole plant is replaced every year.

Pruning is generally done in autumn or winter, but plums, peaches and cherries should be pruned only in summer, because in winter there is a greater risk of disease entering the wound. Large pruning cuts should be protected with a wound-sealing paint.

Trees grown in a restricted form may need both winter and summer pruning.

Raising new stock

A fruit tree raised from seed varies considerably from its parent. The only certain way of perpetuating a variety is by grafting.

Grafting is best left to an expert nurseryman. A portion of shoot – known as a scion – is taken from the variety of tree to be raised and grafted on the rootstock (the root system and part of the stem) of a tree of a different variety. This union between scion and rootstock often shows as a bulge in the stem.

The rootstock influences the size, vigour and fruiting capacity of the tree, and various rootstocks have been standardised and classified. When buying a fruit tree, tell the nurseryman the form in which you want to grow it, and the soil and growing conditions, so that he can provide a tree on suitable rootstock.

Soft fruit canes and bushes are grown on their own roots.

Buying fruit trees

Trees of various ages can be bought for planting. They may be one, two, three or four years old. A one-year-old tree, known as a maiden, consists of a single stem only. If there are a few side-shoots it is known as a feathered maiden.

If you buy a maiden tree, you will need to train it yourself. Two-year-old trees are sold partly trained.

If you do not want to undertake initial training, buy trees that are three or four years old. Do not buy trees any older, as they may be slower to re-establish themselves.

When you buy a tree, ask its age so that you can continue with the correct training. But for most trees the age can be worked out by noting the pattern of side-shoots on the lower branches.

In the first year of a tree's life, only the main stem grows. In the second, side-shoots (branches) grow from the main stem. In the third, side-shoots grow from the first branches, and so on.

If, therefore, the lowest branch of a tree has a side-shoot which also has a side-shoot, you know the tree is four years old. Peaches are an exception to this; they usually produce side-shoots from current year's side-shoots.

Planting fruit trees and bushes

Unless trees have been supplied in containers, plant them between late October and late March, the earlier in this period the better. Trees in containers can be planted at any time, as long as the roots are established, because the soil ball round the roots is planted with them.

Do not plant until the soil is in a suitable condition. It must not be frozen or too wet. Ideally, a handful should hold together when squeezed but fall apart when dropped.

On the day of planting, dig a hole wide enough to take the outspread roots and deep enough (with a 4–6 in. layer of manure in the bottom) for the top ones to be covered with 3–4 in. of soil. Loosen the soil at the bottom of the hole with a fork.

Ideally, fruit trees should not be grown in heavy, waterlogged soils, but if you have no option, put some stones at the bottom of the hole for drainage, and work in a barrowload of sandy soil when refilling. Loosen the sides of the hole with a fork.

Place a stake – tall enough to reach the point where the stem begins to branch – as deeply and firmly in the centre of the hole as possible. Fork 4–6 in. of well-rotted manure or compost into the bottom of the hole. Work it around thoroughly so that roots will not eventually come into contact with large pieces. Mix a compound fertiliser such as Growmore, 4 oz. (4 tablespoons) per heaped barrowload, into the soil that has been removed.

If the tree's roots are dry, soak them in water for about two hours before planting. Cut out damaged roots with secateurs, making a sloping cut. Trim off any stumps of dead wood on the top branches flush with the stem; cut back damaged tips above a bud.

Plant the tree no deeper than it was in the nursery, indicated by the soil mark round the stem. You may need a helper to hold the tree.

Fill in the soil gradually. Shake the tree from time to time to settle the soil round the roots. Once the roots are covered, tread in the soil firmly. Then add the rest of the soil, leaving it loose. Level the surface with a fork. Do not grass over for two or three years. Tie the planted tree to the stake (p. 283).

After planting, the old soil mark should be just visible, and the union between scion and rootstock at least 4 in. above soil level.

In districts where rabbits or hares are a nuisance, protect the tree with plastic anti-rabbit collars or by encircling it with wire netting.

Cordons, espaliers and fans Before planting, set up supporting wires, attaching them with vine eyes and wire strainers to a wall or posts. For cordons, stretch wires at 12 in., 3 ft, 5 ft and 7 ft above ground; for espaliers every 12–15 in., for fans every 9–12 in., starting at the appropriate height above ground.

If planting against a wall, set the stem at least 6 in. from the wall to avoid the dry soil at the base. Lean the stem slightly towards the wall to make it easier to tie to the wires.

The scion on a cordon

Point the stems of cordons towards the north, if possible, to give them the maximum amount of light. Make sure that the scion is uppermost, to prevent it breaking if the cordon has to be lowered. Put the base of the last tree in a row at least 8 ft from the end of the posts or wall, so there is room for lowering.

Other fruits For ways of planting grapes, melons, raspberries, rhubarb and strawberries, see the appropriate section. Blackberries, blackcurrants, blueberries, gooseberries, loganberries and red currants are planted in the same way as shrubs (p. 244). Plant blackcurrants 2 in. deeper than in the nursery.

What to do if you cannot plant at once

If the trees, bushes or canes arrive at a time when you cannot plant them, temporarily cover roots with soil in a trench. This is called heeling in.

The soil must be neither dry nor too wet, so a good site for heeling in during wet weather is against the wall of a house, where the ground is usually only moist. If the site is too dry, it should be watered.

To keep the site moist and to prevent it from freezing, cover it before heeling in – first with plastic sheeting, then with dry straw or bracken and, finally, with more plastic sheeting.

When the trees, bushes or canes arrive, uncover the heeling-in site and dig a spade-deep trench, with one side vertical and the other at a slope of 45 degrees.

Unfasten the bundle and lay the trees along the sloping side of the trench. Heap soil back to cover roots completely. Make sure stems are not covered any higher than the mark indicating the soil level in the nursery. Finally firm the soil.

If the trees arrive at a time when neither planting nor heeling in is possible, unfasten them, place them in an unheated shed or garage, and cover their roots with dry straw or bracken. Do not keep them too long in this way, as the roots may dry out.

HEELING IN

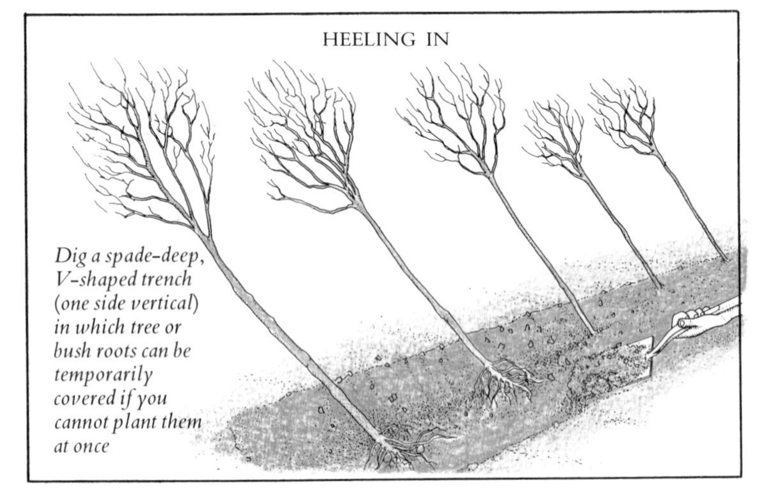

Dig a spade-deep, V-shaped trench (one side vertical) in which tree or bush roots can be temporarily covered if you cannot plant them at once

The space a tree will take up

The planting distances given are a guide only. Find out the distance recommended when buying the tree from the nursery. The more vigorous the rootstock and the more fertile the soil, the further apart trees should be planted. The distances given in the list are mainly for dwarfing or less vigorous rootstocks.

Form of tree	Between trees	Between rows
Bush	8–15 ft	8–15 ft
Dwarf bush	10–12 ft	10–12 ft
Cordon	2½–3 ft	6–10 ft
Espalier	10–15 ft	8–10 ft
Dwarf pyramid	3½–4 ft	7–10 ft
Pyramid	10–12 ft	10–12 ft
Fan	15–24 ft	8–10 ft

Protecting fruit against damage and disease

Fruit buds and growing fruit can be seriously damaged by birds. The only real protection is to cover the trees or bushes with 1 in. mesh nylon or polythene netting.

Soft fruits and trees grown against supports are the easiest to protect by means of temporary cages. Other means of protection are muslin or polythene bags, stockings, newspaper cones or plastic sleeves, put over individual fruits. Less effective are bird scaring devices, bird-repellent sprays or cotton threads tied among the branches.

Fungus diseases and insects, which can seriously damage or kill trees, are the other main problems in fruit growing.

There are many fungicides and insecticides that can be sprayed on fruit, but they should not be used indiscriminately. Regular spraying is not advisable. It kills beneficial insects – such as pollinating ones – as well as enemies, and the pest concerned can develop a resistance to the chemical used. There are now red spider mites that are resistant to all, or most, of the common sprays normally used to combat them.

Researchers are now advocating the use of natural predators to control pests whenever possible. A few are available commercially (p. 398), but, as the supply is limited, some chemical control is necessary.

Keep a keen watch for pests and diseases, and use chemical treatment only when they can be seen or, in some cases, if the plant was attacked the previous year. Confine treatment to the infected tree or bush, and those near by.

Good garden hygiene also helps to keep pests and diseases under control. Never leave old prunings lying about, and in autumn and winter pick off any old, rotting fruit and burn it. Rotting fruit can spread brown rot disease.

Encouraging a reluctant tree to fruit

If a tree is over-vigorous – growing well, but producing little or no fruit – one remedy is to reduce its supply of nitrogen by growing grass round it. Mow in the growing season.

Another remedy is to prune its roots in winter. If the tree is small enough to be lifted, inscribe a circle of 2 ft radius round it, using a stake tied to the tree with string.

Dig a trench along the line of the circle, deep enough to expose the roots. Use secateurs to cut through all thick, thong-like roots. Then work under the tree with a fork, exposing the downward-pointing roots. Some of these may also have to be cut before the tree can be lifted.

Mark the tree in some way before lifting, so that it can be replanted facing in the same direction. After lifting, cut back strong roots, making a sloping cut, but save as many fibrous roots as you can.

Before replanting, make a mound in the bottom of the hole. Get a helper to hold the tree in place on the mound (or tie it loosely to its stake) while you spread out the roots. Then refill the hole, making sure the tree is well firmed in.

For trees too big to lift, inscribe only a half circle, at a distance slightly less than the spread of the branches. Dig a trench along the line as before, cutting through all roots encountered, then replace and firm the soil. The following winter treat the other half similarly.

For apple and pear trees, another remedy is bark-ringing at blossom time. There is, however, a risk of killing the tree if it is not done properly. Use it as a last resort only.

About 6 in. below the point where the branches begin, cut off a narrow strip of bark round half of the tree's trunk, and another round the other half, 3 in. below it. The younger and smaller the tree, the narrower should be the strips. On larger trees the strips should not be more than $\frac{1}{4}$ in. wide.

Use a sharp knife and cut into the surface bark only. Peel off the bark and cover the exposed portions immediately with insulating tape.

Supporting heavily laden branches

Heavily laden branches on bush or standard trees sometimes need to be supported, to prevent them from breaking under the weight. There are three ways of doing this.

The first way is to insert a strong stake, several feet taller than the tree, firmly beside it. Tie ropes to the top of the stake, loop them round the branches, and tie them back to the top of the stake. A second way is to place a stake beside each branch, and tie a loop of rope from the stake round the branch.

With both methods, the point at which the branch is supported must be carefully judged. If the rope is too close to the trunk, the end of the branch may still snap off in a high wind. If the rope is too near the tip, the branch may break between the point of suspension and the trunk. Put some padding between the rope and the branch to keep them from chafing against one another.

A third way is to wedge a stake, with a V-shaped crotch at the top, under each branch needing support; pad between prop and branch.

Branches heavily laden with fruit can be supported individually to prevent them from breaking under the weight. This can be done with loops of rope tied to a stake. Or branches can be propped up with a forked stake. For both methods, use padding between branch and support to prevent chafing

Apples to grow for cooking and desserts

Apple 'Golden Delicious'

Apples are the most widely grown British fruit. They will grow in most soils, but do best in well-drained neutral or slightly alkaline soil that will not dry out in summer.

Apples do not grow well in seaside gardens because salt-laden winds can be damaging.

Most varieties of apple tree need cross-pollinating by another variety that blossoms at the same time (p. 103). But specialist nurserymen now produce 'family trees' that consist of three cross-pollinating varieties growing on a single rootstock. In this way you need plant only a single tree.

For a family of four people who like apples, six bush trees (or four fans, four espaliers, eight dwarf pyramids, or twelve cordons) will provide ample fruit. Fruit matures from August to April, depending on the variety.

The best time to plant is in autumn or in frost-free weather in winter (p. 84). The roots of newly planted trees need plenty of water; if you plant during a dry period, make sure the soil is kept moist.

For the first two or three years, mulch in spring with a layer of straw or well-rotted compost.

Every winter, in late January, feed trees with 1 oz. (1 tablespoon) of sulphate of potash to the square yard. Every third year add 2 oz. (2 tablespoons) of superphosphate to the square yard to the dressing.

Every March feed with 1 oz. (1 tablespoon) of sulphate of ammonia to the square yard. For cooking apples and for other trees grassed round, the amount should be increased to 2 oz. to the square yard.

Sprinkle the fertiliser evenly over the soil, covering an area slightly larger than that overspread by the branches. Let it penetrate naturally. Do not fork it in as this can damage the roots. Remove weeds by shallow hoeing or with a liquid weedkiller.

Mature trees need watering during prolonged dry spells; apply 4 gallons to the square yard to the area overspread by the branches.

Thinning a heavy crop of young apples

The aim of thinning is to allow the remaining apples to grow to full size. Otherwise, too heavy a crop would result in small, poor fruit.

Start thinning a heavy crop of young apples in early June, before the natural drop later in the month.

The June drop is normal and not generally any cause for alarm. But the fall could be very heavy in dry or poor soil conditions. The remedy is proper feeding and mulching.

From each cluster, first remove the central fruit – which is often misshapen at the base – by cutting its stalk with a pair of scissors with pointed blades. Never pull fruit off the tree when thinning, as this can damage the spur. Then cut off any inferior apples, leaving two on each cluster – one if clusters are close.

Thin again in July if there has been a good crop. For the best fruit, thin dessert apples to 4–6 in. apart, cooking apples to 6–9 in. apart. Leave only one apple on each spur.

In early June, thin the fruit to two per cluster

Harvesting apples according to their season

The best way to test if apples are ready for picking is to lift one up to the horizontal in the palm of your hand and twist it gently. It is ready for picking only if it parts easily from the tree, with the stalk remaining on the fruit.

For reaching high fruit, use apple-pickers – nets on long poles. Push the rigid frame of the net against the stalk. If the apple is ready, it will drop into the net.

Harvest apples with as much care as if handling eggs, because they bruise easily. Place ripe apples in a container lined with soft material.

Early apples (ready in August or September) will not keep and are best eaten as soon as they are picked. Mid-season and late varieties are picked in September or October before they are ripe, but mature during storage.

Store mid-season varieties (ready for eating from October to December) separately from late varieties (ready from January onwards), as the gases given off by the earlier apples may unduly hasten the ripening of the later ones.

Some late apples will keep until April or even May if they are stored in suitable conditions.

After picking the apples, place them in a cool well-ventilated room or shed to sweat for two or three days. After they have sweated, sort them out for storing, placing on one side any damaged or diseased fruit (even those only slightly affected) or any without a stalk; those that are suitable can be used immediately.

Apples ready for picking will twist off easily, stalk attached

How to store your apple crop

The ideal storage method is to wrap each apple in oiled-paper or 10 in. squares of newspaper.

Do not make an airtight seal – just fold one corner of the paper over the fruit, overlap this with the opposite corner, then fold over the other two corners. Apples can also be stored without wrapping, but there is a danger of rot spreading, as well as undue moisture loss.

The storage place should be dark, humid and cool, with a temperature of about 3–5°C (37–41°F). Too much ventilation will cause the fruits to shrivel, but too little may cause them to rot internally. To raise the humidity, damp down the store-room floor occasionally. Stand wrapped apples, folds underneath, in a single layer on a slatted shelf or two or three layers deep in a well-ventilated box. Regularly remove any rotting apples.

Instead of being wrapped individually, apples can be placed in a polythene bag (about 150 gauge) holding 4–6 lb. Use small bags so that fewer apples are likely to be spoilt by rot spreading.

The gases given off by apples inside bags delays ripening, but an excess will cause rotting. Use a nail or pencil point to make six small holes in each 24 sq. in. of bag.

Do not store more than one variety in each bag; the gas from the earlier fruits could hasten the ripening of the later ones.

How to keep apples bright and fresh

An old way of improving colour and keeping-ability of apples is 'sun-dewing'. As soon as they are picked, lay the sound apples – stalk down and not touching – on newspaper or polythene outdoors. To keep off birds, enclose the fruit in a cage of netting. Fix polythene round the sides against drying winds, but leave the top uncovered. Leave for three weeks, then store while dry.

What can go wrong with apples

Aphids and codling moths are usually the most common troubles in apple growing. If trees show symptoms not described here, turn to the identification chart on page 377. Look up chemicals on page 398 to find proprietary names.

Symptoms	Cause	Cure
Leaves curled (sometimes red-flushed) and/or shoots distorted, with many small sticky insects present	Aphids (greenfly and several other kinds)	Spray just before blossoming with dimethoate, formothion, fenitrothion or malathion, and after blossoming if necessary
Leaves finely mottled, later turning yellow or rusty brown	Fruit tree red-spider mites	About mid-June, spray with dimethoate, malathion or derris. Repeat later if necessary
Young fruits have a small brown hole in the skin, often with a brown ribbon scar leading from it. When a fruit is cut open, there is an unpleasant odour and a white grub can be seen feeding on the flesh. Fruits often fall prematurely	Apple sawflies	Spray with HCH, fenitrothion or dimethoate immediately after petal fall
From July onwards fruits bear a small hole, but there is no associated scar as with sawfly damage. When cut open, there is no odour; the white caterpillar feeds in or near the core	Codling moths	In mid-June spray with fenitrothion or malathion. Spray again about three weeks later to kill caterpillars before they penetrate fruit
Leaves and young stems are somewhat distorted and covered with a fine white powder; premature leaf-fall may also occur	Apple powdery mildew	In autumn cut out any badly affected shoots. Regularly spray with benomyl, dinocap or thiophanate-methyl
Fruit cracks, or the skin splits	Irregular growth due to erratic water supply	Mulch to conserve moisture, and water trees in dry spells before the soil dries out completely

Symptoms	Cause	Cure
Brown or blackish scabs on fruit, leaves and shoots. These may crack when scabs have coalesced and become corky	Apple scab	From green cluster (after bud scales fall) onwards – until July if necessary – spray with benomyl, captan, thiophanate-methyl, thiram or lime-sulphur. Cut out diseased parts when pruning and burn them
Slightly sunken areas of dead or dying bark on twigs or young stems. Later these areas extend in an elongated oval form, the central tissues cracking and flaking off. Eventually these cankers girdle and kill the stem	Apple canker	Cut out and burn infected spurs and small branches. On larger branches and the trunk, pare away and burn diseased parts, then paint the clean wound with canker paint. If severe, spray with Bordeaux mixture just before leaf-fall, halfway through leaf-fall, and at bud-burst. Improve drainage if there is water-logging. Wet soil may aggravate the trouble for 'Cox's Orange Pippin', 'Lord Suffield', 'James Grieve' and 'Ribston Pippin' particularly
Fruit has small brown areas of tissue throughout the flesh and beneath the skin, showing through as slightly sunken brown spots	Bitter pit	Feed, mulch and water before the soil dries out completely. In mid-June spray with calcium nitrate – ½ lb. to 5 gallons of water. Repeat this treatment three times, at intervals of three weeks
Full-size fruits, both on the tree and in store, show pale brown areas which bear concentric rings of small whitish or yellowish pustules. Sometimes the fruit dries up on the tree and becomes mummified	Brown rot	Destroy rotten and withered fruit on trees, the ground and in store. Cut out dead shoots when pruning. Spray trees with thiophanate-methyl in August or early September, to reduce rotting of fruit in store

Pruning and training apple trees

During the first four years of a fruit tree's life, the aim of pruning is to make it produce a strong, regular framework of branches – to give it a good start in life.

After that the aim is twofold – to keep the tree open to light and air, and to maintain the right balance between growth and fruitfulness.

Winter pruning (November–February) promotes growth by directing energy to growth buds at the expense of fruit buds. Summer pruning (from mid-July to the end of August) promotes the formation of fruit buds.

Fruit buds and growth buds When pruning a fruit tree, you must be able to distinguish between a fruit bud (which will produce a blossom and then fruit) and a growth bud (which will produce a new shoot). Fruit buds are large and round; growth buds are smaller and lie flatter on the stem. Growth buds sometimes develop into fruit buds.

Leaders and laterals A leader is the leading shoot of a branch. A lateral is a side-shoot from a branch.

Spurs and tips Some varieties produce their fruit on short growths known as spurs. Where two or more spurs originate at the same place, they are known as a spur system. Spur-forming trees include 'Cox's Orange Pippin' and 'James Grieve'.

Some varieties produce fruit buds at the tips of the previous summer's shoots, with only a few on spurs. These are known as tip-bearers. Examples are 'Worcester Pearmain' and 'Bramley's Seedling'.

Making a pruning cut Use sharp secateurs, otherwise damage may result and disease enter.

Making a pruning cut

Cut immediately above an outward-pointing bud – do not leave a stump above it, as it will die back and could harbour disease. Slant the cut in the same direction as the bud.

Training Trees bought from a nursery are usually partly trained, and may be up to four years old. Find out the age when you buy, so that you can continue training.

Bearing Ideally, a tree should not be allowed to bear fruit in the first year after planting, but one or two fruits are permissible. A cordon may fruit within a year of planting, a bush on a vigorous rootstock may take five years.

The time a tree takes to reach full bearing capacity may be from five to 15 years, depending on the variety, rootstock and method of pruning. Trees on dwarfing rootstocks reach full bearing earlier, but do not live as long as those on vigorous rootstocks.

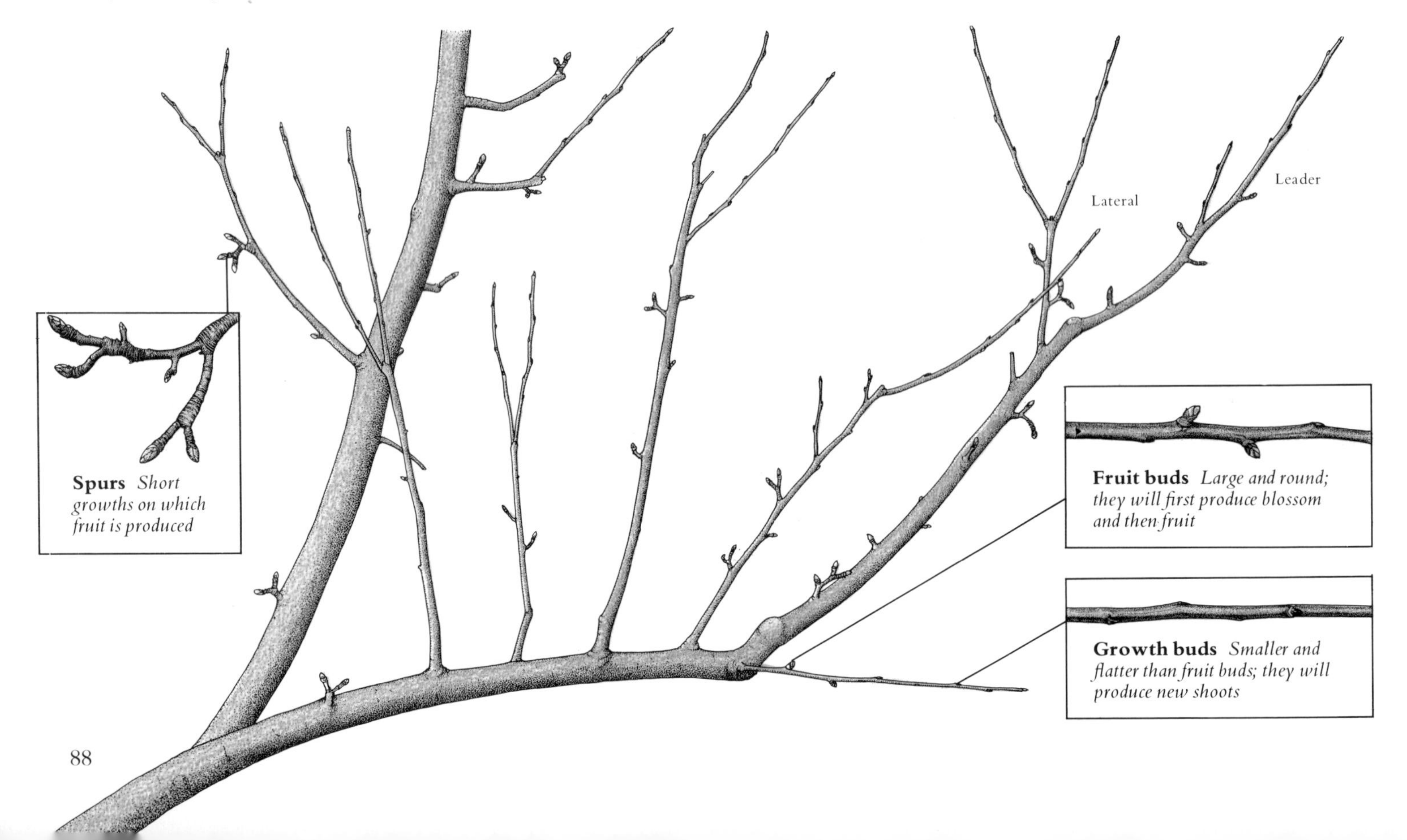

Spurs *Short growths on which fruit is produced*

Fruit buds *Large and round; they will first produce blossom and then fruit*

Growth buds *Smaller and flatter than fruit buds; they will produce new shoots*

Pruning and training a young bush tree

Training a one-year-old bush tree

Grow bush trees 8–15 ft apart, depending on the rootstock (which should be either dwarfing or semi-dwarfing). Check the distance when buying the tree.

If you buy a one-year-old (maiden) tree, cut the stem back to 18–24 in. high, just above a bud, after planting in autumn or winter (p. 84).

The buds or small shoots just below the cut will grow out the following summer. There may be only three or four, perhaps more. Choose three or four to form the first branches. They should be evenly spaced round the stem, none pointing towards the supporting stake. Rub out with your thumb any unwanted buds or shoots.

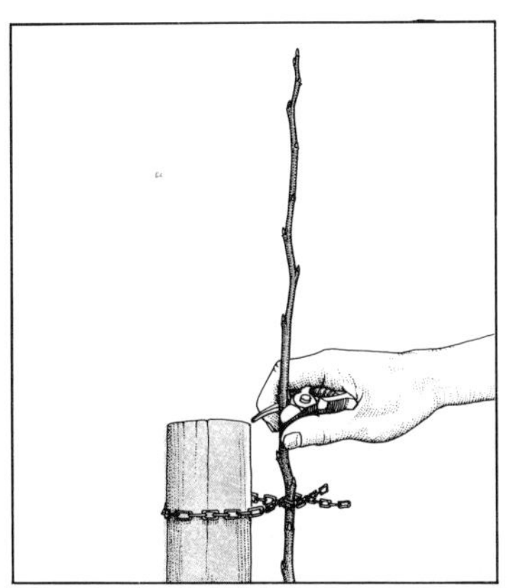

1 *After planting, cut back the main stem above a bud to 18–24 in. above soil level*

2 *Leave three or four well-spaced buds to form branches. Rub out unwanted buds*

Training a two-year-old bush tree

A two-year-old bush tree in winter will have the three or four branches that grew in the summer. Cut back each of the branches to an outward-pointing bud; how far back you cut them depends on their vigour.

If they are thick and vigorous, cut them back by half. If they are thin and weak, cut them back by two-thirds. Rub out with your thumb any inward-pointing buds just below the cuts.

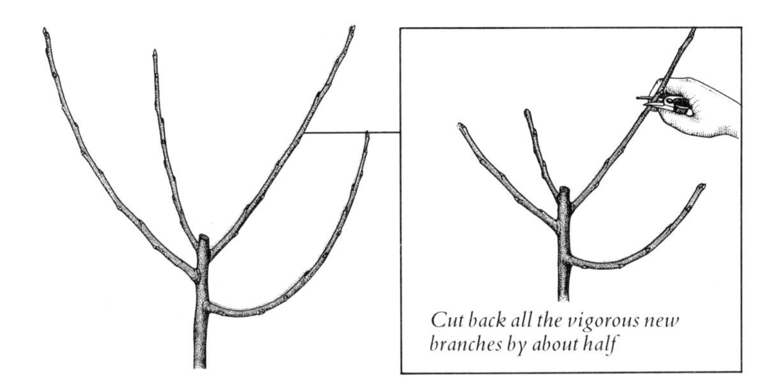

Cut back all the vigorous new branches by about half

Training a three-year-old bush tree

By a tree's third winter, a number of lateral shoots will have grown out from the branches.

Choose some of these laterals to form, with the first branches, the tree's main branches. They should all point outwards and their tips, after pruning, should be at least 18 in. apart.

Cut all main branches back to an outward-pointing bud, shortening new growth on each branch by one-third if the branch is growing vigorously or by a half if it is of average growth. If growth is weak, shorten the new growth by two-thirds.

Each of the laterals not chosen to form main branches should be cut back to four buds from the base.

Cut off any feathers (side-shoots) on the main stem flush with the stem.

After this third-year pruning, the basic shape of the tree is established.

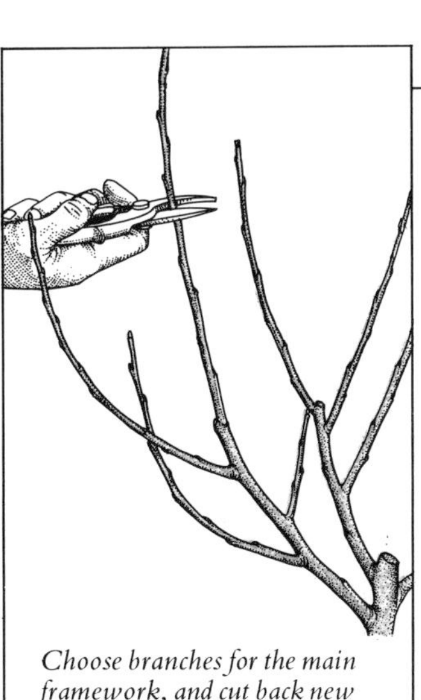

Choose branches for the main framework, and cut back new growth by half

Cut back all other laterals not wanted as main branches to four buds from the base

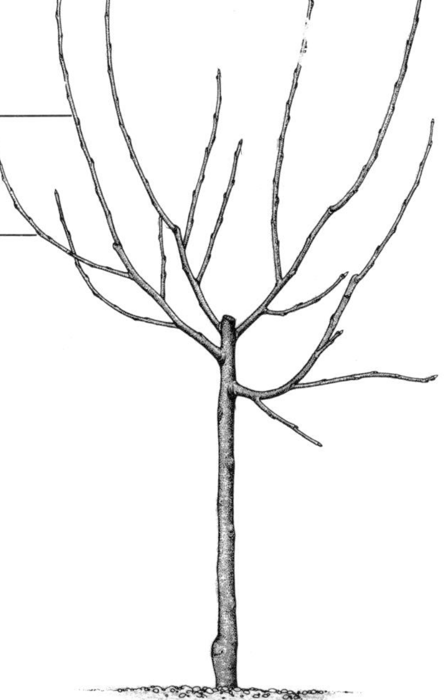

Pruning an established spur-forming bush tree

Established bush trees that bear all their fruit on spurs (such as 'Cox's Orange Pippin', 'James Grieve' and 'Ellison's Orange') are pruned each winter by the method known as the renewal system. The aim of the system is to produce new growth each season to replace some that has already borne fruit. It is based on the three-year cycle of fruiting growth.

During its first summer, a growth bud sends out a shoot. During the second summer this shoot produces fruit buds. During the third summer the fruit buds form spurs and bear fruit that same summer and in following summers.

During its second summer, a shoot not only produces fruit buds, but also new growth from its tip, so that a two-year-old shoot has one-year-old growth extending from it. In the same way, three-year-old growth has two-year-old and one-year-old growth extending from it.

Under the renewal system, a number of two-year-old and three-year-old shoots are cut back. This prevents overcropping and crowding, improves fruit quality, and makes way for new growth.

There is no rule governing how many shoots to prune and how many to leave. Use your judgment to maintain a balance between growth and fruitfulness. Try to prevent the tree becoming overcrowded with branches, but allow sufficient new fruit-bearing shoots to form.

Do not prune one-year-old shoots growing out from a main branch. But you cannot avoid cutting away some one-year-old extension growth when cutting back two-year-old and three-year-old growth. When choosing shoots for pruning, trace back to older wood from one-year-old tips.

On trees of weak growth, cut selected two-year-old growth hard back to two fruit buds. On stronger trees leave more buds. Cut back selected three-year-old growth to the lowest fruiting spur. Growth buds on the spur will produce new shoots the following season, and the cycle of growth will start again.

Branch leaders should have their new growth cut by one-third if the branch is growing vigorously, by one half if it is of average growth, by two-thirds if it is weak. When branches are fully grown (about 8 ft long), prune them in the same way as shoots.

BRANCH LEADERS

Branch leaders of average growth should be cut back by half of their new growth. Cut back stronger ones by one-third of new growth, and weaker ones by two-thirds

Pruning an established tip-bearing bush tree

ONE-YEAR-OLD SHOOTS

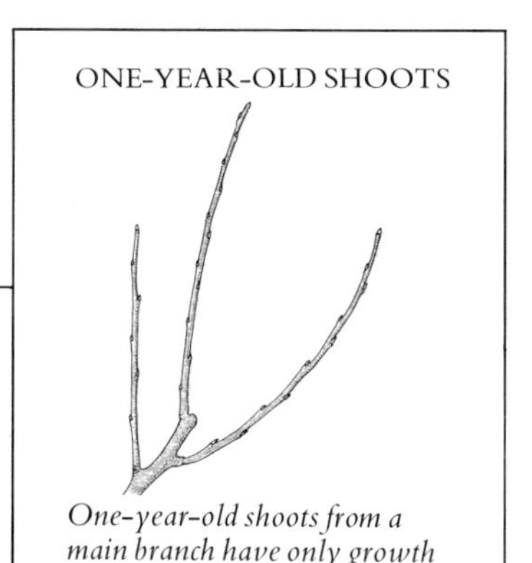

One-year-old shoots from a main branch have only growth buds. Do not prune them

TWO-YEAR-OLD SHOOTS

Two-year-old shoots have fruit buds. Prune some of them. Cut back to two buds on weak growth; leave more buds on stronger trees

THREE-YEAR-OLD SHOOTS

Three-year-old shoots have spurs. Prune some back to the lowest spur to encourage the growth of replacements

There are not as many tip-bearing varieties as spur-forming varieties. Tip-bearers, which include Bramley's Seedling', 'Worcester Pearmain' and 'George Cave', produce some of their fruit buds on the tips of shoots, and some on spurs.

The cycle of growth is the same as for spur-forming trees, but many one-year-old shoots produce a fruit bud at the tip.

Tip-bearing trees need comparatively little pruning. Once a year, in winter, prune back any shoots without a fruit bud at the tip. Cut just above the highest fruit bud, if there is one, otherwise cut back to four or five growth buds from the base of the shoot.

Shoots that have a fruit bud at the tip should not be pruned unless they are crowded – that is, if the tips are less than 12 in. apart. Thin them out by pruning some back to two buds from the base, preferably above a fruit bud if there is one.

Prune branch leaders by removing the fruit bud at the tip, cutting back to a growth bud; this induces the lower growth buds to break and produce more tip-bearing shoots.

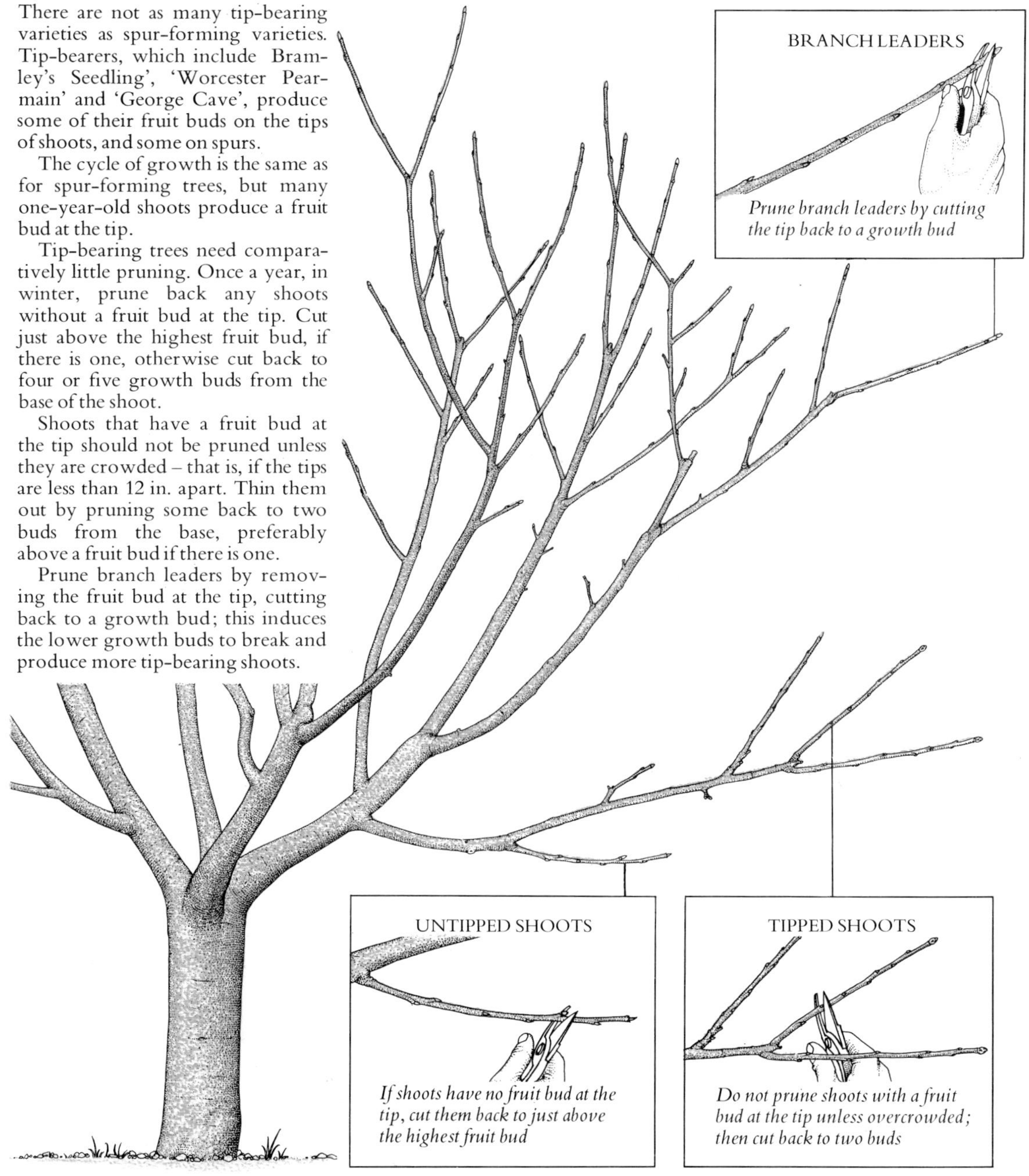

BRANCH LEADERS

Prune branch leaders by cutting the tip back to a growth bud

UNTIPPED SHOOTS

If shoots have no fruit bud at the tip, cut them back to just above the highest fruit bud

TIPPED SHOOTS

Do not prune shoots with a fruit bud at the tip unless overcrowded; then cut back to two buds

Pruning a neglected apple tree

An unpruned standard or bush apple tree can be restored to order in winter. If the tree is making very little new growth, all pruning can be done at once; otherwise, space the work over two or three years.

First remove any dead and diseased branches. Then let in light and air by removing sufficient large branches, particularly in the centre, for those remaining to be 2–3 ft apart in the outer spread where new growth develops. Cut out any crossed or badly placed branches. On very tall trees, shorten the tallest branches back to a lateral.

When removing a whole branch, cut it out as close to the source as possible. Smooth off saw cuts with a sharp knife and cover the wound with wound-sealing paint.

Thin out any complicated spur systems, reducing some in size and removing others entirely. As a general guide, spurs should be spaced 9–12 in. apart. Whether the tree's growth is slow or vigorous, spread spur-thinning over several seasons.

Clear away weeds and grass round the tree base and lightly fork the soil in a circle about 8 ft across.

As order is restored, prune each year according to whether the tree is a spur-forming variety or a tip-bearer (pp. 90, 91).

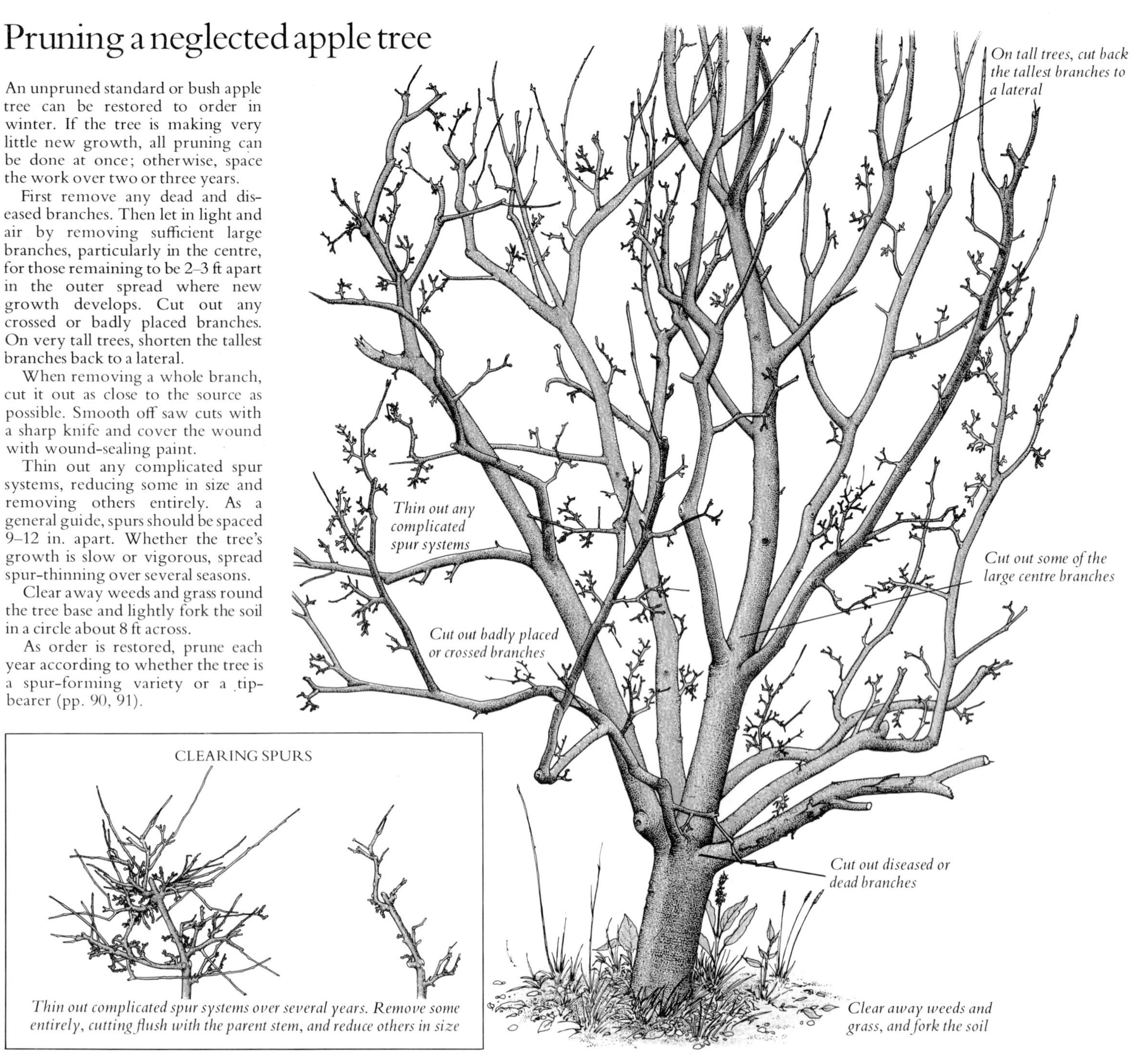

Thin out complicated spur systems over several years. Remove some entirely, cutting flush with the parent stem, and reduce others in size

Pruning and training a cordon tree

Plant cordons $2\frac{1}{2}$ ft apart – 3 ft apart on fertile soil (p. 84). Rows should be at least 6 ft apart.

After planting a tree, whatever its age, wire a bamboo cane, 8–10 ft long, to the horizontal wires – at the same angle as the tree (usually 45 degrees). Tie the stem to the cane with soft string. Remove the cane when the stem of the tree reaches the top wire.

No pruning is necessary at planting time. Prune in the same way each summer as growth becomes mature. This is generally in late July, but may not be until August or September. Mature growth is woody at the base, not less than 9 in. long, and has dark leaves.

Cut back mature laterals to three leaves from the basal cluster. Cut back the mature side-shoots from laterals or spurs to one leaf from the basal cluster. Do not prune the main stem leader.

If you prune in July, there will probably be secondary growth in the following two months. If the summer has been reasonably dry and there is not much growth, cut it all back to one bud in September; after a wet summer that has produced a lot of secondary growth, you may need to continue pruning into early winter.

If the spurs of mature cordons become overcrowded, thin them out in winter (p. 102).

When a cordon grows beyond the top wire, untie it and re-fasten at a more acute angle. But do not lower it to less than 35 degrees from the horizontal, or it will break. Once it cannot be lowered any more, cut back new growth at the tip to $\frac{1}{2}$ in., cutting above a bud. This pruning operation should be done in May.

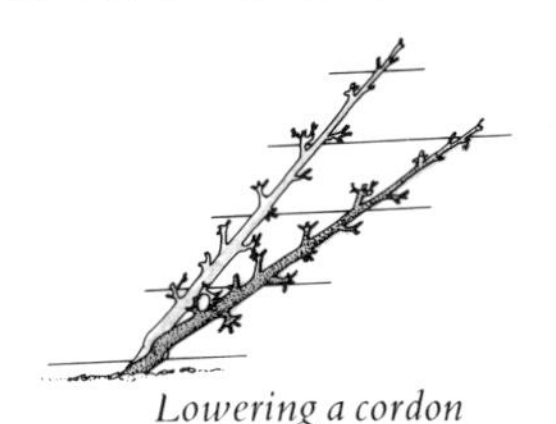
Lowering a cordon

SEPTEMBER PRUNING

Cut back all the small secondary growth from the late-July pruning. Prune it to one bud

In late July prune the mature laterals back to three leaves from the basal cluster

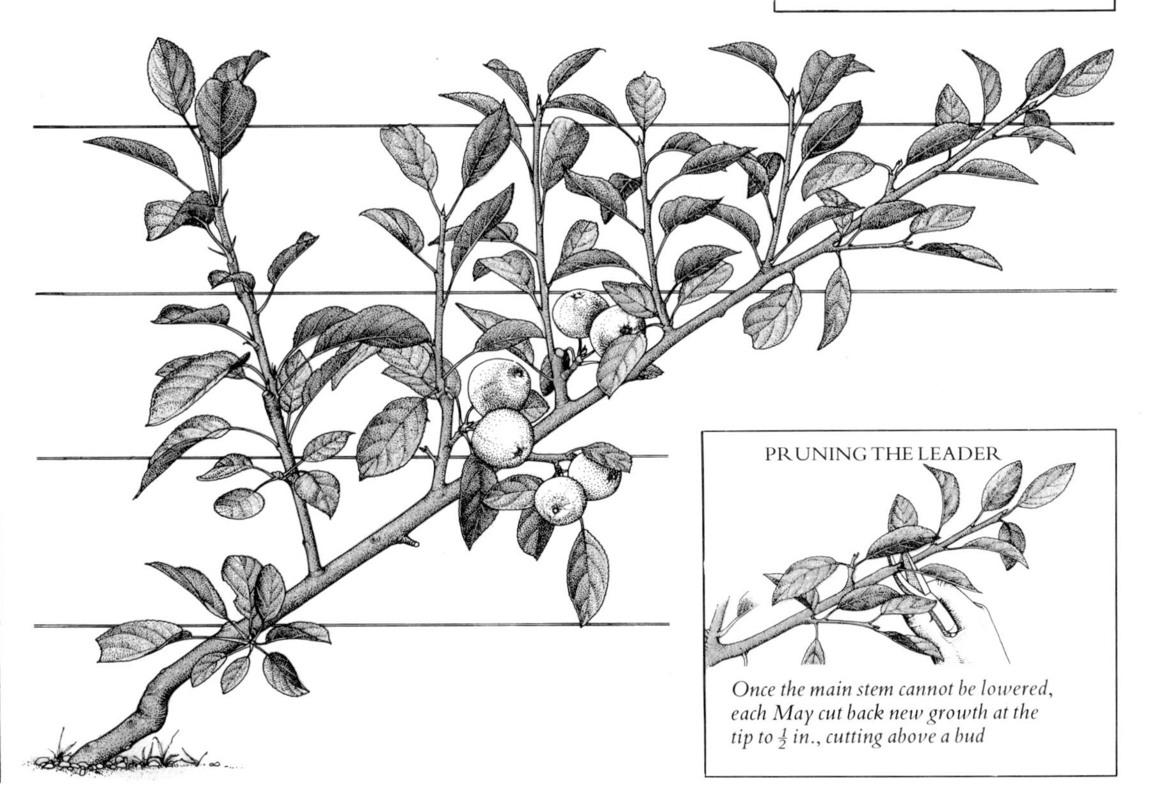

Cut back the mature side-shoots growing from laterals or spurs to one leaf from the basal cluster

PRUNING THE LEADER

Once the main stem cannot be lowered, each May cut back new growth at the tip to $\frac{1}{2}$ in., cutting above a bud

Pruning and training an espalier tree

Training a one-year-old espalier tree

Espaliers should be planted 10–15 ft apart, depending on the rootstock. Ask the nurseryman the correct planting distance when buying. Plant in autumn or winter (p. 84).

If you buy a maiden tree shorten it immediately after planting. Cut it back to a bud or shoot about 14 in. above the ground – 2 in. higher than the first horizontal support wire.

Choose a bud with two other buds or shoots beneath it that are pointing along the line of the wire and are on opposite sides of the stem. The top bud will produce a shoot to grow upright as the main stem, and the two lower buds will produce shoots to form the first tier of opposite horizontal branches. Rub out with your thumb all other buds or shoots.

Notch the bottom bud to stimulate growth. Although the top two buds should grow out strongly, the lowest will probably need encouragement. Use a sharp knife to remove a half-moon of bark from the stem just above the bud.

The following summer, as growth develops, train the three shoots in the required directions by means of canes. The shoot from the topmost bud is trained upright, the two side-shoots diagonally.

Fasten an upright cane to the wires and use soft string to tie to it the shoot from the topmost bud. Then fasten two more canes to the wires on each side of the first cane – both at an angle of 45 degrees. Tie the shoots from the side buds to the two canes with soft string.

You can train the two side branches to grow equally by adjusting the angles of the two canes. If one branch is growing more vigorously than the other, lower its cane – as lowering a branch slows its growth. At the same time, raise the other cane with the weaker shoot – as raising a branch stimulates growth. Adjust the canes in this way as necessary until growth is matched.

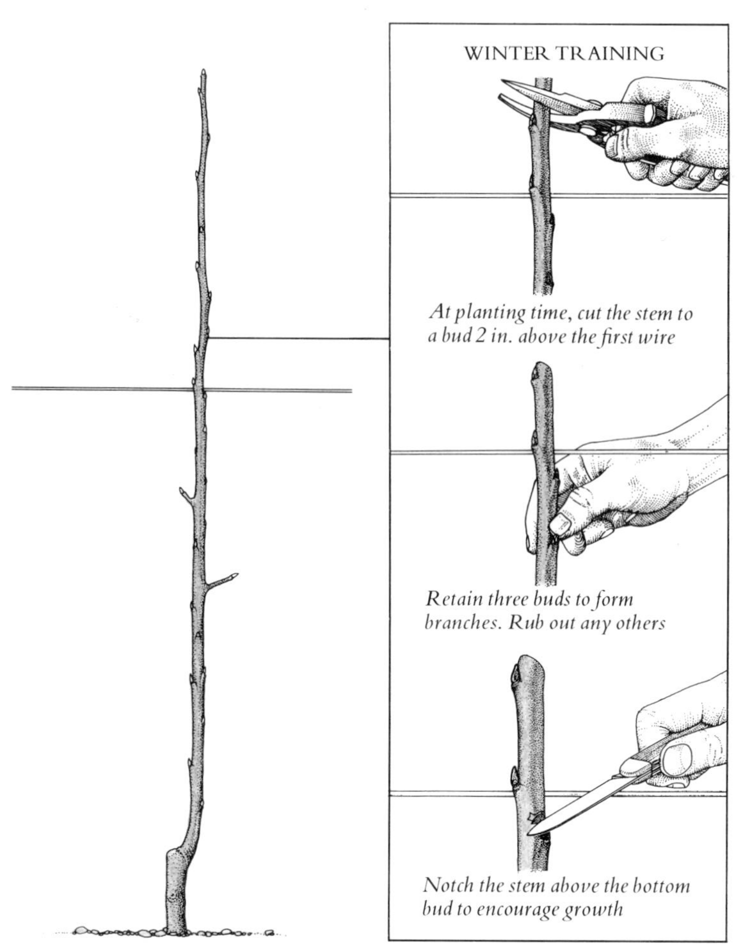

At planting time, cut the stem to a bud 2 in. above the first wire

Retain three buds to form branches. Rub out any others

Notch the stem above the bottom bud to encourage growth

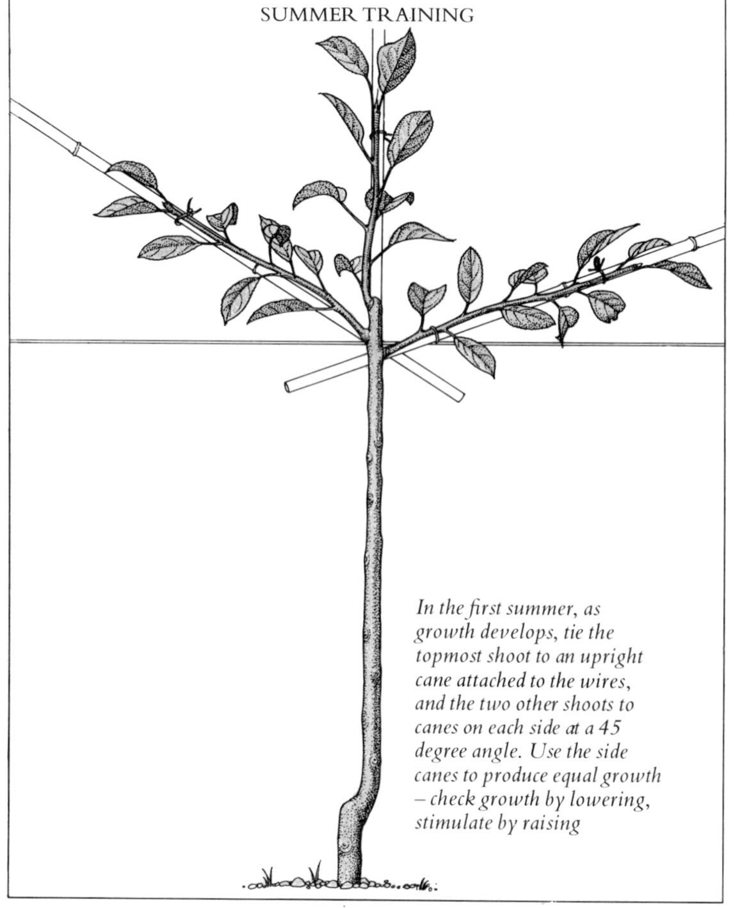

In the first summer, as growth develops, tie the topmost shoot to an upright cane attached to the wires, and the two other shoots to canes on each side at a 45 degree angle. Use the side canes to produce equal growth – check growth by lowering, stimulate by raising

Training an espalier in its second and third years

During the tree's second winter, lower the two side branches to the horizontal on each side of the main stem. Remove the canes and tie the branches to the wire with soft string. This is the age at which many espaliers are bought from nurseries.

Cut back the branch leaders to stimulate the growth of fruiting spurs from them, cutting just beyond a bud. Strong leaders should be cut back by less than half, weak ones by more than half. The aim is to make both branches grow to about the same length eventually.

Cut back the main stem to a bud 2 in. above the second wire. Then select two other buds below it to form a second pair of horizontal branches. Rub out with your thumb all other buds or shoots.

As with the first tier, notch the bottom bud to encourage growth, cutting away a half-moon of bark just above it with a sharp knife.

The following summer, fasten canes to the second-tier side-shoots at an angle of 45 degrees to the main-stem cane. Train the branches in exactly the same way as the first-tier branches the year before.

Tie the extension growth on the first tier leaders to the wires.

Prune the current season's growth as it becomes mature. This is usually in late July, but in some cases – depending on weather or area – in August or September.

Mature growth is not less than 9 in. long, is woody at the base, and has dark green leaves. Cut back mature laterals to three leaves beyond the basal cluster.

If you have pruned in July, there may be new secondary growth springing from the cut wood by September. Cut it all back to one bud. After a wet summer that has produced a lot of secondary growth, you may need to continue pruning into early winter.

In the third winter, cut back branch leaders as before and select buds for the third tier.

In the fourth summer, train the third tier and prune mature growth, as in the third summer. Cut side-shoots from spurs or laterals back to one leaf from the basal cluster.

In late July, cut back mature laterals to three leaves from the basal cluster

In September, cut secondary shoots from the late July pruning back to one bud

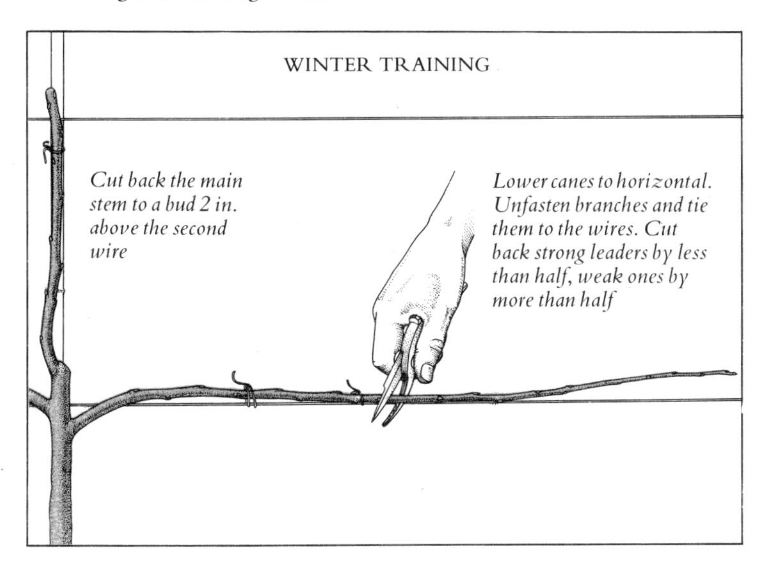

Cut back the main stem to a bud 2 in. above the second wire

Lower canes to horizontal. Unfasten branches and tie them to the wires. Cut back strong leaders by less than half, weak ones by more than half

Finishing off the top tier of an espalier

The top tier of an espalier is created by pruning in winter. Cut back the main stem just above two side buds, rub out unwanted buds below, and leave no upper bud for extending the main stem.

Early in the following summer, when the side buds have put out shoots, tie them to canes at an angle of 45 degrees. Train the growth of the two branches in the same way as for other tiers in previous summers – raise the cane to stimulate the growth of a weaker branch, or lower it to slow the growth of a stronger branch.

In winter, lower branches to the horizontal, remove the canes, and tie the branches to the wires.

Four or five tiers is usually the maximum to which espaliers are grown, resulting in a tree 6–8 ft high; the usual width is about 12 ft (6 ft branches on each side).

However, the tree can be grown to ten tiers if desired; in this case, for a good crop, the total width is usually kept to about 6 ft. Alternatively, trees can be as low as one tier – about 12–15 in. high.

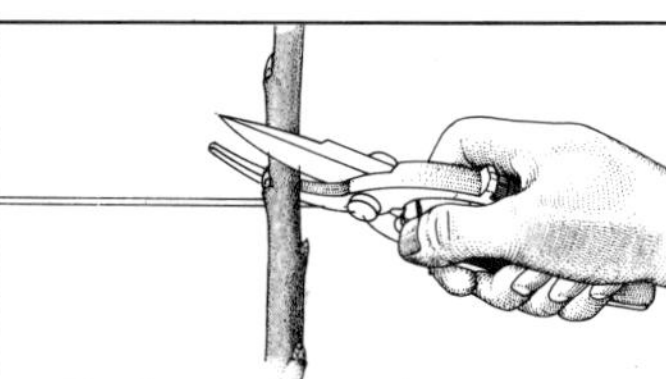

For the top tier, cut the stem to leave two side-branch buds only

Pruning a fully trained espalier tree

Prune the current season's growth each summer as it becomes mature, generally in late July. Mature growth is not less than 9 in. long, its greenish-brown bark has started turning brown at the base, and the leaves are dark green.

Mature laterals growing directly from branches should be cut back to three leaves beyond the basal cluster. Cut back mature side-shoots from laterals or spurs to one leaf from the basal cluster.

If new growth is not mature enough during July, it may be ready for pruning in August. In the North it may not be ready until September.

If you have pruned during July, there will probably be secondary growth by September. If the summer has been fairly dry and there is not much secondary growth, cut it all back to one bud. After a wet summer that has produced a lot of secondary growth, you may have to continue pruning into early winter.

Apart from that, winter pruning is not generally necessary. Once branch leaders have reached a length of about 6 ft – or have reached the extent of the room available – prune them in summer in the same way as mature laterals.

The fruiting spurs may become overcrowded on mature trees. Thin them out in winter by cutting some flush with the parent stem and by reducing the size of others (p. 102).

In late July, cut back laterals to three leaves from the basal cluster

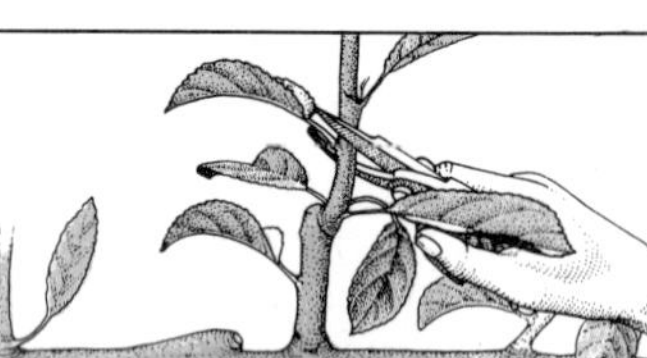

Also in late July, cut side-shoots from laterals to one leaf from the basal cluster

SEPTEMBER PRUNING

In September, cut secondary growth back to one bud

Pruning and training a fan-shaped tree

Training a one-year-old fan-shaped tree

Fans should be spaced 15–20 ft apart, depending on the rootstock. Check the planting distances when buying. Plant in autumn or winter (p. 84).

If you start with a maiden tree cut back the stem to about 24 in. from the ground after planting. Cut above two opposite side buds.

In the following summer, when shoots 9–12 in. long have grown from these buds, tie them to canes attached to the supporting wires at an angle of 45 degrees. Rub out any buds or shoots below them.

Regulate the growth of the two branches – the first ribs of the fan – by adjusting the angle of the canes. If one rib is growing more vigorously, lower its cane to slow growth and raise the other rib cane.

When growth is matched, fix the ribs at an angle of 45 degrees. Remove canes and tie the ribs to the wires when stems are woody.

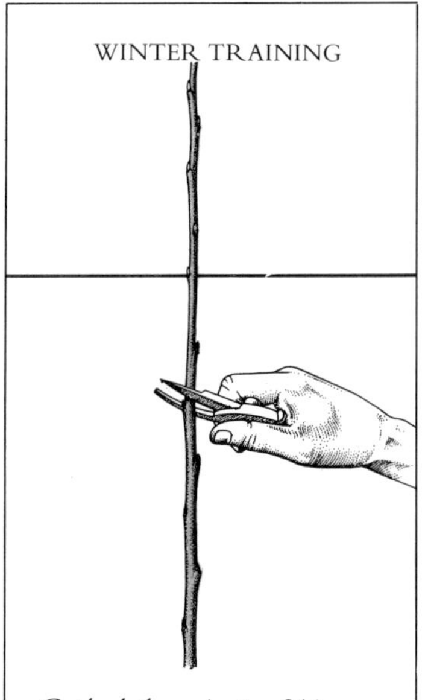

Cut back the main stem 24 in. from the ground, above two buds

When shoots have grown 9–12 in. long, tie them to canes at an angle of 45 degrees. Stimulate growth by raising, slow it by lowering

Training a two-year-old fan-shaped tree

During the second winter, prune each of the ribs back to 12–18 in. long. Cut just above a growth bud.

During the second summer, tie the extension growth from each end bud to a cane at the same angle as the rib. Then, on each rib, select two evenly spaced shoots on the upper side and one on the lower side, and rub out all other shoots.

As the chosen shoots grow long enough, fasten six more canes to the wires and train the shoots to them.

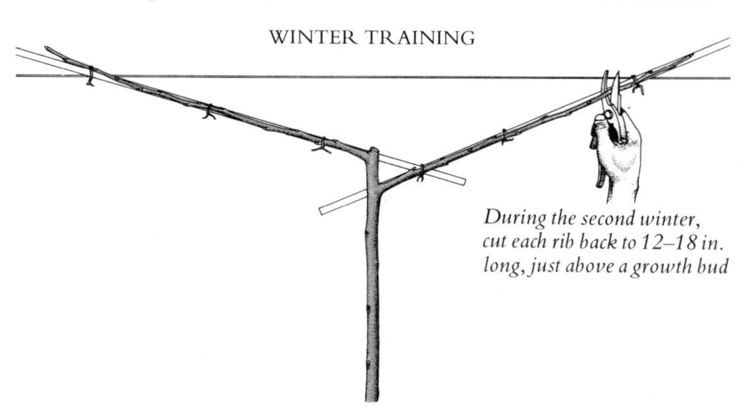

During the second winter, cut each rib back to 12–18 in. long, just above a growth bud

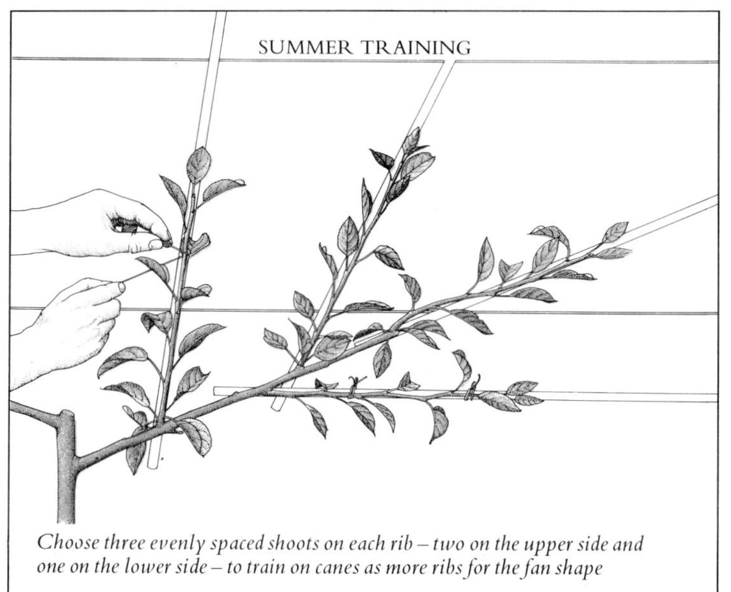

Choose three evenly spaced shoots on each rib – two on the upper side and one on the lower side – to train on canes as more ribs for the fan shape

Training a three-year-old fan-shaped tree

In the third winter, prune each of the eight fan ribs back to 24–30 in., just above a growth bud.

In the following summer, tie the growth from the end bud of each rib on to canes. Choose three evenly spaced shoots from each rib – two on the upper side and one on the lower – for training as more ribs. Cut mature shoots not wanted as fan ribs back to three leaves from the basal cluster.

Tie the 24 new ribs to canes when they are long enough. The fan will now have 32 ribs, probably enough to cover the wall. Remove the canes and tie the shoots to the wires once they have become woody.

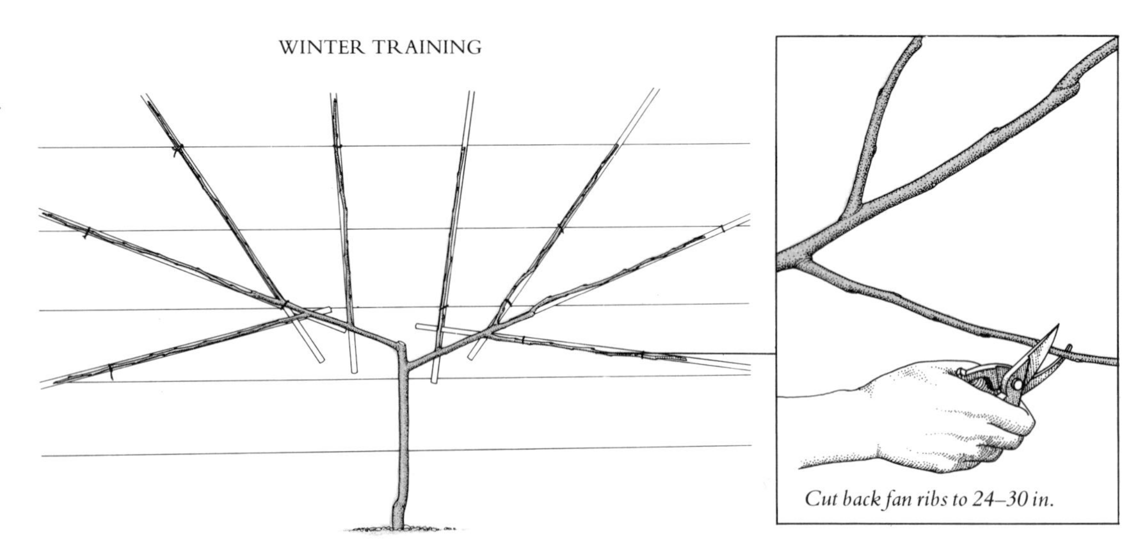

Cut back fan ribs to 24–30 in.

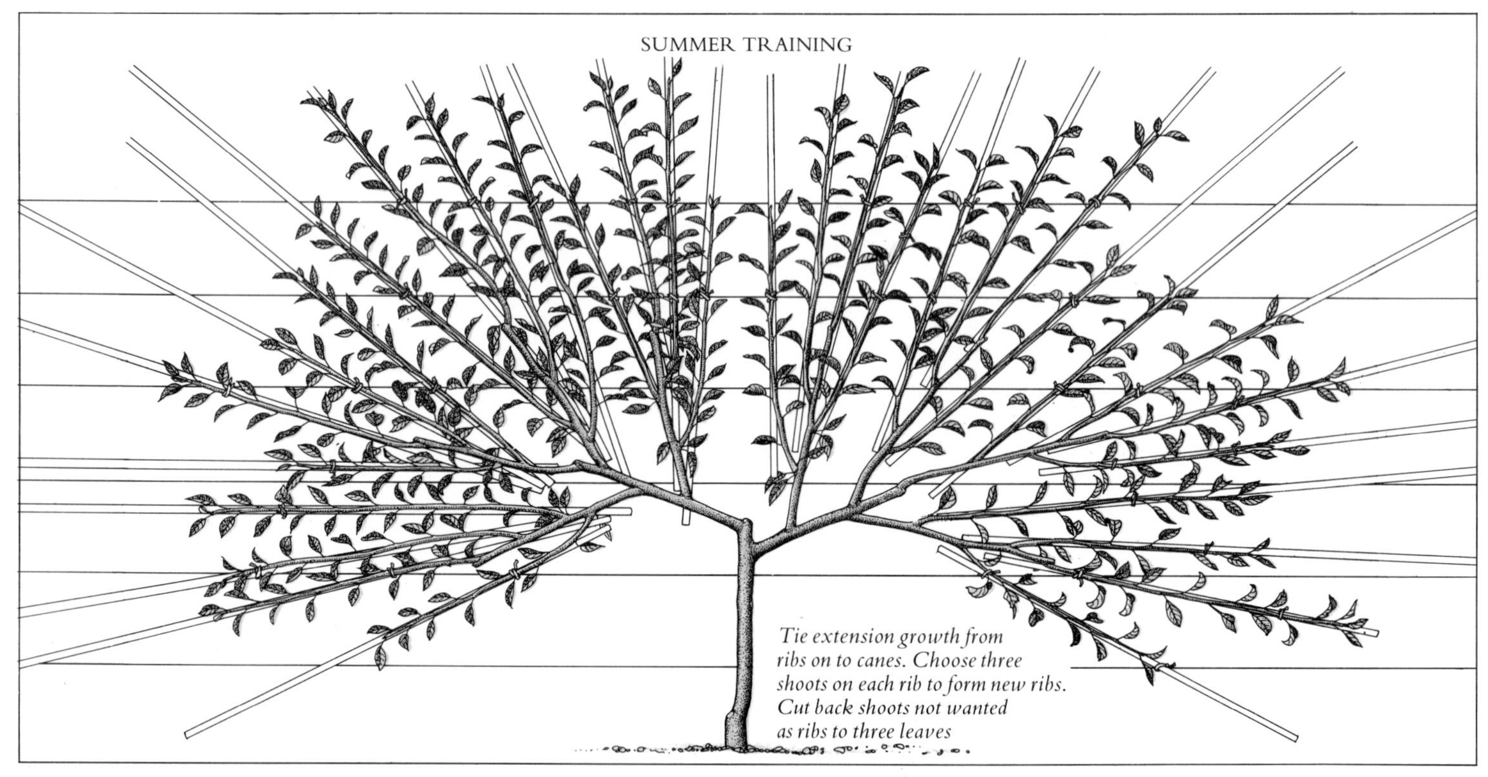

Tie extension growth from ribs on to canes. Choose three shoots on each rib to form new ribs. Cut back shoots not wanted as ribs to three leaves

Pruning a fan after it has been trained

Once the tree's fan shape has been established, the only pruning necessary in winter is the thinning out of overcrowded spurs. This will help the tree to produce regular crops and better-quality fruit.

Remove some of the overcrowded spurs entirely, cutting them off flush with the parent stem, and cut back others to reduce them in size. Carry out no further pruning during the winter.

Prune new growth in summer as it becomes mature – generally starting in late July and perhaps continuing for about a month.

Mature growth is not less than 9 in. long, has turned woody at the base, and has dark green leaves. Cut back mature new side-shoots from ribs to one leaf beyond the basal cluster, unless they are needed as replacements. Tie the replacement shoots to the wires.

If new growth is not mature enough for pruning during July, it may be ready in August. If it is still not mature enough in August – it may not be in the North – wait until September.

If you prune new growth in July, secondary growth may have sprung from the cut wood by September. After a reasonably dry summer that has not produced much secondary growth, cut it all back to one bud in September.

If the summer has been wet and there is a lot of secondary growth, you may need to continue pruning into early winter.

If the ribs of the fan grow beyond the space allotted, cut them back to a strong side-branch and tie it in as a replacement leader.

If ribs outgrow the available space, cut them back to a strong side branch and tie it in as a replacement leader

SUMMER PRUNING

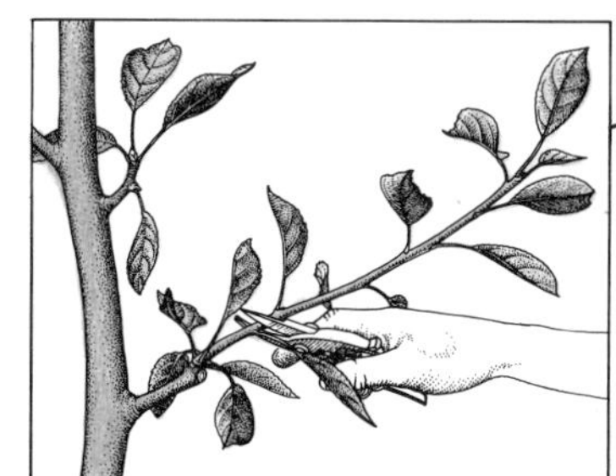

In late July cut back all mature new side-shoots from ribs to one leaf from the basal cluster

Pruning and training a dwarf pyramid tree

Training a one-year-old dwarf pyramid

Dwarf pyramids grow to about 7 ft high, with short branches spreading out round the stem. In early years trees are shaped something like Christmas trees. They should be spaced 3½ ft apart (4 ft on more fertile soils) in rows 7–10 ft apart. Plant in autumn or winter (p. 84).

If you begin with a one-year-old (maiden) tree, cut back the stem to about 20 in. above soil level immediately after planting. Cut just above a bud or side-shoot, and then rub out the bud or shoot second from the top, otherwise it may compete with the topmost bud to produce the leading shoot.

Select three or four of the buds below to form the tree's first branches, so spaced on the stem to grow out in different directions. Rub out unwanted buds or shoots.

The topmost bud will grow upwards to form the tree's central leader, and the second and third should form strong branches, but the fourth and fifth will produce weak branches unless they are stimulated. They therefore need notching; remove a half-moon of bark from above each.

Training a young dwarf pyramid in winter

In the second winter, cut back the central leader to about 18 in. from last year's cut.

To help create a straight stem, make the cut just above a bud facing in the opposite direction from the bud that was chosen during the previous winter.

As in the previous winter, rub out the bud below the top one and choose three or four buds below it suitably spaced for forming another tier of branches. Notch the two lower buds as before, using a sharp knife.

Repeat this training each winter until the main stem has reached a height of about 7 ft.

In the second winter only, cut back the leaders of the first tier of branches to about 9 in. long – above a downward-pointing bud. After this, branch leaders are cut back in summer only.

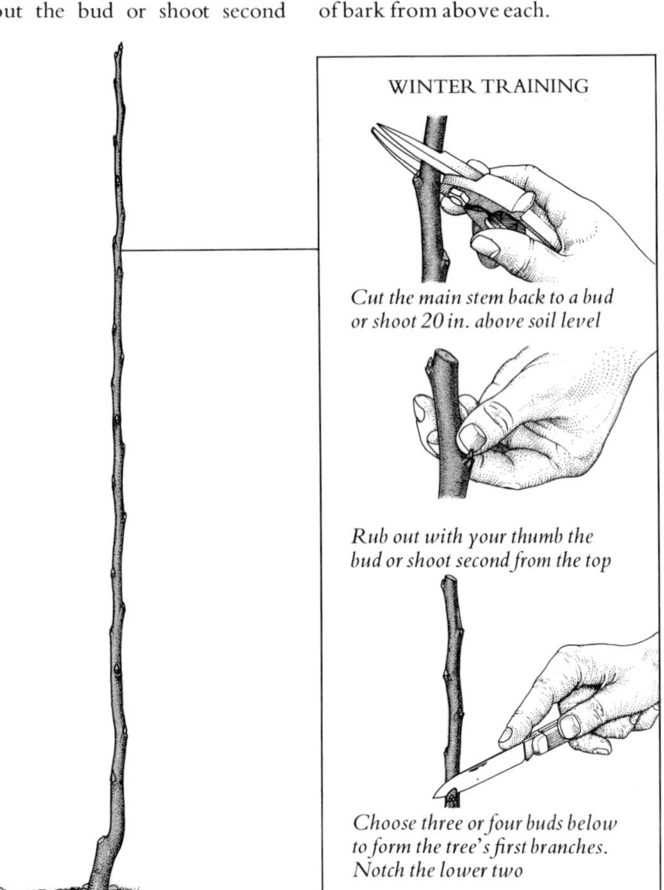

Cut the main stem back to a bud or shoot 20 in. above soil level

Rub out with your thumb the bud or shoot second from the top

Choose three or four buds below to form the tree's first branches. Notch the lower two

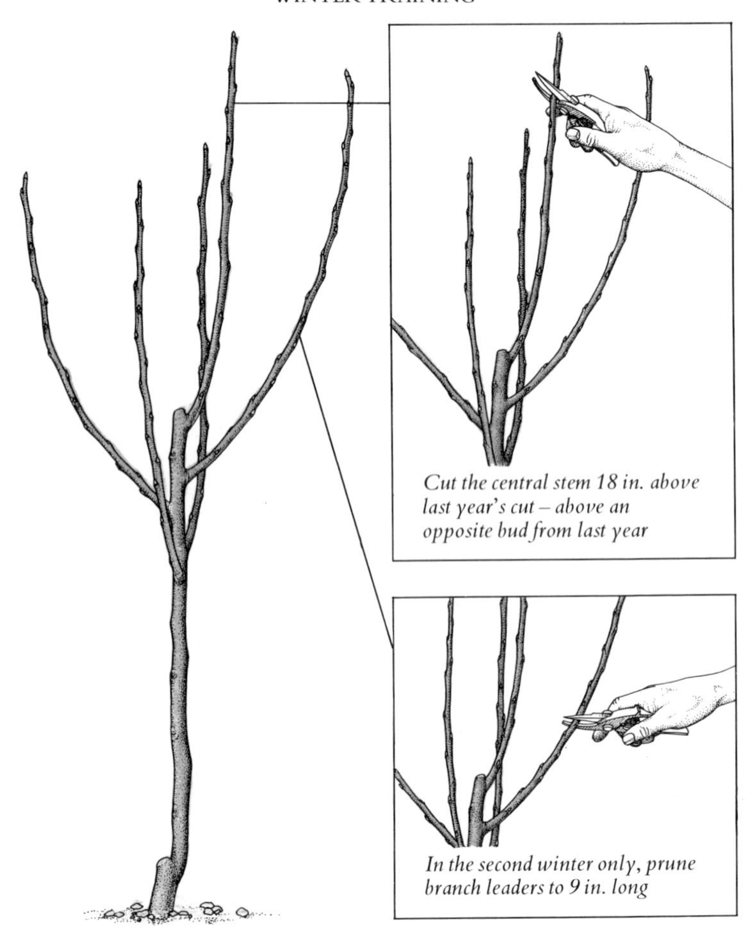

Cut the central stem 18 in. above last year's cut – above an opposite bud from last year

In the second winter only, prune branch leaders to 9 in. long

Pruning a young dwarf pyramid in summer

No pruning is needed in the summer after training a maiden tree. For older trees, prune new growth as it matures, usually starting in late July and perhaps continuing for about a month.

Growth is mature when it is at least 9 in. long, woody at the base, and has dark green leaves.

Cut back extension growth on branch leaders (but not the central leader) to five or six leaves beyond the basal cluster. Cut above a downward-pointing bud.

Cut any mature laterals from branches back to three leaves from the basal cluster.

If there are any mature side-shoots growing from laterals or spurs, cut them back to one leaf from the basal cluster.

Until the fourth summer, remove any new shoots growing from the main stem.

If new growth is not mature enough for pruning in July, it may be ready in August. If it is still not mature enough – it may not be in the North – wait until September.

If you have pruned in July, you may find that secondary growth has sprung from the pruned shoots by September.

If it has been a reasonably dry summer and there is not much secondary growth, cut it all back to one bud from its parent stem during September.

After a wet summer that has produced a lot of such growth, you may have to continue pruning into early winter.

Training a dwarf pyramid to full height

Continue winter training and summer pruning, as in previous years, until the central stem reaches a height of about 7 ft – this will be when the tree is about seven or eight years old. By this time it will have about six tiers of branches from each winter training.

Then in May cut back the central stem by half the previous season's growth. The shape of the dwarf pyramid is then established.

Once the tree reaches about 15 years old, its upper branches will have grown to reach the same spread as the lower ones, consequently the Christmas-tree shape will be lost. Branches should be kept at about 18 in. long.

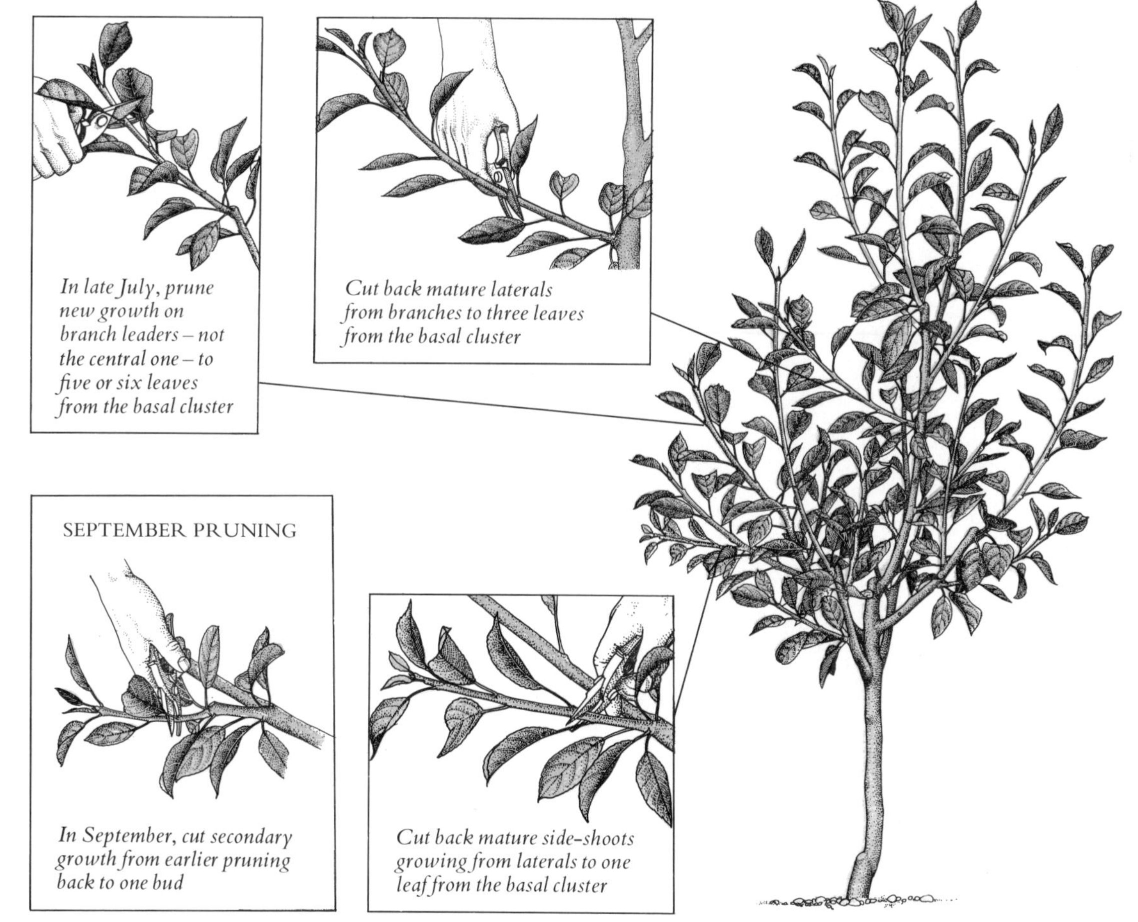

In late July, prune new growth on branch leaders – not the central one – to five or six leaves from the basal cluster

Cut back mature laterals from branches to three leaves from the basal cluster

SEPTEMBER PRUNING

In September, cut secondary growth from earlier pruning back to one bud

Cut back mature side-shoots growing from laterals to one leaf from the basal cluster

CUTTING THE MAIN STEM

When the central leader reaches a height of about 7 ft, cut it back during May by about half the previous season's growth

Pruning an established dwarf pyramid tree

Each May, cut back the central leader above a bud, leaving only ½ in. of the previous season's growth. When branches reach 18 in. long, maintain them at this length.

If branch leaders begin to overlap the branches of neighbouring trees, cut back half of the new growth during one May pruning, and then to only ½ in. of new growth every following May.

As in previous summers, prune growth as it becomes mature in late July. Cut back mature laterals from branches to three leaves beyond the basal cluster. Cut back mature side-shoots from laterals or spurs to one leaf beyond the basal cluster.

If growth is not mature enough for pruning during July, prune in August or September.

Prune any secondary growth from the July pruning back to one bud in September. After a wet season that has produced a lot of such growth, you may have to continue pruning into early winter.

On older dwarf pyramid trees, the fruiting spurs may become overcrowded and need thinning. Do this in winter; remove some entirely, cutting flush with the parent stem, and reduce the size of others.

Thin out overcrowded spurs in winter. Remove some entirely and reduce others in size

Each May cut the central leader to ½ in. of last year's growth

In late July, cut mature laterals to three leaves from the basal cluster

Cut mature side-shoots to one leaf from the basal cluster

Apples: varieties to grow

All these varieties should be available from fruit nurseries. They are listed in the order that they mature.

Pollination groups No apple tree is fully self-fertile, so more than one variety should be grown. Ideally, choose trees from within the same pollination group, although pollination will usually occur between varieties in adjoining groups. The groups relate to flowering time:

1 Early to mid-season
2 Mid-season
3 Mid to late season

Triploids (marked T) are almost sterile varieties and therefore poor pollinators. They need to be grown with two other varieties from the same group – to pollinate both the triploid and each other.

Picking time The approximate time of picking is given as a guide. The exact time will vary according to the season and the locality. All the apples on a tree do not ripen at the same time, and – for the early and mid-season varieties at least – more than one picking will be needed.

Name	Pollination group	Week for picking	Season of use	Colour	Remarks
DESSERT APPLES					
'George Cave'	1	Aug. (2)	Mid-Aug.	Greenish-yellow/red flush	Heavy cropper. Crisp and juicy with a small core. Tip bearing
'Discovery'	2	Aug. (2)	Aug.–Sept.	Bright red	Good crop. May be slow to bear. Some scab resistance. Spur forming
'Worcester Pearmain'	2	Sept. (2)	Sept.–Oct.	Greenish-yellow under bright crimson	Reliable cropper with some frost resistance. Suitable for the North. Susceptible to canker but resistant to mildew. Tip bearing
'James Grieve'	2	Sept. (2)	Sept.–Oct.	Pale yellow/orange-red flush and stripes	Heavy, regular crop. Suitable for the North. Susceptible to apple canker and brown-rot canker. Spur forming
'Ellison's Orange'	3	Sept. (3)	Sept.–Oct.	Yellow with dark-red mottling and stripes	A good cropper, but tends to bear biennially. Suitable for the North. Overripe fruit develops aniseed flavour. Spur forming
'Laxton's Fortune'	2	Sept. (3)	Late Sept.–Oct.	Greenish-yellow/bright-red flush and red streaks	Fine flavour. Tends to bear biennially in some districts. Suitable for the North. Some resistance to scab. Spur forming
'St Edmund's Russet'	2	Sept. (3)	Late Sept.–Oct.	Golden russet	Fine flavour, but fruit tends to be small. Tip bearing
'Egremont Russet'	1	Sept. (4)	Oct.–Dec.	Brown russet	One of the best-flavoured russets. Some scab resistance. Spur forming
'Mother'	3	Sept. (4)	Oct.–Dec.	Yellow/dark-red flush	Recommended for flavour. Some scab resistance. Spur forming
'Sunset'	2	Sept. (4)	Nov.–Dec.	Golden-yellow/light red and speckled russet	Fine flavour. A good garden tree, compact with attractive blossoms. Suitable for the North. Spur forming
'Cox's Orange Pippin'	2	Oct. (1)	Nov.–Dec.	Greenish-yellow/dark-red flush, streaks; some russet	The best-flavoured apple, but it needs good cultural treatment. Susceptible to canker, scab and mildew. Spur forming
'Kidd's Orange Red'	2	Oct. (1)	Nov.–Jan.	Dark red/greyish russet	A good, regular cropper. Recommended for flavour. Spur forming
'Orlean's Reinette'	3	Oct. (4)	Nov.–Jan.	Golden-yellow/red cheek	Recommended for rich flavour. May shrivel in store
'Golden Delicious'	3	Oct. (3)	Nov.–Jan.	Yellow	Easy to grow; a regular cropper. Suitable for the North. Spur forming
'Crispin'	2 (T)	Oct. (3)	Dec.–Feb.	Yellow	Crops heavily. Unsuitable for restricted forms. Spur forming
'Idared'	1	Oct. (4)	Dec.–April	Yellow/crimson flush	A good, regular cropper. Suitable for the North. Spur forming
COOKING APPLES					
'Grenadier'	2	Aug. (2)	Aug.–Sept.	Light green	Suitable for the North. Does not store well. Spur forming
'George Neal'	1	Aug. (3)	Late Aug.–early Oct.	Pale yellow/orange-scarlet flush; russet spots	Flowers early and is sometimes affected by frost. Recommended for quality. Fruit from medium to large in size. Spur forming
'Howgate Wonder'	3	Oct. (1–2)	Oct.–Jan.	Green/red flush, stripes	Regular, heavy cropper; vigorous and upright. Large exhibition fruit of fair flavour. Suitable for the North. Spur forming
'Bramley's Seedling'	2 (T)	Oct. (2)	Nov.–Feb.	Greenish-yellow/red flush and broken stripes	Our best cooker. Unsuitable for restricted tree forms. Tip bearing
'Dumelow's Seedling'	3	Oct. (4)	Nov.–Mar.	Pale yellow/red tinge	Hardy, and suitable for the North. Fruit is from small to medium in size and excellent for mincemeat. Spur forming
'Lane's Prince Albert'	3	Oct. (1)	Dec.–Mar.	Green/crimson stripes	Good crop. Large fruit. Suitable for the North. Spur forming
'Annie Elizabeth'	3	Oct. (3)	Dec.–June	Green/red flush	Suitable for North. Unsuitable for restricted forms. Spur forming

Blackberries and loganberries for summer and autumn treats

Blackberry 'Bedford Giant'

Loganberry 'Clone LY.59'

Blackberries are used for desserts, jam-making and wine-making. They keep well in a freezer. Loganberries, relatives of the blackberry, are grown and used (except for wine-making) in the same way.

Both blackberries and loganberries grow so easily and vigorously that three plants are usually ample for the average garden. They need sun or partial shade, and a well-drained but moisture-retaining soil free of lime. Organic material improves moisture retention.

Blackberries and loganberries are both self-fertilising. Some varieties of each are thornless. Blackberries ripen mainly in August, loganberries in July.

Canes are best planted in autumn (p. 244), but can be put in at any time until March. Position them 8–15 ft apart and, immediately after planting, cut back just above a bud to 9–15 in. above ground level.

The most common problem that is likely to occur is attack by the raspberry beetle, causing small, soft patches on ripe fruits, which contain a small, reddish maggot. To prevent attacks, spray with derris, fenitrothion or malathion as soon as the first fruits start to turn pink.

Plants may also suffer from cane spot (small purplish spots on canes). Cut out and burn badly spotted canes. Spray with benomyl or thiophanate-methyl from bud-burst to petal-fall every 14 days.

Spur blight (dark purple blotches on canes) may attack loganberries. Spray with benomyl, dichlofluanid, thiram or captan soon after the canes emerge, and repeat fortnightly three or four times.

Cultivating and training the plants

Canes are trained up a post or wires in such a way that growing shoots are kept well away from two-year-old shoots, which bear the fruit. This prevents disease spreading.

For training up a post, use 9–10 ft of 4 × 4 in. timber leaving 7 ft above the ground. Train the fruiting canes up the post and tie the new shoots growing from the ground loosely together to one side.

For training canes on wires, use 10–12 gauge wire stretched between posts or against a wall to a height of about 6 ft; place wires 12 in. apart and fasten to vine eyes.

There are three ways of training the canes. With the fan method, the fruiting canes are fanned out on each side and the new growth is temporarily tied to the top wire. The weaving method is similar, except that the fruiting canes are woven round the wires. With the alternate method, fruiting canes are tied in permanently on one side of the wires, and new growth on the other.

Watering and feeding Water only during dry spells in summer. In late January feed with 1 oz. (1 tablespoon) of sulphate of potash per square yard. Add 2 oz. (2 tablespoons) of superphosphate every third year. In March feed with ½ oz. (1 dessertspoon) of sulphate of ammonia per square yard and mulch with rotted manure or compost.

Cutting out the old canes When all the fruit has been picked, cut out the fruited canes at ground level. For thorned varieties, get a helper to hold the old canes as they are cut away. Wear stout gloves.

With post training and fan and weaving systems, untie the current year's shoots from their temporary positions and tie them in to replace the old, cut-down shoots.

THE ALTERNATE METHOD OF TRAINING

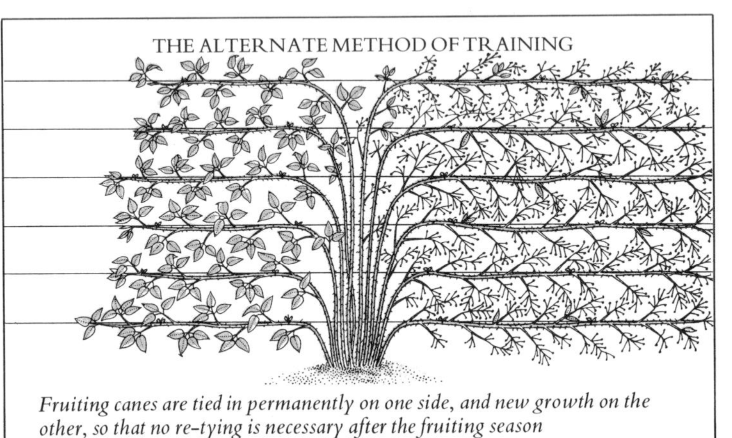

Fruiting canes are tied in permanently on one side, and new growth on the other, so that no re-tying is necessary after the fruiting season

PRUNING

After fruit has been picked, cut out the old canes at ground level

Blackcurrants that thrive in the sun

Raising new blackberry and loganberry plants

Blackberries and loganberries root easily. The best way of raising new plants is to layer the tips of shoots.

At the end of July, bend down a new season's shoot and, where it touches the ground, dig a 6 in. deep hole with a trowel. Plant the tip of the shoot in the hole and firm it in.

By October the tips will have rooted. Sever each new plant from its parent by cutting just above a bud. Do not move the plant yet.

In November transfer each new cane to its permanent bed. It will bear fruit in its second or third year.

1 *At the end of July, bend down a new season's shoot and plant its tip firmly*

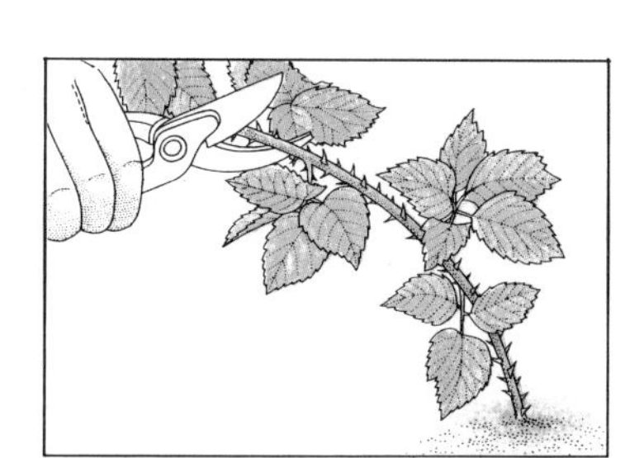

2 *In October, when it is rooted, cut the shoot from its parent just above a bud*

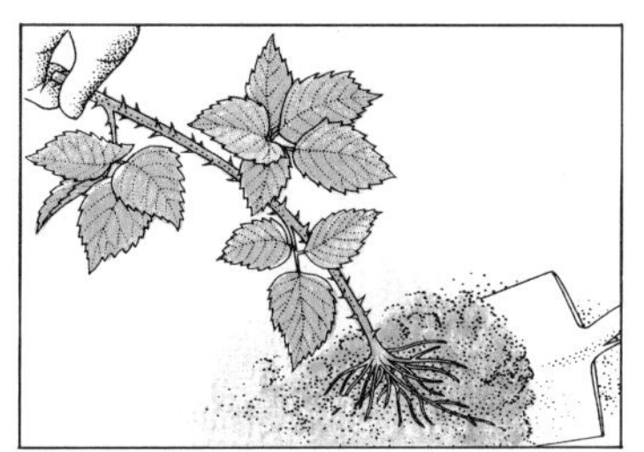

3 *In November lift the new plant and move it to its permanent position*

Varieties of blackberries and loganberries to grow

The season of use given for blackberries and loganberries is for plants grown in the South; ripening will be later in the North. Ripening time is, in any case, an estimate only and will vary according to the growing conditions during the season.

Name	Season of use	Remarks
BLACKBERRIES		
'Bedford Giant'	End July–early Aug.	Strong grower. Large fruits, very sweet. Thorned
'Himalaya Giant'	Mid-Aug.	Heavy cropper. Good flavour. Vigorous. Heavily thorned. Space 15 ft apart
'Oregon Thornless'	Mid-Aug.–end Aug.	Needs a warm position. Sweet with a good flavour. Thornless
LOGANBERRIES		
'Clone LY.59'	July	Good cropper. Needs a warm place. Acid fruits. Mildly thorned
'Clone L. 654'	July	Heavy crop. Needs warmth. Thornless

Blackcurrant 'Blacksmith'

Blackcurrants are used for desserts, jam-making and medicinal drinks. They grow best in an open, sunny position but will tolerate partial shade. Do not plant them in cold, exposed sites or frost pockets.

Any well-drained, moisture-retaining soil is suitable, but blackcurrants thrive best under highly fertile conditions. Before planting, thoroughly work in a generous dressing of well-rotted farmyard manure or good garden compost.

Buy young plants only from places holding a Ministry of Agriculture certificate. For the average family, 9–12 bushes should yield ample fruit. The season is mainly July–August.

Plant between October and March (p. 244), preferably in autumn. Put plants 6 ft apart and 1–2 in. deeper in the soil than in the nursery, so that the new shoots will emerge direct from the soil.

Immediately after planting, cut down all shoots to just above the second bud from soil level. Then mulch with 2 in. of rotted manure, garden compost, leaf-mould or peat.

Every year, in early March, spread well-rotted manure, decomposed lawn mowings or garden compost over the bed. Use two buckets per square yard.

In late January feed with 1 oz. (1 tablespoon) of sulphate of potash to the square yard over the root area. Add 2 oz. (2 tablespoons) of superphosphate every third year. In March feed 2 oz. of sulphate of ammonia to the square yard.

Water thoroughly during dry spells. Roots are shallow, so do not use a fork or hoe to weed. Control weeds with a thick mulch. This also helps to conserve moisture. Protect buds and ripening fruit from birds.

After planting, cut shoots down to just above the second bud

How to harvest a crop of blackcurrants

Do not pick blackcurrants until they are fully ripe. They start to turn black a week or two before they are ready for picking. Not all fruits ripen at the same time; those at the top of a truss are usually ready first. For small quantities it may be better to pick individually rather than cut off a whole truss at a time.

What can go wrong with blackcurrants

Blackcurrant gall mite, which also spreads virus disease, is the most serious problem. For symptoms not described here, turn to the chart of pests and diseases on page 377. Look up chemicals on page 398 to find proprietary names.

Symptoms	Cause	Cure
Buds in winter are several times larger than usual, and wither up in spring	Big bud (blackcurrant gall mites)	Remove and burn affected buds in early March. Spray with malathion or thiophanate-methyl when first flowers open. Repeat spraying about three weeks later
Bush crops poorly and lacks vigour. Leaves are smaller than usual with fewer lobes	Reversion	Dig up and burn. Plant bushes certified to be free of virus. Control the gall mite which spreads the disease
Shoots and/or leaves stunted or crippled. Small sticky insects present	Aphids (black or green)	Spray with a systemic insecticide or malathion, HCH, nicotine or derris

Varieties of blackcurrants to grow

All varieties are self-fertile, so single bushes can be grown. The season of use given is for bushes grown in the South; ripening will be later in the North. Ripening time is, however, an estimate only and it will vary according to the season.

Name	Season of use	Remarks
'Boskoop Giant'	Late June–early July	Large, sweet fruit on a long truss. Thin, tender skin. Spreading bush. Susceptible to frost
'Blackdown'	Mid-July	Good cropper. Sub-acid fruit of good flavour. Lax, very spreading growth
'Wellington XXX'	July	Crops well under a wide variety of conditions. Spreading bush. Does not like lime-sulphur
'Blacksmith'	July	Good cropper. Fairly large fruit of excellent flavour. Thin skin. Large, spreading bush
'Baldwin'	Mid-July–Aug.	Highly recommended. Very rich in vitamin C. Good flavour. Needs generous manuring to produce good crop
'Amos Black'	Aug–Sept.	Moderate cropper. Low in vitamin C. Compact bush. Flowers late, so may miss frosts

Raising new plants from cuttings

Blackcurrants root easily, and the best way of raising new plants is from cuttings about 9 in. long. In early October select some of the current year's shoots that are well ripened, and make sure they are free from disease. Cut off each shoot just above a bud.

Next, trim away the unripened wood at the tip of the shoot, cutting it immediately above a bud. Finally, cut just below a bud at the base to produce a 9 in. long cutting.

Cuttings should be rooted in a prepared trench and later transferred to the blackcurrant bed. With a spade, cut a V-shaped slit (with one side of the V vertical) about 8 in. deep in the ground. Sprinkle sand along the bottom of the slit to help drainage – gritty, washed river sand is the best type.

Insert the blackcurrant cuttings 6 in. apart in the slit, against the vertical face. Only two buds should be showing above soil level. Fill in the trench with soil and press it in firmly with your foot. Keep plants moist during summer.

The cuttings should have rooted a year later. In the following November lift them with a fork and replant them in their permanent positions. Place them 6 ft apart and 2 in. lower in the ground than when they were cuttings.

Immediately after replanting, cut back the plants to the first bud showing above soil level. In the following autumn, unless growth has been strong, cut them down again. Strong shoots can grow on and will bear fruit in the next year.

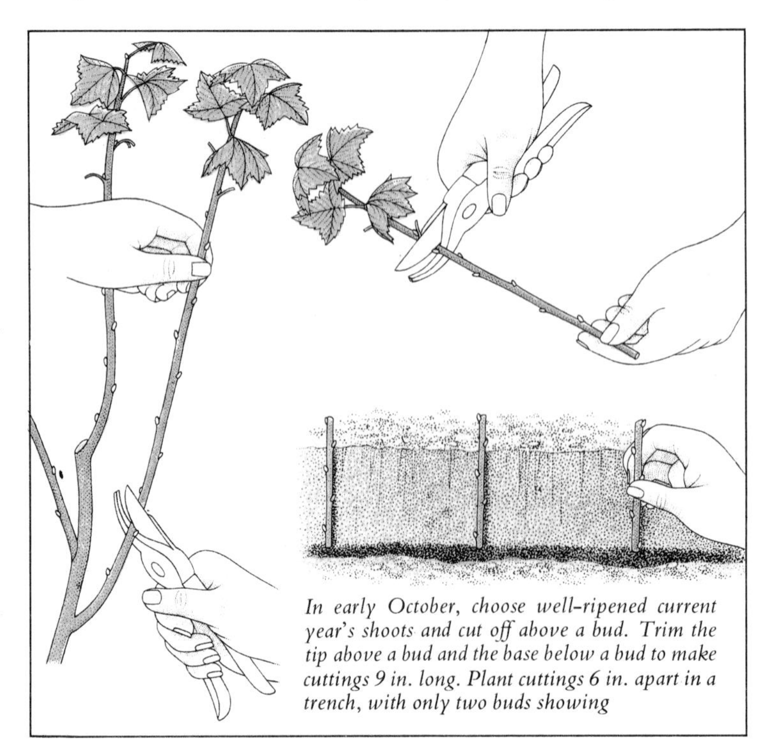

In early October, choose well-ripened current year's shoots and cut off above a bud. Trim the tip above a bud and the base below a bud to make cuttings 9 in. long. Plant cuttings 6 in. apart in a trench, with only two buds showing

Pruning blackcurrants

Pruning in the first autumn after planting

Blackcurrants produce most of their fruit on the previous season's young wood, so the aim of pruning is to remove some older, darker wood to encourage new shoots to grow.

Young wood is either extension shoots from older branches or new shoots springing from or near the ground. A balance has to be kept, so some older wood must be retained for extension growth.

Young plants need little pruning. In the first autumn after planting, cut any weak shoots back to one bud within 2 in. of ground level.

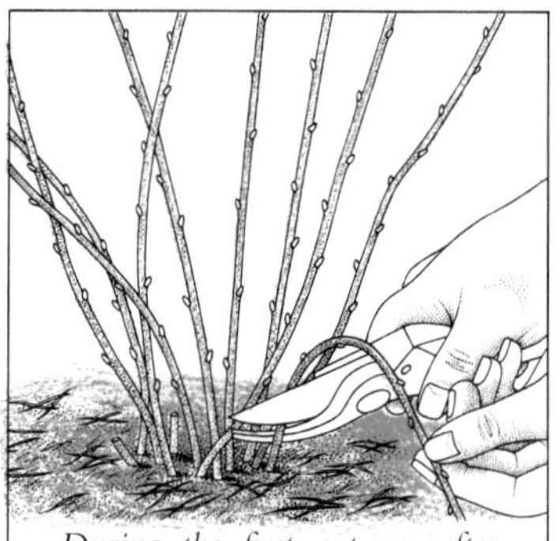

During the first autumn after planting, cut weak shoots back to a bud 2 in. above soil level

Pruning in the second autumn after planting

By the second autumn after planting, the bush will have made considerable new growth. Remove a few – no more than a quarter – of the two-year-old shoots entirely, sacrificing their new extension wood. This will stimulate the development of new shoots from ground level.

In the second autumn, cut out no more than a quarter of the two-year-old shoots entirely

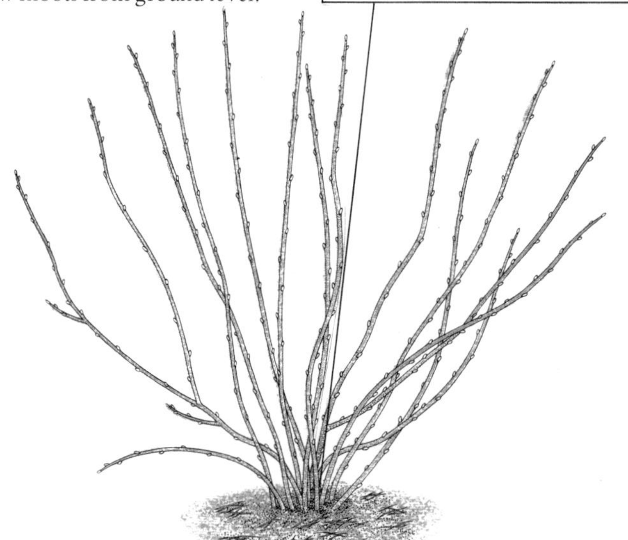

Pruning an established blackcurrant bush

Prune an established bush after picking the fruit or in autumn. Remove some older wood to make way for younger shoots. On regularly pruned bushes, no wood should be older than four years.

A neglected bush with congested growth needs hard pruning to induce new shoots. First cut out entirely any shoots either drooping to the ground or so low that the fruit will be soiled. Next, cut older wood from the centre of the bush to let in light and air. Finally, cut out the oldest of the remaining wood.

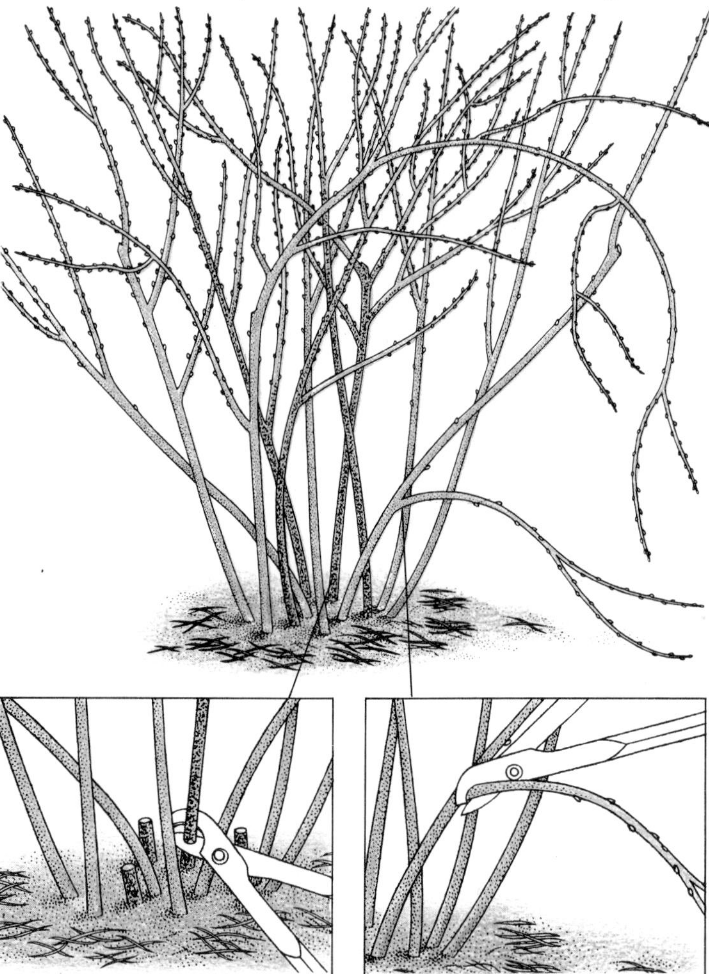

Remove some older wood to make room for new. No wood should be older than four years

Prune neglected bushes heavily to induce new growth. Cut out any drooping shoots entirely

Blueberries–importing a transatlantic flavour

Blueberry 'Jersey'

The blueberry is an imported American relative of the bilberry or whortleberry.

Blueberry bushes are generally bigger than bilberry bushes, bear larger berries, crop more heavily, and are considered to have a better flavour. The berries are suitable for desserts and jam-making.

Blueberries need a moisture-retentive, acid soil – with a pH value no higher than 6 (p. 403). They prefer an open, sunny situation, but can be grown in partial shade. They should be protected from cold winds.

It is useless to try to grow blueberries in an alkaline soil. In such a situation the only way they can be grown is in containers.

Fill the containers with an acid compost such as John Innes acid compost, or a peat-based compost with no lime added. Preferably water them with rain water.

From four to six bushes should provide a good supply of blueberries for the average family. They are ready for picking mainly in August.

Blueberries are not completely self-fertile; to ensure a good yield, plant at least two varieties.

Plants can be propagated by layering (p. 254) in autumn or spring, or by taking semi-hard cuttings in August (p. 250).

How to prune blueberry bushes

Blueberries need no pruning for the first three years after planting. After that, prune each winter. Fruit is borne on the previous year's wood.

To promote new shoots that will fruit the following year, cut from one to four of the oldest shoots from each bush. Either cut them back hard to a strong new shoot or, if there are plenty of young basal shoots, cut them down to soil level.

Cut from one to four of the oldest shoots back hard to a strong new shoot, or down to soil level

Planting and tending blueberries

Plant blueberry bushes between October and March (p. 244). Set the bushes 3–4 ft apart, about 1 in. deeper in the soil than they were in the nursery.

Feed ½ oz. (1 dessertspoon) of sulphate of potash to the square yard in late January, adding 2 oz. (2 tablespoons) of superphosphate to each square yard every third year. Each March give ½ oz. (1 dessertspoon) of sulphate of ammonia to the square yard.

Early each summer mulch with well-rotted manure, garden compost, leaf-mould or peat. Protect plants from birds (p. 85).

Plants may suffer from chlorosis, which is caused by too much lime in the soil. Yellow mottling or patches occur on the leaves, growth is poor and few blueberries are produced. Dig in acidic material such as moss peat and apply a chelated compound (sequestered iron).

For other symptoms, turn to the chart of pests and diseases on page 377. Look up chemicals on page 398 to find proprietary names.

Varieties of blueberries to grow

The season of use given below is for blueberries grown in the South; ripening will be later in the North. Ripening time is, however, an estimate only and will vary according to the growing conditions prevailing during the season.

Name	Season of use	Remarks
'Bluecrop'	Late July–Aug.	Vigorous grower. Large, light-blue fruit. Attractive leaves in autumn
'Berkeley'	Early Aug.–mid-Aug.	Good cropper. Bush has spreading growth of medium vigour
'Jersey'	Mid-Aug.	Reliable cropper. The easiest blueberry to grow. Bush has strong, spreading growth

Cherries to grow for cooking and desserts

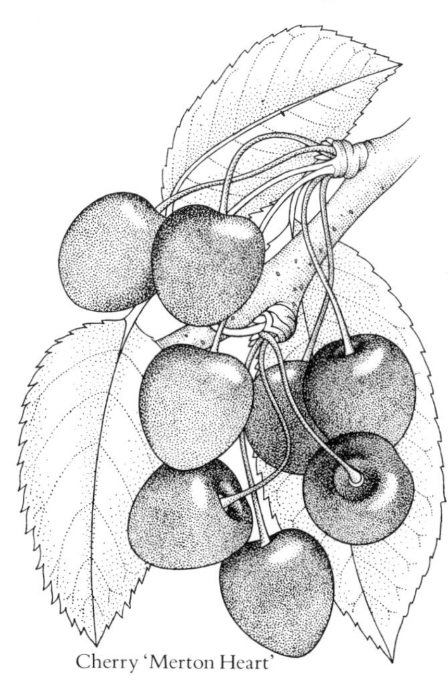
Cherry 'Merton Heart'

There are two kinds of cherry – sweet, eaten fresh, and sour, used for cooking, bottling and making jam.

Both need very deep, well-drained soil, preferably overlying chalk, although sour cherries will thrive on poorer soils than sweet cherries. The two types are cultivated differently, however.

Sweet cherries are very vigorous. Only fan-trained trees are suitable for the average garden, and they take a lot of wall space. No varieties are completely self-fertile, so at least two varieties must be grown for pollination to take place.

Sour cherries are less vigorous and can be grown either as bush trees or as fans. As each tree can pollinate itself, only a single tree need be grown. They are easier to grow than sweet cherries.

For both types, two trees will yield sufficient for the average family. Sweet cherries are ready for picking during July, sour cherries in August and September.

How to grow fan-trained sweet cherries

Sweet cherries are very vigorous; as yet there is no suitable dwarfing rootstock. Fan trees will span 15–20 ft. Plant them 18–24 ft apart (p. 84) against a wall facing towards either the south or west.

In late January feed with ½ oz. (1 dessertspoon) of sulphate of potash per square yard. Let the rain wash it in. Every third year add 2 oz. (2 tablespoons) of superphosphate to each square yard. Every March apply 1 oz. (1 tablespoon) of sulphate of ammonia to the square yard. In late spring mulch with a layer of well-rotted farmyard manure or garden compost.

Water only during dry spells in summer. Remove weeds by shallow hoeing, or with a paraquat weedkiller. If a tree grows vigorously, but produces little or no fruit, it needs root-pruning (p. 85).

In early summer drape the whole tree with netting to protect the fruit from birds.

Do not pick sweet cherries until they are completely ripe; then pull them off by hand. The fruit does not keep well; eat it as soon as possible after picking.

Training and pruning For the first three years after planting a maiden tree, train and prune it like a fan apple (p. 97), but prune in early spring as growth begins – not in winter. After the framework is built up, treatment differs; sweet cherries have more spurs and fewer laterals, and heavy pruning is not necessary.

In early summer rub out current year's shoots that are growing directly towards or away from the wall. Pinch out the tips of others in June or July when they have produced from four to six leaves.

When ribs reach the top of the wall, cut them back to a weak lateral if there is one. Otherwise bend the shoot to the horizontal and tie it to the wire. This will slow growth and encourage new shoots to break. It can then be cut back to a weak lateral.

In September, cut back shoots pinched out in summer to three or four fruit buds. Also cut away any dead wood from the tree, flush with its parent stem.

On older trees, tie new shoots into the fan shape where there is room in June or July. Some may be needed to replace old shoots.

OVERGROWN LEADERS

When ribs reach the top of the wall, cut back to a weak lateral. If there is no lateral, bend and tie to the wires to slow growth

PRUNING AN ESTABLISHED FAN-TRAINED SWEET CHERRY

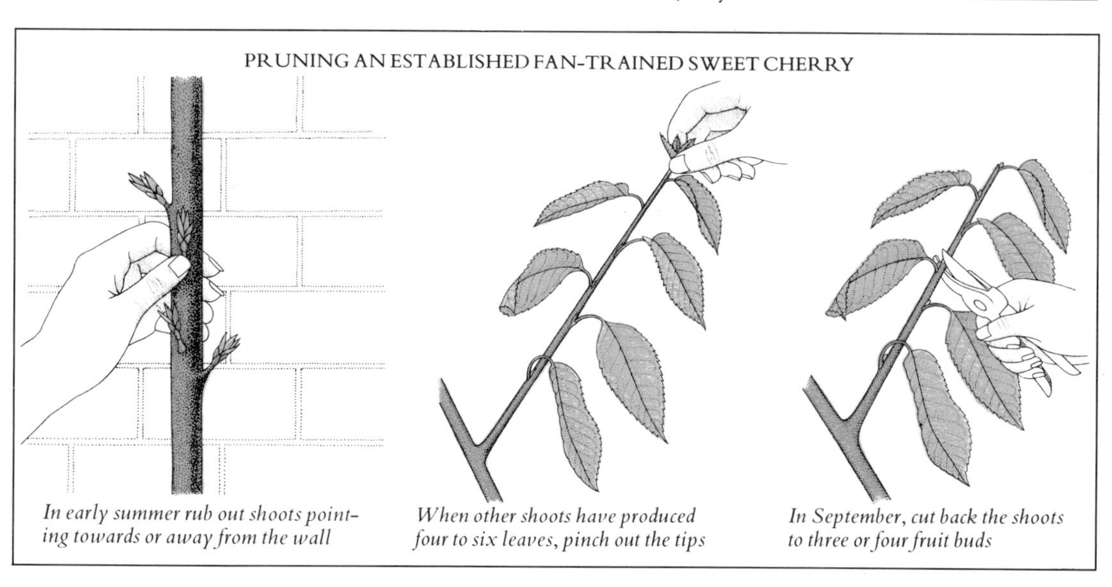
In early summer rub out shoots pointing towards or away from the wall

When other shoots have produced four to six leaves, pinch out the tips

In September, cut back the shoots to three or four fruit buds

How to look after sour cherries

Sour cherries can be grown as either bush trees or fans – these can be grown against any wall, even a north-facing one. Plant both forms of tree 15–18 ft apart (p. 84).

Look after sour cherry trees in the same way as sweet cherry trees. But harvesting is different. Cut off the ripe fruit with scissors, otherwise you may break the spurs, and disease can enter the wound.

Pruning bush trees For the first three years, train and prune bush trees like bush apples (p. 89), but prune in early spring as growth begins – not in winter. After that the annual treatment is different.

Trees bear most fruit on the previous year's growth. The aim of pruning an established tree is the constant stimulation of new wood. Prune in spring, after bud burst.

Once a tree has started to fruit, thin it out to let in light and air, cutting back older shoots to just above one-year-old laterals. Thin out the outer spread occasionally, where new growth develops. No other pruning is needed.

Paint all large pruning cuts on old wood with any type of wood paint or a proprietary sealing compound. This keeps out silver-leaf infection.

Pruning fan-trained trees Prune and train fan sour cherries like fan apples (p. 97), but prune in early spring. Thin out congested fans like sour cherry bush trees.

PRUNING BUSH CHERRY TREES

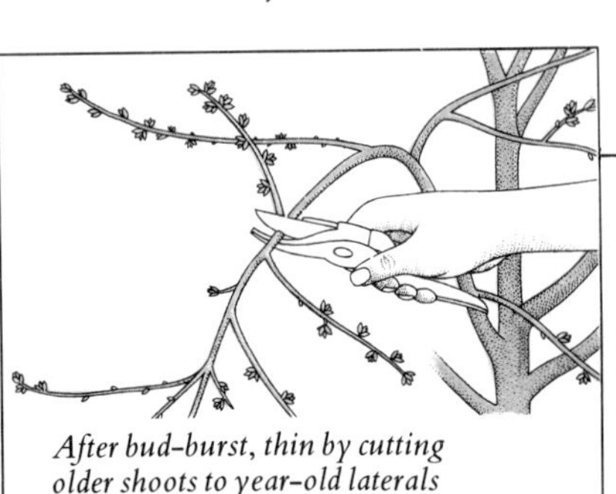

After bud-burst, thin by cutting older shoots to year-old laterals

What can go wrong with sweet and sour cherries

Aphids are the most common problem in cherry growing. If plants show symptoms that are not described here, turn to the identification chart of pests and diseases on page 377. Look up chemicals on page 398 to find proprietary names.

Symptoms	Cause	Cure
One or more branches show silvered leaves. Leaves shrivel, turn yellow and fall prematurely. Branches usually die after two or three years. If cut, the wood shows a brown stain	Silver leaf	Cut back infected branches to 6 in. below unstained wood and burn. Paint wounds. Feed, mulch, water and/or drain as necessary to encourage vigour. If the whole tree is infected, remove and burn it
Shoots and leaves are crippled and covered with small, black insects	Aphids (cherry black-fly)	Immediately after flowering, spray with dimethoate or fenitrothion
Leaves may be discoloured, buds wither, and shoots die back, after which the tree dies rapidly	Honey fungus	Dig up and burn dead or dying trees. Treat soil with dazomet or Armillatox or change it completely before replanting

Varieties of sweet and sour cherries to grow

Sweet cherries need a partner to cross-pollinate at blossom time, so two trees must be grown. Not all varieties flowering at the same time will pollinate each other; the pollination groups below show those that will. Choose two different varieties from the same group. If buying a variety not on the list check with the nurseryman for a suitable pollinator.

Sour cherries are self-fertile so do not need a pollination partner. The variety 'Morello' will pollinate sweet cherries in group 2.

Name	Pollination group	Season of use	Colour
SWEET CHERRIES			
'Merton Heart'	1	Early July	Black
'Merton Glory'	1	Early July	Red
'Merton Favourite'	1	Early July	Black
'Governor Wood'	2	Early July	Bright red
'Roundel'	2	Mid-July	Dark red
'Van'	2	Mid–late July	Dark red
'Bigarreau Napoleon'	2	Late July	Red on yellow
SOUR CHERRIES			
'Morello'		Aug.–Sept.	Dark red

Gooseberries for cooking, jams and desserts

Gooseberry 'Leveller'

Gooseberries can be used for jam-making or desserts. They grow well in any type of well-drained but moisture-retaining soil, and will thrive in full sun or partial shade. Do not plant them in frost pockets – they flower in early March and may be damaged by a severe frost.

Plants can be grown as either bushes – with 6–9 in. stems – or cordons. Double (U-shaped) or triple (trident-shaped) cordons are more common than single cordons. For the average family, 6–9 bushes or 9–12 cordons should provide enough fruit. Gooseberries are self-fertile. Fruit can be available from May (for cooking) to August, and may be green, yellow, red or white, depending on variety.

Preferably, buy plants two or three years old and plant them in any mild period between October and March (p. 244). If your soil is deep enough, double-dig it (p. 405) and work in plenty of manure or garden compost. Plant bushes 5–6 ft apart, single cordons 1½ ft, double cordons 2 ft, and triple cordons 2½ ft, in rows 5 ft apart. Support them upright with 2 × 2 in. stakes about 6 ft high. Single cordons are usually grown 5 ft high, double and triple cordons 3–4 ft high.

Tending and feeding gooseberries

Each spring apply a mulch of well-rotted compost, to prevent the soil from drying out and to keep down weeds. Weeds can also be controlled with paraquat weedkiller; a hoe or fork may damage the roots. Pull away any suckers that grow from the stem or roots. Water only in dry spells during summer.

In late January give a feed of ½–1 oz. (½–1 tablespoon) of sulphate of potash to each square yard. Every third year add 2 oz. (2 tablespoons) of superphosphate to each square yard. In March feed plants with 1 oz. (1 tablespoon) of sulphate of ammonia to the square yard.

In winter, firm in any plants lifted by frost. Birds feed on buds in late winter; protect bushes with netting or cotton threads. At blossom time protect bushes from frost at night with heavy netting, but remove it in the day to allow access to pollinating insects.

Thinning and harvesting gooseberries

Start picking gooseberries for cooking when they are the size of large peas. Thin out on each branch, so that those remaining will reach a good size for desserts or exhibition. Ideally, the thinned fruit should be not less than 3 in. apart. Do not pick fruit for desserts until it is soft and fully ripe.

Pruning a one-year-old gooseberry bush

Fruit is borne on new wood and on spurs on older wood. Prune during autumn or winter, as late as bud-burst (usually February) if birds are likely to damage buds, but no later.

The aim of pruning is to keep the centre of the bush open to light and air. Varieties range from spreading bushes in which branches tend to droop (this can spoil fruit) to very upright bushes. Prune spreading bushes to an upward or inward-pointing bud, upright varieties to an outward-pointing bud. For in-between varieties, or if in doubt, prune to an outward-pointing bud.

On a one-year-old bush, choose the best three or four shoots and cut them back above a bud to about a quarter of their length. Cut out other shoots flush with the stem.

Shorten three or four good shoots by three-quarters, above a bud

Cut out the remaining shoots on the bush, removing them flush with the stem

Pruning a two-year-old gooseberry bush

With a two-year-old bush, choose from six to eight of the strongest shoots. Cut the new growth on these shoots by half if they are growing strongly, by two-thirds if growth is weak. Cut back other shoots to one bud from their base.

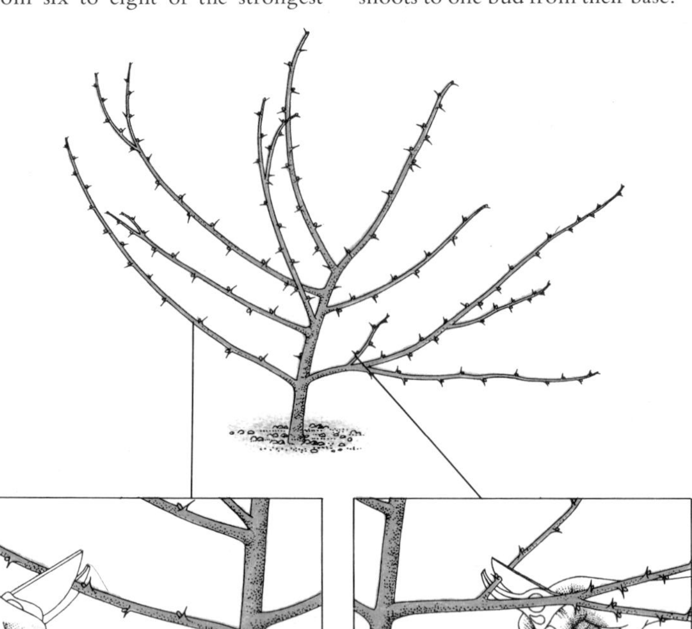

Cut new growth by half on the six to eight strongest shoots

Cut other shoots back to one bud from their base

Pruning an established gooseberry bush

In winter cut back branch leaders by half their new growth. To encourage spur formation, shorten the strongest side-shoots to 3 in. of new growth, and weaker ones to 1 in. Remove the weakest shoots entirely, cutting them flush with the branch.

If a branch has drooped to the ground, choose a new shoot as a replacement and cut back the drooping branch to the source of the new shoot. Prune the new branch by at least half, to ensure sturdy growth. Keep the bush centre open.

In summer – about the third week in June – shorten all side-shoots to five leaves, cutting just above a leaf joint. Do not shorten the branch leaders.

WINTER PRUNING

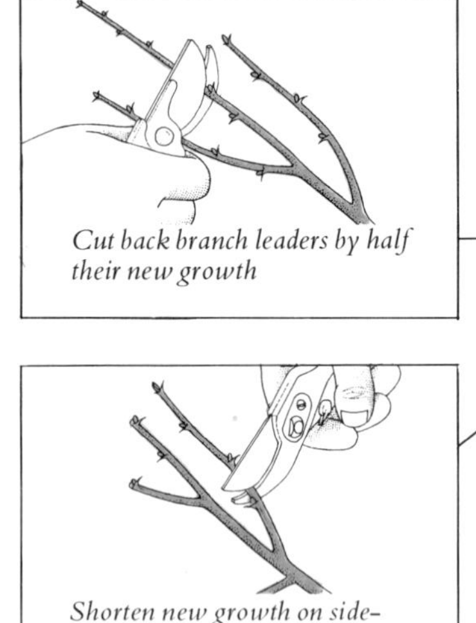

Cut back branch leaders by half their new growth

Shorten new growth on side-shoots to 3 in. (if strong) or 1 in.

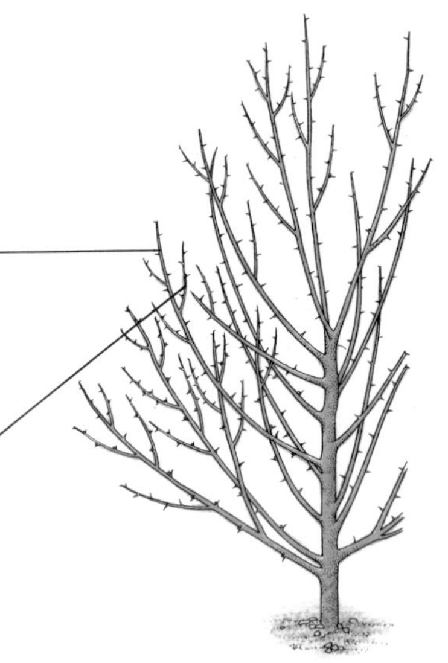

What can go wrong with gooseberries

The most serious problems are gooseberry sawfly and American gooseberry mildew. If plants show symptoms not described here, turn to the chart of pests and diseases on page 377. Look up chemicals on page 398 for proprietary names.

Symptoms	**Cause**	**Cure**
Leaf tissues are eaten by caterpillars	Gooseberry sawflies	When the damage is first seen spray with derris, fenitrothion or malathion
White mealy powder on leaves, shoots and fruits, later becomes brown; shoots become distorted	American gooseberry mildew	Cut out affected shoots in autumn. Spray regularly with benomyl, dinocap or thiophanate-methyl

SUMMER PRUNING

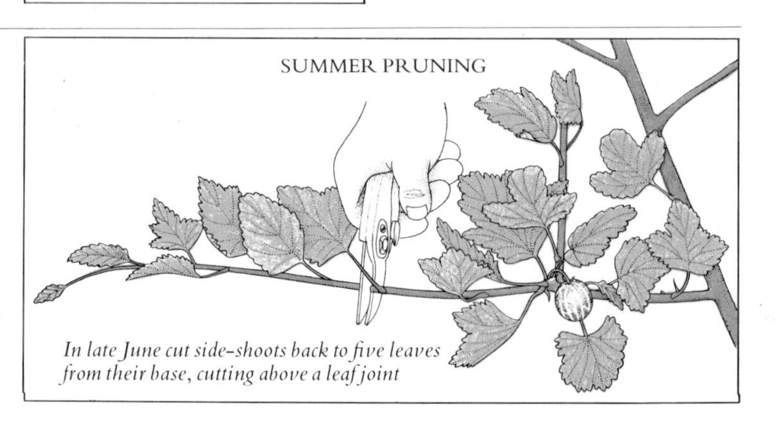

In late June cut side-shoots back to five leaves from their base, cutting above a leaf joint

Raising new plants from cuttings

Gooseberries are raised from cuttings 12–15 in. long, taken in October. Cut out straight shoots of well-ripened current year's wood just above a bud. If the top 1–3 in. of a cutting is soft and unripened, cut it off above a bud – if brown to the tip, leave it. Trim the lower end, just below a bud.

With a spade cut an 8 in. deep V-shaped slit in the ground, with one side vertical and the other sloped at an angle of 45 degrees. Sprinkle sand along the bottom of the slit to help drainage. Gritty, washed river sand is best.

Place the cuttings in the slit 6 in. apart, upright against the vertical face with the top four buds showing above ground level. Fill in the trench with soil and tread it firm.

In early winter the following year, dig up the new plants, which should now have a good root system, and cut off flush with the stem any shoots that have grown from buds that were buried below ground. Then place the plants in their permanent fruiting quarters.

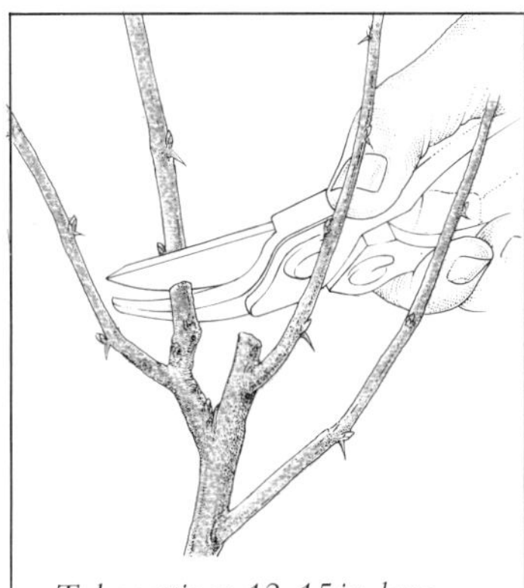

Take cuttings, 12–15 in. long, from well-ripened new shoots

Varieties of gooseberries to grow

The season of use given is for ripe fruit in the South; ripening will be later in the North. It is an estimate only, and will vary according to the conditions during the growing season. Fruit can be picked green for cooking in May and June.

Name	Season of use	Colour	Remarks
'Keepsake'	Early–mid-July	Green	Heavy cropper; susceptible to mildew. Good flavour. Grows large quickly. Bush spreading
'Careless'	Early–mid-July	White	Good cropper. Large, good flavour. Bush tends to spread
'May Duke'	Early–mid-July	Red	Good for gathering green in May. Upright bush
'Whinham's Industry'	Early–mid-July	Red	Good cropper, suits most soils. Good flavour. Large bush
'Leveller'	Early–mid-July	Yellow	Good cropper, excellent flavour. The best gooseberry but needs a fertile soil. Bush spreading, fairly vigorous, but weak on poor soil
'Golden Drop'	Early–mid-July	Yellow	Small, very good dessert fruit. Bush upright and compact
'Lancer'	Late July	Green	Large exhibition fruit, excellent flavour. Spreading bush

Grapes under glass and outdoors

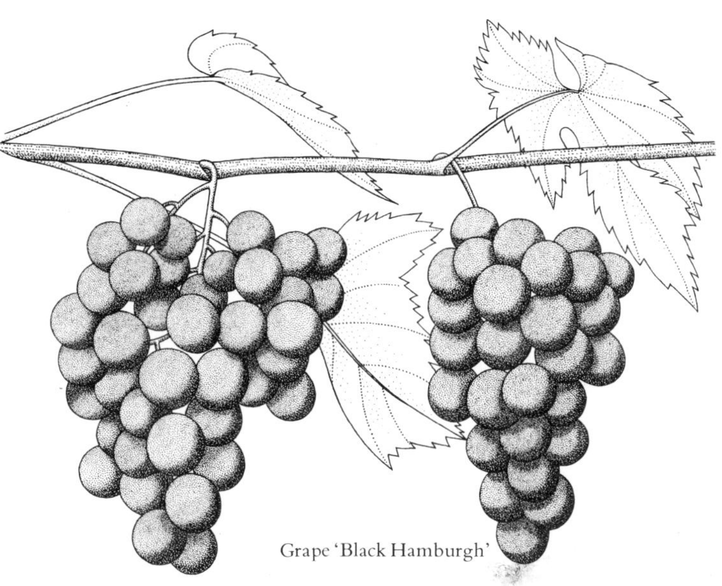

Grape 'Black Hamburgh'

Grapes can be eaten fresh or used for wine-making. Grape vines are hardy enough to grow outdoors, but a great deal of warmth is needed to ripen the grapes. They are therefore usually grown under glass.

The main stem of a vine is known as a rod. From this rod, side-shoots (laterals) branch out and produce spurs on which the bunches of grapes are borne.

It is best to buy one-year-old vines from a nursery in summer or early autumn. You can plant several vines and allow only one rod to develop on each, or plant only a single vine and train two or three rods from it. If you grow single-rod vines, you will have room for several different varieties.

Unless vines are to be grown for wine-making, two single-rod vines should yield sufficient grapes for the average family. The crop is generally ready for picking in September and October. Early varieties may be ready in August.

Grapes will generally ripen in the greenhouse without artificial heat. But a temperature of 10–13°C (50–55°F) from February to April will produce an earlier crop, and also give a longer ripening season for late-maturing varieties. During the growing season, ventilators are the main means of controlling temperatures in heated greenhouses, and the sole means in unheated greenhouses.

The vines will need to be trained against wires running the length of the greenhouse. Position wires 12 in. apart and 18 in. away from the glass. Fix them to the rafters with vine eyes – specially made metal spikes with an eye at one end.

Planting a young vine Make up a bed of 3 parts loam and 1 part rotted manure in the greenhouse border. Ideally, it should be about 5 ft wide, 3 ft deep, and well drained. In summer or early autumn, plant the vine in a hole slightly deeper and wider than the root system. Put single-rod vines 5 ft apart.

Fill in the holes, and firm them with your feet so that there is a saucer-shaped depression at the base of each vine. Fill this with water. Tie each young vine upright to the wires with soft string.

Care and training of young vines

Tending a newly planted vine in autumn and winter

After planting young vines in summer or early autumn, keep them thoroughly watered. Also spray the rods daily with a syringe; this encourages growth. Water and syringe before midday.

When syringeing, spray over the walls and floor with a hose also, particularly on warm days, to keep the atmosphere humid. No artificial heat is needed. Leave the greenhouse ventilated, but avoid draughts or sudden changes of temperature. The greenhouse temperature should be about 10–13°C (50–55°F).

As the new vine grows upwards, tie it to the wires with soft string. In the autumn, before leaf-fall, when a summer planted vine is about 6–10 ft high and an autumn-planted vine about 4 ft high, cut back the rod.

If you want a single-rod vine, cut back the rod by about one-third of its height. If you want to grow several rods from one vine, cut back more – by about two-thirds of the height, or so that it is at about the level of the greenhouse eaves. Cut just above a bud on brown, well-ripened wood.

If any laterals have developed from the rod – this is likely on summer-planted vines – cut them back to two buds from the rod.

Stop watering and syringeing in about October when the leaves start to change colour. In November, after leaf-fall, open the greenhouse to give free ventilation day and night. The temperature should remain below 4°C (40°F) to rest the vines during winter.

In January untie each rod and allow it to arch over. This encourages an even flow of sap, so that side-shoots will break out at even intervals along the rod; otherwise there will be more growth at the top. In February tie the rod back into place.

When growth restarts – in about March in an unheated greenhouse, depending on the severity of the winter – close down the ventilation. But ventilate on warm days, so that growth will be delayed while there is still a risk of frost causing damage to young shoots. Water to keep the soil just moist, and syringe daily before midday.

There is no need to start the vine into growth in February using artificial heat, since it should not be allowed to bear any fruit in its first year.

Training a newly planted vine in spring and summer

In spring, for a single-rod vine, choose the strongest leading shoot from the rod and tie it upright to the wires. Remove other leading shoots with secateurs, cutting them flush with the stem.

If you are growing several rods from one vine, select two or three vigorous leading shoots and remove any others. Shoots tend to grow outwards, and outer rods can be trained along the wires at first, then upwards so that rods grow upright 3 ft apart. Vines with two or three rods usually separate from the main stem just below the roof slope.

Tie laterals from rods horizontally along the wires. You may have to rub out one or two lateral shoots in between wires. Remove any flower trusses that develop, to prevent fruiting during the first year so that the vine will build up strong rods. In summer, pinch back laterals to six leaves from the rod.

SPRING TRAINING

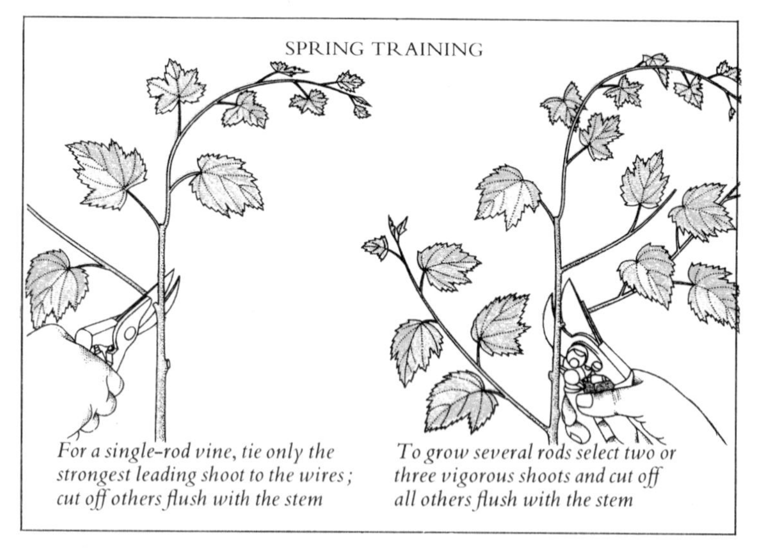

For a single-rod vine, tie only the strongest leading shoot to the wires; cut off others flush with the stem

To grow several rods select two or three vigorous shoots and cut off all others flush with the stem

AUTUMN

Before leaf-fall, cut back the rod by one-third for a one-rod vine

WINTER

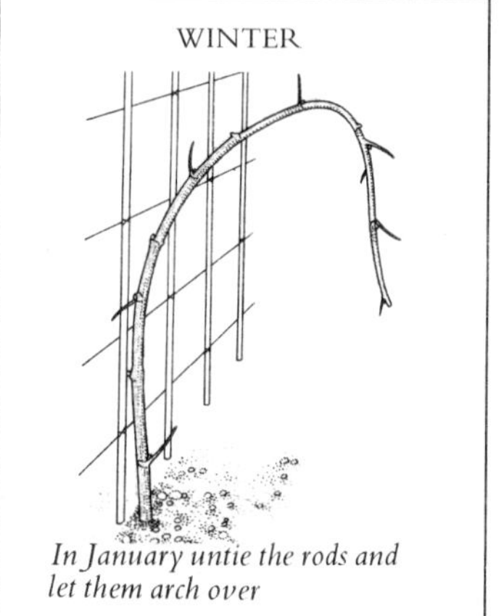

In January untie the rods and let them arch over

REMOVING FLOWERS

In spring remove the flowers to prevent fruiting in the first year

SUMMER TRAINING

In summer pinch the laterals back to six leaves from the rod

Care and training of established vines

As in the vine's first year, stop watering and syringeing when the leaves change colour about October. After leaf-fall open up the greenhouse to rest the vine during winter.

Prune in autumn, after leaf-fall. To build up a strong rod and good fruiting spurs, remove from one-third to one-half of new growth from the leading shoot, cutting back to a bud on brown, well-ripened wood. Cut back laterals to two buds, so that each forms a spur.

During winter remove the top inch of soil in the border and renew it with well-rotted garden compost, farmyard manure, or a proprietary vine manure.

Untie rods in January and lay them on the floor or suspend them from the roof with string. Re-tie them to the wires in February.

In a heated greenhouse, vines can be forced into growth in February by closing down the ventilation and ensuring a night temperature of 10–13°C (50–55°F). In an unheated greenhouse, close the ventilation when growth restarts naturally in about March. Water to keep the soil moist, and syringe the rods daily before midday.

In spring (late March, early April) ventilate the greenhouse if day temperatures rise above 16°C (61°F). When the shoots on spurs are 1–2 in. long, reduce them to the strongest two on each spur by rubbing out the others with your finger. When the two remaining shoots reach a length of 3–4 in., remove the weaker one. Tie the other to the wires when it is about 12 in. long.

When flowering starts – probably in March if vines have been started in February with artificial heat, otherwise in April or May – stop syringeing, or else pollination may not take place. At flowering time the temperature should be about 21–24°C (70–75°F).

Grapes are self-fertile, but to activate more pollen, tap rods from time to time during the flowering season. The best time is at midday; conditions must be dry.

Begin syringeing again after petal-fall, and give plenty of ventilation until the grapes begin to form. Then ventilate only if the temperature rises higher than 21–24°C (70–75°F).

In early summer, when leaves are well developed, pinch back laterals to two leaves beyond a fruit truss. In the first year of fruiting, pinch back to just beyond the first fruit truss – more than one bunch of grapes to each lateral will tend to weaken growth.

In following years, pinch laterals back to two leaves beyond the second or third truss, according to how many bunches you are going to grow on each lateral. Two bunches to each lateral will produce good quality grapes with plenty of flavour. Three is the maximum for grapes of reasonable quality. A vine should carry an average of 1–1½ lb. of grapes to each 12 in. of rod.

AUTUMN PRUNING

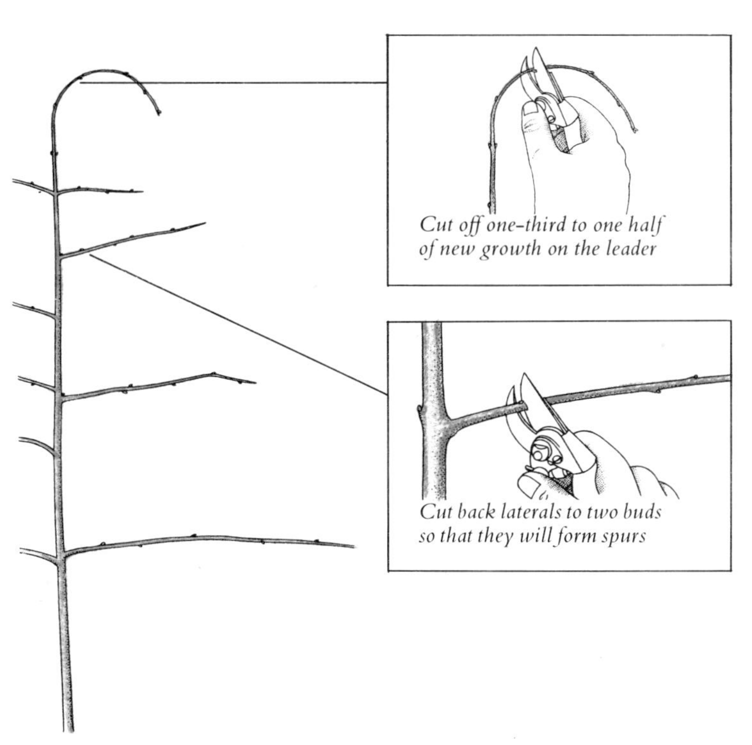

Cut off one-third to one half of new growth on the leader

Cut back laterals to two buds so that they will form spurs

SPRING PRUNING

When shoots on a spur are 1–2 in. long, rub out all but the strongest two. Wait until the two remaining are 3–4 in. long, then remove the weaker one. Tie the other shoot to the wires when it is about 12 in. long

ENSURING QUALITY

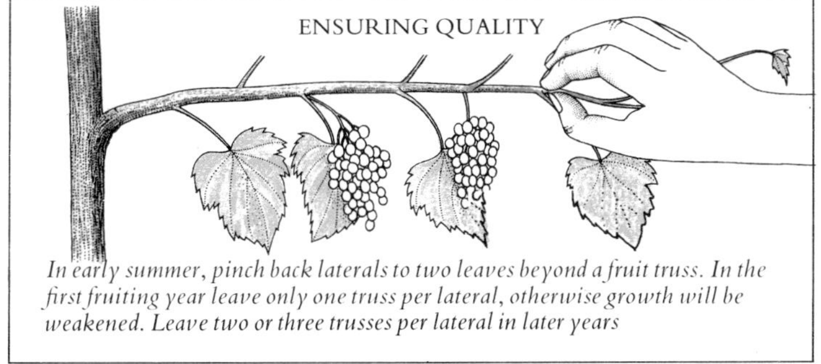

In early summer, pinch back laterals to two leaves beyond a fruit truss. In the first fruiting year leave only one truss per lateral, otherwise growth will be weakened. Leave two or three trusses per lateral in later years

Tending the vine while grapes are maturing

When the grapes begin to swell, cut out with scissors any small, overcrowded fruits in the centre of the bunch. Once grapes are in full growth, about early May, feed with liquid fertiliser (follow the maker's instructions), and dried blood – ½ oz. (1 dessertspoon) per square yard – watered in every ten days.

When grapes are about half size, they stop swelling temporarily while seeds mature. At this time they are particularly vulnerable to too much heat, which may cause scorching of leaf tips and discoloured, sunken areas (scald) on the fruit.

Try to maintain even humidity and an even temperature – no higher than 24°C (75°F) – by opening and closing ventilators, shading the roof, or adjusting artificial heat as necessary. When grapes start swelling again, let the temperature rise to about 29°C (85°F).

In late summer, when the lower leaves on side-shoots growing from laterals are well formed, pinch the side-shoots back to one leaf from the lateral. Leaves are needed to shield the fruit, but should not give too much shade.

Ripening may start from July to September and take from six to nine weeks, depending on conditions and variety. During ripening, ventilate if the temperature rises above 21–24°C (70–75°F). Close the greenhouse down on cold nights.

Stop feeding vines when grapes start to change colour. Cut mature grapes from the stem carefully. If not bruised they will keep in a cool place for up to two months.

THINNING

Thin out small fruits in the centre when grapes start to swell

SUMMER PRUNING

In late summer, pinch side-shoots back to one leaf from the lateral

Stopping the leader at the top wire

When the rod leader reaches the topmost wire, temporarily train it along the wire. In autumn cut back to the bud just above the wire. In following years treat the topmost shoot like a lateral.

On mature vines, laterals usually extend 2–3 ft on each side of the rod, if they have been pinched back regularly.

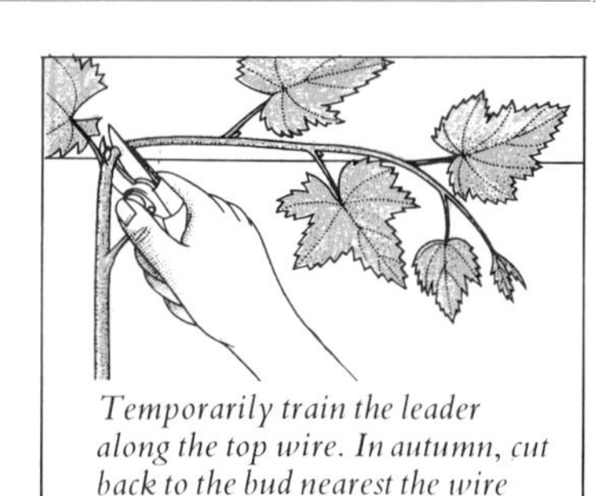

Temporarily train the leader along the top wire. In autumn, cut back to the bud nearest the wire

Raising vines in pots from eye-cuttings

Eye-cuttings are a good method of producing a large number of new vines. Set aside some good shoots from autumn prunings and heel them in (p. 84) in a trench.

Remove the heeled-in shoots the following February, then use secateurs to cut them into 2 in. lengths with a bud (eye) in the middle of each length.

Fill a 3 in. pot with sandy soil or John Innes seed compost and lay one cutting on the surface, bud uppermost. Press the cutting into the compost so that only the bud protrudes above the surface. Then water the soil gently.

Do this with each of the cuttings, then stand the pots in a heated propagator, setting the temperature at 16–18°C (61–64°F). When the cuttings have each put out three or four leaves, they have rooted. Keep them in the propagator for another three or four weeks at a temperature of 13–16°C (55–61°F), then put them on the greenhouse staging.

When each plant is about 12 in. high, pot it into a 5 in. pot. In June or July, remove vines from pots and plant them in the greenhouse border.

Propagating without heat If you do not have a heated propagator, stand the pots in the greenhouse. Because rooting will be slower, take cuttings a month earlier. Plant them in the greenhouse border in July or August, a month later than those raised under heat.

Permanent potting If you want to grow the vines permanently in pots in the greenhouse, pot them into 8–9 in. pots of John Innes No. 2 compost in June or July if they have been raised under heat, in July or August if they have not.

Between the following October and February, pot them into 10–12 in. pots of John Innes No. 3 compost. Then either train them against the wires or against four or five 4–6 ft canes inserted round the edge of each pot.

Every winter, repot plants into fresh compost. A fully established pot-grown plant will produce about six bunches of grapes each season.

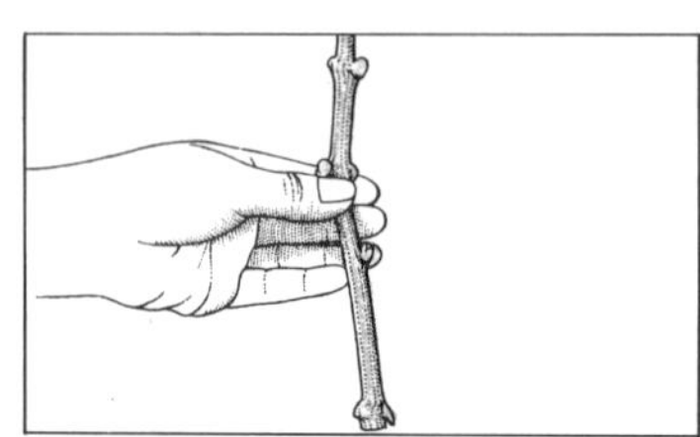

1 *In February choose some good shoots heeled in from last autumn's prunings*

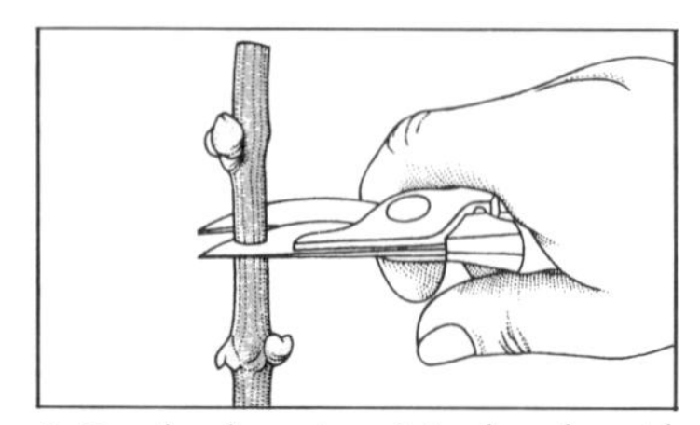

2 *Cut the shoots into 2 in. lengths with a bud in the middle of each length*

3 *Press each eye-cutting into a pot of compost with the bud just showing*

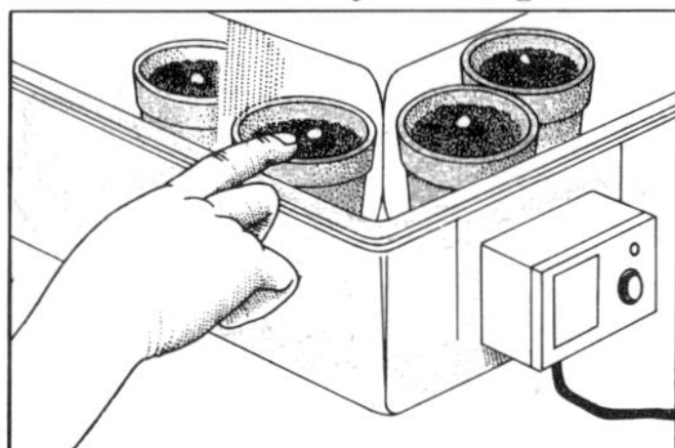

4 *Stand pots in a heated propagator at a temperature of 16–18°C (61–64°F)*

Growing vines outdoors against a wall

Grapes will also grow outdoors. They do best against a sheltered, sunny wall in a well-drained soil, especially on south-facing slopes in the South.

Before planting, enrich the soil with farmyard manure or garden compost – a 2 gallon bucket to the square yard – also 4 oz. (4 tablespoons) of a general fertiliser such as Growmore to the square yard.

Buy one-year-old vines and plant them 4–5 ft apart from October to February, or train several rods from one vine. Train and prune as greenhouse vines, cutting back the rod after planting. Water regularly; in March mulch established vines with well-rotted manure or compost.

Do not allow vines to fruit until they are three years old. Grow only one bunch on each lateral at first – on established vines grow no more than two bunches for grapes of reasonable quality.

Outdoor vines can be increased in two ways. The best way is from hardwood cuttings 8–12 in. long, but eye-cuttings can also be taken in the same way as vines grown in the greenhouse.

If eye-cuttings are taken, the pots will have to be kept in the greenhouse for rooting to take place. In July or August, the young vines (still in pots) can be gradually hardened off to outdoor conditions. They should remain in the pots until they are planted out in their permanent positions in the following October.

Raising outdoor vines from hardwood cuttings

Raise new vines from hardwood cuttings made from autumn prunings.

Select as many prunings as you want new vines. If there is any soft, unripened wood at the top, cut if off just above a bud. Cut at the base, immediately below a bud, to produce a cutting 8–12 in. long.

The cuttings can be planted direct into the position where the vines are to grow. Prepare the soil with farmyard manure or garden compost and fertiliser in the same way as for vines bought from a nursery. Then dig a 6 in. deep V-shaped trench, with one side sloping and one vertical, at the base of the wall. Put a 1 in. layer of sharp sand in the bottom of the trench.

Lean the cuttings 4–5 ft apart against the upright side of the trench with their bases set in the sand. Only the top bud on each cutting should be above soil level. Replace the soil and firm it with your foot.

Then treat the plants as described for growing a young vine outdoors.

1 *In autumn trim prunings to make hardwood cuttings 8–12 in. long*

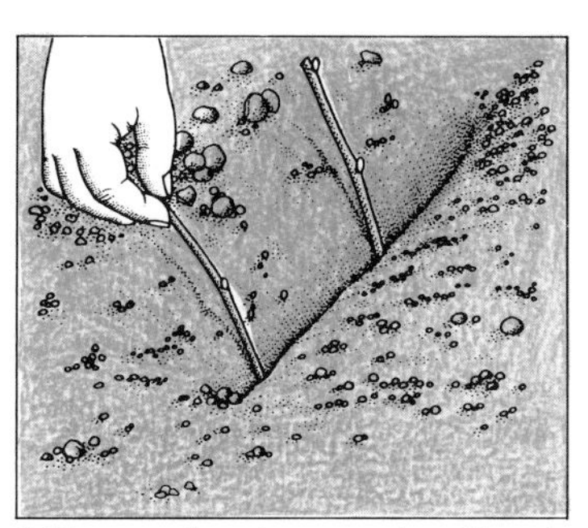

2 *Plant cuttings in a trench with only one bud showing above soil level*

What can go wrong with grapes

Mildew can be a serious problem in cold greenhouses. Honey fungus may kill outdoor vines. Look up chemicals on page 398 for proprietary names. If symptoms are not described here, use the identification chart on page 377.

Symptoms	Cause	Cure
Leaves and young fruits are covered with a fine white powder. Later they become discoloured and fruit splits	Powdery mildew	Cut out severely affected shoots in autumn. Spray regularly with benomyl, dinocap or thiophanate-methyl. Fumigate greenhouse with dinocap smokes
Fruits show sunken and discoloured patches and finally wither, particularly in cold greenhouses	Scald (caused by too much heat)	Cut out affected fruits before they rot. Shade the greenhouse and ventilate it well to prevent trouble
Leaves are discoloured and shoots die back, or flower buds wither. The vine dies rapidly	Honey fungus	Dig up and burn dead or dying vines. Change soil before replanting, or treat with dazomet or Armillatox

Varieties of grapes to grow

Grapes are self-fertile, but some do not pollinate readily and are best grown with another variety. The approximate season of use is given. Ripening time depends on the time the grapes are started into growth, and the conditions during growth.

Name	Season of use	Colour	Remarks
UNDER GLASS			
'Black Hamburgh'	End Aug.	Black	The most popular grape. A reliable cropper, suitable for both cold and heated greenhouses. Highly recommended
'Buckland Sweetwater'	End Aug.	Greeny-white	A good cropper, suitable for cold greenhouses. Sweet flavour
'Muscat of Alexandria'	Sept.-Oct.	White	The finest-flavoured muscat grape. Needs heat. Grow with another variety, such as 'Black Hamburgh', for a good crop
OUTDOORS			
'Seigerrebe'	End Aug.	Golden-brown	The best outdoor grape for eating. Large fruit, excellent muscat flavour
'Riesling Sylvaner' ('Muller Thurgau')	Sept.	White	High-quality wine grape. Good cropper. Suitable for desserts
'Seyve-Villard 5/276'	Late Sept.	White	Very good quality wine grape. A heavy and reliable cropper. Highly recommended

Melons in the greenhouse

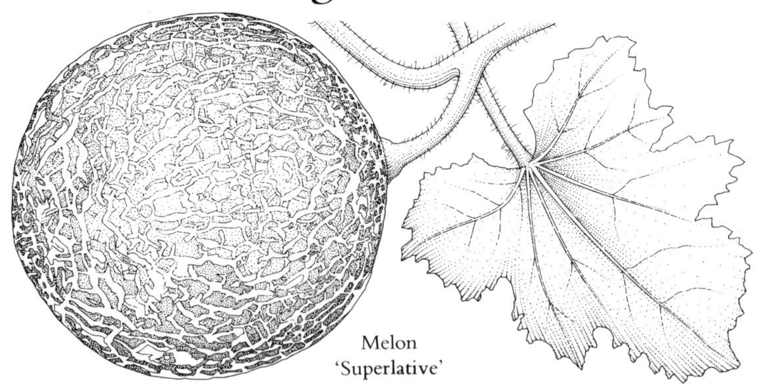
Melon 'Superlative'

All varieties of melon can be grown in the greenhouse. Hardy varieties can also be grown in a cold frame or cloche; however, in all but the warmest parts of the country they still need to be started in a greenhouse or a sunny window.

Half a dozen plants should provide enough fruit for the average family. Melons take four or five months from sowing to harvesting. Seeds sown in March should provide fruit in July – seeds sown in May are ready about September.

Seeds need a minimum temperature of 18°C (64°F) for germination, followed by a minimum temperature of 16°C (61°F) maintained while the seedlings are growing. If these temperatures can be guaranteed, seeds can be sown at any time from January to May. But May is the earliest time for sowing without heat.

Melon seeds should germinate quickly, usually within four or five days of sowing. You may have to place them in a heated propagator.

Fill a 3 in. pot with seed compost and press one seed edgeways into the compost ¾ in. deep. Sow only one seed per pot.

Either stand the pots in a sufficiently warm position (in a greenhouse or on a sunny window-sill in a warm room), or place them in a propagator, covering the heating cables with 2 in. of peat or compost.

Another way of ensuring sufficient heat is to sink the pots in moist peat in a box, stand the box above a radiator or greenhouse heating tubes, and place a sheet of glass over it. As soon as the first growth appears, remove the pots into the light – such as to a shelf just under the roof glass of the greenhouse.

SOWING MELON SEEDS

Sow each seed edgeways ¾ in. deep in a pot of compost. If necessary, sink pots in moist peat in a box placed over heat, and cover with glass

Planting out the seedlings

When four or five true (rough-edged) leaves have formed, the seedlings are ready for planting. The best site is a mound or ridge on a bench or well-drained greenhouse border.

Prepare the soil by forking in well-rotted manure – one or two buckets to the square yard. Cover this with a 9 in. high ridge of good soil, or make several mounds 9 in. high. Do not pack the soil tightly – good drainage is essential.

Alternatively, plant in boxes of John Innes potting compost – 18 in. wide by 12 in. deep – placed on the greenhouse staging. Form the soil into a 6 in. ridge.

Remove seedlings from pots with the soil ball still attached. If space is limited, plant them 15 in. apart and grow each with a single vertical shoot. If you have sufficient space, plant 30 in. apart and train each with twin vertical shoots. Although single-shoot plants produce larger fruits, they take a lot more soil and planting time.

Plant each seedling at the top of the ridge or mound. Do not plant too deeply; the soil ball should only just be covered. Do not firm the soil. Planting on a mound prevents water collecting round the base of the stem and reduces the risk of collar rot.

Another way is to scoop out a small channel round the base of the stem and fill it with clean sand.

Put two canes in the soil on each side of the plant, 15 in. apart. Tie the tops of the canes to a wire running horizontally just above the roof eaves. When the plant is about 6 in. high, pinch out the growing point; it will then form side-shoots. Choose two vigorous side-shoots and pinch off any others completely. Tie both remaining side-shoots to a cane.

For single-stem plants, do not pinch out the growing tip. Allow one stem to grow up a single cane and pinch off any side-shoots.

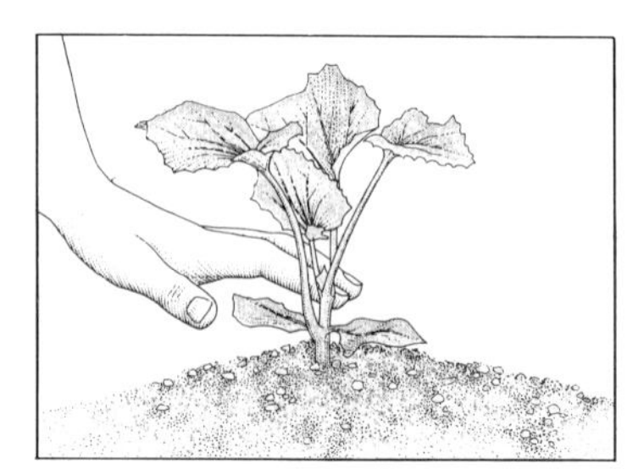

1 *Plant the seedlings 30 in. apart (for growing twin shoots) on mounds*

2 *Instead of a mound, you can make a sand-filled channel round the stem*

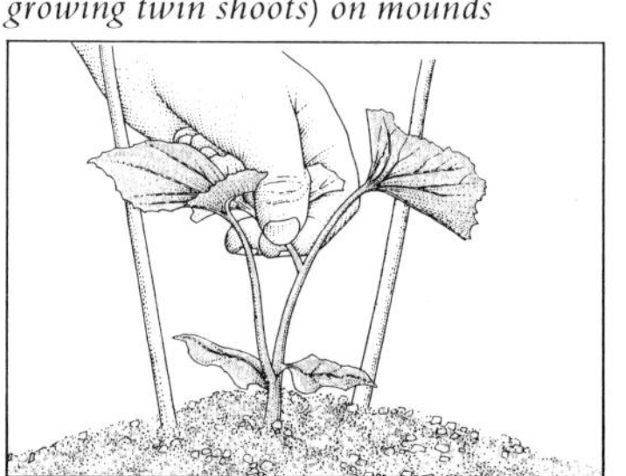

3 *Place canes on each side of the plant. Pinch out the tip when it is 6 in. high*

4 *Choose two vigorous side-shoots and tie each to a cane. Pinch off any others*

Ensuring proper watering and ventilation

Keep the soil evenly moist by daily watering, but do not drench it. The plants must have sufficient water, especially when the fruit is swelling, but too much can result in split fruits or collar rot. Keep water away from the main stem, especially the part just above soil level.

Maintain a humid atmosphere by spraying the leaves lightly with a syringe in the afternoon, also by damping down the ground with a watering can. During flowering, keep the atmosphere drier, as wet pollen makes pollination ineffective.

Whenever the greenhouse temperature is 27°C (81°F), ventilate it freely. At night close up completely.

On hot, sunny days provide temporary shade. On other days let in as much light as possible.

Training the plants to wires

Allow the leading shoots to grow up the inside of the roof, tying them to horizontal wires spaced about 12 in. apart.

When a leading shoot reaches 5–6 ft high, pinch out its growing point. Laterals will not develop strongly from the main stem until its growth has been stopped.

Tie laterals horizontally to the wires. Fasten as many as possible, and leave the others trailing.

When a lateral has produced five leaves – it will be about 12–18 in. long – pinch off its tip. This will encourage the growth of side-shoots that will bear flowers (male and female). The aim is to produce enough female flowers to ensure that four will open at the same time on one plant; this is necessary for pollination. Remove any flowers that grow on the main stem.

1 *When a leading shoot reaches a height of 5–6 ft, pinch out its growing point. Laterals will not develop strongly until growth is stopped on the main stem*

2 *When lateral shoots have made five leaves, pinch off their growing tips to encourage the development of flower-bearing side-shoots*

Pollinating melons by hand

Hand-pollinate greenhouse melons at mid-day when the atmosphere is warmest. The female flower carries an embryo melon – a swelling behind the petals; the male flower has no swelling.

To ensure uniform development of fruit on a plant, pollinate when at least four of its female flowers (on different side-shoots) have opened – usually about a month after planting. One male flower can be used to pollinate four female flowers – it need not be taken from the same plant as the females.

Test the male flower for ripe pollen; it should leave yellow grains when stroked on the palm of the hand. Strip off its petals and press its centre against the centre of each female. Alternatively, transfer the pollen with a dry camel-hair brush or a wisp of cottonwool.

Pollinate each female flower for two or three days in succession.

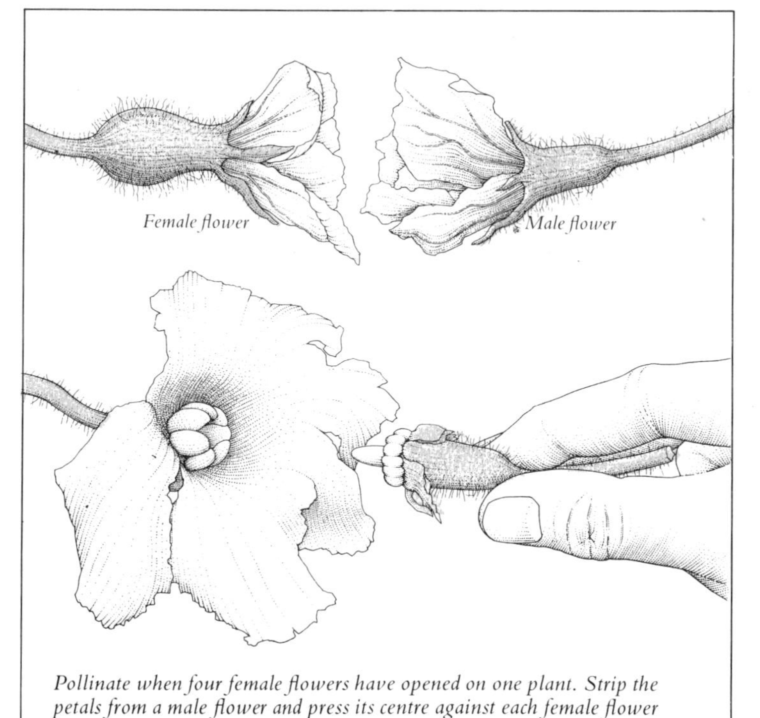

Pollinate when four female flowers have opened on one plant. Strip the petals from a male flower and press its centre against each female flower

Growing melons outdoors

Supporting and cutting the melons

Melons should begin to swell a few days after pollination. When swelling starts, pinch off the shoot beyond the fruit, leaving only one leaf.

Choose four melons of equal size on one plant (whether one or two stems) and pinch off the rest. Uniform size is essential – a larger melon will grow at the expense of the others. If there are only two or three of equal size, grow less than four on the plant. Four is the maximum number for fruit of good size and quality. Never grow more than one fruit on a side-shoot.

Start feeding plants when the melons are as big as a large walnut. Feed about every tenth day instead of watering; use a proprietary liquid fertiliser. Dilute the fertiliser as directed and give 3–4 pints to each plant. Keep the liquid away from the stem, to minimise the danger of collar rot.

When the melons reach the size of a tennis ball, lift those resting on the ground on to a support such as an upturned flower pot, to prevent them from rotting.

As the melons grow, those hanging from the roof wires will need extra support. When they are slightly larger than a tennis ball, support each one in a sling secured to the roof rafters or wires. Special nets are sold at most gardening stores.

When the melon's scent is first detected and it starts to crack round the stalk, stop watering and feeding. Reduce humidity by stopping syringeing and damping down, and by ventilating generously.

The melon is ready for harvesting when the skin yields slightly to pressure from the thumb at the flower end (on the opposite side from the stalk), and when it emits a pleasant smell. Harvest by cutting the laterals at points 2 in. on either side of the fruit stalk. By this time the plant is almost dead.

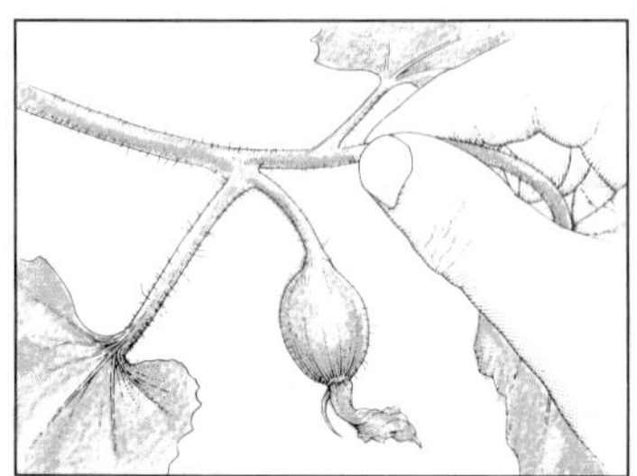

1 *Pinch off the shoot just beyond the swelling fruit, leaving only one leaf*

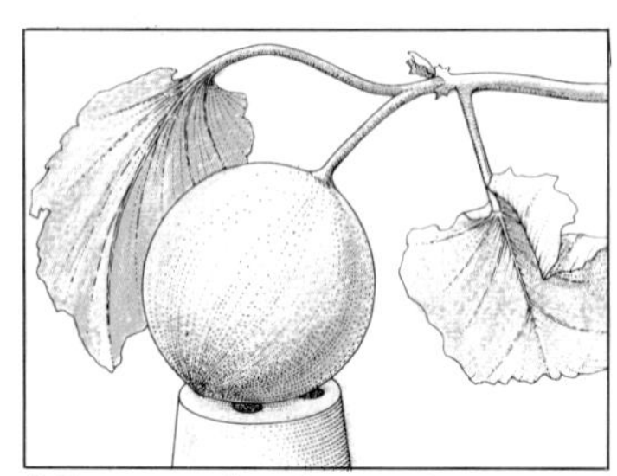

2 *Support each melon growing at ground level on an upturned flower pot*

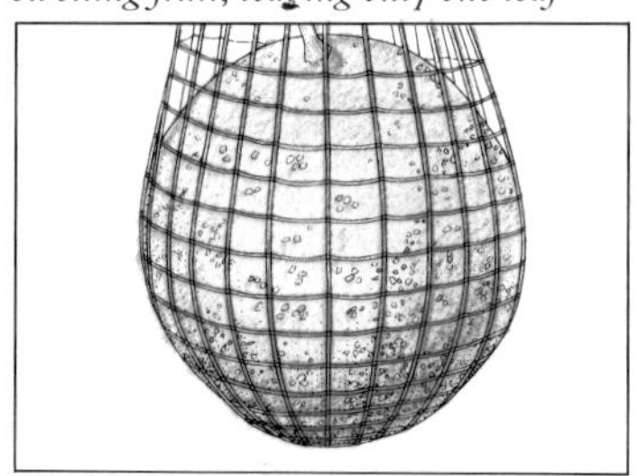

3 *Support each melon growing higher up in a sling secured to the roof wires*

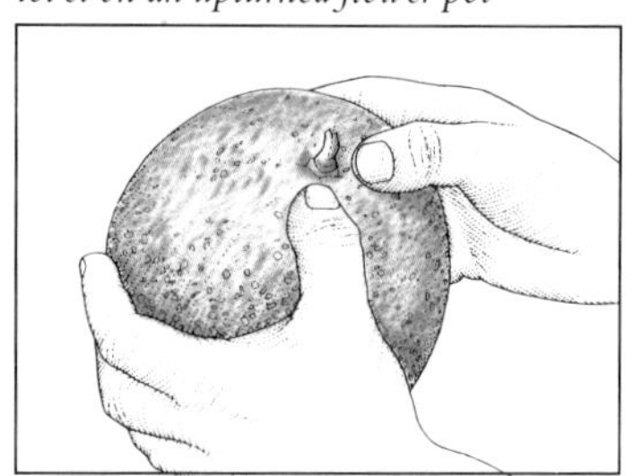

4 *The melon is ready for cutting if it yields to pressure at the flower end*

Sowing the seeds and planting out

Hardier varieties of melon can be grown in a cold frame or under cloches instead of in a greenhouse. However, if a crop is to be guaranteed it must be started in heat in all but the warmest parts of the country.

Sow under heat in early April, in the same way as for melons to be grown in the greenhouse. In the warmest areas you can risk sowing the hardiest varieties direct into the cold frame in early May, to provide melons for picking about September.

In the South, plant out young melons sown under heat into the cold frame or cloche during the third week in May. In the Midlands put them in a week later, and in the North and all cold and exposed places, wait until the first week of June before planting outdoors.

If the melons are to be grown under cloches, place 15–18 in. wide cloches in position a week or two before planting to allow the soil beneath them to warm up.

Prepare the soil in the cold frame or cloche in the same way as for the greenhouse border. If planting in a 6 ft by 4 ft frame, make two 3 in. high mounds about 2 ft from each end and each side. If using cloches, make 3 in. high mounds 3 ft apart.

Plant in the same way as in the greenhouse. If the weather is hot, lightly coat the frame or cloche lights with greenhouse shading wash or lime wash, to prevent the plants from wilting. Once the fruits are set, keep the frame or cloches closed so that the atmosphere is as moist as possible. Water and feed as for greenhouse melons.

Training and pollinating outdoor melons

Pinch out the growing point when four or five true (rough-edged) leaves have appeared. Side-shoots will now develop – select the four strongest and pinch off the others and any more that develop.

In a cold frame, train these shoots towards the corners of the frame; they will grow along the ground and can be pegged in the right direction with sticks. Beneath cloches, train two shoots in each direction along the line of cloches.

In warm weather, leave pollination to insects; open the frame or cloche to attract them. In cold weather, which deters insects, hand pollinate in the same way as for greenhouse plants.

Fruit will be borne on the four main shoots. Grow only one melon on each shoot – pinch it off two leaves beyond the first fruit. As with greenhouse plants, ensure that all melons are equal in size.

After selecting the strongest four side-shoots on a cold-frame plant, train them along the ground towards the four corners of the frame, pegging them with sticks

What can go wrong with melons

Many troubles result from incorrect ventilation or watering. If plants show other symptoms not described here, turn to the identification chart of pests and diseases on page 377. Look up chemicals on page 398 to find proprietary names.

Symptoms	Cause	Cure
Leaves have a pale mottling, sometimes with a rusty tinge, and wither prematurely. In severe cases, leaves are lightly webbed and young shoots fail to grow satisfactorily	Glasshouse red spider mites	Keep greenhouse atmosphere humid. Spraying with derris, dimethoate or malathion may check mites, but they quickly become resistant to chemicals. Predators (p. 398) can be introduced
Leaves are covered with a white floury powder that weakens the plant	Powdery mildew	Cut out severely affected shoots. Spray regularly with benomyl, dinocap or thiophanate-methyl. Fumigate greenhouse with dinocap smokes
Plants wilt, and the lower leaves begin to shrivel and turn yellow	Verticillium wilt	Destroy diseased plants and isolate infected soil. Sterilise greenhouse at end of growing season
Plants collapse due to rotting of the tissue at, or just above, soil level	Collar rot	Remove all decayed tissues. Dust infected areas with dry Bordeaux powder or captan. Give less water. To prevent, use sterilised compost and water carefully

Varieties of melons to grow

The season of use is four or five months after sowing, but depends on the growing conditions, which determine how long the fruit takes to mature. Some varieties mature quicker than others. There are two main types, musk and canteloup, but many varieties are hybrids and the distinction is blurred.

Name	Flesh colour	Remarks
FOR GROWING IN THE GREENHOUSE		
'Hero of Lockinge'	White	One of the easiest to grow. In sheltered areas it will succeed in frames or cloches
'Ringleader'	Green	Large oval fruit. Vigorous
'Superlative'	Red	Very succulent; medium size
FOR GROWING IN FRAMES OR CLOCHES		
'Ogen'	Pale green	Small fruited, quick-maturing canteloup of good flavour
'Sweetheart'	Salmon-pink	Small fruited. Smooth green skin
'Tiger'	Orange	Quick maturing. Has a flattened shape and a green-and-white marked skin

Peaches and nectarines

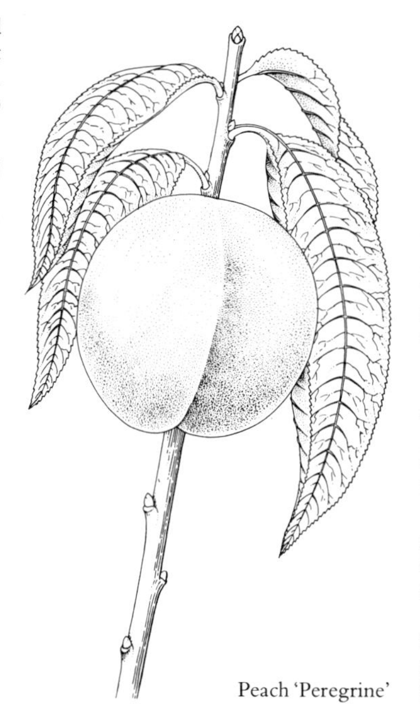

Peach 'Peregrine'

Peach trees are hardier than is generally thought, and can be grown outdoors as far north as Yorkshire, and also in parts of south-west Scotland. Both fan-trained trees and bushes will grow in any situation other than a frost pocket or site exposed to cold winds, but they will of course do best in a warm, sunny position. Fans have the best chance of success, especially when they are grown against a wall facing south or south-west.

Nectarines are a smooth, slightly less hardy variety of peach. They need a warmer situation than other peaches, and should be grown only as fans. Otherwise they can be treated in the same way as peaches.

Both peaches and nectarines are self-fertile – each flower fertilises itself – so only one tree is needed to obtain fruit.

One tree should provide sufficient fruit for the average family. Fruit grown outdoors is usually available in late August or September.

Tending peach and nectarine trees

Any good, well-drained soil is suitable. Good drainage is essential. Plant in the same way as other fruit trees (p. 84) in October or the first half of November.

In late January feed with 1 oz. (1 tablespoon) of sulphate of potash to the square yard. Every third year add 2 oz. (2 tablespoons) of superphosphate to the square yard. In early March give 1 oz. (1 tablespoon) of Nitro-chalk to the square yard, followed by a mulch of well-rotted manure or garden compost.

Water the soil liberally whenever there is a danger of drying out. Nectarines need water more often than peaches while the fruits are swelling, to prevent splitting. Weed round the roots by shallow hoeing, or use a paraquat weedkiller.

To ensure a good crop, assist pollination artificially by lightly dabbing every blossom with a camel-hair paint brush about every third day during the flowering period, which is normally in early March. This is best done on warm, dry days – and about midday is the most effective time.

When the peaches are the size of marbles, start thinning them out, reducing all clusters to single fruits. Remove all fruits that are growing towards a wall, and any that have no room to develop properly.

When the peaches are the size of table-tennis balls, thin them out to a final spacing of 9 in. apart.

Fruit is ready for picking when the flesh round the stalk yields to gentle pressure from the fingers.

Store peaches in a cool place, not touching one another, in containers lined with soft material. The fruits will keep about a month if they are not bruised.

Training and pruning a bush peach tree

Training a one-year-old peach tree

In May, when growth buds have appeared on a one-year-old (maiden) tree planted the previous autumn, cut back the central leader to about 2 ft above the ground. Cut just above a growth bud.

Leave the top three or four buds or side-shoots below the cut to form the first branches.

Remove all the side-shoots lower down the stem.

In May, cut back the central leader to 2 ft above the ground

Leave only the top three or four buds or side-shoots on the tree to form branches. Remove the rest lower down the stem

Pruning the tree in following years

All pruning in following years is also done in May. Remove any branch that crosses over another, cutting it flush with its parent branch. Cut back damaged branches to just above a healthy shoot.

Remove any shoots that are growing from the main stem below the lowest branch; cut them off flush with the stem. Any branch that is dying at the tip (peaches are prone to such die-back) should be cut back to a good side-shoot or outward-pointing branch. If the cut wood shows brown discoloration it is still affected by die-back, so cut it back to healthy wood.

On a well-established bush, cut out any branches drooping to the ground due to heavy fruit-bearing. Also remove older branches as they become unfruitful. This will encourage new wood from the centre.

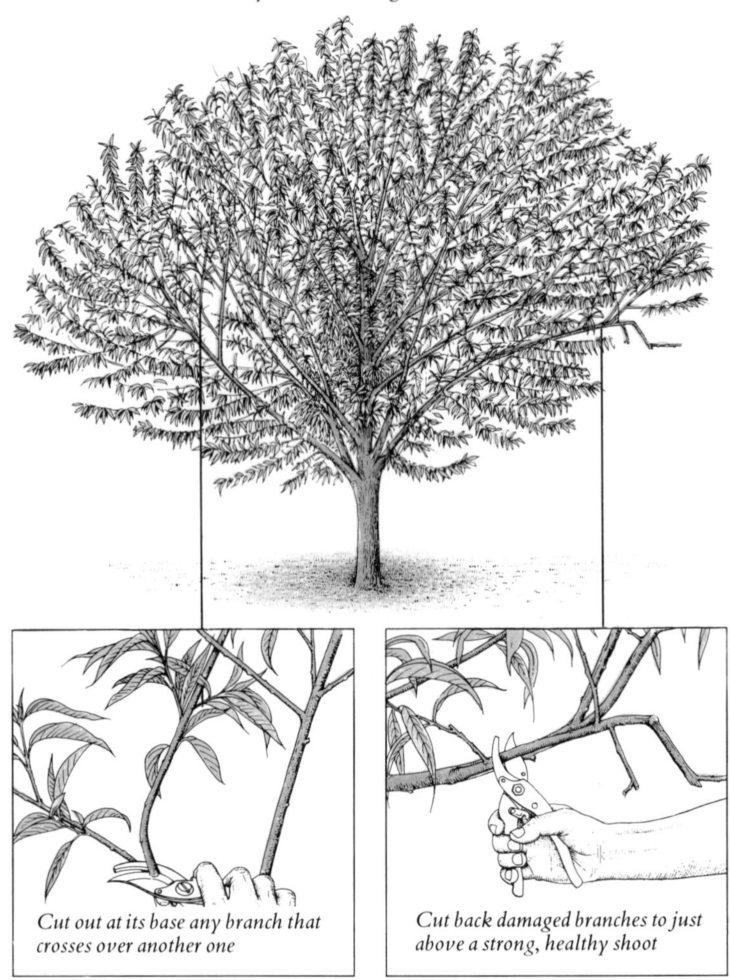

Cut out at its base any branch that crosses over another one

Cut back damaged branches to just above a strong, healthy shoot

Training and pruning a fan-shaped peach tree

Train a young fan peach like a fan apple (p. 97), but prune in early spring as growth begins – not in winter. Unlike apples, peaches produce side-shoots off the current year's growth. Pinch out the side-shoots one bud from their base.

From the fourth spring after planting a maiden tree, when it has 24–32 ribs, pruning differs, as peaches fruit mainly on last year's shoots.

When growth starts in the fourth spring, usually in April, rub or pinch out any buds or shoots pointing towards or away from the wall.

From the buds remaining, select good ones on each side of a rib spaced at 6 in. intervals, and rub out all others except the bud at the tip.

During the fourth summer these buds will produce laterals that will bear fruit the following summer, and the bud at the tip will grow on as a rib leader. Towards the end of the summer, tie both laterals and leaders to the wires. If a lateral grows more than 18 in. long, pinch off its tip.

In the fifth spring, at least two growth buds will have emerged at the base of each of last year's laterals. Allow one to grow on as a replacement, and remove the other (or others) when 2–3 in. long.

Let the tips of fruit-bearing laterals grow on in order to draw the sap and help develop the fruit, but if space is short pinch them back to four leaves when they have made six. Pinch off any side-shoots that grow from them.

In autumn or early winter, after fruit picking, cut back each of the laterals that has borne fruit to its replacement, and tie in the replacement with soft string.

Repeat this process of disbudding, pinching back, cutting out old shoots and tying in replacements every year. On the extension growth from each rib, choose buds to grow out as new laterals, as in the fourth spring. Treat rib leaders reaching the top wire as laterals.

Fill any gaps in the fan structure by keeping some of the old laterals when their replacements are tied in, and growing new shoots from them.

How to raise new peach trees

Peaches are one of the few fruits that grow well from seed. Even imported peaches can be grown in this way.

In autumn sow a stone 2 in. deep in a 3 in. pot of John Innes No. 1 potting compost.

Place the pot in a cold frame or on a window-sill in a cool room. Keep the compost moist.

A seedling should appear six months later. Plant it out in the garden when it is about 6 in. high.

Do not prune the seedling if you want fruit three or four years after sowing. Pruning delays fruiting by one or two years.

Each spring there will be at least two growth buds at the base of each fruiting lateral. Let one grow on as a replacement and remove the other when it is 2–3 in. long

Leave fruiting shoots to grow on. If space is short, pinch them back to four leaves once they have six

After fruit picking, cut back each lateral that has borne fruit to its replacement, and tie in the replacement

Varieties of peaches and nectarines to grow

For growing trees outdoors in the South choose varieties that ripen by early September, for the North by mid-August. Grow fans against a wall facing south or west. For bushes, shelter from the north is ideal but not essential.

Name	Time of ripening	Colour	Remarks
'Duke of York' peach	Mid-July	Cream/red flush	Hardy. Large tender fruit with melting, greenish-white flesh
'Hale's Early' peach	Late July–early Aug.	Lemon/red flush	Hardy. Fruit of fair flavour with melting, pale yellow flesh
'Peregrine' peach	Early Aug.	Crimson	Hardy. Rich flavour with yellowish-white flesh. Highly recommended
'Rochester' peach	Early Aug.	Golden/red flush	Hardy, the best for outside. Large fruit with yellow flesh; fine flavour
'Bellegarde' peach	Early–mid-Sept.	Golden/dark red flush	Large fruit with rich flavour and pale yellow flesh
'Sea Eagle' peach	Late Sept.	Lemon/deep red mottling	Very large, good flavour. Pale yellow flesh. Best under glass
'Early Rivers' nectarine	Mid-July	Greeny-yellow/red flush	Tender, juicy fruit with rich flavour and pale yellow flesh
'Lord Napier' nectarine	Early Aug.	Yellow/red-brown flush	Large fruit, rich flavour. Pale green flesh. Recommended

What can go wrong with peaches and nectarines

Leaf curl and red spider mites are the main problems. If plants show symptoms that are not described here, turn to the identification chart of pests and diseases on page 377. Look up chemicals on page 398 to find proprietary names.

Symptoms	Cause	Cure
Leaves have large reddish blisters, becoming whitish then brown and falling prematurely	Leaf curl	Spray with lime sulphur or Bordeaux mixture in January or early February, repeating a fortnight later and again just before leaf-fall. Burn diseased leaves before they turn whitish
Older leaves gradually turn to a bronzed yellow colour, dry out and die	Red spider mites	Spray with malathion, derris or dimethoate, or introduce a predator (p. 398)
Leaves are eaten and/or spun together; a green caterpillar is usually present	Winter moths	Spray with trichlorphon, malathion or derris as the buds open and leaves develop
Fruits fail to form, or drop off when very small, even after a good blossoming	Frost, or lack of pollination	Protect the tree with netting when frosts are forecast. During cool springs, pollinate with a soft brush

Pears for cooking and desserts

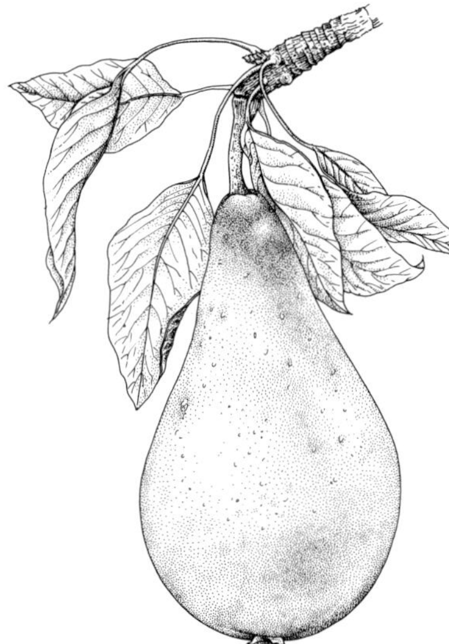

Pear 'Conference'

Pears – which can be used for fresh desserts, cooking or bottling – are almost as easy to grow as apples. Because they blossom earlier, they are more liable to injury by late spring frosts. Plant in a sunny position (p. 84), sheltered from cold winds. There are hardy varieties that are suitable for the North.

Being less tolerant than apples of dry conditions at the roots, pears prefer a deep, loamy soil that will keep its moisture in summer. Like apples, they do not grow well on or near the coast because of damage from salt-laden winds.

Pears can be trained to the same forms as apple trees. Only one or two varieties are tip bearers. More than one tree must be grown for cross-pollination to take place.

As with apples, 'family' trees (those with three varieties on one rootstock) are available.

An average family should get ample pears from four bush trees (or three fans, three espaliers, six dwarf pyramids or eight cordons). The season is from August to January, depending on the variety.

In late January feed with 1 oz. (1 tablespoon) of sulphate of potash to the square yard. Every third year add 2 oz. (2 tablespoons) of superphosphate to each square yard. In March apply 1–1½ oz. (1–1½ tablespoons) of sulphate of ammonia to the square yard. Add an extra ½ oz. for trees grassed round. There is a natural fall of fruit in June, but dry, poor soil can cause the entire crop to fall.

Harvesting the fruit The time of picking is critical. Pears should not be allowed to ripen fully on the tree, or they may become soft and mealy inside.

Harvest early varieties (August-September) by cutting the stalk when the fruit is mature but still hard – before it will twist easily from the stalk by hand. Pick mid-season pears (October-November) and late pears (December onwards) as soon as they will part easily from the stalk, after a gentle lifting and twisting motion.

After picking, place the pears, not touching, in a single layer on a shelf in a cool room or shed, at a temperature of about 3–4°C (38–40°F). The atmosphere should be a little drier than for apples. A larder might be ideal. Inspect pears regularly and remove any that show signs of rot.

To finish off ripening, place the fruits in a warm room, at about 18°C (64°F), for two or three days. If properly stored they should last several months. Use small fruits first.

Pruning and training trees Pruning and training are the same as for apples (p. 88), except that pears can stand much harder cutting back. Never hesitate to remove overcrowded branches.

Pear trees also produce fruiting spurs more easily, and these will need more thinning out than apples. Summer pruning should be done in early July, earlier than for apples.

If you take over a garden where there is a neglected standard or bush pear tree, treat it in the same way as a neglected apple tree (p. 92).

What can go wrong with pears

Aphids and scab are the chief troubles in pear growing. If plants show symptoms not described here, turn to the identification chart of pests and diseases on page 377. Look up chemicals on page 398 to find proprietary names.

Symptoms	Cause	Cure
Shoots and young leaves crippled or stunted; small sticky insects present	Aphids	Spray with a systemic insecticide or malathion, HCH, nicotine or derris
Numerous dark brown pimples appear on both sides of the leaves	Leaf blister mites	Pick off and burn infected leaves and fruits. Spray with thiophanate-methyl at the end of March
Cankers develop at the base of shoots that have died back and are hung with brown and withered leaves	Fire blight	Notify local representative of Ministry of Agriculture, Fisheries and Food, who will recommend suitable treatment, which may mean destroying the tree
Brownish or blackish spots appear on leaves and fruits, and blisters and cracks on spring shoots	Pear scab	Spray with captan, benomyl, thiophanate-methyl or thiram, first when flower buds are nearly open, second at petal-fall, and third three weeks later

Symptoms	Cause	Cure
Slightly sunken areas of dead or dying bark appear on twigs or young stems. Later, these areas extend, the central tissues crack and flake off and the cankers girdle the stem and kill it	Pear canker	This is not as common as apple canker. Cut out or pare off infected parts and burn. Paint wounds with wound paint. Improve drainage if waterlogging occurs, as this may aggravate the trouble
Full-sized fruits, both on the tree and in store, show pale brown areas which bear concentric rings of small whitish or yellowish pimples. Sometimes the fruit dries up on the tree and becomes mummified	Brown rot	Destroy all rotten and withered fruit on the tree, the ground and in store. Cut out any dead shoots when pruning. Spray trees with thiophanate-methyl in August or early September to reduce rotting of stored fruit
Leaf surfaces are eaten, exposing veins which later go brown and die; a small black caterpillar is seen	Pear and cherry slugworms (sawflies)	Spray with malathion or derris when the pest is first seen
Young fruits become deformed and enlarged; often they are elongated or very rounded; later they crack, decay and fall	Pear midges	Spray with malathion or dimethoate at petal-fall as a preventive, and destroy all fallen fruits

Varieties of pears to grow

All the varieties listed are dessert pears. If picked while still firm, most dessert pears will cook well.

More than one variety must be grown for cross-pollination. Choose from within the same pollination group. Varieties in adjoining groups will usually pollinate each other, but some are incompatible.

Varieties are grouped according to their flowering time as follows:
1 Early to mid-season flowering
2 Mid-season flowering
3 Late flowering
Triploids (marked T) need to be grown with two other varieties from the same group – to pollinate the triploid and each other.

The approximate week for picking is given as a guide; it will vary according to locality and season.

Name	Pollination group	Week for picking	Season of use	Colour	Remarks
'Jargonelle'	2(T)	Aug. (1)	Aug.	Greeny-yellow	Heavy, regular crop. Suitable for North. Small fruit. Tip bearing
'William's Bon Chrétien'	2	Aug. (4)	Sept.	Pale yellow	Recommended for sweet, musky flavour. Suitable for bottling. Good, regular cropper. Suitable for North. Susceptible to scab
'Merton Pride'	2(T)	Sept. (2)	Sept.-Oct.	Green	Large fruit, recommended for flavour. Vigorous, upright tree
'Louise Bonne of Jersey'	1	Sept. (3)	Oct.	Pea green/rust-red flush	Regular cropper. Suitable for North. Good flavour and quality. Not suitable as a pollinator for 'William's Bon Chrétien'
'Beurré Superfin'	2	Sept. (2)	Oct.	Yellow/russet patches	Rich flavour. Pick before fully ripe. May rot at core in store
'Conference'	2	Sept. (4)	Oct.-Nov.	Pale green/silver russet	Most reliable cropper, heavy and regular. Suitable for North
'Thompson's'	2	Sept. (3)	Oct.-Nov.	Pale yellow/light russet	Recommended for flavour. Best against a warm wall
'Emile d'Heyst'	1	Sept. (4)	Oct.-Nov.	Pale yellow/brown russet	Good flavour. Suitable for North. Small tree, weeping branches
'Doyenne du Comice'	3	Oct. (1)	Nov.	Pale yellow/fine russet	Our finest pear, but irregular in cropping. Good for bottling. Needs a warm, sheltered position. Subject to scab
'Winter Nelis'	3	Oct. (1)	Nov.-Jan.	Greeny-yellow/russet	Recommended for flavour. Fruits small to medium in size

Plums and apricots to grow as bush trees or against a wall

Plum 'Early Rivers'

Plums can be eaten fresh or used for bottling, cooking or jam-making. Gages are a better-flavoured type of plum for eating and bottling, and damsons, which have a sour taste, are more suitable for cooking and bottling than for eating fresh.

All are cultivated in the same way and will succeed in most soils, but prefer well-drained loam or clay. Plums and gages flower early and should not be planted in areas where spring frosts are likely.

Gages give the best results if they are grown against a wall. Damsons can stand more rain and less sun than plums and gages, and they usually flower a little later.

Trees tend to grow too large for the average-sized garden, unless on semi-dwarfing rootstock. The most suitable restricted forms for the amateur are fans and pyramids. All damsons are self-fertile, but some varieties of plums and gages need to be grown with another variety as a pollinator.

Two or three trees should provide enough fruit for the average family. The fruiting season for plums and gages is from late July to early October, for damsons from September to October.

Preferably plant trees in autumn (p. 84). If the weather is dry, make sure the soil is well watered beforehand. On very acid soils (pH 5 and below) add about 1 lb. of lime to the square yard.

In early spring, mulch with a 2 in. layer of straw, well-rotted garden compost or manure to keep the tree moist. Repeat this every year. Control weeds by shallow hoeing or with a weedkiller. Do not use a fork, as it can damage the tree's shallow root system.

Pull out suckers as soon as they form – remove the soil round them to reveal the root, and tear the sucker from the root. Do not cut them off, as this encourages them to increase.

Wasps may be troublesome in some years. They eat the ripening fruit, especially if it is already damaged. If you can find the nest, apply a proprietary wasp powder. Netting and similar protection against birds (p. 85) helps to deter them.

Apricots are hardy enough to be grown outside, but because they flower early – usually mid-March, but sometimes as early as February – they need a sheltered site to protect the blossom from frost damage.

They are best trained as fan trees against a south-facing wall, but in milder areas can be grown as bush trees if sheltered from cold winds.

One tree should be enough for the average family. The fruiting season is from late July until the end of August, depending on the variety.

Soil and feeding requirements are the same as those of plums. Trees bear fruit on one-year-old and older wood. Train fan and bush trees like apples (pp. 97, 89) until the framework is built up (but prune in early spring as growth begins). Then prune fans like plums, and bush trees like sour cherries (p. 110).

Apricots are self-fertile, but they flower when few pollinating insects are about, so artificial pollination is advisable to ensure a good crop. Dab a small, soft paintbrush over the open flowers every two or three days during the flowering period.

Thinning is necessary only if branches are very heavily laden. Wait until the stones are formed (check by cutting a fruit), as there is often a natural drop just before this. Fruits should be spaced about 5 in. apart on the branch.

Pick apricots when they are ripe and well coloured, and part easily from the tree. Eat or preserve them as soon as possible after picking.

Varieties to grow are 'Hemskerke' and 'Moorpark'. Apricots suffer the same troubles as plums (p. 129).

Feeding plum and damson trees

In late January each year, feed trees with 1 oz. (1 tablespoon) of sulphate of potash to the square yard. Every third year, add 2 oz. (2 tablespoons) of superphosphate to the square yard as well. Each March feed trees with 1–1½ oz. (1–1½ tablespoons) of sulphate of ammonia or Nitro-chalk to the square yard.

Sprinkle the fertiliser evenly over the soil, covering an area a little larger than the spread of the tree's branches. Do not fork it in, as this could easily damage the roots; allow it to penetrate naturally.

Thinning and harvesting the crop

Tree branches are often brittle, and if they snap there is a danger of silver leaf or other diseases entering the wound.

Start thinning a heavy crop at the beginning of June, to take some weight off the branches. Curl a finger round the stalk and snap off the fruit with your thumbnail, leaving the stalk on the tree.

Complete thinning after the natural fall at the end of June. Thin dessert plums to 2-3 in. apart, cooking plums to 2 in. This usually means leaving one to each cluster.

When harvesting, pick fruit by the stalk to avoid bruising. The stalk will snap and come away with the fruit.

Leave plums intended for eating to ripen on the tree as long as possible. Pick plums for cooking or bottling before they are quite ripe.

Plums cannot normally be stored, but 'Coe's Golden Drop' can be kept for several weeks if picked slightly before they are ripe, wrapped in paper, and placed in a cool, well-ventilated room or shed. Remove and burn any rotting fruit, as it may spread disease.

Training and pruning a pyramid plum tree

Training a one-year-old pyramid tree

Pyramid plum trees are similar in shape to dwarf pyramid apple trees (p. 100), but slightly taller – about 9 ft – and much wider (8–10 ft). They are more irregular in outline, because plums generally grow more vigorously and it is difficult to maintain the pyramid shape.

After the basic framework has been established, plums need less restrictive pruning than apples.

If you decide to train a pyramid from a one-year-old tree, cut back the stem to 5 ft above the ground in the April after planting. Cut just above a bud. Cut off flush with the stem any young branches lower than 18 in. from the ground.

If the tree is much less than 5 ft high, let it continue growing for another year before training it.

Training a two-year-old pyramid tree

On a two-year-old tree, cut back the central leader in April to about 18 in. from last year's cut. Make the cut just above a bud.

Cut back from three to five of the strongest side-shoots at the top of the stem to 9 in., pruning to an outward-pointing bud. Cut back all other side-shoots to 6 in. Since the lower growth tends to be weaker, it is cut back harder to encourage even growth. All these side-shoots will now grow on to form the tree's first main branches.

In April prune the central leader to 18 in. from last year's cut

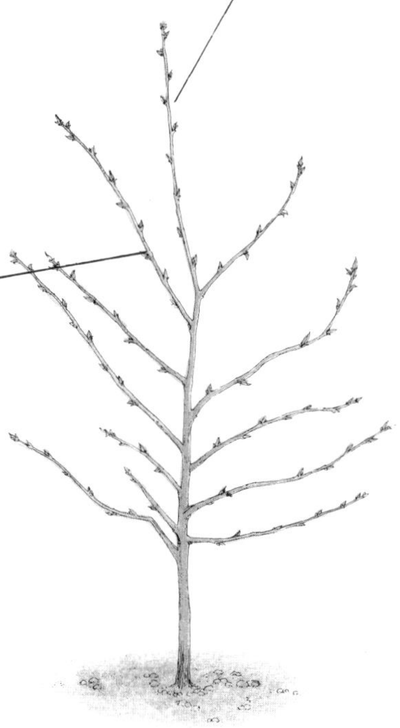

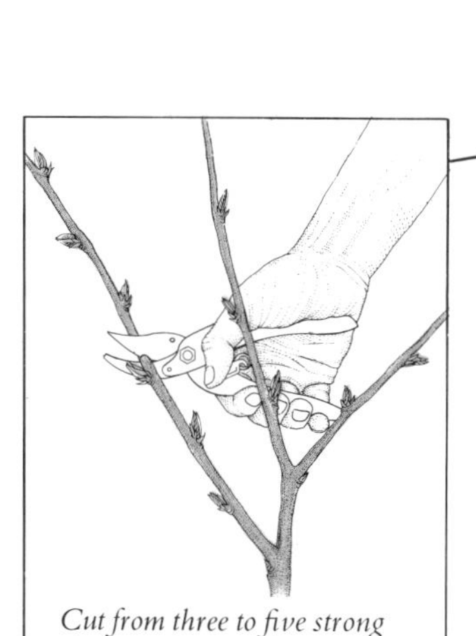

Cut from three to five strong shoots at the top of the stem to 9 in., and all others to 6 in.

Training and pruning from three years old to full height

Each April cut back the central leader to about 18 in. above last year's cut, and just above a bud. Cut back the branch leaders according to their vigour – by one-third of new growth if they are growing strongly, by half if they are of average growth, or by two-thirds if they are weak.

Cut back the strongest laterals from main branches to 9 in. long, and the remaining ones to 6 in. long; always make the cut above an outward-pointing bud.

In April cut back new growth on the branch leaders by half if they are of average growth

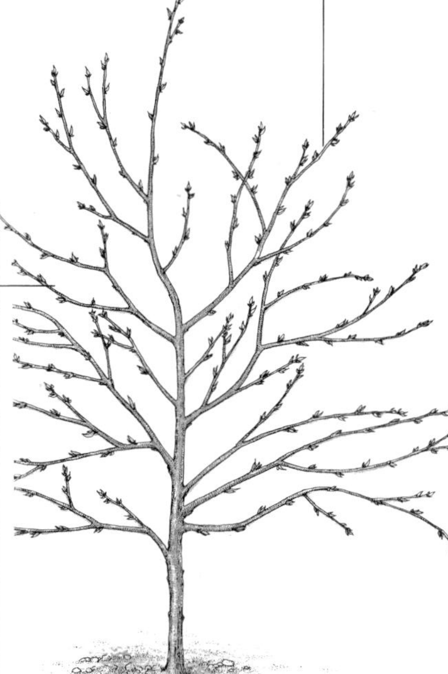

Prune the strongest laterals to 9 in., others to 6 in., above an outward-pointing bud

Pruning an established pyramid tree

Once the tree has reached 9 ft (when it is about six years old), keep it at this height by cutting back the central leader to a strong lateral in the summer. You may need to do this every second or third year, depending on growth.

Established trees should be pruned only in summer – during July. Winter pruning could result in die-back or silver-leaf infection.

Plums bear fruit on the previous season's shoots as well as on spurs on old wood. If the tree is fruiting regularly, prune as little as possible – just pinch vigorous new side-shoots back to six or seven leaves from the parent stem.

Thin out any overcrowded branches as necessary, cutting flush with the parent stem. Similarly, cut away any dead wood.

If branch leaders grow exceptionally long, cut them back to a strong main lateral. Try to keep branches a maximum length of 4–5 ft.

If the tree grows vigorously but does not fruit regularly, root-pruning may be needed (p. 85).

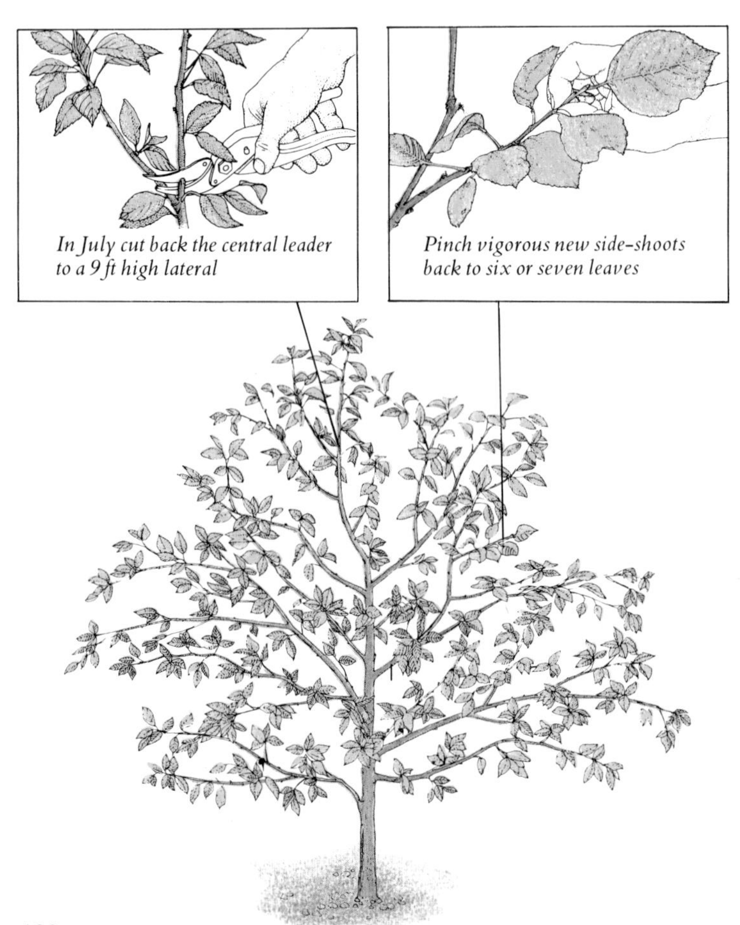

In July cut back the central leader to a 9 ft high lateral

Pinch vigorous new side-shoots back to six or seven leaves

Pruning a fan-trained plum tree

Prune and train fan-shaped plums like apples (p. 97), but prune in early spring as growth begins – not in winter. After the third summer when the framework is built up, treatment is different as plums fruit on old and new wood.

Each spring, as soon as growth starts, rub out all buds that are pointing towards or away from the wall. Early in July, when side-shoots that are not needed as branches have produced six or seven leaves, pinch off their tips.

After the crop has been picked, shorten by half those shoots that were pinched back. Do not allow any shoots to grow strongly upwards, as they may rob lower growth of nourishment. If one is needed to fill up a space or replace an old branch, tie it to a wire.

An unwanted shoot should be cut out flush with the wood from which it springs. Remove any dead wood.

Early in July pinch off the tips of side-shoots not needed as branches, once they have produced six or seven leaves. At the end of the summer, after the crop has been picked, shorten by half those shoots that were previously pinched back

Pruning a neglected bush or standard plum tree

If you take over a garden where there is a neglected standard or bush plum tree, it can be restored to order in the same way as a neglected apple tree (p. 92). But the work must be done in summer, to guard against die-back or silver-leaf infection.

Once the tree has been restored, very little pruning is needed. It is only necessary to thin out overcrowded branches, especially in the centre, and cut away any dead or diseased wood. Prune in summer.

What can go wrong with plums

Apart from wasps and birds, leaf-curling plum aphids are the main pests. If plants show symptoms not described here, turn to the identification chart of pests and diseases on page 377. Look up chemicals on page 398 to find proprietary names.

Symptoms	Cause	Cure
Leaves and young shoots are twisted and stunted; many tiny, sticky insects present	Leaf-curling plum aphids	Spray with a systemic insecticide such as dimethoate or formothion in early spring before the trees blossom, and again after blossoming if necessary
Silvery sheen on leaves, and after one or more years branches die back. When infected branches are cut out, wood shows dark brown staining. Small fungi appear on dead wood	Silver leaf	Cut out affected branches to 6 in. below point where brown stain ceases. Paint all wounds. Feed, mulch, water and/or drain as necessary to encourage vigour. A foliar feed may hasten recovery
Leaves and young shoots, on one or more branches, or the whole tree, wilt suddenly and die	Honey fungus	Dig up and burn dead and dying trees, and sterilise soil with dazomet or Armillatox or change it completely before replanting
Stems and sometimes small branches die back, and general growth lacks vigour	Poor root growth, due usually to unsatisfactory soil conditions	Improve drainage or add lime, as appropriate. (Test the soil for lime content with a soil-testing kit)
Brown spots may appear on leaves, later becoming holes. On the stems and smaller branches, flat cankers develop and branches die back	Bacterial canker	Cut out infected branches and paint wounds in July and August. Spray foliage with Bordeaux mixture in mid-August, mid-September and mid-October
Leaves have a pale or reddish mottling and may fall prematurely	Fruit tree red spider mites	Spray with a DNOC/petroleum winter wash, while trees are dormant, to kill overwintering eggs. Or spray after flowering with dimethoate, malathion or derris
Leaves are eaten and/or spun together; green caterpillars are usually present	Winter moths	Spray with trichlorphon, HCH, malathion or derris as buds open and leaves develop
Branches bare with little or no blossom	Bullfinches	Protect trees with netting or cotton. Spray large trees with bird repellant

Varieties of plums, gages and damsons to grow

Some varieties listed are self-fertile (marked SF). Others need another tree to pollinate them; suitable pollinators are shown by the list number.

With the exception of 'Kirke's' and 'Coe's Golden Drop', all the plums listed are relatively hardy and will grow in a cold area in a sheltered, frost-free position. The gages need a warm, sunny position, and if grown in a cold area are best positioned against a wall facing south or west.

If buying a maiden tree, tell the nurseryman the form in which you intend to train the tree, so that a suitable rootstock is provided.

Variety	Pollinator	Season of use	Colour	Remarks
PLUMS AND GAGES				
1 **'Early Rivers'**	No. 5	Late July–Aug.	Purple	Small fruits with good flavour; fairly small, compact tree
2 **'Oullin's Golden Gage'**	SF	Mid-Aug.	Straw-yellow/red dots	Large fruit, sweet and juicy. Vigorous tree, slow to crop
3 **'Early Transparent Gage'**	SF	Mid–late Aug.	Yellow-green/red dots	Good flavour; good for jam, bottling. Small, compact tree
4 **'Denniston's Superb'**	SF	Late Aug.	Green/red flush	Medium-sized fruit; good flavour. Vigorous, upright tree
5 **'Victoria'**	SF	Late Aug.–Sept.	Pink/red dots	Reliable, heavy crop; good flavour; susceptible to silver leaf
6 **'Old Greengage'**	No. 10	Late Aug.–Sept.	Green/sometimes with red and grey dots	Rich, sweet flavour; the ideal dessert gage, but cropping is light and uncertain. Vigorous tree, slow to bear fruit
7 **'Kirke's'**	Nos. 2, 3	Late Aug.–Sept.	Dark purple	Good flavour, temperamental cropping. Small, spreading tree
8 **'Golden Transparent Gage'**	SF	Early–mid-Sept.	Golden/red dots	Rich flavour. Erratic cropper. Small tree; needs warm position
9 **'Coe's Golden Drop'**	No. 4	Late Sept.	Straw/red-brown marks	Fine, large, high-flavoured fruit; pick when almost over-ripe
10 **'Marjorie's Seedling'**	SF	Late Sept.–Oct.	Purple	Fairly sweet; best used for cooking, bottling. Tall, hardy tree
DAMSONS				
11 **'Merryweather'**	SF	Early Sept.	Dark purple	Large oval fruit. Medium-sized, spreading tree; good cropper
12 **'Prune'**	SF	Sept.–Oct.	Blue-black	Small, tapering fruit; good flavour. Tree of moderate growth

Raspberries for picking from July to October

Raspberry 'Malling Jewel'

Raspberries can be used for fresh desserts, cooking or jam-making, and will keep in a freezer. Some varieties bear fruit in July on the previous season's shoots; others fruit in September or October on the current season's shoots. Canes that have borne fruit are replaced year by year by new canes.

Buy one-year-old canes for planting in late autumn. Raspberries are prone to virus diseases, so buy them from a reputable nursery to ensure that they are disease-free. To avoid the risk of spreading virus diseases, never replenish your stock by raising new plants from those you have; always buy new canes of certified virus-free stock.

Raspberries do best in full sun, but will thrive in partial shade. Do not plant them in positions exposed to frost or strong winds. They grow well in any well-drained but moisture-retaining, slightly acid soil. They will also grow in limy soils if these are enriched with compost or decayed manure.

The average family should obtain a plentiful fruit supply with 18–24 raspberry canes. All varieties are self-fertile.

Preparing the bed and planting the canes

The best way to grow raspberries is in a row, with the canes trained against wires. First clear the site of perennial weeds – either dig them out or use a hormone weedkiller, such as 2,4–D.

In late summer or early autumn, prepare the ground by digging a spade-deep trench about 2 ft 6 in. wide, and fork well-rotted compost or manure into the bottom at the rate of about two 2 gallon buckets to the square yard. At the same time add 1 oz. (1 tablespoon) of superphosphate to the square yard. Then fill in the trench.

The best time to plant is in early November, although it can be done at any time from October to March. Dig a shallow trench about 3 in. deep and 6–9 in. wide. Place the young plants upright in it, 18 in. apart and with roots spread out. Cover the roots with 3 in. of soil and firm it gently with your feet. Leave 6 ft space between rows.

Immediately after planting, cut down each cane to just above a good bud 9–12 in. above ground level.

In late January each year, feed with 1 oz. (1 tablespoon) of sulphate of potash to the square yard. Every third year add 2 oz. (2 tablespoons) of superphosphate to the square yard. Each March feed with ½ oz. (1 dessertspoon) of sulphate of ammonia. Allow these fertilisers to be washed into the soil naturally.

In late March, mulch with a 2 in. layer of garden compost, manure or peat, to conserve moisture. Give plenty of water in warm, dry spells.

Control weeds with a paraquat weedkiller. Do not hoe between the canes, particularly during the growing period, as this may damage the shallow surface roots.

Protect ripening fruit from birds, ideally with netting.

Supporting the long, flexible shoots

In summer, when the canes are making fresh growth, sink an 8 ft high wooden post 2 ft into the ground at each end of the row. Then stretch two galvanised wires between the posts 3 ft and 5½ ft above the ground; or stretch two parallel wires 12 in. apart from cross-pieces fixed at right angles to the posts about 4 ft above the ground. Keep the wires parallel with strong S-shaped hooks. For both methods use 12–13 gauge galvanised wire.

The first August after planting, tie canes individually with soft string to the two-wire system. With parallel wires, simply ensure that all canes are inside the wires.

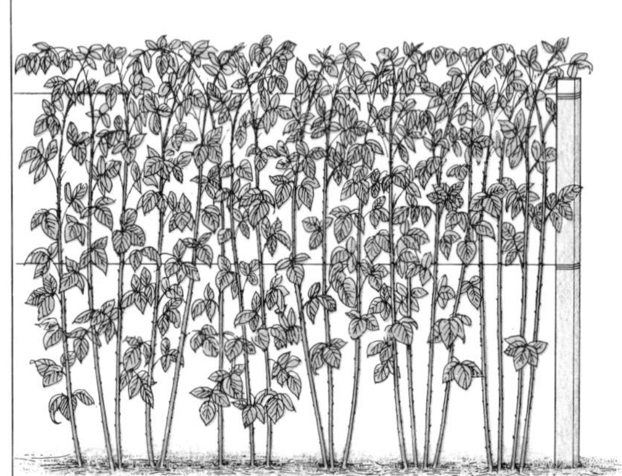

Two-wire system *Stretch wires 3 ft and 5½ ft above the ground between two posts; tie the canes to them*

Parallel-wire system *Stretch two parallel wires between 4 ft high cross-pieces; train canes inside them*

When to gather the ripe fruit

Do not try for a crop the first summer after planting, as this will detract from the vigour of future canes. In the first June after planting, cut off any blossom or fruit on the young canes.

Allow the canes to bear fruit in the second year after planting; summer-fruiting varieties will do so in July, autumn-fruiting varieties in September or October.

Raspberries do not keep fresh for long once they have been picked. Eat or process them as soon as possible after picking.

Replacing old canes with new

In August, when summer-fruiting raspberries have been picked, untie canes that have borne fruit and cut them down to just above soil level leaving only canes of the current year's growth standing.

Choose up to eight of the strongest of the new canes on each plant, and support them on the wires. Cut out unwanted new canes at soil level. Pull out any suckers (shoots direct from the roots) that spring up between rows.

In February cut back each cane growing above the top wire to a bud a few inches above it. This encourages growth on lower buds.

With autumn-fruiting types, cut all canes to the ground in February. New canes will grow up in spring and need support in summer.

1 *In August cut down to soil level all raspberry canes that have borne fruit*

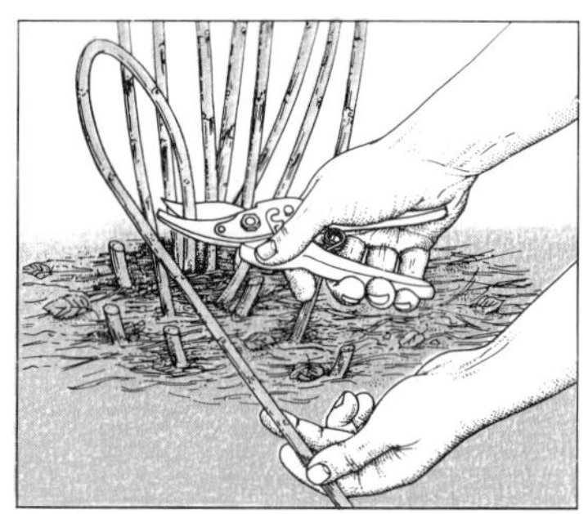

2 *Choose up to eight of the strongest new canes per plant; cut out the rest*

3 *After supporting the new canes, pull out any suckers springing from roots*

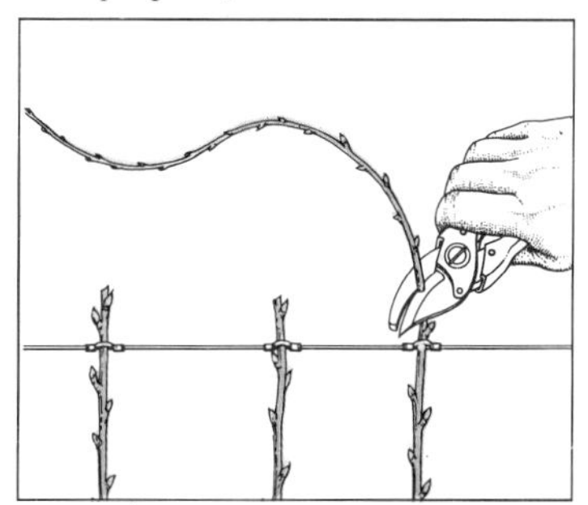

4 *In February trim any canes growing beyond the top wire to a bud just above it*

What can go wrong with raspberries

Raspberry beetle is the most troublesome pest in raspberry growing. If plants show symptoms that are not described here, turn to the identification chart of pests and diseases on page 377. Look up chemicals on page 398 to find proprietary names.

Symptoms	Cause	Cure
Leaves on fruiting canes wilt and wither in summer, and canes may snap off in winds	Cane blight	Cut back diseased canes to below ground. Disinfect knife immediately. Spray with Bordeaux mixture as new canes develop
Canes show purple circular spots which later form small cankers. Leaves may show circular spots with a whitish centre, and some fruits may become misshapen	Cane spot or anthracnose	Cut out and burn badly infected canes. Spray with benomyl or thiophanate-methyl fortnightly from bud-burst to petal-fall
Small grubs feed inside the ripening fruits, making them soft	Raspberry beetles	Spray with derris, malathion or fenitrothion as first fruits turn pink
Young shoots, usually low on canes, wither in April and May. Stems tunnelled by tiny red caterpillars	Raspberry moths	For mild attacks, cut out and burn infected shoots. For severe attacks, spray with malathion
Leaves rolled and/or distorted; sticky insects	Aphids	Spray with dimethoate or pirimicarb
Leaves are mottled and have yellow blotches; they become distorted. Canes become stunted; crop is poor	Virus disease	Dig up and burn all plants. Plant new canes on fresh site. Control aphids, which spread virus disease

Varieties of raspberries to grow

All the varieties listed bear red fruit. There are no yellow varieties available on virus-free stock. The fruiting month given is for the South – ripening will be later in the North. It is an estimate only, and will vary according to the season.

Name	Season of use	Remarks
'Malling Jewel'	Early–mid-July	Heavy, consistent cropper. Sweet flavour. Highly recommended
'Glen Cova'	Early–mid-July	The heaviest cropper. Fruits from medium to small
'Malling Delight'	Early–mid-July	Large, well-flavoured fruits. Has some resistance to virus disease
'Malling Admiral'	Late July–Aug.	Heavy cropper. Good flavour. Some resistance to virus, mildew
'September' (autumn-fruiting)	Late Aug.–Oct.	Fruits medium; very good flavour. Canes only 4–5 ft high

Red and white currants to grow as bushes or cordons

White currant 'White Grape'

Red and white currants are both grown the same way – the white currant is a less common variety of the red. Red currants are used for desserts or jam, jelly or wine-making; white currants for desserts.

They can be grown as bushes (usually on a 9 in. leg) or cordons – single, double or triple. Cordons are grown upright, with each stem tied to a permanent supporting cane.

Almost any moisture-retaining but well-drained soil is suitable, but plants do best in lighter soils. They will thrive in either sun or partial shade. They flower early, so take care not to plant in frost pockets.

For a good, regular supply of fruit, the average family would need four to six bushes or 12–15 cordons. Harvest time is in June and July.

Before planting, dig the bed over and work in 1 oz. (1 tablespoon) of sulphate of potash to the square yard. The plants are very susceptible to potash deficiency, which causes leaf edges to appear scorched.

Plant between October and March (p. 244), ideally in autumn. Place bushes 5 ft apart, single cordons 15 in. apart, double 30 in. apart, and triple 45 in. apart. Cordon rows should be 4 ft apart.

Cordons need 2 × 2 in. stakes for each stem. Use stakes 8 ft long with 5–6 ft above ground level. Alternatively, grow rows against three or four horizontal wires at 2 ft intervals, and tie them to vertical canes fastened to the wires.

In late January feed with 1 oz. (1 tablespoon) of sulphate of potash to the square yard, and every third year add 2 oz. (2 tablespoons) of superphosphate to the square yard. In March feed with ½ oz. (1 dessertspoon) of sulphate of ammonia, and apply a 2 in. mulch of well-rotted manure or garden compost.

Control weeds by mulching, or with a paraquat weedkiller. Do not hoe, as it can damage shallow roots.

Water only during prolonged dry spells. Pull out any suckers that spring from the main stem or the roots. If frost lifts young plants, firm them in with your feet. Strong winds may break off shoots. On young bushes, stake shoots that are important to maintain the shape.

Birds are one of the main problems. They will damage buds and strip the plant of fruit. Netting is the best means of protection.

It is best to pick currants as soon as they are fully ripe.

Pruning bushes and cordons in winter

If bird damage is likely, leave winter pruning until buds begin to swell (usually in February) – but no later – so that you can prune to an undamaged bud. Red currants bear most fruit on spurs on old wood.

Immediately after planting a one-year-old bush, cut each branch back to four buds from the main stem, above an outward-pointing bud.

In the second winter cut out flush with the stem any branches that spoil the over-all bush shape. Shorten branch leaders by two-thirds of new growth if growth is weak, or by half if growth is strong, cutting to an outward-pointing bud. Prune laterals back to one bud from their base so that they will form spurs.

In the third and fourth years leave some laterals to grow into branches where there is room, so that the established bush has eight to ten main branches on a 6–9 in. leg. Otherwise, prune laterals back to spurs each year.

Cut back branch leaders by half the new growth in the third winter, regardless of vigour. In the fourth winter remove about a quarter of new growth. After that prune by about 1 in. yearly.

Keep the centre of the bush open, and as the oldest branches become too spreading or unproductive, replace them with strong new shoots.

On cordons cut back laterals to one bud to form spurs. Until the leader is 6 ft high cut back new growth by 9 in. or two-thirds, whichever is the smaller amount. After the leader reaches 6 ft, remove all new growth each winter – cutting just above a bud.

FIRST WINTER PRUNING

Immediately after planting, cut back branches to four buds

PRUNING IN THE SECOND WINTER

Shorten new growth on leaders by half if growth is strong, by two-thirds if growth is weak

Cut back laterals to one bud from their base, to form spurs

Cut out flush with stem any shoots spoiling bush shape

Pruning bushes and cordons in summer

Cordons and bushes two years old or more are pruned similarly each summer. Start pruning at about the end of June, as the new growth starts to turn pale brown. Cut laterals back to three or five leaves, just above a leaf joint.

Once a cordon has reached 6 ft high, cut back new leader growth to four leaves – preparatory to removing it entirely next winter.

From late June onwards, cut back laterals to three or five leaves

How to raise your own currant bushes

The best way of propagating red currants is from cuttings about 15 in. long. In mid-October select the straightest shoots of the current year's growth and cut them off low down, just above a bud.

Cut off any softwood at the tip (there should not be more than an inch or so), cutting just above a bud; do not cut if the cutting is brown to the tip. Trim the lower end just below a bud to produce a cutting about 15 in. long.

Rub off all but the top four or five buds on the cutting. Buds left on lower down will produce suckers that may prevent the formation of a leg. Dip the lower end of each cutting in hormone rooting powder.

Root the cuttings in a trench prepared in the same way as for gooseberry cuttings (p. 113). Put them 6 in. apart against the upright face of the slit. Do not plant too deeply; the top 9 in. should be above soil level. Fill in and firm the soil.

Cuttings should have rooted by the following November. Lift them with a fork and replant them in their permanent quarters.

Set the young plants 2 in. lower in the ground than they were as cuttings, and immediately after re-planting shorten branches by half. Then treat them as new plants.

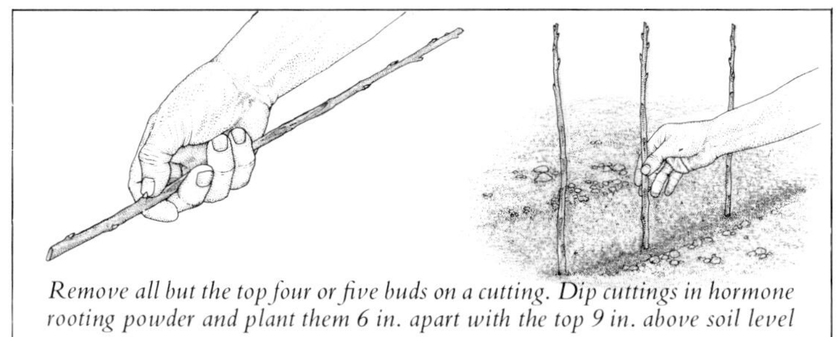

Remove all but the top four or five buds on a cutting. Dip cuttings in hormone rooting powder and plant them 6 in. apart with the top 9 in. above soil level

Varieties of red and white currants to grow

All varieties of red and white currants are self-fertile. The season of use given is for the South; in the North ripening time will be later. Ripening time is an estimate only, and will vary according to the conditions during the season.

Name	Season of use	Remarks
RED CURRANTS		
'Jonkheer van Tets'	Mid–late June	Good cropper. Large fruit. Vigorous, upright growth
'Laxton's No. 1'	End June–early July	Heavy cropper. Good-quality fruit. Growth slightly spreading
'Red Lake'	July	Heavy cropper. Large, good-quality fruit on very long trusses
WHITE CURRANTS		
'White Grape'	End June–early July	Sweet, medium-sized fruits. Good flavour. Vigorous, upright growth

What can go wrong with red and white currants

Aphids and birds are the most common problems in growing red and white currants. If plants show symptoms not described here, turn to the identification chart on page 377. Look up chemicals on page 398 to find proprietary names.

Symptoms	Cause	Cure
Leaves are curled or blistered, often with a reddish tinge; shoot tips may also be distorted	Red currant blister aphids	Spray with a tar oil winter wash in January to kill overwintering eggs. Apply systemic insecticide such as dimethoate or formothion in spring, just before flowering. Repeat after flowering if necessary
Shoots or large branches die back. Coral-red spots appear on dead wood	Coral spot	Cut out all dead shoots to a point at least 2–4 in. below the apparently diseased area and burn. Feed, mulch, water, and/or drain soil as necessary to encourage vigour

Rhubarb – a foretaste of the fruit season to come

Rhubarb 'The Sutton'

Rhubarb can be used for desserts early in the year, before any other fresh fruit is ready. An early, forced crop can be available from January to March. The main crop is from about March to July. Three or four plants will provide enough stems for the average family.

Rhubarb can be grown in the same spot for several years, so fertilise the ground well before planting. If your soil is deep enough, double dig (p. 405) the bed, working farmyard manure or well-rotted garden compost into the second spit. Two weeks before planting, apply a general fertiliser at 3 oz. (3 tablespoons) to the square yard.

Not much is likely to go wrong with rhubarb. Crown rot may occur – buds at the tips of shoots rot and the damage often extends to the rootstock, causing a blackened cavity. If any leaves develop they will be spindly and discoloured and die early. Dig up the plant and burn it; do not put any more plants in the same spot.

Growing rhubarb from seed

Rhubarb can be raised from seed, but the plants may be inferior and stems will not be ready for picking for the first two years. Suitable varieties for sowing are 'Prince Albert' (early) and 'Victoria' (late).

Sow seeds in a frame in early March, in drills ½ in. deep and 12 in. apart, or sow outdoors in April in the same way. Thin seedlings to 6 in. and in the following March transplant to a permanent bed. Then treat in the same way as a rootstock.

Growing rhubarb from rootstocks

March is the best time to plant rootstocks. Either buy them from a nursery, or lift an established plant and divide the roots. Suitable varieties are 'Hawke's Champagne', 'The Sutton' – which is slow to bolt (run to seed) – and 'Timperley Early'.

Dig holes 3 ft apart, deep enough to take the whole of the woody part of the rootstock. New shoots should just be showing above the soil. Plant very firmly by treading the soil round the roots. Water the plant freely if the ground is dry.

Do not pick any of the rhubarb stems in the first year, and in the second year pick only a few stems. Pick rhubarb by holding the stem as low as possible and making a twisting and pulling movement. Do not damage any immature shoots.

Keep the bed well mulched. If any flowering spikes appear, cut them off at once. Always keep the bed well watered; in summer feed regularly with a general liquid fertiliser.

After pulling the last stems at the end of July, dress the ground with a general fertiliser such as Growmore – 4–5 oz. (4–5 tablespoons) to the square yard.

Forcing rhubarb for eating out of season

Shoots are forced into growth for early cropping by excluding light from the plant. This can be done either in a shed or outdoors. A suitable variety is 'Timperley Early'.

In November select and lift with a spade one or two strong plants, two years old or more. Turn them upside-down on the plot to expose their roots to frost and bring on dormancy (winter resting period).

In December put the plants under cover the right way up – the increased warmth will force them into early growth. Place them in a dark shed, in boxes if desired. The roots can be covered with straw or peat, but it is not essential. Keep them moderately moist.

If the shed is not completely dark, cover plants with a deep, upturned box, such as a tea-chest, to keep out the light. The temperature should be 7–18°C (45–64°F).

For a succession of supplies, more plants can be exposed and then put under cover at intervals.

An alternative method of forcing is to put the plants in a greenhouse border beneath the staging. Drape black polythene round the staging and the bed to keep the growth in the dark. Keep the soil dampened. Depending on the temperature, stems should be ready for pulling from four to eight weeks later.

Rhubarb can also be forced in its permanent bed. Cover the roots with a tea-chest or similar box. Weight it or rope it down.

Straw or fresh manure and leaves banked round the box will generate some heat and increase the rate of growth, but this is not essential.

After about two months inspect the rhubarb crowns to check that new growth has started. Pick stems when they are 10–12 in. long.

FORCING RHUBARB

Place roots for forcing in a dark shed. Cover them if necessary, to keep out light

Strawberries – a summer treat that may still be tasted in October

Strawberry 'Royal Sovereign'

There are two types of strawberry, those that carry only one crop each year in late June or early July, and those – known as perpetual or ever-bearing – that produce several crops between June and October. Perpetual varieties are generally less hardy than one-crop varieties.

The average family will need 24–36 plants. Buy stock certified free of virus disease if possible.

Strawberries will grow in all rich, well-drained but moisture-retaining soils, except very chalky ones. Plant in an open, sunny bed, ideally facing south. Put early varieties where they are sheltered from cold winds, and do not grow in frost pockets.

Preparing the ground and planting

For one-crop varieties, the best time to plant is from July to early September. Plant perpetual varieties in the spring.

Double dig the bed (p. 405), if the soil is deep enough, two or three weeks before planting. Remove weeds and add well-rotted manure or garden compost to the top spit – one 2 gallon bucket per square yard for poor soil, half for good loam.

Dig well in, and lightly fork in a general fertiliser such as Growmore at 3 oz. (3 tablespoons) to the square yard; rake to an even tilth.

Plant 18 in. apart in rows 30 in. apart. Soak plants that are in peat pots for an hour first; plant pots so they are just covered with soil. Plant unpotted strawberries in moist soil. Dig a hole 1 or 2 in. deeper than the roots, and put the plant on a mound with its roots spread out.

Place the upper part of the roots (the crown) level with the surface. If it is buried, the crown bud may rot; if its base is exposed, the roots may dry out. Fill in and firm round carefully. Water in dry weather.

Spread roots on a mound so the crown is level with the surface

Tending strawberries from planting to harvesting

Water regularly in dry weather for the first few weeks after planting. Lack of water at this time can retard growth or kill the plants.

In autumn, to conserve plants' energy, clip off any runners that have grown. In January apply ½ oz. (1 dessertspoon) of sulphate of potash to the square yard. If growth is generally poor, spread ½ oz. (1 dessertspoon) of sulphate of ammonia to the square yard along rows in early April. Avoid the foliage. In spring hoe shallowly to control weeds.

In their first season remove the blossoms from one-crop strawberries planted in late autumn or spring. Those planted from the previous July to early September can bear fruit. On perpetual varieties remove flowers until late May, to ensure a good crop later in the year.

When the developing fruits are heavy enough to almost reach the ground (about May for one-crop varieties), scatter slug pellets about 6 in. apart round plants. At the same time tuck clean straw (preferably barley straw) beneath fruit and round plants, covering the pellets. Do not lay straw earlier, as it increases the risk of damage from later frosts.

An alternative is to use strawberry mats – which fit like a collar round the plant – or polythene sheeting. Be sure the soil is moist before laying polythene. Supports can also be made from loops of galvanised wire inserted in the soil beside plants. Hang one stem over each support. This method is useful for plants grown in pots or in a greenhouse.

Protect strawberries from birds by fixing nylon netting over canes inserted in the soil beside plants.

Water during dry spells, and just before ripening, to swell the fruit. During ripening, too much watering can result in grey mould. Pick strawberries complete with stalks. Avoid handling, as they bruise easily.

PROTECTING YOUNG PLANTS AND FRUIT

To keep fruit clean and away from the soil, use special mats or clean straw

Supports can be made with loops of galvanised wire. Hang one stem over each

Clearing out the strawberry bed

On one-crop varieties, as soon as all fruit has been picked, fork the straw well up to the plants and set light to it to burn off the leaves. This will not harm the plants but will destroy old, diseased leaves and kill off any pests. New leaves will soon show through and will now have plenty of light and air.

If burning is not practicable, or cannot be done immediately after picking, cut plants down with shears to about 3 in. above the crown. Pull off any unwanted runners or old, diseased leaves and remove mats or polythene. Rake off litter and burn.

Renew strawberry plants every two or three years. After this they will not crop so heavily and disease is more likely. New plants can be easily raised from existing plants.

Perpetual varieties will carry on cropping until the autumn frosts. Cover them with cloches early in

Cloche for frost protection

October, to ensure fruit for picking up to late October and beyond.

Do not burn leaves off perpetuals as this will destroy new growth, but clear away some of the old leaves. Renew plants after one or two seasons of fruiting.

CUTTING DOWN ONE-CROP STRAWBERRIES

When all fruit is picked, fork straw up to the plant and set light to it to burn off leaves and kill off pests

Alternatively, cut plants with shears to 3 in. above the crown. Pull off old leaves and unwanted runners

Raising new plants from runners

Strawberries can be raised from runners. In June or July choose strong, healthy parent plants that have been cropping well. Select four strong runners from each, and extend them out from the plants.

Runners rooted in pots are easier to transplant. Fill sufficient 3 in. pots with any John Innes or soilless potting compost. On each runner choose the embryo plant – a strong tuft of leaves – nearest to the parent and, with a trowel, dig a hole beneath it big enough to accommodate the pot.

Sink the pot to its rim in the hole, then pin the runner to the compost in the pot. Use a 6 in. piece of galvanised wire bent to a U-shape. Do not sever the runner between the parent and the young plant, but pinch it off just beyond the pot. Ensure the compost never dries out.

Pegged-down runners are ready for planting four to six weeks later. In August sever the runner connecting each new plant to its parent. Continue to water thoroughly, and one week later carefully lift new plants and transfer them to their permanent positions. Then tend them in the same way as newly planted strawberries.

1 *In June or July extend four runners from a strong, healthy plant*

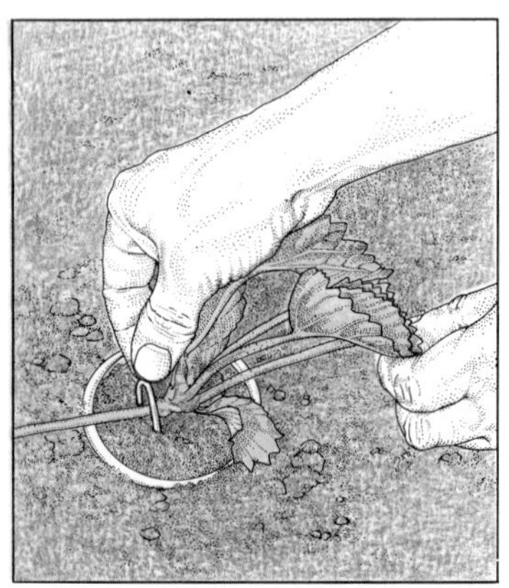

2 *Pin an embryo plant on each runner to a pot of compost buried just beneath it*

3 *Nip off the runner beyond the new plant; do not cut it from its parent*

4 *Sever from its parent four to six weeks later and transplant a week later*

Greenhouse gardening

Even a small greenhouse opens up vast new possibilities – from early vegetables to orchids. Equipment available can give complete, automatic control of cultivation

A greenhouse can free a gardener from the tyranny of the weather. Under cover of glass, he can grow plants that would suffer from cold, heavy rain and wind if they were grown in the open.

Greenhouses may be either heated or unheated. An unheated greenhouse will not keep out frost, but it creates warmer conditions for plants in the growing season. This extra heat speeds the ripening of crops, and improves the flowering of many decorative plants. An unheated greenhouse also protects plants from strong winds and rain and from attacks by birds, animals and some other pests.

Perhaps its most valuable function is to lengthen the growing season. Plants can be started into growth early in the spring, and either kept in the greenhouse or planted out in the garden. In the greenhouse, plants will grow on well into the autumn.

This artificial growing season is achieved in spring by the glass trapping the heat of the sun on clear days, and in autumn by retaining warmth which has built up in the soil and brickwork during summer.

Unheated greenhouses are widely used to grow a crop of tomatoes during spring and summer, and then for growing late-flowering chrysanthemums in autumn, when the tomato plants have been discarded. Many gardeners now also use them for grapes and melons.

For the gardener who is interested in obtaining the finest blooms, an unheated house is invaluable for growing a wide range of half-hardy shrubs, annuals, lilies, gladioli and many other bulbs.

All out-of-season vegetables normally grown under frames or cloches, such as lettuces, carrots, radishes, potatoes and French beans, can be grown just as well in an unheated greenhouse.

When artificial heat is introduced into a greenhouse, the range of plants that can be grown increases greatly, as tender plants which would never survive a British winter can be kept under perfect conditions.

By installing automatic equipment for heating, ventilation, shading and watering, environmental control is almost total.

But before starting greenhouse gardening, decide how much money you are prepared to spend on fuel. A guide to the amount of fuel needed to heat greenhouses of different sizes is given on page 141.

Heated greenhouses are classified according to the minimum temperature maintained. A cool house is kept above 4°C (40°F) and a warm house above 13°C (55°F). Warm houses are now expensive to run because of fuel costs, and are not common. In the past, wealthy gardeners also operated stove houses, kept above 18°C (64°F). However, many plants grown in a stove house will grow well in a warm house, and the stove is now very rare.

A cool house will support a worldwide range of plants, ranging from the less-hardy seedlings to exotic blooms.

Cool house plants that live for many years include pelargoniums, fuchsias, begonias, orchids and perpetual-flowering carnations.

A cool greenhouse is particularly useful for growing flowering plants from seeds or cuttings early in the year, to be planted in the garden at the beginning of summer. This is the technique known as bedding, used widely in public parks. Zonal pelargoniums (geraniums) and the fibrous-rooted begonias are two of the most popular bedding plants.

Strelitzia reginae
(Bird of paradise flower)

How to use a greenhouse – with and without heating

These two greenhouses are both 10 ft × 6 ft in size, but are used for different purposes. The one on the left has no artificial heating and is called a cold house. The one on the right is kept heated in winter to a minimum temperature of 4–7°C (40–45°F) and is called a cool house. Both are illustrated as they would be used in June.

Cold greenhouse To keep a steady stream of fresh air flowing around the plants, there are side ventilators near the base of the wall through which cool air enters. In the roof are four large ventilators, to let out air that has become heated by the sun.

In summer the vents, and perhaps also the doors, are left fully open day and night. In spring and autumn they are opened in the morning if the day promises to be warm or sunny, and closed in the evening.

On hot summer days, however, ventilation is not sufficient. To prevent the temperature rising so high that plants are damaged, the glass is shaded by a rain-resistant electrostatic shading, painted on at the start of warm weather but easily brushed off when the weather cools.

Another aid to cooling is an electric fan placed on the floor or secured to an end wall. It can be turned on to circulate the air.

Along one side of the greenhouse, wooden-slat staging holds a selection of flowering plants in pots. They are standing on trays of wet sand which keeps them constantly watered. The flow of water to the sand is controlled by a cistern attached to the wall.

On the opposite side there is an open border. The existing soil has been dug over and enriched with peat or leaf-mould. On heavy, clay soil, coarse sand would be added. To the left are tomatoes, and to the right a grape vine. A hose from a cistern waters the soil automatically.

Outside the greenhouse, some late-flowering chrysanthemums are growing in pots. They will be brought inside in September when the tomatoes are finished, and will flower in October and November.

Heated greenhouse The greenhouse on the right is heated over winter to 4–7°C (40–45°F). It also has automatic ventilation.

The top ventilator is operated by a special temperature-sensitive device (p. 143) which opens it partially when the temperature inside rises above 21°C (70°F). As the temperature rises even higher, the vent is opened to its full extent.

The shading consists of blinds on the inside of the glass, which are drawn down manually when the sun shines strongly. The blinds are rolled back when the sun is obscured. Automatic blinds, fitted to the outside of the glass, are available, but they are expensive as they have to be made to measure.

Heating is supplied by a 2500 watt fan heater. When the temperature inside the greenhouse falls below 4–7°C (40–45°F), the fan is switched on by a thermostat.

In the left-hand corner is a small mist propagator for rooting cuttings. An alternative would be a heated propagating case without the mist unit. This would be cheaper, but not so effective with difficult-to-root cuttings. However, it is also useful for germinating seeds in February or early March. Later on, most seeds can be germinated in a pot covered with plastic or glass.

Alongside the propagator are rows of cuttings which have rooted. Later, they will be put into a cold frame for hardening off and transplanted into the garden next spring.

The rest of the staging is covered with trays of wet sand, to provide automatic watering for pot plants.

Outside the greenhouse are three frames. The one on the left, heated by electric cables, holds young plants of cineraria, calceolaria and *Solanum capsicastrum*. The two right-hand frames, with no artificial heating, are being used to grow melons.

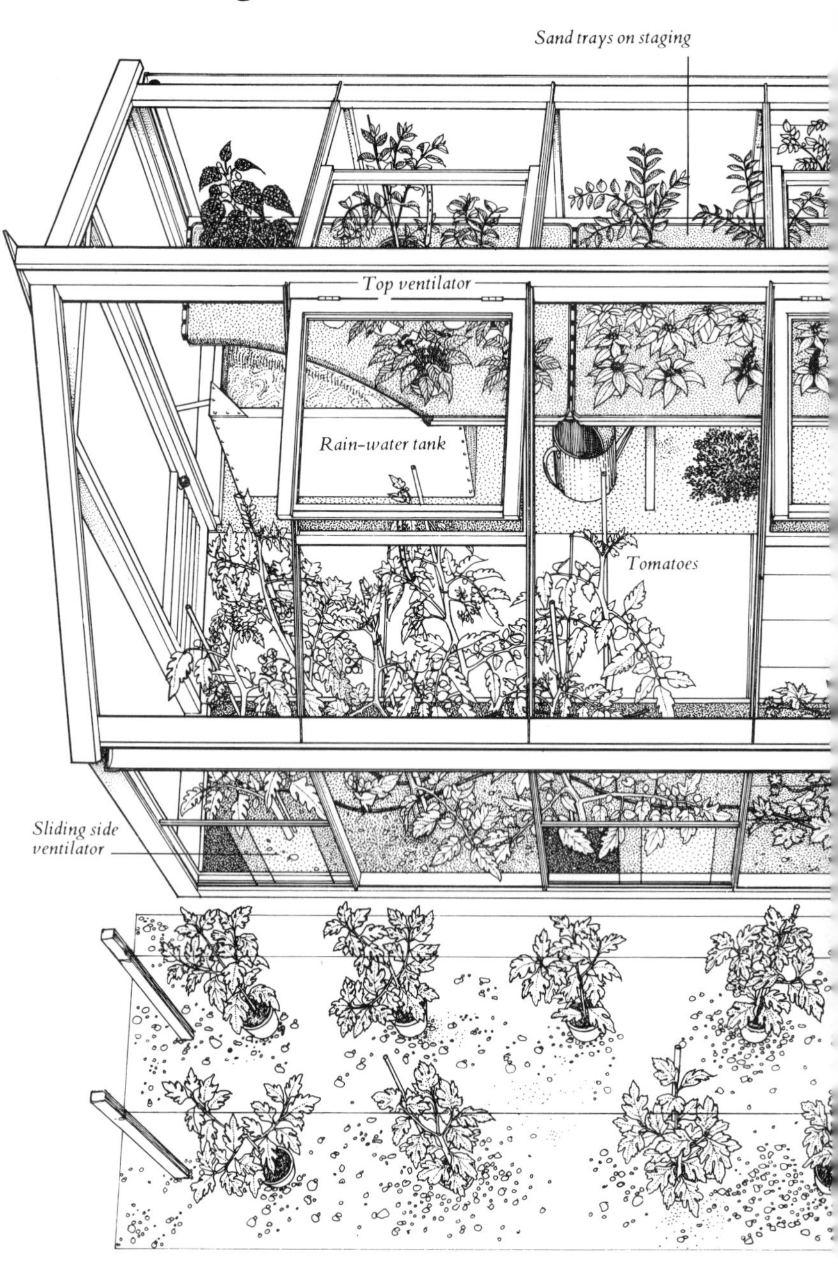

Standing ground for late-flowering chrysanthemums

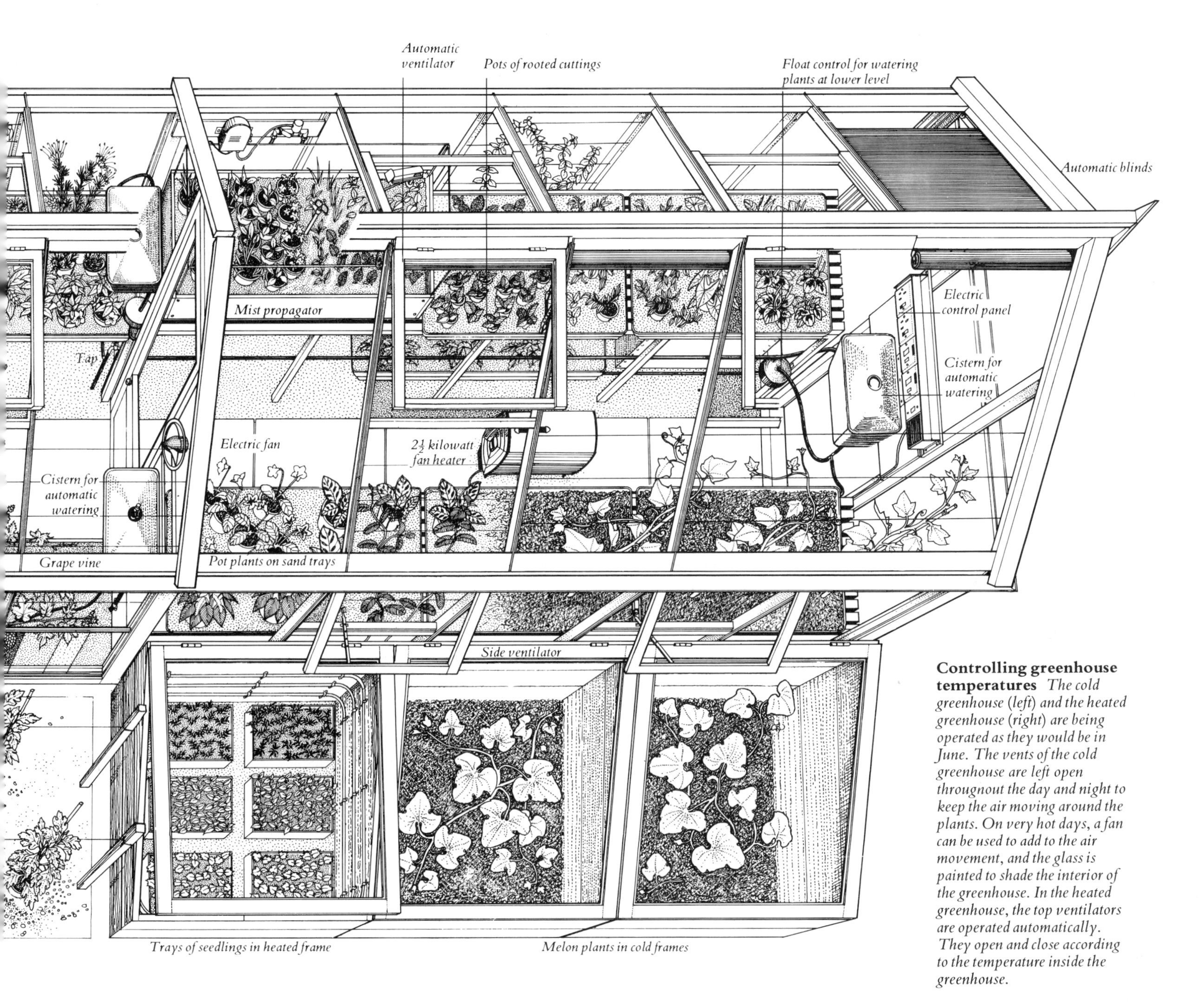

Controlling greenhouse temperatures *The cold greenhouse (left) and the heated greenhouse (right) are being operated as they would be in June. The vents of the cold greenhouse are left open througnout the day and night to keep the air moving around the plants. On very hot days, a fan can be used to add to the air movement, and the glass is painted to shade the interior of the greenhouse. In the heated greenhouse, the top ventilators are operated automatically. They open and close according to the temperature inside the greenhouse.*

How to choose a greenhouse

The first decision when buying a greenhouse, frame or cloche is whether to choose glass or plastic.

The main advantage of glass for greenhouses is that short-wave radiations from the sun pass through it easily, but once they are converted into long-wave heat radiations the glass becomes a barrier, and so the heat is retained inside the greenhouse.

Plastic takes in the rays but does not trap them, so that when the sun goes in the house cools down again very quickly.

Horticultural grades of polythene are available for greenhouses, and these last longer than ordinary plastic sheeting. Corrugated plastic should last about five years and is quite cheap to buy. A recently introduced acrylic plastic is very similar to glass, but is expensive.

Plastic scratches more easily than glass and the scratches become ingrained with dirt.

Condensation can also be a problem because whereas on glass the moisture forms a film, on plastic it collects, obscuring the light and causing drips. This difficulty can be overcome with the efficient use of fan ventilation.

However, for cloches and frames plastic is cheaper, easier to erect and gives excellent results where only temporary protection is needed.

Greenhouse design and shape

There are three basic shapes of greenhouse: the vertical-sided, rectangular or square house; the sloping-sided house (known as the Dutch-light type); and the lean-to. Other shaped houses – round, dome-shaped and hexagonal – are also available. They are useful for displaying ornamental plants, but are not so practical for general greenhouse work or growing a selection of different plants.

A greenhouse with a sloping side or semi-circular roof captures more light and warmth because of the angle at which the glass is set to the sun's rays. The maximum amount of sunlight goes into the greenhouse, and the least is reflected, when the rays strike the glass at a right angle. The more acute the angle at which the rays strike, the more light is reflected and the less absorbed. However, sides that are too severely sloped will interfere with the greenhouse staging and tall plants.

A greenhouse with glass sides down to ground level is the most versatile. Staging can be fitted, and it is possible to grow plants below it as well as on top. Such a greenhouse is ideal for tall-growing plants that need plenty of light, such as tomatoes, chrysanthemums and carnations.

Other greenhouses have a solid base of brick, concrete or wood. Often there is sufficient light under the staging to grow shade-loving plants, or the area may be blacked out for forcing and blanching vegetables.

A lean-to can be more economical to heat than a free-standing greenhouse. If it is set against a brick wall facing south, the wall will act as a heat store, radiating warmth overnight after accumulating it during the day. However, a common fault of lean-to structures is that the roof does not slope enough. A flat roof collects the dirt, dead leaves and other debris.

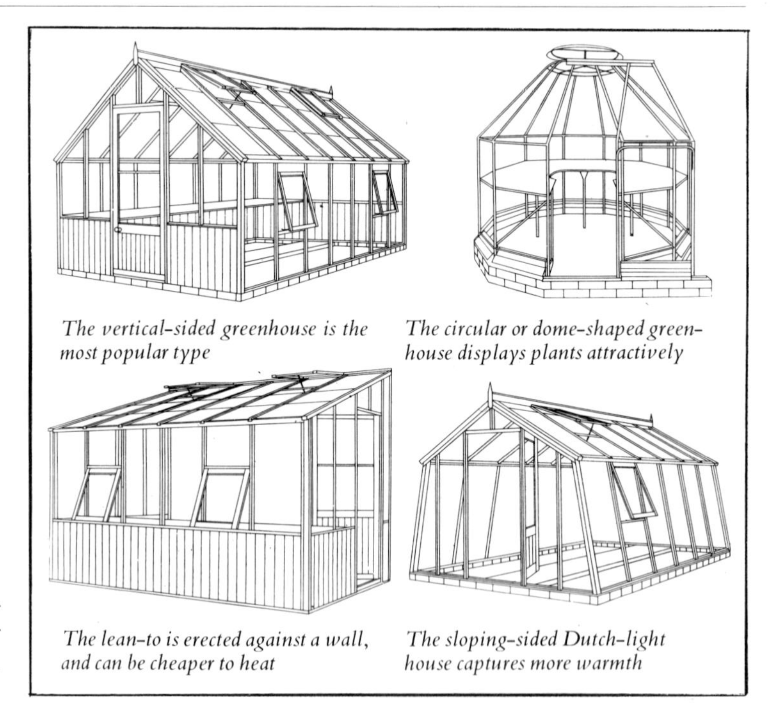

The vertical-sided greenhouse is the most popular type

The circular or dome-shaped greenhouse displays plants attractively

The lean-to is erected against a wall, and can be cheaper to heat

The sloping-sided Dutch-light house captures more warmth

The different kinds of framework

The framework of a greenhouse should have strength, durability and also an attractive appearance. Aluminium alloy, which may be stove-enamelled for a better appearance, is lightweight, strong, needs no painting and cannot warp or rot.

Galvanised iron is also strong, but needs painting occasionally to keep out rust. Painting is best done before glazing, and the framework should be examined every year for signs of wear and tear.

Various woods are used in greenhouse construction. Avoid the cheaper kinds, which have poor weather-resistance and will demand constant rot-proofing treatment. Red cedar lasts well, looks attractive, and is relatively inexpensive. Oak is sometimes used but can warp. Teak is excellent but often costly. Timber framework is available that holds the glass in slots, thus avoiding the use of putty and allowing easy glass removal for roof maintenance. Timber frames should be treated with wood preservatives or water repellents by the supplier before they are delivered.

Prefabricated greenhouses are available for erection by the buyer. It is wise to buy base plinths of concrete, which are generally available as an extra. With timber greenhouses, wooden base walls are usually supplied, but if brick or concrete walls are wanted, the purchaser will usually have to make them. Plans for such walls are supplied by the makers.

When the greenhouse is to be erected without a concrete plinth, the soil can be rammed firm and spread with shingle to make an excellent floor. The shingle, which looks neat, will hold moisture after damping down in summer, and therefore maintain humidity.

What to look for when buying

Examine as many makers' catalogues as possible before buying. Give preference to a greenhouse as large as you can afford, not forgetting maintenance and heating. A greenhouse is so useful and fascinating that space soon becomes filled, and the owner can quickly regret having bought a small one. If you intend to have staging on both sides of the greenhouse it is best to choose one 8 ft wide, to provide working space.

Some of the larger greenhouses have compartments with communicating doors. In this way different temperatures and conditions for a variety of plants can be maintained.

Strength of framework is always important, but especially in windy areas and when the roof is to be used to support hanging baskets of plants. Timber frames should be examined for knot holes which can cause weakness. A boarded base should be strong and thick. The roof should have an adequate slope to run condensation to one side.

Sliding doors are an advantage if they are well fitted. They cannot slam, are adjustable for extra ventilation and are space saving.

Most ventilators are still of the conventional hinged type. Louvred vents are a modern innovation, but some are not close shutting. Always make sure there are at least two ventilators, both side and top. Ideally there should be a side and top ventilator on each side of the house for every 4 ft of glass. They can then be used according to wind direction.

Where to site the greenhouse

A greenhouse should be given an open position where it receives all the light available. Never site a greenhouse next to trees. They cast shade, dirty the glass and can cause damage with falling branches.

Rising ground on the north or east side can shelter a site from cold winds.

It is convenient to have the greenhouse near the house, for easy access and to provide electricity and water.

A rectangular greenhouse is best sited so that its shorter sides face east and west. The longer sides, where the plants are growing, then capture more light in winter, and in summer probably will need shading only on the side facing south.

All these factors make for an ideal site. Lack of some, or even all of them, however, does not rule out the probability of success with a greenhouse. For example, if your only possible site is in almost constant shade, you could specialise in shade-loving plants.

Hints on erecting the greenhouse

All prefabricated greenhouses are delivered with full instructions for erection. Even the larger ones can be put up with only one helper – some can even be erected single-handed. Level and firm the ground some time before erection, and if the greenhouse is larger than 8 ft × 6 ft, make a foundation for it. This need not be elaborate, especially if the house is mounted on concrete. One way of making a foundation is to dig out a shallow trench and fill it with very liquid concrete, which finds its own level by flowing. Any concrete foundation or base supplied with the greenhouse can then be set on this. However, a greenhouse with base walls of brick needs a base and foundation built by a professional. Glass is best handled when it is dry, but not cold. Painting is best done before the glass is put in.

Heating the greenhouse

Fuel costs and heat conservation

In practice there is little difference between the costs of the various fuels. The greater efficiency of electricity, for instance, tends to balance out its slightly higher costs.

It is often more economical to use two fuels rather than one for heating. The cheaper, such as paraffin, is used for background warmth, and the dearer, such as electricity, is used to attain maximum heat with thermostatic control. Unfortunately thermostatic control is difficult on storage heaters that use off-peak electricity, making them unsuitable.

In an open position the winter sun can provide free warmth. A lean-to may be against a wall that will store outside warmth or warmth from the house, and maintain frost-free conditions overnight. Winds carry away heat, and in windy districts a windbreak of trees helps reduce fuel bills.

Many larger greenhouses can be divided into compartments with communicating doors, to provide different temperatures and conditions under the same roof. If there are three compartments, the coolest should be nearest the outside door, and the warmest in the centre.

Fit draught-excluding material to doors and ventilators if necessary.

The correct amount of heat needed

The minimum safe temperature must be maintained during severe cold spells. Consequently, the amount of heat loss during the coldest conditions must be known, and heating equipment capable of compensating for it needs to be installed. Heat loss from all-glass greenhouses is given in the table below.

These figures assume an outside temperature of –7°C (19°F). They give the minimum output of heat needed in watts for electrical equipment and British Thermal Units per hour for oil, gas or solid fuel. The figures apply to all-glass greenhouses. For a house with brick or concrete base walls the figures will be lower. However, it is always safer to assume maximum heat losses.

If you have a greenhouse 6 ft × 10 ft, you will see that a heater with an output capable of 3580 watts or 12,200 BTU/hr is recommended if you want a winter minimum temperature of 13°C (55°F), even during very cold weather.

Greenhouse size (ft)	**Desired temperature (minimum)** 13°C (55°F)		7°C (45°F)		4°C (40°F)	
	Watts	BTU/hr	Watts	BTU/hr	Watts	BTU/hr
5 × 6	2050	7000	1470	5000	1200	4000
6 × 6	2460	8400	1750	6000	1400	4800
6 × 8	2930	10,000	2500	7100	1700	5700
6 × 10	3580	12,200	2550	8750	2000	7000
6 × 14	4310	14,700	3100	10,500	2500	8400
8 × 8	3580	12,200	2550	8750	2000	7000
8 × 10	4000	13,650	2850	9750	2300	7800
8 × 12	4520	15,400	3250	11,000	2600	8800
8 × 14	4790	16,300	3400	11,600	2700	9300
10 × 10	5000	17,100	3600	12,250	2900	9800
10 × 15	6640	22,600	4750	16,100	3800	12,900
10 × 20	7920	27,600	5800	19,700	4700	15,800

Electricity – the most practical heating

The most efficient and useful form of heating for the average greenhouse is electricity.

It is most likely to be trouble-free, gives excellent automatic control, produces no harmful fumes and does not raise humidity in winter. There is no need to transport or store fuel, and equipment is usually compact.

If you intend to use electricity, have a permanent power supply installed by a qualified electrician.

For the amateur's greenhouse, the fan heater is the most popular. It is cheap to install – it plugs into a 13 amp waterproof socket – and is portable.

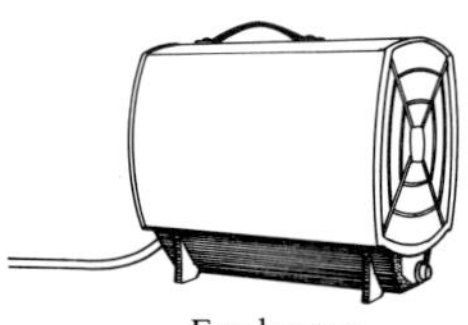

Fan heater

Fan heaters usually incorporate a thermostat which controls the fan and the heat output simultaneously.

The air circulation is good for the plants and reduces fungus diseases. A disadvantage is that if the fan breaks down, heat loss is total.

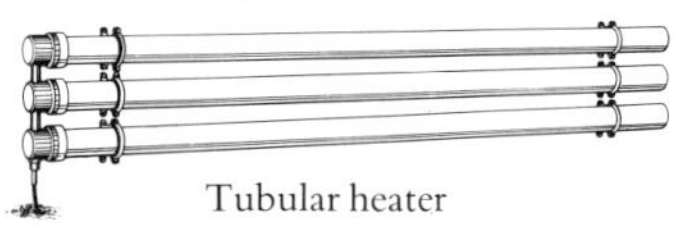

Tubular heater

Tubular heaters – aluminium tubes sealed at both ends and containing a heating element – are also highly efficient. They are screwed to the uprights around the sides of the greenhouse 7 in. clear of the floor and, if they are in banks, with an inch between the tubes. They are often sold in banks of three or four, but the heat distribution is better if they are fitted singly all round the greenhouse. They respond well to thermostatic control, and if one fails, the others should keep out the frost.

Convector heaters, which produce a current of warm air without a fan, are fairly inexpensive and easy to install, but heat distribution is not as good as with fan or tubular heaters. If you are using convectors, have one each end of the greenhouse.

Electric storage heaters, using off-peak electricity, are not really suitable because the heat output cannot be efficiently controlled.

Always use electrical equipment designed for the greenhouse. Domestic equipment is not satisfactory and can be dangerous.

For more economic use of electricity, soil-warming cables, used with air-warming, are invaluable.

Plants will not grow actively during the colder months unless they have a root temperature of 10–13°C (50–55°F). To maintain this by warming the air is very expensive, but cables warm the soil cheaply.

The cables are not expensive to buy and are easy to install. They are operated by mains electricity.

On an open bench for winter-flowering pot plants like cinerarias or calceolarias, the cables should be laid on 2 in. of sand, compost or soil and covered with another 1 in. of the same material.

In a greenhouse border, for tomatoes or other early salad crops, the cables should be buried 9 in. deep so that they will not be disturbed. For details of how to buy and install cables, see page 145.

To provide warm conditions for plants growing actively in cold months, sink pots into peat spread over soil-warming cables. Form a case with sheets of glass. Cables can also be laid 9 in. deep in a greenhouse border to provide warmth for tomatoes and other early crops

Paraffin, gas and hot-water systems

Paraffin heaters are cheaper to buy than electrical heaters, but running costs are about the same. The best kind to use are those that burn with a blue flame.

They produce a certain amount of carbon dioxide and water vapour, which can be beneficial to plants. It is important to use good-quality oil because low-grade oil, when burnt, can give off sulphur fumes which will damage plants. However, with modern paraffin heaters there is a flue which takes the fumes outside the greenhouse. The flue also reduces condensation in the greenhouse, which can harm the plants in winter.

Some paraffin heaters are fitted with an automatic temperature control, but the pilot flame burns continuously and may use the equivalent of 500 watts of electricity an hour, in addition to the fuel for heating.

Paraffin heaters are probably most useful as emergency heating during cold spells to supplement electrical heating, or during power cuts.

Hot-water pipes or natural gas heaters can be used for heating the greenhouse, but they are costly to install.

Aluminium hot-water pipes round the sides of the greenhouse, powered by a solid fuel, oil or gas-fired boiler are good for maintaining higher temperatures, but although they can be thermostatically controlled this is not really efficient. The pipes retain the heat and do not respond quickly to temperature changes.

Heaters that operate on natural gas are perfectly safe for plants, whereas coal gas is poisonous. For natural gas heating a properly installed supply is essential, and can be laid in the same trench as the electricity cable. However, unless the greenhouse is close to the house, this is costly. Natural gas heaters respond well to automatic control, so once installed are quite economical to run.

They are probably best for a lean-to greenhouse where the house itself is heated by gas central heating.

Thermostatic control of heating

Most greenhouse heaters have a thermostat fitted, which regulates temperature to one or two degrees.

Electrical heating allows very accurate control, paraffin and gas slightly less. Hot-water systems are more difficult to control.

The thermostat should be easily adjustable and graduated in degrees. However, it is best set with a minimum/maximum thermometer placed separately in the greenhouse to record the highest and lowest temperatures since the previous day. The heater is adjusted so that the minimum temperature does not drop below the level required.

Installing essential equipment

Greenhouse staging and shelving

The simplest form of staging is the slatted wooden type. To provide humidity in summer, the staging should be covered with a 1 in. layer of moist sand resting on either polythene sheeting or on special sand trays. Pot plants standing on the sand will draw up moisture through their drainage holes by capillary action. The sand can be kept moist manually or automatically by one of the methods described overleaf. In winter, when high humidity is not wanted, the sand should be cleared to allow good air circulation.

In greenhouses heated by hot-water pipes or electric heating tubes, it is sometimes possible to run these under that part of the staging used for propagation.

Oil or electric convection heaters can also be put under the staging but care is obviously needed to avoid overheating: if you use these heaters, install asbestos or metal staging.

Shelves above the staging can be used to provide extra room for pots or seed trays, and to accommodate trailing plants.

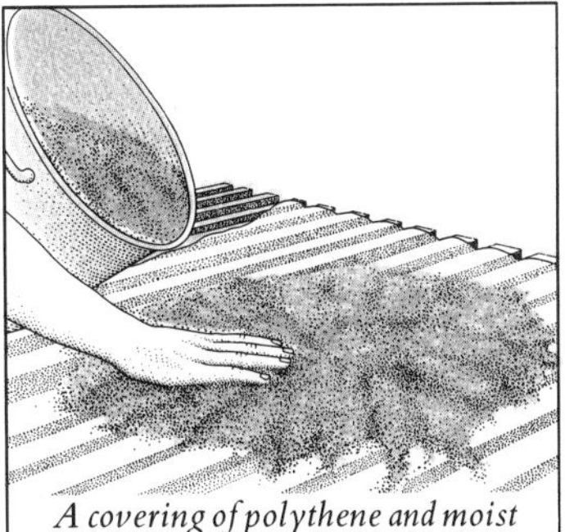

A covering of polythene and moist sand on the staging adds humidity

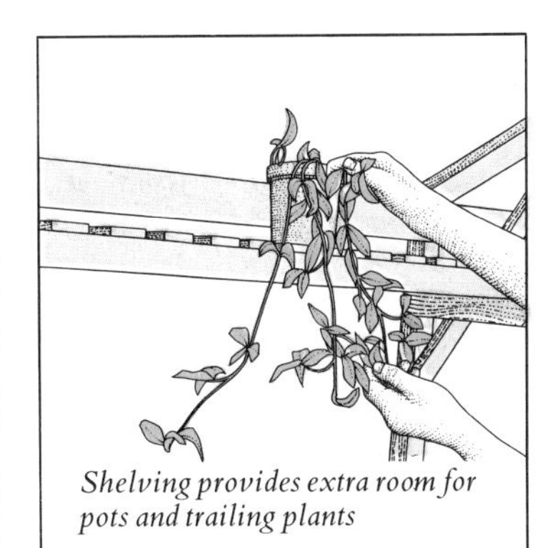

Shelving provides extra room for pots and trailing plants

Providing adequate ventilation

A greenhouse needs at least two ventilators in the roof and some low-positioned ventilators at the side, otherwise it is likely to become too hot in summer. When top vents and side vents are open at the same time a rapid change of air takes place.

Sliding side vents also allow access to the area under staging, for cultivation and the addition or removal of pots or boxes.

Top vents, and sometimes side vents, can be fitted with automatic openers. A compound inside the unit expands or contracts with temperature changes and motivates a piston system of levers.

An alternative form of ventilation is by an electric extractor fan controlled by a thermostat. The fan is best placed in the apex of the roof, at the end of the greenhouse opposite the door. Various sizes of fan are available. As the fan sucks air out of the greenhouse, sufficient air will usually come in under the door and through gaps under the glass. But during very hot weather the door or vents at a distant point from the fan should be left open to give maximum ventilation.

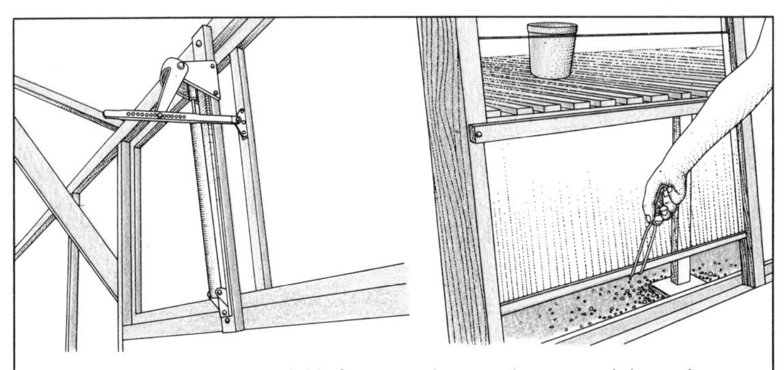

Automatic openers are available for top, and some side, vents. Sliding side vents help to regulate the temperatures inside the greenhouse

Methods of shading the greenhouse

The most efficient method of shading the greenhouse is to use one of the proprietary roller blinds usually made of wood or plastic slats, or woven material such as hessian. These can be lowered on sunny days and rolled back on dull days. They can be fitted to the inside or outside of the roof, and should be set on rails a few inches from the glass.

Automatic blinds are also available but are expensive. Photo-electric cells operate exterior blinds.

An effective, and also cheaper, alternative to blinds is electrostatic shading paint. A concentrate is diluted in water and brushed or sprayed on the outside of the glass. It is waterproof, but will wipe off.

Blinds are usually used only on the greenhouse roof, although they are available to cover the sides as well. A house where the ends face east and west should be shaded on the south side of the roof, one running north and south on both sides.

Electrostatic shading paint can be applied on the side as well as the roof. If the greenhouse runs north-south paint the south, east and west sides, and the roof.

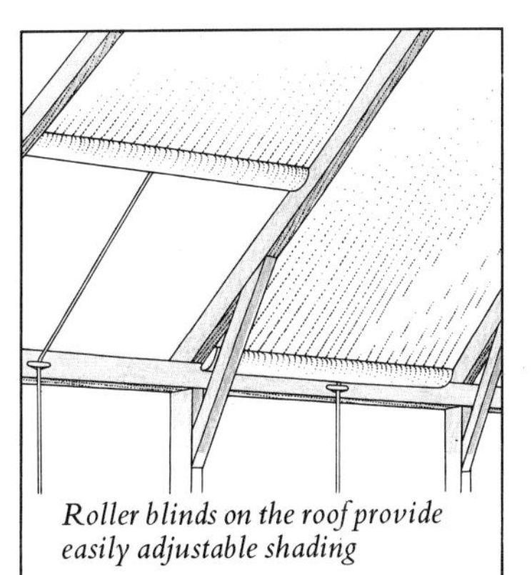

Roller blinds on the roof provide easily adjustable shading

Electrostatic shading paint cannot be washed off by rain

A water supply in the greenhouse

Unless a greenhouse is being erected alongside an existing garden tap, a permanent water supply should be installed. This is work for a plumber, but the expense is justified by the saving in work and time later.

Once a tap has been provided, plants can be watered either by hand, with a hose or automatically.

Automatic watering has several advantages. It is more reliable than hand watering and promotes steady growth of plants. It saves time and enables you to leave the greenhouse unattended for days, or even weeks if suitable equipment is used.

The capillary sand bench is a popular method of automatic watering. Small units are available that can be extended. A unit consists of a plastic tray, a tank or reservoir, and a constant-level float valve.

A layer of sand is placed in the tray according to the supplier's recommendations. Mix the sand with a proprietary non-toxic algicide formulated to prevent the growth of algae. An alternative to sand is a proprietary absorbent mat.

The float valve regulates the level of water in the tray and hence the degree of wetness of the sand.

Use plastic pots with large drainage holes for capillary-bench work. Do not put crocks in when potting.

After potting the plants, press the pots down firmly on the moist sand or matting, so that the compost makes contact with it through the pots' drainage holes.

Water the pots well. This will ensure continued uptake of water from the capillary bench.

Another form of watering is trickle irrigation. This consists of a plastic pipeline with nozzles at intervals which drip water into the pots. The flow of water is usually controlled by a small water tank that siphons over automatically at intervals. The frequency and amount of water supplied is controlled by a valve that has to be adjusted by hand.

This method should not be used for plants which need only occasional and minimal watering, such as cacti.

Nozzles can be held over the pots by wire staples.

The lines can also be used to irrigate sand benches or matting.

A pipeline with misting jets can be fixed permanently over or under staging to provide overhead watering or damping down.

A modern method of automatic watering is by photo-electric control. A photo-electric cell automatically switches on a water valve when the light reaches a certain intensity. The water then runs for a set period. This method can be used to control capillary benches, trickle irrigation and overhead irrigation.

If you find it difficult to know when to water plants a soil-moisture meter is invaluable. It consists of a dial fixed to a long probe. The probe is inserted into the compost in the pot. The dial is calibrated to give 'dry', 'moist' and 'wet' readings. The best meters are also numbered, and have a guide to which numbers are suitable for the various plants.

Capillary bench and moisture meter *The tray of sand is watered by a tank, and pots draw up moisture from the sand. The moisture meter in the pot shows when to water*

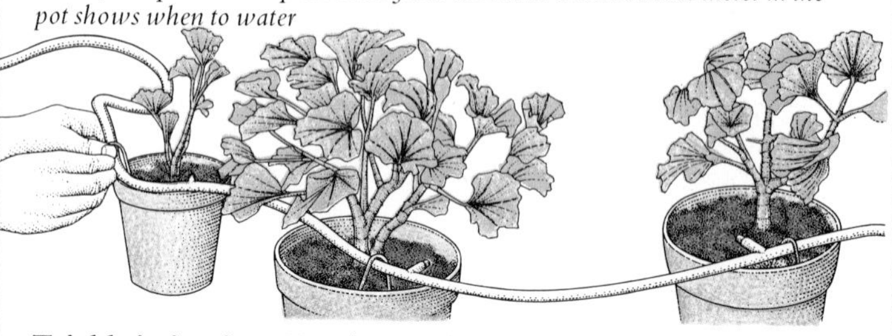

Trickle irrigation *Nozzles on a plastic pipeline drip water on to the compost in pots. Water flow is controlled by a small tank*

Other useful fittings for the greenhouse

There are other fittings that, although not essential, are useful accessories in a greenhouse.

For example, guttering can be fitted to the greenhouse roof to run off rain water. This can be collected in an outside or internal water butt by means of a downpipe, and used for watering plants. A supply of rain water is useful for watering lime-hating plants in hard-water areas. Ensure that an outside butt used for this purpose is covered by a lid to prevent dirt entering. The pipe from the roof should be covered with gauze to trap any debris.

A soil thermometer measures the temperature of soil or compost heated by cables in a propagator, garden frame or greenhouse bed. In a propagating case soil temperatures will need to reach up to 18°C (64°F) for growing plants from seeds and cuttings. Garden frames and greenhouse borders require a winter soil temperature of 10–13°C (50–55°F) for early salad crops.

Artificial lighting is useful for working during dark winter evenings. Moisture-proof electric fittings are available for the greenhouse and should always be installed by a qualified electrician.

Propagators and their uses

A propagator is a box with a transparent cover, which is used for germinating seeds or rooting cuttings. It can be either unheated or heated.

An unheated propagator merely provides a sealed humid environment for cuttings or seeds. A heated propagator also provides bottom heat, which makes rooting and germination more certain. Many storage organs, such as bulbs, corms, rhizomes and tubers, also start into growth earlier if given a little extra warmth.

With large propagators young plants can be kept inside until they are well established. A large unit can also be used as a permanent home for small tropical plants, saving the cost of heating the whole greenhouse to a high temperature.

There are many kinds of propagator. Most are heated by electricity using soil-warming cables. Other propagators using paraffin heaters are less efficient.

The simplest units take one or two seed trays. They can be bought with a heating element fitted into the base and are simply plugged into the mains electricity supply. The trays stand on a layer of sand or gravel. More elaborate versions will take a range of pots and boxes and are thermostatically controlled.

You can make your own propagating case or bench, with a piece of asbestos sheeting slightly narrower than the greenhouse staging and cut to the length you require – 5 ft is a useful size. The asbestos forms a base to stand on the staging, and pieces of board, 9 in. high, are fixed round the sides to make a box. The asbestos sheet can be put directly on to the metal staging supports, saving the cost of the normal top. If this is done the asbestos will need to be supported with wooden or metal cross pieces. Cut three or four drainage holes in the asbestos and spread a 2 in. layer of sand on it. Lay soil-warming cables on this, and cover with a 3 in. layer of moist sand, or 1 in. of sand and 3 in. of peat.

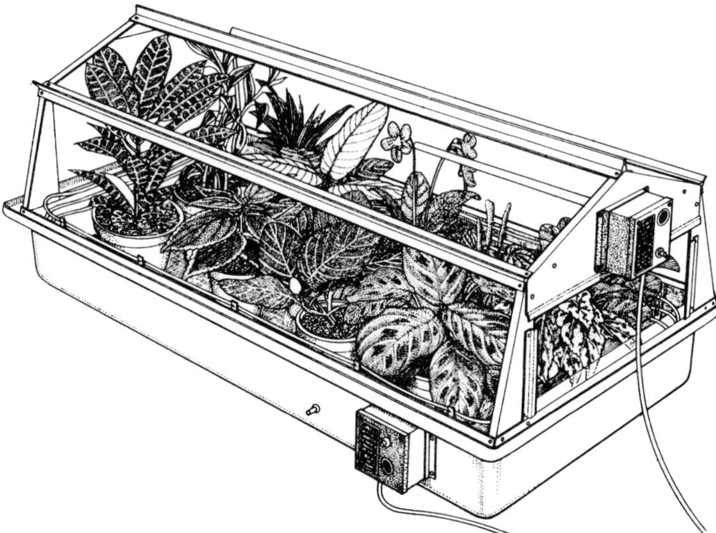

A large heated propagator can be used to house a collection of small tropical plants, saving the cost of heating the whole greenhouse

How to buy and install soil-warming cables

Cuttings root slowly if the soil is cold, and seeds are slow to germinate in cold composts. To heat the soil or compost in a propagator or garden frame by air warmth would be slow and costly. And a high air temperature in winter or spring would tend to produce unwanted top growth in plants being propagated. The simple and economical answer is to use soil-warming cables.

Cables are made in lengths to fit any area and give the correct amount of heat.

To grow early melons or marrows in an outside frame, 5 watts of electricity per square foot will be needed to heat the soil to about 10°C (50°F). For seeds and cuttings in a greenhouse propagator, 15 watts per square foot will give a soil temperature of 18°C (64°F).

The following table shows the wattage and length of cable needed to heat any given area to a soil temperature of 18°C (64°F).

Area (sq. ft)	**Wattage**	**Cable length (ft)**
Up to 6	75	20
12	150	40
25	300	80
50	600	160
100	1200	320
150	1750	470
200	2500	693

Cables are available with a thermostat fitted for economical control of the heat. The wire is fully insulated and usually has a braided metal earthed sleeve for safety. The heating section is usually a distinctive colour and must not be cut.

Cables can be connected direct to the mains supply, or special low-voltage cables can be operated from a transformer – which is safer if there is a risk of damage to cables from garden tools. Those connected to the mains are the most popular.

All mains electrical work should be done by qualified electricians.

Always buy the correct length to fit the area to be heated. Put a 2 in. layer of sand on the base of the propagator and put the cable on this. Lay it backwards and forwards over the whole area to be heated. Avoid sharp bends and lay the cable not less than 4 in. and not more than 8 in. apart. It must never be allowed to cross itself or any adjacent cables. Cover with a further 1 in. of sand and 3 in. of moist peat. Cuttings can be planted directly into the peat, and pots can be sunk in it so that each base is in contact with the sand.

For air warming alone, or in addition to soil warming, cables can be fastened to woodwork around the sides of the frame. With glass-sided frames the cables can be fastened to a row of wooden battens thrust into the ground inside the frame.

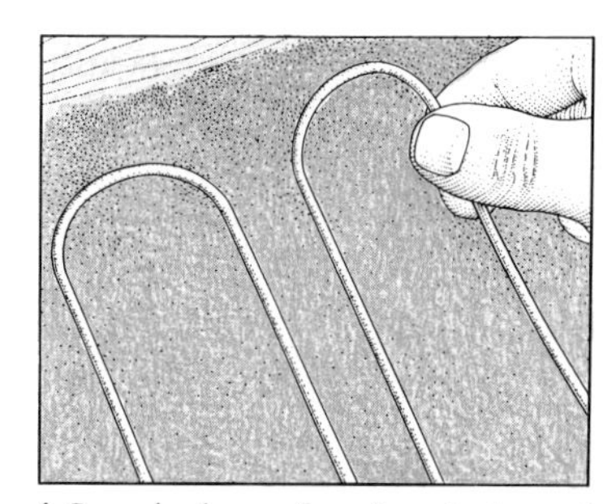

1 *Spread a layer of sand on the base of the case and lay the cable on it*

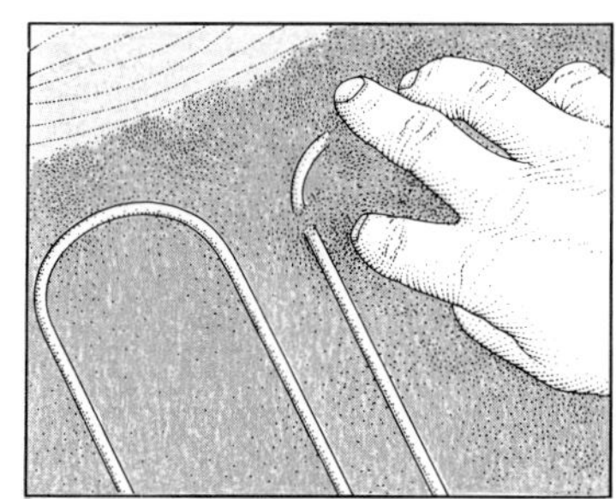

2 *Cover the cable with sand and moist peat to distribute the heat evenly*

Providing the right conditions for plants

Watering, humidity, temperature, shading and feeding can be controlled in the greenhouse to suit almost any kind of plant.

Watering If compost is waterlogged, the roots of the plants rot. Aim for a compost that is just moist. It is always better to be sparing rather than generous with water.

In autumn and winter, when plants are dormant or growing slowly, very little water is required. In spring and summer, when plants are growing strongly, water can be given freely. The amount depends on the size of the plants, their speed of growth, and whether they are bearing fruit or flowering freely. When the weather is cool and daylight poor, plants need far less water than when the temperature is high and conditions are bright.

Generally the best time to water is in the morning. This avoids creating excess moisture at the roots at night, when plants cannot use it, and keeps down overnight humidity.

Always use clean water. If soft water is required for lime-hating plants, collect rain water in a butt, with a lid on it to keep out dirt and leaves.

In warm weather, greenhouse plants benefit from overhead spraying with water. This cleans the foliage, enabling it to breathe.

Humidity and damping down Humidity is the moisture-content of the air. It is increased by spraying plants with water, or by damping down – drenching the walls, floor and staging of the greenhouse (but keeping water off plants with velvety or hairy foliage). The presence of a damp surface, such as a capillary bench, will also raise humidity. Humidity is lowered by watering sparingly and confining water to the area of the plant roots, and by increasing ventilation.

In summer high humidity is usually beneficial to most plants. It reduces the amount of water that foliage loses through transpiration and that compost loses through evaporation. Many popular greenhouse pot plants benefit, in a hot, dry summer, if the greenhouse is damped down at least twice a day, in the morning and evening. However, provided the plants are regularly watered and maximum ventilation given, no popular and 'easy' plant should fail.

In winter, humidity should be kept down; ventilate the greenhouse whenever outside temperature will allow, and water only lightly. High humidity in cold weather creates condensation on the glass (which reduces light), the possibility of fungus diseases and the danger from dripping and waterlogged compost. To keep down humidity in winter, allow capillary watering systems to dry out.

Temperature This should be controlled to suit the type of plants grown. In summer, temperature is reduced by damping down, ventilation and shading. Damping down has a cooling effect because heat is absorbed as the water evaporates, but this will not happen without ventilation. There should be at least two ventilators top and bottom on each side of the house, and in very hot weather the door can be opened.

Shading There are two main reasons for shading a greenhouse.

First, many tropical plants originate from forest areas and thrive best in partially shaded sites.

Second, few plants, however tropical in origin, require a temperature above 29°C (85°F), and for most 24°C (75°F) is adequate. Temperatures above 32°C (90°F) can harm many plants. In warm sunny weather, it is difficult in the average small greenhouse to keep temperatures down with ventilation alone, and shading must also be used.

If possible, shading should be graduated from heavy (an overall solid layer of shading paint) to light (wavy lines in stripes with a space between each line, or sprayed dots), to provide different light requirements for different plants. For example, most cacti need either no shade at all or a very light cover, whereas most ferns need full shade during the brightest, warmest weather. Slatted blinds can be rolled down completely or partially, depending on the amount of sunlight. If shading cannot be graduated, shade-loving plants can be grown under staging or climbing plants.

In general, a part of a greenhouse used for propagation will need shading from mid-March to mid-October. For growing pot plants, shading from mid-April to late September will be adequate.

After winter, plants are often sensitive to a sudden temperature rise caused by sunny spells which, even in cold weather, can make the greenhouse extremely warm. For this reason, light shading may be necessary in spring.

Feeding Overfeeding, like overwatering, is often responsible for the death of pot plants. A build-up of nutrient salts in the compost can damage plant roots. If the correct potting and seed composts are used, plants will need no feeding until they are well established and the pots are filled with roots. As with watering, feeding must be regulated according to the plants' needs. Fast-growing, heavily cropping plants, such as tomatoes, cucumbers or chrysanthemums, can be fed generously. Slow-growing plants, such as rock plants and many cacti, can be ruined by excessive feeding.

Plants absorb nutrients only in solution. For this reason, liquid feeds are best because they are rapid in action and effective. High fertiliser concentrations can damage plants, so never give dry feeds at the roots.

Use properly balanced proprietary pot-plant or greenhouse-plant feeds.

Do not add dried blood, ammonium sulphate or bonemeal to pot plants in a hit-or-miss way. Epsom Salts (magnesium sulphate) can be used to help correct magnesium deficiency in plants prone to it, such as tomatoes and *Solanum capsicastrum*. If the leaves are pale, with yellow margins later becoming brown, and the plant is stunted, water or spray the plants a few times with a solution of ½–1 oz. (½–1 tablespoon) of salts per gallon of water.

Foliar feeds are now sold for plants that need a quick boost to growth or whose root action is slow, such as young, newly transplanted plants.

Plants long established in pots can be given a top dressing of John Innes base fertiliser incorporated with the top couple of inches of compost.

Before going on holiday A greenhouse can usually be left to look after itself for a day – although in summer take care to attend to watering and shading each morning if you are not returning until evening. For periods of a week or more try to get a friend or neighbour to help.

If there is no one to help, automatic equipment is the ideal answer (pp. 143–4). Most automatic watering systems cope for at least a week without attention.

However, if you cannot afford automatic equipment the only thing to do is to carry out the following jobs before going on a summer holiday. Water as thoroughly as possible before leaving. Provide humidity by covering the plants with clear polythene sheeting or bags. If you are not using polythene, thoroughly damp down the greenhouse and leave some pans or baths filled with water inside to maintain humidity. Completely shade the greenhouse. Leave plenty of ventilation, but reduce vents on the same side as the prevailing wind. Check for pests and diseases, and give routine treatment with systemic pesticides and fungicides if necessary. Remove any flowers and buds about to mature. Do any outstanding potting-on or pricking out. Gather any fruit or vegetables almost ready for cropping.

Keeping greenhouse and equipment clean

Cleanliness is vital for success in the greenhouse. It reduces pests and diseases and encourages general plant vigour and health. Keep all pots and containers clean. Try to use equipment made of plastic, metal or glass, which cannot harbour disease organisms.

Regularly wash grime and algae from both sides of the greenhouse glass. Wash down staging and interior structures, using clean water with detergent. Proprietary algicides are also available to keep greenhouse floors, benches and the various forms of automatic watering systems free from slimes and algae.

In an empty house, where there is no risk of fumes damaging plants, a sterilant, such as Jeyes Fluid can be added to the water before washing down.

In areas with hard water, deposits of lime will often form on watering equipment, impairing its efficiency. To remove these, use a diluted solution of a proprietary kettle descaler or bath stain remover containing formic acid. This can also be used for cleaning grimy glass.

The greenhouse should not be used to store garden tools or other equipment. These harbour pests. Regularly inspect plants and remove any dead flowers or decaying foliage. Isolate unhealthy plants by taking them out of the greenhouse or putting them in a polythene bag. Use only sterilised composts.

Fumigation is an easy and efficient method of killing pests. It should be done twice a year, in October and March. Certain pesticides sold for spraying, such as malathion and HCH, are also available to be used as fumigants.

Before fumigation, water plants but keep foliage dry. Do not carry out the operation in strong sunlight and when temperatures are high. It is best done in the evening, after which the greenhouse should be kept completely shut until morning, and then should be ventilated freely.

To keep fumes and vapours in the greenhouse, block any gaps with wet sacking or masking tape. Do not fumigate on a windy day.

To give the recommended amount of fumigation, it is necessary to know the cubic capacity of the greenhouse. This is ascertained by multiplying width by length and by average height.

If the greenhouse has contained plants badly infected by disease, sterilise the empty house by burning sulphur at the rate of 1 lb. per 1000 cu. ft. The sulphur is ignited with wood shavings to burn with a blue flame. The sulphur dioxide produced is poisonous and will kill all plants. It must not be inhaled.

The correct way to pot your plants

Plastic pots have generally replaced clay ones, because they are easy to clean, lightweight and not so easily broken. Also, as they are non-porous, less watering is needed.

When pot plants have to be plunged in moist peat or sand, however, clay is preferable, as it allows moisture to pass through the pot to the roots. Plants that prefer dry growing conditions also do better in clay pots.

The most popular sizes for general greenhouse use are $2\frac{1}{2}$ in. (for seedlings), $3\frac{1}{2}$ in. and 5 in. (all measurements refer to the inside diameter of the top of the pot). Large plants, shrubs and climbers may need correspondingly larger pots. Ensure that all pots have adequate drainage holes.

For short plants such as rock plants, some succulents, and small bulbs, half-pots or seed pans can be used, which are only half the depth of normal pots. They give a better balanced appearance to the potted plant and use less compost. Before use, all pots should be scrupulously clean. Scrub them thoroughly, if necessary, to remove any dirt and encrustations.

Thoroughly soak the clay pots, especially new ones. Otherwise they will dry out the compost.

Plastic pots need no drainage material in the bottom. Clay pots up to 5 in. need no drainage material either, but if you are potting a plant in a clay pot larger than 5 in., first cover the drainage hole with a few pieces of broken pot or clean pebbles. Even this should not be done if the pots are to be stood on a capillary sand bench.

To pot a plant, place moist potting compost in the pot and tap it down gently on the bench. Hold the plant in the pot so that the roots are resting on the compost, and the base of the plant comes to about 1 in. below the top rim of the pot.

Position the plant centrally and run more compost around it, leaving 1 in. between the top of the compost and the top of the pot. Always take care not to damage the roots. A few taps of the pot on the bench will be sufficient to anchor them firmly. Do not firm the compost with the fingers, as this may cause it to become waterlogged.

After potting, water the plant. Be careful not to water too much. If roots have been damaged, they may rot if the compost is excessively wet. It is usually sufficient to fill the space on top of the compost and allow the water to drain through.

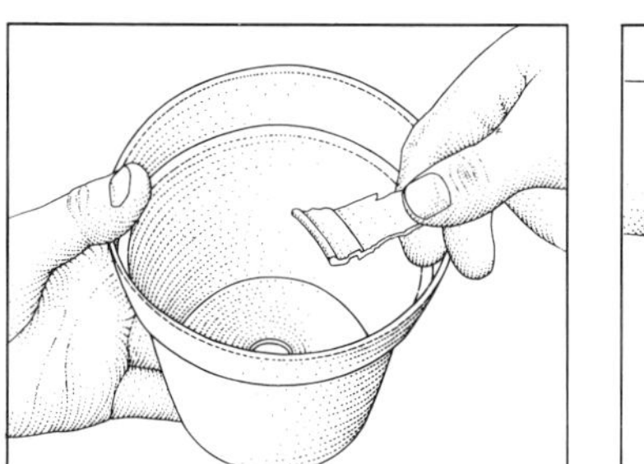

1 *Place drainage material in the base of a clay pot larger than 5 in.*

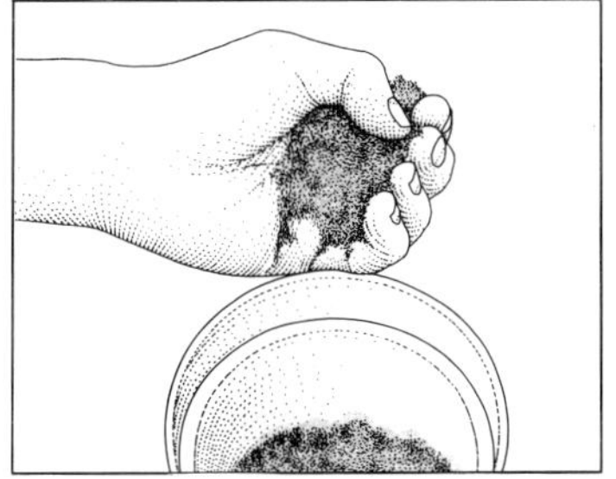

2 *Put moist potting compost into the pot and tap it down gently*

3 *Position the plant centrally, add more compost and tap the pot on the bench*

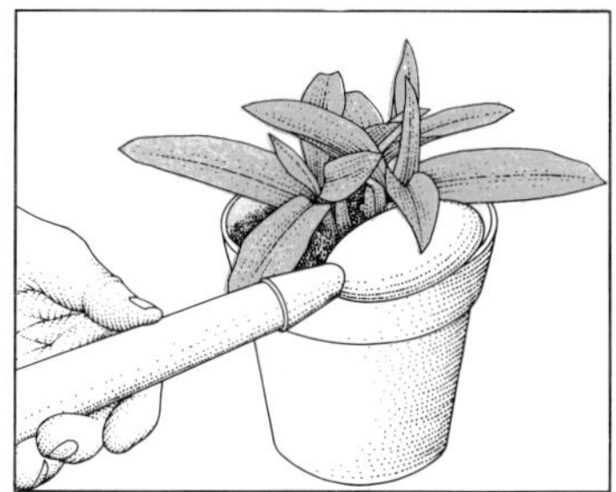

4 *After potting, water by filling the 1 in. space between rim and compost*

A succession of plants to grow throughout the year

By taking care over the individual plants' lighting, heating or humidity requirements, and by fitting a greenhouse with compartments or accommodating smaller plants in propagating cases, a surprisingly varied selection of plants can be grown successfully in one greenhouse.

Even so, you will make things easier for yourself if you avoid combinations involving plants with very different requirements, for example, cacti and ferns.

It is best to keep members of the following groups of plants in separate sections of the greenhouse: fruit and vines; vegetables and salad crops; plants to be propagated; specialist plants such as chrysanthemums and alpines; and decorative plants. And for good show or exhibition results, the crop or flowers should be given a greenhouse of their own. The right conditions and pest and disease control can then be maintained without having to worry about any other plants.

Try to choose decorative plants that provide year-round interest. whether for attractive flowers, foliage or fruit or for pure curiosity value.

Plants grown in succession In an unheated greenhouse, a succession of plants with different growing periods can be grown through the year. For example, climbing French beans can be sown in the greenhouse border in February for cropping in April and May; these can be followed by tomato plants when the beans are cleared; and late-flowering chrysanthemums can be brought in when the tomatoes are finished in autumn.

An unheated greenhouse can be used to shelter practically all the favourite outdoor ornamental plants from spring to autumn. But remember that the purpose of the unheated house is to give weather protection only, so always provide maximum ventilation and just enough shading to prevent sun scorch. Special favourites for a house of this kind are plants giving flowers for cutting and for flower shows: for example, roses, border carnations, sweet peas, dahlias, bulbs of most kinds and gladioli.

An unheated house can also be used in winter to protect hardy plants that are difficult or susceptible to damage by excessive wet, such as *Lobelia cardinalis*, some agapanthus varieties, many rock plants, and not quite hardy bulbs.

Another use is the protection of early-flowering hardy shrubs, such as camellias, grown in pots.

Annuals with alpines A greenhouse devoted entirely to alpines, with airy and bright conditions, is also excellent for summer-flowering annuals. Many of the ordinary garden annuals will give remarkable results grown in an alpine house in pots of good compost. After the alpines flower in spring, they can be put in frames outside for the summer to give more space inside the greenhouse for the annuals.

A cool greenhouse – kept at a minimum of 4–7°C (40–45°F) in winter – is commonly used for saving plants such as pelargoniums and fuchsias. In early spring it can be used to display most of the favourite greenhouse plants, such as calceolarias, cinerarias, primulas, schizanthus and salpiglossis, grown on from the previous autumn's sowings. At this time innumerable bulbs can also be brought into the greenhouse for forcing (p. 41).

In the spring, when summer-flowering plants such as pelargoniums and fuchsias are coming to life, you can also start many summer-flowering bulbs such as sinningias (gloxinias), smithianthas, gloriosas, achimenes and lilies. All will follow the spring display and keep up colour well into the autumn.

For giving a winter display, perpetual-flowering carnations (p. 58), gerberas, zonal pelargoniums, browallias, some fibrous begonias and even the exotic *Strelitzia reginae* (commonly thought to be suited only to a warm house) are invaluable. Space under the staging can be used in winter for forcing rhubarb, endives and chicory.

In warmer conditions – a winter temperature of 13°C (55°F) – gloxinias, streptocarpus, saintpaulias, columneas and achimenes grow well together and provide winter blooms as well as additional colour at other times of the year.

When the greenhouse is kept at an even higher temperature, 16°C (61°F) in winter, a great range of sub-tropical and tropical foliage plants can be grown together.

There are many beautiful shrubs and perennials for the greenhouse, and many greenhouse species will allow vigorous pruning to keep them compact. Rampant climbers, such as *Passiflora caerulea*, are best avoided, especially when they are almost hardy outdoors anyway.

House-plant shops are excellent sources of greenhouse plants, and most house plants are at their best after being kept under glass for some time. Some will flower and even fruit in a greenhouse, whereas in the home they may well provide only decorative foliage.

Foliage plants, such as coleus, monstera, peperomia, philodendron, saxifrage or tradescantia, provide year-round pleasure in the greenhouse. These foliage plants can also be brought in for display in the house.

Growing plants in hanging containers

Trailing plants are best displayed in hanging containers, which can be fixed to the greenhouse roof or walls. Some cheaper, ready-made greenhouses will not take the weight of large baskets, but small pots should be quite safe.

The old-fashioned wire basket is now covered with plastic to prevent rusting. Ordinary plastic pots can also be used. Drill holes round the rim of the pot and pass wires through.

Before putting plants in baskets, first line the baskets with sphagnum moss or black plastic sheeting.

Then fill the basket with potting compost and put in the plants evenly around the edge. Pierce holes in plastic sheeting to take each plant's roots. Hanging containers dry out quicker than ordinary pots in dry weather, and need a daily soaking.

Plants effective in baskets include pendulous begonias, ivy-leaved pelargoniums, fuchsias, nasturtiums, lobelias and tradescantias.

Sometimes bulbs, such as lachenalia, are pushed between the meshes and through the moss. They will grow out in a ball-like mass of bloom.

1 *Line a hanging basket with sphagnum moss to contain the compost*

2 *Fill the basket with potting compost and put in the plants*

Starting off young plants to stock the greenhouse

Seeds: the cheapest way for a mass of bloom

Growing from seed is a cheap and easy way of stocking a greenhouse and filling it with colour all year round. Buy seed from a reputable firm and sow at the earliest correct time. Do not sow old seed, which may have deteriorated.

Use 5 in. pots or seed pans or small plastic seed trays. Half fill each with slightly moist seed compost. Before sowing very fine seed, sprinkle the surface with a little seed compost rubbed through a fine sieve. Gently level and firm the surface.

Sow the seed as thinly and evenly as possible by tapping it out of the packet with the forefinger. More even distribution can be attained if very fine seed is mixed with a little fine silver sand before sowing. If seed is known to take six months or more to germinate, incorporate a fungicidal seed dressing with it, to prevent it rotting in the compost.

Many seeds are now available in pelleted form. A coating increases their size, and enables you to space them accurately.

After sowing, cover the seed with about its own depth of sifted compost. Do not cover excessively, since the seed needs air for germination and the emerging seedling needs light and air to develop sturdily right from the start. Do not cover very fine seeds or those that germinate best if exposed to the light, such as sinningias (gloxinia), streptocarpus, smithianthas and saintpaulias. Spray the compost with a fine mist until it is thoroughly moist.

Label each seed tray with a waterproof plastic label.

To keep the compost moist, cover the seed trays with a sheet of glass or plastic. But first cover the tray with a piece of absorbent white paper to prevent condensation dripping back on to the seed. The paper allows some light through if seeds need it.

For satisfactory germination the seed must have a suitable temperature. The seeds of most greenhouse plants will germinate well at 13–18°C (55–64°F). The more tender the plants, the higher the temperature required. Warm-greenhouse plants may need 18–24°C (64–75°F). If the temperature in the greenhouse is not high enough – perhaps in early spring – put the seed tray in a heated propagator.

Seed varies considerably in the time it takes to germinate, so never discard seed that appears to have failed before giving it plenty of time to break and produce roots.

Pricking out As soon as the two seed leaves appear on each seedling, the seedlings must be pricked out.

Transfer the seedlings individually to 2½ in. pots of John Innes No. 1 potting compost or in a group to large seed trays (8½ in. × 14 in.).

Many slow-growing greenhouse pot plants are best put in seed trays first, as trays do not dry out as quickly as small pots.

Set seedlings 1–2 in. apart, according to their size.

As a precaution against damping-off disease, water in with Cheshunt Compound, diluted according to the maker's instructions.

After pricking out, the seedlings need a well-lit part of the greenhouse, but not excessive sunlight.

Pot on greenhouse-plant seedlings into 3½ in. pots when the pots are filled with roots, or when seedlings in boxes touch each other.

Plants for bedding out in the garden need hardening off (p. 30).

1 *Sow the seed thinly on moist seed compost in pots or small trays*

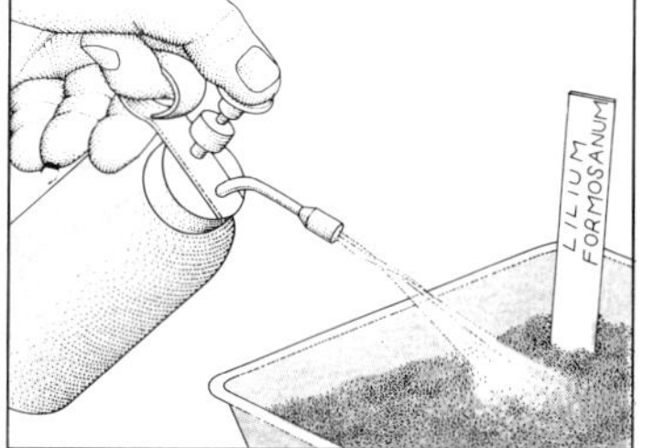
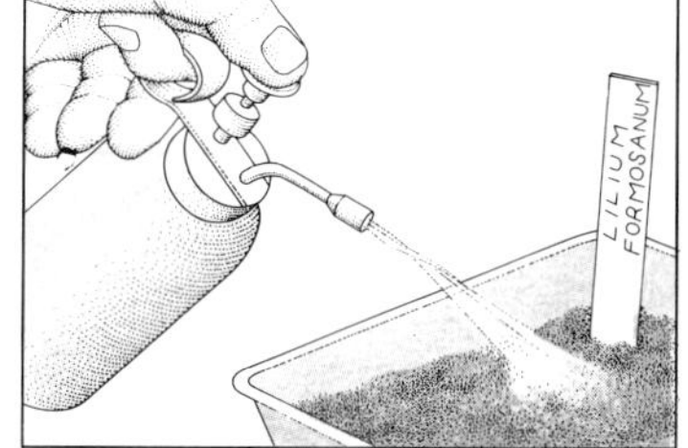

2 *After covering seed with compost, label it and spray with water*

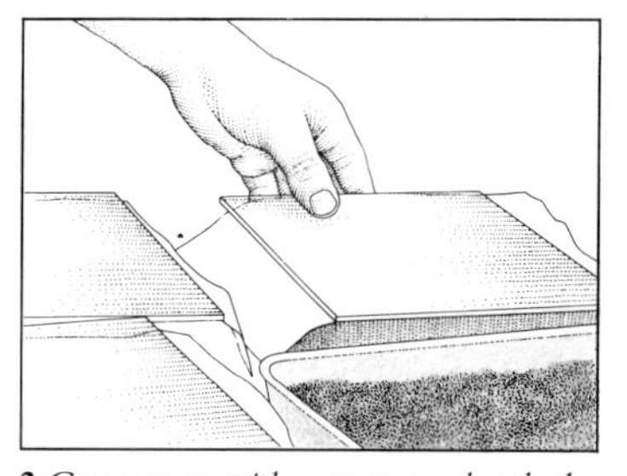

3 *Cover tray with paper, to absorb the condensation, then a sheet of glass*

4 *Immediately leaves appear, prick out the seedlings to pots or trays of compost*

Bulbous-rooting plants for early flowers

Many greenhouse plants are grown from storage organs – bulbs, tubers, corms and rhizomes. For early results, they are best started in 3–5°C (5–10°F) more heat than their normal growing temperature. Examples include hippeastrums, tuberous begonias, gloriosas, achimenes, smithianthas, sinningias (gloxinias), gesnerias, and many of the summer-flowering bulbs and corms that can be started in late winter or early spring for early flowers.

Most bulbs can be potted direct into pots and then placed in a warm propagator. However, it is not always easy to see on tubers, corms and rhizomes which end should be uppermost, and they should first be immersed in moist peat in a suitable container placed in a warm propagator or on the greenhouse bench. Inspect them every few days, and when shoots or roots are visible take them out of the propagator and pot them the correct way up in potting compost. Gloxinias and begonias, in particular, should be treated in this way.

In autumn, after the foliage has begun to fade, allow plants from bulbs and other storage organs to go dry. When the pots are quite dry, tip out the contents and separate the bulbs from the compost. Clean away any compost and remove any dead roots. Store the bulbs in dry sand in a frost-free, dry place. If the greenhouse becomes damp in winter, store somewhere else.

Do not tip out and clean plants with fragile tubers or rhizomes, such as gloriosas and smithianthas, as they can be damaged. They are best left in their pots, which should be set on their side, to avoid accidental watering, in a dry, frost-free place.

They should be removed from their pots and repotted in fresh compost just before they are due to restart into growth. In most cases they will have multiplied. Divide up and pot the pieces separately.

How to increase your greenhouse plants

There are several simple ways of growing new greenhouse plants from existing ones, and some plants respond to one method better than another. However, softwood cuttings and division are the easiest methods. They also produce new plants identical to the parent plant.

In all cases, make sure that you propagate only from completely healthy plants. Never use plants with yellow or mottled foliage, deformities or striped or distorted flowers – they may be suffering from virus diseases, and these will be passed on to the cuttings too.

Also, always avoid taking cuttings from plants that you know to have been affected by pests of any kind, as they may fail to root.

Softwood cuttings – an easy method

One of the most popular and easy methods of propagating greenhouse plants is by softwood cuttings. This is used for such widely grown plants as fuchsias, regal pelargoniums and zonal pelargoniums (or geraniums). It can be done at any time except winter, but spring is best.

Choose a healthy shoot without flowers or flower buds. Cut off a few inches with a sharp knife, cleanly and immediately below a leaf joint.

Gently pull or cut away the lower leaves and any stipules, or 'whiskers'.

Dipping the base of each cutting in hormone rooting powder can hasten rooting and make it more certain, but is by no means essential. Fill a 2½ or 3 in. pot with John Innes seed compost or a compost of equal parts peat and sand. The compost should be moist.

Press the cutting gently into the compost to just below the lowest leaf. If you are taking more than one cutting, several can be put round the side of a slightly larger pot.

Now cover the pot to keep the plant in a moist, warm atmosphere and shade it to prevent loss of moisture through its leaf surfaces. Special pots with a transparent dome are available for this purpose. Alternatively, ordinary pots or seed trays can be placed in a closed propagating case, or a polythene tent can be constructed over each pot or tray. Do this by inserting bent lengths of wire into the compost, the ends next to the rim of the container, and putting a plastic bag or sheet of polythene over them. Tuck the polythene in under the base. The pots can be put on greenhouse staging but away from strong light.

1 *At any time except winter cut off a few inches of a healthy shoot without buds or flowers. Cut cleanly, immediately below a leaf joint on the stem*

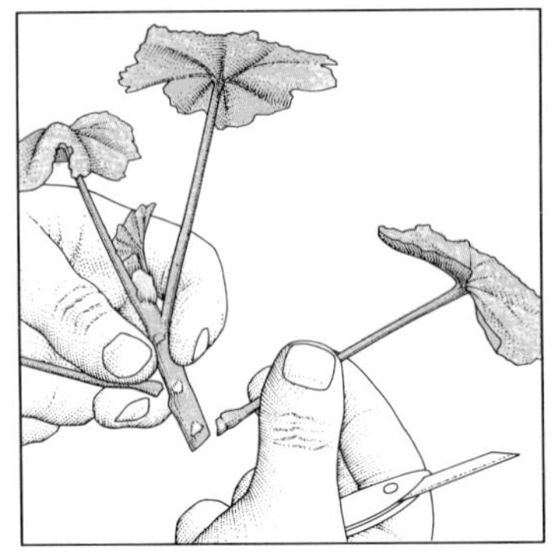

2 *Gently pull the leaves away from the lower part of the cutting*

3 *Press the cutting into moist compost, and cover to keep humid*

Cuttings from many easily grown pot plants can also be rooted in polythene bags. Place a little compost at the bottom of the bag, insert the cuttings in this, seal the top of the bag and hang it in a warm place – in a kitchen would be ideal.

With all methods, keep the compost moist by spraying occasionally with a fine mist of water.

Bottom heat is essential for the rooting of some warm greenhouse plants. This is best provided by soil-warming cables in a greenhouse propagator (p. 145).

The formation of top growth is a sign that rooting has occurred. This should take about three weeks. The plants must then be potted on into 3½ in. pots of John Innes No. 1 or 2 compost or a proprietary potting compost.

Most young plants from rooted cuttings should not be exposed to direct sunlight even if they are sun lovers. Full light should be given to them only very gradually as their roots develop.

Keep the compost moist, but not wet – waterlogging may prevent formation of roots in many cases, although some plants, such as *Impatiens sultanii* (busy lizzie), will root simply by putting cuttings in a glass of clean water.

Leaf cuttings for popular pot plants

Many widely grown pot plants, such as foliage begonias, saintpaulias, streptocarpus, gloxinias and sansevierias, can be propagated from leaf cuttings in various ways.

One method, often successful with begonias, is to pick a leaf and remove the stalk, then carefully cut across the veins in several places.

Fill a seed tray with seed compost and lay the leaves flat on the surface of the compost.

Weigh them down with stones, or peg with bent wire to keep the veins in contact with the soil. Place a sheet of glass or polythene over the tray to retain moisture, and put the covered tray in a warm propagator at a temperature of 18–21°C (64–70°F). After a few weeks, roots should form where the slits were made. Each rooted part can then be separated and potted individually in 3½ in. pots of potting compost. Put them on greenhouse staging, shaded from strong light for a few days.

Another method, used for begonias and peperomias, is to cut the leaves into small triangular sections with a piece of the stalk at the apex of each. The triangles are inserted apex down in the compost, covered and treated as before.

The long leaves of plants such as sansevierias and streptocarpus can be cut into sections about 2 in. long. Each section is inserted vertically in the compost.

The best method for saintpaulias, and other small-leaved plants is to cut off leaves with ½–1 in. of stem.

Insert the stalks individually in a 2½ in. pot, or three in a 3½ in. pot, of seed compost so that the base of each leaf just touches the compost. Cover the containers and place them in warmth. Bottom heat of 16–18°C (61–64°F) will produce rooting in 10–14 days, and new growth should appear above the surface about one month after insertion.

Saintpaulias: taking leaves with stems attached *Cut off cleanly the required number of leaves, each with ½–1 in. of stem attached. Insert the stalks in a pot of seed compost so that the base of each leaf just touches the surface. Cover the pot and place it in warmth*

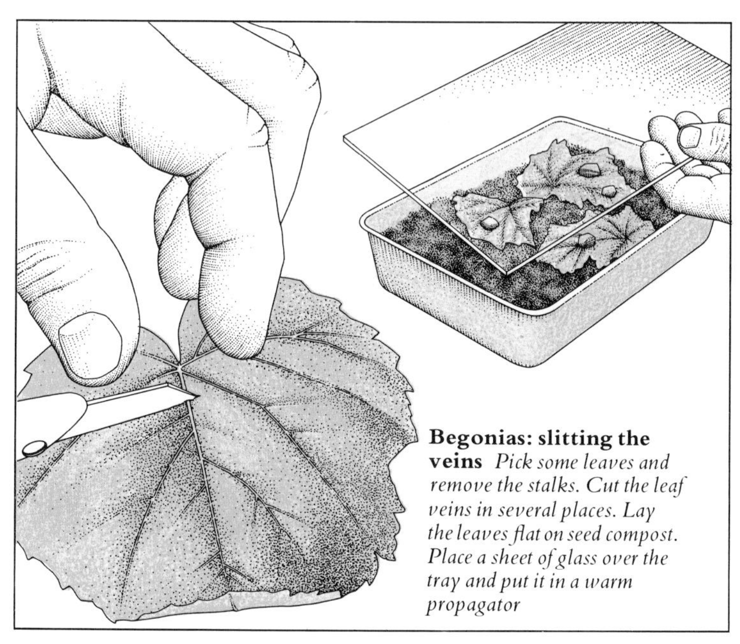

Begonias: slitting the veins *Pick some leaves and remove the stalks. Cut the leaf veins in several places. Lay the leaves flat on seed compost. Place a sheet of glass over the tray and put it in a warm propagator*

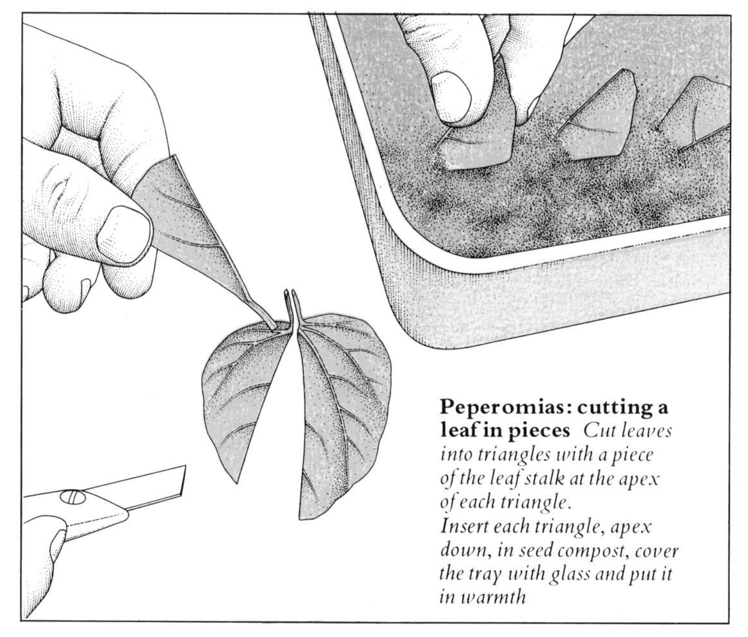

Peperomias: cutting a leaf in pieces *Cut leaves into triangles with a piece of the leaf stalk at the apex of each triangle. Insert each triangle, apex down, in seed compost, cover the tray with glass and put it in warmth*

Mist – for quicker and better results

Intermittent mist propagation is a more expensive but more efficient alternative to keeping cuttings in a closed case or in a bag.

A thin film of moisture is maintained over the leaf surfaces using a water jet controlled automatically by an electronic leaf element or detector unit. This switches itself on only when the cuttings begin to dry.

With this method, propagation can be carried out in full sunlight, and the normal processes involved in plant food formation – known as photosynthesis – can take place.

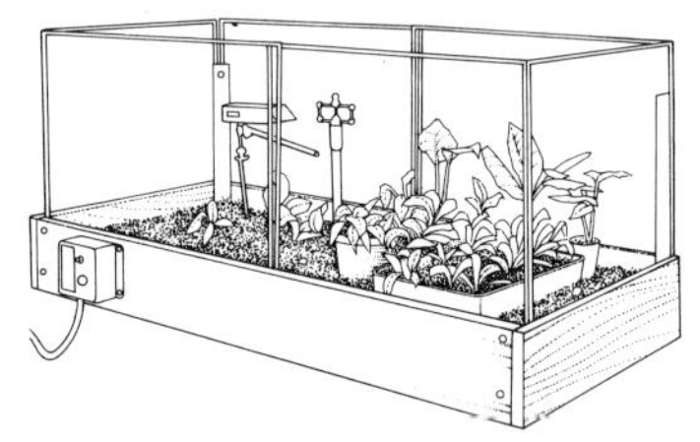

A mist unit with surround

Bottom heat is usually needed to balance the cooling effect of moisture passing constantly through the compost and to encourage healing, callus formation and rooting.

With mist propagation rooting is more rapid and certain, and cuttings, that with other methods root with difficulty only or not at all, usually succeed. Also there is usually less disease (particularly grey mould), because spores are washed away before they can do any damage.

The only drawback to mist propagation is that cuttings rooted by this method are more tender than those raised under glass in the ordinary way and need to be hardened off with great care.

Small misting units, with a surround to keep the mist within bounds, can be bought for slightly more than a heated propagator.

Increasing perennial pot plants by division

Division is an easy way of propagating perennial greenhouse plants. It should be done in early spring, before new season's growth begins.

Tap the plant, with its compost, out of its pot. If the compost is dry and difficult to dislodge, water it.

Examine the top of the plant to discover where stems or tufts of growth arise. With a very sharp knife, cut firmly down through the plant between the tufts of growth.

It does not matter if roots are not cut cleanly, but the less damage done to them the better. Old or dead roots, or those that are damaged, can be cut away.

Pot each segment separately in potting compost. Water the plants moderately and keep them in shade for a few days. Most plants will flower the same year.

Many greenhouse bulbs, including hippeastrums, form offsets – small bulbs that sprout from the parent bulb. They can be pulled away during repotting and potted individually in 3–5 in. pots. Use the same compost and the same heat as for the adult plants. It is often necessary to grow these small bulbs for two years or more until they have reached flowering size.

1 *In early spring cut down through the plant between the tufts of growth*

2 *After removing old or dead roots, pot each segment separately*

PRODUCING NEW PLANTS FROM OFFSETS

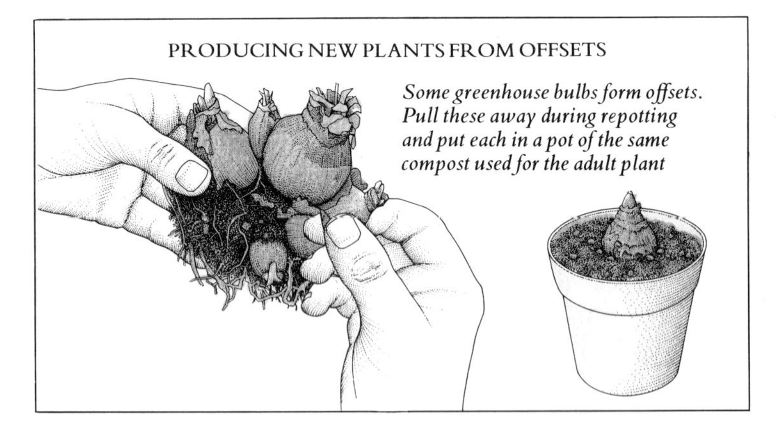

Some greenhouse bulbs form offsets. Pull these away during repotting and put each in a pot of the same compost used for the adult plant

Some other methods of increasing plants

Layering is an effective method of propagating some climbing and trailing plants. Bend down a branch so that its stem touches some seed compost placed in a 3–4 in. pot. Slit the stem at this point or peel away a tiny piece of the outer skin. Keep the wound in contact with the compost with a staple made from bent wire, or a weight such as a small stone. When roots have formed, which should usually take between three and six months, cut the stem carefully away from the parent plant.

Greenhouse shrubs that do not root easily from cuttings can be propagated by air layering. Examples are gardenia and stephanotis. Air layering is also used to shorten leggy plants such as the rubber plant, *Ficus elastica*. The method is given in full on page 255.

Sometimes, seed can be saved as a means of propagation. It is no use saving seed from hybrid plants as it cannot be relied on to yield identical plants, but species plants will come true to type. Make sure seed is ripe before collecting, and sow as soon as possible afterwards. The technique is explained on page 149. Popular plants which provide good results from seed are: celosia, eccremocarpus, freesia, *Solanum capsicastrum* and torenia.

Some greenhouse plants, such as *Saxifraga stolonifera*, produce runners with plantlets. These can be pegged down on to compost between spring and autumn in the same way as strawberries (p. 136).

Passiflora can be propagated by detaching the suckers it throws up, each with some roots attached, and planting them.

Growing plants under other forms of glass

Frames – for small-scale greenhouse gardening

A garden frame consists of a framework of wood, metal, concrete or brick covered by hinged, removable or sliding panes of glass called lights. It can be unheated – known as a cold frame – or heated.

Lights can also be bought separately to place on top of existing brick sides or over a pit.

A frame enables those without a greenhouse to carry out some greenhouse gardening on a small scale. For a gardener with a greenhouse, it is an essential adjunct.

Aluminium alloy framework is lighter and more durable than wood.

A portable frame is the most convenient type. It can be moved to sunny or shady positions, depending on the plants grown or the time of year, and can be mounted on a low base of bricks or concrete blocks to provide extra height.

A row of frames can be built along one side of a greenhouse that has a brick or concrete base, so that they benefit from its warmth. The frames should be placed on the shadier side of the greenhouse, to avoid excess heat and sunlight. Portable frames can be similarly sited

To accommodate pot plants, the floor of a frame can be covered with shingle or weathered ash. This prevents worms entering the pots and the compost from becoming soggy, as well as keeping down the weeds.

A cold frame is popularly used to harden off plants raised in the greenhouse, or on a window-sill, before they are planted out in the garden.

It can also be used to raise early crops of low-growing vegetables such as lettuces, radishes and spring onions; thus leaving tomatoes, climbing French beans and other tall plants to make use of the greenhouse height.

Tender biennials such as cineraria, calceolaria, primula and cyclamen can be sown in a cold frame in summer, and kept there in pots through winter before being transferred to the greenhouse staging in the spring.

Cuttings of hardy shrubs and perennials taken in summer can be kept in the frame over winter, before planting out in spring.

The provision of heating by soil-warming cables enlarges the scope of a frame by enabling even earlier vegetables to be grown, and a wider range of plants from seeds.

A frame with air-warming cables is used for overwintering tender plants like fuchsias and pelargoniums, more efficient propagation and growing melons and cucumbers.

Soil-warming and air-warming kits are available for frames, and all that is then needed is for a qualified electrician to provide an outdoor electric supply. A thermostat should be incorporated (p. 145).

Cloches – for vegetables and cut flowers

Cloches are glass or plastic tunnels placed over rows of plants to keep out frost and cold winds. They speed up growth and extend the growing season at both ends, particularly in the vegetable garden.

They should be placed in position to warm the soil about a week before the seeds or plants are put in.

Other uses of cloches include: overwintering hardy crops such as lettuces and carrots; obtaining early yields of strawberries; and, in colder areas or cool summers, growing early ridge cucumbers. Hardy melons can also be grown under cloches. Several plants grown for cut flowers – for example, anemones, violets and gladioli – can be advanced or protected under cloches.

Cloches can also be used for the outside rooting of cuttings and the germination of seeds.

FRAMES AND CLOCHES

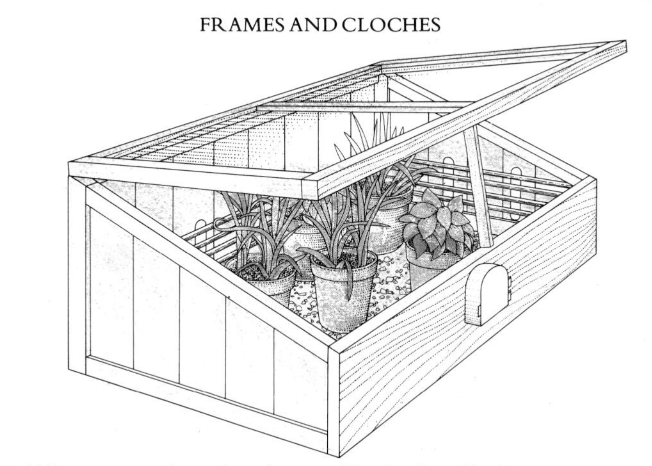

Cold frames are used to raise early vegetables, harden off bedding plants raised in the greenhouse and raise plants from cuttings and seeds. Heated frames provide even earlier vegetables and widen the range of plants raised from seeds. They can also house tender plants in winter

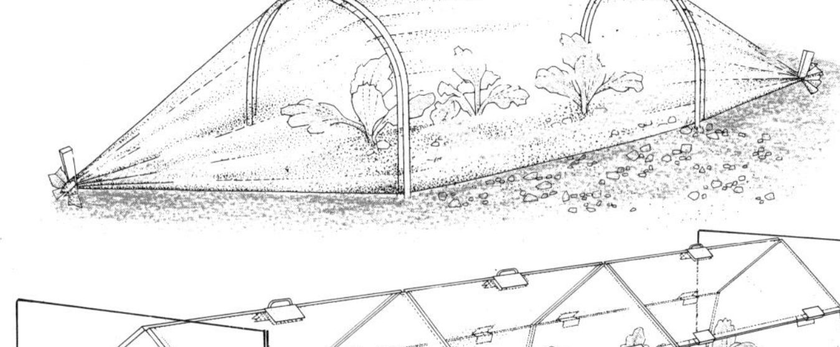

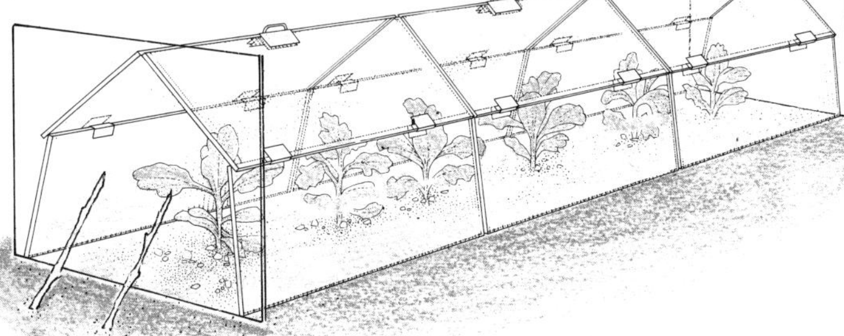

Cloches protect plants, speed up their growth and extend their growing season at both ends. They can also be used to overwinter hardy crops, obtain early strawberries, grow hardy melons and early ridge cucumbers in cold areas, and for propagation. Glass cloches trap heat efficiently when each end is sealed with a sheet of glass. Plastic tunnel cloches supported and secured at intervals with loops of bent wire, are cheaper but less efficient.

Two special uses for a greenhouse

Raising bedding plants for the open garden

Many greenhouse plants can be put out in the open garden to flower during summer. This technique, called summer bedding, can be used with plants needing a minimum temperature of up to 16°C (61°F).

Using the greenhouse or a frame to raise summer bedding plants from seeds can save a considerable amount of money each year, and enable you to experiment with new varieties. Raising greenhouse plants from seeds is described on page 149.

In the greenhouse most half-hardy plants can be sown from January to March. Fast-growing plants, such as African marigolds, should not be sown until April: plants sown earlier would be spoilt by being starved in boxes until the temperature was suitable for planting them out – mid to late May, according to the area. Slow-growing plants, such as fibrous begonias, need sowing in January.

Prick out the seedlings into trays or boxes as soon as the two seed leaves appear.

Plants that do not like root disturbance, such as zinnias and column stocks, are better pricked straight out into individual small pots and then potted on until ready for planting out.

Some popular bedding plants can be raised from cuttings. Examples are zonal pelargoniums (geraniums), fuchsias, shrubby calceolarias, heliotropes and all chrysanthemums, except annual types.

All plants for bedding out must be hardened off gradually before full exposure to the weather. First put plants in cooler parts of the greenhouse, then transfer them to closed unheated frames. Gradually increase the ventilation of the frames until they are left fully open all the time.

Half-hardy bedding plants should not be planted out until all danger of frost has passed.

Growing climbers and wall shrubs

A few climbing plants or wall shrubs, trained up into the roof on wires, can give a greenhouse an attractively mature appearance in a fairly short time. They also make use of the upper half of the greenhouse, which is often wasted space.

Climbers, and especially wall shrubs, are particularly useful in a lean-to greenhouse where a bare supporting wall can be effectively covered. They also give shade in the summer, partially covering the greenhouse roof so that shade-loving plants can be grown below.

Many climbers and wall shrubs can be planted permanently in the greenhouse border, where they will flower for many years and need little attention apart from an annual top-dressing of well-rotted manure or garden compost, and some cutting back in the autumn.

Ideal for growing in the border are *Abutilon megapotamicum*, *Bougainvillea glabra*, *Lapageria rosea*, *Passiflora caerulea*, *Plumbago capensis*, and tibouchina.

Some climbers are more suited to growing in pots to contain their growth and, like *Jasminum polyanthum* which flowers in the winter, can be stood outside in summer.

Other climbers suitable for pots include *Cobaea scandens*, dipladenia, gloriosa (glory lily), *Eccremocarpus scaber* and ipomoea (morning glory).

They should be planted in 10–12 in. pots of John Innes No. 3, or a peat-based compost.

All the climbers mentioned can be grown in a cool greenhouse where the winter temperature does not drop below 4–7°C (40–45°F).

However, *Abutilon megapotamicum*, *Jasminum polyanthum*, lapageria and *Passiflora caerulea* can all be grown in a sheltered spot in a cold greenhouse. Additional warmth is not necessary unless the temperature outside drops below –7°C (19°F).

Month-by-month in the greenhouse

January

Clean the panes to let in maximum light. Ventilate a cool or cold greenhouse on mild and sunny days. Water sparingly, especially during dull, cold or foggy weather. Remove dead and dying leaves and flowers before they become a source of disease; overwintering cuttings, especially of zonal pelargoniums (geraniums), should be regularly picked over.

Ventilate a warm greenhouse if the temperature exceeds 21°C (70°F) and give it a light damping down.

Take cuttings of late-flowering chrysanthemums. Cuttings taken in December will be ready for potting at the end of the month.

Ventilate perpetual carnations on mild and sunny days. Water and feed sparingly. Cuttings can be taken. Pot rooted cuttings taken earlier. Watch out for aphids and carnation rust.

Water all orchids only when absolutely necessary. Damp down only on sunny days. Paphiopedilums which have finished flowering can be repotted.

February

Ventilate cool and cold greenhouses on sunny and mild days; lightly damp down paths and benches with a fine-rosed watering can around midday. Do not over-water plants, but give special attention to mature plants which dry out quickly.

Ventilate a warm greenhouse if the temperature exceeds 21°C (70°F); damp down lightly.

Move dormant plants of heliotrope, fuchsia and bouvardia on to the greenhouse staging and lightly water. Spray over with water each day, and as growth commences increase watering. Maintain a minimum of 7–10°C (45–50°F).

Seeds of half-hardy and tender annuals and perennials, such as tuberous and fibrous begonias, celosia, coleus and streptocarpus, can be sown if a minimum temperature of 13–16°C (55–61°F) can be maintained. Sow schizanthus now to provide flowers for late spring and early summer.

Tomatoes for planting out under glass in April should be sown about the middle of the month. They will

June

Pay particular attention to watering during hot spells, as well-rooted pot plants can dry out in a few hours. Ventilate freely on all warm days, and damp down the paths and benches once or twice daily.

Take softwood cuttings of abutilon, begonia, coleus, fuchsia, pelargonium and tibouchina. Leaf cuttings can be taken of streptocarpus and *Begonia rex*.

Give exhibition incurved and single varieties of chrysanthemums a second stopping about the middle of the month.

July/August

Sow seeds of cineraria early in July and calceolaria from mid-July onwards in cold frames. Softwood and leaf cuttings can still be taken. Water, ventilate and damp down as for June.

In August take cuttings of *Campanula isophylla*. Rest hippeastrum bulbs by reducing watering.

Late chrysanthemums grown for exhibition should have the stems reduced to the strongest two or three to each plant.

Freely ventilate perpetual carnations at all times, and lightly shade on the hottest days. Continue to disbud. Water and feed regularly.

Continue to water orchids freely. Begin to expose cymbidiums to full light. Large plants may be stood outside in a sheltered position.

need a temperature of 16°C (61°F).

At the end of the month, a batch of achimenes may be started into growth. Place the scaly rhizomes about 1 in. apart each way, in moist peat, at a temperature of 13–16°C (55–61°F). When the shoots are about 1–2 in. tall, place four or five together in a 5 in. pot and put it on the greenhouse staging for growing on.

Passiflora and plumbago can be pruned towards the end of the month. Cut back previous season's shoots to within 3 in. from their base.

Pot chrysanthemum cuttings taken in January, and keep all young plants moist.

Ventilate perpetual carnations on mild and sunny days. Water and feed sparingly. Disbud flowering stems as necessary. For indoor use cut the flowers immediately they open. Take more cuttings. Pot those already rooted.

Ventilate orchids in mild or sunny spells. Water sparingly, but make sure that the plants do not dry out and the bulbs shrivel. Cymbidiums, dendrobiums and paphiopedilums that have finished flowering may be repotted.

March

Ventilate, damp down and water as necessary (see February). Some shading may be needed. Pot on over-wintered annuals and established plants that are pot-bound. Congested specimens may be divided.

Sow seeds of half-hardy and tender annuals and perennials. Prick off seedlings from earlier sowings. Complete pruning of climbers.

Begonias, achimenes and other plants with dormant fleshy roots should be started into growth at a temperature of 13–16°C (55–61°F). Hippeastrum (amaryllis) bulbs may be started in gentle warmth. Begin watering when leaves appear.

Prick out tomato seedlings.

Rooted cuttings of late chrysanthemums should be put in a cold frame from the end of the month. Protect with matting if frost is likely.

Pot on and make a first stopping of perpetual carnations. Ventilate freely on warm days.

In long, sunny periods, shade orchids during the hottest part of the day. Damp down daily, except in cold weather. Continue repotting.

April

Increase ventilation as the weather gets warmer, and make sure plants do not dry out. Shade the glass during long sunny spells. Damp down the greenhouse regularly during warm periods.

Complete potting up of begonia tubers, gesnerias and other dormant fleshy roots. Sow seeds of *Solanum capsicastrum* and *Campanula pyramidalis* at a minimum temperature of 13–16°C (55–61°F).

Divide overgrown orchids which have finished flowering. Shade the house during sunny spells and damp down regularly. Water more freely, but unless plants are growing vigorously allow them to dry out between waterings.

May

Ventilate freely during the day; damp down and water plants daily, and give special care to shading young plants. Pinch out young plants of fuchsia, plumbago and bouvardia to promote bushy growth. Pot on at regular intervals, so that plants do not get pot-bound and suffer a check.

Put chrysanthemums in their final pots before the end of the month. Support with canes. A week to ten days later, move the pots to a standing ground outside.

Ventilate perpetual carnations freely. Shade lightly. Damp down regularly. Pot on young rooted cuttings. Second-year plants in 6 in. pots should be moved on to 8 in. pots. Make a second stopping.

Shade orchids and damp down frequently. Water freely.

September

Continue to ventilate, damp down and water as during the summer, unless the weather turns cold. Reduce feeding towards the end of the month, ceasing it entirely for plants that have finished growing. Bring in young plants of cineraria and calceolaria from cold frames.

Sow cyclamens and annuals for spring flowering under glass. Begin potting spring-flowering bulbs.

Towards the end of the month, bring late-flowering chrysanthemums into the greenhouse. Ventilate freely unless frost is forecast.

Plant tender bulbs such as lachenalia in a cool greenhouse.

Give cymbidiums full sunshine. Water all orchids more sparingly and give more light and air.

October

Cease feeding by the end of the month and remove permanent shading, except over ferns. Ventilate and damp down on warm days, but prepare to turn on heating if cold spells or frosts are forecast.

Thin out overgrown climbers to admit light.

Ventilate chrysanthemums during the day, but a little heat will be needed on frosty nights. Disbud later flowering varieties.

Cuttings of perpetual carnations can be taken from now until March.

Reduce damping down and watering of orchids. Remove shading by the end of the month. Odontoglossums that have finished flowering may be repotted or divided.

November

Ventilate cool and cold greenhouses on sunny days, but shut the ventilators early in the afternoon. Complete potting on of autumn-sown annuals, like salpiglossis, lobelias and schizanthus, for a spring display, and cuttings of pelargoniums, fuchsias and heliotropes.

Several hardy perennials, such as astilbe and polyanthus, will flower during late winter in a cool greenhouse if lifted from the garden now. Pot them but leave them outside.

Maintain a minimum temperature of 7°C (45°F) for perpetual carnations, and ventilate on mild or sunny days. Disbud flowering stems, and feed and water sparingly.

Restrict ventilation of orchids to mild and sunny days.

December

Do any necessary watering and ventilating on mild and sunny days. Remove dead or dying leaves and flowers regularly.

Astilbe and polyanthus plants in pots for early flowering can be brought into a cool greenhouse. Clean the glass so that the weak winter light is not further diffused.

Water stools of late chrysanthemums and increase temperature. Begin taking cuttings towards the end of the month.

Continue to disbud perpetual-flowering carnations; water and feed sparingly. Maintain a minimum temperature of 7°C (45°F).

Ventilate orchids for a few hours on sunny days only. Water mature plants only once a fortnight.

What can go wrong with greenhouse plants

This chart describes the most common problems likely to occur in the growing of greenhouse plants. If your plants show symptoms not described here, turn to the full-colour identification chart starting on page 377.

For trade names of chemicals, see page 398.

Symptoms	Cause	Cure
Leaves have brown margins and appear scorched or have a bleached appearance. Plants are often checked in growth	Usually a combination of too much heat and lack of shade	Except for most cacti and many succulents, plants under glass should not be allowed to suffer temperatures above 29°C (84°F) without either ventilation or shading, or both. Plants that have suffered excess heat should be shaded and watered sparingly for three to four days. If they are pot-bound, apply a liquid or foliar feed
Flower buds yellow, wither and often drop prematurely; the growing point may also be shrivelled and the leaves somewhat flaccid and lack lustre. The plants are inclined to wilt readily	Persistent under-watering, sometimes as a result of too little space between pot rim and soil level	To give enough room for adequate watering, there should be a gap between soil level and pot rim at least one-tenth of the pot depth. Plants showing symptoms should be watered thoroughly, if necessary by standing them in a bucket of water for several minutes. Subsequently, water normally, making sure that at each watering a little trickles out of the drainage holes
Plants in pots or containers produce thin growth and lack vigour; leaves are small and often yellowish	If no signs of pest or disease present, then probably starvation	Apply a liquid feed, and possibly also a foliar feed, according to maker's instructions. If the container is choked with roots, repot into a larger pot. Plants that respond to division should be divided and potted separately
Leaves and young shoots have a fine powdery white coating, often accompanied by distortion. Later, the powdery areas may take on purplish or reddish hues; the leaves may fall prematurely	Mildew	Fumigate with dinocap smokes or spray with benomyl, dinocap or thiophanate-methyl
Leaves finely mottled and yellowing, eventually shrivelling or falling prematurely; in severe attacks, the shoots are weakened and become covered with a fine webbing	Red spider mites	Spray with derris, malathion or dimethoate
Leaves and petals mottled or with bleached areas	Thrips	Spray or dust with HCH, malathion, nicotine or derris
Young shoots and leaves stunted or malformed; covered in greenish, pink or black insects	Aphids	Spray with derris, malathion dimethoate or pirimicarb
Leaves often mottled yellow and young shoots less vigorous. When lightly shaken, insects like minute white moths take wing	Glasshouse white flies	Spray repeatedly with malathion, HCH or pyrethrum. A difficult pest to eradicate. Fumigate with HCH
The stems and leaf axils are infested with clusters of small insects covered with a waxy white wool. Plant and leaves sometimes yellow and leaves fall early	Mealy bugs	Spray with malathion, nicotine or a systemic insecticide, repeating at regular intervals until the pest has gone. If the attack is slight, wipe off the insects with a soft brush or cloth soaked in soapy water
The plant lacks vigour and looks yellowish, often wilting, even when the soil is moist. When knocked out of pot or dug up, the roots are covered with small soft insects under a waxy whitish wool	Root mealy bugs	Soak root system with malathion, diazinon or nicotine
Stems and leaves bear small, soft, pale brown insects shaped like shields. Plant vigour may be reduced, the leaves yellow and fall prematurely	Scale insects	Spray with malathion, nicotine or a systemic insecticide. If the attack is slight, wipe off the pests with a soft brush or cloth soaked in soapy water
Leaves, and sometimes flowers, become puckered or distorted, the tissues brittle; growing points may die out	Tarsonemid mites	Apply finely powdered sulphur, making sure it gets into leaf axils and growing points
Stems, leaves, flower buds and flowers show brown dead patches of tissue that become covered with a fluffy, greyish-white mould during particularly cool, humid conditions	Botrytis or grey mould	Fumigate with tecnazene smokes or spray with benomyl or thiophanate-methyl
Seedlings, particularly those sown thickly in pots or pans under glass, rot at ground level and topple over	Damping-off disease	Water with quintozene or captan. To prevent this disease, sow seed thinly in a sterilised compost and water in with Cheshunt Compound
Rhododendrons and azaleas in pots show yellow mottled leaves, and may flower poorly	Chlorosis	Repot into an acid compost such as John Innes acid compost or a peat-based compost without lime, and water with clean rain water

Eight of the most popular greenhouse plants

Begonias

With their beautiful flowers and foliage, the many begonia species and hybrids make excellent greenhouse plants.

Tuberous-rooted begonias The large double-flowered begonias grow from tuberous roots, rather like dahlias. They include the trailing varieties popular for growing in hanging baskets.

Start the tubers into growth in damp peat (p. 149) whenever a minimum of 16°C (61°F) can be maintained. When immersing the tubers in the peat, check that the flat or concave side of each is at the top and just level with the surface.

Inspect the tubers every few days. As leafy shoots are produced pot them into 3½ in. pots of John Innes No. 2 or similar potting compost. As the roots fill these pots, pot on into 5 in. or 7 in. pots.

Begonia stems and foliage are usually brittle, so tie the stems to a cane at an early stage.

When the plants are well established in their final pots, give regular liquid feeds.

To obtain deep colours, and to keep the greenhouse cool during summer, shade the glass during sunny weather. Larger blooms can be produced by allowing only one shoot to develop from each tuber. Remove the other shoots and use them as cuttings (p. 150). Remove also the female flowers, which have a winged capsule behind the bud and form only single blooms.

Sow begonia seed in January at a temperature of about 16°C (61°F) to get a colourful display the same year. Tubers will be formed and can be saved for subsequent years.

At the end of the year, when the foliage of tuberous begonias begins to yellow, gradually reduce watering until the pots are dry. Turn out the contents of the pots, separate the tubers from adhering compost and store in dry sand in a frost-free place for the winter.

Tuberous-rooted begonias can be put out as summer bedding plants.

The winter-flowering Lorraine varieties are grown from cuttings taken in the spring for flowering the following November at a temperature of 10°C (50°F).

Fibrous-rooted begonias The smaller-flowered *Begonia semperflorens*, popular for bedding out, are grown from seed and have normal, fibrous roots. They are half-hardy perennials often grown as annuals.

They flower well in 3½ in. pots, but the large-flowered forms will do better in 5 in. pots. For the maximum flowering period, sow them in early January at a temperature of 16°C (61°F).

No stopping, staking or tying is necessary. Flowering is prolonged if faded flowers and seed pods are regularly removed.

Foliage begonias The Rex begonias are grown for their leaves, which are patterned in silver, cream, red and purple. *B. masoniana* (iron cross) is another foliage type with bronze-purple markings.

Give foliage begonias humidity and shade in summer. In winter, keep them just moist at a temperature of 13°C (55°F). Pot on in April and increase by division at the same time. They can also be increased by leaf cuttings (p. 151).

Calceolarias

Calceolarias have long been favourite greenhouse pot plants. They have exotic pouch-like blooms in a wide range of colours, often with vividly contrasting patterns or spots.

There are large-flowered and many-flowered types. Recently, F1 hybrids have been introduced that are easy to grow and fast flowering.

To grow calceolarias as bedding plants, sow seed in March at 10–13°C (50–55°F). Plant out in the garden at the end of May. Discard plants after flowering.

For Christmas and winter flowering, sow seed in May or June. No artificial warmth is required.

For convenience, seedlings can first be transferred to seed trays, about 20 per tray. Keep the trays in cold frames shaded from direct sunlight. See that the plants do not become dry at any stage, and keep a constant watch for greenfly, to which calceolarias are prone. When the plants are large enough, pot them individually in 5 in. pots, the more compact types in 3½ in. pots. When they begin to show buds, give them regular liquid feeds. The taller varieties will need to be supported with canes.

Bring the plants into the greenhouse in mid-September and overwinter them at 7°C (45°F).

Plants flowering from late winter to early spring need protecting from sudden temperature rises and strong sunlight which will cause wilting. Shade the greenhouse.

During winter, ventilate whenever the weather permits, to lessen the risk of fungus disease attack. Do not use HCH or DDT smokes for controlling pests, since these can blacken calceolarias. Do not spray the plants when in bloom because this can cause rotting of the flowers.

Cinerarias

The daisy-like flowers of cinerarias are borne profusely during half the year in a cool greenhouse – from December to June. They are often richly coloured and sometimes banded with white. Cineraria varieties are divided into the following groups: Hybrida Grandiflora (large, broad-petalled flowers); Multiflora Nana (broad-petalled flowers); Stellata (narrow-petalled flowers); and Double-flowered.

Sow and grow cinerarias as described under calceolarias, with this exception: most varieties will need a final 5 in. pot, and large-flowered varieties may require a 7 in. pot. For

Begonia semperflorens

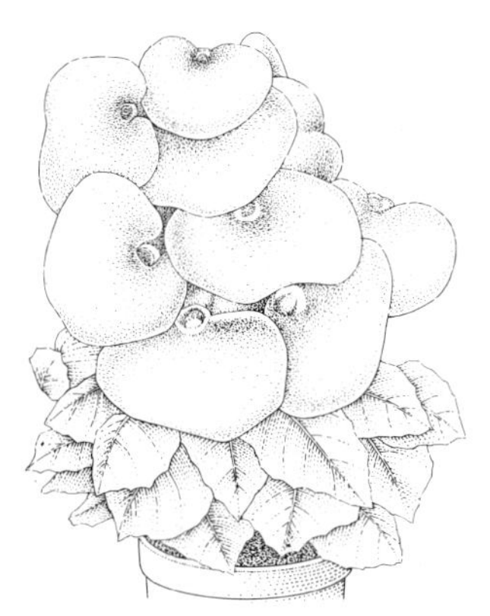

Calceolaria × herbeo-hybrida

Cineraria

Cyclamen

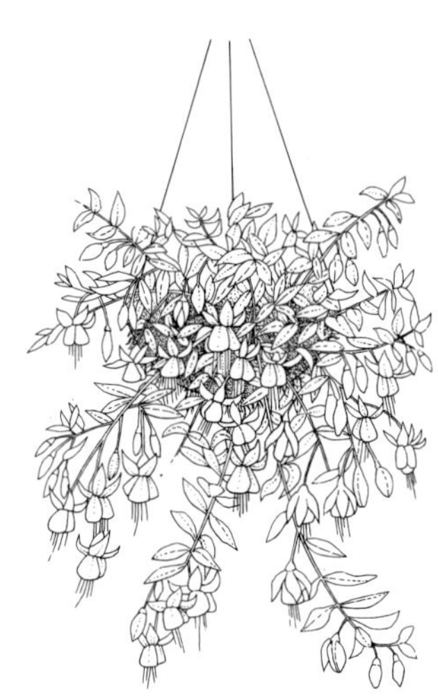

Fuchsia (pendulous)

early and Christmas flowering, sowing should be brought forward earlier than for calceolarias, to about April. Discard the plants after they have flowered.

Cyclamens

Cyclamens are graceful, sometimes sweetly scented plants. The foliage often has beautiful silver markings. Miniature varieties and varieties with frilled flowers and double flowers have been introduced.

Cyclamens react to wide differences in temperature, erratic watering or draughts, by wilting and failing to produce flowers; buds and corms may also rot.

Repot new plants in summer and place the pots in a shady frame. Water lightly until a root system has developed, then begin to water more generously. In late September return the plants to the greenhouse. A temperature of about 13°C (55°F) kept reasonably steady, should be maintained. In districts where low autumn temperatures are likely, put the plants in the greenhouse earlier. Flowering can be expected from winter to spring. Feed and water regularly during late spring and early summer. Later in the summer rest the plants by keeping the compost almost dry, preferably in a shady cold frame.

The following September repot, using the same size container and fresh compost. After some years the corms usually (but not always) begin to produce fewer flowers.

Cyclamens can also be grown from seeds, but buy them from a reliable seedsman. They are large and can be sown individually. Sow them in pots on the surface of any seed compost and cover them with a ¼ in. deep layer of moist peat rubbed through a sieve to remove lumps. The best time for sowing is from August to November. After sowing, place the containers in a propagator where a steady temperature of about 18°C (64°F) can be maintained, to avoid erratic germination. As the seedlings appear above the peat, prick them out promptly into 2½ in. pots of John Innes No. 2 compost.

Retain the seedlings in their initial pots at a temperature of about 18°C (64°F). Keep the compost moist. When the plants are established and making strong growth, lower the temperature to about 16°C (61°F). In April pot on the plants to 5 in. pots and, when the weather is warm enough, transfer them to a shady frame outside.

When potting on at any stage be sure that the top of the corm, however tiny, protrudes above the compost.

In September – or earlier, according to temperature – bring the plants into the greenhouse. Remove premature flower buds to conserve the plants' resources for their major display from December to spring. Give liquid feeds when the flower buds first form.

Corms obtained from seed can be treated in the same way as a bought plant.

Fuchsias

The fuchsia has many merits. It is relatively easy to grow and has a long flowering season – through summer and autumn. It can be trained to form various shapes and is a good summer bedding plant. Varieties differ widely – some trail or hang, others are erect, some have variegated foliage and *Fuchsia procumbens* has decorative berries.

Buy the plants as rooted cuttings in early spring and pot them in 2½ in. pots of John Innes No. 2 potting compost. Pot on the plants to final 5 in. pots in April or May.

Most fuchsias need some form of training. The simplest is the bush form, which is produced merely by stopping (pinching out) some shoots to induce bushy growth. Rooted cuttings can be stopped when a few inches high to encourage more shoots to rise from the lower parts of the stem.

Trailing plants in hanging baskets also need their growing tips pinched out when the leading shoot is just over the basket edge. Large baskets or hanging containers will need about three plants symmetrically placed in them.

The standard is a beautiful form. In this case, do not remove the growing tip. Encourage the plant to grow a single stem by removing all side-shoots but retaining leaves that spring directly from the stem. As the stem increases in length, tie it to a cane to ensure upright growth. When the desired height has been reached, pinch out the growing tip. As the side-shoots near the top develop, pinch them out when they are a few inches long to encourage more strong growth. Eventually a bushy head will develop.

During the period of active growth remove any weak shoots and give liquid feeds. After pinching out, plants should take six to eight weeks to form flowers as long as they are not stopped again.

Most of the named varieties of greenhouse fuchsias are not hardy and must be kept in a frost-free greenhouse. Give them just enough water in winter to keep the compost slightly moist. In cool conditions some plants may lose their foliage and become dormant, in which case keep them fairly dry. In spring, when new growth appears, begin watering and repotting. When it is seen where new growth comes from, cut away all dead shoots. Unwanted new shoots, removed to develop a shape, can be used for cuttings, which usually root easily (p. 150).

During summer, fuchsias need a cool, moist atmosphere and some ventilation. They should also be slightly shaded. Remove promptly any faded flower heads and their seed pods to ensure the maximum flower production.

Primulas

The vast primula genus includes three popular greenhouse pot plants. *Primula malacoides*, which in spring produces dainty circular tiers of flowers, is raised as a biennial. *P. obconica* is a perennial notable for hardly ever being without flowers. It will flower in its first year if the seeds are sown in January or February. *P. sinensis*, best raised as a biennial, has a thick stem bearing two or three whorls of brightly coloured flowers from late February to March. These last two plants have hairy leaves that can irritate sensitive skins.

Sow *P. malacoides* and *P. sinensis* from May to August. A temperature of only about 10°C (50°F) is necessary for germination. Sow *P. obconica* from January to June at a temperature of about 16°C (61°F). In all cases, prick out into 2½ in. pots. Use John Innes No. 2 compost or a peat-based potting compost. Pot on as required, keeping the plants well shaded and the compost evenly moist. *P. obconica* needs a final 5 or 6 in. pot, the others 4–5 in. Overwinter them at a minimum temperature of about 7°C (45°F).

Pelargoniums (geraniums)

The most common pelargoniums are zonal pelargoniums, better known as geraniums. Recently, some fine F1 hybrid strains of seeds have been introduced.

Sow zonal pelargoniums as early in the year as possible at a temperature of about 16°C (61°F), for flowering during summer and autumn. After germination transfer the seedlings to small pots and later pot them on into 5 in. pots. Early-sown plants can be used for bedding out.

To obtain winter flowers, take cuttings (p. 150) early in the year from last year's plants retained in the greenhouse. Pot on and during summer sink the pots in soil out of doors in a sunny position; keep the compost moist.

Encourage bushy growth by pinching out the tips of the rooted cuttings when they are a few inches high. Remove any premature flower buds and in autumn take the plants into the greenhouse. With a winter minimum of 10°C (50°F), a dry atmosphere, the minimum of water and as much sunlight as possible, the plants should flower well in winter.

Regal or show pelargoniums are the greenhouse pelargoniums proper. These have a very wide colour range, but flower for a much shorter period than zonals. Regals are best obtained as named varieties from a specialist nursery, but cuttings from existing plants can be taken in early spring or during July and August (p. 150).

Pinch out the growing tips of young plants at an early stage to promote bushy growth. To avoid straggly specimens, cut back old saved plants when they show signs of growth in spring. Use the pieces cut off as further cuttings.

Ivy-leaved pelargoniums are mostly trailing plants. They are ideal for hanging baskets, but can also be trained up trellis or wires on the wall of a lean-to.

They have a long flowering period, like zonals, and should be grown in the same way. They need an initial pinching out to promote branching.

The scented-leaved pelargoniums produce less showy flowers. They include a number of species and varieties named after their leaf scent: nutmeg, lemon, orange, rose. The foliage is attractive and fragrant and they can be kept as evergreen ornamentals.

All these pelargoniums need a moist, but never waterlogged, compost at all times during their growing period. In winter most prefer to be kept rather dry and in a dry atmosphere. Cold and damp can cause root and basal stem rot, and frost is usually fatal to the plants. Ventilate freely in winter whenever weather permits.

All pelargoniums root readily from cuttings taken during spring and summer. Rooted cuttings can be kept growing on over winter with a minimum temperature of about 10°C (50°F).

Regal pelargoniums need some shade under glass, but in general pelargoniums prefer plenty of light. Shading is only necessary to prevent scorching and excessively high temperatures under glass.

Schizanthus

This dainty annual, which produces masses of colourful flowers, is usually grown as a biennial in the greenhouse, to flower in spring.

Choose giant-flowered varieties such as Sutton's Giant Pansy-Flowered and Sutton's Giant Hybrids. These strains have large, richly coloured flowers usually veined with gold.

Sow in autumn. Pinch out the growing tips of the plants when they are a few inches high and do the same with side-shoots. Do this twice so that good bushy growth develops. By February the plants should be in 5–7 in. pots.

Schizanthus benefit from generous liquid feeding as they grow. Each plant should be tied to a cane.

In winter schizanthus need only frost-free conditions and all the light possible. In summer, shade them to prevent scorching.

To grow schizanthus as an annual, use the dwarf compact varieties described in the seed catalogues. 'Dwarf Bouquet' and 'Hit Parade' are especially good. These can be grown without any stopping and will flower well in 3½ in. pots. If preferred, they can be stopped once and potted on to 5 in. pots to make larger plants. Sow in early spring at about 10°C (50°F).

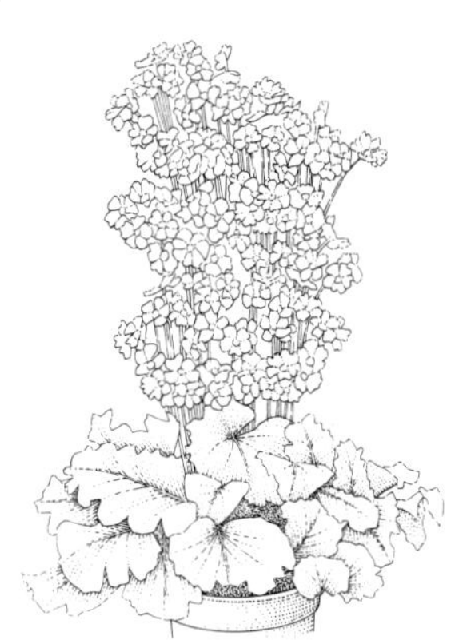

Primula malacoides

Regal pelargonium

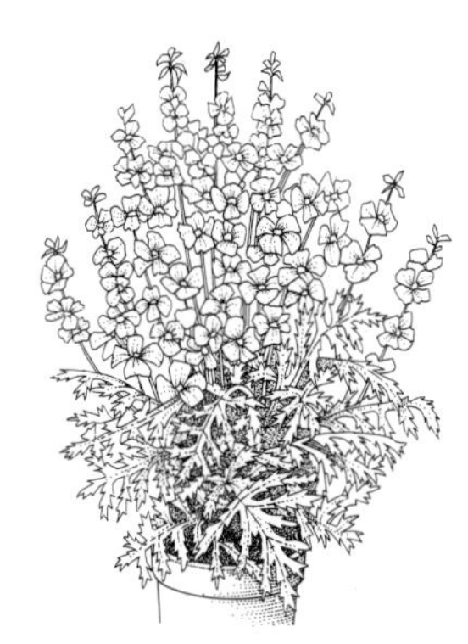

Schizanthus

Heathers for colour

Heathers are among the easiest garden plants to grow. Some flower in summer, some in winter – and some give brilliantly rich foliage when the frosts come

Heathers can provide the nearest most people will get to a trouble-free garden, colourful all the year.

They evoke the refreshing qualities of open moorland, at the same time exhibiting the refinements of nursery-bred varieties. In addition, they can be easily propagated.

There are about 630 species of heather in the world, but over 600 grow only in southern Africa.

However, there are plenty of heathers that thrive in Europe, all belonging to three genera – calluna, erica and daboecia.

'Heather' and 'heath' both refer to the same broad group of plants, but tradition is confused when it comes to particular plants. Calluna is called heather, or ling, and never heath, and all the others are heaths, except *Erica cinerea*, which is usually called bell heather.

Heathers are broadly grouped according to when they flower – some in summer and autumn, and the rest in winter and spring. Summer and autumn-flowering heathers mostly need a lime-free soil, but the winter-flowering ones will tolerate lime.

Heathers can also be divided into two groups according to size: tree heathers which grow up to 8 ft tall, and the rest, which vary from pincushion size to 4 ft high.

Tree heathers are valuable for adding height to what can be otherwise a comparatively featureless expanse. Pure heather gardens need artifice to prevent this. Slopes, gulleys, banks and rocks help, but best of all is the judicious admixture of non-heathers. A standard addition, dwarf conifers, can be beautiful but may fail to give contrast.

There are many other shrubs which combine well, especially rhododendrons. Even annuals can be used, before the young heaths have grown and filled the gaps.

It is also standard practice to grow groups of several of each sort of heather. In a large garden this makes the proportions better. Even in a small one, single plants can look straggly, so three is a wise minimum, but make a drift of at least six when you can.

Heathers can also enhance shrub borders, mixed borders or rock gardens, either as an edging or intermingled with other plants.

The dead flower heads of summer and autumn-flowering species can glow in the winter sun as richly as the flowers did earlier. Certain varieties of *E. vagans* do this superbly, but equally good are *E. ciliaris* 'Maweana', and some hybrids of *E. cinerea* and *E. terminalis*.

Many of the summer-flowering heathers, particularly callunas, provide a second display in winter, when their foliage turns into the richest colours as the frosts intensify. It may glow crimson, scarlet, bronze, gold, orange, yellow, silver, grey or green and every mixture between, the shades changing with the season.

FINDING YOUR WAY THROUGH THE HEATHERS

Calluna The supreme moorland heather, commonly called ling. It grows wild on moorland throughout the country, from mountain tops to sea cliffs, and is very hardy.

Calluna produces its flowers mainly in August and September, on spikes up to 12 in. long. The flowers are usually white or various shades of red, purple and pink.

Calluna vulgaris

There is only one species, *C. vulgaris*, which has many named varieties, varying from tight pincushions to plants $2\frac{1}{2}$ ft tall.

Many newer varieties have foliage in remarkable shades of red, yellow, orange and bronze.

Calluna will not grow in a soil containing lime.

Daboecia *Daboecia cantabrica* (St Dabeoc's heath) produces the largest flowers of all our heathers – $\frac{1}{3}$ in. across. They bloom from June until autumn in white, pink, crimson or purple. After the flowers fade, the corollas drop off. The deep green leaves are silvery underneath. Heights range from 6 in. to $2\frac{1}{4}$ ft.

Daboecias will not stand limy soil, and they need protection from frosts in very cold areas. However, the hybrid *D. cantabrica* × *azorica* is hardier and longer flowering.

Daboecia cantabrica × azorica

Erica (summer flowering) *Erica ciliaris* (Dorset heath). A decorative and long-flowering heather that adds colour (mainly pinks and whites) from July to early winter. The plants are rather lax and do not grow well in cold areas. Most varieties are 12 in. high with a spread of 9 in. They need an acid soil if they are to thrive.

E. cinerea (Bell heather). The gayest of all the heathers, with flowers ranging from the palest pinks through every sort of red to black-purple. All varieties flower well from June to August, and some

Erica cinerea

last into the autumn. They do not grow well in cold areas. Varieties range in height and spread from 6 to 18 in. They need an acid soil.

E. tetralix (Cross-leaved heath). A good heather for silver-grey foliage, with flowers either pink or white from late June to August. Very hardy, but needs an acid soil. Height and spread is 9–12 in.

E. vagans (Cornish heath). A bush heather, up to 4 ft high and 8 ft across, which can have very long thick flower spikes, especially when young. It can stand a little lime and a considerable amount of frost. It flowers from July through to the winter in purple, pink and white.

Erica (winter-spring flowering) All the following grow in limy soil.

E. carnea (syn. *E. herbacea*) (Winter or mountain heath). One of the most widely grown heathers, excellent for ground-cover. It is very hardy. The light green or bright yellow leaves give a pleasant display in summer, and the red, pink or white flowers open between October and February. All varieties are at their best in February and

Erica carnea

March, and flowering lasts until May. Height and spread is 6–12 in.

E. mediterranea (syn. *E. erigena*). The tallest of the winter-flowering, lime-tolerant species – up to 6 ft or more high and 3 ft across. The purple, pink or white flowers may appear in December and last until summer.

E. × darleyensis (Darley Dale heath). A fairly tall-growing heather – about 2 ft high – which often starts flowering in December and lasts into early summer. The flowers range through purple, pink or white and are at their best in March and April. The flower spikes can be long and extremely elegant.

Tree heathers *E. arborea* (Tree heather). The tallest of the heathers, growing up to 12 ft in warm conditions, but rarely exceeding 8 ft. It will not grow well in exposed sites or on limy soil. The white flowers appear from March to June.

E. terminalis (Corsican heath). A very hardy tree heather which will stand

Erica arborea *Erica terminalis*

some lime in the soil. It grows up to 8 ft high. The pink or purple flowers bloom from June to winter, and the dead heads turn a rich russet colour in winter.

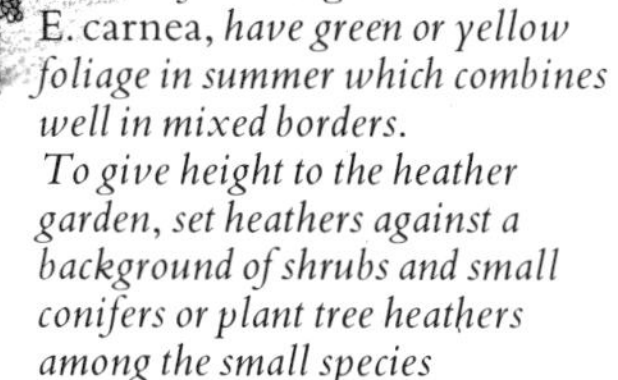

Heathers can provide colour in the garden all year round. Calluna vulgaris, *which flowers in late summer, also gives a brilliant display in winter when its foliage changes to red, yellow, orange or bronze.* Erica tetralix, *another summer-flowering heather, has silver-grey foliage.*
Winter-flowering heathers, such as E. carnea, *have green or yellow foliage in summer which combines well in mixed borders.*
To give height to the heather garden, set heathers against a background of shrubs and small conifers or plant tree heathers among the small species

How to grow, and increase, your heathers

Planting and general treatment

Heathers need an open position in full sun. All species do best in peaty, acid soils. Winter and spring-flowering species will tolerate a limy soil; but most summer and autumn-flowering types can stand no lime.

A mulch of peat or garden compost may be applied each spring, but no annual fertiliser is required.

Established heathers need only be watered during long droughts.

Heathers bought in containers can be planted at any time of the year, although autumn or spring are best.

Prepare for planting by digging the ground thoroughly and removing every trace of perennial weeds.

With lime-free soils, spread a layer of peat, an inch or so thick, on the ground and lightly fork it in. Limy and heavy soils need more.

On very poor soils, sprinkle 2 oz. (a shallow handful) of dried seaweed over every square yard.

Next, decide on the spacing of the plants. The small varieties should be planted 9 in. apart, the taller, spreading ones 18 in., to obtain quick ground-cover. To produce fine individual plants these distances can be at least doubled. For tree heathers allow about 3–4 ft. Heathers usually look best when planted in groups. Mark out the spacing with stakes.

With a trowel, dig a hole slightly deeper than the container holding the heather. Remove the plant from the container, and tease the roots apart so they are not in a ball.

Lower the plant into the hole and fill up with peaty soil. Except for tree heathers, ensure that the whole stem is buried, so that the foliage rests on the soil.

Firm the plant with your fingers. When planting is finished, water thoroughly. Then apply a top-dressing of peat to cover the entire surface of the soil. This conserves moisture and keeps down weeds.

For the first months after planting, ensure the soil never dries out. March winds are a special danger.

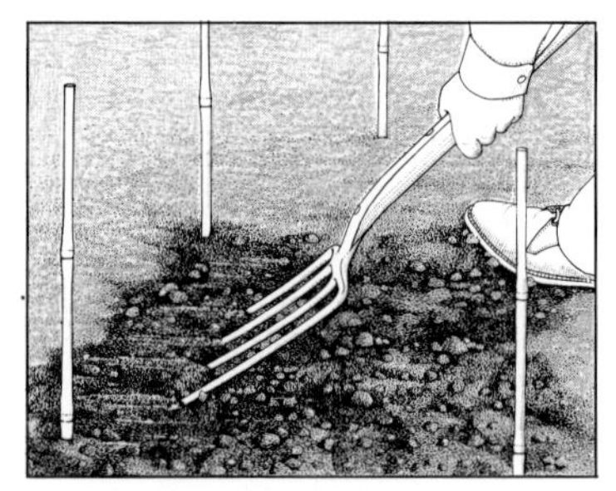

1 *Thoroughly dig the soil, remove any weeds, and fork in a layer of peat*

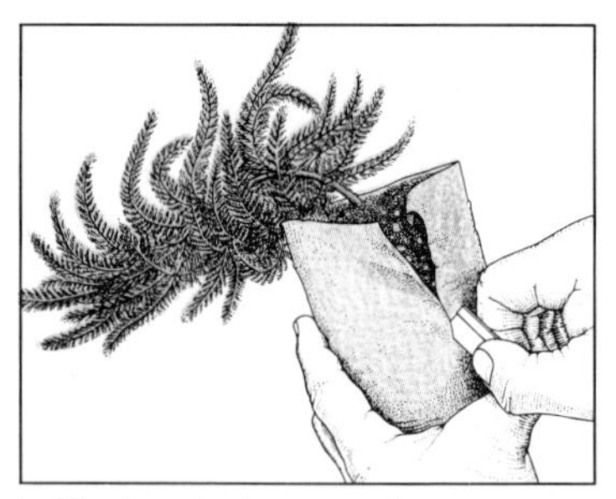

2 *Slit the polythene container to remove the young plant*

3 *Plant the heather so that the foliage rests on the soil*

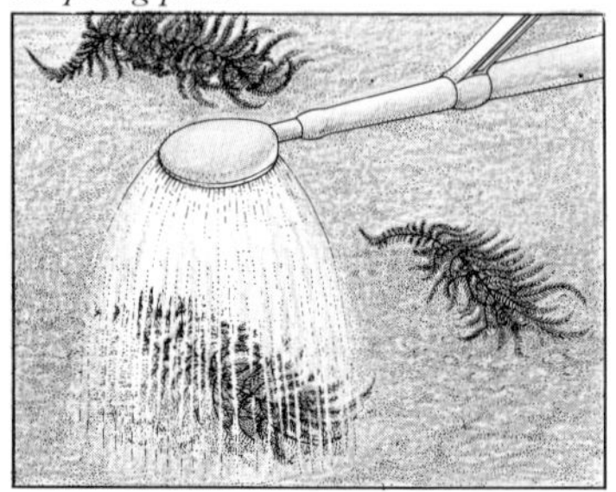

4 *Water thoroughly and top-dress the area with another layer of peat*

Dead-heading and pruning established plants

Winter and spring-flowering heathers, and dwarf forms of others, rarely need pruning.

Remove the dead flower heads with scissors immediately after they have faded. Cut the growth just below the faded flower spikes.

The dead flower heads of summer and autumn-flowering heathers can often provide attractive colour in winter, so leave dead-heading until the spring.

Summer and autumn-flowering heathers may in time become straggly with age and lose the vigour of their flower spikes. In spring, cut back the old woody stems with secateurs. They can be cut back as far as you like, and no damage will be done to the plant. Make the cut diagonally.

Cut off old flowers of winter and spring-flowering heathers after they fade. Dead-head summer-flowering plants in spring

What can go wrong with heathers

This chart describes the common problems that are likely to occur in growing heathers. For symptoms not described here, turn to the chart on page 377.

Trade names for the various chemicals are listed on page 398.

Symptoms	Cause	Cure
Plant looks unhappy (not growing well, leaves brown) a month or so after planting	Faulty planting	Lift the plant. If the roots are in a tight ball, pull them apart carefully. Replant and saturate with water
Foliage, particularly the young tips, becomes suffused or mottled yellow, and may turn brown and die	Chlorosis	Too much lime in the soil; water the plants with chelated compounds (sequestered iron) and mulch with moss peat. Preferably, avoid the lime-hating species, including *Calluna vulgaris*
Foliage takes on a greyish tinge, wilts and finally browns and dies	Wilt or die-back	No cure for infected plants. Keep remaining plants vigorous by applying a general fertiliser and mulching with moss peat

How to layer an established heather

The best methods of growing new heathers from established plants are by layering in spring and by taking cuttings in late summer.

Any well-established plant can be layered at any time of the year, but the quickest results are produced in spring.

First, separate a low-lying branch from the rest of the plant.

Over the main stem of the branch place several handfuls of a mixture of equal parts of peat and coarse sand. Alternatively, cover with a proprietary peat-based compost.

Press the layer down with a heavy stone and leave in place. Repeat the operation with as many branches as required.

Spring layers should have rooted by autumn, and autumn layers in 12 months' time. Sever the old stems with secateurs and lift the new heathers with a trowel. Plant in the normal way.

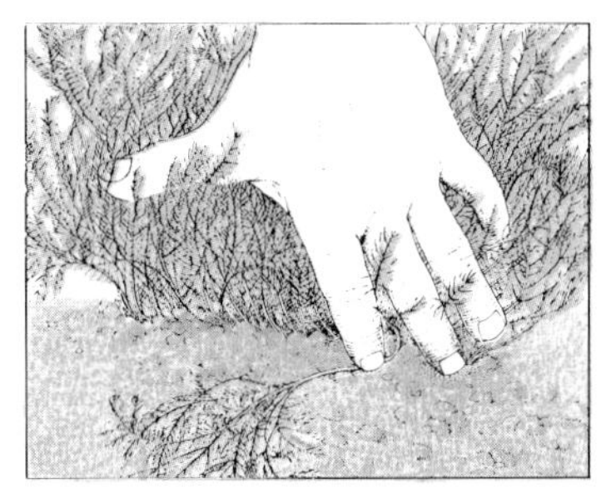

1 *In spring, separate a low branch, and cover with peaty compost*

2 *Anchor with a heavy stone, and repeat with other branches*

Growing new heathers from cuttings

In August or September, snip off branches that include side-shoots of the current year's growth. This is softer, thinner and a paler green than the old growth. In the case of summer-flowering heathers, take only shoots that have no flowers.

Cover the base of a 5 in. pot with a layer of gravel (or coarse peat) and almost fill the pot with a compost of 2 parts moss peat, 1 part coarse sand. Moisten well and firm down with the base of another pot.

Finish off by spreading a thin layer of dry coarse sand over the surface of the compost.

Pull a side-shoot of current year's growth from the branch. Trim the tip of the shoot so that the cutting is 1 in. long. A 5 in. pot will take about 20 cuttings $\frac{3}{4}$ in. apart.

Make planting holes with a pencil or a sharp stick to half the depth of the cuttings. Insert the cuttings and firm them in with your fingers.

Now make a cover with two pieces of bent wire inserted in the pot. Place a plastic bag over the wire and fasten it with an elastic band.

Put the pot in a shady part of the greenhouse or frame. When new growth appears, the cuttings have rooted. Raise the polythene to let in some air. A week later remove the polythene altogether.

Keep the cuttings in a cold greenhouse or frame through the winter.

In April, the cuttings should be ready for potting into their own 3 in. pots in a compost of 3 parts moss peat and 1 part coarse sand, or a moist peat-based compost.

Ensure that the growth is clear of the surface of the compost and stand the pot outside in a partly shaded place. Take care that the soil never begins to dry out.

In autumn, the heathers should be ready to plant out.

1 *In August or September, snip off a branch with pale green side-shoots*

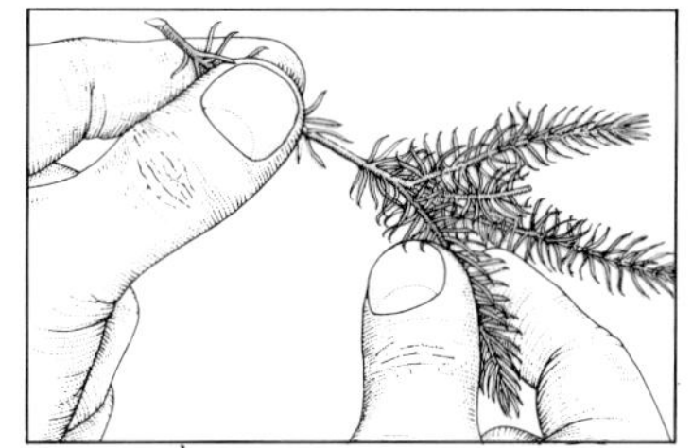

2 *Pull off the side-shoots and trim the tips to make cuttings 1 in. long*

3 *Plant in holes $\frac{1}{2}$ in. deep and $\frac{3}{4}$ in. apart. A 5 in. pot takes about 20 cuttings*

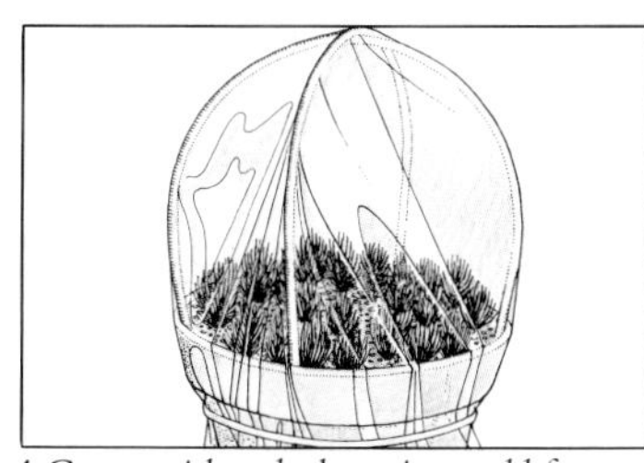

4 *Cover with polythene in a cold frame. Remove polythene when growth starts*

5 *In spring, remove from the frame and tease out the tiny plants*

6 *Put each plant in a 3 in. pot, with the foliage clear of the compost*

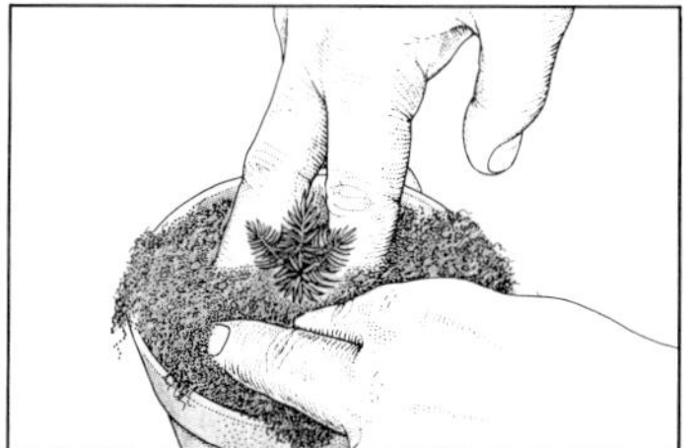

7 *Firm the plant, water and stand in a lightly shaded spot. Plant in autumn*

House plants

The secret of growing house plants is to give each one the right conditions of light, heat and humidity. So choose the right plants for each part of the house

During the past 20 years house plants have increased enormously in popularity, partly because homes today provide better conditions for indoor plants, and partly because there is now a much greater range of plants available for every situation.

With the introduction of central heating, better insulation and large picture windows, many more colourful and interesting plants can be grown in the home. These range from hardy and easily grown hederas (ivy) and philodendrons, through more exacting plants such as dizygothecas and peperomias, to the difficult group which includes the red-flowered anthuriums and the popular but sensitive saintpaulias (African violet).

Types of house plants Broadly speaking, house plants fall into two main categories: foliage plants and flowering plants (including flowering pot plants). Foliage plants are either green-leaved or variegated, often with strong, dominating colours. The green-leaved plants are the hardier, and therefore easier to grow, although there are some exceptions, such as adiantums (maidenhair fern) and some of the varieties of ficus (rubber plant).

Coloured foliage plants often need higher temperatures and more humid conditions, which may be difficult to maintain in the home. Calatheas and marantas, which have brilliantly coloured leaves, may fail after a few months, unless their exact growing conditions can be met. On the other hand, the Rex begonias, with their distinctive and colourful leaf markings, and the silvery-banded, purple-backed zebrinas are easily grown.

Variegated leaf plants – chlorophytums, sansevierias, peperomias and tradescantias – are mainly as easy to grow as green foliage plants, but they require a position with better light.

Flowering house plants, such as aphelandras, anthuriums and impatiens (busy lizzie), will flower indoors year after year under the correct conditions, which include annual repotting. Some plants, such as cyclamens and *Euphorbia pulcherrima* (poinsettia), are sometimes difficult to keep from year to year, usually because they are brought straight into a living-room that is too warm and dry while they are in flower. They are then often overwatered and neglected when the flowers have finished.

Bromeliads are a special type of plant, grown as much for their unusual foliage as for their flowers. Aechmeas (urn plant), for example, have grey-green leaves and a rose-pink flower spike. In their natural environment, many bromeliads grow on tree trunks, where their roots absorb nourishment from the leaf-mould and other debris which collects there. They therefore need a

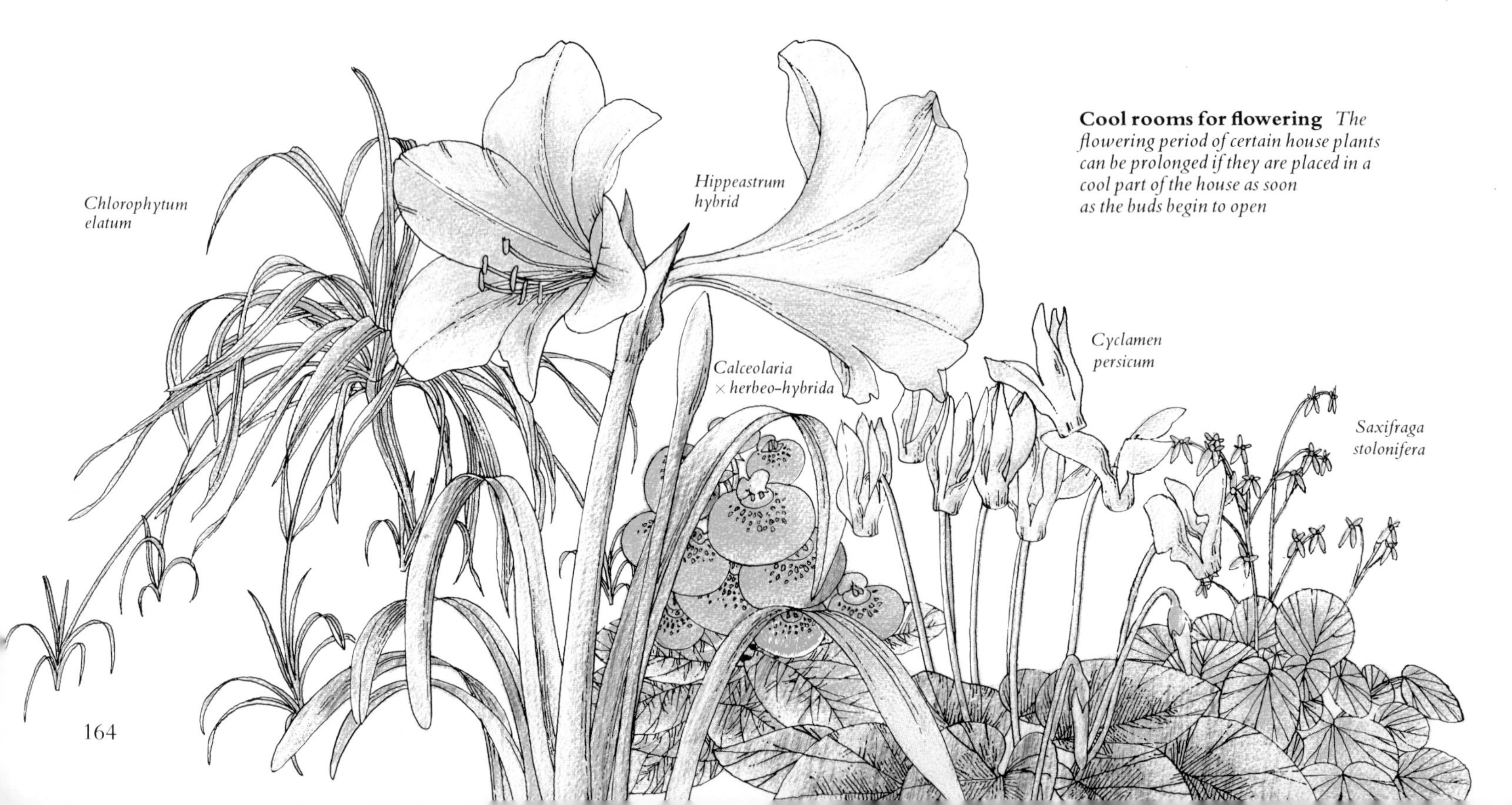

Cool rooms for flowering *The flowering period of certain house plants can be prolonged if they are placed in a cool part of the house as soon as the buds begin to open*

different compost from other house plants, usually one consisting of peat and sphagnum moss, kept barely moist. Watering is given by topping up the 'vase' formed by the leaves in the centre of the plant.

Flowering pot plants are garden or greenhouse plants that have been specially grown to flower indoors, chiefly in winter and spring. They are sold when the buds have formed, and may flower for several weeks. They need no special care beyond watering, removing dead flowers and providing a suitable atmosphere. Chrysanthemums, calceolarias and azaleas are the most popular indoor-flowering pot plants, but once they have finished blooming they must either be discarded or planted out in a greenhouse border or, if they are hardy, in the garden.

The shapes of house plants Shape is a factor to be considered in selecting house plants. They may be erect like *Ficus elastica* (rubber plant) or climbing like *Cissus antarctica* (kangaroo vine), both of which will eventually grow to a height of 6 ft or more. Others, like pileas and peperomias, are small and bushy. Tradescantias and zebrinas are trailing, requiring little headroom, but plenty of space to display their drooping stems.

Bear in mind the eventual height and shape of the plant, as well as the climatic atmosphere of each of the rooms, when choosing plants for the home.

Selecting the right plants Plants are rarely successful if you try adapting them to your home. It is far better to choose plants that will thrive naturally in the rooms where you intend to grow them. Central heating, which provides almost constant warmth, nevertheless has its drawbacks. If it is controlled by a time switch, the contrast between night and day temperatures may be too great – in fact, a drop during the night of more than 8°C (15°F) may slow down growth of the more delicate plants.

Central heating also creates a dry atmosphere which is harmful to some indoor plants, and in particular to tropical and semi-tropical plants which need a high degree of humidity. Humidity can be increased by setting the plants in trays of damp peat or in saucers of water.

All plants need freely circulating air, but few will tolerate cold draughts. Their growth may slow right down and they may die. Fumes from coal fires, oil and coal gas, can also be damaging, but plants are not affected by natural-gas fumes.

Well-lit areas, such as living-rooms and bedrooms, will suit most house plants provided they are given reasonably humid conditions. South and west-facing rooms provide the best light. Direct sun, however, is not recommended – it should be filtered through net curtains or venetian blinds. During the hottest parts of the day, plants near south-facing windows may need to be moved away from the glass to avoid scorching and wilting.

Unless the window is insulated with double-glazing or heavy curtains the plants should be moved into the room during winter nights, even in centrally heated homes,

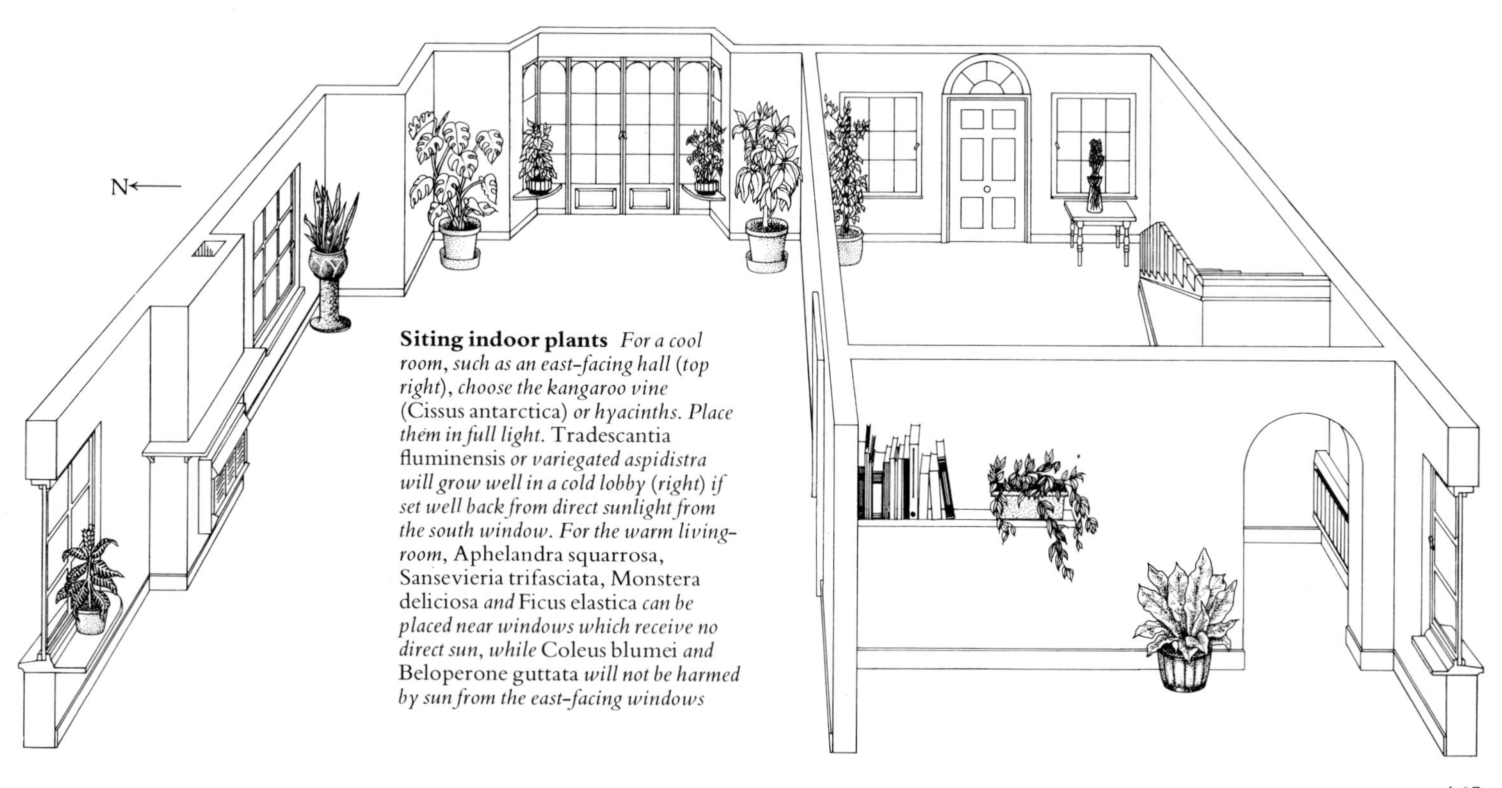

Siting indoor plants *For a cool room, such as an east-facing hall (top right), choose the kangaroo vine* (Cissus antarctica) *or hyacinths. Place them in full light.* Tradescantia fluminensis *or variegated aspidistra will grow well in a cold lobby (right) if set well back from direct sunlight from the south window. For the warm living-room,* Aphelandra squarrosa, Sansevieria trifasciata, Monstera deliciosa *and* Ficus elastica *can be placed near windows which receive no direct sun, while* Coleus blumei *and* Beloperone guttata *will not be harmed by sun from the east-facing windows*

because of the drop in temperature close to the glass. Do not leave plants in the space between glass and curtains at night.

Plants needing a degree of humidity, such as saintpaulias (African violet) and many of the indoor ferns, do particularly well in warm, moist rooms such as bathrooms and kitchens, provided the day and night temperature variations are not too extreme.

Even for badly lit, draughty places such as stairs and landings, there is a good choice of house plants. Most hederas (ivy), aspidistras, fatsias, fatshederas and several of the philodendrons do extremely well in such conditions.

For the best results, select your house plants according to the requirements you can provide in your home, bearing in mind the amount of light as well as the heat they will enjoy in the chosen position.

Difficult house plants do not thrive in homes without central heating, because of the cooler conditions or bigger variation in temperatures, but both the intermediate and easy groups are perfectly suitable for houses without central heating.

Arranging and grouping plants
Many foliage house plants are seen to their advantage when several are grouped together. Very tall plants, such as *Cissus antarctica*, fatsias, ficus and hederas, are best on their own, for they may dwarf their companions. Rosette-shaped and bushy plants with vivid foliage, as well as flowering pot plants, are also best displayed on their own.

Fast-growing climbers are ideal against room-dividers and bare walls. Many trailing plants, such as tradescantias, zebrinas and *Pelargonium peltatum*, are suitable for hanging on walls – but if possible they should be removed from their wall supports when being watered.

Many florists sell ready-grouped arrangements of three or four plants. They have been removed from their pots and set in a deep container, in a compost of loam, peat and sand with a little added charcoal to prevent the compost going sour.

Such a grouping should include plants that contrast in colour and shape, but they must all have the identical cultural requirements. Tall, erect plants should be kept to the rear, bushy and spreading ones in the centre, and trailing plants to the front of the container. Alternatively, a number of plants, in their pots, can be grouped together in a shallow tray. Stand the pots on pebbles in the tray and pour water between the pebbles so that extra humidity can be provided without the plants' roots being kept too moist.

Plant troughs are ideal for the grouping of foliage plants. They are made from wood, metal, plastic or pottery, and may be free-standing, supported by legs, or ordered to fit an indoor window-sill.

An additional advantage of a plant trough is that it can easily be moved away from too strong a light, or cold windows, to a more shaded or warmer position.

Set the pots closely together in the trough to obtain the best contrast or harmony in height, shape, colour, texture and growth habit. The pots can easily be changed around and a few flowering house plants will give additional colour.

The atmosphere immediately around the plants can be kept more moist than that of the room generally, by standing all the pots on pebbles in saucers of water or, ideally, sinking them in moist peat.

Buy plants that will thrive naturally in the position you intend to grow them. The amount of light or shade a plant requires, and its tolerance to draughts or fumes, varies from plant to plant. Plants with thick, dark foliage will tolerate shade; those with variegated leaves need more light. Few plants do well in a draught.

Warm-room plants *Leaf growth of many foliage plants can be stimulated when they are grown in a warm and humid atmosphere*

How to get the best out of house plants

Repotting plants that have outgrown their containers

All house plants need to be repotted if they become pot-bound. This happens when a plant has filled its pot with roots and has exhausted the soil in which it is growing.

You can easily tell a pot-bound plant: it makes little or no new growth, and it dries out quickly even after frequent watering. Sometimes the roots penetrate through the drainage holes in the bottom.

Generally, young plants should be repotted into larger pots once a year, in spring or early summer.

Established plants need repotting less frequently, every two to three years or even longer. They can usually be repotted in the same-size pot, with fresh compost.

Because of their confined space, pot-grown plants require more attention to soil, water and light than plants grown in the open. The soil – or compost – must contain the right proportions of essential plant foods: nitrogen, potash and phosphate. It should be free of pests and diseases and sterilised before use. This is a lengthy process, but many ready-mixed, sterilised composts are available.

The John Innes potting composts come in three grades, each consisting of the same proportions of loam, peat and sand, with added fertilisers. No. 3 contains three times as much fertiliser as No. 1.

Other suitable composts include the comparatively new soil-less or loamless composts, sold under brand names. They are largely of peat with fertilisers, and added sand for drainage.

All soil-less composts are suitable for growing house plants; alternatively, use John Innes No. 1 potting compost for young plants and No. 2 or No. 3 for established plants.

Repotting should be done when the compost in the pot is just moist.

To dislodge a pot-bound plant, place one hand over the compost, with the fingers either side of the plant stem. Invert the pot with the other hand and tap it firmly on the base to shake out the soil ball. If necessary, tap the pot against the edge of a table.

If there is a mass of intermingled roots with the soil ball, the plant needs moving into a larger-size pot. If not, return the plant to its pot with fresh compost.

With established plants, reduce the size of the soil ball by carefully easing the soil away and pulling away some of the roots.

If the pot is a clay one with a large drainage hole, place a crock – that is a piece of broken clay pot – over the hole, curved side up, to stop the compost falling through. Alternatively, use perforated zinc discs.

Plastic pots have several small drainage holes in their base and do not need any crocking.

Both types of pot should be scrubbed in water, especially on the inside, to eliminate disease organisms. New clay pots should be soaked in water for at least 12 hours, or they will draw moisture out of the compost.

Depending on the depth of the root ball, put a 1–2 in. layer of compost over the base of the pot.

Set the root ball on the compost so that the top is about ½ in. below the bottom of the rim of the pot.

Hold the plant steady in the centre with one hand, and with the fingers of the other hand trickle more compost into the space between root ball and pot. Cover the top of the ball with compost until it reaches the lower rim, then lightly thump the pot down on the working surface to settle the compost.

Top up with more compost to leave at least ½ in. space between compost and the top of the pot. Water in thoroughly, and firm lightly with the fingertips.

1 *Invert a pot-bound plant and shake out the soil-and-root ball*

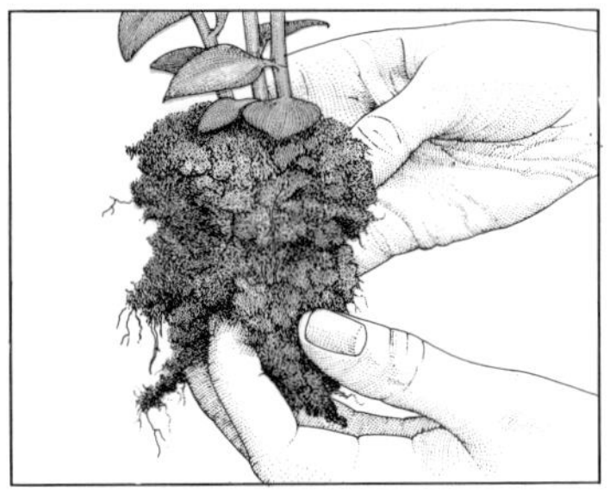

2 *Before putting the plant in a larger pot, ease away some of the old soil*

3 *Set the root ball on fresh compost and trickle more compost around it*

4 *Water the plant thoroughly and firm the compost lightly with the fingers*

How to keep leaves shiny and free from dust

Plants breathe and absorb moisture from the air through their leaves. Both sides of the leaves should be kept clean to prevent clogging of the pores. Give small-leaved plants fine overhead sprays of clean water once a month, particularly during the growing season and if the plants are kept in coal-fired rooms.

Wipe both sides of large-leaved plants with a damp pad of cottonwool from time to time. Dust-repelling liquids are available which impart a glossy sheen to the leaves at the same time as cleaning them.

Soft rain water is better than tap water both for watering and for cleaning. Set the house plants outdoors during soft warm rain showers, but bring them indoors again before nightfall.

Plants with soft hairy leaves, such as saintpaulia, must not be cleaned with water or proprietary leaf cleaners, as the leaves will become spotted. Use a fine paintbrush to remove any dust.

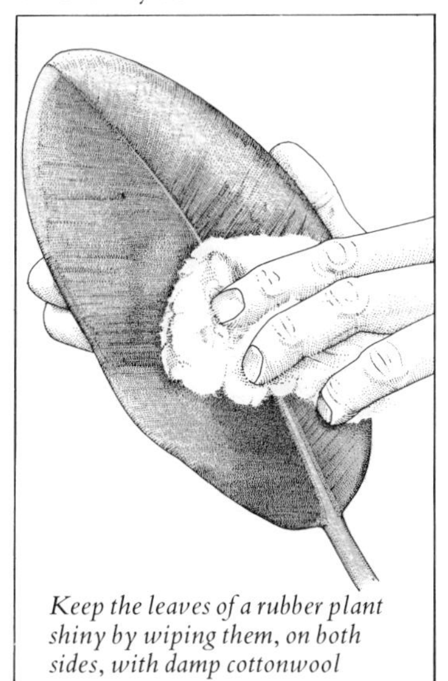

Keep the leaves of a rubber plant shiny by wiping them, on both sides, with damp cottonwool

Watering and feeding correctly

More house plants are killed by over-watering than by any other factor. The amount of water to be given depends on the type of plant, the room temperature and the time of year. Generally, house plants need more water during the growing or flowering season – late spring and summer – than during the resting period – autumn and winter. Narrow-leaved plants need more water than broad-leaved plants.

A copious watering once a week is better than a few drops every day. Tap water is normally quite satisfactory. But azaleas may develop yellow leaves if they are permanently watered with hard tap water, so use rain water whenever possible.

Long-stemmed and woody plants may be watered from the top of the pot, but tap water will eventually leave a lime deposit on the compost.

Rosette-type plants whose leaves grow straight from a low rootstock or corm, for example saintpaulia and cyclamen, should preferably not be watered from the top as this may cause rotting of the roots. Pour the water into the plant tray or saucer on which the pot stands and allow the compost to draw it up.

A badly dried-up plant can sometimes be revived by giving it a bath to ensure the root ball becomes thoroughly moist. Set the plant in a deep container and fill with water until this reaches the compost. As soon as air bubbles stop rising, the plant has had enough water.

Always avoid drops of water on hairy-leaved plants, such as gloxinia and saintpaulia. They cause discoloration and rotting of the leaves.

Liquid feed should be given during the growing season after the plants have been watered. Dissolve the feed in water according to the manufacturer's instructions, and water this on to the moist compost. One pint is generally sufficient to feed a dozen plants at a time. Many plants with poor root systems can get a boost from a foliar feed – a special spray of soluble fertiliser.

WATERING HOUSE PLANTS

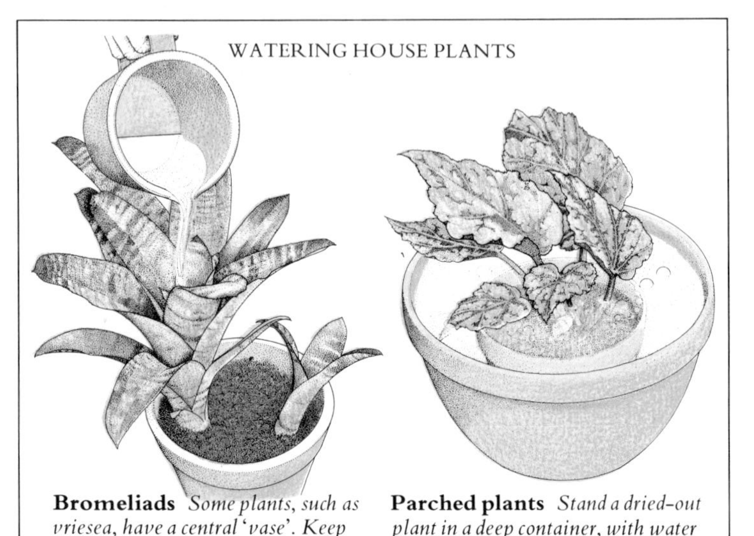

Bromeliads *Some plants, such as vriesea, have a central 'vase'. Keep this topped up with rain water*

Parched plants *Stand a dried-out plant in a deep container, with water to the top of the compost*

Creating a moist growing atmosphere

Many house plants originated in tropical jungles and rain forests, where the atmosphere is always moist. Although they have in most cases adapted themselves to drier climates, they grow better when artificial humidity is provided, even during the dormant winter season.

Central heating creates a dry atmosphere in the house. To overcome the problem, provide humidity by placing shallow trays of water beside your house plants. Alternatively, set plant pots in a larger pot or decorative container and fill the space between them with peat kept moist all the time. This does not preclude regular watering of the plants themselves. Single pots can also be stood on trays or saucers of gravel. Small polished stones are sold as an alternative. Pour water over the gravel as required, but do not let the water reach the base of the pots or rotting of the roots may occur.

Spraying with water also improves humidity as well as keeping the leaves clean. On hot summer days a daily spraying is advisable.

Some plants, particularly those with hairy or soft leaves, benefit from an occasional steam treatment. Stand the pot in a large bowl supported on a bad heat conductor, such as a brick or a pudding basin, so that the leaves are kept clear of the bowl.

Steam treatment for hairy-leaved plants

Pour boiling water into the bowl and leave the plant until the water no longer gives off steam. A well-lit, warm bathroom is the ideal place for growing saintpaulias and other hairy-leaved plants.

TWO METHODS OF PROVIDING HUMIDITY

Pebbles *In shallow water they prevent roots from being soaked*

Damp peat *Set a plant (in its pot) in damp peat inside a larger pot.*

Cutting back overgrown plants and training climbers

House plants need little or no pruning, but if they are growing straggly, shoots may be cut off cleanly just above a leaf joint.

Rubber plants and monstera that have grown too tall cannot be cut back without encouraging unwanted side-shoots. However, they can be restarted by cutting off the top shoot, about 12 in. long, below a node and inserting it in a pot of cuttings compost (p.173).

To encourage the bushy or trailing habit of plants, pinch out the tips of young shoots in spring just above a leaf joint.

This will produce side-shoots from the leaf axils.

Bushy and single-stemmed plants need no support, but climbing plants – such as the ivies and philodendrons – should be trained as soon as they are growing strongly. Insert bamboo canes in the pot and tie the shoots loosely into place with soft raffia or plastic rings, obtainable from florists' shops.

Triangular, square and circular trellis frames made of bamboo or plastic are also available.

Philodendrons and some other climbers develop aerial roots through which the plants obtain part of their nourishment. Such climbers are best trained on moss sticks – poles or circular frames filled with moss or other fibrous material. The moss must be kept constantly moist.

Looking after house plants during summer holidays

Before you go on holiday, arrange with a friend to look after your plants. If this is not possible, a few simple precautions will ensure that the plants will remain healthy for two or three weeks.

Remove all flowers and flower buds, pinching them off cleanly with the fingernails. This reduces the amount of water the plants will need while unattended.

Move the plants away from south or west-facing windows, out of direct sunlight.

Water the plants well, then pack them in deep boxes, surrounding them with wet, screwed-up newspaper or thoroughly soaked peat.

Or, alternatively, water each plant thoroughly and cover with a polythene bag. Blow into the bag to extend it and keep it away from the leaves. Seal the bag around the pot with a rubber band.

Several automatic watering systems are available. However, the simplest watering for a number of plants is a home-made capillary system, using 1 in. lamp wicks.

Set a bucket of water on a brick or box on the draining board, or on a kitchen table. Arrange as many plants as possible round the bucket. Tie a small stone to one end of a lamp wick, and drop it into the bucket. Insert the other end of the wick in the soil of a pot. (One wick for each plant.) The water will seep through the wicks and into the pots.

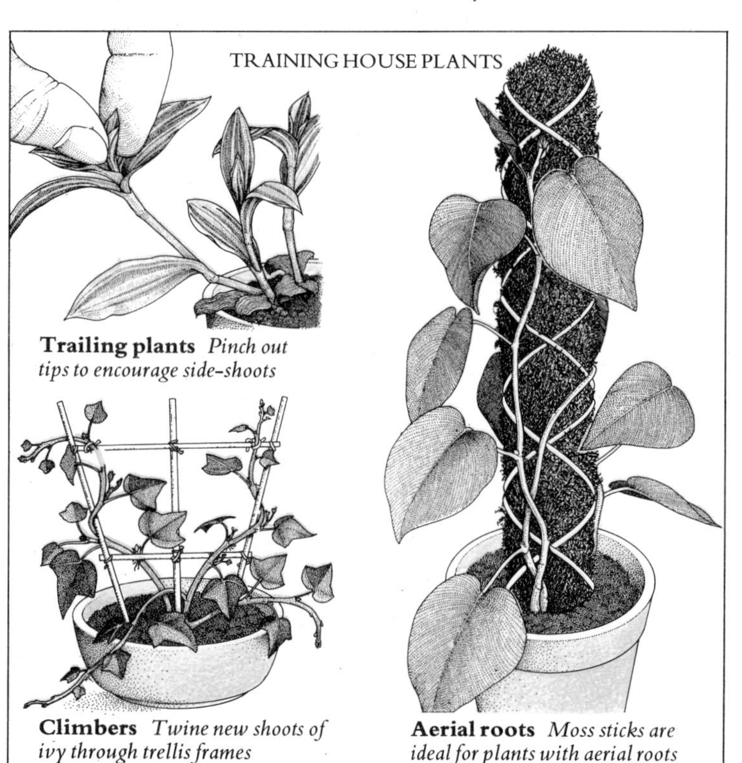

TRAINING HOUSE PLANTS

Trailing plants *Pinch out tips to encourage side-shoots*

Climbers *Twine new shoots of ivy through trellis frames*

Aerial roots *Moss sticks are ideal for plants with aerial roots*

THREE WAYS OF KEEPING PLANTS MOIST

Wet newspaper *Pack wet newspaper or peat round pots in a box*

Plastic bag *Cover the plant with a plastic bag held by a rubber band*

Lamp wicks *Push a 1 in. lamp wick into the compost, with the other end in a bucket of water. This method lasts several weeks*

What can go wrong with house plants

House plants are not often attacked by pests and diseases. Lack of healthy vigorous growth and poor leaf and flower production are more often caused by wrong growing conditions, including incorrect watering, poor light and a dry atmosphere.

Symptoms	Cause	Cure
Poor or absent blooms, weak and elongated stems, leaves smaller and paler than usual	Light deficiency	Increase existing light – if necessary with warm-white fluorescent tubes for flowering plants, and daylight fluorescent tubes for foliage plants
Lopsided growth, with stems and leaves bending to one side	Light deficiency	Give the pot a quarter turn every other day to provide even light
Pale or brownish mottling, particularly on young leaves	Red spider mites, thrips	Spray with malathion
Plants stunted and with poor roots, often rotting or browning	Usually over-watering	Let plants dry out completely between waterings
Slow stem and leaf growth even when fed; soil dries out quickly, even after frequent watering; roots growing through drainage holes in pot	Pot-bound	Move plants into larger pots
Plants growing slowly or not at all	Under-feeding, over-watering or pot-bound	Feed regularly, reduce watering or pot on
Wilting	Soil or atmosphere too dry, too much sun or heat, over-watering, pot-bound	Spray leaves frequently, reduce watering and check on drainage, or move into larger pots
Sudden drop of buds, flowers and leaves	Usually a shock to the plant's system caused by a sudden change in temperature, light, increase of coal-gas fumes, prolonged cold draught or dryness of roots	Improve cultural conditions
Variegated leaves revert to green	Light deficiency or over-feeding	Cut off green leaves and move plant to a lighter position; reduce feeding
Brown edges or spots on leaves	Hot dry air, draughts, paraffin, coal-gas fumes, over-watering, sun-scorch, water splashes, over-feeding, pot-bound	Improve cultural conditions, pick off badly affected leaves
Yellow leaves which stay firm and healthy	Lime in compost, or tap water used for lime-hating plants	Repot in John Innes acid potting compost or a loamless compost, and water with rain water

Unusual house plants from fruit

Growing plants from fruit stones

Exotic and unusual additions to house-plant collections can be grown from the stones of many fruits, such as avocado pears, peaches and dates.

Peach and date stones can be put in 2–3 in. pots of seed compost, covered with black polythene and left to germinate at a temperature of 18°C (64°F). Peach stones should first be subjected to a temperature of 4°C (39°F) for several weeks before being planted.

To grow an avocado plant, insert three matchsticks to half their length into the soft stone. The object of bruising the stone is to stimulate rooting. Germination from stones is quickest in late summer.

Suspend the stone over the mouth of a jar of water. The water should reach to about $\frac{3}{4}$ in. below the base of the stone.

After six to eight weeks, thick white roots will appear from the base of the stone. Pot the stone, 2–3 in. deep, in a large pot of John Innes No. 1 compost and keep it in a well-lit, warm and humid place. Eventually, a single shoot will come up through the compost and develop long slender leaves.

Avocado plants grow rapidly and need repotting annually; pinch out the growing shoot when the required height is reached.

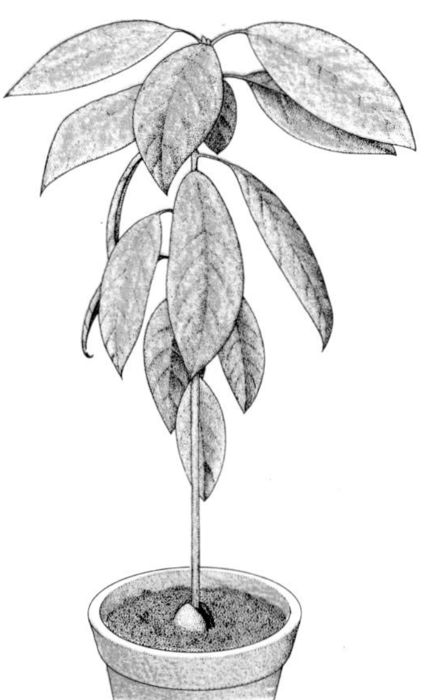

Avocado plant grown from a stone

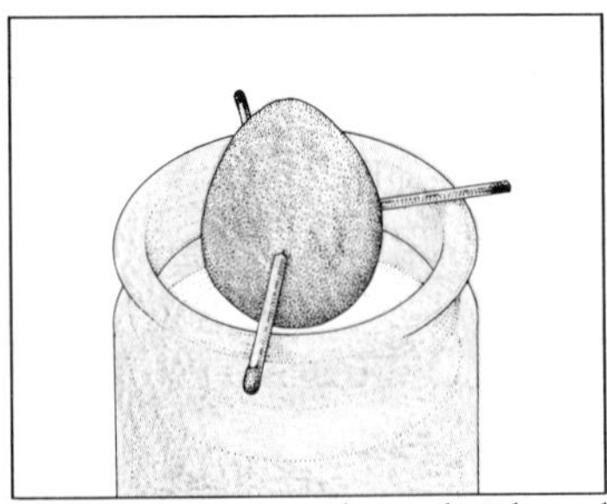

1 *Pierce the stone with matchsticks and suspend it over a jar of water*

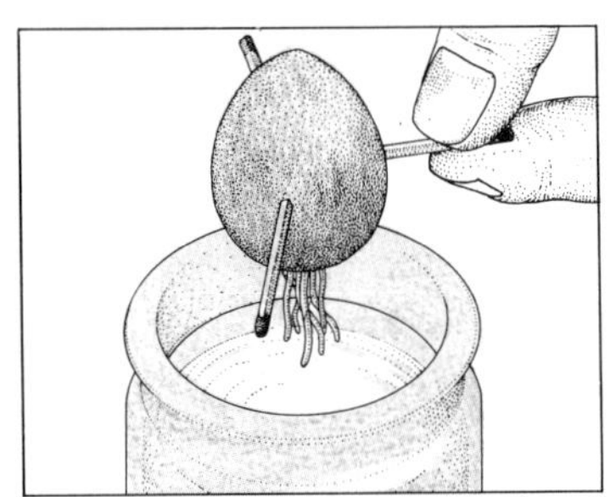

2 *After six to eight weeks, a number of brittle roots appear from the base*

3 *Pot the stone, roots down, 2–3 in. deep in moist compost*

House plants from pips of citrus fruit

Plants can be grown from the pips of grapefruit, lemons and oranges. The plants may flower but are unlikely to fruit. Plant the pips as soon as they are removed from the fruit.

Fill a 4 in. pot to within ½ in. of the top with a proprietary seed compost, or a compost made of 1 part loam and 1 part peat.

Water the compost thoroughly and bury the pips, four to six to each pot, ½ in. deep. Cover the pot loosely with a small sheet of polythene and secure with adhesive tape or a rubber band.

Germinate the pips at a temperature of 18°C (64°F); rooting should occur within a few weeks, and leaf-bearing shoots will appear through the compost.

Remove the polythene and leave the pot at the same temperature. When the plantlets are well established, plant them singly in 3–4 in. pots of John Innes No. 1 compost. They will eventually grow into 3–4 ft short-stemmed, bushy plants.

1 *Fill a 4 in. pot with seed compost, water thoroughly and leave to drain*

2 *Bury four to six fresh fruit pips and top with ½ in. of compost*

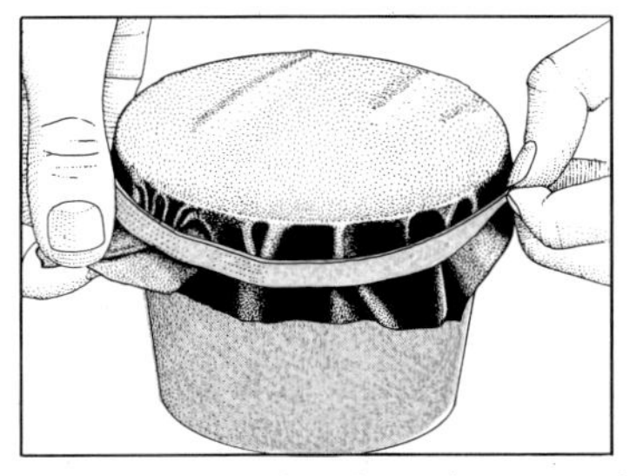

3 *Cover the pot loosely with a piece of polythene and secure with tape*

Pip-grown lemon tree

Growing a pineapple plant from a fresh leaf top

Slice the green, leafy top from a fresh pineapple, together with a narrow piece of flesh containing the top row of 'pips' on the skin. Dry off the top for one or two days.

Fill a 3½–4 in. pot to within ¾ in. of its top with moist potting compost; sprinkle a thin layer of coarse sand on top.

Set the pineapple crown on the sand, and sprinkle a little more compost over the fleshy part.

Cover the pot with a polythene bag and put in a shaded position, at a temperature of 18°C (64°F). Rooting generally takes place in about eight weeks, and is indicated by the fresh appearance of the leaf tuft and possibly by new leaves.

Once growth is well established, remove the polythene and repot the plant in a larger pot.

The plant may grow to 2 ft high, but is unlikely to fruit unless given considerable humidity and warmth.

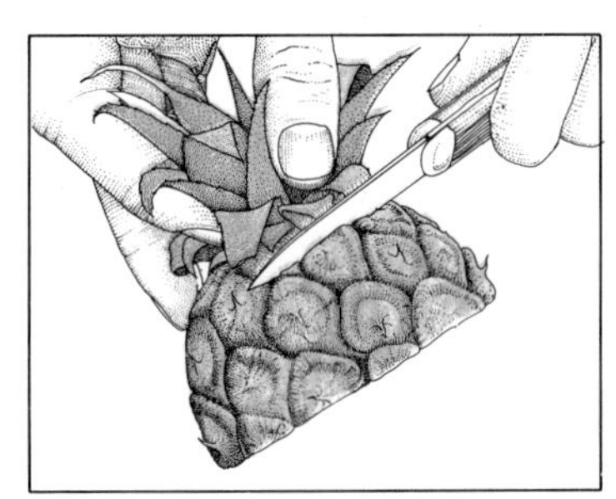

1 *Cut the crown and the top row of 'pips' from a fresh pineapple*

2 *Set the top on a shallow layer of coarse sand sprinkled over compost*

3 *Sprinkle fresh compost over the pineapple and firm with the fingers*

4 *Pull a clear polythene bag over the pot and secure with an elastic band*

Young pineapple plant

How to grow new house plants from old

Most house plants can be increased, some by simply dividing the plant into two or more pieces or by taking quick-rooting tip or leaf cuttings, or by removing offsets from suckering plants. Other plants may be increased by more complicated methods requiring artificial heat and moisture.

The following are the main propagation methods: division, air layering, cuttings of tip or side-shoots, leaf cuttings, offsets and plantlets.

Many house plants can also be raised from seeds. Most seedsmen and nurseries stock seeds of popular plants, such as begonias and impatiens, and some have seeds of more exotic plants, such as dizygotheca and fatsia. Most seeds germinate easily, but the plants will take a couple of years to reach maturity and need close attention and care during the early stages.

Sow the seeds during late spring or summer, in pots of seed compost.

Cover the seeds with a thin layer of sand or compost, and leave them to germinate, preferably at a temperature of 16–18°C (61–64°F).

As soon as the seedlings have developed two pairs of leaves, pot them singly into $2\frac{1}{2}$–3 in. pots of John Innes No. 1 compost.

Keep the young plants well watered in a shaded, draught-proof place until new growth is evident. Gradually move the plants into more light, but away from draughts. Provide extra humidity and, when the plants are growing strongly, move them to their permanent positions.

Dividing multi-stemmed house plants

Division or splitting of a plant is the easiest method of propagation.

Only certain types of plants, however, can be increased in this way. Each plant must have at least two, and preferably several, stems arising from or below ground level, each stem with an independent, well-developed root system.

Suitable plants for division include adiantum (maidenhair fern), asparagus (asparagus fern), chlorophytum (spider plant), aspidistra, fittonia, cyperus (umbrella grass), nephrolepis, peperomia and sansevieria (mother-in-law's tongue).

House plants can be divided at any time during the growing period, from late spring to early autumn.

Knock the plant out of its pot, and tease away the soil round the crown and root ball, using a small stick or your fingers. This will expose the rootstock and the points at which the plant can be divided.

Grasp the base of the plant in both hands and pull it gently but firmly apart. If the crown or rootstock is thick and tough, sever the largest roots or the underground stems with a sharp knife.

Pot the separated pieces at once in John Innes No. 2 compost.

Water sparingly at first and keep the pots in a shaded warm position for a few weeks.

Certain house plants, especially beloperone, tradescantia, pilea and zebrina, are often grown commercially from three or more cuttings in the same small pot. As the cuttings grow, they form one single plant which can later be divided by pulling it carefully apart. Pot up the separate pieces.

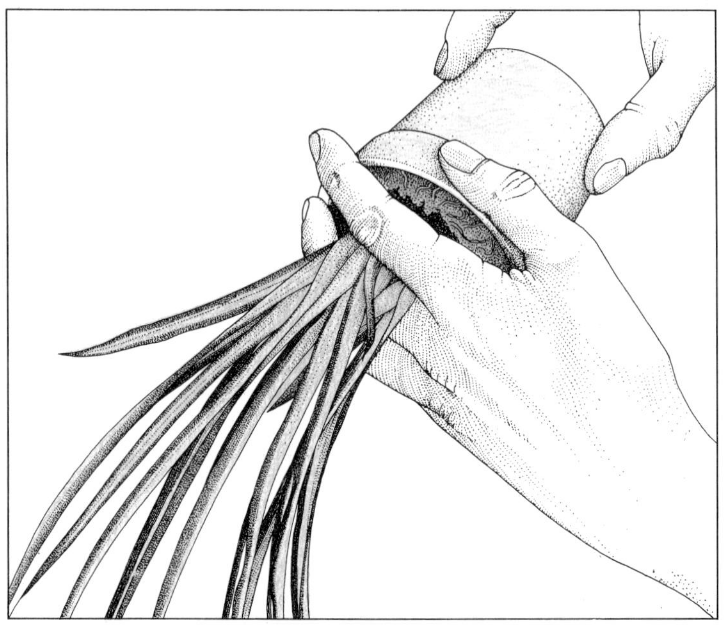

1 *Invert the pot and place your fingers around the stems; knock the rim of the pot against the edge of a table to dislodge the compost and the roots*

2 *Ease away the compost and carefully pull the roots of the plant apart*

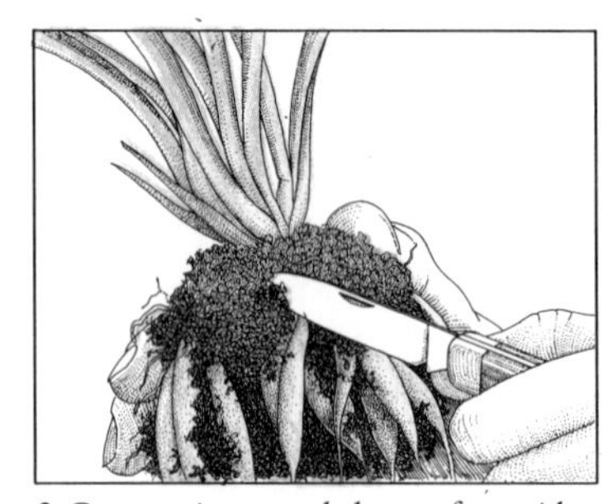

3 *Cut any intertangled roots free with a sharp knife or a razor blade*

4 *Set each division in a pot of John Innes No. 2 potting compost*

5 *Fill up with more compost, and level it $\frac{1}{2}$ in. below the top of the pot*

Taking tip cuttings from non-flowering stems

Cuttings from hollow-stemmed plants, such as impatiens and tradescantia, and from ivy root extremely easily.

Take cuttings from the tips of young, non-flowering stems or side-shoots, between June and August. Strip the lower leaves from a 3–4 in. cutting, and trim it cleanly just below a leaf node. Stand the cutting in a glass of tap water; roots will appear within 10–14 days and the cutting can then be potted up.

With other house plants, insert the cuttings at once in a rooting medium.

Fill a 3½ in. pot to just below the rim with a mixture of equal quantities of peat and coarse sand, or a proprietary cuttings compost.

Using a sharp knife, cut off the top 3–4 in. of a stem or side-shoot. Pull off the lower leaves and make a clean cut across the stem, just below a leaf node.

With a small dibber or stick make a number of 1–1½ in. deep planting holes in the compost – a 3½ in. pot will accommodate four to six cuttings. Make the holes round the edge of the pot so that the stems are supported on the rim.

Firm the compost gently round each cutting. Fill the pot to the rim with water and leave to drain.

Cover the pot loosely with a polythene bag and secure with a rubber band. Set the pot in a shaded position where a temperature of 18°C (64°F) can be maintained. Keep the compost moist.

After three or four weeks the cuttings should have rooted, and the tips will be showing fresh growth.

Remove the polythene bag, and carefully invert the pot. Separate the rooted cuttings carefully, and pot singly in 3–3½ in. pots of John Innes No. 1 compost.

Water carefully, and keep the plants in a shaded, draught-free place until they are growing well.

HOW TO TAKE TIP CUTTINGS

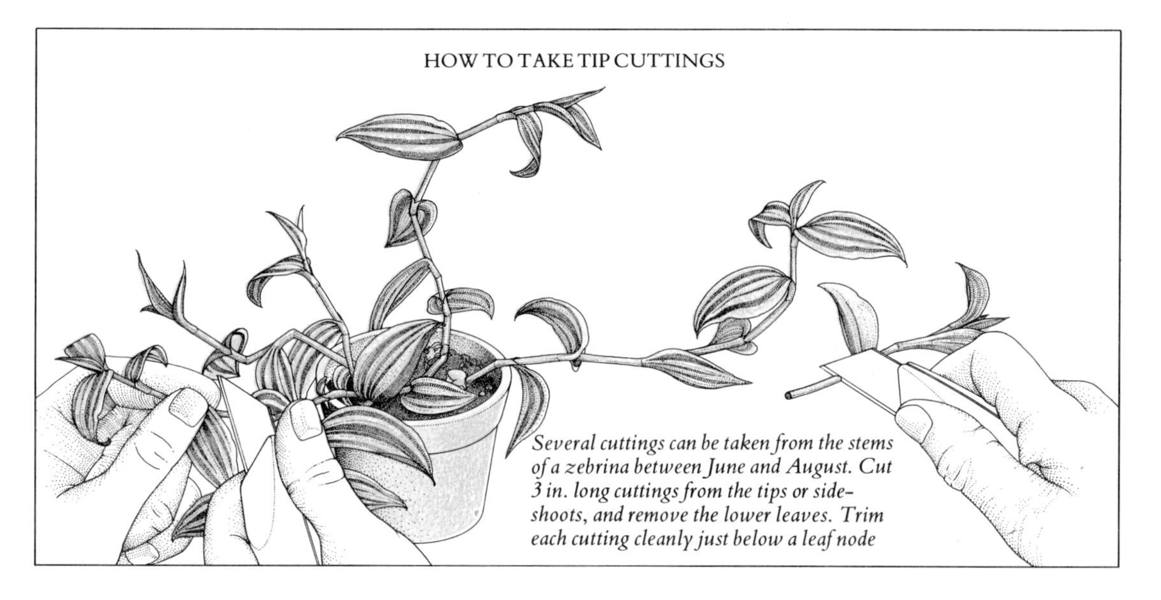

Several cuttings can be taken from the stems of a zebrina between June and August. Cut 3 in. long cuttings from the tips or side-shoots, and remove the lower leaves. Trim each cutting cleanly just below a leaf node

ROOTING TIP CUTTINGS

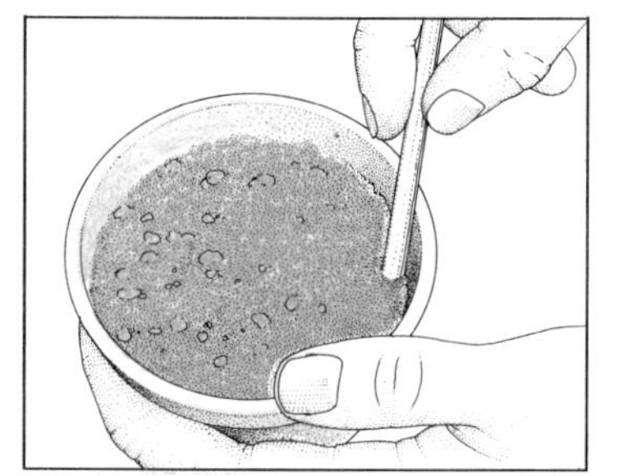

1 *Make four to six planting holes round the edge of a 3½ in. pot*

2 *Insert each cutting so that the stem rests against the pot*

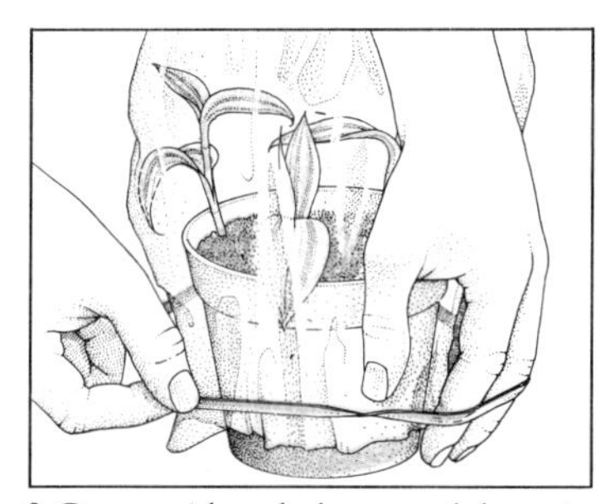

3 *Cover with polythene, and keep in shade until the cuttings are rooted*

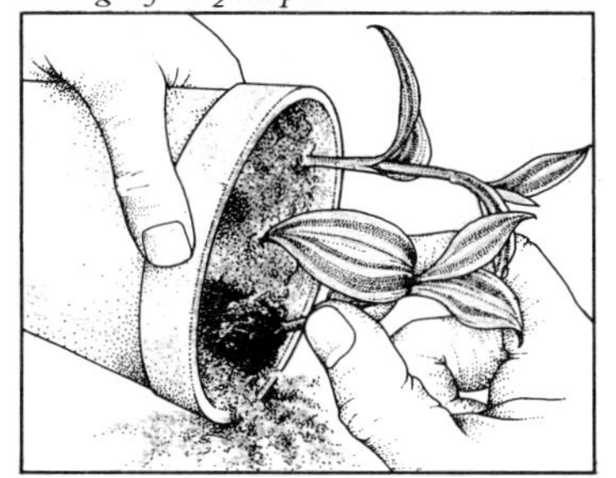

4 *Tip up the pot, and carefully separate the rooted cuttings*

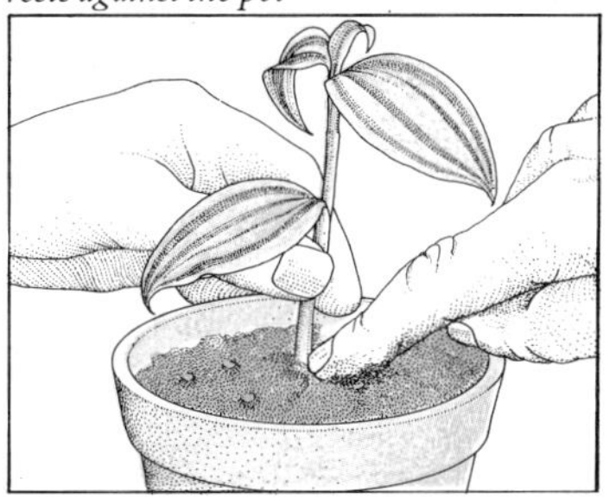

5 *Pot the new plants singly in 3–3½ in. pots of John Innes No. 1 compost*

6 *Water the potted cuttings and keep in a shaded place for a few weeks*

Removing rooted offsets from suckering plants

Most of the bromeliads, such as billbergia, aechmea and vriesea, as well as other house plants (fatsia, hippeastrum and aglaonema) readily produce offsets or suckers. These small plants, which appear at the base of the parent, either close to it or a short distance away, may eventually overcrowd the pot.

Offsets which have reached about half the height of the parent plant can be easily removed and potted up separately. The best time for this type of propagation is between June and August.

Knock the plant from its pot, placing the fingers of one hand round the stems and inverting the pot with the other hand. If necessary, tap the pot against the workbench to loosen the root ball.

Remove the plant from the pot and crumble away the soil.

Hold the root ball, stems up, in one hand and tear or cut away the offset complete with roots, but take care not to break them.

Put a layer of moist John Innes No. 2 compost in a 3–4 in. pot, and set the offset on top so that the top of the crown is ½ in. below the rim of the pot. Trickle in more compost and firm with the fingertips.

Fill the pot with water and allow to drain thoroughly.

Tall offsets will need staking for one or two months, until the root systems are well established. Insert a bamboo cane close to the plant and secure with one or two ties.

Set the plant in a well-lit position, but out of direct sunlight for a couple of weeks. A north-west-facing window-sill is the ideal place. Keep the compost moist.

1 *Knock pot of congested billbergia firmly to loosen the root ball*

2 *Pull the rooted offset away without damaging the roots*

3 *Insert the offset in a 3–4 in. pot of compost; firm with the fingers*

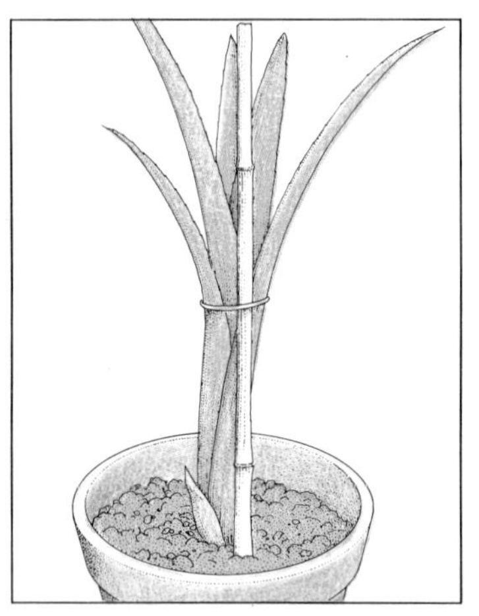

4 *Tie tall offsets to bamboo stakes for a few weeks; keep moist*

Detaching and rooting plants from runners

Some plants, notably saxifraga and chlorophytum, produce small plants either on the flowering spikes or on thin runners from the parent plant.

On saxifraga detach the thread-like runners, each of which bears a plantlet, from the parent plant. Nip off the runner from the plantlet.

Fill a 2½ in. pot with moist John Innes No. 1 compost to within ½ in. of the rim.

Make a shallow depression in the surface and set the plantlet in it. Firm the compost round the base of the plant.

Do not water, but place a polythene bag over the pot and secure with a rubber band.

Keep the pot out of direct sunlight and at a temperature of 18–21°C (64–70°F). Keep the compost moist.

After about ten days, the plantlet should have rooted. Remove the bag and set the pot in a lighter and cooler place.

Chlorophytum often bears a number of plantlets on tough stalks. These can be layered into individual 2 in. pots of John Innes No. 2 compost and secured with wire staples. After about three weeks, the plantlets should have rooted and the stalks can be severed.

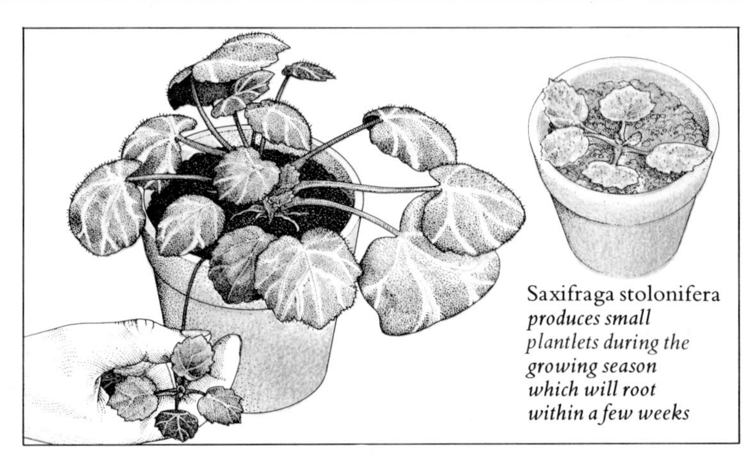

Saxifraga stolonifera *produces small plantlets during the growing season which will root within a few weeks*

Leaf cuttings from hairy or fleshy-leaved plants

House plants with thick, hairy or fleshy leaves, such as saintpaulia, begonia, sinningia (gloxinia) and peperomia, are increased by leaf cuttings.

The best time for this propagation method is from June to September.

To grow new plants from old, cut two or three healthy leaves, each with a 1–1½ in. stalk, from the plant.

Almost fill a 3½ in. pot with a mixture of equal quantities of peat and coarse sand, or a proprietary cuttings compost. Make two or three planting holes, slightly less deep than the stalks.

Trim the end of each leaf stalk cleanly across with a sharp knife.

Insert the leaf stalks into the holes. The base of each stalk should just touch the bottom of the hole, but the leaf itself must be clear of the compost, or rotting may occur.

Firm the cuttings gently with the fingertips, taking care not to bruise the slender stalks.

Ideally, the cuttings should be left to root in a propagating unit with additional heat, but a close and warm atmosphere can easily be provided in the home. Fill the pot to the top with water and let it drain thoroughly, then enclose it in a polythene bag. Secure the bag with a rubber band, and take care not to let the compost dry out. A moist compost, however, may cause condensation on the inside of the bag. If this happens, remove the bag and turn it inside out before replacing it.

After three to five weeks, roots should have formed, and new leaves will appear from the base of the leaf stem. Invert the pot and separate the rooted cuttings carefully, without breaking the fine roots. Pot the cuttings singly in 2½ in. pots of John Innes No. 1 compost. Water and drain thoroughly. Keep the plants in a shaded, warm position for two or three weeks.

HOW TO TAKE LEAF CUTTINGS

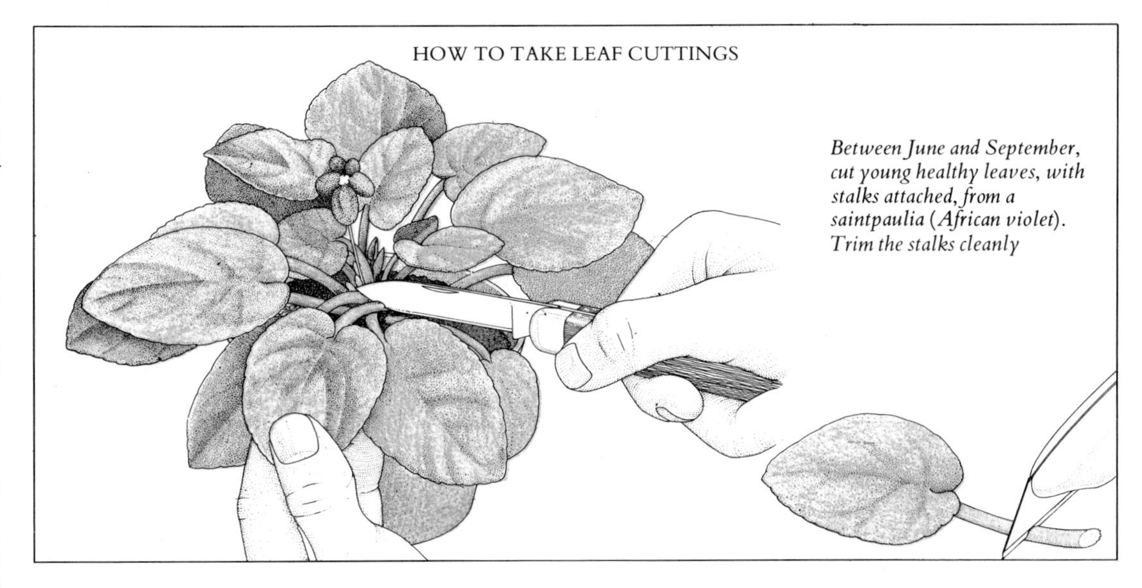

Between June and September, cut young healthy leaves, with stalks attached, from a saintpaulia (African violet). Trim the stalks cleanly

ROOTING LEAF CUTTINGS FROM SAINTPAULIAS

1 *With a small stick make a few planting holes in a pot of compost*

2 *Insert each cutting so that the leaf blade is just touching the compost*

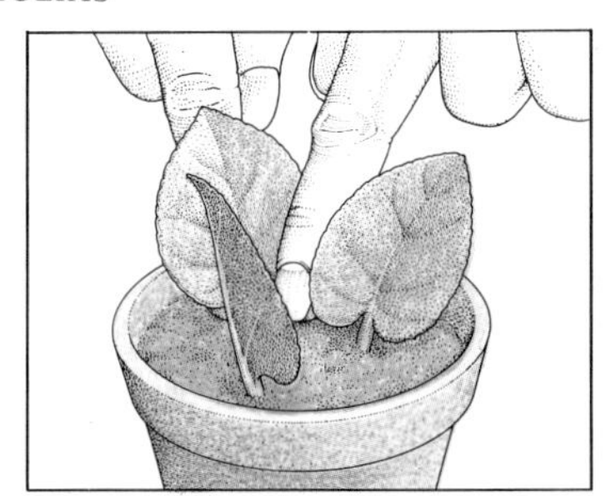

3 *Firm the compost with the fingers, avoiding damaging the stalks*

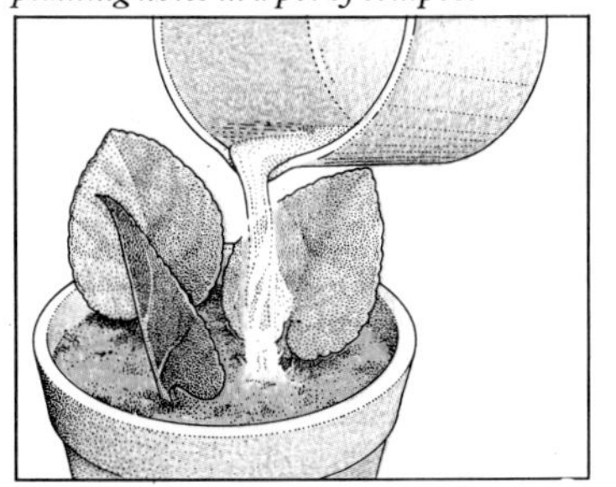

4 *Fill the pot with water to the top and let it drain completely*

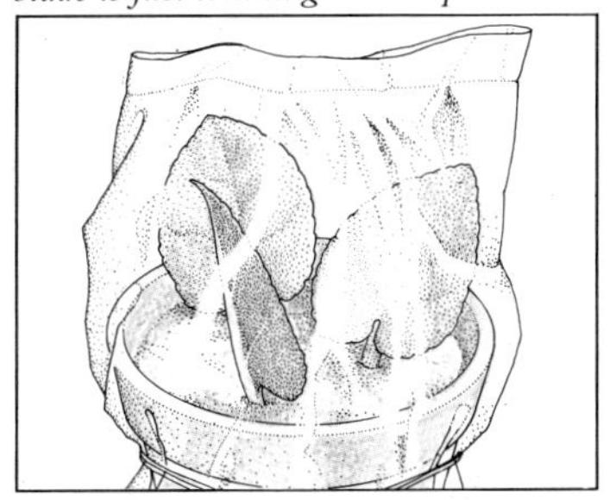

5 *Cover the pot with a polythene bag, secured with a rubber band*

6 *When new leaves have grown, pot each cutting in potting compost*

Raising several new plants from one leaf

Several new plants can be grown from one leaf, if it is large enough, as in the case of *Begonia rex*.

At any time between June and September, detach a mature leaf and trim the stalk to within $\frac{1}{2}$–1 in. of the leaf base. Using a sharp knife, make a number of cuts on the underside where the main veins join.

Place the leaf, cut side down, on a seed pan of moist John Innes No. 1 potting compost. Secure the leaf to the compost with pebbles or crocks. Cover the pan with polythene and place it in a temperature of 21°C (70°F).

After about four weeks, small plantlets will appear from the cuts.

Remove the polythene, and leave the pan in a warm, shady place for another two or three weeks.

Pot the rooted plantlets individually in $2\frac{1}{2}$ in. pots of potting compost.

1 *Increase* Begonia rex *and other begonias from leaf cuttings*

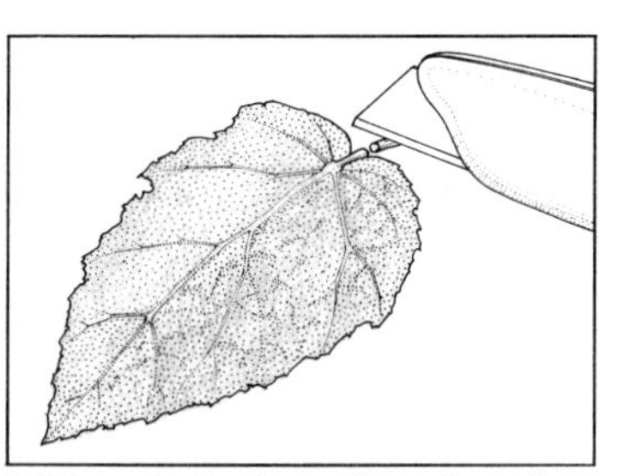

2 *Select a leaf and trim the stalk to about $\frac{1}{2}$ in. from the leaf base*

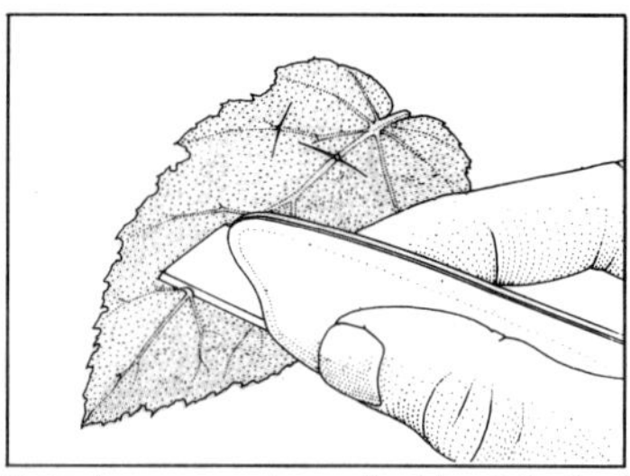

3 *Make cuts on the underside of the leaf where the main veins meet*

4 *Lay the leaf, cut side down, on the compost and weight it down with crocks*

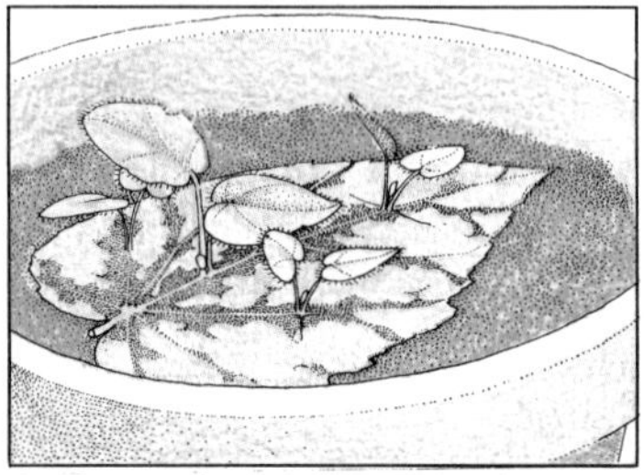

5 *After a few weeks, plantlets will appear from the cut intersections*

Increasing sansevieria from leaf sections

The leaves of sansevieria can be cut into horizontal sections, each of which will produce a new plant.

During spring or summer, select a one-year-old healthy leaf and cut it away close to the crown.

Fill a 5 in. pot with moist John Innes No. 1 compost.

Using a sharp knife, cut the leaf crossways into 1 in. deep sections.

Insert three or four sections, lower side down, in the compost to half their depth.

Spray the cuttings with tepid water, and place a polythene bag over the pot. Keep the cuttings in a shaded position at a temperature of 21°C (70°F).

When each section begins to produce a leaf, after about six weeks, remove the polythene and pot the young plants singly in 3 in. pots of John Innes No. 1 compost.

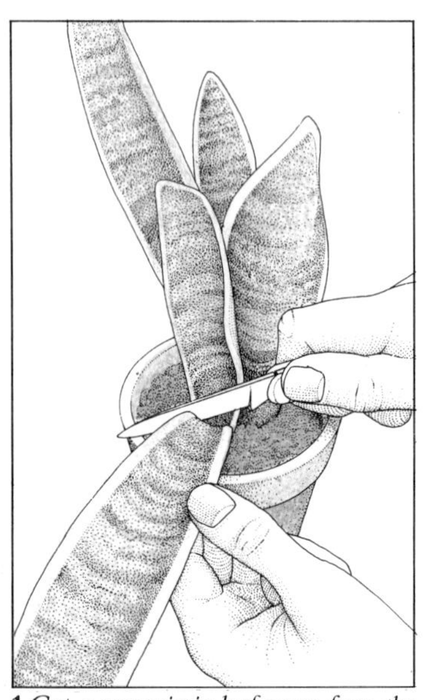

1 *Cut a sansevieria leaf away from the crown of the parent plant*

2 *Using a sharp knife, cut the leaf into 1 in. deep horizontal sections*

3 *Insert the sections, lower side down, in a pan of moist potting compost*

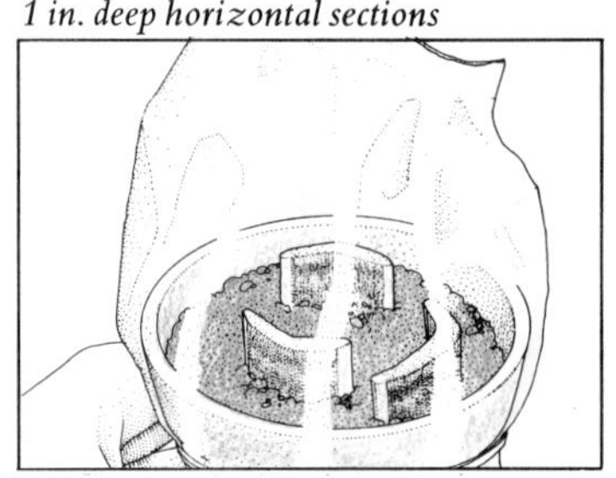

4 *Cover with a polythene bag to create a humid atmosphere*

5 *After six weeks the leaf sections will develop into young plants*

Propagating plants by air layering

After some years dizygothecas and rubber plants (ficus) may grow too tall, and will often lose their lower leaves. Rather than throw the plant out, propagate it by the air-layering method in spring to produce a new, shorter-stemmed plant.

Using a sharp knife, remove the leaves 6–9 in. below the growing tip. Cut them flush with the stem, without damaging the tissues.

Then make an upward-slanting cut about 1½ in. long, starting below a leaf node. Tie the stem to a stake above and below the cut.

Prop the cut open with a piece of slate, and brush both sides with hormone rooting powder.

Remove the slate and fold clear polythene around the cut. The polythene should be about 6–7 in. wide and long enough to come 3–4 in. below and above the cut. Seal with adhesive tape below the cut, to create a tube or sleeve.

Fill the tube with thoroughly moistened sphagnum moss or peat, pressing it into and around the cut with a small stick. Seal the top of the tube with tape, so that the rooting medium will remain moist.

After eight to ten weeks the cut should have produced roots.

Sever the shoot below the tube and carefully free the roots from the polythene and moss. Discard the old plant or let it grow on to produce side-shoots.

Pot the new plant in a 4 in. pot of John Innes No. 2 compost. For the first two or three weeks, until the new root system is established, grow the plant in a temperature of 18–21°C (64–70°F) and syringe the leaves daily with water.

1 *In spring, remove any leaves about 6–9 in. below the top cluster on an overgrown rubber plant. Cut the leaves flush with the stem*

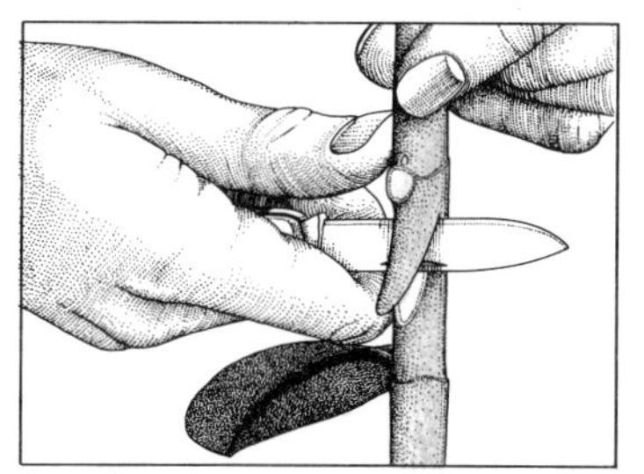

2 *Make a slanting, upward cut, 1½–2 in. long, from below a leaf node*

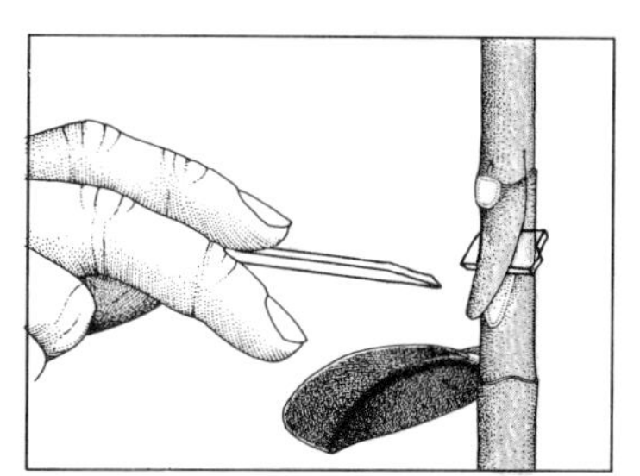

3 *Open out the cut carefully and brush with hormone rooting powder*

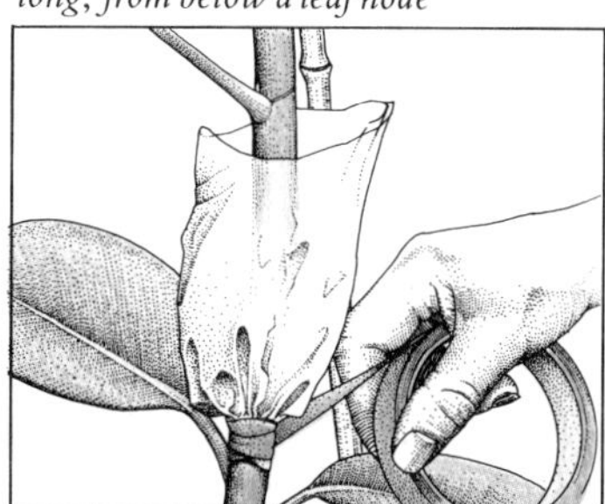

4 *Secure a polythene tube over the cut with adhesive tape*

5 *Pack the polythene with moist sphagnum moss and seal the tube*

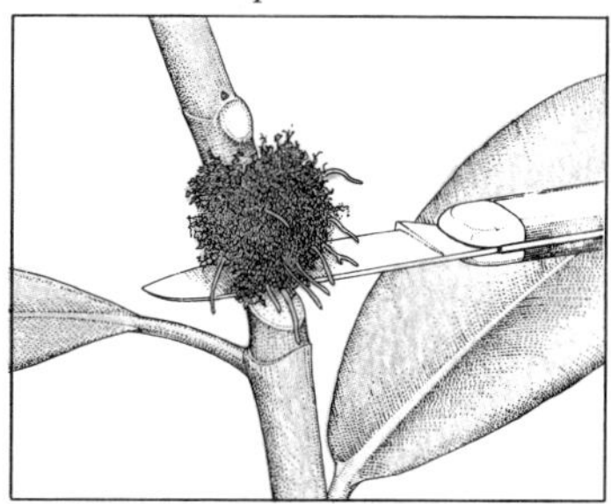

6 *When roots become visible, sever the shoot just below them*

7 *Pot the new rubber plant in John Innes No. 2 potting compost*

Irises

From the stately bearded iris – long known as the flag iris – down to tiny plants that grow from bulbs, the iris provides a delicate beauty throughout the year

Irises are ancient garden plants that were cultivated in Asia well before the birth of Christ.

There are two groups – those that grow from rhizomes (thick, underground stems) and those that grow from bulbs.

The most popular rhizomatous types are the bearded irises which have fleshy hairs like a beard on the outer petals, or 'falls'.

The bearded irises, also called flag or German irises, are classified according to their height – tall bearded (28 in. and over), intermediate bearded (10–28 in.) and dwarf bearded (under 10 in.). All have thick, creeping rhizomes with a fan of broad leaves growing from the ends, from which also grows the single flower stem or spike. Flower colours include white, pink, blue, purple-black, gold, red and many combinations.

Ideally, tall bearded irises should be planted in separate beds or in groups at the front of herbaceous or shrub borders. They bloom in early June when there are few other bold flowers, and their foliage makes a pleasant contrast to the leaves of other plants.

Intermediate bearded irises flower from early to late May and are suitable for the front of iris beds, or beds of low-growing shrubs or perennials. They may also be used in large rock-garden pockets.

Dwarf bearded irises will not stand much competition, and are best kept to rock-garden pockets or in groups in front of small plants. They flower in late April, and several varieties clumped together provide a striking effect.

Apart from the bearded types, there are non-bearded, but equally beautiful irises. The main ones are the sibiricas, or Siberian irises, which grow 3–4 ft high. Their leaves are narrow and grassy, and flowers are produced in mid-June on tall slender stems which are ideal for cutting.

Sibiricas can be used as mid-border plants in most soils, but they prefer a position which gets plenty of moisture.

Pacific Coast hybrids are smaller plants with slim, evergreen leaves. Flowers appear from early May to early June in white or shades of yellow, orange and blue. They grow on wiry stems which range in height from 9 to 18 in. Pacific Coast hybrids flourish in sun or semi-shade in a lime-free soil, and are best planted in the front of a border or in front of shrubs. They are commonly grown from seeds or seedlings bought from a specialist iris nursery.

Other beardless irises include the spuria, stylosa and crested types.

The spurias are suitable for the back of the border, since they grow to 3–4 ft. They are long-lived, and have fine, reedy, mid-green foliage. Several flowers are carried on one stem in late June.

The winter-flowering stylosa iris, *Iris unguicularis*, likes a hot, dry position against a south-facing wall. It flowers from October to March, and its straggly foliage can be trimmed back to 12 in. for neatness as soon as flowering starts.

The crested irises, or evansias, which include *I. japonica*, *I. milesii* and *I. tectorum*, have orchid-like flowers, with crests rather like a cock's comb on the falls instead of beards. The broad, glossy leaves are evergreen.

There are other irises that will grow only in boggy soil or submerged beneath water.

The kaempferi and louisiana hybrids can be planted in a bog garden, but not directly in water. The

'Galilee', a pure blue and white tall bearded iris

kaempferi types have deciduous foliage with very large flowers in July. The louisianas have evergreen foliage, and carry flowers on their zigzag stems during late June and early July.

The English, American and Japanese water irises, *I. pseudacorus*, *I. versicolor* and *I. laevigata*, are very vigorous plants. They should be planted in 2–4 in. of water, either in pots or baskets, or directly into the bed of the pond. They flower in June and July. For cultivation of water plants, see page 327.

The bulbous irises, which are grown like daffodils or crocuses, are the only irises that will grow well in pots indoors. There are three types – reticulatas, xiphiums and junos.

The reticulatas (4–8 in. high) are quite distinctive, with their square-section foliage. They flower between December and March, and some of the blooms are pleasantly perfumed. They are useful plants for growing both indoors in pots and outside in the rock garden.

The xiphiums (18–24 in.) include the well-known Dutch, Spanish and English irises. Both Dutch and Spanish irises like a warm, dry soil, but the English irises prefer moist, cool soil.

The Dutch irises flower first, starting in early June. Then follow the Spanish, and after them the English in late June and continuing into July.

The Dutch and Spanish irises produce foliage in the autumn – unlike the English, whose new leaves appear in spring.

Juno irises (12–24 in.) grow from bulbs which have fleshy storage roots, and if they are to be pot grown, deep pots should be used to accommodate these roots. The most easily grown juno, *I. bucharica*, carries up to seven cream-white and yellow, scented flowers on each stem in April and early May.

Bearded irises *The most widely grown irises of all. They are also known as flag or German irises. They flower in every shade of colour*

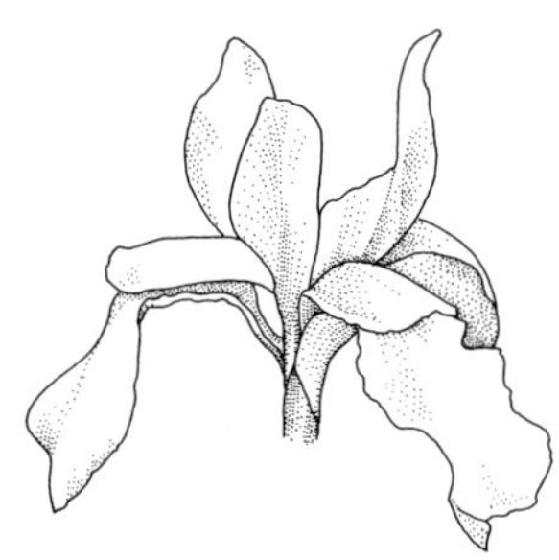

Sibiricas *Popular beardless irises that flower in mid-June. They can be grown either in the border, round the edge of a garden pool or beside a stream*

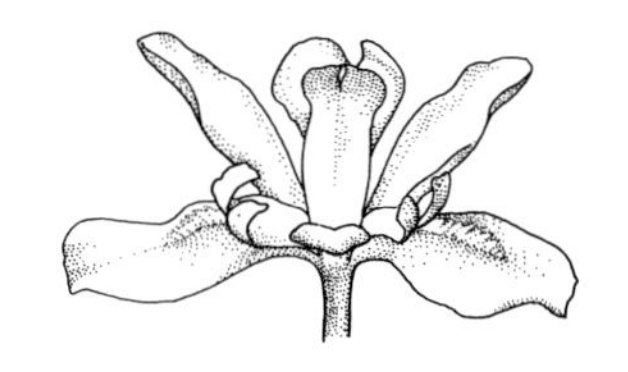

Crested irises *These carry orchid-like flowers with cock's-comb crests. They are evergreen, and flower in delicate shades from April to May*

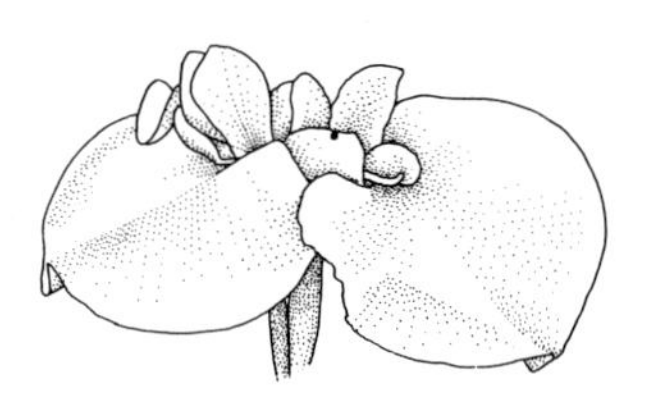

Water irises *Flowering between May and June, they can adapt to border conditions, but their true stature appears when planted in pools*

Dwarf bearded irises, which are less than 10 in. high, flower profusely in April. They make ideal groups in a rock garden, or in front of small plants and dwarf shrubs. Several varieties grown together can produce an attractive display

Reticulatas *These small bulbs flower between December and March. Nearly all are hardy, and are suitable for rockeries or the fronts of borders*

Dutch, Spanish and English irises *Popular bulbous plants – excellent for cut flowers – they provide a colourful display between early June and July*

Irises that grow from rhizomes

Preparing a well-drained, rich soil

Many irises are perennial plants that grow on rhizomatous rootstocks.

The most popular group of all, bearded irises, have thick, fleshy rhizomes that lie half-exposed on the surface of the soil.

The beardless and crested irises have thinner rhizomes and should be planted below the surface.

Soil preparation for all rhizomatous irises is similar, except for crested irises and Pacific Coast hybrids.

Irises grow best in a rich soil containing plenty of humus. Select a site for planting that is not overshadowed by trees or tall shrubs, and that receives plenty of sun, as the rhizomes thrive in warm soil.

Good drainage is essential, so dig clay soil over thoroughly and add plenty of sand, weathered ashes or straw to break it up. Drainage will also be improved if the bed is raised about 2–3 in. above the surrounding soil level.

Prepare the bed before planting by spreading plenty of organic matter over the surface, ideally 1½ in. of peat, 2 in. of well-rotted garden compost and 2 in. of farmyard manure. Single dig the plot, pushing the manure into each trench as it is dug. Add two handfuls of sterilised bonemeal to the square yard; incorporate it in the top spit.

Although most irises will grow in soil that is slightly acid, they do best in a neutral one. If the soil is strongly acidic, spread hydrated lime or, better still, ground chalk or limestone over it at a rate of two handfuls to the square yard.

Pacific Coast hybrids and crested irises, which differ from the rest, will not tolerate thin, chalky soils. Therefore, the ground should be left slightly acid in beds where they are to be planted. If the ground is chalky, dig in plenty of peat or leafmould to provide acid conditions.

Planting bearded irises on the surface

Bearded iris rhizomes are best planted in late June or early July, but they can be safely planted up to September. Set the irises in groups of three or four, allowing 18 in. between tall bearded varieties, 9–12 in. between intermediates, and 6–9 in. between dwarfs.

Before planting, trim the leaves to a fan shape. If any roots are damaged, cut off the broken parts.

Dig a fan-shaped hole with a trowel, with the point of the fan towards the sunniest direction. The hole should slope from surface-level at the pointed end to a depth of about 4 in. at the semi-circular end. Place the rhizome at the point of the fan with the leafy end lowest, and spread the roots down into the hole.

Fill the soil back over the roots, but leave the top of the rhizome exposed. Firm the soil with your hands. Label and water the plant.

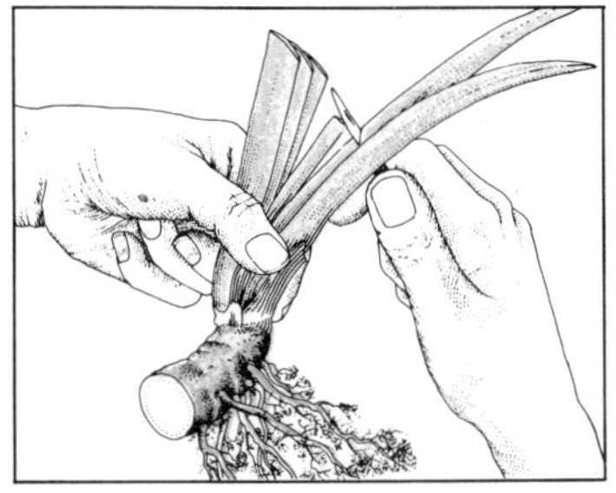

1 *Before planting, trim the long leaves of bearded irises to a neat fan shape*

2 *Dig a sloping fan-shaped hole, with the point towards the sun*

3 *Place the rhizome at the point. Spread the roots below the leafy end*

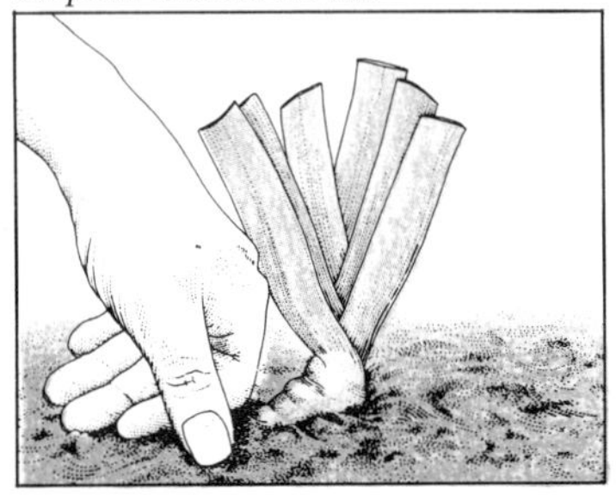

4 *Leave the top of the rhizome exposed, but firm the soil round the roots*

Watering and feeding bearded irises

After planting, do not let the ground round the rhizomes dry out. Water as necessary for three weeks, after which the rhizomes will have established themselves.

In October, sprinkle potassium sulphate over the bed at 1 oz. (1 tablespoon) to the square yard to harden the rhizomes for winter.

If late-planted rhizomes are lifted by frost during winter, do not press them down as this will break their roots. Build up around the rhizomes with sand or light soil, or lift and replant properly.

Peel off dead foliage during winter to discourage slugs.

In March, carefully fork in a general fertiliser, such as Growmore; use about 3 oz. (3 tablespoons) to the square yard over the iris bed.

FROST HAZARD

Frost may lift the rhizomes, but do not press them back. This could break their roots and weaken them. Instead, bank up sand or soil around the sides

WINTER TRIMMING

In winter, peel off dead leaves that might harbour slugs, and trim back the foliage to prevent wind damage, which could loosen or break the roots

Planting beardless irises below the surface

The rhizomes of beardless irises are more slender than those of the bearded. The true beardless are the sibiricas, spurias, Pacific Coast hybrids and water irises.

Crested irises can also be included within this group for cultivation purposes, as their rhizomes are planted beneath the ground, and not on the surface.

Sibiricas, which flower in June, are hardy and easy to grow. Nursery plants, each one consisting of a rhizome with the foliage trimmed back, usually arrive in September. Plant them 1 in. deep in soil that is not too dry, with the roots well spread. Pick a sunny position and set the rhizomes 18–24 in. apart. Water them thoroughly after planting and keep the soil around them moist.

Plant the fibrous rhizomes of spurias in clumps, 2 in. deep, in late October. Any fertile soil is suitable, as long as the position is sunny. The rhizomes will not withstand drying out, so keep them damp while they are out of the ground. New plants may take time to establish themselves, and may not flower until the second season after planting.

The Pacific Coast hybrids, which flower from early May to mid-June, are usually supplied as seedlings by the nursery. Plant them in October. Make a hole large enough to take the soil ball, and put some peat in it. Plant the seedlings fairly firmly, and keep them well watered.

Among the water irises, pseudacorus, versicolor and laevigata types can be planted immersed in ponds. Others, such as the kaempferis and louisianas, respond better to waterside or bog conditions. For methods of planting rhizomatous water plants, see page 327.

The slender rhizomes of crested irises are planted in May or June, just below soil level, singly or in groups. They need moist soil with peat or leaf-mould added, and a sheltered, semi-shaded position.

1 *Trim leaves of beardless and crested irises to 9 in. before planting*

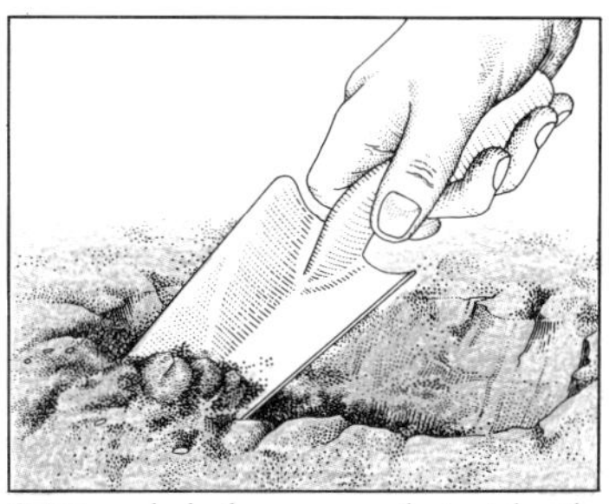

2 *Dig a hole large enough to take the roots, with the rhizome 1 in. deep*

3 *Spread the roots out well, return the soil, and firm it with the fingers*

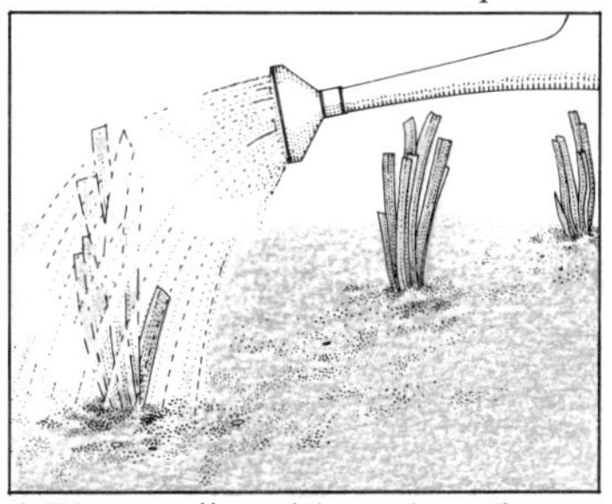

4 *Water well, and keep the soil moist until the plants are established*

Keeping beardless irises healthy all year

During winter the leaves of sibiricas die right down. Clear them up to prevent slugs and other pests wintering in the rotted foliage, and to let light and air reach the roots.

Avoid hoeing and cultivating around the plants, as the roots are near the surface and easily damaged. For safety weed by hand or, better still, spread a 2 in. mulch of well-rotted manure, peat or garden compost around the plants in spring. This will discourage weeds and conserve moisture.

After sibiricas have flowered in June and the blooms have faded, break off the seed heads, as these deprive the plants of energy and could choke the surrounding soil with seedlings.

These cultivation procedures are common to most irises with underground rhizomes. However, there are certain special requirements.

Sibiricas may produce only sparse blooms in their first season, but by the second, the plants will flower freely, and clumps of them will start to increase in size.

To preserve their height and lush green colour, apply a general fertiliser in early spring using it as recommended by the manufacturer.

Spurias become active in spring and do well in herbaceous border conditions. They usually flower better the following year if they are not watered in the late summer, after the flowering season.

Both Pacific Coast hybrids and crested irises favour a moist but well-drained soil. They dislike alkaline conditions, so in spring mulch them with a 1–2 in. layer of leaf-mould.

SPRING MULCHING

In spring, spread a mulch of manure, peat or garden compost around beardless irises

SEED-POD REMOVAL

In summer, after sibiricas have flowered, remove seed pods to prevent seedlings choking the bed

Dividing the rhizomes of bearded irises

Divide bearded iris rhizomes every three years to increase the stock and improve the quality of the blooms. The best time is immediately after flowering, but it can be done up to late September, when new growth will show that clumps have become overcrowded.

One rhizome will branch several times over the years, developing into a criss-cross clump of rhizomes, which exhaust the soil, exclude sun and air from the roots, and consequently result in poor flowering or no flowers at all.

Lift the clump by loosening the soil round it with a fork, and gently prise it from the ground.

Using a sharp, strong-bladed knife, cut off the younger rhizomes from the edge of the clump – each one should have one or two strong leaf fans growing from it. Shake off the soil from the roots. Take care to leave the new white ones intact. Discard the old, centre section of the clump, which consists of old and exhausted rhizomes.

Peel off withered leaves and trim the remainder into a fan shape. Replant them (p.180).

1 *When bearded irises become overcrowded, they will cease to flower*

2 *Loosen the soil round the clump and prise it from the ground carefully*

3 *Cut young rhizomes from the edge – each with one or two leaf fans*

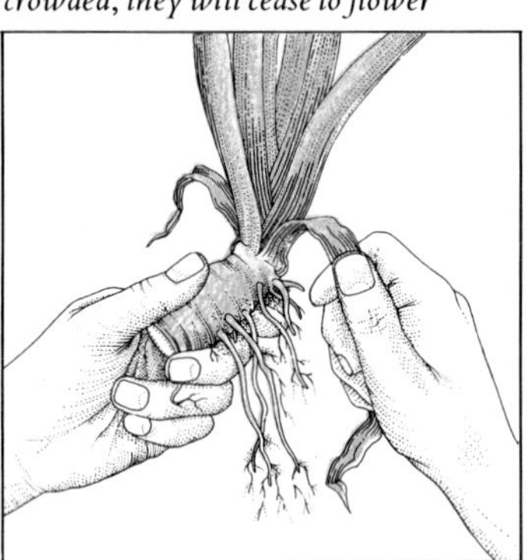

4 *Peel withered leaves from the young rhizome, retaining only fresh foliage*

5 *Trim the fresh foliage to a fan shape and replant the rhizome*

6 *Fill in with soil round the rhizome, but leave its top exposed*

Dividing beardless, crested and water irises

Beardless, crested and water irises may also become overcrowded after three to five years and need to be divided. More care is needed with some of the rhizomes, as they are not as fleshy as the bearded ones and often resent disturbance.

Large clumps of sibiricas tend to grow hollow in the centre, where the soil has been exhausted. Divide them about every three years, either in autumn or in April.

Trim back the foliage to about 9 in. and clean out dead foliage from the centre of the clump.

Loosen the soil round the clump with a fork and carefully lever it from the ground. Chop the clump into about eight pieces with a spade. Trim each piece, so that about six leaf spikes remain, and replant.

Spurias need to be divided only every four or five years.

Divide the rhizomes in autumn and replant them immediately.

Treat Pacific Coast hybrids in the same way, dividing them when the new roots appear in September.

Crested irises should be split after they have flowered.

Divide water irises in July, when the clumps become too big for the size of the pool.

1 *Before lifting sibiricas, cut back the foliage and clean away debris*

2 *Lift the clump, chop it into about eight sections with a spade, then replant*

Irises that grow from bulbs

The best-known bulbous irises are the English, Dutch and Spanish (hybrids of the xiphium group).

They provide a continuity of flowers for the summer border. Dutch irises are the first to bloom – from early to mid-June – followed by Spanish irises two weeks later and continuing to late June. The last to flower are the English in July.

The stems are about 2 ft in height and are ideal for cutting.

Almost as popular are reticulata irises, which flower between Christmas and early March. They make excellent rock-garden plants.

The third group, the junos, such as *Iris bucharica*, are not well known, but are fairly hardy. Blooms appear between March and May.

Siting and planting bulbous-rooted irises

Choose a sunny, well-drained site and dig plenty of well-rotted compost or farmyard manure into it.

Plant Dutch, Spanish and English irises in September or October. Set them about 4-6 in. deep.

English irises prefer soil that will not dry out too quickly in hot weather. They are the easiest to grow, as they favour rich, damp soils, and do not require lifting after flowering. Plant them 6-8 in. apart, and they will soon be established.

Dutch irises are also set 6–8 in. apart, preferably in a light soil.

Spanish irises are more effective if they are placed 4 in. apart in lighter soil and in a warmer and drier position than Dutch iris bulbs.

Plant reticulata bulbs 2-3 in. deep and 2-4 in. apart in clumps, in September or October. Select a light, well-drained soil in a sunny position. Avoid heavy soils – the bulbs may not come up a second year. Lighten heavy soils by working in compost and sand before planting.

Juno bulbs have thick storage roots attached to them, from which feeding roots develop during the growing season. Plant the bulbs singly or in clumps in a spot sheltered from summer rain – in the rain-shadow area of a wall or shrubs – or else in well-drained soil. Set them 2 in. deep and 6-9 in. apart in the ground during September.

Cultivation and care of bulbous irises

Lightly fork well-rotted compost into beds of English irises after the foliage has died down. They are quite hardy, and will not need lifting in the autumn until they become overcrowded.

If the soil is wet and heavy, lift and store Dutch iris bulbs after the foliage has died down in late summer. Replant them in September. If the soil is light, they can be left in the ground throughout the year.

To help ripen Spanish iris bulbs, lift them annually after the foliage has died down. Let them dry and replant them in September.

When storing bulbs, keep them in a dry, airy shed to prevent rot or mould affecting them.

It is a good idea to soak bulbs with a systemic or captan fungicide just before replanting them. This will prevent the bulbs rotting when they are in the ground.

After reticulatas have flowered, feed them with a general liquid fertiliser fortnightly until the leaves yellow, to ensure good bulbs for the following season.

Do not lift juno bulbs unless they become very congested. Fork well-rotted compost into the bed, taking care not to damage the roots. If the ground lacks lime, dress the soil annually with about 1 oz. (1 rounded tablespoon) of ground chalk or limestone to the square yard.

Propagating bulbous irises by division

All bulbous irises are increased by the natural division of the bulbs.

Lift and divide English and Dutch irises when the clumps become overcrowded. Divide Spanish irises when they are lifted annually – also Dutch irises if it is necessary to lift them each year.

Remove the bulbs carefully from the ground with a fork, after the foliage has died down. Dry them for a few weeks, clean them, and divide them into single bulbs. Replant in September or October.

Large bulbs will flower the following year. Small offsets, however, should be planted in 1 in. drills in a seed bed. Rake the soil to a fine tilth, and incorporate a handful of sterilised bonemeal to each square yard. The bulbs will reach maturity in about two years.

If reticulata beds become overcrowded, carefully lift the bulbs after the foliage has yellowed – about June. Dry off the bulbs and replant in September or October.

Propagate juno bulbs after the foliage has died down and dried out. The storage roots will then be limp and less likely to break off. If they do, the bulb will be weakened and will not flower until new roots have developed. During this time, two flowering seasons may be lost.

Gently remove the soil surrounding each bulb. Lift them with a hand fork, and separate them carefully. Make sure each bulb has at least one storage root attached. Replant them immediately after lifting.

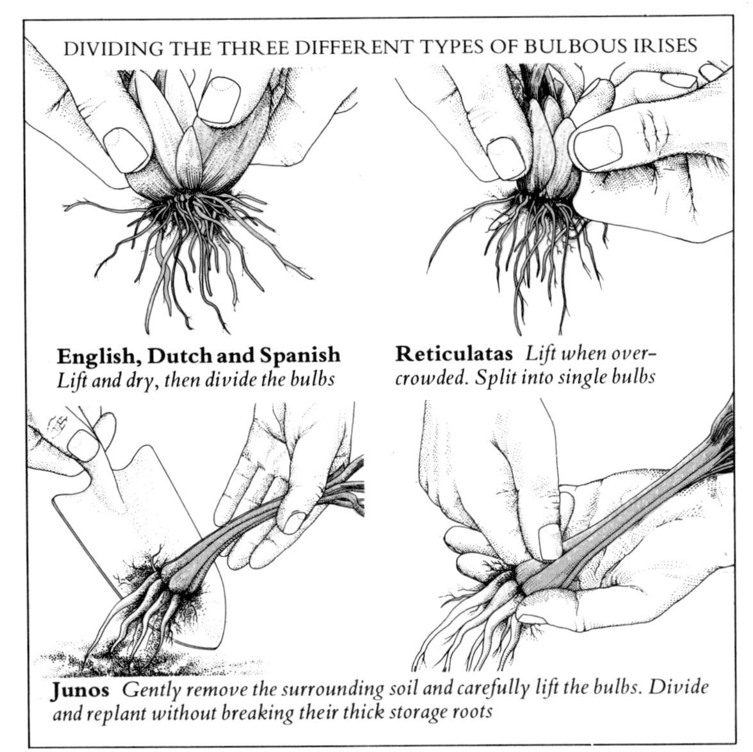

DIVIDING THE THREE DIFFERENT TYPES OF BULBOUS IRISES

English, Dutch and Spanish *Lift and dry, then divide the bulbs*

Reticulatas *Lift when overcrowded. Split into single bulbs*

Junos *Gently remove the surrounding soil and carefully lift the bulbs. Divide and replant without breaking their thick storage roots*

Lawns for hard wear or to please the eye

The most characteristic feature of the traditional English garden is the lawn. It provides both a recreation area and a foil for the bright colours of borders and beds

Grass is basically a crop, whether it grows as a fine lawn or a farm meadow. The farmer must feed the grass in his meadow, keep weeds under control and ensure it is not over-grazed if he wishes to keep it in good condition and yield a maximum crop of good-quality grass. Similarly, a lawn needs regular care if it is to become and remain first-class turf in both appearance and texture.

The basis of a good lawn is careful preparation of the site before sowing or turfing. Adequate drainage is essential, although the soil itself must be moisture-retentive. By judicious feeding, elimination of weeds, and watering regularly in dry weather, the grass will soon become established. But even an established lawn can soon deteriorate if it does not receive careful attention.

Regular mowing is the most important requirement – an operation similar in effect to pruning. If it is carried out frequently in late spring, when growth is at its most vigorous, it will encourage a thick, firm but resilient turf to develop, which will be resistant to drought and invasion by weeds and moss.

If mowing is infrequent, the coarser grasses become dominant, and will sometimes smother the finer and more desirable grasses completely.

Feeding is another important spring activity. As the grass begins to grow again, its vigour must be maintained. A well-fed lawn will also recover quickly from any set-back such as drought or heavy use.

Nor should the lawn be forgotten in autumn, when the gardener should try to correct conditions which may have developed during the summer, such as compaction, wear, thin patches, or fibre build-up in the turf.

Types of lawn There are three basic types of lawn, depending on their use. They are: the utility lawn, fine lawn and games lawn.

The utility lawn, the normal family lawn, has coarser, broad-leaved grasses predominating. It should be able to withstand both hard wear and considerable neglect.

A fine lawn is one grown from fine-leaved grasses of compact growth. Its main purpose is to be visually attractive. Normally it will not stand hard wear, but where a lawn is wanted for the occasional game of bowls or croquet, and the grass does not get heavy wear, a fine lawn is suitable.

A games lawn, such as the carefully maintained bowling-green turf in a public park, arouses great envy, but considerable skill is needed to keep it in this condition. Sea marsh turf (Cumberland turf) is normally used. If not carefully treated and maintained, Cumberland turf can deteriorate very quickly, as it may contain grasses that die out under inland conditions.

Types of lawn-seed mixtures The growing conditions under which individual grasses thrive vary considerably. Most lawn-seed mixtures are selected from grasses that will tolerate a broad span of conditions though, in time, one species may become dominant in one particular type of soil.

If you have difficulty in establishing a good lawn, it is useful to know how various types of seed react to particular soils or situations. The following grasses are the main ones found in lawn-seed mixtures.

Fine lawn grasses Browntop bent (*Agrostis tenuis*) has a creeping method of growth, spreading by runners. It is usually found on acid soils, but will tolerate all soils, even quite dry ones.

Chewing's fescue (*Festuca rubra-commutata*) is a tufted grass. It will grow on both acid and alkaline soils, even when they are dry.

Utility lawn grasses Crested dog's-tail (*Cynosurus cristatus*) is compact and tufted. It grows well on heavier chalky soil, but does not like drier, sandy, acid soil. Do not mow closely.

Creeping red fescue (*Festuca rubra rubra*) is rhizomatous in growth, sending out rooting tendrils along the surface. It will grow in most soils, but some strains cannot be mown closely.

Rye grass (*Lolium perenne*) is tufted in habit. Though it grows in any type of soil, it does best on heavier ones. Choose compact leafy strains for good coverage.

Smooth-stalked meadow grass (*Poa pratensis*) is another tufted type. It spreads quickly by means of creeping underground stems. It grows best on medium or light soils, and is quite tolerant of shade.

Rough-stalked meadow grass (*Poa trivialis*) is tufted, and can be grown successfully on wet, heavy soils. It is the best grass for shady situations.

For the gardener who wants to make up his own lawn-seed mixtures, a good, hard-wearing, drought-resistant turf, suitable for a fine lawn or games area, can be obtained from 80 per cent Chewing's fescue and 20 per cent browntop bent. Both these grasses will grow on acid or alkaline soils.

If a quick-growing and hard-wearing utility lawn is wanted, containing coarser, broad-leaved grasses, the best mix is 40 per cent Chewing's fescue, 30 per cent rye grass (S23 strain), 20 per cent crested dog's-tail, and 10 per cent rough-stalked meadow grass.

For a lawn that receives a lot of shade, use a mixture of 50 per cent rough-stalked meadow grass, 30 per cent smooth-stalked meadow grass and 20 per cent creeping red fescue. These grasses cannot be closely mown. It is best never to cut them lower than about $1\frac{1}{2}$ in.

However, garden centres and shops usually stock ready made-up seed mixtures, supplied by reputable seedsmen under trade names. They will include the best strains available to meet the particular requirements for which the mixture is formulated. All the gardener needs to do is to calculate from the instructions on the packet the quantity of seed required for the area to be sown.

Selecting turf for a lawn If you are laying your lawn from turf, check the turves before purchase.

Make sure they are free of all coarse grasses, such as cocksfoot and Yorkshire fog. These cannot be eradicated with weedkillers or by routine mowing. Heavily weed-infested turf should also be avoided, as the grass will be weak.

Thickness of turves is no guide to quality (though all turves should be of equal thickness). Thin turves, as a rule, under suitable conditions, root into a prepared bed more rapidly than thick ones. Greenkeepers usually use turves which are 1 ft $\times$ 3 ft, and $1\frac{1}{4}$–$1\frac{1}{2}$ in. thick.

Meadowland turf is often offered for sale, usually as a result of local building operations. It is likely to contain a high percentage of coarser grasses and will be suitable only for utility areas.

If you can obtain it, old parkland turf is probably the best quality for a fine lawn. A good alternative is downland turf, originating from upland pastures and hillsides, and although it may be fibrous and matted, when lifted thinly it establishes well, although slowly.

Sea marsh turf (Cumberland turf) is used for bowling greens, and is a mixture of sea marsh bent and fescue grasses. It needs expert maintenance and is unsuitable for fine lawns.

How to make a new lawn

Clearing and tidying the site

A new lawn often has to be put down in the garden of a newly built house on ground which is covered by builder's rubble. Sometimes the subsoil from foundation digging covers the topsoil.

Start preparing the ground in summer when the soil is reasonably dry. First tidy up any debris, then clear away any subsoil that has been left behind by builders. Either spread it thinly over the site or, if possible, bury it.

A lawn need not be perfectly level. Grass on a gentle slope, even if irregular, is easily manageable – as long as there are no sharp bumps and hollows, so that the mower will run over the surface without scraping it. If a flat surface is desired, drive in pegs 6 ft apart and level their tops, using a straight-edged plank and a spirit level. Paint a line on the pegs 4 in. from their tops. Add or remove soil from between the pegs until the surface is level with the painted line on each peg.

Where only slight changes in level are needed, the soil can be levelled with a rake, provided that at least 6 in. of topsoil is retained.

If necessary, topsoil can be bought from a nursery and spread over the site as needed.

For larger levelling or grading operations, a lot of soil will have to be moved. First remove the topsoil and put it to one side. After forking out the subsoil, return the topsoil and spread it evenly. (The topsoil is always darker and richer than the paler subsoil.)

If the underlying land is heavy clay or some other sticky soil, the drainage will probably be poor: the soil particles cling together and act as an impermeable barrier to prevent water seeping away.

To overcome this, the texture of the soil must be improved. This can be done by digging in organic matter such as well-rotted farmyard manure, garden compost or peat, and also inorganic matter such as gritty sand or weathered ashes. There are also various chemical preparations available from garden suppliers to break up clay soil.

As a general guide, allow about one bucketful to each square yard of soil when digging in organic matter, and two bucketfuls for inorganic matter.

About three months before seeding or turfing, turn the ground over with a fork or cultivator. This will allow time for weed seeds to germinate and be removed with a paraquat weedkiller, and for heavy soils to be broken down by weathering. When digging, take care not to bring the subsoil to the surface.

Remove stones and roots of perennial weeds such as nettles, docks, thistles and brambles. Do not leave pieces of root behind, as these will grow again.

Improve the drainage and aeration of a heavy top-soil by working in coarse sand with a fork. Apply it at a rate of about half a bucketful to the square yard.

To improve moisture retention in light soils, work damp peat into the top 6 in. at a rate of about a bucketful to the square yard. Alternatively use well-rotted manure, garden compost or leaf-mould at the same rate of application.

Preparing the surface for turf or seed

Whether you are using turf or sowing seed, a firm soil bed is an essential foundation.

Leave the site to weather for three months or so, giving a further treatment with paraquat to control weeds. The rough surface must now be made level and firm for either seeding or turfing. For seeding, the tilth must be rather finer than for turfing. Break down clods of earth with your feet if the site is small. On larger areas use a roller, but only when the soil is dry.

After breaking down clods, rake the surface to get it roughly even, and remove stones. Rake diagonally across the plot, first from left to right and then from right to left. Roll it again, in two directions at right angles to each other.

Next, tread the ground firm. This involves close-treading and putting the weight on the heels, to find the soft spots. Do this only when the soil is dry enough not to stick to the boots, otherwise it will become too compact and drainage will be affected. Tread thoroughly, so that the soil will not sink afterwards.

Follow this with another raking and another treading, at right angles to the first.

When raking, make the surface even, eliminating all bumps and shallow depressions.

Seven to ten days before turfing or sowing, apply a general fertiliser such as Growmore at 2–4 oz. (2–4 tablespoons) to each square yard. Work this in with a rake, removing any remaining stones, while giving a final level to the site.

At this stage of preparation, turf can be laid or seed sown.

1 *Break down the clods, then rake the ground and remove any stones*

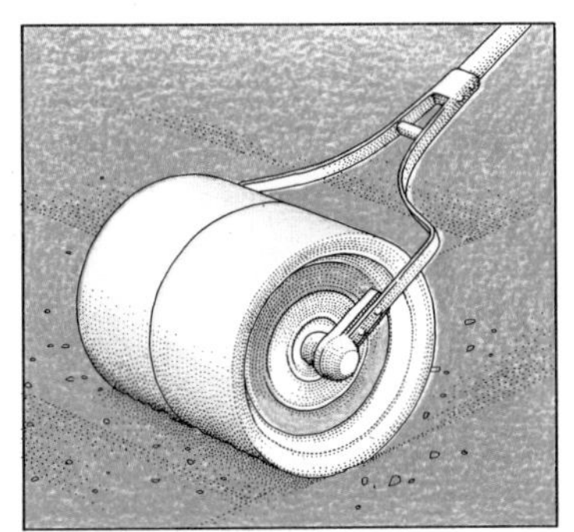

2 *Roll the surface in two directions at right angles to each other*

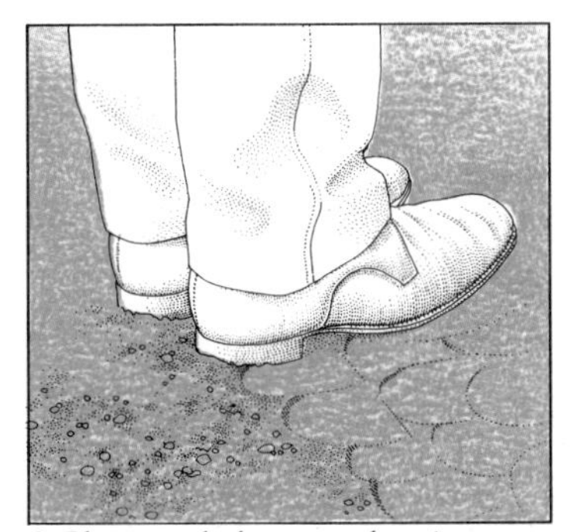

3 *Close-tread the ground, using your heels; then rake again*

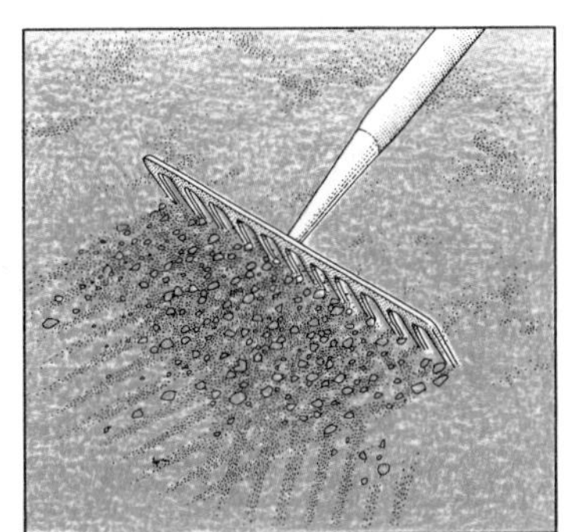

4 *A week to ten days before sowing or turfing, rake in a general fertiliser*

Laying a lawn with turf for quick results

Laying turf is best done between September and early February. This gives the turves time to settle and develop a good root structure, so that the grass can make a good start in spring.

Turves are usually cut in 3 ft × 1 ft sections. Do not leave them stacked for more than a day or two, otherwise decomposition may set in. If they cannot be laid immediately, set out the turves singly in a shady position and water if necessary.

Start laying the first row of turves from one side or one corner of the site. Work in a forward direction to prevent disturbing the levelled surface. At the edges of the lawn allow an overlap, which can be cut later.

Position the first row of turves roughly in place.

Open each turf out and press it firmly into position against the preceding one. Brush the surface with the flat of the hand to raise the compressed blades of grass and also remove loose debris. If there are any obvious weeds in the turves remove them by hand.

Place a plank on the first row and stand on it to lay the second row of turves, staggering them against the first row like brickwork. Lay them as the first row, roll the plank over, and begin the next row.

When the site has been completely turfed, roll it twice – the second time at right angles to the first.

Sweep the turf with a stiff brush to remove loose material and lift the flattened grass. Finally, water thoroughly with a sprinkler.

Leave the grass for about 10–14 days before mowing with the blades set at $1\frac{1}{2}$ in., except in winter when no mowing should be necessary.

With a half-moon edging tool, trim the turf along paths and borders. Use a plank to ensure a straight edge. Where the lawn meets a border, a sloping cut looks neater.

If curved edges are required, mark out the curve using a knife on a piece of string tied to cane.

MAKING A CURVED EDGE

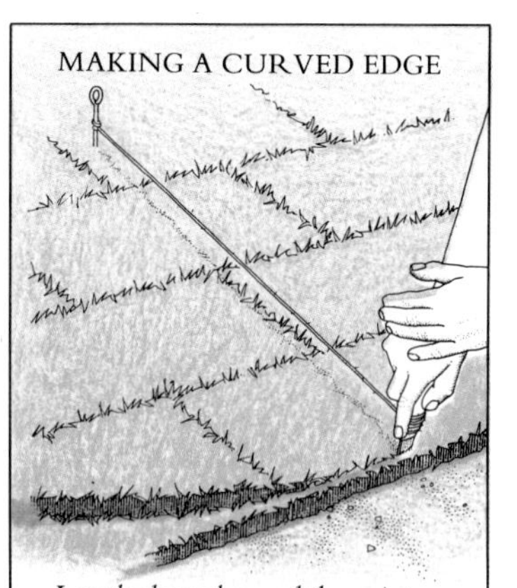

Lay the lawn beyond the point where a curved edge is required. Mark out the curve using a piece of string attached to a cane. Hold the end of the string and a knife in one hand and inscribe an arc. Use a half-moon turfing iron to cut the turf along the mark

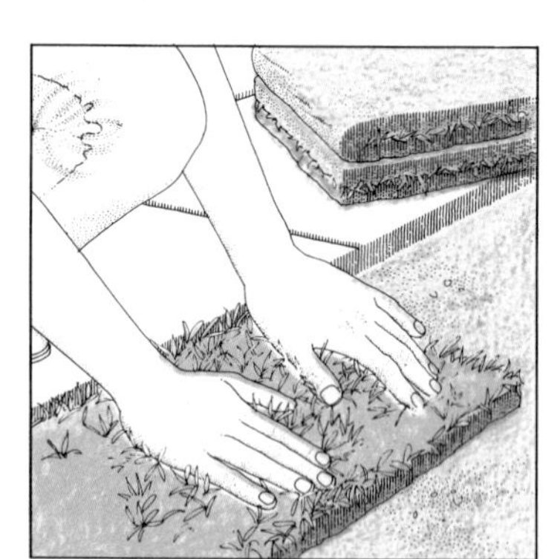

1 *Open out each turf and press it firmly into position*

2 *Stand on a plank on the first row and lay the second, staggering the turves*

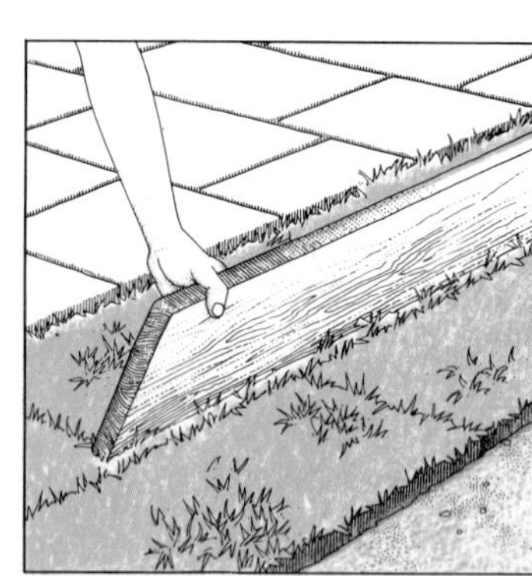

3 *Roll the plank over on to the second row and lay the third row the same way*

4 *Roll the lawn twice, the second time in a direction at right angles to the first*

5 *Brush the lawn to remove debris and to lift the flattened grass*

6 *Trim the edges with a half-moon turfing iron, making a sloping cut*

After-care of the new turf

Water the new turf once or twice a week with a garden sprinkler. This will prevent shrinkage and cracks appearing between the turves. Do not flood the new lawn.

If any cracks do appear between the joints of the turves, fill them with sandy soil.

Do not roll the new turf again until it has taken root, and then use only a light roller.

Inspect the turf in early spring and replace any turves that have failed. Alternatively, seed these dead patches once the soil has warmed up in late April.

Turf laid in autumn or early winter will need no mowing until spring, when new growth begins.

In spring – or early summer for a spring-laid lawn – apply a lawn feed or a general fertiliser according to the maker's instructions.

Growing a new lawn from seed

Seeding is best done in late April or August in the north-east, and in April or September in all other parts of the country.

Leave the prepared ground fallow during the summer to allow dormant weed seeds to germinate. These can be removed by hoeing and raking, or by watering with a contact weedkiller such as paraquat.

Choose a windless day for sowing the seed, when the surface of the soil is dry and the soil below it is moist. Lightly rake the surface to a fine tilth, at least 1 in. deep. If a rough surface is left, it will result in reduced germination.

Sow fine lawn mixtures at $1\frac{1}{2}$ oz. to the square yard. Seed for shady areas and for hard-wearing and general-purpose lawns can be sown at 1 oz. to the square yard, as stronger growing and thicker-bladed types of grass are used. When using proprietary mixtures, follow the manufacturer's instructions. Sow the seed either by hand or with a seed distributor. Mark a 3 ft wide strip along one side of the site, with two lengths of string attached to pegs. Sow the seed along the strip, then move one piece of string to create the next strip.

To ensure even coverage, sow half the seed across the plot, and the remainder up and down it. After sowing, rake in the seeds so that they are just below the surface.

Do not roll. Unrolled surfaces are less prone to caking, and the corrugations help to protect the seedlings in bad weather.

Most seeds are treated with a bird repellant, but if birds are very troublesome, criss-cross thin black cotton, 2–3 in. above the surface, between pegs, or lay light brushwood on the ground. Remove it as soon as the seedlings appear.

1 *Remove any weeds by hoeing, or with a paraquat weedkiller*

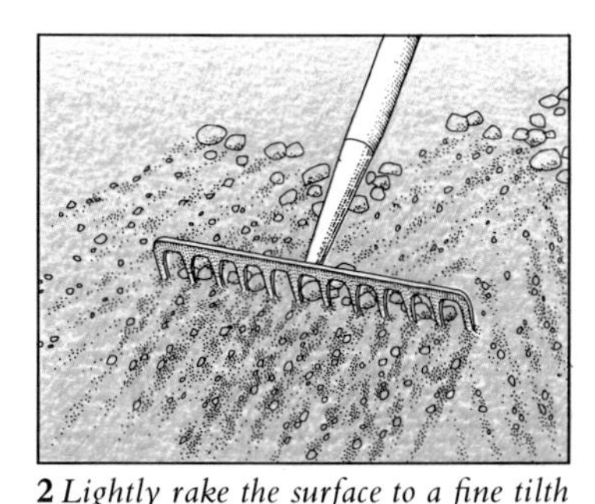

2 *Lightly rake the surface to a fine tilth at least 1 in. deep*

3 *Mark a 3 ft wide strip down one side of the plot with string*

4 *Sow seed along the strip at 1–$1\frac{1}{2}$ oz. to the square yard*

Rolling and cutting the young grass

When the grass is about 1–$1\frac{1}{2}$ in. high, brush off any wormcasts and roll with a light roller or the rear roller of a mower. This firms the soil and encourages better rooting.

About six weeks after sowing, depending on the weather, the grass will be $1\frac{1}{2}$–2 in. long. Remove wormcasts and debris by brushing lightly, and mow the grass with the mower blades set 1 in. high.

Allow a further $\frac{1}{2}$ in. of growth, then cut the grass again, reducing the height of the blades to $\frac{3}{4}$ in. Gradually reduce the height of the cut until mowing regularly with the blades set at about $\frac{1}{2}$ in.

1 *When the new grass is about $1\frac{1}{2}$ in. high, brush off all debris and wormcasts*

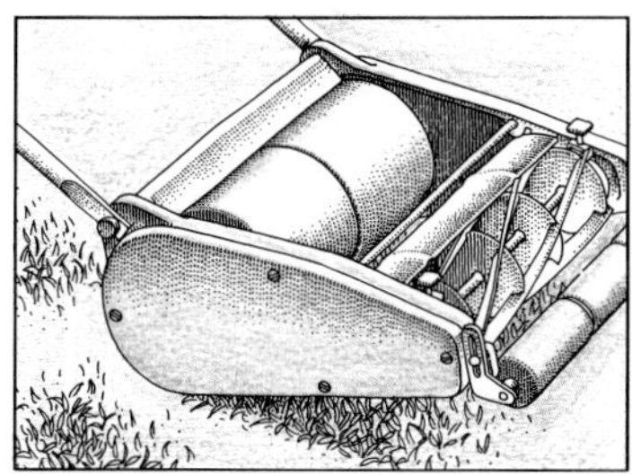

2 *Roll with a light roller or the back roller of a mower*

Watering and weeding a newly seeded lawn

Watering is essential if a dry spell occurs at any time after sowing. There is a danger, however, that artificial watering will dislodge young seedlings if applications are too heavy or too prolonged. Use a fine spray if possible.

Several types of lawn sprinkler can be used. The oscillating type waters a rectangular area, and can be adjusted to spray a limited area from left to right, to one side only, or a full sweep to both sides.

A rotating sprinkler will cover a circular area, and can be adjusted to produce a spray pattern from mist to full jet. Take care not to leave unwatered patches between the circular areas, as the sprinkler is moved.

Selective weedkillers should not be used in the first six months of growth as they may damage the young grass. Instead use a proprietary form of ioxynil to control quick-growing annual weeds, but apply it to the lawn only after the seedling grasses have developed at least two fully opened leaves.

Oscillating sprinkler

Weed grasses, such as perennial ryegrass, and other grasses, such as annual meadow grass, may appear among the seedlings. Remove these by hand as soon as they are seen, and do so gently, to avoid disturbing the sown grasses.

Looking after an established lawn

Mowing and trimming the edges

To maintain healthy growth, colour and texture, a lawn should be carefully mown and rolled, aerated regularly, brushed and raked, top-dressed, weeded, and kept free of fungi and pests.

The frequency of mowing depends on the amount of growth. This can be two or three times a week in the height of the growing season – May and June.

The mowing season is from March to October, but an occasional light topping may be needed during mild winters when there is late or early growth.

Do not mow when the grass is very wet. Very close mowing weakens the grass. Cutting to about $\frac{1}{2}$ in. gives the best results. On lawns for rougher use, $\frac{3}{4}$–1 in. is adequate.

Leave the grass slightly longer in dry weather and in spring and autumn when growth is slow.

Before mowing the lawn, remove wormcasts with a stiff brush. If casts are not removed they will form uneven humps, rot the grass and cake the mower blades. Brushing encourages the finer grasses.

If you mow the lawn in parallel strips, change direction at successive mowings so that the new mowing is made at right angles to the previous one. This prevents ridging.

During very dry periods leave the grass cuttings on the surface, provided the lawn is free from weeds. This will help to conserve moisture.

Otherwise use the grass box on the mower. A continual return of cuttings leads to soft, weak turf and encourages worms and fungi.

Trim the edge of the lawn with long-handled shears.

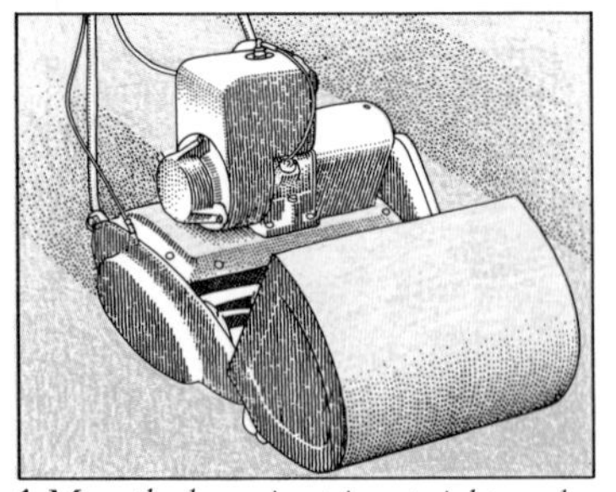

1 *Mow the lawn in strips at right angles to the previous mowing*

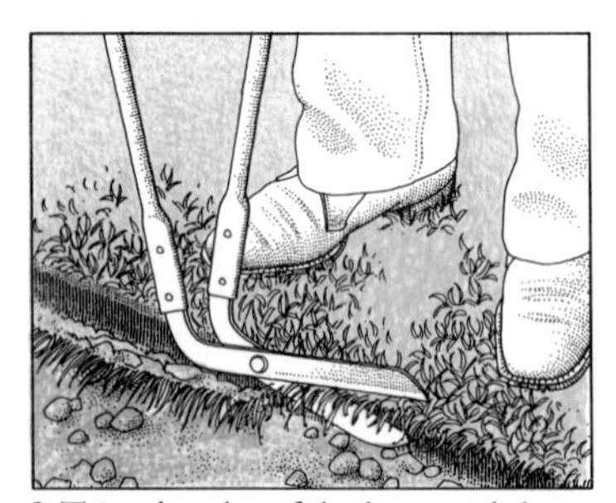

2 *Trim the edge of the lawn with long-handled shears*

CHECKING THE HEIGHT OF THE BLADES

To check the height of the blades place a straight edge across the front and rear rollers of the machine. The height of the cut is the distance from the straight edge to the bottom fixed blade. Make sure each side of the machine has the same setting

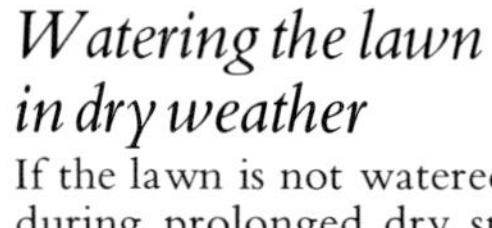

Watering the lawn in dry weather

If the lawn is not watered regularly during prolonged dry spells it can deteriorate seriously.

Use a sprinkler, preferably an oscillating one, to obtain maximum coverage. Soak the grass well at weekly intervals in hot, sunny weather. If the soil is sandy, water every four or five days.

The equivalent of about 1 in. of rain is needed. Gauge this roughly by positioning a straight-sided can underneath the spray. Note the tap setting and then find the time taken to fill the bottom inch of the can. Use the same tap setting and time for all future watering.

Brushing and raking the lawn

In spring, lightly brush or rake the lawn with a wire-tined lawn rake to remove winter debris, particularly before mowing.

In mid-September, scarify (rake thoroughly and vigorously) with the lawn rake or with a wheeled lawn sweeper to clear debris. Remove the rakings with a stiff brush.

Remove debris from the lawn with a wire-tined lawn rake

Spreading fertiliser on the lawn

Apply a liquid or granular general-purpose fertiliser such as Growmore (2 oz. or 2 tablespoons to the square yard) in early April, when the soil is moist and the grass is dry.

Even distribution of fertilisers is important, so that the grass is not scorched and regular growth is obtained over the whole surface. Mix powdered fertiliser with four to eight times its weight of sand before spreading it on the lawn.

Divide the mixture and apply half up and down the lawn and the other half working across the lawn.

Granular fertiliser is much easier to spread. A wheeled mechanical spreader will spread it at the correct rate. If spreading by hand, use pegs and string to mark out the site.

Water in solid fertilisers with a garden sprinkler to avoid any risk of scorching the grass and to feed the roots as quickly as possible.

Apply liquid fertilisers with a large watering can, using a rose or dribble-bar attachment. Avoid overlapping and double application, which may scorch the grass.

Do not use nitrogenous fertilisers after August. Autumn feeding will only be necessary if the lawn has suffered compaction or drought. Use a fertiliser high in phosphates (but low in nitrogen) to redevelop a strong root system. A suitable mixture is 7 lb. of sterilised bonemeal and 3 lb. of sulphate of potash, applied at 2 oz. (2 tablespoons) to the square yard.

Mechanical spreader

Spiking and top-dressing in autumn

Spiking the lawn in early autumn is essential on heavy soils where drainage is poor. It is also necessary where soils have been compacted by heavy use and wear. Spiking also assists root growth.

On small areas and lighter soils use a garden fork. Push it in at 3–4 in. intervals and 3–4 in. deep.

Use a straight, in-and-out action with the fork – do not pull back on it, as this will make a ridge.

Mechanical spiker

Specially designed spikers are made which have interchangeable tines. They are easier to use than a garden fork and give better aeration on all types of soils.

The solid tines can be replaced by hollow ones, which remove a core of soil. These are best on heavy ground. Sweep up the cores after spiking and brush a sandy top-dressing into the holes.

Alternatively, wedge-shaped blades can be attached. These are most effective for compacted areas. They will also prune the roots and thereby encourage stronger root growth. For large areas, wheeled spikers are available. These also have interchangeable sets of tines.

In autumn, after aerating the lawn, apply a light top-dressing to it. This will smooth out slight surface irregularities and, used annually, will form a layer of moisture-retaining material.

The composition of the dressing can be varied according to the soil and material available – sieved loam, leaf-mould, peat, sieved compost and sharp sand. An ideal dressing can be formed of alternate layers of 6 in. thick loamy soil and 4 in. thick well-rotted manure left to stand for a year or more, after which it should be sieved. Mix sand with it for heavy clay soils, but leave it as it is for light, sandy soils. Apply the dressing at about half a bucketful to the square yard.

Do not exceed the rate of application ($\frac{1}{4}$ in. or less), otherwise the turf will be smothered.

Aeration *To aerate a lawn, spike it with a fork – making 3–4 in. deep holes – or a wheeled spiker*

Top-dressing *Place half a bucketful of dressing on each square yard of lawn. Rake the heaps level*

Controlling weeds in the lawn

Check surface-creeping weeds such as clover and yarrow by raking or brushing upright before mowing. This also helps to control annual weeds such as the lesser yellow trefoil, and mat weeds such as mouse-ear chickweed.

Use the grass box when mowing, and destroy the clippings.

Use a small hand fork to remove isolated weeds before they develop into a serious infestation.

Selective weedkillers, in the form of powders or liquids, are effective against most weeds.

Apply a fertiliser a fortnight before the weedkiller to give the grass an extra boost. Mow the lawn two or three days before applying the weedkiller and try to pick a warm, still day for application, when the grass is dry and the soil is moist. Follow the maker's recommendations closely.

Selective weedkillers are based on a hormone substance which over-stimulates weed growth, causing the leaves to twist and curl. Finally, the weeds die and rot away. The amount of hormone absorbed by the grass is not enough to do any harm.

Do not mow the lawn for at least three days after using the weedkiller. Compost the clippings for at least six months before using them.

Dry fertiliser/weedkiller combinations are available, but the weedkiller may be less effective than when applied after a fertiliser.

Selective weedkillers are best applied in May, June and July, but can be used up to September.

For treatment of isolated weeds, special packs of spot weedkiller, in powder or liquid form, are available. The chemical is puffed, dabbed or injected into the crown of each weed.

Various lawn-sand preparations are available as alternatives to hormone weedkillers for controlling daisies and other broad-leaved weeds. Lawn sand is also an effective moss killer, though mercurised moss killers give more lasting control.

The lawn sands contain sulphate of ammonia and sulphate of iron. The chemicals have a corrosive effect on broad leaves, but are absorbed to a much lesser extent by the narrow-leaved grasses.

Apply lawn sand in spring or early summer. Follow the maker's instructions and do not overdose. The best time is when the grass is moist with dew and the soil damp.

Water the lawn if rain has not fallen after two days. After three weeks, rake up dead undergrowth. Apply a further dressing if necessary.

Temporary blackening of the older grass often occurs. However, once the chemicals have been washed down, the grass will recover rapidly.

Remove isolated weeds from the lawn with a small hand fork, or treat them individually with a spot weedkiller

What can go wrong with lawns

This chart describes the most common problems that are likely to occur in the cultivation of lawns.

For other symptoms of lawn pests and diseases not described here, turn to the full-colour identification chart on page 397.

Trade names for the various chemicals are listed on page 398.

Symptoms	Cause	Cure	Prevention
Small, irregular mounds (casts) of soil scattered over the lawn. On heavy soils, and when flattened down hard by walking or the mower roller, these can stifle the smaller grasses and make an uneven surface	Earthworms	Remove casts by regular sweeping. Apply a worm killer such as chlordane according to maker's instructions if worms are persistent	Fewer large cast-forming worms are found in acid soil, so dressing the lawn with sulphate of ammonia, sulphate of iron and organic substances such as peat will help to prevent this trouble
Yellowish grass, usually in irregular patches, but sometimes more extensive after a wet autumn	Leatherjackets	Dust soil with HCH	Make sure the lawn is well drained
Patches of yellow, dying grass which later brown over. In moist weather the patches may be covered with a cottony, white mould. Often seen after long-lying snow has melted, or when nitrogen has been applied later than August	Fusarium patch or snow mould	Apply quintozene according to maker's instructions. Sulphate of iron, at ¼ oz. to ½ gallon of water to the square yard, will also cure mild attacks	Keep the lawn well aerated
Pink or reddish gelatinous growths, particularly on fine-leaved grasses	Red thread	Apply quintozene according to maker's instructions	Aerate the lawn regularly and apply sulphate of ammonia at 1 oz. (1 tablespoon) to the square yard, but not in late autumn or winter
Large areas of grass show very little growth, and leaves have a lack-lustre appearance	Drought	Soak thoroughly, preferably with a sprinkler, putting on 2 gallons to the square yard	Maintain a moist soil by regular watering until the drought is over
Patches or whole lawn looking very thin, the grass growing sparsely and lacking vigour. Daisies, yarrow and moss may invade the thin areas	Neglect and starvation, usually showing most noticeably on thin, sandy soils	Kill weeds with a lawn weedkiller such as 2,4-D, and apply a top-dressing of well-rotted compost or good loam, with a lawn fertiliser mixed in dry; then water well	Top-dress and feed annually in autumn
Large heaps of loose soil, joined just under the turf by tunnels	Moles	Use a proprietary mole trap or place smoke pellets in the runs	
A slippery gelatinous layer develops over the grass	Algae and gelatinous lichens	Drain and spike the soil. Apply mercurised lawn sand or sulphate of iron (4 rounded tablespoons to 1 gallon of water) or copper sulphate (1 rounded dessertspoon to 10 gallons of water). Top-dress and feed	Keep the lawn well drained

Month-by-month lawn care

January Brush off fallen leaves.

February If wormcasts appear, remove, and apply a worm killer.

March As soon as the ground is firm, brush off surface debris. Roll when dry, to consolidate ground lifted by frost.

Rake thoroughly to lift up grass and weeds and mow lightly with the blades set about 1–1½ in. high. Two cuts are generally enough in March.

April Apply a fertiliser, followed a week or two later by a selective lawn weedkiller or lawn sand.

Mow often enough to keep the grass down, but not lower than ¾ in.

Dig out patches of coarse grass or resistant weed. Fill holes with sifted soil and re-seed, or else re-turf.

May Increase the frequency of mowing as necessary. Cut at ¼ in. above the summer level. This is the best month to eradicate weeds.

June, July and August Mow to normal summer level, two or three times a week. Rake before mowing.

Water well during prolonged dry periods. Destroy isolated weeds with spot weedkiller.

If persistent weeds such as yarrow are present, apply a selective weedkiller at three to four week intervals.

September Increase intervals between mowing, and raise the height of the cut by ¼ in. above the summer cut. Control worms, which may become active this month. Watch out for fusarium disease. Rake, spike and top-dress the lawn.

October Regular mowing comes to an end. Use a high blade setting for the last cut or two.

November If the weather is not frosty or wet, and the surface is firm, mow once with the blades set high. Brush off any leaves.

December Brush away the last of the autumn leaves, but keep off the lawn if it is very wet or frozen.

Levelling humps and hollows

Simple levelling work is best done in the non-growing period – between October and March.

Use a half-moon turfing iron or spade to cut a cross through the centre of the hollow or hump. Then make parallel cuts on each side of one line of the cross.

With a spade, peel back the turves so that all the soil is uncovered.

Fork the soil to a depth of 3–4 in., break it up well, tread it down and rake it level.

Then add or remove soil, according to whether you are levelling a hollow or a hump.

Fold the turves over the soil, and press them firm by rolling or treading. Fill cracks with fine soil.

1 *Cut a cross over the centre of the hollow or hump, then make parallel cuts on each side of one line of the cross. With a large area, make extra cuts*

2 *Lift the turves with a spade and peel them back carefully*

3 *Fork the soil 3–4 in. deep, tread and rake it. Add or remove soil*

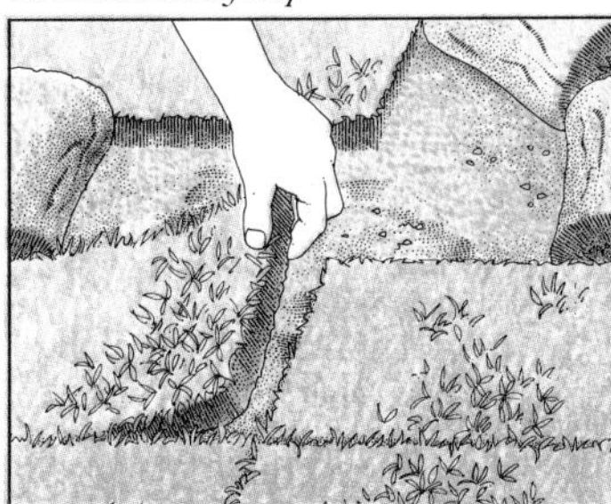

4 *Fold back the turves and press them firmly into position*

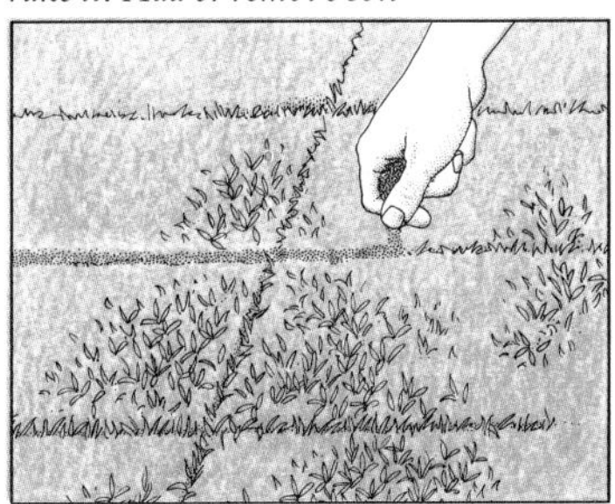

5 *Brush fine soil into the cracks between the turves*

Repairing broken edges round a lawn

Cut out a rectangle of turf around the broken edge, using a half-moon turfing iron or spade. Lift the turf with a spade and reverse it so that its straight edge replaces the damaged edge of the lawn.

Fill the hole formed by the damaged edge with fine soil. Press it in firmly and then, finally, sow it with grass seed.

1 *Cut out a square of turf around the broken edge. Lift the turf*

2 *Reverse it so that the straight edge replaces the damaged edge*

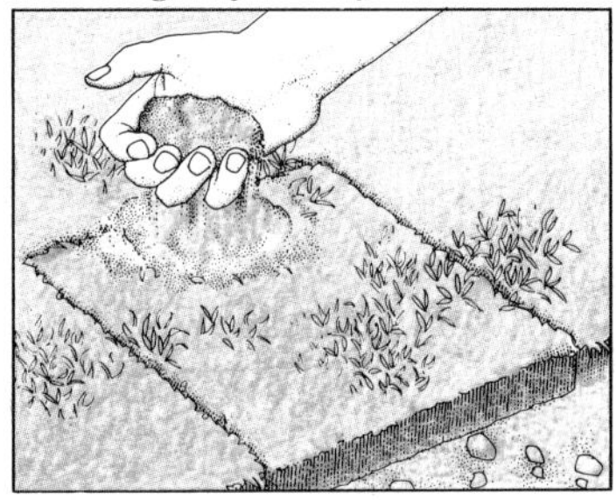

3 *Fill the hole with fine soil, firm it and sow with grass seed*

How to renovate a neglected lawn

Examine the grass and weeds covering the lawn. If very coarse grass, moss, pearlwort and other persistent weeds are dominant, the best plan is to lay a new lawn.

If desirable grasses still make up the main part of the lawn, carry out the following programme, starting in spring.

Cut down tall grasses and weeds to about 2 in. above the ground. Use a rotary mower, a billhook or a pair of shears, depending on the area to be cleared. Rake off all the cut vegetation.

Rake and brush the surface thoroughly to remove all dead vegetation and debris. Mow the grass with the blades set as high as possible. Subsequent mowings should be carried out regularly.

Feed and weed the lawn in late spring or summer, using a general fertiliser first, and then a selective weedkiller about a fortnight later.

Apply a calomel-based (mercurous chloride) moss killer or lawn sand to get rid of moss.

Attack the remaining troubles in autumn, using an autumn feed, worm killer and fungicide. Dig out clumps of 'weed' grasses.

A little later, during September, spike the surface and apply a top-dressing of well-rotted manure, garden compost or leaf-mould. If the lawn is thin, mix in seed with the top-dressing at a rate of $\frac{1}{2}$ oz. to the square yard.

Re-seed or else re-turf any bare patches which may appear after the weedkilling operations.

Begin the normal lawn management programme during the following spring.

Lilies

Famous since earliest history, lilies are among the most varied of plants in their colour, size and flowering time, and the conditions in which they will grow

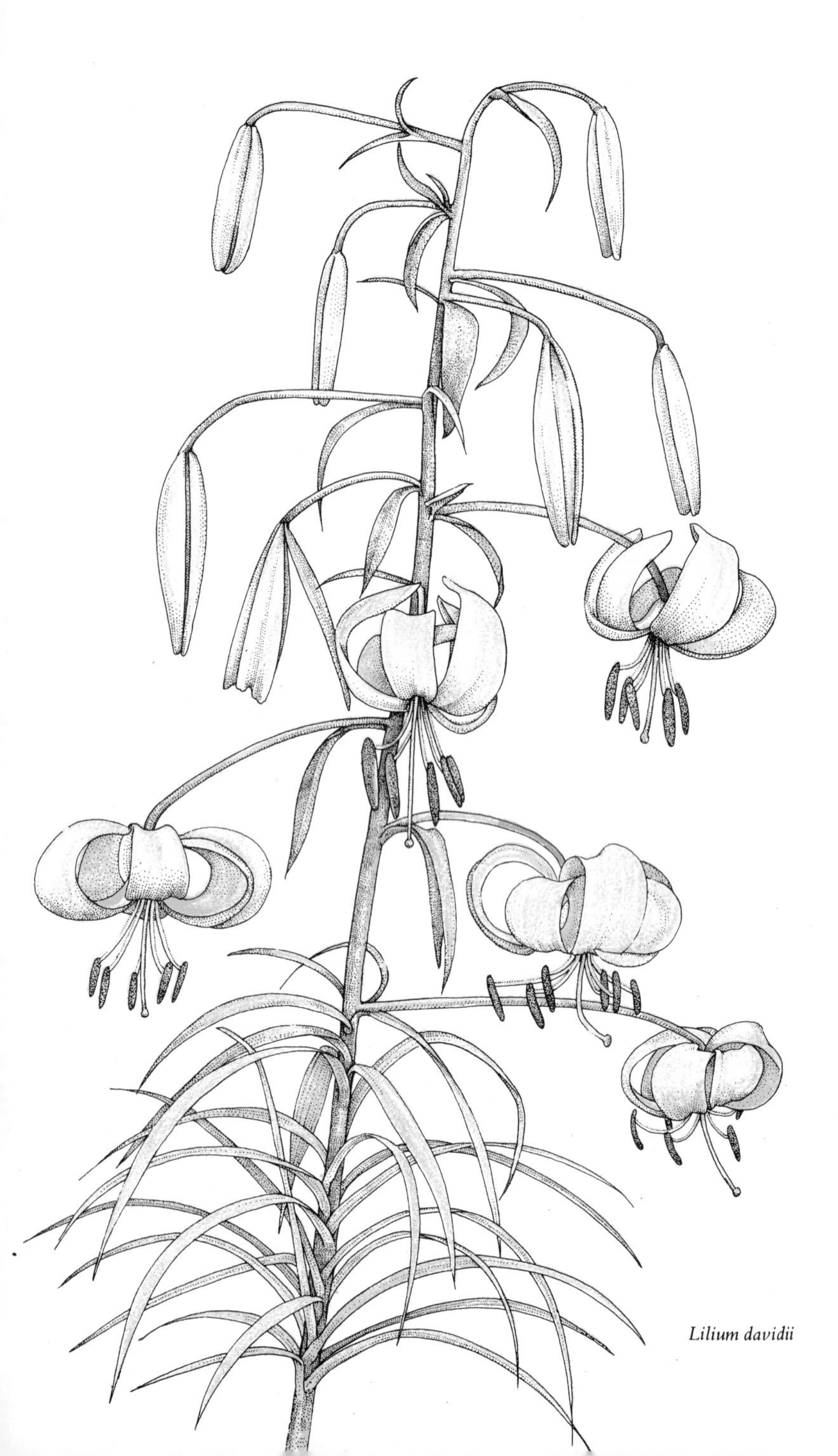

Lilium davidii

One of the oldest cultivated flowers, the lily has been cherished for at least 3000 years in ancient Egypt, Rome, Greece, China and Japan. For centuries only a few species were known, the most famous being the gleaming white Madonna lily (*Lilium candidum*) – traditionally a symbol of purity – from the eastern Mediterranean. Another species fairly widespread in Europe was *L. martagon*, with dark-spotted pink-mauve flowers that open in July.

Few plants are as versatile as the lily, a genus of mainly hardy bulbs with about 90 species. All are perennials, but they vary widely in size, colour, flowering period, and the conditions in which they will thrive.

Because some lilies, including the Madonna, can be difficult to grow, lilies were once considered flowers for the skilled gardener only. But many will grow well outdoors in Britain. And in the past 100 years easier-grown species have been discovered, and many hybrids have been developed that are robust, disease-free, and outshine their parents in vigour and variety of colour. There are even hybrids that grow reasonably true from seed, like the Olympic hybrids, the Empress strain and the Imperial strain. It is worth saving seeds and sowing them every year, particularly with short-lived lilies like *L. regale* which does not produce very many offset bulbs. Growing from seed is also an asset because virus disease, the great lily enemy, can be spread by vegetative propagation. The oldest hybrid, and one of the finest, is the unusual, apricot-coloured Nankeen lily (*L.* × *testaceum*), derived from *L. candidum* and *L. chalcedonicum*, a tall, scarlet species from Greece.

Lilies can be divided into two main flower shapes – the trumpet and the turk's-cap. Very wide trumpets are sometimes called bowl shaped, and some trumpet and turk's-cap types have flowers facing upwards.

Trumpet lilies, such as the regal lily (*L. regale*) and the Easter lily (*L. longiflorum*), have fairly large flowers. The trumpet flowers come in various shapes, from the narrow white flower of *L. formosanum* to the elongated white trumpet of *L. giganteum* with its purple flecks. As the name implies, this is a tall lily that can grow up to 12 ft.

Turk's-cap lilies, such as *L. martagon*, have smaller, pendent flowers about 1½ in. long with petals normally curving backwards at the tips.

An outstanding example of the bowl-shaped lily is the spectacular golden-rayed lily of Japan, *L. auratum*; this has flowers 10 in. across, coloured white with a bright yellow central band on each petal, and a covering of crimson spots.

Upward-facing lilies have flowers clustered together in fine heads – like the orange lily from central Europe, *L. bulbiferum croceum*, which flowers in June and July.

There are lilies of almost every colour, except blue. They vary from the pure whites of *L. longiflorum* and *L. candidum*, through many pastel shades, pinks, purples, yellows and oranges to the deep crimson of the popular hybrid 'Paprika'. Many flowers are streaked or spotted, such as the creamy-white, crimson-spotted, beautifully scented *L. speciosum*.

The flowering season outdoors ranges from May to September or October. One of the earliest species is *L. pyrenaicum* from the Pyrenees, a hardy greenish-yellow turk's-cap lily with purple spots. Unfortunately it has a rather overpowering smell at close quarters, as do a few other species (including *L. martagon*) and is better planted well away from paths. These heavy lily perfumes are pleasant when they are not too strong. One lily that does have a very pleasant, fragrant scent is *L. cernuum*, which is pale pink with red spots, and flowers from June to July. One of the latest to flower is the tiger lily (*L. tigrinum*) from Japan, which has orange turk's-cap flowers flecked with black.

Lilies vary in height from about 1½ ft to 12 ft. Among the tallest are the North American species *L. superbum* and *L. pardalinum* (the panther lily), particularly the variety 'Red Giant', and *L. henryi* from China. The smallest include *L. concolor* with its upward-facing, deep crimson blooms, and *L. pumilum* which has scarlet turk's-cap flowers.

Lilies originate from such varied situations in nature that at least one species or hybrid can be found to suit almost any garden.

Some, including *L. pardalinum* and *L. auratum* need peaty, acid soil. Others, including *L. longiflorum* and *L. bulbiferum croceum* and most of the hybrids, are tolerant of lime. Some prefer lime – examples are *L. candidum* and *L. × testaceum*.

Many lilies are happiest in full sun, but some like partial shade, such as *L. superbum* and the Paisley hybrids – so named because of their multi-colouring, which resembles the pattern of a Paisley shawl. All prefer their roots cool, so they need small ferns or shrubs to shade the base of the stem.

A species that thrives in most soils or positions is the tall regal lily *L. regale*, with white trumpet flowers coloured red-purple outside. Others that are fairly easy to grow include *L. martagon* and some of its offspring, the Backhouse hybrids; and the colourful Mid-Century hybrids, which include the upward-facing, nasturtium-red 'Enchantment'.

These robust and easy-to-grow species and hybrid lilies will thrive in mixed borders, as long as they are not crowded out. Their variety of colours and shapes makes it easy to mix them with other plants, and the many June and July-flowering lilies provide colour after irises and paeonies have faded.

Lilies are not really suitable for bedding out, but they can be grown in individual pots and planted – in their pots – when ready to flower.

It is safest to grow some of the tender lilies as pot plants. Lilies like *L. longiflorum* and *L. formosanum* that must be treated as tender will thrive in a pot or container under glass and regularly give a good display.

Another species for pot-growing is *L. davidii* from China, a turk's-cap bloom with a profusion of bright orange flowers.

A border composed entirely of lilies can flower from May to October. But most need protection from wind, and some of the taller plants need support. A background of shrubs, particularly rhododendrons and azaleas, will give wind protection and set off the lilies to advantage. Taller plants can be grown among the shrubs, so that they can be supported naturally without staking.

Lilies particularly suitable for woodlands or wild gardens include the Bellingham hybrids from America. The flowers grow in shades of red, orange and yellow, spotted with maroon or black. Other woodland lilies include *L. auratum* and the fragrant *L. monadelphum* (the Caucasus lily).

Lilies that do well in roomy pockets in rock gardens include *L. cernuum*, with its fairly short-lived upward-facing flowers, and *L. pumilum*, with scarlet turk's-cap flowers. Both need moist, well-drained soil containing plenty of organic material.

Some species, such as *L. candidum*, *L. tigrinum* and *L. testaceum*, are likely to carry virus disease and should be isolated from other lilies.

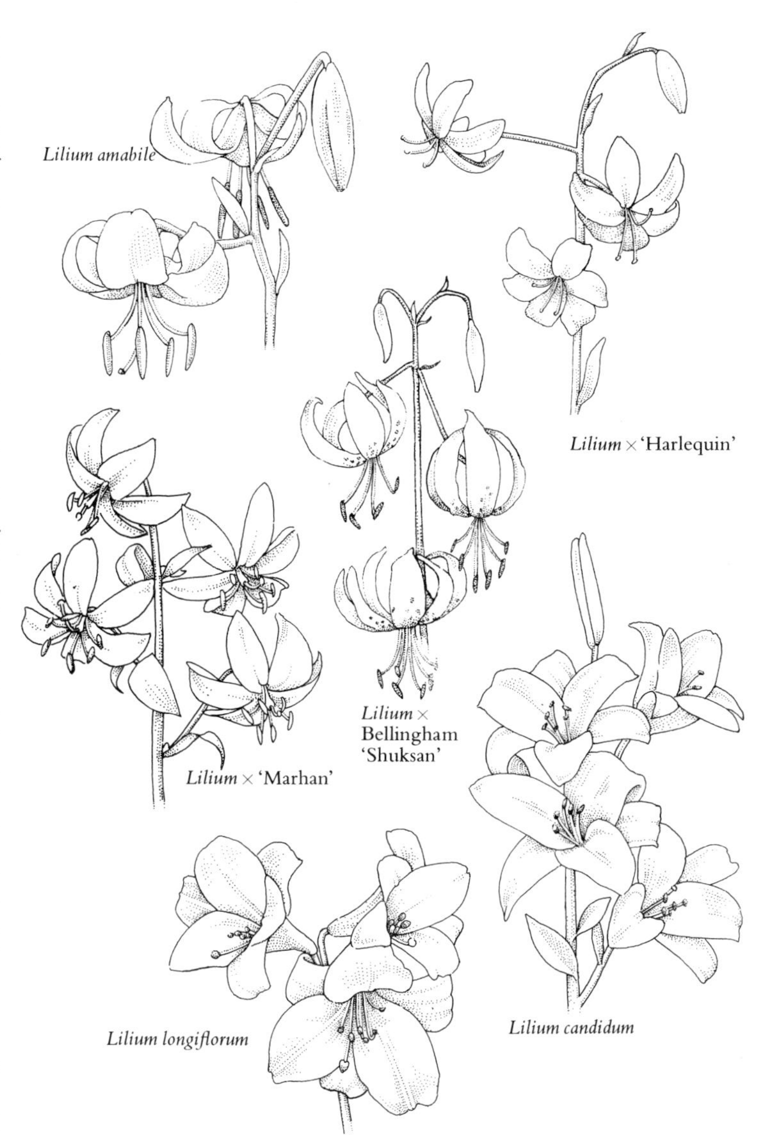

Lily flower shapes *There are two main groups into which the flower shapes are divided. Turk's-cap types have pendent flowers about 1½ in. long. Their petals are rolled and curved backwards at the tips. Examples include* Lilium amabile, *and hybrids* L. × *'Harlequin',* L. × *'Marhan' and* L. × *Bellingham 'Shuksan'. Trumpet lilies range from narrow trumpets to bowl shapes. The group includes* L. candidum *and* L. longiflorum

Planting and caring for lilies

Choosing the bulbs and preparing the soil

Most lilies will grow in any well-drained soil. If possible, choose a south-facing position, on a slight slope to help drainage.

There should be shrubs or small trees near by to provide shelter from strong winds. Most lilies do well in sunny positions but some, such as *Lilium canadense* and *L. superbum*, prefer dappled shade.

Lilies look very attractive beside streams and ponds, but keep them above possible flood level.

Dig the soil well in advance of planting, to a depth of 2 ft or more, breaking it up well.

If the soil is light, fork in some leaf-mould, well-rotted garden compost or peat (a large bucketful to the square yard). For heavy soils, add coarse sand at the same time.

Never use fresh manure around the roots of lilies, as it can rot them.

Ensure that the bed is well drained, as lilies will die in stagnant conditions. If the garden is flat and tends to flood, make raised beds of prepared soil about 12 in. deep, ideally with peat-block walls.

It is safest to buy bulbs from a reputable nursery or garden shop. Buy only plump, healthy-looking specimens. They should have firm, closely packed scales and a good root system. Never plant a bulb with withered, loose scales (the scales should be plump and firm). Avoid, too, any with roots trimmed close to the bulb. If you have been tempted by bargain lots of late-season bulbs, which may be bruised or limp, remove the outer scales, bury the bulbs in moist peat for a day or two, then plant them in the normal way.

Young bulbs are best, because they form roots that pull the bulbs down to the most suitable level.

Some lilies are treated with paraffin wax to prevent them drying out. Examine these closely before buying to ensure that they are healthy. The scales should be plump and firm – not withered, bruised or soft.

How and when to plant out the bulbs

Most lilies can be planted at any time between late summer and early spring, provided the ground is not frost-bound.

Try to plant the Madonna lily (*L. candidum*) as soon as possible after the stem dies down in autumn, and certainly before it grows its winter rosette of leaves.

Some lilies root only from the base (as do hyacinths and daffodils); others produce roots from the base of the stem just above the bulb as well. The base-rooting type should be planted as early in the autumn as possible.

If planting is delayed because of bad weather or soil conditions, grow the bulbs temporarily in pots, described on the opposite page. If the delay will be brief, store the bulbs in shallow boxes of slightly damp peat in order to prevent them drying out.

For most lilies, dig the planting hole two and a half times the depth of the bulb. The exceptions are *L. candidum*, *L. giganteum* and *L. testaceum*, which should be planted only just below the surface.

Line the base of the hole generously with coarse sand or fine gravel to help drainage.

Spread out the roots of the bulb. Apply more sand over the roots, then fill in the hole with soil. Insert a label or stick to mark the exact position of the bulb.

After planting, prick in with a small fork a handful of sterilised bonemeal to every square yard.

1 *Spread the roots of the bulb on a good layer of drainage material*

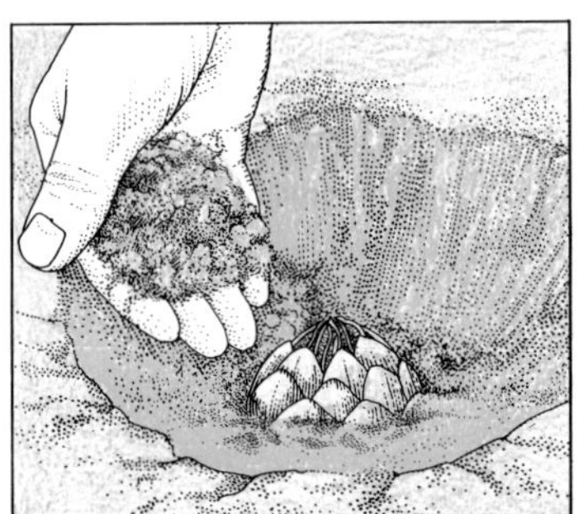

2 *Spread more sand over the roots, fill the hole with soil. Label the bulbs*

Staking, watering and feeding

Lilies that flower in late summer may be spoilt by autumn gales if they are not staked.

Those with arching stems, such as *L. henryi*, look better if supported. But there is no need to stake lilies that are less than 3 ft high.

Stake in March, using a bamboo cane for each plant. The cane should be about two-thirds of the estimated eventual length of the stem. As the lily grows, tie the stem to the cane.

The soil must never be allowed to dry out. During dry spells in the growing season, thoroughly water the soil and, if possible, apply a mulch of leaf-mould.

Most lilies are hardy, but in March newly emerged lilies should be protected from frost by placing them under cloches.

Cutting blooms for vase arrangement

Lilies are superb for flower arrangement, but the same plants should not be cut in successive years, as this weakens them. Take blooms from one-third of the plants each year, giving each plant two years' rest.

When cutting lilies, sever only the top one-third to a half of the stem, using scissors or secateurs. Cut them when the blooms are half open. Water the plants well the day before and do the cutting before the sun gets on them, when the stems are full of moisture.

The blooms will last longer if they are stood up to their necks in cold water for 12 hours before arranging.

When arranging lilies, strip the lower leaves from the stems. Any leaves that are under water in a vase will turn the water brackish.

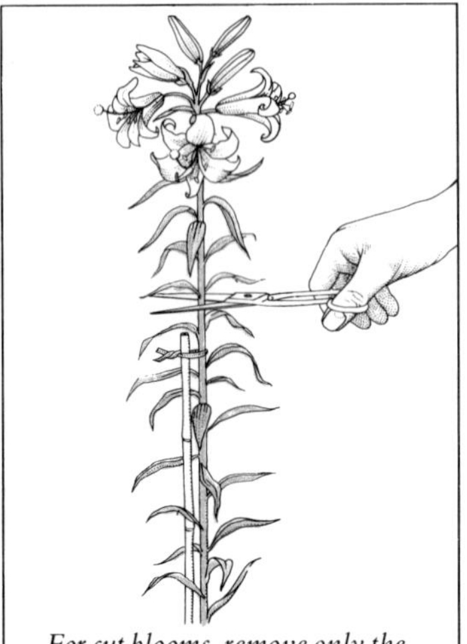

For cut blooms, remove only the top one-third to a half of the stem every third year

Dead-heading to stop seeds forming

Pinch off the flowers after they have faded to prevent seeds forming, and so weakening the plant.

In autumn, allow the stems to die down naturally. When they are dead, cut them off at soil level and burn them. Do not use them as compost material – if they have a disease, it will spread. If you want to increase certain varieties, leave one or two seed pods on each plant.

The seed capsules, cylindrical or spherical in shape, contain between 500 and 700 seeds.

Harvest them when they are ripe, that is when they turn yellow, and dry them off indoors. If left too long on the plants the capsules will burst open, dispersing the seed.

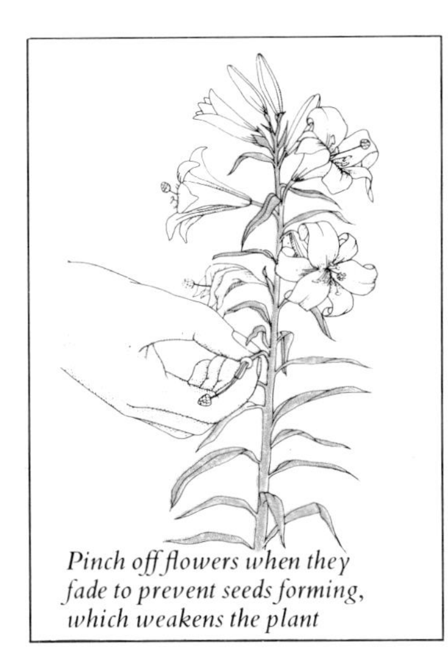

Pinch off flowers when they fade to prevent seeds forming, which weakens the plant

What can go wrong with lilies

This chart describes the most common problems that are likely to occur in the growing of lilies. If your plants show symptoms that are not described here, turn to the full-colour identification chart of pests and diseases starting on page 377. Look up the relevant chemical on page 398 for lists of trade names.

Symptoms	Cause	Cure
Growing tips of shoots and young flower buds covered with greenish or pinkish insects; leaves beneath sticky; sometimes buds and leaves are malformed	Aphids	Spray with derris or malathion
Leaves and shoots eaten, slime trails present around the plant	Slugs or snails	Apply pellets of metaldehyde or methiocarb
Water-soaked areas in leaves which later turn grey or white. The fungus may spread into the stem and cause a brown rot which topples the stem	Lily disease (grey mould)	Spray with benomyl, Bordeaux mixture or liquid copper
Leaves with a pale or yellow striping or mottling, getting worse over several years with weakening and finally stunting of the stem. The flowers are often severely crippled or non-existent	Virus	There is no cure, and plants must be destroyed to prevent the virus spreading

Growing lilies in pots and tubs

Lilies can be grown in pots either as indoor plants, or simply to start them off when conditions are too bad for outdoor planting. Shorter, earlier-flowering kinds are best, such as the Mid-century hybrids 'Enchantment' (red), 'Cinnabar' (maroon), and 'Harmony' (orange).

Potting can be done between October and the end of March, but the earlier the better.

Use a 6 in. pot for a medium-sized bulb (about 2 in. across).

Place about 1 in. of drainage material at the bottom of the pot.

With base-rooting lilies, half fill the pot with John Innes No. 2 potting compost. Make a mound on the compost, place the bulb on top and spread out its roots. Cover the roots with compost and firm them in with the fingers. Fill the pot with compost to within $\frac{1}{2}$ in. of the top and then label it.

Bury the pot to the rim in sand or peat outdoors, and cover it with about 4 in. of the same material.

With stem-rooting lilies, only quarter fill the pot with compost before inserting the bulb, so that the bulb is deep in the pot. Just cover it with compost. Place it in an unheated greenhouse or frost-proof shed. When the shoot reaches the top of the pot, fill with compost to within $\frac{1}{2}$ in. of the top.

In early spring – when the young growth of base-rooting lilies has pushed through – either plant the bulbs outside or bring them inside into a light position with a temperature of 12–16°C (54–61°F). Do not bring them into a warmer room until the flowers start to open.

Regular and moderate watering should now start. Over-watering is harmful – the aim being to keep the compost constantly moist. Once a fortnight, feed potted lilies with weak liquid manure.

When they have finished flowering, indoor plants can be either planted out in the garden or kept in the same pots for another year. In this case, the top $1\frac{1}{2}$ in. of compost should be renewed, and the pots kept during winter under sand or peat outdoors. Keep moist.

Lilies can also be grown in tubs outdoors. Plant them in the same compost as used for pots, but look after the plants in the same way as those growing in the open garden.

POTTING TWO TYPES OF LILY

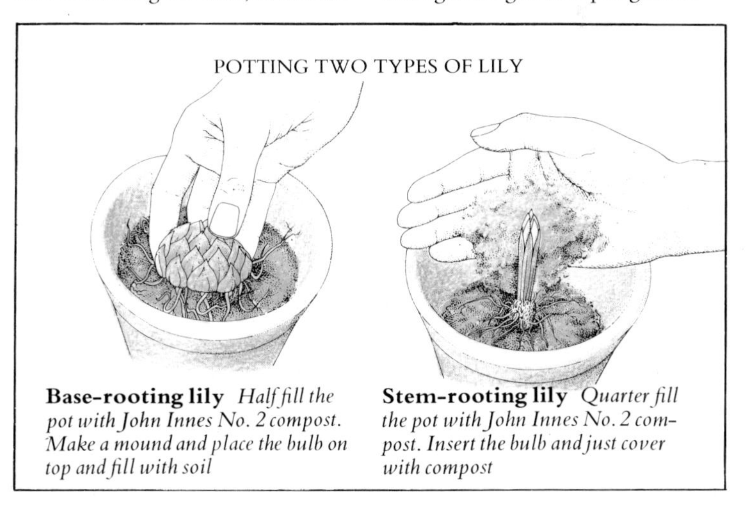

Base-rooting lily *Half fill the pot with John Innes No. 2 compost. Make a mound and place the bulb on top and fill with soil*

Stem-rooting lily *Quarter fill the pot with John Innes No. 2 compost. Insert the bulb and just cover with compost*

How to propagate your own lilies

Producing plants from scales

The easiest and most widely practised method of increasing lilies is by propagating from the scales of bulbs. Flowering plants can be produced two to five years later, according to species.

The best time is early autumn when flowering has finished, although scales can be planted at any time between August and January. Use only plump, healthy bulbs fresh from the garden, or there is a risk of passing on infection.

Fill a pot or seed tray to within ½ in. of the top with well-moistened John Innes No. 1 potting compost or a seed compost.

Pull away any withered or damaged outer scales from each bulb, until plump, unbruised scales – the ones to be planted – are revealed.

Detach as many of these as are required. A bulb of average size yields roughly 12–24 scales.

Pull each scale away gently but firmly, removing it as close to its base as possible.

If the bulb is wanted for replanting, remove only about one-third of its total bulk of scales. The papery scales at the heart of the bulb are not so likely to yield good results.

Make a hole in the compost with a finger and insert a scale, base down, to half its depth. Then firm in with your fingers.

Repeat with all the scales, planting them ½–1 in. apart.

Put a propagating case or plastic bag over the container. If the scales have been taken early, this container can go into a cold frame or cold greenhouse, or indoors on a cool window-sill.

If taken in late autumn or winter, bottom heat of 10–13°C (50–55°F) will hasten growth. Within six weeks of planting, one or more bulblets, or tiny bulbs, should have formed at the base of each scale. Check this by gently removing the soil around one or two scales. If bulblets have formed, remove any heat.

Shoots will soon appear above the compost. The young plants may now be either planted outside, or potted individually into 2½–3 in. pots of John Innes No. 1 potting compost.

Sink the pots into sand or peat outside and cover them with about an inch of the same material.

Alternatively, place the pots in an unheated greenhouse, cold frame or frost-proof shed.

The following autumn, the bulbs of all vigorous hardy hybrids will be ready for planting out. Less vigorous varieties will not be ready for planting out until the following autumn. Keep them in the same pot or plant in rows in the garden.

Lifting and dividing the bulbs in summer

Some lilies, like *L. pyrenaicum* and *L. bulbiferum croceum*, increase their bulbs so quickly that they need to be lifted and divided every three or four years. *L. regale* can also be propagated in this way.

When the stems have died down in late summer, loosen and lift the clump carefully with a garden fork.

Any scales that come away from the bulbs can be collected and used for propagation.

Gently separate the bulbs and replant them in fresh soil.

Some vigorous lilies, such as *L. pardalinum*, have elongated bulbs joined together like a rhizome. These need to be divided even if you do not want to propagate, otherwise flowering gradually deteriorates.

Sever these bulbs from one another with a sharp knife. Then plant the bulbs in their new positions in the normal way.

Since lilies may take more than a year to recover from division, divide only some of your stock each year.

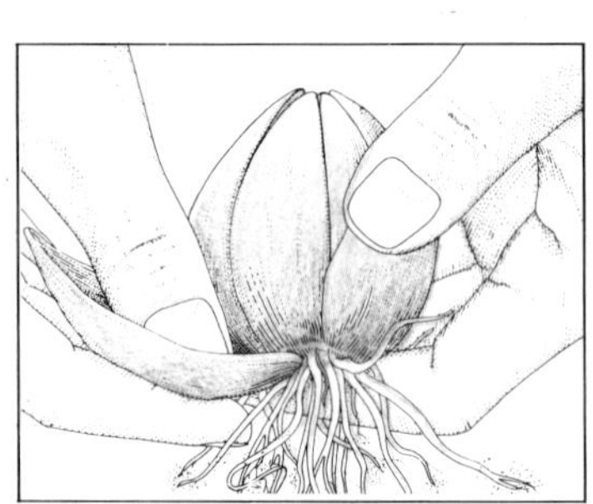

1 *Pull away any withered or damaged outer scales from each bulb*

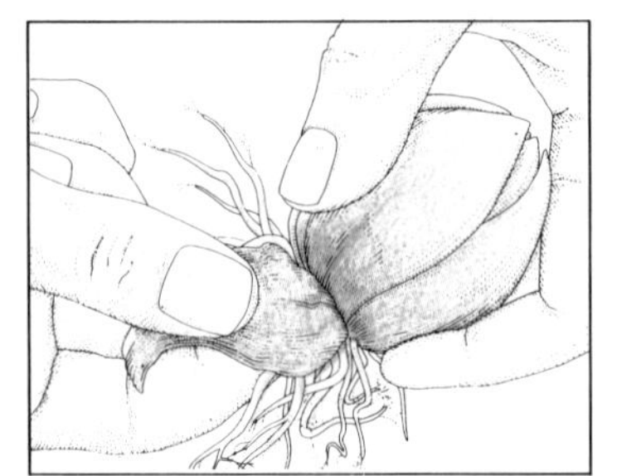

2 *Gently pull away as many of the plump scales as are needed*

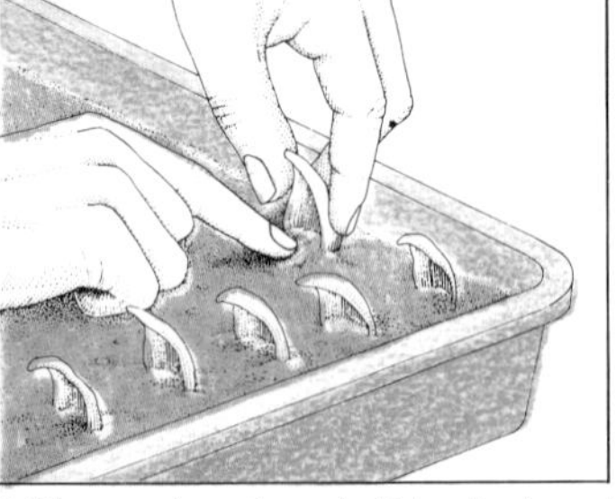

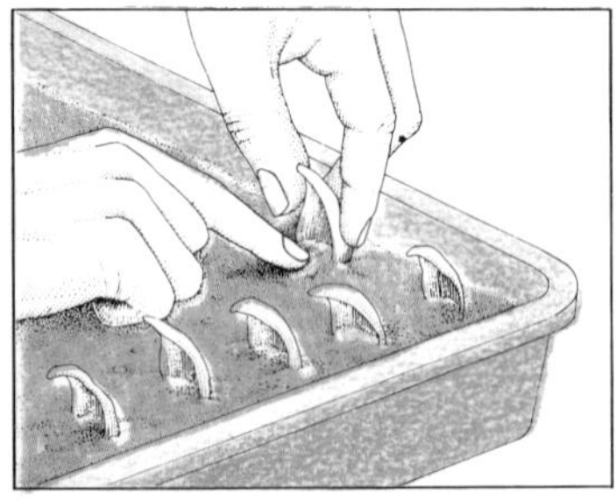

3 *Plant each scale to half its depth and cover the container with a plastic bag*

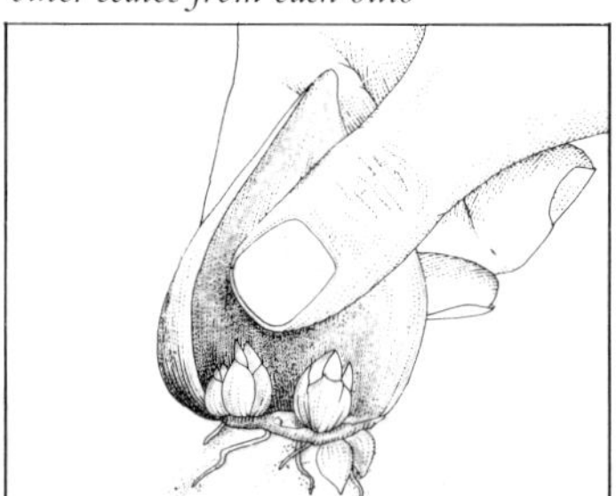

4 *Within six weeks, check to see that miniature bulbs have formed*

5 *When shoots appear, pot each new plant in a 2½–3 in. pot*

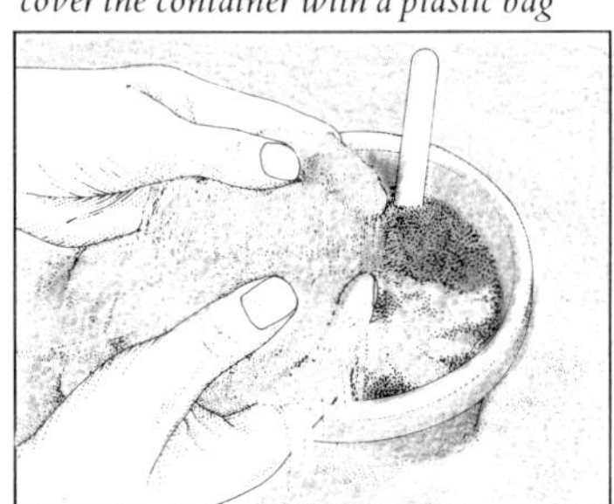

6 *Sink the pots in sand or peat outdoors. Cover with an inch of sand.*

DIVIDING BULBS

Use a sharp knife to separate the rhizomatous bulbs formed by some vigorous lilies; then plant them in new positions

Producing tiger lilies from bulbils

Bulbils are the tiny green or black-purple bulbs that grow on the stem in the leaf axils of some species of lilies, such as *L. bulbiferum* and *L. tigrinum* (tiger lilies).

Detach them when they will come away easily without pulling – about flowering time.

Place a layer of crocks or gravel in the bottom of a pot or seed tray. Then fill the container with seed compost.

With a dibber make a planting hole ½ in. deep in the compost, put in the bulbil and cover it with compost. Sow them 1 in. apart.

Put the container in a cold frame and plant out the young lilies the following autumn.

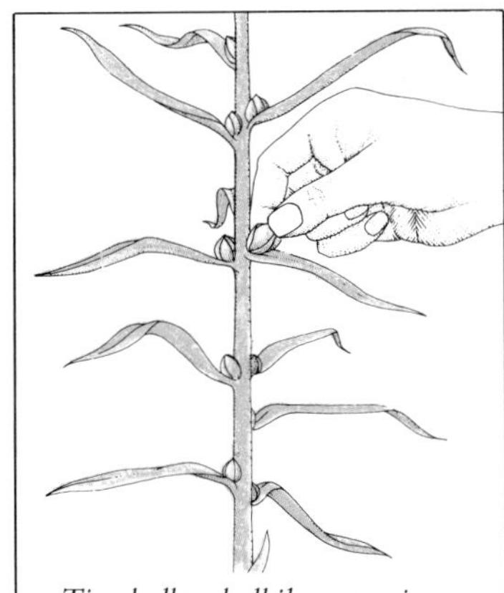

Tiny bulbs – bulbils – grow in the leaf axils of some species. Remove them in late summer and plant them in seed compost

Obtaining new plants from bulblets

Bulblets are offsets that grow on some lilies, such as *L. wardii* and *L. nepalense*, just below ground level, either among the stem roots or from the base of the bulb. They should not be confused with bulbils.

In late summer, carefully remove the soil around the stem and gently detach the bulblets. Then plant them straight into the ground. Make the planting hole two and a half times the depth of the bulblet and line the hole with moist peat.

Alternatively, the bulblets can be started off in a greenhouse in 3 or 4 in. pots of John Innes seed compost or a proprietary seed compost. Plant them out in their permanent positions a year later.

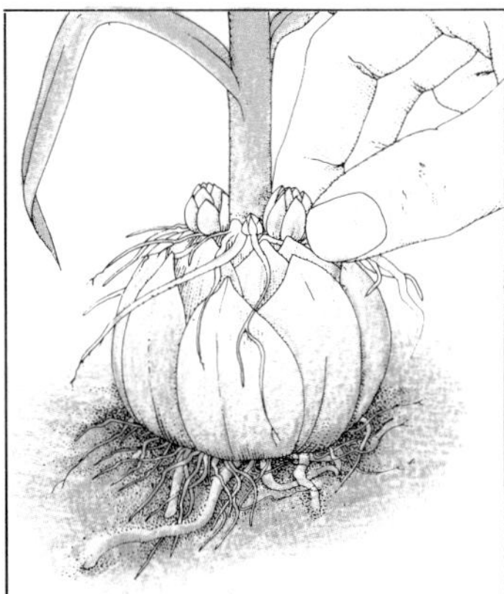

Offsets, which grow among the stem roots or on the base of some lilies, can be detached and planted out in late summer

Growing lilies from seed

Sowing seeds is another way of producing a large collection of lilies. It also creates a disease-free stock. However, hybrid lilies will not breed true with this method and, as with scales, you must wait at least two years for flowers.

Harvest the seed capsules in autumn when they turn yellow and sow the seeds immediately, or in early spring, in seed compost.

Using pots or trays, sow the seeds at least 1 in. apart and ½ in. deep. Put the containers in a cool greenhouse or on a window-sill.

A minimum temperature of 10–13°C (50–55°F) will hasten germination but is not essential. Make sure that the compost never dries out.

Lily seeds can be divided into two groups – epigeal (examples are *L. regale* and *L. tigrinum*) and hypogeal (examples are *L. canadense* and *L. superbum*). Epigeal seeds germinate quickly and produce top growth in a few weeks, before the bulb has formed. Hypogeal seeds produce a bulb first, and it may be many months before the first shoots appear above the compost.

As soon as the second leaf appears on epigeal seedlings, transplant them into pots, pans or 3 in. deep boxes, 1 in. apart each way.

When hypogeal seedlings produce their first leaf, move them individually into 2½ in. pots. In both cases, use John Innes No. 2 potting compost or a peat-based compost.

Place the containers in a cold frame, or sink them in sand or peat outdoors. At the end of the first growing season, one year after the seeds were sown, remove the young bulbs from the containers and plant them in rows in a sheltered spot.

Let them grow on for another year; by then some species and hybrids will have produced flowering-sized bulbs.

The seeds of vigorous lilies, such as *L. regale*, may be sown directly into the open ground in spring. Sow the seeds ½ in. deep in drills 12 in. apart. Leave them for two summers before transplanting them to their permanent sites.

TWO TYPES OF LILY SEED

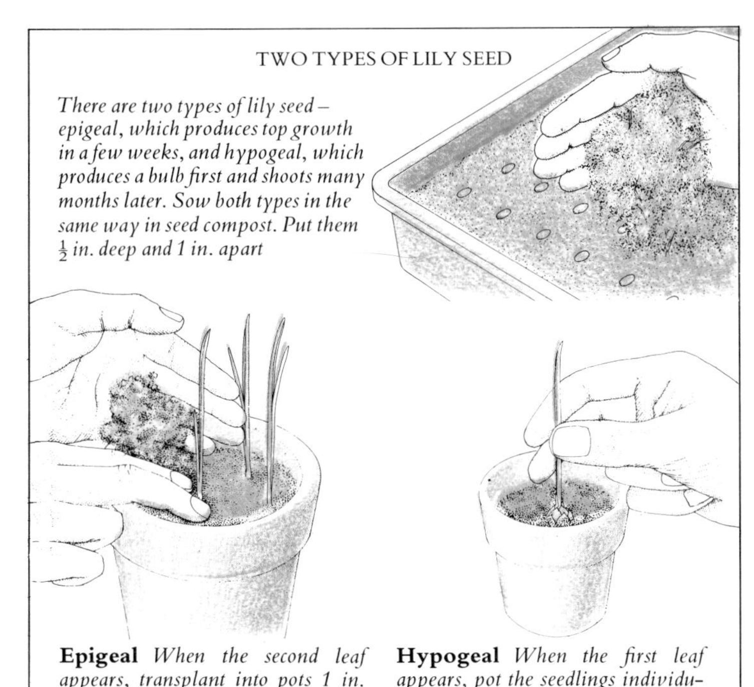

There are two types of lily seed – epigeal, which produces top growth in a few weeks, and hypogeal, which produces a bulb first and shoots many months later. Sow both types in the same way in seed compost. Put them ½ in. deep and 1 in. apart

Epigeal *When the second leaf appears, transplant into pots 1 in. apart each way*

Hypogeal *When the first leaf appears, pot the seedlings individually into 2½ in. pots*

Orchids for a greenhouse or the home

A wide range of orchids will grow in a cool greenhouse without any special equipment. And tropical orchids can be added to the collection inside a heated glass frame

The ideal greenhouse for orchids is a conservatory built against a house wall. It will draw heat from the wall, and if the house has central heating an extra radiator could probably be fixed inside the conservatory to provide cheap heating.

If you are buying a new greenhouse, choose a small, extendable model. To start with, 10 × 8 ft is ideal, but 6 × 8 ft is quite adequate.

The staging along the sides and end of the greenhouse should be at waist height – about 3 ft above the ground.

The central path should be 2 ft wide, and is best made of cement or stone flagging. The area under the staging should be open ground, possibly covered with stone chippings, shingle or plastic granules for cleanliness.

An electric extractor fan, 10–12 in. in diameter, is the best way of ventilating the greenhouse and should be installed in the wall opposite the entrance door, about 6 ft from the ground. There should also be a bottom ventilator – covered with wire mesh to keep out pests – in the base of the entrance door. It will need a sliding shutter to help control air flow.

A small number of tropical orchids, which need very warm conditions, can be grown economically in a cool greenhouse by keeping them in a fairly tall glass frame on the staging.

A frame with bottom heating should provide enough heat, but if necessary it can be lined on the inside with plastic sheeting during winter for extra insulation. Fix the plastic to wooden supports around the sides and top of the frame, leaving 1 in. of space between plastic and glass. In summer, remove the plants from the frame and keep them in the warmest part of the greenhouse. At least six tropical orchids would fit into a frame 2 × 3 × 3 ft tall.

An alternative is to erect a glazed partition at the end of the greenhouse, forming a cubicle which can be kept warmer and more humid. This can provide quite a large area for tropical orchids. During the winter, line the area with plastic sheeting mounted on wooden frames. Remove the plastic in the spring when sunlight is needed.

Another place to grow tropical orchids is indoors, in a miniature greenhouse. The 'greenhouse' is a small garden frame standing on a window-sill over a central-heating radiator. If possible the frame should be kept in a north or east-facing window in summer, and a south or west-facing window in winter. Cultural requirements are the same as for normal-size greenhouses, but ventilation will require care as temperature changes are more rapid in such a small space.

Providing heat Most orchids can be divided into either 'cool-house' or 'warm-house' types.

The cool-house plants need a minimum temperature of 7°C (45°F) in winter and 14°C (57°F) in summer. Tropical plants need a minimum temperature of 16°C (61°F) in winter (although they will tolerate brief, cooler periods) and 22°C (72°F) in summer.

To provide the heat, an electric fan heater with a thermostatic control is ideal, as it keeps the air moving. A 3 kilowatt heater will keep a 10 × 8 ft orchid house warm enough for cool-house orchids. A 4½ kilowatt heater is needed in the same size greenhouse for warm-house orchids.

Keep a paraffin heater as a safeguard against an electrical power failure.

To grow tropical orchids in a separate section of a 10 × 8 ft coolhouse, you would need an additional smaller heater in this section.

Damping down In their natural habitat, many orchids grow in positions where water vapour rises from the damp ground or foliage around them. They absorb the moisture through their leaves.

This humidity is produced in the greenhouse by spraying water frequently on the flooring of the house and on the staging where the plants stand. Light but frequent dampings are more effective than occasional flooding.

In summer, damp the orchid house at least once a day, in the morning, and preferably twice a day. If the weather is particularly hot, three or four dampings may be necessary.

In winter, two or three dampings a week are sufficient, before midday. Do not damp if the outside temperature drops below freezing.

If your soil is light and sandy, more frequent or heavier dampings may be necessary.

The easiest method of damping is to use tap water applied through a hose with a fine-spray nozzle.

Do not spray the tap water on the plants themselves. This can be avoided by standing them on upturned pots.

When warm-house orchids are grown in a frame, damp down with a syringe containing rain water.

Regulating air flow Fresh air is essential to all orchids, but it must be provided without causing a draught, and without lowering the temperature or the humidity.

A 10–12 in. extractor fan will draw in enough air through gaps around the door to ensure ventilation, but a ventilator at the bottom of the greenhouse can be opened to increase air flow in hot weather.

Fans can be connected to a thermostat, so that they come on automatically when the temperature of the greenhouse becomes too high.

The cheapest form of ventilation is by the traditional ventilators fitted to the top and bottom of the greenhouse on both sides. It is preferable to have one top vent and one bottom vent on each side of the orchid house for every 4 ft of the length.

During summer, open the top ventilators on the leeward side 4–6 in., day and night. On very hot days, also open the bottom ventilators on the same side. When the temperature drops below average, close all ventilators.

In winter, close the top ventilators to preserve the warm air, and open the bottom ventilators on the leeward side to allow fresh air into the greenhouse.

Bottom ventilators should be at least 12 × 24 in., and covered with wire netting to keep out pests.

Shading plants To prevent the temperature inside the greenhouse from rising too high in summer, the greenhouse needs to be shaded.

The best – but most expensive – form of shading is provided by roller blinds made of wooden or plastic laths.

Cheaper shading is provided by plastic blinds which are run up and down the roof.

An air space should be left between the glass and the blinds, to allow the air to circulate over the glass and to keep an even temperature in the house.

Unroll the blinds on the sunny side of the greenhouse whenever the sun shines brightly during late spring and summer.

A less satisfactory method of shading is to paint the greenhouse glass with synthetic whitewash. In late February apply two wavy vertical stripes of whitewash, a few inches apart, to each pane. Use a sprayer or a 4 in. brush. In April fill in each pane with three more stripes.

Wash off the whitewash in late September.

Slat staging is ideal for orchids that need freely circulating air, such as dendrobiums and cattleyas. Solid staging covered with damp gravel is best for orchids that need greater humidity in their growing season, such as cymbidiums and paphiopedilums. An alternative to both types is to suspend dummy staging, covered with damp gravel, 12 in. below the slat staging. Keep the gravel moist when damping down the greenhouse

The week-to-week care of orchid plants

How orchids produce their flowers

The orchids grown by amateur gardeners in Britain mostly lead an aerial existence in their normal habitat – growing above ground on tree branches. Plants that grow in this way by means of specially adapted roots are called epiphytes.

Most epiphytic orchids flower in Britain from autumn to late spring, and the flowers grow from swollen stems known as pseudobulbs. These sometimes grow in clumps, and may occur at intervals along prostrate stems, or rhizomes.

A few epiphytic orchids do not produce pseudobulbs – for example, vandas, which have erect, woody stems, with the flowers growing from the leaf axils, and paphiopedilums which are tufted plants with flower stems growing from the base.

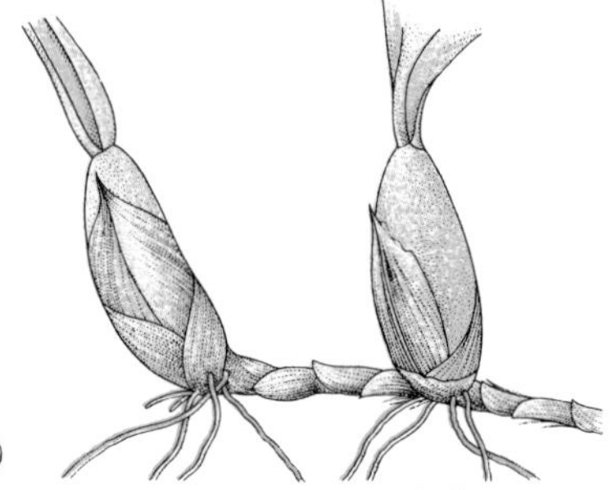

Two types of pseudobulbs *Cymbidiums (left) have stout pseudobulbs 3–4 in. high and covered with leaves. The old, leafless bulbs are called back-bulbs. The pseudobulbs of coelogyne (right) grow along a creeping, horizontal rhizome*

How to water and feed orchid plants

Orchids should not be watered with very cold or limy water. So keep a tank of rain water inside the greenhouse, where it will be kept warm. A tank holding 60–100 gallons would be right for an orchid house measuring 10 × 8 ft.

Before starting to wash down the outside of the greenhouse, block the inlet gutter to the tank with a wad of cloth to stop dirty, lime-containing water from running in.

A tap-water supply to the greenhouse is valuable for topping up the tank in dry spells, as limy water is better than none at all.

Examine plants once a week to see if the compost is moist, or lift the pot to test the weight.

When the compost has become reasonably dry, water thoroughly, until it is saturated. Do not water if the compost is wet; leave the plant until the next week.

Hanging plants should be placed in a bath of water, until bubbles stop rising from the compost.

If you are doubtful whether the compost is dry enough to water, leave the plant alone.

After orchids have been in the same compost for over a year, feed them with a liquid fertiliser about once a fortnight during the growing season – late spring to late summer. Water the plants first, as fertiliser can damage dry roots.

HANGING PLANTS

Submerge in water until bubbles stop rising from the compost

The resting period when watering is rarely needed

Many orchids require a resting period, usually from late summer to mid-autumn. During this period they may lose their leaves, leaving only the pseudobulbs from which new growth will emerge.

When the leaves have fallen, or the pseudobulbs have grown stout and healthy, move the plant to a shelf in better light and in a cooler part of the greenhouse. Reduce humidity to a minimum.

During the resting period, orchids with pseudobulbs need no water unless the compost dries out completely. Then drench thoroughly. Orchids without pseudobulbs may need an occasional watering.

When growth begins again, return the plant to its normal place and resume watering.

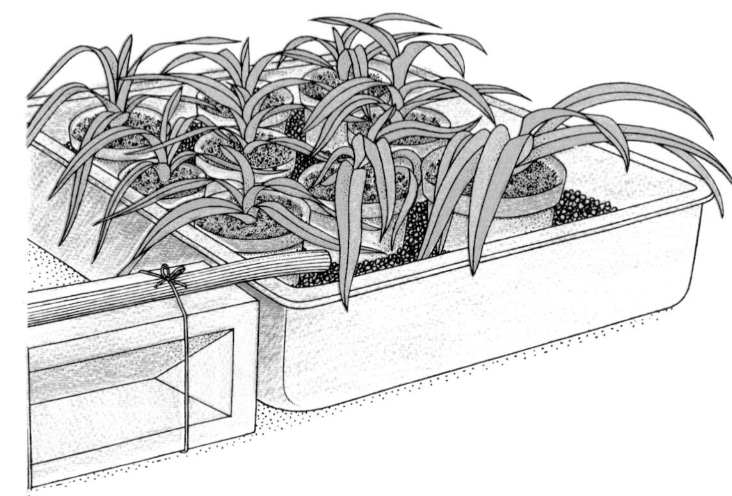

Watering unit for long holidays *Sink the pots in a tray filled with an equal mixture of coarse sand and peat, and insert a hose connected to a tap that has been adjusted to drip very slowly. Keep the greenhouse shaded*

Caring for orchids at holiday time

Before you go away on a summer holiday, soak the plants thoroughly. This should last for three weeks.

If the holiday is longer, keep plants in a capillary watering unit. The units can be bought, but are easy to make. Fill a gravel tray with coarse sand mixed with an equal quantity of peat, and sink the pots in it to halfway up their sides. Put a hose in the tray, and allow water to trickle in extremely slowly.

Control temperature by keeping the greenhouse shaded.

Ventilation is the most difficult problem. Preferably get a friend to look after it for you, or buy automatic ventilation. If neither is possible, open the ventilators to the average you have been using recently – and hope for the best.

Supporting top-heavy orchid plants

Some orchids such as cattleyas and dendrobiums can be top heavy, and need support after potting until they have produced strong new roots. So insert a cane at the back of each plant. The cane should be as tall as the eventual height of the plant.

Pass a piece of green string around two or three of the rear growths, halfway up, and tie it to the stake.

Repeat with the other growths.

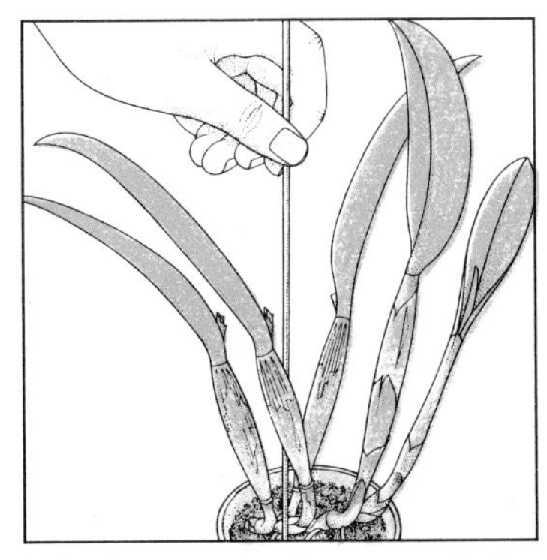

1 *Cattleyas need to be supported after potting, or they may topple over*

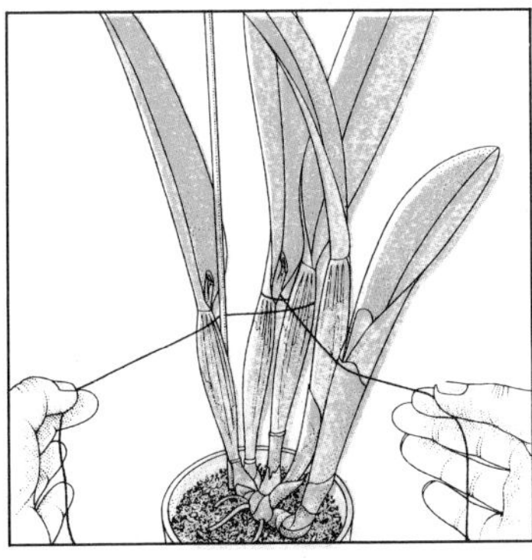

2 *Wind pieces of green string around the growths, and tie to a stake*

Supporting flowers on long stems

Flowers that grow on tall stems, such as some species of paphiopedilums, can be supported by means of galvanised wire. Bend the wire into a U-shape at the end, and then bend the U over at right angles.

Support long flower spikes by inserting a cane at an angle, and fixing the stems to it with pieces of raffia.

WIRE AND CANE SUPPORTS

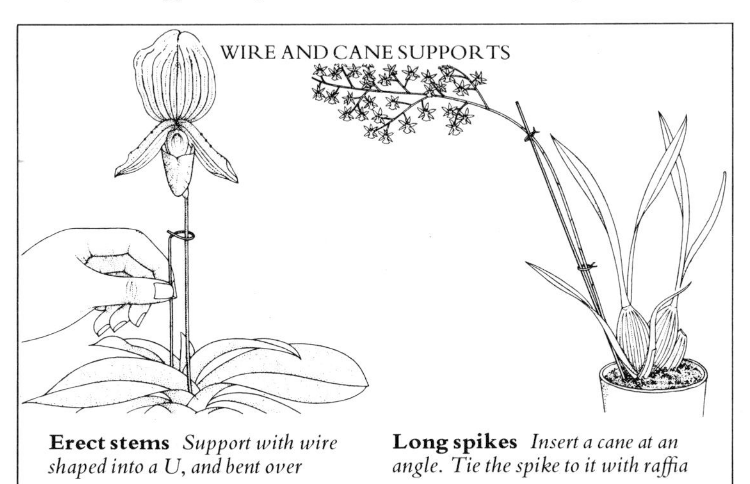

Erect stems *Support with wire shaped into a U, and bent over*

Long spikes *Insert a cane at an angle. Tie the spike to it with raffia*

What can go wrong with orchids

This chart describes the most common problems that you are likely to encounter when growing orchids.

It is not, however, an exhaustive list, and if your plants show symptoms that are not mentioned here, you will find further information in the full-colour identification chart of pests and diseases starting on page 377.

Turn to page 398 for lists of trade names for the chemicals.

A MALATHION BATH

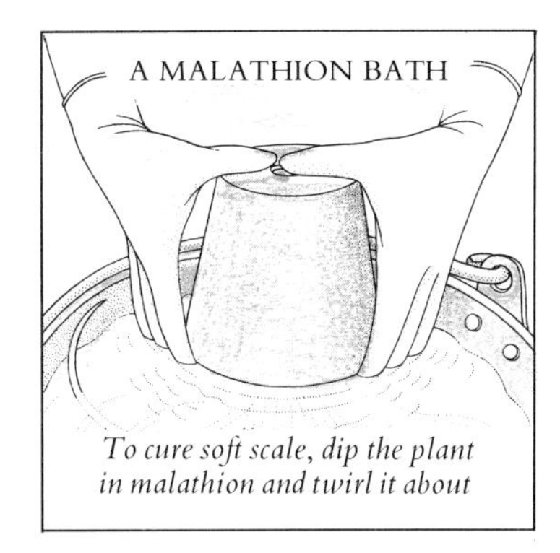

To cure soft scale, dip the plant in malathion and twirl it about

Symptoms	Cause	Cure
Small, brown, flattened ovoid scales on leaves and pseudobulbs (severe attacks weaken the plant)	Soft scale – an infestation by scale insects	Dip entire plant in malathion solution
Whitish, cottonwool-like tufts on leaves and pseudobulbs (severe attacks yellow leaves and weaken the plant)	Mealy bug	Remove with a soft brush wetted with methylated spirit, or spray with malathion
Yellowish or brownish mottling on leaves, later causing premature yellowing and death	Red spider mite or thrips	Spray with malathion
Flowers deformed and leaves with semi-transparent patches	Virus disease	No cure. Burn the plants
Brown speckling on petals and young leaves	Excessively high humidity	Give more ventilation on warm days and reduce damping down
Leaves or bulbs begin to rot	Damping-off disease	Spray with carbendazim
Small or poor yellowish leaves and pseudobulbs, with few or no flowers	Starvation, or compost too wet	Repot in new compost, dividing if necessary. Water carefully
Leaves suffused yellow or yellowish-brown, sometimes with brown dying patches	Scorch due to lack of shading and proper ventilation during hot spells	Make sure the greenhouse roof is shaded in late spring and summer and pay close attention to ventilation
Young leaves or flower buds eaten off	Slugs and sometimes snails	Sprinkle slug pellets around plants while young growths are forming
Flower buds fail to develop properly, usually withering or falling early	Too cold, or too hot and dry	Make sure that the right cultural regime is being carried out. A minimum/maximum thermometer will keep a check on rising and falling temperatures

Shortening vandas and other single-stem plants

Some orchids, such as vandas, grow vertically on a single stem. They will eventually become too tall and floppy for the greenhouse, and will need to be cut in half.

These orchids have aerial roots growing out of the stem. Every year the roots develop laterals, which begin as green points. When the laterals start to grow in the spring, the plant can be cut and repotted.

Fill a 5–6 in. pot with crocks or gravel to one-third its depth. Add a 1 in. layer of orchid compost and a sprinkling of slow-release general fertiliser, such as Vitex or Magamp.

With secateurs, sever the stem beneath a group of aerial roots.

Remove any dead leaf bases from the severed section.

Twirl this section into the pot so that the roots coil around the inside.

Fill the pot with compost.

If you have used osmunda compost, surface it with a mixture of equal parts of sphagnum moss and osmunda (or asplenium) fibre. Pack the mixture tightly into the compost in vertical wedges, using a dibber.

The base of the original stem will later produce lateral shoots. These can be severed and potted separately when roots have formed.

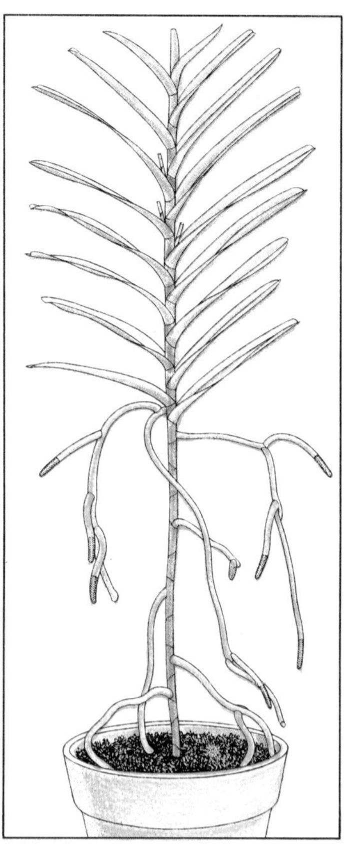

1 *Vanda stems eventually become too tall and must be shortened by half*

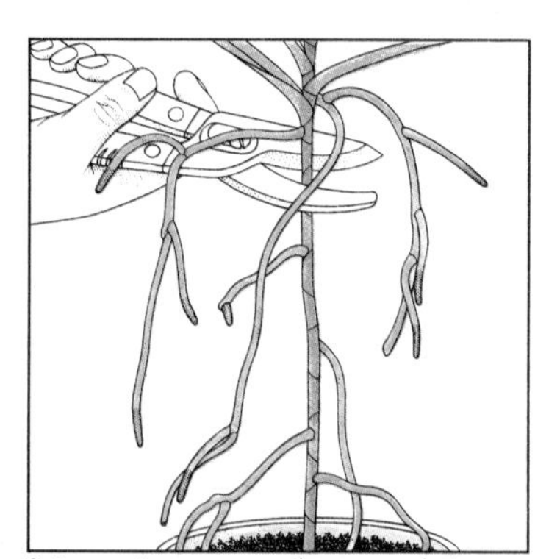

2 *In spring, sever the stem below a group of sprouting aerial roots*

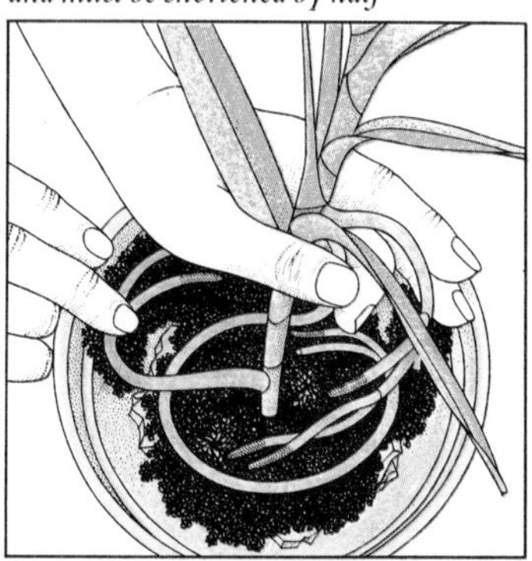

3 *Twirl the top part of the stem into a 5–6 in. pot and fill with orchid compost*

Special containers for orchids

Orchids can be grown in ordinary plant pots, but the pots must have a good layer of crocks at the bottom to allow for rapid drainage.

Special orchid pots or pans are perforated and need no drainage material.

Wooden baskets are more suitable for pendulous plants. When planted, they are hung up in the greenhouse, allowing the plants to droop down.

Alternatively, pendulous orchids can be grown on sections of tree-fern stems, or on thick pieces of rough bark. The orchid roots are wrapped in compost, and pinned to the support with galvanised wire staples or plastic-covered garden wire. The plant is then hung up in the greenhouse so that it can follow its natural drooping habit.

Upright orchids can be grown in perforated clay pots. Orchids with trailing flowers grow best in hanging wooden baskets or on sections of tree-fern stem

A choice of composts for growing orchids

The best compost for orchids is made partly from the root fibres of osmunda ferns, and can be bought from specialist nurseries.

A cheaper alternative is fir bark, which comes in various sizes, according to the size of the plants which have to be potted.

If you want the best-quality compost in large quantities, it is cheaper to make it yourself than to buy it ready-made. The ingredients can be bought from specialist nurseries.

The compost consists of equal parts of osmunda fibre, sphagnum moss and $\frac{1}{8}$ in. plastic nodules.

Chop the osmunda fibre into $1\frac{1}{2}$ in. chunks. Sheep shears, obtainable from a garden centre, are a useful tool for this job.

Sieve the fibre to get rid of dust.

Clean the sphagnum moss by removing any stalks, leaves or grass, and chop it into 1 in. lengths.

Mix the fibre, the moss and the plastic nodules together in equal quantities.

Orchids will grow in this compost for four or five years.

How to grow new orchids

Bringing old bulbs back to life again

The most common method of propagating orchids is from back-bulbs. These are old pseudobulbs that have lost their leaves. They are found behind the new leafy bulbs.

The best time to remove them is in the autumn, at the end of the resting period, or when an overlarge plant is being divided and repotted in the summer.

Remove the plant from its pot or basket, and cut off the largest back-bulbs with their roots.

Ensure that there are at least four bulbs – either old or new – left on the original plant.

Place a layer of crocks or gravel in the bottom of a 3 in. pot and half fill with moist orchid compost (see previous page).

Cushion the base of the back-bulb in some compost, and put it on the compost in the pot. Fill in around it with more compost.

Insert a label with the name of the plant.

Stand the pot in a propagator containing moist sand or peat, and preferably with bottom heat of 16–18°C (61–64°F).

Put the propagator in a shaded part of the greenhouse, with maximum heat.

When shoots begin growing from the base of the bulb, remove it from the propagator and stand it on the greenhouse staging – still in its pot. The new shoots may take as little as a month or longer than a year to appear. Sometimes no growth occurs at all and the back-bulb just yellows and withers away.

Successful new plants will need to be moved into the next larger size of pot within a year of sprouting.

A large cymbidium back-bulb, 3–4 in. high, will flower in three or four years.

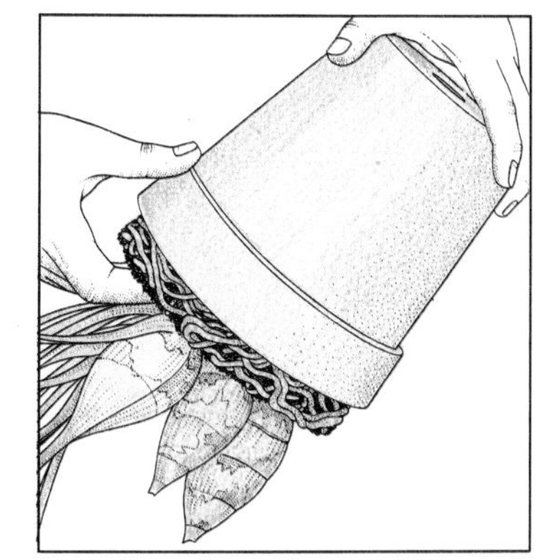

1 *In autumn, or when a plant needs repotting, take it from the container*

2 *Cut off the largest back-bulbs with roots, leaving four bulbs on the plant*

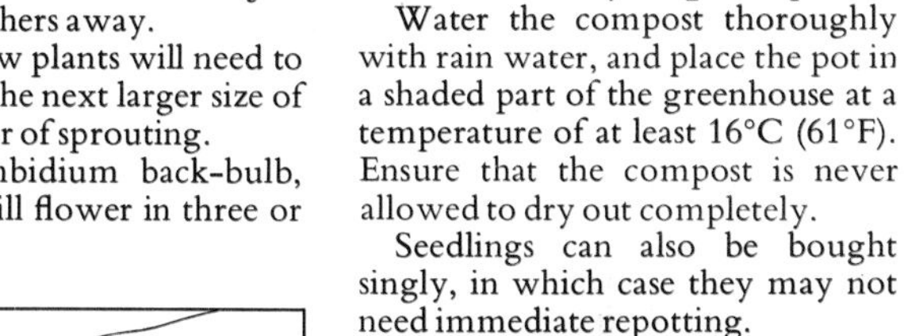

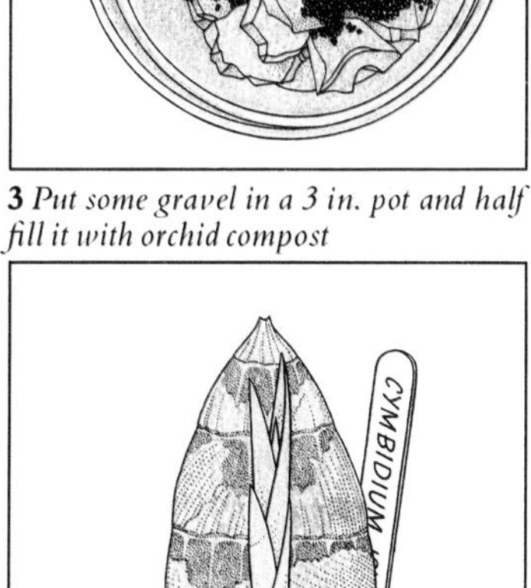

3 *Put some gravel in a 3 in. pot and half fill it with orchid compost*

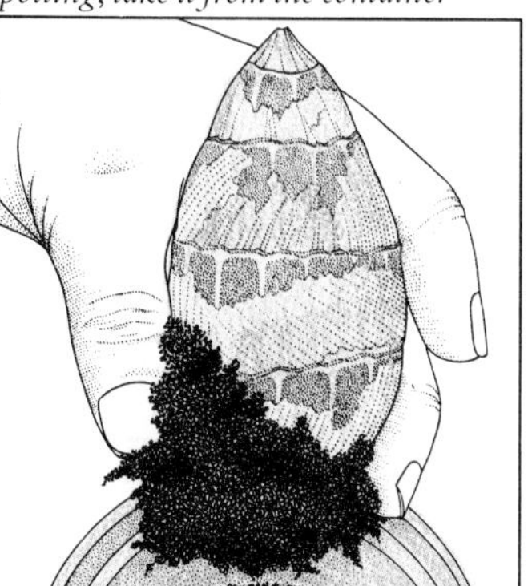

4 *Cushion the base of the back-bulb in compost and plant in the pot*

5 *Stand the pot on moist sand inside a propagator, preferably heated*

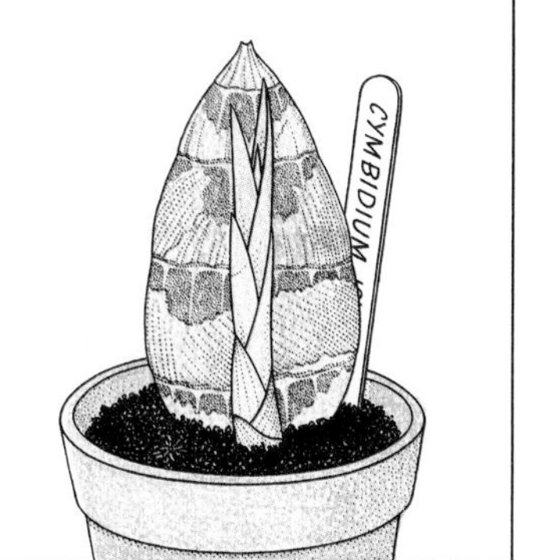

6 *When shoots grow, remove from propagator. Pot on within a year*

Buying 'community pots' of seedlings

A cheap way of obtaining orchids is to buy community pots of seedlings from a specialist nursery. However, you will have to wait two or three years before they flower.

When the seedlings arrive, pot them individually in 1½–2 in. pots.

Water the compost thoroughly with rain water, and place the pot in a shaded part of the greenhouse at a temperature of at least 16°C (61°F). Ensure that the compost is never allowed to dry out completely.

Seedlings can also be bought singly, in which case they may not need immediate repotting.

Six to eight months later, move the seedlings into 2½–3 in. pots.

Two to four months after that, check whether the roots have reached the outside of the compost ball. If they have, the plant needs repotting into a 4 in. pot.

This time, put a few grains of a slow-release general fertiliser, such as Vitex or Magamp, on the compost around the rim of the pot.

Water the plant and put it in a shady part of the greenhouse at a temperature which is not allowed to fall lower than 10°C (50°F).

Keep the compost moist, but never waterlogged.

Eighteen months later, pot the plant on into a 6 in. pot.

The plant is then at flowering age.

STARTING SEEDLINGS

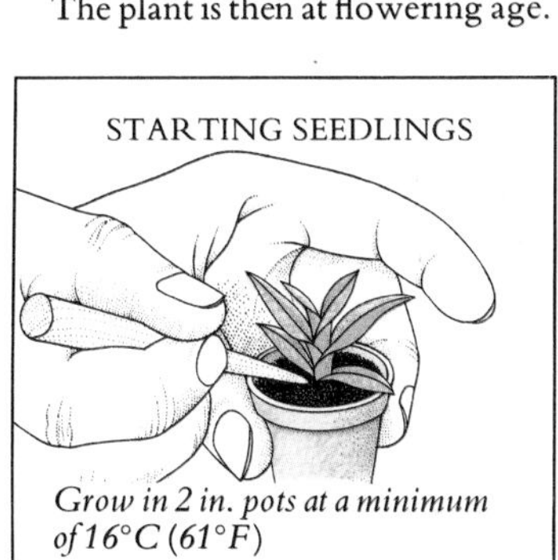

Grow in 2 in. pots at a minimum of 16°C (61°F)

Perennials

Many of our best-loved flowers are hardy herbaceous perennials which spring up afresh year after year. They make outstanding features in borders or tubs

Whether a garden is a cramped back yard, a typical rectangular plot, or generous tract around a country house, there are hardy perennials to provide all the flowers, foliage and character it needs.

The terms 'hardy perennial' and 'herbaceous plant' are both shortened forms of hardy herbaceous perennial, meaning a plant that comes up year after year, and dies down to dormant roots in winter, when the lifeless stems can be removed. Lupins, delphiniums, phloxes and oriental poppies are popular examples. Others, such as flag irises, garden pinks and kniphofias (red-hot pokers), are termed and treated as herbaceous plants by gardeners, even though their leaves remain green and alive all the year.

Some perennials, such as hollyhocks, centranthus, delphiniums and linums, have short lives of only four or five summers – something overlooked by gardeners who never think of plants growing old. Others, such as michaelmas daisies, coreopsis and anthemis, bloom with much greater freedom if dug up and divided every two years. A few, such as paeonies, thalictrums and Christmas roses (*Helleborus niger*) may outlast the lifetime of a man.

Hardy perennials were introduced into formal British garden design in the late 19th century, using wide beds – the herbaceous border. They were usually backed by tall, clipped yew hedges, with the tallest plants ranged along the back of the bed and the shortest at the front.

To be really effective, a herbaceous border needs to be at least 10 ft wide and 30 ft long, so it was never seriously adopted in suburban gar-

The emergence of the herbaceous border during the 1870's has been attributed to William Robinson, influential editor of The Garden. *Until that time there had been little scope for hardy perennials which, with their infinite variety, did not fit into the formal style of decorative gardening*

dens. A strictly herbaceous border also has the drawback that it presents almost bare soil between October and April, when plants die down.

However, in recent years, hardy perennials have become popular with small-garden owners.

One reason is the development of the mixed border in which other types of plants – annuals, roses, biennials, bulbs and shrubs – are mixed in to give a greater continuity of display and winter interest.

Secondly, island beds have become popular in gardens where long borders do not fit conveniently into a design. These are ideal for the majority of short and medium-growing herbaceous plants. The tallest plants should fill the centre, with shorter ones towards the edges. Informal shapes, such as dumb-bells or kidneys, look more effective than circles or ovals. Stars or diamonds should be avoided, as their angles are awkward to plant.

A natural development of island beds are mini-borders. These are simply smaller versions filled with short, compact-growing perennials.

A third modern use of herbaceous plants is as ground-cover, in which vigorous, spreading and fairly short kinds are planted close together to form a dense, continuous mass hiding any bare ground. Ground-cover is very useful for covering banks or, if the plants are shade-lovers, for carpeting ground beneath shrubs, perhaps inter-planted with naturalised bulbs. Theoretically, ground-cover plants smother weeds, but in the initial stages they need careful weeding and always need some hand-weeding afterwards, as no hoe can be used between them. For a list of ground-cover plants, see page 246.

A pleasing variation of ground-cover is a chess-board area of paving with some squares filled with soil and holding plants chosen both for foliage and for flowers, such as bergenias and paeonies.

Herbaceous perennials can be planted informally in a great variety of different places. Around the edges of garden pools or streams they mingle with aquatic plants. On the edges of woodland and in open glades they can be planted in drifts. Beside steps and over the edges of paths, wispy or spreading plants such as *Gypsophila paniculata* 'Rosy Veil' or laced pinks can spill out. Large upright, vigorous, or high-growing perennials may even be set formally in groups in grass, keeping the different kinds separate from one another and choosing them so that their foliage contrasts with the mown turf. The clumps need to be bold and the soil around them requires forking over until the plants are established.

Even on balconies of town flats carefully selected herbaceous plants can be grown in tubs.

In recent times plants with good foliage have become much appreciated for their textural qualities and long-season effects, notable among them being anaphalis, artemisias, *Brunnera macrophylla* 'Variegata', eryngiums, hostas, variegated irises, pulmonarias and sedums. Silver, gold and purple-leaved varieties are particularly sought after, not only by gardeners but by flower arrangers who make considerable use of hardy perennials. Seed heads of *Papaver orientale*, flowers of achilleas, anaphalis, eryngiums, echinops, gypsophilas, limoniums and physalis can be dried for indoor decoration.

An attractive border depends much upon how the plants are arranged. Later-flowering or foliage plants should conceal gaps left by earlier flowers; colours should blend and everything should be in scale. Colour scheming might be based on the rainbow, beginning at one end with violet merging into blue, and graduating through green to yellow, then orange, and finishing with red. Some plants lend a light wispy appearance – for instance, astilbes, gypsophilas, heucheras, limoniums and linarias. Others, such as bergenias, rheums, ligularias and rodgersias, create heavy blends of foliage.

The perennials opposite form part of a traditional herbaceous border: small plants in front, then medium sized, and tall ones at the back

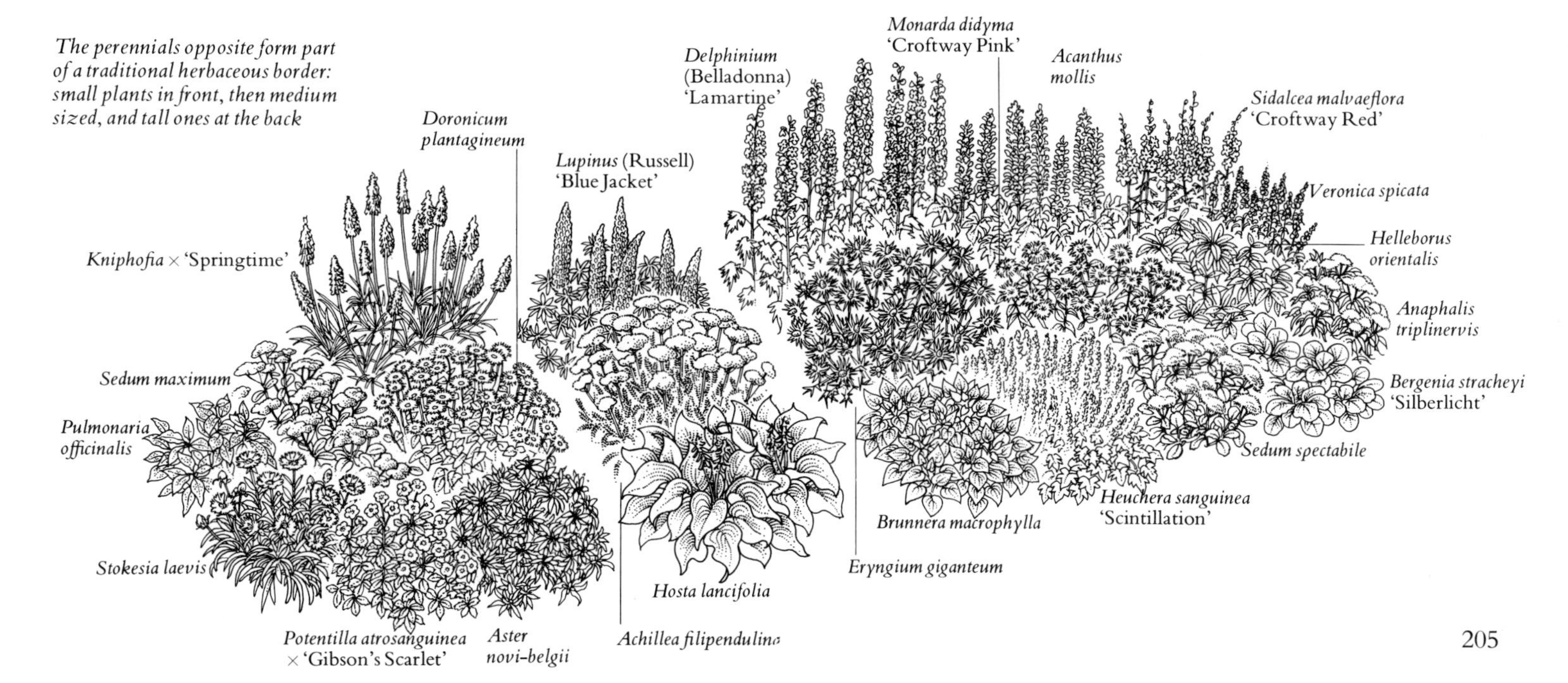

Giving herbaceous perennials a good start

Preparing the herbaceous border for planting

The best time for planting perennials is early autumn – late September to late October – when the soil is still warm. Alternatively, plant perennials in spring. The soil is then drier, and the plants will often need to be watered in.

Several weeks before planting, make a plan for the bed; order the plants you need, for delivery by late September or October.

Double dig the bed (p. 405) in September to give the soil time to settle, adding in a bucketful of peat or garden compost to the square yard. Just before planting, break up any large clumps of soil and tread the surface of the bed. Finally sprinkle on two handfuls of general fertiliser, such as Growmore, to each square yard and rake it in.

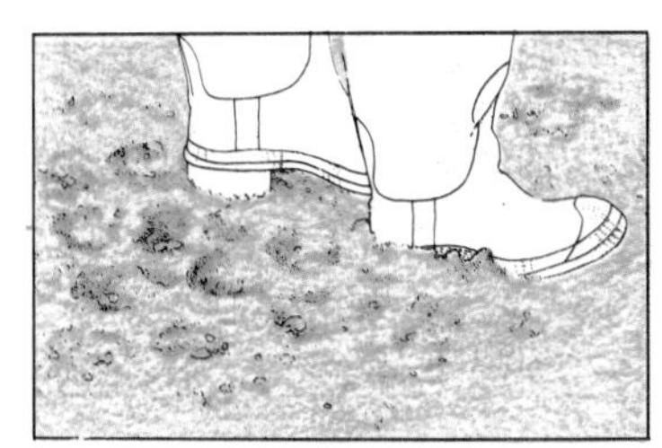

1 *Firm the soil by treading it, putting the weight on your heels*

2 *Rake a general-purpose fertiliser into the top few inches of soil*

Planting out herbaceous perennials

Container-grown perennials can be planted at any time of the year, except when the ground is frozen. They are best planted in dull weather and must be kept thoroughly watered in summer until they are established.

Dormant plants may arrive from the nursery before it is convenient to plant them out. If they have to be kept for several days, remove them from their wrappings, and water the roots or pack damp peat round them. Leave them in a shaded place, out of drying winds.

Following the planting plan, draw guide-lines on the bed with the corner of a hoe. If the bed is large, the guide-lines are easier to follow if they are marked out with sand. They will remain, even if rain should postpone planting.

Working from the centre of the bed outwards, lay out the plants in one section at a time. Space them evenly, allowing room for the eventual spread of the foliage.

For plants with a small root system, use a trowel to take out circular planting holes.

Set each plant upright in the centre of the hole, ensuring that the hole is deep and wide enough to accommodate the spread-out roots. Firm in the plant with your fingers and the back of the trowel, levelling the planting hole $\frac{1}{2}$–1 in. below the surface of the bed so that it will collect water.

Use a spade to dig holes for plants with large root systems. After filling in the holes with soil, firm with your feet.

Plant prostrate perennials, such as artemisia and omphalodes, which are intended for spreading ground-cover, in groups of three or four plants. Bunch the roots and stems together to form one plant and insert them as a clump.

After the bed has been planted, prick the soil with a fork, using only the tips of the prongs.

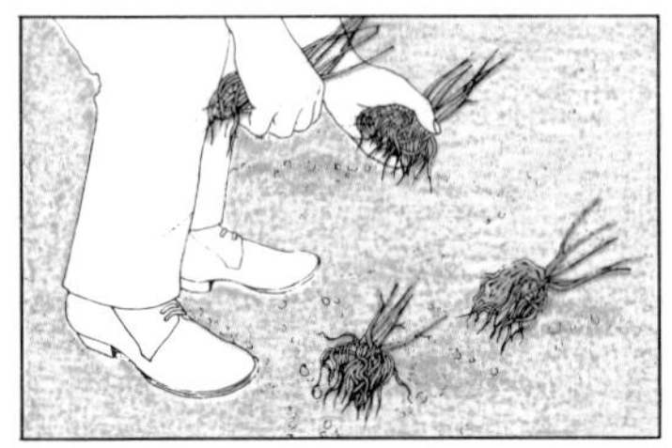

1 *Space the plants out evenly within a marked-off section of the bed*

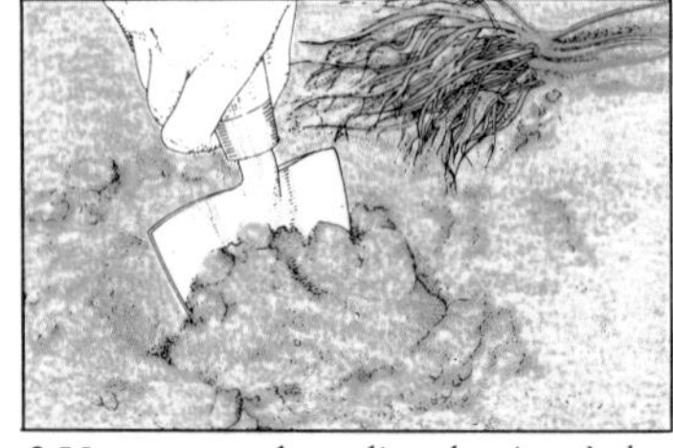

2 *Use a trowel to dig planting holes, deep and wide enough for the roots*

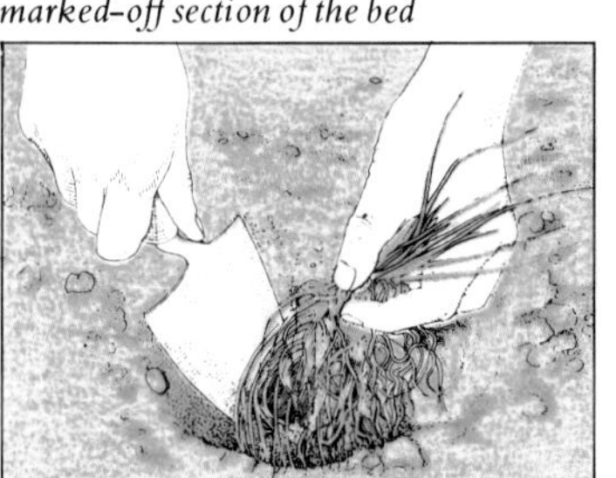

3 *Set the plant in the centre of the hole, spread out the roots, and return the soil*

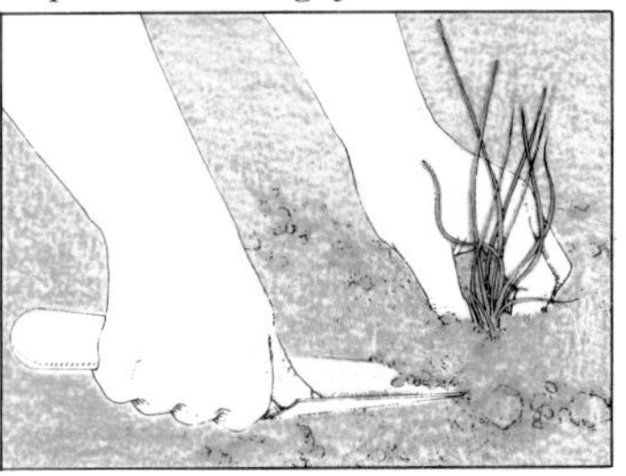

4 *Firm in the plant with the back of the trowel and with the fingers*

PLANTING BIG ROOTS

Large-rooted plants *Use a spade to dig out a deep hole, wide enough to accommodate the roots. Set the root ball in the centre and fill the hole with soil. Firm in with the heels*

SPACING PROSTRATES

Small ground-cover plants *Prostrate perennials usually arrive from the nursery in compact bunches. Separate them into groups of three or four and insert as a single plant*

Jobs to be done as spring arrives

Keeping the ground clear of weeds

Begin weeding as soon as growth starts, and keep weeds down by regular hoeing or by spraying the soil with propachlor (Ramrod) to kill germinating weed seeds. Keep a bucket at hand, and drop weeds in it as you remove them. Burn any persistent weeds that are hard to control; the others can be put on to the compost heap.

In small beds, weeding can be done by hand, but for normal garden work a Dutch hoe, a short-handled onion hoe and a border fork are all useful tools.

Use an onion hoe where plants are growing close together, as in seed beds and rock gardens. Cut off the weeds with a chopping motion, drawing the hoe towards you and being careful not to chop off the tops of any of the young ornamental plants.

For general surface hoeing, and between rows of plants, use the Dutch hoe. Avoid unnecessary stooping by choosing a hoe about the same height as yourself. Draw the hoe, with a skimming motion, backwards and forwards through the soil to cut off the weeds and also to remove the roots.

Where persistent, deep-rooted weeds are growing around the base of a plant, loosen them with a border fork and remove them by hand. It may be necessary to dig up the plant and split it apart to get at weeds, such as couch and ground elder, that have become entangled among its roots. Replant the divisions of the plant after the weeds have been completely removed.

REMOVING SURFACE AND DEEP-ROOTED WEEDS

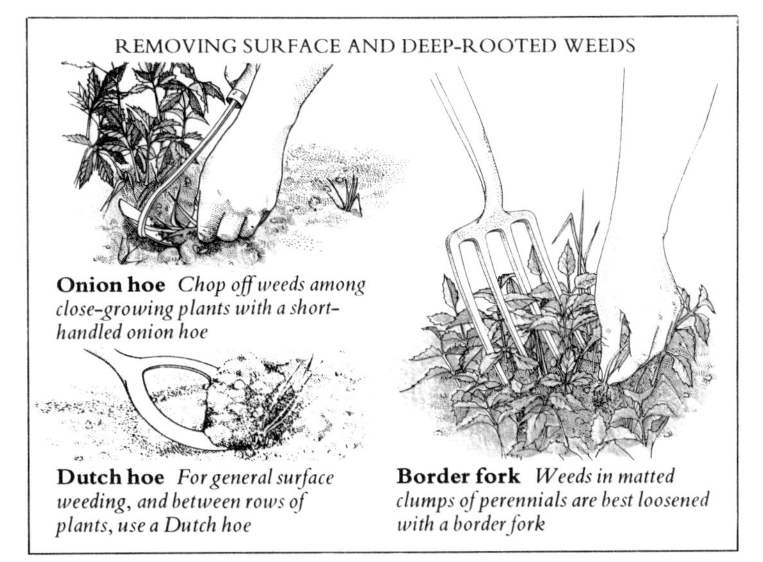

Onion hoe *Chop off weeds among close-growing plants with a short-handled onion hoe*

Dutch hoe *For general surface weeding, and between rows of plants, use a Dutch hoe*

Border fork *Weeds in matted clumps of perennials are best loosened with a border fork*

Loosening the soil in established beds

At the start of the growing season, and again in late autumn, the soil in established beds should be loosened. This is particularly important on heavy soil or on one compacted after prolonged rain. Loosening allows air and moisture to penetrate to the roots of plants, and at the same time exposes weeds.

A fork can be used, but a long-handled, tined cultivator is ideal.

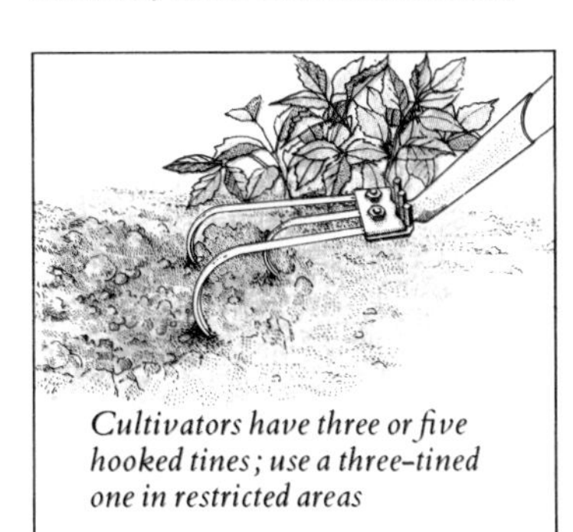

Cultivators have three or five hooked tines; use a three-tined one in restricted areas

Supplying plant food and constant moisture

Mulching is the application of a layer of organic material over the soil. A mulch conserves moisture in the soil by reducing evaporation; it supplies plants with nutrients as it decomposes, and it helps to suppress weed seedlings.

For herbaceous borders, rotted garden compost, leaf-mould, peat or farmyard manure are the most suitable materials.

Apply the mulch in late spring after the ground has been weeded, but before growth is well advanced.

In dry weather, give the soil a good soaking before mulching.

Spread a layer of the mulching material, 2–3 in. deep, over and around the roots of the plants, levelling it with the back of a rake. Ideally, the whole surface of the bed should be mulched, but if this is not possible it is better to mulch the area around the plants thickly than to spread the layer of mulch to a shallower depth over the whole bed.

The health of plants can be maintained or improved, and growth encouraged, by the application of a balanced fertiliser.

Organic fertilisers are particularly suited to perennials, as the nutrients are released slowly. In early spring, before mulching, apply a mixture of equal quantities of hoof and horn and sterilised bonemeal at 4 oz. per square yard. Alternatively, use a general fertiliser such as Growmore at 2–3 oz. per square yard.

From May to July, the plants are better fed with a quick-acting liquid foliar spray used every three or four weeks.

Watering should not be necessary if the bed has been mulched, except during prolonged spells of dry weather. If watering is needed, use a sprinkler system which gives a steady and even spray of water. Water during late afternoon or early evening to lessen evaporation by the sun. Heavy soils, which compact under strong rain, should have the surface soil loosened before being watered.

MULCHING

Use a garden fork to lift the mulching material. Spread it evenly, 2–3 in. deep, over the entire root area of the plants. Rotted garden compost, leaf-mould, peat or farmyard manure are suitable mulches. Level it off with the back of a rake

How to support top-heavy perennials

Perennials that have a naturally floppy habit, or become top-heavy when in flower, need some support. This can be in the form of bamboo canes, galvanised wire mesh or pea sticks. Put the supports in position in April before the growth has become too advanced.

Both single plants and clumps can be supported by pea sticks, but tall-growing plants are best staked with canes or wire mesh.

The supports should be tall enough to reach just below the flower spikes, and you must therefore know in advance the eventual height of a plant.

Plants supported by pea sticks and wire mesh need no tying in, but tall stems should be tied to their cane supports with strong raffia or garden twine, or with one of the proprietary ties that are available

These are usually of metal, covered with green plastic, and clip on to the stake and stem.

Wire-mesh supports for tall-growing plants

Exceptionally tall-growing plants (5–6 ft), such as filipendulas, some heliopsis, polygonums and rudbeckias and the very tall delphiniums, can be supported with wire-mesh cylinders. Once the mesh is in position, no tying in is necessary. Use 8 in. square galvanised mesh (this is also available in green) to make a cylinder that is wide enough to just enclose the whole group of plants.

Insert three tall bamboo canes upright in the ground inside the cylinder. Tie each cane to the wire mesh, just above ground level, halfway up, and again at the top of the cylinder.

For even taller plants, it may be necessary to fit a second cylinder on top of the first. Overlap the two cylinders by one mesh square and tie them together with twine.

1 *Push canes into the soil inside the mesh, and tie in with tarred twine*

2 *For 6–8 ft plants, overlap the mesh cylinder with another one*

3 *As the plants grow, the stems are held securely within the framework*

Supports of bamboo canes and twine

Use bamboo canes to support single stems, or groups of plants with a height above 2 ft and up to 4–5 ft maximum, such as most delphiniums, malvas and thalictrums.

For a single-stemmed plant, insert one bamboo cane firmly in the ground close to the plant and tie the stem to it with raffia, twine or wire rings. As the stem grows, add further ties at 6–9 in. intervals.

For a group of plants, insert three bamboo canes firmly in the ground at equidistant intervals around and close to the plants; tilt the canes slightly outwards.

Knot twine to one cane, 6–9 in. above ground, then loop the twine round the other two canes. Pull the twine taut and tie it in place.

As growth advances, tie one or more lengths of twine to the canes, 9 in. above the first.

1 *Support a clump of delphiniums with bamboo canes and twine*

2 *As the plants grow, add another piece of twine, 9 in. above the first*

3 *At the ultimate height, several circles of twine will enclose the plants*

RING SUPPORT

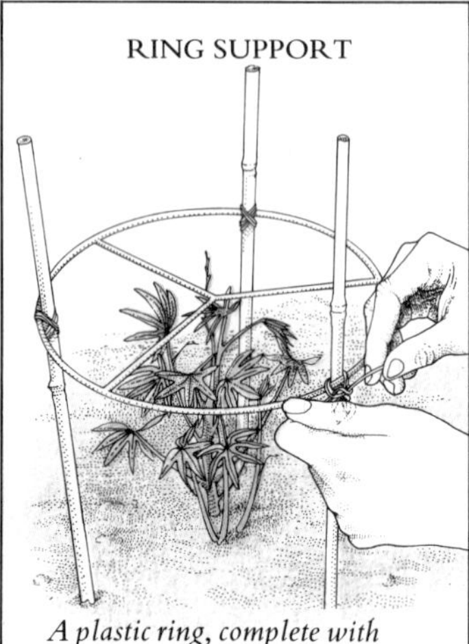

A plastic ring, complete with spokes, can be raised as the plant increases in height. Insert three bamboo canes round the plant and place the ring over them, tying it to the canes

Late-season care of perennials

Keeping floppy plants up with pea sticks

Use pea sticks to support plants up to 2 ft which tend to be floppy, or which may be exposed to wind damage.

Pea sticks are sold by many garden centres, and are usually the trimmings from small trees or hedges that have been cut back. Almost any tree or shrub provides good pea sticks, particularly hazel, elm, chestnut and oak.

Before inserting the pea sticks, make sure that the soil is soft and permeable. The sticks cannot be hammered into the ground, and too much pressure will break them.

Insert two or three pea sticks as near to the centre of the plants as possible. Push them in deep enough to remain firm. Two or three sticks in one group of plants are usually sufficient, but if the plants are known to sprawl badly after heavy rain or storms, insert pea sticks around the outside of the groups as well to give extra support.

At the height of the eventual base of the flower spikes, break the tops of the sticks and bend them inwards. Intermesh them to form a firm top to the frame.

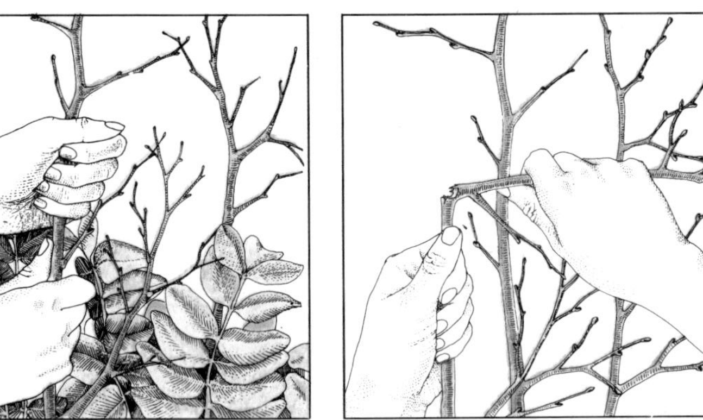

1 *Push two or three pea sticks into the centre of a clump of plants*

2 *Break the tops of the sticks, turning them to the centre of the plants*

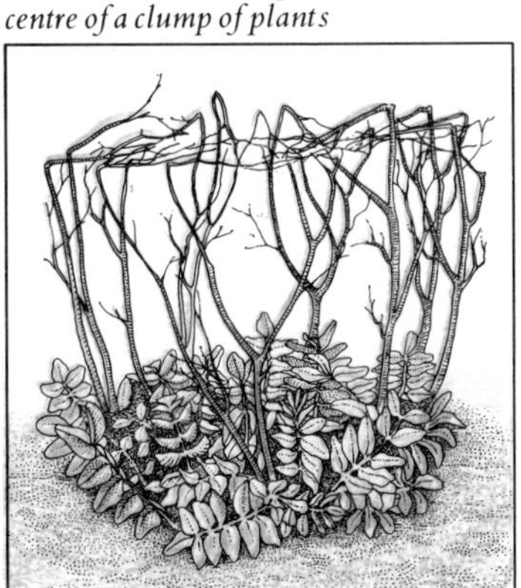

3 *Interlace the tops so that they form a close framework over the plants*

4 *As the plants grow, stems and leaves will hide the supports*

Removing faded flowers and stems

When flowers have faded, remove the dead heads and their stems. Dead-heading prevents the plants from setting seeds and thus diverting their energy away from producing new flowers.

Dead-heading of early-flowering perennials, such as delphiniums, lupins and violas, will often encourage a second show of flowers.

Cut back plants with single, bare flower stems, such as red-hot pokers, as close as possible to the base.

On plants where the lower parts of flower stems have leaves growing on them, cut off the stems just below the top leaves.

From mid-summer onwards, dead-head only plants whose faded flowers are unsightly. The heads of some plants, such as achilleas and sedums, are attractive well into autumn and winter.

Plants with bare flower stems should be cut to ground level (left). Trim flower stems with foliage on them (right) to just below the top leaves

Using chemical weedkillers in a perennial border

Deep-rooted perennial weeds can be treated with a chemical weedkiller, for example aminotriazole or dalapon, before a bed is planted.

In established beds it is difficult to spray on chemicals without harming decorative plants. In these cases, paint the weeds with a selective weedkiller recommended for broad-leaved lawn weeds, for example mecoprop, 2,4-D or dichlorprop.

Alternatively, dip the growing tips of the weeds into a container of the weedkiller. The chemical will be absorbed into the plant sap.

To avoid a lot of weedkiller being left over, treat border weeds at the same time as the lawn.

KILLING BINDWEED

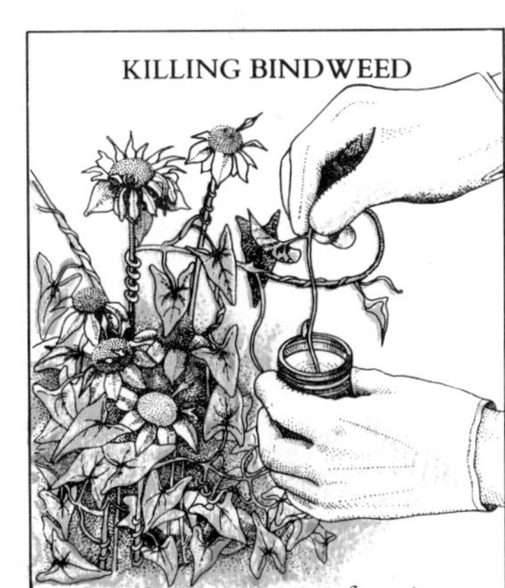

Dip the growing tips of persistent weeds into a selective lawn weedkiller

Cutting plants back after flowering

Little pruning, apart from dead-heading, is needed.

Cut or pull off dead or shrivelled leaves, as they may harbour diseases.

Some plants, such as anthemises and gaillardias, which have one flower display of great profusion, make little or no new growth.

To make them look tidy, they can be cut hard back to near ground level as soon as flowering is over.

Mat-forming plants, such as aubrietas and artemisias, which are used as edging plants, grow straggly after flowering in early summer. They need hard pruning with scissors or hedging shears. Cut them back to just above ground level. This hard pruning promotes healthy new growth and often a second show of flowers.

MAT-FORMING PLANTS

Aubrietas and artemisias can be kept tidy and induced to flower again by hard pruning after the first show of flowers

Cutting plants back before winter

Herbaceous borders should be tidied when autumn frosts stop growth.

Continue dead-heading where necessary and cut down unsightly dead stems with secateurs.

Divide and replant any overgrown clumps of perennials (p. 211) and fork over the soil.

Apply bonemeal, at two handfuls to the square yard, and rake it in.

To protect the crowns of half-hardy plants during winter, lay the severed top growth over the plants and cover with a 2–3 in. layer of leaf-mould. By March, when new growth will be starting, the protective covering should have rotted. For plants needing protection, see the tables beginning on page 329.

1 *Cut down dead stems of half-hardy plants to just above ground*

2 *Cover the crown with the severed stems and a layer of leaf-mould*

What can go wrong with perennials

If your plants show symptoms that are not described here, turn to the full-colour identification chart of pests and diseases on page 377.

For a comprehensive selection of the trade names of recommended chemicals, turn to page 398.

Symptoms	Cause	Cure
Flower buds fail to develop properly, withering or dropping before opening	Drought	Soak thoroughly at the rate of 2 gallons to the square yard, and repeat at least once a week during dry spells. Mulch with peat, garden compost or decayed manure
Stem tips and flower spikes covered with small greenish sticky insects. In severe cases, growth of the plant may be distorted and the flowers fail to open	Aphids	Spray with derris or malathion
Young leaves, flower buds or stem tips distorted, the leaves sometimes with small irregular holes	Capsid bugs	Spray with HCH or fenitrothion
Leaves eaten	Caterpillars	Spray with derris or dimethoate
Young shoots eaten, and slime trails present	Slugs or snails	Put down pellets of metaldehyde or methiocarb
Young stems wilting and falling over after having been eaten through below ground level	Cutworms	Soak the crowns of affected plants with malathion or rake in HCH dust
Leaves and young shoots, and sometimes flowers, covered with waxy white powder and sometimes distorted or withering	Mildew	Spray with dinocap, benomyl or sulphur
Leaves and soft tips of stems wither, yellow and hang down; sometimes whole plant infected (particularly michaelmas daisies)	Verticillium wilt	Remove infected shoots and spray with thiram
Leaves, and sometimes young stems, show brownish or reddish pustules, which later erupt to show the powdery spores. Infected leaves often yellow and die	Rust	Not always easy to cure, but spraying with zineb or copper will reduce the infection
Leaves wilting, especially on hot days, the lower ones yellowing and dying prematurely; stems thin and often crowded, flowers small	Starvation and drought	Soak thoroughly with water, spray on a foliar feed and mulch with decayed manure or garden compost. Divide the following autumn
Plant not growing well and leaves brown, a month or so after planting	Faulty planting	Lift the plant and see if the roots are in a tight, dry ball. If so, loosen the soil around the roots, replant carefully and water

Increasing your stock by dividing perennials

Lifting overgrown plants from the soil

Division is the simplest form of propagation for most perennials. A clump of plants, complete with roots and growth buds, is lifted from the ground and pulled or cut into separate pieces, each of which will grow into a new plant identical to the parent.

Division should be carried out in the dormant period between October and March, except during frosty weather. Slow-growing perennials and those that flower early in the year are best divided in autumn.

The methods of division vary, according to the size and type of rootstock. After lifting, small clumps of young perennials can easily be pulled apart by hand. Older and overgrown plants, however, whose roots have formed an entangled mass, must be levered apart with two garden forks or severed with a sharp knife. Rhizomatous plants are divided by separating young root pieces from the main rhizome, and tuberous plants are split into single tubers, provided each has a strong growth bud on it.

Choose a day for lifting when the soil is neither frozen nor sticky. Push a garden fork into the ground alongside the clump of plants to be lifted. Lever the clump upwards and remove the fork, repeat this operation on the other three sides of the clump and then lift it carefully out of the ground.

Ease away as much soil from the roots as possible with your fingers, being careful not to damage any fleshy roots or tubers. It may be necessary to wash the clump in a bucket of water so that the growth buds become clearly visible.

Dividing rhizomatous-rooted plants

Plants which grow from rhizomes are easily lifted, as the rootstock, which is really a swollen underground stem, grows just below the surface of the soil. Bergenias, monardas, physalis and polygonatums are all rhizomatous, and each plant can be separated into several new ones. Ideally, this should be done in the early spring just as the new growth buds are beginning to emerge.

After lifting, prise away all the soil so that the old main rhizome can be seen, together with the younger underground stems coming from it. Select a number of these side growths, each showing two or three strong growth buds or vigorous young shoots, as well as having healthy roots.

Any 2–3 in. long side growth is suitable for replanting, and can be broken away from the main rhizome by hand. However, to avoid damaging the tissues it is advisable to cut off these side growths using a sharp knife.

Discard the old rhizome and trim the new growths back, cutting to just below a cluster of healthy fibrous roots.

Cut off any stumpy and rotten parts from the chosen pieces, and remove dead leaves and leaf stalks.

Plant the young rhizomes at once, vertically, with the root cluster downwards and fairly deep, so that the rhizomes are well anchored in the soil and are at about the same depth as was the original plant.

1 *Bergenias usually need dividing every three years, preferably just as they are starting into growth in spring. Choose healthy young rhizomes growing off the old one. Make sure that each rhizome contains at least two growth buds or young shoots, and that the thin fibrous roots are undamaged. Having selected the new growths, which should be 2–3 in. long, next remove them*

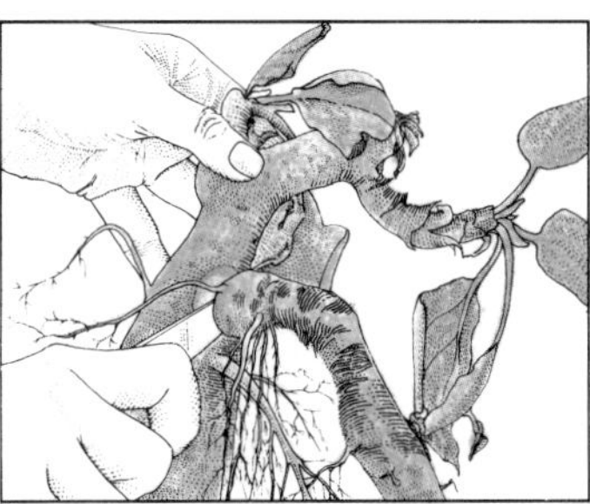

2 *Cut off the side growths flush with the old rhizome, which can be discarded*

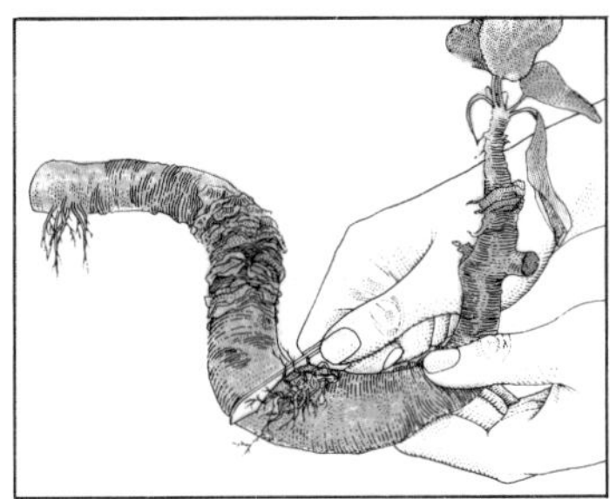

3 *Trim the cut pieces to just below a cluster of fine healthy roots*

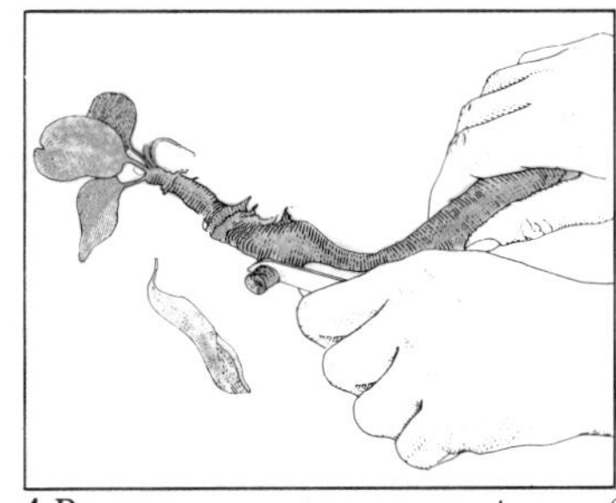

4 *Remove any stumps or pieces of rotten stem, and any dead leaves*

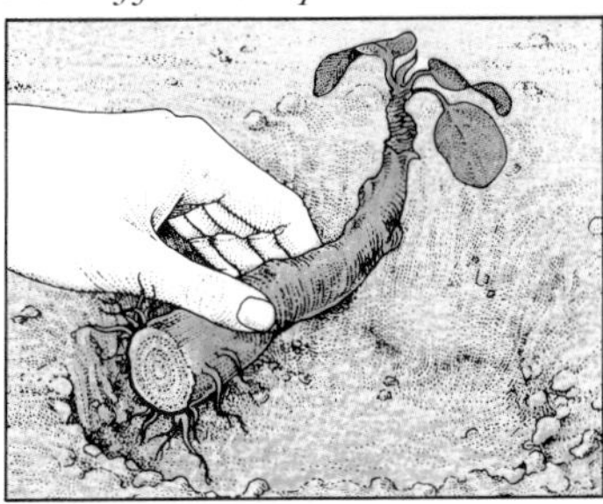

5 *The young trimmed rhizome is now ready for planting*

Division of young perennials

Young, tufted perennials that have fibrous roots, such as heleniums, rudbeckias and michaelmas daisies, are easily divided. After lifting, the plants can be pulled apart by hand or with a small fork so that each section contains healthy roots and strong growth buds. Cut off any dead roots and leaves. Replant the divisions at once in their permanent positions or, if they are very small, grow them on in a spare piece of ground until the following autumn, when they can be planted out in their permanent positions in the garden.

1 *Divide plants with small root systems by pulling them apart*

2 *Trim off with a knife any roots which are rotten, dead or damaged*

3 *Plant out pieces with six shoots in the border, smaller ones in spare ground*

Division of fibrous and fleshy-rooted perennials

Large, overgrown fibrous-rooted perennials, such as heleniums and phlox, are sometimes difficult to divide as both the crowns and shoots form a solid mass. Having lifted the clump, force the prongs of two strong garden forks, back to back, into the centre of the clump. Lever the clump apart first by forcing the handles of the forks together, and then pressing them away from each other. Repeat until the clump splits in half. Divide each half again.

With a sharp knife, cut away and discard the central woody part of each portion; separate the remainder into healthy pieces, each containing about six buds or shoots. Remove dead or rotten roots and growths before planting the divisions out. Water them if it is dry.

Plants with tough, woody crowns, such as baptisia and rheum, cannot be split with forks. Cut through the crowns with a sharp knife, so that each severed portion has both roots and growth buds. Replant the divisions at once.

Fleshy-rooted plants, such as agapanthus and hosta, are divided in the same way as young perennials.

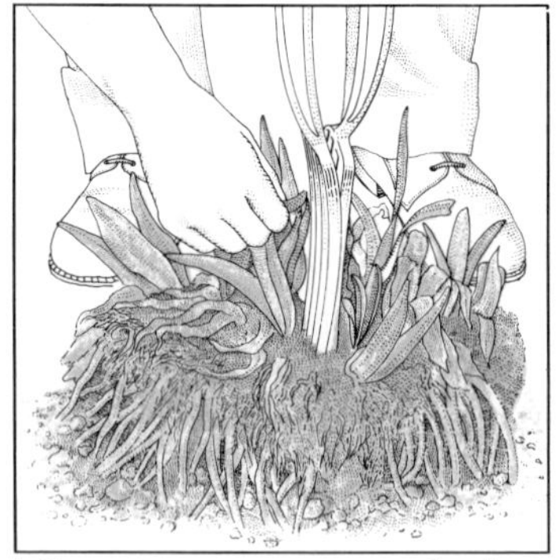

1 *Separate overgrown matted plants with two forks, back to back*

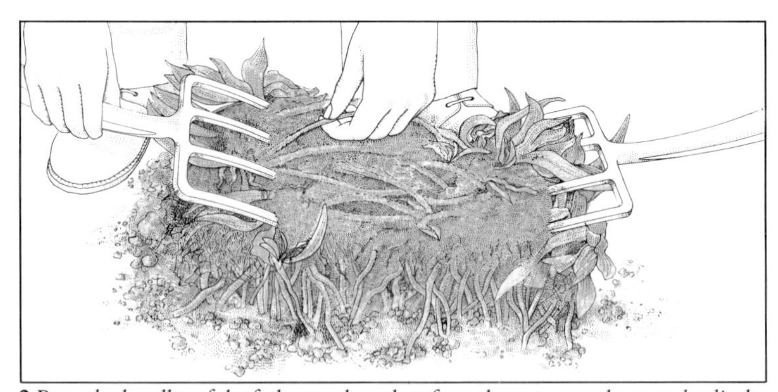

2 *Press the handles of the forks together, then force them apart to lever and split the clump into two. Split the two sections in half in the same way*

3 *Cut away any woody shoots and dead roots from the divisions*

4 *On fleshy-rooted plants, trim rotten or damaged roots back*

5 *Plant out the divisions at once in their permanent flowering positions*

How to grow new perennials from cuttings

Division of plants with tuberous roots

The method of dividing tuberous-rooted plants varies according to the type of tuber.

Dig up the clump of plants and carefully prise away the soil without breaking the tubers. If necessary, wash the plants in a bucket of water so that the growth buds then become clearly visible.

Root tubers, such as hemerocallis and paeonies, have growth buds in the crown, where the tubers join together. Slice through the clump, from the crown downwards, to divide the plant into several pieces, complete with tubers and growth buds. Plant the divisions at once. Pieces of a single tuber with only one bud generally take longer to become established than sections with three or four tubers and buds.

Paeonies often resent root disturbance and may take a season or more to recover. When division becomes necessary, due to overcrowding, it should be carried out in autumn.

The small claw-like tubers of anemones and liatris can be pulled apart by hand. Any large tubers can be cut into pieces with a knife, provided each piece has a strong growth bud.

DIVIDING A PAEONY

Cut the rootstock into pieces, each with several tubers and buds; trim off rotten stumps

Taking tip cuttings in summer and autumn

Some perennials, notably shrubby plants such as *Centaurea gymnocarpa*, penstemons, sedums, some of the saxifrages, as well as foliage perennials such as anthemis and rutas, are best increased from tip cuttings.

These should be taken from the ends of non-flowering lateral shoots during late summer and early autumn. The rooted cuttings generally need protection during winter in a cold frame.

Take the cuttings, 3–4 in. long, from the tips of healthy, leafy stems, ensuring that each cutting has at least three leaf joints.

Fill a pot to just below the rim with equal parts of peat and coarse sand, John Innes seed compost or a proprietary cuttings compost. A 4 in. pot will take about six cuttings.

Trim each cutting just below the lowest leaf node, using a sharp knife or a razor blade. Pull off or cut away the lowest pair of leaves.

Make shallow planting holes in the compost with a pencil. Insert the cuttings so that the base of each stem touches the bottom of the hole, without burying the leaves. Firm in with the fingers.

Water the pot thoroughly from overhead, and label the cuttings. Cover the pot with a plastic bag and secure with a rubber band. To prevent the plastic coming into contact with the cuttings, erect a framework of sticks or looped wires before putting the plastic in place. Set the pots of cuttings in a shaded cold frame to root.

Alternatively, insert the cuttings straight into a propagating case with a bottom heat of 16°C (61°F).

After four to six weeks (less in a propagating case), the cuttings should have rooted. Tug them gently. If they do not yield, they have rooted and can be removed from the plastic covering or propagator. Leave the pot of cuttings in the frame for four or five days, then remove by turning the pot upside-down and dislodging the compost, together with the rooted cuttings, in one piece.

Separate the rooted cuttings carefully, and pot them up singly in 3–3$\frac{1}{2}$ in. pots of John Innes No. 1 potting compost. Firm in each cutting and water thoroughly, then leave them to drain.

Place the pots in the shaded cold frame for about a week, then pinch out the growing tip of each cutting. This will encourage the plants to develop a strong root system instead of making top growth.

Overwinter the cuttings in a closed cold frame. Plant out in their growing positions in spring, when all danger of frost is over.

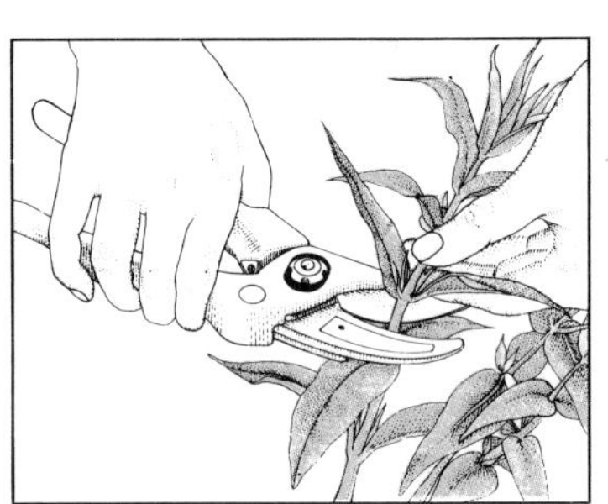

1 *Snip off non-flowering side-shoots, 3–4 in. long, in September*

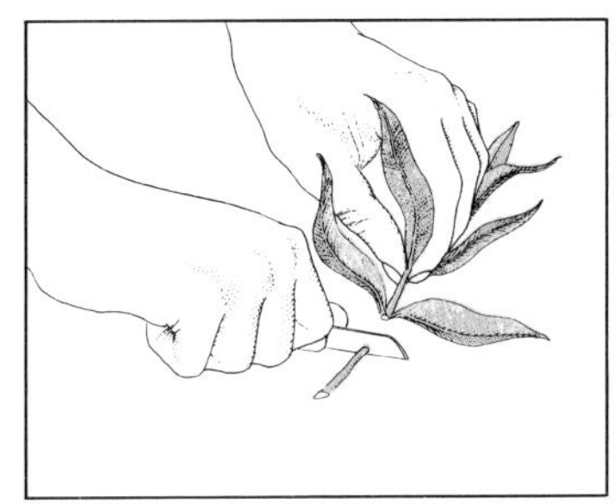

2 *Trim the cuttings straight across the stem, just below a leaf node*

3 *Make planting holes in a 4 in. pot of compost; insert cuttings*

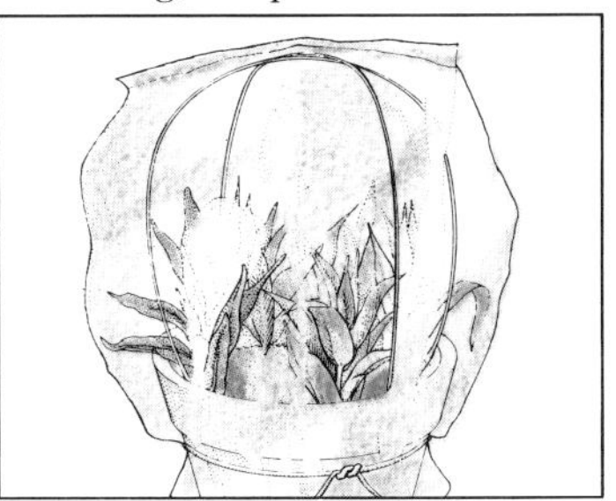

4 *Criss-cross two wire loops to make a framework, and cover with plastic*

5 *After five or six weeks, plant each rooted cutting in a 3 in. pot of compost*

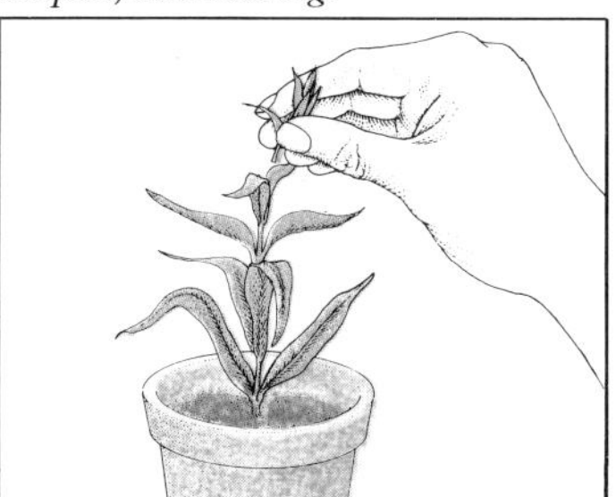

6 *Pinch out the tip of each cutting. Overwinter in a cold frame*

Taking basal cuttings in spring

Most clump-forming perennials, such as anchusas, armerias, delphiniums, hypericums, lupins, scabiosas and many others, are propagated not only by division, but also from the young shoots appearing from the base of the plants in spring.

Cut off some of these basal shoots when they are 3–4 in. long, at crown level or just below.

Insert the cuttings directly into the soil in a cold frame, or simply in 3 in. pots containing a compost of equal parts peat and sand, or a proprietary cuttings compost. The pots are then put into the cold frame.

The advantage of putting the cuttings into pots, as opposed to directly into the soil in the cold frame, is that it allows them to be transferred from the frame at any time, perhaps for hardening off after rooting, without transplanting. Keep cuttings well watered by spraying them from overhead, and keep the frame closed. As new growth starts to show, increase ventilation by gradually opening the frame.

After about six weeks, pot the cuttings singly in $3\frac{1}{2}$ in. pots of John Innes No. 1 compost.

Plant them out in their permanent positions during autumn.

1 *Scrape away the soil from the crown and sever the young shoots*

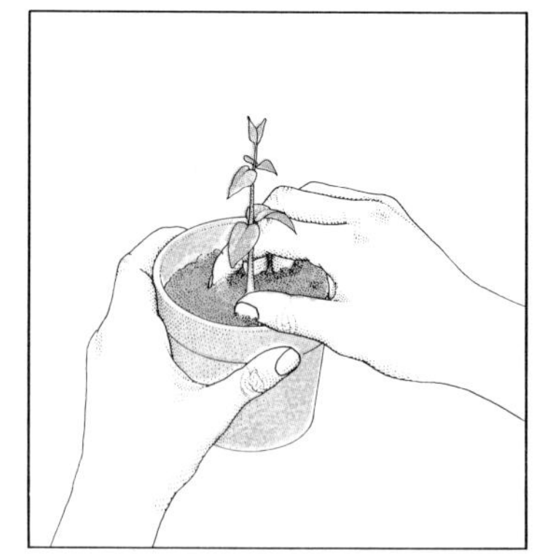

2 *Insert in cuttings compost and place in a closed cold frame*

Growing perennials from pieces of root

Perennials that are too small to divide can be grown from root cuttings from autumn to early spring.

Thick or fleshy roots, such as those of dicentras, oriental poppies and romneyas, are cut into 2–3 in. pieces. Cut the top end (nearest the crown of the plant) straight across, and the lower end at a slant, so that you will not confuse top and bottom.

Fill large pots or deep boxes with a compost of equal parts peat and sand. Make a number of planting holes, 2 in. apart and 2–3 in. deep. Insert the cuttings vertically, so that the flat top of each is level with the compost; cover with $\frac{1}{4}$ in. of sand.

Thin perennial roots, for example phlox and verbascums, are cut into slightly shorter lengths, about 2 in. Lay the cuttings flat on the compost and cover with $\frac{1}{4}$–$\frac{1}{2}$ in. of compost.

Leave both types of cuttings in a closed cold frame during winter.

In spring, when the cuttings have rooted and developed three or four pairs of leaves, pot them singly in 3 in. pots of John Innes No. 1, or a proprietary cuttings compost.

Stand the pots outdoors during summer and plant out in autumn.

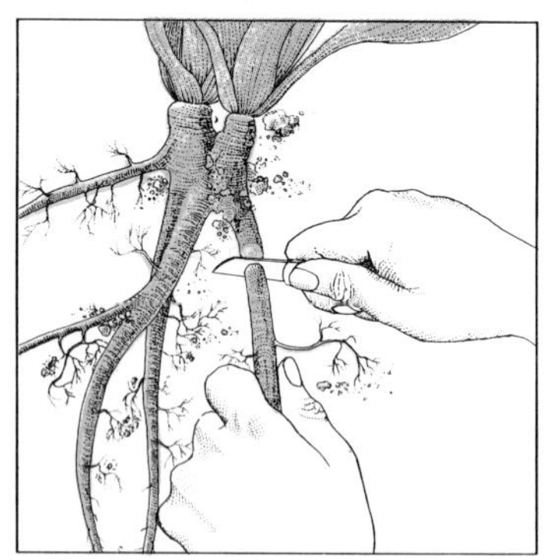

1 *In autumn, cut thick roots into 2–3 in. lengths*

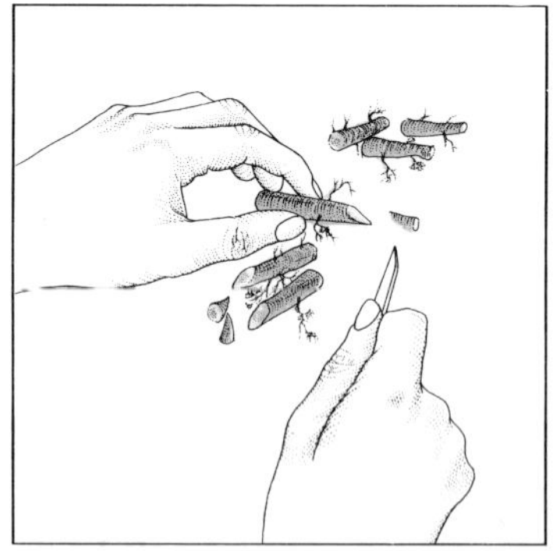

2 *Cut lower end of cutting at a slant, to distinguish base from top*

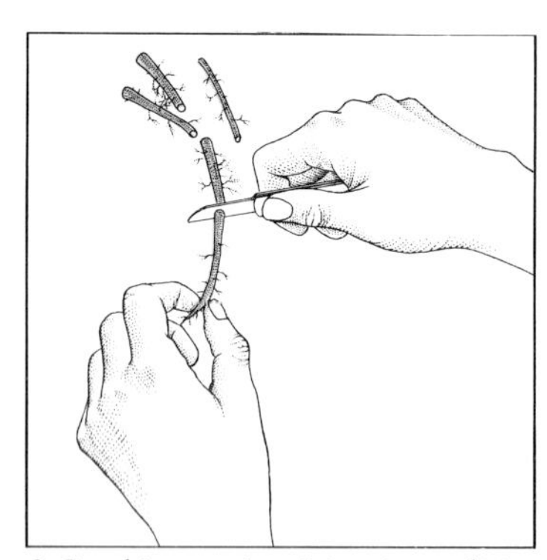

3 *Cut thin roots into 2 in. pieces, slicing them straight across*

4 *Insert thick root cuttings, angled side down, in pots of compost*

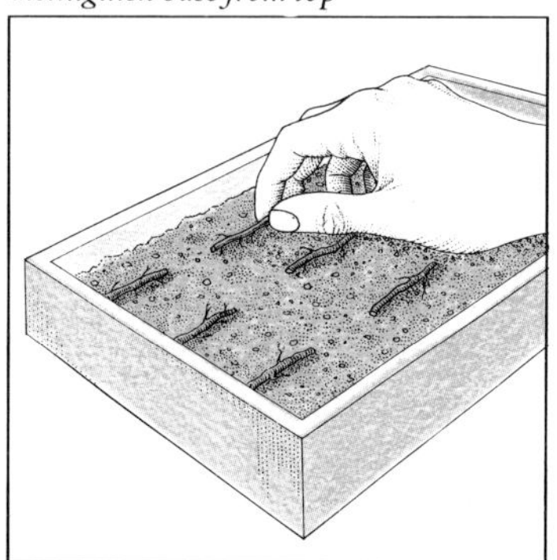

5 *Lay thin root cuttings flat on the compost and cover with more soil*

6 *In spring, when the cuttings have formed leaves, pot them singly*

Growing new plants from seed

How to gather seeds from the garden

In nature, all flowering plants reproduce themselves by seeds which fall to the ground when ripe, spend the winter under the cover of dead leaves, and begin to germinate when warmer weather arrives in spring.

Cultivated plants can also be propagated from seeds, but results are varied. Although most of our garden plants originated from species growing in the wild, they have been cross-bred and hybridised to produce larger, more showy plants.

Seeds gathered from cultivated plants will not produce plants identical to the parent. They can, however, be grown on in a spare piece of ground for a year or two so that the strongest and most attractive seedlings can be selected. To perpetuate a seed-raised strain, subsequent plants must be vegetatively propagated – by cuttings or division.

Packaged seeds from reputable nurserymen can usually be relied on to produce true seedlings, and they provide an inexpensive means of raising a large number of plants. Seeds which are gathered from existing plants should be stored in a cool, airy place until late winter.

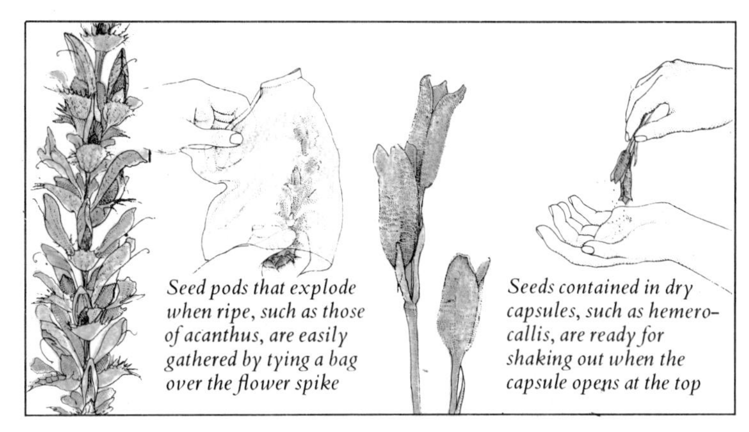

Seed pods that explode when ripe, such as those of acanthus, are easily gathered by tying a bag over the flower spike

Seeds contained in dry capsules, such as hemerocallis, are ready for shaking out when the capsule opens at the top

Sowing and germinating the seeds

Seeds may be sown outside in a sheltered bed, but it is generally more successful to raise seedlings under glass in January and February.

Fill a seed box, pan or a 3 in. pot with John Innes seed compost or with a proprietary seed compost, so that the surface is about 1 in. below the rim. Water the container and leave it to drain thoroughly.

Sprinkle the seeds evenly but thinly over the surface, and cover with a $\frac{1}{4}$ in. layer of compost.

Very fine seeds should just be sprinkled evenly over the surface.

Cover the seed containers with a plastic bag to provide the initial conditions for germination – moisture and warmth. Put the containers in a closed cold frame, in a cold greenhouse, or propagating case with a bottom heat of 15–18°C (59–64°F).

Three to six weeks later the seedlings should appear. Remove the plastic bag and gradually admit air and light by ventilating the frame or greenhouse on mild days.

When the seedlings, especially those in shallow boxes and pans, have developed their first two pairs of leaves, they must be transplanted (pricked out) into boxes, to give them more room for development. Fill the boxes with John Innes No. 1 potting compost and moisten it thoroughly. Make a number of shallow planting holes, 2 in. apart and about 3 in. between the rows. Using a spare plant label, carefully prise up the seedlings and set them in the holes, firming them gently.

Seedlings that have been sown well apart in deep pots can be left longer and transplanted straight into individual pots. Invert the pot to dislodge them. Tease the young plants apart, and pot them up singly in 3 in. pots of moist John Innes No. 1 potting compost or a proprietary soil-less potting compost.

Handle the seedlings carefully. Fill in with compost to $\frac{1}{2}$ in. below the rim. Water after 24 hours.

Grow all seedlings on in the cold frame, gradually admitting more light and air, and making sure the compost does not dry out.

Vigorous perennials in boxes will often need to be potted up as already described. Provided they are growing strongly, all young plants benefit from being planted out in a sheltered spot during summer and left to grow. The following autumn, set the plants in permanent sites.

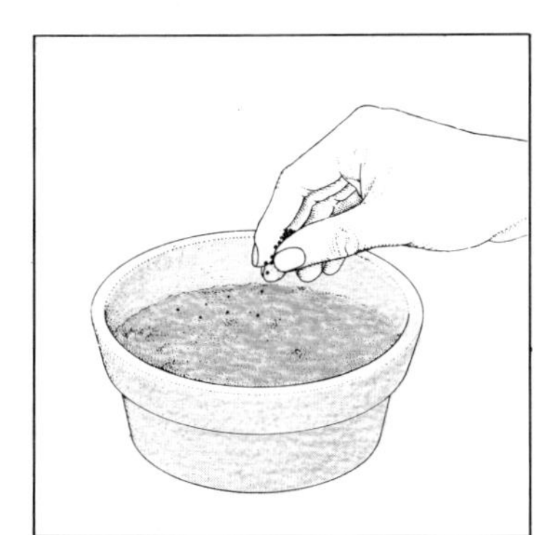

1 *In late winter, sprinkle seeds on moist compost and cover them thinly*

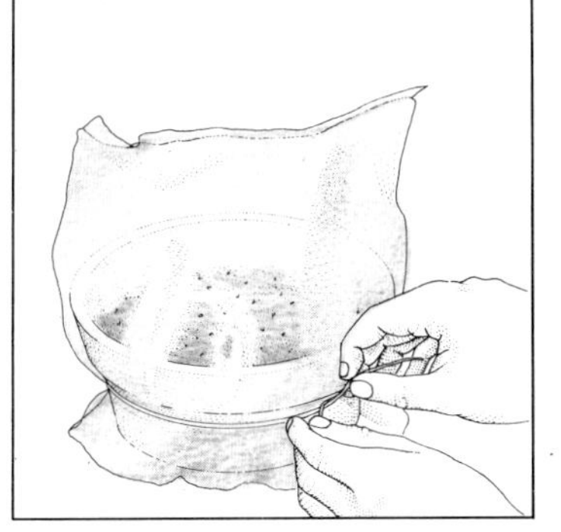

2 *Cover with a polythene bag and put in a closed cold frame*

3 *When the seedlings have two pairs of leaves, prick them out into boxes*

4 *One or two months later, move vigorous plants into 3 in. pots*

Rhododendrons & azaleas

The vivid displays produced by rhododendrons and azaleas can last from spring to high summer. There are plants to fit any size of garden – but the soil must be right

Rhododendrons can provide one of the most popular features in modern gardens. Varying in size from mat-like dwarf shrubs only a few inches high to trees higher than 40 ft, they can be used for any size of garden and any suitable position.

The rhododendron derives its name from the Greek – *rhodon* (rose) and *dendron* (tree). The first wild species to be introduced into cultivation in Britain was the Alpine rose, *Rhododendron hirsutum*, which was brought from central Europe in 1656. In 1753 Linnaeus, the Swedish botanist, officially established and named the genus. At the same time, he created the separate genus of azalea. Then, in the 19th century, another botanist, George Don, realised that there was no botanical difference between rhododendrons and azaleas, and the two species were classified in the same genus. They remain so today, although gardeners still prefer to talk of rhododendrons and azaleas as two separate types of plants. Rhododendrons are mainly evergreen shrubs; azaleas are mostly deciduous, although one popular group, the Japanese or Kurume azaleas, are evergreen.

The flowers of rhododendrons and azaleas have a wide range of colour: white, pink, lavender, violet, purple, yellow, crimson, scarlet and orange. And the shapes of the flowers range through tubular, starry, funnel, bowl and bell-shaped, varying in size from $\frac{3}{4}$–6 in. wide and $\frac{3}{4}$–4 in. long.

To give the best results, rhododendrons and azaleas need to be

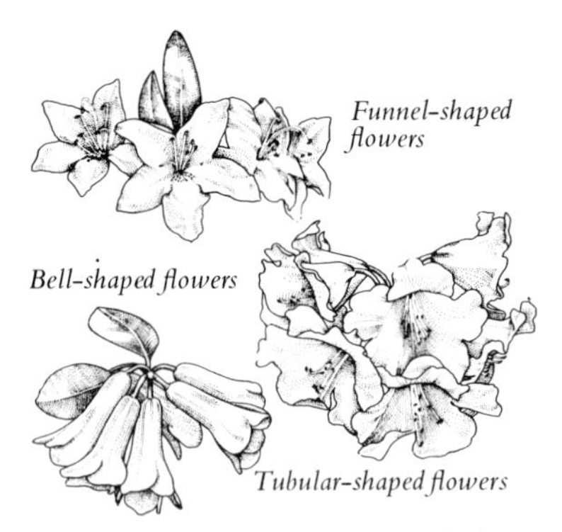

grown in dappled or light shade. The soil should be moist and acid – the plants will not thrive in soil containing chalk or lime. Given the right conditions, a succession of varieties can be in flower for several months of the year.

The large-leaved, tree-like species and their hybrids are best suited to sheltered woodland gardens in southern England and to the western side of Britain from Cornwall to Argyll, whereas the smaller-leaved, shrubby kinds will thrive in exposed conditions over a very wide area. Best results are obtained from varieties whose branches shade their own roots; any which tend to grow tall and leggy should be avoided. The dwarf species will grow well in rock and peat gardens and in narrow borders. Varieties which flower before the end of May should be planted in positions sheltered from early-morning sun, because of the bad effect this has on flowers subjected to late spring frosts. It is best to avoid hollows, as frost 'flows' and gathers at the lowest points.

Ideally, rhododendrons should be grown with other plants, both flowering and foliage, which will ensure the maximum decorative effect during the long periods when the evergreen rhododendrons are out of flower, and the deciduous kinds have not reached their autumn-colouring stage.

The soil which suits rhododendrons allows for a very wide range

Rhododendron indicum, *which grows about 4 ft high, is excellent for a tub on a shaded terrace. Red or pink flowers are borne in June*

of plants to be grown with them.

Heaths and heathers also thrive in acid soil and are of great ornamental value, and there are sizes to suit all gardens. The foliage colours range from glowing red, russet, orange, yellow and bronze, to green and grey. The flowers are small, in shades of pink, purple, red or white. Many varieties are at their best in late winter and spring.

The shrub *Pernettya mucronata* has white flowers in late May and early June, and bears clusters of colourful fruits from October to March. It thrives well in sun or shade. It is unisexual, so male and female plants must be grown together, otherwise no berries will be formed.

Pieris japonica 'Variegata' is a shrub with white flowers in March and April and dense and attractive variegated foliage, which contrasts well with the leaves of rhododendrons and azaleas.

Lilies produce a magnificent show of flowers in most colour ranges, except blue, from May to September. Some, such as *Lilium auratum*, *L. henryi* and *L. speciosum*, which flower in June and July, are suitable for woodland gardens.

Hostas are very suitable herbaceous perennials, both for their foliage and their flowers, and once planted they can be left undisturbed for years.

Another perennial, *Gentiana asclepiadea*, has willow-like, mid-green leaves and deep blue flowers from late July to September. It likes a damp, partially shaded site. *G. sino-ornata*, considered to be the finest autumn-flowering gentian, produces sheets of brilliant blue flowers, striped deep blue and green-yellow. They are 2 in. long and open from September to November.

Camellias, particularly varieties of *Camellia × williamsii* which flower from November to April, are also ideal for growing with rhododendrons. They have glossy, dark green foliage, and flowers ranging in colour from white and pale pink to rich rose-purple.

Many ground-cover plants can also be grown with rhododendrons to provide additional colour. Ideal are lily-of-the-valley, flowering April to May, *Gaultheria procumbens*, July to August, epimedium, May to July, and primula, January to May. Hardy ferns provide fine contrasting foliage, and the tall agapanthus – particularly the Headbourne hybrids – produces large heads of blue flowers from July to September.

THE WIDE CHOICE, FROM GIANTS TO DWARFS

As rhododendrons and azaleas range in size from tree-like giants to prostrate dwarfs, first decide on the space you have to fill before buying your shrubs.

The size of plants can vary considerably according to the rainfall of the area where they are grown. The heights given here are a guide for an average rainfall area.

Tree-like plants (over 15 ft) The biggest rhododendrons are evergreens, growing to 25 ft and more, and mainly found in southern and western Britain. They are suitable only for large woodland gardens sheltered from north and east winds.

R. arboreum

They include *Rhododendron falconeri*, which bears large cream flowers blotched with red in April and May, and *R. sinogrande*, with huge leaves, 20 in. long, coloured silver underneath. Yellow flowers bloom in April. *R. arboreum*, one of the biggest rhododendrons grown in Britain, reaches a height of 40 ft but is suitable only for mild areas. There are also the hybrids 'Albatross' (white flowers in June), 'Loderi King George' (pink flowers in May), and 'Polar Bear' (white flowers, July–August).

Large bushes (8–15 ft) Evergreens suitable for smaller gardens include

R. thomsonii

R. yunnanense, which produces numerous pink flowers in May. It tolerates dry conditions and is useful for screening. *R. thomsonii* has red flowers in March and April.

Of the evergreen hybrids, 'Cynthia' is very reliable in the open garden, and bears crimson flowers in May. Other evergreen hybrids are 'Azor' (salmon flowers, June–July), 'Faggetter's Favourite' (scented, pink flowers in May), and 'Lady Clementine Mitford' (pink flowers in May, and silver-grey foliage).

Medium bushes (4–8 ft) The deciduous azaleas are all medium-sized bushes, which makes them popular in gardens of average size.

Ghent azaleas are very hardy and grow 4–8 ft tall. The flowers are small, tubular and fragrant. The most popular Ghent hybrid is 'Coccinea Speciosa', which carries brilliant orange-red flowers in May.

Occidentale azaleas, up to 8 ft tall, produce masses of scented pink flowers in late May and early June.

The Knap Hill and Exbury azaleas grow 4–8 ft high, with large, trumpet-shaped flowers, sometimes double, that open in May. Flower colours range through red, orange, pink and white.

Mollis azaleas also grow 4–8 ft high. The flowers appear in May, before the leaves, and the colour range is mainly yellow and orange.

The Rustica hybrids are a race of double-flowered azaleas, mainly in shades of pink, that open in late May and early June. The shrubs grow 6 ft high and up to 6 ft across.

Small bushes (2–4 ft high) Small evergreen hybrids which make compact bushes are 'Blue Diamond' (lavender-blue flowers in April), 'Cilpinense' (white, rose-flushed flowers, March–April), and 'Elizabeth' (crimson flowers, April–May).

The evergreen azaleas, called Japanese or Kurume azaleas, are particularly suitable for small gardens, rarely growing over 4 ft high. They bloom in April and May, mostly in shades of pink and red. 'Kuri-no-yuki' is white.

Dwarf bushes (1–2 ft high) Dwarf evergreen hybrids, suitable for rock gardens, include 'Chikor' (yellow flowers, April–May), 'Prostigiatum'

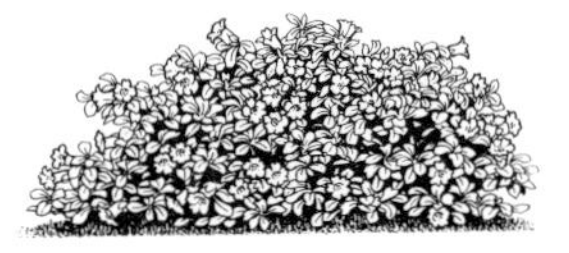

R. forrestii repens

(purple flowers in April) and 'Ptarmigan' (white flowers in April).

Prostrate evergreens Low-growing rhododendrons with a wide spread can be grown as ground-cover on acid soil in a lightly shaded place. They include *R. forrestii repens* (crimson flowers, April–May) and the hybrid 'Jenny' (red flowers, May–June).

Growing healthy rhododendrons and azaleas

The two essentials for successful cultivation of rhododendrons are an acid soil – soil with a pH content of no more than 6 (p. 403) – and one that is rich in humus. Neither rhododendrons nor azaleas will thrive in limy or chalky soil.

A thin, sandy soil will need the addition of plenty of humus-forming material, such as peat or garden compost.

Plant rhododendrons that flower before late May in positions shaded from early-morning sunlight. Sudden thawing after frost can damage buds and young growth.

Every year or two after planting, mulch the bed with more compost or peat. No artificial fertiliser is needed.

If you are growing a rhododendron in a tub and live in an area with limy (hard) water, do not water it from a tap. Use rain water collected in a barrel or another container fed from a drainpipe.

After they have flowered, remove the dead flower heads. (The easiest way is to snap them off with finger and thumb.) This will help to ensure a good crop of flowers the following year.

REMOVING DEAD FLOWERS

After flowering, break off the entire flower head with finger and thumb. This will help to produce the maximum number of flowers next year

Pruning young and old rhododendrons

Rhododendrons do not need regular pruning. Spindly young plants may be lightly pruned to make them bushy. In spring, before new growth starts, prune the stems by about one-third of their length, cutting just above a bud. The buds may be very small and rather difficult to see.

Straggly plants, or old neglected ones in need of rejuvenation, may be cut back in March with a saw to any point about 3 ft above the ground. No buds will be visible, but shoots will grow from the stumps.

After this severe pruning, they will take three more years before they will flower again.

SPINDLY YOUNG PLANTS

If young plants are too spindly, prune the stems in spring. Cut just above the small green buds

A STRAGGLY OLD BUSH

Straggly old bushes can be cut back with a saw in March to within 3 ft of the ground

What can go wrong with rhododendrons and azaleas

This chart describes the most common problems that are likely to occur in growing rhododendrons.

If your plants show any symptoms not described here, turn to the full-colour chart of pests and diseases starting on page 377.

Trade names for the various chemicals are given on page 398.

Symptoms	Cause	Cure
Leaves show yellow patches between veins or are suffused all over. If severe, they may brown and wither	Chlorosis	Treat with chelated compounds (sequestered iron) and mulch with peat. Rhododendrons must have an acid soil to thrive well
Leaves have a rusty brown mottling, sometimes falling prematurely, particularly on the sunny side of a bush	Rhododendron bug or Japanese lace-wing fly	Spray with malathion at the first signs of attack
Flower-bearing buds fail to develop in spring and turn blackish, often with a greyish or silvery cast. Later, small, black, pinhead-shaped foreign bodies appear	Bud-blast, spread by the rhododendron leafhopper – a jumping insect about $\frac{1}{4}$ in. long, bright green above with two contrasting red stripes	Spray with malathion as soon as the insect is noticed
Leaves roll into cigar-shaped cylinders and usually hang down	Cold or drought	This usually occurs during frosty spells, and recovery is natural when warmer weather returns. If it happens during a warm spell, drought may be the cause. Water thoroughly and mulch with moss peat

Increasing your stock of plants

Layering: the easiest and fastest way

The simplest way of propagating rhododendrons and azaleas is by layering. This is also the fastest way of producing a new flowering plant.

It is more easily done with old plants, on which the branches have become flexible, than on new growth of young plants.

In October, bend a branch until it reaches the ground 9–12 in. from the tip. Strip off the leaves at this point.

Cut a sliver off the branch on the underside, or twist the branch to injure the surface tissue.

Dig a 3–4 in. hole and half-fill it with moist seed compost, or equal parts of moist peat and coarse sand.

Bend the branch as near as possible to a right angle at the wound and push it into the hole. Secure the branch with a bent 8–10 in. long piece of galvanised wire, and fill the hole with compost. Stake the upright tip of the branch.

Cover the ground around it with 1 in. of compost to act as a mulch.

Repeat the operation with other branches to produce more plants.

Water the area thoroughly and be sure the soil never dries out.

After two years, if roots have grown from the wound, sever the young plant, lift it out of the ground with a good ball of soil, and plant it in position.

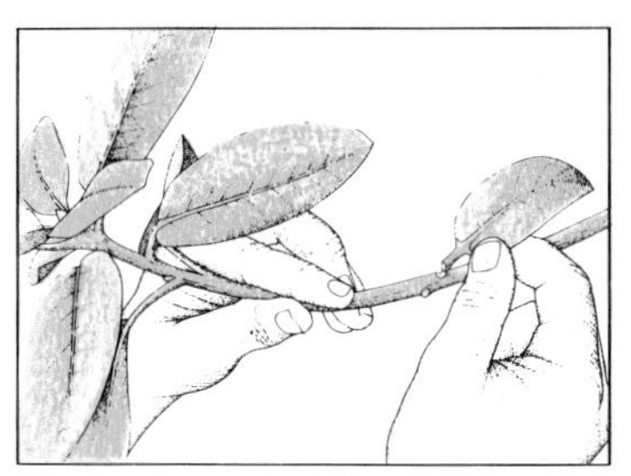

1 *In October, strip off leaves about 9 in. from a branch tip*

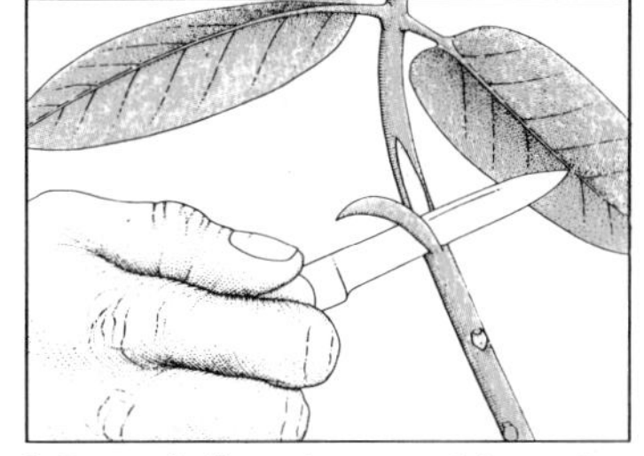

2 *Cut a shallow slice out of the underside of the branch*

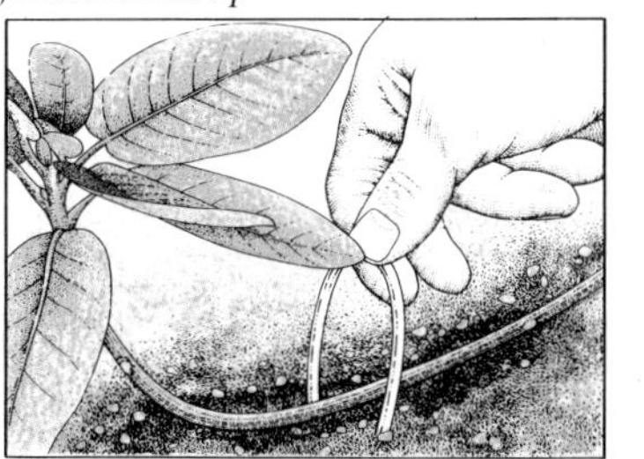

3 *Bend the branch into a shallow hole half-filled with compost. Pin down*

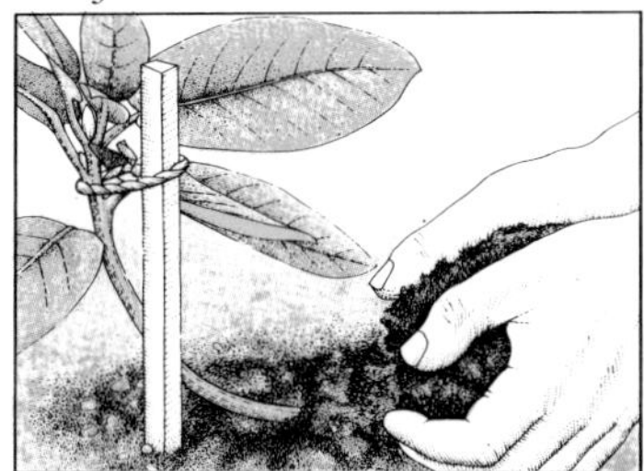

4 *Stake the upright tip of the branch and cover with more compost*

5 *After two years, the layers should have rooted. Sever the young plants, lift with a ball of soil and plant out. They may flower next summer*

Semi-hard cuttings: for the maximum number

To produce the greatest number of new rhododendrons and azaleas, take semi-hard cuttings between July and September.

With secateurs, cut off 6 in. shoots which have formed in the current year. Each shoot will have a small flower bud at the tip. Sever the shoot close to its parent stem.

Remove all the leaves from the lower part of the shoot and cut it straight across, just below a leaf node, so that the resultant cutting is about 2–4 in. long.

Wound the cutting by paring off a narrow sliver of bark about 1 in. long. If the leaves are more than 3 in. long it is better to shorten them. Place the leaves on top of one another and cut them straight across the middle with a sharp knife or razor blade. This reduces the surface exposed to the air and cuts down loss of the moisture they need for successful rooting.

Now follow the procedure for semi-hard cuttings (p. 250).

Between July and September, cut off 6 in. shoots of current year's wood. If the leaves are longer than 3 in., cut them in half. Remove a sliver of bark

Rock plants—beauty in miniature

A successful rock garden re-creates the wild outcrops of rock on mountain slopes. Plant it with flowers that thrive in rugged stony terrain

With their delicate detail and exquisite form, alpines and rock plants have a particular fascination – the wonder of the miniature.

As their original habitat is the mountainous and rocky regions of the world, they are mainly hardy and can tolerate thin, stony soils and drying winds. And, provided their natural conditions of sharp drainage are imitated for them, they are easy to grow.

Their brilliant colours enhance any garden and, since their size allows them to grow happily in sinks, troughs or other ornamental containers, no garden, however small, need be without them. Once planted they need little attention, except to be kept clear of weeds in order to prevent them from being smothered.

In their natural habitat most mountain plants are covered by an insulating blanket of snow each year, and do not suffer the low temperatures and the damp conditions which they may have to endure under cultivation.

For this reason, some plants are best grown in pots in an alpine house. This is simply a cold greenhouse with added ventilation.

Most rock plants, however, grow well in the open, and are most commonly used in specially prepared rock gardens.

Ideally, a rock garden should be on a slope, but a flat site can be quite suitable if it is provided with adequate drainage.

Rock gardens are most economically constructed by the 'outcrop' principle – the use of a small quantity of rock on top of the soil to give the impression of more beneath the surface. The outcrop system is possible with all types of rock, and is an important consideration as the cost of rock from quarries increases.

When planting a rock garden, select a variety of plants so as to have a constant show of colour throughout the year. For instance, dwarf bulbs, which can be planted under carpeting plants, will provide colour during the winter.

Other places to grow rock plants on a flat site are paved areas or alpine lawns. To grow plants between paving, the slabs are laid on sand, with gaps between to accommodate aromatic plants which give off fragrance when they are walked on. The alpine lawn consists of low-growing rock plants with bulbs growing through them, and can be placed on the lower parts of the rock garden.

Alpines and rock plants (which are almost synonymous terms) can also be grown in raised beds. In this way, plants with different requirements – lime-lovers, lime-haters or sun-lovers that require good drainage – can all be grown in separate beds filled with different soil mixtures. A system of raised beds can be constructed from several types of material. The best material is rock or paving built up like a drystone wall with soil between the pieces. Plants can then be planted to trail down the sides of the beds.

Bricks can also be used to build raised beds. They can be cemented in place and holes left for drainage. Peat blocks can be used, but only for low beds, as peat dries out quickly if it is built too high.

Breeze blocks can also be used, but although they are strong they are very ugly.

The height of a raised bed can vary from 6 in. to about 3 ft. The higher ones are an advantage to older gardeners, and those who find it difficult to bend or stoop.

Alpines and rock plants can also be mixed with other plants in the garden. The front of a shrub border, particularly if it is raised or has a stone edging, can be attractively filled with trailing plants and dwarf shrubs.

Many of the taller rock plants associate well with herbaceous perennials. In fact, many gardens have all these plants mixed in an attractive medley.

Despite their versatility in the garden, rock plants are not suitable for cultivation as house plants, as they need sunshine in summer and cold, dry conditions in winter.

Before attempting to build a rock garden, the gardener should have in his mind (if not on paper) a plan of the basic design for the garden he wishes to create. To get an idea of this, it is advisable to visit a rock garden in one of the large botanic gardens throughout the country, such as Kew and Wisley in Surrey, Oxford, Cambridge, Edinburgh, and the University of Liverpool's garden at Ness in Cheshire. Smaller rock gardens, which might be more appropriate to the owner of a small garden, can be seen in some of the gardens that are open under the National Gardens Scheme, and also at National Trust properties.

To build a successful, natural-looking rock garden it is as well to remember a few basic principles. Certainly no attempt should be made to copy an actual mountain in a garden. The scale would be quite out of proportion. It is better to try to simulate an outcrop of rock, which will look far more effective.

All rock begins as a solid lump in the earth's crust. Then, due to various strains and stresses, the lump begins to crack – not diagonally, but vertically and horizontally.

Further cracking takes place, aided by climatic conditions, and the lump takes on a different shape. The most exposed parts crumble away,

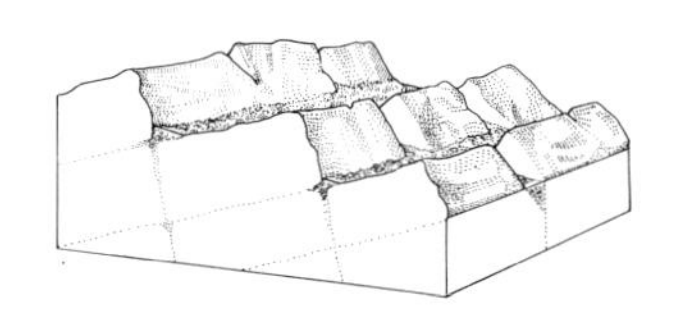

Natural outcrops in the making

and the main bulk of the rock becomes hidden beneath soil formed by the crumbled rock particles. Only corners of rock remain in view, as outcrops protruding from the soil.

If this principle of construction is remembered, a rock garden will look more natural.

If there has been some geological upheaval, the rocks will have been tilted – which is another feature that can be incorporated into the building of the garden. However, once an angle has been determined it must not be broken.

If a rock garden is to be constructed on a mound, it is best to keep the stones flat in order not to give a broken-back effect.

Height in proportion to width is also a factor that must be taken into account.

For every foot the garden is to be raised, the bed should be 4–5 ft wide at the base.

Once the basic rock garden has been built, it can be extended in various ways. Water is always an attractive feature, but when constructing a waterfall care must be taken not to make it look too artificial.

The most important factor to consider when designing the rock garden is the angle from which it is to be primarily viewed – whether it is to make an impact on the passer-by, to be looked at from an upstairs window, or to be admired from close quarters.

With this point in mind, maximum effect can be achieved both in the positioning of the rocks and the placing of the plants.

How to build a rock garden

The first step in planning a rock garden is to check that rocks are available locally. In areas a long way from quarries they may be difficult to obtain.

Sandstone and limestone are the best types of rock, and they can be bought quite reasonably from a quarry. But haulage charges are expensive, and for every mile the rock has to be transported so the price of the rock is increased.

Some large garden centres may stock a supply of rock, or take orders for delivery from a quarry. Your nearest specialist nurseryman or garden centre should be able to advise you on sources of supply.

If possible, choose the pieces of rock you wish to use, or at least tell the supplier the maximum and minimum sizes that you need for the job.

On a 15 ft × 10 ft site, $1\frac{1}{2}$–2 tons of rock should be sufficient. It is not possible to forecast how many pieces will come to the ton, but 1 ton of sandstone is roughly equal to 14–16 cubic feet, and 1 ton of limestone to 13–14 cubic feet.

You will also need to order $\frac{1}{4}$ in. rock chippings to top-dress the finished garden and for mixing with the soil.

There are two main types of chippings: gravel and limestone. Gravel chippings are the more easily obtainable. They are paler than limestone chippings and blend in with most rock.

Limestone chippings are, of course, particularly suitable for use with limestone rocks.

Some garden centres and builders' merchants keep rock chippings in stock, but with others it may be necessary to order a supply of chippings in advance.

The ideal position for a rock garden is a warm, gentle slope facing south or south-west, and protected from strong winds.

A semi-open site is best, with dappled sunlight coming through a tree a few yards away, to prevent certain plants being scorched during very hot sunshine.

Do not build a rock garden beneath a tree, which could drip water on to the plants, or in a dry corner where the roots would get insufficient moisture. And do not choose a wet site, which could cause the roots to rot.

Before a rock garden is built, all perennial weeds must be completely removed from the site, either by pulling them out by hand, digging them out, or else using chemical weedkillers.

If the ground is infested with horsetail, every trace must be removed before construction is started – if necessary by several applications of dichlobenil weedkiller.

If the rock garden is being built on a lawn, remove the turf from the site and lay it carefully to one side. It can be used as turf elsewhere or can be stacked upside-down in a heap to provide loam for potting composts or material for mulching.

Good drainage is essential for a rock garden, as most rock plants will not survive damp conditions. A light

1 *Form an L by placing the largest rock at the corner and making the arms from progressively smaller rocks. Fill with a free-draining soil mixture*

2 *Extra outcrops can be added by building them either behind or to one side of the first. Small stones can be laid at random on each outcrop*

3 *If the rock garden is being built on sloping ground, the stones should be tilted so that rain water runs into the soil rather than down the slope*

4 *Extra tiers can be added as far as space allows, remembering that the rock garden should be four to five times wider than it is high*

soil on a gravelly subsoil will have sufficient natural drainage. But a clay soil, or heavy soil with a subsoil of clay, will need to be given artificial drainage.

Drainage is particularly important if the site is flat.

To provide drainage, dig trenches about 18 in. deep and 3–6 ft apart, depending on the density of the clay. Fill the bottom half with large stones, broken bricks or rubble. Then place a layer of upturned turf (or gravel or coarse peat a couple of inches deep) on top to prevent the upper soil from falling between the rubble and blocking the drainage. Finally, fill up with soil.

Sandy soil that is not being drained needs to be dug over only one spade deep before the rocks are laid.

When the site has been cleared of weeds, and any trenches have been completed, building of the rock garden can begin.

Start by placing rocks (weighing up to ½ cwt each) along two sides of the prepared ground to form an L-shaped outcrop.

Use the largest rock as the keystone, or corner, of the L. Place progressively shallower rocks to form the two arms of the L, with the final rocks almost disappearing into the soil. The finished result should give the appearance of an outcrop of rock protruding from the earth, with a much larger mass of rock below ground level.

A south-facing slope can be created on a north-facing slope by placing rocks on top of one another at the corner of the L to tilt the bed towards the south.

Place the rocks so that all joints line up horizontally and vertically. Do not overlap a joint with the rock above, like bricks in a wall.

All stones have strata lines. Lay the stones so that the strata lines run horizontally.

Generally, a rock garden should be four to five times wider than it is high.

Take care to set the rocks firmly and securely. When the rocks have all been placed in position, fill the space between the arms of the L with free-draining soil.

Prepare a mixture of 2 parts ¼ in. rock chippings, 1 part loam (preferably sterilised), and 1 part moss peat.

Fill the inside of the L with the mixture, flush with the top of the rocks, and gently firm it by treading lightly.

The mixture will settle, so keep some in reserve for topping up later.

Rake the surface flat.

After about ten days, or earlier if there has been heavy rain, the soil will have subsided and can be topped up with the mixture which was held in reserve.

Finally, apply a top-dressing of ¼ in. rock chippings, ½–1 in. deep, raking them flat.

The chippings prevent loss of moisture from the soil, protect the neck of a plant from rotting, and prevent rain from splashing soil on to the flowers.

When the bed has been completed, further beds can be laid if the rock garden is to be extended – either behind the first bed or to one side of it.

If the construction is on a slope the stones should be positioned so that water runs back into the soil, rather than being lost by running away down the slope.

There are various ways in which a rock garden can be built up further. A waterfall or pool for aquatic plants will enhance the garden's attractiveness. For details of how to construct your own water garden, see page 326.

Each builder of a rock garden will have his own ideas as to the kind of effect he wishes to achieve, and provided the basic principles of construction are adhered to – correct placing of joints and strata lines kept horizontal – he can follow his own design.

WAYS OF EXTENDING THE ROCK GARDEN

There are various ways of extending a rock garden. Above, a paved area has been laid in front of the garden, which has been built on a slope. Plants growing between the paving stones make an attractive foreground. A scree could be laid instead of the paving

Another attractive way of extending a rock garden is by the use of water – either by creating a waterfall or adding a pool with perhaps fish or aquatic plants. Care must be taken not to make the effect look too artificial or contrived. Details of building a water garden are on page 326

Planting a rock garden

Rock plants are always grown in pots by nurserymen, and so can be planted at any time of year (except during severe frosts) as the roots will not be disturbed.

To remove the plant, hold it upside-down with the stem between two fingers and pull or tear away the pot.

If the pot is a plastic one, tap the rim sharply on a hard surface to dislodge the plant.

With a trowel, dig a hole in the soil to the depth of the root ball and insert the plant.

Fill the hole with soil and firm the plant in with the fingers or the trowel handle.

Re-cover the area with chippings, and water moderately.

Home-grown seedlings which are ready for potting on can be put directly into the rock garden.

Plant in the same way, making sure the planting hole is large enough for the seedling's root system.

Upright shrubs or conifers look best when they are planted at the base of a rock.

Prostrate shrubs or conifers, on the other hand, are best grown on top of a rock, over which part of their growth can cascade.

Rosette-forming plants which need to be protected from wet can be grown in a vertical crevice, so that rain does not gather in the rosettes and rot them.

After taking the plant from its pot and removing the crocks from the bottom of the compost, test that the plant fits into the crevice. If it does not, tease its soil ball into the right shape.

Wedge the soil ball into the crevice, and firm in with soil underneath the plant.

Finally, fill in the crevice from above the plant with a mixture of soil and chippings.

Ideally, crevice plants should be planted at the same time as the rocks are placed in position, but this is not always practicable and planting may have to be done later.

Large, well-established plants will give a mature effect to a new planting. They can be transplanted from a temporary bed, or from another part of the rock garden. A good position for large specimens is in the angle between rocks.

Dig up the plant during wet weather in autumn or early spring, ensuring that plenty of soil is taken up with the roots.

Plant it in the rock garden in the normal way.

After planting, tread it in firmly with the feet.

Take care, when planting, to confine rampant plants to an area of the rock garden where they will do least harm to their neighbours.

Before planting, consult the chart of plants beginning on page 329 to discover a plant's potential spread and its ideal habitat.

1 *Dig a hole large enough to take the whole root ball, and insert the plant*

2 *Fill hole with soil. Firm in plant. Cover with chippings, then water*

FOUR TYPES OF ROCK PLANTS

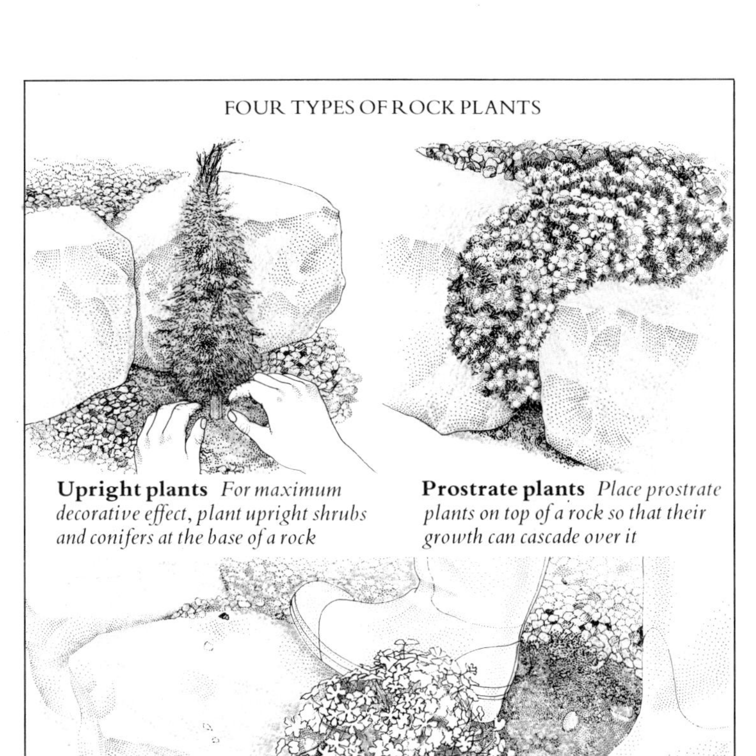

Upright plants *For maximum decorative effect, plant upright shrubs and conifers at the base of a rock*

Prostrate plants *Place prostrate plants on top of a rock so that their growth can cascade over it*

Large specimens *Large plants, transplanted from temporary beds or other parts of the rock garden, can be planted in the angle between rocks. Plant in the usual way, then firm the plants in well with the feet*

Rosette-forming plants *Plant rosette-forming plants in a vertical crevice. Wedge the soil ball into the crevice. Firm in with soil underneath the plant, then fill in from above with soil and chippings*

Roses

The earliest roses go back into unrecorded time, before man himself. This best-loved flower grows in hundreds of varieties, and over 30 million roses are planted every year

Fossil remains found in Europe and America show that the rose was established on earth before man evolved. It has been found growing wild in most of the countries in the temperate zone of the Northern Hemisphere.

During its evolution, it developed shapes and habits ranging from small, shrubby bushes to robust tree-climbers soaring up from the forest floor to reach the light.

These wild roses are the true species, of which there are at least 150, the great majority originating from Asia. With few exceptions, all grow single flowers, each with a whorl of five petals.

Throughout the ages, gardeners cultivated the rose, developing the double flower and, eventually, the high-pointed, modern hybrids in which the ancestral floral characteristics are almost totally submerged.

Amongst the earliest species, the gallica rose, *Rosa gallica*, is believed to be the parent from which all European garden roses are descended. At some stage, *R. gallica* was crossed with another species to produce *R. damascena*, and this was probably brought to England from the Damascus region of Syria by the early Crusaders.

But at the end of the 15th century, records show that only 14 kinds of rose were being grown in England and for the next 200 years there were no important innovations.

By this time there were several forms or varieties of the original species but none had been created artificially. They originated as 'sports', which are chance offshoots

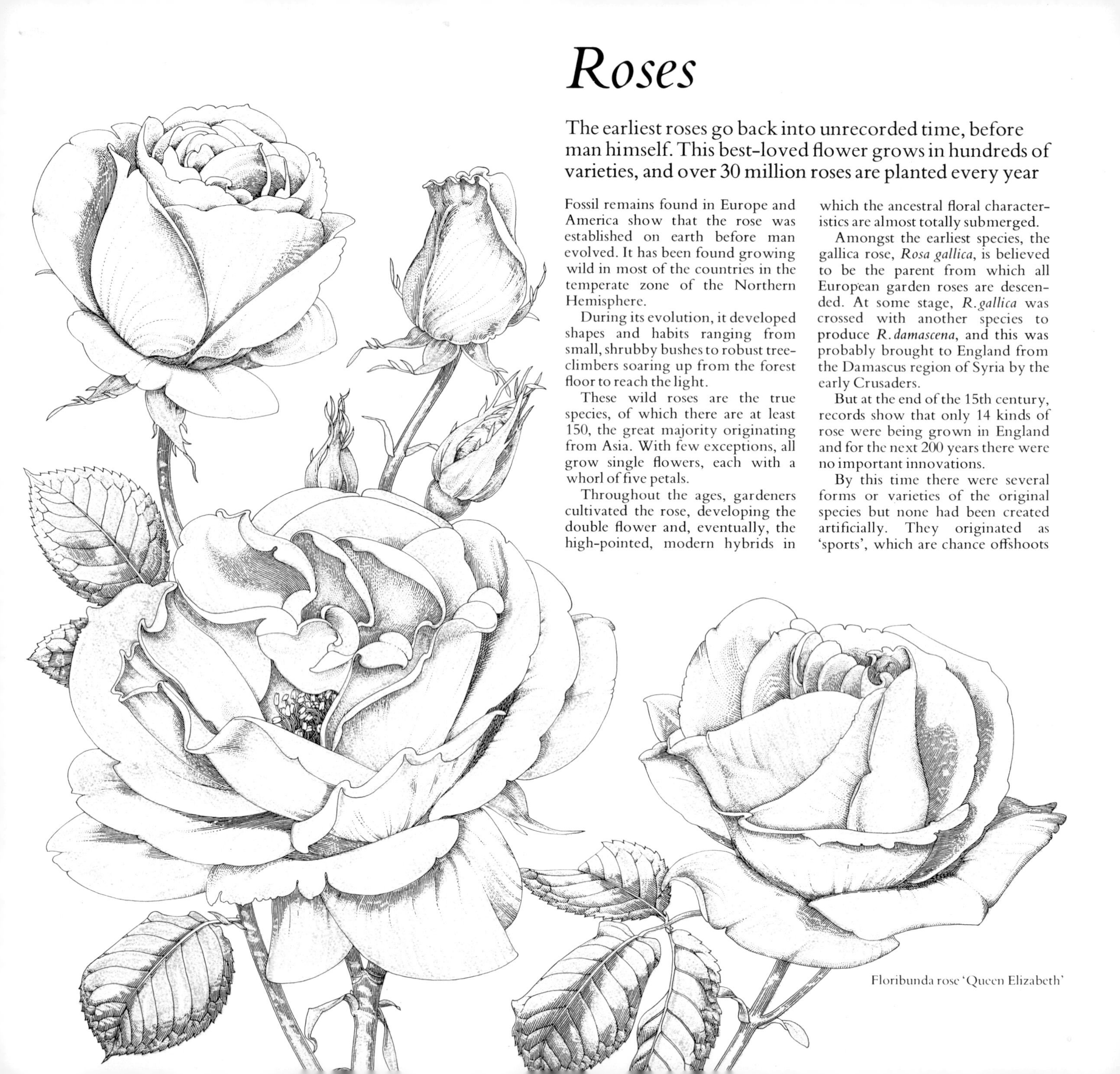

Floribunda rose 'Queen Elizabeth'

different from the flower of the parent rose. For example, a pink flower might appear on a rose usually bearing white blooms. These sports were propagated by grafting, budding or cuttings – all quite ancient skills – and became new varieties or cultivars.

It was the arrival in Europe of the China rose, at the end of the 18th century, which changed the course of rose history. By now gardeners had learned how to breed roses, and from crossing the old with the new, tea roses and hybrid perpetuals were developed. These were dominant in gardens until the end of the 19th century.

The hybrid tea roses, probably the most popular with gardeners, are a fairly recent development, not being grown very widely in this country until after the First World War. They were developed in France at the end of the 19th century – the result of crossing tea roses with hybrid perpetuals.

A little later, and also from France, came polyantha-pompons, which were produced from the Japanese *R. multiflora* crossed with a China rose. These in turn led to the floribunda roses so popular today.

Many Old roses (hybrids of original species) also came from France. Empress Josephine made them fashionable with a rose garden of all the species and varieties available at the time.

As roses became more highly bred, their use in gardens became more formal. During the 19th century it became fashionable to separate roses from other plants, and plant them in geometric formal beds of their own. Often, only roses of one variety would be grown in each bed.

Although roses are still often grown on their own, there is now a move back to a more natural style of rose growing, for two reasons. Firstly, the segregated rose bed is dead space for at least five months of the year, and contributes nothing to the garden. Secondly, the bare soil around the roses produces many more weeds than soil that is covered with other plants.

To a modern eye, many roses look far better when treated in a freehand style – in particular the species roses, the Old roses and many of the modern floribundas.

Mixing roses and other plants

Roses can be mixed with other shrubs or herbaceous perennials, placed individually in a chosen position, or used to fill a corner, flank a doorway or adorn a house wall. For instance, tall, arching modern shrub roses like 'Nevada', 'Frühlingsgold' and the species *R. moyesii* look splendid behind a bank of hydrangeas or other shrubs of moderate size, or behind some of the hybrid teas or floribundas.

When mixing roses, or growing them among other plants, keep in mind the size and flowering seasons of the plants in the mixture. If hybrid teas and floribundas are grown, make sure that short varieties will not become hidden by the larger ones such as 'Queen Elizabeth', 'Sutter's Gold', 'Fred Gibson', or 'Fragrant Cloud'. The nursery catalogues should give the ultimate height of the plant.

Floribundas are ideal roses to mix with other plants – to create a fine visual effect, to prolong the flowering season, or to fill gaps in the flowering period.

They merge well with dwarf azaleas, which they follow in flowering, or with any small shrubs. Floribundas are the best roses to mingle in a herbaceous border, covering gaps after the delphiniums have been cut down, or filling blank spaces before the autumn display.

Dedicated rose growers usually frown on mixing hybrid teas with any other kind of plant. However, many gardeners will find the appearance of the garden greatly improved if they conceal the inelegant legs of their hybrid teas with various other low-growing plants.

Ground-cover for the rose beds

The following low-growing plants may help to keep down weeds as well as looking attractive.

Blue violas are especially good for growing beneath hybrid teas – in particular the dense, bushy types such as *Viola gracilis* and *V.* × *williamsii*, also known as violetta.

An even better weed suppressor is the Labrador violet, *V. labradorica*, which spreads by both underground runners and seed. Its purple-tinted foliage quickly provides a dense and attractive carpet.

Other good ground-cover plants are the small, bright blue speedwell, *Veronica prostrata* (synonymous with *V. rupestris*), the annual lobelias and ageratums, and the dwarf, herbaceous types of potentilla (*Potentilla verna* and *P. tonguei* for example), which flower continuously from June to September.

The numerous dwarf, hardy geraniums (crane's-bill) all make good decorative cover that is not excessively invasive. Among them are the Lancaster crane's-bill, *Geranium sanguineum lancastriense*, the Dalmatian geranium, *G. dalmaticum*, and the Balkan, *G. cinereum subcaulescens*.

A few dwarf shrubs also provide good cover around the feet of

Blue violas grown beneath hybrid tea roses not only look attractive but also help to suppress weeds and conceal the bare, lower stems of the roses

hybrid teas, such as *Gaultheria procumbens* (if the soil is acid) and the grey-leaved *Hebe pinguifolia* 'Pagei'. Care must be taken not to damage these woody evergreens when walking between the roses.

The Old roses flower for only four weeks in June and July and are fairly drab for the rest of the season. They can be mixed with other flowering shrubs, or with herbaceous perennials which will provide colour and interest at other times of the year.

As Old roses tend to be taller than hybrid teas, larger perennials can be grown beneath them. Hostas are a good choice, particularly those with variegated or blue-tinted foliage. Lilies, in many glowing colours, add their splendour for a short spell. The larger, hardy geraniums will also clothe the legs of Old roses.

The beautiful *Aster × frikartii* gives a long season of blue-and-gold daisies. The blue orbs of agapanthus, the slim spires of *Campanula persicifolia*, the mauve, shrub-like *Salvia superba*, oenotheras of any kind, and the myriad white stars of gypsophila – all make excellent successors to the Old roses. The roses can be preceded in spring by a display of primulas, columbines (aquilegia), anemones and hellebores.

Roses for hedges Several types of roses make fine floral hedges, though they are bare in winter. Compared with the usual hedging plants, they occupy a lot of space laterally, except for floribundas.

Good results can be obtained by planting them only slightly closer together than normal and pruning them lightly.

The best all-rounders are the rugosa roses (Old roses), because of their dense foliage. Most of them have a long flowering period. The royal purple 'Roseraie de l'Hay', the white 'Blanc Double de Coubert' and the single mauve 'Scabrosa' make fairly tall hedges. The hybrid white 'Schneezwerg' ('Snow Dwarf') makes a good 4 ft high hedge.

For lower hedges (but with a shorter flowering period), the most dramatic patterns are made by a few of the very old gallica roses – especially the popular, crimson and white-streaked 'Rosa Mundi' (*R. gallica* 'Versicolor'), which can be trimmed with garden shears.

The thorny Scotch rose, *R. spinosissima*, makes a very efficient barrier against animals. The variety 'Stanwell Perpetual' grows to 6 ft with masses of scented pink flowers.

The smaller spinosissima roses give thick, low hedges, like *R.s. lutea*, which will grow to 4 ft, and the old 'Double Yellow', 'Double White' and 'William III', all about 2 ft.

Among climbing roses, 'New Dawn' makes an excellent dense hedge. When regularly pruned, it behaves as a shrub rose. It is well branched and strong, and is covered almost continuously with blush-pink, sweetly scented flowers. It will easily grow to a height of 7 ft and requires only regular clipping to keep it in shape.

The white, scented floribunda 'Iceberg' makes a fine hedge up to 5 ft or more. 'Dorothy Wheatcroft' is equally good, with red flowers.

The floribunda 'Queen Elizabeth' makes a good hedging rose. Planted at 2 ft intervals and trimmed in winter or early spring it will grow to 6 or 8 ft high.

For a shorter, thicker hedge, cut the plants back to 18 in. from the ground every winter.

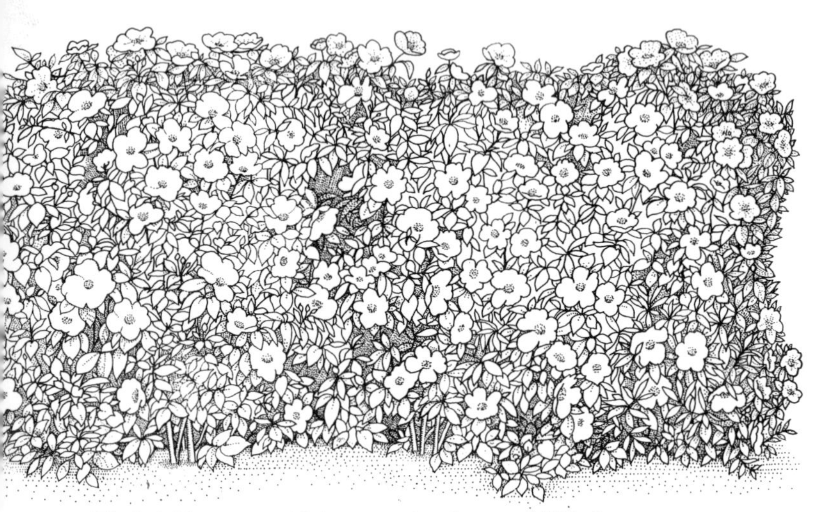

The hybrid rugosa rose 'Schneezwerg' makes a good 4 ft hedge

Roses to provide ground-cover A few roses hug the ground closely and are excellent for clothing bare earth and, when established, suppressing weeds. They can also be used to cover awkward banks where other plants would be difficult to cultivate.

The best roses for ground-cover include 'Max Graf', a rugosa hybrid with scented flowers like a large dog rose. It flowers around midsummer and spreads widely, taking root as it goes. An even wider spread is provided by *R. × paulii*, which is white, and its deep pink sport 'Rosea'. Both of these provide a spectacular mass of blooms in June.

'Raubritter', a hybrid of the species rose *R. macrantha*, is less prostrate, and builds up to a mound, with its arching stems covered in pink flowers during July and August.

'King's Ransom', a hybrid tea rose grown as a standard

R. wichuraiana, which is quite flat, may extend to 20 ft in length; it carries scented, creamy-white flowers in August.

The standard rose Standard roses have a slim, erect, bare stem, on top of which roses of various breeds may be budded – usually hybrid teas or floribundas. They add formal elegance to the rose garden.

Standard roses are normally about $3\frac{1}{2}$ ft high, plus their top growth. There are also half-standards, which are slightly shorter than the full standard rose.

Weeping standards have a stem of 5–6 ft and are budded with one of the flexible rambler roses, which hang down to the ground.

THE SEVEN TYPES OF ROSE

Species roses All wild roses, as well as hybrids between two wild roses of different types, are grouped as species roses.

A species rose usually has a single flower of five petals only, though some double forms do occur. Most flower for a short period during May, June or July.

Popular species: *R. moyesii* (red), *R. primula* (yellow), *R. rugosa* (pink).

Old roses Outstanding for their fragrance, most Old roses have double flowers with many more petals than the species roses. They were bred from sports (mutants) or hybrids of species, and were highly popular before the introduction of the hybrid tea roses.

Old roses include the albas, Bourbons, Chinas, damasks, dwarf polyanthas, gallicas, the hybrid musks, hybrid perpetuals, hybrid rugosas, hybrid sweetbriars, moss, Portland, Provence or cabbage, and Scotch roses.

The flowering season is generally in June and July.

Hybrid teas These are the successors to the hybrid perpetuals of the Old rose section. They produce flowers freely between June and October, and are excellent for cutting. The flowers measure 4–6 in. across and are generally double. They have high-pointed centres and many are richly scented.

Popular varieties: 'Fragrant Cloud' (red), 'Fred Gibson' (orange), 'King's Ransom' (yellow), 'Peace' (pale yellow) and 'Super Star' (red).

Floribunda roses The modern floribunda roses have large clusters of flowers, smaller than hybrid teas.

The flowers may be single, semi-double or double and bloom from June till October. A few are fragrant.

Floribunda roses are basically a cross between dwarf polyanthas and the early hybrid teas.

Popular varieties: 'Allgold' (yellow), 'Elizabeth of Glamis' (orange-pink), 'Goldgleam' (yellow), 'Iceberg' (white) and 'Masquerade' (gold and flame).

Modern shrub roses These are chiefly hybrids between species roses and Old roses. They are bushy plants, reaching an average height and spread of 6 ft. The flowers are 2–4 in. wide, single or double. They are generally repeat flowering, and bloom from June to September.

Popular varieties: 'Chinatown' (yellow), 'Fred Loads' (red), 'Fritz Nobis' (pink), 'Frühlingsmorgen' (pink and yellow), 'Cocktail' (red and yellow) and 'Nevada' (white).

Climbing and rambling roses There is a vast range of ascending roses – some of which are descendants of the true climbing species, while others are sports of hybrid teas or floribundas.

Several climbers are very vigorous, and will climb 20–50 ft through old trees or up house walls. Single, fragrant flowers are carried in June and July.

The less-vigorous climbers, which grow from 10 to 15 ft, are ideal for pillars, fences and screens. Flowers, basically of the hybrid tea type, are borne from June to July.

Popular varieties: 'Bantry Bay' (pink), 'Danse du Feu' (red), 'Golden Showers' (yellow), 'New Dawn' (pink) and 'Schoolgirl' (orange).

Ramblers are supple-stemmed compared with climbers. They are best-suited to pergolas and pillars. On walls, they are prone to mildew.

With few exceptions, they all flower on long, flexible canes grown the previous year. Large trusses of single, semi-double or double flowers form in June and July.

Popular varieties: 'Albertine' (pink), 'Dorothy Perkins' (pink), 'Easlea's Golden Rambler' (yellow) and 'Excelsior' (crimson).

Miniature roses These are roses that average 6–12 in. in height and are almost thornless. The $\frac{3}{4}$–$1\frac{1}{2}$ in. diameter flowers – semi-double or double – are carried in June and July. Many are repeat flowering. A few climbing varieties are available.

Popular varieties: 'Baby Masquerade' (flame and gold), 'New Penny' (orange), 'Perla de Montserrat' (pink) and 'Yellow Doll' (yellow).

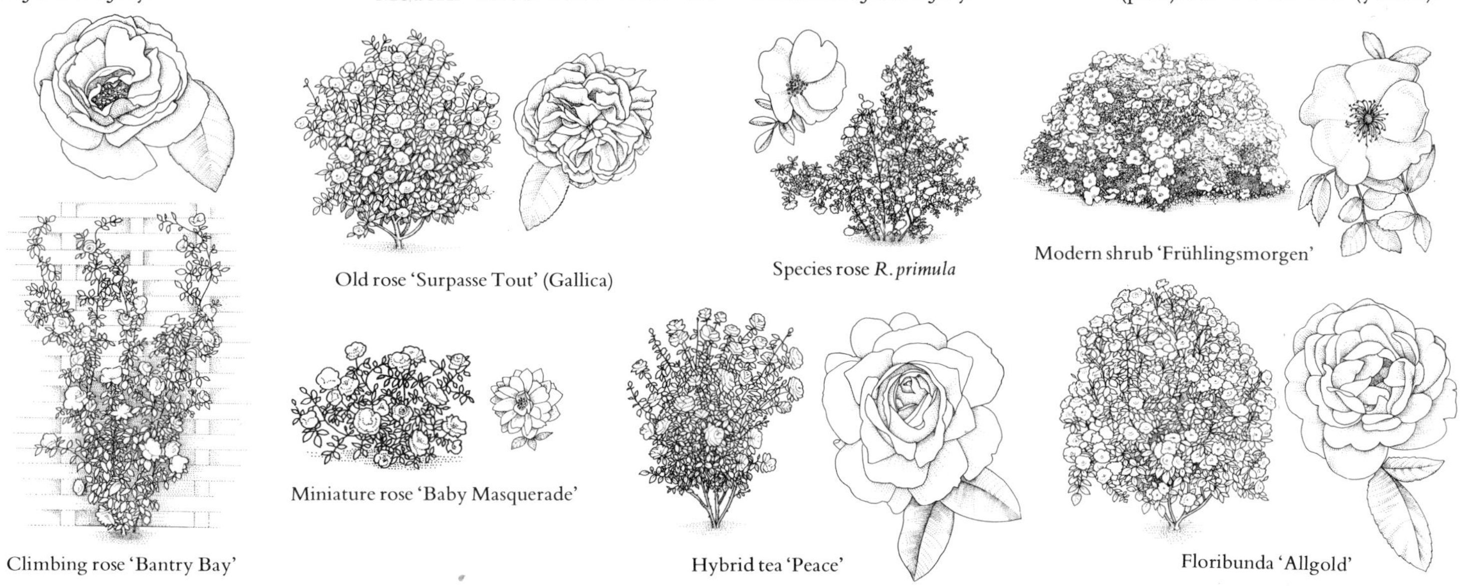

Old rose 'Surpasse Tout' (Gallica)

Species rose *R. primula*

Modern shrub 'Frühlingsmorgen'

Miniature rose 'Baby Masquerade'

Climbing rose 'Bantry Bay'

Hybrid tea 'Peace'

Floribunda 'Allgold'

Step-by-step guide to rose planting

Creating the conditions roses like best

Roses will grow in a wide variety of soils and situations, and they will survive in even the most unfavourable conditions. But, ideally, they prefer an open, sunny situation, combined with a fairly rich, loamy, slightly acid soil. Clay, if well broken up, is excellent. Drainage must be free, though roses need ample watering either by rain or by sprinkler.

Soils become rose sick, so avoid planting roses in beds where other roses have been growing for more than about ten years. If this is unavoidable, import fresh soil or, in the summer before planting, sow the bed with rape or annual lupins and dig them in before they flower. Once planted, roses will survive happily in the same bed for many years if the ground is regularly mulched and fed.

Dig the ground to a spade's depth at least a month before planting the roses. If the ground has a tendency to become waterlogged it should be double dug (p. 405). Dig in 3–4 in. of animal manure, garden compost or leaf-mould. When doing this, do not break up the lumps of soil too much and do not tread the soil in after turning it over. This will keep it loose and allow air to circulate through it.

Chalk and sandy soils need particularly large quantities of organic matter. Chopped-up turf is good, as it will rot down into humus quite quickly and the nutrients will not be leached out of the soil as rapidly as manure. Repeated top-dressings of manure or garden compost are needed in chalk and sand.

If the soil is very light, blend the top 6–10 in. with a bucket of peat and a double handful of general-purpose fertiliser to every square yard. It is also worth forking well-rotted manure into the sub-soil.

Rake the bed to a level mound, but do not tread on it, as this will compact the soil.

When to plant The best time to plant roses is from about the middle of October to the end of November – the earlier the better in the North. They can, however, be planted any time up to the end of March if the weather is free from frost. A little surface frost is acceptable, but do not plant if the ground is frozen hard and deep, or if it is waterlogged. In areas of high rainfall, it is often best to plant in spring.

If the plants arrive during a hard spell of frost, and they are packed in sacking, put them in a garage or shed. Partially open the bundle and water the roots and stems occasionally. If they are packed in a polythene bag, put some damp peat in it to cover the roots.

Though roses can usually be left in their packing for up to ten days, it is better to plant them at once, if conditions are right, or at least to bury the roots in a shallow trench and water them well. They will then be safe indefinitely.

Plants bought in containers from garden centres can be planted at any time of the year — provided the ground is not frosty or waterlogged.

The planting mixture First, prepare a planting mixture consisting of two spadefuls of peat to one spadeful of natural soil and one large handful of sterilised bonemeal.

Next, mark out the positions of the roses in the bed (see below). Place pegs at the correct distances for each type.

Planting distances Plant each rose not less than 15 in. from any path or lawn. The distance between each plant for each type is:

Miniatures, 12 in.

Standards, not less than 3 ft.

Hybrid tea and floribunda bushes of moderate growth, 18 in.; those of stronger growth, 2 ft or more; 'Queen Elizabeth', at least 4 ft.

Shrub roses, 5 ft.

Climbers and ramblers, at least 7 ft.

Preparing the roses before planting

When you are ready to plant, bring the roses out a few at a time. If there is a cold, drying wind, cover the roots with a sack.

If the roots seem at all dry, make a mud puddle and swill them in it.

If the stems are dry and shrivelled, the plants may recover after total immersion in water. If not, return them and ask for replacements.

Using sharp secateurs, cut out all dead wood. Cut off any flower buds, leaves and weak or damaged shoots left on by the nursery.

Check that each stem is pruned back to just above an outward-facing eye or incipient bud, or die-back will occur in the stem.

Trim back any excessively long roots with secateurs to about 10 in.

Cut away any thick, coarse root that appears to be an old tap root. Trim back any damaged roots to a point just above the damage. Preserve the thin, fibrous roots.

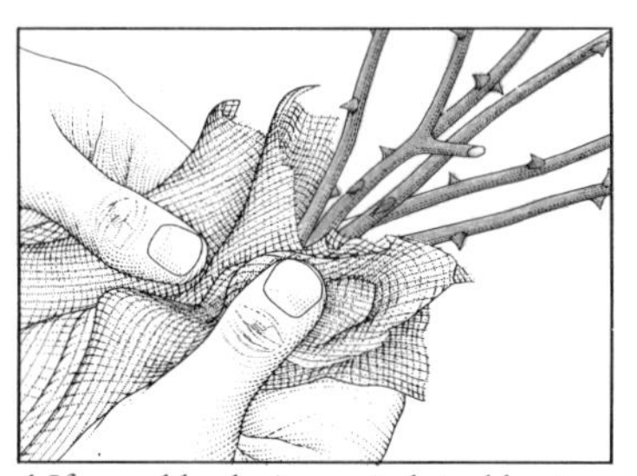

1 *If a cold, drying wind is blowing, protect the roots with sacking*

2 *If roots seem dry, make a mud puddle and swill them in it*

3 *Cut off dead stems, flower buds, leaves and weak or damaged shoots*

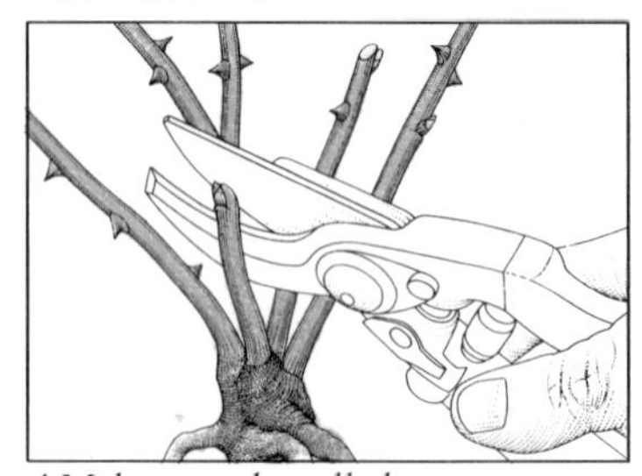

4 *Make sure that all the stems are cut back to an outward-facing bud*

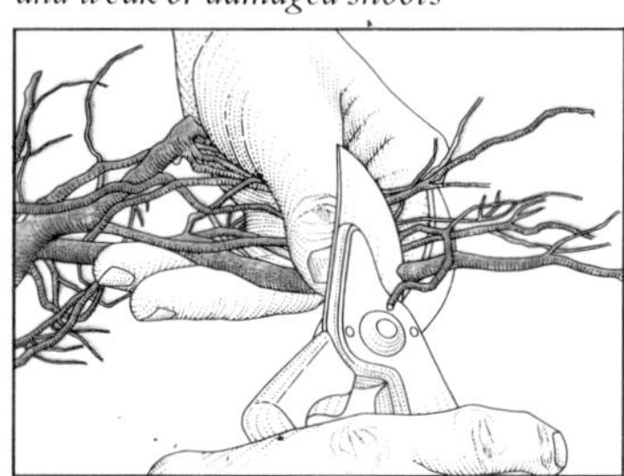

5 *Trim back any long or damaged roots to about 10 in.*

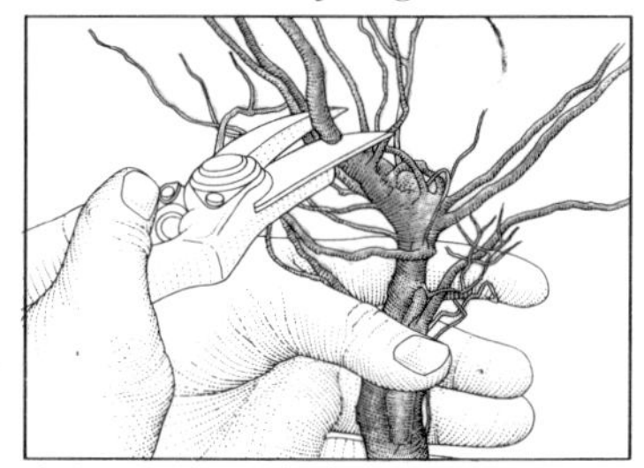

6 *Cut out any thick, coarse root which appears to be an old tap root*

Shaping the hole to fit the roots

Dig a hole to fit the natural shape of the roots. If they spread out in all directions, the hole will need to be about 2 ft in diameter and 10 in. deep, with a mound at its centre.

If, as is most common, the nurseryman has laid in his stocks so that the roots all run more or less in one direction, make the hole in the shape of an open fan about 12 in. long. It should be about 4–5 in. deep at the handle of the fan, where the main stem will be placed, and 6–8 in. deep at its outer edge.

Spread the prepared planting mixture about 1 in. deep over the bottom of the hole, before inserting the roots. Lay a cane across the hole to mark the natural level of the soil, and use this to judge the correct planting depth.

BEFORE AND AFTER PLANTING THE ROSE

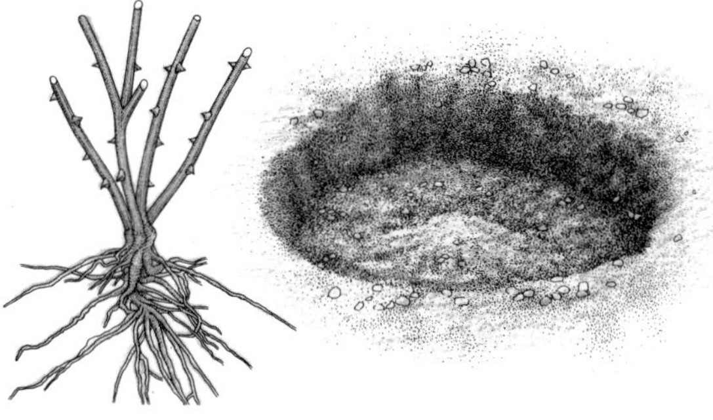

Digging the hole *If the roots spread out in all directions from the main stem, dig a round hole about 2 ft in diameter and 10 in. deep. If the roots run in one direction, make the hole fan-shaped and slightly shallower*

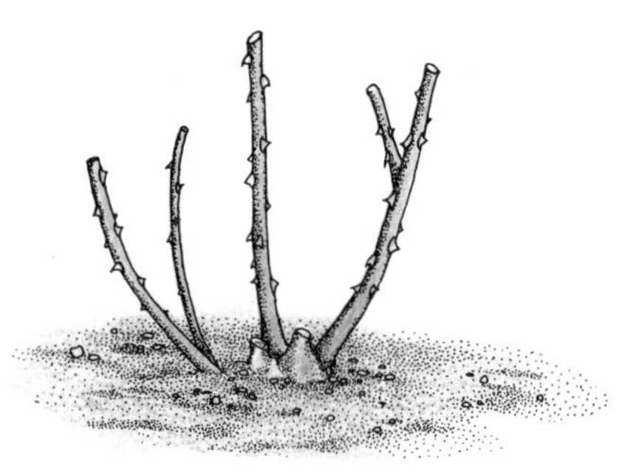

Planting the rose *Spread the prepared planting mixture about 1 in. deep in the hole before spreading out the roots. After the earth has been filled in, the stem of the rose should be buried to its original depth*

Planting bush roses at the right depth

In heavy soil, plant so that the union between rootstock and branches is level with the surface of the bed. In light soil, plant the union about 2–3 in. below the surface. This will help to conserve moisture round the shoots (as light soil is less retentive) when they start to grow.

Spread out the roots as much as possible in the hole, and try to prevent them crossing each other by combing them out with the fingers. They should not be coiled around

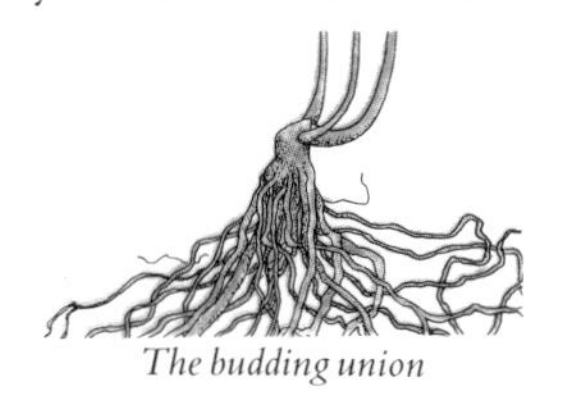

The budding union

the circumference of the hole. If necessary, extend the diameter of the hole so that the roots can run straight. Add more planting mixture round the roots, and then partially fill the hole with natural soil.

Move the rose gently up and down to make sure that the mixture and the soil fill the root space completely, eliminating any air pockets. Check that the union is at the correct level. It is a mistake to plant too deeply.

Firm the soil round the roots (lightly in heavy soils and fairly firmly in light soils), treading down the soil with the toe to avoid compacting it too much. Tread round the hole, working towards the centre. This will avoid upsetting the level of the plant in the hole.

Fill up the hole with more natural soil. Do not tread a second time, unless it is necessary to make sure the union is firmly set in the ground. Finally, label the rose.

Watering in should not be necessary if the bush is planted between October and March. However, if the soil is very dry it should be soaked before the rose is planted.

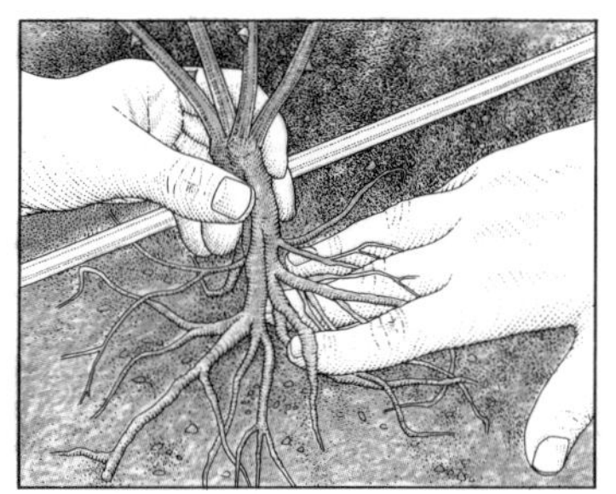

1 *Mark the soil level with a cane. Hold the rose so that the union is at soil level*

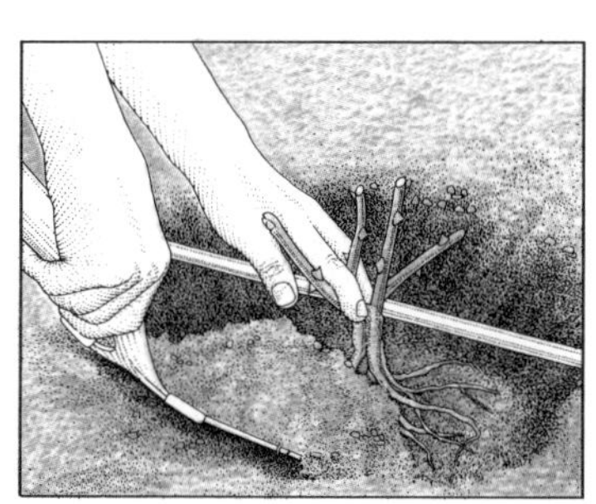

2 *Put some planting mixture over the roots, then partially fill with soil*

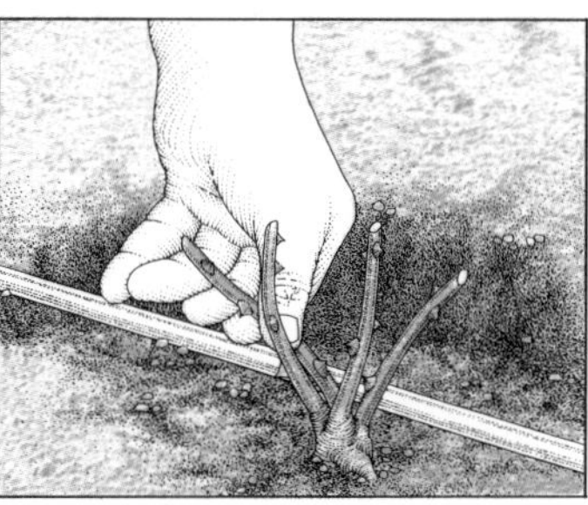

3 *Move the plant up and down to make sure the soil fills the root space*

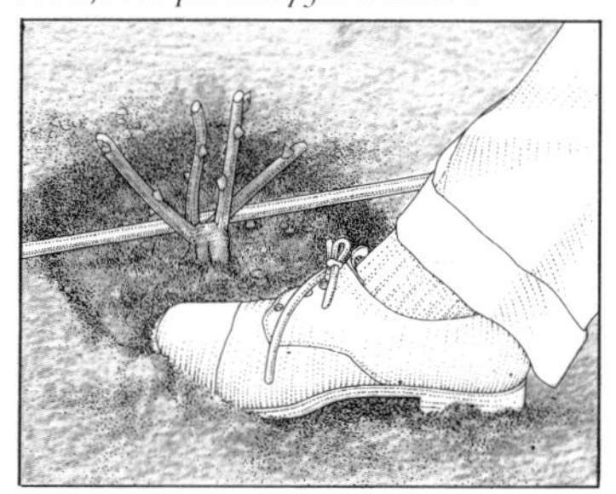

4 *Tread the soil round the roots and, finally, fill the hole*

Planting and staking a standard rose

As with bush roses, trim off any long roots with secateurs, so that the root system is of a fairly even length – 10–12 in. Cut back damaged roots.

If the stem is matted with many small thorns, the rose will have been budded on to a *Rosa rugosa* stock, and this will usually have two or more layers of roots. Retain the basal roots, and cut off the upper layers of roots close to the stem.

Cut off any leaves and flower buds, and remove weak shoots and wood that has died back.

Trim branches to just above an outward-facing eye.

Standards must be staked. Use a 1 in. by 1 in. stake and cut it to allow 2 ft below the ground, and about 6 in. above the union to allow for future growth. Paint the section to be buried with wood preservative, one or two days before planting.

Dig a hole about 12–15 in. in diameter. Sharpen one end of the stake and hammer it firmly into the ground, in the middle of the hole, up to the 2 ft mark.

Trees that have been budded on to the common briar – a relatively smooth stem with few or no thorns – should be planted with the root tips about 6–8 in. deep. Those budded on to the thorny rugosa should have their roots about 4 in. deep. Spread about 1 in. of planting mixture in the hole.

Place the rose against the stake, as close and as straight as possible. The point at which the stem grows out of the roots should be level with the surface of the soil. Spread the roots out well all round the hole.

Either hold the standard firmly in position against the stake, or tie it temporarily while covering the roots with planting mixture. Move the standard up and down slightly to allow soil to fill the root spaces.

Partially fill the hole with natural soil and gently firm with the toe. Add more natural soil to fill the hole completely, but do not firm.

Secure the standard to the stake with rubber or plastic ties, which can be bought from garden centres.

Alternatively, tie with garden twine, but bind sacking round the stake to act as a buffer. Watch out for pests wintering in these ties – red spider is a common one.

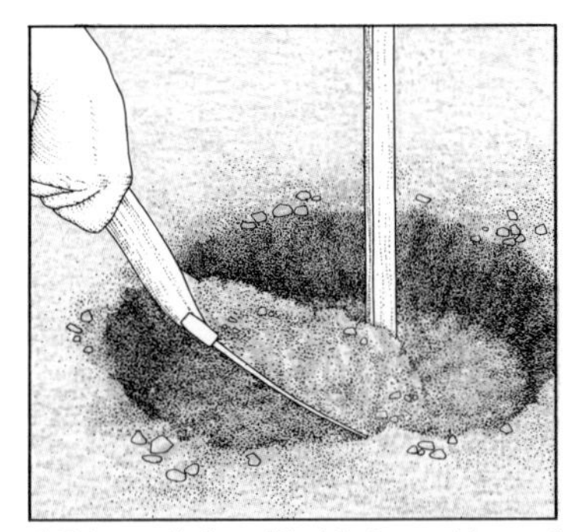

1 *Dig a hole, 12–15 in. wide and hammer in stake. Add planting mixture*

2 *Hold the rose upright. Spread roots out, and cover with planting mixture*

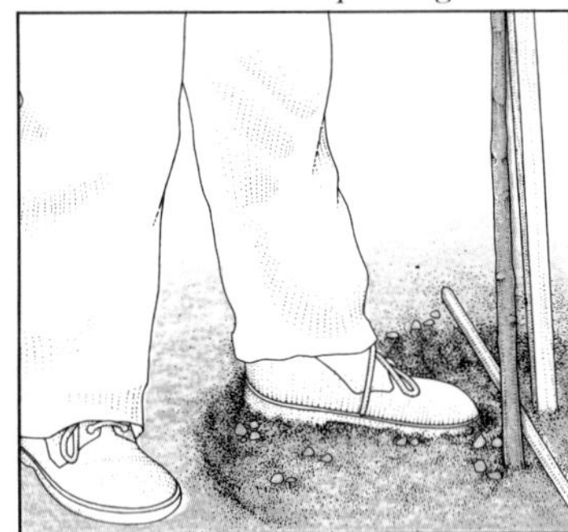

3 *Partially fill the hole with soil and gently firm with the toe. Top up with soil*

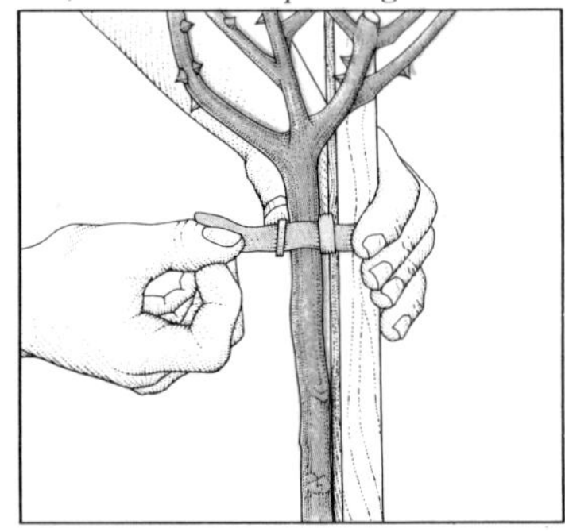

4 *Secure standard to stake with rubber tie, or sacking and twine*

Planting climbers against a wall

The basic planting method is the same as for bush roses.

Where the rose is to be trained against a wall, fix wires horizontally at 15 in. intervals on the wall. Use plastic-coated straining wire, stretched between two vine eyes and tightened with straining bolts.

Dig the hole for the roots at least 12 in. away from the wall. Spread the stems out fan-wise, so that when they grow they can be trained on to the wires.

There is usually more dead wood on young climbers than on bush or standard roses. This should be cut back to just above a bud point.

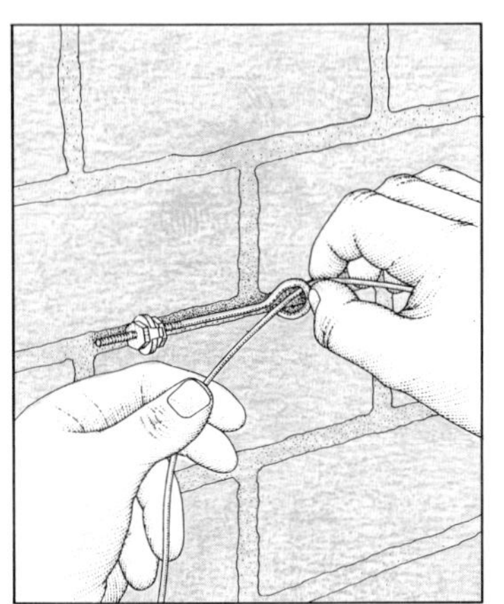

1 *Fix plastic-coated wire horizontally on the wall at 15 in. intervals*

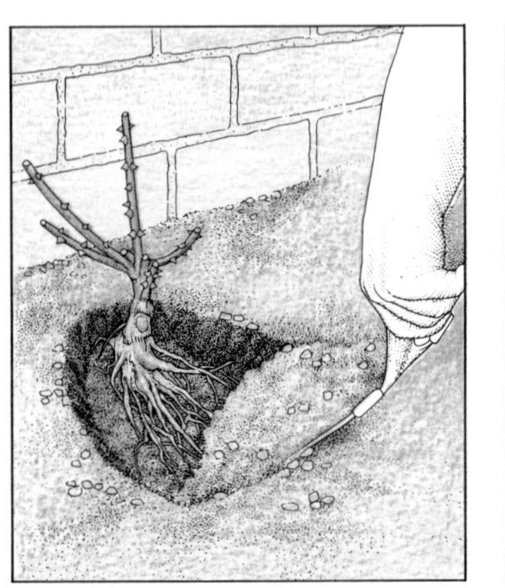

2 *Plant the rose 12 in. from wall, with roots pointing away from it*

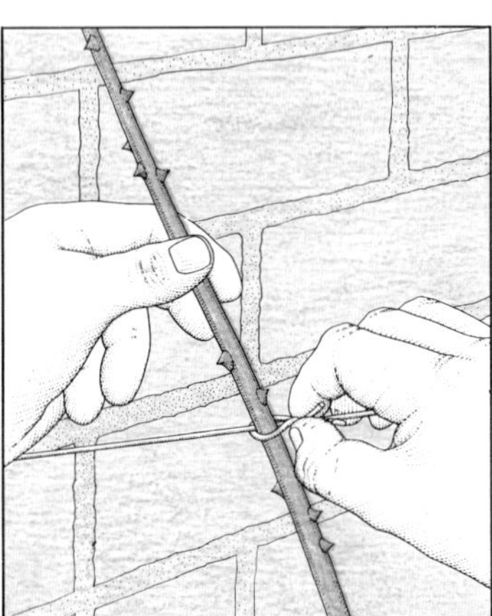

3 *As the stems grow, spread them out fan-wise and attach to the wires*

Propagating hybrid teas by budding

Preparing the rootstock and the bud wood

The best way of propagating hybrid tea roses is to graft an eye of a growth bud on to a wild rootstock.

The rootstock can be raised from seed (a slow process), from cuttings, or it may be bought in from specialist nurseries.

On fertile soil, the wild dog-rose, *R. canina*, is best. Before it is planted, the lateral stems can be removed and grown on as cuttings. Alternatively, use a variety of *R.multiflora* or *R.laxa*.

For standards, *R. rugosa* 'Hollandica' is the most favoured stock.

In November, plant the wild rootstocks in rows, 12 in. apart, the collar of each plant barely covered.

By July, the rootstocks will be ready for budding.

Select the bud wood from the variety to be propagated. Choose a strong, healthy stem with firm wood, about 12 in. long, on which the flowers have just faded.

To make it easier to handle, remove the thorns from the stem.

Remove the faded flowers by severing the stem just above a bud or leaf axil. Cut off the leaves, but leave about ½ in. of leaf stalk. Place the stem in a deep container full of water.

Now hold the stem of the rootstock to one side with your foot. Carefully dig out the soil on the other side, so that the top roots are completely exposed.

Wipe the collar of the stem above the roots perfectly clean.

Using a sharp knife, make a T-shaped cut about 1 in. long in the bark close to the roots.

Do not cut into the woody tissue below the bark. Cut the top of the T first, about ½ in. long, and then cut the tail slightly longer with an upward stroke to meet the top cut.

With the back of the knife blade, gently prise open the bark and fold it outwards.

PLANTING A ROOTSTOCK

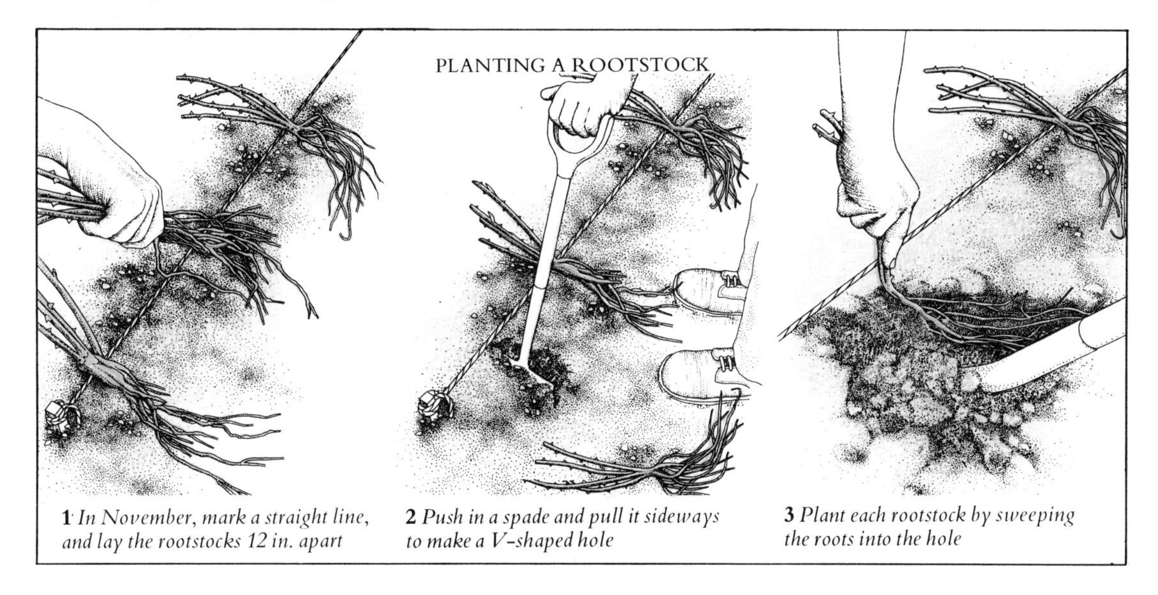

1 *In November, mark a straight line, and lay the rootstocks 12 in. apart*

2 *Push in a spade and pull it sideways to make a V-shaped hole*

3 *Plant each rootstock by sweeping the roots into the hole*

PREPARING THE BUD WOOD AND ROOTSTOCK

1 *In July, choose as bud wood a strong 12 in. stem from the rose to be propagated*

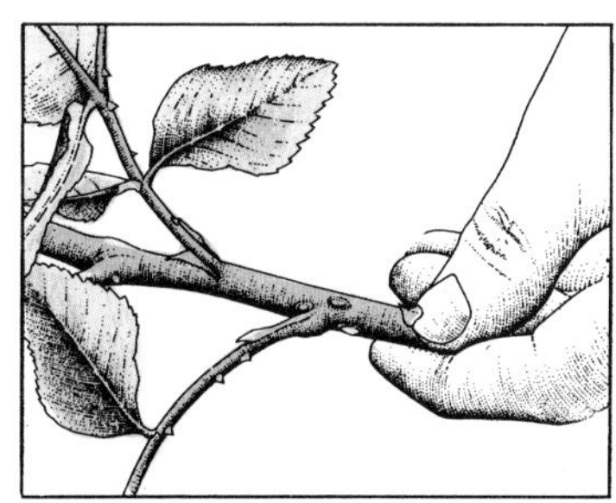

2 *Remove thorns from stem with sideways pressure of the thumb*

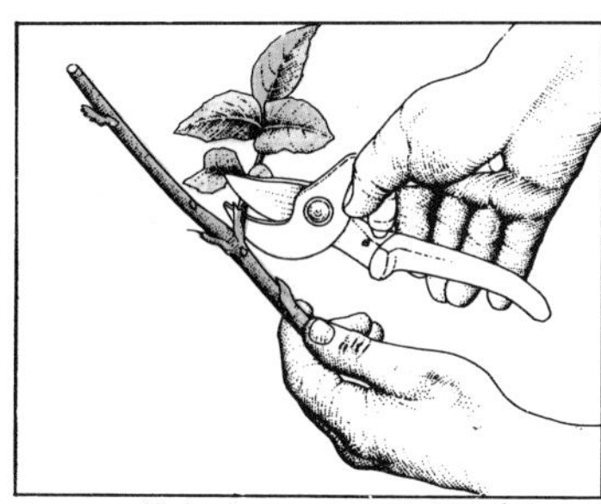

3 *Cut off the leaves, retaining ½ in. of the leaf stalk*

4 *Push the rootstock stem aside with your foot and remove soil*

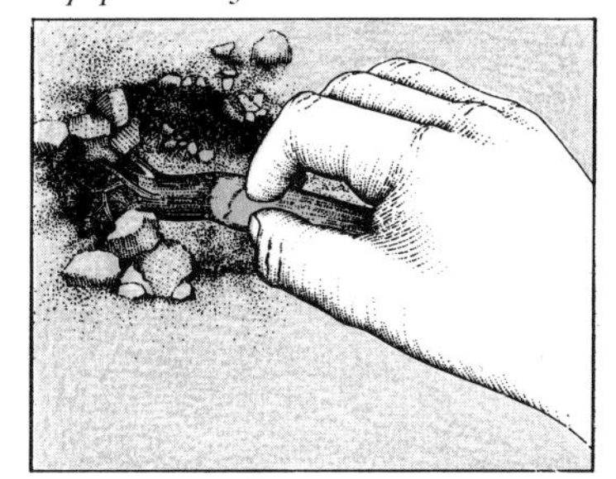

5 *Wipe clean the collar of the rootstock stem above the roots*

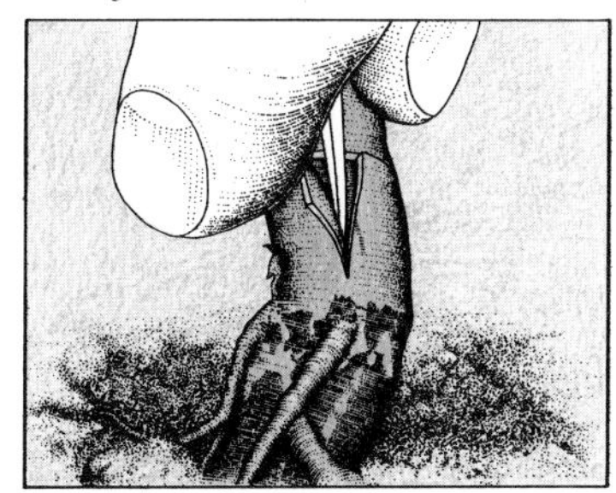

6 *Make a T-shaped cut in the bark of the rootstock and prise open the two flaps*

Arranging the marriage of bud and rootstock

Once the rootstock has been prepared with a T-shaped cut in the bark, remove the stick of bud wood from the water and slice out one of the eyes within a leaf axil.

Begin the cut ½ in. above the eye, draw the blade behind it, and come out ½ in. below it. Use a shallow scooping motion, so that a sliver of the wood behind the bark is also removed. This whole piece is called a 'shield'.

Hold the shield with one hand, and peel back the strip of bark until the sliver of wood sticks out well. Take this sliver between finger and thumb, ease it out smoothly from the bark with a slight overhead twist, and discard it.

If the sliver of wood has been satisfactorily removed, the embryo of the latent bud will appear as a tiny pimple on the inner side of the piece of shield.

Hold the piece of shield by the stump of the leaf stalk and slide it into the T-cut on the rootstock. Trim off the upper end of the inserted portion of shield. Close the flaps of the cut around the shield.

Tie the insert in place firmly, but not too tightly, with damp raffia, passing two turns below and three turns above the leaf-stalk stub. Knot the raffia on the opposite side of the stem to the bud.

If the tie is too tight, about three weeks later you will find a swelling has appeared below the bud. If this does happen, carefully cut a few strands of the raffia.

Finally, carefully put back the soil around the rootstock until it is level with the base of the grafted bud.

The sign of a successful budding is a patch of fresh green colour which appears on the stem of the rootstock.

About the middle of February, cut off all the top growth of the rootstock immediately above the new bud.

When the new growth is a few inches long, pinch it back to two buds from the grafting point to encourage further growth. Plant out the developed 'maiden' rose in its bed in autumn.

Standard roses can be created by grafting a hybrid tea on to the main stem of rugosa or of cultivated briars grown from seed or cuttings.

On hedgerow briars, the budding must be made on the upper sides of the young side-shoots, as close as possible to the main stem. Make two or three buddings on each briar.

BUDDING A STANDARD

Grow R. rugosa *or* R. canina *for a year until it reaches 2–3 ft for half-standards or 4–5 ft for standards. The following summer, bud on to the main stem or, preferably, on to the upper sides of three shoots at the top*

GRAFTING THE BUD ON TO THE ROOTSTOCK

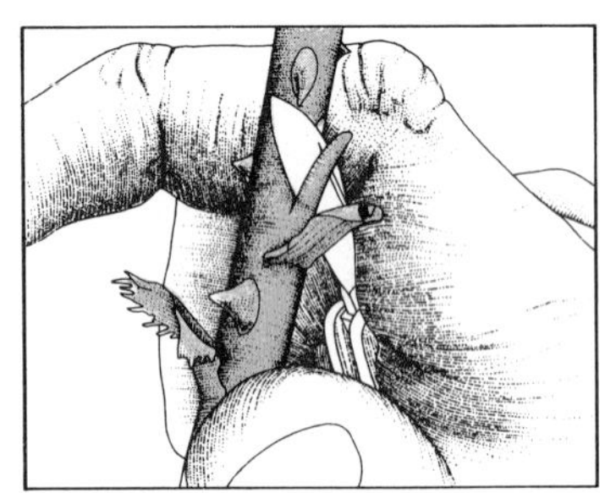

1 *Scoop an eye from the bud wood, beginning ½ in. above*

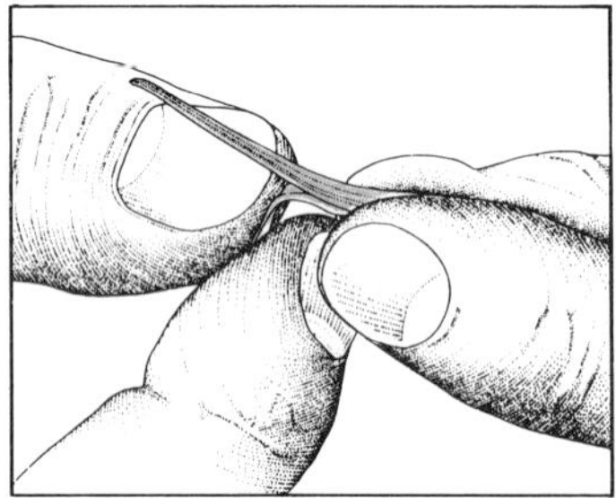

2 *Peel back the bark of the 'shield'; remove and discard sliver of wood*

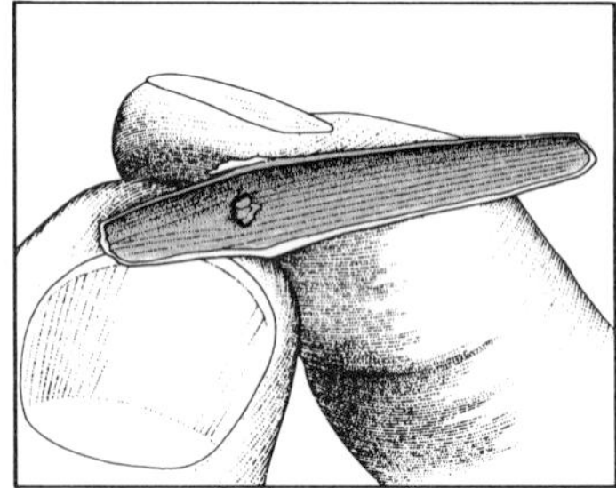

3 *Embryo of bud will appear as tiny pimple on inner side of the shield*

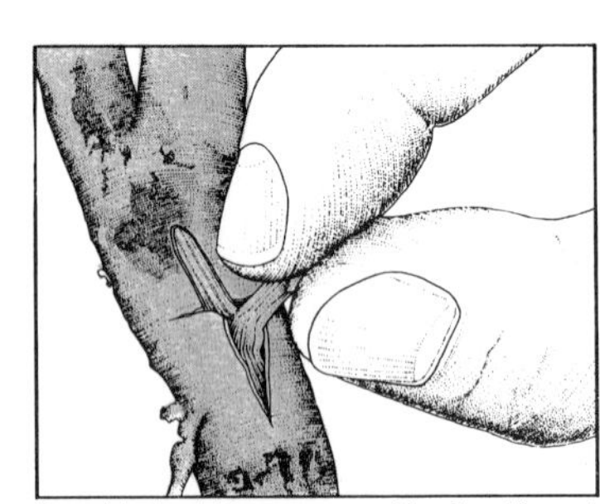

4 *Hold shield by stump of leaf stalk and slide it into the T-cut*

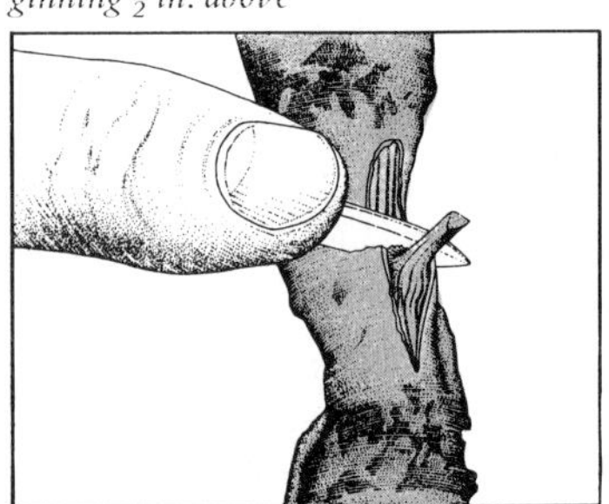

5 *Trim off upper end of the shield. Close the bark flaps around shield*

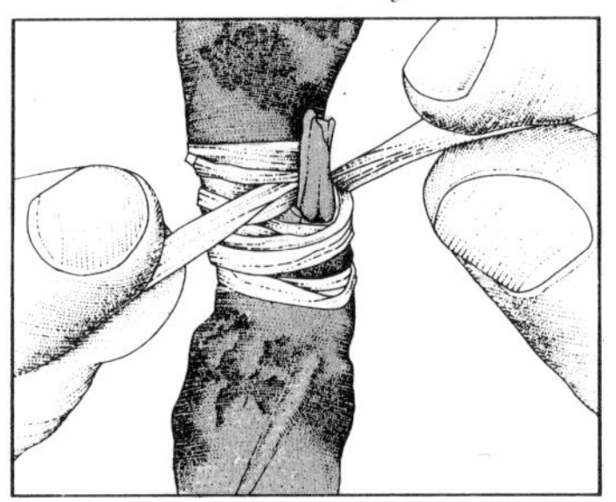

6 *Secure shield with raffia, knotted on the opposite side of the stem*

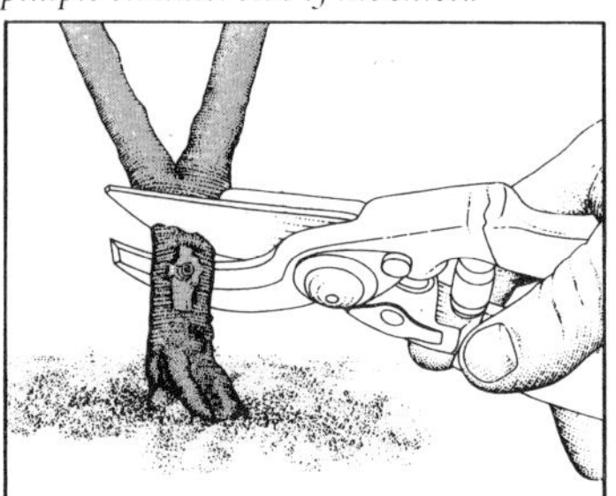

7 *In mid-February cut off top growth of rootstock, above the new bud*

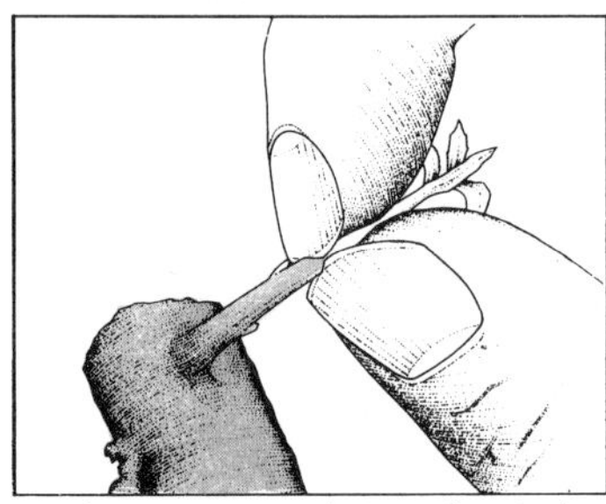

8 *When new growth is a few inches long, pinch back to two buds*

Looking after roses through the year

How to identify and remove suckers

From early May onwards, watch for shoots that come from below ground level, and also from the stems of standard roses.

These suckers grow from the rootstock below the point of union, and can usually be identified by their leaves and thorns, which are different from those of the cultivated scion. The sucker leaflets are narrower than those of the garden rose and its thorns are needle-like. It is commonly thought that suckers have seven leaflets on each leaf and that the scion has only five, but this is not always so.

The surest test is to trace the suspect growth to the point of origin which, if it is a sucker, will be below the union of rootstock and branches. Wrench the sucker off from the point of origin – this may be difficult to find if the root is deep. Never cut it, as this is merely a form of pruning, which will encourage more suckers to grow.

Dead-heading roses to encourage more flowers

As soon as hybrid tea blooms wither, cut them off with secateurs to a point just above a strong shoot or outward-facing bud. This will encourage a second flowering.

Many people simply cut back to the first leaf with five leaflets. But this may result in the loss of several potential flowering stems.

Towards the end of the season, dead-head more lightly – to the first bud below the flower – as young growth that will not harden before winter should be discouraged.

Finally, in autumn, cut off only the foot stalk of the flower.

With floribundas, dead-heading must be ruthless. There are no eyes on the bloom stems, so the whole truss must be cut back to the first eye below it. Seed heads should not be allowed to form unless the hips are wanted for decoration or seed and, even then, not until the rose is two years old.

Bush roses *Dig away soil, find junction and wrench sucker off*

Standard roses *Remove shoots on stem below grafting point*

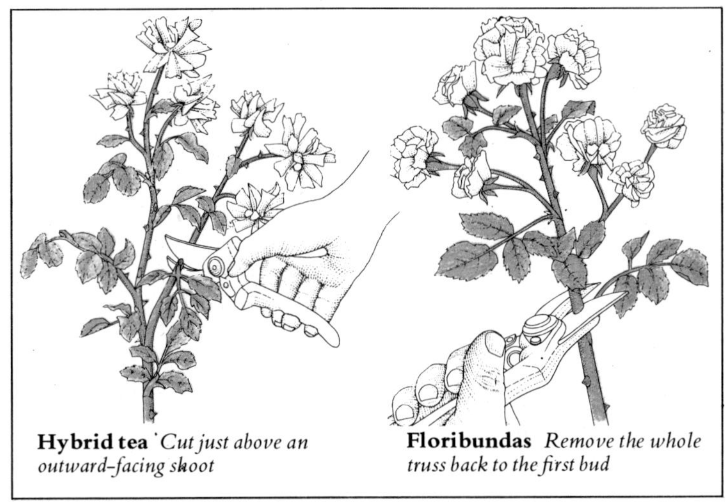

Hybrid tea *Cut just above an outward-facing shoot*

Floribundas *Remove the whole truss back to the first bud*

Creating larger blooms by disbudding

Some of the flower buds can be removed from hybrid teas, so that the remaining flowers grow larger.

As new stems develop on hybrid teas, clusters of side buds appear just below the central terminal bud. Nip out these side buds with the fingers, for a distance of about 6 in. below the terminal bud.

Some exhibitors remove the larger centre buds and the smallest buds from each cluster on floribunda roses, to achieve the same result.

For bigger blooms, pinch off buds just below the large one

When to water and spray roses

Watering is dictated by the weather and the nature of the soil. Sandy and chalky soils need abundant water. In other soils most roses, other than newly planted ones, will not suffer, even during a drought of two or three weeks.

Do not water roses when they are in full flower, unless a trickle irrigator can be used to apply the water only round the roots. Water will damage the blooms.

At other times, use a sprinkler that gives a fine, mist-like spray. Avoid drenching the plants heavily from coarse nozzles. Give a long and thorough wetting with the tap turned down low.

In early May, and again in July, spray your roses with a systemic insecticide which will protect them against most insects. To guard against fungus disease use a general-purpose fungicide designed for roses. Begin spraying in May and repeat every two or three weeks until September – July being the most important time. Spray the soil around them as well as the plants.

A simple feeding and mulching routine

In the first year after planting, roses should not be fed.

In all subsequent years the annual feeding routine begins in April.

Apply a 2–3 in. cover of animal or vegetable manure over the rose bed. This mulch conserves moisture, feeds the plants, improves the soil, and keeps down weeds.

Cow or horse manure is probably the best mulch, but it is untidy and contains weed seeds. Peat has many advantages, but it is expensive. Garden compost is usually the easiest mulch to obtain. In May, apply a proprietary rose fertiliser over the bed, according to the manufacturer's instructions. Blanket this with 2 in. of wet peat. Make sure the ground is moist before you lay the peat – all mulches should be applied on damp soil, to conserve moisture during dry spells in summer.

Early in July, apply more fertiliser to help the plants prepare for their second display of flowers.

In late August, apply sulphate of potash at 1 oz. to the square yard, to toughen stems before winter. Do this earlier in a wet season.

MULCHING

In April, apply a 2–3 in. mulch of well-rotted manure or peat

FEEDING

In May and early July, apply a fertiliser and cover with peat

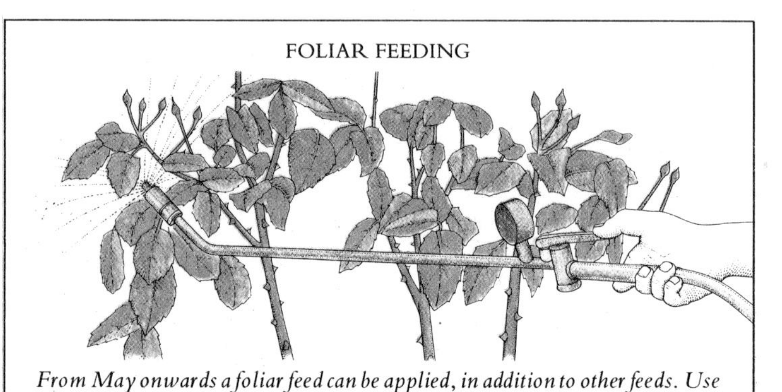

FOLIAR FEEDING

From May onwards a foliar feed can be applied, in addition to other feeds. Use a long-lanced spray, to ensure thorough cover of the tops and bottoms of the leaves. Foliar feeds can also be mixed with pesticides and fungicides for roses

What can go wrong with roses

If your plants show symptoms that are not described here, turn to the full-colour identification chart of pests and diseases starting on page 377. Look up chemicals on page 398, for a selection of trade names by which they can be bought.

Symptoms	**Cause**	**Cure**
Young shoots and flower buds covered with small, greenish, sticky insects. Severe attacks cause malformation of stems, leaves and buds	Aphids	Spray with dimethoate, formothion or malathion
Leaves and flower buds may be severely distorted, the leaves often having a tattered or holed appearance	Capsid bugs	Spray with HCH, malathion or diazinon
Leaves eaten, sometimes also rolled	Caterpillars of moths and sawflies	Spray with derris or trichlorphon
Leaves with a pale mottling. Severe attacks result in leaves yellowing and falling prematurely. Small, jumping and flying insects on the plant	Leaf hoppers	Spray with malathion or HCH
Flowers somewhat malformed, the petals covered with minute, elongated black insects – particularly in sheltered warm areas	Thrips	Spray with derris, malathion or dimethoate
Leaves and young shoots covered with a waxy-white powder and sometimes distorted	Mildew	Spray with dinocap or benomyl
Leaves with sooty irregular spots. A severe attack causes leaves to fall prematurely	Black spot	Spray with carbendazim, zineb or mancozeb
Shoots twisted or malformed and covered with an orange powder in spring or summer. Small yellow spots on the undersurfaces of leaves, which may fall prematurely	Rust	Not always easy to control properly, but spray with zineb or mancozeb at the first signs of attack
Shoot tips blackened or purplish, often slightly distorted patches on young leaves	Frost or cold winds	If this happens regularly, make sure final pruning is delayed until March so that young shoots are produced later
Leaves yellow and fall early, flowers are few and short-lived, general growth thin and poor	Starvation or drought, or a combination of both	Usually occurs on thin, gravelly soil or against walls sheltered from prevailing rain. Make sure the soil does not dry out, and mulch annually with well-decayed manure or garden compost plus a general proprietary rose fertiliser

Growing better roses by good pruning

When to prune and how to do it

The best time to prune roses, under average climatic conditions, is in January and February. If there is a prolonged spell of severe frost, wait until it has cleared before starting to prune the plants.

In colder areas, such as eastern Scotland, the usual pruning time is during April.

Exceptions to this rule are climbers, ramblers and weeping standards. Climbers are given a light pruning when they finish flowering, before the main pruning in winter. Ramblers are pruned in early autumn. Weeping standards (which are ramblers grafted on to tall stems) are also pruned in autumn.

Terms used in pruning roses A stem or branch of the current year's growth is called new wood. Hybrid teas, floribundas and most other modern roses flower on it.

Old wood is a stem of some previous year's growth. Ramblers and most climbers (except the climbing sports) flower on old wood, the shoots growing one year and bearing flowers the next.

An eye is a young or incipient growth bud, found in the axil of a leaf. In winter, it appears as a mere pin-head on a stem, from which a shoot may grow.

There are two types of bud. One is a growth bud (or eye, as above) from which a stem will form. The other is a flower bud.

The shoots by which the main stems of roses extend themselves are known as leaders. Laterals are stems that grow from a leader.

A snag is a dead stump resulting from a pruning cut being made too far above a bud, or too far from the junction of one limb with another.

How to make a pruning cut Use strong, sharp secateurs to cut the stem cleanly with no ragged edges. Cut no more than $\frac{1}{4}$ in. above an eye or growth bud. Angle the cut so that it slopes slightly back and away from the bud, to allow moisture to drain away.

The bud should face outwards to

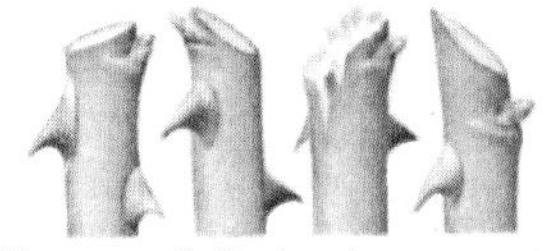

Correct cut (left); the others are wrong

allow growth to spread out from the centre, and keep the bush uncrowded. This applies to all roses except ramblers and climbers, which must be encouraged to grow along a support, and prostrate types, which are trained along the ground.

Do not cut too close to the bud, as it may be damaged. Alternatively, if the cut is made too high above the bud, the stem may die back.

If more than one growth bud develops at the same point after pruning, pinch out the weaker of the two. Do this carefully with your thumb nail or the point of a sharp knife.

When removing a complete stem, cut as close as possible to the parent stem with secateurs, then trim the stump flush with the stem, using a sharp knife.

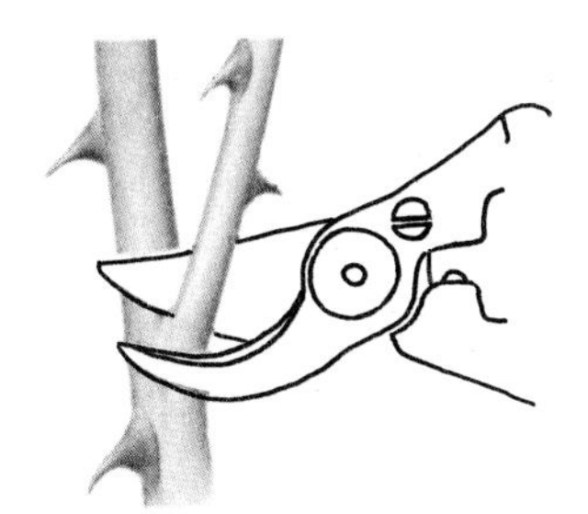

Remove whole stems flush with a branch

Do not try to cut thick stems with secateurs. Instead use long-handled 'loppers', and for old, hard wood use a narrow-bladed pruning saw. Saw cuts should be pared clean with a sharp knife.

Pruning newly planted roses

Bush and standard roses, if planted between mid-February and early March, must be pruned immediately. If they are planted in autumn, wait until spring.

With all newly planted roses, start by carrying out the first three steps of pruning shown on page 237, even if no pruning is recommended. Then treat each rose according to type.

Hybrid teas and hybrid perpetuals are cut back to buds about 4 in. from the ground.

Do the same with floribundas, but prune them to 5–6 in. above the ground. On short varieties, such as 'All Gold', prune rather lower. Prune dwarfs to 2–3 in.

Do not prune newly planted Old roses, because they flower on the wood produced in the previous season. Retain all available wood for the next year's flowers.

Climbers, ramblers and species roses and their hybrids also require no pruning in their first year, other than tipping the shoots by about 3 in. The same applies to modern shrub roses.

Cut polyanthas back by one-third in spring after planting, and prune miniature roses back to within 2 in. of the ground.

PRUNING A NEWLY PLANTED HYBRID TEA

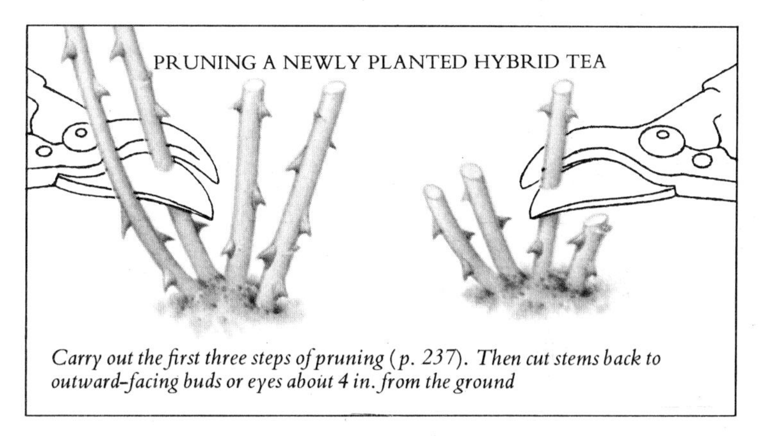

Carry out the first three steps of pruning (p. 237). Then cut stems back to outward-facing buds or eyes about 4 in. from the ground

PRUNING A NEWLY PLANTED FLORIBUNDA

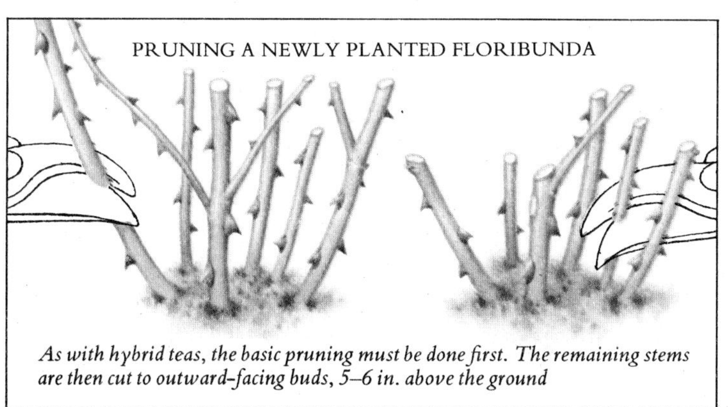

As with hybrid teas, the basic pruning must be done first. The remaining stems are then cut to outward-facing buds, 5–6 in. above the ground

How to prune hybrid teas, floribundas and miniatures

Roses that grow in a bush-like fashion should be pruned in January or February, with the aim of building up a cup-shaped structure, which is fairly open at the centre. This produces a well-balanced shape, and also allows air and light to penetrate.

Roses of this type include hybrid teas (and hybrid perpetuals), floribundas (and polyanthas), standards that are budded with hybrid teas and floribundas, and miniatures.

Make pruning cuts on bush-shaped roses just above an outward-facing growth bud, so that the cup-shaped structure develops from outward-growing stems.

After carrying out the three basic pruning steps (opposite page), prune each rose according to type.

With hybrid teas, cut back about one-third of the growth annually. This is moderate pruning for garden display. If fewer but possibly larger flowers of good individual shape are required for exhibition or indoors, prune back hard to about three buds above the base of each stem.

Generally, weak varieties should be pruned harder than more vigorous varieties, so that strong growth is encouraged. Exceptionally vigorous hybrid tea varieties, however, must occasionally be cut back very hard when they become too gaunt and leggy, otherwise the roots may be damaged in high winds.

Floribundas and polyanthas are generally more vigorous and free-flowering than hybrid teas, so prune them less severely – only by about a quarter.

Standard roses may be either hybrid teas or floribundas and are pruned in the same way as the bush types. Miniature hybrid teas and floribundas are also treated in the same way.

On taller bush-type roses, trim the top growth in autumn by about a quarter, to prevent high winds rocking the plants and loosening or breaking their roots.

A bush-type rose, ready for pruning in January or February, will have a mixture of wood on it. It may carry dead or old and unproductive stems. There may be some stems that are diseased and others that cross and rub together. Thin or weak shoots may also occur

THE THREE BASIC PRUNING STEPS

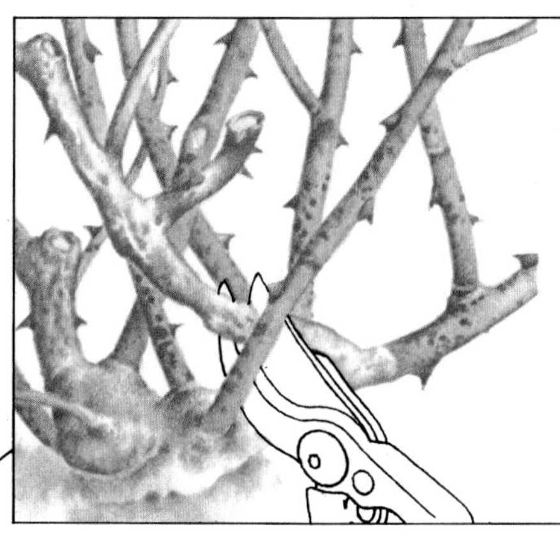

1 Cut back dead stems *Cut back any dead stem to the point where it meets a healthy stem or, if necessary, cut it all the way back to the union between bud wood and root-stock. Cut back any part of a stem which is diseased to just above a bud on healthy wood*

2 Cut out thin or weak stems *To allow more nourishment to reach vigorous wood, cut out completely all very thin or weak stems. Cut them back to their point of union with a strong stem or with the rootstock. Feeble wood will merely waste the plant's strength, and probably produce no flowers*

3 Cut out stems that cross or rub *When two stems cross, cut back the weaker of the two to a growth bud below the point where they cross. This prevents overcrowding of new growth, and allows air and light to penetrate. With climbers and ramblers this is not practicable. Simply train their stems so they do not rub*

HOW HARD SHOULD YOU PRUNE?

Weak varieties and thin shoots should always be cut back harder than vigorous varieties and strong shoots. Prune standard roses harder than bushes, and hybrid teas harder than floribundas

Lightly pruning a bush-type rose *If your plant is of average growth, prune it lightly each year if you want to produce a good display*

Hard pruning a bush-type rose *If you want to grow large, well-formed roses, though few in number, prune your plant hard back annually*

Pruning climbers and pillar roses

Climbers are varieties of great vigour, developing thick, stiff stems, which are suitable for training up walls or on large screens. They flower on the previous year's wood. Pillar roses are simply short climbers that do not normally grow more than 9 ft. Special forms of climber are the sports of hybrid teas and floribundas, which flower on the new wood – that is, stems that have grown during the current season.

Most climbers do not shoot readily from the base – new wood usually appears higher up the old stems of the leaders.

To prune climbers, first trim back the flowered twigs to selected buds after they have bloomed.

Second, in early winter, remove all dead wood and weak or spindly stems. Then cut back leaders to a strong new shoot. If no new growth has formed, cut back leaders, and those laterals that have flowered, by about half.

If possible, train the new shoots horizontally when pruning. This will encourage the development of flowering laterals.

The very vigorous tree climbers, such as 'Kiftsgate' and *R. longicuspis*, need no pruning except to remove dead or diseased wood.

SUMMER PRUNING

After the climber has bloomed, trim back the flowered twigs to a selected new bud. Do not let seed pods form, as these will deprive the rose of energy, which will be better used in producing new growth. Remove all prunings and burn them. Do not cut new shoots, as these will flower the following season

After its flowered twigs have been trimmed back in summer, a climbing rose is pruned in early winter. The rose may contain dead or spindly wood, all of which is removed. New shoots are retained to form the framework for the following season's flowers

Pruning the lax ramblers

The true ramblers develop long, flexible canes from the base of the plant. These canes produce no flowers until their second year. Examples of this type include 'Dorothy Perkins' and 'Excelsa'. Weeping standards, which are lax ramblers budded on to an upright stem, are pruned the same way.

The aim when pruning ramblers is to remove old wood in proportion to the amount of new wood that develops. This preserves the form of the rose on its supporting frame.

Pruning is done in early autumn.

Where new growth springs liberally from the base of the rose, such as with 'Dorothy Perkins' and with 'Excelsa', cut the old flowered canes right down to the ground.

If new stems are usually produced from a point halfway or lower on the old stems, as with 'American Pillar' and sometimes with 'Crimson Conquest', cut back the old stems to that point.

When a rambler produces little new basal growth, retain the strongest old canes, and prune laterals to two buds from their base.

WINTER PRUNING

Clearing old wood *After removing dead, diseased and spindly wood, cut back the leaders to strong new shoots. By this method, older wood is constantly being replaced by young wood*

Encouraging new wood *If no new shoots have grown from a leader, prune it and its laterals by about half. When an old stem ceases to throw out new shoots, cut it out completely to encourage new growth from the base*

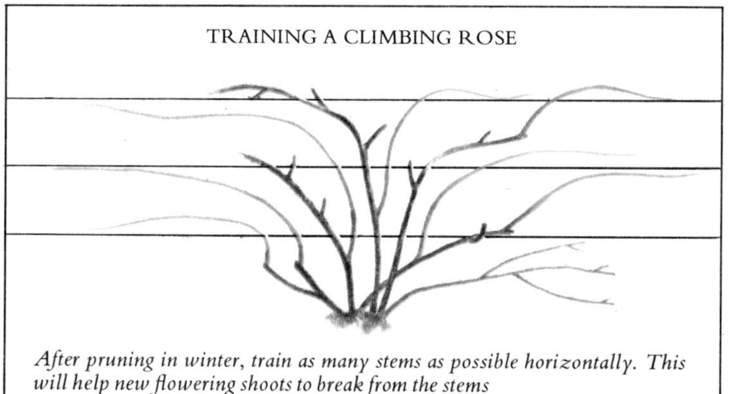

TRAINING A CLIMBING ROSE

After pruning in winter, train as many stems as possible horizontally. This will help new flowering shoots to break from the stems

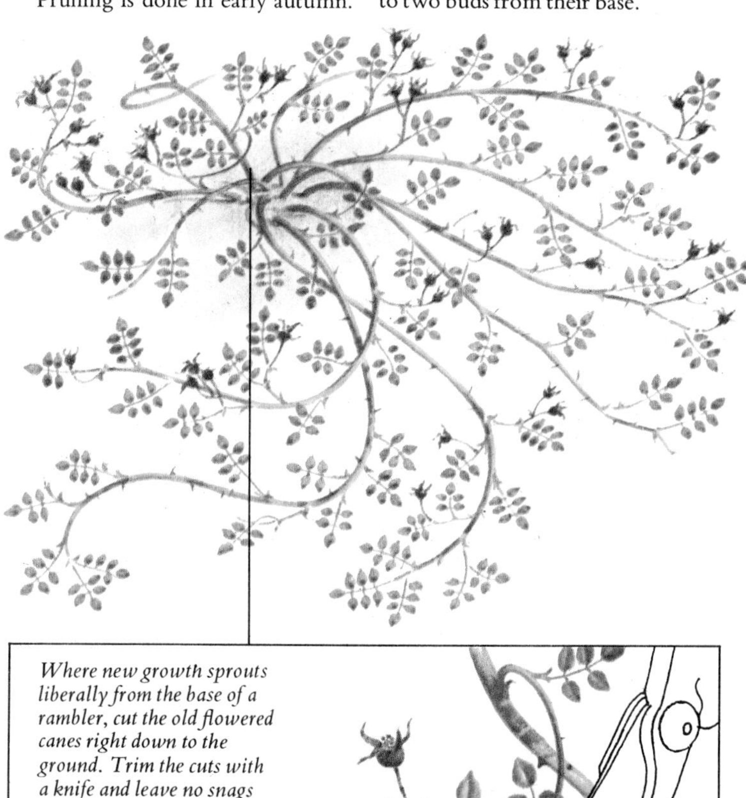

Where new growth sprouts liberally from the base of a rambler, cut the old flowered canes right down to the ground. Trim the cuts with a knife and leave no snags

Pruning species, 'Old' and modern shrub roses

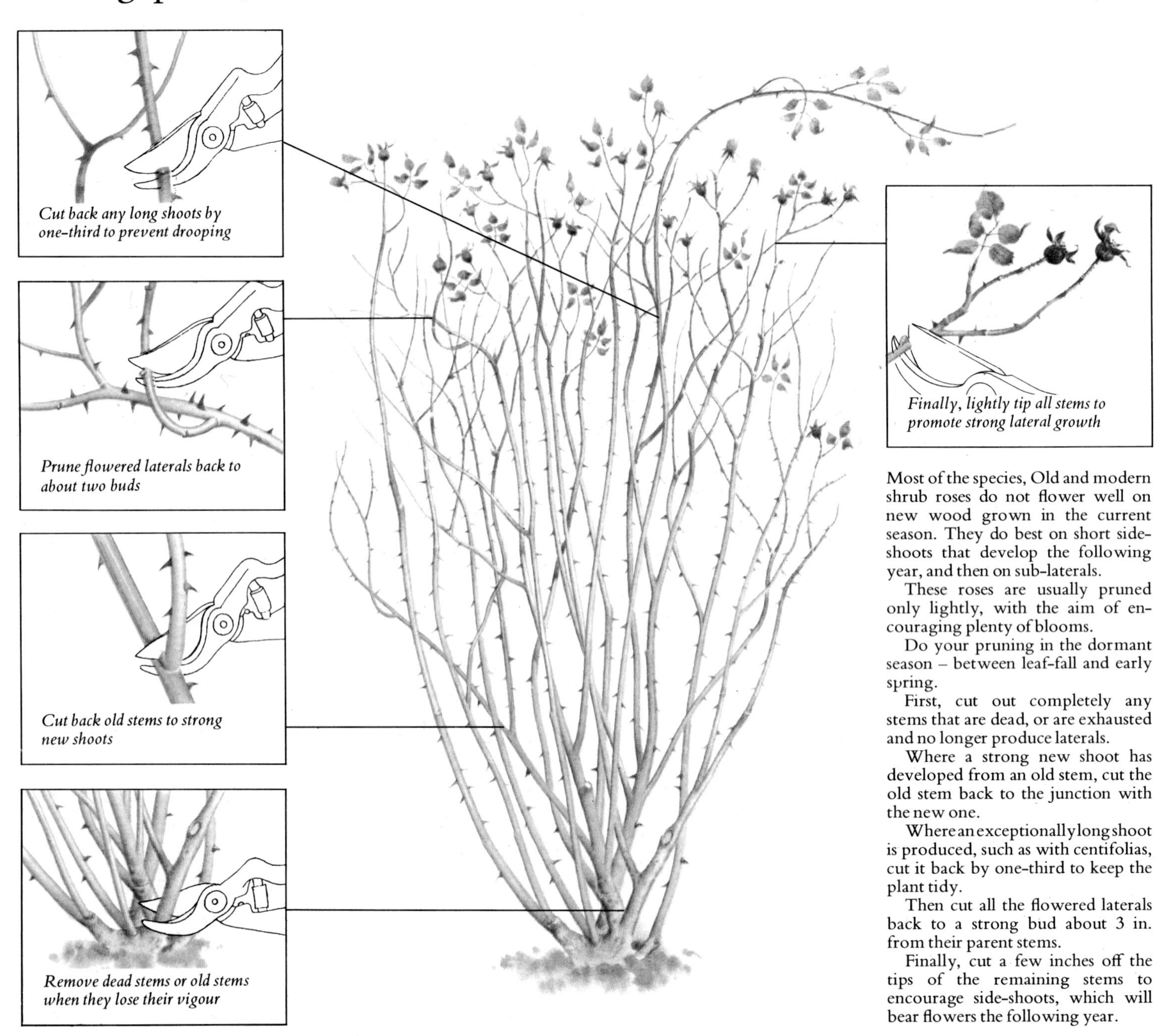

Most of the species, Old and modern shrub roses do not flower well on new wood grown in the current season. They do best on short side-shoots that develop the following year, and then on sub-laterals.

These roses are usually pruned only lightly, with the aim of encouraging plenty of blooms.

Do your pruning in the dormant season – between leaf-fall and early spring.

First, cut out completely any stems that are dead, or are exhausted and no longer produce laterals.

Where a strong new shoot has developed from an old stem, cut the old stem back to the junction with the new one.

Where an exceptionally long shoot is produced, such as with centifolias, cut it back by one-third to keep the plant tidy.

Then cut all the flowered laterals back to a strong bud about 3 in. from their parent stems.

Finally, cut a few inches off the tips of the remaining stems to encourage side-shoots, which will bear flowers the following year.

Shrubs & climbers

Shrubs are among the garden's most versatile plants, not only as a background to other displays, but also adding their own colour and interest all the year round

Magnolia is a large, spectacular shrub which grows up to 15 ft high and has a profusion of fragrant, white flowers, usually in spring

Shrubs play a vital part in the process of turning a patch of ground into a garden. They are the permanent framework around which other plants are interwoven. A garden without shrubs and climbers lacks emphasis and variation in height, as well as the unity that can be created by their linked branches.

In winter, when most plants die back to ground level, the garden can be flat and lifeless. But with their leaves, flowers, berries and bark, shrubs can provide colour all year round. They also have the practical use of providing privacy.

Unlike many other garden plants, shrubs grow stout, woody branches that remain alive all year round. The difference between a shrub and a tree is not simply a matter of height: a shrub produces its branches at, near or below ground level, whereas a tree has a single, woody trunk that branches some distance from the ground. The philadelphus, for instance, is a shrub even though it grows up to 10 ft high. A Japanese maple, which may be only 8 ft high, is nevertheless a tree. Many climbing plants are also shrubs, in that they form permanent, woody branches. They are invaluable for creating a visual link between a house and its garden, uniting them into one.

As shrubs are long-lived, they should be carefully chosen before being given a place in the garden.

The first point to consider is whether they are to be evergreen or deciduous. Evergreens do not drop their leaves in the autumn and, although they shed some the following spring, they are always clothed with foliage.

Deciduous shrubs lose all their leaves in the autumn, become bare-framed and dormant in winter, and break into new leaf the following spring. They often make up for their winter drabness with a more spectacular show of flowers than the evergreens produce.

The value of evergreens Evergreens were favourite shrubs of Victorian gardeners, but by the first half of the 20th century they were considered too dull.

Examples of some of the most popular Victorian shrubs – spotted laurel, euonymus, holly and privet – have survived in thousands of shaded inner-suburban gardens, into an era when they are again recognised as having valuable uses. They provide colour in winter, many grow well in shady places, and the size and texture of their leaves can provide an interesting contrast to the more flamboyant deciduous shrubs.

Whereas the Victorians planted their shrubs close together, today the plants are given enough space to grow to their natural shape and size.

Closely planted shrubs must be clipped back each year into a similar, anonymous shape. Shrubs that are allowed to grow naturally have far greater individuality.

There are four main shapes: rounded, upright, spreading and weeping. If a tall plant is needed as a feature in the corner of a small garden, there is no point in choosing a rounded shape; it will have outgrown its elbow-room well before it reaches the desired height. So an upright shrub is necessary. To shield a compost heap, a rounded evergreen would be much more suitable than a narrow, upright deciduous shrub.

Deciding a colour scheme Shrubs are a major part of a garden's colour scheme. Evergreens provide patches of greenery all year round, but a deciduous shrub changes in its appearance almost month by month.

In winter it is a skeleton of bare stems. In spring it will be covered with young leaves. Then come the flowers. They are followed by a further period of all-green foliage, possibly deeper in colour as the leaves grow older. Then may come berries, and the change in leaf colour to orange, russet and reds in the autumn. In winter, the bark may provide yet another variation of colour. The possible combinations of colours on all the shrubs in a garden are infinite, and in making his choice the gardener comes into his own as an artist.

Clever use of colour not only achieves fine visual effects, but can also alter the perspective of a garden.

For example, soft colours used towards the end of the garden disguise boundary limits and give an illusion of greater distance. This effect is heightened if brighter-coloured shrubs are used near to the house and in the middle distance.

If a shrub is being used to disguise an unsightly shed or rubbish heap, it is a good idea to choose one with muted colours – too bright colours will just draw attention to what you are trying to hide.

Gardeners must decide, before planting, whether adjacent shrubs should or should not be in flower at the same time, or whether both should be leafless in winter. They must judge which colours make a pleasant combination.

The choice of colour is obviously a matter of the individual gardener's preference. However, certain colour combinations will look particularly attractive in any garden.

The association of grey and white near water is effective, and grey-foliaged shrubs are also useful for dividing up brighter-coloured ones that would otherwise clash.

A combination of blue and white shrubs grown against a mellow wall provides a pleasant contrast. *Cotoneaster lacteus* and *Pyracantha crenulata* 'Rogersiana', both with white flowers, with a blue-flowered ceanothus between them, could be used for this effect.

Rather than grouping shrubs in very strong colour contrasts, it is often better to choose a toning sequence of colours, like shades of silver, grey and pink, or blue, mauve, purple and white.

However, brighter effects should not be dismissed altogether. The combination of *Erica carnea*, with its purple flowers, grown as ground-cover under hamamelis, which has

Wistaria, one of the finest and most popular climbers, can grow to 100 ft. It has racemes of fragrant flowers in May and June

yellow flowers, provides a spectacular splash of colour in January.

Finally, in making your choice, take into account the site where the shrub is to grow. Some shrubs, like callistemon (bottle brush) and embothrium (Chilean fire bush) will grow in warm, coastal regions, or sheltered inland sites, but die elsewhere. In cold areas, hardier shrubs such as cotoneaster, berberis and spiraea grow happily.

Shady parts of a garden should not be regarded as problem areas. Some plants actually prefer light shade – hamamelis (witch hazel) and hydrangeas, for example. Many others do perfectly well without sun – daphnes, magnolias, skimmias and many viburnums.

Soil varies from garden to garden throughout the country. It can consist of sand, chalk, clay or peat; it may be naturally damp or dry, acid or alkaline. These factors influence the choice of shrubs for any site.

The difficult task of choosing the right shrub for a particular soil or situation is simplified by the chart starting on page 360, which gives the characteristics and requirements of trees, shrubs and climbers.

Gardening by the sea brings the special problem of sea-spray. Many shrubs will be killed by salt deposits on their leaves. Others, such as *Hippophae rhamnoides*, *Euonymus japonicus*, *Olearia haastii* and escallonias have leathery foliage, resistant to salt. Before deciding on shrubs for a seaside garden, visit a garden centre in the area which specialises in seaside varieties.

Plants to disguise ugly corners Shrubs and climbers are immensely useful for disguising ugly parts of a garden or house. A prostrate juniper will spread over a manhole cover, and still allow it to be removed when necessary. *Cotoneaster × watereri* or lonicera (honeysuckle), fan-trained over trellis, will hide the dustbins or compost heap, and a chain-link fence will disappear under *Clematis montana*.

Below windows, or around them, is the place for planting scented shrubs and climbers. Lavender, choisya, philadelphus, viburnum and honeysuckle can fill a room with their fragrance.

The easiest way to obtain most common shrubs is to buy them from a local nursery or garden centre, already growing in pots or plastic bags. They can then be planted into the garden in summer, as the root growth is unchecked, but keep them well watered until autumn especially during dry spells.

Many shrubs and climbers will need to be ordered from a specialist nursery, for delivery in the dormant season from November to March.

Evergreen shrubs, not bought in containers, should be planted out in October or April when the soil is warm, as they have no completely dormant period.

Many garden centres guarantee a replacement if a plant dies, provided it has been well treated. Choose plants that have a deep green, healthy look and reject any that have withered, brownish leaves, which may mean they are suffering from lack of food or water.

Ideally, buy plants from reputable nurserymen who have grown their stock in containers for several months, to get them established before being sold.

Different-shaped shrubs can be used to create harmonious forms in a garden. An attractive arrangement is to group a rounded shrub with a severely upright one and a spreading or low, weeping one. The three shapes work well together and can be repeated throughout the garden

Planting and supporting shrubs

How to space and plant free-standing shrubs

Shrubs are supplied by nurseries in three ways: with balled roots, with bare roots, or in a container.

Balled-root shrubs have some soil around the roots, kept in place by hessian. Plants which have difficulty in establishing themselves after transplanting are sold in this way to keep the root system intact.

Shrubs that grow on easily after transplanting are often sold with bare roots.

Container shrubs are established shrubs growing in plastic or 'whalehide' pots of compost.

Shrubs bought in containers can be planted out at any time of the year. But if you plant in summer be careful to keep the soil moist until the autumn. Newly planted shrubs may die if the soil dries out.

Balled-root and bare-root shrubs can be planted between early October and late April if evergreen, and between late October and the end of March if deciduous.

First remove any perennial weeds, such as bindweed, from the bed with a garden fork. Then dig over the soil to one spade's depth and, if possible, let the soil settle for about two weeks. But for immediate planting, firm the whole bed thoroughly by treading the soil down.

The space between shrubs should be at least half the total of their ultimate spread. For example, two shrubs expected to spread 4 ft and 6 ft should be planted 5 ft apart.

Work out the spacing beforehand, and mark the planting positions with bamboo canes.

If several weeks elapse before planting, and annual weeds spring up, cut them down with a hoe. Dig out any remaining perennial weeds. Finally, level off the soil.

Remove one of the markers and dig a hole as deep as, and slightly wider than, the shrub's container or its root ball.

Check the hole for depth. With a container shrub, the surface of the compost should be level with that of the surrounding soil. With a balled-root or bare-root shrub, the mark indicating the old soil level on the stem should be level with the surface of the surrounding soil.

Break up the soil at the base of the hole with a fork.

Mix the soil from the hole with well-rotted garden compost, manure or peat. The ideal mixture is 2 parts of the soil and 1 part of the organic material. If the shrub is in a container or pot, water it thoroughly before planting. Remove the container. Sacking round a balled-root shrub should not be cut away until after the plant has been placed in the hole.

Check that a container shrub has an extensive root system. If it lacks one, return it to the nursery.

With a bare-root shrub, cut back any damaged or diseased roots to healthy growth.

With all shrubs, use secateurs to remove any stumps of old wood, cutting flush with the stem. Remove any diseased or damaged wood, cutting just above a bud.

Hold the plant by the base of its stem, and insert it in the hole. With a balled-root or container shrub, fill in the hole with the prepared soil. Tread it firmly. Top up with more soil and tread again.

Soak the soil thoroughly around the base of the plant with water.

With a bare-root shrub, lift the plant up and down, gently shaking the roots so that the soil will settle all around them. Firm with the feet, several times, to eliminate any air pockets between the roots.

1 *Check hole for depth. The base of the stem should be at soil level*

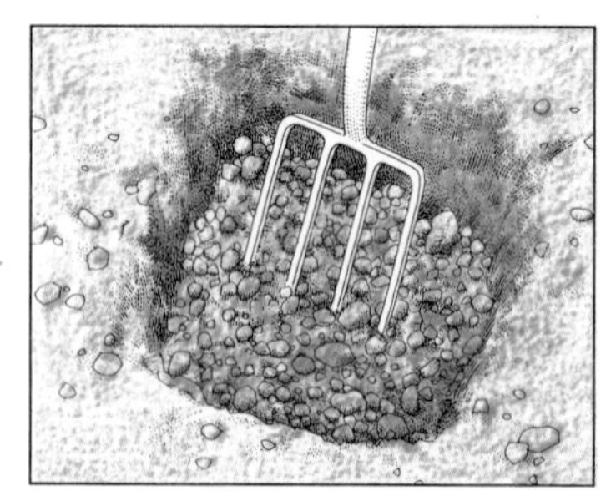

2 *Fork over the base of the hole. Add peat to excavated soil*

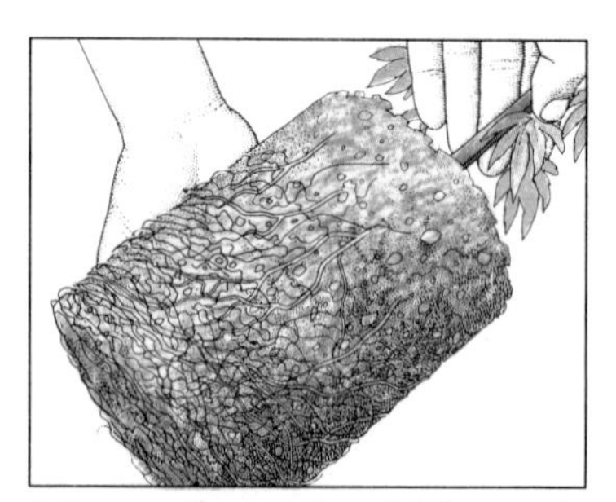

3 *Remove the container. Make sure the shrub's roots are extensive*

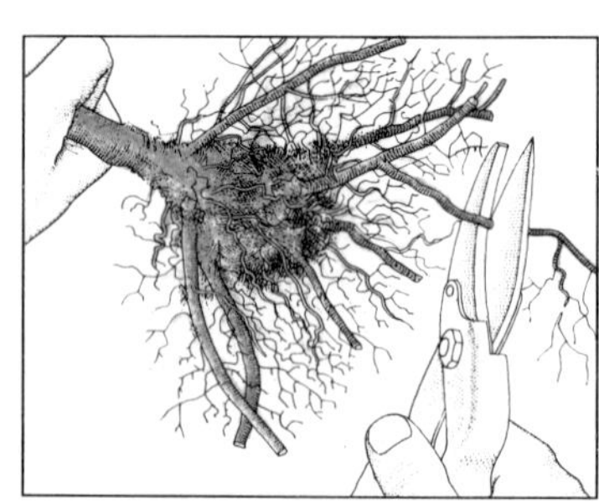

4 *With a bare-root shrub, cut back any damaged or diseased roots*

5 *With all shrubs, cut off stumps of old wood flush with the stem*

6 *Remove any damaged or diseased wood, cutting just above a bud*

7 *Hold the plant by the stem, place in the hole and replace the soil*

8 *Fill the hole and tread the soil firmly. Soak the soil thoroughly*

Healthy shrubs all year round

Watering and feeding the shrubs after planting

Soon after planting, when the soil is moist, spread a mulch over the soil. Use peat, leaf-mould, spent hops, garden compost, manure or pulverised bark. This retains the moisture in the soil and keeps down weeds. The mulch also feeds the plants in later years, as it is eventually absorbed into the soil.

Apply the mulch, about 2 in. thick, with a fork, covering all the soil between the shrubs. Spread a fresh layer each year, in spring.

If the shrub is planted in autumn, winter or early spring, watering – other than the first watering-in after planting – is unnecessary, unless the plant wilts during a long dry spell.

If you plant in late spring or summer, water liberally in dry weather during the first few weeks.

If the soil is poor, apply a general-purpose fertiliser, such as Growmore or John Innes base, each February. Sprinkle the granules around the plant, at 1 oz. (1 tablespoon) to the square yard. Work the granules into the soil with a hoe.

After planting, and whenever pests appear, spray the shrub with a pesticide. Do this during a dry period, but not in bright sunshine. During spraying, point the nozzle upwards so that the undersides of the leaves and the tops are covered.

Spread garden compost, peat or manure around shrubs after planting to retain moisture

After planting, spray with a pesticide – direct the nozzle to soak the undersides of leaves

Protecting tender shrubs in winter

Several decorative shrubs are not hardy enough to withstand severe weather outdoors in the British Isles, but they can be grown successfully if they are sheltered from extreme cold. Freezing or very cold winds cause the most damage.

The ideal situation for tender shrubs is on the south side of a wall or fence, 6 ft or more high.

A dense evergreen hedge can also provide enough shelter. Shrubs that tolerate shade will usually be protected from the worst winds if planted among trees.

Shelter is not enough during severe weather; further protection will be necessary.

During a severe spell, wrap straw or bracken around the branches and bind it in place with sheets of hessian, tied with twine.

Wall shrubs and climbers can be protected by mats made of bracken or straw sandwiched between two sheets of chicken wire. Simply squeeze a 4–5 in. layer of material between two pieces of chicken wire, then join the four edges by twisting the wires together. Hang the mats in front of the plants in bad weather.

Free-standing shrubs can be protected by using a strip of the same construction. Stand it on end around the plant like a collar. During the coldest weather a lid of similar material can be placed on top.

Bamboo canes and a plastic bag with the bottom slit open will also give a fair amount of protection. Insert four canes around the plant in a square. Lower the plastic bag over the canes to cover the shrub.

Plants which regularly produce shoots from the base, either below or just above ground level, such as fuchsias, should be protected in this vital area. Put a 6–9 in. layer of straw, bracken, weathered ashes, coarse sand or peat around and over the plant in late autumn. Clear away this layer in spring.

An alternative is to use canes and bracken. Form a wigwam of canes by inserting about six at equal distances around the plant and tying them together at the top. Also loop string halfway down each cane, all around the wigwam.

Stuff bracken into this framework and, if necessary, tie it with more string. Another method is to tie hessian around the wigwam.

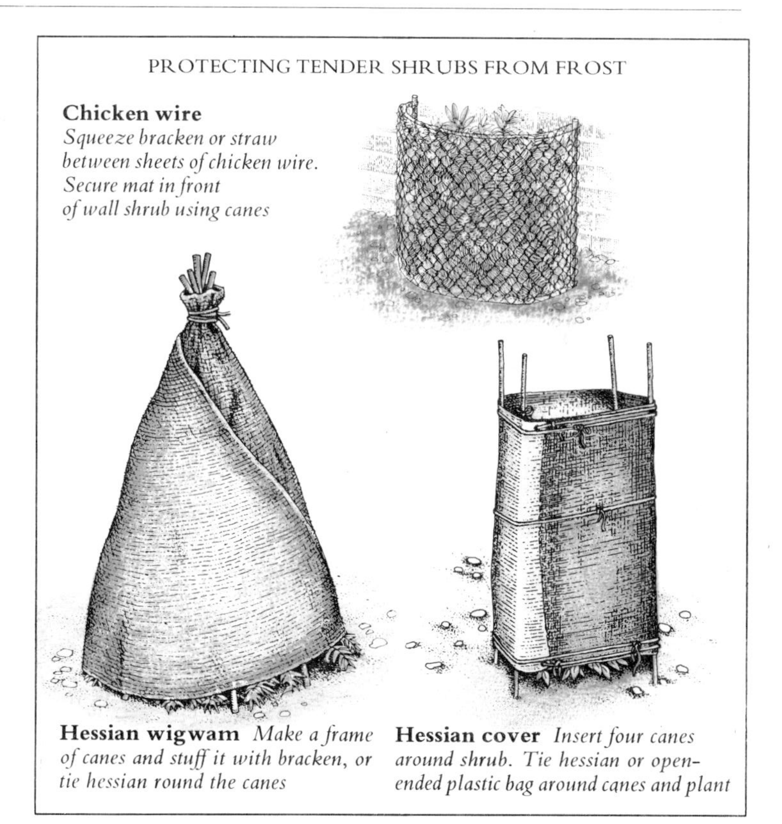

PROTECTING TENDER SHRUBS FROM FROST

Chicken wire *Squeeze bracken or straw between sheets of chicken wire. Secure mat in front of wall shrub using canes*

Hessian wigwam *Make a frame of canes and stuff it with bracken, or tie hessian round the canes*

Hessian cover *Insert four canes around shrub. Tie hessian or open-ended plastic bag around canes and plant*

Keeping down the weeds

Regular hoeing and use of weedkillers

Once the shrubs have grown, it is usually too shady beneath them for weeds to be much of a problem. Until this does happen, however, any weeds that do appear must be removed regularly.

Use a hoe when the weeds are still very small, but take care not to damage shrubs with shallow roots.

Weedkillers can be used between shrubs, but be careful not to splash the foliage. A piece of cardboard or a sheet of wood can be used to protect the leaves of shrubs as you apply the weedkiller by watering can or by sprayer. A paraquat or diquat weedkiller such as Weedol will not damage the roots of shrubs, as it becomes inactive on contact with the soil. For established perennial weeds, such as bindweed, repeated treatment over a couple of years may be necessary.

To smother annual weeds, the ground can be mulched in spring with a 1–2 in. layer of garden compost, or an organic material that is sterile or weed-free, such as peat.

Ground-cover plants are another solution to the weed problem. If chosen with care they enhance the beauty of the shrubs, providing a carpet of foliage and flowers.

Controlling weeds with ground-cover

An alternative to controlling annual weeds by hoeing or using weedkillers is to plant ground-covering plants, which smother the weed seedlings, underneath the shrubs.

These plants can also improve the look of the garden. For example, the rose bed is normally attractive only from about early July to mid-October. But low-growing plants with flowers or handsome foliage can make the bed interesting all the year round.

Another advantage is that most ground-cover plants, once established, need little maintenance.

Ground-cover plants will not control perennial weeds, such as bindweed, ground elder, couch grass and dandelions, and any area to be planted with ground-cover must first be free of them.

Where roses are underplanted with ground-cover they need to be fed more generously than usual, to provide sufficient for the ground-cover plants as well.

Either increase the normal application of rose fertiliser, or replace it in spring with a granular general-purpose fertiliser such as Growmore.

The following chart provides a selection of low-growing perennials and shrubs suitable for ground-cover in various soil conditions.

All the perennial ground-cover plants listed are easily increased by division between October and the end of March (p. 211).

For methods of propagating the shrubby plants see page 249.

PLANTS SUITABLE FOR SMOTHERING WEEDS

Name	Type	Height/Spread	Position
Bergenia			
All varieties	Evergreen perennial	*H* 12 in.	Sun or shade
Brunnera			
B. macrophylla	Deciduous perennial	*H* 12–18 in. *S* 18–24 in.	Sun or shade
Cornus			
C. canadensis	Perennial	*H* 4–6 in. *S* 24 in.	Sun or shade
Cotoneaster			
C. dammeri	Evergreen shrub	*H* 2–3 in. *S* 4–6 ft	Sun or partial shade
Erica			
Dwarf types	Evergreen shrub	*H* and *S* 9–24 in.	Sunny position
Euphorbia			
E. robbiae	Evergreen perennial	*H* 18 in. *S* 2–3 ft	Tolerates dry soil. Sun or shade
Geranium			
G. endressii	Semi-evergreen perennial	*H* 12–18 in. *S* 18–24 in.	Tolerates dry soil. Sun or shade
Hedera			
H. helix and varieties	Evergreen climbers	*H* 3–6 in. *S* 4–6 ft	Sun or shade
Hosta			
H. sieboldiana	Deciduous perennial	*H* 24 in. *S* 3–4 ft	Tolerates moist soil. Sun or shade
Hypericum			
H. calycinum	Evergreen sub-shrub	*H* 12–18 in. *S* 18–24 in.	Tolerates dry soil. Sun or shade
Juniperus			
J. horizontalis	Evergreen shrub	*H* 12 in. *S* 4–5 ft	Tolerates dry soil
Lamium			
L. maculatum	Perennial	*H* 12 in. *S* 18 in.	Sun or shade
Pachysandra			
P. terminalis	Evergreen sub-shrub	*H* 12 in. *S* 18–24 in.	Sun or shade
Polygonum			
P. affine	Perennial	*H* 6–9 in. *S* 18–24 in.	Sun or partial shade
Pulmonaria			
P. saccharata	Deciduous perennial	*H* 12 in. *S* 18 in.	Needs moist soil. Sun or shade
Stachys			
S. lanata	Evergreen perennial	*H* and *S* 12–18 in.	Tolerates dry soil. Sunny position
Symphytum			
S. grandiflorum	Deciduous perennial	*H* 8 in. *S* 18 in.	Sun or shade
Vinca			
V. minor	Evergreen sub-shrub	*H* 2–4 in. *S* 3–4 ft	Sun or shade

Care and protection of shrubs

Removing any unwanted suckers from shrubs

A sucker is a shoot arising from the base of a plant, or below ground.

Suckers on most shrubs can be left, as they are simply part of the plant; but suckers on shrubs that have been grafted on to a different rootstock must be removed to prevent weakening the plant. Shrubs that produce this sort of sucker include ilex, magnolia, camellia, rhododendron and syringa.

An unwanted sucker always appears from below the union – the point where the plant has been grafted on to the rootstock. With shrubs the union is usually planted below the surface, so that the suckers spring from below ground.

Unwanted suckers found above ground usually occur on fruit trees.

In all cases, trace the sucker to its point of origin and wrench it off by hand. Do not cut it off above ground, as more suckers will form.

UNWANTED SUCKERS

Dig to where the sucker joins the plant, and wrench it off

How to grow a good crop of berries

Many shrubs and some trees are grown primarily for the coloured fruits they produce in autumn or winter. Poor crops of berries or fruit can be caused by various factors.

In the first place, buy the plants from a reputable nurseryman and ask him to advise on varieties that fruit abundantly.

Some shrubs and trees are dioecious, that is the male and female flowers grow on separate plants, and cross-pollination has to occur before berries will grow. Examples are holly, sea buckthorn, skimmia and aucuba. Plant dioecious shrubs in groups of three or more female plants with a male plant in the centre of the group.

Weather conditions can affect each year's crop of berries. If the plant suffers drought at flowering time or just as the berries are forming, the berries may fall off prematurely. Frost at flowering time may prevent the fruit forming.

If the weather is dull and cold at flowering time bees and other pollinating insects are sluggish, and the crop will be poor.

The right growing conditions are important for good berry crops. If a sun-loving shrub such as pyracantha is grown in shade it will flower and fruit poorly. A lime-hating shrub, such as pernettya, will die if it is grown in a limy soil.

Birds can have a severe effect on berry crops. In winter, bullfinches eat the buds that would flower in the following year. Blackbirds and thrushes eat the ripening fruits. If birds are a problem, spray a repellent over the plants, or cover them with netting or a network of black cotton.

The fruits of Cotoneaster × *'Cornubius' grow in large, red bunches, which appear in autumn, weighing down the long branches, and often lasting well into winter*

When to transplant an established shrub

A shrub can be transplanted between early autumn and late spring, provided the soil is neither frozen nor waterlogged.

Dig a circular trench around the shrub – well away from it to avoid damaging the roots.

When the trench is completed, dig under the shrub and lever it out.

Crumble away some of the surplus soil around the roots. This lightens the load to be moved and will reduce the size of the new planting hole.

Plant the shrub as though putting in a newly received balled-root shrub (p. 244). Water thoroughly.

1 *Dig a trench around the shrub, to avoid root damage, and lever it out*

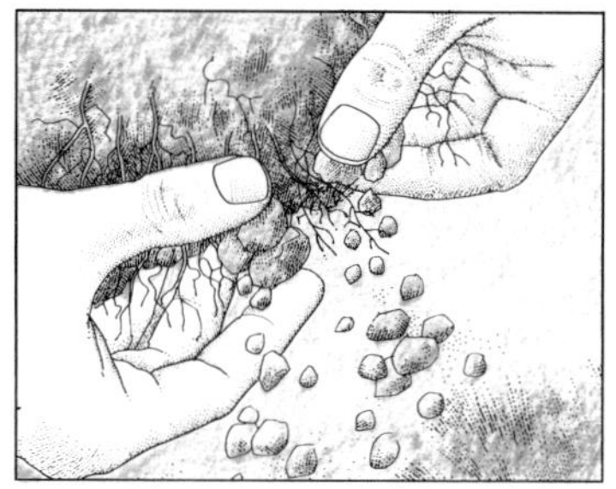

2 *Crumble away some of the soil from the roots before replanting*

Growing shrubs in containers

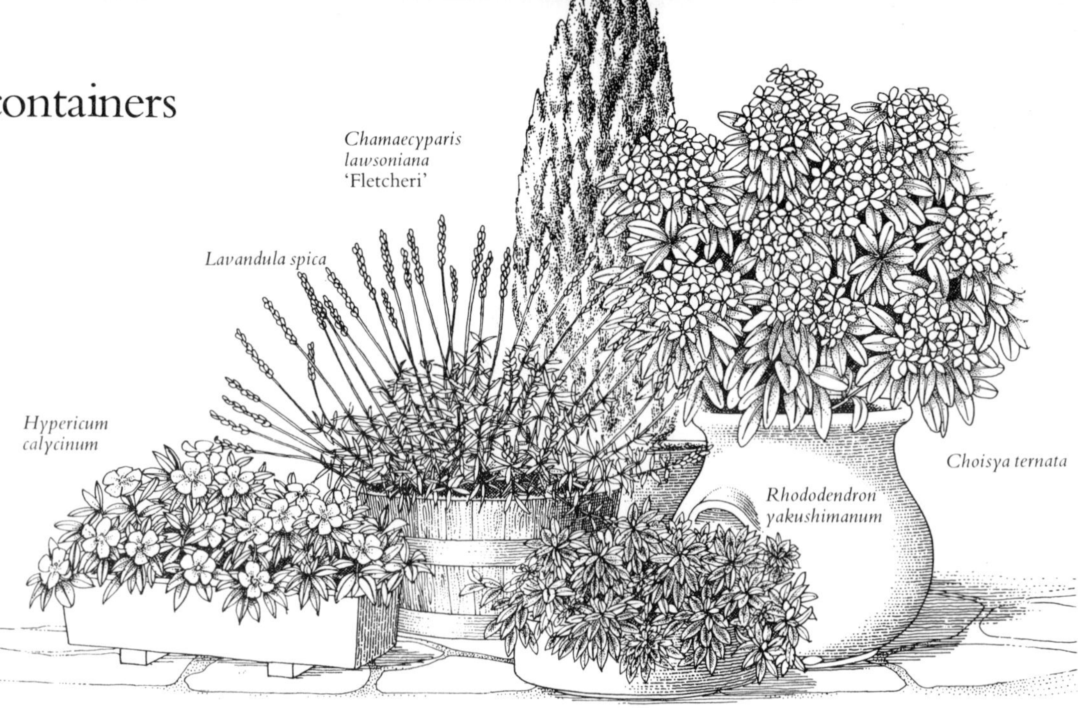

Many of the most decorative shrubs can be grown in large pots or tubs, and are particularly effective on paved areas. The root restriction caused by the tub often results in more profuse flowering.

Shrubs that grow particularly well in containers include: aucuba, berberis, camellia, caryopteris, chamaecyparis (dwarf forms), choisya, cistus, clematis, cotoneaster (smaller forms), deutzia, escallonia, euonymus, forsythia, hebe, hypericum, jasminum, kerria, laurus, lavandula, lonicera, mahonia, passiflora, pernettya, prunus, pyracantha, ribes, rosmarinus, spiraea, syringa, tamarix, vitis, weigela and wistaria.

Not all shrubs respond to container culture. Magnolia, cercis (Judas tree) and daphne (large forms) are not suitable. In general, avoid species with thick, fleshy roots.

A tub $2\frac{1}{2}$ ft wide by $1\frac{1}{2}$ ft deep will be adequate for the healthy growth of a shrub 4–5 ft tall and 3–4 ft wide.

Ensure that the tub has drainage holes in its base.

Put in a $1–1\frac{1}{2}$ in. deep layer of drainage material – broken clay pots, or gravel and coarse sand.

Add a layer of John Innes No. 3 potting compost, or a mixture of 3 parts peat, 1 part coarse sand. Add 4 oz. (4 tablespoons) of John Innes base fertiliser to every bushel of the mixture used.

Check that the shrub is placed on the compost with the base of the stem level with the rim of the tub.

Ensure the root ball is moist, then take it from its container. Check that there is a good root system.

Place the shrub in the tub and fill the compost in around it.

Firm the compost with a piece of wood. Then fill the tub with more compost to $\frac{1}{2}$ in. below its rim.

Water thoroughly after planting, then again whenever the surface of the soil begins to dry out.

One year after planting, apply a liquid fertiliser to the compost. Repeat whenever the leaves of the shrub look small and discoloured, or when the growth seems short.

To maintain a healthy shrub at about the same size, prune the stems and roots at four to six year intervals.

In autumn or early spring, remove the shrub from its container and strip about 4 in. of roots and soil from all round the root ball. Scrub out the container, return the shrub and fill in with fresh compost.

Shrubs that grow large can be kept small – and healthy – by yearly or two yearly root pruning.

PLANTING IN A TUB

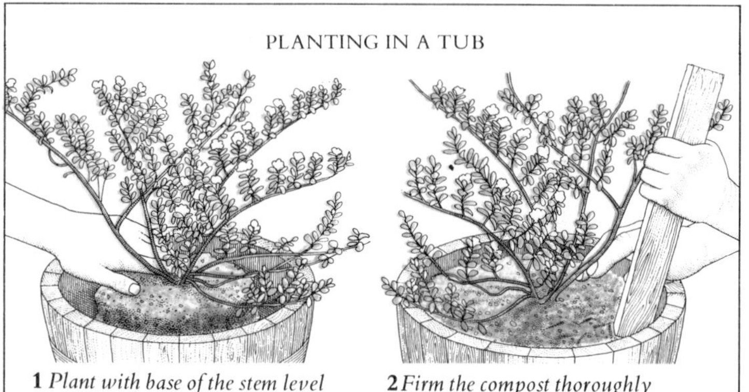

1 *Plant with base of the stem level with the rim of the tub*

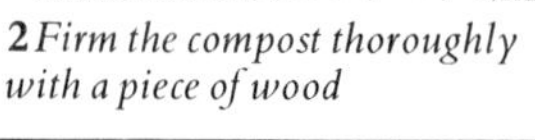

2 *Firm the compost thoroughly with a piece of wood*

PRUNING THE SHRUB

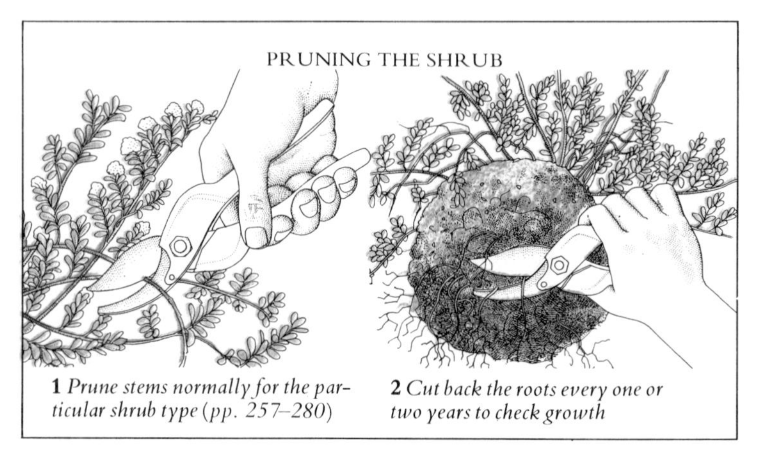

1 *Prune stems normally for the particular shrub type* (*pp.* 257–280)

2 *Cut back the roots every one or two years to check growth*

How to grow new shrubs from cuttings

Hardwood cuttings – the easiest way

The simplest way of propagating a large range of popular hardy shrubs – and trees – is by taking hardwood cuttings in late autumn and early winter. Except for watering in dry spells, and weeding, no further attention is needed for 12 months. The young shrubs are then ready for planting in their permanent quarters.

Hardwood cuttings are vigorous stems which have just completed their first season's growth and have become hard and woody. They bear buds all along their length and these will grow into new shoots the following spring.

Preferably take the cuttings in October, when they have just stopped growing and are beginning the winter period of dormancy. Some shrubs will grow from hardwood cuttings taken at any time in late autumn or winter. However, careful timing is important for success with others.

Cut the stem with secateurs near its base and then trim it to about 10–12 in. in length. If the shoot is a long one, two or more cuttings may be made from it. Avoid using the soft thin tip, as it will produce a weaker plant or may not root at all.

Sever each cutting cleanly just below a bud or joint at the base, and just above a bud at the top end.

Cut evergreens below and above a leaf and remove all the leaves on the lower half.

Shrubs with large leaves, such as cherry laurel, should have each leaf reduced by half, using a razor blade or sharp scissors. This reduces water loss until the cutting is rooted.

Cuttings from difficult-to-root shrub species often respond to wounding – the removal of a thin sliver of bark on one or opposite sides near the base of the cutting.

Some shrubs that are difficult to root can be encouraged by dipping the base of the cutting into a rooting powder, making sure to cover the wounded area.

Before taking the cuttings, choose a site sheltered from north and east winds and dig it thoroughly. If the soil is heavy, work in coarse sand or weathered ashes to help drainage and aeration.

Make a narrow slit-like trench by pushing in a spade to its full blade depth and then pulling it forwards for several inches.

Place a layer of coarse sand 1–2 in. deep in the bottom, and stand the cuttings on the sand so that the lower half or two-thirds is below ground.

Plant the cuttings 3–4 in. apart with 2 ft between the rows.

Push soil into the trench and firm it with the foot.

After severe frosts, cuttings can become loosened. Push each cutting down with the thumb or finger so that the base is again in close contact with the soil or sand.

In early spring, firm the soil again.

Hoe regularly during the summer, and water during long, dry spells.

One year later, all the easier-rooting cuttings will be ready for lifting and setting in their permanent quarters in the garden.

Species that are slower to root or to grow should be left in the ground for a further year.

Protecting with plastic spray Hardwood cuttings of evergreen trees and shrubs may die because of rapid, excess water loss through the leaves.

This can be averted by spraying the cuttings with a liquid plastic, S600, which forms a transparent plastic film on the leaves.

It can also be used on softwood or semi-hardwood cuttings of both deciduous and evergreen plants, particularly those with large leaves.

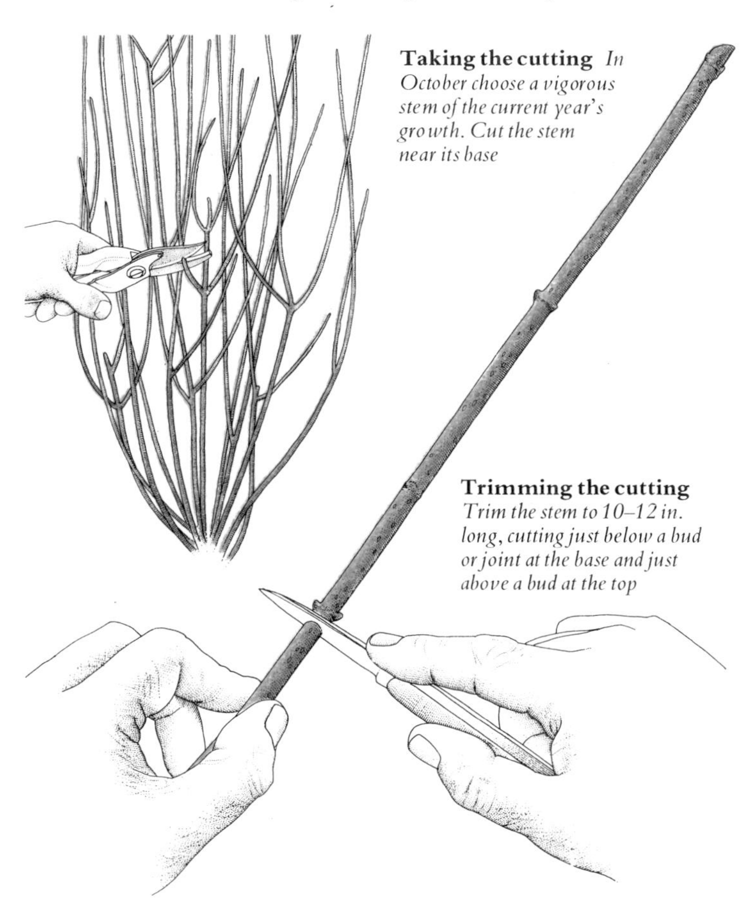

Taking the cutting *In October choose a vigorous stem of the current year's growth. Cut the stem near its base*

Trimming the cutting *Trim the stem to 10–12 in. long, cutting just below a bud or joint at the base and just above a bud at the top*

PLANTING

1 *To aid rooting, remove a thin sliver from near the base*

2 *Plant the cuttings to at least half their length*

3 *A year or two later, the cuttings are ready to be transplanted*

Semi-hard cuttings taken in summer

Some trees and shrubs root poorly from hardwood cuttings, but respond well when semi-hard material is used instead.

Examples are: actinidia, aucuba, caryopteris, choisya and lavandula.

Semi-hard cuttings are the current year's growth which has become moderately firm and woody towards the base but is still growing, so the tips of the shoots will be soft. The best time to take semi-hard cuttings is from mid-July to the end of August, but in very hot summers they will be ready sooner than this.

Semi-hard cuttings require some attention from the time they are set out until they are well rooted. The essentials are some sort of propagating frame – with or without bottom heat – regular watering, and shading from the sun.

When rooted, the young plants can either be set outside in a nursery bed or potted.

Either way, a year or two must elapse before the plants are ready for permanent quarters.

Take the cuttings by choosing 6–8 in. long side-shoots of the current season's wood – easily identified, as the shoots will have leaves growing on them.

With a knife or secateurs, cut off a shoot close to the main stem.

Remove the leaves from the lower part of the shoot and sever it just below the lowest leaf node. Trim off the soft tip above a leaf so the cutting is 2–4 in. long.

Heeled cuttings Semi-hard cuttings often root more surely if they are removed with a sliver of the parent stem. Some species will root very poorly, or not at all, if this heel-like sliver is missing. Examples are pyracantha and ceanothus.

The inclusion of a heel encourages roots to form, as it prevents the sap, which flows down from the leaves to help form the roots, from draining away into the soil.

First, cut off a main shoot carrying several side-shoots, preferably without flowers.

With a sharp knife make a slanting cut into the main shoot beneath the junction with the side-shoot. Then cut in the opposite direction to remove the shoot.

Heel cuttings should be 2–3 in. long. If longer, trim from the tip.

Now treat the cuttings in the same way as shown for other hardwood or semi-hard cuttings.

Where to take the cutting *Between mid-July and the end of August choose 6–8 in. side-shoots of current year's growth – any shoots with leaves on them – and cut close to the main stem*

Trimming the cutting *Remove the lower leaves and sever the shoot just below the lowest leaf node. Trim off the soft tip of the shoot just above a leaf so the cutting is 2–4 in. long*

TAKING HEELED CUTTINGS

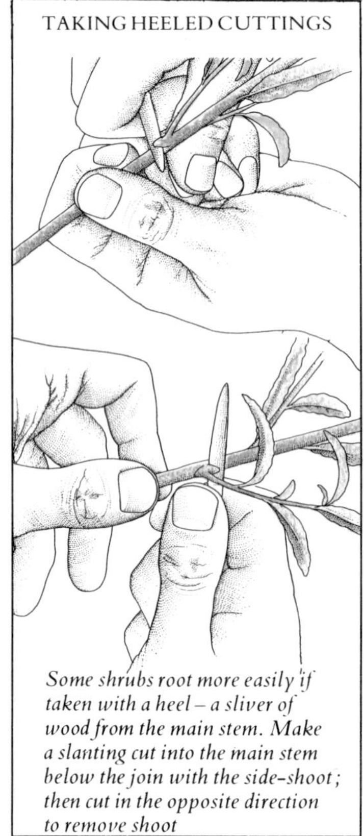

Some shrubs root more easily if taken with a heel – a sliver of wood from the main stem. Make a slanting cut into the main stem below the join with the side-shoot; then cut in the opposite direction to remove shoot

Planting and care of semi-hard cuttings

Once the cuttings have been taken, fill a pot to just below the rim with a seed compost or a mixture of equal parts of peat and coarse sand.

The size of the pot will depend on the length and number of the cuttings. A 3 in. pot will be big enough for up to five cuttings, a 5 in. pot for five to ten.

Make a hole in the compost, about one-third the length of a cutting.

Insert the cutting and firm it with a dibber and finger. Plant the other cuttings, and water them generously with a sprayer or a watering can with a fine rose.

The cuttings need a humid atmosphere to prevent them drying out. One simple method is to construct a cover from two 12–15 in. long pieces of galvanised wire and a sheet of polythene.

Bend one piece of wire, and insert both ends into the compost. Insert the other, bent in the same way, to form a cross-shaped support.

Drape a sheet of polythene or a plastic bag over the pot, fasten it in place with an elastic band or string, and trim off the spare material.

A box is best for a large number of cuttings. A polythene-and-wire frame can also be made for this.

The propagating container should be placed in a shaded greenhouse or frame. Warmth is essential, but direct sunshine on the cuttings may cause overheating.

The best rooting conditions are created if a source of heat is supplied from beneath. This can be done by placing the propagating container on the greenhouse heating pipes, or using soil-warming cables. Propagating frames or units can be obtained with heating cables or wires built in.

The compost above the heating source should be maintained at a steady heat of 16–18°C (61–64°F) for most hardy plants.

Although bottom heat usually hastens the rooting of most plants, it is not essential.

Even the complete novice can expect success, as long as the cuttings are taken early in the recommended rooting period (the end of July to mid-August), and suitable compost and treatment are adopted.

To balance any loss of difficult-to-root plants, it is wise to take a few extra cuttings.

Under the conditions described, rooting usually takes place in two or three weeks.

After rooting, harden off the cuttings. This entails acclimatising them to the drier or colder conditions they will meet outside, by keeping them in a greenhouse or frame and raising the polythene, or piercing a few holes in it, to let in air. Keep them away from strong light.

A week later, raise the polythene still higher or increase the number of holes in it.

A further week later, remove the polythene altogether, and a week after this the cuttings are ready for potting individually.

Shake rooted cuttings from pot or box, and gently separate them.

Place potting compost in the bottom of a $3\frac{1}{2}$ in. pot. Stand the young plant on this and then fill the pot with compost to just below the lowest pair of leaves.

Firm the compost so that the surface is about $\frac{1}{2}$ in. below the rim. Water generously.

Keep the pot in a greenhouse or frame. Never let the compost dry out.

In three weeks, the roots should have reached the outside of the compost. If the plant is of a hardy genus, it can now be planted out in the open. A non-hardy plant should first go into a larger pot and be kept in the greenhouse or a frame until it is planted out in the spring.

1 *Insert cutting one-third of its length in a pot of peat-and-sand compost*

2 *Water generously with a sprayer, or a watering can with a fine rose*

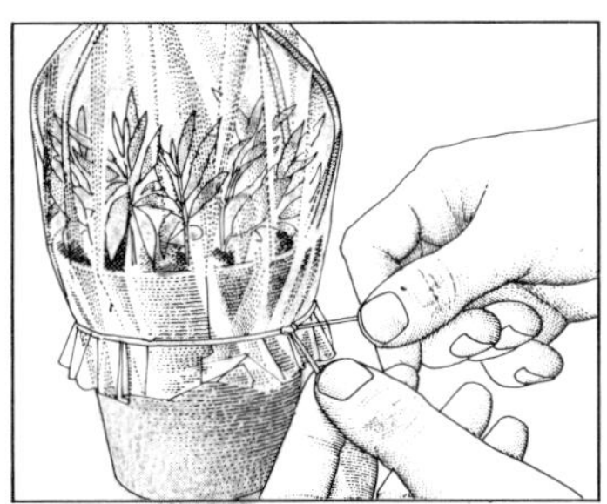

3 *Make a frame of galvanised wire and polythene to create humidity*

4 *After rooting, harden off by raising the polythene to let in air*

5 *About three weeks later, shake out the cuttings and gently separate them*

6 *Pot up cuttings singly in $3\frac{1}{2}$ in. pots containing potting compost*

7 *When the plant is established, it is ready for planting out*

Softwood cuttings taken from the shoot tips

Although commonly used for hardy herbaceous perennials and greenhouse plants, taking softwood cuttings is the least convenient method of propagating trees and shrubs. However, if you wish to take cuttings in early summer, this is the method to use. Softwood cuttings are the immature, soft shoot tips, taken before they have become hard.

From the time of insertion until rooting and potting take place, constant care is needed.

A warm propagating case, preferably with heating cables in the bottom, is required. Watering, shading and general hygiene are critical, though a mist propagation unit will help to simplify the procedure (p. 152). Plants will not be ready for planting out for one or two years.

Softwood cuttings should be young and non-flowering, firm but not hard and 2–4 in. long. Cuttings should be taken in June or July.

Cut off a shoot with four or five pairs of leaves.

With a sharp knife or razor blade, sever the bottom of the shoot immediately beneath the pair of leaves closest to the main stem. Cut cleanly and diagonally.

Remove the first and second pair of leaves close to the stem. Be careful not to tear the stem.

Take about ten cuttings for planting in a 5 in. pot. Fill the pot to just below the rim with a cuttings compost, or a mixture of equal parts of peat and coarse sand.

With a dibber make holes in the compost about one-third the length of the cutting. Insert the cutting and firm with the fingers. Then continue as for semi-hard cuttings (p. 251).

Growing shrubs from pieces of root

Some plants, both herbaceous and woody, readily produce shoots direct from their roots, particularly at a point where damage has occurred. Consequently, pieces of root can be used as cuttings.

One advantage is that root cuttings require less attention than soft or semi-hard cuttings. Shrubs that grow well from root cuttings are rhus, cotinus, spiraea and rubus.

These fleshy root cuttings are taken in autumn, winter or spring.

Lift the plant with a garden fork, or unearth part of the root system of a large plant. Then with secateurs cut off the thicker roots close to the main stem or root.

Using a knife, cut pieces about $1\frac{1}{2}$ in. long from these roots. Cut each piece straight across at the top (nearest to the main root or stem), and at an angle at the base.

Fill a pot to just below the rim with a cuttings compost, or equal parts of peat and coarse sand.

Make a hole in the compost to the same depth as the cutting, using a dibber or piece of tapering wood.

Insert the cutting, flat top uppermost, so that the top is flush with the surface of the compost. Put about six cuttings into each 5 in. pot.

Cover the cuttings with $\frac{1}{4}$ in. of coarse sand and spray with water. (Thinner roots can be used, but should be 2–3 in. long and planted horizontally about $\frac{1}{2}$ in. deep.)

Keep the cuttings in a greenhouse or a frame.

Six months later, shake out the rooted cuttings from their pot and gently separate them. Pot them and care for them in the same way as semi-hard cuttings (p. 251).

TAKING A SOFTWOOD CUTTING

Using a sharp knife, cut off a shoot with four or five pairs of leaves. Cut the bottom of the shoot diagonally, just below the first pair of leaves. Remove the first and second pair of leaves. Put about ten cuttings in a mixture of equal parts of peat and coarse sand in a 5 in. pot

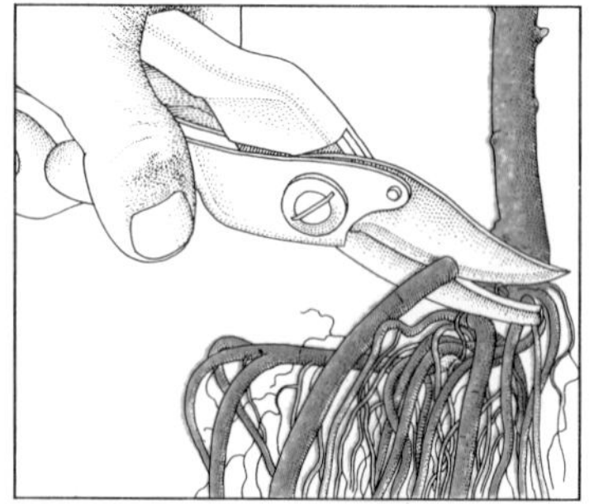

1 *With secateurs, cut off a thick root close to the main stem of the shrub*

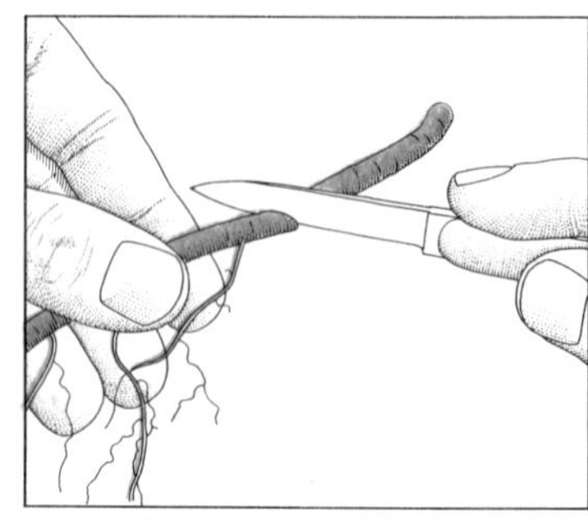

2 *Cut $1\frac{1}{2}$ in. pieces straight across at the top, but angled at the base*

3 *Plant in peat and sand so that the top is flush with the compost*

4 *Six months later, move the plants into $3\frac{1}{2}$ in. pots of potting compost*

Leaf-bud cuttings for speed and quantity

If several plants are required from a limited amount of propagating material, leaf-bud cuttings can be taken. Provided the propagating material is taken at the right time, individual buds can root and break into growth more quickly than those on a traditional cutting.

Nevertheless, hardwood or semi-hardwood cuttings usually make a bigger plant a year after rooting.

In August or September, cuttings can be taken from semi-hard lateral shoots – shoots that began growing in the spring. Each shoot will have several leaves, with a growth bud in each leaf axil.

With secateurs, cut off the shoot near its base. Then with a sharp knife, cut through the shoot at an angle, about $\frac{3}{4}$ in. below the lowest leaf.

Sever the shoot just above the bud in the leaf axil. Cut straight across. Three or four leaf-bud cuttings can be made this way.

Scrape some bark off the cutting with a knife. Then dip the end and the wounded part of the cutting in rooting powder.

Fill a pot to just below the rim with a proprietary cuttings compost, or one made with equal parts of peat and coarse sand.

Insert the cutting so that the bud just shows above the surface.

Take about 12 cuttings for each 6–7 in. pot.

Water the cuttings lightly after insertion. Use a small hand sprayer, or shake water on with the fingers. Cover the pot with a wire-and-polythene hood (p.251), to provide a humid atmosphere, and place it in the greenhouse or a frame.

Six months later, shake out the rooted cuttings from the pot and gently separate them.

Place potting compost in the bottom of the necessary number of $3\frac{1}{2}$ in. pots – one for each cutting.

Stand the rooted cutting centrally in the pot, and then top up with compost so that the cutting is covered to just below the original leaf.

Firm the compost so that the surface is about $\frac{1}{2}$ in. below the rim, to allow for watering. Water generously. Keep the pot in a greenhouse or frame. Never allow the compost to dry out.

In three to six weeks, the roots should reach the outside of the compost. If the plant is of a hardy genus, it can now be planted out in the open. Non-hardy plants should first go into a larger pot in the greenhouse, or a frame, for the following summer and winter before being planted out in the spring.

1 *In August or September cut off a shoot with several leaves*

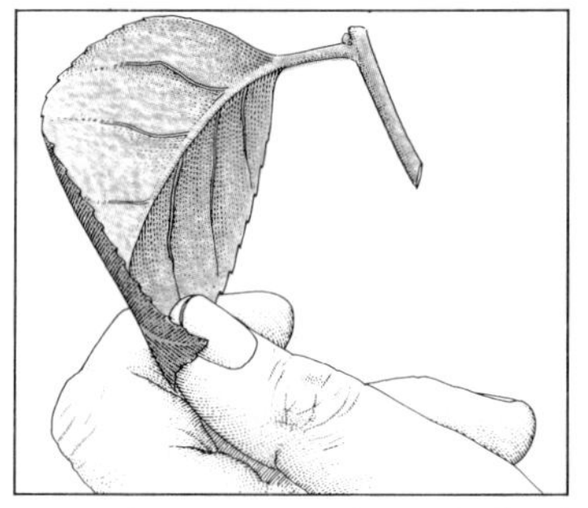

2 *Trim by cutting just above a leaf axil and about $\frac{3}{4}$ in. below it*

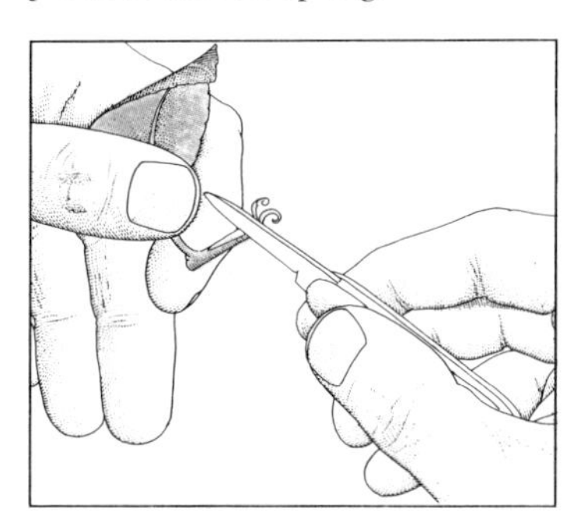

3 *Scrape off some bark, then dip the wounded part in rooting powder*

4 *Insert the cutting in peat and sand so that the leaf axil just shows*

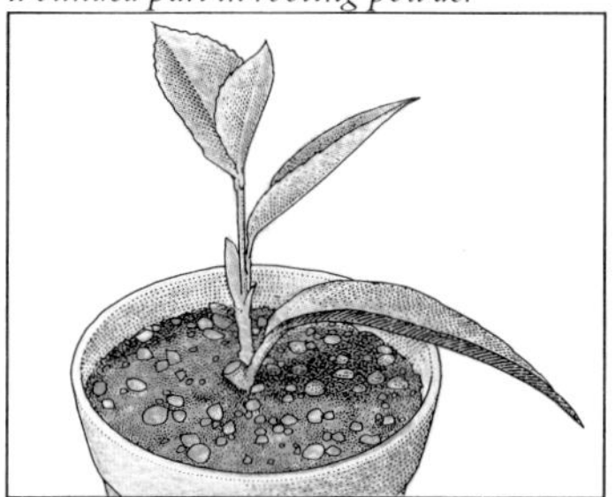

5 *Six months later, plant the cuttings in $3\frac{1}{2}$ in. pots of potting compost*

Grey mould – the main enemy of cuttings

The main enemy of cuttings is botrytis or grey mould.

It is a fluffy, greyish-white covering on stems, leaves or flower buds, and requires dead or dying plant tissues to grow on. Once established, it will kill the rest of the cuttings.

Grey mould thrives in cool, moist conditions, and is most troublesome from autumn to early spring.

Good hygiene will greatly reduce the incidence of the disease. Look carefully at batches of cuttings at least once a week, and remove all dying and dead leaves or whole cuttings. A fungicidal powder, such as quintozene or dinocap, may be applied (chart, p.398).

Using rooting powder to promote growth

Rooting powders or liquids contain growth-promoting substances (hormones) which, when applied to the base of a cutting, stimulate root formation.

These hormones are present in the plants themselves, but often in such minute quantities that natural rooting is very slow. By applying a dose of hormone, rooting is either speeded up or made more certain for plants that are difficult to root, such as chimonanthus, parrotia and dizygotheca.

However, where a plant normally roots readily, hormone treatment usually has a negative effect.

The proprietary brands of rooting powders and liquids come in different strengths; weaker for softwood and stronger for hardwood cuttings. There are also general-purpose formulas. If large-scale propagation is contemplated, it is worthwhile using a specific rooting preparation, but if small numbers of hard or soft cuttings are taken, then use a general-purpose preparation.

Layering – new plants from a growing shoot

Ordinary layering – the basic method

Layering is a simple method of propagating shrubs without a greenhouse or frame. It is based on the fact that a plant that has been cut, scraped or fractured is likely to produce roots from the wound if this portion of the shrub is in contact with soil.

The best branches for layering are non-flowering ones that have grown in the current year; that is, the freshest, smoothest shoots.

Deciduous plants are best layered in autumn or winter; evergreens in autumn or spring.

First, fork over the surface of the soil around the plant.

Choose any flexible branch and bend it down until it reaches the ground 9–12 in. from the tip. Strip the leaves off the branch where it touches the soil.

Wound the underside by cutting a shallow tongue with a knife, cutting towards the growing tip. Or twist the branch to injure the tissue.

Dig a hole 3–4 in. deep beneath the wound and part-fill with seed compost or equal parts of peat and coarse sand.

Push the wounded part of the branch into the hole, forming a right-angle at the wound.

Peg the branch to the ground with a bent piece of galvanised wire, 6–8 in. long, and stake the upright tip. Fill the hole with compost.

Repeat with other branches. Water the area thoroughly, and ensure that it never dries out.

Most plants should have rooted 12 months later.

Check the new roots by carefully scraping away the soil. If roots are well established, sever the new plant from the parent, lift with a good ball of soil and plant in position.

If the roots are not well grown, but the layer is healthy, replace the soil and leave a few more months before re-examining the layer.

A flexible branch that has grown in the current year is bent to the ground a few inches from the tip, slit with a knife and buried in moist compost. Twelve months later, roots should have grown from the wounded portion

1 *Bend a flexible branch and strip off the leaves 9–12 in. from the tip*

2 *Cut a shallow tongue into the underside of the branch, cutting towards the growing tip. Alternatively, twist the branch sharply to break the surface tissue*

3 *Bend the branch at the wound and peg into the ground with a piece of wire*

4 *Stake the upright tip and cover the wound with compost. Water well*

5 *A year later check roots have grown. If so, sever branch and plant out*

Serpentine layering for climbing shrubs

A handy method of propagating climbing shrubs with long pliable stems, such as honeysuckle and jasminum, is called serpentine layering. It should be done at the same time as ordinary layering. Use long, trailing shoots that have grown during the current year.

Bend a shoot to the ground carefully and, where it reaches the soil, dig a 2 in. deep hole beneath it. Wound the shoot underneath as for ordinary layering.

Peg the shoot into the hole with a piece of bent twig or wire.

Fill in the hole with a mixture of equal parts peat and coarse sand, or seed compost.

Cover with soil and firm with the fingers. Leave the next two pairs of leaves above ground and repeat the operation. Continue this way along the entire length of the shoot.

One year later, the layer should have rooted.

Scrape the soil away from each buried section of the layer and, if it is well rooted, sever it from the preceding section with secateurs. (If it is not well rooted, bury the whole layer again and check it a few months later.)

Each rooted section is now ready to plant out in the normal way.

Transplanting is made easier if, instead of pegging the shoots into holes in the ground, they are pegged into pots of peat and sand sunk into the ground. When the layer has rooted it can then be moved without disturbing the new roots.

1 *Bend down a shoot, peg into a 2 in. hole and fill the hole with seed compost*

2 *Repeat the operation leaving two pairs of leaves above the ground*

Air layering for stiff or high branches

When branches are too stiff or too high to be layered at soil level, they may be 'layered in the air'. This can be done between May and July.

Select a stretch of branch of the current year's growth and strip off the leaves in the middle. Then cut off a shallow slice of wood and put rooting powder on the cut.

Wrap a sheet of polythene around the area of the cut and tie the bottom of it with raffia or string.

Fill the open-topped tube with a mixture of equal parts moist peat, coarse sand and sphagnum moss. Fasten the top.

About ten weeks later, remove the polythene and cut off the new plant below the roots. Pot into a $4\frac{1}{2}$–6 in. pot containing potting compost.

Place the potted shrub in a closed frame for two weeks and keep it moist. Then harden it off. This entails opening the frame during the day, gradually admitting more air until the frame is left open entirely. Plant out the following spring.

1 *Select a branch of current year's growth and strip off a pair of leaves*

2 *Cut off a slice of wood and dab rooting powder on to the wounded area*

3 *Wrap polythene around cut, tie the bottom and fill with rooting mixture*

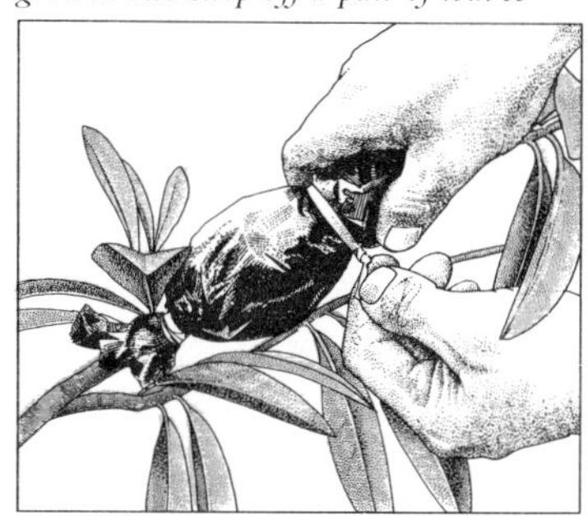

4 *Fasten the top of the tube and leave the plant for at least ten weeks*

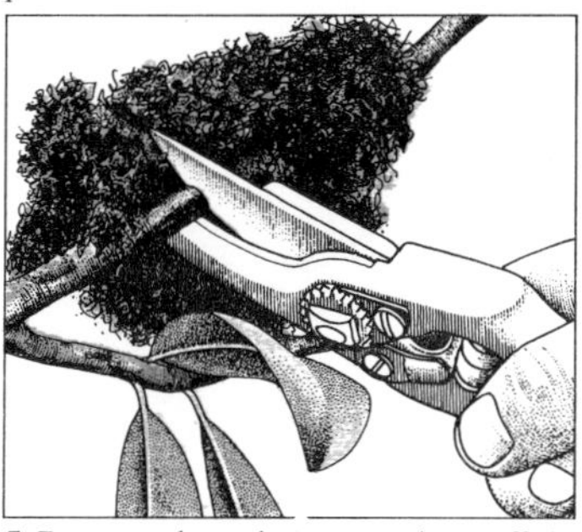

5 *Remove the polythene and cut off the new plant below the roots*

6 *Pot into a $4\frac{1}{2}$–6 in. pot with a potting compost of coarse sand and peat*

New shrubs from seeds, suckers and division

Collecting and storing seeds for spring sowing

Shrub seeds ripen at different times of the year, but usually in autumn.

Berries are ready to collect for propagation when they are changing colour. Seeds in pods or capsules are ready when their containers are turning brown or splitting open.

It is best to sow seeds immediately. Sprinkle them on a layer of seed compost in a pot, and cover with more compost. Put the pots in a sheltered spot until the spring, when the seeds will germinate.

Seeds can be stored, although berries and oily seeds keep only a few months. Dry ones will keep for several years. Berries and oily seeds, such as those of the paeony, can be kept in moist sand; dry seeds in an airtight jar.

The traditional way to store berries, used in nurseries where large numbers of shrubs are to be propagated, is to place a layer of moist sand in a pot; squash some berries with moist sand, then fill the pot with alternate layers of plain sand and the sand-and-berries mixture.

With oily seeds, simply put alternate layers of moist sand and the seeds in pots. Store the containers in a moist, cool, rodent-free place.

Sow no later than early March, or seedlings may grow in the sand.

Mix together the sand and seed in the container and sow the mixture.

For the complete method of growing plants from seed, see p. 215.

Shrub seeds *Oily seeds (left) of the tree paeony are best sown at once, otherwise store them in moist sand. Seeds of* Leycesteria formosa *(centre) can be stored dry. Japanese quinces (right) can be stored whole until spring*

STORING BERRIES IN SAND

Berries can be stored by putting a layer of sand into a pot and adding a layer of berries squashed with sand. Alternate the layers until the pot is full

Using suckers from below ground to grow new shrubs

Several kinds of trees and shrubs produce shoots from below ground, known as suckers. These produce roots suitable for propagation.

Examples include forsythia, deutzia, philadelphus, species roses, rhus, rubus, spiraea and weigela.

Trees that grow from suckers are ailanthus (tree of heaven), ulmus (elm), and various kinds of prunus.

Between October and March remove soil from the base of the sucker to check that roots have formed.

Cut the sucker close to its point of origin (a stem or a root) and lift.

Plant well-rooted specimens in permanent sites, and poorly rooted ones in a nursery row to grow on.

Plants to be propagated by suckers must be growing on their own roots. Suckers from grafted plants, such as some roses, hamamelis, rhododendrons and viburnums, only reproduce the rootstock.

PROPAGATION BY SUCKERS

In autumn or winter, remove soil from the base of the sucker to check that roots have formed. Then cut off the sucker close to its point of origin with stem or root

Simple division to produce large new plants

Many shrubs produce their main branches from underground buds. Subsequently, the buried bases of the branches produce roots. These shrubs resemble woody herbaceous perennials and can be divided in the same way. This is an easy way to obtain large new plants instantly.

An existing shrub is lifted and divided into several equal-sized pieces, each with plenty of roots attached. The pieces can then be planted out separately at once.

This method is best carried out in spring, but it can be done at any time between October and April. The shrub should be at least three years old before it is divided.

Shrubs propagated in this way include romneya, ruscus, *Kerria japonica*, *Rubus cockburnianus*, *Ceratostigma plumbaginoides* and *Clerodendrum bungei*.

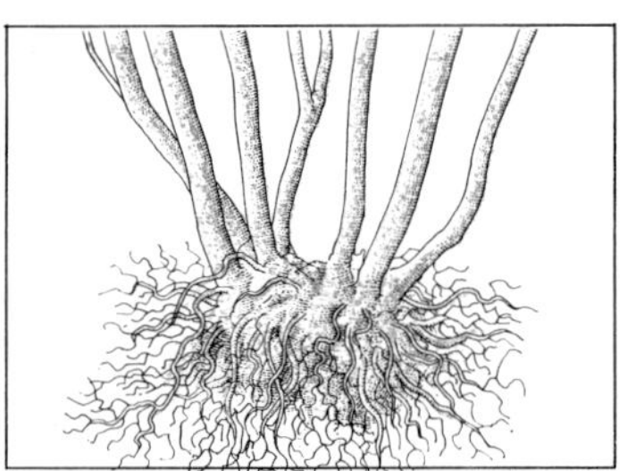

1 *Plants to be divided must produce the main branches from below the ground*

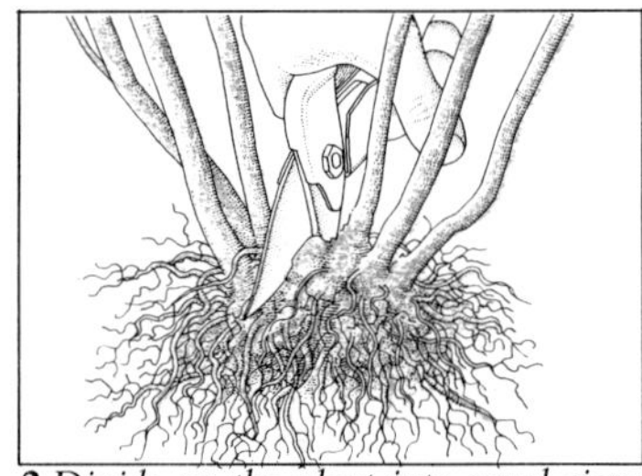

2 *Divide up the plant into equal-sized pieces with roots, and replant*

Six ways of pruning shrubs and climbers

A shrub will rarely suffer if it is left unpruned. However, you may wish to control the size of a shrub, or to remove straggly branches which spoil its appearance. And dead or diseased branches should be cut away to prevent the spread of infection. On some shrubs, growth may be improved if light is let into the centre by cutting away old branches. And some shrubs will produce larger – but generally fewer – flowers if pruned each year.

Three tools are used in pruning: secateurs for removing shoots and small stems; long-handled loppers for larger stems; and a pruning saw for large branches.

A sharp knife may also be needed for trimming large wounds.

When shortening branches, cut just above an outward-facing bud or shoot. Cut diagonally, parallel with the angle of the bud or shoot.

When removing entire branches, cut flush with the trunk or main branch. Then trim the raw area with the sharp knife and paint it with a wound-sealing compound, or any household paint. This will prevent disease spores entering the shrub through the wound.

Shrubs which have been hard pruned – especially when this is an annual operation – benefit from a 2 in. thick mulch of garden compost or decayed manure after pruning, plus 2 oz. (2 tablespoons) to the square yard of a general fertiliser, such as Growmore.

Method 1 Removing dead and straggly wood only

This method of pruning applies to most shrubs, and may only involve the removal of a small piece of damaged branch.

It can be done at any time of year. You will probably carry it out when a shrub develops a long straggly branch, or after a storm when a branch has been damaged. Or you might prefer to carry out a routine examination of all shrubs in the garden every spring.

Remove any dead or damaged wood, cutting back to a healthy shoot or bud, facing outwards. Then remove shoots that are particularly weak, cutting right back to a main branch. If any branches have grown straggly and unsightly, prune them by half to a strong shoot or bud facing outwards.

Do not remove any well-formed, healthy wood, or you are likely to cut off many of the buds that would produce flowers later.

A few of the most popular shrubs pruned in this way are camellia, cistus, daphne, euonymus, hebe, potentilla and viburnum.

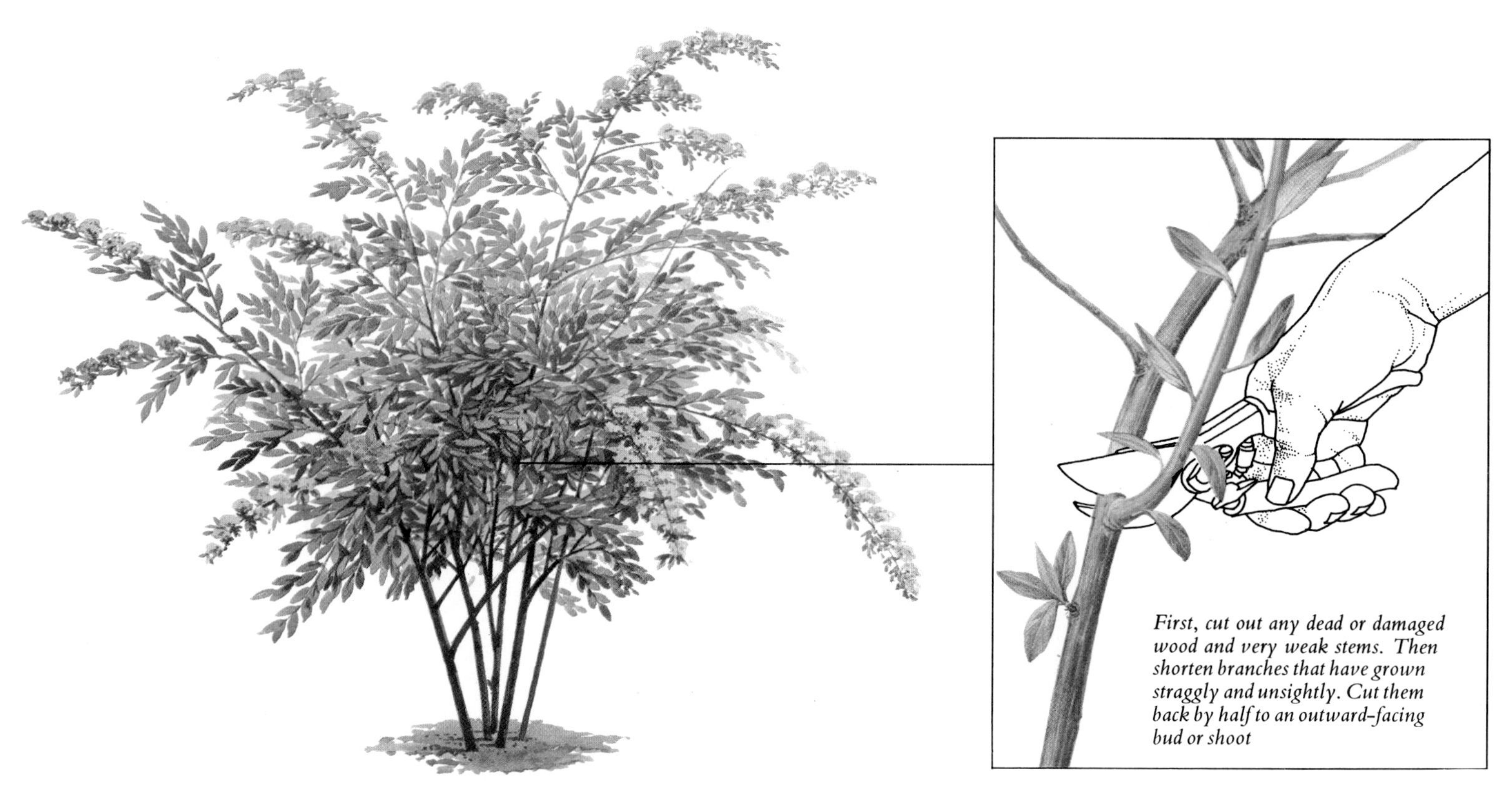

First, cut out any dead or damaged wood and very weak stems. Then shorten branches that have grown straggly and unsightly. Cut them back by half to an outward-facing bud or shoot

Method 2 Cutting down large overgrown plants

Some shrubs, particularly evergreens, should not be pruned at all until, after many years, they become overgrown or bare at the base. Then, in spring, cut all the main branches down to within a few inches of the ground with a saw. Mulch with garden compost or rotted manure and apply 2 oz. (2 tablespoons) to the square yard of general fertiliser, such as Growmore. The shrub will not flower the following summer.

SHRUBS THAT CAN BE PRUNED BY THIS METHOD	
Aucuba (Spotted laurel)	Pieris
Olearia (Daisy bush)	*Prunus laurocerasus, P. lusitanica* (Cherry laurels)
Pernettya	
Philadelphus (Mock orange)	

Begin pruning an old, overgrown shrub by clearing away the top growth with loppers

Saw off branches a few inches from the ground. Paint stumps with wound-sealing compound

Method 3 For shrubs that flower on last year's wood

Some shrubs flower on shoots grown the previous year. These can be pruned each year immediately they finish flowering, whether in spring, summer or in winter. The pruning is aimed at keeping the shrub in bounds, or promoting larger but fewer flowers.

Cut each shoot that has borne flowers back to two or three shoots or buds from its junction with the parent stem. The new shoots will produce flowers next season.

SHRUBS THAT CAN BE PRUNED BY THIS METHOD	
Buddleia alternifolia	*Prunus glandulosa, P. triloba*
Cytisus (all species except *C.* × 'Porlock')	Rubus
Deutzia	*Spiraea* × *arguta*
Kerria	Weigela
Mahonia aquifolium (as ground-cover)	

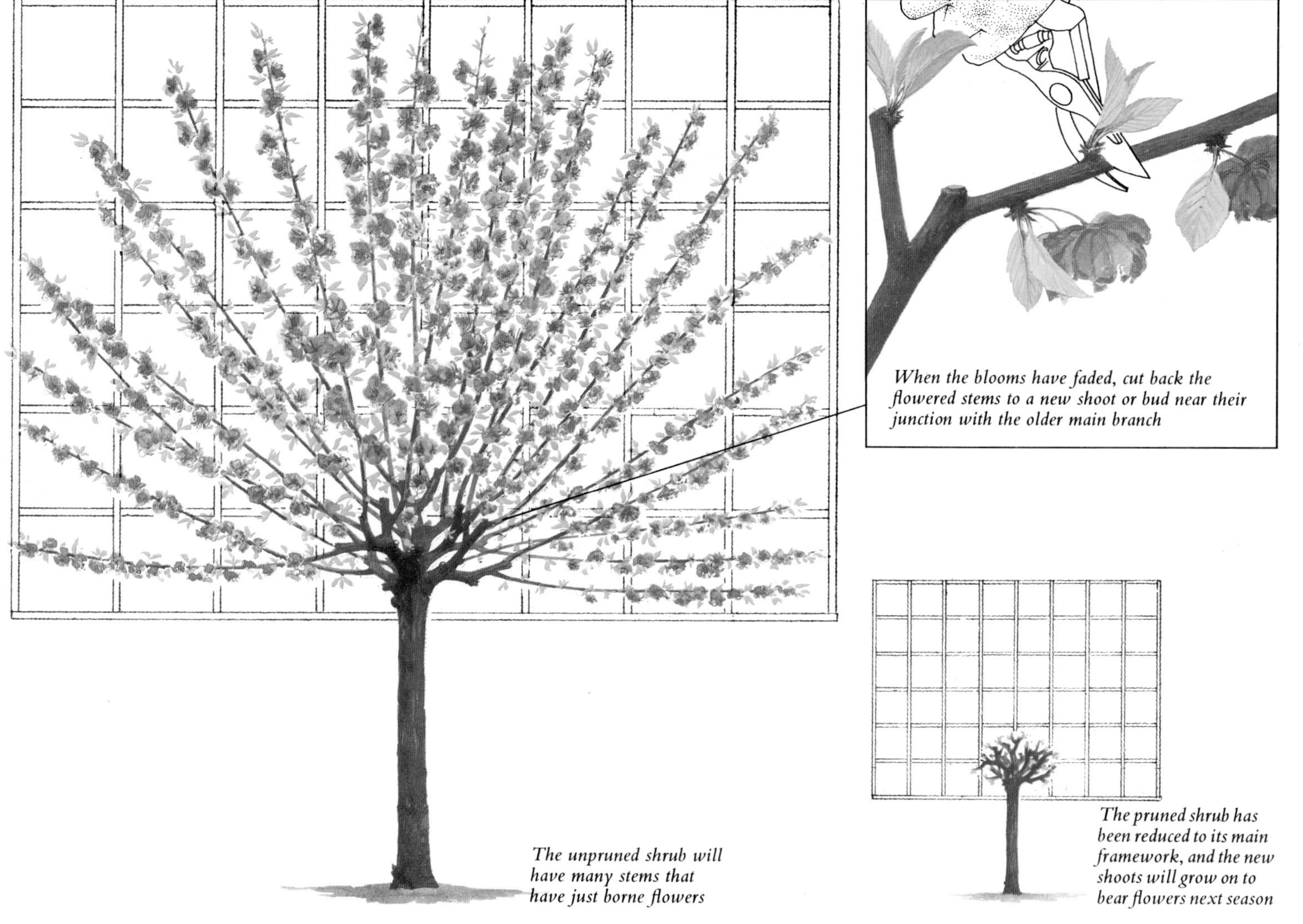

When the blooms have faded, cut back the flowered stems to a new shoot or bud near their junction with the older main branch

The unpruned shrub will have many stems that have just borne flowers

The pruned shrub has been reduced to its main framework, and the new shoots will grow on to bear flowers next season

Method 4 For shrubs that flower on new shoots

Some shrubs flower on shoots that have grown in the current season.

To restrict their size, or to encourage larger but fewer flowers, they can be pruned in spring, as growth is beginning.

Cut all last year's shoots back to two or three buds or shoots from their base. Unless you want to remove a branch altogether, do not cut back into the older wood, as new shoots might not grow.

After pruning, mulch with a 2 in. layer of garden compost or rotted manure and apply 2 oz. (2 tablespoons) to the square yard of general fertiliser, such as Growmore.

SHRUBS THAT CAN BE PRUNED BY THIS METHOD

Buddleia davidii
Caryopteris
Ceanothus (deciduous)
Ceratostigma
Colutea
Cytisus × 'Porlock'
Fuchsia
Indigofera
Lippia
Passiflora
Santolina
Solanum crispum
Spartium
Spiraea bullata, S. × *bumalda, S. douglasii, S. japonica, S. menziesii, S. salicifolia*
Tamarix pentandra

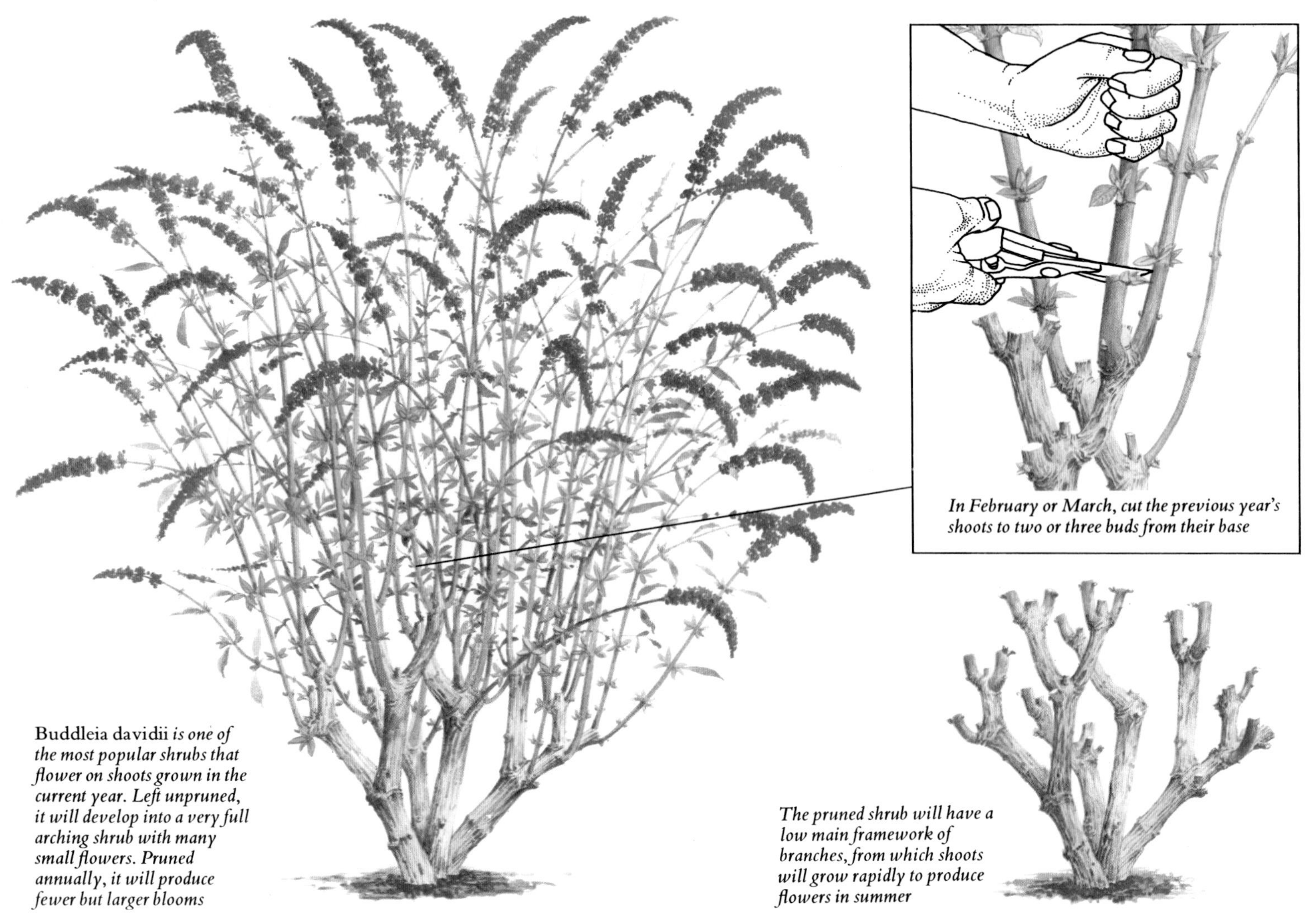

In February or March, cut the previous year's shoots to two or three buds from their base

Buddleia davidii *is one of the most popular shrubs that flower on shoots grown in the current year. Left unpruned, it will develop into a very full arching shrub with many small flowers. Pruned annually, it will produce fewer but larger blooms*

The pruned shrub will have a low main framework of branches, from which shoots will grow rapidly to produce flowers in summer

Method 5 Clearing out old wood from the centre

Some shrubs, most notably the common *Hydrangea macrophylla*, benefit from having some of the oldest growth removed almost at ground level each year.

In spring, cut out the three-year-old stems, which are rough-looking and have sub-laterals as well as laterals. Make the cut within an inch or two of the ground. You may also cut away some of the two-year-old stems, which have laterals but no sub-laterals.

For pruning *Hydrangea paniculata*, see page 269.

SHRUBS THAT CAN BE PRUNED BY THIS METHOD

Hydrangea macrophylla
And overgrown specimens of:
Berberis
Clethra
Cotoneaster
Forsythia
Genista
Hebe
Kolkwitzia
Potentilla
Ribes sanguineum
Symphoricarpos

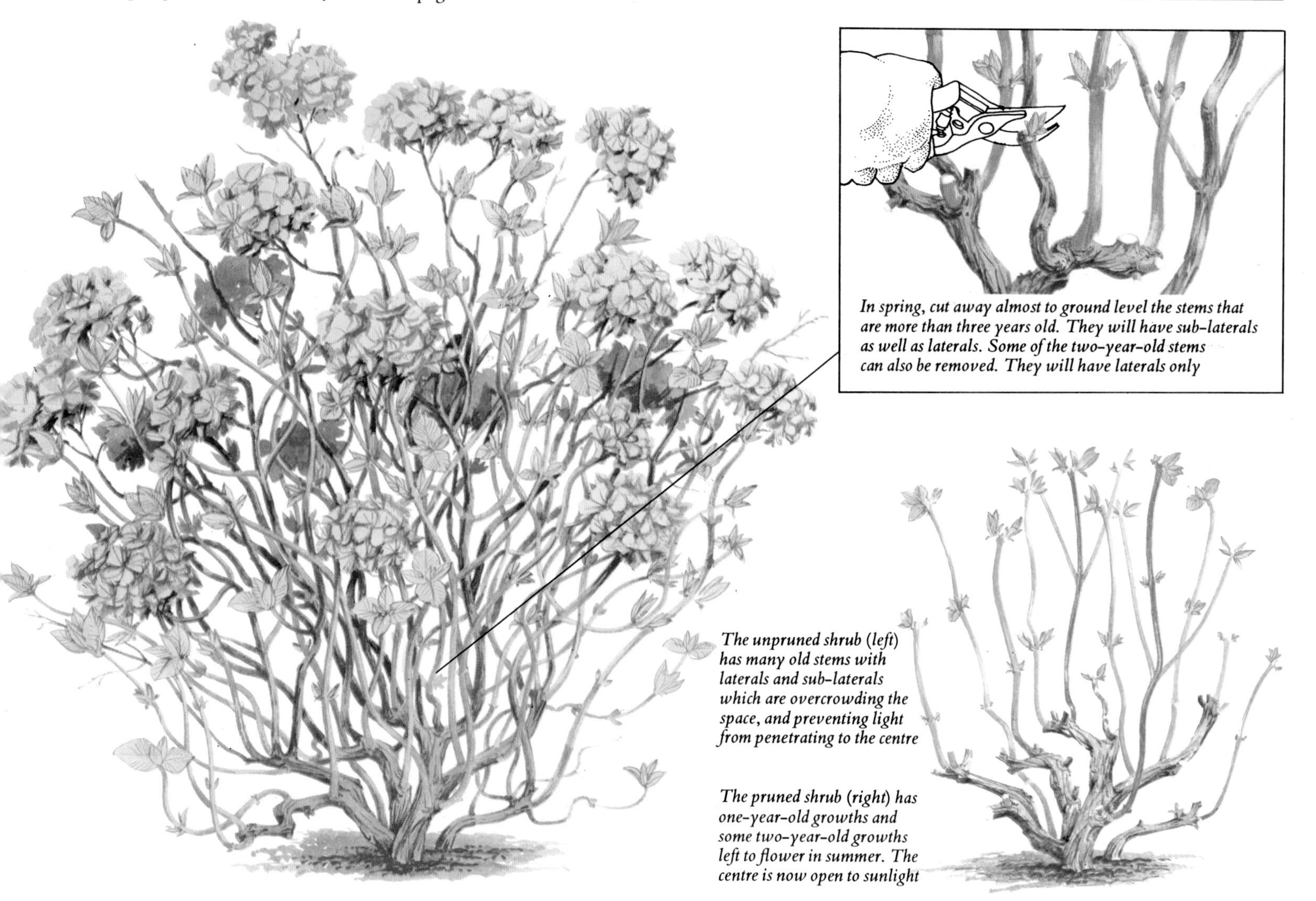

In spring, cut away almost to ground level the stems that are more than three years old. They will have sub-laterals as well as laterals. Some of the two-year-old stems can also be removed. They will have laterals only

The unpruned shrub (left) has many old stems with laterals and sub-laterals which are overcrowding the space, and preventing light from penetrating to the centre

The pruned shrub (right) has one-year-old growths and some two-year-old growths left to flower in summer. The centre is now open to sunlight

Method 6 Restricting the size of climbing plants

Leave most climbers unpruned until they get too large, then prune after flowering. Prune non-flowering climbers in spring or summer.

Self-clinging climbers, such as ivy or climbing hydrangea, can be trimmed as necessary on the wall.

Climbers that use supports, such as honeysuckle and clematis, should first be detached from the supports. Then remove all lateral growths, just leaving the main stems.

If the main stems look extremely old, remove them and keep some of the younger ones – either shoots growing from ground level or from low down on the old stems.

For clematis also see page 265, and for wistaria see page 280.

SHRUBS THAT CAN BE PRUNED BY THIS METHOD

Actinidia
Campsis
Clematis armandii, C. macropetala, C. montana
Hydrangea petiolaris (Climbing hydrangea)
Lonicera japonica, L. periclymenum (Honeysuckle)
Parthenocissus (Virginia creeper)
Polygonum baldschuanicum (Russian vine)
Vitis (Ornamental grape vine)

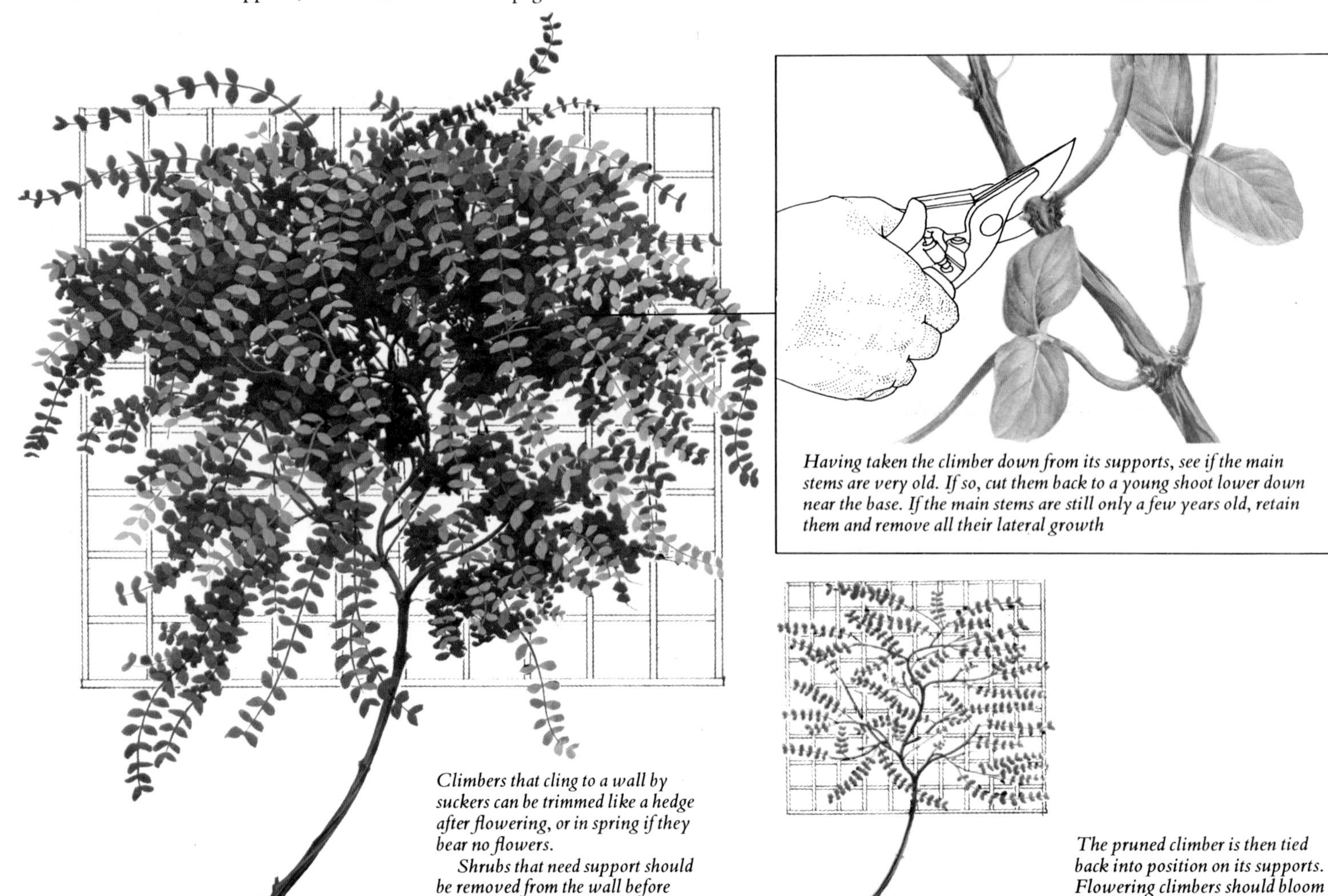

Having taken the climber down from its supports, see if the main stems are very old. If so, cut them back to a young shoot lower down near the base. If the main stems are still only a few years old, retain them and remove all their lateral growth

Climbers that cling to a wall by suckers can be trimmed like a hedge after flowering, or in spring if they bear no flowers.

Shrubs that need support should be removed from the wall before pruning is started

The pruned climber is then tied back into position on its supports. Flowering climbers should bloom again next year

Pruning 36 popular shrubs – in close-up

Buddleia alternifolia After flowering, remove old shoots to encourage new ones

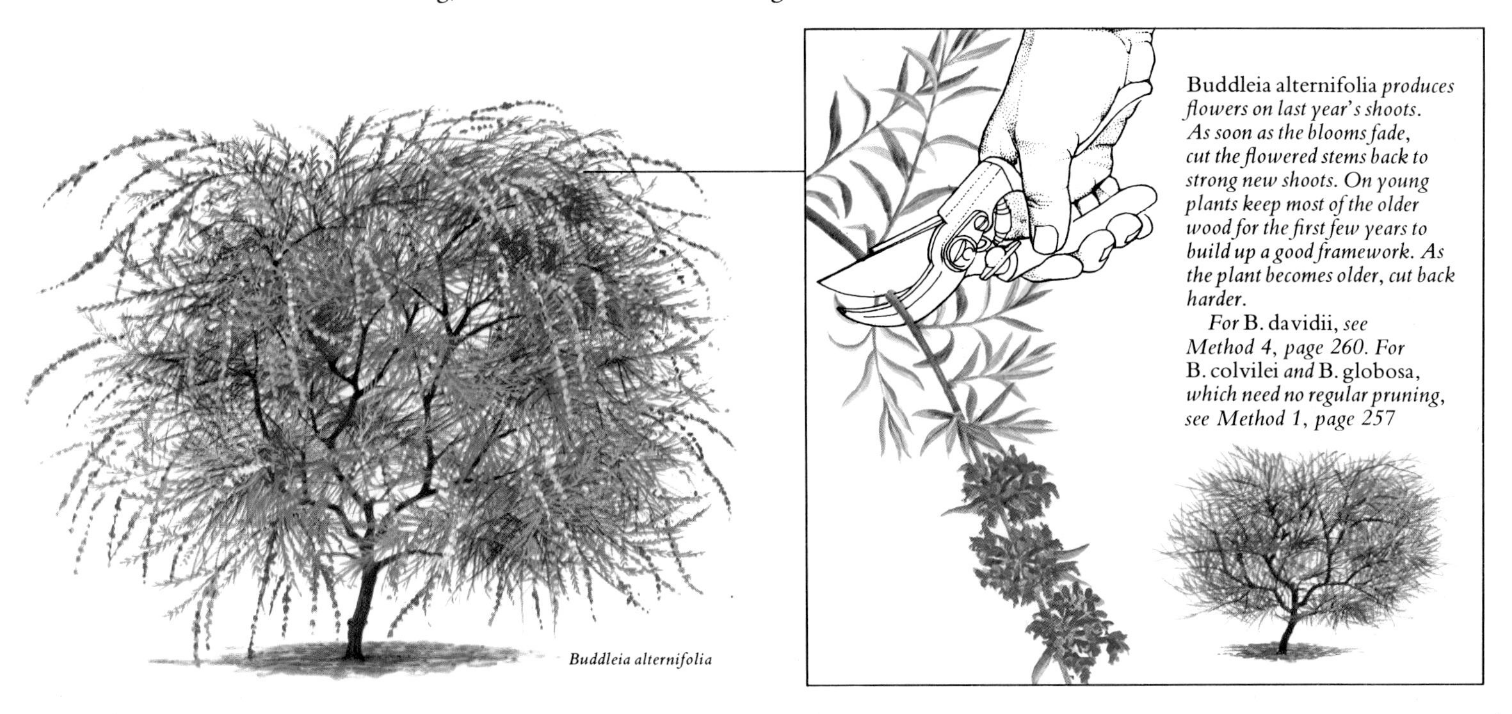

Buddleia alternifolia

Buddleia alternifolia *produces flowers on last year's shoots. As soon as the blooms fade, cut the flowered stems back to strong new shoots. On young plants keep most of the older wood for the first few years to build up a good framework. As the plant becomes older, cut back harder.*

For B. davidii, *see Method 4, page 260. For* B. colvilei *and* B. globosa, *which need no regular pruning, see Method 1, page 257*

Caryopteris The bush becomes twiggy, with small flowers, unless it is pruned each spring

Caryopteris × clandonensis

In February or March, cut the previous year's shoots back to a new shoot 1 in. from the old wood. Remove all dead, weak or crowded shoots

Ceanothus (Deciduous types). Prune in late March or early April; the new shoots will flower in late summer

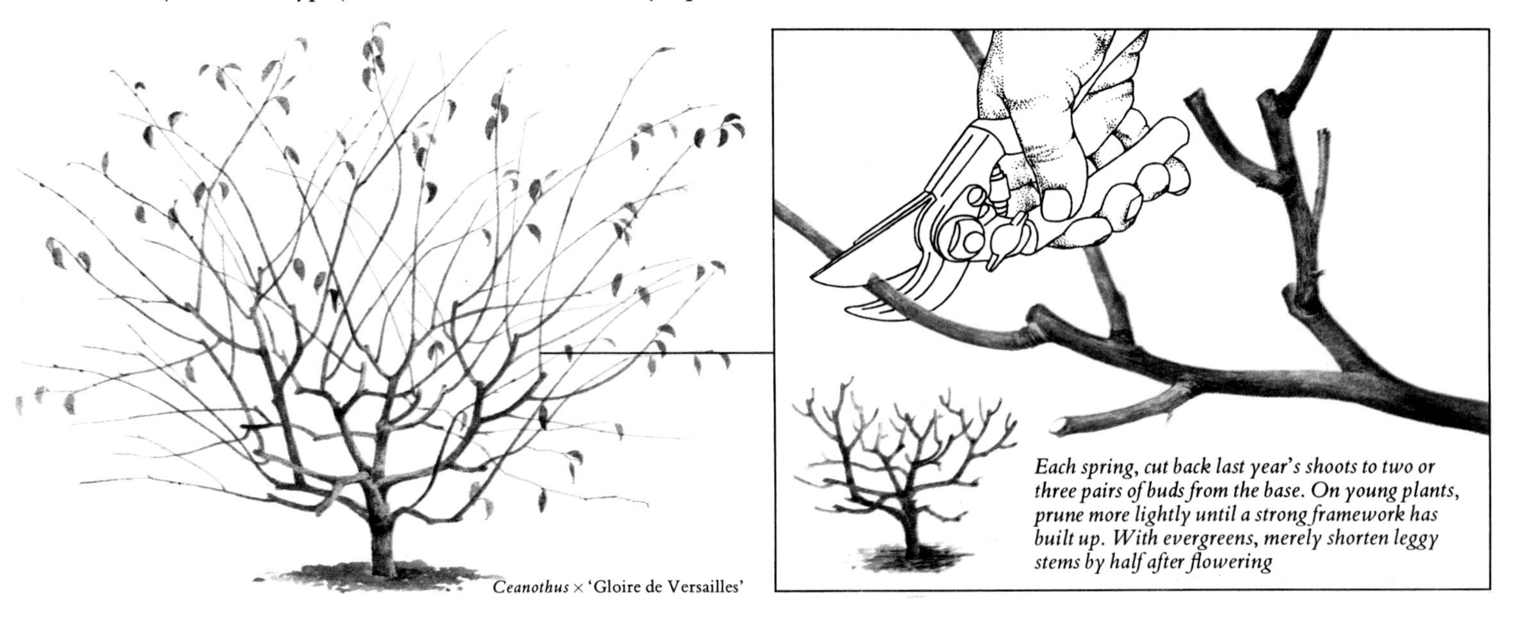

Each spring, cut back last year's shoots to two or three pairs of buds from the base. On young plants, prune more lightly until a strong framework has built up. With evergreens, merely shorten leggy stems by half after flowering

Ceratostigma Cut to the ground in late March or early April for flowers on the new season's wood

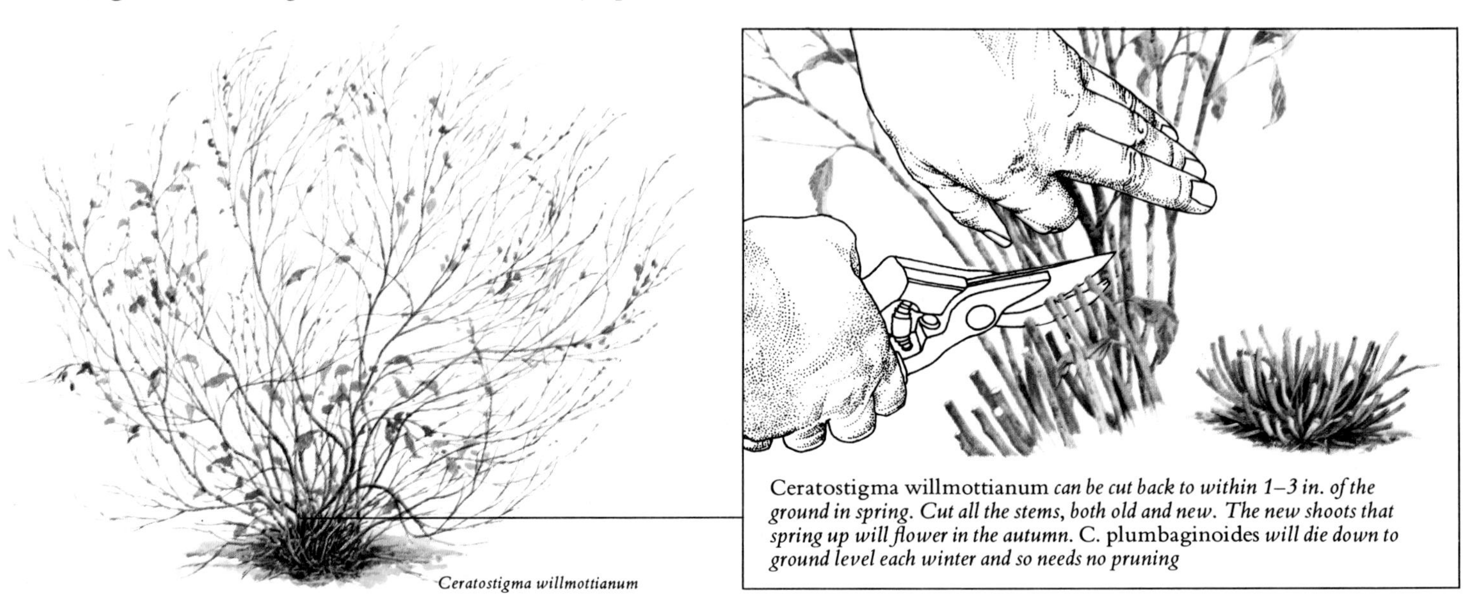

Ceratostigma willmottianum *can be cut back to within 1–3 in. of the ground in spring. Cut all the stems, both old and new. The new shoots that spring up will flower in the autumn.* C. plumbaginoides *will die down to ground level each winter and so needs no pruning*

Chaenomeles (Japanese quince, japonica or cydonia). Prune a wall-trained shrub in summer to keep it within bounds

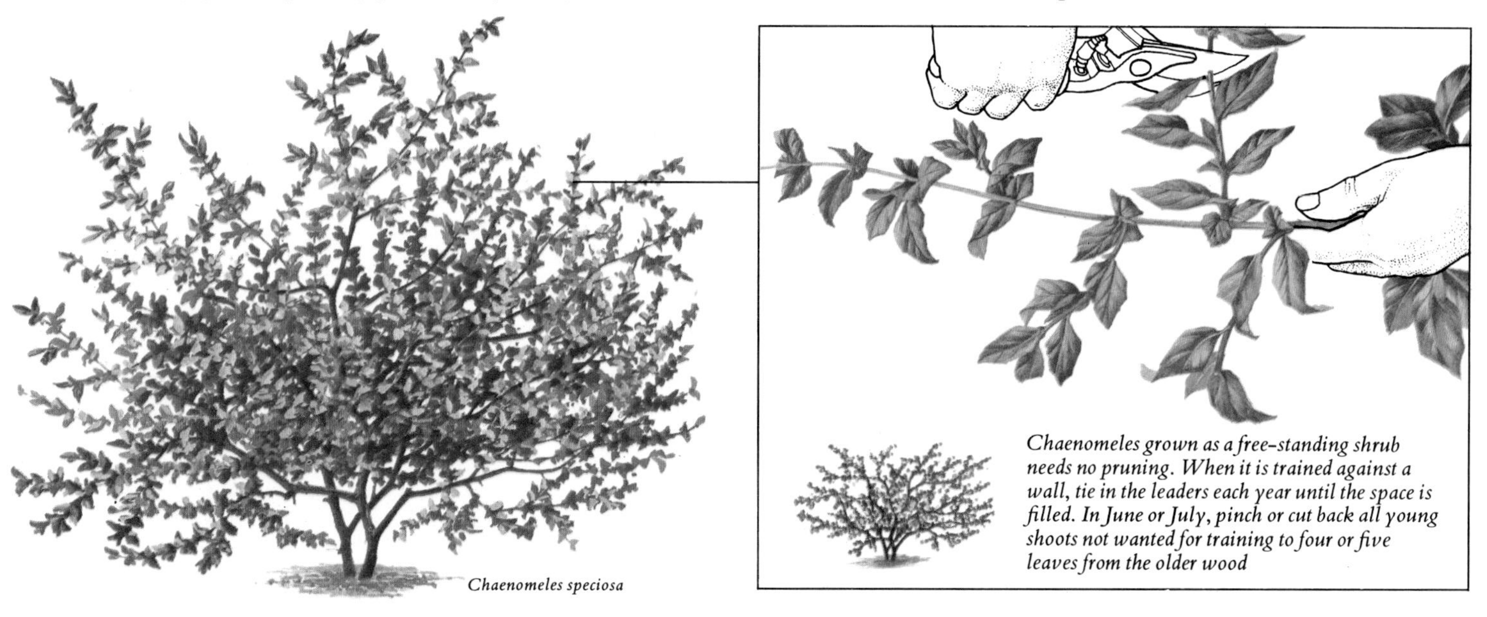

Chaenomeles speciosa

Chaenomeles grown as a free-standing shrub needs no pruning. When it is trained against a wall, tie in the leaders each year until the space is filled. In June or July, pinch or cut back all young shoots not wanted for training to four or five leaves from the older wood

Clematis For the greatest show of flowers no pruning is necessary, but eventually the tangled shoots may need to be cut back

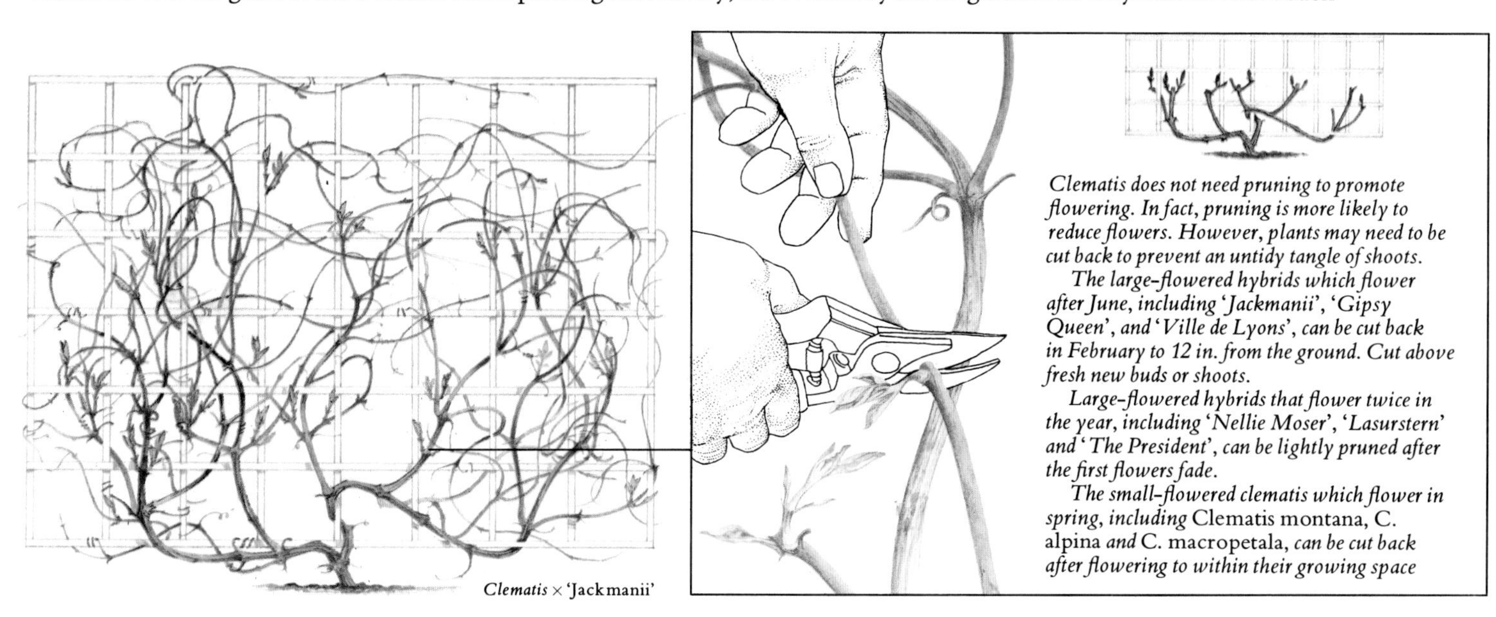

Clematis × 'Jackmanii'

Clematis does not need pruning to promote flowering. In fact, pruning is more likely to reduce flowers. However, plants may need to be cut back to prevent an untidy tangle of shoots.

The large-flowered hybrids which flower after June, including 'Jackmanii', 'Gipsy Queen', and 'Ville de Lyons', can be cut back in February to 12 in. from the ground. Cut above fresh new buds or shoots.

Large-flowered hybrids that flower twice in the year, including 'Nellie Moser', 'Lasurstern' and 'The President', can be lightly pruned after the first flowers fade.

The small-flowered clematis which flower in spring, including Clematis montana, C. alpina *and* C. macropetala, *can be cut back after flowering to within their growing space*

Cornus (Dogwood). For coloured stems in winter, hard prune *Cornus alba* and *C. stolonifera* 'Flaviramea' in February or March

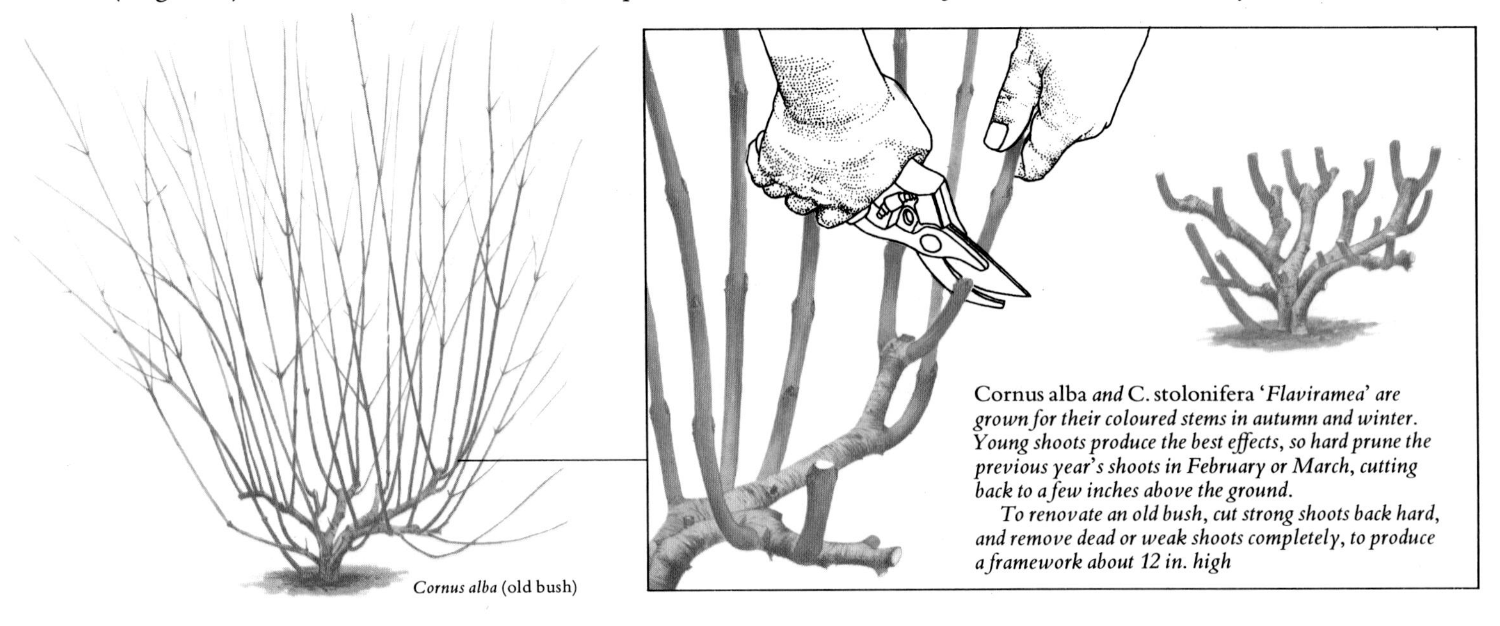

Cornus alba (old bush)

Cornus alba *and* C. stolonifera *'Flaviramea' are grown for their coloured stems in autumn and winter. Young shoots produce the best effects, so hard prune the previous year's shoots in February or March, cutting back to a few inches above the ground.*

To renovate an old bush, cut strong shoots back hard, and remove dead or weak shoots completely, to produce a framework about 12 in. high

Cytisus (Broom). Prune after the flowers fade to prevent the shrub becoming leggy

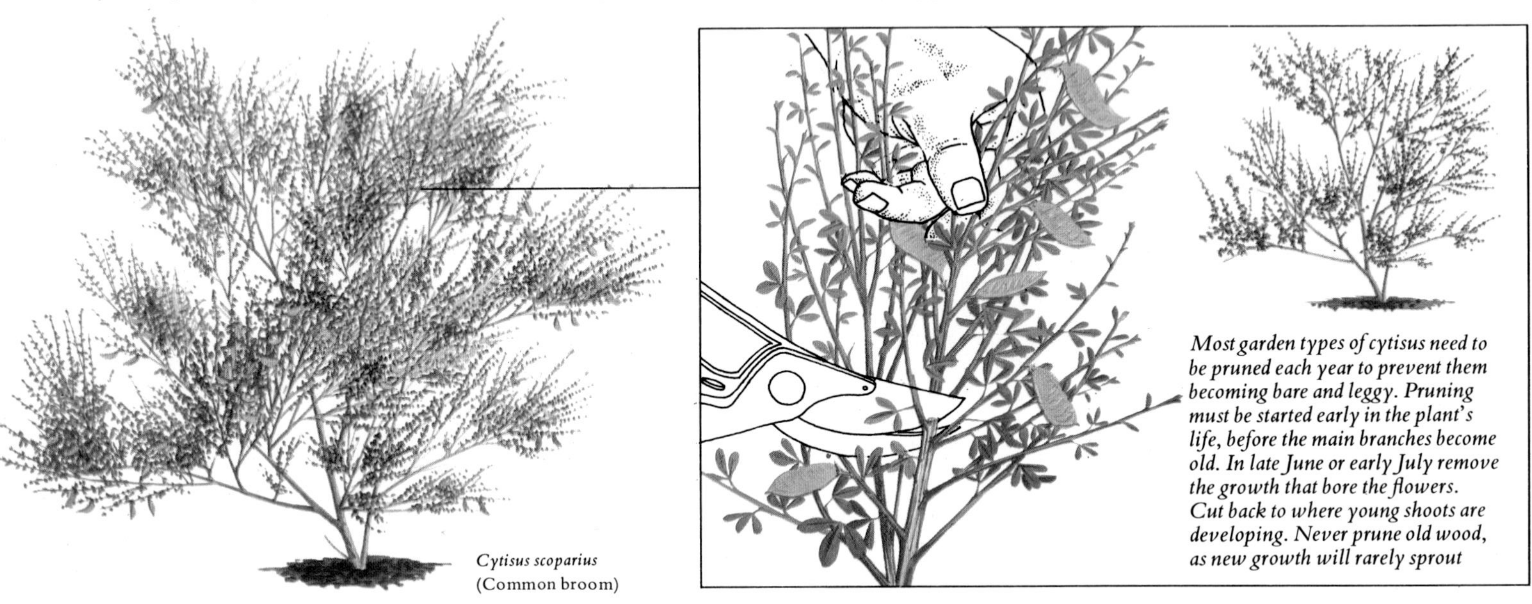

Cytisus scoparius (Common broom)

Most garden types of cytisus need to be pruned each year to prevent them becoming bare and leggy. Pruning must be started early in the plant's life, before the main branches become old. In late June or early July remove the growth that bore the flowers. Cut back to where young shoots are developing. Never prune old wood, as new growth will rarely sprout

Deutzia Remove the flowered stems in July to prevent the shrub becoming untidy

Deutzia × hybrida

Left unpruned, deutzias will become dense and untidy, with progressively fewer flowers. After the flowers fade, usually in July, cut the flowered stems back to a point where new shoots are developing. Some deutzias have attractive flaking bark on the old wood; if this is wanted as a winter feature, leave some old shoots unpruned on the shrub

Forsythia Replace poor-flowering wood regularly; prune in April after flowering

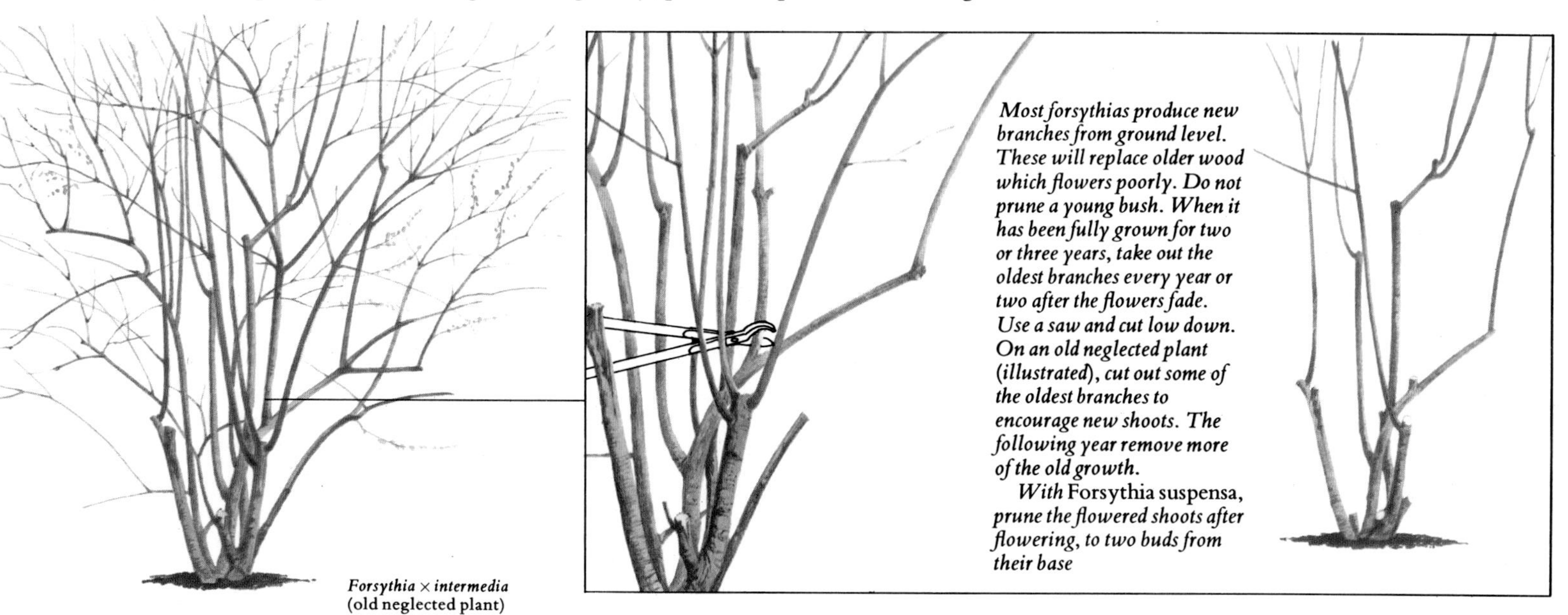

Forsythia × intermedia
(old neglected plant)

Most forsythias produce new branches from ground level. These will replace older wood which flowers poorly. Do not prune a young bush. When it has been fully grown for two or three years, take out the oldest branches every year or two after the flowers fade. Use a saw and cut low down. On an old neglected plant (illustrated), cut out some of the oldest branches to encourage new shoots. The following year remove more of the old growth.

With Forsythia suspensa, *prune the flowered shoots after flowering, to two buds from their base*

Fuchsia (Hardy types). Cut back hard in February or March to encourage strong new shoots

Fuchsia magellanica

Hydrangea macrophylla To restrict the size of an old shrub, prune out the oldest stems in March

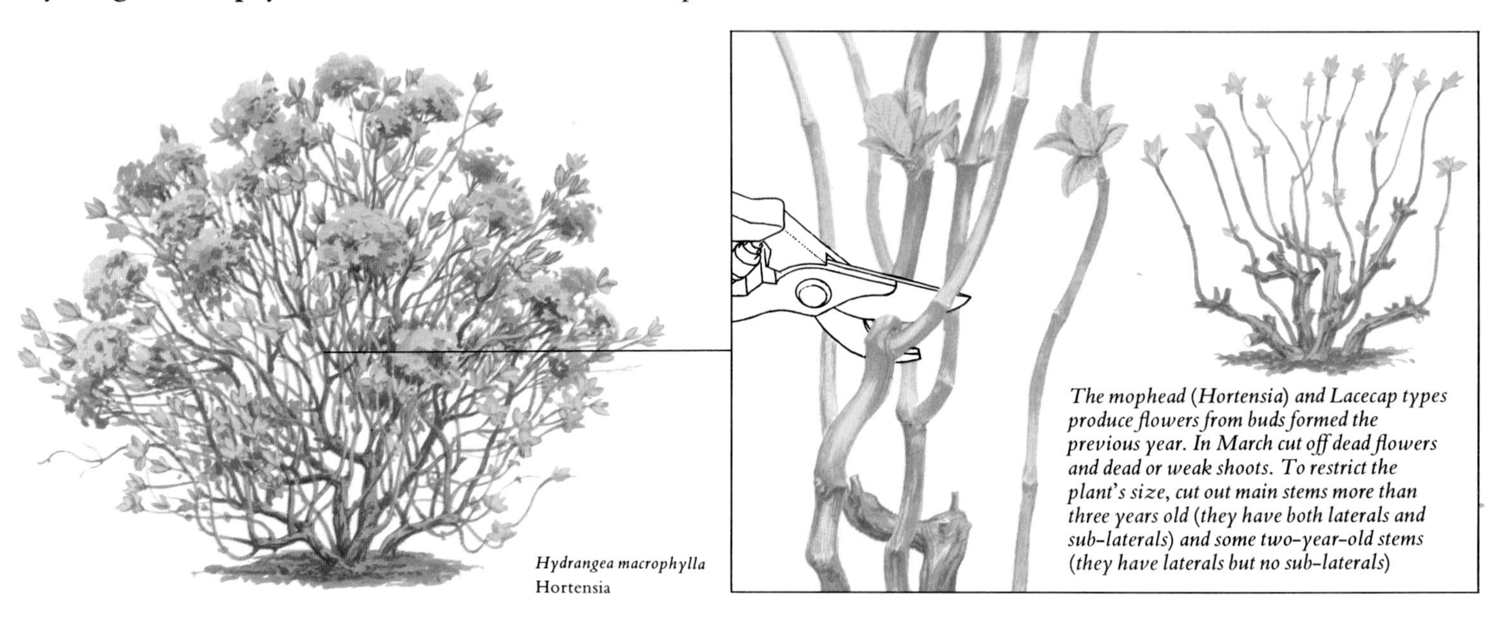

Hydrangea macrophylla
Hortensia

Hydrangea paniculata The tall hydrangea with white, pyramidal flowers is pruned hard back in February or March

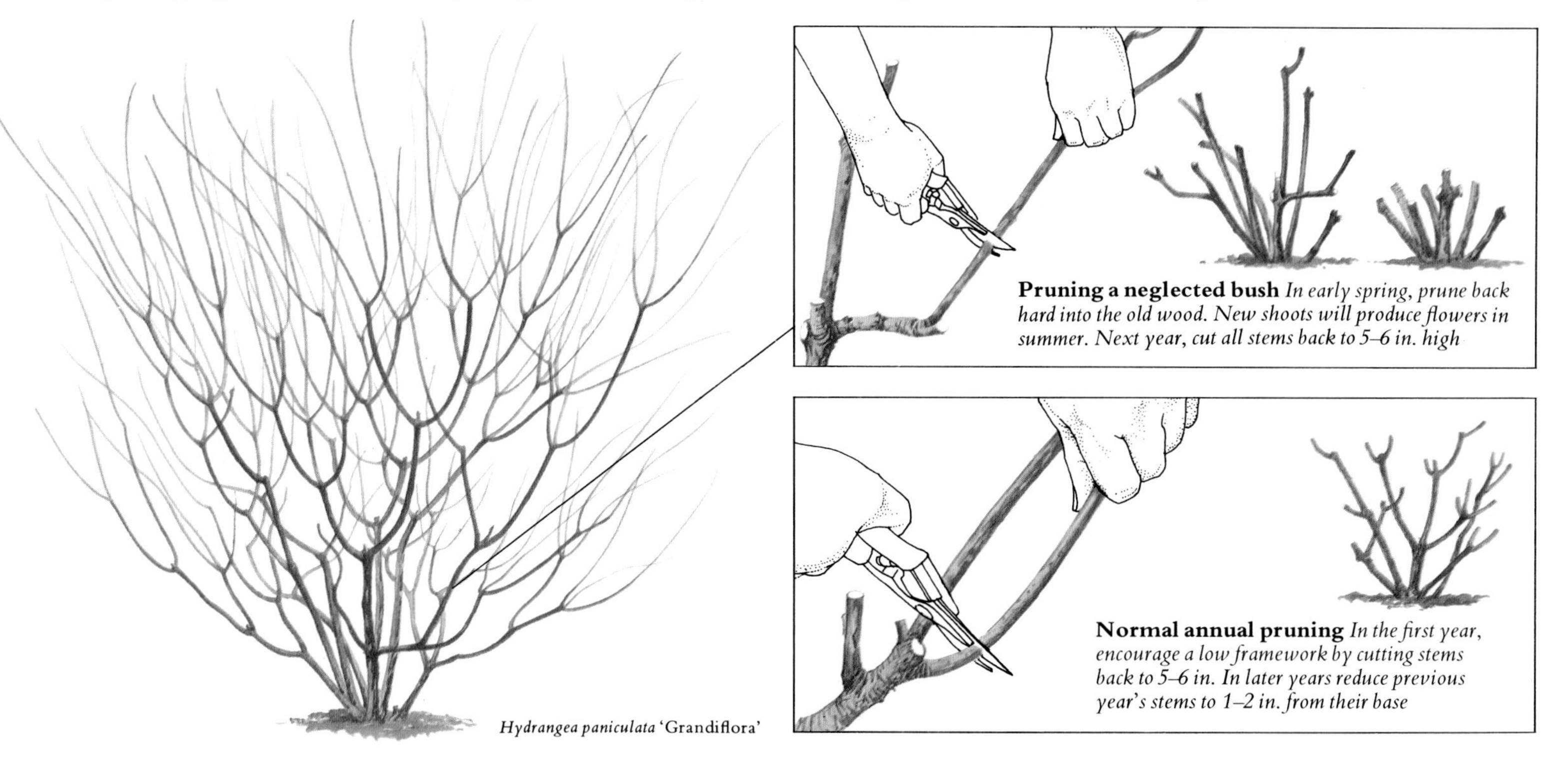

Pruning a neglected bush *In early spring, prune back hard into the old wood. New shoots will produce flowers in summer. Next year, cut all stems back to 5–6 in. high*

Normal annual pruning *In the first year, encourage a low framework by cutting stems back to 5–6 in. In later years reduce previous year's stems to 1–2 in. from their base*

Hydrangea paniculata 'Grandiflora'

Hypericum calycinum (Rose of Sharon). Cut back with shears in early spring to produce dense, low cover

Use garden shears to cut the old shoots back to within 2–3 in. of the base in late February or March. At the same time, clear away dead leaves and garden debris. Young shoots will quickly develop and flower in summer

Hypericum calycinum

Hypericum (Shrubby types). Prune the tall-growing hypericums in March to remove dead and spindly wood

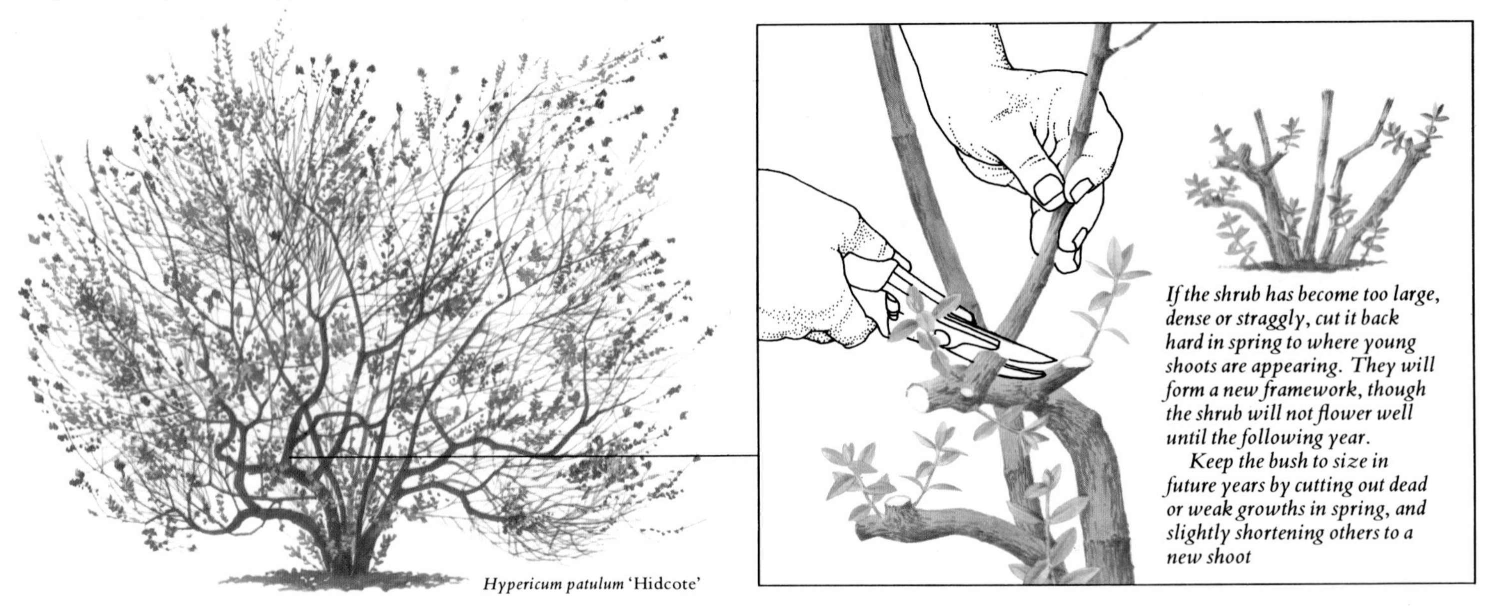
Hypericum patulum 'Hidcote'

If the shrub has become too large, dense or straggly, cut it back hard in spring to where young shoots are appearing. They will form a new framework, though the shrub will not flower well until the following year.

Keep the bush to size in future years by cutting out dead or weak growths in spring, and slightly shortening others to a new shoot

Indigofera Winter frosts may do the pruning for you; if not, cut hard back in spring

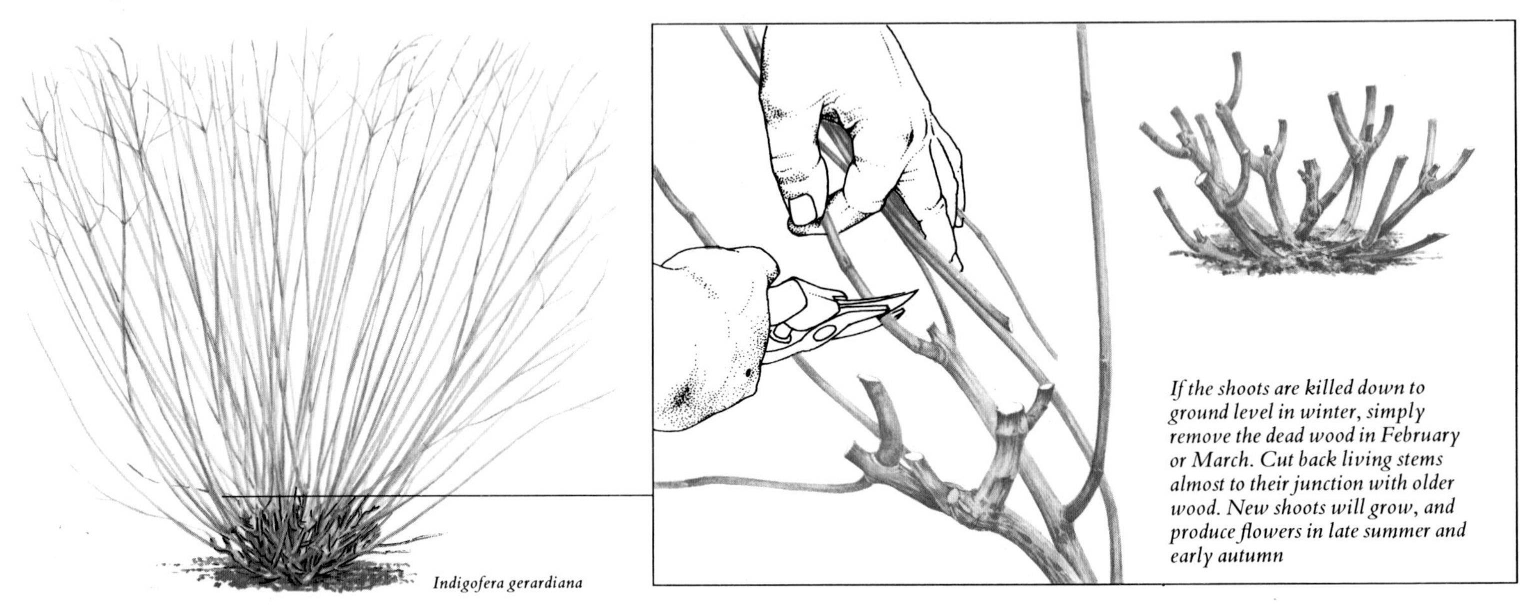
Indigofera gerardiana

If the shoots are killed down to ground level in winter, simply remove the dead wood in February or March. Cut back living stems almost to their junction with older wood. New shoots will grow, and produce flowers in late summer and early autumn

Jasminum nudiflorum (Winter jasmine). After flowering, cut back flowered shoots and thin out weak stems

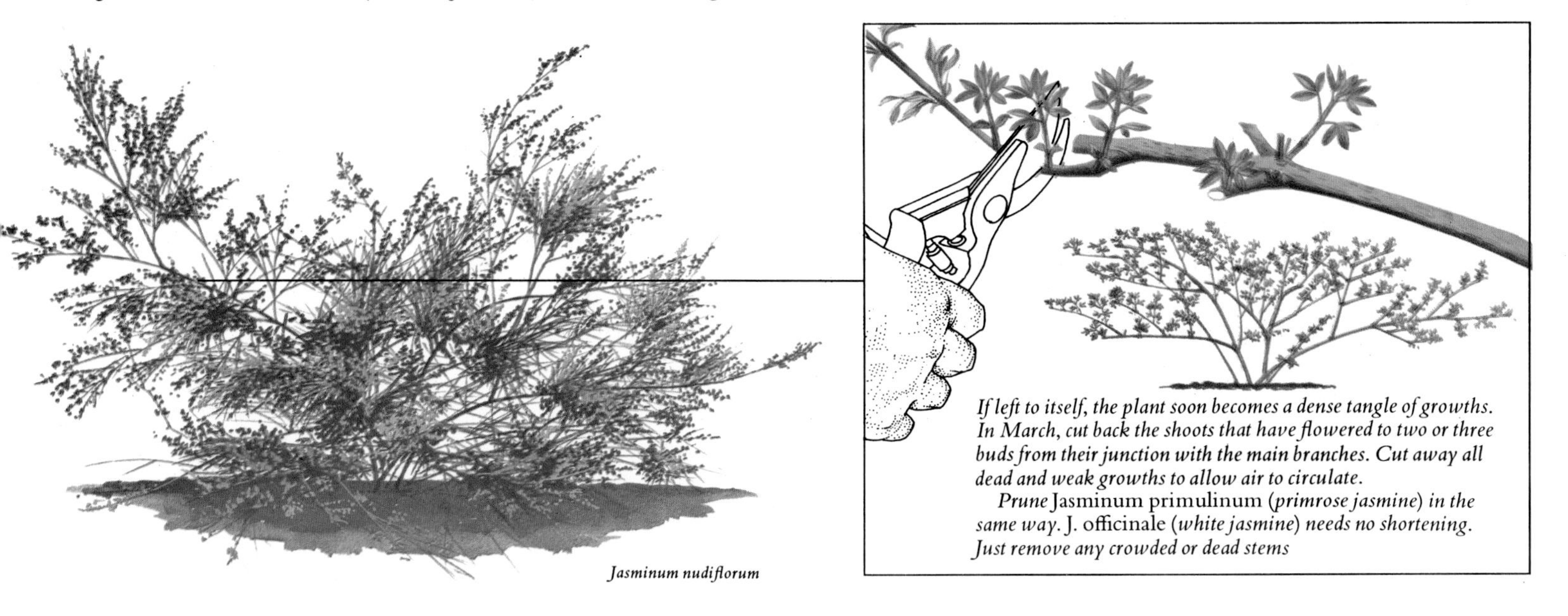

If left to itself, the plant soon becomes a dense tangle of growths. In March, cut back the shoots that have flowered to two or three buds from their junction with the main branches. Cut away all dead and weak growths to allow air to circulate.

Prune Jasminum primulinum *(primrose jasmine) in the same way.* J. officinale *(white jasmine) needs no shortening. Just remove any crowded or dead stems*

Jasminum nudiflorum

Kerria Flowers best on young growths; prune after the flowers fade in May or June

Kerria produces new shoots from ground level each year, which flower the next season and then often die back. Encourage this habit by removing the old flowered stems when the flowers fade in May or June. Cut right back to near the ground or, on stronger stems, to where new shoots are developing. 'Plenifora' will probably need to have all stems cut down to ground level

Kerria japonica

Lavandula (Lavender). Prune in late March or April to prevent the plant becoming leggy

With no pruning, the shrub will become leggy and bare-stemmed. In late March or early April, cut down the dead flower spikes plus about 1 in. of top growth. Use either secateurs or hedging shears. Do not cut back hard into old wood as die-back can result. To tidy the plant for winter, old flowers can be cut off in autumn.

When plants are still young, prune them hard to encourage a bushy shape

Lavandula spica

Leycesteria Promote strong, flowering stems by pruning hard in March

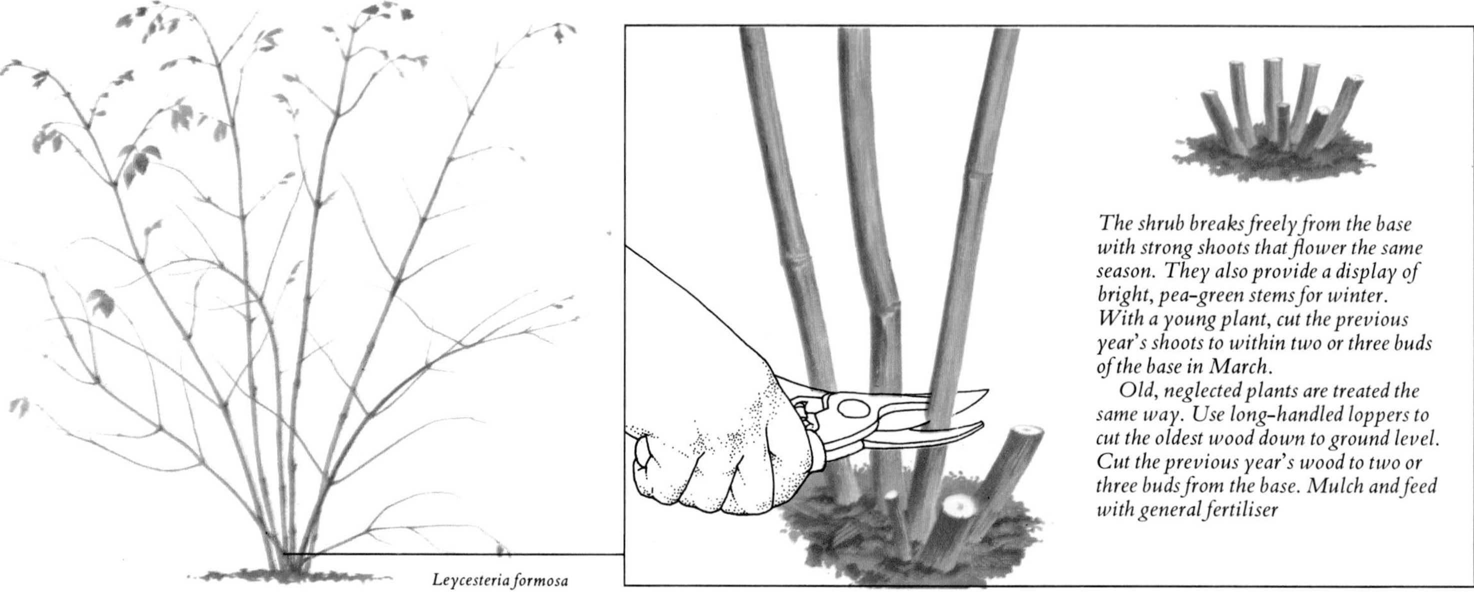

The shrub breaks freely from the base with strong shoots that flower the same season. They also provide a display of bright, pea-green stems for winter. With a young plant, cut the previous year's shoots to within two or three buds of the base in March.

Old, neglected plants are treated the same way. Use long-handled loppers to cut the oldest wood down to ground level. Cut the previous year's wood to two or three buds from the base. Mulch and feed with general fertiliser

Leycesteria formosa

Lippia If the branches survive the winter, hard prune in April for larger flowers

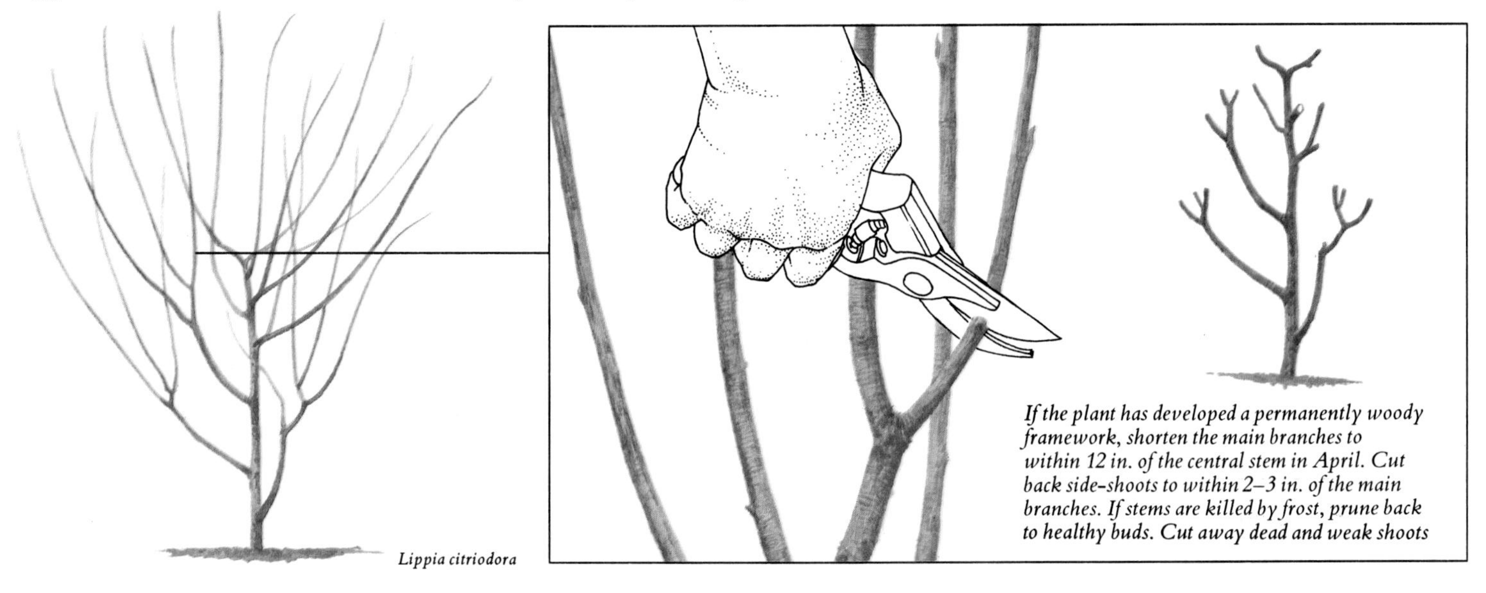

Lippia citriodora

If the plant has developed a permanently woody framework, shorten the main branches to within 12 in. of the central stem in April. Cut back side-shoots to within 2–3 in. of the main branches. If stems are killed by frost, prune back to healthy buds. Cut away dead and weak shoots

Philadelphus (Mock orange, syringa). Cut out the oldest branches to keep the plant young

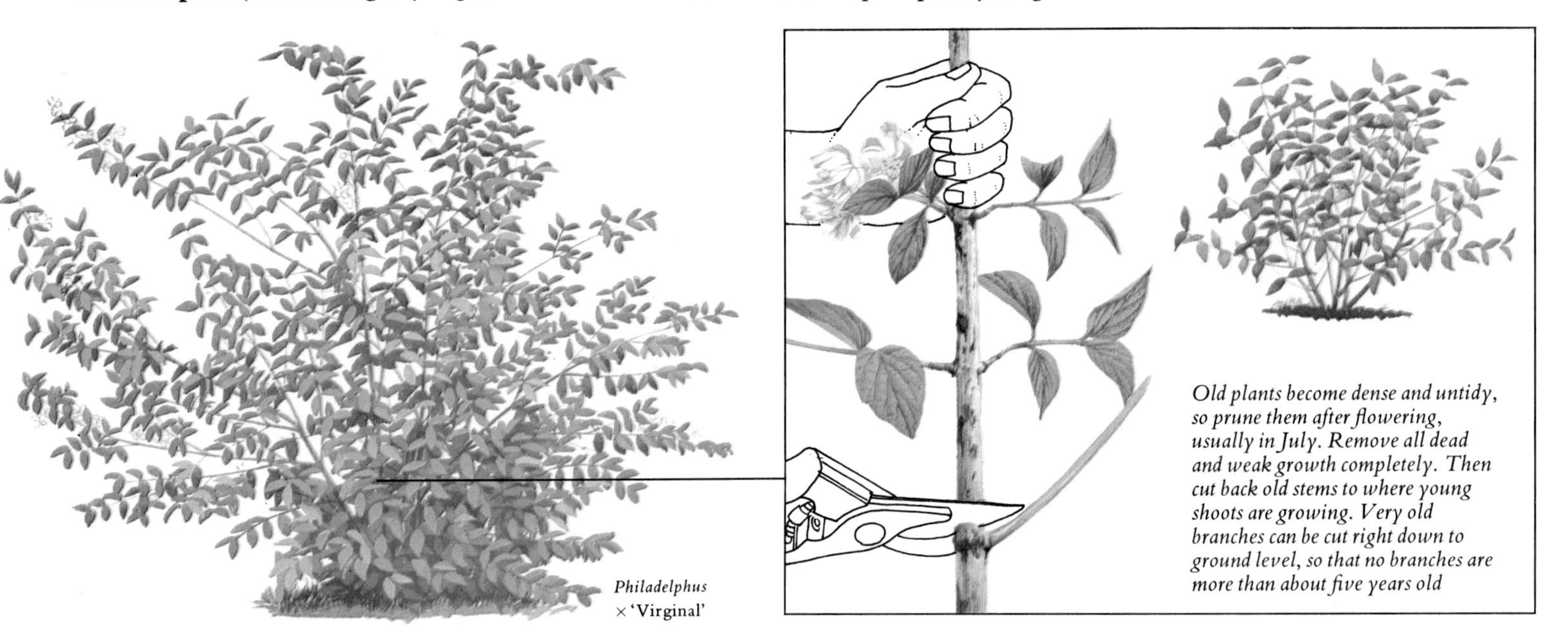

Philadelphus × 'Virginal'

Old plants become dense and untidy, so prune them after flowering, usually in July. Remove all dead and weak growth completely. Then cut back old stems to where young shoots are growing. Very old branches can be cut right down to ground level, so that no branches are more than about five years old

Rhus (Sumach). Prune *Rhus typhina* and *R. glabra* to produce large ferny leaves

The attractive ferny leaves of Rhus typhina *and* R. glabra *turn fiery orange in autumn. To get a good display, with extra-large leaves, cut the previous year's growths back to within 4 in. of the old wood in February. By this method, a low, well-structured framework will gradually be built up*

Ribes (Flowering currant). Regularly replace old wood with new by pruning after the flowers fade

If a plant becomes too large it can be cut back immediately after flowering, generally in April. Cut the old stems hard back to where live buds are emerging from the bark near the ground

Young shoots that grew last year need only be shortened to strong shoots appearing lower down. In future years remove one-third of the older stems each year

Rubus Cut out old stems after flowering to encourage new shoots from the base

Rubus cockburnianus

Rubus cockburnianus *is grown for its white stems in winter. In July, cut out the stems that have flowered. The young stems that remain will be white in winter and will flower next summer. Other species can be pruned in the same way, either after flowering or after fruiting.* R. × tridel *and* R. deliciosus, *however, need a framework of older wood*

Salix alba (White willow). Prune hard in February for orange or yellow ornamental stems the following winter

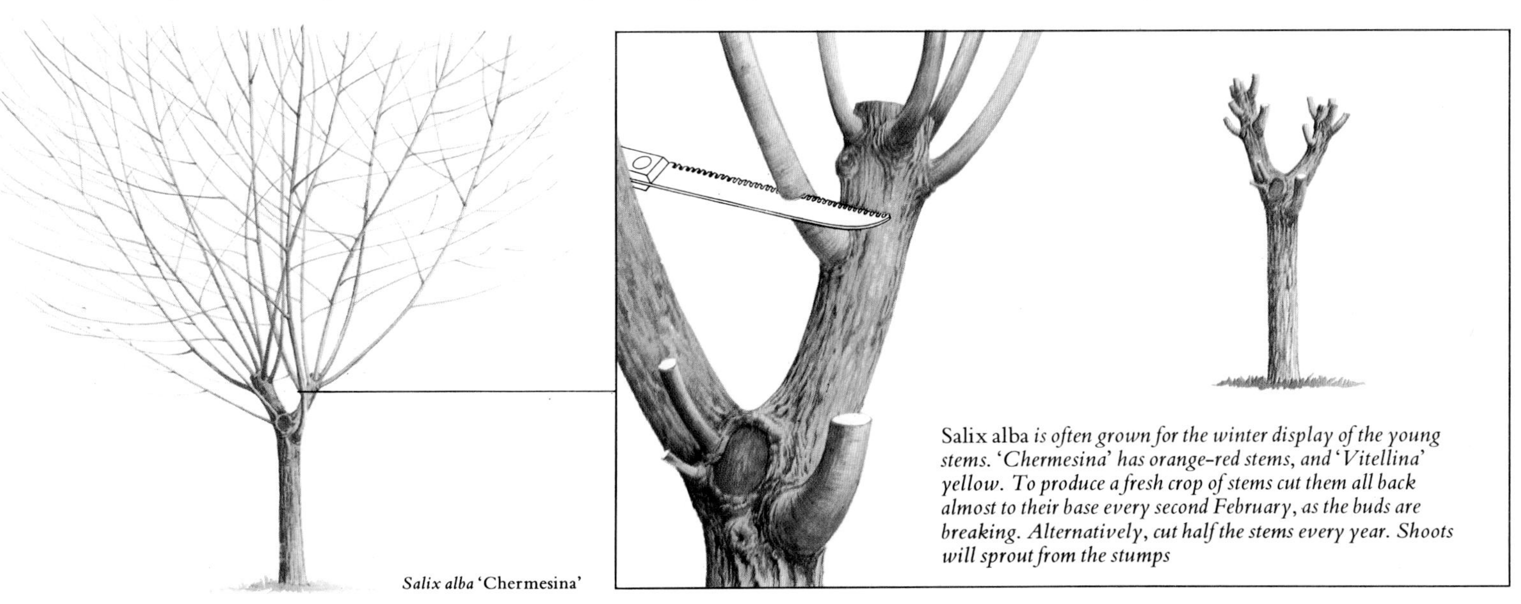

Salix alba 'Chermesina'

Salix alba *is often grown for the winter display of the young stems. 'Chermesina' has orange-red stems, and 'Vitellina' yellow. To produce a fresh crop of stems cut them all back almost to their base every second February, as the buds are breaking. Alternatively, cut half the stems every year. Shoots will sprout from the stumps*

Sambucus (Elder). Cut the stems right down in winter for brilliant summer foliage

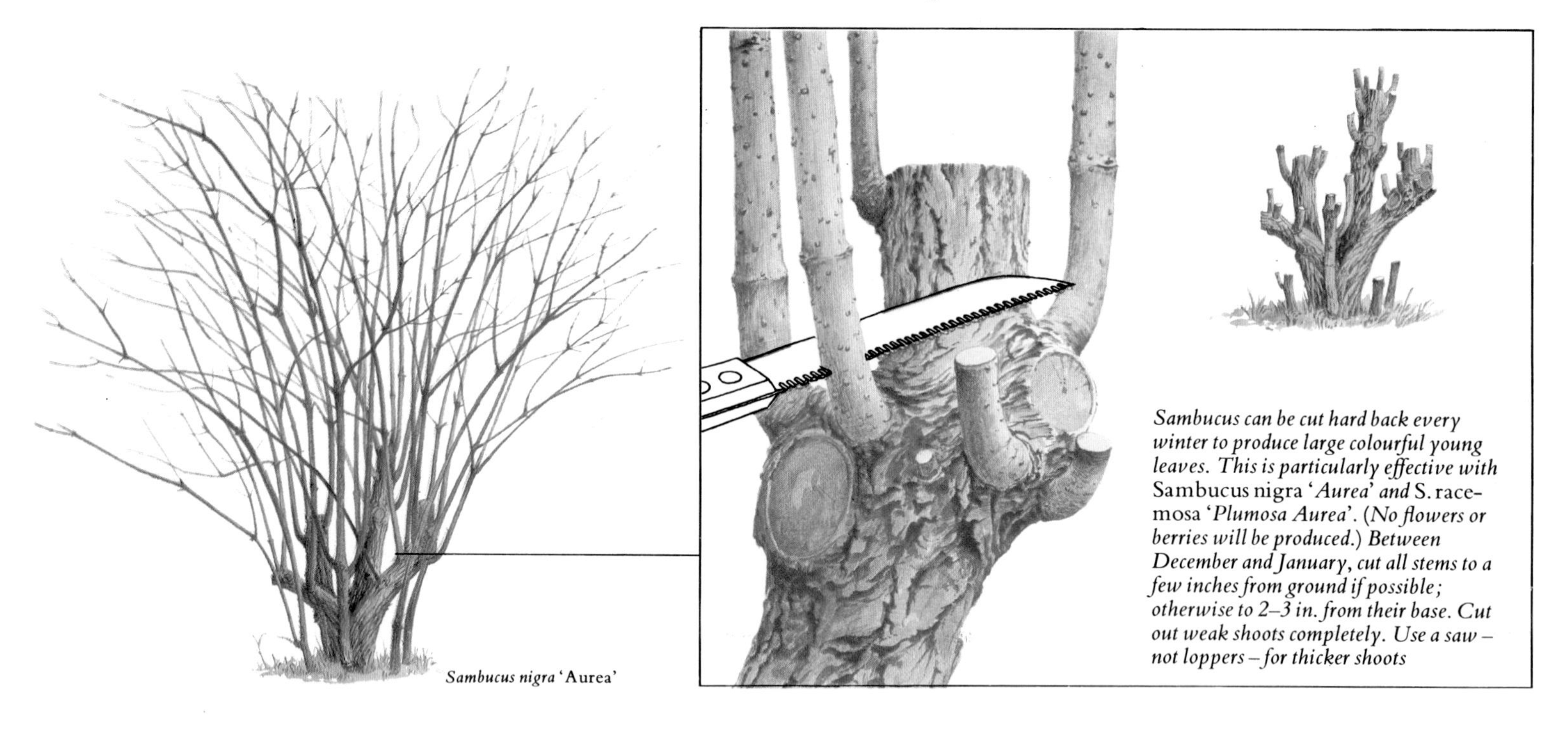
Sambucus can be cut hard back every winter to produce large colourful young leaves. This is particularly effective with Sambucus nigra '*Aurea*' *and* S. racemosa '*Plumosa Aurea*'. *(No flowers or berries will be produced.) Between December and January, cut all stems to a few inches from ground if possible; otherwise to 2–3 in. from their base. Cut out weak shoots completely. Use a saw – not loppers – for thicker shoots*

Sambucus nigra 'Aurea'

Santolina (Cotton lavender). Prune in April to prevent the plant becoming unkempt and straggly

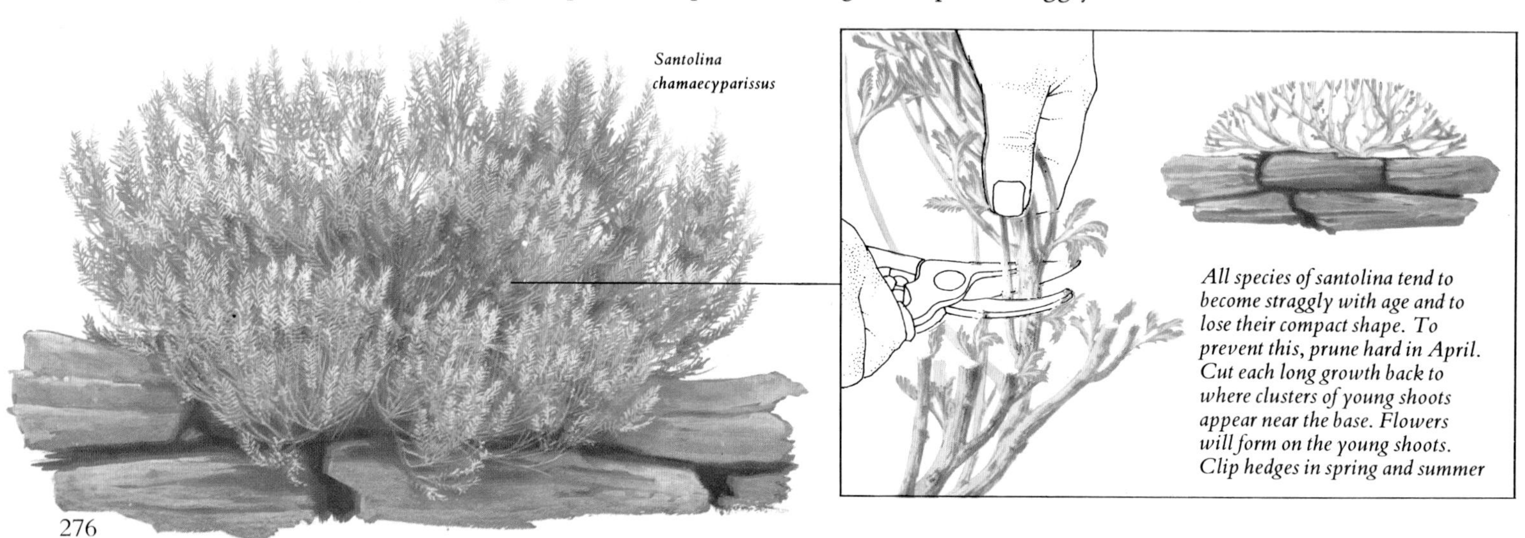
Santolina chamaecyparissus

All species of santolina tend to become straggly with age and to lose their compact shape. To prevent this, prune hard in April. Cut each long growth back to where clusters of young shoots appear near the base. Flowers will form on the young shoots. Clip hedges in spring and summer

Sorbaria For better foliage and larger flowers, cut down the stems in winter

Sorbaria arborea

Between December and February, prune all stems back hard – to within 4–9 in. of the base. New shoots will develop quickly and produce larger leaves and flower heads. Most species of sorbaria produce many suckers, which have to be removed to keep the plant within bounds

Spartium (Spanish broom). Old, untidy plants can be cut back as hard as you like

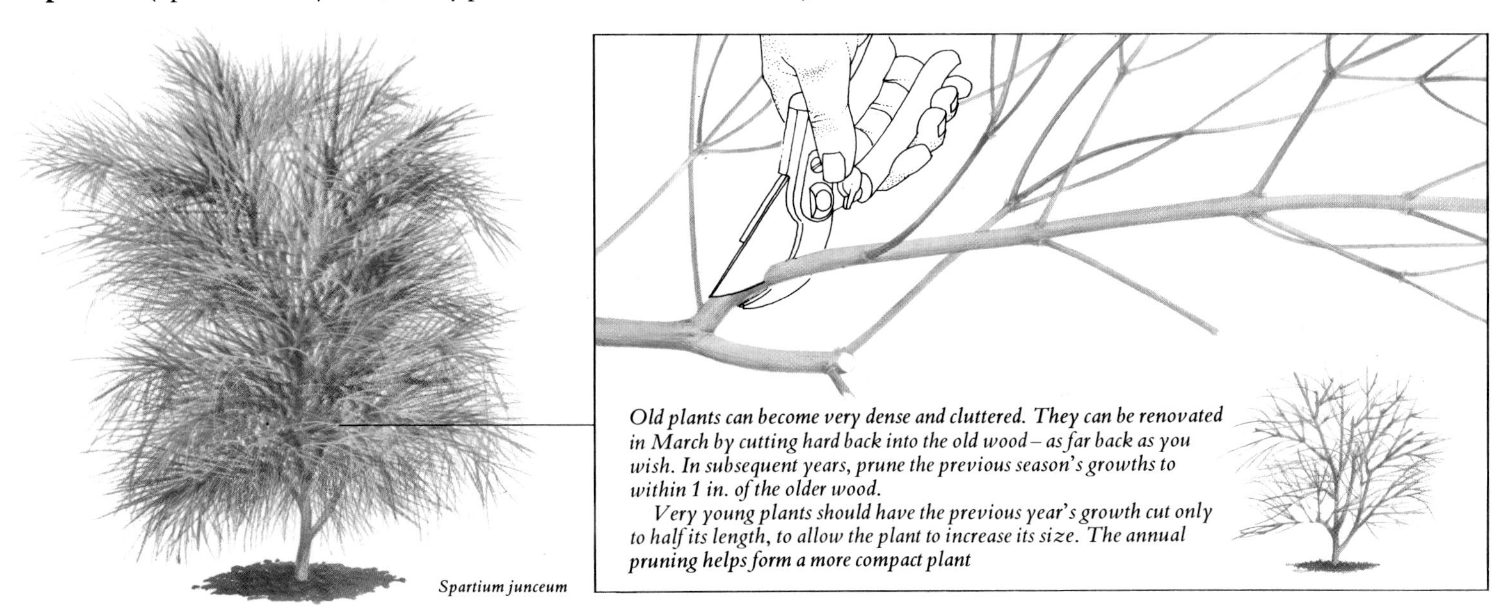

Spartium junceum

Old plants can become very dense and cluttered. They can be renovated in March by cutting hard back into the old wood – as far back as you wish. In subsequent years, prune the previous season's growths to within 1 in. of the older wood.

Very young plants should have the previous year's growth cut only to half its length, to allow the plant to increase its size. The annual pruning helps form a more compact plant

Spiraea × arguta (Foam of May, bridal wreath). Renovate an overgrown plant by cutting back old stems when the flowers fade

Spiraea japonica Prune almost to ground level in spring, and flat heads of pink flowers will bloom in late summer

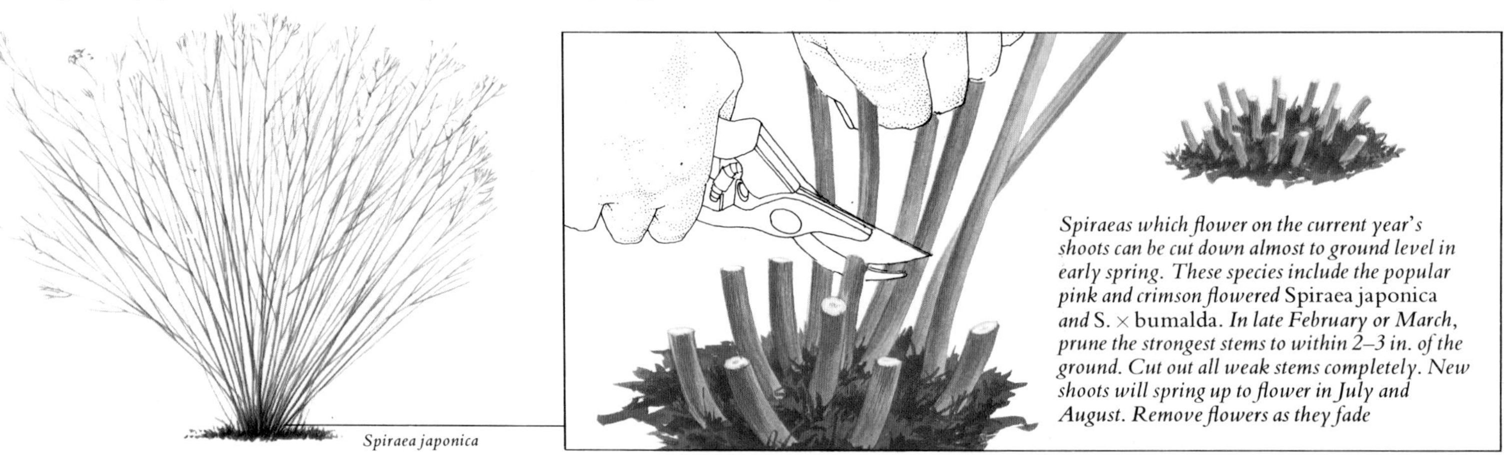

Stephanandra Prune hard in summer to encourage brightly coloured leaves and stems

Stephanandra tanakae

Stephanandra is grown for its autumn leaves and for the stems which are brightly coloured in winter. Pruning produces a new supply of stems, and lets light into the bush to colour the leaves.

After the plant has flowered in June or July, cut the flowered stems down to strong, young shoots sprouting lower down the stem, or right down to the ground. Remove weak stems completely

Tamarix (Tamarisk). To keep plants compact, prune the summer-flowering species hard each spring

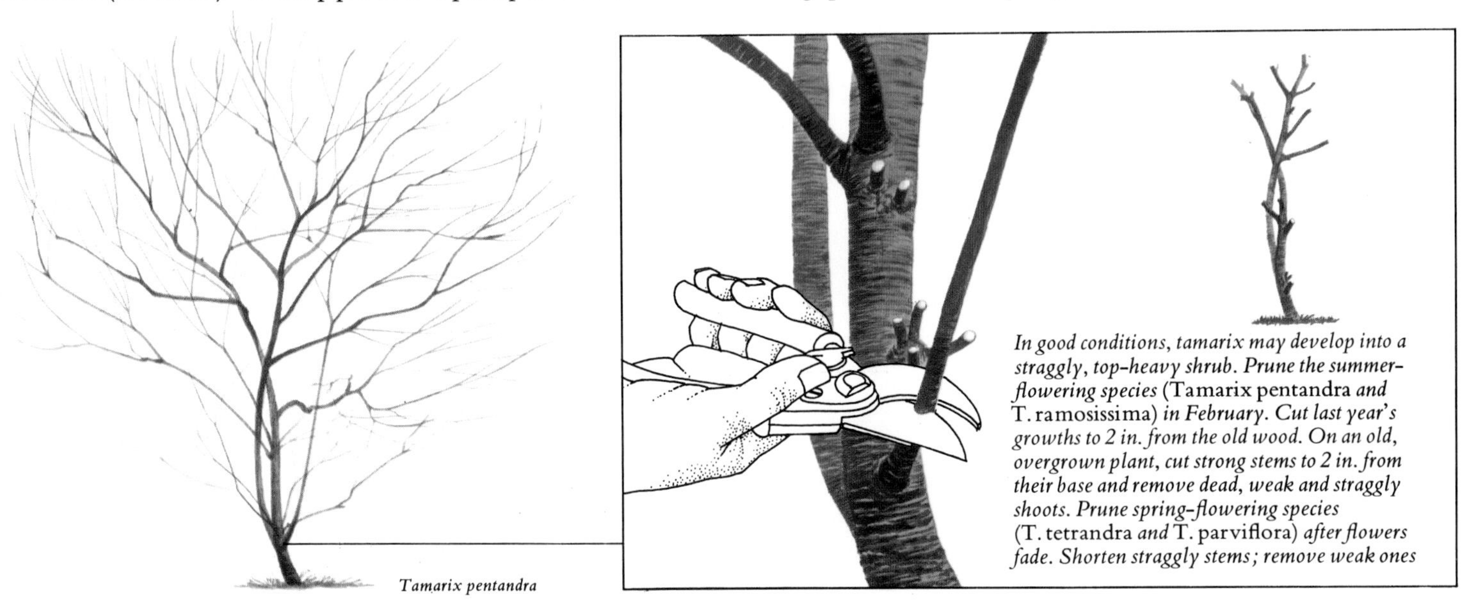

Tamarix pentandra

In good conditions, tamarix may develop into a straggly, top-heavy shrub. Prune the summer-flowering species (Tamarix pentandra *and* T. ramosissima) *in February. Cut last year's growths to 2 in. from the old wood. On an old, overgrown plant, cut strong stems to 2 in. from their base and remove dead, weak and straggly shoots. Prune spring-flowering species* (T. tetrandra *and* T. parviflora) *after flowers fade. Shorten straggly stems; remove weak ones*

Weigela To prevent plants from becoming overcrowded, prune away the flowered shoots in June or July

Weigela florida

Wistaria To promote flowers, cut back the fast-growing shoots in summer

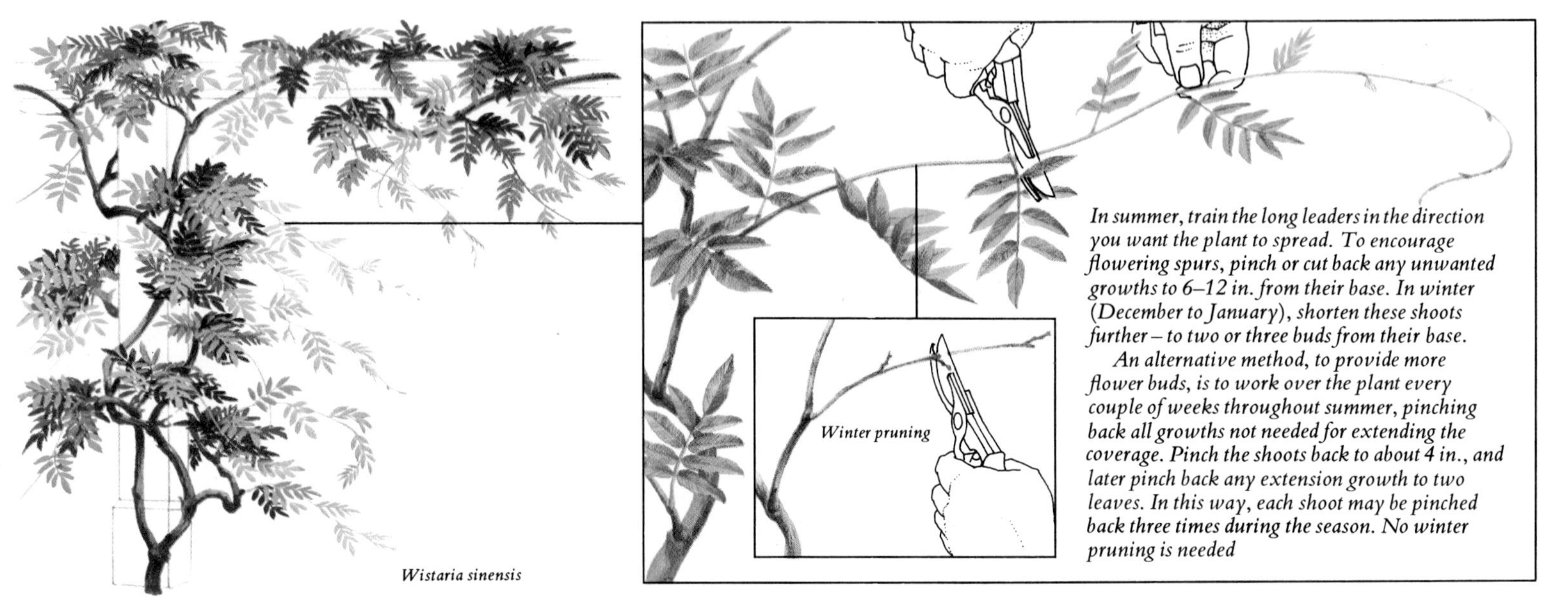

Wistaria sinensis

Trees

Few plants provide as much personal pleasure as the young tree you plant yourself. As it grows to maturity it creates an aura of tranquillity over the garden

The Swedish birch, like many other trees, is most effective planted in a group

Trees give an air of maturity and permanence to a garden. They add height and depth to even simple garden designs, and provide shelter and privacy. Deciduous trees give shade in summer, while in winter the naked branches have a stark beauty outlined against the sky. Evergreen trees maintain their attraction throughout the year, and are especially appreciated in the drab months when there is little other colour in the garden.

Most people select trees for their foliage, flowers and forms, or for a specific purpose, such as to provide a windbreak. As trees have to be lived with for many years, it is vitally important to choose, from the beginning, the right tree for the right purpose or place.

The imposing chestnut tree, equally attractive for its shape, leaves, flowers and autumn colours, is as out of proportion in the small suburban garden as is an isolated crab apple in parkland. However, it is quite possible for a big tree to thrive in the suburbs, and a flowering tulip or one of the large cherries would be a good choice.

One reason for planting trees is to create a shelter-belt against the wind. Dense evergreen or coniferous trees do this best. If shade is desired, do not plant erect and columnar trees, such as the incense cedar. Instead, use wide-spreading or weeping trees, like beech, birch and willow. If a tree is to be planted in the foreground, open shapes such as the silver Swedish birch or cedar provide a frame for the rest of the garden. For a boundary, the more solid shapes of a sycamore or oak, or the dark, pyramid shape of a fir will give a feeling of privacy by obscuring the houses beyond.

Evergreen trees are becoming more popular, not only for their screening and hedging value, but also for their beauty of shape. Many evergreens, and especially conifers, are both wind and drought-resistant once established. They are ideal as specimen trees on lawns, and even the smallest garden can accommodate a dwarf conifer. It is during winter that evergreens are truly outstanding. The green leaves bring welcome colour to a dull scene, and this can be made even more scintillating by evergreens with golden, silver or blue-green leaves.

Choosing the planting sites As a general rule it is not advisable to plant trees close to the house. Not only may the roots eventually damage the foundations and drains, but fast-growing trees can also quickly exclude light and air from the house. Avoid planting any but dwarf evergreens or extremely slow-growing deciduous trees in small gardens. Trees should be in harmony with the house, not overshadow it.

Where room allows, a group planting of three is more effective than a single specimen tree. The best effects come from letting one shape dominate the group – one tall, thin tree, one triangular-shaped fir and one bowl-shaped tree will just look messy. No set pattern can be given for this, but the trees should belong to the same genus and have roughly the same dimensions and shapes.

The spacing between trees in a group depends on the varieties, but as a basic guide the space between two trees should equal half the eventual total spread of both trees.

Boundary screens in the early stages are often made up of fast-growing deciduous trees and slower-growing conifers. As the conifers become effective, the deciduous trees are removed.

How to plant a tree

Preparing and digging the hole

Late October to late March is the ideal planting time for deciduous trees. Evergreens are best planted in October and November, or in March and April when the soil is warm and moist. Conifers, which are apt to shed their foliage after planting unless the roots have adequate moisture, are best planted in March and April.

The ground must not be frozen or waterlogged. If necessary, store young trees newly arrived from the nursery in a cool but frost-free shed until planting is possible.

Trees that have been ordered from a nursery arrive with the roots in a ball of soil and tied in polythene or hessian, or with bare roots. Remove the covering.

If you collect a tree direct from a nursery or garden centre, it may already be growing in a container. In this case it may be planted at any time of year – soil and weather permitting. But if you plant it in summer, be sure to keep the soil thoroughly watered until autumn.

Most trees are sold at three or four years old. They must be planted to the same depth as they were growing in the nursery – the soil mark is clearly visible on the lower stem. The average planting hole should be 3 ft across and 18 in. deep.

If you are planting in grass, mark a circle on the grass before digging the hole. Tie a length of string to a strong peg, insert the peg in the ground, and measure off 18 in. on the string. Tie another sharpened peg to the string at this distance and scratch a circle in the grass with it.

Chop round the marked line with a spade, and then cut through the turf in sections. Remove the pieces with the spade and stack them on one side.

Begin digging the hole from the centre of the circle. A change in colour of the soil indicates that the subsoil has been reached; this is usually clay coloured and infertile, and should be kept in a separate heap from the darker topsoil.

Loosen the soil at the bottom of the hole with a fork to aid drainage and aeration and to make it easier for the roots of the tree to penetrate.

On heavy soils, it is advisable to break up the sides of the hole with a fork for the same reasons.

All trees must be staked during the early years of growth. Stout wooden stakes, treated with a wood preservative, are usually obtainable from nurseries. The stake should reach to just below the point where the tree begins to branch, and should be positioned before planting.

Make a hole for the stake in the centre of the planting hole. Insert the stake as deeply as possible, firm it in with your heels and hammer it securely in place with a mallet.

On heavy, wet soils put a 6 in. layer of rubble over the base of the planting hole to aid drainage.

Chop up the removed turves and place them in the hole, grass side down. Next, fork in a 4–6 in. layer of well-rotted farmyard manure, garden compost or leaf-mould. Begin filling in the hole with the excavated soil. If any subsoil has been dug up, fill in with mixed subsoil and topsoil.

When the hole is about half full, tread down the soil firmly.

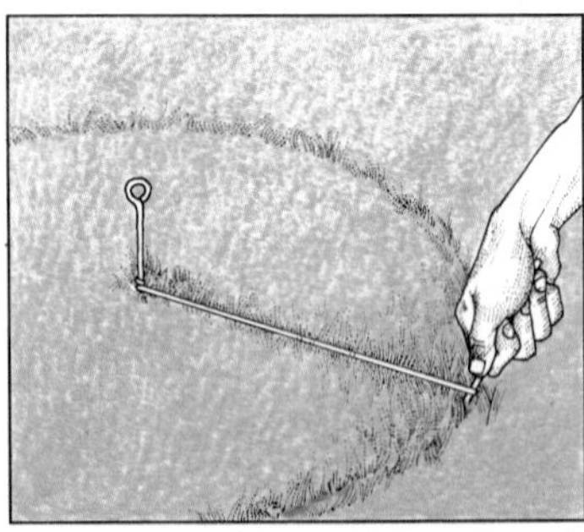

1 *In grass, mark out a 3 ft circle with two pegs and a piece of string*

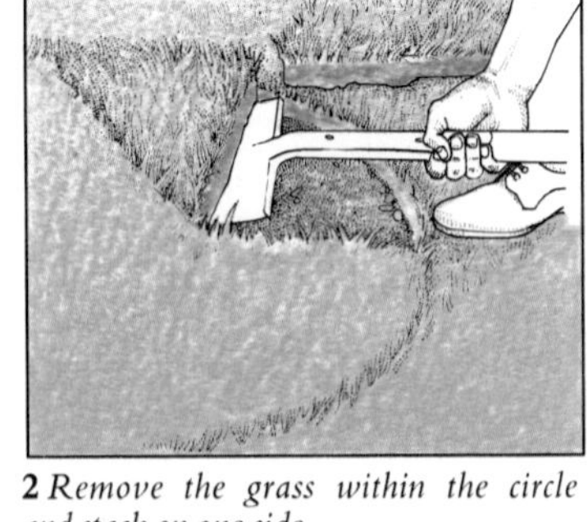

2 *Remove the grass within the circle and stack on one side*

3 *Dig the hole 18 in. deep and loosen the bottom soil with a fork*

4 *On heavy soils, break down the sides of the hole as well*

5 *Drive in a stout stake. On clay soil, add rubble to help drainage*

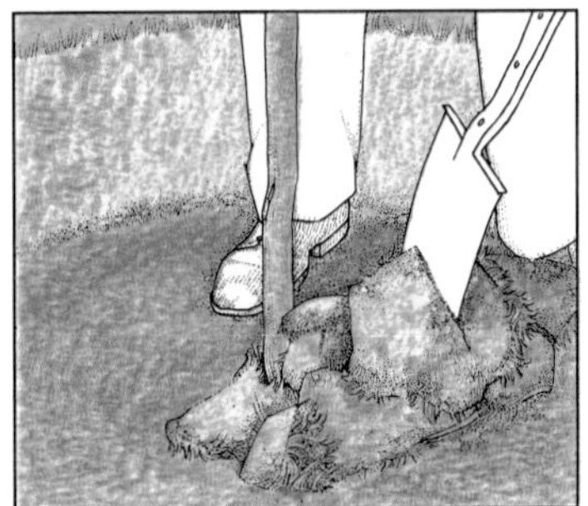

6 *Chop the turves into 3–4 in. pieces and put them in the hole, grass down*

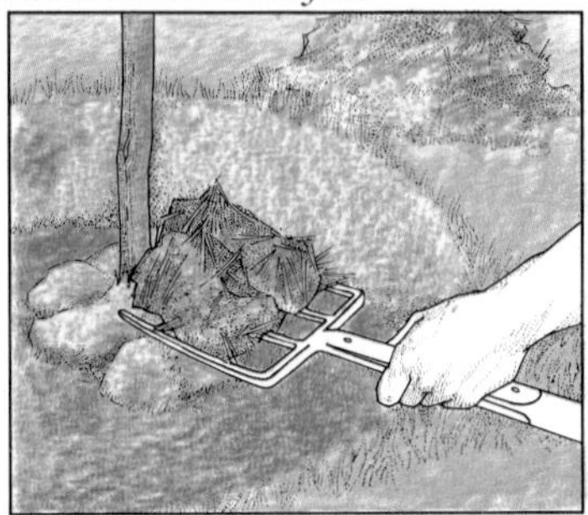

7 *Add a layer of manure or garden compost to provide a slow fertiliser*

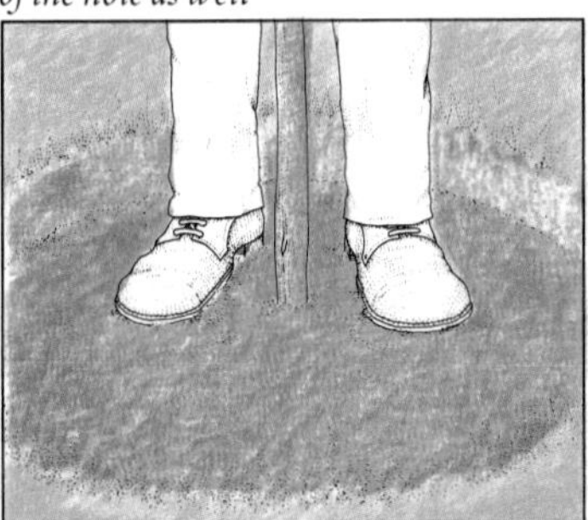

8 *Half fill the hole with soil and tread it down firmly*

Planting and staking a young tree

Before planting out nursery-grown trees, the top branches may need to be lightly trimmed. Examine the branches, and cut off any stumps of old wood, flush with the stems. Remove the tips of any branches which may have been damaged in transit, cutting back to healthy growth, just above an outward-facing bud.

In the case of bare-rooted trees, examine the roots and cut back any damaged or dead parts to healthy tissue, to stop infestation by spores of fungal diseases.

Planting is easier if it is done by two people. While one person holds the tree in position, the other places a flat piece of wood across the top of the hole. The old soil mark on the stem should be level with the wood; remove or add soil accordingly.

Hold the tree upright against the stake and start filling in the hole with the remaining soil. Shake the tree occasionally to make sure the soil is settling amongst and around the roots to eliminate air pockets.

As the soil is added, tread it down from time to time, particularly around bare-rooted trees. When the roots have been covered, scatter two generous handfuls of slow-acting sterilised bonemeal over them and mix in a bucket of peat.

Fill in the rest of the hole, treading from time to time to firm the soil. When planting is completed, the old soil mark should be just visible.

Level the soil with a fork, and leave the surface bare for two or three years, otherwise grass roots will compete with the roots of the tree for nourishment.

The tree must now be tied firmly to the stake. There are several proprietary tree ties available, the best being made of strong plastic or webbing straps with rubber buffers.

Loop the strap, about 4 in. below the branches, round the stem of the tree and through the buffer, which provides a cushion between tree and stake. Pull the strap tight and fasten it against the stake, not the tree. Nail the tie to the stake.

If there is a crook in the stem which is likely to rub on the stake, put on another tie.

An alternative method is to wrap hessian round the stake several times, and then wrap it round the stem and stake so there is a thick protective cushion between stem and stake. Tie the covering in place with one or two pieces of strong, tarred string.

Inspect the tie several times during the year, particularly after strong winds, and re-tie or renew if necessary. As the main stem thickens, loosen the tie to prevent the tree from being strangled.

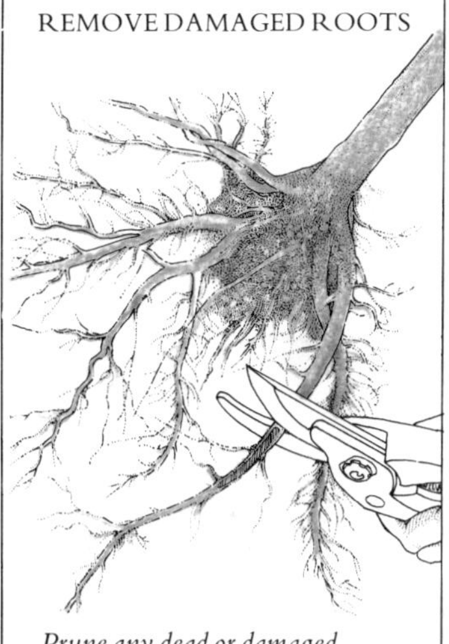

Prune any dead or damaged roots back to healthy tissue, to avoid fungal diseases

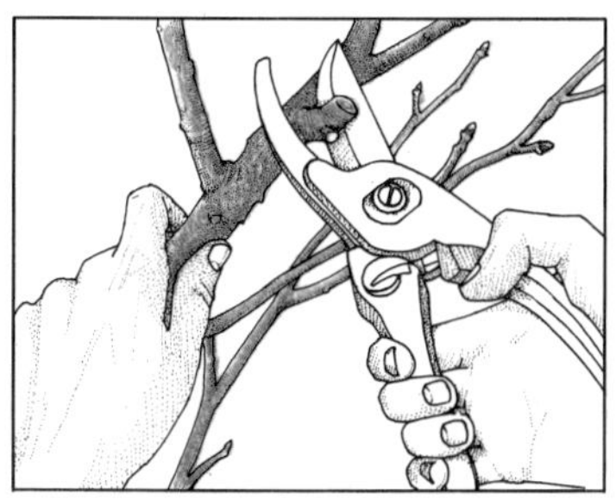
1 *On top branches, cut off dead stumps of wood, flush with stems*

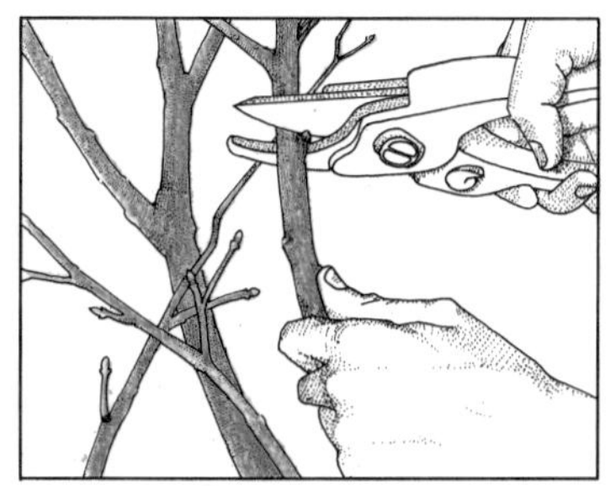
2 *Trim any damaged tips back to outward-facing buds*

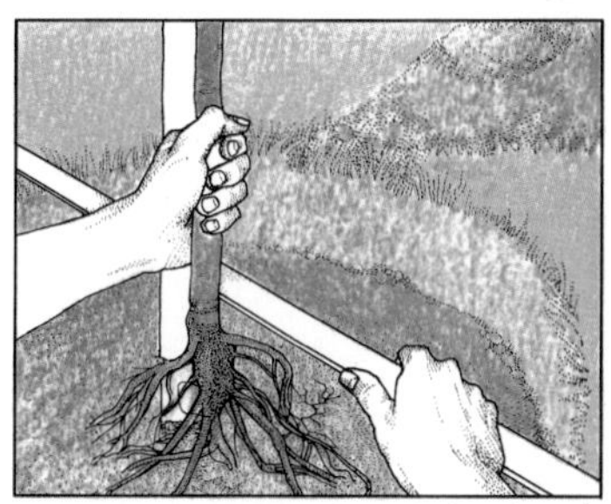
3 *Line up the old soil mark level with the surface, using a piece of wood*

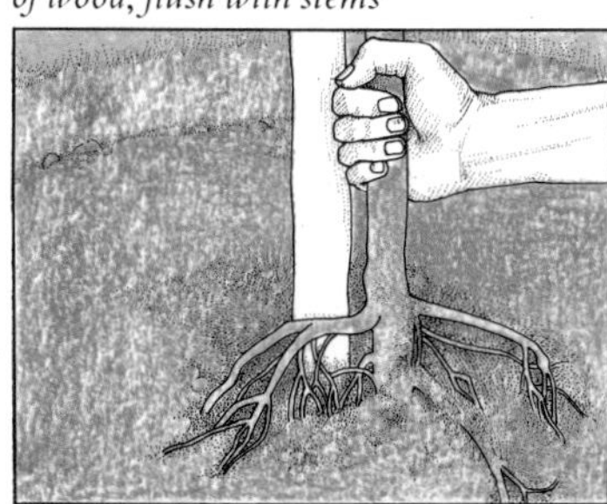
4 *Begin filling in the hole, and shake the tree to settle the soil*

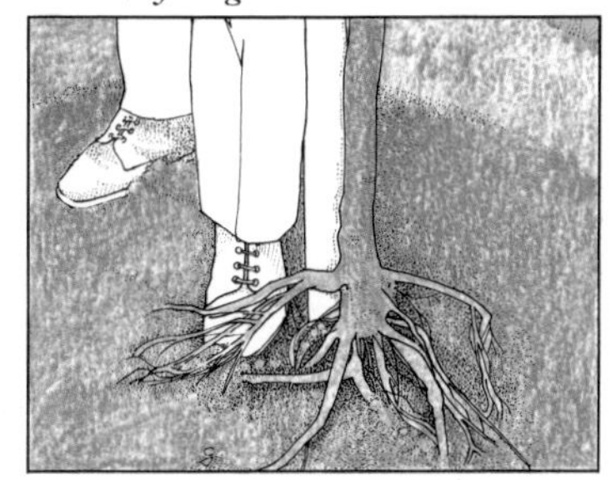
5 *Tread and level the soil; measure the depth against the soil mark*

6 *Level the surface with a fork and leave it bare for two or three years*

Tree ties *Fix the strap around stem and stake, with the rubber buffer in between*

Hessian *Wrap around stake, then around stem and stake*

Vegetables

Garden-grown vegetables have a flavour rarely matched by those bought from a shop. And even a small garden can produce small luxury vegetable crops each season

Many gardeners grow vegetables only if they have space to spare. Yet vegetables not only provide fresh, full-flavoured food, but can also be a money saver, particularly if you have a greenhouse or cold frame to help grow early and late crops when they are out of season and usually expensive to buy.

Pick a light, airy spot for the vegetable plot – one that gets plenty of sun and is not overhung by trees or shaded by fences. You may prefer to have only lawns and flower beds in view from the house, but do not, for this reason, relegate the vegetable plot to an unsuitable portion of the garden.

Water is vital for growing vegetables, not only to increase the yield and prevent crop failure, but also to make seed sowing practicable. If the plot is some way from the mains water supply, it is worth installing a standpipe.

One good path of a solid material, such as concrete, is useful. Other paths should be narrow, temporary ones made by treading down the soil firmly; they can be dug over when needed.

Site the cold frame on a border facing west or south at the eastern end of the plot, which should get plenty of sun. This is also the best end for permanent seed beds.

The compost heap should be about 5 ft square (p. 402) and, ideally, sited in a shady spot.

Some form of windbreak may be needed round the vegetable plot if it is exposed to prevailing winds. A dwarf hedge about 2 ft high is adequate. Dividers between different sections of vegetables are a waste of space in a small garden.

Water, cold frame and compost heap *Water is necessary for growing vegetables. If there is none close at hand, it is worth installing a standpipe.*

The cold frame should be facing south or west on a sunny border. The compost heap should, ideally, be in a shady spot

Windbreak and paths *One good path of solid material is useful – others can be made by treading down the soil. A windbreak – such as a hedge – will protect the plot from prevailing winds*

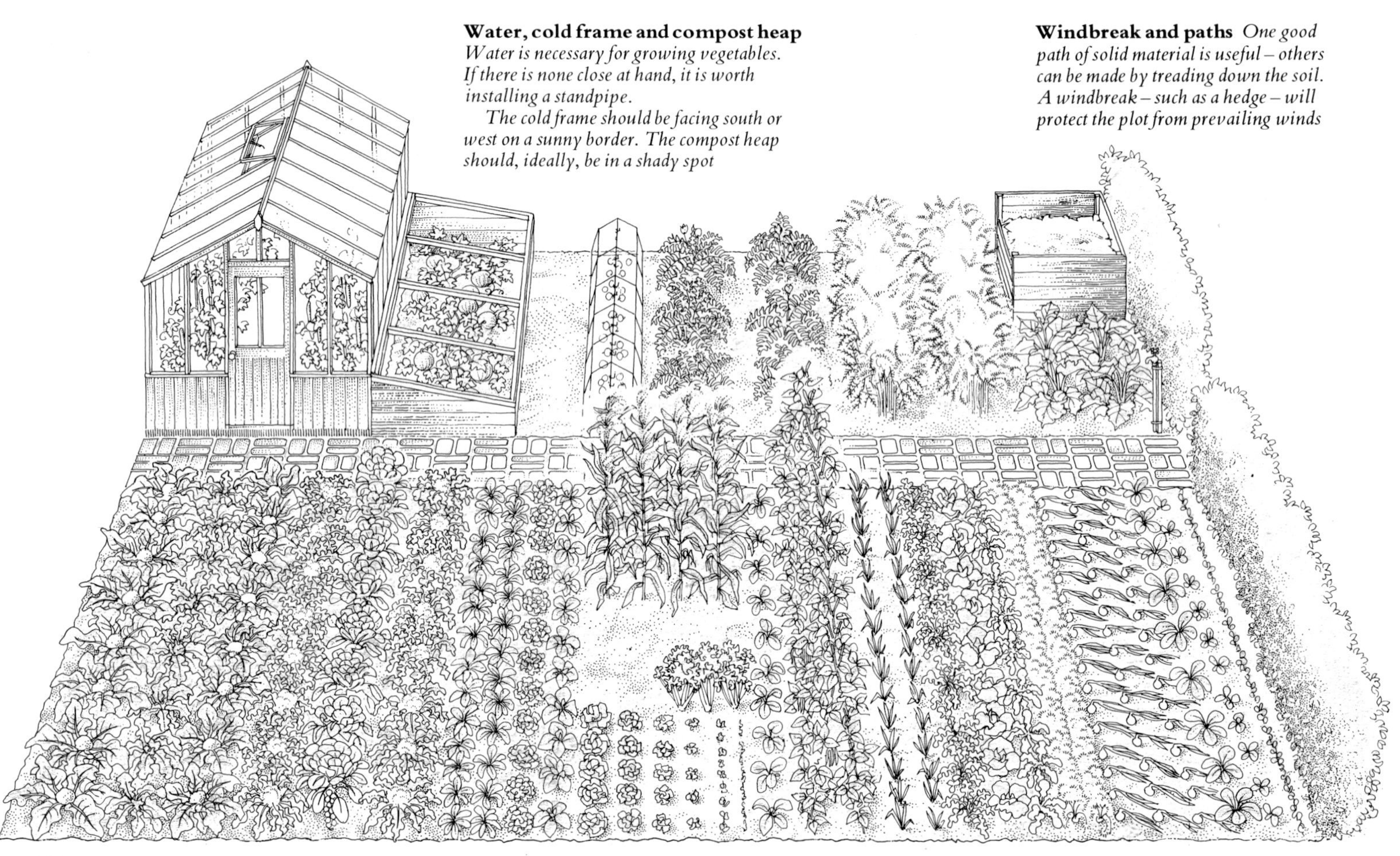

Preparing the ground for a new vegetable plot

Clear and prepare the site for a new vegetable garden in autumn, or during a dry and frost-free period in winter. It will then be ready for planting the following spring.

If the site has run wild or has not been cultivated before, clear away all rubbish, burning it where possible; bricks and rubble can be used as foundations for a path.

If builders have been on the site, the subsoil may have been left on the surface; distribute it as evenly as possible over the garden.

Use a bagging hook or a rotary grass cutter to cut down tall grass, coarse weeds and brambles – make sure there are no thick, protruding roots to foul the blades.

Next skim off the turf surface with a spade – or a turfing iron if you can borrow one. First sharpen the blade with a file, then mark out the surface in strips with 1 in. deep spade cuts, the width of the spade apart. Make similar cuts at right angles, about 12 in. apart.

Insert the spade (or turfing iron) into the cuts and push it horizontally to lift 1 in. thick pieces of turf.

Stack the turf in an unused corner of the garden, grass side downwards. Dust the layers alternately with lime and sulphate of ammonia, until the stack is complete. It will eventually rot down into loam for potting or planting mixtures.

If possible, double dig (p. 405) the ground, adding manure or well-rotted garden compost into the top spit at the rate of a 2 gallon bucket to the square yard.

If the plot is thick with perennial weeds – particularly couch grass, ground elder, docks, dandelions and nettles – lift the roots and burn them, returning the ashes to the soil.

1 *Cut down tall grass, coarse weeds and brambles with a bagging hook*

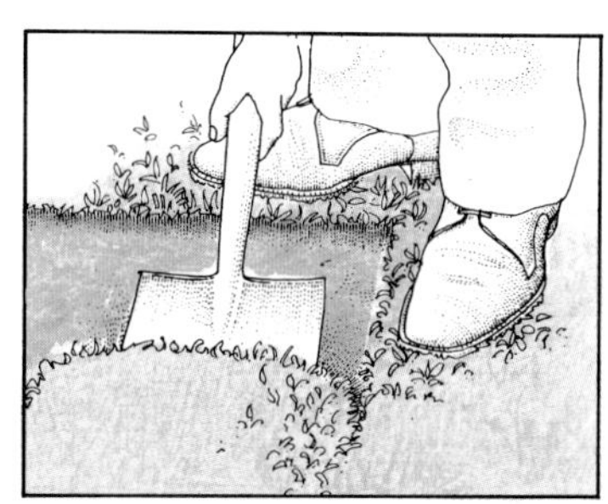

2 *Cut the turf into sections, and slice them out with a spade or turfing iron*

3 *Stack turf, dusting layers alternately with lime and sulphate of ammonia*

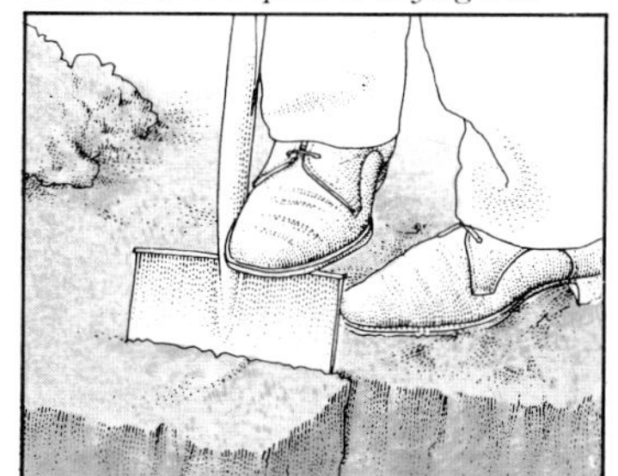

4 *Double dig, working in well-rotted garden compost or farmyard manure*

Preparing your type of soil

The ideal soil for vegetables is loam – a mixture of sand, silt, clay and humus. Good loam has these in sufficient proportions to ensure that it does not dry out quickly, does not get waterlogged and has an open, spongy texture.

Good loam is easily worked, and needs only the regular replacement of plant food in the form of manure and fertilisers.

Soil may be acid or alkaline, whatever its type. Most vegetables grow best in soil that is neutral – neither too acid nor too alkaline – or slightly acid. Over-acid soils need dressings of lime, the amount depending on the degree of acidity, which can be measured with an inexpensive soil-testing kit. Ideally, the measurement should be between pH 6.5 and pH 7.0. Alkalinity can be counteracted by adding acid material such as moss peat or poultry manure to the soil.

Sandy soil is light and dry. It warms up rapidly in spring in time for early crops, and also dries out quickly. Essential plant foods are consequently washed out at a steady rate in the drainage water, so it is often lacking in nutrients. Feed with small amounts of artificial fertiliser at regular intervals and dig in manure and compost.

Clay soil is heavy, slow to warm up, and very retentive of moisture. It may be rich in plant food but poorly drained, so that roots are starved of oxygen.

The best way to lighten it and to improve drainage is to dig in manure, compost, peat and grit or sharp sand. Add lime if it is acid.

Chalky soil is often shallow and, like sandy soil, will drain very quickly, with consequent loss of plant foods. Like clay, it may be sticky and hard to dig, but do not add lime as chalky soil is already alkaline. Work in plenty of well-rotted garden compost, farmyard manure or peat. Feed regularly with artificial fertilisers. Do not double dig if the topsoil is very shallow.

Peaty soil is usually acid and may be badly drained. Surplus water can be carried away by drainage trenches, but it is worth the cost of consulting a drainage expert.

Spread a heavy dressing of lime to deal with the acidity in the soil – as much as $\frac{1}{2}$ lb. to the square yard may be needed yearly. Dress with a general fertiliser regularly, as peaty soil is usually lacking in phosphates and potash.

Using growing space to the full

The main crops grown within the rotation plan do not make full use of the space available for the whole year – there is room for other crops to be fitted in. These are known as catch crops and succession crops.

Catch crops include quick-growing vegetables sown in the early part of the season, before a main crop is sown or planted in the plot.

A catch crop of salad onions, for example, can be sown in March in the brassicas plot, before the winter cabbage is planted out in July.

Catch crops can also be grown between rows of slower-growing vegetables, and lifted before the slower ones need more space. For example, lettuces, radishes or summer spinach, can be grown between rows of peas – or summer turnips between rows of runner beans.

Do not use a vegetable that will cover the whole area with its foliage, as the main crop will be smothered.

Succession crops are those planted after a main crop has been cleared. A main crop of spinach, for example, sown in February and picked after two months, can be followed by lettuces, sown from April to July.

Rotating crops to make the best use of the garden

Divide the vegetable garden into three plots, and grow different groups of vegetables in each plot each year in a three-year cycle.

A simple rotation system ensures the most effective use of manures. It also reduces attacks by pests and diseases. As two years will always elapse before a vegetable is grown in the same soil again, pests are less likely to be carried over.

In the first year, use Plot One for peas, beans, celery, chicory, cucumbers, endives, leeks, lettuces, marrows, radishes, spinach, spinach beet, sweet corn and tomatoes. These crops need rich, freshly manured soil. Most are sown in spring and early summer, and some can be cleared in time for a second crop later in the year.

Use Plot Two for root vegetables – beetroots, carrots, parsnips, swedes and turnips – and potatoes. These crops do best in soil manured for a previous crop, and dressed with fertiliser. They are mostly sown in spring and early summer, and harvested in time for the plot to be manured in readiness for sowing peas, beans, etc. the next year.

Use Plot Three for brassicas – broccoli, brussels sprouts, cabbages, savoy cabbages, cauliflowers and kale. These also prefer land manured for a previous crop, and dressed with lime as well as fertiliser. They are mostly sown in spring in a seed bed within the plot, planted out in summer, and harvested from autumn to spring.

Each year move the crops along to the next plot, so that the rotation in each plot is peas, beans, etc., then brassicas, then roots.

Onions and shallots will grow in any reasonably good soil. There is probably more room in the root-crop plot, but for larger bulbs, grow in rich soil in the pea plot.

Artichokes and asparagus are grown permanently in one bed, and do not fit into the rotation system.

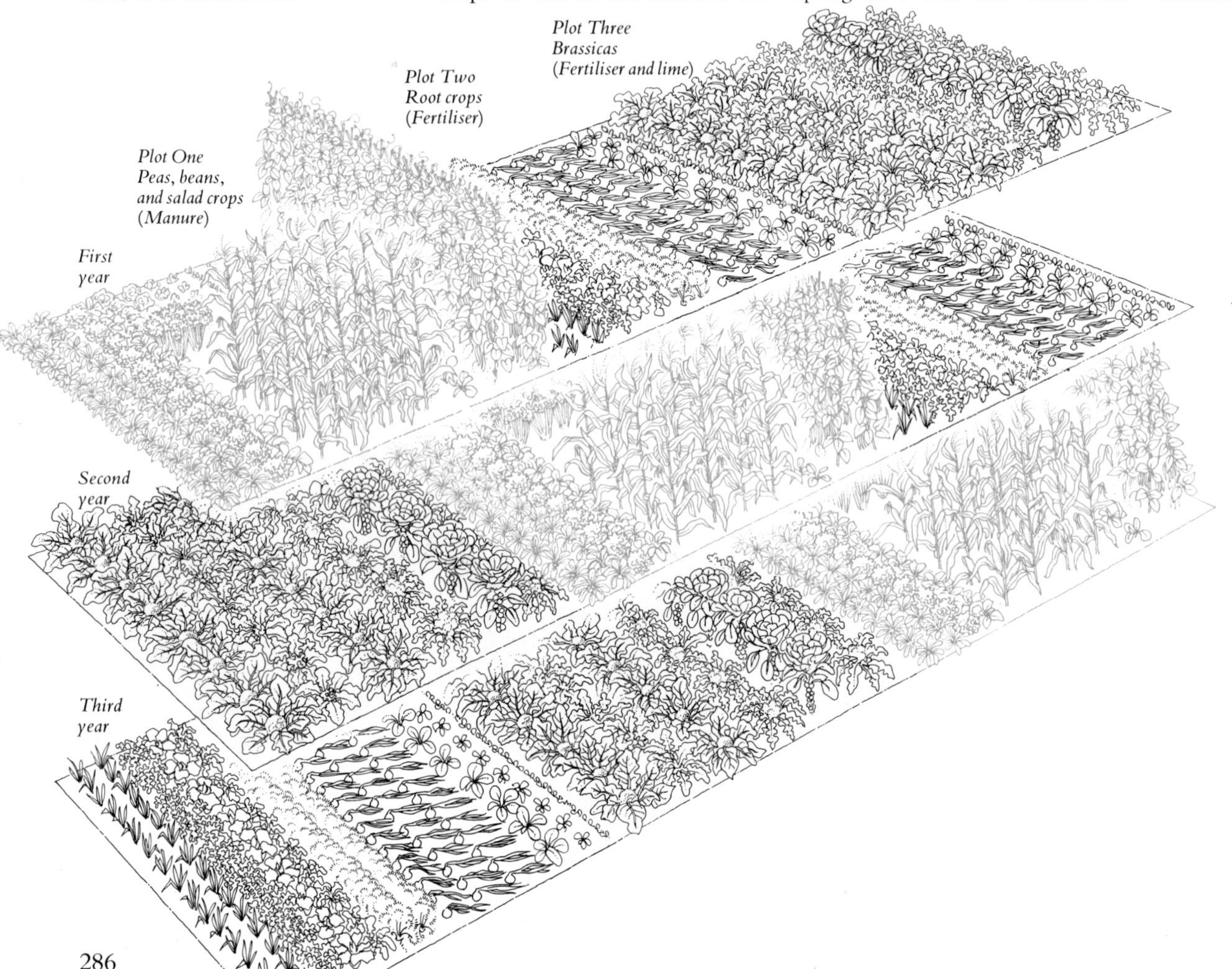

First year *Double dig Plot One, work in plenty of well-rotted garden compost or farmyard manure, and grow peas, beans and salad vegetables. Dress Plot Two with fertiliser only, and grow root crops. Dress Plot Three with lime and fertiliser only, and grow brassicas*

Second year *Double dig and manure Plot Two for the peas, beans and salad crops, which follow the root vegetables. Dress Plot Three with fertiliser for the root crops, and apply fertiliser and lime to Plot One for the brassicas*

Third year *Double dig and manure Plot Three in which peas, beans and salad crops will follow last year's root crops. This year dress Plot One with fertiliser only for the root crops, and prepare Plot Two with fertiliser and lime for the brassicas*

Techniques used in the vegetable garden

Preparing a seed bed The seed bed must be moist and firm, and of a fine tilth if seeds are to germinate. Prepare it carefully.

Dig the seed bed over in autumn or winter. In spring, when it is dry enough to walk over without soil sticking to your boots, hoe or lightly fork over the ground to a depth of about 3 in. This will allow the soil to dry out so that it will crumble easily.

When the soil is dry, tread it firm – this breaks up lumps and also makes it easier for roots to get moisture. Then rake it over to make a fine tilth and at the same time remove any large stones or clods.

Drawing a drill Rows of vegetables will get maximum sunshine if you run them from north to south. But in a small garden, do not worry if this is not convenient.

Short rows, each with a different kind of vegetable, are simpler to cultivate than long rows each with several different kinds, which may also present spacing problems.

Growing plants in straight rows makes hoeing easier. Mark out rows with a peg at each end, and stretch a garden line between them as a guide.

Use the edge of a draw hoe to make the drill. Make sure the drill is straight by placing one foot on the line to keep it taut while drawing the blade of the hoe against it.

The depth of a drill generally depends on the size of the seeds – the smaller they are, the shallower the drill. Draw very shallow drills – $\frac{1}{4}$–$\frac{1}{2}$ in. – with a pointed stake.

Seed sowing Buy fresh seed each year. Old seeds, or those saved from previous crops, may not germinate or may produce inferior plants.

Many seedsmen now sell pelleted seeds. These can be spaced more accurately, and thinning is easier. With pelleted seeds, the soil must be kept thoroughly moist until the seedlings emerge.

If the weather is dry, water the seed bed thoroughly the day before sowing. Always sow thinly, as plants will have to be thinned eventually. Do not sprinkle seeds direct from the packet – there are two ways in which they can be sown by hand.

One method is to place them in the palm of the hand and dribble them into the drill with the thumb and forefinger. Very small seeds can be mixed with a little fine, dry sand to ensure thin, even distribution.

If any seeds are left over, sow them at the end of a row; the seedlings can be used to fill any gaps later when you are transplanting or thinning.

Another method is to sow small pinches of seed at regular intervals; this is known as station sowing. It wastes fewer seeds and saves effort at thinning time.

The spacing between stations depends on the type of vegetable. Beetroot, for example, is sown in stations about 4 in. apart, because it is usually thinned to 4–5 in. apart.

The only thinning needed is to remove all but the strongest plant at each station. This method allows catch crops of, say, radishes to be sown between stations in the row.

If a vegetable is wanted for pulling when half grown – onions for salads, for example – sow the seeds at half stations. When the seedlings appear, remove all but one at each half station; when they are half grown lift alternate plants, leaving one to every station.

Closing the drill To cover the seeds, return the soil carefully with the back of the rake, working along the line of the drill – not across it. Then lightly firm the soil with the back of the rake.

Another method that can be used is to return the soil with your feet by shuffling along either side of the drill, then lightly raking the soil. But you must be careful not to cover the seeds too deeply, or tread them into heavy soils too hard.

Thinning Start thinning seedlings early, as soon as they can be handled without damage. At this stage the roots will be undeveloped, so their removal will cause little disturbance to their neighbours.

If the weather is particularly dry, thin seedlings in the evenings and water the bed afterwards. Thin in successive stages, as there may be losses caused by pests or disease.

Always thin out weak or malformed seedlings. At first, thin the row so that seedlings are spaced at half the final distance required. Later

SOWING SEEDS

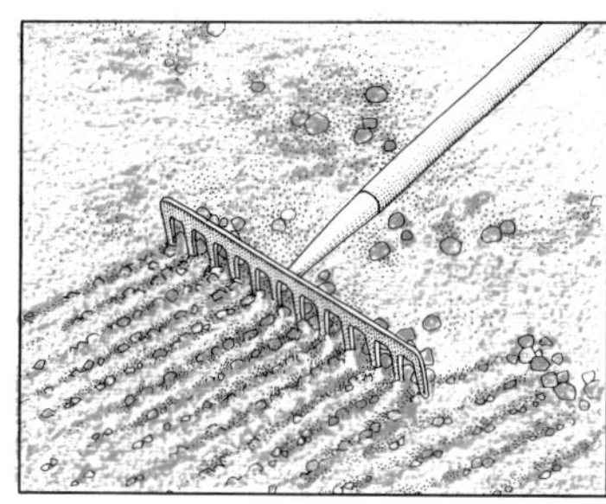

1 *Rake the seed bed to a fine tilth and remove any large stones or clods of earth*

2 *Mark out the rows with a line and pegs, and use a draw hoe to make a drill*

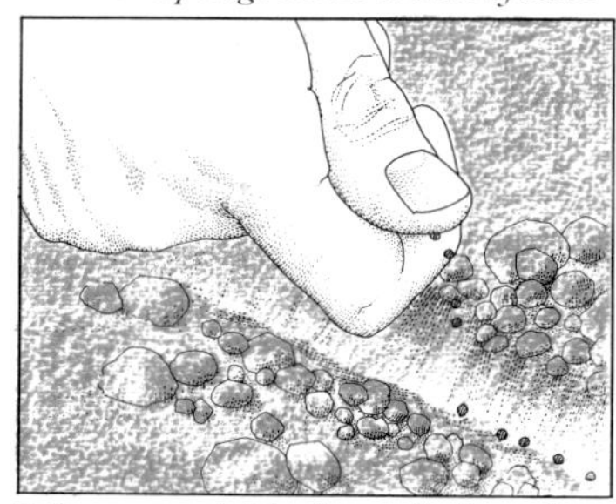

3 *Do not sprinkle the seeds direct from the packet. Sow them thinly by hand*

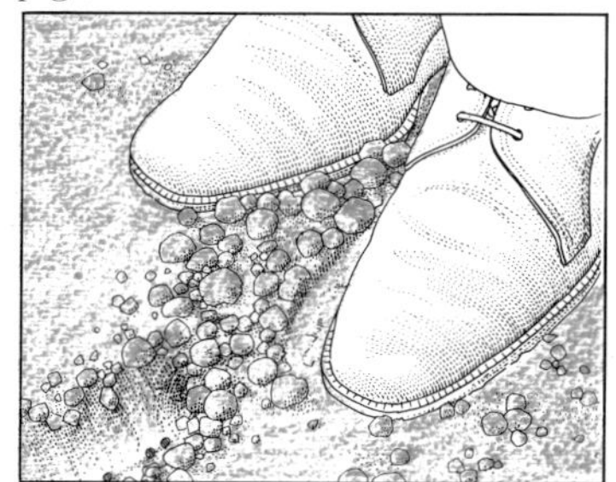

4 *If you close the drills with your feet be careful not to firm the soil too hard*

PRICKING OUT SEEDLINGS

Prise seedlings out carefully with a seed label so that roots are not damaged

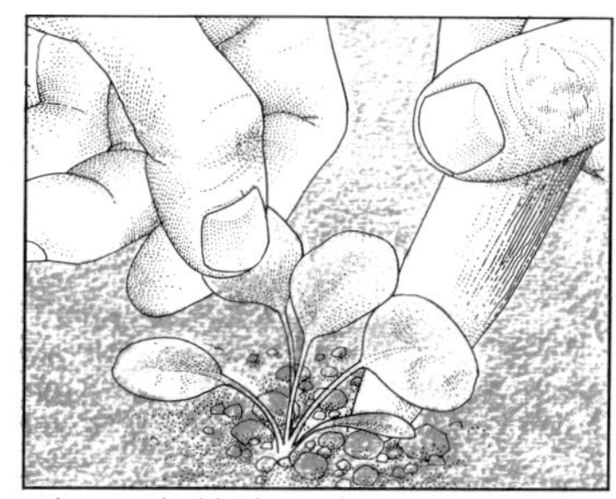

Always hold them by an expendable seed leaf. Do not hold them by the stem

take out alternate seedlings to leave the rest at the full spacing.

Fill any gaps by transplanting seedlings from thinnings, or from surplus seeds sown at the end of a row. But crops with tap roots – such as beetroots and carrots – cannot usually be successfully transplanted.

Do not leave thinnings lying on the ground; they will attract pests. Put them on the compost heap.

Pricking out If seeds have germinated in boxes, or clay or plastic pots, seedlings must be transplanted to other boxes or pots when quite fragile to give the roots room to develop. Do this when the first true (rough) leaves appear.

Prise them carefully from their container with a plastic seed label, so that as little damage as possible is done to the roots. Hold them by an expendable, first-formed seed leaf – never by the stem. Seedlings in peat pots do not need to be pricked out.

Hardening off Plants that have been grown from seed in a greenhouse or cold frame must be introduced gradually to a cooler temperature before they can be planted outdoors.

Transfer greenhouse plants to the coolest part of the greenhouse, then after about a week to a cold frame.

Gently introduce plants to outdoor conditions by raising the light of the cold frame and allowing air to circulate. Remove it altogether on fine, warm days, and at night open the frame on the side sheltered from the prevailing wind. If the change in temperature is made too quickly, plants become stunted and perhaps discoloured.

Transplanting Some crops, such as leeks, cabbages and other greens, are usually raised in small nursery beds, then finally transplanted into permanent beds.

Soak the nursery bed thoroughly the night before transplanting. The young plants will then be fresh with stiff leaves, and the roots will come away easier than if the soil is dry.

Firm the new bed, and water it overnight if the weather is dry.

Lift the plants with a garden fork or hand fork, taking care not to damage the roots. Protect them from the sun or drying winds until they are replanted. Make holes with a trowel or dibber, and plant as soon as possible.

To ensure firm planting, push the trowel or dibber into the ground alongside the plant and lever the soil firmly against the roots.

Test for firmness by holding a leaf between finger and thumb. If the leaf tears when you pull it the plant is firm enough, but if you pull the plant out of the ground, replant it more firmly. Water plants thoroughly after transplanting.

TRANSPLANTING SEEDLINGS

Firm the plant by levering soil against the roots with a trowel or dibber

Pull a leaf between finger and thumb; if it tears, the seedling is firmly planted

What can go wrong with vegetables

Below are the main troubles likely; those peculiar to any one kind of vegetable are given in the relevant section. If you are still uncertain, consult the identification table on page 377. Look up chemicals on page 398 to find proprietary names.

Symptoms	Cause	Cure
Leaves and stems crippled and stunted. Small green, yellowish, pinkish or black insects present	Aphids	Spray with one of the systemic insecticides, such as dimethoate, with malathion or derris
Leaves eaten – usually rounded areas from the margin inwards	Caterpillars	Locate and remove if possible. Spray with trichlorphon, malathion or derris
Leaves eaten – usually an irregular or grazed area, often with faint silvery trails	Slugs or snails	Cultivate thoroughly, and clear up accumulations of decaying plant material. Avoid heavy dressings of organic manures and mulches. Use methiocarb or metaldehyde slug baits
Plant collapses, with the stem eaten through at or below ground level	Cutworms, leather jackets or wireworms	Control weeds, which encourage cutworms. Protect susceptible plants by working a little HCH dust or bromophos into the soil. Seed dressings also give some protection
Roots with holes, usually more than ⅛ in. diameter	Soil-dwelling slugs	Damage is usually found when it is too late to cure. Fork in slug pellets at planting time, or water with a liquid slug destroyer
Roots with holes, usually less than ⅛ in. diameter, often with yellow grubs	Wireworms	Work a little HCH dust or bromophos into the soil
Leaves covered with fine, white mealy powder, sometimes with slight discoloration or distortion	Mildew	Cut out severely affected shoots. Spray regularly with benomyl, dinocap or thiophanate-methyl
Leaves or young shoots eaten or damaged	Birds	Protect young plants with wire-netting guards or criss-crossed black cotton
Leaves wilt and may turn orange, sometimes with other tints	Drought	Mulch and water before soil dries out. A foliar feed may help recovery
Young leaves are a pale yellowish-green; later light tints of yellow, red, orange or purple develop	Nitrogen deficiency	Apply sulphate of ammonia in the following spring. Foliar feeds may temporarily alleviate the problem
Seedlings rot and collapse at ground level	Damping off	Water with Cheshunt compound or zineb. Prevent by use of sterilised compost, clean pots, thin sowing and careful watering

Asparagus, the prince of vegetables

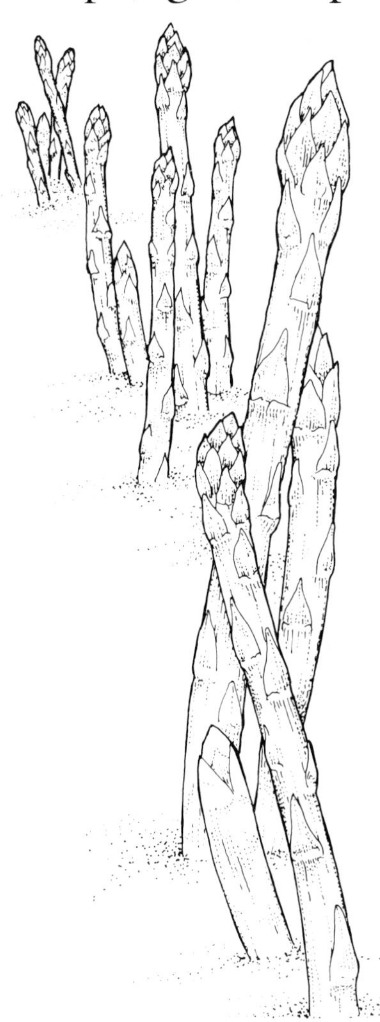

Asparagus 'Connover's Colossal'

An expensive vegetable to buy, asparagus is economical to grow since the same plants will provide crops year after year. Plants are grown in a permanent bed where they can remain for 20 years. There is no need to divide them to supply new growth. A mature plant will give a crop for about six weeks, beginning late April or early May.

Planting asparagus crowns

Asparagus will grow on most soils, but good drainage and freedom from perennial weeds are essential. In the autumn before planting, dig in manure or garden compost, one bucket to the square yard, to enrich the site. Next February, fork over the soil to make a fine tilth for planting.

Plant asparagus crowns early in April. Two and three-year-old crowns are sometimes offered by nurserymen, but one-year-old crowns are cheaper and less liable to be damaged in transplanting, so growth is less likely to be retarded.

Asparagus roots must not dry out, so while preparing to plant protect them from drying winds with a damp sack. Plant as soon as possible.

Prepare trenches 12 in. wide and 8 in. deep, spaced $4\frac{1}{2}$ ft apart. Mix gritty sand into the excavated soil to give the roots good aeration and drainage. Replace enough of this soil in the bottom of the trench to make a rounded ridge 3 in. high, so that the top is 5 in. below ground level.

Stand the asparagus crowns on this ridge, with their roots spread out on either side. Space them 18 in. apart. Do not fill in the trench, but lightly cover the crowns with 2–3 in. of soil so that the roots do not show.

Gradually fill in the trench later in the season as growth develops, drawing in a little more soil to keep the crowns covered each time you hoe. This will form a ridge that will force roots to grow deeply.

Growing asparagus from seed Sow thinly in a seed bed in March or April, in drills $\frac{1}{2}$ in. deep and 18 in. apart. Thin seedlings to 6 in. apart. In March or April the next year, plant out in the same way as crowns.

Harvesting the stems and tending the plants

Although the first shoots will be ready towards the end of April or early May, do not cut any shoots in the first season after planting. Cut some of the thicker stems in the second season, but not more than one from any plant.

In the third season, cut all the stems that appear, but stop cutting five weeks after the first cut. In the fourth and following seasons, continue cutting for six weeks.

Cut shoots when they are 3–4 in. above the ground. Never leave them to grow any higher, whether thick or thin – they will not get any thicker, only taller and woodier.

Make the cut as low as possible – well below soil level. A curved asparagus knife is ideal, but you can use a bread knife.

If the shoots are not wanted for cooking immediately, or if several cuts are needed to fill a dish, stand the stems in ice-cold water for a few hours. They can then be stored for a few days in a refrigerator at a temperature between 0°C (32°F) and 4°C (40°F). Stems can also be deep-frozen for longer storage.

When asparagus cutting ends, let stems grow to their full height. In exposed places, support them by running a string fixed to stakes down each side of the row. If stems rock, roots are loosened and water can penetrate and rot them. In summer, pick berries from female plants before they fall and germinate.

When foliage turns yellow in late October, remove the supporting stakes and strings and cut off the stems at ridge level. This will promote new shoots in late April. Rake up foliage and burn or compost it.

In March spread a general fertiliser, such as Growmore, over the row at the rate of 3 oz. (3 tablespoons) to the square yard. Gently stir it into the surface with a fork; a hoe or rake may injure shoots just below the surface. Use a hoe to draw up a little soil over the stems. Hand weed the bed in spring.

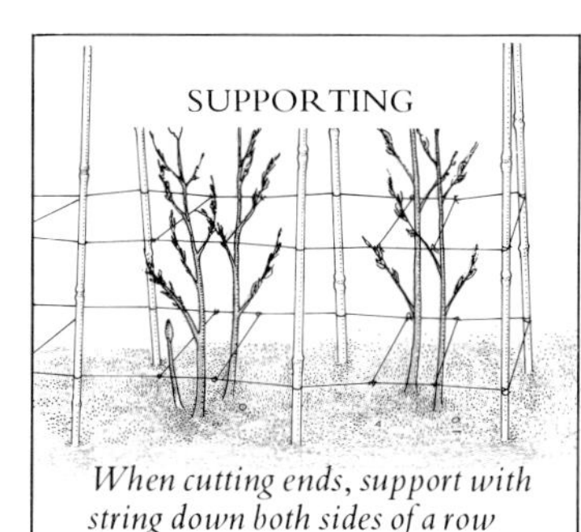

When cutting ends, support with string down both sides of a row

What can go wrong with asparagus

Asparagus beetle These can strip foliage completely. Spray with derris at once if you see any greyish grubs.

Violet root rot A web of violet-purple fungus may attack root tips, causing plants to go yellow and die. Remove and burn affected plants. Isolate the infected area with pieces of polythene or corrugated iron for the rest of the life of the bed.

Frost Late frosts can cause plants to go black and shrivel. Plants ridged with soil, with only the tips showing, should be all right, but if severe frosts are likely, cover them with paper, straw or sacking.

Other troubles Cutworms and slugs may eat young plants (p. 288).

Varieties of asparagus to grow

FROM PLANTS
'Connover's Colossal'
'Kidner's Pedigree'
'Giant Mammoth'

FROM SEED
'Brocks Imperial'
'Connover's Colossal'
'Martha Washington'

Beans—runners for late season flavour

Runner beans (scarlet runners) are heavy croppers and easy to grow, but they repay careful cultivation. They are larger and better flavoured than french beans, but not so hardy. The cropping season is during late summer and early autumn. These beans are noted for their decorative scarlet flowers, but there are also white-flowered varieties.

The form that most gardeners know is the tall-growing type that needs stakes or wires for support, but there are dwarf varieties that need only tomato canes for support.

The plot must be well manured during autumn or winter. If possible within your rotation system, choose a sheltered site to encourage plenty of insects for pollination.

Sowing outdoors under glass

The first outdoor sowing can be made under cloches in mid or late April for a late July crop. Put the cloches in position a fortnight before sowing to warm up the soil.

Make a pair of drills 2 in. deep and 12 in. apart. Sow the seeds 9–12 in. apart. Place a few extra seeds at the end of each row for transplanting into any gaps.

Cover with cloches immediately after sowing. Leave the cloches in position until all danger of frost has passed. Remove them about mid-May – late May or June in colder parts – and fix up supports for the plants to climb.

Runner bean 'Hammond's Dwarf Scarlet'

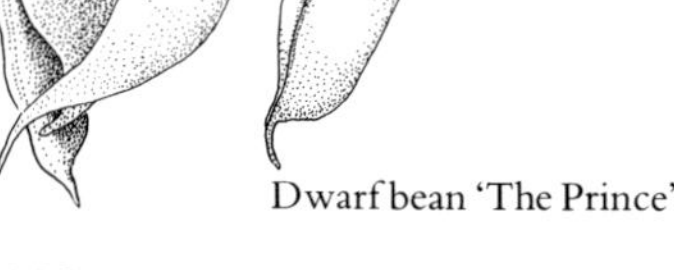

Dwarf bean 'The Prince'

Growing an early crop of runner beans

Sow an early variety in early April, using heat to force germination, for an early July crop. Sow seeds singly, 1 in. deep, in peat pots filled with seed compost, and place the pots in a heated propagator or a warm cupboard until germination takes place.

As soon as the seeds have germinated, transfer them to an unheated greenhouse or cold frame, or an inside window-sill. Frost is the great enemy.

Gradually harden the plants off (p. 288). If they are in a cold frame, allow the air to circulate on warm days, but close the frame at night if there is danger of frost.

If the plants are sturdy, it is a reasonable risk, in warmer parts of the country, to plant them out in the open about the second week in May. In colder parts it is wiser to wait until the end of May, or even the first week in June.

Before planting, place in position the stakes or other forms of support you intend to use.

Use a trowel to dig holes for each peat pot. Place them close to the supporting pole or netting, on the inner side of the support. Space the plants at 12 in. intervals for the best results. If pressed for space, 6 in. is the minimum distance apart.

Fix a sheet of clear plastic to the outside of the supports, to a height of about 2–3 ft. This will protect the plants from cold ground winds.

Sowing the main crop in succession

Make the first sowing for the main crop about mid-May. No cloches are needed. Use an early, quick-growing variety to prolong the season. Sow the rest of the main crop – using any preferred variety – in succession until the end of June.

Runner beans are usually grown in double rows spaced at least 12 in. apart. If more than one double row is sown, allow a minimum of 5 ft between each. Sow in drills 2 in. deep with 9–12 in. between each seed.

Tending and harvesting the plants

After sowing, scatter slug pellets over the bed, as slugs can ruin seedlings. Put crossed stakes in the ground when the first leaves appear.

As the seedlings mature, mulch with strawy manure, garden compost or peat before the ground becomes dry.

Water thoroughly round the roots when the flower buds are green, or when the first flowers open. Syringe the flowers every evening to assist fertilisation. Pinch out the growing tips when the plants reach the top of their supports. This encourages side-shoots and increases flowering.

Pick runner beans while they are young and tender, before the seeds begin to swell. To avoid damage, hold the stem with one hand and pull pods downwards with the other.

Runner beans germinated under heat will be ready in early July. The cloche-grown April crop will be ready in late July, and the main crop during August and September.

After the last pods have been picked, cut the foliage at the base. Leave roots in the ground, as they are a source of nitrogen. Stems are too woody for composting; burn them.

ENSURING A GOOD CROP

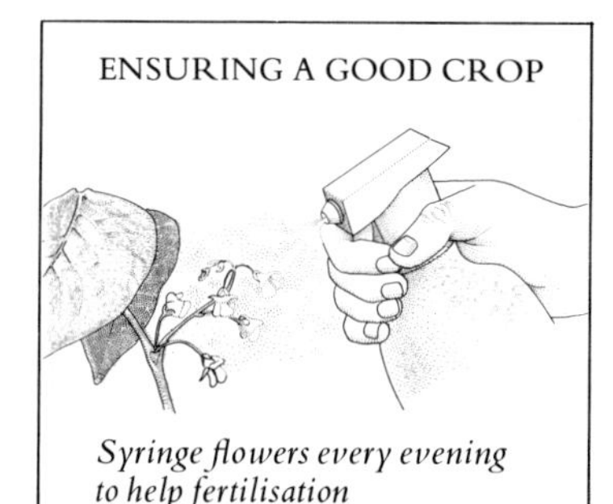

Syringe flowers every evening to help fertilisation

INCREASING FLOWERING

Pinch out the growing tips when plants reach the top of the support

Beans – dwarfs for early treats

How to support runner beans

Both tall and dwarf types of runner beans need support to keep the crop clear of the ground. Dwarfs need only a 3 ft stake, to which they are tied as they grow.

Tall types need longer stakes and a much firmer structure, as a full-grown row of runner beans has considerable wind resistance. Hazel poles, about $7\frac{1}{2}$ ft long, are best. Stout bamboos are an alternative.

The usual method is to set the stakes 12 in. apart on both sides of each row, or double row, as soon as the plants appear. Push them firmly into the ground, about 12 in., and cross opposite pairs at the top. Lash them securely to a horizontal pole where they meet. Opposite poles can be crossed halfway, so that about half the crop hangs above the crossing point, clear of the foliage.

As plants grow, twine the runners round the stakes. Tie them with soft string if necessary.

Another method is to sow seeds in a circle about 5 ft in diameter, with an 8 ft stake driven into the centre and a number of pegs round the edge. Loop strings from the pegs to the pole top, like a tent.

Yet another way is to use large-mesh, plastic-coated wire netting along each row. Support it with 8 ft stakes (with diagonal struts) placed 10 ft apart and pushed 12 in. deep. Erect it before planting.

METHODS OF SUPPORTING BEANS

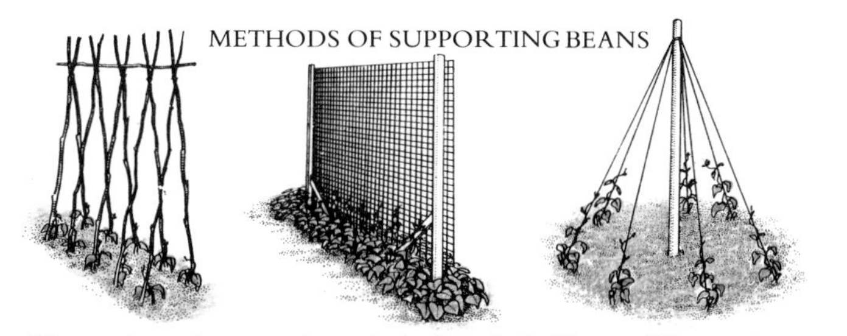

The usual way is to set stakes on both sides of a double row. Wire netting can also be used, or alternatively a pole, string, and pegs in a tent shape

The dwarf or french bean is popular because it is easy to grow and does not need staking. There is also a climbing variety. Dwarf beans are similar to runner beans, but smaller and hardier, and can be sown earlier. A March or April sowing under glass will give a crop at the end of June.

Dwarf beans are picked when they are young and green, and the whole pod is eaten. Some are pencil-podded (stringless) and others are flat-podded. Some pods can be left to ripen fully and the beans dried, stored and used as haricot beans.

Sowing under glass and outdoors Deep dig the plot before planting. Dwarf beans do best in ground fed with farmyard manure or garden compost during autumn and winter.

Start an early crop in late March or early April for picking in late June. Place seeds 2 in. apart in 4 in. deep boxes of potting compost in a cold frame. Gradually harden off seedlings (p. 288) during May. Raise the frame light to allow air to circulate; leave it off altogether on fine, warm days. Transplant the seedlings towards the end of May in rows 18 in. apart with 9 in. between plants.

Make the first sowing outdoors in April under cloches, for picking in early July. Put the cloches in place about a fortnight before sowing to warm up the ground. Sow seeds 2 in. deep and $4\frac{1}{2}$ in. apart in drills 18 in. apart. Remove the cloches at the end of May.

Sow the next crop in May without glass, followed by another three weeks later. This will give a succession of pickings throughout the summer.

Sowings of quick-growing (early) varieties can continue into early July for picking in the autumn.

Tending, harvesting and storing

Hoe regularly and water if necessary. Apply a liquid fertiliser if the soil is poor. When the plants are about 4 in. high, thin them to 9 in. apart. When pods are formed, push in a few twiggy sticks as support.

Pick beans regularly when young and tender; this encourages more pod formation. Do not let pods grow longer than 4 in., as they become tough. To avoid damage and uprooting when picking, hold the stem steady with one hand and pull the pod downwards with the other.

If you want dried beans for winter, leave a few plants unpicked. When pods are quite ripe at the end of summer, cut plants at ground level.

Hang them upside-down to dry in the sun (or under cover in bad weather). When pods are absolutely dry and crisp, pick and shell them. Store in airtight containers.

What can go wrong with runner beans

Small crop If beans flower well but little or no crop follows, the cause may be dryness at the roots or lack of pollinating insects. Ensure that roots are always moist at budding time, and the site is sheltered enough to encourage insects.

Foot rot A fungus causes plants to rot at the base of the stem. Water with Cheshunt compound. Avoid by rotating crops.

Other troubles Blackfly (aphids) or slugs may attack (p. 288).

Varieties of runner beans to grow

TALL
'Kelvedon Marvel' Very early
'Sunset' Early; pink flower
'Enorma'
'Achievement'
'Prizewinner'
'Streamline'
'Cookham Dene'
DWARF
'Hammond's Dwarf Scarlet'
'Hammond's Dwarf White'

What can go wrong with dwarf beans

Anthracnose This causes blackish spots and sunken areas on stems and pods. It will usually kill off young plants. Spray with half strength Bordeaux mixture, captan or zineb before flowering.

Foot rot Symptoms and control are the same as for runner beans.

Other troubles Blackfly (aphids) may attack the plants. Small seedlings may be eaten by slugs (p. 288).

Varieties of dwarf beans to grow

FLAT-PODDED
'The Prince'
PENCIL-PODDED
'Tendergreen'
'Sprite'
'Phenix Claudia'
'Glamis'
Recommended for the North
'Chevrier Vert'
Early: good for cooking whole

Beans—hardy broad beans for early crops

Broad beans are hardy and will give a heavy yield with little attention. They can be sown both under glass and outdoors to provide crops from early June to August. Generally, only the seed, not the pod, is eaten, but early beans can be eaten whole.

Preferably, sow broad beans in soil that has been well manured in winter, but any well-dug piece of land will do. Before sowing, break up the soil and rake it to a fine tilth.

Sowing the main crop outdoors Make the first outdoor sowing early in March. Follow with sowings in late March and early April.

Sow in either single or double rows, depending on the space and layout of your plot. A double row allows a heavier yield per plot without impairing the plants. Allow at least 2 ft space between broad beans and the adjoining crop on the plot.

For single-row sowing, draw drills 18 in. apart and 2 in. deep. For double rows, draw drills in pairs 9 in. apart with 2 ft between rows.

Before sowing, dust the beans with a seed dressing to prevent disease. Reject any that have small holes (the exit holes of bean beetles).

Sow seeds 9 in. apart, with positions staggered in each double row. Sow a few extra seeds at the end of each row, to provide replacement plants for any gaps that occur. Rake over drills to cover the seeds.

Cover rows with cloches to protect seeds from birds. The cloches can be removed when the seeds germinate. If no cloches are available, criss-cross between the rows with cotton tied to pegs. Set traps in areas where field mice are prevalent.

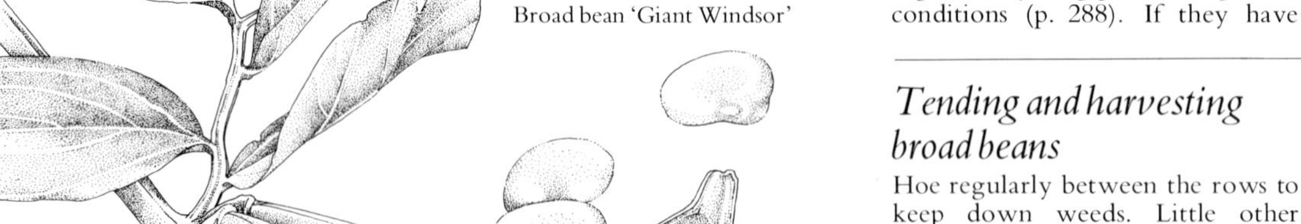

Broad bean 'Giant Windsor'

Sowing an early crop of broad beans

Make the first sowing of broad beans under glass in an unheated greenhouse or cold frame in early January in colder areas, or in February in warmer southern areas. This will give a crop in early June.

Fill a seed box with seed compost and place the beans 2 in. apart each way. Cover them with 1 in. of seed compost. Do not make the compost too firm.

Cover the box with a piece of glass and place a newspaper over it. Remove both glass and newspaper as soon as germination starts.

An alternative method is to sow the beans in 3 in. peat pots in John Innes seed compost. Plant one bean in each pot, $\frac{3}{4}$ in. deep. Stand the pots in a seed tray in a slightly warm place to germinate. Do not let the compost dry out completely, but water it only sparingly.

At the end of March start hardening off the young plants to open-air conditions (p. 288). If they have been grown in an unheated greenhouse, first of all transfer them to a cold frame.

Plant outdoors in early April. If the seeds have been planted in peat pots, stand the pots in water for a few minutes immediately before you plant them.

Use a trowel to make holes 9 in. apart, and plant the peat pots in them so that the rims are just covered with soil. Do not leave the edge of the pot protruding, as it acts like a wick – drying in the wind and sucking moisture from the surrounding soil.

Treat the plants in the same way as a crop sown outdoors.

An early crop in warm areas In warm, sheltered localities with well-drained soil, it is worth chancing an autumn sowing of broad beans outside in late October or early November. This will provide an early summer crop the following June.

Choose a longpod variety, which is hardy but not so sweet in flavour. Sow and cultivate in the normal way, fitting cloches over the rows to protect seeds from birds and frost.

Tending and harvesting broad beans

Hoe regularly between the rows to keep down weeds. Little other attention is necessary until the beans start flowering.

When the plants are in full flower pinch out the growing points – the tuft of leaves on the top of each plant. This will not only prevent extension growth, but will also discourage blackfly, which often infect this part of the plant. It will also concentrate nutriment in the developing pods.

Broad beans do not normally need staking. However, some of the longpod varieties, which can reach about 4 ft high, may need staking on windy sites.

Place stakes about 3 ft high at regular intervals on each side of the rows, and stretch string from stake to stake at a suitable height to support the plants. A second row of string can be used if necessary.

Harvesting Early broad beans can be picked in late May or early June, before the beans inside the pods have formed. The pods will be 2–4 in. long; cook and eat them whole.

The main outdoor-sown crop will be ready for picking in late June and through July into August.

Pick when the beans are of good size and well formed, but before the pods become tough. Pick a few at a time from each plant, starting with the bottom clusters. This will encourage the development of the remaining pods.

After the crop has been harvested, cut down the foliage and compost it. Dig in the roots, which contain nitrogen and will feed the soil.

Beetroot for salads, soups and storing

What can go wrong with broad beans

Blackfly If blackfly (aphids) appear – often unnoticed at first on the underside of leaves – spray with insecticide. If the pods are ready, or nearly ready, for picking, use a safe insecticide such as malathion. If you use a systemic insecticide, be sure to allow the full period of time recommended by the makers between spraying and picking.

Pea and bean weevils Seedlings may be attacked by the pea and bean weevil, which eats small, circular pieces from the leaf margins, creating a scalloped effect. Spray with derris or malathion at the first signs of attack.

Chocolate spot This disease is mainly encouraged by a potash deficiency and may occur after severe weather – beans become covered in blotches of chocolate colour. Spray with Bordeaux mixture.

Other troubles Seedlings may also be eaten by slugs (p. 288).

Varieties of broad beans to grow

FOR AUTUMN AND VERY EARLY SOWING
'Aquadulce Claudia'
'Monarch Aquadulce'
'Colossal'
'Green Masterpiece'
'Imperial White Longpod'
Remarkably long pods; heavy cropper; white seeds
'Imperial Green Longpod'
FOR SPRING SOWING
(Less hardy but sweeter flavour)
'Dreadnought'
'Imperial White Windsor'
'Imperial Green Windsor'
'Giant Windsor'
'Masterpiece Green Longpod'
'Unrivalled'
DWARF
'The Midget'
'The Sutton'

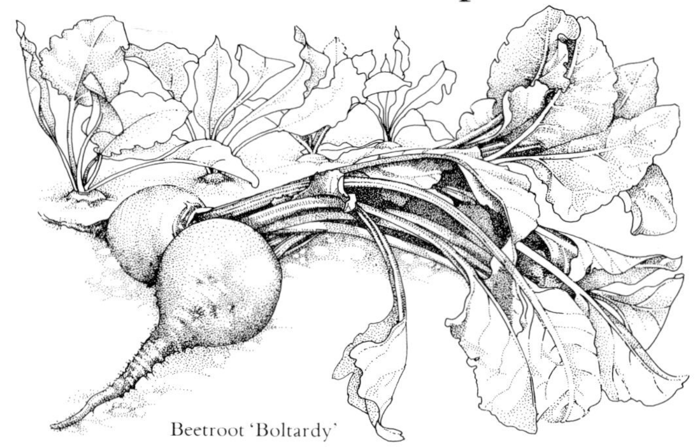

Beetroot 'Boltardy'

Beetroot do not need much space and are simple to grow. They are easily stored, so that a supply can be available all year round.

Do not sow beetroot in freshly manured ground. If the soil is not very fertile, apply a general fertiliser, before sowing, at the rate of 2 oz. (2 tablespoons) to the square yard.

The three main types of beetroot are globe, long-rooted (which may be up to 12 in. in length), and intermediate – also known as 'tankard' because of its squat shape.

Globe beetroot are sown in early spring and lifted in June ready for summer salads. The long-rooted and intermediate types are sown in May and early June. They can be lifted in autumn, and stored for use in winter through to April and May.

Sowing an early crop Sow globe beetroot in late February or March. Prepare a seed bed in a cold frame or beneath a cloche. Make shallow drills $\frac{1}{2}$ in. deep and 6 in. apart and sow thinly. Cover by lightly raking over the drill.

Thin seedlings to 5–6 in. apart before they become crowded. Harden them off gradually (p. 288), finally removing the frame light or cloches by mid-April. Keep the bed moist.

Sowing the main crop Sow long-rooted or intermediate beetroot successionally from mid-May to early June. It is also worth making a sowing of globe beetroot in July, for pulling in autumn and winter.

Make drills 1 in. deep and 12 in. apart. Sow seeds thinly and cover by lightly raking over the drill.

When the first rough leaf appears, thin seedlings to about 2 in. apart, leaving only one plant in each place. Continue thinning during July, removing every other plant for use while young. This will leave the remaining beetroot 4–5 in. apart.

Beetroot need little watering, except when seedlings. Hoe regularly to keep down weeds, but take care not to damage roots, as they will bleed, and lose colour and flavour.

Beetroot are susceptible to some mineral deficiencies. Yellowing between the veins of older leaves indicates a manganese deficiency. Spray with manganese sulphate – 2 oz. to $2\frac{1}{2}$ gallons of water (plus a spreader or a little detergent) – or water the soil with up to 10 oz. to $6\frac{1}{4}$ gallons. Alternatively, apply a chelated compound (sequestered iron). Roots with greyish or brown patches in the flesh indicate a boron deficiency. Apply 1 oz. (1 tablespoon) of borax (bulked with light sand) to 20 square yards of soil.

Cutworms and other general soil pests may attack, and seedlings may suffer from damping off (p. 288).

Lifting and storing beetroot

Lift globe beetroot in June, when they are the size of a cricket ball. If allowed to grow any larger, they will become hard and woody. Store them if they are not wanted for use immediately.

Lift early successional sowings when they are large enough for eating – from about early August onwards. Maincrop roots for storage should be lifted in October.

Lift beetroot carefully. If you use a fork, take care not to bruise or damage them. Do not store damaged or pest-infested roots – they will rot in storage.

After lifting, twist off the leaves, not too close to the crown. Twisting closes the pores in the stems and seals juices in the roots, reducing bleeding when they are cooked. Never cut off the leaves.

Store in a cool place. Put the roots on a layer of damp sand in a box or barrel, or against a wall. Cover them with more sand.

Further layers of beetroot can be added to the store when they have grown large enough. These should also be covered with damp sand.

Varieties of beetroot to grow

GLOBE
'Boltardy'
'Detroit Red'
'Crimson Globe'
'Early Bunch'
'Little Ball'
'Ruddigore'
'Golden'
Yellow-flushed. It does not bleed when cooked
INTERMEDIATE
'Cylindra'
LONG-ROOTED
'Cheltenham Green Top'
'Long Blood Red'

Brussels sprouts for winter meals

Brussels sprout 'Peer Gynt'

Brussels sprouts will provide a crop from late August until February if early and late varieties are grown. Pickings can be made from one batch of plants continually for a considerable time.

To develop well, sprouts need a long season of growth (about eight months), so should be sown early in the year. They are first raised in a seed bed, and later transplanted to a permanent bed for cropping.

Sprouts prefer ground that is firm; prepare the permanent bed in winter or early spring so that it can settle thoroughly. Dress the soil with 3 oz. (3 tablespoons) of superphosphate mixed with 1 oz. (1 tablespoon) of sulphate of potash to the square yard just before planting out the young plants.

Sowing and planting for early and late crops

Sow an early variety under glass in February for picking in late August. Sow thinly into the bed of a cold frame, in drills ½ in. deep and 6 in. apart. Thin seedlings to 3 in. if rows become overcrowded. Thinnings can be transplanted if the roots are not damaged. Gradually harden off seedlings (p. 288).

Alternatively, sow thinly in seed boxes of John Innes seed compost and cover with glass and newspaper until the seeds germinate. Prick out (p. 288) and transplant seedlings into trays or a cold frame bed in early April, when the first true leaves have formed, and harden off.

Make the first maincrop sowing in mid-March, either in the bed of the cold frame or outside in a sheltered position. Then sow in succession in a prepared seed bed (p. 287) – thinly in drills ½ in. deep and 6 in. apart – from mid-March to mid-April. Use late-cropping varieties for the final sowings.

Transplant young plants (p. 288) to their permanent bed when they are about six weeks old and 4–6 in. tall – before they become either woody or tall and spindly. Early varieties will be ready in May, and successional sowings through May and into June. Reject weak plants or those without a growing point.

Sprouts must be planted firmly, as deep as the first seed leaves. Space them 2½ ft apart, in staggered rows 2½ ft apart. Water after planting.

How to tend and harvest brussels sprouts

Hoe regularly to keep down weeds and open the surface of the soil. Water freely if the weather is dry. About a month after planting, draw a little soil round stems to stabilise plants against wind damage. Large plants in exposed places should be staked. Break off the lower leaves of the plant when they begin to turn yellow – not before.

Sowings of early varieties will be ready for picking by late August or early September. The crop is at its best in November and December, but pickings of late varieties can continue into February, sometimes into March.

Pick sprouts when they are a good size and in tight buttons – before they develop into loose, over-blown buds. Pick a few at a time from the bottom of the stem. When the bottom sprouts are ready for picking, cut off the cabbage-like top of the plant (it can be cooked as greens) to encourage the sprouts at the top of the stem to swell.

What can go wrong with brussels sprouts

Loosely knit sprouts If sprouts are not firm and tight, it may be due to poor seeds, soil that is not firm enough, a potash deficiency or an excess of nitrogen. It should not occur if reliable seeds are used and plants properly cultivated.

Other troubles Sprouts suffer the same problems as cabbages (p. 296) – also from birds, caterpillars and aphids (p. 288).

Varieties of brussels sprouts to grow

EARLY
'Peer Gynt'
'Indra'
MID-SEASON—LATE
'Prince Askold'
'Rollo'
'Vremo Inter'
LATE
'Sigmund'
'Bastion'

Cabbages – the all-year-round vegetable

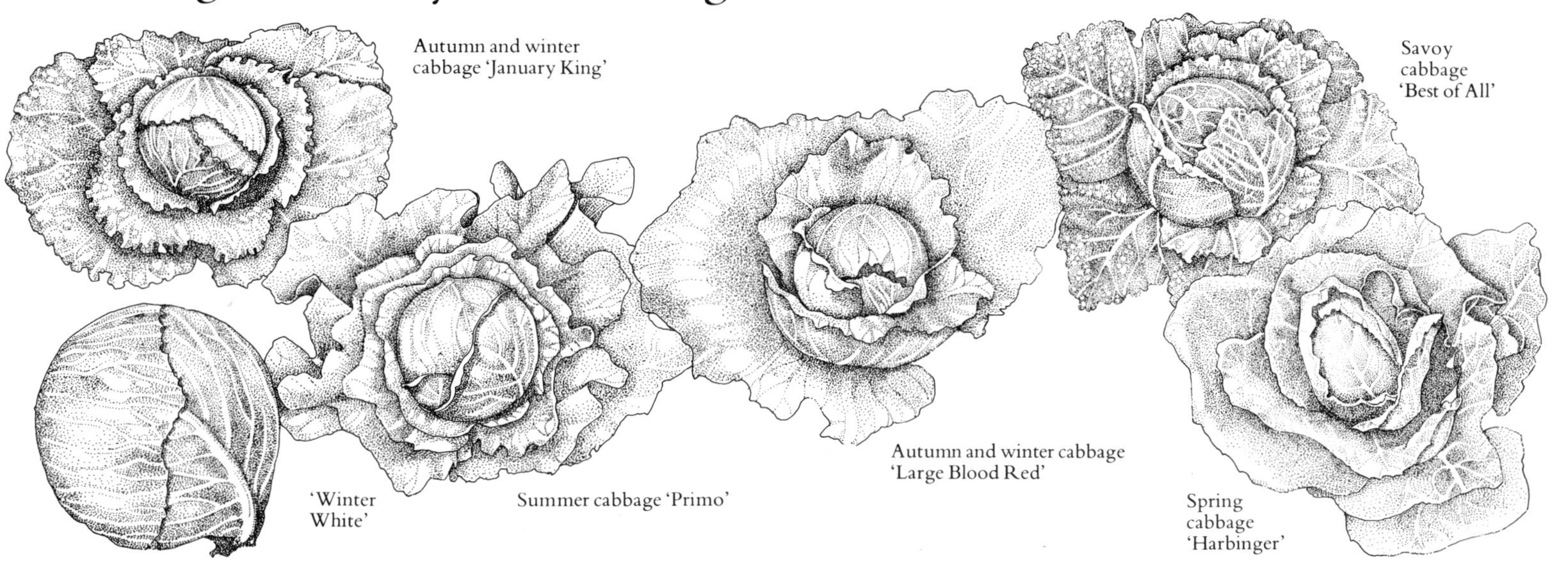

Cabbages can be harvested all the year round if different varieties are sown in succession. There are three main groups – quick-growing summer cabbages sown in spring, slower-growing autumn and winter cabbages sown in late spring, and spring cabbages sown during late summer and autumn.

Cabbage heads (hearts) vary in size and may be round, pointed (conical) or drumhead – very solid and almost flat.

There are also savoy cabbages, a hardy type with crinkled leaves. They are sown at the same time as autumn and winter cabbages, but are generally cut later.

Cabbages are sown in prepared beds (p. 287), and later transplanted to a permanent bed (p. 288). in a sunny, open position for cropping. Do not manure the bed. Plant them in soil that was well manured for the previous crop – peas, beans – in the rotation system. Dig the ground as it becomes vacant, but leave it rough until planting time. Then break it down and firm it.

Just before planting, dress the ground with a mixture of 3 oz. (3 tablespoons) of superphosphate and 1 oz. (1 tablespoon) of sulphate of potash to the square yard. Or as an alternative use a general fertiliser such as Growmore according to the maker's instructions.

Summer cabbages Sow quick-growing varieties for summer use in late February or March, for cutting from June to October. If sown earlier, they may flower early and run to seed (bolt) prematurely.

Sow direct into the bed of a cold frame, or into a prepared seed bed under cloches. Sow seeds thinly in drills $\frac{1}{2}$ in. deep and 6 in. apart. Thin seedlings to 3 in. if rows become crowded. Alternatively, seeds can be sown in seed boxes in a cold greenhouse in the same way as brussels sprouts (p. 294).

Gradually harden off the seedlings (p. 288) ready for planting out in April or May.

Plant firmly up to the first seed leaves; space 18 in. apart in staggered rows 18 in. apart.

Autumn and winter cabbages Sow thinly in a prepared seed bed, in the same way as summer cabbages. Sow in succession throughout April and May so that plants are ready from November to February.

Transplant the young cabbages in June or July, placing them 18 in. apart with 2 ft space between rows. Rows need to be wider apart than for summer cabbages, because autumn and winter cabbages have to stand longer in their final beds.

Spring cabbages Sow in a prepared seed bed, with the same spacings as for summer cabbages, in drills $\frac{1}{2}$ in. deep and 6 in. apart. In the North, sow during the first and second weeks of August; in the South, during the last two weeks of August. Water lightly if there is no rain after four or five days.

Cabbages should be ready for cutting from April to June the following year.

Transfer the young cabbages to their final quarters in either September or October – about six weeks after sowing.

By the time the plants are six weeks old, they should have developed a good, fibrous root system, essential if they are to survive the winter. It also prevents them running to seed prematurely (bolting). Lift them carefully from the seed bed, pushing a hand fork well under the roots to bring them up intact.

Every alternate plant can be used for spring greens in March before the crop matures, and the remainder left as the main crop for cutting in April. If you want spring greens, put plants in rows 16 in. apart with 9 in. between each plant. If you want all hearted cabbages, space them 18 in. apart in rows 18 in. apart.

Firm the soil surface round the stems with the thumbs – frost may lift them if they are not planted very firmly. Water each plant after planting. In case the crop should fail, plant some of the seedlings in a cold frame or under cloches. Place the seedlings 12 in. apart in staggered rows that are also 12 in. apart.

Savoy cabbages Sow in seed boxes or a cold frame in the same way as other cabbages. Sow in April for a crop from September to December, in May for a crop from January to March, and in July for cutting in April and May. Transplant savoy cabbages when they are about six weeks old, placing them 18 in. apart in rows 2 ft apart.

Tending and harvesting cabbages

Hoe regularly between rows to keep down weeds. Remove any decaying leaves in autumn and late winter; water freely if the weather is dry.

Spring cabbages should be encouraged to heart early. After removing spring greens, dress the soil with 2 oz. (2 tablespoons) of nitrate of soda or sulphate of ammonia to the square yard.

Cabbages are ready for cutting when they have a good, firm heart. Leave the lower stem and roots in the ground to form new shoots which can be used as greens later.

After the crop has finished, clear old stumps from the ground, dry and burn them. Composting may carry over pests to future crops.

SPRING GREENS

In March thin out every other spring cabbage to use as greens

What can go wrong with cabbages

Club root (Finger and toe). Leaves wilt and may be discoloured, roots become swollen and distorted, then smell and decay. The cause is a soil-borne fungus that thrives in acid soils. Lift and burn affected plants. Improve drainage if necessary, and dress the soil with hydrated lime – about one bucket to every 30 square yards. Rotating crops lessens the risk of attack, so does calomel dust. When planting, put 4 per cent calomel dust in holes, or dip roots in a paste of dust, water and a little flour.

Cabbage root fly Young plants wilt and collapse, due to white maggots that eat roots and tunnel into stems. Burn affected plants and soil round the roots. Protect transplants by mixing bromophos in the soil, or water with a spray-strength solution of diazinon or trichlorphon.

Cabbage whitefly These gather on the undersides of leaves and suck the sap. Spray young plants regularly with malathion, pyrethrum, dimethoate or fenitrothion. Destroy old plants that may harbour flies.

Flea beetles These pit new leaves with tiny holes. Water daily until seedlings grow freely. Dust weekly with HCH or derris until rough leaves form.

Other troubles Caterpillars, aphids, birds, damping off (p. 288).

Varieties of cabbages to grow

SUMMER CABBAGES
'Derby Day'
Recommended for sowing under glass
'Greyhound'
'Primo'
AUTUMN AND WINTER CABBAGES
'Winter White'
Can be stored in a cool, airy place
'Autumn Pride'
'January King'
'Large Blood Red'
SPRING CABBAGES
'Harbinger'
'Early Offenham'
'First Early Market'
SAVOY CABBAGES
'Best of All'
'Ormskirk Late'

Carrots, the versatile root vegetable

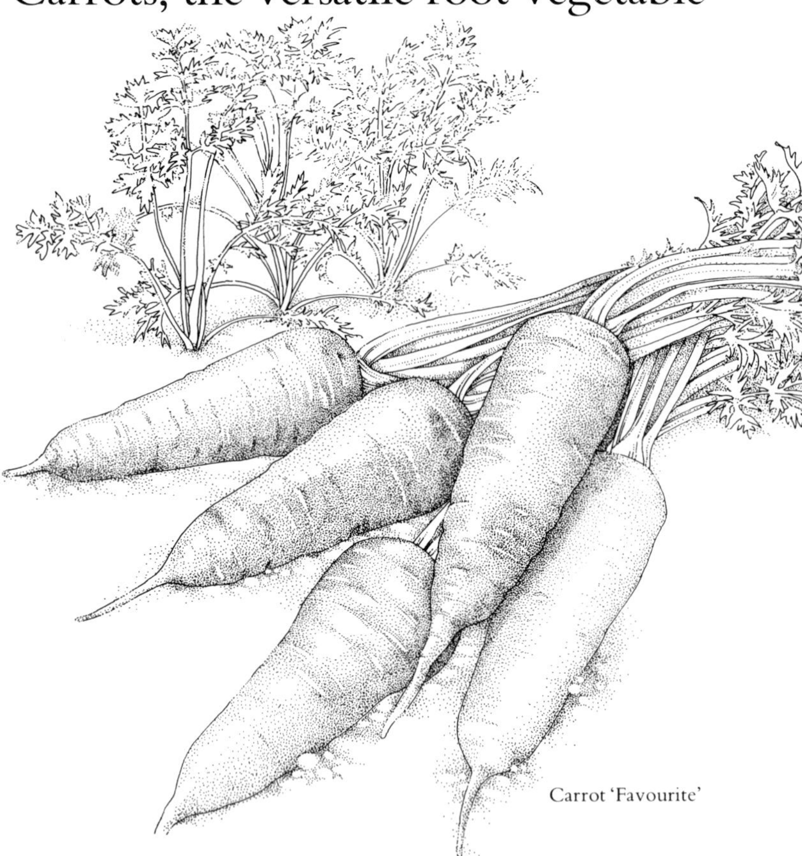

Carrot 'Favourite'

Carrots are valuable for their high vitamin A content, and a crop can be available from June until spring of the following year by means of successional sowing and storing.

Roots may be termed short, intermediate or long. In shape they may be cylindrical (some short ones are round) with a stump end, or tapering to a point.

Stump-rooted types are the most popular, but tapering types are favoured by exhibitors. Short stump-rooted varieties are very good for forcing in cold frames or under cloches.

The intermediate and long varieties (either stump-rooted or tapering) are best for later sowing and for storing.

All varieties do well on light, easily worked soil that is reasonably rich. Use a site that has been manured for a previous crop, and prepare the bed with fertilisers only.

A few days before sowing, rake in a mixture of 3 oz. (3 tablespoons) of superphosphate, 1 oz. (1 tablespoon) of sulphate of potash, and 1 oz. (1 tablespoon) of sulphate of ammonia to the square yard.

Make sure that the soil is as fine as possible, as any lumps or stones can cause forking of the roots. Grow only short or intermediate varieties on heavy or rough ground.

Sowing early and maincrop carrots

Sow the first crop of carrots (a stump-rooted variety) in February. Prepare a seed bed in a cold frame or beneath cloches – put the cloches in place a fortnight before sowing to warm up the soil.

Make shallow drills ½ in. deep and 6 in. apart in the seed bed. Sow the seed thinly, and cover it lightly.

Do not thin the seedlings when they appear. Remove the frame light or cloches in mid-April, and keep the bed moist if there is no rain. Carrots will be ready for pulling in June. Use the largest first, leaving the rest to grow on.

Make the first outdoor sowing – a short, stump-rooted variety – in March if the ground is not wet or cold. If it is, wait another three or four weeks. After the first sowing, sow any preferred variety in succession until the end of July.

Make drills ¾ in. deep and 9–12 in. apart, and sow as thinly as possible. Cover the seeds by returning the soil with the back of a rake, or by shuffling your feet along either side of the drill (p. 287). Lightly rake over the soil afterwards.

Thin on a dull, cool day, or in the evening – there is less smell from crushed foliage, which attracts the carrot fly. Water afterwards, and do not leave thinnings lying about.

Make the first thinning to 1 in. apart when the first rough leaves appear. Continue thinning the short-rooted varieties until they are 2 in. apart, and the larger-rooted varieties until they are 4 in. apart. Thinnings from the larger varieties are large enough for eating.

What can go wrong with carrots

Carrot fly Leaves turn red, then yellow and wither, and roots are infested with maggots. Early crops in a sheltered position and main crops sown in mid-June or early July often escape attack. Eggs are laid in late May and early June; grubs hatch out about a week later.

If carrot fly is prevalent, sow early or late, and thinly to avoid thinning. Use a seed dressing. If you have to thin, water afterwards.

Protect established plants by watering a spray-strength solution of diazinon or trichlorphon along the rows, two or three times in August and September.

Split roots This may be caused by drought followed by heavy rain. Avoid irregular growth by watering before the soil dries out completely.

Other troubles Slugs, cutworms and wireworms may attack (p. 288).

Varieties of carrots to grow

SHORT (STUMP)
'Amsterdam Forcing'
'Early Gem'
'Early Nantes'
'French Forcing'
'Nantes Tip Top'
'Champion Scarlet Horn'

INTERMEDIATE (STUMP)
'Favourite'
'Scarla'
'Berlicum Cylinder'

INTERMEDIATE (TAPERING)
'James's Intermediate'
'Autumn King'

LONG (TAPERING)
'New Red Intermediate'
'St Valery'

LONG (STUMP)
'Scarlet Perfection'

Harvesting and storing a carrot crop

Pull carrots from early sowings as soon as they are large enough for eating. Keep the late sowings for winter storage.

Carrots for storage should be lifted during the first half of October – no later, or bad weather will damage the crop. Roots that are left in the ground too long will get woody and crack, and are of little use for storing.

If carrots are in good condition, and are properly stored, they will keep until March or April of the following year.

Lift roots for storing with a fork, taking care not to damage or bruise them. Sort out damaged roots, and put them aside for immediate use. Damaged roots are subject to soft rot, which attacks through wounds and causes a slimy decay, spreading outwards from the centre.

Before storing, cut off the leaves as near as possible to the crown without damaging it. Remove any soil, and store the carrots in layers of slightly damp sand placed in boxes or heaps in a dry, well-ventilated, frost-proof shed, removing them as required.

An alternative method is to store them in a clamp in the open. The clamp should be on a dry site in a sheltered position.

Make a conical mound of the carrots, piling them in layers with the top (leaf) end outermost. Then cover the heap with clean, dry straw and build up a skin of slightly damp soil about 2 in. thick over the straw. Firm the soil on the clamp, to prevent it from being washed away by rain.

If carrots are stored in very damp conditions, they are likely to get sclerotinia rot – a fluffy fungus that soon causes them to become black and hard.

STORING CARROTS IN A CLAMP

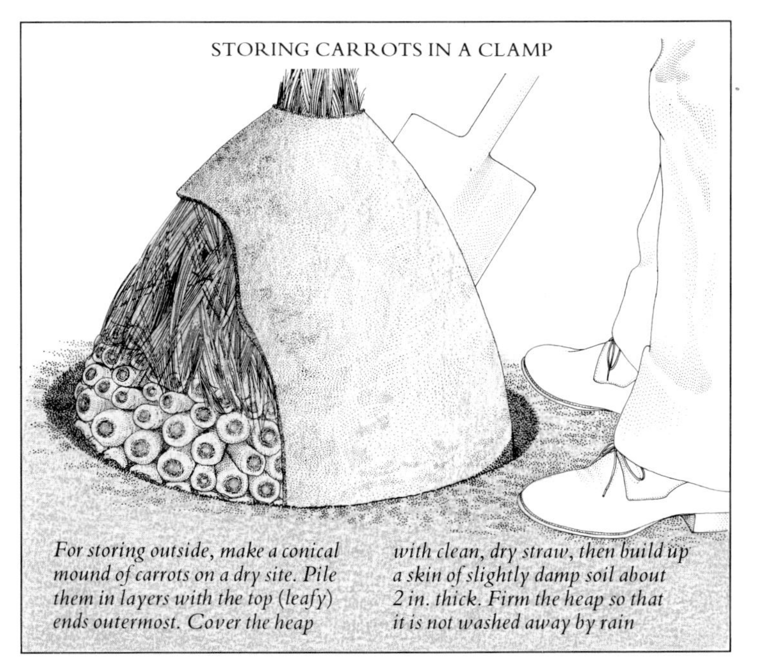

For storing outside, make a conical mound of carrots on a dry site. Pile them in layers with the top (leafy) ends outermost. Cover the heap with clean, dry straw, then build up a skin of slightly damp soil about 2 in. thick. Firm the heap so that it is not washed away by rain

Cauliflowers and broccoli for winter and summer

Cauliflowers and broccoli are both grown for their heads of immature flowers, known as curds. Broccoli are hardy; cauliflowers need more care in growing and are the most difficult of all the brassica crops to grow successfully.

The two main types of broccoli are heading broccoli (sometimes known as winter cauliflower), which has a compact white head like a cauliflower, and sprouting broccoli, which produces many small heads on separate shoots.

There are three kinds of sprouting broccoli – the hardy purple or white-headed type, the less-hardy green-headed type (sometimes known as calabrese), and a perennial type, which will produce small heads every year for three or four years.

A supply of either cauliflowers or broccoli can be available all year round. Cauliflowers are sown mainly during spring for harvesting from June to October. Both heading and sprouting broccoli are sown mainly from mid-April to late May, and harvested from September to the following June – except for calabrese, which matures in late summer or autumn.

Cauliflowers have a fairly short season of growth, so it is essential that they are not retarded in any way. If, for example, seedlings grown under glass are not properly hardened off (p. 288) before planting out, or plants are not watered sufficiently, they will produce only small, almost useless curds.

Both cauliflowers and broccoli are grown from seed in a seed bed, and later planted out (p. 288) to a permanent bed for cropping. It should be in an open, sunny position, but not too exposed.

They do best in ground that is firm but has been deeply dug, so prepare the bed well in advance, or else leave it rough from the previous crop. It should have been well manured for the previous crop.

A fortnight before planting out, hoe into the soil a mixture of 3 oz. (3 tablespoons) of superphosphate and 1 oz. (1 tablespoon) of sulphate of potash to the square yard.

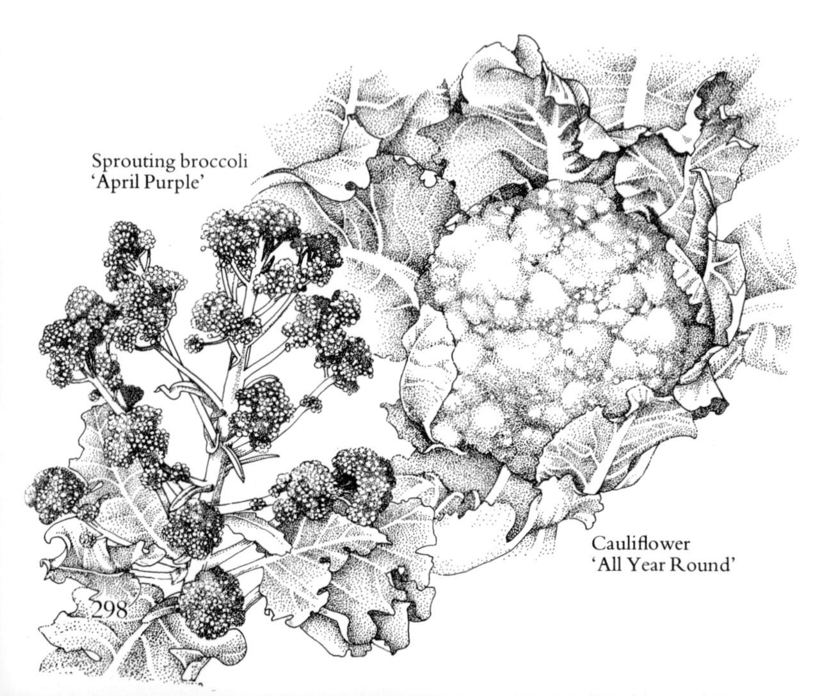

Sprouting broccoli 'April Purple'

Cauliflower 'All Year Round'

How to sow for a continuing supply

To ensure a continuing supply of cauliflowers, sow in succession in small batches, otherwise plants all reach maturity at the same time.

For a continuing supply of broccoli, choose early and late-maturing varieties, and sow them all within a few weeks. Choose varieties carefully, as they vary in hardiness. Some are not suitable for colder or exposed areas.

Early cauliflowers Plants for cutting during June can be started in two ways – either sown outdoors in late summer and wintered in a cold frame for planting out about March, or sown in seed boxes in a heated greenhouse or frame in January and planted out in April.

In August, for late summer sowings, choose a sheltered corner of the garden and make drills ½ in. deep and 6 in. apart. Use a summer-cutting variety, and sow thinly – try to space one seed every ½ in.

In October, transfer the seedlings to a cold frame. Water the seed bed the night before lifting the seedlings. Lift them with care, using a hand fork, and take care not to damage the roots. Put them 2-3 in. apart, in rows 6 in. apart. Water them in, and keep the frame closed.

Leave them in the frame during winter, regularly checking the soil for dryness; water if necessary. Start to harden off (p. 288) in February.

If sowing under glass in January, sow thinly in a tray of seed compost and lightly cover the seeds with sieved compost. Maintain a temperature of 13°C (55°F) for germination and afterwards if possible. In February, when seedlings are large enough to handle, prick them out (p. 288).

Replant them individually, using a small dibber, into 3 in. pots of John Innes No. 1 compost. Use peat pots to simplify planting out in April.

Early broccoli In late February or March sow early-maturing varieties of heading broccoli, such as 'Veitch's Self-protecting', for September cutting. Sow in boxes in a cold greenhouse, or direct into a cold frame.

If sowing in a cold frame, put seeds in drills ½ in. deep and 6 in. apart. Thin seedlings to 3 in. apart if they become crowded. If sowing in a box in a greenhouse, cover the box with glass and newspaper until germination occurs.

In early April, when greenhouse seedlings have formed their first real leaves, prick them out (p. 288). Put them in a cold frame 3 in. apart, either in trays or in the soil, and gradually harden them off (p. 288).

When hardened off, seedlings can be transferred to a sheltered nursery bed outside. The aim is to get sturdy, well-rooted plants for putting out in the open in May.

Maincrop sowings From early March to early May, sow the maincrop of cauliflowers in succession for cutting in late summer and autumn. Make the first March sowing in the bed of a cold frame, or in seed boxes in a cold greenhouse. Transfer the greenhouse seedlings to 2½–3 in. peat pots when they are large enough. Plant out seedlings when they are six weeks old.

Later sowings of cauliflowers can be made in a seed bed outdoors and later planted in the permanent bed.

From mid-April to late May, make the main sowings of heading and sprouting broccoli outdoors for cutting from November to June. Sow early-maturing varieties first, followed by later-maturing varieties.

Sow outdoor cauliflowers and broccoli in a prepared seed bed (p. 287), in drills ½ in. deep and 6 in. apart. Sow very thinly, and rake over the surface lightly to cover the seed. Label rows clearly with the variety and sowing date.

If the broccoli become crowded, thin them to 3 in. apart to ensure sturdy, well-rooted plants for planting out. Thinnings can be transplanted into a separate row.

Planting out and looking after the young plants

Young plants grown in a greenhouse or cold frame should be hardened off (p. 288) before planting out.

Plant out cauliflower seedlings when they are about six weeks old. Broccoli should be planted out at about the same age, before they become either hard and woody, or tall and spindly; strong plants are needed to survive the winter.

Early cauliflowers sown in a greenhouse or cold frame can be planted out in late March, if the weather is reasonably mild. If it is bad, wait until April. If put out too early in windy conditions, growth can be set back by weeks.

Water the seed bed the night before lifting young plants. If they are in peat pots, place the pots in water for a minute or two before planting. Lift young plants from the seed bed with a fork, taking care not to damage the roots. Discard any without a growing point in the centre; they will not produce heads.

Plant early cauliflowers 18 in. apart, in staggered rows 18 in. apart. Maincrop sowings, which will be longer growing, should be placed further apart. Plant summer cauliflowers 2 ft apart in rows 2 ft apart; autumn cauliflowers (in June and July) 2-2½ ft apart each way.

Early varieties of broccoli will be ready for planting out in May. The main sowings should be put out in June (in warmer areas) or July. Plant them 2 ft apart, in staggered rows 2 ft apart.

For both cauliflowers and broccoli, make planting holes with a dibber and plant seedlings up to the lowest seed leaves. Be sure to firm them in. Push a dibber or trowel into the ground 2 in. from the plant and press soil towards the stem.

Water the young plants in after planting, and test for firmness by pulling the tip of one of the leaves. It should tear off. If the plant is lifted, replant it.

If plants are in peat pots, plant them with a trowel so that the rim is just below soil level.

Hoe between cauliflowers regularly to keep down weeds. If growth is slow, rake in 1 oz. (1 tablespoon) of nitrate of soda or sulphate of ammonia to the square yard. Water plants freely if the weather is dry; occasionally use a weak liquid fertiliser instead.

If broccoli have been planted firmly, they need little more than regular hoeing. About a month after planting, draw up a little soil round the stems, to just below the lowest leaves. This causes fresh roots to form, and gives the plants better anchorage and growth.

When the curds of both cauliflowers and broccoli begin to form, break a leaf or leaves over them. This will protect them from sun, which turns them yellow, and frost, which turns them brown.

What can go wrong with cauliflowers and broccoli

Pests and diseases Cauliflowers and broccoli suffer from the same pests and diseases as cabbages (p. 296), and are more susceptible to club root. The club-root fungus thrives in acid soil, so before growing cauliflowers or broccoli check the acidity with a soil-testing kit; add lime if needed.

Poor crop Cauliflowers need steady, rapid growth. They will fail if growth is retarded by poor soil or lack of water. Broccoli need steady, slow growth. They will become spindly and not winter hardy in over-rich conditions.

Loose planting may cause both types of plant to be lost through wind or frost damage.

Whip tail In acid soils, plants may produce thin, strap-like leaves with ruffled and irregular growth. If this occurs, water with a solution of 1 oz. (1 tablespoon) of sodium molybdate in 2 gallons of water for every 10 square yards of soil.

Varieties of broccoli to grow

HEADING BROCCOLI
(With approximate cutting dates for mid-April to late May sowings)

SUITABLE FOR THE NORTH AND EXPOSED AREAS
'Veitch's Self-protecting' Nov.
'Reading Giant' Mar.-April
'Thanet' late April
'May Star' late April-May
'Matchless' April-June
'White Cliffs' early May
'May Blossom' mid-May
'Progress' May
Extremely hardy
'June Market' late May-June
Recommended for North

SUITABLE FOR SOUTHERN ENGLAND
'Early Feltham' Jan.-Feb.
'Westmarsh Early' Feb.-Mar.
'Snow White' Mar.-April
'Late Feltham' April-May
'Extra Late Feltham' May-June
'Summer Snow' June

SUITABLE FOR THE SOUTH COAST
'St Gwithian' Nov.-Dec.
'St Agnes' Dec.-Jan.
'St Buryan' Jan.-Feb.
'St Keverne' Mar.
'Seale-Hayne No. 5' April-May
'St Mark' late May

SPROUTING BROCCOLI
'Christmas Purple' Dec.
'Early Purple' Jan.-Feb.
'Late Purple' Mar.-April
'April Purple' April
'Early White' Feb.-Mar.
'Late White' Mar.-April

GREEN SPROUTING BROCCOLI
'Green Comet' Sept.-April
'Late Corona' Sept.-April

PERENNIAL BROCCOLI
'Nine Star' or **'Bouquet'** Mar.

Cutting cauliflower and broccoli curds

Curds are ready for cutting when they are well developed but have not begun to open. In mild weather check daily, as they develop quickly.

Daily cutting is probably necessary. Cauliflowers are best cut in the early morning with the dew still on them. Cut sprouting broccoli curds to within 2 in. of their base, so that more will develop. Cut them while they are young and tender.

If a number of cauliflower or heading-broccoli curds are ready at the same time, breaking leaves over them will hold them back for a day or two. If this is not long enough, pull them up by their roots and hang them upside-down in a dry, cool place for up to three weeks.

After the crop is finished, dig up the stumps and dry and burn them.

Varieties of cauliflowers to grow

SUMMER CUTTING
'Classic'
'Early Snowball'
'Delta'
'Dominant'
'Snow King'
'Alpha'
'All Year Round'
Produces heads over a long period, according to the time of sowing

AUTUMN CUTTING
'Autumn Giant'
'Superlative'
'Nova'
'Beacon'
'White Chief'

LATE-AUTUMN CUTTING
'Boomerang'
'South Pacific'
'Snowcap'

Celery for subtle salads and hot dishes in autumn and winter

Celery 'Avonpearl'

Celery is a versatile vegetable. It can be eaten raw with cheese or chopped in salads, braised and served hot or used as a flavouring in soups and casseroles. It is in season from mid-September to March.

There are two types – trench-grown celery, which is earthed up as it grows so that the stems are blanched, and self-blanching celery, which is grown on level ground.

Self-blanching varieties are not as hardy as the trenching varieties, and should be used for the early crop, ready from mid-September. Trenching celery is ready for use from about late September through to March.

Both types need very good soil and a lot of moisture during growth, and good drainage. The celery bed or trench therefore needs plenty of well-rotted manure dug in deeply, or good garden compost together with leaf-mould and peat. Before planting out rake in 2–3 oz. (2–3 tablespoons) of a general fertiliser to the square yard.

Sowing celery seeds under glass

In early March sow celery, for planting out in May and using from September, in a heated propagator, at about 13–16°C (55–61°F).

Sow seeds thinly in a pot, pan or seed box of John Innes or other seed compost. Use a sieve to cover seeds with a fine sprinkling of compost.

Cover the seed container with glass overlaid with newspaper. As soon as the seedlings appear, remove both glass and newspaper.

When seedlings are large enough to handle, prick them out (p. 288) into a separate seed box. Using a dibber, make holes 2 in. apart and fairly deep to take the long roots.

Place the seedling roots in the hole and gently firm the compost round them with the dibber.

During April, remove seedlings to a cold frame for hardening off (p. 288) ready for planting out.

Make a second sowing in a cold frame or greenhouse in mid-April, for planting out in June and using from about October.

Preparing trenches and planting celery

In April, dig a trench in readiness for planting out in May or June. The trench should be either 15 in. wide to take a single row of celery, or 1½–2 ft wide to take two rows 12 in. apart.

Mark out the position of the trench with pegs and garden line. Dig out the soil from the trench to a depth of 12 in. at least, throwing the excavated soil on either side.

If the subsoil is very poor and you want the best results, dig out another 12 in. of soil from the trench and remove it to another part of the garden. Replace it with topsoil from wherever you can spare it.

Fork over the bottom of the trench so that it is thoroughly broken up, then work liberal amounts of well-rotted manure, or garden compost and leaf-mould, into the bottom. One level wheelbarrow to each 6 ft run of double-row trench is not too much.

Return most of the topsoil evenly from either side of the trench, but do not replace it all. When the ground has settled, the trench should be about 6 in. below the general garden level with a 3 in. ridge of soil on either side.

This hollow will give the young celery plants valuable shelter from winds when they are first put out, as well as channelling the rain water they need. The ridges on either side will eventually be used for earthing up the celery.

In the meantime, do not waste this space. Either plant out a row of lettuce seedlings 12 in. apart along the top, or sow lettuces or stringless dwarf French beans.

Early seedlings should be completely hardened off and ready for planting out in late May. April-sown seedlings, from the cold greenhouse or frame, will be ready for planting out in June.

Use a hand fork to loosen and lift the young plants from their seed box. Plant them with a trowel.

For single-row planting, space the plants at 10 in. intervals down the middle of the 15 in. wide trench.

If planting double rows in a trench 1½–2 ft wide, space the rows 12 in. apart with 10 in. between each plant. Do not stagger plants – set them in pairs so that they will be easier to earth up later. Complete by watering liberally.

GROWING CELERY IN TRENCHES

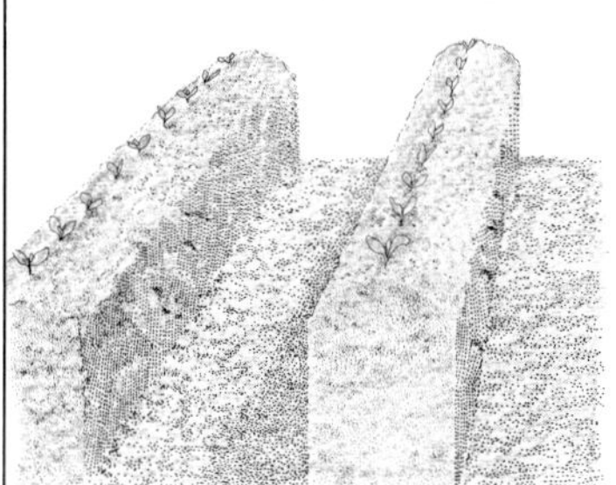

Dig trenches in April. Work well-rotted manure or garden compost into the bottom, and return most of the topsoil. The final trench should be

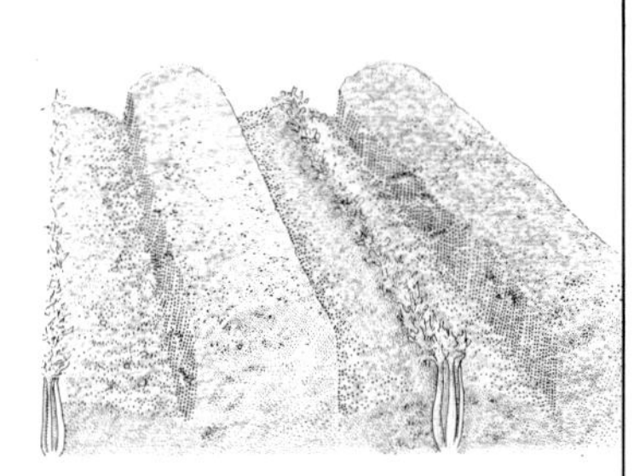

6 in. deep, giving young plants protection from winds. The soil ridge on each side is for earthing up later. Meanwhile grow lettuces on ridges

Cultivating celery grown in trenches

To encourage steady growth, water freely if the weather is dry.

Begin earthing up when the plants are about 12–15 in. high. For May-planted celery this will be about early August, and for the June-planted crop it will be about September or early October.

Before earthing up, cut off any suckers that may have grown from the base of the plants, then tie the stems loosely just below the leaves. Thoroughly moisten the ground.

Do not earth higher than the base of the leaves, and do not let any soil fall into the heart of the plants.

Make the first earthing very slight, drawing some soil from the ridges on each side of the trench with a spade. Make a second earthing in the same way three weeks later, taking more soil than before.

For the third and final earthing after another three weeks, the soil will probably have to be excavated from each side of the row. Cover all the stems right up to the leaves, sloping the soil away neatly.

It takes from six to eight weeks from the first earthing to blanch celery properly. After this time, dig it up when needed. If snow or very hard frost threatens, lay bracken or straw along the ridge tops of late celery to give it some protection.

To pick celery, open the ridge at one end and remove a few sticks with a fork. Then bank up the soil again as a protection from frost.

When the plants are 12–15 in. high, make the first slight earthing. Make the second and third earthings more generously at three-week intervals

Planting and cultivating self-blanching celery

Self-blanching celery does not need trenching. It is not as hardy as trench-grown celery, and will be damaged by a succession of sharp frosts. Grow it as an early crop, for use from about mid-September.

Plants are grown on level ground, positioned close together in a block so that the shade from their leaves helps them to blanch each other. The plants on the outside, which are not completely shaded, need some covering, but the square formation gives the least number of unshaded plants for a set area.

Alternatively, plants can be grown in the bed of a cold frame (with the light removed), so that the outer plants will be shaded by the walls of the frame.

Prepare the bed in April by digging in plenty of well-rotted farmyard manure or garden compost with leaf-mould or peat. Seedlings sown in early March should be hardened off and ready for planting out in May.

Use a garden line and a stick to mark out the bed in 9 in. by 9 in. squares, and set plants where the lines cross, so they are 9 in. apart each way. Water in after planting.

Water generously every week if the weather is at all dry. No earthing is necessary, but when the celery is 12–15 in. tall cut off basal side-shoots to encourage vigorous growth in the main shoots.

If plants are grown in an open bed, bank straw round the stems of the outer plants so that light is excluded and the stems are blanched.

Lift plants with a fork when they are needed, and pack the straw back round the exposed plants.

COVERING SELF-BLANCHING CELERY

If the plants are grown in an open bed, outer plants in the block need a covering of straw banked round the stems to shade and blanch them

What can go wrong with celery

Slugs These are the most troublesome pests. Put down slug baits, keep the bed well weeded, and do not leave organic matter on the surface.

Celery fly or leaf miner The grubs cause brown blisters on leaves from May onwards. Pinch off affected leaves and burn them, or crush the blisters with your fingers. To stimulate growth, feed plants with 1 heaped teaspoon of nitrate of soda to the square yard, and water it in immediately. Do not overfeed, or the roots will be scorched. If attacks persist, spray with malathion, dimethoate or trichlorphon.

Leaf spot This is a fungal disease which appears as brown spots on leaves and stems. Spray with Bordeaux mixture or mancozeb. Repeat spraying weekly if necessary.

Varieties of celery to grow

TRENCHING	*SELF-BLANCHING*
'Giant White'	**'Avonpearl'**
'Clandon White'	**'Golden Self-blanching'**
'New Dwarf White'	**'Lathom Blanching'**
'Superb Pink'	**'American Green'**
'Unrivalled Pink'	**'Tendercrisp'**
'Giant Red'	**'Greensleeves'**
'Standard Bearer Red'	**'Utah'**

Chicory for braising or winter salads

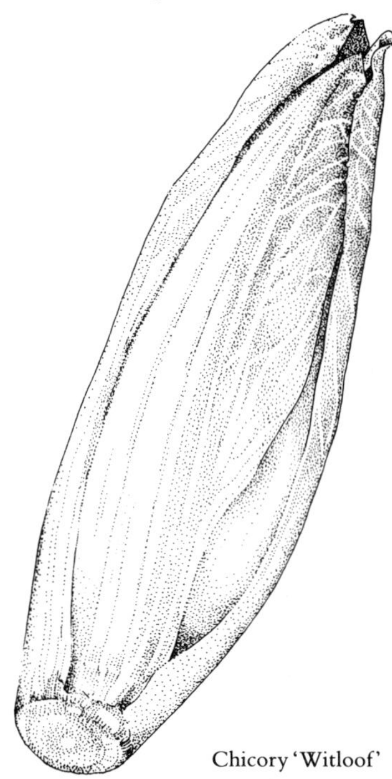

Chicory 'Witloof'

Chicory is grown for use in winter salads or for cooking (braised with butter and seasoning). Ready for use from November, it can be available until about February.

It is sown in early summer, and its roots are lifted in batches from November onwards and taken indoors for forcing and blanching in warmth and darkness. This produces tightly folded bunches of white leaves about 6 in. high, which are known as chicons.

During summer, the leaves of the variety 'Sugar Loaf' – which are similar in appearance to a cos lettuce – can be picked and cooked like spinach, or else finely chopped and used raw in salads.

Before sowing, dig the ground well, working in well-rotted manure or garden compost. Follow this with a top-dressing of superphosphate, using 2 oz. (2 tablespoons) to the square yard.

Sowing, tending and forcing chicory

Sow very thinly in April or May, in drills ½ in. deep and 15 in. apart. When the first true leaves (rough-edged) appear, thin the seedlings to 6 in. apart.

Hoe and weed between plants regularly. By November, the roots should be well formed, 12 in. or more in length, and like narrow-shouldered parsnips in appearance.

From November onwards, when the leaves die down, batches of chicory roots can be lifted with a garden fork.

Cut off the leaves 1–2 in. above the top of the root, taking care not to damage the growing point. If the roots cannot be forced immediately, store them temporarily in a shallow trench, covering them loosely with a layer of soil.

To prepare roots for forcing, use a sharp knife to shorten them to 8 in. long, so they can be fitted into a 9 in. pot.

Put some soil in the bottom of a 9 in. pot, and place four or five roots in it. Fill the pot to the rim with more soil, keeping the crowns about 1–2 in. apart and just above the pot rim. Thoroughly water the soil.

Fill another 9 in. pot with peat, and invert it over the pot containing the roots, so that all light is excluded. The pressure of the peat on the terminal bud will make it grow into a tight chicon.

Instead of pots, deep boxes can be used. The method of forcing is the same; cover the box of roots with about 9 in. of peat to apply pressure to the terminal buds, and invert another box over it.

If roots can be kept in a warm spot indoors, they will sprout faster. The temperature should not be below 7°C (45°F) or above 16°C (61°F).

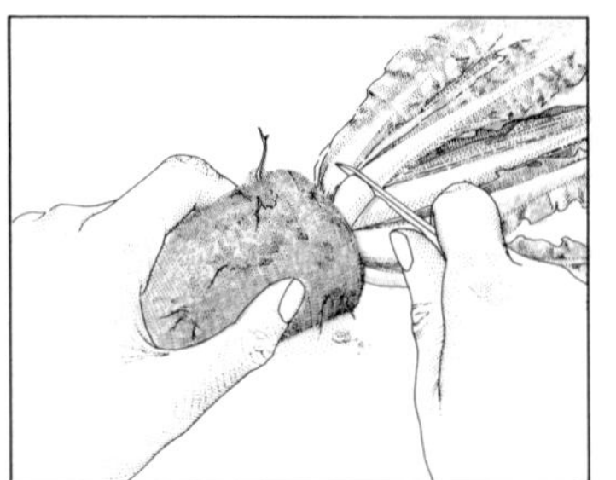

1 *From November, when the leaves die down, cut them off 1–2 in. above the root*

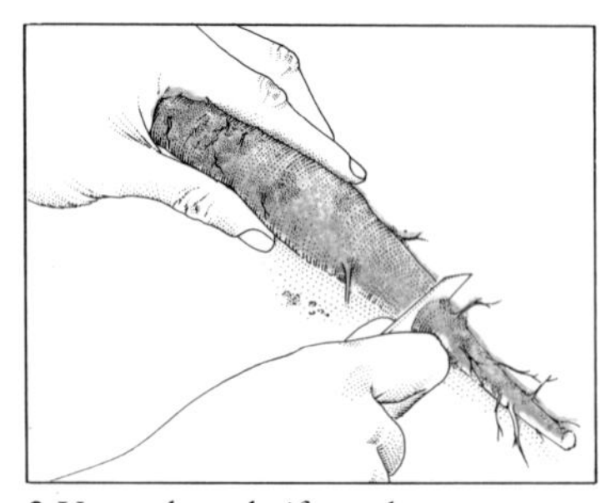

2 *Use a sharp knife to shorten roots to 8 in. so they will fit into a 9 in. pot*

3 *Put soil in the bottom of a 9 in. pot and place four or five chicory roots in it*

4 *Fill with soil and keep crowns 1–2 in. apart. Cover with a peat-filled pot*

Harvesting the blanched chicons

The blanched chicons are ready for use when they are about 6 in. tall, while growth is still quite tight and has not started to open out. They are usually ready about four weeks after being placed in pots.

Cut them off at soil level, just before they are wanted for use. After the shoots have been forced, put the roots on the compost heap.

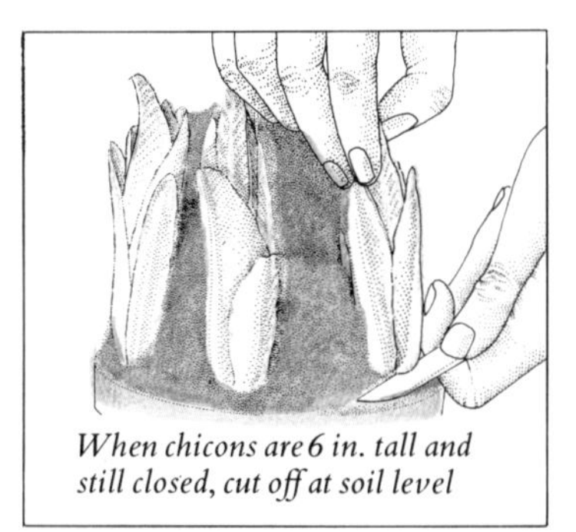

When chicons are 6 in. tall and still closed, cut off at soil level

What can go wrong with chicory

Pests and diseases Chicory seldom suffers from disease. Roots may be attacked by slugs and snails (p. 288), or by swift moth caterpillars (long, dirty-white caterpillars with brown heads), wireworms and cutworms. Bromophos can be worked into the soil as a safeguard, but do not use HCH as it may taint the chicons.

Varieties of chicory to grow

'Witloof'
Also known as 'Brussels Chicory'
'Sugar Loaf'
Leaves can be eaten in summer
'Red Verona'

Cucumbers to grow under glass and in the open

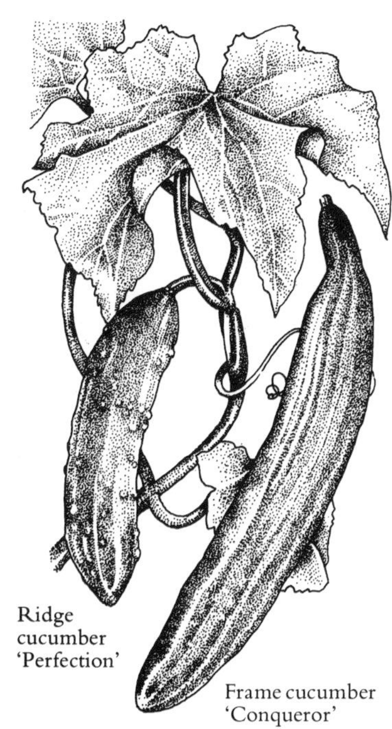

Ridge cucumber 'Perfection'

Frame cucumber 'Conqueror'

There are two types of cucumber: frame cucumbers, which need a good deal of warmth and are grown under glass (in a greenhouse or cold frame), and ridge cucumbers, which are hardier and can be grown outdoors in summer in a sunny, sheltered position.

Cucumbers grown without artificial heat are in season from about August to October. Those grown in a heated greenhouse are ready from about May.

Cucumbers are climbing plants. In greenhouses they need to be trained along wires; in cold frames or in the open they can be left to trail along the ground.

All cucumbers need rich soil. If growing them in a greenhouse border, make a bed of 3 parts good loam and 1 part well-rotted manure. If growing them in a cold frame or outdoors, dig the bed well and enrich it with plenty of well-rotted manure or garden compost.

Growing frame cucumbers in a greenhouse

A high temperature is needed for the seeds to germinate. They can be started in boxes or pots in an electrically heated propagator in the greenhouse, with the propagator thermostat set at 24°C (75°F).

If no propagator is available, stand seed containers above the source of greenhouse heat.

Make a first sowing in February and a second in April. Sow either singly in 3 in. peat pots filled with seed compost – pushing them in edgeways until covered by about ½ in. of compost – or else 1 in. apart in boxes of seed compost.

Cover the pots or boxes with glass, and place a folded sheet of newspaper on top. Then place them in the propagator or over the source of heat.

After germination, night temperatures should not fall much below 16°C (61°F) for about a month. For all-female F1 (first generation) hybrids, the night temperature must not be less than 21°C (70°F) – so growing these varieties is not usually feasible for the amateur.

Before planting out seedlings, fix horizontal wires for training laterals (side-shoots) along the wall and under the roof where the plants will grow. Place them about 12 in. away from the glass.

When seedlings have two rough leaves, transfer them to a bed made up on the greenhouse border or bench, or into 10 in. pots of John Innes No. 3 potting compost. Fix a vertical wire, string or cane beside each plant for it to grow up.

When the plants have grown up to a height of about 8 ft (or the limit of the space available) pinch out the growing tips of the leading shoots. This will encourage the growth of laterals, which should be tied to the horizontal wires with twine.

If no cucumbers have appeared on laterals by the time they are about 2 ft long, pinch out the growing tips. If laterals do produce fruit, pinch out their growing tips at a point 1–2 leaves beyond the first cucumber. If laterals put out side-shoots that bear fruits, pinch out side-shoots 1–2 leaves beyond the first fruit.

Cucumbers carry both male and female flowers (except for F1 hybrids which have only female flowers). Female flowers have an embryo cucumber behind them. Pick off the male flowers as soon as they develop, so that the female ones are not fertilised. If they are, the cucumbers will have seeds and be unpalatable.

Shade the plants from strong sunshine, and water copiously. Damp down the floor of the greenhouse with a hose at least twice a day to maintain humid conditions. If white roots appear on the surface of the beds, cover them with fresh potting compost.

There is no need to support the fruit as it develops. If the plants have grown well, the first cucumbers can be cut 12–14 weeks after sowing. Pick them when they are a reasonable size, but before they start to yellow. If picked too young they will taste bitter.

TRAINING GREENHOUSE CUCUMBERS

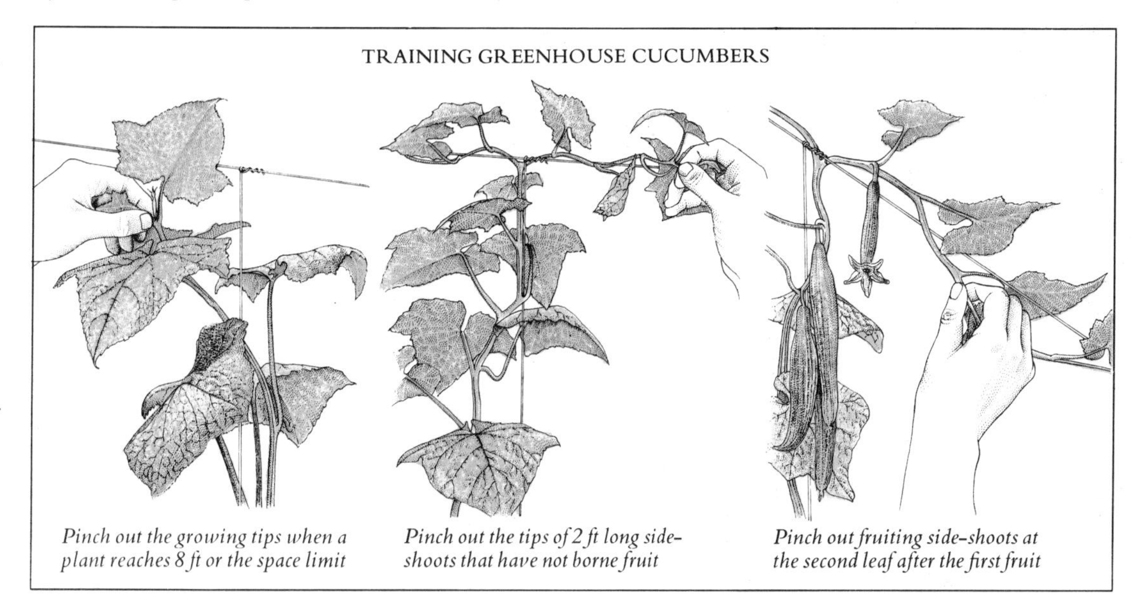

Pinch out the growing tips when a plant reaches 8 ft or the space limit

Pinch out the tips of 2 ft long side-shoots that have not borne fruit

Pinch out fruiting side-shoots at the second leaf after the first fruit

Growing frame cucumbers in a cold frame

Prepare the cold-frame bed by digging in well-rotted manure, then cover the surface with 4–5 in. of topsoil from the garden.

In late May, sow seeds in pots or boxes, in the same way as for greenhouse cultivation, but put them in the cold frame to germinate.

When the seedlings are growing well, plant out one under each frame light, setting each plant at the back of the frame. Tear off the rims of peat pots before planting. Make sure there is a slight mound round the stem of the plant; this will prevent water settling round the collar of the plant and rotting it. Scatter slug pellets round plants.

Put the frame light on and paint it with greenhouse shading or limewash. Open the light 2 in. on the sheltered side during the day, and leave it open very slightly at night. Support it with a rectangular block of wood. The length, breadth and width of the block should provide varying heights. Alternatively, you can use a stepped block of wood.

Water the plants frequently and during very hot weather syringe the inside of the frame at least twice a day. This helps to maintain the humid conditions needed.

When plants have made four or six rough leaves, pinch out the growing point to promote the growth of laterals (side-shoots). When the laterals have made four leaves each, pinch them out also.

Spread the laterals evenly over the floor of the frame. As with greenhouse cucumbers, remove the male flowers as they develop. Pinch out all fruiting shoots 1–2 leaves beyond the first fruit. When any growth reaches the front edge of the frame, pinch it out also.

If the crop is growing well, cutting can start in late July and early August. Harvest in the same way as for greenhouse plants.

FRAME TRAINING

Pinch out the main shoot at four leaves. Repeat for laterals

Pinch out fruiting laterals 1–2 leaves beyond the first cucumber

What can go wrong with cucumbers

Cucumber mosaic virus Plants are stunted and leaves and fruits are mottled and puckered. Remove and burn affected plants immediately.

Glasshouse whitefly This small, moth-like insect with white wings may suck the sap from plants grown under glass. It is found on the undersides of young leaves, or as flat yellow scales on older leaves. Spray infested plants with pyrethrum, malathion, dimethoate or formothion. Do not use HCH, as it will quickly kill plants. Introducing a parasite (p. 398) has been found particularly successful.

Foot rot This causes plants to rot at the base of the stem, which may be discoloured; roots are usually dead. It may be due to badly drained soil. It should not occur if crops are well cultivated and rotated.

Other pests Slugs, snails (p. 288). Glasshouse red spider mite (p. 381).

Growing ridge cucumbers outdoors

Start an early crop in a cold greenhouse or cold frame in late April. Sow the seeds ½ in. deep in 3 in. peat pots filled with seed compost.

Harden off seedlings (p. 288) during May, and plant them out in the first week in June. Using a trowel, set the young plants 2–2½ ft apart in rows 3 ft apart. Scatter slug pellets round each plant.

Make later sowings directly into the cropping bed – under cloches in mid-May (removing them after mid-June), or in the open in late May.

Sow the seeds in stations (p. 287), 2–2½ ft apart, in groups of three 6 in. apart and 1 in. deep. If you sow more than one row, set the rows 3 ft apart. Scatter slug pellets round each station. When the plants have made from two to four leaves, thin each station to the strongest plant only.

An alternative method of sowing, which saves space, is to put seeds 9 in. apart in a 1 in. deep drill and train plants up a wire trellis.

When the young plants have made four or five leaves, pinch out their growing tips. They will then put out three or four side-shoots.

Water plants freely during dry weather, and scatter slug pellets regularly to protect new shoots.

Do not pick off the male flowers (as with frame cucumbers), because the female blooms need fertilising. Help pollination by picking some fully developed male flowers and shaking the pollen on the female flowers. Pinch out at the seventh leaf any shoots that do not bear young cucumbers.

Cut cucumbers while they are young, to encourage more cropping. Heavy cropping is possible during August and September, but the autumn frosts will kill the plants.

TRAINING OUTDOORS

Pinch out the growing tip when the plant has four or five leaves

Pinch out beyond the seventh leaf shoots without cucumbers

Varieties of cucumbers to grow

FRAME VARIETIES
'Butcher's Disease Resister'
'Telegraph'
'Conqueror'

F1 HYBRIDS THAT PRODUCE ONLY FEMALE FLOWERS
'Femstar'
'Rocket'
'Femspot'

RIDGE VARIETIES
'Bedfordshire Prize'
'Long Green'
'Perfection'
'Nadir'

F1 HYBRIDS THAT MATURE EARLIER AND ARE HARDIER
'Baton Vert'
'Burpee Hybrid'
'Burpless Tasty Green'

Leeks – the hardiest of winter vegetables

Leeks are one of the easiest of the onion family to grow. They are hardy and will withstand even the severest winters.

Sow them from late January to early April to produce crops from late August to the following May. They are sown under glass or in a seed bed outdoors and later transplanted to a permanent bed.

There is no need to aim for giant, prize-winning specimens, as the smaller ones are more economic and better flavoured for soups and stews.

Although they repay the effort of thoroughly digging the soil, leeks are not as exacting in their requirements as onions. Either plant them on the land manured over winter for peas, beans and onions, or dig in some well-rotted manure or garden compost when turning the ground over after the previous crop is cleared.

Leek 'Early Market'

Sowing early and maincrop leeks

Sow at the beginning of the year to produce large plants for transplanting in April and harvesting in late August. Large plants are easier to handle and will make longer stems.

Towards the end of January, sow leeks under glass. Artificial heat is not essential unless you want to grow particularly large-stemmed leeks for exhibition.

Fill a seed tray with seed compost, into which has been mixed a little ground chalk or limestone.

Space the seeds 1 in. apart. To do this, place them in a sheet of paper folded about halfway along its length to make a V-shape and roll the seeds on to the seed bed with the point of a pencil.

Sift a little compost over the seeds, using a fine-meshed sieve.

Gently firm the compost – use the bottom of a pot or a flat piece of wood. Finally, cover the seed box with glass and a sheet of newspaper.

If large stems are required, germinate at 13–16°C (55–61°F); but leek seeds will germinate easily in a cold greenhouse or cold frame.

Start to harden off (p. 288) the plants about mid-March, and plant them outdoors during the first two weeks of April.

For the main crop, prepare a seed bed outdoors (p. 287) and sow in late March or early April for harvesting from September to April.

Rake the bed thoroughly and work in 2 oz. (2 tablespoons) of superphosphate to the square yard immediately before sowing.

Take out drills $\frac{1}{2}$ in. deep and 6 in. apart. Sow the seeds thinly, and when the seedlings are at an early stage of development, thin them to at least $1\frac{1}{2}$ in. apart. Plant out in June or July.

Transplanting seedlings into final beds

Plant out the seedlings when they are about 6–8 in. high. This will be about early April for seedlings sown under glass, and June or July for those from outdoor seed beds. The earlier they can be transplanted the better, as they do best with a long season of growth.

If the soil is dry, soak the seed bed before lifting the seedlings. Lift them carefully with a hand fork.

Trim off the top quarter of the leaves with scissors or a knife.

Make holes with a dibber, 6 in. deep and 9 in. apart, with 15 in. between the rows.

Drop the seedlings into the holes so that the tips of the leaves are just showing. Planting them deeply in this way helps to blanch the stems. Do not try to cover the roots with soil, or firm them in or fill the holes with soil.

Just pour water from the watering can into each hole. This will wash some soil round the roots and be enough to tighten the plants. The holes will fill up gradually after rain, and when the bed is hoed.

Plant leeks for exhibition 12 in. apart in trenches prepared in the same way as for celery (p. 300).

WATERING IN SEEDLINGS

Do not fill the hole with soil. Just pour in water directly

Cultivating and harvesting the leek crop

Hoe regularly to aerate the soil and keep down weeds. Water in dry weather to keep the bed moist.

No feeding is necessary, except for exhibition plants. Feed these plentifully with weak liquid manure, and occasionally hoe in small dressings of nitrate of soda.

When the holes in which the leeks are planted have filled up, draw some soil up to the stems with a hoe. This will help to make a good length of blanched stem.

Earth up in this way gradually over a period of a few weeks. If too much is done too quickly, the plants may rot.

For exhibition leeks planted in trenches, draw soil up round the stems in the trenches and gradually form a steep ridge. In this way long, thick stems about 8 in. round and with about 12–20 in. blanched can be grown.

Storing Leeks are among the hardiest of vegetables, and may be left in the ground during autumn and winter and lifted as required.

If, by April, there are any plants remaining, lift them, complete with roots. Loosen the soil with a fork.

Dig a shallow trench in a shaded spot – such as the north side of a wall, hedge or fence – and lay the plants with their roots in the trench.

Return the soil to the trench, covering all but the green parts of the leaves.

Using this method, a late supply of leeks can be preserved for a few more weeks. This is especially useful for a household at this time of the year, when fresh vegetables are often scarce and expensive.

BLANCHING STEMS

For a good length of blanched stem, draw up earth with a hoe

What can go wrong with leeks

Onion fly Maggots may feed on the roots and lower stem, causing the plant to wilt. Apply calomel dust to the soil before sowing or shortly afterwards. Water a spray-strength solution of trichlorphon into the roots of established plants on two or three occasions during their growth.

Diseases Leeks are normally free from diseases, although they are subject to those common to onions (p. 311). They may suffer from rust; powdery masses of orange spores appear on the leaves. Remove and burn the affected leaves.

Varieties of leeks to grow

EARLY
'The Lyon'
Also known as 'Prizetaker'. Popular for autumn exhibitions
'Marble Pillar'
'Early Market'
'Malabar'
MID-SEASON
'Musselburgh'
One of the hardiest varieties
'Walton Mammoth'
LATE
'Giant Winter'
Also known as 'Royal Favourite'
'Empire'
'Winter Crop'

Lettuces for successional cropping

Cos lettuce 'White Heart'

Cabbage lettuce 'Fortune'

Lettuces can be grown all the year round, but producing crops for winter and early spring is not easy.

From late March until late July, sowings can be made in the open for harvesting from about June until mid-October. Seeds are sown directly into the place where the lettuce crop is to grow.

Sowings for harvesting in November and December can also be made in the open in early August, but in early September the lettuce seedlings are transplanted to a cold frame to crop.

Hardy varieties sown outdoors in late August or early September can be grown in the open throughout the winter in milder areas, for cutting at about the end of April.

In mid-October, varieties for maturing under glass (known as forcing varieties) can be sown in the open or under cloches. They are transplanted under glass in early December, either to a cold frame or under more cloches. They are ready for cutting in April.

Sowings under glass can be made during January and February for cutting in spring and early summer.

All lettuces should be grown quickly, with as little check to growth as possible. They do best on rather rich, well-watered, light soil that has been manured during autumn or winter. Dig the ground thoroughly and leave it rough until planting time. Then break up lumps and rake the soil to a fine tilth.

Before sowing rake in 2–3 oz. of general fertiliser per square yard.

Lettuces can also be grown as a catch crop or a succession crop (p. 286), such as in the spinach plot once the spinach has finished.

A sunny position is best for early and late lettuces, but midsummer crops will need less watering if grown in a little shade

Sowing lettuces for crops all year round

Sow lettuces in small batches so they are available in succession. They are best used as soon as they are ready. For March to July sowings, some firms offer packets of mixed varieties that take different times to mature, so that lettuces can be cut for about a month from one sowing.

There are three main types: cabbage, cos and loose-leaf. Cabbage types are round and can be crisp or soft (butterhead). Cos types grow upright, have oblong leaves and are usually crisp; they generally take longer to mature and need more watering than cabbage lettuces. There are intermediate varieties between cos and cabbage types. Loose-leaf lettuces have no hearts.

Sowing the main crop outdoors Make the first outdoor sowing in late March, and continue at fortnightly intervals until the end of July. This will provide a succession of lettuces from about June to mid-October.

Sow seeds in their permanent places, half a row at a time, in drills ½ in. deep and 12 in. apart.

Thin the seedlings when the first pair of true leaves is well established. Remove the weakest seedlings and thin in stages – first to 3 in. apart, then to 6 in., and finally to 12 in. apart. Then re-firm the soil.

Thinnings can be transplanted to fill gaps, or moved to any other available space in the garden. But thinnings transplanted later than April are likely to bolt (flower prematurely) in dry weather, unless kept well watered.

An autumn or early winter crop Sow a forcing variety (such as 'May King') in a prepared seed bed (p. 287) in the open, not later than the first week in August.

Make drills ½ in. deep and 6 in. apart and sow seeds thinly. When seedlings are established (in early September), move to a cold frame.

Mark out the frame bed in 8½ in. squares. Plant each seedling where two lines cross. This prevents overcrowding, which can lead to disease.

Use a dibber to make holes large enough to take the roots. Put the seedlings in the holes and firm the soil round them. Do not plant too deeply, as this can also lead to disease. Wait until mid-September before putting on the frame light.

Alternatively, leave the seedlings in the seed bed and thin them to 9–12 in. apart. Cover them with cloches in mid-September, with glass over the ends of the row. They should be ready in November or December.

A forcing variety can be sown in a greenhouse border in late August. Sow thinly in drills ½ in. deep and 12 in. apart. Keep plants watered and thin in stages until they are 12 in. apart. Maintain a minimum temperature of 7–10°C (45–50°F). They should be ready in December.

An early spring crop under glass Sow a forcing variety in mid-October for harvesting in April. Sow in the open or under cloches.

For open beds, sow thinly in drills ½ in. deep and 6 in. apart. For cloches, sow thinly in drills ½ in. deep and 4 in. apart; put a cloche or cloches over rows (two or three rows to a cloche); close the ends with glass.

Transplant the seedlings from early December onwards, when they are well established. Put cloche-sown seedlings under more vacant cloches, and outdoor-sown seedlings into a cold frame.

Put seedlings under cloches 12 in. apart in rows 10–12 in. apart. Put seedlings in the cold frame 8½ in. apart each way, in the same way as for an autumn or winter crop. If you can get cheap straw, pack it round the frame to help keep out the cold.

A spring crop grown in the open In milder areas it is worth taking a chance and growing some of the hardier varieties, such as 'Arctic King' or 'Winter Density', in the open without the protection of cloches or frames. These varieties are better able to withstand autumn frosts, and will survive the winter if the weather is not too harsh.

Sow seeds in pinches 3 in. apart in late August or early September, in drills ½ in. deep and 12 in. apart.

In October thin seedlings to one every 3 in. Use the thinnings to make another row, if space allows. In early spring thin the plants by stages, so that they are finally 9–12 in. apart. They will be ready for cutting in late April or May.

An early summer crop under glass Sow forcing varieties in succession either under cloches or in a cold frame from mid-January to the end of February. These sowings will be ready for salads in late April.

Under cloches, sow and transplant in the same way as for the early spring crop. In a cold frame, sow thinly in drills ½ in. deep and 6 in. apart. When seedlings are well developed, transplant them 8½ in. apart back into the cold frame.

Gradually harden off seedlings (p. 288). If using cloches, harden off plants by removing every other cloche. Remove the frame light or cloches completely in mid-April. Keep the bed moist if there is no rain.

Starting a summer crop under glass In January or early February, sow cabbage lettuces (not forcing varieties) in a cold greenhouse or cold frame to provide a crop for cutting about mid-May.

Sow seeds broadcast (scattered over the surface) in a box of seed compost. Sift fine compost over them so they are just covered.

Cover the seed box with glass to prevent moisture loss. Place a folded sheet of newspaper over the glass to keep out light and to help insulate the seeds against cold.

Check regularly to see if seeds have germinated (it takes six to ten days). As soon as germination occurs remove the paper, or the seedlings will become spindly and weak.

Prick out (p. 288) seedlings when they are three or four weeks old and replant in a deeper box of John Innes No. 1 compost. Water them in.

Start hardening off (p. 288) seedlings about the third week in March, ready for planting out in April.

Cultivating and harvesting the lettuce crop

Hoe regularly between the rows to aerate the soil and keep down weeds. Water outdoor crops in dry weather, do not let the soil get thoroughly dry. Once you start watering, do it regularly as long as the weather is dry, otherwise the lettuces will bolt (flower prematurely) before they have time to form hearts.

Birds will damage or peck out seedlings. Protect plants with black cotton stretched between sticks at the ends of rows. Or cover rows with wire-netting pea guards (p. 313).

Once the lettuces reach the top of the pea guards, they are safe from pecking and the guards can then be moved to protect later sowings.

Protect young seedlings from slugs, whether in the open or under glass, by scattering slug pellets along rows after sowing or transplanting.

Lettuces grown in frames or cloches during winter should be watered as little as possible. If watering is needed, do it early in the day and make sure there is sufficient ventilation. Ventilate cloches or frames as often as possible in suitable weather. If cloches have no ventilators, remove every other cloche, replacing them at night.

Harvest full-hearted lettuces early in the morning when the dew is still on them. Use a sharp knife to cut them away from the lower stem and leaves. Lift and compost the remains.

What can go wrong with lettuces

Bolting Lettuces easily bolt (flower prematurely), shooting up long, thick stems that are bitter and useless for eating. Prevent bolting by avoiding any check to growth, such as late transplanting, overcrowding, or shortage of water. If plants bolt, do not leave them in the bed; put them on the compost heap.
Downy mildew This should not occur if plants are properly watered and ventilated, and crops rotated. It is a greyish or whitish furry coating on the under surfaces of leaves, and yellow blotches on upper surfaces. Spray affected plants with zineb.
Grey mould This is a fungus that causes plants to rot at ground level, where they are covered with a grey, velvety mould. Plants wilt, and the top growth is easily separated from the roots. To prevent, dust quintozene into the soil before sowing or transplanting. Spray affected plants outdoors with benomyl, carbendazim, zineb, thiram, dichlofluanid or thiophanate-methyl. Fumigate those under glass with tecnazene smokes.
Root aphids Colonies of white, wax-covered aphids sometimes infest the roots. This may occur at any time under glass, or in late summer and autumn outdoors. Water the roots of affected plants with a spray-strength solution of malathion or diazinon. Do not leave old stumps or roots in the ground.
Other troubles Aphids (greenfly) may attack. Seedlings may be eaten by slugs or birds, or suffer from damping off (p. 288).

Varieties of lettuces to grow

FOR GROWING IN THE OPEN IN SUMMER
CABBAGE (BUTTERHEAD)
'Soft Cabbage'
'Suzan'
'Avondefiance'
'Hilde'
'Fortune'
'Unrivalled'
'All the Year Round'
'Cobham Green'
'Tom Thumb'
The smallest lettuce
'Continuity'
CABBAGE (CRISPHEAD)
'Webb's Wonderful'
'Windermere'
'Avon Crisp'
'Great Lakes'
COS
'Lobjoit's Green Cos'
'Little Gem'
Small, compact, and very early
'White Heart'
INTERMEDIATE
'Winter Density'
'Buttercrunch'
'Sugar Cos'

FOR GROWING IN THE OPEN IN WINTER
CABBAGE
'Valdor'
'Arctic King'
'Imperial Winter'
'Winter Crop'
COS
'Hardy Winter White'
INTERMEDIATE
'Winter Density'

FOR GROWING UNDER GLASS IN WINTER (FORCING)
CABBAGE
'Kloek'
'Knap'
'Kwiek'
'May King'
'Seaqueen'
'Emerald'
'Delta'
'Unrivalled'
A good variety for cloche-growing

FOR STARTING UNDER GLASS IN JANUARY
'Premier'
'Blondine'

Marrows and courgettes

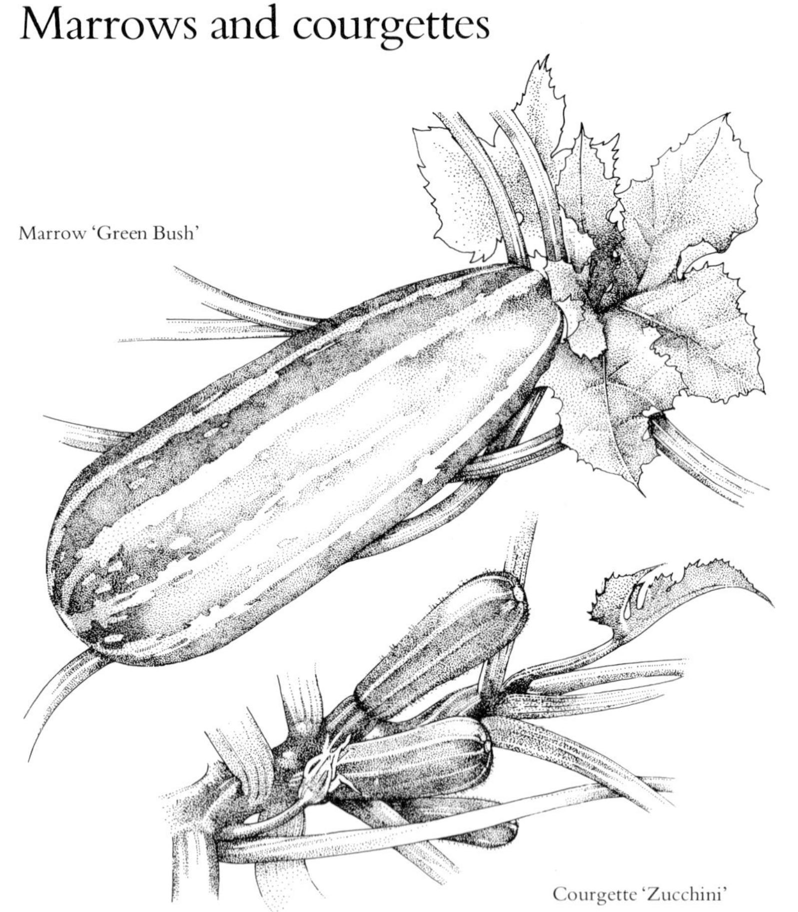

Marrow 'Green Bush'

Courgette 'Zucchini'

Marrows need a lot of space, which in a small garden may be more sensibly employed growing a more productive crop. However, if you have a spare patch in a sunny corner of the garden, use it to put in two or three marrow plants.

There are two types, bush and trailing. Bush marrows, which are grown 2 ft apart, take less space than trailing marrows, which spread out along the ground and are grown about 3–4 ft apart.

The courgette is also a kind of small marrow. Plants are similar in size to other marrows, and are planted 2 ft apart, but the fruit is cut when it is only about 4 in. long.

Marrows are in season from about July to October. They are half-hardy and will not survive frost. Early sowings in April or early May must be made under glass, and plants put out in late May or early June. Later May sowings can be made direct in the permanent bed.

Plants need rich soil and plenty of moisture. Take out a spit depth of soil where each plant is to be grown, and enrich the soil by working two or three buckets of well-rotted manure or garden compost into the second spit.

Replace the top spit, and leave a ridge about 2 in. high ringing each planting site. This will help to concentrate moisture when watering the plants.

Sowing seeds under glass and outdoors

During April or early May, sow seeds singly 1 in. deep in 2½ in. pots filled with seed compost. Peat pots are best, as the seedlings can be planted without removing the pots, so that roots are not disturbed.

Cover the pots with glass and a folded sheet of newspaper, and place them in a cold greenhouse or cold frame. Remove the paper as soon as the seeds have germinated.

Alternatively, seeds can germinate in pots or trays on a shady window-sill or close to the southern wall of a centrally heated house.

If frost threatens at night, cover seedlings with a cardboard box or put sacking over the frame light.

Harden off the seedlings (p. 288) gradually during May, and plant them out at the end of the month.

If the seedlings have been grown in clay or plastic pots, knock them gently out of the pots.

Using a trowel, make holes in the prepared bed for the peat pots, or the soil ball round the roots of each seedling.

Make sure the rims of peat pots are sunk below the soil level, to prevent them acting like wicks and sucking moisture from the ground on windy days. The tops of soil balls should be ½ in. below soil level.

Plant bush marrow and courgette seedlings 2 ft apart. Plant trailing marrows 3–4 ft apart.

Sow seed outdoors about mid-May under cloches, and remove the cloches at the beginning of June. Alternatively, sow seed in the open at the end of May.

Sow bush and courgette marrow seeds in stations 2 ft apart, with three seeds 1 in. deep and 6 in. apart at each station. Thin each station to one strong plant.

Sow trailing marrows also in stations. If possible allow 4 ft between stations, certainly not less than 3 ft. Put seeds in groups of four or five, 1 in. deep and 6 in. apart at each station. When the seedlings are well established, thin them to the strongest plant.

Harvesting marrows and courgettes

Marrows and courgettes should be cut continuously from the plant while they are young. This encourages more fruit to form.

Start cutting courgettes in July, as soon as the withered flowers fall. They should be about 4 in. long. Cut them off with a sharp knife.

Cut bush and trailing marrows from the plant for summer use when they are 6–8 in. long. The skins should yield to gentle pressure.

Towards the end of the season, leave a few marrows to grow to full size and ripen thoroughly for storage. As the larger fruits develop, place a slate, tile or brick beneath each one to keep it off the ground. This will prevent injury to its skin and safeguard it from slugs.

In September, before the first frosts arrive, cut the mature marrows and hang them in netting for storage. If the marrows are firm and undamaged they can be kept in this way for many weeks.

In ideal storage conditions, there should be free circulation of air, no possibility of frost, and a temperature of about 16°C (61°F). A kitchen larder may be the best spot.

HARVESTING MARROWS

Start cutting courgettes in July, when about 4 in. long

Cut mature marrows in September, and store them in nets

Tending marrow plants

After sowing seeds or planting seedlings outdoors, scatter slug pellets round the bed. Renew the bait regularly while the plants are young.

When trailing marrows have produced four or five leaves, pinch out their growing tips. Each plant will then produce three or four side-shoots. A plant with a number of side-shoots is generally more convenient in a small garden than a plant with one long, trailing shoot, and is likely to give a heavier crop.

Marrows need plenty of moisture. In dry weather, water them frequently. Soak the surrounding soil with a watering can. Apply liquid fertiliser once a fortnight. Do not use it more frequently, otherwise there will be too much leafy growth.

If a plant does develop too much leafy growth, clip back some of the leaves to allow more air to circulate round the flowers and young fruits.

Plants bear flowers continuously throughout the season, and have both male and female flowers. To produce a crop, the female flowers (which have an embryo marrow behind the bloom) must be fertilised by a male flower (which has no swelling behind it).

In cold, dull or wet weather, when there are few insects about to carry pollen, help fertilisation by pollinating flowers by hand.

Pick off a ripe male flower and strip off the petals, then press the pollen-bearing centre of the male flower into the middle of a fully open female flower. Each male flower can be used to pollinate two or three female flowers.

What can go wrong with marrows

Virus disease Marrows are very susceptible to virus disease, which causes stunted plants and blotched and distorted leaves and fruit. No chemical cure is known. Remove and burn affected plants at once.

Foot rot This is rotting at the base of the stem, and the roots are usually found to be dead. The disease may result from badly drained soil. It should not occur if crops are well cultivated and not grown continually in the same spot.

Other troubles Slugs and snails may eat seedlings and fruit (p. 288).

Varieties of marrows to grow

BUSH MARROWS
'Prokor'
'Tender and True'
'Green Bush'
'White Bush'
'Epicurean'
'Golden Zucchini'
'Custard White'
'Custard Yellow'

TRAILING MARROWS
'Long Green Trailing'
'Long White Trailing'
'Long Green Striped'
'Table Dainty'

COURGETTES
'Courgette'
'Green Bush'
'Zucchini'

Onions and shallots

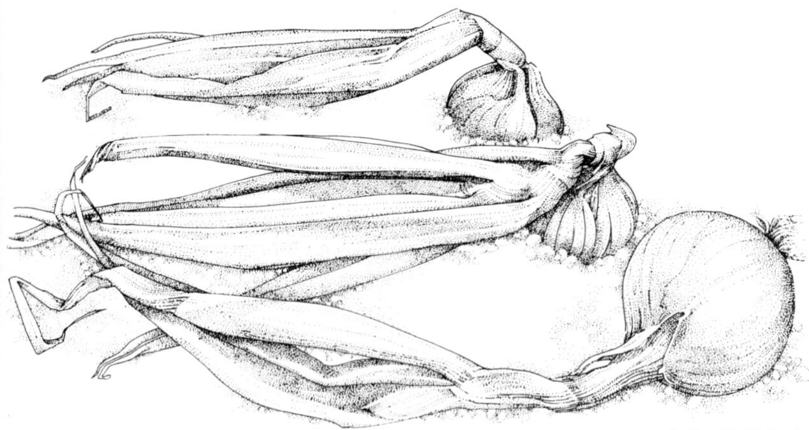

Onion 'Solidity'

Onions are in season all year round. The main crop is sown in mid-August to stand over winter, then transplanted to the permanent bed in spring for pulling from June or July.

Another crop, for lifting in late September and storing for use through to about June, can be grown from seed sown in January or February under glass, or in March in the open. Alternatively, it can be grown from onion sets – immature bulbs – planted out in April.

For spring onions (about March), sow hardy varieties of salad onions in September, or use some of the August-sown main crop pulled young. Salad onions can also be sown in succession from late February to September for pulling from June to mid-November.

The thinnings of most varieties can be used for salads, but salad varieties are more suitable. Some varieties are also good for pickling.

Shallots are grown in the same way as onions, but are easier to grow. They are usually grown from sets put out in April, as seed-grown shallots tend to bolt (flower prematurely). They are harvested in late July or August, and can be stored.

Onions of a suitable size and quality for normal kitchen use can be grown in any average soil. But they will grow better and larger in a plot deeply dug and well-manured the previous autumn.

Before sowing or planting, rake in 3 oz. (3 tablespoons) of superphosphate and 1 oz. (1 tablespoon) of sulphate of potash per square yard.

Sowing a crop at the start of the year

Onions for autumn harvesting can be sown in January or February. Sow in trays or pots of seed compost in a cold greenhouse, a cold frame, or under cloches with closed ends.

Place seeds on a sheet of folded paper, then use a pencil point to space them 1 in. apart. Sift a little compost over them.

Firm the compost with the bottom of a pot or a flat piece of wood. Then cover the seed box with glass and a folded sheet of newspaper.

The temperature for germination should be 13–16°C (55–61°F). As soon as germination occurs, remove the newspaper. Take away the glass just before the seedlings reach it.

Start to harden off the seedlings (p. 288), about mid-March. Prick them out (p. 288) and plant them during the first two weeks of April. Use a trowel to set them 6 in. apart in rows 12 in. apart. About ½ in. of white stem should be covered. Water them in if the soil is dry.

Sow outdoors into the permanent bed without glass protection in early March if the soil is workable. Sow in drills ½ in. deep and 12 in. apart.

When seedlings are 2 in. high, thin them to 1 in. apart. When they are 4–6 in. high, thin again to 4 in. apart and use the thinnings for salads. Lift for storing in late September.

Growing a crop from onion sets

Onion sets can be planted in April as an alternative to sowing seed. They are easier to handle and no thinning or transplanting is needed.

Sets are particularly popular with gardeners in the North, and with those whose soil tends to lie very wet in winter, as they generally give better results than growing from seed. But sets are likely to bolt (flower prematurely), if they are kept short of water while they are developing. Some strains are more resistant to bolting than others.

The sets are sold by the pound, which may contain from 120 to 160, according to the variety. If you get your sets before you are ready to plant, do not leave them in their bag. Spread them out in full light in a cool, dry place, to prevent them from sprouting prematurely.

Choose a sunny site for planting and prepare the soil well, breaking it down finely. Make sure the soil is fairly moist before planting.

Make drills 12 in. apart, just deep enough to cover the sets so that their tips just show above the surface. Space them 6 in. apart.

Fill in the drills, making sure the sets are fairly firm. Cover the rows with pea-guards (p. 313), as birds are attracted by the green tips, and will pull the sets from the ground if they are not protected. Tend plants in the same way as those raised from seed.

Sowing the main crop in August

In mid-August, sow seeds in a seed bed. The soil should be well-drained and worked to a fine tilth. If it tends to become waterlogged during winter, draw up a little soil into ridges and make the drills on top of them. Sow seeds fairly thickly in drills ½ in. deep and 9 in. apart.

Do not thin seedlings. In the following spring – in March if the soil can be worked easily – transplant to the permanent bed.

Put them in fairly deep, with about ½ in. of white stem covered, 6 in. apart in rows 12 in. apart. If you grow a large-bulbed variety, allow 12 in. between plants. Onions can be pulled from June, and stored from late July or August.

Sowing spring or salad onions

Sow a hardy variety of salad onion in September, in drills ½ in. deep and 9 in. apart. No thinning is needed. The crop should be ready for pulling about March.

In late February, sow a crop in a cold frame or beneath cloches for pulling in June. Make drills ½ in. deep and 6 in. apart. Leave plants unthinned. Remove the frame light or cloches by about mid-April, and keep the bed moist if there is no rain.

Sowings can be made in the open at intervals from March to September as required. Salad onions can be sown as a catch crop – between rows of peas, for example, or in the cabbage plot before the winter cabbage is planted out in July.

Tending and harvesting for storage

Hoe and hand weed between rows regularly. Keep plants watered, especially in dry periods.

When the outer leaves begin to turn yellow, bend over the tops. This encourages early ripening and can give a large increase in weight.

A fortnight later, loosen the bulbs and break their roots by pushing a fork underneath them and lifting slightly. This also assists ripening. In another fortnight, lift the bulbs with a fork and spread them to dry.

After a few days of drying, cut off the tops, remove loose skin, taking care not to bruise the bulbs, and store in a cool, dry place. Lay them on slatted shelves, or hang them up – in net bags or in plaited strings.

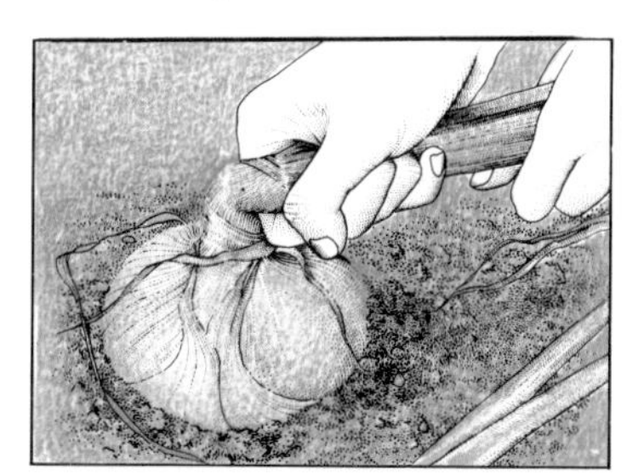

1 *When the outer leaves begin to turn yellow, bend over the tops*

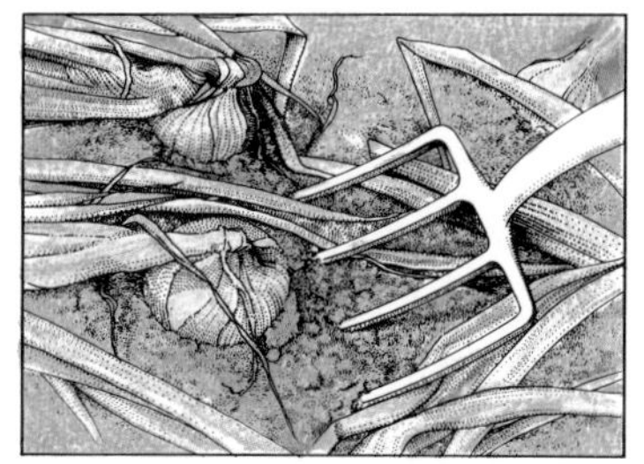

2 *A fortnight later, loosen bulbs by lifting them slightly with a fork*

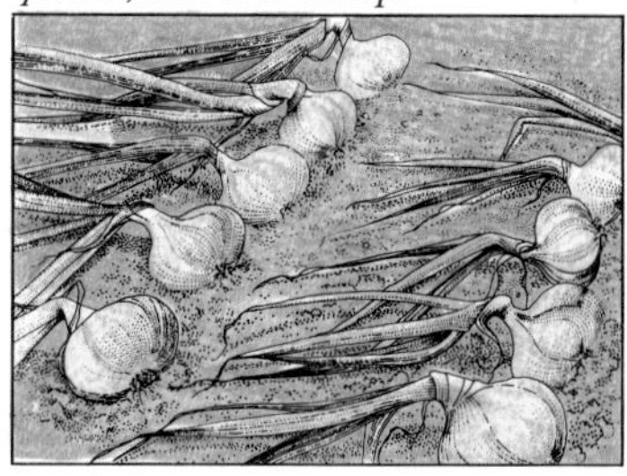

3 *Lift the onions with a fork a fortnight later and spread them out to dry*

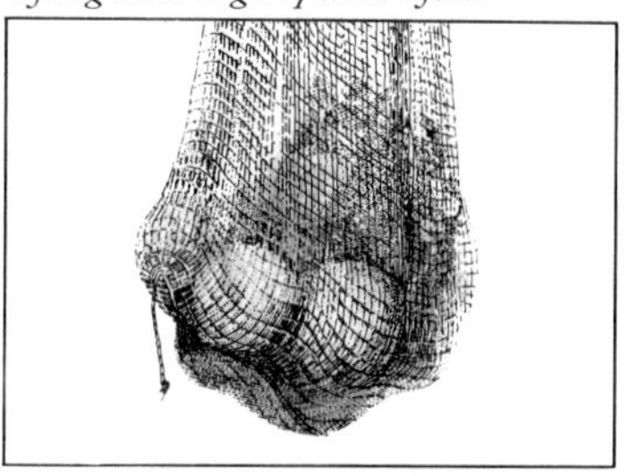

4 *Store in net bags hung from a shed or garage roof, or in plaited strings*

How to plait a string of onions

The traditional string of onions has a central core of thin rope or straw about 2 ft long. If you use straw, tie it together with string every 3 in. along its length.

Bind the onions to the rope or straw with a continuous length of string. Start at the bottom of the truss and work upwards. Bind each onion round its neck so that its roots face outwards.

PLAITING ONIONS

Bind the onions with string to a rope core. Start from the bottom

Varieties of onions and shallots to grow

FOR SOWING IN JANUARY
'Ailsa Craig'
Very large. Does not store well
'A 1'
Large and flat. Stores well

FOR SOWING IN SPRING
'Bedfordshire Champion'
'Wijbo'
Heavy cropper. Keeps very well
'Dura'
Pale skin. Remarkably good keeper
'James Long Keeping'
'Giant Zittau'
'Blood Red'
'Ailsa Craig'

FOR SOWING IN AUGUST
'Reliance'
'Solidity'
'Autumn Queen'
'Express Yellow'

FOR SALADS
'White Lisbon'
'Barla'
'White Lisbon Winter Hardy'
For August sowing

FOR PICKLING
'Paris Silverskin'
'Barla'
'White Lisbon Winter Hardy'

ONION SETS
'Stuttgart Giant'
'Sturon'
'Rijnsburger'

SHALLOTS
'Yellow Dutch'
'Giant Red'
'Longkeeping Yellow'
'Hâtive de Niort'

What can go wrong with onions and shallots

Onion fly The grubs of this fly eat into the bulbs, causing them to become soft, and to rot. The grubs are more active in dry soil. Lift and burn affected plants, making sure no grubs are left in the soil.

To prevent, apply calomel dust to the soil before or shortly after sowing, and water the roots of established plants with a spray-strength solution of trichlorphon on two or three occasions during growth. HCH dust is an alternative, but it can affect growth and taint bulbs.

Onion eelworm These very tiny worms are hatched in the bulb tissues, causing leaves to become swollen and bloated. Remove the affected plants and burn them or bury them deeply. Grow future crops from seeds rather than sets, if possible. To avoid the risk of attack, keep to a three-year crop rotation.

White rot This white, fluffy fungus covers rotting roots and the base of the bulb, causing leaves to turn yellow. Spring onions are usually affected. Burn diseased plants. Prevent attack by rotating crops and dusting seed drills with 4 per cent calomel dust. Once the disease appears, the soil remains contaminated for at least eight years.

Downy mildew In wet seasons particularly, this may cause greyish or purplish streaks or spots on leaves. At the first signs of mildew, spray with zineb, or dust plants when moist with Bordeaux powder. Raise seedlings on a fresh site every year.

Neck rot This attacks stored onions, a grey, velvety mould appearing near the neck. Store only well-ripened onions in good condition; those with thin necks are less likely to attack than those with thick, soft necks. Burn any diseased onions.

Grey mould Maincrop onions sown in mid-August may suffer from greyish, velvety mould on rotting leaves. Spray with benomyl, carbendazim, dichlofluanid, thiophanate-methyl, zineb or thiram.

Parsnips, the hardy root crop of winter

Parsnip 'White Gem'

Parsnips are an extremely hardy root crop, and can be left to stand over winter in places too cold for turnips and carrots. But they are slow growers and need a good start if they are to produce large roots.

For this reason, the earlier the seeds can be sown, the better. They are usually sown in late February or early March, ready for use from late October.

If the ground is wet and sticky, however, it pays to wait until April or even early May. For the best results parsnips need a seed bed that is reasonably dry and crumbly.

There are three types of parsnips – long, intermediate and short-rooted. Short-rooted varieties are similar to turnips in shape, and are useful for growing on shallow soils.

Grow parsnips on ground that was well manured for a previous crop. Freshly manured ground is likely to cause roots to fork. Avoid stony ground; it may deflect roots.

Dig deeply, and leave the plot rough until sowing time, then break it down to a fine tilth. If you want to grow parsnips for exhibition, you will need to double dig to about 2 ft (p. 405). But large exhibition roots are often coarse in texture, with a poor flavour.

Before sowing, rake in a mixture of 3oz. (3 tablespoons) of superphosphate, 1oz. (1 tablespoon) of sulphate of ammonia, and 1oz. (1 tablespoon) of sulphate of potash to the square yard.

Make drills 1 in. deep and 12 in. apart, and sow seeds in pinches of three or four. Keep your hand close to the drill when sowing, as seeds are large but winged and light, and blow away easily.

Rake the soil lightly over the drill to cover the seeds. They generally germinate in about three weeks, but the time taken varies.

When seedlings are large enough to handle, thin them to 6 in. apart. Do not try to replant thinnings as they will not grow good roots.

How to sow successfully in stony soil

In gardens where the soil is stony, and unfavourable for long roots, prepare individual stations for each plant. This method can also be used for growing exhibition roots.

Make holes with a crowbar 2–3 ft deep as soil conditions permit, spacing the holes 12 in. apart. Fill the holes almost to the top with moist, sifted garden soil, and make it reasonably firm with the crowbar.

Sow three or four seeds at each station, and cover them with $\frac{1}{2}$ in. of sifted soil. Sowing too deeply is a frequent cause of failure. Thin to one strong seedling at each station.

Make full use of the parsnip row by sowing a pinch of lettuce seed (a small variety) between each crowbar hole. Cover with a little sifted soil.

Thin the lettuces to one between two parsnips. They will be ready before the parsnips need all the space.

Cultivating and harvesting the roots

Hoe between the plants regularly. Water if the weather is very dry – do not let the soil dry out completely.

Parsnips can be left in the ground after the top growth dies down during winter. Lift them as needed.

About November, however, lift a few roots as a standby supply for use if the ground becomes frozen.

Cut off the green tops and lay the roots on a bed of dry sand or soil in a box. Cover each layer of roots with more sand or soil.

If you still have some roots left in the ground by the following February, lift and store them.

Dig a trench alongside the row to make it easier to extract the roots without breaking them.

Stack them on the north side of a wall where there is complete shade, otherwise they may start to sprout. As an added protection against sprouting, cover them with plenty of soil.

What can go wrong with parsnips

Parsnip canker A reddish-brown canker may form on the shoulder of a root. This should not occur if crops are rotated and grown in deep, loamy soil with balanced fertiliser and lime (if necessary) added. Sow seeds early and thin to 6 in. apart. If the trouble persists grow a variety resistant to canker.

Cracking Roots may split lengthwise, usually due to drought. Make sure the soil never dries out.

Celery leaf flies or leaf miners Maggots burrow into leaves, causing brown blisters on them. Crush the blisters, or pick off and burn the affected leaves. If the damage is extensive, spray with malathion, dimethoate or trichlorphon.

Other troubles Wireworms may attack, also cutworms (p. 288).

Varieties of parsnips to grow

SHORT-ROOTED
'Avonresister'
Small. Resistant to canker
'Evesham'

INTERMEDIATE
'Offenham'
'White Gem'
'The Student'

LONG
'Tender and True'
'Improved Hollow Crown'
'Lisbonnais'

Peas to pick from May to October

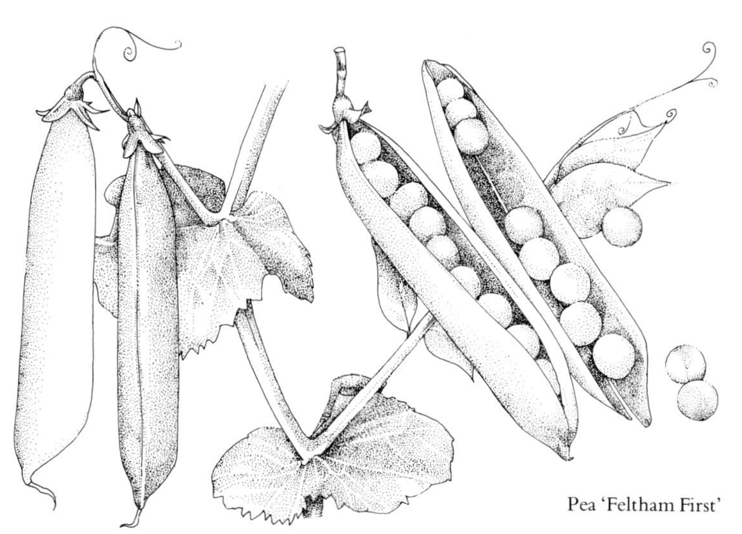
Pea 'Feltham First'

Green peas are in season from about May to October. For a continuous supply, sow a range of varieties in succession from about March to July. Some can also be sown in late autumn to crop the following May.

Varieties are grouped into early, second-early, maincrop and late. Later varieties need more heat in which to mature. If sown after March, some early varieties may crop poorly before they are fully grown, but some can be sown in June or July to crop in autumn.

Peas vary in height from dwarf (about 1½ ft) to tall (about 6 ft). Some are round-seeded; these are hardier and best for late autumn and early spring sowings. Others are wrinkled-seeded (called marrowfat) and are better flavoured.

Select an open and sunny site, and manure it well in the autumn or winter before sowing. Peas grow best in rich soil.

Before sowing, dress the soil with 3 oz. (3 tablespoons) of superphosphate of lime and 1½ oz. (1½ tablespoons) of sulphate of potash per square yard.

Sowing an early crop under glass

An early crop can be started under glass and later planted out. In February sow early, wrinkled-seed varieties in 2½ in. peat pots filled with seed compost. Put one pea ¾ in. deep in each pot.

Stand the pots in a seed tray, and induce germination in slight warmth – about 7–10°C (45–50°F). Cover the tray with glass and a sheet of folded newspaper. Remove both as soon as germination takes place.

Do not let the compost dry out, but water only sparingly.

At the end of March, move the seedlings to a cold frame for hardening off (p. 288).

In April, plant them out in the open 9 in. apart. Use a trowel to make a hole for each pot. Ensure that the pot rim is just below the soil surface, otherwise it will act as a wick and draw moisture up from the soil, which will then rapidly dry out.

In mild areas, the peas will be ready for picking in early June.

Sowing outdoors in succession

Outdoor sowing can start in late February or March, provided the soil is neither waterlogged nor frozen, and is workable. Then make sowings in succession about every three weeks until June or July.

Sow early varieties in late February and March, and a second-early in late March. Sow maincrop varieties in April and May, and late varieties in June and July.

Some early varieties can also be sown in late June and July for an autumn crop, but not all are suitable, being susceptible to mildew in late summer and autumn.

The first outdoor-sown peas should be ready for picking in late June, and crops often continue in succession until mid-October.

Dig a flat-bottomed drill about 6–8 in. wide and 1–1½ in. deep in heavy soil, or 2 in. deep in light soil.

The distance between drills depends on the heights of varieties sown in adjoining drills. Take an average between heights. For example, a 2 ft variety and a 4 ft should be grown 3 ft apart.

Sow the seeds about 1½ in. apart each way, in three rows on the bottom of the drill. Trials held at the Royal Horticultural Society's garden have shown that there is no adverse effect on cropping when peas are sown as thickly as this.

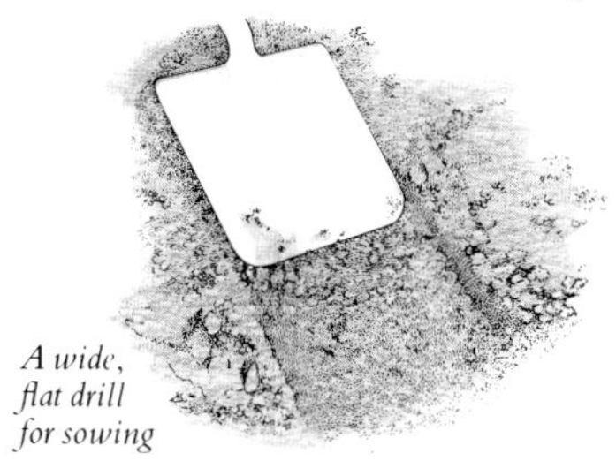
A wide, flat drill for sowing

Sow a few spare seeds at the end of each row, to fill any gaps.

Return the soil to the drill. Do not compact it, but leave it loose.

In gardens where mice are a nuisance, set a few traps after sowing.

Provide some protection against birds also, as they can quickly clean up a crop of seeds. Make pea-guards from wire netting fixed over a simple wooden frame, or over wire hoops (coat-hanger wire will do). Alternatively, criss-cross black cotton between sticks down the sides of the drills.

PROTECTION AGAINST BIRDS

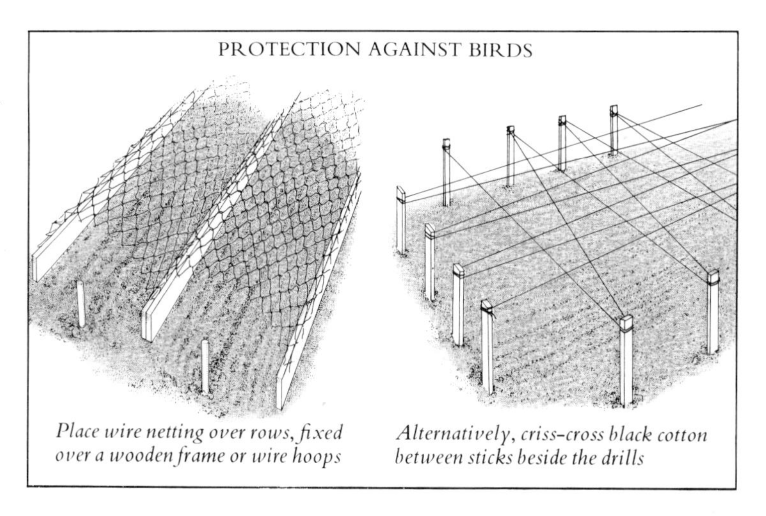
Place wire netting over rows, fixed over a wooden frame or wire hoops

Alternatively, criss-cross black cotton between sticks beside the drills

Autumn sowing for early summer cropping

Gardeners who are prepared to take a chance can sow a crop of peas outdoors under cloches in early November for picking in late May.

An autumn sowing of peas is possible even in the North, but sow the seeds earlier – in the last two weeks of October.

Use a round-seeded early variety, and before sowing treat seeds with an anti-disease seed dressing. Put the seeds in a paper bag or a tin, and puff in the seed dressing so that each seed is thinly coated.

Then sow in the normal way. Cover the row with cloches immediately after sowing. This will protect the plants from birds and cold, and reduce the risk of losing the crop from foot rot.

Keep plants covered until spring – or, if the height of the cloches will permit it, until the peas are ready for picking.

Hardy varieties recommended for sowing in autumn are 'Meteor' and 'Feltham First'.

Tending and harvesting the pea crop

When seedlings are about 2 in. high, hoe down the rows to keep the soil open and well aerated.

As soon as two pairs of leaves have formed, start staking all but dwarf plants with twiggy pieces of brushwood. Alternatively, support them on large mesh plastic netting fixed to stakes, or even large-mesh galvanised wire netting.

Peas need plenty of moisture. Water the crop regularly in dry weather, particularly when the first flowers appear, and again when the young pods start to form.

Use a mulch of peat or strawy manure between the rows to help conserve moisture in the soil.

Harvest peas when they are well developed but before they become tight in the pod. Pull the pod downwards with one hand, holding the stem with the other. This prevents the plant being uprooted, or the stem being snapped off. Pick pods regularly as they become ready, to encourage further cropping.

If you want peas for drying for winter use, keep a few plants and allow all the pods to ripen well before picking. If the weather turns damp before they have finished ripening, lift each plant. Hang plants in bundles in a dry, airy place to finish drying.

STAKING TALLER VARIETIES

When plants have made four leaves, give them twiggy sticks to climb

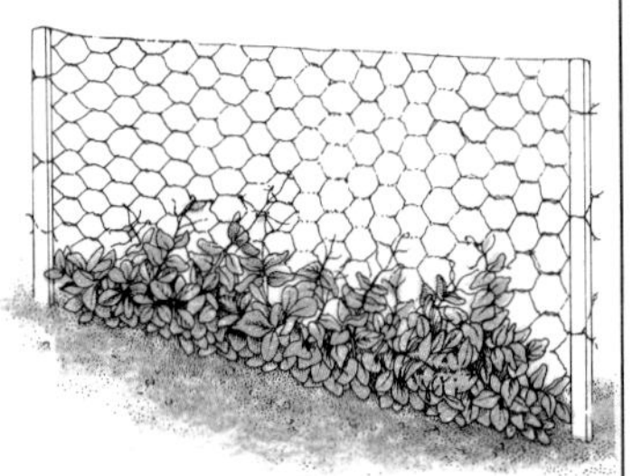

Alternatively, large-mesh netting fixed to stakes gives good support

What can go wrong with garden peas

Foot rot Peas are prone to this disease, which causes rotting round the base of the stem, followed by wilting of the whole plant. Make sure the ground is well cultivated and drained, and that crops are rotated.

Mildew A white fungus may grow on the leaves of later crops, especially if early plants are not removed after cropping. Clear early plants away and spray the later crops with dinocap.

Pea and bean weevils These eat leaf edges of young plants in a scalloped pattern. Apply HCH dust or fenitrothion.

Thrips and pea moths Thrips feed on leaves and flowers, leaving them with a finely mottled, silvery appearance. The danger period is from June to September, especially in hot, dry weather. Pea moth maggots may infest main and late crops. For both pests, spray with fenitrothion ten days after flowers appear.

Other troubles Aphids, birds and slugs may all damage plants (p. 288).

Varieties of peas to grow

Approximate heights of plants are given in brackets, but they vary with soil, situation and seasonal conditions.

EARLY (ROUND-SEEDED)

'Feltham First' (1½ ft)
Suitable for autumn or spring sowing, with or without cloches
'Feltham Advance' (2 ft)
'Meteor' (1½ ft)
Popular for autumn sowing; recommended for exposed gardens
'Improved Pilot' (3 ft)
'Histon Mini' (1 ft)
Valuable for growing under cloches

EARLY (WRINKLED-SEEDED)

'Sweetness' (3 ft)
'Little Marvel' (1½–2 ft)
'Kelvedon Wonder' (1½ ft)
Very popular variety
'Gradus' (4 ft)
'Pioneer' (1½–2 ft)
'Progress No. 9' (1½ ft)
Also known as 'Early Bird'
'Early Onward' (2 ft)

EARLY VARIETIES FOR JUNE/JULY SOWING
(Resistant to mildew)

'Kelvedon Wonder' (1½ ft)
'Progress No. 9' (1½ ft)
'Pioneer' (1½–2 ft)

SECOND-EARLY
(All wrinkled-seeded)

'Onward' (2½ ft)
Probably the most widely grown pea
'Victory Freezer' (2½ ft)
Also known as 'Kelvedon Monarch'
'Achievement' (4–5 ft)
'Miracle' (4½ ft)
'Hurst Green Shaft' (2½ ft)
Produces pods on the top 10 in. of foliage, making picking easier

MAINCROP
(All wrinkled-seeded)

'Alderman' (5 ft)
'Sleaford Three Kings' (2½ ft)
Bears pods in groups of three
'Recette' (2 ft)
Bears pods in threes. Long season

LATE
(All wrinkled-seeded)

'Lord Chancellor' (3–4 ft)
'Gladstone' (4 ft)
Has good drought resistance

LESS COMMON TYPES

'Asparagus' (or winged pea) (1½ ft)
Sow early April–May. Eat pods whole when 2–3 in. long
'Gullivert' (3 ft)
Sow March–June. The true French *petits pois*
'Purple Podded' (5 ft)
Has decorative purple pods, but peas are green. Sow March–May

SUGAR PEAS
(Also known as *Mangetout*. Sow March–June, and eat pods while still young)

'Carouby de Maussane' (5 ft)
'Dwarf de Grace' (2½ ft)
'Dwarf Sweetgreen' (1½–3 ft)

Potatoes – choosing varieties of a staple crop

Potato 'Home Guard'

Potatoes are grown from small tubers which are set out in trays to sprout before planting. There are first-early, second-early, and maincrop varieties.

First earlies are planted in mid-March for use as new potatoes in June and July. Second earlies are planted in early April, for lifting from July to September to supply a continuing crop of fresh potatoes. Maincrop varieties, which take longer to mature, are planted in late April, lifted in September or early October, and stored for winter.

A potato crop takes up a lot of space – about 30 ft by 14 ft for eight rows, yielding about 500 lb. If space is limited, it is better to grow a small crop of early (new) potatoes for use when shop prices are high.

Or you can grow a small main crop of varieties to suit your own taste. Many of those sold in the shops are chosen for their heavy cropping rather than their quality.

Potatoes may be round, oval or kidney shaped, with red, white or yellow skins. The flesh may be white or yellow and the texture either floury or waxy.

Grow them in an open plot with plenty of light. Shade encourages tall top-growth and light cropping. Potatoes grow reasonably well in most soils, but prefer a light, easily worked loam.

If the soil is heavy, lighten it by digging in well-rotted garden compost, leaf-mould or peat, and grit or sharp sand. If the soil conditions are good, just add well-rotted manure, unless the plot has already been manured within the three-crop rotation system.

In any case, dress the ground at planting time with a mixture of 2 parts of superphosphate, 1 part of sulphate of ammonia, and 1 part of sulphate of potash, using the mixture at a rate of 4 oz. (4 tablespoons) to the square yard. Alternatively, use a general fertiliser as recommended by the manufacturer.

Preparing the seed tubers for planting

Tubers weighing 2–3 oz. (about the size of a large hen's egg) are best. Large ones must be cut in two, lengthwise, at planting time. Buy seed potatoes at the end of January; set them out in trays immediately.

Tubers usually have most of their 'eyes' (from which the sprouts grow) concentrated near or at one end. This is called the rose end.

Place the tubers in a seed tray with the rose ends uppermost. Folded newspaper placed between rows helps to keep them in position.

Save space by using tomato trays. These have a 6 in. post at each corner, so they can be stacked one on top of another.

The trays need to be kept in frost-free conditions with plenty of air circulating, such as in a room or greenhouse. The temperature should be 5–7°C (41–45°F).

For healthy sprouting, some light is necessary to green the shoots, but full light is not required. High humidity should be avoided.

The aim is to start the tubers sprouting about four or five weeks before planting time. Not only will this provide a longer season of growth, resulting in a heavier crop, but you can also check that every tuber is viable and not affected by any fungal or virus disease.

By planting time, the sprouts should be short and sturdy and ideally about $\frac{1}{4}$–$\frac{1}{2}$ in. long. If tubers are kept too dark and too warm, long spindly sprouts will result. Longer sprouts – about 3–4 in. – can be planted successfully if care is taken not to damage them.

SPROUTING TUBERS

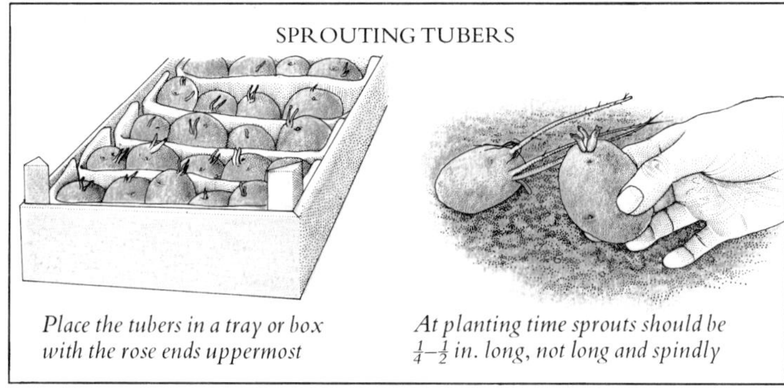

Place the tubers in a tray or box with the rose ends uppermost

At planting time sprouts should be $\frac{1}{4}$–$\frac{1}{2}$ in. long, not long and spindly

Growing an early crop in pots

If there is space available in the greenhouse in January or February for a small, luxury crop, plant some tubers in 10 in. pots and force them into early growth.

Crock the pots well, and cover the crocks with about 2 in. of John Innes No. 3 potting compost.

Place one tuber in each pot, with the sprouts or eyes uppermost. Pack more compost round and over it, so that the tuber is covered to a depth of about 1 in.

Later, as growth progresses, add more compost at intervals until it reaches 1 in. below the pot rim.

Water regularly, using a weak liquid fertiliser. About 12–14 weeks after planting, knock the soil ball out of the pot and pick off the largest potatoes. The plant and soil ball can then be replaced in the pot, to continue growing.

How to grow new potatoes

In warm, sheltered gardens plant first-early varieties from mid-March to the beginning of April, to provide 'new' potatoes in June and July. In colder parts of the country wait until mid-April, as the young growth will stand no more than a few degrees of frost.

Using a draw hoe, take out a drill 4 in. deep on light soil, or 6 in. deep on a heavy one. If you are planting more than one row of new potatoes, space drills 2 ft apart.

Select well-sprouted tubers, and set them 12 in. apart in the bottom of the drill with the sprouts uppermost.

Return the soil to the drill with your feet (p. 287), but do not press down on the tops of the tubers, as the young shoots may be damaged. Rake up a little soil from between the rows to make a slight ridge.

To protect early potato growth against frost, hoe up a little soil over the shoots as they appear above the ground.

When the shoots get too tall for this, scatter dried bracken or straw over each tuft of leaves.

As an extreme measure, well-advanced early potatoes can be covered temporarily with sheets of newspaper. Peg the paper at the corners with twigs to prevent it blowing away.

Earthing up When the top growth of early potatoes reaches about 9 in., begin earthing up.

The object of this is to increase the depth of the soil over the roots, so encouraging them to spread and form tubers. It also lessens the risk of the tubers being exposed to light and becoming green and inedible. The hoeing action involved in earthing keeps down weeds.

Start by breaking up the soil between the rows with a hoe or cultivator, then scatter a dressing of a general-purpose fertiliser, such as Growmore, over the cultivated soil. Use the manufacturer's recommendations for rate of application – usually about 1 oz. (1 tablespoon) to the square yard.

Use a draw hoe to pull up the loose soil and fertiliser from between the rows, forming a slight ridge along the line of plants.

A week later, repeat the hoeing, drawing up a little more soil. When the plants are at least 12 in. tall, make a final earthing so that the ridge height is 6 in., but no higher.

Make the ridge fairly wide at the top, but with steep sides. If the weather is very dry, make the top flat or even slightly indented. The shallow hollow will collect and concentrate any water from rain or a garden sprinkler. But if a prolonged wet spell is forecast, round off the top of the ridge to throw off excess water.

Harvesting The earliest potatoes should be ready about June. Remove a little soil with your fingers from the side of the ridge to examine the crop. The largest potatoes suitable for picking should be about the size of a hen's egg.

By careful picking, suitable tubers can be removed for a first dish of new potatoes, leaving the remainder to increase in size.

When the complete crop has reached maturity – about late June or early July – start lifting them. Lift only as many as are required for use at a time.

First cut off the top growth of the plants with shears. This makes it easier to lift them. Then insert a garden fork well clear of the plant. Push it well in, so that the plant can be lifted and thrown sideways between the rows in one operation.

Dry off any potatoes that are not wanted for cooking immediately.

In dry weather, make ridge tops indented to concentrate water

In wet weather, round the ridge top to throw off excess water

Growing second-early and maincrop potatoes

In early April plant second-early varieties, and towards the end of April plant maincrop varieties. Using a draw hoe, take out trenches about 4 in. deep and 3 in. wide, spacing the trenches 27 in. apart. Plant the seed tubers 15 in. apart.

Cover them with soil and make it into a slight ridge with a rake. This will prevent light getting to the tubers and turning them green.

When the top growth is about 9 in. high, spread fertiliser between the rows and earth them up in the same way as early varieties. Keep down the weeds by regular hoeing.

During early July spray the crops with maneb, zineb or Bordeaux mixture, to prevent potato blight. Make sure that the undersides of the leaves are sprayed, as well as the tops.

Second earlies will be ready for lifting from July to early September. Some can be stored if necessary. Maincrop varieties will be ready in September or early October when the foliage dies. Lift them in the same way as earlies; take care not to bruise or damage them.

After lifting, spread the potatoes to dry – put them under cover if rain threatens. They must be thoroughly dry before they are stored.

How to store potatoes for winter use

After the main crop has been lifted and allowed to dry, the potatoes can be stored either in clamps in the open or in boxes in a frost-proof shed. If they are stored in a shed, they must be kept in total darkness to prevent them from turning green.

To make a clamp, dig a shallow trench about 4 ft wide, 3 in. deep, and long enough to take the crop when heaped. Lay straw over the bottom of the clamp.

Carefully pile the potatoes on top of the straw to a height of 3 ft, and cover the mound with a 6 in. layer of straw. Next heap a 6 in. layer of soil taken from round the clamp over the straw, but leave the top of the mound open for about a week to allow for sweating.

When excavating the covering soil, leave a trench round the clamp. This will carry off excess moisture.

When closing the open top of the clamp, leave an air-shaft into the mound by twisting a 4 in. thick tuft of straw, and passing it through the covering soil. A long clamp will need these tufts every 6 ft.

Open one end of the clamp to remove potatoes as they are needed. Be sure to seal it again with soil and sacking to protect against frost.

Radishes for summer and winter

Radish 'Scarlet Globe'

There are two main types of radish: the small varieties that are grown for summer salads, and the large winter kind that can be eaten raw or boiled. Either type may be round, oval or long in shape.

Summer radishes can be sown from early March to September for pulling from mid-April to October. Winter radishes are sown in July or August and are ready for lifting from about November.

Any well-cultivated ground of fine tilth is suitable. Improve light, sandy soils by forking peat or finely chopped leaf-mould into the surface. This will help to retain moisture, which is very important as radishes are tender and crisp only if they are grown quickly with no check.

Early sowing under cloches or in cold frames

From late February to early March, sow summer varieties of radish in small batches in a cold frame or under cloches.

Make drills $\frac{1}{2}$ in. deep and 6 in. apart. Sow seeds very thinly (not touching) and cover drills by returning the soil with the back of a rake. Lightly water the bed and put the frame lights or cloches in position.

Plants will not need thinning, unless you sowed too thickly.

The first radishes will be ready for lifting in late March. Remove the frame lights or cloches in April, once the weather is suitable. Keep the bed moist if there is no rain.

Growing salad radishes in the open

Between early March and September, make small successional sowings at intervals of two or three weeks, according to your requirements.

Summer sowing – June, July and August – should be done in a cool, shady position. During this period radishes sown in dry ground in full sun will bolt (flower prematurely), and be dry and hot-flavoured.

Sow the seeds in the same way as for cloche and cold-frame radishes.

Radishes can be used as a catch crop between rows of other vegetables such as peas, beans or carrots. They can also be sown in pinches between other slower-developing plants such as lettuces.

Do not allow radishes to suffer from lack of moisture. Water regularly in dry weather.

Thin the crop as it develops, and pull the plants while they are young and tender. Plants are ready four to six weeks after sowing.

Growing for use as winter vegetables

Sow winter radishes in mid-July in the North, or mid-August in the South. Sow seeds thinly, in drills 1 in. deep and 9 in. apart. A month after planting, thin them to one plant every 6 in.

Dust seedlings with HCH or derris for the first three weeks, to prevent attack by flea-beetles. Hoe regularly to keep down weeds. Water occasionally to stop the plants running to seed. Plants are ready about three months after sowing.

Leave the crop in the ground during winter, lifting as needed.

What can go wrong with radishes

Flea beetles These eat the leaves of young plants, pitting them with very small holes. Attacks are worst in dry weather in May. Dust seedlings with HCH or derris.

Boron deficiency This may cause discoloured patches on the flesh, or browning of the interior. Apply 1 oz. (1 tablespoon) of borax – bulked with light sand – to every 20 square yards of soil.

Other troubles Radishes may be attacked by wireworms or cutworms (winter crops only). Seedlings may suffer from damping off (p. 288).

Varieties of summer and winter radishes

All varieties are red unless otherwise stated

SUMMER (ROUND)

'Cherry Belle'

'Scarlet Globe'

'Saxa'
Good for growing under glass

'Red Forcing'

'Sparkler'
Bright red with white base

SUMMER (OVAL)

'French Breakfast Forcing'

'Red White-tipped'

'Yellow Gold'
Yellow skin, white flesh

SUMMER (LONG)

'Icicle'
All white

WINTER RADISHES

'Black Spanish'
Available in round or long shapes; both very hardy, with black skin and white, very pungent flesh

'China Rose'
Oval; hardy, with pink skin and white flesh; pungent flavour

Spinach for picking round the year

Spinach 'Greenmarket'

There are three main types of spinach: round or summer spinach, prickly or winter spinach, and spinach beet (also known as perpetual spinach). All are grown for their leaves, which are picked continually to encourage more growth.

Summer spinach is in season from May to September, and winter spinach from mid-October to April. Spinach beet crops all year.

Sow summer and winter spinach in small batches, otherwise plants run to seed before they can be used, especially if the weather is hot and dry. Summer spinach can be used as a catch crop between rows of peas and beans, or before planting out cabbages and leeks.

Spinach is tastier if grown quickly, so should be well manured and watered. All spinach grows best in rich, deep, moist soil. Grow in the plot prepared for beans and peas in the annual rotation system. The soil should have been deeply dug in winter, with plenty of well-rotted manure or compost worked in.

Growing a summer crop of spinach

Make the first sowing in late February or early March, when the soil is workable and can be broken down to a fine tilth. Then sow every ten days until mid-July.

Early sowings should be in a sunny site, but later sowings – from May to July – should be in a shady spot so that plants will need less watering and will not bolt (flower prematurely). 'New Zealand' spinach will tolerate hot, dry soil.

Using a hoe, make drills 1 in. deep and 9 in. apart. Sow seeds thinly, and return the soil to the drills with your feet. Rake the surface over lightly.

A few weeks after sowing, when seedlings are large enough to handle, thin them to 3 in. apart.

About two weeks later thin the seedlings again, removing every other plant for use.

Keep the plants well watered in dry weather, or they will bolt. Hoe between rows regularly.

Start picking spinach as soon as the leaves are a reasonable size, usually about the end of May. Take only the largest leaves from each plant, pinching them off between finger and thumb. Careless pulling may loosen the roots and spoil the chances of a further yield.

Pick regularly and quite hard, but never take more than half the leaves from one plant at a single picking.

How to grow spinach for winter

Sow winter spinach at fortnightly intervals from early August until about the third week of September. Choose a sheltered and sunny position, and sow in the same way as summer spinach.

Good drainage is important. If the garden tends to lie rather wet in winter, hoe up a little soil into 3 in. high ridges and make the drills on top of them.

Thin in the same way as summer spinach, and hoe regularly between the rows to keep down weeds.

From mid-November onwards, protect the plants from frost with cloches, or with a thick layer of bracken or straw placed between the rows.

Winter spinach is usually ready for picking from mid-October onwards. Gather the leaves as they become ready. Do not pick plants as hard as summer spinach. If they are over-picked, growth will cease.

Spinach beet – a useful substitute

Spinach beet is often grown as a substitute for summer and winter spinach. It is a kind of beetroot grown only for its foliage.

Make drills 1 in. deep and 9 in. apart. Sow seeds thinly in April for a summer and autumn crop, and in late July or early August for a winter and spring crop.

Thin seedlings to 8 in. apart. Keep rows free of weeds, and water plants occasionally during dry spells.

Pick the leaves, together with their stems, when they are a usable size. Any coarse leaves not wanted for use should be picked and put on the compost heap.

Do not pick too many leaves from autumn-sown spinach beet, as plants should be allowed to build themselves up before winter.

Seakale beet is grown in the same way as spinach beet. Its leaves have a white midrib that can be separated and used in the same way as seakale – as a choice spring vegetable that is cooked like asparagus.

The rest of the seakale beet leaf is used as spinach.

What can go wrong with spinach

Downy mildew The upper sides of leaves have yellow blotches, the undersides a greyish or white furry coating. Thin out the plants and spray with zineb. Make sure crops are rotated.

Virus disease This may cause striped, blotched, mottled or distorted leaves. Burn affected plants.

Leaf spot Leaves develop round or oval brown spots, sometimes with a black pinpoint. Remove and burn affected leaves; spray with benomyl, dichlofluanid, mancozeb, zineb or thiophanate-methyl as necessary.

Other troubles Birds or aphids may attack (p. 288).

Varieties of spinach to grow

SPRING AND SUMMER

'Long Standing Round'
'Victoria'
'Sigmaleaf'
'Cleanleaf'
'New Zealand'
Crops over a long period; only one sowing needed

WINTER

'Long Standing Prickly'
'Greenmarket'
'Virkade'
'Sigmaleaf'

SPINACH BEET

May appear in lists as Perpetual Spinach or Leaf Beet

Tomatoes for growing outdoors and under glass

Tomato 'Alicante'

Tomatoes are very sensitive to frost and cold, and are generally grown in greenhouses in Britain. But there are varieties that can be grown outdoors from June to September in a sunny, sheltered position.

As they take four or five months from sowing to ripening, depending on conditions, plants need to be sown in late March or early April. They can be started in a cold greenhouse if the weather is suitable, but stand a better chance if started in heat.

Tomato plants can usually be planted out in a cold greenhouse or frame about mid-April, under cloches about mid-May or in the open garden in June.

You can also buy plants from a nursery ready for planting out. They should be sturdy, dark green, and about 8 in. high. Do not buy plants that look weak, fern-like or diseased. Avoid light green plants, with large gaps between the leaves, which have been grown in poor light; also purplish-green plants, as they will have been grown under too cold conditions. If planting outdoors, make sure you buy an outdoor variety.

Tomatoes are usually grown as a single stem (cordon), which, if not stopped, can grow to a height of about 6 ft. All greenhouse plants are grown as cordons. Dwarf or bush varieties are also available for growing outdoors. Dwarfs spread along the ground and are no higher than 6 in. Bushes have a drooping growth.

Raising seedlings in a greenhouse or indoors

In late March or early April, sow seeds in a heated propagator – temperature 15–18°C (59–64°F) – or indoors on a sunny window-sill. If you sow indoors, you must have enough room to grow the plants until they can be planted out.

Sow seeds in boxes or pots of seed compost. If you sow in boxes, sow 1 in. apart. Hold the seeds in a piece of paper folded in a V-shape, and guide each one into the box with a pencil point.

Sift $\frac{1}{8}$ in. of compost over the seeds and stand the box in a bowl of water until the compost is thoroughly moist. Cover the seed box with glass and a sheet of folded newspaper. Remove the glass and newspaper as soon as the seedlings appear (after eight to ten days). Then stand the seedlings as close to the light as possible.

As soon as the first pair of leaves has formed, prick off (p. 288) the seedlings separately into $2\frac{1}{2}$ or 3 in. pots of John Innes No. 1 potting compost. Leave the pots in the greenhouse or on the window-ledge, and keep moist.

If you sow in pots, put seeds $\frac{1}{8}$ in. deep and $\frac{1}{4}$ in. apart. Water and cover them in the same way as boxes. Thin to one strong seedling per pot.

About mid or late May, start hardening the plants off (p. 288) ready for planting out.

PUTTING INTO POTS

Hold seedlings by the seed leaves when pricking off into 3 in. pots

Planting out young tomatoes in the open

Choose a warm, sheltered spot for planting – preferably a border beside a wall or fence. Dig the ground thoroughly and add plenty of well-rotted manure or garden compost. Do this well before planting, or at the same time as applying fertiliser.

A fortnight before planting out, apply a general fertiliser, such as Growmore, at a rate of 3 oz. (3 tablespoons) to the square yard.

When all danger of frost is over – usually late May in the South and early June in the North – plant out in the prepared bed.

Knock each plant gently out of its pot, keeping the soil ball intact, and plant it so that the top of the ball is $\frac{1}{2}$ in. below soil level. Firm the soil round each plant. Space plants 18 in. apart in rows 30 in. apart – 2 ft apart for dwarf and bush varieties.

Immediately after planting, push a 5 ft chestnut stake or stout bamboo cane deep into the ground alongside the root ball. Dwarf and bush varieties do not need staking.

Water plants thoroughly and scatter slug pellets round them.

PLANTING OUT

Knock the plant gently out of its pot, keeping the soil ball intact

Greenhouse growing for a longer season

If you have enough space, growing plants in a cold greenhouse will give the extra length of season and warmth needed to ripen tomatoes.

There are a number of methods that can be used. All depend on adequate and regular watering, so you will need a neighbour's help when you go on holiday.

To plant pot-grown seedlings into the greenhouse border, prepare the soil in winter by digging in well-rotted manure or garden compost.

To improve drainage in a heavy soil or where tomatoes have been grown previously, dig in straw or a bucket of coarse peat to the square yard. Every three to five years the top 6 in. of soil at least, more if possible, should be renewed.

When the seedlings are 5–6 in. tall, knock them out of their pots, keeping the soil balls intact, and plant them 15 in. apart in staggered rows 2 ft apart.

Water in after planting. Afterwards, a good soaking once or twice a week will be sufficient. Do not over-water, but be guided by the appearance of the plants.

Use a proprietary liquid tomato fertiliser at the rate recommended by the manufacturer. Do not over-feed before the flowers have set, as this may cause them to drop off.

Growing a crop in plastic bags

A modern method of tomato growing is to use specially prepared plastic bags. These are available from most garden suppliers.

The bags are filled with a peat-based compost, plus fertilisers and trace elements. They provide plants with sufficient nutrients to last until the fruit is set.

Lay each bag out flat on the floor or staging of the greenhouse, and cut a rectangular panel out of the top. Plant directly into the hole. If you want tomatoes of good size, put four plants to each bag and allow no more than six trusses of fruit per plant. For a larger crop of smaller fruits, put four plants to each bag and allow more than six trusses per plant.

Do not over-water the bags and do not make drainage holes in them. To test the moisture content, press a small piece of newspaper on the surface of the compost. If it is moistened, the compost is wet enough; if the paper remains dry, or almost so, more water is needed.

As soon as the fruit has set, start to feed plants with a liquid tomato fertiliser, following the manufacturer's instructions.

These bags can also be used outdoors where soil is unavailable – on patios, balconies and flat roofs.

GROWING IN BAGS

Cut a panel from the top of the bag and plant into the hole

Check the moisture content of the compost with a piece of newspaper

Ring culture in the greenhouse

Ring culture is a method of growing tomatoes in open-ended pots or rings, which stand on a bed of moist aggregate (crushed, graded stone or similar material). The plants establish themselves in compost inside the rings and then send roots down into the aggregate.

The advantage of this method of culture is that a relatively small amount of soil is needed, and the bed can easily be flushed out with a soil disinfectant, such as Jeyes Fluid or permanganate of potash, each autumn after the crop has been gathered. The bed should be renewed every three to five years.

Dig a trench about 6 in. deep in the floor of the greenhouse. Line it with polythene sheeting, and make a good drainage hole in each yard of sheeting. Alternatively, the bed can be set up on the greenhouse bench, boxed in with 6 in. wide planks.

Fill the trench or bed with a free-draining aggregate of weathered boiler ash or fine clinkers. As an alternative, use a mixture of 3 parts of $\frac{1}{2}$ in. washed gravel and 1 part of coarse-grade vermiculite.

Make cylinders 9 in. high and 9 in. in diameter by stapling together roofing felt or linoleum. Or buy them from a garden supplier.

Stand rings 18 in. apart on the prepared bed. Half fill them with John Innes No. 3 compost. Place a plant on the compost and pack more compost round it, to within 1 in. of the top.

After planting, water the plants through the rings, but after that water only through the aggregate.

Encourage root development by watering sparingly in the first ten days. After this, water more often to keep the aggregate moist.

After fruit has formed on the first flower truss, feed the plants with liquid fertiliser watered into the aggregate bed.

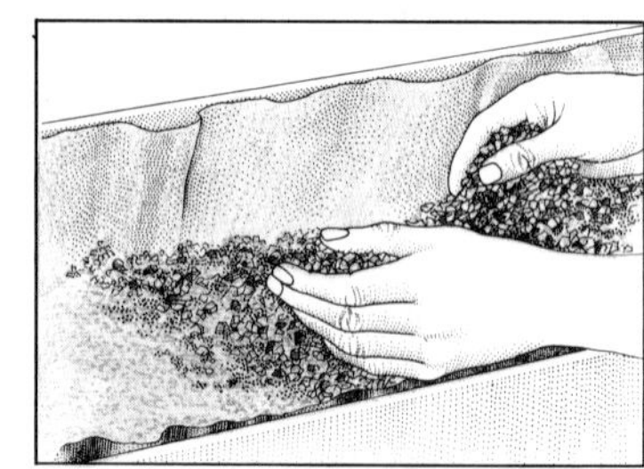

1 *Line a 6 in. deep trench or bed with plastic sheeting and fill with aggregate*

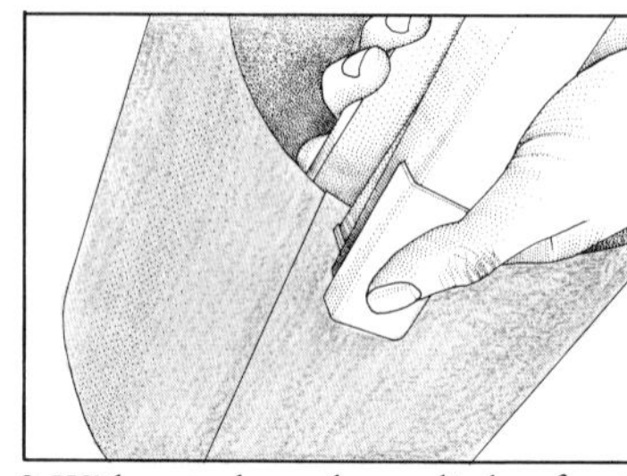

2 *With a stapler make a cylinder of roof felt, 9 in. high and 9 in. across*

3 *Place the plant in the ring and pack compost to within 1 in. of the top*

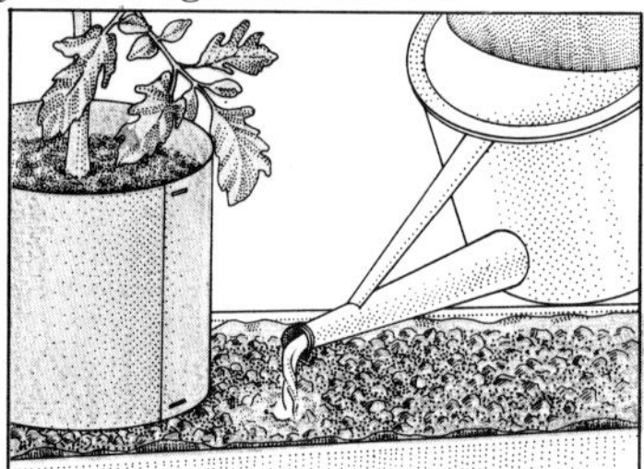

4 *Except for watering in after planting, water only into the aggregate*

Looking after plants growing outdoors

In very dry weather, tomatoes need regular and frequent watering. In normal conditions they should not be over-watered. Irregular watering can cause split fruits.

If you have any doubts about how often and how much to water, use the 'flower-pot' method of watering. When planting out, sink a 6 in. flower pot up to its rim alongside the soil ball. Top it up regularly once a week; this should be adequate.

There is no need to pollinate the flowers artificially – wind and insects will do the job naturally. After fruit has formed on the first truss of flowers, feed plants once a week with a liquid tomato fertiliser placed in the watering pot. Follow the maker's instructions for the amount of fertiliser to use.

For cordon plants, tie the stem to the stake with soft garden string or raffia as the plant grows. Wrap the string twice round the stake, make a loose loop round the plant, and tie the string against the stake. This will allow the stems to expand without being damaged.

Remove all side-shoots that appear within the leaf axils before they reach 1 in. in length. They can be pinched out between finger and thumbnail, but it is safer to cut them off with a clean, sharp knife.

When the tomatoes have set four trusses of fruit – some time during August – cut off the growing point two leaves above the top truss to prevent further flowering and to encourage the fruit to swell.

Dwarf and bush varieties do not need staking, and side-shoots and main shoots are left to branch freely.

Lay straw or similar material, or plastic sheeting, beneath plants to prevent fruit on the lower trusses from coming into contact with the soil. It will also keep down weeds and conserve moisture round roots.

TYING THE PLANT

Wrap the string twice round the stake and loop it loosely round the stem

STOPPING TOMATOES

1 *Cut side-shoots growing in leaf axils before they are 1 in. long*

2 *When four trusses of fruit have set, cut off the growing point*

Ripening and harvesting the outdoor crop

Pick tomatoes as they ripen. Hold in the palm of your hand and with your thumb press the slight swelling on the stalk just above the fruit, where it will break cleanly.

Before the first frost arrives, probably about the middle of September, cut all the green trusses still unripened and lay them on an inside window-sill. Or fruits can be individually wrapped in paper and put in a dark cupboard or drawer at a temperature of 7–10°C (45–50°F).

Another method is to lift the plants complete with roots, remove the leaves, and hang them upside-down in a greenhouse.

Growing tomatoes in pots or boxes

If you have no suitable garden space and no greenhouse border, you can grow tomatoes in containers. These can be placed on sunny window-ledges either indoors or else outside, on the greenhouse staging, or on a sunny balcony or patio. They need watering regularly, so you will need the help of a neighbour if you go on holiday.

Use 10 in. pots or boxes, and fill them with a mixture of 2 parts of good soil to 1 part peat, or use John Innes No. 3 compost. Leave a 4 in. space between the mixture and the top of the container, to allow for a top-dressing to be added later.

If seedlings have been germinated in boxes, prick them out (p. 288) into 3 in. pots and grow them on for about three weeks before transferring them to the permanent container.

With a trowel, dig a hole in the soil of the container large enough to take the unbroken soil ball round the roots of the young plant. After planting, firm the soil with your fingers. Then water the plant in.

Pot plants need more watering and manuring than plants grown in open beds or the greenhouse border.

Plants should be staked and stopped in the same way as cordon plants grown outside.

When fruit begins to appear on the trusses, give a top-dressing of 2–4 in. of John Innes No. 3 compost. Water the plant well after the dressing to settle the soil.

Stopping and supporting greenhouse plants

Whichever method is used for growing tomatoes in a greenhouse, all side-shoots growing from the leaf axils should be carefully cut out with a clean, sharp knife before they are 1 in. long.

Dense foliage, particularly yellowing leaves, may be thinned to allow air and sunlight to penetrate to the fruit.

It is not necessary to use any artificial methods to pollinate the flowers. There is enough air movement and insect life in a greenhouse to do the job naturally. But you can assist the process by tapping the canes or supports – this will release pollen from the stamen tips of the open flowers so that it will fall to the stigma below.

When six trusses of fruit have formed, stop the plant by cutting out the growing point.

Greenhouse tomatoes can be tied to canes inserted beside each plant. Another simple method is to attach lengths of string to overhead wires stretched tightly from one end of the greenhouse to the other, about 6 ft from the ground. Tie the other end of each string to the base of a plant, or to a short bamboo cane driven in near its base. Support the plant by twisting the string round it as it grows.

Turnips and swedes – root crops for summer and winter

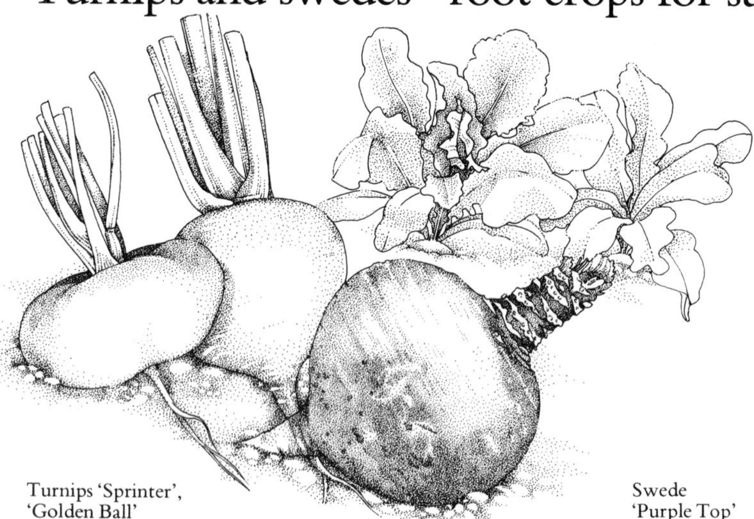

Turnips 'Sprinter', 'Golden Ball'

Swede 'Purple Top'

Turnips and swedes are grown in the same way, except that swedes are larger and need to be grown further apart. There are three main shapes of turnip – globe, flat-round (oblate), and long (similar to a parsnip). Swedes are globe shaped.

Turnips are in season for most of the year. Two crops are normally grown: an early crop for summer, sown in succession from April until early July, for use from July to October; and the main crop for winter, sown in late July for use from about mid-October to April. Swedes are sown in May or June for use from about mid-October to April.

Turnips are best grown no bigger than tennis balls. At this stage they are tender and well flavoured. The garden swede has a more delicate flavour than the turnip, and is often preferred as a winter crop because it is hardier.

Swedes take longer to mature, and keep in the soil better than turnips, although many people prefer to lift them before they become too big and coarse in texture.

Both vegetables are sown direct into the bed where they are to crop. Summer turnips make a useful catch crop between peas, as they are ready for lifting from six to eight weeks after sowing. They are not an easy crop to grow where the topsoil is sandy and thin – they need rich, well-manured soil so that they grow quickly and without check, otherwise they tend to be tough, and harsh in flavour.

For early summer turnips, choose ground manured the previous season. In addition, dust the surface with 3 oz. (3 tablespoons) of superphosphate, 2 oz. (2 tablespoons) of sulphate of ammonia, and 1 oz. (1 tablespoon) of sulphate of potash to each square yard.

For swedes and the winter crop of turnips use ground that has been cleared of an early crop. Lightly dig over the plot, and hoe in a fertiliser dressing similar to that recommended for early turnips.

Winter turnips are lifted and stored in about mid-October. Swedes can be left in the ground over winter and lifted as required. A few can be lifted and stored, in case the ground becomes frozen hard.

Turnips can also be grown for their leaves. An August sowing provides a nutritious crop of greens in early spring. The roots can also be eaten if desired.

Sowing and tending turnips and swedes

One early turnip, 'Jersey Navet', can be sown under cloches or in a cold frame from February to May for a very early crop. Generally, sow the first early summer turnips in early April. Then sow about every three weeks until early July.

In late July sow maincrop varieties for storage over winter.

Make drills $\frac{3}{4}$ in. deep and 15 in. apart and sow seeds thinly.

As soon as the first rough leaves appear, thin seedlings to 3 in. apart. About three weeks later thin to 6 in.

Sow swedes in May or June, in drills $\frac{3}{4}$ in. deep and 18 in. apart. When seedlings are 1 in. high thin them to 12 in. apart.

Hoe regularly to keep down weeds, and in dry weather water regularly.

Sow turnips for spring greens at the end of August. Make drills $\frac{3}{4}$ in. deep and 9–12 in. apart. Do not thin. Cut leaves when they are 8 in. high.

Harvesting and storing the roots

Pull summer turnips when they are about the size of a tennis ball. Use them within a few days.

In early November, lift all winter turnips and some swedes for storing. Use a fork and do not bruise roots, or they will rot in store. Do not store damaged or pest-bitten roots.

Twist the leaves off sound roots, and put them in layers on a bed of sand or dryish soil in a box, covering each layer with sand or soil. Put the box in a cool, dry, frost-proof shed.

Alternatively, store in outdoor clamps like carrots (p. 297).

What can go wrong with turnips and swedes

Flea beetles These can be a serious pest in dry weather, eating small holes in the leaves of young plants. Dust seedlings with HCH or derris weekly until rough leaves appear.

Split roots These are caused by drought followed by heavy rain. Avoid irregular growth by watering before the soil dries out completely.

Club root Roots become swollen and distorted due to a soil-borne fungus. Burn affected roots. To prevent, improve drainage if necessary, and spread one bucket of hydrated lime to every 30 square yards of soil. Rake in 4 per cent calomel dust before sowing.

Boron deficiency This may cause discoloured patches or browning of the flesh. Apply 1 oz. (1 tablespoon) of borax – bulked with light sand – to every 20 square yards of soil.

Other troubles Wireworms or cutworms may attack (p. 288).

Varieties of turnips and swedes to grow

TURNIPS

EARLY (FLAT-ROUND)
'Purple Milan'
'Sprinter'

EARLY (GLOBE)
'Snowball'
'Early Six Weeks'
'Tokyo Cross'

EARLY (LONG)
'Jersey Navet'
Suitable for frames or cloches

MAINCROP (GLOBE)
'Golden Ball'
Hardy; keeps well
'Manchester Market'
'Red Globe'
'Green-top White'
Suitable for spring greens

SWEDES
'Purple Top'
'Chignecto'
Resistant to club-root disease

Herbs fresh for the kitchen pot

Herbs can be grown in their own part of the garden—preferably close to the kitchen door—or they can be mixed with the other flowering plants. If sage is grown at the edge of a border within bruising distance of a passing lawnmower, it will throw out a rich scent to mix with the smell of the new-mown grass. Thyme can be grown between paving stones to release its perfume when stepped on in summer. Or a terracotta parsley pot, smothered in crinkly green heads of parsley, can be mixed with other pot plants on a sunny patio.

Almost all herbs grow best in a sunny position. They thrive on a light, fertile and well-drained soil, but most will do well even in poor soil. Except for sorrel, all like an alkaline soil. Give a light dressing of lime in autumn, and a general-purpose fertiliser in spring.

Planting, sowing, thinning, watering and propagating are all carried out in the same way as for other annuals, perennials and shrubs – see the appropriate sections of the book.

When planting herbs together, make sure that taller types are at the back, so that they do not overshadow low-growing ones.

Plant garlic in a sunny, moist position in October and February. The bulbs can be used whole or split up into their cloves. Plant 6 in. apart in light, well manured soil. Pinch off flower heads as they appear. Crop in summer and late summer.

Growing herbs in the kitchen
Winter supplies of fresh herbs can be grown in pots or boxes on a sunny window-sill in the kitchen.

The best results indoors are obtained with perennials grown either from cuttings or divisions taken in autumn. Chives, marjoram, mint, rosemary, sage and winter savory are all suitable for growing in the kitchen. They will not last indefinitely indoors, so take fresh cuttings each autumn.

Some herbs, such as basil, dill and parsley, can be raised from seed outdoors in late summer, and transplanted into pots in the autumn for wintering in the kitchen.

Ordinary garden soil can be used for growing herbs in pots if it is moderately rich and free draining. But a potting compost such as John Innes No. 1 is better.

Water plants regularly, and keep them away from draughts. If possible, stand the pots in gravel on a shallow tray, and keep the gravel wet.

Choice for the garden

SHRUBS: Bay, rosemary, sage, savory (winter), thyme (common), thyme (lemon).

PERENNIAL: Angelica, chives, fennel, horseradish, marjoram (pot), mint, sorrel, tarragon.

BIENNIAL: Caraway, parsley.

HARDY ANNUAL: Borage, chervil, coriander, dill, savory (summer).

HALF-HARDY ANNUAL: Basil, marjoram (sweet).

BULB: Garlic.

Home-grown herbs provide a constantly available source of fresh culinary flavouring, which can be used with a wide variety of foods. They are also attractive plants for the garden where, if crushed, they will release their rich scent

Water plants

Water adds life to the garden, in the fish that live in it and the birds that come to drink. Any site can have a water garden – be it a wine cask or a chain of pools

Making a water garden can be an exciting adventure that everyone can enjoy, for the smallest of gardens can have a pool, stream or waterfall.

Even a tiny patio or balcony can have its pool. This can be made from a sawn-down wine cask and will usually be large enough to hold a water lily, a few smaller plants and two or three fish.

Any receptacle capable of holding water is a potential pool – there are even water lilies small enough to survive in a washing-up bowl.

Larger gardens, of course, provide greater scope, as water can combine with rock to create a chain of pools.

In a town garden there will probably be space to sink a prefabricated glass-fibre shell into the ground, and with the aid of electricity and a small pump, install a fountain. The same water is used over and over again for streams, waterfalls and fountains, and the only running cost is for electricity.

In a suburban or country garden, a larger pool can be made at reasonable cost with heavy-duty plastic sheeting. Any shape or size is possible, and any depth – or series of depths. Pools may also be on different levels, linked by waterfalls made of glass fibre or plastic liners.

Glass-fibre shells and plastic liners have superseded concrete for pool

construction. Concrete pools are notorious for developing leaks, due either to soil settlement or to frost damage. Plastic liners are sometimes used for lining existing concrete pools that have cracked.

Pools can also be made from odd containers such as obsolete baths, cisterns or horse troughs. These can be part-filled with soil, sunk into the ground and their edges masked with plants or pieces of rock.

Water is an attraction to children and care should be taken to prevent accidents, which can easily happen if there is no supervision.

A water garden can be either a pool containing deep-water plants in the centre and shallow-water plants on the margins, or a bog garden containing moisture-loving plants which do not need to grow actually in the water.

All water gardens need plenty of light, otherwise the plants will not flower. The water should be clear, with half or two-thirds of its surface free from vegetation so that it is possible to see, and feed, the fish and enjoy the reflections in the water.

To maintain clear water, it is necessary to achieve a balance between plant and animal life. If this is not done, the water will become murky and evil-smelling and the fish will die.

The culprits which cause murky water are algae – microscopic plants that thrive on sunlight and feed on mineral salts in the water.

The mineral salts are introduced into the water by the breakdown of organic materials such as leaves or peat. Consequently, it is essential to keep the pool completely clear of leaves and to make sure the soil is free from peat or garden compost.

The only sure way to keep water clear is to use plenty of oxygenating plants in the pool. These are plants which live beneath the surface of the water, feeding on the mineral salts and so starving out the algae. They also rob the algae of light by creating shady pockets in the pool.

The oxygenators also breathe in the carbon dioxide which is given off by fish and other creatures in the pool. In turn they release oxygen (hence their name) into the water, where it becomes available for fish to breathe. Thus, a perfect cycle is effected: the oxygenators and the fish each utilising the waste products of the other.

Some oxygenators are much more efficient than others, and also grow more rapidly. Provided they do not choke other plants or look unsightly, you can scarcely have too many of these useful plants.

Besides their aesthetic value and their role in the pool cycle, fish have other uses. They keep down mosquitoes by devouring their larvae, they consume snail eggs, aphids and caddis worms, and they eat a certain amount of algae and submerged vegetation. In addition, their droppings manure the soil.

Some species of fish are better than others for small ornamental pools. The most satisfactory are golden orfe, goldfish, comets and shubunkins. These are brightly coloured, stay near the surface and can be trained to come for food.

Some fish, for example tench and mirror carp, have a tendency to grub around for food in mud, which keeps the water constantly agitated and murky.

A pool can contain four types of plants. Deep-water plants grow in the centre of the pool; oxygenators below the surface help keep the water clear; shallow-water plants live in the marginal water; and bog plants grow in the moist soil around the edge

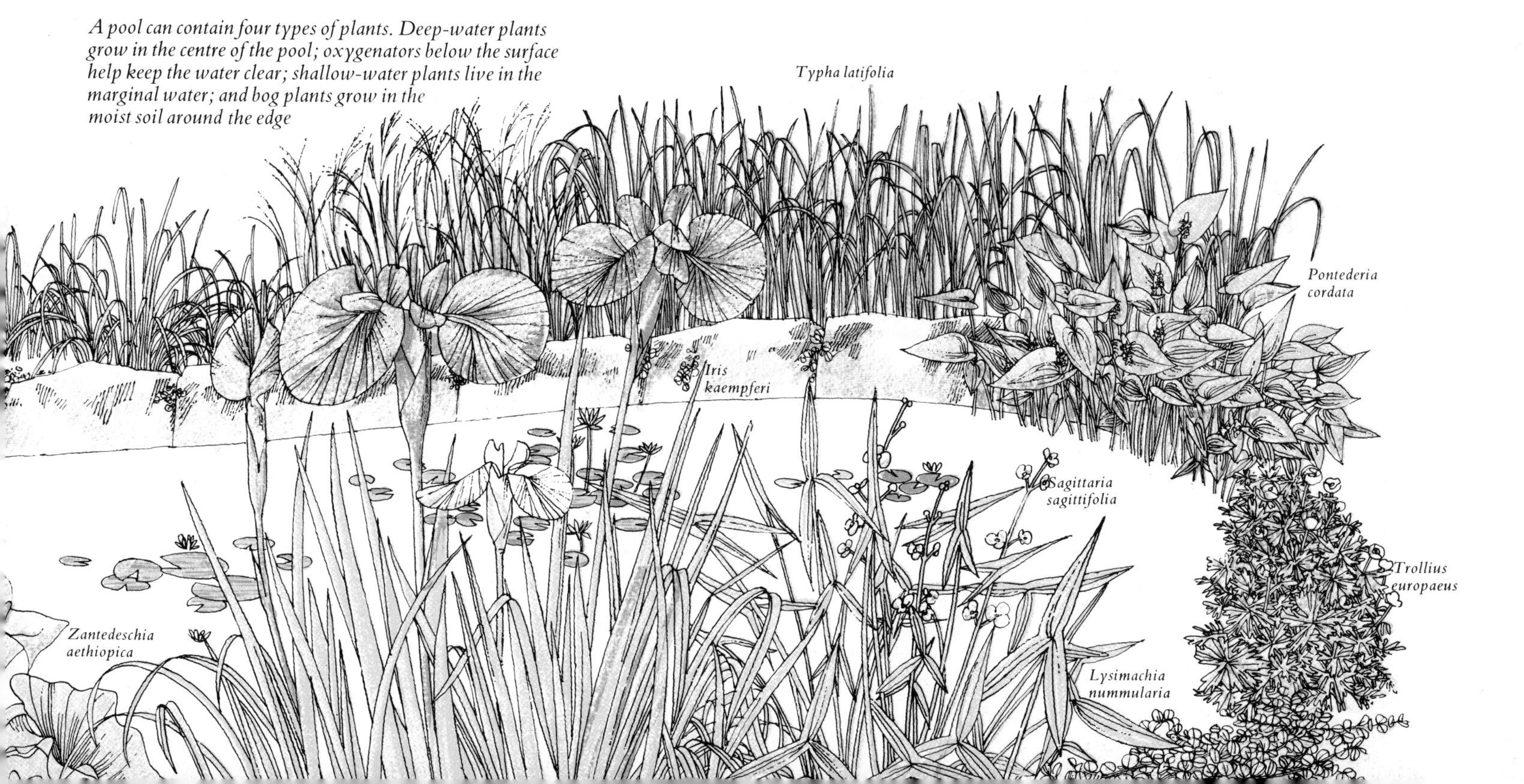

Planning and installing a garden pool

Select a sunny, open site, within easy reach of your garden hose.

Decide on the shape of the pool, avoiding narrow necks, dumb-bell shapes, and crosses which waste space that could be used for plants.

Mark out the shape of the pool with a piece of rope. Plan a shallow ledge in the pool for growing marginal (shallow-water) plants. But place the ledge so that the view of the water is not obscured by tall marginals such as reeds.

Glass-fibre pools Dig a hole the shape of the pool, but a few inches wider. Compact the base of the hole very firmly, removing all stones, then cover with an inch of sand or sifted soil. Place the pool in position.

Make quite sure the pool edge is level, using a plank and spirit level.

Fill in the gap between the pool and the excavation. Ram the soil firmly, particularly underneath the shelves, checking at intervals that the pool edge is still level.

Finish by laying paving, projecting an inch or so over the edge, or cover the edge with turf. Planting can be done immediately.

Plastic liners Ordinary polythene or PVC liners are short-lived, so it is worth investing in a stronger material. Butylite, a synthetic rubber, will last for about 50 years. Flexilene, nylon-reinforced PVC, has a lifespan of about ten years.

Measure the maximum length and width, and add twice the maximum depth required to both these measurements. The resultant figures give the size of liner required. For example, if the maximum length is 12 ft, the maximum width 6 ft, and the depth 3 ft, you would need 18 ft × 12 ft of liner. There is no need to make any allowance for shelves or overlap round the edges. The elasticity of the liner will provide the surplus required.

Dig a hole, making the sides sloping rather than vertical. Cut out deep and shallow-water areas. Check that all edges are horizontal.

Remove all sharp stones from the hole and spread an inch of sand or sifted soil over the bottom. If the walls are very rough, face them with damp sand or damp sifted soil.

Unfold the liner carefully in the hole and allow at least 6 in. of material to overlap the edge. Weigh down the overlap with smooth stones.

Run water into the pool slowly, pleating and tucking the liner into shape to give a neat finish.

Fill completely, and check the depths of the margins – between 2 in. and 9 in. is reasonable. Correct where necessary by adding sand beneath the liner. The water will now hold the liner in place, so the stones can be removed.

Trim off any surplus liner round the edges with a sharp knife, but leave at least 6 in. of overlap. Finish by laying paving slabs or rockery stone, overlapping the pool by about 1–2 in. No part of the liner should show after completion.

Keep the pool full of water at all times, as strong sunlight shining directly on to the fabric may cause it to deteriorate.

MAKING A GARDEN POOL FROM PLASTIC SHEETING

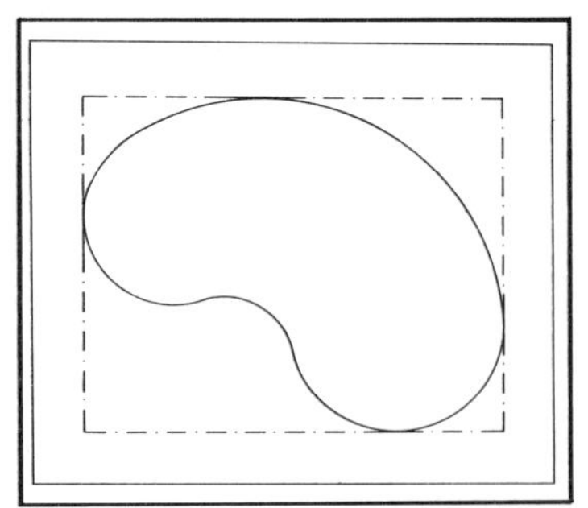
1 *Measure the maximum width and length and add twice the depth*

2 *Dig the hole, remove stones and lay an inch of sand or soil on the bottom*

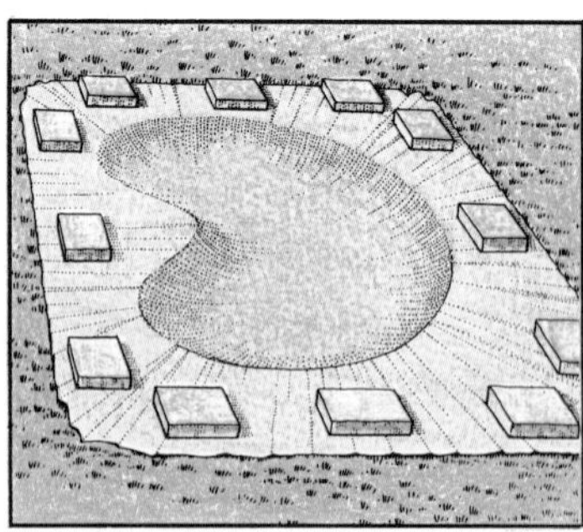
3 *Unfold the liner in the hole and hold it down with stones*

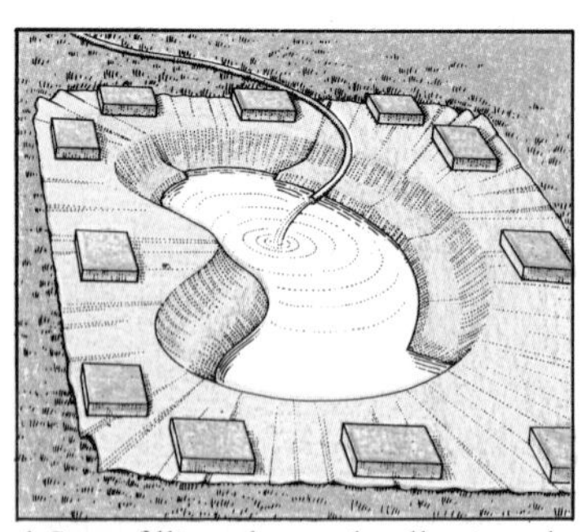
4 *Start filling the pool, allowing the liner to adapt to the shape of the hole*

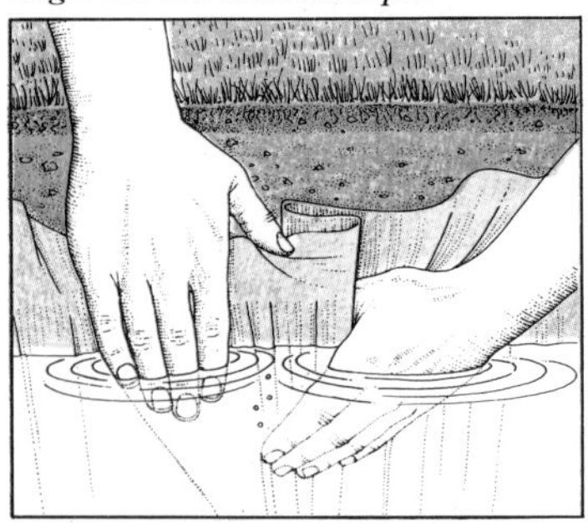
5 *Pleat the liner into shape and add more sand to marginal areas if necessary*

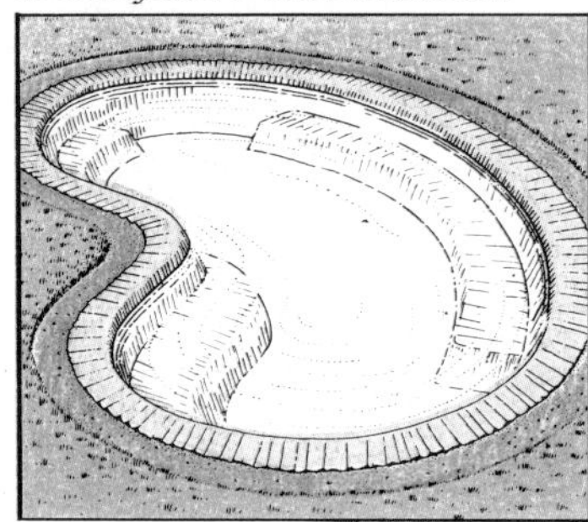
6 *When the pool is full, trim the liner edges leaving a 6 in. overlap*

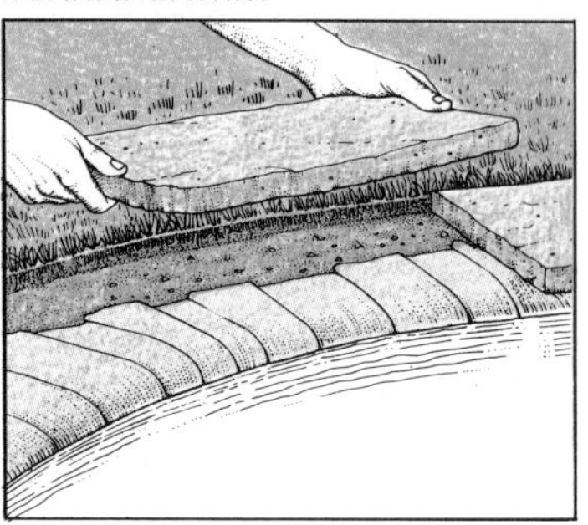
7 *Cover the edges with stones or slabs slightly overlapping the pool*

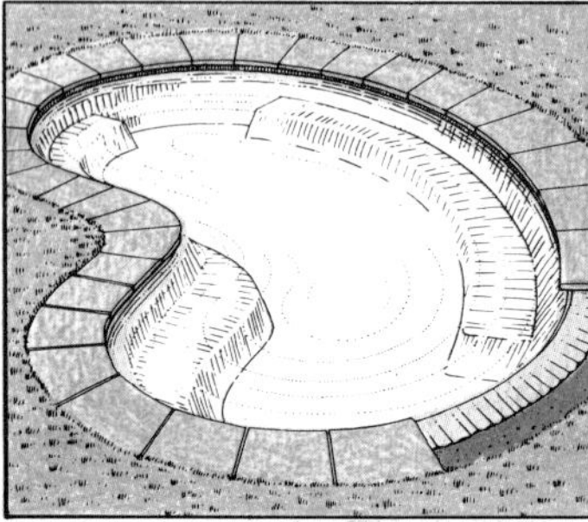
8 *Ensure that no part of the liner is visible when the pool is complete*

Introducing water plants in a pool

Plastic baskets for water lilies

Water lilies (nymphaea) are the main deep-water flowering plants used in most pools. The best way of planting them is in plastic baskets made for the purpose. The baskets make it easier to restrict growth, and reduce the risk of fish stirring up mud.

Water lilies and other deep-water plants can be bought as established plants in containers, and can be put into the pool at any time of the year.

But it is cheaper to buy plants just starting into growth in early spring. In this case you can begin planting towards the end of April, if the weather is reasonably warm. If not, wait until May.

Select a good, heavy loam from the garden and remove all obvious roots from it. Do not introduce any of the organic materials normally used in potting composts, as they will charge the water with mineral salts during their breakdown. This will encourage algae, while toxic substances may be formed which could suffocate the fish in the pool.

Mix sterilised bonemeal into the loam at a rate of one double handful to one bucket of loam, or superphosphate at one handful per bucket. Add enough water so that when a compressed handful is tossed in the air, it falls back in the hand without breaking up into particles.

Line the baskets with clean, coarse hessian or sacking.

If plastic baskets cannot be obtained, drill several $\frac{1}{4}$ in. holes in 10 in. plastic pots.

Alternatively, while the pool is still empty, build brick pockets on the bottom, with spaces between the bricks to allow water to enter, and line the pockets with hessian or clean sacking.

If you decide against using any sort of basket, you can put a 6 in. layer of loam in the bottom of an empty pool, so that plants can be put directly into it. But to prevent fish from stirring up the mud, spread a layer of sand or pea-sized shingle over the loam.

Water lilies with rhizomatous rootstocks, such as *Nymphaea alba*, have sturdy white roots, which are used for anchorage, and thinner hairy roots which are the feeding roots. In April and May, there will also be new leaf shoots growing from the rhizomes. If the nursery has not trimmed the plants, or if they have been damaged in transit, use a sharp knife to cut off dead and broken leaves, and remove the older brown anchorage roots. Cut back the new, white anchorage roots to about $3\frac{1}{2}$–4 in. to fit the containers.

Carry out the same operation with those lilies that have a rootstock of a tuberous kind, such as *N. tuberosa*. These also have thick, fleshy anchorage roots and finer, hairy, feeding roots.

Place lilies with rhizomatous roots horizontally in the partially filled container. Top up with the prepared soil mixture, so that the growing points of the shoots protrude above the surface. Gently lift the plant to allow the loose soil to fill in around the roots.

Plant tuberous types up to the base of the stems, with the roots going straight down into the soil.

Firm the soil with the fingers and, if necessary, add more soil to fill any spaces. Make the soil firm with a section of broomhandle, but do not pack it too tight. Take care not to damage the plant.

If fish are to be placed in the pool, top-dress the container with clean pea-sized shingle. This will stop the fish disturbing the plants, or uprooting them.

Do not immerse newly planted lilies immediately – this may prevent flowering the first season, and the shock may even kill weaker varieties in a cold summer.

Instead, run in enough water to just cover the container. Raise the water level gradually, following the growth of the shoots, until, after six to eight weeks, the pond is full.

If a pond is already filled, place the plants just below the surface, on brick supports, and gradually lower the supports until, after about two months, the plant is finally on the bed of the pool.

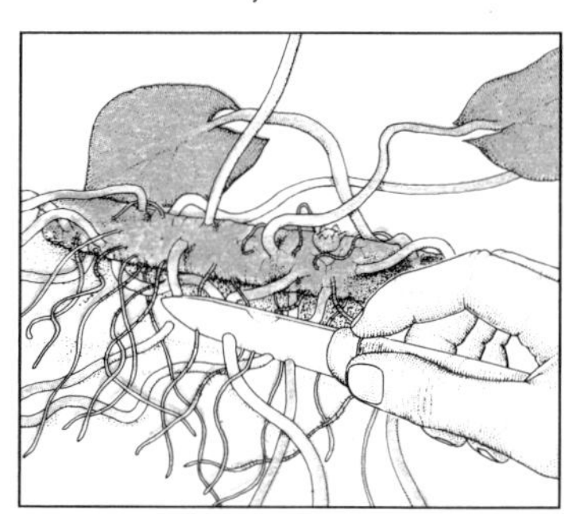

1 *Cut off old brown roots, and trim new white roots to $3\frac{1}{2}$–4 in.*

2 *Plant in containers lined with hessian and partly filled with loam*

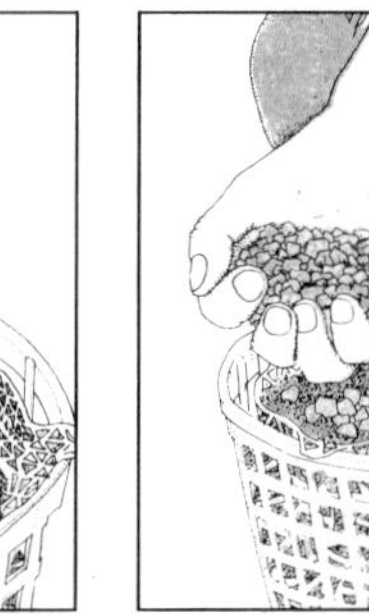

3 *Top-dress with shingle to stop fish uprooting plants*

4 *Fill the pool so that the shingle is just below the water surface*

An annual bonemeal feed for lilies

Water lilies planted in containers will not last indefinitely without the help of artificial feeding. In such a limited amount of soil the roots will soon remove the nourishment from the planting mixture. If they are to survive in good health they will need an annual feed each spring.

Starvation signs are indicated by small, yellowing leaves, meagre blooms and a general lack of vigour. Apart from repotting, the position can be helped by feeding the plants with special bonemeal 'pills'.

Make bonemeal pills by mixing a 3 in. flower pot full of sterilised bonemeal with enough clay to bind it together. Roll this into two round pills. Provide two pills for a large lily, and one for a medium-sized lily. Lift the container from the pond, push the pill into the soil near the roots, and then return the lily to the pond.

Marginal plants for the edge of the pool

Marginals are shallow-water plants that prefer no more than 2–3 in. of water over their roots. Pools should be designed with a shelf around the edge to accommodate them. Alternatively, the containers can be raised on bricks to bring them to the required level.

First remove dead leaves and old brown roots from marginals with a creeping rhizomatous rootstock, such as the bog arum (*Calla palustris*). Plant in a container of a size to match the rootstock, with the rhizome horizontal and exposed.

Pack the soil firmly round the roots with the fingers. Do not pack it too tight.

Cover the surface of the soil with pea-sized shingle, and sink the container so that the roots are covered by about 2–3 in. of water. Do not sink them any deeper.

Marginals with a celery-type root system, such as pickerel weed (*Pontederia cordata*), should have dead and discoloured leaves removed, and any large shoots trimmed back with a sharp knife.

Remove old brown roots, and trim other roots back to about $2\frac{1}{2}$–3 in.

Make a hole in the soil deep enough to plant the marginal so that the soil comes up to the base of the shoots and the roots go straight down into the soil.

Pack the soil very firmly round the plant, add pea-sized shingle to the surface, and sink in water to a depth of 2–3 in.

TWO TYPES OF MARGINALS

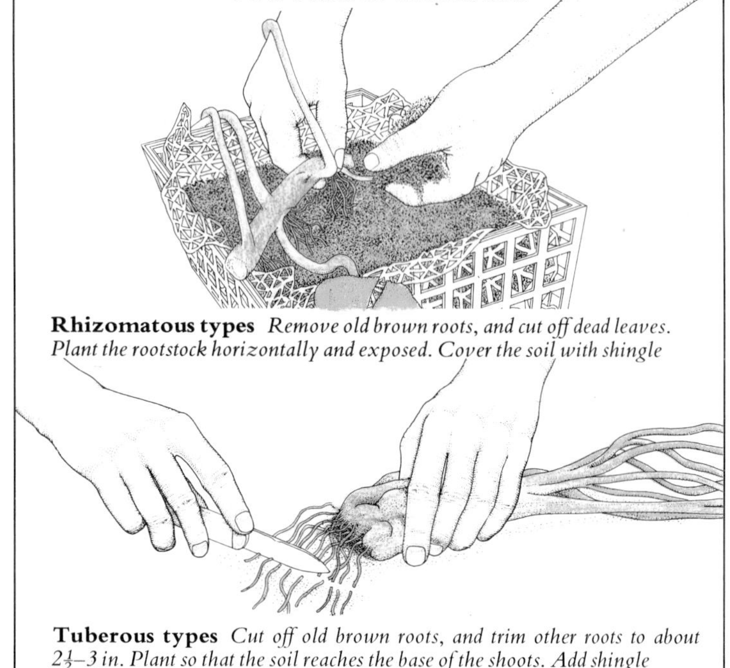

Rhizomatous types *Remove old brown roots, and cut off dead leaves. Plant the rootstock horizontally and exposed. Cover the soil with shingle*

Tuberous types *Cut off old brown roots, and trim other roots to about $2\frac{1}{2}$–3 in. Plant so that the soil reaches the base of the shoots. Add shingle*

Why oxygenators are needed

Oxygenating plants that grow on the bottom of a pool are essential in any water garden. They maintain water clarity by competing with algae for food and light; they supplement the oxygen in the water and use up some of the carbon dioxide exhaled by fish; and they encourage the growth of beneficial microscopic animal life.

They also provide shelter for fish, and somewhere for them to spawn.

Since their rootstocks are small, the oxygenators – such as the Canadian pondweed (*Elodea canadensis*) – need only be weighted with a strip of zinc and dropped in if the bottom of the pool is soil-covered. They are suitable for a water depth of 1–3 ft.

Most of these plants are sold as bunches of unrooted cuttings. Plant one bunch of cuttings for every 2 sq. ft of water surface in pools up to 100 sq. ft in size.

Oxygenators may also be grown in the same way as lilies and marginals – in soil-filled containers.

POOLS WITH SOIL

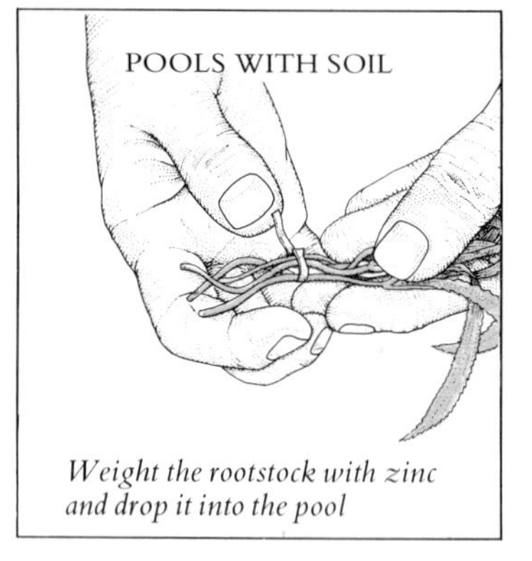

Weight the rootstock with zinc and drop it into the pool

POOLS WITHOUT SOIL

Place in the pool in small soil-filled, perforated containers

Floaters that need no soil

Floating water plants, such as the water soldier (stratiotes), which float under the surface of the pool, are planted simply by placing them in the water. They obtain their nourishment through their trailing roots, which absorb the dissolved nutrient material from the soil containers of other plants in the pool.

Similarly, the water hyacinth (eichhornia), which floats on the surface of the pool, is simply placed in the water, from which its roots will absorb dissolved nutrients. It will also grow in mud.

Water soldier (*stratiotes*)

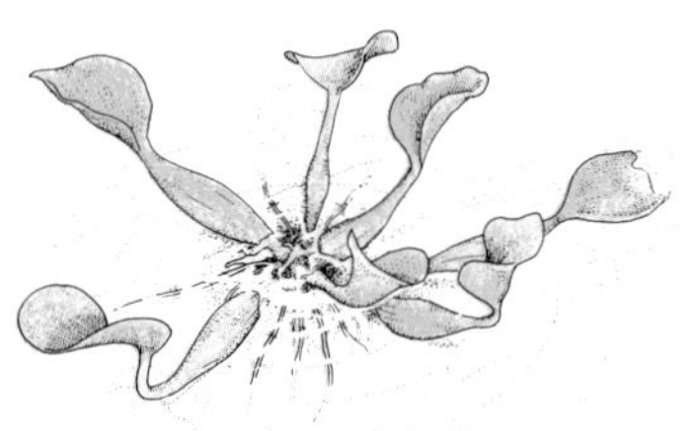

Water hyacinth (*eichhornia*)

Guide to plants and flowers

A selection of plants and bulbs that will give colour to your garden for most of the year – and some that will thrive indoors even in the darkest winter days

All the plants listed here are recommended. Most are at their best in beds or herbaceous borders, but some are more suitable for shrubberies, rock gardens, pools or boggy ground, as indicated in the list.

Perennials can be left in the same spot to flower year after year, although many of them are the better for lifting and dividing every few years. Biennials are sown in spring or summer and planted out in the autumn to flower the following year. Hardy annuals are sown in the open in spring to flower the same year. Half-hardy annuals also flower the same year, but need to be grown in some warmth before planting out when the frosts are over.

Mulching, which is often recommended here, means covering the roots and base of the plant with peat, compost, leaf-mould or manure. The same materials, dug in, make enriched soil. Dead-heading means removing faded flowers to encourage further flowering. A cultivar is a variety of plant created by human cultivation.

The figures in brackets after the name of each plant indicate height and spread. Thus (H2 ft, S9 in.) means a height of 2 ft and a spread of 9 in.

ACANTHUS

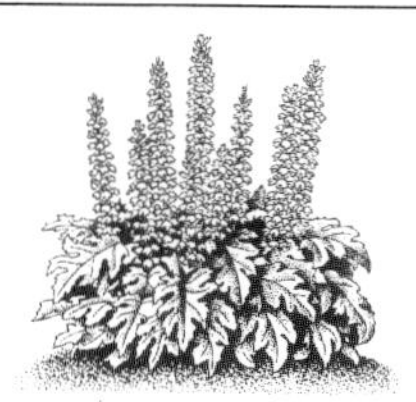

Acanthus mollis

Perennial: Statuesque, long-lived plants with handsome, deeply divided leaves. Tubular flowers in tall spikes above the foliage.
Species *A. mollis* (H3 ft, S2–3 ft), purple or white flowers, July-Aug. *A. spinosus* (H3–4 ft, S3 ft), purple or white flowers, July–Aug.
Planting Singly or in groups of three, Oct.–May, in good, well-drained soil. Mixed or herbaceous borders. Alkaline, dry soils.
Care After flowering, cut stems back almost to ground; avoid root disturbance, and lift and divide only when overcrowded. Mulch in spring.
Propagation By division, Oct.-Mar.; by root-cuttings in spring; by seeds in cold frame, Mar.

ACHILLEA
Yarrow

Perennial: Tall with pungent, fern-like leaves. Flowers in clusters or

Achillea filipendulina

broad, flat heads. Good for cutting. *A. filipendulina* can be dried for winter decoration.
Species *A. filipendulina* 'Gold Plate' (H3–4 ft, S2 ft), plate-like heads of deep yellow flowers, July-Sept. *A. ptarmica* 'Perry's White' (H2–2½ ft, S3 ft), clusters of double, button-shaped white flowers, June–Aug.
Planting In small groups Oct.–Mar. in any well-drained soil, with compost or peat added. Thrives on alkaline soils. In borders or among shrubs.
Care Mulch in late spring. Dead-head. Cut all stems to ground in Nov.
Propagation By division, Oct.–Mar. Poor flowering indicates need for division and feeding.

ACONITE, WINTER
Eranthis

Tuberous perennial: Heart-warming display of bright yellow flowers in Jan.–Mar. Often grown under trees. Associates well with snowdrops.
Species *E. hyemalis* (H4 in., S3 in.), lemon-yellow, Jan.–Feb. *E. × tubergenii* (H4 in., S4 in.), robust hybrid, rich yellow, Mar.
Planting 1 in. deep, Aug.–Sept., in loamy, well-drained soil.
Propagation Divide tubers in late spring and replant at once. Sometimes difficult to establish due to lack of water in spring.

ACONITUM
Monkshood

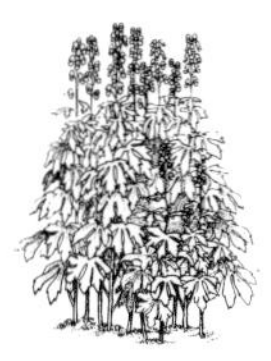

Aconitum napellus

Perennial: Long spikes of hooded flowers, excellent for cutting. All parts of the plant are poisonous.
Species *A. napellus* (H3½ ft, S1½–2 ft), deep blue, July–Aug. 'Bicolor', blue and white; 'Bressingham Spire', violet-blue.
Planting In groups of three to five, Oct.–Mar., in moisture-retentive soil, with compost or peat added. Lightly shaded borders, but will grow in sun if soil does not dry out.
Care Mulch in late spring, and water in dry spells. Cut back flowering parts of stems when flowers fade. Cut all stems to ground in Oct. Stunted growth probably due to too dry, sunny site; replant in moist, shady spot.
Propagation By division, Oct.–Mar., or by seeds sown in cold frame Mar.–April.

ADIANTUM

Fern: Deciduous, hardy plant, suitable for rock gardens, shrub borders and under trees.
Species *A. pedatum* (N. American maidenhair fern) (H18 in., S18 in.), for neutral soil. *A. venustum* (H9 in., S2 ft), for any soil.
Planting In light shade.
Propagation Division or spores.

AETHIONEMA

Aethionema pulchellum

Spreading sub-shrub: Good rock-garden plants with freely produced pink flowers.

Agapanthus – Anchusa

Species *A. pulchellum* (H6–9 in., S15 in.), dark pink, May–July. *A.* × 'Warley Rose' (H4–6 in., S15 in.), deep rose-pink, April–May.
Planting In sunny site, well-drained soil. Dry wall, scree, trough, alpine house.
Propagation Seeds in cold frame or greenhouse in Mar. Cuttings of non-flowering shoots in cold frame, June–July. Seedlings must be over-wintered in pots and may take two years to reach flowering size.

AGAPANTHUS
African lily

Agapanthus orientalis

Perennial: Evergreen plant, fully hardy only in South and West. Trumpet-shaped flowers on long stems are good for cutting. Seed heads are dried for winter decoration.
Species *A. orientalis* and 'Headbourne Hybrids' (H2–2½ ft, S2–2½ ft), light blue to violet-blue and white, July–Sept.
Planting In groups of three or more in April. Well-drained soil with manure, compost or peat. Sheltered spot required, preferably at foot of south or west-facing wall.
Care Mulch in late spring. Water freely in dry spells. Cut stems to ground after flowering unless seed heads required. In all but mildest areas protect against frost, late Oct.–April, with 6–9 in. layer of bracken, sand or ashes.
Propagation By division, April–May. Dividing necessary to improve flowers on older plants. By seeds, sown in cold frame or cold greenhouse in Mar.–April.

AGERATUM

Ageratum

Half-hardy annual: Widely grown for edging. Mainly blue flowers like powder puffs.
Species *A. houstonianum* (H3–9 in., S6–9 in.), 'Blue Chip', 'Blue Blazer', 'Blue Angel', various shades of blue; 'Summer Snow', white; 'Fairy Pink', salmon-rose. June until frosts.
Planting Sunny, sheltered position. Moist but not wet soil.
Care Dead-head.
Propagation Sow Mar.–April, 16°C (61°F).

Althaea see Hollyhock

ALYSSUM, SWEET

Alyssum

Hardy annual: Well-established favourite for edging and growing between paving, in rock gardens and in stone walls.
Species *Lobularia maritima* (H3–4 in., S12 in.), 'Little Dorrit', white; 'Rosie O'Day', pink; 'Lilac Queen', deep lilac; 'Oriental Night', purple, June–Sept.
Planting Sow outdoors April–May and plant out in ordinary, well-drained soil. Full sun.

ALYSSUM
Gold dust

Perennial bedding and rock plant: Sprawling, shrubby plant, producing mass of striking yellow in late spring.
Species *A. saxatile* (H9–12 in., S12–18 in.), April–June.
Planting Well-drained, sunny site. End of bed, top of dry wall, paving, rock garden.
Propagation 2–3 in. cuttings of non-flowering shoots inserted in peat/sand (50/50) in cold frame in June.

AMARANTHUS
Joseph's coat

Half-hardy annual: Foliage plant mainly grown for its scarlet or crimson leaves overlaid with bronze or green. Not suited to cold or exposed areas.
Species *A. tricolor* (H1½–3 ft, S12–18 in.).
Planting Singly, to give height to bedding schemes, in moist but not wet soil enriched with compost or manure. Sunny position. Take care to avoid root disturbance when transplanting.
Propagation Sow in Mar., 15°C (59°F).

ANAGALLIS
Pimpernel

Half-hardy annual: Compact plant smothered with gentian-blue or red flowers. Suitable for edging borders and for rock gardens. Makes attractive winter pot plant.
Species *A. linifolia* (H6 in., S12 in.), 'Phillipsii' and *A. monelli*, blue; *A. arvensis* 'Mixed', June–Sept.
Planting In well-drained soil. Full sun.
Propagation Mar.–April, 16°C (61°F). On a warm site, anagallis may seed itself from year to year.

ANAPHALIS

Anaphalis triplinervis

Perennial: Grown for its silvery or grey foliage and flat, clustered, pearly white flower heads. Good for cutting or for dried winter arrangements.
Species *A. triplinervis* (H12 in., S18 in. or more), white flowers, Aug.
Planting In groups, Sept.–April, in any well-drained soil. Sunny place to front of borders.
Care Mulch in late spring. Cut all stems to ground in late autumn.
Propagation By division, Sept.–April. Spread by underground rhizomes may have to be checked by lifting plant and cutting back before replanting. Alternatively, contain root system with vertical slates, tiles, etc.

ANCHUSA

Biennial and perennial: Species described is excellent in groups at back of borders.

Androsace – Aquilegia

Anchusa azurea

Species *A. azurea* (H3–5 ft, S12–18 in.), bright blue, June–Aug. 'Loddon Royalist', gentian-blue; 'Opal', sky-blue.
Planting Oct.–Mar., in sunny position. Fertile, well-drained soil.
Care Mulch in late spring. Support with canes. Remove faded flower sprays. Cut stems to ground in autumn. If ground becomes water-logged, transplant or dig in sand or ashes.
Propagation By root cuttings or division in Mar.

ANDROSACE
Rock jasmine

Perennial rock plant: Attractive, ground-hugging dwarfs in pinks and white.
Species *A. chamaejasme* (H1–2 in., S6 in.), white, June. *A. helvetica* (H2 in., S4–6 in.), white, April–May. *A. lanuginosa* (H1½ in., S12–18 in.), pink, white, June–Oct. *A. sarmentosa* (H4 in., S up to 2 ft), rose-pink, April–June. *A. sempervivoides* (H2 in., S9–12 in.), bright pink, May–June.
Planting In sharply drained soil, preferably with rock chippings, in sun or light shade. Scree, dry wall, trough, alpine house. *A. helvetica*, alpine house or frame only. *A. lanuginosa*, also level bed or rock garden.
Propagation Sow seeds in Jan.–Feb., allow to freeze and bring in to 7°C (45°F). Detach rosettes in June and insert in sand in a cold frame. For *A. lanuginosa* take 2 in. basal shoots and treat as for rosettes.

ANEMONE

Anemone coronaria De Caen

Perennial: Cheerful flowers on stems 6–12 in. high, ideal for cutting.
Species *A. blanda* (H6 in., S4 in.), white and pastel shades of blue and mauve-pink, Feb.–April. *A. coronaria* (including single De Caen and double or semi-double St Brigid anemones) (H6–12 in., S4–6 in.), crimson, scarlet, pink, lavender, mauve and white. By successive planting will flower Feb.–Oct.
Planting 2 in. deep in any well-drained soil. Sun or light shade. *A. blanda*, plant early autumn. *A. coronaria*, Nov.–April.
Care Apply nitrogen fertiliser to *A. coronaria* as buds appear and protect with cloches in winter.
Propagation *A. blanda*, by offsets or division of rhizomes in late summer. *A. coronaria*, lift and divide every two years.

ANTHEMIS
Chamomile

Anthemis tinctoria

Perennial: Easily grown plant with yellow or white daisy-like flowers. It tends to sprawl. *Anthemis nobilis* can form a small, fragrant lawn.
Species *A. nobilis* (Common chamomile) (H6–9 in., S12–15 in.). 'Treneague', non-flowering, good as a lawn. *A. tinctoria* hybrids for beds (H2½ ft, S1½–2 ft), 'E. C. Buxton', deep yellow; 'Wargrave', cream, June–Aug.
Planting In groups Sept.–Mar. in well-drained soil. Likes a sunny place and thrives at seaside.
Care Mulch in late spring and support with pea-sticks on windy sites. Dead-head regularly and cut flowering stems to ground in Oct.
Propagation By division, Sept.–Mar.; by cuttings of basal shoots, April.

ANTIRRHINUM
Snapdragon

Antirrhinum

Half-hardy annual: Justly one of the most popular flowers, bearing tall spikes of blooms in many beautiful colours from July to the frosts. If flowers are squeezed, they open like the jaws of a dragon.
Species *A. majus* and its hybrids in a dazzling range from 'Tom Thumb' (H6 in.) to 'Maximum' (H3–4 ft). Dwarf (H up to 12 in.), 'Floral Carpet', mixed; 'Pixie', mixed; 'Sweetheart', mixed, double flowers; 'Little Darling' and 'Wedding Bells', mixed, with open penstemon-like flowers. Medium (H up to 2 ft), 'Coronette', sturdy, mixed colours; 'Fantasy', mixed, including rust-resistant cultivars. Tall (H up to 4 ft), 'Rocket' and 'Madame Butterfly', mixed.
Planting Sow Feb.–Mar., 16°C (61°F). Plant out, when frost danger over, in any soil in open, sunny position.
Care Pinch out centres to encourage bushy habit. Dead-head to prolong flowering. Tall cultivars may need staking in positions exposed to wind. For best results dig in well-rotted manure.

AQUILEGIA
Columbine

Aquilegia vulgaris

Perennial: Colourful and graceful plants for the border. The flowers have a funnel-shaped centre and prominent spurs; good for cutting. The leaves are grey-green and fern-like.
Species *A. vulgaris* (H3 ft, S12–18 in.), short-spurred, blue, pink, white flowers, May–June. 'McKana Hybrids', long-spurred, white, cream, yellow, pink, red, blue.
Planting In groups of six or more, Sept.–Mar., in any fertile, well-drained but moist soil. Thrives on alkaline soil. Sunny or shady borders.
Care Mulch in late spring and water during dry spells. Dead-head. Cut stems to ground after flowering. Spray with systemic insecticide if aphids appear.
Propagation By division Oct.–Mar. or by seeds sown in cold frame or open ground in April. Self-sown seedlings usually differ from parents.

Arctotis–Astilbe

ARCTOTIS
African daisy

Arctotis

Half-hardy annual: Big, daisy-like flowers in brilliant colours are borne on long stems from July to autumn. Flowers close in the afternoon and in dull weather.
Species *A. × hybrida* (H1½–2 ft, S12 in.), *A. s. grandis*, white, cream, primrose, buff, around blue discs; 'Large-flowered Hybrids', mixed.
Planting Sow Mar., 18°C (64°F). Plant out in open sunny position. Medium soil.
Care Pinch out centres of plants when 5 in. high to encourage bushy habit. Support with twiggy sticks. Dead-head.

ARMERIA
Thrift

Armeria maritima

Evergreen perennial: Suitable for front of borders and rock gardens. Masses of small, globular, pink flower heads.
Species *A. caespitosa* (H1–3 in., S6–9 in.), May. *A. maritima* (H6–12 in., S12 in.), May–July.
Planting Well-drained soil in sunny position; dry wall, scree. *A. caespitosa* also in trough or alpine house.
Propagation 2 in. basal cuttings in peat/sand, in cold frame, July–Sept.

ARTEMISIA

Artemisia ludoviciana

Perennial: Chiefly grown for its silvery-grey, feathery and/or aromatic foliage. The plants described have long flower plumes, which can be dried for winter decoration. Excellent background in mixed borders.
Species *A. lactiflora* (H4–5 ft, S1–2 ft), cream-white flowers, Aug.–Sept. *A. ludoviciana* (H2–4 ft, S15–18 in.), off-white flowers, Sept.–Oct.
Planting In small groups, Oct.–Mar., in any well-drained but moisture-retentive soil. Sun or partial shade.
Care Mulch with compost or peat in late spring. Cut plants back almost to ground level in autumn. If growth is stunted, water thoroughly before mulching.
Propagation By division, Oct.–Mar.

Arum lily see Zantedeschia

ARUNCUS

Perennial: Graceful, damp-soil plants with attractive leaves made up of several small leaflets. Long, fluffy flower clusters rise above foliage. Especially effective at margins of pools.
Species *A. sylvester* (H4–6 ft, S2–2½ ft), long plumes of cream-white flowers, June–July.
Planting In groups, Oct.–Mar., in loamy, moist soil. Partial shade.
Care Mulch in late spring and water freely in dry spells. Cut stems to ground level in autumn.
Propagation By division in Oct. or spring.

ASTER

Aster

Half-hardy annual: One of the most delightful late-summer and autumn flowers with chrysanthemum-like blooms.
Species *Callistephus chinensis.* The type plant has been replaced by numerous named cultivars, mainly sold in mixed colours. Dwarf (H up to 10 in.), 'Colour Carpet', mixed; 'Dwarf Queen', mixed; 'Thousand Wonders', mixed. Tall (H up to 2½ ft), 'Super Sinensis', mixed, with big almost single flowers; 'Ostrich Plume', 'Californian Giant', 'Powder Puff', 'Giant Comet', 'Totem Pole', all double mixed.
Planting Sow Mar.–April, 16°C (61°F), and plant out after frosts in sunny, well-drained position. In warm areas, seeds can be sown outdoors in April. To avoid aster wilt, do not plant successive years in same bed.
Care Bigger, taller cultivars may need staking. Dead-head to obtain more flowers.

ASTER
Michaelmas daisy

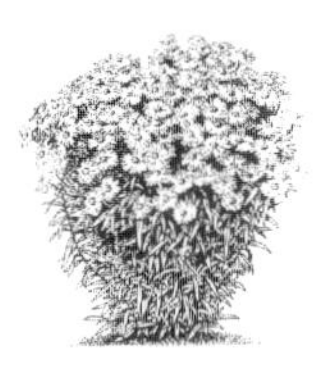
Aster novi-belgii

Perennial: A large group of plants with a wide range of colour. All have daisy-like flowers and are excellent and long-lasting when cut.
Species *A. amellus* (H1½–2 ft, S1½–2 ft), 'King George', violet; 'Sonia', pink, Aug.–Sept. *A. novae-angliae* (H4–5 ft, S18 in.), 'Lye End Beauty', blue; 'September Ruby', crimson, Sept.–Oct. *A. novi-belgii* (H1–4½ ft, S12 in.), 'Audrey', semi-double, blue; 'Orlando', semi-double, pink, Sept.–Oct.
Planting In groups Oct.–Mar. in any well-drained soil open to sun.
Care Mulch annually in late spring and water freely, particularly in late summer. Support tall types with canes. Dead-head regularly and cut stems to ground level after flowering. Many cultivars are prone to mildew and should be treated periodically with fungicide spray. Poor flowers may indicate presence of tarsonemid mites and need for division every two years.
Propagation By division, Oct.–Mar. Replant only outer parts of the clump.

ASTILBE

Perennial: Graceful plants with deeply cut, dark green and often copper-tinted foliage. Elegant plumes of dainty flowers, suitable for cutting and drying.
Species *A. × arendsii* (H2–3 ft,

Athyrium–Bluebell

Astilbe × arendsii

S1–2 ft), feathery plumes, 12–15 in. high, white, pink, red, June–Aug.
Planting In groups, Oct.–Mar., in moist, fertile soil. Sunny or shady borders or the margins of pools with bog plants like irises and primulas.
Care Mulch in late spring and water freely in dry weather. Poor growth is usually caused by inadequate moisture. Cut stems to ground level in autumn.
Propagation By division, Mar.–April. Divide every three years in spring, discarding old centre of clump.

ATHYRIUM
Lady fern

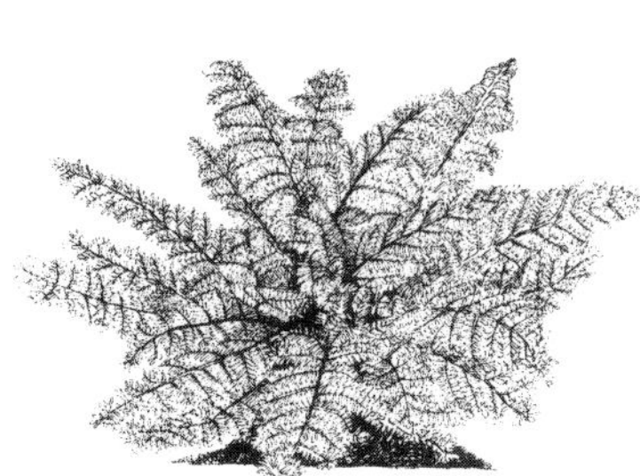

Athyrium filix-femina

Deciduous fern: Called 'lady' because of its dainty, fresh green fronds. But this is a very hardy plant.
Species *A. filix-femina* (H1½–3 ft, S2–3 ft). Several cultivars, all suitable for shady gardens.
Planting In ordinary, moderately moist soil. Light shade, cool position.
Propagation By division or spores. (Cultivars by division only.)

AUBRIETA

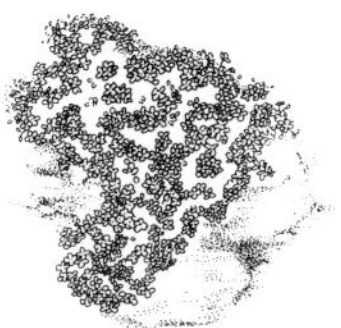

Aubrieta deltoidea

Perennial rock plant: Low-growing, hardy evergreen that brings gaudy splashes of purple to spring gardens.
Species *A. deltoidea* (H3–4 in., S1½–2 ft), 'Barker's Double', rose-purple, double; 'Dr Mules', violet-purple; 'Godstone', bright purple; 'Gurgedyke', bright purple; 'Magician', red-purple, Mar.–June.
Planting In well-drained, limy soil in full sun. Dry wall, paving.
Care After flowering, cut back rock-garden plants to encourage neat habit of growth, but do no more than remove old flowering stems from plants trailing over dry walls.
Propagation By seeds in cold frame, Feb.–Mar. By 2 in. basal cuttings in summer.

Autumn crocus see Colchicum and Crocus

BEGONIA

Begonia

Grown as half-hardy annual: The perennial, fibrous-rooted begonia produces a mass of small flowers from June to autumn, quite unlike the big, fleshy blooms of the tuberous sorts. Plants potted from the garden in autumn will continue to flower in a sunny window.
Species *B. semperflorens* (H6–18 in., S6–15 in.), in many shades of red and pink and in white with bright green, copper or purple-flushed leaves.
Planting Sow Jan.–Feb., 16°C (61°F). Plant out in rich, moist soil. Partial shade.

BELLIS

Bellis

Biennial: Giant or double forms of the common daisy make attractive plants for edging, and with spring bulbs. Flowering in spring and early summer. Useful in window-boxes.
Species *B. perennis* (H4–6 in., S3–6 in.), 'Fairy Carpet', rose and white; 'Pomponette', mixed; 'Super Enorma', mixed.
Planting Sow May–June. Any fertile soil. Sun or partial shade.
Care Dead-head regularly.

BERGENIA

Perennial: Evergreen plants thriving on all soils. Leathery leaves often turn red in autumn. Flower sprays rise above foliage.
Species *B. cordifolia* (H12 in., S18 in.), drooping heads of pink-purple flowers, Mar.–April. *B. crassifolia* (H12 in., S18 in.), pale pink, Dec.–April. *B.* × 'Ballawley' (H18 in., S2 ft), bright red, April–May. *B.* × 'Silberlicht' (H12–15 in., S15 in.), white, flushed pink, April–May. Leaves may turn red-bronze in autumn.
Planting Oct.–Mar. in any well-drained soil to front of borders. Excellent ground-cover for shrubs and trees. Thrives in alkaline soil.
Care Mulch in late spring. Remove faded flower stems. If brown spots occur, due to fungus, spray with captan or zineb and give foliar feed once fortnightly, April–Sept. Poor growth and flowers usually due to inadequate moisture at roots.
Propagation By division of rhizomes after flowering or in Sept.–Oct. But leave undisturbed as long as possible, dividing only when overcrowded.

BLUEBELL
Endymion

Endymion hispanicus

Bulbous plant: Good for naturalising under trees and in woodland.
Species *E. hispanicus* (Giant bluebell) (H12 in., S6 in.), deep and clear blue. 'Mount Everest', white; 'Myosotis', sky blue; 'Queen of the Pinks', deep pink, April–June.
E. nonscriptus (English bluebell: Wild hyacinth in Scotland) (H12 in., S4 in.), purple-blue, April–June.
Planting 4 in. deep in rich, moist soil, late summer or early autumn. Sun or light shade.
Propagation Multiplies by self-sown seedlings. Can be divided after leaves have withered.

Bulrush–Carnation

BULRUSH
Scirpus

Tall rushes for margins of ponds or streams.
Species *S. lacustris* (H3–4 ft), red-brown spikelets, July–Aug. Invasive: best in deep or running water.
Planting In water 6–18 in. deep.
Propagation By division.

BUSY LIZZIE
Impatiens

Impatiens

Half-hardy annual: Popular pot-plant that grows well in shady spots in garden. Profusion of spurred blooms, June to autumn.
Species *I. balsamina* and hybrids (H6–15 in., S6–15 in.), in wide selection of shades of red, pink, orange and purple, some striped with white. The new hybrids are especially good.
Planting Sow Mar.–April, 16°C (61°F), in sun or partial shade. Harden off slowly to avoid damage to plants.

Calendula see Marigold

CALLA
Bog arum

Perennial: Attractive, flowering plant for growth in wet mud, ideal for masking edge of pool. Pollinated by snails.
Species *C. palustris* (H6–9 in.), white arum-lily-like flowers, June; red berries later.
Planting Mud to 6 in.
Propagation By division.

Callistephus see Aster

CAMPANULA
Canterbury bell

Canterbury bell

Biennial: Sturdy, upright plant with big, bell-shaped flowers.
Species *C. medium* (H15 in.–3 ft, S12 in.), May–June. 'Bells of Holland', mixed pink, blue, white, mauve; 'Cup and Saucer' (semi-double), pink, blue, white or mixed.
Planting Sow April–June. Plant out in well-drained soil in sunny position.
Care Dead-head regularly. Support taller cultivars in exposed sites.

CAMPANULA
Bellflower

Perennial: A large group of popular border plants with erect, leafy stems carrying bell-shaped flowers. Those described are good as cut flowers.
Species *C. lactiflora* (H3–5 ft, S18 in.), white, pale pink, blue flowers, June–Sept. *C. latifolia* (H4–5 ft, S1½–2 ft), white, blue, purple, in spikes, June–Aug. *C. persicifolia* (H2–3 ft, S12–18 in.), evergreen, white, blue, purple flowers, June–Aug.

Campanula persicifolia

Planting In well-drained soil, preferably with decayed manure or compost, in groups of about six, Oct.–Mar. Sunny or lightly shaded borders or among shrubs.
Care Mulch in late spring. Support with pea-sticks on exposed sites. Dead-head regularly. If brown or black spots on leaves show rust infection, remove affected leaves and spray with thiram or zineb every two weeks.
Propagation By division Oct.–April or by basal cuttings in April–May. *C. persicifolia* spreads quickly and produces poor flowers unless divided and replanted every three years.

CAMPANULA

Perennial rock plant: Also used in front of borders.
Species *C. arvatica* (H2 in., S12 in.), blue, July. *C. barbata* (H3–18 in., S6–12 in.), purple to white, June. *C. carpatica* (H9–12 in., S12–15 in.), blue, purple, white, July–Aug. *C. cochlearifolia* (syn. *C. pusilla*), (H4–6 in., S12 in.), blue, white, July–Sept. *C. garganica* (H5–6 in., S12 in.), blue, May–Sept. *C. pulla* (H3–4 in., S9–12 in.), rich purple, June.
Planting In well-drained soil–gritty for *C. arvatica*–sunny site. Dry wall, scree, paving, trough, alpine house.
Propagation By seeds in cold frame Oct.–Mar. or April; by division Mar.–April; cuttings of non-flowering basal shoots in peat/sand April–May.

CANDYTUFT
Iberis

Candytuft

Hardy annual: Quick-growing edging plant, easily grown in towns as it tolerates polluted atmosphere. Roughly cross-shaped flowers borne in broad clusters.
Species *I. amara* (H15 in., S6 in.), white, pink, red-purple. 'Giant Hyacinth-Flowered White', dense racemes, June–Aug. *I. umbellata* (H9–18 in., S6–18 in.), 'Fairy Mixed', mixed; 'Red Flash', carmine; 'Rose Cardinal', mixed, June–Aug.
Planting Sunny position. Poor soil acceptable.
Care Dead-head regularly.
Propagation Sow Mar.–May or Sept.

Canterbury bell see Campanula

CARNATION

Half-hardy annual/perennial: Although perennial, carnations grown from seeds produce their double, scented flowers the same year. Plants lifted from garden in autumn will continue to flower in

Catananche – Cimicifuga

Carnation

pots in sunny window. Not recommended for cold areas in North.
Species *Dianthus caryophyllus* (H12 in.–2 ft, S12 in.), pink, red, yellow, purple, white, July–Sept.
Planting Sunny position in borders or pots. Ordinary, well-drained soil with added manure or compost and general fertiliser.
Care Stake tall plants. Disbud flower stems in June.
Propagation Sow in Jan.–Feb., 15°C (59°F).

CATANANCHE

Perennial: Cornflower-like plants with slender leaves. Excellent for cutting and drying.
Species *C. caerulea* (H1½–2½ ft, S12–18 in.), purple-blue, lavender or white, June–Sept.
Planting In groups, Sept.–April, in light, well-drained soil. On heavy soils plants seldom last more than two years. Full sun essential.
Care Mulch in late spring. Support with pea-sticks. Cut flower stems to ground in autumn.
Propagation By root cuttings in Mar. or by seeds sown in cold frame in April. Seedlings raised in warmth in Feb. and hardened off in cold frame will flower same year.

CELOSIA

Half-hardy annual: Spectacular bedding plant with flowers standing erect in plumed or crested heads. Tall cultivars useful for cutting.
Species *C. argentea* Plumosa, 'Golden Feather', rich yellow; 'Fire Feather', red; 'Fairy Fountains', mixed. *C. argentea* Cristata, 'Chanticleer', mixed; 'Jewel Box', mixed. Both species (H9 in.–3 ft, S9–12 in.).
Planting Sheltered, sunny position in rich soil.
Propagation Sow Mar.–April, 18°C (64°F). Ensure seedlings are hardened off and frost danger over before planting out.

CENTAUREA

Perennial: Cornflower-like blooms, good as cut flowers.
Species *C. dealbata* (H1½–2 ft, S12–18 in.), pink, June–July and again in autumn. *C. macrocephala* (H3–5 ft, S12 in.), yellow, July–Sept. *C. montana* (H1½–2 ft, S12–18 in.), white, pink, purple, May–July.
Planting In groups Oct.–Mar. in any good, well-drained soil. Sun or light shade.
Care Mulch in late spring with compost. Support tall species with pea-sticks. Dead-head. Cut all stems to ground in autumn. If infected with powdery mildew, spray fortnightly with dinocap, benomyl or thiophanate-methyl.
Propagation By division Oct.–Mar. Lift and divide every three or four years.

Cheiranthus see Wallflower

CHINESE LANTERN
Physalis

Perennial: Easily grown, unspectacular, white flowers which develop into papery, orange-red 'lanterns' in autumn. Excellent for

Physalis franchetii

dried winter arrangements.
Species *P. franchetti* (H2–2½ ft, S3 ft), July–Aug.
Planting Singly or in groups of three, in ordinary, well-drained soil. Sandy or chalky soils need compost or peat. Sun or partial shade. Best in informal or wild gardens, as rather invasive.
Care Mulch in spring. Water in dry spells. Cut 'lantern' stems for drying in Sept., and cut down other stems to ground in autumn. To prevent creeping roots invading other beds, dig round crowns in autumn and remove severed root pieces, or surround with slates buried vertically.
Propagation By division, Oct.–Mar.

CHRYSANTHEMUM, ANNUAL

Chrysanthemum

Hardy annual: Daisy-like flowers, often with distinct concentric zones of contrasting colours making surprising patterns.
Species *C. carinatum* (syn. *C. tricolor*), *C. coronarium* (H9 in.–2ft, S9–12 in.), June–Sept. 'Double Gaiety', mixed (scarlet, orange, rose, pink); 'Cecilia', yellow, white; 'Monarch Court Jester', mixed; 'Catherine Wheels', mixed.
Planting Sunny position. Light well-drained soil. Excellent for mixed borders where the rich colours stand out well.
Care Pinch out young plants grown for cutting to encourage long-stemmed side-shoots.
Propagation Sow Mar.–April. For flowers in spring and early summer, sow in autumn in cold greenhouse and pot seedlings.

Chrysanthemum, *border and greenhouse*, see p. 60

CIMICIFUGA
Bugbane

Cimicifuga foetida

Perennial: Tall, graceful and slow-growing plant with fern-like leaves for moist, shady spots. Plume-like flower-spikes are good for cutting.
Species *C. americana* (H3–4 ft, S12–18 in.), cream-white, Aug.–Sept. *C. foetida* (H4–5 ft, S1½–2 ft), drooping spikes of starry cream or white flowers, July–Aug.
Planting Plant singly or in groups of three or four in deep, moist soil enriched with compost, manure or leaf-mould. Light shade, at back of borders or among trees and shrubs.
Care Mulch with compost or leaf-mould in Mar. Support with canes in exposed sites. Cut stems to ground in autumn. Stunted growth and small flower spikes likely on shallow, dry soils. Transplant to moist, shady site.
Propagation By division, Oct.–Mar. But plants should be left undisturbed for several years.

Cineraria maritima–Crocus

CINERARIA MARITIMA

Half-hardy annual: An almost hardy shrub, grown as an annual for its silvery foliage.
Species *Senecio maritima* (H9–12 in., S12 in.), yellow flowers, July–Sept.
Planting Sunny position in any ordinary soil. Very wind-firm, especially by the sea.
Propagation Sow Feb.–Mar., 16°C (61°F).

CLARKIA

Clarkia

Hardy annual: Popular and easily grown, with flowers on long spikes.
Species *C. elegans*, *C. pulchella* (H1½–2 ft, S12 in.), red, pink, purple, white. Flowering early summer onwards.
Planting Sunny position. Medium to light, slightly acid soil.
Care Avoid heavy feeding which encourages leaf growth. Support with short pieces of brushwood.
Propagation Sow in open, Mar.–April.

COLCHICUM
Autumn crocus

Bulbous plant: For display from Sept. to Nov., under light tree cover and among shrubs or grass.
Species *C. autumnale* (H6 in., S9 in.), rose-lilac, single, double, Sept.–Nov. *C. speciosum* (H6–10 in., S9–12 in.), rose-purple, white, purple veined, Oct.–Nov.
Planting In any well-drained soil, July–Aug. Sun or partial shade. *C. autumnale*, 3–4 in. deep; *C. speciosum*, 4–6 in. deep.
Propagation Separate corms in June–July and replant at once.

COREOPSIS
Calliopsis

Hardy annual: Free-flowering bushy plant with daisy-like flowers, good for cutting.
Species *C. drummondii* (H2 ft, S12 in.), yellow or crimson, July–Sept.
Planting Sunny position in fertile, well-drained soil.
Care Cut back early-sown plants after flowering to encourage second flush. Tall plants need staking.
Propagation Sow in open, Mar.–June.

COREOPSIS

Coreopsis grandiflora

Perennial: Popular border plant, free-flowering over long period. The big, daisy-like flowers are good for cutting.
Species *C. grandiflora* (H12–18 in., S18 in.), bright yellow, June–Sept. *C. verticillata* (H1½–2 ft, S18 in.), clear yellow, June–Sept.
Planting In groups in light, fertile and well-drained soil. Full sun.
Care Mulch lightly in late spring, and water freely during dry spells. Support with pea-sticks in exposed sites. Cut back stems after flowering and cut down to ground in autumn.
Propagation By division Oct.–Mar., or by seeds in cold frame or on flowering site Mar.–April. *C. grandiflora* often deteriorates after two seasons, but seeds itself freely.

CORNFLOWER

Cornflower

Hardy annual: Easy-to-grow flowers in blue, pink, red, purple and white. There are two sizes of plant, tall and dwarf.
Species *Centaurea cyanus*, Tall (H3 ft, S2 ft), 'Blue Diadem', blue; and Ball strains, various colours. Dwarf (H12 in., S9 in.), 'Rose Gem', red; 'Jubilee Gem', blue; 'Polka Dot', mixed, June–Sept.
Planting Sunny position in any fertile, well-drained soil.
Care Dead-head. Support with twiggy sticks in windy positions.
Propagation Sow in open, April–May.

Cortaderia see Pampas grass

COSMOS
Cosmea

Half-hardy annual: Showy plant with filigree foliage and bearing

Cosmos

many flowers, like single dahlias, from late summer onwards. Excellent for cutting. Best results in warm, dry seasons.
Species *C. bipinnatus*, *C. sulphureus* (H1½–3 ft, S1½–2 ft), 'Sunset', orange-red; 'Bright Lights', scarlet, orange, yellow; 'Sensation', mixed, Aug.–Sept.
Planting Sunny position in light, well-drained soil, not recently manured.
Care Avoid over-rich soil, which produces too much foliage. Dead-head.
Propagation Sow Feb.–Mar., 16°C (61°F), or outdoors as hardy annual in April–May in mild areas.

Crocosmia see Montbretia

CROCUS

Crocus (Spring flowering)

Bulbous plant: Remarkable range of species, flowering in the open between Aug. and April. They thrive in rough grass, at the edge of borders, between shrubs and beneath small, deciduous trees. Ideal for rock gardens.
Species
WINTER FLOWERING *C. chrysanthus* and hybrids (H3 in., S3 in.), white,

Cynoglossum – Dictamnus

golden-yellow, mauve, blue, bronze, some striped with contrasting colours, flowering Feb. Large-flowered cultivars, such as 'Blue Pearl', pale blue and white; 'E. A. Bowles', rich yellow and bronze; 'Snow Bunting', white, purple and orange; *C. tomasinianus* 'Whitewell Purple', purple-blue, all excellent for indoor pot cultivation.
SPRING FLOWERING *C. vernus* (H4–5 in., S4 in.), white, lavender, blue, silvery-white, red-purple, with stripes, flowering Mar. 'Little Dorrit', pale lilac; 'Queen of the Blues', lavender blue; 'Negro Boy', red-purple; 'Snowstorm', white; 'Striped Beauty', silver and mauve; *C. aureus* 'Yellow Giant', yellow.
AUTUMN FLOWERING *C. speciosus* (H4–5 in., S3–4 in.), lilac-blue, rose, white, lavender, flowering Oct. 'Albus', pure white; 'Artabir', pale blue striped with dark blue.
Planting In any well-drained soil in a sunny position, 2–3 in. deep. Plant autumn-flowering sorts in Aug.–Sept.; others in Sept.–Nov.
Propagation Lift when leaves turn brown and replant corms at once, the biggest in permanent sites. Replant smaller cormlets in spare ground for about two years to reach flowering size.

CYNOGLOSSUM

Perennial: Long-lived, clump-forming plant with intensely blue forget-me-not-like flowers.
Species *C. nervosum* (H1½–2 ft, S12–18 in.), flowering June–Aug.
Planting In groups of four or five, in fertile, well-drained soil. Sunny or lightly shaded borders.
Care Mulch in late spring. Support with pea-sticks. Cut flower stems to ground in autumn.
Propagation By division, Oct.–Mar. Spreads quickly and may need to be divided and replanted every two years. Also grown from seeds in cold frame, Mar.–April.

Dahlia see p. 71

DELPHINIUM

Delphinium × Belladonna

Perennial: Elegant border plants of great popularity, bearing tall, tapering spikes of spurred flowers, usually with different coloured centres.
Cultivars Elatum Hybrids. Dwarf (H3–4½ ft, S1½–3 ft), 'Blue Tit', indigo; 'Cinderella', purple. Tall (H4½–6 ft, S2½–3 ft), 'Butterball', cream; 'Mullion', blue; 'Swan Lake', white, June–Aug. Belladonna Hybrids (H3½–4½ ft, S1½–2 ft), 'Bonita', blue; 'Moerheimii', white; 'Pink Sensation', pink, June–Aug.
Planting In groups of three to six in rich, well-drained but moisture-retentive soil. Full sun, sheltered from winds.
Care Mulch in early spring. Water freely in dry spells. Support Belladonna cultivars with pea-sticks, the tall Elatum cultivars with a stout cane to each stem. Maintain healthy growth by cutting away at crown level any weak shoots in April. Remove faded flower spikes back to a good leaf to encourage second show of flowers. Cut all dead flower stems to ground in autumn.
Propagation By division of woody crowns, Sept.–Mar. Divide and replant after four years to maintain vigour. Also by basal cuttings in April.

DIANTHUS
Annual pink

Dianthus

Half-hardy annual: Beautiful and scented border flowers related to carnations and perennial pinks. Tolerant of salt-spray, alkaline soil and smoky atmosphere.
Species *D. chinensis* and hybrids (H6–15 in., S6–15 in.), 'Baby Doll', white, rose, crimson; 'Queen of Hearts', scarlet; 'Merry-go-round', white with scarlet centre, June to autumn.
Planting In sunny position. Soil not too acid.
Care Pinch out growing tip of young plants to promote strong basal and side-shoots.
Propagation Sow Jan.–Mar., 15°C (59°F).

DIANTHUS
Pink

Perennial rock plant: Cousin of the carnation, studded with bright flowers.
Species *D. alpinus* (H4 in., S6 in.), pink to purple, May–Aug. *D. deltoides* (H6–9 in., S12 in.), carpeting habit, red, pink, white, June–Sept. *D. gratianopolitanus* (H4–12 in., S2 ft), carpeting habit, pink, May–July. *D. haematocalyx* (H6–12 in., S4–6 in.), cushion habit, rose-purple, yellow reverse, July onwards. *D. neglectus* (H4–9 in., S6 in.), cushion habit, July–Aug.
Planting Sunny site in well-drained limy soil. Light shade tolerated. Dry wall, paving, scree, trough, alpine lawn, alpine house. *D. deltoides* not suitable for alpine house. *D. gratianopolitanus* not suitable for alpine house or trough.
Propagation By tip cuttings in peat/sand in a cold frame, June–Aug.; by seeds in spring.

DICENTRA
Bleeding heart

Dicentra spectabilis

Perennial: Bears heart-shaped flowers on arching stems above grey-green, fern-like leaves.
Species *D. formosa* (H12–18 in., S15 in.), pink, May–June. *D. spectabilis* (H1½–2½ ft, S1½–2 ft), deep pink and white, Mar.–May.
Planting In groups of three or four in well-drained but moisture-retentive soil enriched with compost, leaf-mould or peat. Front of sunny or lightly shaded border; or use as ground-cover beneath trees and shrubs. Needs shelter from wind.
Care Mulch in late spring.
Propagation By careful division of the brittle, fleshy roots, Oct.–Mar. Once established, leave undisturbed for as long as possible.

DICTAMNUS
Burning bush

Perennial: A handsome and usually long-lived plant with pink or white flower spikes over

Doronicum–Eichhornia

Dictamnus albus

strongly aromatic leaves.
Species *D. albus* (H2 ft, S1½–2 ft), fragrant, white spider-like flowers; *D. purpurea*, pink, red-striped, June–July.
Planting In groups of three, Oct.–Mar., in well-drained, fertile, limy soil. Add 2–4 oz. (2–4 tablespoons) ground limestone to each square yard in acid soils. Site in sunny borders or on banks.
Care Mulch in late spring. Cut stems to ground in autumn. Leave plants undisturbed; they do not transplant well.
Propagation By seeds sown in cold frame as soon as ripe in late summer. Seedlings reach flowering size in two to three years.

DORONICUM
Leopard's bane

Doronicum

Perennial: Very useful plant providing long display of big, yellow, daisy-like flowers in spring and early summer, before the annuals bloom. Makes good cut flowers.
Species *D. orientale* 'Spring Beauty' (H3 ft, S12–18 in.), bright yellow, double, May–July. *D. plantagineum* (H2 ft, S12–18 in.), single, golden-yellow, April–June.
Planting In groups of three or four, Oct.–Mar., in well-drained, fertile soil. Sun or light shade, in borders or under trees.
Care Mulch in early spring. Support with pea-sticks in exposed sites. Dead-head to encourage second crop of flowers. Cut all stems to ground in autumn. If affected by powdery mildew, spray with benomyl or dinocap.
Propagation By division, Oct.–Mar. Divide and replant every three years to maintain vigour.

DRABA

Perennial rock plant: Domes of closely packed rosettes, from which rise wiry stems bearing short racemes of yellow flowers.
Species *D. aizoides* (H4 in., S6–9 in.), lemon-yellow, April. *D. mollissima* (H1 in., S6 in.), bright yellow, May–June. *D. polytricha* (H2 in., S6–9 in.), pale yellow, April.
Planting Well-drained gritty soil in a sunny site. With exception of *D. aizoides*, best in an alpine house.
Propagation Cuttings of rosettes in peat/sand in a cold frame, June–July. Seeds, Mar.–April.

DRYAS

Perennial rock plant: Evergreen, mat-forming plant bearing white, saucer-shaped flowers, followed by graceful, fluffy seed-heads.
Species *D. octopetala* (H3–4 in., S2 ft), June–July.
Planting In well-drained, limy soil on sunny site. Paving, scree, rock garden, alpine lawn, with bulbs.
Care Do not disturb roots once established.
Propagation 1½–2 in. heel cuttings of side-shoots in peat/sand in cold frame, Aug. or Mar.

DRYOPTERIS

Dryopteris cristata

Fern: Hardy plants that will grow in most sites.
Species *D. cristata*–Crested buckler fern (H2–3 ft, S2 ft), deciduous. *D. dilatata*–Broad buckler fern (H3–4 ft, S3–4 ft), deciduous. *D. filix-mas*–Male fern (H3–5 ft, S2½–4 ft), deciduous or semi-evergreen. *D. sieboldi* (H18 in., S18 in.), deciduous. *D. pseudomas* (syn. *D. borreri*)–Golden-scaled fern (H2–5 ft, S2–5 ft), evergreen or semi-evergreen.
Planting In shade (*D. filix-mas* in light shade). Acid to neutral soil. (*D. dilatata*, damp, woodland soil.)
Propagation Division or spores.

ECHINACEA
Purple coneflower

Perennial: Easily grown border plants bearing daisy-like flowers with rounded, cone-like centre. Good for cutting.
Species *E. purpurea* (H3–4 ft, S1½–2 ft), crimson-purple, July–Sept.
Planting Singly or in groups of three, Oct.–Mar., in well-drained soil enriched with manure, compost or leaf-mould. Full sun.
Care Mulch in early spring. Support with pea-sticks in windy sites. Dead-head. Cut stems to ground in autumn. Stunted growth usually due to dry soil: give monthly foliar feed in summer.
Propagation By division, Oct.–Mar.

ECHINOPS
Globe thistle

Echinops ritro

Perennial: Thistle-like plant bearing globular flower-heads with metallic sheen, dried for winter decoration. Deep-rooted.
Species *E. ritro* (H3–4 ft, S1½–2 ft), metallic blue flowers, July–Aug.
Planting Singly or in groups of four, Oct.–Mar., in deep, well-drained soil. Thrives on alkaline soil. Sunny site.
Care Mulch lightly in spring. Cut stems to ground in autumn.
Propagation By division, Oct.–Mar.

EICHHORNIA
Water hyacinth

Eichhornia crassipes

Floating plant: Free-floating, with orchid-like flowers, suitable for any depth of water, provided bottom soil is fertile. Trailing roots useful for fish to lay eggs on.
Species *E. crassipes* (syn.

Elodea–Forget-me-not

E. speciosa), pale violet with gold and blue petal marks, flowering in summer.
Care Must be removed from pool, potted in moist soil and brought into greenhouse by end Sept. Replace in pool early June.
Propagation New plants, produced on stolons June–Sept., may be detached when showing several well-formed leaves.

ELODEA
Canadian pondweed

(syn. *Anacharis*) Pool oxygenator: Flowers insignificant.
Species *E. canadensis* (planting depth 6–18 in.).
Propagation By cuttings or division.

Endymion see Bluebell
Eranthis see Aconite

ERIGERON
Fleabane

Erigeron speciosus

Perennial: Easily grown plants with prolonged display of daisy-like flowers. Similar to Michaelmas daisies but earlier flowering. Good as cut flowers.
Species *E. speciosus* hybrids (H1½–2 ft, S12–18 in.), violet-blue, pink, lavender, single or semi-double, June–Aug.
Planting In groups of about five, Oct.–Mar., on well-drained soil preferably enriched with manure or compost. Sunny border.
Care Mulch in early spring. Support with pea-sticks may be needed. Dead-head. Cut stems to ground in autumn.
Propagation By division, Oct.–Mar. Reduced flower production usually indicates need for division. Replant only outer, vigorous parts of clump.

ERYNGIUM

Eryngium bourgatii

Perennial: Somewhat spiny-leaved plants bearing metallic-blue flowers surrounded by spiky collars. Dry for winter decoration.
Species *E. bourgatii* (H18 in., S12 in.), blue-green, July–Aug. *E. maritimum* (sea holly) (H18 in., S18 in.), silver-blue, July–Sept. *E. tripartitum* (H2½ ft, S1½–2 ft), grey-blue, July–Sept. *E. variifolium* (H2–2½ ft, S12–18 in.), blue with white collars, July–Aug.
Planting Singly or in groups of four to six, Oct.–April, in ordinary, well-drained soil. Sunny border.
Care Mulch lightly in spring. Support *E. tripartitum* with pea-sticks. For drying, cut flowers before they fade. Cut stems almost to ground in autumn.
Propagation By division of fleshy roots, or by root cuttings in Feb. in cold frame.

EUPATORIUM

Perennial: Tufted, erect plants bearing clusters of small flowers in heads 4–5 in. wide. Too vigorous for small gardens.

Eupatorium purpureum

Species *E. purpureum* (H4–6 ft, S2–3 ft), rose-purple, Aug.–Sept.
Planting In groups of four, Oct.–Mar., in any good, moist soil. Sun or partial shade. Best grown in wild garden, with room to spread.
Care Mulch in spring. Cut stems almost to ground in autumn.
Propagation By division, Oct.–Mar.

EUPHORBIA

Euphorbia griffithii

Perennial: Thriving on poor soil and grown for its brightly coloured bracts, surrounding insignificant flowers. *E. characias* good for cut flowers.
Species *E. characias* and *E. wulfenii* (H3–5 ft, S3 ft), evergreen, yellow-green flowers, May–June. *E. griffithii* (H2–3 ft, S1½–2½ ft), flame red, May–June. *E. robbiae* (H18 in., S2 ft or more), pale yellow-green, April–July.
Planting Singly or in groups of three, Sept.–April, in well-drained soil. *E. characias* and *E. griffithii* in sunny, sheltered borders; *E. robbiae* ideal ground-cover in shade.
Care Mulch in spring. Cut flower stems to ground in autumn. Avoid disturbing *E. characias* and *E. griffithii*.
Propagation By division, Sept.–April; or by basal cuttings rooted in cold frame, April–May. *E. characias* and *E. wulfenii* best from seeds in spring or when ripe.

FILIPENDULA

Perennial: Erect, clump-forming plants with fluffy sprays of tiny flowers. Make good cut flowers.
Species *F. hexapetala* (H1½–2 ft, S18 in.), cream tinged with pink, June–July. *F. purpurea* (H3–5 ft, S1½–2 ft), rose-pink, July–Aug. *F. ulmaria* (meadow sweet) (H3–4 ft, S6 in.–2 ft), cream, double, June–Aug.
Planting Singly or in groups of four, preferably in moist soil with added compost or manure. Sun or light shade. *F. purpurea* and *F. ulmaria* ideal beside water.
Care Mulch in late spring. Water *F. purpurea* and *F. ulmaria* freely in dry spells. Cut all stems to ground in autumn.
Propagation By division, Oct.–Mar.

FORGET-ME-NOT
Myosotis

Myosotis

Biennial: Easily grown, moisture-loving plant, bearing dense masses of small blue flowers. Can be perennial, but usually removed after flowering.
Species *M. alpestris* (H5–12 in., S4–9 in.), 'Blue Ball', indigo-blue;

Foxglove–Geranium

'Carmine King', rose-carmine, April–June. *M. sylvatica* (H12–15 in., S6 in.), 'Blue Bird', deep blue, May–June.
Planting Almost any position where soil does not dry out. Waterlogging may kill off plants in badly drained sites in winter. Dig in compost or peat. Partial shade.
Propagation Sow in seed beds or cold frame, April–May, and plant out in September. Forget-me-nots are often self-seeding.

FOXGLOVE
Digitalis

Digitalis

Biennial: The familiar woodland plant has been developed into magnificent strains bearing massive spikes of richly coloured flowers. Suitable for cutting.
Species *D. purpurea* (H3–5 ft, S18 in.), 'Excelsior' (tall), white, cream, pink-to-purple flowers; 'Foxy' (shorter), white, cream, pink, red, June–July.
Planting In partial shade in any ordinary garden soil that does not dry out in summer.
Care Remove central spike when it has flowered to encourage flowering side-shoots.
Propagation Sow seeds outdoors May or June, scattering on surface and gently raking in. Move to flowering sites Sept. Thin covering of damp peat helps germination. 'Foxy' may be grown as half-hardy annual, sown Feb.–Mar.

GAILLARDIA
Blanket flower

Gaillardia

Half-hardy annual: Showy, red-yellow, daisy-like flowers for border and cutting.
Species *G. pulchella* (H12 in.–2 ft, S9–18 in.), 'Lollipops' (double), red, yellow and mixed; 'Picta Lorenziana' (double), yellow, bronze, red, June to autumn.
Planting In sunny site with light, well-drained soil. Light shade acceptable.
Care Support taller cultivars. Dead-head.
Propagation Sow Feb.–Mar., 15°C (59°F).

GAILLARDIA
Blanket flower

Perennial: Valuable contributor to the border display, blooming for long period and good for cutting. Flowers 3–4 in. across.
Species *G. aristata* (H1½–2½ ft, S18 in.), 'Dazzler', orange-yellow with maroon-red centre; 'Goblin', bright flame-red tipped with yellow; 'Wirral Flame', deep red, gold-tipped petals, June–Oct. Dwarfs (H9 in.).
Planting In groups of three or six, Mar.–May, in light, well-drained soil. Sunny border.
Care Mulch lightly in spring. Support with pea-sticks. Cut stems to ground in autumn. Plants deteriorate after about three years.
Propagation By seeds sown in cold frame or open ground in summer. Plant out following spring. Seeds sown in warmth, early spring, often flower same year.

Galanthus see Snowdrop

GENTIAN
Gentiana

Gentiana acaulis

Perennial rock and border: Mainly alpine plants with trumpet-shaped flowers in white, yellow, purple and blue. Taller types suitable for borders.
Species *G. acaulis* (H3 in., S18 in.), deep blue, May–June. *G. septemfida* (H9–12 in., S12 in.), deep blue, July–Aug. *G. sino-ornata* (H6 in., S12–15 in.), rich blue, Sept.–Nov. *G. asclepiadea* (H1½–2 ft, S12 in.), blue, July–Aug. *G. lutea* (H3–5 ft, S12 in.), star-shaped, yellow, in spikes, July–Aug.
Planting Group in well-drained but moisture-retentive soil with added compost or manure. Alpines suitable for peat bed, alpine lawn, trough and alpine house. Sun or partial shade.
Care Mulch in spring. Support *G. asclepiadea* with pea-sticks. Water in dry spells. Leave undisturbed once rooted.
Propagation Except for *G. acaulis*, which is best divided in June, all gentians may be divided in Mar. *G. asclepiadea*, *G. lutea* and *G. septemfida* may be raised from seeds, sown in cold frame when ripe or in autumn.

GERANIUM
Crane's bill

Geranium sanguineum

Perennial border: Free-flowering, tufted plants with open, saucer-shaped blooms. Not to be confused with pelargoniums–tender pot plants popularly known as geraniums.
Species *G. endressii* (H12–18 in., S1½–2 ft), 'A. T. Johnson', 'Rose Clair', 'Wargrave Pink', shades of pink, May–Aug. *G. macrorrhizum* (H15 in., S1½–2 ft or more), 'Walter Ingwersen', pink, May–July. *G. pratense* (H1½–2 ft, S18 in.), 'Album', white; 'Florepleno', double, blue, July–Sept. *G. sanguineum* (H6–9 in., S18 in.), crimson, magenta, June–Sept.
Planting In groups of three or four, Sept.–Mar., in well-drained soil with added compost, peat or leaf-mould. Sun or light shade to front of borders.
Care Mulch in spring. Support *G. pratense* with pea-sticks. Cut faded flower-stems almost to ground to encourage second flowering. Cut all stems to ground in autumn. Put down slug pellets to prevent damage to young plants in moist, shady sites.
Propagation By division, Sept.–Mar. By seeds sown in cold frame, Mar.–April.

GERANIUM
Crane's bill

Perennial rock plant: Alpine varieties of border geranium.
Species *G.* × 'Ballerina' (H6–9 in.,

Geum–Grape hyacinth

S12 in.), pink, June–Sept. *G. cinereum* (H4–6 in., S9–12 in.), crimson-magenta, May–Oct. *G. dalmaticum* (H6 in., S9–12 in.), light pink, July–Aug. *G. renardii* (H9 in., S12 in.), white heavily veined with purple, May–July. *G. subcaulescens* (H4–6 in., S12 in.), crimson-magenta, May–Oct.
Planting Well-drained but moisture-retentive soil in sun or partial shade. Scree, paving, trough.
Propagation By division, Sept–Mar. By seeds sown in Mar.

GEUM

Geum reptans

Perennial: Showy plant, generally short-lived. Unless divided, will seldom flower more than three seasons. The bright, saucer-shaped flowers are good for cutting.
Species *G. chiloense* (H1½–2 ft, S12–18 in.), semi-double or double, yellow, orange, scarlet, June–Sept. *G. reptans* (H9–12 in., S12–15 in.), yellow, May–July, is suitable for growing in rock gardens.
Planting In groups of five or six, Sept.–Mar., in moist but well-drained soil enriched with leaf-mould, peat or compost. Sun or light shade.
Care Mulch in spring. Support with pea-sticks in exposed sites. Cut back almost to ground after flowering.
Propagation Divide every two or three years in autumn or spring. Or sow seeds in cold frame in Mar. Grow seedlings in spare ground until Sept. Then plant out.

GLADIOLUS

Gladiolus (Primulinus)

Half-hardy bulbous plant: Many hundreds of cultivars range over almost all colours of the spectrum. New, fascinating cultivars are introduced every year. Excellent for cutting.
Cultivars
LARGE-FLOWERED HYBRIDS (H3–5 ft, S4–6 in.), full colour range, many bi-coloured or with throat markings. 'Aristocrat', rich red; 'Eurovision', vermilion; 'Green Woodpecker', lemon-green, July–Sept.
BUTTERFLY HYBRIDS (H2–4 ft, S4–6 in.), full colour range with attractive throat markings. 'Donald Duck', lemon and orange; 'Madame Butterfly', pink and violet; 'Summer Fairy', red and maroon, July–Sept.
PRIMULINUS HYBRIDS (H1½–3 ft, S3–6 in.), full colour range, smaller, hooded flowers. 'Ivory and Mauve', cream and carmine; 'Joyce', rose and yellow; 'Red Star', scarlet, July–Sept.
MINIATURE HYBRIDS (H1½–3 ft, S4–6 in.), full colour range; like primulinus but smaller. 'Bo Peep', apricot; 'Graceful', orange; 'Greenbird', green and crimson.
Species *G. byzantinus* (H2 ft, S6 in.), wine-red, June. *G. × colvillii* (H18 in., S5 in.), white, pink, red, purple, June–July.
Planting 4–6 in. deep in well-drained soil. Open, sunny site except for *G. colvillii*, which needs sheltered site. Plant hybrids in fortnightly succession in Mar.–April to obtain continuous display. Plant species gladioli in Oct. All kinds at their best in groups in herbaceous borders.
Care Stake bigger cultivars.
Propagation Lift all hybrid corms in Oct. Dry quickly in warmth (24°C (75°F) for first three days, 13–15°C (55–59°F) for following ten days). Separate and store at not less than 10°C (50°F) during winter. *G. byzantinus* is fully hardy and can be left undisturbed. *G. colvillii* is half-hardy and needs protection from frost with bracken or cloches.

GODETIA

Godetia

Hardy annual: A garden favourite similar to clarkia. Bushy plants carry single or double, funnel-shaped flowers of vivid reds, pinks and white.
Species *G. amoena* and *G. grandiflora* hybrids (H9 in.–2 ft, S6–12 in.), 'Kelvedon Glory', salmon-orange; 'Sybil Sherwood', salmon-pink.
Planting Sunny position on light, moist but well-drained soil.
Propagation Sow Mar.–April or Sept. Autumn-sown seedlings need cloche protection in cold areas.

GOLDEN ROD
Solidago

Perennial: The familiar tall, hardy invader, bearing plumes of gold in late summer, now has striking garden hybrids, including dwarf forms. Plume-like flower heads make a vivid display and are good for cutting.

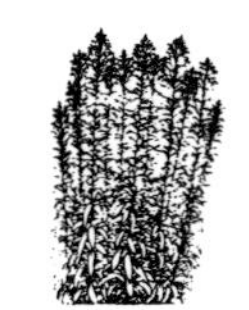

Solidago × hybrida

Cultivars *S. × hybrida* (2½–6 ft, S1–2 ft), 'Goldenmosa', 'Mimosa', 'Peter Pan'; (H12 in.–2 ft), 'Golden Thumb', 'Lemore', shades of yellow, July–Sept.
Planting In groups of three to four in well-drained, ordinary soil. Sun or light shade. Herbaceous or mixed borders.
Care Mulch lightly in spring. Support with pea-sticks in windy sites. Water during dry spells. Cut stems to ground in autumn.
Propagation Divide and replant every three years, Oct.–Mar., to maintain vigour.

GRAPE HYACINTH
Muscari

Bulbous plant: Hardy dwarf for rock gardens and border edges, bearing conical heads of tiny blue flowers like miniature bunches of grapes. Good as pot plants.
Species *M. armeniacum* (H8 in., S4 in.), deep blue, white edges, April–May. *M. botryiodes* (H7 in., S4 in.), sky-blue, Mar.–May. *M. comosum* (H10–18 in., S4–6 in.), blue to mauve, May–June. *M. tubergenianum* (H8 in., S4 in.), light and dark blue, Mar.
Planting 3 in. deep in any free-draining soil, Aug.–Nov. Sunny site.
Propagation Division every three years when leaves turn yellow. *M. armeniacum* seeds itself.

Grasses–Helichrysum

GRASSES, ORNAMENTAL

Hardy annual: Increasingly used for flower arrangements and dried for winter display.
Species Some of the best types are briza, cortaderia, lagurus, pennisetum, phalaris, polypogon, setaria, stipa and tricholaena (H9 in.–2 ft).
Planting Sunny position in ordinary soil.
Care If needed for winter decoration, cut before seed heads ripen.
Propagation Sow in Mar.–April.

GUNNERA

Perennial bog plant: For big gardens only, because of its giant, rhubarb-like leaves. Greenish flower-spikes, like fat cigars.
Species *G. manicata* (H6–10 ft, S10–15 ft). Late spring to early summer.
Care Best protected with straw or its own dead leaves in winter.
Propagation Division, or seeds in Mar.–April.

GYPSOPHILA

Gypsophila

Hardy annual: Slender, erect plant bearing a mass of small, star-shaped flowers giving effect of coating of foam.
Species *G. elegans* (H9–18 in.), 'Covent Garden', white; 'Monarch', white; 'Rosea', pink.
Planting Sunny position. Any well-drained soil. Dress acid soil with 2–4 oz. (2–4 tablespoons) of lime per square yard.
Care Support taller plants with twiggy sticks.
Propagation Sow in Mar.–April or Sept.

GYPSOPHILA

Gypsophila paniculata

Perennial: Clouds of white or pink blossom on slender stems.
Species *G. paniculata* (H3 ft, S2–3 ft), single white flowers or doubles in pink and white, June–Aug.
Planting In groups of three, Oct.–Mar., in well-drained, limy soil. Dress acid soil as for annual (above). Choose site where plants can be left undisturbed for years.
Care Mulch in spring. Support with pea-sticks. Cut stems to ground in autumn. Roots resent being moved.
Propagation By seeds sown in cold frame Mar.; or by basal cuttings Mar.–May or in July. Double cultivars also by grafting.

GYPSOPHILA

Rock plant: Evergreen perennial for dry wall, paving, scree, trough or alpine house. Masses of miniature flowers in pink and white.
Species *G. cerastioides* (H3 in., S12–18 in.), white, June–Oct. *G. repens* (syn. *prostrata*) (H6 in., S2 ft), white, deep pink, June–Aug.
Planting In well-drained soil on sunny site.
Propagation 2 in. basal shoots in peat/sand in cold frame, April–May. *G. cerastioides* also by division, Mar.–Sept.

HELENIUM

Helenium autumnale

Perennial: Easily grown, long-lived plants. Daisy-like flowers of yellow, maroon, red and bronze shades. Long-lasting as cut flowers.
Species *H. autumnale* (H2½–3½ ft, S1½–2 ft), shades of yellow, orange, bronze, copper and mahogany-red, July–Sept.
Planting In groups of three or four, Oct.–April, in any ordinary, well-drained soil. Sun or light shade.
Care Mulch in spring, and water in dry spells. Support with canes in exposed sites. Dead-head. Pull off weak shoots from crowns in May to leave about six healthy shoots on each clump.
Propagation Divide and replant every three years to retain vigour.

HELIANTHEMUM
Rock rose

Perennial rock plant: Reasonably hardy, colourful evergreen that needs careful siting as it may swamp less-vigorous plants.
Species *H. alpestre* (H3–4 in., S12 in.), yellow, June–July. *H. lunulatum* (H6 in., S9 in.), gold, neat, compact habit, June–July. *H. nummularium* (H4–6 in., S2 ft), pink, yellow, brown, June–July.
Planting In well-drained, limy soil on sunny site. Dry wall, paving.
Care Dead-heading of all cultivars induces second flowering Aug.–Nov.
Propagation 2–3 in. non-flowering lateral shoots with heel, in pots of peat/sand in cold frame, June–Aug.

Helianthus see Sunflower

HELICHRYSUM

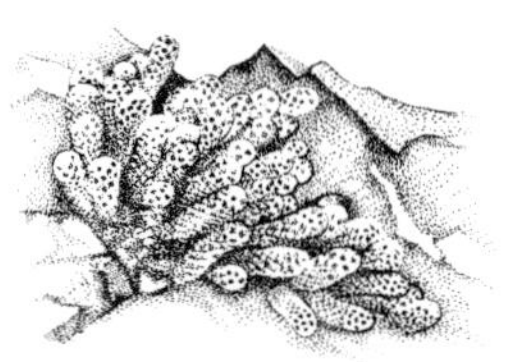

Helichrysum selago

Perennial rock plant: Mainly cultivated for its attractive, grey-green or white woolly foliage. Flowers small and groundsel-like.
Species *H. bellidioides* (H3 in., S12 in.), mat-forming evergreen. Leaves dark green above, white woolly beneath. White flowers, May–July. *H. milfordiae* (H2 in., S9 in.), silver leaves forming cushions, cinnamon buds, white flowers, May–June. *H. selago* (H6–9 in., S6–9 in.), wiry shrublet, silver-grey leaves, insignificant off-white flowers, June–Aug.
Planting In moist, well-drained soil with peat or leaf-mould and grit. *H. bellidioides*, peat bed, paving, rock garden in sun, trough, alpine house. *H. milfordiae*, scree, alpine house. *H. selago*, alpine house, dry wall, sheltered scree.
Propagation Cut lateral shoots of *H. selago* and detach small shoots of *H. bellidioides* and *H. milfordiae*. Insert in 3/1 sand/peat in cold frame, April–July. Plant out April–May.

Heliopsis–Honesty

HELIOPSIS

Heliopsis scabra

Perennial: Tall, showy plants with yellow, daisy-like flowers on erect, branching stems.
Species *H. scabra* (H3–4 ft, S1½–2 ft), in yellow and gold, single, semi-double and double, July–Aug.
Planting In groups of four or five, Oct.–Mar., in ordinary, well-drained soil. Full sun.
Care Mulch in spring. Cut stems to ground in autumn.
Propagation By division.

HELIOTROPE

Half-hardy annual: Tightly packed clusters of small, fragrant flowers from June to autumn. Not for cold, windy areas.
Species *Heliotropium × hybridum* (H9–18 in., S12–15 in.), 'Marine', purple; 'Monarch Royal Marine', deep blue.
Planting Any good, well-drained soil. Full sun.
Care Best results in cool greenhouse, but also satisfactory for summer bedding.
Propagation Sow Mar.–April, 16°C (61°F). Bed out late May.

HELLEBORUS
Christmas rose and Lenten rose

Perennial: Winter and early spring flowering. The saucer-shaped flowers are long-lasting in water.

Helleborus niger

Species *H. niger* (Christmas rose) (H12–18 in., S18 in.), white, gold centre, continuous Dec.–Mar. *H. orientalis* (Lenten rose) (H1½–2 ft, S1½–2 ft), white, pink, crimson, purple, Feb.–Mar.
Planting In groups of three or four, Sept.–Oct., in deep, well-drained but moist soil with added compost, leaf-mould or peat. Light shade or sun on edges of shrub or mixed borders. Decorative ground-cover beneath tall trees.
Care Mulch in autumn. Water in prolonged dry spells. In cold districts protect opening blooms of *H. niger* with cloches. Cut stems to ground after flowering.
Propagation By division; but helleborus dislike disturbance and should be left alone for years. Also by seeds sown in cold frame as soon as ripe.

HEMEROCALLIS
Day lily

Hemerocallis fulva

Perennial: Handsome lily-like plants increasing in popularity as original yellow plants are replaced by colourful varieties.
Species *H. fulva* (H2½–3 ft, S1–2 ft). This species has been crossed with several others to create the modern hybrid cultivars, which are now available with single and semi-double flowers in pink, yellow, apricot, red, purple and bronze shades, June–Aug.
Planting In groups of three to five, Oct.–April, in moisture-holding soil enriched with manure or compost. Sunny or lightly shaded borders, or by edge of pools.
Care Mulch in spring. Cut stems almost to ground after flowering. Water freely in dry weather. Each flower lasts one day only, but many follow in succession.
Propagation By division of tuberous roots, Oct.–April. But leave undisturbed until overcrowding makes division necessary.

HEUCHERA
Coral flower

Perennial: Slender stems carry airy clusters of small, bell-shaped flowers above evergreen leaves. Useful as edging to paths and borders or as ground-cover. Good for cutting and drying.
Species *H. sanguinea* hybrids (H1½–2 ft, S12 in.), 'Pearl Drops', white; 'Red Spangles', blood-red; 'Scintillation', coral-tipped pink, June–Sept.
Planting In groups of four or five, Oct.–April, in moisture-retentive soil with manure or compost. Sun or light shade.
Care Mulch in spring. Cut stems almost to ground after flowering.
Propagation By division, required every third year, when crowns tend to rise out of ground. Divide and plant more deeply.

HOLLYHOCK
Althaea

Perennial: Popular cottage-garden plant with tall spikes of widely

Althaea rosea

funnel-shaped blooms, grown at back of borders. Best treated as annual or biennial.
Species *A. rosea* (H6–8 ft, S2 ft), single or double flowers 4 in. across, white, yellow, pink, red. 'Chater's Double', double yellow, pink, red and white, July–Sept.
Planting Singly or in groups, Oct.–April, in rich, heavy soil with compost or manure. Sunny, sheltered position.
Care Stake in late spring before mulching. Water freely in dry spells. Cut down to 6 in. above ground after flowering. Protect in winter with bracken or cloches in cold areas. Older plants produce poorer flowers, and should be discarded.
Propagation By seeds sown outdoors in June–July. In cold areas, overwinter seedlings in cold frame. As an annual, sow early spring in warmth.

HONESTY
Lunaria

Honesty

Biennial: The small, purple flowers are fragrant and make an attractive

Hosta – Inula

display in spring and early summer. But honesty is grown mainly for its silver, disc-like seed-pods, used for indoor decoration.
Species *L. annua* (syn. *L. biennis*) (H2 ft, S12 in.), in pale purple, deep purple and white shades, May–June.
Planting In ordinary garden soil, ideally with partial shade.
Care Cut seed-pods in Aug., before autumn gales.
Propagation Sow May–June.

HOSTA
Plantain lily

Hosta sieboldiana

Perennial: Grown as much for its attractive, often variegated leaves as for its spikes of trumpet-shaped flowers.
Species *H. fortunei* (H1½–3 ft, S2 ft or more), lilac, July. Grey-green leaves. *H. lancifolia* (H2 ft, S2 ft), lilac, July–Sept. Mid-green leaves. *H. sieboldiana* (H2 ft, S3 ft), white, purple-tinged, July–Aug. Big, green, strongly veined leaves. *H. undulata* (H2 ft, S2 ft or more), lilac, Aug. Wavy leaves with white markings.
Planting In groups of three to five or more, Oct.–Mar., in well-drained but moisture-retentive soil, enriched with manure, compost or peat. In light shade in borders at edge of pools, and as ground-cover.
Care Mulch in spring. Water freely in dry spells. Cut faded flower stems to near ground. Put down slug pellets to protect young leaves. Burn leaves affected with brown blotches due to grey mould.
Propagation By division in Mar. But leave plants undisturbed for as long as possible.

HOTTONIA
Water violet

Hottonia palustris

Perennial: Useful oxygenator for pools, bearing pale lilac flower spikes (8–10 in.) in May–June.
Species *H. palustris*.
Planting In 6–10 in. of water.
Propagation By division.

HYACINTH
Hyacinthus

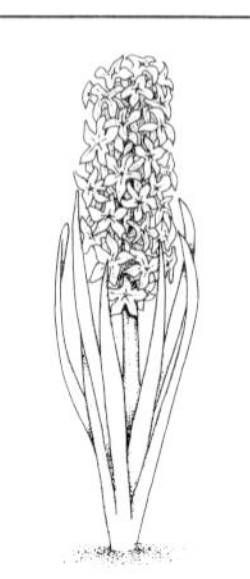

Hyacinthus (Large flowered)

Bulbous plant: Most hyacinths sold every year are for indoor pot culture, but they are also suitable for growing in sheltered spots in the garden and in window-boxes. Exquisite perfume.
Cultivars Large-flowered hybrids (Dutch hybrids) (H8–9 in., S6–8 in.), for both garden and indoor cultivation: 'L'Innocence', white; 'City of Haarlem', yellow; 'Gipsy Queen', apricot; 'Jan Bos', cerise; 'Pink Pearl', pink; 'Delft Blue', blue; 'Ostara', purple-blue, April–May. *H. orientalis albulus* (Roman hyacinth) (H6 in., S6–9 in.), white, pink and blue; more fragrant than Dutch hybrids; usually grown in bowls, April–May.
Planting 5–6 in. deep in light, well-drained soil during autumn. Sunny or partially shaded site. Pot prepared bulbs for forcing in Aug.–Sept.
Propagation By slitting or scooping out the base of bulb to encourage growth of bulblets. Roman hyacinth also propagated by offsets.

HYPERICUM
St John's wort

Hypericum polyphyllum

Shrubby perennial: Vigorous, low-lying plant bearing handsome golden-yellow flowers.
Species *H. calycinum* (Rose of Sharon) (H12–18 in., S indefinite), golden-yellow, June–Sept. Forms dense carpet. *H. coris* (H6 in., S12 in.), clear gold, July. Rock plant. *H. olympicum* (H9–12 in., S12 in.), gold, July–Aug. Rock plant. *H. polyphyllum* (H6 in., S12 in.), gold, July–Sept. Rock plant.
Planting *H. calycinum* as ground-cover in border or shrubberies. Any well-drained soil. Other species in rock gardens, paving, dry walls. Sunny site. *H. coris* grows best in poor soil.
Care Cut *H. calycinum* to within few inches of base in Mar., annually or every two years, to keep compact. Trim to shape each Mar.
Propagation *H. calycinum* by division, Oct.–April. For rock plants take 2 in. cuttings and plant in cold frame in peat/sand, June–Aug., overwintering in cold frame.

Iberis see Candytuft
Impatiens see Busy Lizzie

INCARVILLEA

Perennial: Easily grown with clusters of big, foxglove-like flowers. The leaves are cut into several pairs of narrow leaflets.
Species *I. delavayi* (H18 in., S1½–2 ft), rose-red, May–June.
Planting In groups of three to five, Mar.–April, in rich, well-drained soil. Set the crowns just below soil surface. Sunny borders.
Care Mulch lightly in autumn. Remove faded flower stems and dead leaves in autumn. New growth does not appear until late spring; avoid damage when hoeing by marking site with sticks.
Propagation By seeds sown outdoors in April; transplant to permanent position after two years. Division possible in autumn, but crowns are difficult to split.

INULA

Perennial: Free-flowering plant with big, daisy-like flowers. Varieties described suitable for borders or rock gardens.
Species *I. acaulis* (H2–4 in., S12 in.), golden-yellow, April–May. *I. hookeri* (H1½–2 ft, S1½–2 ft), pale yellow, fragrant, Aug.–Sept. *I. royleana* (H2 ft or more, S1½–2 ft), golden-yellow, Aug.–Oct.
Planting In groups of three or

Kingcup – Leontopodium

four in fertile, moisture-retentive soil. Good on clay. Sun or light shade.
Care Mulch in spring. Water during dry spells. Cut dead stems to ground in autumn.
Propagation Divide and replant every three years, Oct.–Mar., to contain spreading habit.

Ipomoea see Morning glory
Iris see p. 178

KINGCUP
Caltha, Marsh marigold

Caltha palustris 'Plena'

Water-margin plant: Hardy perennial providing splendid display of yellow blooms in spring.
Species *Caltha palustris* (H9–15 in.), single, gold, Mar.–June. 'Plena', double, gold on branching stems, April–June, long-lasting.
Planting In mud to 4 in. water depth.
Propagation By division. Wild species also by seeds when ripe.

KNIPHOFIA
Red-hot poker

Kniphofia galpinii

Perennial: Popular plant with sedge-like leaves and long spikes of tubular flowers. Excellent eye-catcher at focal points.
Species *K. galpinii* (H1½–2 ft, S1½–2 ft), orange, Sept.–Oct. *K. uvaria* hybrids and cultivars (H2½–5 ft, S2–4 ft), 'Alcazar', orange; 'Gold Else', yellow; 'Maid of Orleans', cream; 'Samuel's Sensation', scarlet, July–Oct.
Planting Singly or in groups of three or four, Oct. or April, in well-drained, ordinary soil. Avoid rich, wet or badly drained soil. Sunny border.
Care Mulch in late spring. Water freely until well established. Cut flowering stems down as they fade. In cold areas tie leaves together to protect crown in winter, or cover with bracken, straw or peat.
Propagation By division. But leave fleshy roots undisturbed as long as possible. Also by seeds sown in cold frame or in open, April.

KOCHIA
Burning bush

Kochia

Half-hardy annual: Bushy plant of striking pale green that looks like a feather duster. Turns russet-crimson in autumn. Can be used to form a low, temporary hedge.
Species *K. scoparia trichophylla* (H2–3 ft, S12 in.–2 ft), flowers insignificant.
Planting Open, sunny position, preferably in light soil.
Propagation Sow Mar.–April, 16°C (61°F). In warm areas in open ground, April.

LARKSPUR
Annual delphinium

Larkspur

Hardy annual: Vigorous, quick-growing, with single or double blooms in long, tapering spikes of many colours.
Species *D. ajacis, D. consolida* (H9 in.–3 ft, S12–15 in.), shades of blue, red, violet, white.
Planting Sunny position in ordinary, well-drained soil.
Care Stake tall cultivars. Dead-head.
Propagation Sow seeds Mar.–April. Even better results by sowing Sept. for flowering June.

LAVATERA
Mallow

Lavatera

Hardy annual: Tall, bushy plant with open, trumpet-like flowers. Good for temporary screen. Useful for cutting.
Species *L. trimestris* (H2½–3 ft, S2 ft), 'Loveliness', deep rose; 'Splendens Alba', white.
Planting Sheltered, sunny position. Soil fertile but not too rich.
Care Needs supporting in exposed sites.
Propagation Sow in open, Mar.–April.

LAVATERA
Mallow

Perennial: Shrubby plants, best cut back each year and treated as herbaceous perennials. Species and cultivars described have attractive grey, hairy foliage and wide, funnel-shaped blossoms.
Species *L. bicolor* (B3–6 ft, S2–4 ft), lilac-pink with purple eye and veining, Aug.–Oct. *L. olbia* 'Rosea' (H4–7 ft, S2–4 ft), satin pink, June–Oct.
Planting Singly in Sept. or Mar.–April (the latter best in cold areas), in well-drained soil preferably on south side of wall or hedge. Sun or light shade.
Care Cut back all one-year-old stems to within 6 in. of their bases, Mar.–April.
Propagation By basal cuttings, May–June. By seeds sown Mar.–April, in cold frame or greenhouse.

LEONTOPODIUM
Edelweiss

Leontopodium alpinum

Perennial rock plant: The much-sung alpine. Flower heads and undersides of leaves covered with white, woolly hairs. Grows readily from seeds.

Lewisia – Loosestrife

Species *L. alpinum* (H8 in., S9 in.), grey-white, June–July.
Planting Well-drained soil on sunny site. Scree, paving, dry wall, alpine house.
Propagation Seeds in John Innes No. 1 compost and grit (50/50) in cold frame, Feb.–Mar.

Leopard's bane see Doronicum

LEWISIA

Perennial rock plant: Semi-succulent evergreen with showy flowers.
Species *L. brachycalyx* (H2–3 in., S6–9 in.), white, tinged pink, May. *L. cotyledon* (H12 in., S6 in.), white, pink, apricot, May–June. *L. tweedyi* (H6 in., S9 in.), pink, apricot, April–May.
Planting In well-drained soil, sunny site. Scree, dry wall, alpine house. *L. cotyledon* does well in peat bed.
Propagation Offsets in sand/peat (50/50) in cold frame, June. Pot on and overwinter in frame. Seeds in cold frame, Mar., but may not come true to type.

Lily see p. 192

LIMONIUM
Sea lavender, Statice

Perennial: Tall variety gives attractive late-summer display in borders. Dried, it makes ideal everlasting flowers. Dwarf variety useful in rock garden. Both types evergreen.
Species *L. latifolium* (H2½ ft, S1½–2 ft), lavender-blue, July–Sept. *L. bellidifolium* (H6–12 in., S6 in.), white, Aug.–Oct.
Planting In well-drained soil in full sun. Thrives by sea. *L. latifolium* does well in poor, dry soil. *L. bellidifolium* suitable for scree, dry wall, trough and alpine house.
Propagation Seeds in cold frame, Mar. *L. latifolium* also by root cuttings in Feb.–Mar., and *L. bellidifolium* by division in spring.

LINARIA
Toad flax or bunny rabbits

Linaria

Hardy annual: Bushy plant producing dainty spikes of small flowers like antirrhinums with spurs. Ideal for edging.
Species *L. maroccana* (H9–18 in., S6–18 in.), 'Excelsior', mixed; 'Fairy Bouquet', mixed.
Planting Sunny position in ordinary, well-drained soil.
Care When first flush of flowers is over, trim back with shears to promote autumn display.
Propagation Sow in permanent site, Mar.–April.

LINUM
Flax

Hardy annual: One of the most prolific flowering annuals, best grown in masses. Shallow, funnel-shaped flowers in clusters throughout summer.
Species *L. grandiflorum* (H9 in.–2 ft, S5–12 in.), 'Album', white; 'Rubrum', red.
Planting Full sun, ordinary soil.

Linum

Propagation Sow in open, Mar.–April. For spring flowering in pots, sow Sept., and grow five or six seedlings in each 5 in. pot of John Innes No. 1. Move to cold greenhouse, Oct.

LINUM
Flax

Linum flavum

Perennial rock plant: Colourful in level bed, scree, paving or alpine house.
Species *L. flavum* (H12–18 in., S9 in.), golden-yellow, June–Aug. *L. narbonense* and *L. perenne* (H1–2 ft, S12 in.), rich blue, May–Sept.
Planting In well-drained soil. Sunny site.
Propagation Seeds in John Innes seed compost in cold frame, Mar.–April. Prick out into garden rows or pot singly.

LITHOSPERMUM

Perennial rock plant: Hardy, mat-forming, notable for freely produced funnel-shaped, true blue flowers. Makes good ground-cover.
Species *L. diffusum* (H4 in., S2 ft), deep blue, June–Oct. *L. oleifolium* (H6 in., S12 in.), pink buds, blue flowers, May–Aug.
Planting In moist, well-drained soil with leaf-mould or peat. Sun or partial shade. Peat bed, dry wall, open space in rock garden. *L. oleifolium*, trough also.
Propagation 1½–2½ in. soft lateral shoots with heel, in sand/peat (50/50), July–Aug. Keep just moist. *L. diffusum* mid to late July; water well.

LOBELIA

Lobelia

Half-hardy annual: Very popular edging plant. Trailing cultivars also grown in hanging baskets as foil for other flowers. Forms mass of blooms from May until first frosts.
Species *L. erinus* (H4–6 in., S6–12 in.), 'Cambridge Blue', light blue; 'Crystal Palace', deep blue; 'Rosamund', red; 'String of Pearls', mixed; 'White Gem', white.
Planting Fertile, moist but well-drained soil in partial shade.
Propagation Sow seeds Feb.–Mar., 16°C (61°F). Prick out seedlings in groups of three or four. They are too small and delicate to separate.

LOOSESTRIFE
Lythrum

Perennial: Water-loving plant suitable for moist borders, bogs and sides of pools. Showy and long-flowering. Clump-forming.

Love-lies-bleeding – Marigold

Lythrum salicaria

Species *L. salicaria, L. virgatum* (H2–5 ft, S18 in.), purple, rose-pink, red, June–Sept.
Planting In groups of three, Oct. or Feb.–April, in moist soil enriched with manure, compost or peat. Sun or partial shade.
Care Mulch in spring. Cut dead stems to ground in autumn. Water freely if grown in ordinary borders.
Propagation By division, Oct.–Mar.

LOVE-LIES-BLEEDING

Love-lies-bleeding

Hardy annual: Popular cottage-garden annual, prized for its drooping, crimson tassels. In autumn, stems turn crimson.
Species *Amaranthus caudatus* (H3–4 ft, S18 in.), crimson; 'Viridis', pale green.
Planting Sunny position. Any fertile soil.
Care Leave the dead flower heads on plant for their display. No staking needed.
Propagation Sow in open, Mar.–May, or earlier under glass.

LUPIN

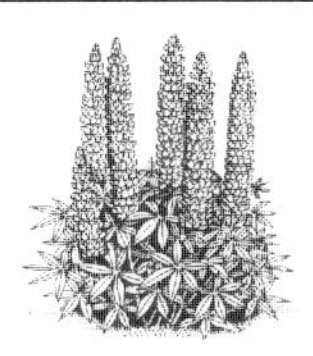

Lupinus polyphyllus

Perennial: Among the most popular border plants. Easily grown. Elegant spires of pea-shaped flowers in delicate combinations of colour.
Species *Lupinus polyphyllus* hybrids, Russell strain (H3–4 ft, S18 in.), 'Blue Jacket', blue and white; 'Bressingham Sunshine', yellow; 'Lady Fayre', pink; 'Lilac Time', lilac; 'Mrs Micklethwaite', pink and gold; 'Serenade', orange, gold and crimson, May–July.
Planting In groups of three to six, Oct.–Mar., in well-drained soil enriched with manure, compost or peat, and a general fertiliser. Sun or light shade.
Care Mulch in spring and top-dress with general fertiliser. Water in dry spells. Remove spikes of seed-pods as soon as flowering ceases. Cut dead stems to ground in autumn. If virus diseases produce mottling of leaves and browning of stems, destroy infected plants. Put down slug pellets to stop slugs damaging young shoots.
Propagation By basal cuttings, Mar.–April. By selected seeds sown in cold frame in spring. Discard self-seeded plants, as these tend to produce inferior colours.

LYCHNIS
Campion

Perennial: Brilliantly coloured plants that make a vivid border display. Good for cutting.
Species *L. chalcedonica* (H3 ft,

Lychnis coronaria

S18 in.), scarlet, July–Sept.
L. coronaria (H1½–2 ft, S12 in.), crimson-magenta, white, July–Sept.
Planting In groups of four, Oct.–Mar., in ordinary, well-drained soil. Sunny borders.
Care Mulch lightly in spring. Water during dry spells. On windy sites support with pea-sticks. Dead-head. Cut plants to ground in autumn or spring.
Propagation By basal cuttings in April; or by seeds sown in cold frame, Mar.–April. *L. coronaria* easily raised from seeds, flowering the first year. It rarely lasts more than two or three seasons.

LYSICHITON

Perennial bog plant: Hardy, producing big, arum-lily-like flowers in late spring. Massive foliage appears later.
Species *L. americanum* (H12–18 in.), yellow.
L. camtschatcense (H6–9 in.), white.
Planting In rich, wet soil.
L. americanum can be planted in 2–3 in. water. Full sun or partial shade.
Propagation By division in spring, or by seeds when ripe.

LYSIMACHIA

Perennial: Useful for moist borders. The plants are erect, with clusters or spikes of white or yellow flowers in summer. Invasive, spreading rapidly.
Species *L. clethroides* (H3 ft, S2 ft or more), white, July–Sept.
L. punctata (H2–3 ft, S2 ft or more), yellow, June–Aug.
Planting In groups of three, Oct.–Mar., in ordinary, moisture-retentive soil, particularly moist borders at edge of pools. Sun or light shade.
Care Mulch in spring. Support with pea-sticks on windy sites. Water freely in dry spells. Cut all stems to ground in autumn.
Propagation By division of roots, Oct.–Mar. Divide and replant to contain spread every two or three years.

Mallow see Lavatera

MARIGOLD, POT
Calendula

Calendula

Hardy annual: Old cottage-garden favourite with mainly orange flowers up to 4 in. across and leaves having sweetly pungent aroma. One of easiest of all flowers to grow.
Species *C. officinalis* (H9 in.–2 ft, S6–12 in.), 'Art Shades', mixed; 'Kelmscott Giant', and 'Geisha Girl', bright orange; 'Pacific Beauty', apricot, cream, pink or mixed.
Planting Any soil in sun or light shade.
Propagation Sow seeds in open, Mar.–April or Sept. Calendulas self-sow, but modern strains are best grown from selected seeds.

Marigold–Narcissus

MARIGOLD
African and French

French marigold

Half-hardy annual: Provides dazzling mass of gold, orange or bronze-red from June to autumn. The African marigolds have big, carnation-like flowers up to 6 in. across. The French varieties have smaller, often bi-coloured flowers.
Species *Tagetes erecta* (African) (H2–3 ft, S12–18 in.). Hybrid cultivars have increased bloom size and prolonged flowering. *Tagetes patula* (French), singles and doubles in many patterns.
Planting In open, sunny position. Well-drained, fertile soil. Africans make imposing backdrop of colour for other annuals in borders.
Care Dead-head to prolong display.
Propagation Sow seeds Feb.–Mar., 18°C (64°F).

MATRICARIA EXIMIA

Half-hardy annual: Small bedding or pot plant bearing little pompom or daisy-like heads, July–Sept.
Species *Chrysanthemum parthenium* (H9 in., S9 in.), 'Golden Ball', yellow; 'Snow Dwarf', 'Snow Puffs' and 'White Gem', white.
Planting Sunny position in light, well-drained soil. If soil is too rich, plants will lose their compact shape.
Propagation Sow Mar.–April, 13°C (55°F).

MESEMBRYANTHEMUM
Livingstone daisy

Mesembryanthemum

Half-hardy annual: A low, spreading plant with glistening, pale green leaves. The bright, daisy-like flowers open only in strong sunshine.
Species *M. criniflorum* (H4 in., S12 in.), mixed.
Planting In full sun on light, well-drained soil. Suitable for border edges, banks and rockeries.
Propagation Sow Mar.–April, 15°C (59°F).

Michaelmas daisy see Aster

MIMULUS
Monkey flower

Perennial grown as half-hardy annual: Shade and moisture-lover, particularly useful by pools. Can be grown in beds if never allowed to dry out. Spotted flowers, like open snapdragons, June–Sept.
Species *M. cupreus*, *M. luteus* (H9 in., S9 in.), mixed colours; often persists as perennial in sheltered areas.
Propagation Sow Mar., 13°C (55°F).

MONARDA
Bergamot

Perennial: Clump-forming plants with mint-like, sweetly aromatic leaves. The dense whorls of tubular flowers attract bees and butterflies.
Species *M. didyma* and hybrids (H2–3 ft, S2 ft), scarlet, rose-pink, purple, June–Sept.
Planting In groups of four to six, Oct.–Mar., in enriched, moisture-retentive soil. Sun or light shade in borders, near water or in woodland gardens.
Care Mulch in spring. Water freely during dry spells. Cut dead stems to ground in autumn.
Propagation By division. To maintain vigour, divide and replant every two or three years.

MONTBRETIA
Crocosmia

Montbretia

Bulbous plant: Brings display of orange-copper to late summer gardens. Hardy except in coldest districts.
Species *C.* × *crocosmiiflora* (H2 ft, S4–6 in.), shades of orange, red and yellow, July–Sept.
Planting 2–3 in. deep in sandy, well-drained soil. Warm, sunny site.
Care Leave foliage as protection until Mar.
Propagation Spreads freely on growing site. Divide overgrown clumps after flowering or in spring and replant at once.

MORNING GLORY
Ipomoea

Half-hardy annual: One of the loveliest climbers with delicately coloured, trumpet-shaped flowers, which open in the morning and close in the afternoon. July–Sept.

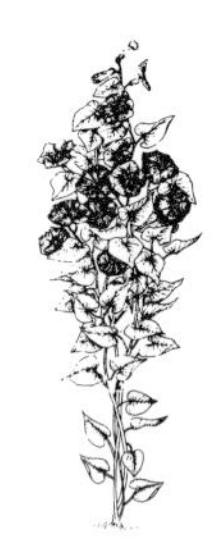

Ipomoea

Species *I. purpurea*, *I. tricolor* (H8 ft or more, S12 in.), 'Early Call', rose; 'Flying Saucers', striped blue and white; 'Heavenly Blue', blue; 'Wedding Bells', mauve; 'Early Tots' (dwarf) mixed.
Planting Sheltered, sunny spot. Light, rich soil.
Propagation Sow Mar.–April, 18°C (64°F). Soak seeds overnight to aid germination. In mild areas can be sown outdoors as hardy annual, late April–May.

Muscari see Grape hyacinth
Myosotis see Forget-me-not

NARCISSUS

Narcissus (Daffodil)

Bulbous plant: Heralds of spring from the earliest days of gardening, the narcissi are known to have at least 8,000 cultivated varieties. They include the daffodils and jonquils.
Cultivars
DAFFODIL (H14–18 in., S6–8 in.), has a trumpet at least as long as its

Nasturtium–Nigella

petals and one flower to each stem. 'Dutch Master', 'Golden Harvest', 'King Alfred', yellow; 'Queen of Bicolors', white petals, yellow trumpet; 'Beersheba', 'Cantatrice' and 'Mount Hood', white, Mar.–April.

LARGE-CUPPED NARCISSUS (H14–22 in., S6–8 in.), has a cup more than one-third the length of its petals and one flower to each stem. 'Carlton', yellow, frilled cup; 'Fortune', orange-red cup, yellow petals; 'Flower Record', red cup, white petals; 'Silver Lining', all white, Mar.–April.

SMALL-CUPPED NARCISSUS (H14–18 in., S6 in.), has a cup less than one-third the length of the petals and one flower to each stem. 'Ardour', orange-scarlet cup, yellow petals; 'La Riante', deep orange-red cup, white petals; 'Chinese White' and 'Polar Ice', all white, Mar.–April.

DOUBLE-FLOWERED NARCISSUS (H12–18 in., S6 in.). Cup and petals indistinguishable, one flower per stem. 'Golden Ducat', deep yellow; 'Mary Copeland', orange and white; 'Van Sion', golden-yellow; 'Yellow Cheerfulness', yellow, Mar.–April.

TRIANDRUS NARCISSUS (H8–16 in., S6 in.). Drooping cup and swept-back petals. White, cream, deep yellow. 'Rippling Waters', white; 'Thalia', cream and white, Mar.–April.

CYCLAMINEUS NARCISSUS (H8–15 in., S3–6 in.). Long, pendent cup with petals strongly reflexed. Yellow, white, orange. 'February Gold', yellow; 'Peeping Tom', yellow, Mar.–April.

JONQUIL (H7–14 in., S4–6 in.). Petals longer than cup; fragrant flowers, three or four on each stem. Pale lemon to rich gold, single or double. 'Golden Sceptre', golden yellow; 'Trevithian', buttercup yellow, April.

TAZETTA NARCISSUS (H14 in., S6–8 in.). True tazetta types have short cup and several flowers to a stem. Not fully hardy, but good for growing in pots. Lemon cups, white petals. 'Paper White', white, Jan.–Mar. Poetaz types similar shape but with frilled cups. Hardy. Red cups, cream petals. 'Geranium' is good variety, April.

POETICUS NARCISSUS (H17–20 in., S6 in.). Cup is short with red fringe and white petals. 'Actrea', yellow and crimson cup, April–May.

DWARF NARCISSUS (H3–8 in., S2–3 in.), (wild daffodil). *N. bulbocodium*, all yellow. *N. triandrus albus*, cream-white, Feb.–April.

Planting With exception of true tazettas, which are suitable only for indoor or greenhouse cultivation, plant all narcissi (including poetaz types) in Aug.–Oct. Any fertile, free-draining soil. Sun or light shade. Plant dwarf narcissus at least three times depth of bulb. All others about 6 in. deep. Site in groups in herbaceous or shrub borders or under trees. Cyclamineus narcissus, jonquil and dwarf narcissus ideal for rock gardens.

Propagation Remove offsets after lifting in early summer. Replant at once, or from Aug. onwards, in spare ground. Flowering size reached in one to three years. Species can also be propagated by seeds, collected in early summer as soon as the seed capsule splits; but three to seven years needed to reach flowering size.

NASTURTIUM

Hardy annual: Highly popular in all its three forms as a climber, trailing dwarf and dwarf bedding plant. Produces a long succession of spurred, funnel-shaped flowers in brilliant yellows, oranges and reds. Climbers are useful for hiding unsightly fences. Trailing dwarfs are popular for hanging baskets.

Nasturtium

Species *Tropaeolum majus* (H6 in.–8 ft, S6 in.–2 ft). Climber: 'Tall Mixed'. Trailing dwarfs: 'Golden Gleam', yellow; 'Scarlet Gleam', red. Bushy dwarfs: 'Cherry Rose', mixed; 'Empress of India', scarlet.

Planting In poor, dry soil. Sun or partial shade.

Propagation Sow in open, April–May.

NEMESIA

Nemesia

Half-hardy annual: Quick-flowering, compact plant with obliquely funnel-shaped blooms, often with spotted and bearded throats. The flowers are borne through summer.

Species *N. strumosa* and forms (H9–18 in., S4–6 in.), 'Blue Gem', blue; 'Fire King', crimson; 'Sparklers', mixed.

Planting In sunny position in enriched soil with added fertiliser.

Care Pinch out growing centre when young to encourage branching. Water well in hot, dry weather. Dead-head regularly.

Propagation Sow Feb.–April, 15°C (59°F). In mild areas sow outdoors, Mar.–April.

NICOTIANA
Tobacco plant

Nicotiana

Half-hardy annual: Petunia-like flowers with evening fragrance, therefore often sited near windows. Easily grown. Free-flowering, June–Sept.

Species *N. affinis*, *N. × sanderae* (H9 in.–3 ft, S9–12 in.), 'Crimson Bedder', red; 'Lime Green', greenish-yellow; 'White Bedder', white.

Planting In sunny position. Fertile, well-drained soil.

Care Stake tall cultivars in exposed places. Dead-head.

Propagation Sow Feb.–April, 18°C (64°F).

NIGELLA
Love-in-a-mist

Hardy annual: Erect plant with feathery foliage and blue, pink or white flowers. Good for cutting. The dried pods are used for winter decoration.

Species *N. damascena* (H9–18 in., S9–12 in.), 'Miss Jekyll' (semi-double), blue; 'Persian Jewels', mixed.

Nuphar – Paeony

Nigella

Planting Ordinary, well-drained soil. Full sun.
Care Dead-head.
Propagation Sow in open, Mar.–April or Sept.

NUPHAR
Yellow water lily

Water plant: Vigorous and not for use in small pools as all nuphars can be rampant. Floating leaves and flowers.
Species *N. advena* (planting depth 2 ft), rich yellow flowers, summer. *N. pumila* (*N. minima*) is a miniature version of *N. advena*.
Propagation By division.

NYMPHAEA
Water lily

Nymphaea × marliacea 'Rosea'

Water plant: Elegant and sometimes sweetly scented blooms, providing shade for fish and helping to inhibit the growth of algae. Most hardy species and cultivars are long-lived, and require little attention.
Species and cultivars About 70 varieties are commonly available from specialist growers, in shades of red, white, yellow and pink.
Planting Pygmy cultivars in 4–6 in. of water; medium cultivars in 12–18 in.; deep-water cultivars up to 2½ ft.
Propagation By division in spring.

OENOTHERA
Evening primrose

Oenothera lamarckiana

Perennial: Herbaceous or semi-evergreen, long-flowering plant. Funnel-shaped blossoms have satiny petals. Good for cutting.
Species *O. lamarckiana* (H4 ft, S15 in.), yellow spikes, June–Sept. *O. missouriensis* (H4–6 in.), trailing habit, large yellow flowers, May–Sept. *O. speciosa* (H18 in., S12 in.), white, fading to pink, May–Sept. *O. tetragona* (H18 in., S12 in.), yellow, June–Sept.
Planting In groups of five, Oct.–Mar., in ordinary, well-drained soil. *O. speciosa* thrives on poor, dry soils. Sun or light shade at front of borders. *O. missouriensis* good for rock garden or dry wall.
Care Mulch in spring. Water freely during dry spells. Cut dead stems to ground in autumn. On heavy, wet soils, root rot may occur. Transplant to drained site.
Propagation By division, Oct.–Mar. *O. missouriensis* by basal cuttings or seeds in spring.

OMPHALODES
Navelwort

Perennial rock plant: In addition to rock gardens, omphalodes is

Omphalodes verna

suitable for the front of borders and woodland planting. Five-petalled flowers are like big forget-me-nots.
Species *O. luciliae* (H4–6 in., S18 in.), soft blue, May–Sept., leaves grey-green. *O. verna* (H6 in., S12 in.), bright blue, Feb.–May.
Planting Moist soil with peat or leaf-mould. Sun or partial shade.
Propagation By division: *O. luciliae*, June–July; *O. verna*, Mar.–April or after flowering.

ONOCLEA
Sensitive fern

Fern: Good waterside plant of creeping habit. Often used as ground-cover to stabilise banks of streams.
Species *O. sensibilis* (H1½–2 ft).
Planting Acid to neutral, wet soil. Light shade.
Propagation Division in spring.

ORONTIUM
Golden club

Orontium aquaticum

Water-margin plant: Suitable for water 1–2 ft deep (when the leaves float), or for wet mud (when they stand upright). Bears very attractive white spadix covered with small, yellow flowers. Big, waxy leaves.
Species *O. aquaticum* (H1–2 ft) (planting depth 2–9 in.), flowering May–June.
Propagation By division in spring or seeds when ripe.

OSMUNDA
Royal fern

Fern: Wet-soil deciduous plant. Its fertile frond-tips resemble those of astilbe seed heads. Clump-forming.
Species *O. regalis* (H4–10 ft), green and brown fertile fronds in summer.
Planting In wet, fertile soil or in shallow water.
Propagation By division in spring.

PAEONY
Paeonia

Paeonia mlokosewitschii

Perennial: Popular, long-lived tuberous plants, bearing many big, bowl-shaped flowers, delicately tinted. Not difficult to maintain if left undisturbed once established.
Species and cultivars *P. lactiflora* hybrids (H2–2½ ft, S2 ft), 'Augustus John', red; 'Bowl of Beauty', semi-double, pink and gold; 'Globe of Light', single, pink and yellow; 'Karl Rosenfeld', double, red; 'The Bride', white and yellow, May–July. *P. mlokosewitschii* (H2 ft, S1½–2 ft), single, pale yellow, April–May. *P. officinalis* (H2 ft, S1½–2 ft), 'Alba-plena',

Pampas grass–Phlox

pink; 'Rosea-plena', deep pink; 'Rubra-plena', crimson, May–June.
Planting In groups of three or four, Oct.–Mar., in deep, enriched, moisture-retentive soil. If enriched only with peat, add John Innes base fertiliser at 2–3 oz. (2–3 tablespoons) per square yard. Sometimes takes several years to establish. Do not transplant.
Care Mulch in spring. Support with canes, pea-sticks or wire loops. Water in dry spells. Dead-head. Cut all stems to ground in autumn.
Propagation By division of roots, Sept. to early Mar. Species also by seeds when ripe in a cold frame; takes several years to reach flowering size.

PAMPAS GRASS
Cortaderia

Cortaderia selloana

Perennial: Stately plumes, up to 9 ft tall, lending dignity to gardens in autumn.
Species *C. selloana* (H6–9 ft, S4–6 ft), silver-cream plumes on 5 ft stems, Sept.–Oct.
Planting Singly in April in well-drained, fertile soil. Full sun and sheltered from wind. Allow room for expansion.
Care Mulch and remove dead leaves in late spring. Cut down flowering stems when they become 'thin on top' in early winter. Beware sharp leaves, and wear gloves.
Propagation By division, April.

Pansy see Viola
Papaver see Poppy

PENSTEMON

Penstemon × gloxinioides

Perennial: Semi-evergreen, short-lived plant with flower-spikes composed of colourful foxglove-shaped blooms. Fully hardy only in mild districts.
Species *P. barbatus* (H3 ft, S18 in.), pink to carmine, white, June–Aug. *P. × gloxinioides* (H12–18 in., S12–18 in.), pink, red, June–Aug.
Planting In groups of four, Mar.–April, in well-drained, enriched soil. Sunny, sheltered spot near the house; herbaceous border in mild districts.
Care Mulch lightly in spring. Water in dry spells. Dead-head. Cut stems to ground in autumn and protect crowns against frost.
Propagation By cuttings of non-flowering side-shoots, Aug.–Sept., rooted in a cold frame. Best raised from cuttings annually, and planted out in spring.

PENSTEMON

Perennial rock plant: Low-lying shrubs and sub-shrubs with purplish flowers in summer.
Species *P. menziesii* (H9 in., S15 in.), violet-purple, June. *P. newberryi* (H9 in., S15 in.), rose-purple, June. *P. rupicola* (H3–4 in., S12 in.), rose-carmine, May. *P. scouleri* (H12 in., S18 in.), rose-purple, June–July.
Planting In well-drained, sunny site. Scree, raised bed, paving, peat bed, alpine lawn.
Propagation $1\frac{1}{2}$–$2\frac{1}{2}$ in. non-flowering shoots in peat/sand (50/50), July–Aug. Pot on, overwinter in cold frame.

PETUNIA

Petunia

Half-hardy annual: Small plant producing big, funnel-shaped flowers in profusion from June until autumn. Very small cultivars suitable for borders, window-boxes and hanging baskets. Wind and heavy rain can damage flowers; choose weather-resistant types for exposed positions.
Cultivars Multiflora: bushy plants 6–12 in. tall with freely borne, weather-resistant flowers. Grandiflora: similar to multiflora but bigger and fewer flowers, sometimes double and/or frilled. Ruined by bad weather. Nana Compacta: dwarf, neater form of multiflora, less than 6 in. tall. Pendula: plants with long, trailing stems, very suitable for hanging baskets or summer ground-cover. The four groups embrace all colours and many types have two-colour combinations.
Planting In sheltered, sunny position. Not over-rich soil.
Care Dead-head regularly.
Propagation Sow Jan.–Mar., 15°C (59°F).

PHLOX

Half-hardy annual: Long-lasting bedding plant, bearing dense heads

Phlox

of flowers, June–Sept. Useful for window-boxes and cut flowers.
Species *P. drummondii* (H6–15 in., S9 in.), 'Large-flowered Mixed'; 'Nana Compacta' (low-growing), mixed; 'Twinkling Stars' (dwarf), mixed.
Care Dead-head. On poor soil feed with liquid fertiliser.
Propagation Sow Mar.–April, 15°C (59°F).

PHLOX

Phlox maculata

Perennial: Large trusses of showy flowers in late summer. Good for cutting.
Species *P. maculata* (H2–3 ft, S18 in.), purple, July–Sept. *P. paniculata* (H3–4 ft, S18 in.), 'Brigadier', salmon-scarlet; 'Dorothy Hanbury Forbes', pink; 'Fairy's Petticoat', mauve; 'Graf Zeppelin', red and white; 'Harlequin', bright, variegated foliage, purple flowers, July–Oct.
Planting In groups of four to six, Oct.–Mar., in enriched, well-drained, moisture-retentive soil. Light shade or sun.
Care Mulch in spring, heavily if drooping flowers of poor quality are being produced. Water freely in dry spells. Support with pea-

Phlox–Primula

sticks on exposed sites. Cut all stems to just above ground in autumn. Eelworm can cause stunted shoots with pale leaves. Destroy affected plants.
Propagation By division of fibrous roots, Oct.–Mar.; by root cuttings, Feb.–Mar.

PHLOX

Perennial rock plant: Very decorative alpine.
Species *P. adsurgens* (H12 in., S12 in.), salmon-pink, June–July. *P. douglasii* (H2–4 in., S18 in.), lavender, May–June. *P. subulata*, purple, pink, April–May.
Planting Well-drained soil with peat or leaf-mould. Sunny site. Dry wall, paving, scree. *P. adsurgens*, peat bed, alpine house.
Propagation 2–2½ in. basal shoots in peat/sand (50/50) in cold frame, July.

Physalis see Chinese lantern
Pink see Dianthus
Polyanthus see Primula

POLYGONUM

Perennial: Vigorous, spreading plant forming big mats. Leaves are narrow, sometimes red-tinted. Dense spikes of closely set flowers over long period.
Species *P. affine* (H12 in., S2 ft or more), pink, June–Oct. *P. amplexicaule* 'Speciosum' (H3 ft, S2 ft), claret-red, June–Sept. *P. bistorta* 'Superbum' (H1½–2½ ft, S2 ft or more), pink, July–Sept.
Planting In groups of three, Oct.–Mar., in enriched, moisture-retentive soil. Sun or partial shade. Good as ground-cover. *P. amplexicaule* and *P. bistorta* thrive on edge of pools and streams.
Propagation By division.

POLYSTICHUM

Fern: Several beautiful forms suitable for all soils. Hardy.
Species *P. aculeatum* (Hard shield fern) (H2–3½ ft, S2–3½ ft), evergreen. *P. setiferum* (Soft shield fern) (H3–4 ft, S3–4 ft), semi-evergreen. 'Acutilobum' ('Proliferum'), dense plumy fronds–the best garden form.
Planting In light shade. *P. aculeatum* also in sun.

PONTEDERIA
Pickerel weed

Water-margin plant: Broad, lily-like leaves with spikes of purple-blue florets, Aug.–Sept.
Species *P. cordata* (H18–30 in.).
Planting Start in shallow water (2–3 in.). Increase depth later if necessary to 9 in.
Propagation Divide in spring.

POPPY
Papaver

Poppy

Hardy annual: Dainty, free-flowering plant. Cup-shaped flowers, formed of four overlapping petals in single blooms. Suitable for cutting.
Species *P. rhoeas*, *P. somniferum* (H1½–3 ft, S12 in.), scarlet and mixed pastel shades, singles and doubles.
Planting In any ordinary soil. Sunny position.
Care Dead-head to prevent self-seeding.
Propagation In open, Mar.–April or Sept.

POPPY
Papaver

Papaver alpinum

Perennial rock plant: Showy-coloured blooms in mid-summer.
Species *P. alpinum* (H4–10 in., S4–10 in.), white, yellow, red, orange, June–July.
Planting Well-drained soil on sunny, open site. Paving, scree, trough, alpine house.
Propagation Sow seeds in flowering position, Mar.–April or Sept.

Primrose see Primula

PRIMULA
Primrose

Primula denticulata

Perennial: Many species, sizes and colours for borders where soil can be kept moist.
Species *P. denticulata* (Drumstick primrose) (H12 in., S12–18 in.), lilac-purple, white, Mar.–May. *P. pulverulenta* (H2–3 ft, S12–18 in.), crimson, June–July. *P. × variabilis* (*P. × polyantha*, *P. × tommasinii*) Polyanthus (H12 in., S12 in.), 'Pacific Strain' and 'Mother's Day', large blue, purple, yellow, pink, red and white; 'Giant Bouquet' and 'Goldlace', smaller, yellow-edged, Mar.–May. *P. vulgaris* (H6 in., S9 in.), common primrose, now available in many colours, including blue.
Planting In groups of four, Sept.–Mar., in enriched, moisture-retentive soil. Sun or partial shade.
Care Mulch freely. Water freely in dry spells. Dead-head.
Propagation By division after flowering or in spring; by seeds sown in cold frame on ripening, or in Mar.–April. Keep seedlings moist and shaded. Named varieties do not come true.

PRIMULA
Primrose

Primula auricula

Perennial rock plant: Many delightful variations for spring flowering.
Species *P. auricula* (H6 in., S6 in.), evergreen, yellow, purple, Mar.–April. *P. clarkei* (H2 in., S6 in.), pale lavender, Mar. *P. edgeworthii* (H3–4 in., S9 in.), rose-lilac, Jan. *P. marginata* (H4 in., S6–9 in.), evergreen, lavender-blue, April–May. *P. rosea* (H6 in., S6–8 in.), rose-pink, Mar.–April.
Planting Moist but well-drained

Primula–Ranunculus

soil with leaf-mould or peat. Partial shade or sun. Peat bed, paving, trough, alpine house. *P. auricula* and *P. marginata* do best with at least half-day sun.
Propagation *P. auricula* and *P. marginata*: 1–2 in. cuttings or rooted shoots (suckers), June–Aug. *P. clarkei* and *P. edgeworthii*: seeds as soon as ripe. *P. rosea*: division after flowering.

PRIMULA
Primrose

Primula florindae

Bog plant: Vigorous, flowering from early spring to early summer.
Species *P. beesiana* (H2 ft), rose-carmine. *P. florindae* (H2–3 ft), yellow (will grow in shallow water). *P. japonica* (H18 in.), white, rose, purple (very vigorous).
Propagation By division in spring or by seeds sown when ripe.

POTAMOGETON

Potamogeton crispus

Water oxygenator: Useful and entirely submerged. Avoid floating species, *P. natans*.
Species *P. crispus* (Curled pondweed) and *P. densus* (Frog's lettuce). Flowers insignificant.
Planting In 6–24 in. water.
Propagation By cuttings or division.

PULSATILLA
Pasque flower

Pulsatilla vulgaris

Perennial: Long-lived once established, with fern-like foliage. Related to anemones. Cup-shaped flowers emerge before or with young leaves.
Species *P. vulgaris* (H6–12 in., S12–15 in.), purple, white, April–May.
Planting In groups of six, Sept.–Mar., in light, well-drained soil. Sunny border.
Care Mulch in spring. Attractive seed-heads may be left until early autumn. Resents root disturbance and should not be moved unless absolutely necessary.
Propagation Sow seeds in cold frame as soon as ripe, or from autumn to spring.

PYRETHRUM

Pyrethrum roseum

Perennial: Popular, clump-forming, border plants. Big, daisy-like flowers excellent for cutting.
Species *P. roseum* (syn. *Chrysanthemum coccineum*) (H2–3 ft, S18 in.), cerise, pink, red, crimson, single or double, May–June, sometimes later.
Planting In groups of four or five, Oct.–Mar., in light, well-drained soil. Sunny border.
Care Mulch in spring. Support with pea-sticks. Water in dry spells. Cut faded flowering stems almost to ground to encourage further blooms.
Propagation Divide woody roots and replant every two or three years. Poor flowers usually result from overcrowding. Divide in July, or Oct.–Mar.

RANUNCULUS
Buttercup

Ranunculus acris

Perennial: Bushy plant with double buttercup flowers, good for cutting.
Species *R. aconitifolius* 'Flore-Pleno' (Fair maids of France) (H2 ft, S18 in.), white, May–June. *R. acris* 'Flore-Pleno' (H1½–2 ft, S18 in.), yellow, June–Aug. or later.
Planting In groups of four, the roots 2 in. deep, Oct.–Mar., in any ordinary garden soil that is moist. Plant the roots 'claws' down. Sun or light shade in herbaceous or mixed borders or in rock gardens.
Care Mulch in spring. Support with pea-sticks on windy sites. Dead-head. Cut dead stems to ground in autumn. Poor flowers usually due to too dry soil. Transplant to moister site.
Propagation By division, Oct.–Mar.

RANUNCULUS
Buttercup

Ranunculus calandrinioides

Perennial rock plant: Evergreen for sheltered site.
Species *R. calandrinioides* (H4–6 in., S4–6 in.), white, flushed pink, Mar.–April (scree); Dec.–Mar. (alpine house).
Planting In sharply drained soil. Sheltered sunny spot. Scree, alpine house.
Propagation Seeds in cold frame, Feb.–Mar.

RANUNCULUS
Spearwort

Ranunculus lingua

Water-margin plant: Golden, buttercup-like flowers, May–July. Narrow, greyish foliage persists in winter and spreads.
Species *R. lingua* (2–4 ft). 'Grandiflora' is giant form.
Planting In 4–12 in. of water.
Propagation Division of underground rhizomes. Will spread itself unassisted to form large masses of growth.

Red-hot poker see Kniphofia

Rodgersia–Saxifrage

RODGERSIA

Bog plant: Can also be grown in border if kept moist.
Species *R. pinnata* (H2–3 ft), red, white or pink, summer. *R. tabularis* (H3 ft), yellowish-white, summer.
Planting In light shade.
Propagation Division in spring.

RUDBECKIA

Half-hardy annual: Popular, late-summer plant with big, daisy-like flowers, usually yellow or bronze with black centre.
Species *R. bicolor*, *R. hirta* (H9 in.–3 ft, S12 in.–2 ft), yellow, bronze, orange and mahogany, single and double.
Planting Open, sunny position. Any well-drained soil.
Care Stake taller sorts. Protect with slug pellets.
Propagation Sow Feb.–Mar., 15°C (59°F).

RUDBECKIA

Rudbeckia fulgida

Perennial: Tall members of the daisy family, with yellow and bronze flowers in late summer.
Species *R. fulgida* (H2–3 ft, S2 ft), orange to yellow, star-shaped, July–Sept. *R. hirta* (Black-eyed Susan) (H1–3 ft, S1½–2 ft), bronze, mahogany, golden-yellow, single and double, Aug.–Oct.
R. laciniata (H6–7 ft, S2–3 ft), golden-yellow, single or double, Aug.–Oct.
Planting Singly or in groups of three to five in enriched, reasonably moisture-retentive soil. Sun or light shade.
Care Mulch in spring. Support with strong canes. Water in dry spells. Dead-head. Cut dead stems to ground in autumn. *R. hirta* is short-lived. Best regularly grown from seeds.
Propagation By division of fibrous roots, Oct.–Mar.; by seeds sown in cold frame Mar.–April. (Seeds from cultivars do not come true.)

RUSH, FLOWERING
Butomus

Butomus umbellatus

Water-margin plant: Umbels of rose-pink, July–Sept.
Species *B. umbellatus* (H2–4 ft).
Planting In mud with up to 6 in. water. Flowers more freely if water is shallow.
Propagation By division.

SAGITTARIA
Arrowhead

Water-margin plant: Double flowers like a white stock in July–Aug.
Species *S. sagittifolia* 'Flore Pleno' (H12–18 in.).
Planting In 6–9 in. water.
Propagation Division of underground tubers. Remove and replant smallest of young plants around parent growth.

SALPIGLOSSIS
Painted tongue

Salpiglossis

Half-hardy annual: Brightly coloured, funnel-shaped flowers for borders or pots July–Sept. Suitable for cutting.
Species *S. sinuata* (H1½–2½ ft, S12 in.), 'Grandiflora', 'Monarch', 'Bolero', 'Shalimar', 'Splash', all mixed. F1 hybrids recommended for poor soils.
Planting Open, sunny position in fairly rich soil.
Care Pinch out when young to induce branching. Support with twiggy sticks. Dead-head.
Propagation Sow Feb.–Mar., 18°C (64°F).

SALVIA

Salvia

Half-hardy annual: Favourite in municipal parks. Flowers, usually bright red, borne in densely packed spikes, June to autumn.
Species *S. splendens* (H9–18 in., S9–18 in.), red, pink, salmon. *S.* × *horminum* (H18 in., S9 in.), grown for coloured bracts in white, red, rose, blue and purple.
Planting Ordinary, well-drained soil. Sunny position.
Care Pinch out when 2–3 in. high to develop bushy plants.
Propagation Sow Jan.–Mar., 18°C (64°F).

SALVIA

Salvia haematodes

Perennial: Erect plants with spikes of tubular, two-lipped flowers, particularly effective by grey-leaved neighbours.
Species *S. haematodes* (H2–3 ft, S1½–2 ft), purple, June–Sept. *S.* × *superba* (H2–3 ft, S1½–2 ft), blue-purple, July–Sept.
Planting In groups of four, Oct.–Mar., in enriched, well-drained soil. Sunny mixed borders.
Care Mulch in spring. Support with pea-sticks in exposed sites. Dead-head. Cut all stems to ground in autumn.
Propagation Divide woody rootstocks of *S.* × *superba* and replant every three years Oct.–Mar. *S. haematodes* is short-lived and resents root disturbance. Increase from seeds sown in cold frame, Mar.–April.

SAXIFRAGE
Saxifraga

Perennial rock plant: Compact, low-lying, bearing masses of mainly yellow, white and pink flowers. The leaves are formed into

Scabious – Shasta daisy

grey-green or silvery rosettes encrusted with lime.
Species
EUAIZOONIA SECTION *S. paniculata* (syn. *S. aizoon*) (H12–15 in., S12–15 in.), white, June. *S. cochlearis* (H8 in., S9–12 in.), white, June. *S. cotyledon* (H2 ft, S12–15 in.), white, June–Aug. *S. longifolia* (H18 in., S12 in.), white, June.
KABSCHIA AND ENGLERIA SECTIONS *S. apiculata* (H4 in., S12–18 in.), yellow, Mar.–April. *S. burseriana* (H2 in., S12 in.), white, Feb.–Mar. *S.* × 'Cranbourne' (H1 in., S9–12 in.), clear pink, Mar.–April. *S.* × 'Elizabethae' (H3 in., S12 in.), light yellow, Mar.–April. *S. grisebachii* (H6–9 in., S9–12 in.), pink, Mar.–May.
Planting In well-drained, gritty soil. Sun or shade. Dry wall, paving, scree, trough, alpine house. Euaizoonia species especially suitable for rock crevices.
Propagation Strike non-flowering rosettes in May–June. Insert lower leaves in pan of peat/sand, watering from below. Also by division for *S. cotyledon* and *S. longifolia* when possible.

SCABIOUS
Pincushion flower

Scabious

Hardy annual: Late flowering with daisy-like blooms in full colour range. Good for cutting. Seed-heads may be dried for winter decoration.
Species *Scabiosa atropurpurea* (H1½–3 ft, S9 in.), 'Monarch Cockade', mixed; 'Tom Thumb', dwarf, mixed.
Planting Any fertile soil. Sunny position.
Care Dead-head if seed-heads not needed.

SCABIOUS

Scabiosa caucasica

Perennial: Handsome plants with narrow leaves and frilled, daisy-like flowers, usually pale blue. Good for cutting. Seed-heads may be dried.
Species *Scabiosa caucasica* (H1½–2 ft, S18 in.) in various shades of blue, also white, June–Sept.
Planting In groups of four or five, Oct.–April, in enriched, well-drained soil. Thrives on limy soil. Sunny borders.
Care Mulch lightly in spring. Dead-head. Cut down dead stems in autumn.
Propagation By division, Mar.–April.

SCILLA

Bulbous plant: Relative of the bluebell, producing mass of blue flowers from Feb. onwards.
Species *S. bifolia* (H6 in., S3 in.), mauve-blue, Feb.–Mar. *S. sibirica* (H6 in., S4 in.), brilliant blue, Mar.–April. *S. tubergeniana* (H4 in., S4 in.), silvery-blue, darker veined, Feb.–Mar.
Planting 4 in. deep in late summer or early autumn, in sun or

Scilla tubergeniana

partial shade. Any rich, moist soil. Irregular groups in narrow borders, at edges of beds and in rock gardens. Good for naturalising in short grass. *S. sibirica* is best sort for indoor pot cultivation, but must be kept cool.
Propagation Separate offsets when foliage dies down; replant at once for flowering in one to three years.

Scirpus see Bulrush

SEDUM
Stonecrop

Sedum spectabile

Perennial: Attractive, fleshy-leaved plants. Dense heads of small, starry flowers.
Species *S. maximum* 'Atropurpureum' (H1½–2 ft, S12 in.), rose-purple, leaves flushed with red-purple, Aug.–Oct. *S. spectabile* and *S. telephium* (H12–18 in., S12 in.), pink, red-purple, Aug.–Oct. *S. caeruleum* (H4–6 in., S6 in.), annual, blue, July. *S. dasyphyllum* (H½ in., S12 in.), carpeting perennial, white, June. *S. roseum* (H12–15 in., S12–15 in.), perennial, yellow, May–June.
Planting In groups of four or five, Oct.–April, in ordinary well-drained soil. Avoid heavy wet soils which would cause root and crown rot. Sedum thrives on poor, dry soils with exception of *S. maximum*. Sunny border.
Care Light mulch in spring. Attractive seed-heads may be left on until spring.
Propagation By division, Oct.–April. Even small, rootless pieces will usually take.

SEMPERVIVUM
Houseleek

Perennial rock plant: Easily grown, sun-loving plant. Thrives in poor soil, provided it is well drained. Rosettes of fleshy leaves, green, purple or red. Flowers in summer, red, pink, yellowish or purplish.
Species *S. arachnoideum* (H½–1 in., S12 in.), bright rose-red, June–July. *S. erythraeum* (H1–2 in., S6–9 in.), deep rose, July. *S. montanum* (H1 in., S6–9 in.), pale red-purple, June–Aug. *S. tectorum* (H2–3 in., S12 in.), rose-purple, July.
Planting Well-drained soil. Sunny site. Dry wall, scree, paving, alpine house.
Propagation Remove and replant offsets Sept.–Oct. or Mar.–April.

SHASTA DAISY

Perennial: Popular and easily grown border plant, with graceful, daisy-like flowers, white or pink. On fading, white blooms turn grey and should be removed.
Species *Chrysanthemum maximum* (H2½–3 ft, S12–18 in.), 'Esther Read', double, white; 'Everest', white; 'Mayfield Giant', cream-white; 'Wirral Pride', semi-double, white, June–Aug.

Sidalcea – Stock

Planting In groups of six, Oct.–Mar., in any well-drained, good soil, preferably limy. Sun or light shade.
Care Mulch in late spring. Support *C. rubellum* with pea-sticks. Dead-head. Cut dead stems to ground in autumn.
Propagation Divide and replant every two or three years in spring. Poor flowers usually indicate need for division. Also by cuttings of basal shoots in cold frame in spring.

SIDALCEA

Perennial: Tall, handsome plant bearing funnel-shaped, mallow-like flowers in slender spikes. Easily grown in borders.
Species *S. malvaeflora* (H2½–4 ft, S18 in.), crimson, pink and salmon, June–Sept.
Planting In groups of four or five, Oct.–Mar., in fertile, well-drained soil. Sun or light shade.
Care Mulch in spring. Support with pea-sticks on windy sites. Cut faded flower stems back to 12 in. Cut all stems to ground in autumn. If flowers are poor, transfer to moister, enriched site.
Propagation By division, Oct.–Mar., using healthy, vigorous pieces from outside of clump and discarding centre.

SILENE

Perennial rock plant: Densely tufted green carpeting plant with stemless blossoms.
Species *S. acaulis* (H2 in., S12–18 in.), vivid pink, May–June.
Planting In well-drained soil. Sun or light shade. Scree, paving, dry wall, alpine house.
Propagation 1–1½ in. vigorous shoots in peat/sand, July–Aug.

SNOWDROP
Galanthus

Galanthus nivalis

Bulbous plant: Sometimes difficult to establish, requiring moisture during growing period. But afterwards needs little attention in bringing splendour to coldest winter.
Species *G. elwesii* (H6–10 in., S4–6 in.), *G. nivalis* (H4–6 in., S4–6 in.), both white and green, Jan.–Feb.
Planting 4 in. deep in early autumn or immediately after flowering, in partially shaded site. Groups under trees, among ivy, or together with muscaris, chionodoxas and winter aconites. Also in rock gardens.

Solidago see Golden rod

STACHYS

Perennial: Mat-forming plant with whorls of tubular flowers.
S. lanata grown mainly for its evergreen, silvery leaves.
S. macrantha has more showy flowers.
Species *S. lanata* (H12–18 in., S18 in.), purple flowers, July. Not hardy. *S. macrantha* (H12 in., S18 in.), rose, pink, purple, May–July.
Planting In groups of three or four, Oct.–Mar., in ordinary, well-drained soil. Sun or light shade in borders. *S. lanata* also as border edging or ground-cover.
Care Mulch in spring. Dead-head. Cut off dead stems in autumn.
Propagation By division, Oct.–Mar.

St John's wort see Hypericum

STOCK

Stock

Half-hardy annual: Colourful, delightfully scented flowers for summer, ranging from 12 in. dwarfs to giant Column type. Single and double.
Species *Matthiola incana* (H12 in.–2½ ft, S9 in.–2 ft), in shades of yellow, pink, red, lavender and white.
Planting In ordinary, well-drained soil, preferably slightly alkaline. Enrich if soil is poor. Full sun or partial shade.
Care Stake tall cultivars in exposed sites. Dead-head.
Propagation Sow Feb.–Mar., 13°C (55°F). Plant out only strong, healthy seedlings. In mild areas can be sown outdoors, April–May.

STOCK
Brompton or Winter

Biennial: Over-wintering cultivars of *Matthiola incana*, producing flowers on sturdy, branching plants Mar.–May.
Propagation Sow June–July in cold frame or greenhouse. Except in mild areas, keep in frame over winter and plant out in spring.

STOCK
Night-scented

Night-scented stock

Hardy annual: Spikes of single, lilac flowers, pleasantly scented in evening.
Species *Matthiola bicornis* (H15 in., S9 in.), lilac, April.
Planting In sun or light shade. Soil fertile and slightly alkaline.
Propagation Sow in open, April.

STOCK
Virginian

Virginian stock

Hardy annual: Pretty, mixed colours on slender stems. Very easy to grow and often given to children for their first attempt at gardening. Scented.
Species *Malcolmia maritima* (H8 in., S4–6 in.), mixed colours.
Planting Any site or soil, but best in sun.
Propagation Sow in open, Mar.–

Sunflower – Tradescantia

July, or in Sept. for spring flowering. Sow thinly and periodically for succession of blooms.

SUNFLOWER

Sunflower

Hardy annual: Garden giant with flowers often as big as dinner plates.
Species *Helianthus annuus, H. debilis* (H2–10 ft, S12 in.–2½ ft), generally yellow, but also primrose, bronze and maroon.
Planting In full sun. Rich, well-drained soil.
Care Tall cultivars need support.
Propagation Sow two or three seeds in each flowering position in April. Thin to one seedling later.

SUNFLOWER
Helianthus

Helianthus decapetalus

Perennial: Tall border plant with daisy-like flowers, good for cutting.
Species *H. decapetalus* (H4–6 ft, S1½–2½ ft), shades of yellow and gold, single, semi-double or double.
Planting In groups of three to five or singly, Oct.–Nov. or April, in well-drained, fertile soil. At back of sunny border.
Care Mulch in spring. Support with canes. Dead-head. Cut dead stems to ground in autumn.
Propagation Divide and replant every three years in autumn to prevent double flowers reverting to singles. Sow seeds in cold frame or open ground, Mar.–April.

SWEET WILLIAM

Sweet william

Biennial and half-hardy annual: Favourite cottage-garden plant with densely packed, flattened heads of single or double flowers.
Species *Dianthus barbatus* (H12 in.–2 ft, S8–10 in.), shades of pink, salmon, red, white, double and single.
Planting Sunny position preferably in alkaline soil.
Care Dead-head.
Propagation Sow biennials May–June, and plant out in flowering positions in autumn. Sow annuals Feb.–Mar., 20°C (68°F), or in open, April.

Tagetes see Marigold

THALICTRUM
Meadow rue

Perennial: Greyish leaves that resemble maidenhair ferns, and

Thalictrum aquilegifolium

big, loose heads of tiny flowers that are good for cutting.
Species *T. aquilegifolium* (H4 ft, S2 ft), mauve to purple, May–July. *T. dipterocarpum* (H4–5 ft, S2 ft), lavender-purple, June–Aug. *T. speciosissimum* (H5 ft, S2 ft), lemon-yellow, July–Aug.
Planting In groups of four or five, Oct.–Mar., in enriched, moisture-retentive soil. Sun or light shade at back of borders or among shrubs.
Care Mulch in spring. Support with canes. Water freely in dry spells. Cut dead stems to ground in autumn.
Propagation By division Oct.–Mar., but resents root disturbance and should be lifted only when absolutely necessary.

THYMUS

Rock plant: Carpeting sub-shrub with attractive flowers, good for chinks between paving stones.
Species *T. nitidus* (H8 in., S12 in.), lilac-pink, May–June. *T. serpyllum* (H1–3 in., S2 ft), pink, white, June–Aug.
Planting Sunny site with well-drained soil. Paving, scree, dry wall, trough, alpine house, alpine lawn.
Propagation Division, Mar.–Sept.

TIARELLA

Rock plant: Heart-shaped leaves and fluffy spires of white flowers April–June. Evergreen perennial.
Species *T. cordifolia* (H6–12 in., S12 in.), cream-white, May–June. *T. wherryi* (H6–14 in., S12 in.), cream-white, May-June. Forms attractive clumps.
Planting Moist soil with leaf-mould or peat. Sun or shade. Ground-cover. *T. wherryi*, peat bed. *T. cordifolia* can be invasive.
Propagation Divide *T. cordifolia* Oct.–April. Sow seeds of *T. wherryi* in seed compost in cold frame, Mar., or divide carefully.

Tobacco plant see Nicotiana

TRADESCANTIA
Spiderwort, Trinity flower

Tradescantia virginiana

Perennial: Hardy relative of tradescantia house-plants. Smooth, erect stems grow rapidly each spring with grassy leaves and clusters of three-petalled flowers at the top.
Species *T.* × *andersoniana* (*virginiana*) (H1½–2 ft, S18 in.), purple, mauve, blue, violet, cerise or white, June–Sept.
Planting In groups of four or five, Oct.–April, in fertile, moisture-retentive soil. Sun or partial shade.
Care Mulch in spring. Support with pea-sticks in windy places. Cut dead growth to ground in autumn. Protect with slug pellets.
Propagation By division, Oct.–April. Divide every three or four years. Seeds may be sown in March but named cultivars do not come true from seed.

Trollius–Veronica

TROLLIUS
Globe flower

Perennial: Bold, buttercup-like plants with globular, deeply cleft, rounded leaves. Good for cut flowers. Moist site required.
Species *Trollius × hybridus* (H2–3 ft, S12–18 in.), 'Earliest of All', mid-yellow; 'Golden Wonder', deep yellow; 'Lemon Queen', pale yellow; 'Orange Princess', orange, May–July.
Planting In groups of five, Oct.–April, in deep, enriched, moist soil. Sun or light shade. Moist borders, bog or waterside.
Care Mulch in spring. Water freely in dry spells. Dead-head. Cut dead stems to ground in autumn.
Propagation By division of fibrous roots, Oct.–April; by seeds sown in cold frame, Sept.–Mar.

TULIP
Tulipa

Tulipa (Single early)

Bulbous plant: Hundreds of different cultivars of tulip are produced for sale. They brighten our gardens from Mar. to May.
Cultivars
SINGLE EARLY (H8–14 in., S4 in.). Flowers that open out flat. 'Brilliant Star', scarlet; 'Couleur Cardinal', orange-red; 'Keizerskroon', red and yellow; 'Pink Perfection', bright pink, April. Also suitable for forcing to flower indoors in Feb.
DOUBLE EARLY (H12–15 in., S6 in.). Paeony-like, often frilled. 'Electra', pinkish-mauve; 'Marechal Niel', bright yellow; 'Orange Nassau', orange; 'Peach Blossom', pink, April.
TRIUMPH (H16–20 in., S6 in.). Angular flowers on sturdy stems, excellent for mass planting. 'Dutch Princess', gold and orange; 'Korneforos', red; 'Pat', white; 'Virtuoso', rose-lilac. Late April–May. Can also be forced under glass.
DARWIN (H2–2½ ft, S6–8 in.). Big, rounded flowers on strong stems. 'Charles Needham', scarlet, 'Clara Butt', pink; 'Niphetos', yellow; 'Queen of Night', purple; 'Snowpeak', white, May.
DARWIN HYBRIDS (H2–2½ ft, S6–8 in.). Big brilliant flowers. 'Apeldoorn', red; 'Golden Oxford', yellow; 'Holland's Glory', scarlet; 'Apeldoorn's Elite', red and orange. Early May.
LILY FLOWERED (H1½–2 ft, S6 in.). Long-waisted flowers with pointed petals that bend outwards at tips. 'Arkadia', yellow; 'China Pink', pink and white; 'Queen of Sheba', red and orange, April–May.
COTTAGE (H2–3 ft, S6–8 in.). Rounded flowers on tall stems. Good as cut flowers. 'Bacchus', violet-blue; 'Golden Harvest', deep yellow; 'Greenland', green and pink, April–May.
PARROT (H2 ft, S8 in.). Big, fringed flowers, often with twisted, bi-coloured petals. Good for cutting. 'Black Parrot', purple; 'Fantasy', pink; 'Red Parrot', red; 'White Parrot', white, April–May.
KAUFMANNIANA HYBRIDS (H6–10 in., S5 in.). Flowers open into six-pointed star. Ideal for rock gardens. 'Shakespeare', scarlet and salmon, yellow base; 'Stresa', red and yellow; 'The First', carmine and yellow-white (the first tulip to bloom in spring and popular in window boxes), Mar.
FOSTERIANA HYBRIDS (H12–18 in., S6 in.). Big, blunt-pointed, brilliant flowers. Best grown in borders where they can be left undisturbed. 'Easter Parade', yellow; 'Red Emperor', deep red; 'Princeps', scarlet-orange; 'Purissima', cream, April.
GREIGII (H7–14 in., S5 in.). Blunt, pointed petals opening to reveal black or brown centres. Good for sunny rock gardens. 'Margaret Herbest', red; 'Oriental Beauty', orange-red; 'Red Riding Hood', bright red, purple-mottled leaves; 'Lamba', yellow and bronze-green. Early April–May.
Planting 6 in. deep in a sunny, sheltered site in well-drained, preferably alkaline soil. Plant in Nov.–Dec. Earlier planting is not advisable as emerging shoots may suffer frost damage. Parrot tulips need protection from wind.
Propagation Tulips can be lifted annually when leaves start to wither. Remove offsets and store bulbs and offsets in dry, warm place until replanting in autumn. Alternatively most tulips, with exception of the earlies, can be left in the same place for several years provided all dead and decaying foliage is removed.

TYPHA

Typha minima

Water-margin plant: Rush, producing poker-like stems with brown flower-heads the shape of poker handles at the top. Used for winter decoration. Spreads vigorously.
Species *T. angustifolia* (H4 ft) (Cat-tail). *T. minima* (H12–18 in.) (Dwarf reed mace).
Planting *T. minima* in 2–6 in. water. Others in 4–6 in.
Propagation By seeds or division.

VERBASCUM
Mullein

Verbascum bombyciferum

Perennial: Erect plant with small flowers borne on imposing spikes 1–2 ft or more long.
Species *V. bombyciferum* (H4–6 ft, S1½–2 ft), sulphur-yellow, June–July. *V. olympicum* (H5–8 ft, S2–3 ft), yellow, purple-centred, June–Sept. *V. phoeniceum* hybrids (H3 ft, S12–18 in.), white, biscuit, pink, mauve, yellow, May–Sept.
Planting In groups of four, Sept.–Oct., or Mar.–April in enriched, well-drained soil. Sunny borders and island beds. Avoid moist soils.
Care Mulch lightly in spring. Support with canes in windy sites. Cut off faded spikes below lowest flower. Cut all stems to just above ground in autumn.
Propagation By root cuttings, Feb.–Mar., in cold frame. By seeds sown in Feb. at 13°C (55°F). Cultivars do not come true.

VERONICA

Perennial: Clump or mat-forming plants bearing mainly blue flowers in tapering racemes, from 6 in. to 9 in. long.
Species *V. exaltata* (H4–5 ft,

Veronica–Zinnia

Veronica spicata

S18 in.), pale blue, July–Sept. *V. gentianoides* (H9–15 in., S12 in.), pale blue, May–June, sometimes later. *V. spicata* cultivars (H12–18 in., S9–12 in.), shades of blue, white, pink, June–Aug.
Planting In groups of four or five, Oct.–Mar., in well-drained but moisture-retentive soil, enriched. Sun or light shade. *V. exaltata* is best at back of border or among shrubs.
Care Mulch in spring. Water in dry spells. Support tall species with canes or pea-sticks. Remove faded flower spikes at base to promote further blooming. Cut all stems almost to ground in autumn. If affected by powdery mildew, spray with dinocap at fortnightly intervals.
Propagation By division, Oct.–Mar. Divide every three years to retain vigour.

VERONICA

Rock plant: Carpeting perennial, flowering in summer.
Species *V. cinerea* (H4 in., S12–15 in.), pale blue, June–Aug. *V. pectinata* (H3 in., S12–18 in.), deep blue, May–June. *V. prostrata* (H3–8 in., S12–18 in.), deep blue, May–July. *V. satureioides* (H3 in., S12–18 in.), dark blue, April–Aug.
Planting In well-drained soil. Sun or light shade. Paving, scree, dry wall. *V. pectinata* is an invasive plant.
Propagation 2 in. cuttings of lateral shoots in peat/sand in cold frame, July–Aug. Division in Mar.–April.

VIOLA
Pansy

Pansy

Perennial: One of the most popular garden flowers. Short-lived, lasting only two or three years, it is best treated as biennial. Mass of big blooms in striking colours.
Cultivars *Viola × wittrockiana* (H6–9 in., S9–12 in.). Many cultivars in wide selection of colours.
Planting Sun or partial shade. Well-drained, ordinary soil. Ideal for edging.
Care Dead-head, and spray against aphids.
Propagation Sow in June–July, either in damp, shaded site or in boxes in cold frame. Can also be sown Feb.–Mar. in cold frame or greenhouse to flower same year.

VIOLA
Pansy or violet

Viola cornuta

Perennial rock plant: Free-flowering for bold effects.
Species *V. aetolica* (H2 in., S9–12 in.), yellow, May–June. *V. biflora* (H2–3 in., S12 in.), vivid yellow, April–May. *V. cornuta* (H4–12 in., S12–15 in.), deep violet, June–July. *V. cucullata* (H3–6 in., S12 in.), violet or white, May–June.
Planting In moist, well-drained soil. Sun or light shade. Paving, peat bed, trough, alpine house.
Propagation Sow seeds in John Innes seed compost and place in shade in Mar. Divide spring or autumn.

WALLFLOWER

Wallflower

Biennial: Well loved for its beautiful display of yellow and russet flowers in spring and early summer. Fragrant.
Species *Cheiranthus cheiri* (H8 in.–2 ft, S8–12 in.), wide range of red, orange, yellow, bronze and purple, in giant, dwarf and early-flowering strains, April onwards. *C. × allioni* (Siberian wallflower) (H8–18 in., S10–15 in.), similar appearance to wallflower but later flowering, May–June.
Planting Sunny position in any well-drained soil. Dress acid soils with 4 oz. (4 tablespoons) of hydrated lime per square yard.
Propagation Sow seeds in May, and plant out in nursery bed 12 in. apart, about July, in showery weather. Transfer to flowering positions early Oct. Pinch out growing points of plants when they are 4 in. high to encourage bushy growth.

Water lily see Nuphar and Nymphaea

ZANTEDESCHIA
Arum lily

Bog plant: Green, glossy, arrow-shaped leaves and big, white flowers in spring, summer and early autumn.
Species *Z. aethiopica* 'Crowborough' (H$2\frac{1}{2}$ ft).
Planting In full sun. Cover tubers with mound of peat and sand in autumn. Can also be grown in water up to 12 in. deep, where it is rarely killed by low temperatures.
Propagation By seeds or division of the rhizomes.

ZINNIA

Zinnia

Half-hardy annual: Brilliant daisy-like flowers, single and double, tall and dwarf, July–Sept. They last well in water.
Species *Z. elegans* (H9 in.–$2\frac{1}{2}$ ft, S6–12 in.), 'Persian Carpet', multi-colour shades; 'Giant' and 'Dwarf Double', mixed.
Planting Sunny, sheltered spot in enriched soil. Change planting position if grown from year to year.
Care Blooms can be damaged by heavy rain. Pinch out growing tips of young plants to encourage branching. Dead-heading improves subsequent flowering.
Propagation Sow in Mar.–April, 16–18°C (61–64°F), harden off May, and plant out early June. Or sow outdoors early May.

Guide to shrubs and trees

How to make the most of your garden, whatever its size, by planting the essential framework of trees and shrubs for all-the-year-round colour and interest

Whatever sort of garden you have, the trees, shrubs and climbers need to be chosen with care. Once established, they are likely to be with you for many years and occupy a considerable amount of space. Owners of small gardens, in particular, should beware of planting a pretty, little sapling that will grow into a forest giant.

Each species listed here is followed by figures in brackets to show its height and spread. Thus (H12 ft, S6 ft) means a height of 12 ft and a spread of 6 ft. In the case of trees, double sets of figures are given to indicate height and spread after ten years, and then ultimate height and spread.

There are species and cultivars to suit every sort of garden—cold, wet, dry, chalky, sandy, acid, alkaline, seaside, windswept or air-polluted. The list tells you which to choose to meet your particular needs.

Mulching, which is often advised here, means covering the roots and base of a plant with peat, compost, leaf-mould or manure.

ALMOND
Prunus

Vigorous ornamental tree, suitable for all soils. Erect branches when young, spreading later.
Species *P. dulcis* (Common almond) (H12 ft, S8 ft/H20 ft, S15 ft), clear pink flowers cluster along naked branches in Mar.–April.
Planting In site sheltered from cold winds. For effect, plant against dark background.

AMELANCHIER
Shadbush, Juneberry

Amelanchier canadensis

Hardy, deciduous shrub. Outstandingly attractive both in bloom and autumn colour.
Species *A. canadensis* (H10 ft, S10 ft), *A.* × *grandiflora* (H25 ft, S15 ft), arching branches decked April–May with starry, white flowers, followed by crimson to black edible fruits.
Planting In moist, neutral to acid soil. If soil is poor, enrich with humus and add general fertiliser. Light shade or sun.
Propagation By layering; or from seeds sown when ripe.

ARBUTUS
Strawberry tree

Arbutus andrachne

Handsome evergreen shrub or small tree that bears strawberry-like fruits in autumn, edible but tasteless. Pitcher or urn-shaped white or pink flowers. Attractive bark. Hardy in South and West.
Species *A. unedo* (H15 ft, S8–10 ft), will tolerate limy soil. Flowers Mar.–April. *A. andrachne* (H15 ft, S10 ft), has bark that peels off in spring in cinnamon-red scrolls. Flowers Oct.–Dec.
Planting Warm site in full sun or light shade. Best planted Oct. or spring. Stake if exposed to high wind, especially by sea. Protect against frost for three or four winters after planting.
Propagation By layering in Mar. Seeds can be sown Sept.–Oct.

ARUNDINARIA
Bamboo

Arundinaria

Evergreen that spreads rapidly once established. Either plant in place where this does not matter, or keep within bounds by annual pruning with spade.
Species *A. simoni* (H15–20 ft), noble appearance, long, broad leaves. *A. japonica* (H10–15 ft), useful for sun or shade, and forms a quick screen.
Planting In April–May in moist but not wet soil.
Propagation By division in late spring.

ASPEN
Populus

Ideal specimen tree for towns and coastal areas.
Species *P. tremula* 'Pendula' (H12 ft, S6 ft/H20 ft, S12 ft), long grey catkins in Feb.
Planting Good on any soil.

Azalea see p. 216

Bamboo see Arundinaria and Phyllostachys

BAY
Laurus

Laurus nobilis

The sweet bay has aromatic leaves used for flavouring fish and other dishes. Hardy evergreen.
Species *L. nobilis* (H10–18 ft, S10–18 ft), tiny yellow-green flowers, April.
Planting In rich, well-drained soil, Mar.–April. Sun or light shade. Mulch root area in North and East to prevent frost damage.
Care Water in dry spells. Feed with general fertiliser in late spring if growth is slow. Mulch late April.
Propagation By heeled cuttings of semi-hard shoots, Aug.–Sept.

BEECH
Fagus

Generally too large for gardens, the beech makes an excellent

Berberis – Caryopteris

Beech

windbreak or hedge if trimmed once a year in late summer. Autumn russet-brown leaves retained through winter.
Species *F. sylvatica* 'Fastigiata' 'Cuprea', copper-coloured leaves; 'Purpurea', purple-red leaves.
Planting For hedges, set 18 in. apart Oct.–Mar. Remove upper quarter of all shoots after planting.
Care Trim once a year late in the summer. The hedge will grow to a height of 4 ft after three years, 5–8 ft after six years.

BERBERIS
Barberry

Berberis × stenophylla

A big group of shrubs with brightly coloured flowers and berries. Several deciduous types end the year in a flame of scarlet and orange leaves. The spiny leaves and stems make an effective hedge. Small forms suitable for larger rock gardens. Most species are hardy and easy to grow.
Species *Berberis aggregata* (H6 ft, S5–6 ft), deciduous, yellow flowers July, red berries. *B. buxifolia* (H6 ft, S6 ft), evergreen, yellow flowers, Mar.–April, blue-black berries. *B. darwinii* (H8–10 ft, S8–10 ft), evergreen, bright orange flowers, April–May, blue-black berries. *B. × stenophylla* (H8–10 ft, S10–12 ft), evergreen, golden-yellow flowers, April, blue-black berries. *B. thunbergii* 'Aurea' (H3–4 ft, S3–4 ft), golden foliage, yellow flowers, June–July, scarlet berries.
Planting Evergreens flourish in sun or light shade, but deciduous sorts colour well only in full sun. Plant evergreens Sept.–April, deciduous Oct.–Mar. Most soils suitable. For hedges, site 12–15 in. high plants 18–24 in. apart. After planting, cut all shoots by a quarter.
Care Water plentifully if there is dry spell after planting. Mulch in spring. In cold winters *B. buxifolia* needs protection in exposed sites. Wrap straw or plastic round branches. Clip hedges once a year, evergreens after flowering, deciduous in late summer.
Propagation By seeds sown in open, Nov.; by semi-hard cuttings, July–Sept.; by hardwood cuttings from deciduous shrubs, Oct.–Dec.

BIRCH
Betula

Deciduous. Silver lady of the woodlands.
Species *B. pendula* 'Dalecarlica' (Swedish birch) (H18 ft, S8 ft/H60 ft, S15 ft), silver-white bark, weeping branches. 'Youngii' (Young's weeping birch) (H8 ft, S6 ft/H16 ft, S16 ft), branches hang almost to ground.
Planting On any soil. Thrives in cold. 'Youngii' recommended for lawns in fairly small gardens.

Broom see Cytisus, Genista and Spartium

BUDDLEIA

Buddleia davidii

Big group of shrubs, including the butterfly bush (*B. davidii*) which attracts butterflies. Produce profusion of flowers. *B. alternifolia* can be trained on a wall.
Species *B. alternifolia* (H12–20 ft, S14–20 ft), deciduous, lavender-blue flowers, June. Scented. Hardy. *B. colvilei* (H10–18 ft, S6–10 ft), semi-evergreen, rose-pink flowers, June–July. Not fully hardy. *B. davidii* 'Black Knight' (H9 ft, S7–12 ft), deciduous, deep violet-purple flowers, July–Oct. Scented. Hardy. *B. globosa* (H10–12 ft, S10 ft), semi-evergreen, orange-yellow flowers, May–June. Scented. Half-hardy.
Planting In Oct.–Nov. or Mar.–April in almost any soil. Tender sorts need shelter from frost.
Care Feeding needed only on very poor soil as it encourages too much leaf growth. *B. davidii* can be cut back to lowest buds in spring. Remove flowered shoots of *B. alternifolia* after flowering. Others need no regular pruning.
Propagation By hardwood cuttings Oct.–Mar.; by semi-hard cuttings with a heel, July–Aug.

CAMELLIA

Popular evergreen shrub with big, brilliant flowers, needing neutral to acid soil. Except for *C. reticulata*, the species described here are reasonably hardy.
Species *C. japonica* (H6–12 ft, S6–8 ft), 'Adolphe Audusson', semi-double, scarlet; 'Alba Simplex', single, white; 'Arejishi', salmon; 'Contessa Lavinia Maggi', double, pink; 'Latifolia', semi-double, red; 'Nobilissima', paeony-flowered, white, Feb.–May. *C. reticulata* (H10–15 ft, S8–12 ft), 'Captain Rawes', turkey-red, Feb.–April. *C. saluenensis* (H10–15 ft, S6–12 ft), 'Merryn Galsworthy', single, flat, pink, Mar.–April. *C. × williamsii* (H6–8 ft, S4–6 ft), white to rose-purple, Nov.–April.
Planting In enriched lime-free soil. Choose sheltered spot in sun or light shade. Plant Sept.–Oct. or Mar.–April. *C. reticulata* does best fan-trained against warm wall facing west. Regular feeds of sequestered iron needed on slightly limy soil to prevent yellow-edged or mottled (chlorotic) leaves.
Care Prevent damage to flower buds by late spring frost by covering with polythene. Shorten straggly shoots back to sturdy side-shoots in spring before buds break. Annual pruning not needed. Mulch with leaf-mould in spring to keep the roots cool.
Propagation Semi-hard cuttings, July–Sept., preferably applying bottom heat of 13–16°C (55–61°F); leaf-bud cuttings, July–Sept. For *C. reticulata*, layer whippy shoots Sept., to root in 18 months.

CARYOPTERIS

Deciduous shrub with aromatic, grey-green foliage and clusters of blue flowers, Aug.–Sept. Forms rounded hummock if pruned hard annually. Hardy in most districts.
Species *C. × clandonensis* (H2–4 ft, S2–4 ft), 'Ferndown', deep mauve-blue; 'Heavenly Blue', deep blue; 'Kew Blue', bright blue, Aug.–Sept.
Planting In most soils, but prefer

Cedar – Choisya

Caryopteris × clandonensis

enriched sandy loam or chalky soil. Dry site in sun or light shade. Plant Sept.–Oct. or Mar.–April, against sheltered wall in cold areas.
Care In light soils, give summer feed of potash fertiliser to intensify blue of flowers. In spring, prune previous year's growth to within an inch of the older branches. Remove overcrowded shoots.
Propagation By semi-hard cuttings, 3–4 in. long with a heel, Aug.–Sept. Apply rooting powder. Or by hardwood cuttings, Oct.–Nov.

CEDAR, JAPANESE
Cryptomeria

Japanese cedar

Excellent fairly slow-growing specimen tree for small gardens. Low, sweeping branches with bright green leaves in summer, purple or bronze in winter.
Species *C. japonica* 'Elegans' (H5 ft, S18 in./H15 ft, S6 ft).
Planting In any moderately fertile, damp but well-drained soil. Full sun or very light shade.
Care Responds well to light pruning, but this spoils its naturally pleasing shape.

CHAMAECYPARIS
False cypress

Graceful, evergreen conifers, varying from cigar-shaped to broad-crowned forms. Easy-to-grow varieties used for eye-catching lawn specimens or for hedging and screening.
Species *C. lawsoniana* (Lawson cypress), 'Allumii' (H10 ft, S2 ft/H50 ft, S10 ft), narrow, spire-like, blue-grey foliage, brown cones; 'Columnaris' (H8 ft, S18 in./H25 ft, S3 ft), slender with pale grey to blue-green foliage; 'Green Hedger' (H7 ft, S18 in./H50 ft, S15 ft), narrow pyramid outline, bright green foliage, used for hedging or as single specimen; 'Pembury Blue' (H7 ft, S2 ft/H30 ft, S10 ft), silver-blue foliage, one of the most popular blue cypresses for small gardens; 'Winston Churchill' (H7 ft, S2½ ft/H25 ft, S10 ft), rounded crown, dense, brilliant gold leaves; 'Wisselii' (H8 ft, S2 ft/H45 ft, S12 ft), ascending branches with blue-green leaves. *C. obtusa* (Hinoki cypress), 'Tetragona Aurea' (H6 ft, S18 in./H25 ft, S6 ft), dense, moss-like, golden-yellow foliage, extremely slow-growing; ideal as dot plant in lime-free heather gardens.
Planting All cypresses thrive in ordinary soil, in full sun or light shade.

CHAENOMELES
Japanese quince or Japonica

Vigorous grower, producing brilliant display of white, pink or red flowers in early spring. Ideal for clothing north-facing wall, as it will thrive in fairly dense shade. Quinces formed in summer are edible and make pleasant jelly. (Best gathered in late autumn.)
Species *C. speciosa* (H6 ft, S4–6 ft), 'Moerloosii', pink and white; 'Nivalis', pure white; 'Simonii', scarlet, Jan.–April. *C. × superba* (H6 ft, S4–6 ft), 'Crimson and Gold', crimson; 'Rowallane', blood-red, Jan.–April.
Planting In most soils, including chalk, in full sun or shade. Most varieties do best when trained against wall or fence. *C. speciosa* spreads into tangled bush and is best used in less-formal parts of garden. Chaenomeles thrives in conditions that most other shrubs dislike. It tolerates fairly dry soil at planting time and excessive wetness in winter.
Care Remove dead or crowded branches after flowering. Shorten side-shoots of wall-grown bushes, June–July. Water with sequestered iron if chlorosis occurs in chalky soil.
Propagation By semi-hard cuttings with a heel, July–Aug.; by layering flexible shoots, Aug.; by seeds, ripened on plant and sown Sept.–Oct.

CHERRY, JAPANESE FLOWERING
Prunus

Japanese flowering cherry

Vigorous, very decorative trees. Several varieties excellent for small gardens. Any soil.
Cultivars *P.* 'Amanogawa' (H12 ft, S2 ft/H18 ft, S5 ft), erect, narrow habit with dense clusters of pink flowers, April–May; suitable for restricted sites. *P.* 'Kanzan' (H14 ft, S8 ft/H30 ft, S20 ft), double purple-pink flowers, April; rich autumn tints. Most popular flowering cherry with stiff, ascending branches. *P.* 'Kiku-shidare Sakura' (Weeping cherry), (H10 ft, S6 ft/H15 ft, S10 ft), double deep-pink flowers, Mar.–April; pendent branches; slow growing. Fine specimen tree for small gardens. *P.* × 'Pink Perfection' (H12 ft, S6 ft/H20 ft, S10 ft), long clusters of double pink flowers, April. Excellent for small gardens.

CHOISYA
Mexican orange

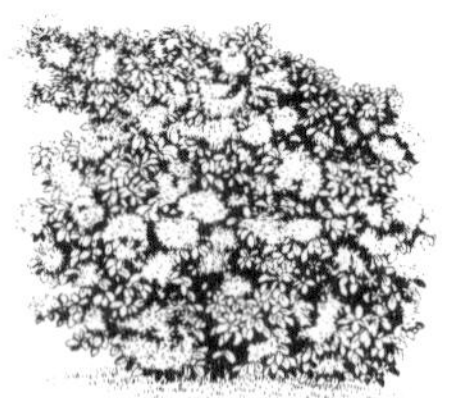

Choisya ternata

One of the brightest flowering spring evergreens, with sweet orange scent.
Species *C. ternata* (H8–12 ft, S6–8 ft), white flowers, April–May.
Planting Equally happy in full sun or light shade, but prefers light, well-drained soil. Plant when soil is warm, Sept.–Oct. or April–May.
Care Water in dry spells and mulch to conserve moisture. If exposed to wind, cover young shrubs with hessian or plastic sheeting in winter.
Propagation By semi-hard cuttings, 4 in. long, July–Sept.; or by softwood cuttings, June–July, preferably with bottom heat.

Cistus–Cornus

CISTUS
Rock rose

Cistus × purpureus

Evergreen shrub with dazzling, paper-thin flowers; ideal for sunny, quick-draining sites. *C. × corbariensis* and *C. laurifolius* are fairly hardy, but most other species and hybrids need protection from frost except in South.
Species *C. × corbariensis* (H3–4 ft, S6–9 ft), white flowers, May–June. *C. laurifolius* (H6–8 ft, S4–6 ft), dark, leathery leaves, white flowers, June–Aug. *C. × purpureus* (H4–5 ft, S4 ft), rose to purple, May–July.
Planting In open, sunny position, sheltered from north and east winds. Tolerates chalk, sand and sea air. Cistus do not transplant well, so buy container-grown plants to prevent undue root disturbance. Plant April–May.
Care Mulch early spring. Stake tall plants if exposed to wind. Avoid pruning except for light trim after flowering if plant becomes straggly.
Propagation By semi-hard cuttings with a heel July–Aug.; or by seeds sown Mar. under glass.

CLEMATIS

Climbers that cover walls, trellises or pergolas with flamboyant blooms. There are small-flowered species to bloom in succession from spring to late autumn, and even in winter if the

Clematis montana

weather is mild. Large-flowered hybrids bloom only from early summer to mid-autumn.
Species *C. alpina* (H3–4 ft), violet-blue, April–May. *C. armandii* (H30 ft), white or pink, April–May. *C. montana* (H40 ft), white or pink, May. *C. viticella* (H12 ft), purple, July–Sept. *C. tangutica* (H30ft), yellow, lantern-shaped flowers late summer to autumn, followed by decorative, silky seed-heads.
HYBRIDS, EARLY FLOWERING (H10–20 ft), 'Barbara Jackman', red-purple; 'Belle of Woking', mauve; 'Lasurstern', blue; 'Marie Boisselot', white; 'Nellie Moser', pink; 'The President', purple-blue, May–June.
HYBRIDS, LATE FLOWERING (H8–15 ft, S4–8 ft), 'Duchess of Albany', pink; 'Gipsy Queen', purple; 'Jackmanii', purple; 'Lady Betty Balfour', purple; 'Perle d'Azur', blue; 'Ville de Lyon', red, June–Sept.
Planting In deep, enriched soil, Oct.–Mar. Sunny site with root area shaded from excessive heat, for preference a west-facing wall with low shrubs or ground-cover over roots. 'Nellie Moser' does well against north-facing wall. Set a cane against young plant to help it grow up to trellis, wire, or other support.
Care Water in dry spells. Mulch in spring. *C. armandii* needs protection against severe frost. Generally, avoid pruning except to prevent untidy tangle of shoots. But late-flowering hybrids can be cut back to 12 in. from ground in Feb.
Propagation By semi-hard cuttings, July; by layering in Mar., using serpentine method, if several plants required, to root within 12 months. Species clematis can be raised from seeds, sown in Oct. and raised in cold frame or greenhouse.

CLERODENDRUM

Big, scented, deciduous shrub. The hardiest species, *C. trichotomum*, bears striking blue berries with red calyces in autumn. Grows best in South and West.
Species *C. bungei* (H6–8 ft, S6–8 ft), pink, Aug.–Sept. *C. trichotomum* (H10–15 ft, S10–15 ft), white, Aug.–Sept.; turquoise berries. *C. t. fargesii*, fruits more abundantly, Aug.–Sept.
Planting In fertile, well-drained soil, Sept.–Oct. or Mar.–April. Full sun and shelter from cold winds.
Care No regular pruning needed. Thin crowded and frost-damaged shoots, Mar.–April. Pull off suckers: do not cut them.
Propagation By pulling up rooted suckers after leaves have fallen, and replanting; by semi-hard cuttings with a heel, July–Aug.

COLUTEA
Bladder senna

Prized by flower arrangers for its bladder-like pods, which are flushed red or copper. Hardy and easy to grow. Flowers produced on current year's growth.
Species *C. arborescens* (H8 ft, S8 ft), deciduous, yellow pea flowers, June–Sept.
Planting In Nov.–Mar. in any soil. Needs little nourishment.
Care In Mar. shorten all previous year's shoots to within a few buds of main framework.
Propagation By seeds sown in open, Mar., transplanting seedlings to permanent quarters, Oct.; or by semi-hard cuttings, 3–4 in. long with a heel, July–Sept.

CORNUS
Dogwood

Cornus alba

Deciduous shrub grown for decorative foliage or coloured bark in winter. Hardy.
Species *C. alba* 'Sibirica' (H5 ft, S7 ft), red, shiny stems in winter. *C. mas* (H8–12 ft, S6–10 ft), golden-yellow flowers, Feb.–April, red berries. *C. stolonifera* (H8 ft, S7–10 ft), red bark in winter. 'Flaviramea' greenish-yellow bark.
Planting In any garden soil that is not too dry during mild spells in winter. *C. alba* and *C. stolonifera* can be planted by a pool or stream. All thrive in sun or light shade.
Care Water freely in hot, dry spells the year following planting. Cut stems of species grown for bark to few inches from ground in spring. Flowering dogwoods seldom need pruning.
Propagation By semi-hard cuttings, 4 in. long, July–Sept., or 12 in. hardwood cuttings, Oct.–Nov. *C. alba* and *C. stolonifera* by suckers removed to growing site in autumn.

Cotinus–Cytisus

COTINUS

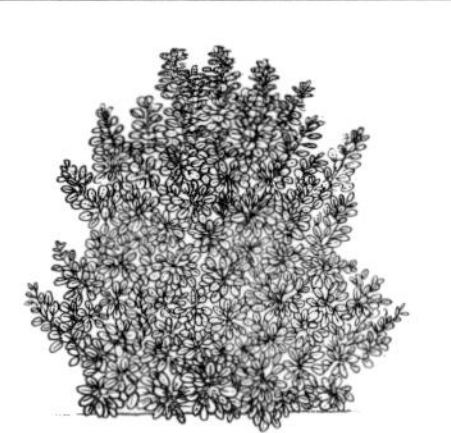

Cotinus coggygria

Deciduous shrub with leaves brilliantly coloured in autumn. Haze of wispy, pinkish, hairy flower stalks gives smoke effect in summer to *C. coggygria*.
Species *C. americanus* (H10 ft, S7–8 ft), green-white flowers, July. Fiery tints in autumn. *C. coggygria* (Smoke bush) (H8 ft, S8 ft), 'Purpureus', reddish-purple flowers, July; 'Foliis Purpureis' and 'Royal Purple', plum-purple foliage turning bright red.
Planting In ordinary, well-drained but not too dry soil. Light, acid loam for best autumn colours. Full sun, sheltered from icy winds. *C. americanus* grows well in light shade.
Care Water freely in dry springs. Mulch in April. Shorten straggly branches Mar.–April.
Propagation By layering flexible shoots in gritty soil, Sept.; by 4 in., semi-hard cuttings, July–Sept.

COTONEASTER

Cotoneaster horizontalis

Shrub grown for bright, autumn berries in red, orange and gold. All species and cultivars are hardy.
Species *C. horizontalis* (H2 ft, S6–7 ft), deciduous, pink flowers, June, red berries. Useful for covering unsightly banks or bare rocks. *C. lacteus* (H10–15 ft, S8–12 ft), evergreen, creamy-white flowers, June–July, red berries. Makes neat, evergreen hedge. *C. × watereri* (H12–15 ft, S12–15 ft), semi-evergreen, white flowers, June, profuse red berries.
Planting In most soils, Oct.–Mar. Sun or light shade.
Care Cut out straggly shoots from evergreens April, deciduous Feb. No annual pruning needed. Trim hedges, Aug.
Propagation From semi-hard cuttings with a heel in July–Aug.; from seeds sown when berries are ripe, Sept.–Oct.; from layers spring or autumn.

CRAB APPLE
Malus

Crab apple

Ornamental tree giving a bonus of fruit for making jelly and jam.
Species *M. coronaria* 'Charlottae' (H12 ft, S6 ft/H20 ft, S12 ft), scented, semi-double, pink flowers, May–June, rich autumn tints; 'Golden Hornet' (H12 ft, S6 ft/H18 ft, S10 ft), white flowers, May, big crop of fruit persisting into Dec.; 'John Dawnie', white flowers, colourful orange and red apples, the best all-purpose crab.
Planting In any good soil. Sun or light shade. Grow well in towns and coastal areas.

Crataegus see Hawthorn

× CUPRESSOCYPARIS
Leyland cypress

Lawson cypress

Hardy, fast-growing conifer, making a tall, broadly columnar tree. Widely used for making big hedges and windbreaks.
Species *C. × leylandii* (H30 ft, S4 ft/H70 ft, S15 ft), dense columnar habit, grey-green leaves, brown, rounded cones in small clusters.
Planting In any deep, well-drained soil. Sun or light shade. For hedges plant Oct. to late April, 2–3 ft apart.
Care Hedges can be clipped or pruned, May–Aug.

CYPRESS
Cupressus

Cypress

Noble conifer making excellent specimen tree where space is limited.
Species *C. glabra* 'Pyramidalis' (Arizona cypress) (H12 ft, S4 ft/H40 ft, S15 ft), blue-grey foliage, clusters of purple-brown cones. *C. macrocarpa* 'Goldcrest' (H10 ft, S4 ft/H40 ft, S15 ft), feathery, rich yellow foliage.
Planting In any soil. Full sun. *C. macrocarpa* used for screens and hedges in coastal districts.
Care Protect from cold winds in early stages.

CYTISUS
Broom

Cytisus scoparius

Shrubs grown for their profusion of yellow-bronze, red or white pea flowers in early summer. Thrive in poor, dry soil. Deciduous.
Species *C. battandieri* (H9–15 ft, S8 ft), fragrant yellow, May–June. *C. beanii* (H1½–2 ft, S3 ft), yellow, May. *C. scoparius* (H6–8 ft, S6–8 ft), various colours, May–June.
Planting In moist peat during mild spell, autumn or early spring. Full sun or light shade. *C. battandieri* does best in deep, rich loam against warm, south-facing wall.
Care Cut back flowered stems in summer to where new shoots are developing.
Propagation By seeds sown in pots in cold frame, April; by semi-hard cuttings with a heel, Aug.–Sept.

Daphne–Euonymus

DAPHNE

Daphne mezereum

Fragrant shrubs which flower in winter, spring or summer. Most effective in rock gardens and narrow borders.
Species *D. cneorum* (H6 in., S2 ft), evergreen, rose-pink, May–June, strongly fragrant. *D. collina* (H2½ ft, S2½ ft), evergreen, rose-purple, May–June. *D. mezereum* (H5 ft, S2–4 ft), deciduous, pink to purple or white, Feb.–April, strongly fragrant; attractive red berries.
Planting In Sept. or Mar.–April in ordinary or chalky soil. Nestle roots in peat. Sun or light shade. Shield from cold winds.
Propagation By semi-hard cuttings with a heel, July–Aug.; or sow ripe seeds not later than Oct. Evergreen species can be layered in spring.

DAVIDIA

Davidia

Spectacular deciduous specimen tree, producing big, pendulous, cream-white flower bracts in May.
Species *D. involucrata* (H10 ft, S4 ft/H45 ft, S20 ft).
Planting On any soil, but avoid frost pockets.

DEUTZIA

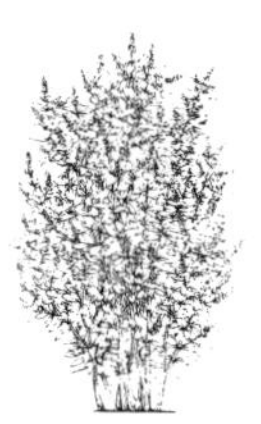

Deutzia scabra

Easily grown shrubs, flowering when young. Propagated readily from cuttings. Deciduous.
Species *D. × elegantissima* (H4–5 ft, S4–5 ft), pale rose-purple flowers, May–June. *D. scabra* (H6–10 ft, S4–6 ft), double white flowers tinted pink, June–July.
Planting In any ordinary soil, Oct.–Mar., during mild spell. Tolerant of polluted city air.
Care Water freely in dry spells. Mulch in late spring. If shoots of young plant grow slowly, feed with general fertiliser in spring.
Propagation By semi-hard cuttings, July–Aug.; by hardwood cuttings, Oct.

ELDER
Sambucus

Hardy, deciduous, rounded bushes needing plenty of room. Masses of black and red fruit can be made into elderberry wine.
Species *S. nigra* (H12–15 ft, S12–15 ft), cream flowers, June, black berries. *S. racemosa* (H8–10 ft, S9–10 ft), yellow-white flowers, April–May, scarlet berries. 'Plumosa Aurea', finely cut golden leaves.

Sambucus racemosa

Planting In any soil during mild spell, Oct.–Mar. Full sun, particularly golden-leaved cultivars.
Care Water in dry spells and mulch to conserve moisture. Cutting back stems to within a few inches of ground in winter will encourage strong new growth, but at the expense of flowers and fruit.
Propagation By hardwood cuttings, 9–12 in. long, Oct.–Feb.; by semi-hard cuttings, 4–6 in., July–Sept.

ESCALLONIA

Escallonia × iveyi

Ideal shrub for seaside gardens, protecting other plants against salty winds. Swathes of pink, red and white flowers on arching branches in late summer.
Species *E. × iveyi* (H10 ft, S6–8 ft), evergreen, white, July–Aug. *E. macrantha* (H6–10 ft, S5–6 ft), big clusters of crimson flowers, June–July; *E.* hybrids: 'Donard Star', rose-pink; 'Pride of Donard', rich red.
Planting In well-drained, but moisture-retentive, fertile soil, Sept.–Oct. or Mar.–April. Full sun. *E. × iveyi* is rather tender, and is best grown against warm, sunny wall. 'Donard' cultivars thrive in chalky soils and exposed sites near sea.
Care Feed with general fertiliser in early spring after planting.
Propagation By semi-hard cuttings with a heel, Aug.–Sept.

EUCRYPHIA

Tall shrub, richly covered with white, cup-shaped flowers, July–Sept. Leaves turn red and yellow in autumn. Hardy if sheltered against cold winds.
Species *E. glutinosa* (H10 ft, S6–8 ft), white with yellow stamens, July–Aug. *E. × nymansensis* (H10 ft, S4–6 ft), cream with pink stamens, Aug.–Sept.
Planting In fertile, acid soil, preferably cool and peaty, Sept.–Oct. or April–May. *E. × nymansensis* will grow well on limy soil with plenty of humus.
Care Water freely in dry spells, and mulch annually with peat or leaf-mould if in light soils. In unsheltered places, protect against frost with straw or plastic sheeting round branches in winter. Do not prune, but pinch out growing tips of young plants in late spring.
Propagation By semi-hardwood cuttings with a heel from young shoots, Aug.–Sept. Layer long, whippy stems, Aug.

EUONYMUS

Deciduous and evergreen shrubs valued for pink and red, berry-like fruits and scarlet-tinted, autumn leaves. Deciduous types hardier than evergreens, which do best in South and West. *E. japonicus* makes good seaside hedge.

False Acacia – Genista

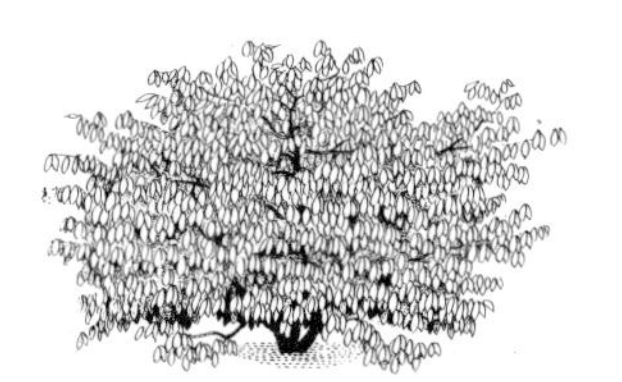

Euonymus alatus

Species *E. alatus* (H6–8 ft, S6–8 ft), deciduous, red autumn leaves. *E. fortunei* 'Silver Queen' (H6 ft. S4–6 ft), evergreen, silver-variegated leaves. *E. japonicus* 'Aureopictus' (H10–15 ft, S5 ft plus), evergreen, gold-variegated leaves.
Planting In most soils, including chalk. Plant evergreens Sept.–Oct. or April–May, deciduous during mild spells in autumn and winter. Full sun or light shade for species mentioned.
Care Water young plants in dry spells, especially *E. fortunei* if used as ground-cover beneath shrubs. Feed in spring with general fertiliser if growth is poor. No regular pruning, but overcrowded shoots of deciduous species may be thinned out, Feb. Trim *E. japonicus* hedges April, and possibly again Aug.–Sept.
Propagation By semi-hardwood cuttings with heel, Aug.–Sept.; by seeds, Sept., germinated in cold frame or greenhouse.

FALSE ACACIA
Robinia

Hardy, deciduous trees and shrubs with pea-like flowers, growing well in dry soils.
Species *R. pseudoacacia* 'Bessoniana' (H15 ft, S8 ft/H30 ft, S15 ft), globular tree with thick clusters of pale pink flowers, June; 'Frisia' (H14 ft, S7 ft/H25 ft, S12 ft), grown for its golden-yellow leaves persisting spring to autumn.
Planting In any soil. Full sun.
Care Prune out annually any shoots of 'Frisia' which revert to producing green leaves.

FORSYTHIA

Forsythia × intermedia

Much loved for its dazzling display of yellow in spring, when few other flowers are out. Deciduous, hardy, easy to grow.
Species *F.* × 'Beatrix Farrand' (H18 ft, S18 ft), big, golden flowers. *F.* × *intermedia* (H8 ft, S8 ft), 'Lynwood', big, yellow flowers; 'Spectabilis', yellow. *F. suspensa* (H8–10 ft, S8–10 ft), lemon-yellow. All Mar.–April.
Planting Will thrive in any soil in full sun or partial shade. Plant in mild spells, Oct.–Mar. Too-rich soil will produce leaves at expense of flowers. *F. suspensa* can be fan-trained against wall.
Care Water freely if plants wilt in hot weather. Mulch in late spring. Any trimming should be done immediately after flowering. On a well-established plant, remove oldest branches near ground level.
Propagation By hardwood cuttings, Oct. Pendulous forms of *F. suspensa* often root their branches at tips where they touch soil. Detach and replant, Oct.

FUCHSIA

Most species have been superseded by hybrids with blooms of

Fuchsia magellanica

remarkable shapes and colour combinations. Frosts often kill all stems above ground, but new shoots appear in spring.
Species *F. magellanica* (H4–6 ft, S2–4 ft), crimson and purple. 'Gracilis', slender habit and flowers, the hardiest Fuchsia; 'Riccartonii', crimson, July–Oct. HYBRIDS (H1½–3 ft, S1½–2½ ft), 'Abbe Farges', cerise-lilac; 'Alice Hoffman', rose-white; 'Brutus', red-dark purple; 'Empress of Prussia', red-scarlet; 'Howletts Hardy', scarlet-violet; 'Lady Thumb', red-white; 'Margaret', carmine-purple; 'Mrs Popple', scarlet-deep purple, July–Oct.
Planting In deep, rich soil, May or June, when frosts are over. Sun or light shade. Water freely. *F. magellanica* 'Gracilis' and 'Riccartonii' make good informal hedges.
Care Water in dry spells. Mulch late spring. Feed with general fertiliser when new shoots appear in spring. Protect roots in winter with ashes, peat or leaf-mould. Cut back frost-affected branches to near ground level, Mar.–April.
Propagation By softwood cuttings of shoots in early spring; semi-hard cuttings, Aug.; by division of rootstocks, late spring or autumn.

GAULTHERIA

Hardy evergreen shrubs for moist, but not wet, lime-free soils. Low-growing form of *G. procumbens* is one of finest carpeting plants for peaty, shady spots beneath trees and shrubs.
Species *G. procumbens* (H3–6 in., S3 ft), white or pink flowers, July–Aug., red autumn berries. *G. shallon* (H4–6 ft, S4–6 ft), white or pink flowers, May–June.
Planting In cool, acid, peaty soil, in partial shade, Sept.–Oct. or April–May.
Care Water in dry spells and feed with general fertiliser in late spring if growth is slow.
Propagation By semi-hard cuttings with a heel, July–Aug.; by seeds sown Oct.; by division autumn or spring.

GENISTA
Broom

Genista pilosa

Deciduous shrubs covered with bright, golden flowers in spring or summer, ranging from ground-hugging types to 20 ft high Mount Etna broom.
Species *G. aetnensis* (H15–20 ft, S12–15 ft), golden-yellow, July–Aug. *G. hispanica* (H2–4 ft, S6 ft), golden-yellow, May–June. *G. pilosa* (H1–2 ft, S2–3 ft), bright yellow, May–July.
Planting In hot, sunny positions even in poorest of soils. Plant in holes lined with moist peat in mild spells, Oct.–April. *G. hispanica* good for ground-cover. *G. pilosa* effective spreading over drystone wall.
Propagation By semi-hard cuttings with a heel, Aug.; by seeds sown Mar.

Hamamelis–Holly

Ginkgo see Maidenhair tree

HAMAMELIS
Witch hazel

Hamamelis mollis

The bare branches of these hardy, deciduous shrubs carry a mass of spidery flowers, Nov.–Feb., when there is little other colour in the garden. Leaves usually colour well in shades of yellow and/or red before falling. Cut flowering shoots last for days in water.
Species *H.* × *intermedia* (H6–10 ft, S6–10 ft), 'Hiltingbury', coppery-red flowers, Feb. *H. mollis* (H6–8 ft, S6–8 ft), golden-yellow. 'Pallida', lemon-yellow, Jan.
Planting In well-drained, moisture-retentive, neutral to acid soil in mild spells, Oct.–Mar. Add moist peat to planting holes. Full sun or light shade. Tolerates polluted city air.
Care Water freely. Apply general fertiliser in spring if growth is poor. Mulch. Pruning not needed.
Propagation By expert grafting or seeds. The latter may take 18 months to germinate.

HAWTHORN
Crataegus

All hawthorns thrive in any good soil in an open position, and are excellent hardy trees for town and seaside. Flower display, May.
Species *C. monogyna* (Common hawthorn, May) (H25–30 ft,

Hawthorn

S15–20 ft), white flowers.
C. oxyacanthoides (*C. laevigata*) (H14 ft, S8 ft/H20 ft, S12 ft), 'Rosea Flore-Pleno', double pink flowers, crimson haws; 'Plena', double white, crimson haws; 'Coccinea Plena' (Paul's double scarlet), double scarlet, crimson haws.
Planting In any soil at any time during winter when weather permits. *C. monogyna* planted mainly as tough, thorny hedge. As hedge use 12–18 in. high plants at intervals of 12–15 in. For screening use plants 3–4 ft high, 2–3 ft apart.

HEBE
Veronica

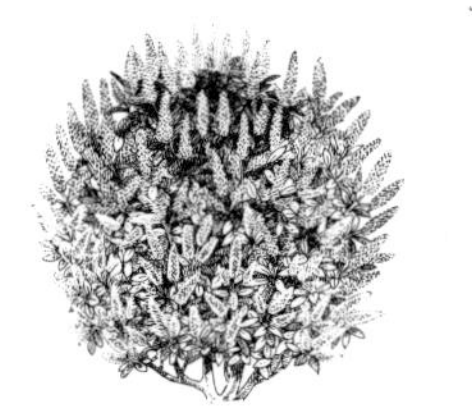

Hebe speciosa

Evergreen, flowering shrubs, best grown in sites sheltered from cold.
Species *H.* × 'Carl Teschner' (H12 in., S2–2½ ft), violet-blue, June–July, very hardy.
H. cupressoides (H3–5 ft, S2–4 ft), pale blue, June, very hardy.
H. speciosa (H5 ft, S4–5 ft), 'Great Orme', bright pink;
'La Seduisante', red, July–Sept.
Planting In any well-drained, fertile soil, Sept.–Oct. or Mar.–April. Sun or light shade.
H. speciosa hybrids less hardy than other species and cultivars and should be planted near warm wall. 'Carl Teschner' makes good ground-cover.
Care Mulch early spring. Protect *H. speciosa* hybrids with straw or plastic sheeting in winter.
Propagation By semi-hard cuttings of young, non-flowering shoots, July–Sept.

Hedera see Ivy

HIBISCUS
Tree hollyhock

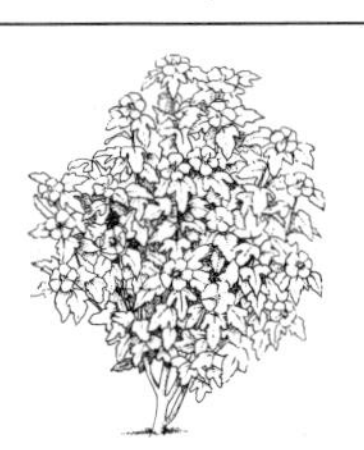

Hibiscus syriacus

One of the finest late-summer flowering shrubs. Cup-shaped flowers, fully 3 in. across, resemble flamboyant hollyhocks on upright branches. Hardy, but needs protection against frosty spring winds. Deciduous.
Species *H. syriacus* (H6–10 ft, S4–6 ft), 'Blue Bird', mid-blue, red-centred; 'Dorothy Crane', white, crimson-centred; 'Duc de Brabant', double, rose-purple; 'Hamabo', pink, red-eyed; 'William R. Smith', white, July–Oct.
Planting Plant Oct.–Mar. in fertile soil that drains well. Sunny border. In North plant against south or west-facing wall. Take care not to damage roots while planting. Water freely in summer.
Care Apply general fertiliser early spring. Mulch late spring.
Propagation By semi-hard cuttings with a heel, July–Aug. Use rooting powder. Bottom heat helpful.

HIPPOPHAE
Sea buckthorn

Hardy deciduous shrub ideal for coastal gardens exposed to gales and salt-spray, or for arid, sandy gardens inland. Bright orange berries among grey-silver leaves. Used for hedges.
Species *H. rhamnoides* (H8–10 ft, S8–10 ft).
Planting To get berries, plant up to six females to one male shrub. Male should be to windward of females. Ordinary soil, Oct.–Feb. Add bonemeal or superphosphate at planting time. Water well after planting. For hedges, set plants at 2–3 ft intervals.
Care Mulch late spring if soil sandy. Clip hedges to shape, Aug.
Propagation Sow seeds, Oct.

HOLLY
Ilex

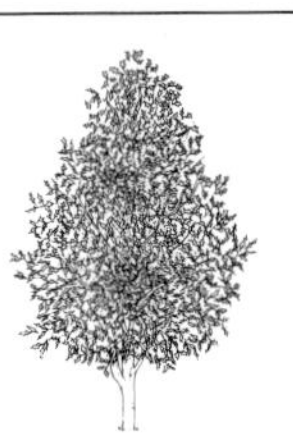

Holly

Hardy evergreen shrub making spiky hedge. Accepts pollution of city air. Male and female bushes have to be planted together to produce berries, except for *I. aquifolium* 'Pyramidalis', which produces male and female flowers on same bush.
Species *I.* × *altaclarensis* 'Golden

Honeysuckle – Judas tree

King' (H18–30 ft, S8–15 ft), gold-edged leaves, scarlet berries. *I. aquifolium* (H18–25 ft, S10–15 ft), 'Argenteo-marginata', variegated leaves, red berries; 'Pyramidalis', dark green leaves, red berries.
Planting In peat-lined holes, April–May or Sept.–Oct. Sun or partial shade: variegated forms full sun. For hedges, plant 2 ft apart.
Propagation By semi-hard cuttings with a heel, Aug.; by layering, detaching from parent plant after two years.

HONEYSUCKLE
Lonicera

Lonicera periclymenum

One of the best-loved climbing plants for covering walls, arbours and arches with fragrant, attractive flowers. *L. fragrantissima* produces mass of white flowers in winter.
Species *L. fragrantissima* (H4–6 ft, S4–6 ft), semi-evergreen, creamy-white, Dec.–Mar. *L. nitida* (H5–6 ft, S5–6 ft), evergreen, dark green leaves; 'Baggesen's Gold', golden leaves, flowers insignificant. *L. periclymenum* (H15–20 ft, S15–20 ft), deciduous climber; 'Belgica' (Early Dutch), reddish-purple and yellow flowers; 'Serotina' (Late Dutch), rich purple-red and cream, May–Oct.
Planting In any fertile, well-drained but not dry soil. Add moist peat and bonemeal to planting hole. Plant *L. fragrantissima* April–May, others during mild spells, Sept.–Mar. For hedging, set *L. nitida* 9–12 in. apart.
Care Water in dry spells. Mulch annually. Apply general fertiliser if growth is slow, spring or summer. Prune lightly; heavy cutting back delays flowering. Trim hedges spring and summer.
Propagation By semi-hard cuttings, 4–5 in. long, July–Sept.; by hardwood cuttings, Sept.–Nov.; by serpentine layering of whippy shoots, Aug.–Sept.; by seeds of climbing varieties sown in Oct. in cold frame.

HYDRANGEA

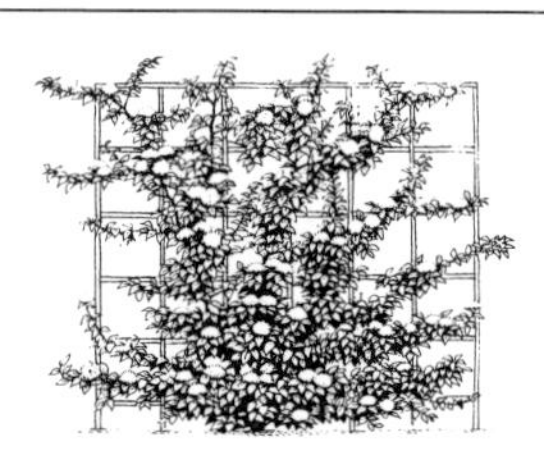

Hydrangea petiolaris

Deciduous shrubs and climbers, hardy in South and West but elsewhere needing sheltered spot.
Species *H. macrophylla* (H4–6 ft, S4–6 ft), pink or blue (Hortensias with mop-like flower-heads, or Lacecaps with flattened heads), July–Sept. *H. paniculata* (H12–15 ft, S8–10 ft), white flower cones, Aug.–Sept. *H. petiolaris* (H60 ft, S30 ft), self-clinging climber, white flowers, June.
Planting In well-drained but moisture-retentive soil, Oct.–Nov. or Mar.–April. Pick site sheltered from early-morning sun, which would cause damage after night frosts.
Care Mulch annually. Feed with aluminium sulphate when flower buds are forming, to enhance colour of blue cultivars. Ground limestone will stop pink varieties turning bluish. Leave faded blooms on plant to protect new buds from frost. Remove old stems of *H. macrophylla*, Mar. Cut *H. paniculata* hard back, Mar. Cut back unwanted growth of *H. petiolaris*, summer.
Propagation By semi-hard cuttings, Aug.–Sept.; softwood cuttings of climbers, 3 in. long, June–July.

Ilex see Holly

IVY
Hedera

Popular climbing plant thriving where others would fail – on shady walls and dry, sunless areas beneath trees. Attractive leaves can brighten gloomiest spots. Evergreen.
Species *H. canariensis* 'Gloire de Marengo' (H15–20 ft, S15–20 ft), creamy-white, variegated leaves. *H. helix* (H10 ft, S10 ft), 'Glacier', silver-grey leaves; 'Goldheart', small leaves with golden, central blotches.
Planting In any soil, Sept.–Oct. or Mar.–April. Plant with moist peat and sprinkling of bonemeal. Variegated kinds colour best against south or west-facing wall or fence.
Care Tie leading stems of young plants to canes wedged against wall, fence or tree.
Propagation By semi-hard cuttings, July–Aug.; by 6 in. long hardwood cuttings, Oct.–Nov.

JASMINE
Jasminum

Flowering wall shrubs needing support. Splendid for covering old tree stumps, walls and arbours. Winter jasmine is heart-warming sight in mid-winter. Summer-flowering jasmine has strong fragrance.

Jasminum nudiflorum

Species *J. nudiflorum* (H10 ft, S10 ft), deciduous, yellow flowers, Nov.–April. *J. officinale* (H30 ft, S18 ft), deciduous, white, fragrant, June–Oct.
Planting Oct.–April, during mild spell. Ordinary soil. Sun or light shade.
Care Thin crowded shoots of *J. officinale* after flowering. Cut back flowered stems of *J. nudiflorum* after flowering. On sandy soils mulch in April to check drying in summer.
Propagation By semi-hard cuttings with a heel, July–Sept.; by layers of whippy shoots, Sept.–Oct., cut from parent after 12 months; by seeds in cold frame, Sept.–Oct.

JUDAS TREE
Cercis

Judas tree

Good specimen tree for most gardens, bearing rose-purple pea flowers along main stems, April–May.
Species *C. siliquastrum* (H10 ft, S8 ft/H25 ft, S15 ft).
Planting In any well-drained soil. Full sun. Avoid frost pockets.

Juniper–Leycesteria

JUNIPER
Juniperus

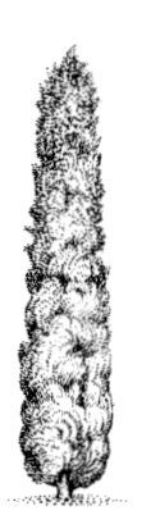

Juniper

Narrow column of blue-grey leaves. Ideal conifer for small gardens and as focal point among heathers. Spreading or prostrate species are also very useful.
Species *J. virginiana* 'Skyrocket' (H8 ft, S12 in./H25 ft, S18 in.), blue-grey spire. *J. squamata* 'Meyeri' (H5 ft, S6–8 ft), has bluest foliage of any juniper. Spreading form. *J. horizontalis* (H12 in., S6 ft or more), blue-green leaves, good ground-cover. *J. sabina* 'Tamariscifolia' (H2½ ft, S5 ft), attractive prostrate form.
Planting On any soil. Junipers require site in full sun.

KALMIA
Calico bush

Lime-hating evergreen, producing umbrellas of crinoline-shaped, pink flowers in June. Leaves are poisonous to cattle.
Species *K. latifolia* (H6–10 ft, S6–8 ft).
Planting In moist, well-drained peaty soil in cool, lightly shaded position. Not for limy soil.
Care Water and mulch in dry spells.
Propagation By layering slender shoots, Aug.–Sept., removing them a year later; by semi-hard cuttings with heel, Aug.

KERRIA
Jew's mallow

Kerria japonica 'Picta'

One of the hardiest shrubs for a cold, bleak aspect, with handsome display of yellow flowers in spring. Good for covering walls, arches, fences. Deciduous.
Species *K. japonica* (H4–6 ft, S4–6 ft), orange-yellow flowers; 'Picta', low-growing (1½–2 ft), silvery, variegated leaves; 'Pleniflora', double flowers.
Planting In any soil, in sun or shade, Oct.–Mar., in a mild spell.
Care Water in dry spells in spring. Mulch late April after soaking ground. Cut back flowered shoots to vigorous new stems after flowering.
Propagation By division, Oct.–Mar.

KOLKWITZIA
Beauty bush

Graceful, arching shrub with mass of soft pink, yellow-throated foxglove-like flowers in early summer. Deciduous.
Species *K. amabilis* (H6–12 ft, S4–10 ft), pink; 'Pink Cloud', deeper pink, May–June.
Planting In any enriched, well-drained soil, Oct.–Nov. or Mar. Sunny spot.
Care Water in dry spells. Mulch late April. Apply general fertiliser spring and early summer if growth is slow. Cut out older flowered stems after flowering.
Propagation By semi-hard cuttings, July–Aug. By seeds in cold frame when ripe or in spring.

LABURNUM

Laburnum

Widely grown for its long, pendulous racemes of rich yellow pea flowers in early summer. Good lawn tree. Seeds are poisonous. Deciduous.
Species *L.* × *watereri* 'Vossii' (H15 ft, S7 ft/H25 ft, S15 ft), May–June.
Planting In any well-drained garden soil, Oct.–Mar. Sun or partial shade. Young trees need staking for first two years.

Laurus see Bay

LAVENDER
Lavandula

Lavandula spica

Scented shrub thriving in hot, dry conditions. Purple-blue spikes attract butterflies. Grows well by sea. Evergreen.
Species *L. spica* (H3–4 ft, S3–4 ft), pale grey-blue, July–Sept. *L. stoechas* (French lavender) (H2 ft, S2 ft), dark purple, May–July, not reliably hardy. *L. vera* (Dutch lavender) (H18 in., S2–3 ft), blue-purple, July–Sept.
Planting In any well-drained soil, including chalk, during mild spells, Sept.–Mar. Enrich poor soil. For hedges plant 9–12 in. apart.
Care In light soil, mulch roots. Feed with general fertiliser spring and summer. In Mar.–April cut back faded flowers plus an inch of top growth. Replace old, woody specimens with young plants.
Propagation By semi-hard cuttings after flowering; by hardwood cuttings, 6–9 in. long, Sept.–Oct.

Lawson cypress see Chamaecyparis

LEYCESTERIA
Flowering nutmeg

Leycesteria formosa

Bamboo-like shrubs, profusely decked with tassels of flowers in summer. Deciduous.
Species *L. formosa* (H6 ft, S5 ft), white flowers with red-purple bracts, July–Aug.
Planting In any soil, sun or shade, in mild periods, Sept.–Mar.
Care To obtain pea-green stems for winter display, cut all shoots back to two or three buds from base in Mar.
Propagation By seeds, Feb.–Mar., in cold frame. Softwood cuttings, 3–4 in. long, June–Aug., with bottom heat.

Lilac–Maple

Leyland cypress see × Cupressocyparis

LILAC
Syringa

Syringa vulgaris

Sweetly scented flowering shrub with upright cones of flowers, good for cutting. Tolerates smoky atmosphere. Deciduous.
Species *S. × josiflexa* 'Bellicent' (H12–15 ft, S12 ft), rose-pink, May–June. *S. microphylla* 'Superba' (H4–6 ft, S4–5 ft), rose-pink, May–Oct. *S. vulgaris* (H8–12 ft, S5–10 ft), 'Blue Hyacinth', lavender-blue; 'Maud Notcutt', white, May–June.
Planting In any soil, Oct.–Mar. Sun or partial shade. *S. microphylla* makes fine low hedge.
Care Give young plants good start by removing most of flowers in first year as soon as they appear. Mulch April. Water freely in dry spells. Apply general fertiliser spring and summer. Dead-head. Remove crowded shoots when leaves fall. Shorten and thin out stems of mature bushes to encourage new shoots.
Propagation By semi-hard cuttings 4–5 in. long with a heel, July–Sept.

LIPPIA
Lemon-scented verbena

Lippia citriodora

Crushed in the hand, leaves emit strong lemon fragrance. Deciduous shrub, hardy only in South and West. Panicles of tiny, pale mauve flowers, Aug. Good for tubs in patios.
Species *L. citriodora* (H5 ft, S4 ft).
Planting In well-prepared soil, May, away from north and east winds. Full sun. In cold areas, plant in tubs which can be moved into greenhouse late autumn.
Care Water freely in dry spells. Mulch in spring. Apply general fertiliser, April–Aug., if growth is slow. In April shorten previous season's stems to 6–12 in.
Propagation By softwood cuttings, 3–4 in. long, July, preferably with bottom heat.

Lonicera see Honeysuckle

MAGNOLIA

Magnolia grandiflora

Magnificent shrub or tree, bearing exotic flowers. Spectacular as specimen tree or grown against walls.
Species *M. grandiflora* (H10–15 ft, S6–10 ft), evergreen, big white flowers, July–Sept. *M. × soulangiana* (H10–15 ft, S10–18 ft), deciduous, white flowers, April–May. *M. stellata* (H8–10 ft, S8–12 ft), deciduous, starry white flowers, Mar.–April.

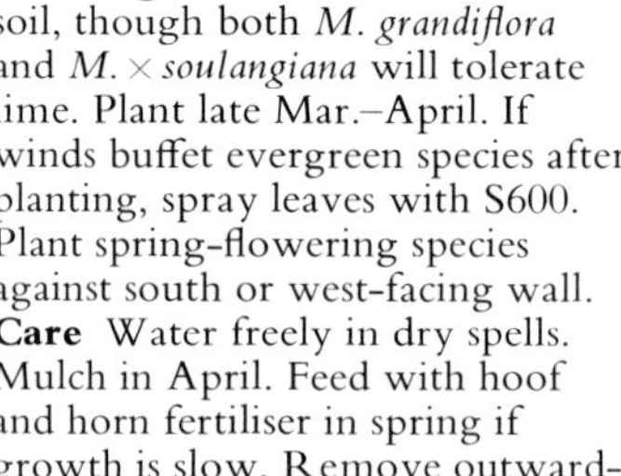

Planting Best in neutral to acid soil, though both *M. grandiflora* and *M. × soulangiana* will tolerate lime. Plant late Mar.–April. If winds buffet evergreen species after planting, spray leaves with S600. Plant spring-flowering species against south or west-facing wall.
Care Water freely in dry spells. Mulch in April. Feed with hoof and horn fertiliser in spring if growth is slow. Remove outward-growing shoots, April, from *M. grandiflora* if being trained against a wall.
Propagation By seeds sown, Oct., in lime-free compost in cold frame; by layering whippy shoots, early spring.

MAHONIA

Mahonia lomariifolia

Statuesque evergreen with sprays of yellow bell flowers, winter or spring, followed by blue-black berries. Foliage is eye-catching all year round.
Species *M. aquifolium* (Oregon grape) (H3–5 ft, S5–6 ft), yellow flowers, Mar.–April. *M. lomariifolia* (H10–12 ft, S6–8 ft), yellow flower spikes, Jan.–Mar. *M. japonica* (H8–10 ft, S8–12 ft), racemes of scented, yellow flowers, Jan.–Mar. *M. ×* 'Charity' (H8–10 ft, S6–8 ft), fragrant, yellow racemes, Nov.–Feb.
Planting In fertile soil, Sept.–Oct. or April–May. *M. aquifolium* makes good ground-cover beneath shrubs and trees. *M. lomariifolia* ideal for patio tubs.
Care Feed with potash spring and summer to intensify flower colour. Keep soil moist in drought. Mulch April. Clip *M. aquifolium* to within 6 in. of ground in April, if being grown as ground-cover. This will induce more new stems from base.
Propagation By seeds in cold frame, Aug.; by semi-hard cuttings, July–Sept., applying rooting powder; by rooted suckers, removed in spring.

MAIDENHAIR TREE
Ginkgo

Maidenhair tree

Fine specimen for big gardens and industrial areas. Deciduous leaves, fan-shaped like the maidenhair fern, turn golden-yellow in autumn. Distant relative of conifers.
Species *G. biloba* (H8 ft, S2 ft/H70 ft, S25 ft).
Planting In warm, sunny position, early April, in enriched soil.

MAPLE
Acer

Wide selection of this deciduous tree offers beautiful displays of strikingly coloured leaves and bark. Some suitable for quite small gardens.

Monkey Puzzle – Paeony

Maple

Species *A. palmatum* (Japanese maple) (H10 ft, S8 ft/H30 ft, S15 ft), red, orange, yellow autumn tints; 'Atropurpureum' (H8 ft, S6 ft/H15 ft, S8 ft), red to purple leaves, spring and summer. *A. platanoides* 'Drummondii' (Norway maple) (H15 ft, S6 ft/H30 ft, S15 ft), white-bordered leaves. *A. griseum* (Paperbark maple) (H10 ft, S6 ft/H35 ft, S20 ft), peeling bark, brilliant red and orange autumn leaves. *A. negundo* 'Auratum' (H16 ft, S10 ft/H30 ft, S18 ft), golden-yellow foliage, spring to autumn.
Planting Japanese maples need lime-free soil and sheltered position. Others are suitable for most soils in open, sunny position.
Care Cut out any shoots of *A. platanoides* 'Drummondii' that revert to producing green leaves.

MONKEY PUZZLE
Araucaria

Monkey puzzle

Conifer of fascinating appearance, with sweeping branches in symmetrical whorls. Female trees bear round cones. Suitable only for big gardens and parks.
Species *A. araucana* (H10 ft, S5 ft/H60 ft, S35 ft).
Planting In Oct. or early Nov. on light soils; in Mar. on heavier ground. Badly drained soil not tolerated.

MOUNTAIN ASH
Rowan

Mountain ash

Most species thrive in open sites and any moisture-retentive but well-drained, fertile soil. Colourful autumn foliage and pink, red, orange or white berries.
Species *Sorbus aucuparia* (H14 ft, S8 ft/H40 ft, S25 ft), yellow and orange autumn leaves, orange-red berries. *S. cashmiriana* (H12 ft, S6 ft/H20 ft, S14 ft), drooping, pink flowers in May, white berries. *S.* 'Embley' (H16 ft, S8 ft/H30 ft, S18 ft), brilliant red autumn foliage, orange-red berries. *S. vilmorinii* (H10 ft, S8 ft/H20 ft, S15 ft), fern-like leaves, red to purple in autumn, rose-red to pink or white berries.
Planting In sunny position. *S. aucuparia* suitable for seaside. Others can be grown in fairly small gardens.

MULBERRY
Morus

Hardy, deciduous, slow-growing tree, cultivated for its ornamental appearance and edible red berries. Long-lived.
Species *M. nigra* (H10 ft, S5 ft/H25 ft, S20 ft).
Planting On any soil in open position. Good for milder industrial areas.

MYRICA
Sweet gale

Deciduous shrub suitable for damp areas. The wood and leaves are fragrant and were once used for flavouring beer.
Species *M. gale* (H2–4 ft), yellowish catkins in spring.
Propagation By seeds or by layers.

OLEARIA
Daisy bush

Olearia macrodonta

Very useful evergreen shrub, flowering June–Aug., with blooms like Michaelmas daisies. Some varieties are resistant to salt-laden gale-force winds and do well in shady town gardens.
Species *O. haastii* (H6–8 ft, S8–10 ft), white flowers, July–Aug. *O. macrodonta* (H8–12 ft, S6–8 ft), white, June–July.
Planting In good, enriched soil, Oct. or Mar.–April. Full sun. Species listed here are hardy and suited to windswept coasts.
Propagation By 3–5 in. semi-hard cuttings with heel, July–Sept. Apply rooting powder.

PACHYSANDRA

Pachysandra terminalis

One of the best evergreens for a very shady site, even under trees. Low-growing, creeping plant with deep green leaves and clusters of small white flowers in spring.
Species *P. terminalis* (H12 in., S18 in.), small white flowers, April; 'Variegata', white-edged leaves.
Planting In any fertile soil, moist but not wet, Oct.–Mar. Shady site. Not happy in shallow, chalky soils.
Propagation By division, Mar.

PAEONY, TREE
Paeonia

Paeonia lutea

Shrub for sheltered gardens only, producing exotic, highly fragrant flowers year after year. Site should be shaded from early-morning sun. Deciduous.
Species *P. lutea ludlowii* (H4–6 ft, S4–6 ft), yellow, June. *P. suffruticosa* (H5–6 ft, S5–6 ft), 'Beni Tukasa', scarlet; 'Comtesse de Tudor', salmon-pink; 'Hamadaijin', double purple;

Parthenocissus – Pieris

'Lactea', white with purple centre, May.
Planting In soil enriched with leaf-mould, peat or manure and bonemeal, Sept.–Mar. Ensure graft union between rootstock and scion is buried 3 in. below surface. Good site is among other shrubs, which will screen young leaves and flower buds against frost.
Care Mulch in May.

PARTHENOCISSUS
Virginia creeper

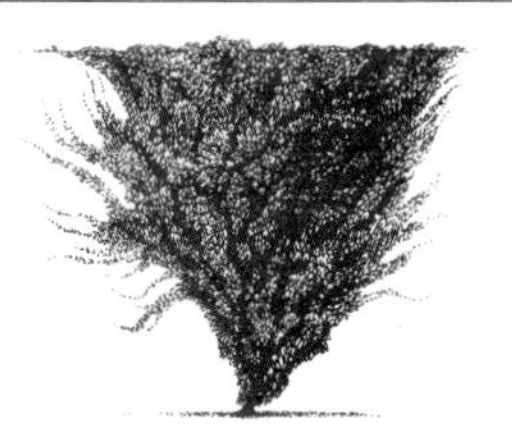

Parthenocissus tricuspidata

Spectacular, self-clinging, deciduous climber with flame-tinted leaves in autumn. Ideal for covering walls, rough-barked trees, fences and rubbish areas. Creepers protect brickwork rather than damage it. But keep growth below gutters.
Species *P. henryana* (H25–30 ft). *P. himalayana* (H25–30 ft). *P. quinquefolia* (H70 ft), fiery scarlet leaves. *P. tricuspidata* 'Veitchii' (H50 ft), deep blue, silver-coated fruits in summer.
Planting In enriched soil, Oct.–Mar., during mild spells. *P. tricuspidata* 'Veitchii' tolerates chalk. *P. henryana* and *P. himalayana* need shelter from cold winds and frost. Train all young shoots up canes until they can cling to wall or tree.
Care Top-dress in spring with slow-release fertiliser, like bonemeal. Water in dry spells. Cut out congested or unwanted stems in summer.
Propagation By semi-hard cuttings, 4–6 in. long, July–Sept.; by hardwood cuttings, 9–12 in., Sept.–Nov.; by layering whippy shoots, spring or autumn.

PASSIFLORA
Passion flower

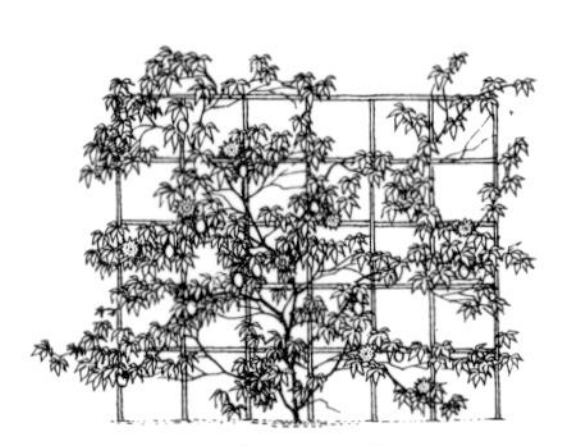

Passiflora caerulea

Flowering climber for warm, sunny districts in South and West. Edible fruits form after long, warm summer. Deciduous.
Species *P. caerulea* (H20–30 ft), white and purple, 'Constance Elliott', pure white, June–Sept. *P. umbellicata* (H15–20 ft), violet, July–Sept.
Planting In enriched soil, May. Water well in dry spells after planting. Support plants against wire or netting framework until clinging tendrils take hold.
Care Water well and mulch, May. Apply general fertiliser late spring and summer if growth is slow. Protect against frost by thick layer of peat or leaf-mould around base, and plastic sheeting over plant in late autumn. Prune out weak or dead shoots in spring, and shorten side-shoots to 6 in.

Periwinkle see Vinca

PERNETTYA

Low-growing evergreen making excellent ground-cover for acid soils. Clusters of white bell flowers are followed by colourful berries. Deters rabbits, which dislike spiny-tipped foliage. Very hardy.
Species *P. mucronata* (H2–3 ft, S2–3 ft), 'Bell's Seedling', crimson berries; 'Alba', white berries; 'Davis's Hybrids', mixed colours; flowers May–June.
Planting In holes lined with moist peat during mild weather, Sept.–May. Sun or light shade. Grow one male to three berry-bearing females, with females at front of clump.
Propagation By semi-hard cuttings, 3–4 in. with heel, Sept. Apply rooting powder.

PHILADELPHUS
Mock orange

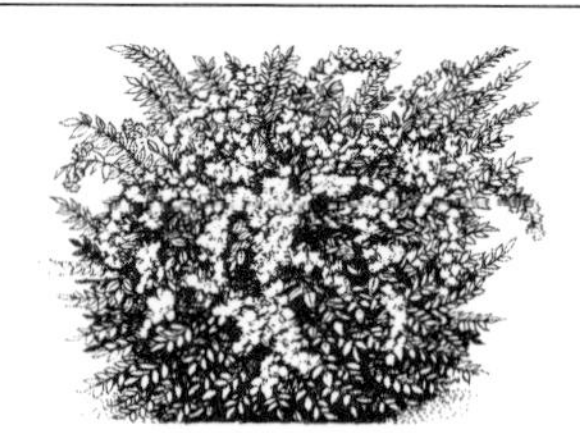

Philadelphus × 'Avalanche'

Splendid deciduous shrub, covered with fragrant white flowers in midsummer. Hardy. Philadelphus is often called syringa, the botanical name for lilac.
Species *P. coronarius* (H6–9 ft, S6–8 ft), creamy white, 'Aureus' golden-yellow leaves, June–July. HYBRIDS (H8–10 ft, S6–10 ft), 'Avalanche' (H3–5 ft), single, white; 'Belle Etoile', white with purple blotch; 'Virginal', double white, June–July.
Planting In well-drained soil, Oct.–Mar. Tall sorts make perfect back-of-border plants.
Care Little attention needed once established. Mulch late spring. Remove old shoots when flowers fade. Cut old, overgrown plants to within 12 in. of ground in spring.
Propagation By semi-hard cuttings, July–Aug.; by hardwood cuttings, 10–12 in. long, Sept.–Nov.

PHYLLOSTACHYS
Black bamboo

Clump-forming bamboo of graceful, arching habit, suitable for damp places in garden. Canes are green first year, then turn black. Young shoots are edible.
Species *P. nigra* (H8–15 ft).
Propagation By division in spring.

PIERIS
Lily-of-the-valley tree

Scarlet-hued, young leaves of some varieties so resemble flowers that whole bush seems decked in blooms. In fact, flowers are white lily-of-the-valley blooms which cascade from every branch in spring. Pieris likes same acid soil conditions as rhododendrons. Evergreen.
Species *P. floribunda* (H4–6 ft, S4–6 ft), white flowers, April–May. *P. formosa* 'Forrestii' (H6–12 ft, S10–15 ft), creamy-white, April–May. *P. japonica* 'Variegata' (H6–10 ft, S6–10 ft), creamy-white, Mar.–April.
Planting In peat-lined holes, Oct. or Mar., on site sheltered from frosty winds. Partial shade. Lime-free soil. *P. floribunda* makes good hedge on acid, peaty soil.
Care In dry spells, water and mulch. Plants can be cut back to 12 in. from ground in spring, but only if overgrown.
Propagation By layering or by air layering in spring; by seeds in cold frame Nov. or Mar.

Plum–Ribes

PLUM, ORNAMENTAL
Prunus

Ornamental plum

Handsome tree for fairly small garden, bearing rich display of pink flowers in spring.
Species *P.* × *blireiana* (H10 ft, S5 ft/H15 ft, S8 ft), rose-pink, April, purple foliage. *P. cerasifera* 'Nigra' (Cherry plum) (H12 ft, S8 ft/H20 ft, S15 ft), pink, Mar.–April, black-purple leaves.
Planting In any soil, preferably in full sun. *P.* × *blireiana* may be grown as big, multi-stemmed shrub or single-stemmed tree. Cherry plum makes good lawn tree; also used for hedging.

POLYGONUM

Polygonum baldschuanicum

Widely used deciduous climber. Most vigorous species, *P. baldschuanicum*, is known as mile-a-minute vine. In fact it grows 10–15 ft a year and can rapidly cover wall, arch or old shed.
Species *P. baldschuanicum* (H40 ft, S40 ft), sprays of white, pink-tinted flowers, July–Sept.
Planting In holes enriched with organic manure, Mar.–April. Sunny site.
Care Nip out growing tips of young shoots several times after planting to encourage branching. Water in dry spells, and mulch.
Propagation By 9–12 in. hardwood cuttings, Sept.–Oct.; by 4–6 in. semi-hard cuttings with heel, July–Sept.

POTENTILLA

Potentilla arbuscula

Dwarf shrub with mass of white, yellow or tangerine blooms. Flowers for almost six months of year, from early summer to autumn. Deciduous and hardy in all localities including seaside. *P. fruticosa* makes ideal, low hedge for dividing garden.
Species *P. arbuscula* (H2 ft, S5 ft), rich yellow, June–Oct. *P. fruticosa* 'Katherine Dykes' (H4 ft, S5 ft), primrose-yellow, May–Sept.
Planting On any well-prepared soil, including chalk, during mild spell, Oct.–Mar. Sunny position. Sea air tolerated. For hedges space at 1½–2 ft intervals. *P. arbuscula* is perfect carpeter among shrubs or on bank.
Care Water during dry spells and mulch in spring.
Propagation By semi-hard cuttings with heel, July–Sept.; by 6–9 in. hardwood cuttings, Oct.–Nov.

Prunus see Almond, Cherry and Plum

PYRACANTHA
Firethorn

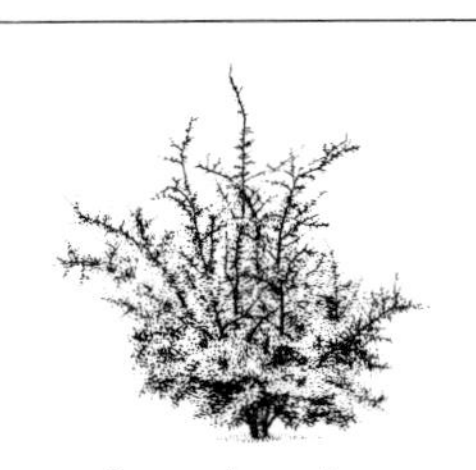

Pyracantha coccinea

Evergreen, covered with scented, hawthorn-like flowers, early summer, and orange, yellow or scarlet berries in autumn and winter. Needle-sharp spines make it effective hedge. Suitable for all soils.
Species *P. angustifolia* (H10 ft, S6–8 ft), creamy-white flowers, June–July, orange berries. *P. coccinea* (H10–15 ft, S8–12 ft), white flowers, June, bright red berries.
Planting In mild spell, Oct.–Mar. Can be trained against wall or fence with trellis or wires for support. For hedging, plant at 2 ft intervals. Stake free-standing shrubs.
Care Mulch in April and water freely in dry spells. Trim hedges May–July. Remove straggly or forward-growing stems of wall-trained plants in spring or summer.
Propagation By semi-hard cuttings, 4 in. long with heel, July–Sept. Use rooting powder and bottom heat.

Rhododendron see p. 216

RHUS
Sumach

Hardy deciduous shrub grown for its ferny leaves, which turn fiery orange in autumn. *R. typhina* forms coppery, velvety crimson to

Rhus typhina

copper-brown seed-heads. Not a good lawn shrub, as it throws up suckers.
Species *R. glabra* (H5–9 ft, S5–6 ft), light red flowers, July. *R. typhina* (H10–15 ft, S10–15 ft), pale red, June–July.
Planting Oct.–Mar. in any soil, but colours best in light, sandy loam. Full sun.
Care Dig up suckers.
Propagation Transplant suckers autumn or spring.

RIBES
Flowering currant

Ribes sanguineum

Versatile shrub for covering a wall or planting as free-standing bush. Happy against north or east wall, and makes fine flowering hedge. Deciduous.
Species *R. alpinum* (H3–6 ft, S3–4 ft), flowers insignificant, red berries. *R. sanguineum* (H6–9 ft, S5–7 ft), red flowers, Mar.–May.
Planting Oct.–Mar. in any soil including chalk. Sun or light shade. *R. alpinum* makes good hedge. *R. sanguineum* will grow in shady corner; its colour contrasts well with forsythia.

Rosemary – Sorbaria

Care Mulch April–May, and water in dry spells. Thin out old stems to near ground after flowering.
Propagation By 9–12 in. hardwood cuttings, Sept.–Nov.

ROSEMARY
Rosmarinus

Rosmarinus officinalis

Aromatic leaves are used to flavour many dishes. Attractive pink, lavender, blue or white flowers in spring. Evergreen.
Species *R. lavandulaceus* (H3–4 in., S3–4 ft), pale blue, April–Sept. *R. officinalis* (H6–7 ft, S5–6 ft), mauve, 'Albus', white; 'Blue Spire', blue, Mar.–April and sporadically until Sept.
Planting In holes lined with peat and sprinkling of bonemeal or superphosphate, April–May. Full sun in any soil. *R. lavandulaceus* is mat-forming, ideal for cascades over rock gardens, but needs warm, sheltered site. *R. officinalis* is hardy and thrives at seaside.
Care Do not let soil dry out in summer. Mulch April. Cut out dead shoots, Mar.–April.
Propagation By 8–12 in. hardwood cuttings, Sept.–Oct. or Feb.–Mar.; by 4 in. semi-hard cuttings, July–Sept.

RUBUS

Deciduous shrub related to raspberry. *R.* × *tridel* has big, eye-catching white blooms. In winter, *R. cockburnianus* produces thicket of ghostly white canes. *R. phoenicolasius*, the Japanese wineberry, will sprawl gaily over pergolas and produce edible fruit.
Species *R. cockburnianus* (H7–9 ft, S5–6 ft), small purple flowers, June, white stems. *R. phoenicolasius* (H6–8 ft, S8–10 ft), climber with pink inflorescences, June, and edible fruit. *R.* × *tridel* 'Benenden' (H6–8 ft, S8–10 ft), white flowers, May.
Planting In well-drained, enriched soil, Oct.–Mar. Fruiting sorts best grown fanned out against fence or wall, or over pergola.
Care Mulch in spring. Feed fruiting kinds with 1 oz. (1 tablespoon) sulphate of potash to square yard in winter, and ½ oz. sulphate of ammonia to square yard, Mar.–April. Cut back old flowered or straggly shoots to near base, Mar.–April.
Propagation By dividing clumps, Sept.–Mar.; by tip-layering, late summer.

Salix see Willow
Sambucus see Elder

SANTOLINA
Cotton lavender

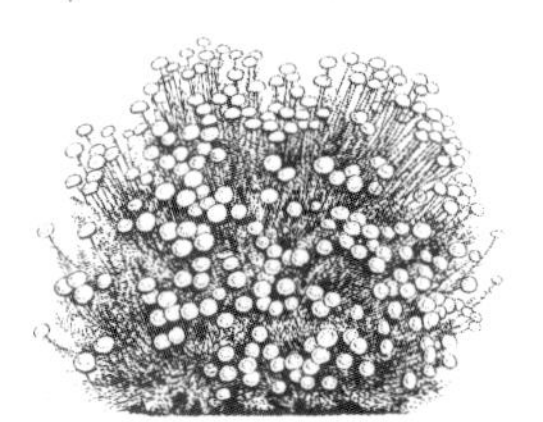

Santolina virens

Evergreen shrub grown for its feathery, silvery leaves. Yellow button flowers. Thrives in dry soils and tolerates salt-spray. Makes informal, low hedge.
Species *S. chamaecyparissus* (H18–24 in., S18–24 in.), lemon-yellow flowers, July, silvery-white leaves. *S. virens* (H2 ft, S3–4 ft), yellow flowers, July, green, thread-like leaves.
Planting In any well-drained soil, Sept.–Oct. or Mar.–April. Full sun. For hedge, plant at 9 in. intervals.
Propagation By semi-hard cuttings, 3–4 in. long, July–Sept.

SENECIO

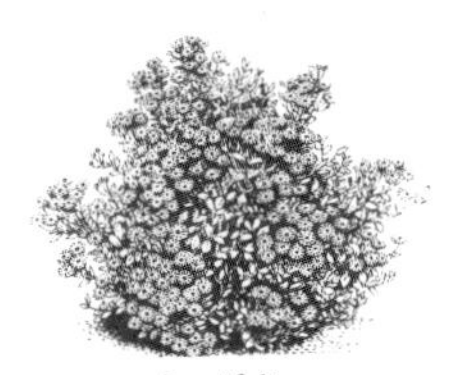

Laxifolius

Showy evergreen foliage plant with bright yellow, daisy-like flowers, at their best in full sun. Hardy and strong-growing, makes effective informal hedge with white-felted leaves.
Species Plants sold as *S. greyi* and *S. laxifolius* are almost always the same hybrid 'Dunedin Sunshine' (H3–4 ft, S4–6 ft), yellow flowers, June–July, very hardy.
Planting In peat-lined holes in well-drained, enriched soil, Oct.–April. Ideal for exposed coastal sites. Plant hedges at 18 in. intervals.
Care Mulch in April, and water in dry spells. Trim hedges April.
Propagation By 3–4 in. semi-hard cuttings, July–Sept. Rooting powder is beneficial but not essential.

SKIMMIA

Attractive, hardy evergreen with white, scented flowers and scarlet berries. Male and female flowers usually on different plants.
Species *S. japonica* (H3–5 ft, S5–6 ft), creamy-white flowers, Mar.–April, scarlet berries, female. 'Fragrans', scented white flowers, Mar.–April, male. *S.* × 'Foremanii' (H3–4 ft, S3–4 ft), creamy-white flowers, Mar.–April, scarlet berries, bisexual.
Planting In ordinary, well-drained but moisture-retentive soil, Sept.–Nov. or Mar.–April. Light shade. Leaves discolour in hot, dry places. For display of *S. japonica* berries, set one male with three or four females. *S.* × 'Foremanii' will fertilise itself.
Care Mulch April–May, and water in dry spells.
Propagation By 4 in. semi-hard cuttings with heel, July–Sept.

SORBARIA

Sorbaria aitchisonii

Hardy, deciduous shrub with elegant, feathery leaves and creamy-white plumes of flowers. For back of border, where it will vigorously develop attractive, arching shoots.
Species *S. aitchisonii* (H8–10 ft, S8–9 ft), creamy-white, Aug.–Sept.
Planting In holes lined with moist peat in ordinary soil, during mild spell, Oct.–Mar. Full sun or light shade.
Care Mulch in spring, and water in dry spells. To restrict size, cut previous year's shoots hard back in winter.

Spartium – Vinca

Propagation By digging up rooted suckers and replanting, autumn or spring.

SPARTIUM
Spanish broom

Reasonably hardy, deciduous shrub, ideal for dry gardens on chalky or sandy soil. Showy display of yellow, pea-like flowers in summer.
Species *S. junceum* (H8–10 ft, S6–8 ft), bright yellow, June–Aug.
Planting In any well-drained soil, Sept.–Oct. or Mar.–April. Full sun.
Care Mulch in April. Cut off faded flowers to prevent seeding. Old plants can be cut back hard in Mar.
Propagation Sow seeds in cool greenhouse or cold frame, early spring.

SPIRAEA

Spiraea japonica

Hardy, deciduous shrub bearing discs or plumes of flowers. Makes informal hedge. Thrives at waterside.
Species *S.* × *arguta* (H6–8 ft, S6–8 ft), white, April–May. *S.* × *bumalda* (H3–4 ft, S4–5 ft), bright crimson, July–Aug.; 'Anthony Waterer', variegated leaves. *S. japonica* (H3–5 ft, S4–6 ft), pink, July–Aug.
Planting In any ordinary soil during mild spell, Oct.–Mar. If soil is poor, pack moist peat round roots and add bonemeal or superphosphate. Sun or shade. For hedges plant 15–24 in. apart.
Care Mulch in spring. Dead-head. For fewer but much larger flower clusters, cut back *S.* × *bumalda* and *S. japonica* to within 2–3 in. of ground in Feb. To make compact growth, shorten flowered shoots of *S.* × *arguta* in summer.
Propagation Detach suckers, autumn or spring, and replant.

SPRUCE
Picea

Handsome specimen conifers from the Christmas-tree family.
Species *P. pungens* 'Kosteri' (Blue spruce) (H6–10 ft, S3–4 ft/H30 ft, S10 ft); short, stiff needles shading from silver-blue to blue-green; cones after 20 years. *P. omorika* (Serbian spruce) (H10–15 ft, S3–4 ft/H60 ft, S15 ft); narrowly spire-shaped with shiny, dark-green needles, white-banded underneath; dark purple cones.
Planting On well-drained but moisture-retentive soil in sun or light shade.

STACHYURUS

Hardy, deciduous shrub for winter garden. Bare shoots decked, Feb.–April, with chains of waxy, golden-yellow bells. Requires site that stays moist in summer.
Species *S. chinensis* (H8–10 ft, S8–10 ft), soft yellow catkins, Mar.–April. *S. praecox* (H8–10 ft, S8–10 ft), pale yellow, Feb.–April.
Care Mulch in late April to help conserve moisture in dry spells.

Sumach see Rhus
Syringa see Lilac

TAMARISK
Tamarix

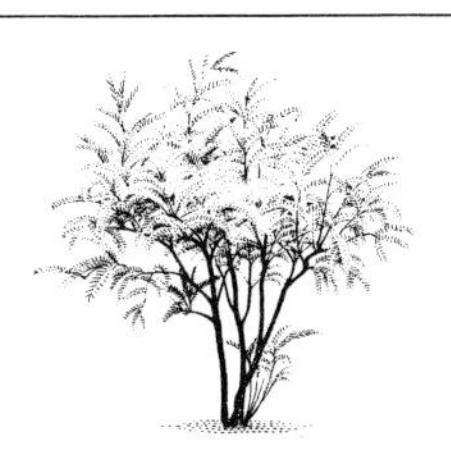

Tamarix pentandra

One of the finest deciduous, wind-resisting shrubs for exposed seaside gardens and cold districts inland. Feathery sprays of pink flowers on delicate branches.
Species *Tamarix gallica* (H8–10 ft, S8–10 ft), pink, July–Sept. *T. pentandra* (H12–15 ft, S12–15 ft), rose-pink, Aug. *T. tetranda*, (H10–15 ft, S10–15 ft), light pink, May.
Planting Oct.–Mar. in any well-drained soil. Full sun. For hedges, plant 2 ft apart.
Care Mulch if soil dries out the first summer after flowering. Prune summer-flowering types Feb., and spring-flowering types after flowering.
Propagation By 9–12 in. hardwood cuttings, Oct.–Nov.; by 4–6 in. semi-hardwood cuttings, July–Sept.

VIBURNUM

Viburnum opulus

Shrubs valued for profuse and showy blooms in winter and spring, for decorative autumn fruits and for leaf colour.
Species *V.* × *bodnantense* 'Dawn' (H9–12 ft, S9–12 ft), deciduous, white-flushed rose, Dec.–Feb. *V. davidii* (H2–3 ft, S4–5 ft), evergreen, white, June. *V. opulus* (H up to 15 ft, S12–15 ft), deciduous, white, May–June. *V. rhytidophyllum* (H10–15 ft, S10–12 ft), evergreen, makes effective screen.
Planting In any well-drained soil, including chalk. Plant evergreens Sept.–Oct. or Mar.–April; deciduous, Oct.–Mar. Site winter-flowering sorts in sheltered spot. Place berrying types in groups of two or three for good set of fruit. *V. davidii* excellent for larger rock garden. Sun or shade.
Care If soil is sandy, top-dress with hydrated lime in spring. Mulch in April. Apply general fertiliser in spring if growth is poor.
Propagation Layer shoots in spring or autumn; take semi-hard cuttings with heel, July–Sept.

VINCA
Periwinkle

Hardy, evergreen, mat-forming shrub, making ground-cover in mixed borders or wild gardens. Plentiful blue flowers.
Species *V. major* (H6–12 in., S3–4 ft), purple-blue, April–June and sometimes Sept.–Oct. *V. minor* (H2–4 in., S3–4 ft), blue, Mar.–June, often continuing sporadically until Oct.
Planting In ordinary, well-drained soil, Sept.–Mar. Best results if site is partially shaded.
Propagation By division of clumps, Sept.–April; by layering trailing stems, Sept.

Vine, Grape see Vitis

Vitis–Yucca

VITIS
Grape vine

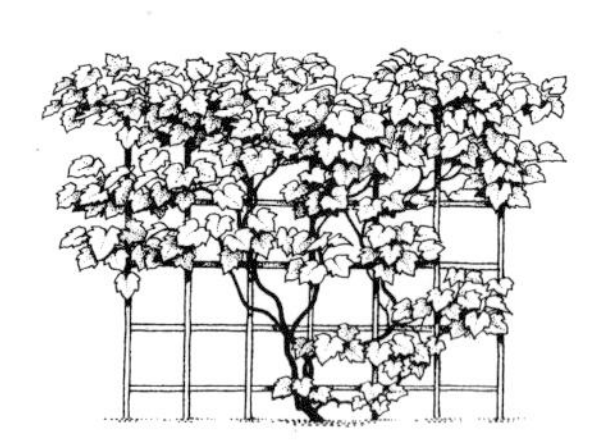

Vitis coignetiae

Group of deciduous climbers, including the wine-producing grape, grown for decorative autumn leaf tints as well as for fruit.
Species *V. amurensis* (H50 ft, S20–35 ft), downy, red young growths; leaves crimson and purple in autumn. *V. coignetiae* (H90 ft, S30–60 ft), very vigorous, needing plenty of space; leaves turn orange-red, purple and crimson in autumn. *V. vinifera* (H30 ft, S15 ft) (for grapes), thrives on south or west-facing wall, where fruit can ripen.
Planting In fertile, humus-rich soil in sheltered spot during mild spell, Nov.–Mar. South or west-facing position preferable.
Care Water freely, and feed fortnightly with liquid fertiliser in spring. Mulch in spring to keep soil moist in summer. Remove old, leggy shoots of ornamental vines in July. For tending vines grown for fruit, see p. 113.
Propagation By 9–12 in. hardwood cuttings, Oct.–Nov.; by single-bud or eye cuttings, late winter under glass.

WEIGELA

Popular summer-flowering shrub, which bears small, foxglove-like flowers in clusters, May–June. Hardy and deciduous. Tolerates lime.
Species *W. florida* (H6–10 ft, S5–8 ft), rose-pink, 'Foliis Purpureis', pink; 'Variegata', pink, creamy edges to leaves. Hybrids (H5–8 ft, S4–7 ft), 'Bristol Ruby', ruby-red; 'Eva Rathke', bright red.
Planting In holes lined with peat during mild spell, Oct.–Mar. Enrich sandy soil. Sun or light shade.
Care Water young plants in dry spells. Mulch April–May.
Propagation By 9–12 in. hardwood cuttings, Oct.–Nov.; by semi-hard cuttings with heel, July–Sept.

WILLOW
Salix

Willow

Very attractive tree, thriving on any soil except those that are dry and shallow. The popular golden weeping willow makes a beautiful specimen in a small garden in its early stages, but grows so fast that it has to be replaced every eight to ten years.
Species *S. aegyptiaca* (H12 ft, S8 ft/H16 ft, S8 ft), ideal 'pussy willow' for smaller gardens. *S. alba* 'Vitellina' (Golden willow) (H16 ft, S10 ft/H45 ft, S30 ft), bright yellow shoots in winter, particularly when young; 'Sericea' (Silver willow) (H14 ft, S7 ft/H40 ft, S20 ft), silvery foliage. *S. daphnoides* (Violet willow) (H15 ft, S10 ft/H30 ft, S15 ft), purple-violet shoots covered with white, waxy bloom in winter. *S. × chrysocoma* (Golden weeping willow) (H20 ft, S15 ft/H45 ft, S40 ft), long, pendent, yellow branches, golden-yellow. *S. matsudana* 'Tortuosa' (H10 ft, S6 ft/H30 ft, S12 ft), twisted and contorted branches. Slow growing.
Planting Most willows do best in moist conditions and in open sites, but will thrive in most gardens.

WISTARIA

Wistaria sinensis

Dramatic climbing shrub, covering a wall, tree or pergola. Long racemes of mauve or white flowers, May–June. Hardy and deciduous.
Species *W. floribunda* (H30 ft, S30 ft), violet-blue. *W. sinensis* (H up to 100 ft); 'Alba', white; 'Plena', mauve. *W. venusta* (H up to 30 ft), white with yellow blotch.
Planting In fertile, humus-rich loamy soil, during mild spell, Oct.–Mar. Sheltered site needed, such as against warm wall. Stick canes or brushwood by young stems to guide them to climbing supports–horizontal wires, trellis or tree.
Care Water freely in dry spells, and mulch. Top-dress with general fertiliser spring and summer, as wistarias are gross feeders. If flower buds get frozen, spray with water to prolong thawing. To restrict growth, reduce current season's shoots to 6 in. from base in summer. In winter, shorten these shoots to two or three buds from their base.
Propagation Easily done by layers pegged down, spring or autumn.

YEW
Taxus

Fine, slow-growing evergreen, making impressive, tall hedge or handsome specimen. Leaves poisonous.
Species *T. baccata* (English yew) (H7–10 ft, S3–5 ft/H40 ft, S35 ft), dark green, short, needle-like foliage, 'Fastigiata' (Irish yew) (H8 ft, S2 ft/H25 ft, S7 ft), dense columnar growth, dark green foliage; 'Fastigiata Aurea', golden foliage.
Planting Thrives on any well-drained soil in sun or deep shade. Irish yew much used for formal landscapes, and best in sunny site.

YUCCA

Leathery-leaved evergreen, called 'Candles of the Lord' in California because of the huge spires of big, creamy flowers growing high above the main plant. Also known as 'Adam's needle' on account of the narrow, often spine-tipped leaves. Hardy, thriving in exposed positions and salty wind.
Species *Y. filamentosa* (H4–6 ft, S3–4 ft), July–Aug. *Y. recurvifolia* (H3–6 ft, S3–6 ft), Aug.–Oct.
Planting In any well-drained soil or tubs, April or Oct.
Care Water only if soil is very dry. Feed only if leaves discolour and turn yellowish.
Propagation Transplant rooted suckers, preferably in spring, but also in summer and autumn.

Plant disorders

Most troubles that affect plants can be treated successfully. First identify the complaint from these illustrations and then apply the remedy recommended

This section will enable you to recognise and control the pests, diseases and physiological disorders that most commonly affect cultivated plants. Although they present a formidable picture when seen in a mass, only a small proportion is likely to attack a single garden.

Keep a constant eye on all your plants to see whether the leaves, stems or flowers are in any way unhealthy – distorted or discoloured, for example. Take remedial action as soon as possible.

Plants that have been regularly attacked in the past by certain pests and diseases should be protected against them in advance, and soils that are known to harbour pests should be cultivated regularly with a fork or hoe.

The best time to spray plants is in dull, still weather.

Do not spray flowers when they are open, as you may kill the insects that pollinate them.

Dahlia

Leaves with tattered holes

Shoots rotting and disfigured by grey mould

Roots eaten by caterpillars

How to use the chart

On the left is an ailing dahlia. The leaves have tattered holes in them, the shoots are rotting and covered in places with a grey, velvety mould, and the roots have been damaged by large, white caterpillars.

To discover what is wrong with the leaves look through the illustrations under the heading 'Leaves with holes' starting on page 378, until you find the one that most closely resembles the damage.

The correct illustration is the top picture on the right, which shows the damage caused by capsid bugs. This appears on page 379.

The illustrations of symptoms are set out in the following order: leaves, shoots, flower buds, flowers in bloom, fruit (including tomatoes, peas and beans), root structures and finally, lawns. The picture will not necessarily show the particular plant affected in your garden, but the caption lists the plants most commonly affected. It also gives the symptoms and the danger period.

By turning to the section 'Shoots discoloured', you will find that the shoots of the dahlia are suffering from grey mould (p. 386).

When a plant is obviously ailing, but no symptoms are visible above ground, dig it up and examine the roots. This would reveal that the dahlia's roots are being attacked by swift moth caterpillars (p. 396).

Treatments recommended will usually involve a chemical. Consult the list of pesticides and fungicides on page 398 to discover what forms are available, and their brand names.

Capsid bugs

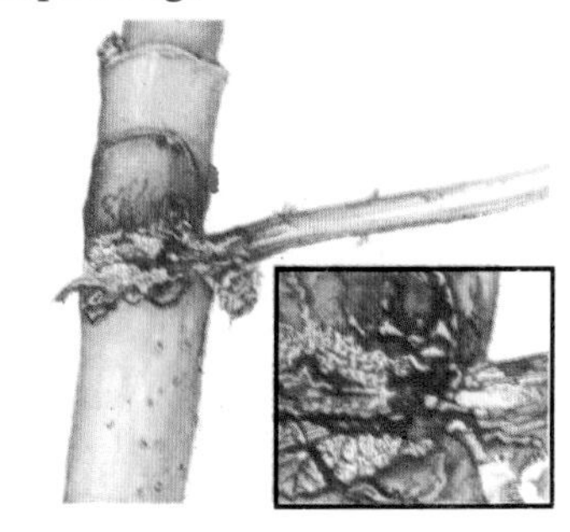

Grey mould (or botrytis)

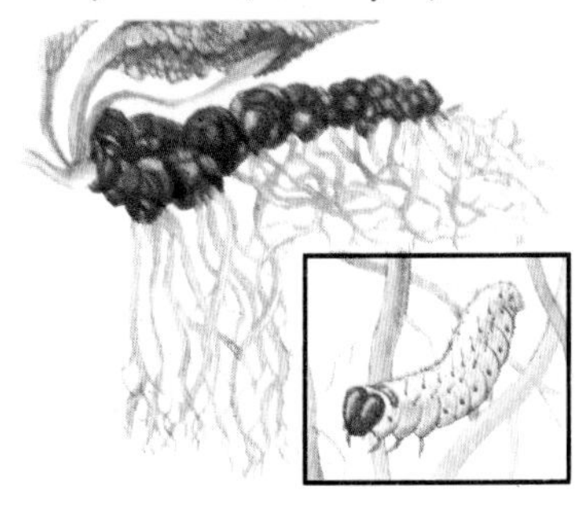

Swift moth caterpillars

Leaves with pests visible

Aphids

Plants affected Almost any cultivated plant growing out of doors, in greenhouses or in houses.
Symptoms Colonies of small, round-bodied, black, green, pink, red, yellow or variously coloured aphids, mostly wingless but often with some winged individuals present.
Danger period Spring and early summer out of doors, but any time of year under glass.
Treatment Spray thoroughly with systemic insecticides such as dimethoate, formothion, oxydemeton-methyl or menazon, or with non-systemic insecticides such as malathion, HCH or derris. Pirimicarb gives good results on most ornamental plants, and pirimiphos-methyl can be used to control aphids on fruit and vegetables. Greenhouses may be fumigated with HCH or dichlorvos if necessary.

Glasshouse and cabbage whiteflies

Plants affected Cabbages, brussels sprouts and other brassicas outside; many plants inside.
Symptoms Whiteflies beneath leaves.
Danger period May to September outside; all year in heated greenhouse.
Treatment Spray infested plants with HCH, pyrethrum, malathion, dimethoate or formothion. Fumigate greenhouses with HCH or dichlorvos. Destroy old plants.

Mealy bugs

Plants affected Many different greenhouse and house plants, especially succulents, hippeastrums, vines, camellias, citrus, coleus and orchids.
Symptoms Small, pink insects covered with woolly or mealy white wax on leaves.
Danger period Any time of year.
Treatment Spray thoroughly with systemic insecticides such as dimethoate or formothion or with non-systemic insecticides such as malathion.

Scale insects

Plants affected Many different plants, especially bay laurels, camellias, citrus and ferns. Particularly troublesome in greenhouses.
Symptoms Flat or rounded brown scales, mainly on the undersides of the leaves and generally lying alongside the veins.
Danger period Late spring and early summer outdoors, but any time of year under glass.
Treatment Spray outdoor plants with malathion, nicotine or a systemic insecticide such as dimethoate or formothion in late May, repeating about three weeks later. Use the same treatment for greenhouse plants whenever scale insects are active. Hand-treat house plants, if possible, by wiping off the scales with a soft cloth dipped in soapy water or petroleum emulsion.

Leaves with holes

Caterpillars

Plants affected Many different plants, especially shrubs and trees.
Symptoms Irregular pieces of leaf eaten, often leaving large holes.
Danger period From March onwards out of doors, but any time of year in greenhouses.
Treatment Locate and remove caterpillars, if possible, or spray thoroughly with trichlorphon, HCH, malathion or derris as soon as symptoms are seen.

Earwigs

Plants affected Clematis, dahlias and some other plants.
Symptoms Irregular, tattered holes eaten in leaves.
Danger period May to October.
Treatment Spray or dust with HCH.

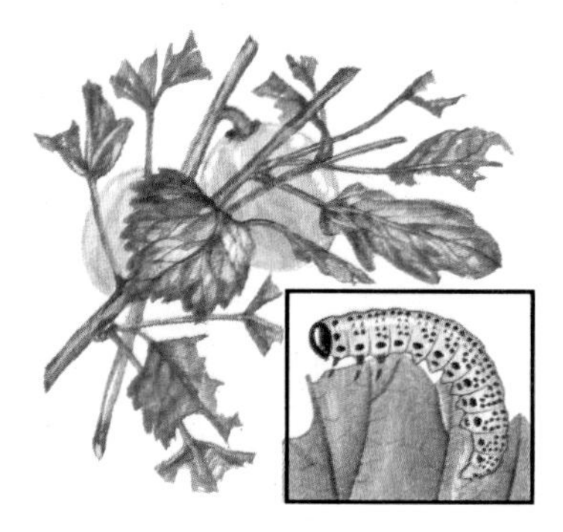

Gooseberry sawflies
Plants affected Gooseberries.
Symptoms Leaf tissues eaten away, with many leaves reduced to a skeleton of veins.
Danger period April to August.
Treatment Spray thoroughly with derris, fenitrothion or malathion early in May or when damage first occurs.

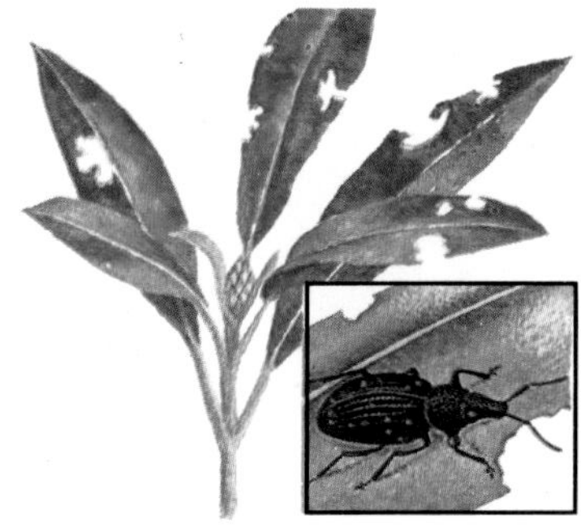

Vine weevils
Plants affected Rhododendrons, primulas, camellias, clematis, vines and some other plants.
Symptoms Small, irregular notches eaten out of leaf edges at night.
Danger period Spring and summer out of doors, any time of year under glass.
Treatment Remove accumulations of leaves and other plant debris, where the weevils rest by day, and spray or dust affected plants with HCH.

Slugs and snails
Plants affected Tulips, lilies, delphiniums, sweet peas, lettuces and many other plants.
Symptoms Irregular holes eaten in leaves; slime tracks present.
Danger period July to October.
Treatment Cultivate thoroughly and clear up accumulations of decaying plant material. Avoid heavy dressings of organic manures and mulches, and use methiocarb or metaldehyde slug baits.

Pea and bean weevils
Plants affected Peas and beans.
Symptoms Leaf edges eaten in a scalloped pattern.
Danger period March to June.
Treatment Apply HCH dust or fenitrothion spray to young plants as soon as symptoms are seen. Older plants are not seriously affected.

Leafcutter bees
Plants affected Roses, lilacs, privet, laburnum and some other ornamental plants.
Symptoms Regular, roughly semi-circular pieces cut out of leaf edges.
Danger period June, July and August.
Treatment Spray affected plants with HCH to kill or repel bees. Locate and destroy nests.

Shothole
Plants affected Plums, peaches, cherries and other prunus species.
Symptoms Brown patches on leaves become irregularly shaped holes.
Danger period The growing season.
Treatment Feed trees annually, mulch and never allow the soil to dry out. Apply a foliar feed to small trees. If trouble occurs the following season, spray with half-strength copper fungicide during summer, and full-strength solution at leaf-fall.

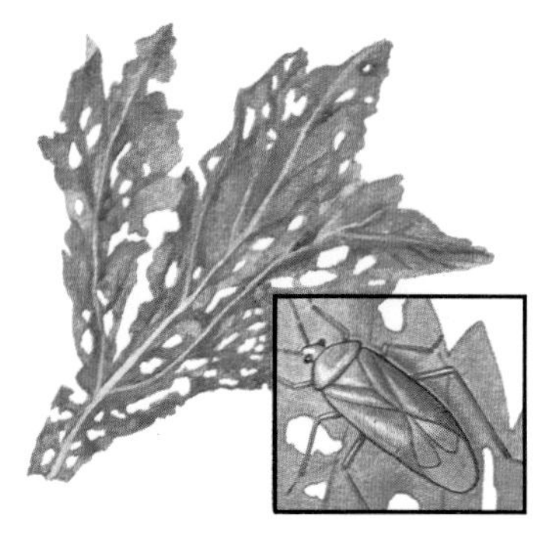

Capsid bugs
Plants affected Apples, currants, beans, dahlias, buddleia, forsythia, hydrangea and some other plants.
Symptoms Tattered holes appear in younger leaves.
Danger period April to August.
Treatment Good garden hygiene and weed control may reduce capsid damage. Protect susceptible plants by spraying with HCH, malathion or diazinon as soon as the first symptoms are seen.

Tortrix caterpillars
Plants affected Shrubs, trees and herbaceous plants – especially chrysanthemums, heleniums, perennial phlox and various greenhouse and house plants.
Symptoms Irregular, small holes eaten in leaves, which are drawn together with silk webbing.
Danger period May and June out of doors, any time of year under glass.
Treatment Spray thoroughly and forcibly with HCH, derris or trichlorphon, or remove caterpillars by hand.

Leaves with holes (cont'd)

Rose slugworms
Plants affected Roses.
Symptoms Holes eaten partly through leaf tissues, leaving transparent membranes.
Danger period June to September.
Treatment Spray thoroughly with HCH or derris when symptoms first appear.

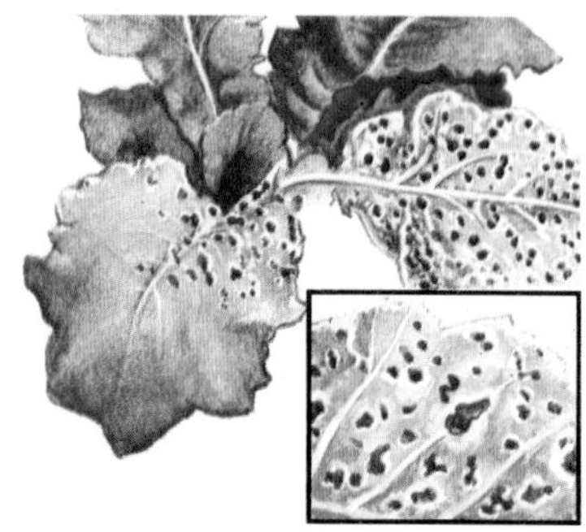

Flea beetles
Plants affected Cabbages, radishes, turnips, wallflowers and related plants.
Symptoms Youngest leaves pitted with very small holes.
Danger period During dry spells in May.
Treatment Dust susceptible seedlings with HCH or derris. Good garden hygiene will reduce the risk of attack and seed dressings will give some protection.

Leaves discoloured

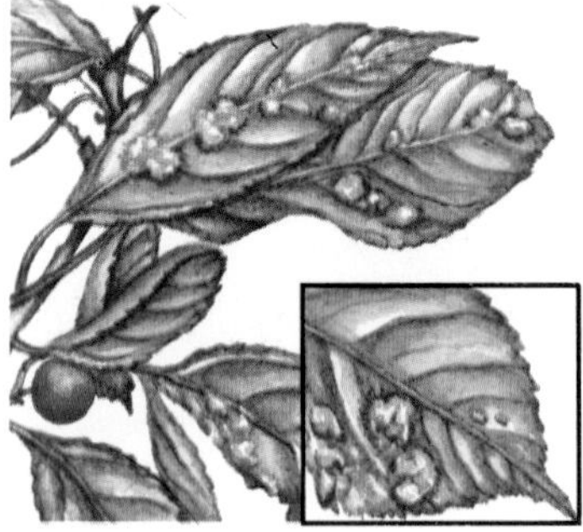

Scab
Plants affected Apples and ornamental malus species, pears and pyracanthas.
Symptoms Olive-green blotches of fungal growth on leaves, which fall prematurely.
Danger period Throughout the growing season.
Treatment Spray regularly, starting when young flower buds are visible, and until July if necessary, with benomyl or carbendazim (except on sulphur-shy varieties and pears), thiophanate-methyl or thiram. Start spraying pyracanthas when leaves are half-grown.

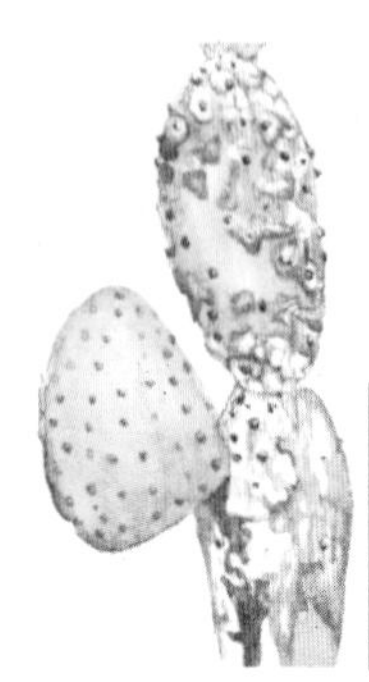

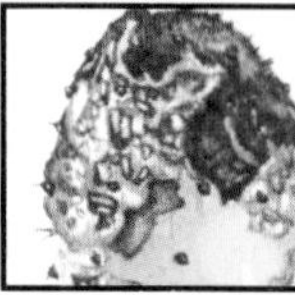

Corky scab
Plants affected Cacti, especially epiphyllums and opuntias.
Symptoms Irregular rusty or corky spots that may become sunken.
Danger period Throughout the growing season.
Treatment Improve cultural conditions. Destroy badly affected plants.

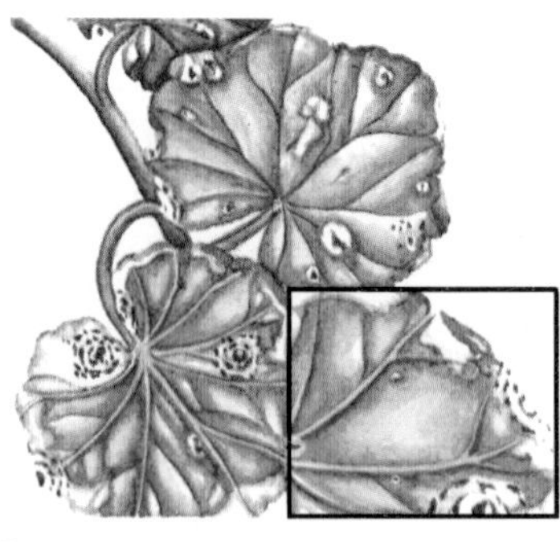

Rusts
Plants affected Many types, but especially roses, hollyhocks, *Hypericum elatum* 'Elstead', pelargoniums, sweet williams, mint and plums.
Symptoms Brown, orange or yellow powdery masses of spores develop on affected leaves and stems, and occasionally flowers and seed pods.
Danger period Throughout the growing season for hollyhocks, pelargoniums, hypericums and mint; late summer for roses and plums; autumn for sweet williams.
Treatment Remove and burn diseased leaves on all types of plants, and burn over the mint bed in autumn. For plants under glass, reduce the humidity by ventilating, and spray pelargoniums with zineb at weekly intervals; other plants with mancozeb, thiram or zineb at 10–14 day intervals. These fungicides should also be used on roses and hypericums, and on young sweet williams before the disease becomes troublesome. They could also be tried on hollyhocks, but it is better to raise new plants every other year. Control measures are not usually necessary for plum rust, apart from encouraging vigour in affected trees by good cultural treatment. Grow rust-resistant antirrhinums.

Leaf mould
Plants affected Tomatoes under glass.
Symptoms Purple-brown mould on the under surfaces of leaves, yellow blotches on upper surfaces.
Danger period The disease can occur in April or May, but is more common from June onwards.
Treatment Grow resistant varieties. Ventilate the greenhouse well and spray with a copper fungicide, maneb or zineb.
Treatment Grow resistant varieties. Ventilate the greenhouse well and spray with a copper fungicide, mancozeb or zineb.

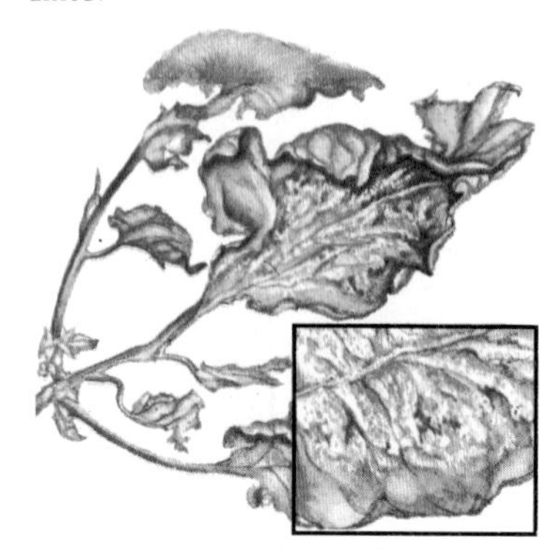

Grey mould (or botrytis)
Plants affected All types, but particularly tomatoes, chrysanthemums and lettuces under glass.
Symptoms Grey, velvety mould on rotting leaves.
Danger period Growing season.
Treatment Remove and burn infected parts. Ventilate the greenhouse well, and fumigate with tecnazene smokes or spray with benomyl, captan, thiram or zineb.

Rose black spot
Plants affected Roses.
Symptoms Distinct black or dark brown spots, either small and diffuse or up to ½ in. across, on leaves which soon turn yellow and fall prematurely.
Danger period Throughout the growing season, but most serious from June onwards.
Treatment Spray with benomyl, dichlofluanid, mancozeb, thiophanate-methyl or zineb, beginning as the first leaves unfold and repeating as necessary throughout the summer. Rake up and burn diseased leaves. Encourage vigour in rose bushes by spraying them with a foliar feed and by good general care through the growing season.

Glasshouse red spider mites
Plants affected Many different greenhouse and house plants, but also plants growing out of doors in summer. Fuchsias, roses, peaches, cucumbers, dahlias, violets and strawberries are particularly susceptible.
Symptoms Very fine, light mottling of upper leaf surfaces, followed by general yellow discoloration.
Danger period Any time under glass, June to August outdoors.
Treatment Maintain a humid atmosphere in greenhouses, spraying plants with water if necessary. Thorough spraying with derris, dimethoate or malathion may check infestations.

Powdery mildew
Plants affected Many types, but especially begonias, euonymus, michaelmas daisies, roses, gooseberries and apples.
Symptoms A white, floury coating on the leaves and shoots, and sometimes on the flowers.
Danger period Throughout the growing season.
Treatment Cut out severely affected shoots on trees and shrubs in autumn. Spray regularly with benomyl, dinocap or thiophanate-methyl. Copper and sulphur sprays can be used on herbaceous plants and shrubs.

Leafhoppers
Plants affected Roses, pelargoniums, primulas and other plants, both out of doors and under glass.
Symptoms Coarse white flecks on leaves; insect skins often present on the undersides.
Danger period April to October outdoors, but any time of year in greenhouses and houses.
Treatment Spray thoroughly with HCH or malathion, repeating at fortnightly intervals if necessary.

Pear leaf blister mites
Plants affected Pears and mountain ash.
Symptoms Numerous dark brown pustules appear on both sides of the leaves.
Danger period April to August.
Treatment Pick off affected leaves and burn, or spray with lime sulphur at the end of March.

Thrips
Plants affected Privet, gladioli, peas and some other plants.
Symptoms Leaves finely mottled with a general silvery appearance.
Danger period June to September, especially during hot, dry weather.
Treatment Spray or dust with HCH, malathion or derris when symptoms are first seen.

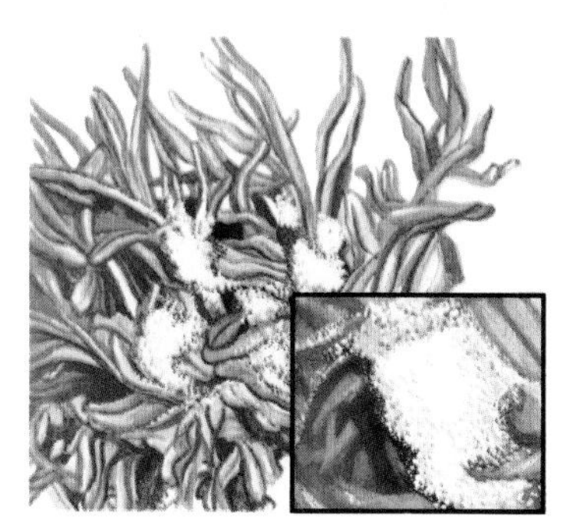

Froghoppers
Plants affected Lavender, chrysanthemums, roses, solidago, perennial asters and many other plants.
Symptoms Frothy masses of 'cuckoo spit' covering small pink insects.
Danger period June and July.
Treatment Wash off 'cuckoo spit' with a powerful jet of water from a garden hose and then spray with malathion or HCH.

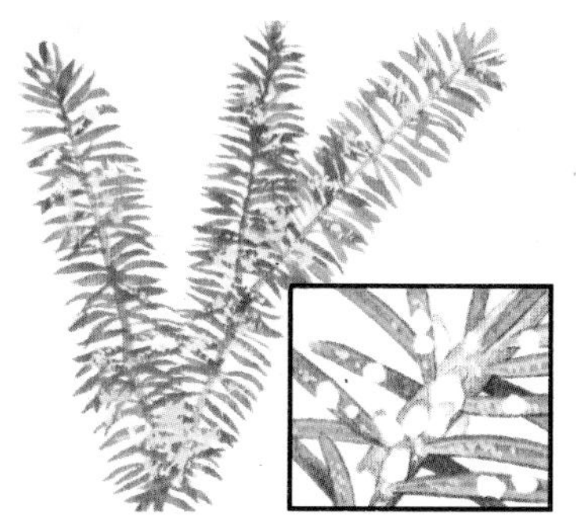

Adelgids
Plants affected Pines, larches, spruces, firs and some other conifers.
Symptoms Colonies of small, dark aphids partially covered by tufts of white woolly wax infest undersides of leaves and leaf axils.
Danger period April and May.
Treatment Spray thoroughly with HCH in early May and repeat about three weeks later.

Leaves discoloured (continued)

Lime-induced chlorosis

Plants affected Many different plants, but particularly hydrangeas, ceanothus, raspberries and acid-loving plants, such as rhododendrons and camellias, growing on alkaline soils.
Symptoms Yellowing between veins; most obvious on younger leaves.
Danger period Growing season.
Treatment Dig in acidic materials such as peat. Apply a chelated compound or fritted trace elements.

Silver leaf

Plants affected Peaches, plums, cherries and other prunus species; apples, pears, lilacs; other trees and shrubs.
Symptoms Some leaves become silvered. When a cross-section of an affected branch 1 in. or more across is moistened, a brown or purple stain appears. A flat, purple fungus eventually develops on dead wood.
Danger period September to May.
Treatment Cut out affected branches to 6 in. below the point where the stain in the wood stops. Paint all wounds with a protective paint.

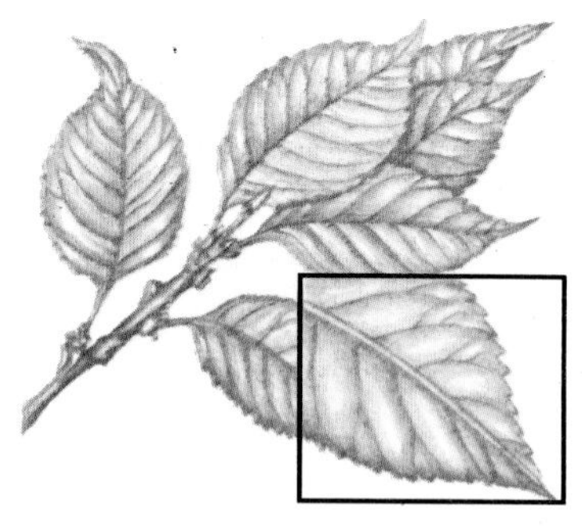

Magnesium deficiency

Plants affected All types, particularly tomatoes and apples.
Symptoms Orange bands between the veins, later becoming brown. Affected leaves may wither.
Danger period Throughout the growing season, or after applications of a high-potash fertiliser.
Treatment Spray with a solution of magnesium sulphate (8 rounded tablespoons to $2\frac{1}{2}$ gallons of water), plus a few drops of liquid detergent.

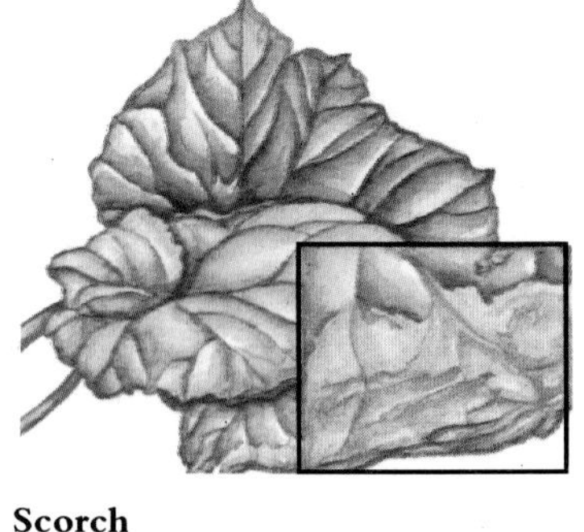

Scorch

Plants affected Most types of house and greenhouse plants, beeches and acers.
Symptoms Pale brown spots appear on the leaves of affected plants, but sometimes whole leaves become papery.
Danger period Spring for trees and shrubs, summer for house plants and greenhouse plants.
Treatment Shade the greenhouse or remove plants from glass, especially if there are flaws in the panes. Ensure that plants do not suffer from dry soil.

Virus

Plants affected All types, but in particular daffodils and lilies (striped leaves), raspberries and marrows (blotched leaves).
Symptoms Yellow striping, blotching or mottling of leaves, which may be distorted.
Danger period Throughout the growing season.
Treatment Dig up and burn. In the case of soft fruits, plant only stocks certified to be free of virus.

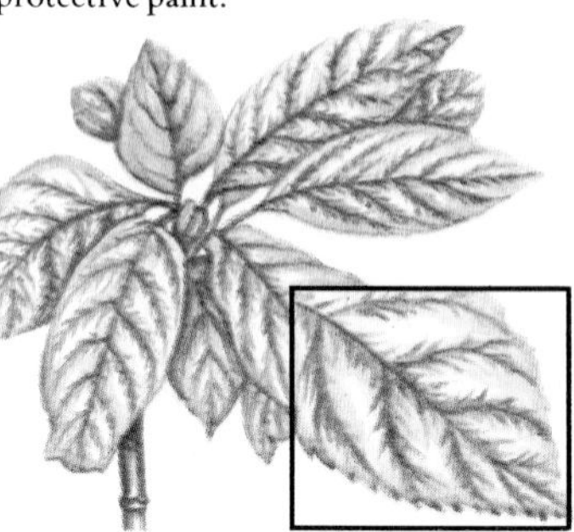

Manganese deficiency

Plants affected Many types of plants.
Symptoms Yellowing between the veins of older leaves.
Danger period Throughout the growing season.
Treatment Spray with a solution of manganese sulphate (2 tablespoons to $2\frac{1}{2}$ gallons of water plus a few drops of liquid detergent) or apply chelated or fritted compounds.

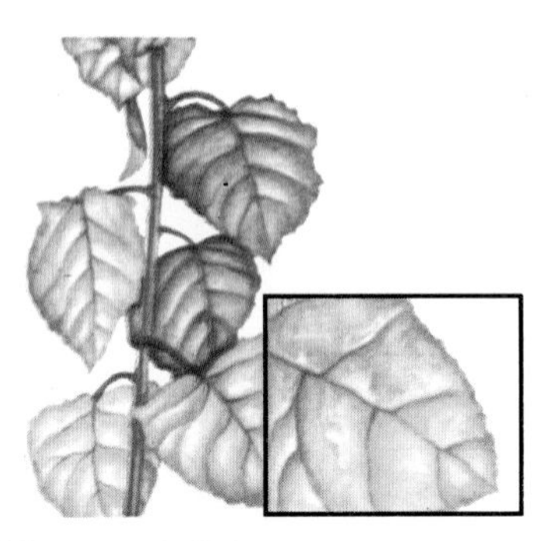

Nitrogen deficiency

Plants affected All types can be affected, but the trouble is most common on fruit trees and vegetables.
Symptoms Young leaves turn pale yellow-green, later developing yellow, red or purple tints. Plants small and lack vigour.
Danger period Throughout the growing season.
Treatment Apply nitrogenous fertiliser, such as sulphate of ammonia, next spring. A foliar feed may help.

Blight

Plants affected Tomatoes and potatoes.
Symptoms Brown blotches on leaves, with a white, furry coating on the undersides. The leaves quickly turn completely brown, then rot.
Danger period July onwards.
Treatment Spray at 10–14 day intervals, particularly in a wet season, with Bordeaux mixture, liquid copper, mancozeb or zineb. Spray potatoes before their tops meet and tomatoes soon after the first fruits set.

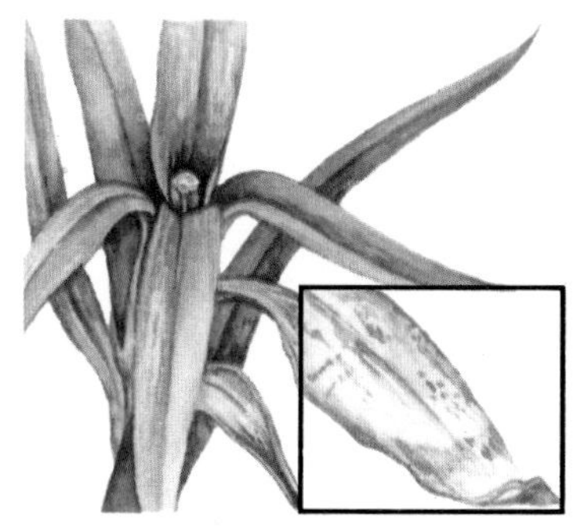

Fusarium wilt
Plants affected Many types, particularly carnations, other dianthus species, sweet peas, peas and beans.
Symptoms Leaves become discoloured and plants wilt. The stem bases may also be discoloured.
Danger period Growing season.
Treatment Remove and burn affected plants. Grow susceptible plants on a fresh site each year, or sterilise the soil. Propagate dianthus species only from healthy plants.

Powdery mildew
Plants affected Strawberries.
Symptoms Purplish discoloration of leaflets, which curl upwards, exposing their under surface.
Danger period Throughout the growing season.
Treatment Immediately before blossom time, dust with sulphur or spray with $1\frac{1}{2}$ per cent lime sulphur or dinocap. Repeat this at 10–14 day intervals until one or two weeks before harvest time. Alternatively, at an early blossoming stage spray three times at 14 day intervals with benomyl or thiophanate-methyl.

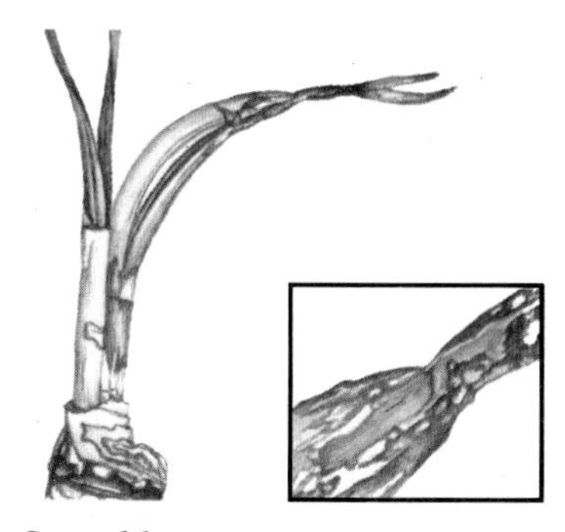

Smoulder
Plants affected Narcissi.
Symptoms Leaves rotting and covered with a grey, velvety mould.
Danger period Spring.
Treatment Store bulbs in a cool, dry place. Destroy affected bulbs. Remove and burn affected plants during the growing season as soon as any symptoms are seen on the foliage. Spray the rest with zineb at 10 day intervals.

Fruit tree red spider mites
Plants affected Apples, plums and pears, and some related ornamentals.
Symptoms Older leaves gradually turn to a bronzed yellow colour, dry out and die.
Danger period May to September.
Treatment Spray thoroughly with a DNOC/petroleum winter wash while the trees are still dormant to kill over-wintering eggs, or spray immediately after flowering with dimethoate, malathion or derris.

Leaves distorted

Leaf-curling plum aphids
Plants affected Plums and damsons.
Symptoms Young leaves puckered and curled.
Danger period April to July.
Treatment Spray thoroughly with a systemic insecticide such as dimethoate or formothion in early spring, before the trees blossom, and again after blossoming if necessary.

Cherry blackflies
Plants affected Flowering and fruiting cherries.
Symptoms Leaves at tips of young shoots are curled and twisted.
Danger period May to July.
Treatment Spray thoroughly with a systemic insecticide such as dimethoate immediately after flowering.

Tarsonemid mites
Plants affected Begonias, dahlias, fuchsias, gerberas, pot cyclamens, ferns and other greenhouse plants.
Symptoms Leaves distorted in severe infestations, or slightly curled at edges; slightly thickened and brittle.
Danger period Any time of year under glass.
Treatment Apply sulphur dust.

Leaf-rolling rose sawflies
Plants affected Bush and climbing roses.
Symptoms Leaves tightly rolled down along their whole length.
Danger period May, June and July.
Treatment Remove and burn affected leaves in May and early June if possible, or spray with trichlorphon, HCH or a systemic insecticide at fortnightly intervals in May.

Leaves distorted (continued)

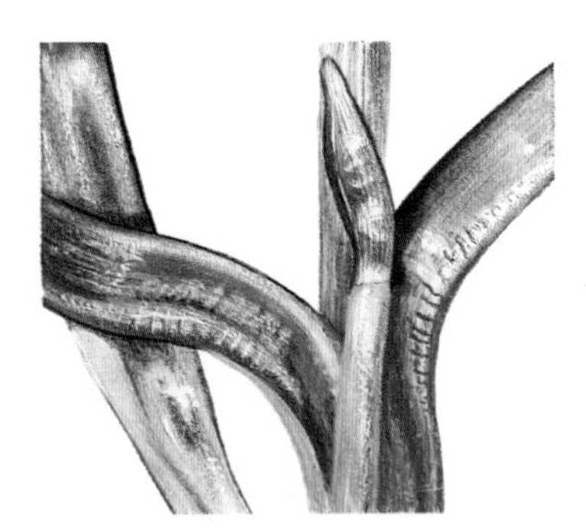

Bulb scale mites

Plants affected Narcissi and hippeastrums.
Symptoms Leaves twisted and malformed, with rusty brown or red scars.
Danger period January to April on narcissi, especially when forced. Any time on hippeastrums under glass.
Treatment Destroy severely affected plants. Expose dormant bulbs to frost for two or three nights, or immerse them for one or two hours in water heated to 43°C (109°F).

Stem and bulb eelworms

Plants affected Daffodils, tulips, hyacinths and some other bulbs.
Symptoms Leaves stunted and distorted, with small yellow bumps on them.
Danger period January to May.
Treatment Remove and burn affected plants. Do not replant bulbs in affected areas of soil for at least three years.

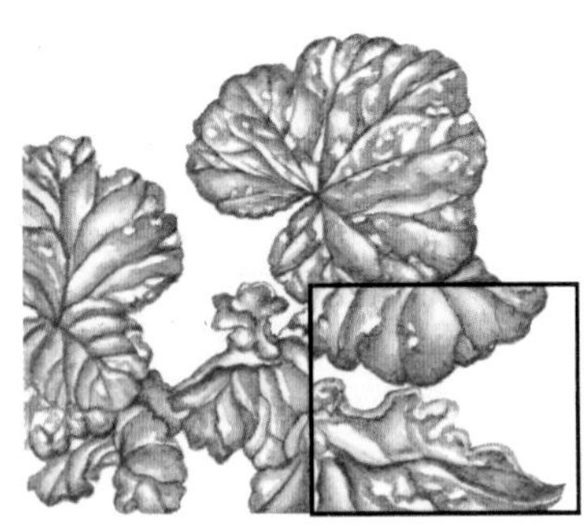

Virus

Plants affected Many types of plant, but particularly strawberries, pelargoniums and marrows.
Symptoms Leaves are crinkled, small and sometimes irregularly shaped.
Danger period Throughout the growing period.
Treatment Burn diseased plants.

Verticillium wilt

Plants affected Cotinus, rhus and acer species, tomatoes and carnations in greenhouses, michaelmas daisies.
Symptoms Wilting of the leaves on one or two shoots (on tomato plants all leaves affected, but recovering at night), affected branches eventually dying back.
Danger period Throughout the growing season.
Treatment On trees and shrubs, cut affected branches back to living tissue and paint wounds. If trouble persists, dig up the plant, burn it, and grow a less susceptible plant in that position. Destroy diseased plants in the greenhouse, isolate infected soil from adjacent healthy plants and sterilise the greenhouse at the end of the season. Take tip cuttings of diseased michaelmas daisies, and burn old plants.

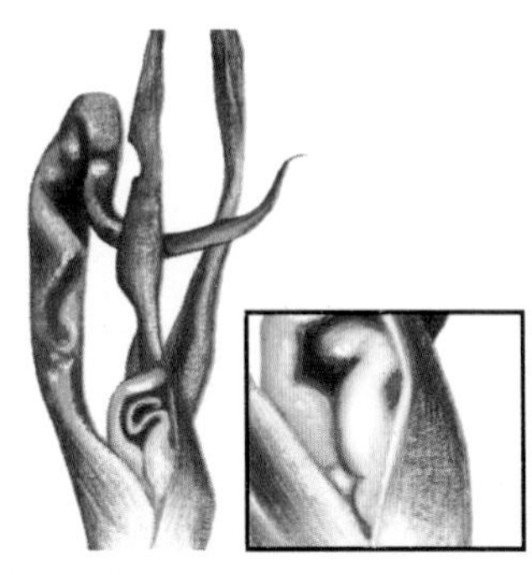

Onion eelworms

Plants affected Onions, shallots, chives and garlic.
Symptoms Leaves swollen and bloated.
Danger period June to August.
Treatment Remove affected plants and burn or bury deeply. Keep to a three-year rotation, and grow from seed rather than from sets if possible.

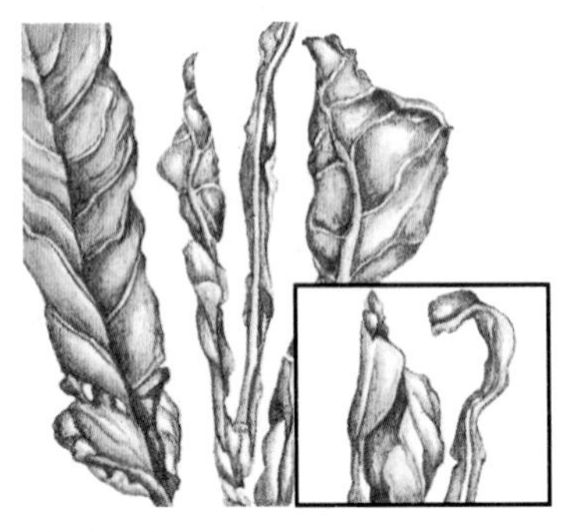

Whiptail

Plants affected Broccoli and cauliflowers.
Symptoms Leaves ruffled, thin and strap-like.
Danger period Throughout the growing period in acid soils.
Treatment Water with a solution of sodium molybdate (1 rounded tablespoon in 2 gallons of water for every 10 sq. yds of soil).

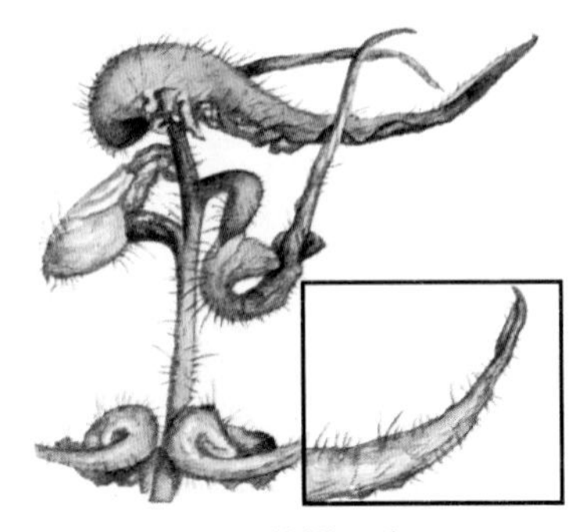

Hormone weedkiller damage

Plants affected All types, but tomatoes and vines are very susceptible.
Symptoms Leaves narrow, fan-shaped, and frequently cupped.
Danger period Growing season.
Treatment None once damage has occurred, as plants usually recover. To prevent damage, do not use weedkiller sprays on a windy day or weedkiller equipment for any other jobs, and destroy mowings from a freshly treated lawn.

Club root
Plants affected Brassicas, wallflowers and stocks.
Symptoms Wilting of leaves, which may be discoloured.
Danger period Throughout the growing season.
Treatment See under Club root on page 397.

Willow anthracnose
Plants affected Weeping willows.
Symptoms Leaves curl, become spotted and fall prematurely.
Danger period As leaves unfold in spring, sometimes in a wet summer.
Treatment Spray small trees as leaves unfold with a copper fungicide such as Bordeaux mixture, and repeat at least twice in summer. Burn any fallen leaves.

Gall wasps
Plants affected Oaks, some species of roses and willows.
Symptoms Many different galls resembling peas, cherries, silk buttons and spangles growing out of leaves. Sometimes solitary, often numerous.
Treatment Remove and destroy if possible, but gall wasps seldom cause serious damage.

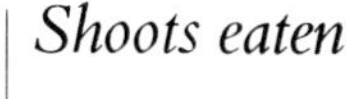

Shoots eaten

Aphids
Plants affected Many different plants, but especially roses and broad beans.
Symptoms Colonies of aphids develop on young shoots.
Danger period May to July outdoors, but almost any time of year in greenhouses.
Treatment See Aphids on page 378.

Reversion
Plants affected Blackcurrants.
Symptoms Leaves are smaller and with fewer lobes than normal. Affected bushes fail to produce a good crop.
Danger period Only obvious on long basal shoots in June or July.
Treatment Dig up and burn. Plant bushes certified to be free of virus. Control the blackcurrant gall mite that spreads the disease.

Red currant blister aphids
Plants affected Red and blackcurrants.
Symptoms Leaves with raised, irregular red or green blisters.
Danger period May and June.
Treatment Spray with tar-oil winter wash in January to kill overwintering eggs, and apply systemic insecticides such as dimethoate in spring, just before flowering. Repeat after flowering if necessary.

Peach leaf curl
Plants affected Peaches, nectarines, almonds, including ornamental types.
Symptoms Leaves with large red blisters become white, then brown, and fall prematurely.
Danger period Before bud-burst.
Treatment Spray with Bordeaux mixture in January or early February, repeating a fortnight later and again just before leaf-fall. Remove and burn diseased leaves before they whiten.

Leopard moths
Plants affected Apples and pears, both fruiting and ornamental, ashes, birches, cherries, cotoneasters, hawthorns, lilacs, maples, oaks, rhododendrons, sorbus and willows.
Symptoms Branches tunnelled by caterpillars, causing wilting of leaves beyond the tunnel.
Danger period Throughout the year.
Treatment Kill the caterpilllars by introducing HCH into the tunnels.

Shoots eaten (continued)

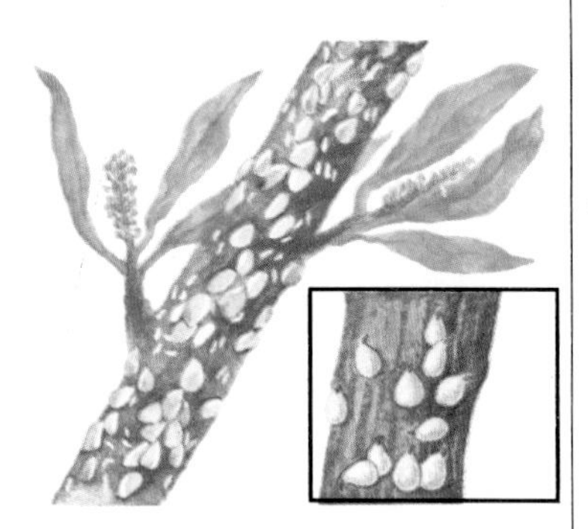

Scale insects

Plants affected Many different plants, both under glass and outdoors, especially beeches, ceanothus, cotoneasters and horse chestnuts.
Symptoms Colonies of brown, yellow or white scales on older shoots.
Danger period Most times of year, but particularly late spring and summer.
Treatment See Scale insects on page 378.

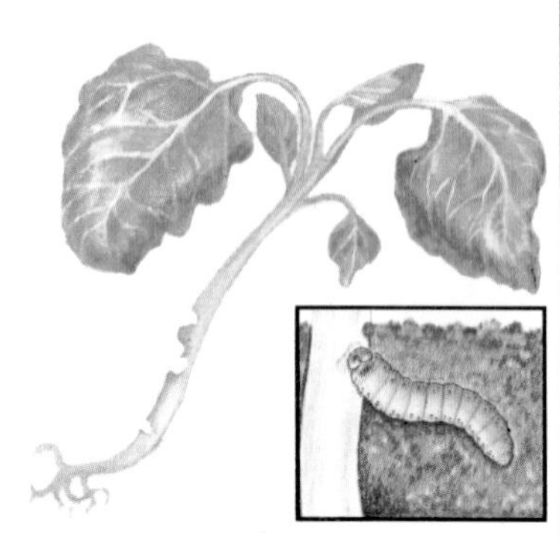

Cutworms

Plants affected Lettuces, other vegetables and young ornamental annuals.
Symptoms Shoots eaten through at soil level; fat caterpillars in soil.
Danger period Early spring and late summer.
Treatment Control weeds, which encourage cutworms, and protect susceptible plants by working a little HCH dust or bromophos into the soil. Seed dressings also give some protection in the early stages.

Shoots discoloured

Woolly aphids

Plants affected Apples, cotoneasters, pyracanthas, crataegus and sorbus.
Symptoms Woody swellings and tufts of white wool on trunks and branches.
Danger period April to September.
Treatment Where possible, brush a spray-strength solution of malathion or HCH on to affected areas when wool first appears, or apply one of these as a spray. Systemic insecticides such as dimethoate may also be used.

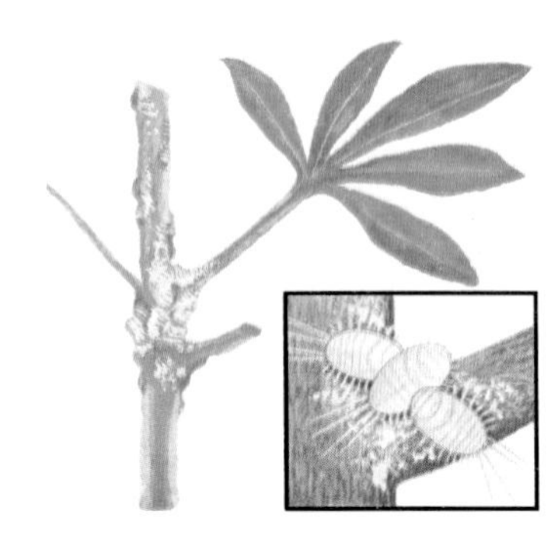

Mealy bugs

Plants affected Greenhouse and house plants, especially cacti, other succulents and climbers.
Symptoms Colonies of mealy bugs covered with white mealy or waxy wool usually concentrated around buds and leaf axils.
Danger period Most times of year, but particularly late summer and autumn.
Treatment See Mealy bugs on page 378.

Spur blight

Plants affected Raspberries and loganberries.
Symptoms Canes bear purple blotches that later become silver, spotted with black. Spurs on these die back.
Danger period Spring and summer.
Treatment Cut out old infected canes after fruiting, and remove young thin surplus canes early. Spray with benomyl, dichlofluanid, thiram or carbendazim soon after canes emerge, and repeat three or four times at fortnightly intervals. Thiophanate-methyl can also be used, the first application being given at bud-burst and repeated at 14 day intervals until the end of flowering. A less effective alternative is to spray with a copper fungicide at bud-burst, and again when the tips of the flowers are just showing white.

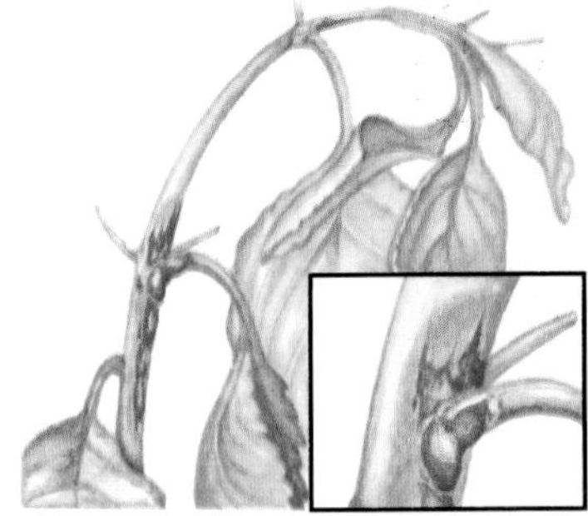

Bacterial canker

Plants affected Cherries, plums, gages, damsons and ornamental prunus species.
Symptoms Elongated, flattened, canker-bearing exudations of gum on shoots that are dying back; leaves yellow and wither prematurely.
Danger period Autumn and winter, but symptoms do not appear until the following spring or summer.
Treatment Cut out infected branches and paint all wounds with a wound-sealing compound.
Spray the foliage with Bordeaux mixture.

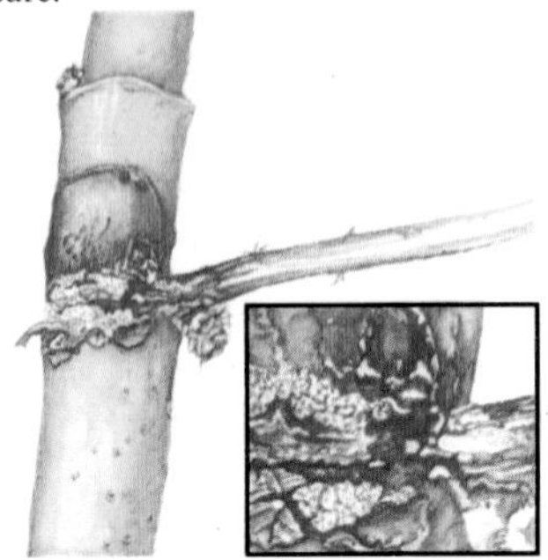

Grey mould (or botrytis)

Plants affected Clarkias, godetias and zinnias in particular, also other types.
Symptoms Rotting stems covered with a grey, velvety mould.
Danger period Throughout the growing season in wet weather
Treatment Cut out affected shoots and spray with benomyl, carbendazim, thiram or zineb.

Shoots distorted or wilted

Witches' brooms

Plants affected Prunus species and birches.
Symptoms Several shoots, sometimes bearing blistered foliage, growing from one point and crowded together on infected branches.
Danger period Throughout the life of the tree.
Treatment Cut out the affected branch to a point 6 in. below the broom and paint the wound with a protective paint.

Gumming

Plants affected Cherries and other prunus species.
Symptoms Gum exudes on branches and trunks and gradually hardens.
Danger period All the year round, but the disease is worst in summer.
Treatment With good feeding, mulching and watering, the gumming should stop, but gum may have to be removed so that dead wood beneath can be cut out. Cover the wound with protective paint.

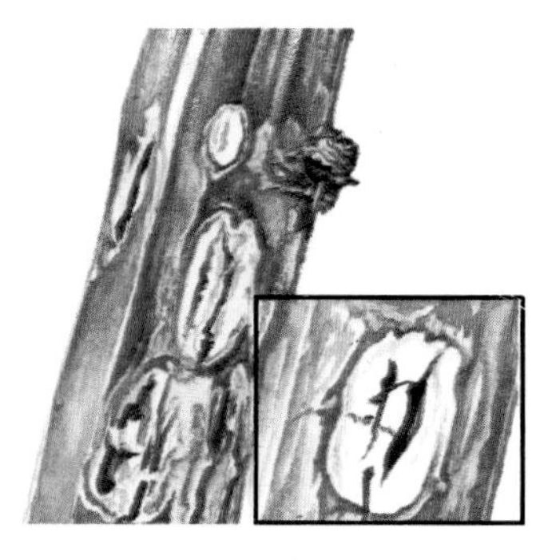

Cane spot

Plants affected Raspberries, loganberries and hybrid berries.
Symptoms Small circular, purple spots, enlarging to become elliptic white blotches with a purple border, about $\frac{1}{4}$ in. long. These eventually split to form small pits, which give the canes a rough cracked appearance. Leaves may also be spotted and fruit distorted.
Danger period May to October.
Treatment Cut out and burn badly spotted canes. Spray raspberries with 5 per cent lime sulphur at bud-burst and $2\frac{1}{2}$ per cent lime sulphur immediately before blossom time. Alternatively, use copper or thiram (except on fruit to be processed) at these times, or use benomyl or thiophanate-methyl from bud-burst to the end of blossoming, at 14 day intervals. For loganberries, apply a copper fungicide or thiram (except on fruit to be processed) both before blossom time and as soon as the fruit has set, or use benomyl or thiophanate-methyl as for raspberries.

Rose rust

Plants affected Roses.
Symptoms Swellings on stems that burst open to reveal a mass of bright orange, powdery spores.
Danger period Symptoms appear in spring.
Treatment Cut out and burn affected shoots. See also Rusts on page 380.

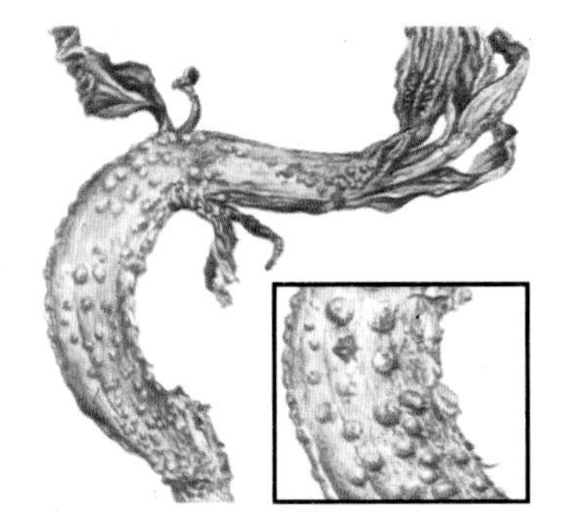

Mint rust

Plants affected Mint.
Symptoms Swollen, distorted shoots bear orange-coloured spore pustules.
Danger period Symptoms appear in spring, but affected plants are permanently diseased.
Treatment Cut out and burn affected shoots; burn over the mint bed at the end of the season. See also Rusts on page 380.

Petunia wilt

Plants affected Petunias, salpiglossis, zinnias, other bedding plants.
Symptoms Plants wilt, often as they are about to flower. Stem bases may be discoloured.
Danger period Growing season.
Treatment Rotate bedding plants so that susceptible ones are grown on a fresh site each year. Water planting holes with Cheshunt compound, and drench plants with it weekly. Burn diseased plants.

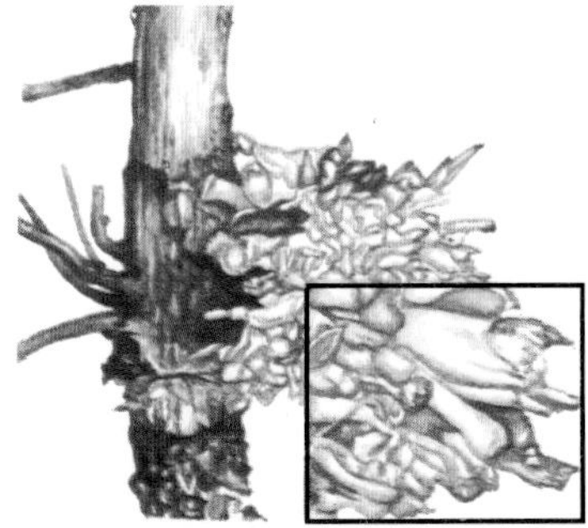

Leafy gall

Plants affected Many types, but in particular sweet peas, pelargoniums, dahlias, chrysanthemums, carnations, gladioli and strawberries.
Symptoms Abortive, often flattened, shoots with thickened, distorted leaves develop at ground level.
Danger period During propagation and throughout the growing season.
Treatment Destroy infected plants. When replanting, grow a non-susceptible type of plant.

Shoots distorted or wilted (continued)

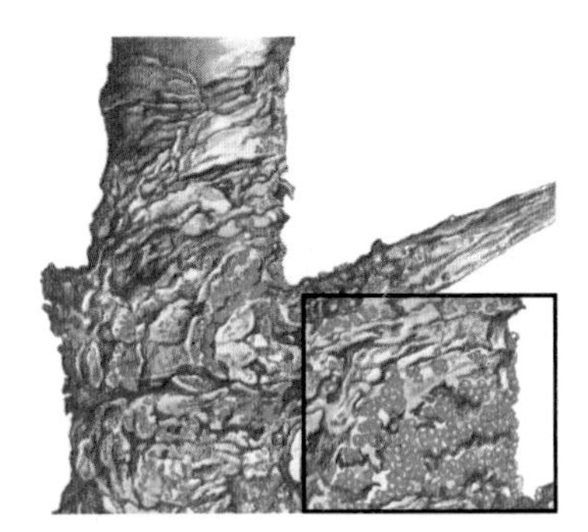

Apple canker

Plants affected Apples, and less commonly pears, beeches, ash, poplars and sorbus.
Symptoms Elliptical cankers, with the bark shrinking in concentric rings until the inner tissues are exposed. Girdling of the shoot or branch by the canker causes die-back.
Danger period Any time.
Treatment Cut out and burn infected spurs and small branches. On larger branches and main trunks, pare away all diseased material (which should be burnt) until a clean wound is left. Coat this with a canker paint. In severe cases, spray with Bordeaux mixture just before leaf-fall and at bud-burst.

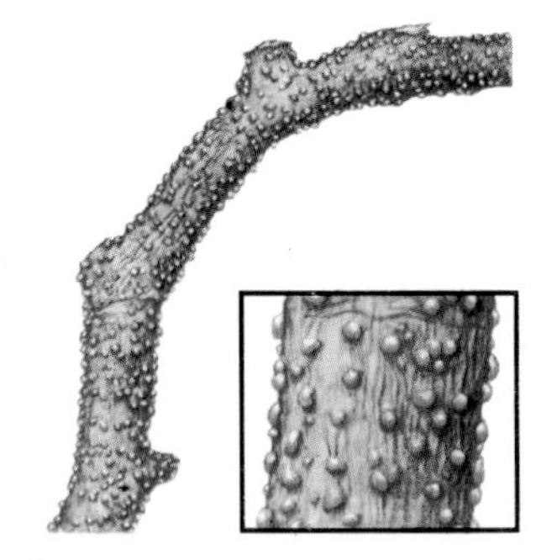

Coral spot

Plants affected Many trees and shrubs, particularly acers, magnolias, red currants, figs.
Symptoms Die-back of shoots or large branches caused by coral-red, spore-filled pustules on dead wood. Sometimes the whole plant dies.
Danger period Any time.
Treatment Cut out all dead shoots to a point at least 2–4 in. below the apparently diseased area, and burn. Feed, mulch, water and/or drain soil as necessary to encourage vigour.

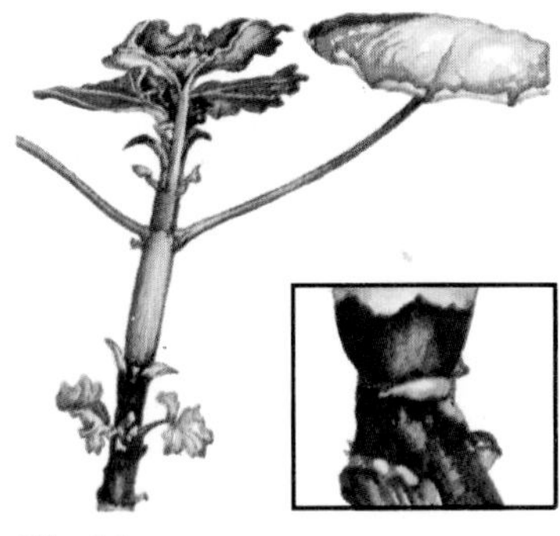

Black leg

Plants affected Pelargoniums and potatoes.
Symptoms A black rot develops at the base of cuttings or at the stem base, and the affected tissues become soft. Leaves yellow and whole cutting or stem dies.
Danger period For pelargoniums, soon after cuttings are taken; for potatoes, June.
Treatment Destroy badly affected plants. No other treatment is required for potatoes, apart from planting healthy seed tubers. Prevent the disease on pelargoniums by using sterilised compost, maintaining strict greenhouse hygiene and watering carefully with mains water.

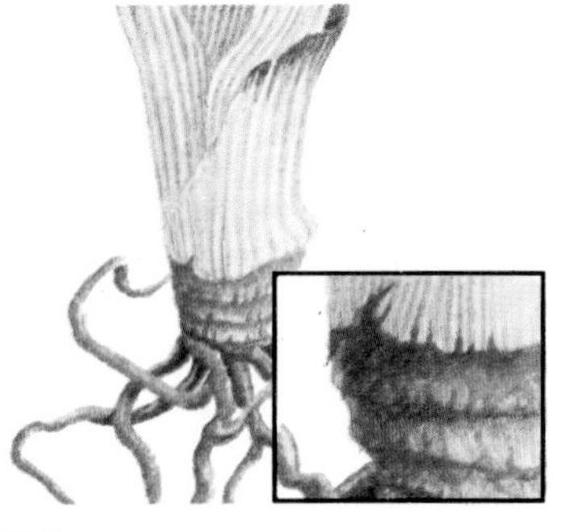

Rhizome rot

Plants affected Rhizomatous irises.
Symptoms A soft, yellow, evil-smelling rot of the rhizome at the growing point causes the fan of leaves to collapse at ground level.
Danger period Any time, but particularly in wet weather.
Treatment Improve drainage if necessary, and control slugs and other pests. Destroy badly affected plants, but on others cut out rotting parts and dust with dry Bordeaux powder.

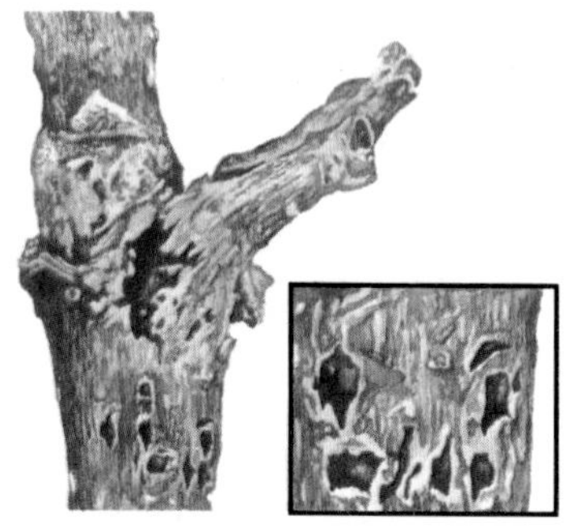

Scab

Plants affected Apples and pears.
Symptoms Small blister-like pimples develop on young shoots, later burst the bark and then show as ring-like cracks or scabs.
Danger period Growing season.
Treatment Cut out cracked and scabby shoots when pruning. Spray as for Scab on page 380.

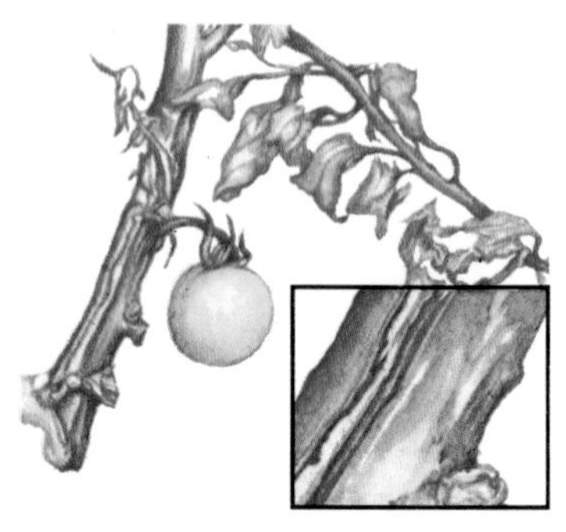

Virus

Plants affected Sweet peas and tomatoes.
Symptoms Wilting of plants that show streaks on leaf stalks and stems.
Danger period Throughout the growing season.
Treatment Dig up and burn affected plants as they are seen.

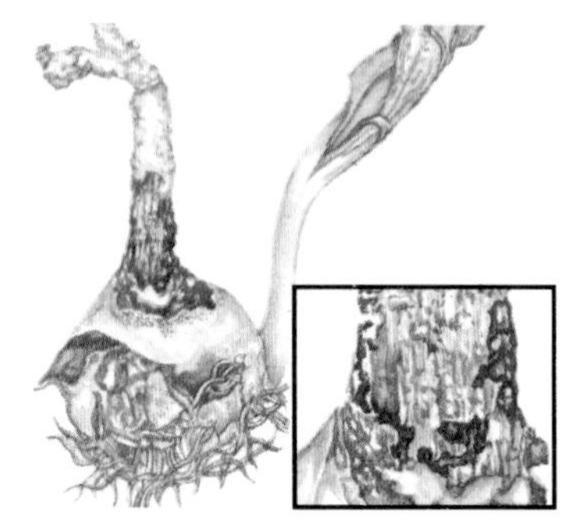

Tulip fire

Plants affected Tulips.
Symptoms Young shoots are crippled; they rot above ground and become covered with a grey, velvety mould.
Danger period Spring.
Treatment See Tulip fire on page 395.

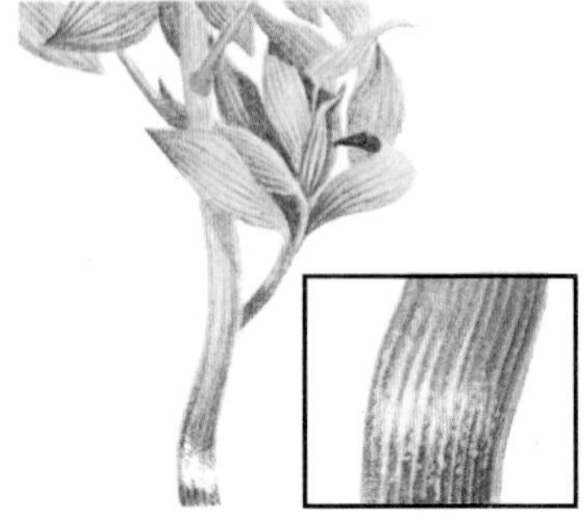

Paeony wilt

Plants affected Paeonies.
Symptoms Affected shoots collapse at ground level.
Danger period Growing season.
Treatment Cut out affected shoots to below ground level and dust the crowns with dry Bordeaux powder. Spray with carbendazim, dichlofluanid, thiram or zineb soon after the leaves appear.

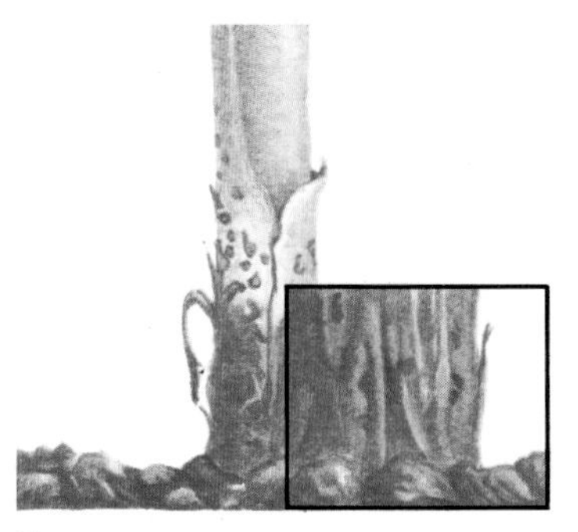

Foot rot
Plants affected Tomatoes, bedding plants, sweet peas, peas, beans.
Symptoms Stem bases, which may be discoloured, rot and roots usually die.
Danger period Growing season.
Treatment Rotate vegetables and bedding plants, and always use sterile compost for pot plants. Water bedding plants grown in seed boxes with Cheshunt compound when they are put in their planting holes and, if trouble occurs, at weekly intervals.

Crown rot
Plants affected Rhubarb.
Symptoms Rotting of the terminal bud, followed by progressive rotting of the crown, in which a cavity may develop. Any leaves which develop will be spindly and discoloured, and die down early.
Danger period Throughout the growing season.
Treatment Dig up and burn. Do not plant rhubarb again in the same position.

Grey mould of lettuce (or botrytis)
Plants affected Lettuces.
Symptoms Wilted plants are found to be rotten at ground level, where the tissues are covered with a grey, velvety mould. Top growth separates easily from the roots.
Danger period Throughout the growing season but worse on winter lettuces.
Treatment Dust quintozene into the soil before planting out. Under glass, fumigate with tecnazene smokes or remove and burn diseased plants and decaying leaves and spray indoors or out with benomyl, carbendazim, dichlofluanid, thiophanate-methyl, thiram or zineb.

Dry rot
Plants affected Gladioli, but acid-antheras, crocuses and freesias are also susceptible to infection.
Symptoms A dry rot of the leaf sheaths at soil level makes the top growth topple over. Affected tissues are covered with minute black resting bodies, just visible to the naked eye.
Danger period Growing season.
Treatment See Dry rot on page 395.

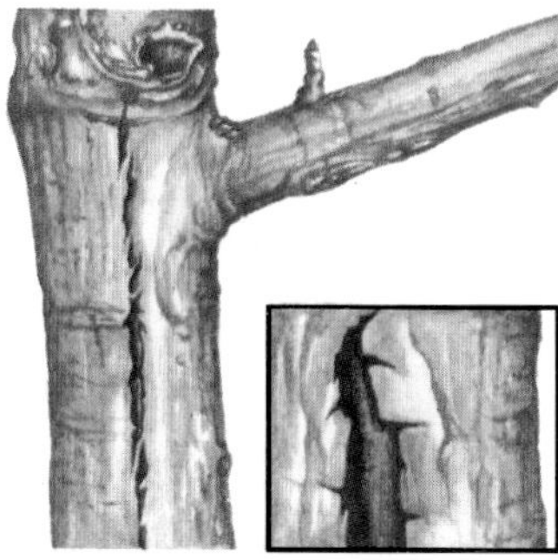

Bark splitting
Plants affected Many types of tree, including fruit.
Symptoms Bark splits, and the cracks open up.
Danger period Throughout the year.
Treatment Cut out any dead wood and remove loose bark until a clean wound is left. Coat with a wound-sealing paint. If the tree is then fed, mulched and watered properly, the wound should heal naturally.

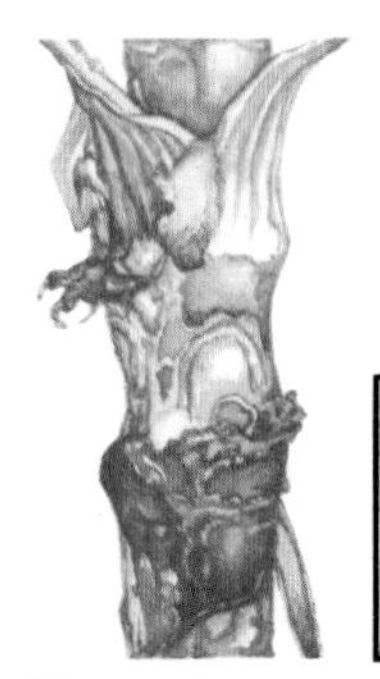

Stem rot
Plants affected Tomatoes, godetias, lobelias and carnations, each of which is affected by a different disease.
Symptoms Rotting of stems, but no very obvious fungal growth is visible on the affected areas.
Danger period Growing season.
Treatment Where possible, cut out affected parts and dust or spray with captan. Alternatively, destroy diseased plants.

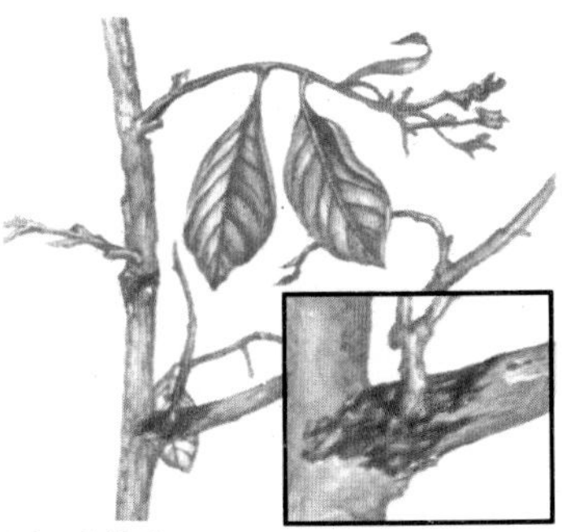

Fire blight
Plants affected Cotoneasters, hawthorns, sorbus species, pears, apples, other related ornamentals.
Symptoms Shoots die back, particularly flowering spurs, their leaves turn brown and wither, and cankers develop at their base.
Danger period Flowering time.
Treatment Notify the local representative of the Ministry of Agriculture, Fisheries and Food, who will recommend treatment, possibly destruction of plant.

Flower-bud disorders

Caterpillars

Plants affected Roses, chrysanthemums, apples and some other plants.
Symptoms Holes eaten into buds.
Danger period March to June outdoors, but almost any time of year under glass.
Treatment Spray with HCH, derris or trichlorphon when the pests are present.

Bullfinches

Plants affected Plums, pears, gooseberries, flowering cherries and forsythias.
Symptoms Flower buds eaten.
Danger period November to April.
Treatment Spray developing buds with a bird repellent or use netting to protect susceptible plants.

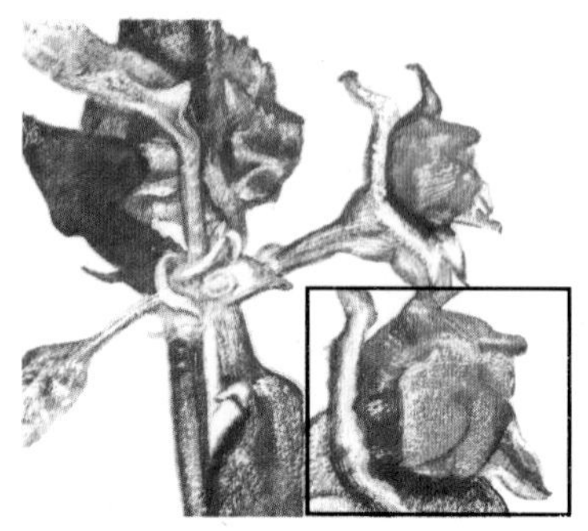

Apple blossom weevils

Plants affected Apples.
Symptoms Flower buds almost reach maturity but fail to open.
Danger period April and May.
Treatment Spray with HCH, fenitrothion or a systemic insecticide just before buds start to open.

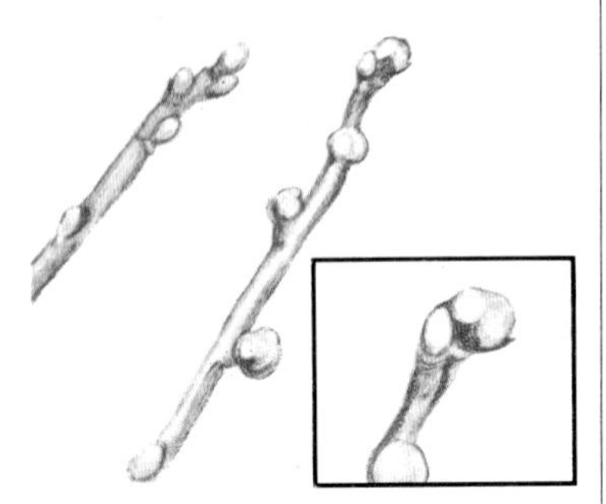

Blackcurrant gall mites

Plants affected Blackcurrants.
Symptoms Buds greatly enlarged.
Danger period February and March.
Treatment Remove and burn affected buds in early March and spray with lime sulphur when the first flowers open, repeating after about three weeks.

Flowers attacked after opening

Earwigs

Plants affected Clematis, chrysanthemums, dahlias and some other plants.
Symptoms Ragged pieces eaten out of the petals.
Danger period May to October.
Treatment Reduce earwigs before plants flower by spraying or dusting plants and soil with HCH. Earwigs can also be trapped in rolls of corrugated cardboard, in old sacking, or in flower pots stuffed with straw.

Virus

Plants affected Viola species, wallflowers, tulips, lilies, dahlias, chrysanthemums and many other types of herbaceous plants.
Symptoms Flowers distorted, or flower colour broken: white streaks, or stripes in a lighter or darker shade of the background colour.
Danger period Throughout the growing season.
Treatment Destroy affected plants.

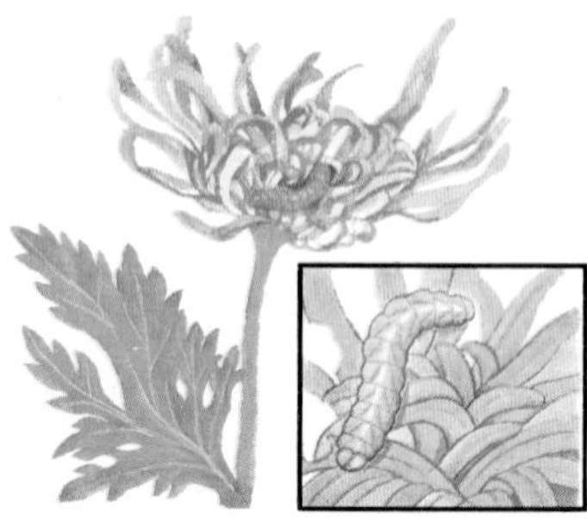

Caterpillars

Plants affected Chrysanthemums, carnations and greenhouse plants.
Symptoms Petals eaten; caterpillars often inside the blooms.
Danger period Any time of year.
Treatment If relatively few blooms are affected, remove the caterpillars by hand. Alternatively, spray with HCH or trichlorphon – preferably before plants are in full bloom, as flowers may be marked by spraying.

Capsid bugs

Plants affected Chrysanthemums, dahlias and many other ornamental annuals and perennials.
Symptoms Flowers distorted.
Danger period June to October outdoors, but continuing later under glass.
Treatment Spray with HCH, malathion or diazinon as soon as the first signs of damage appear.

Petal blight

Plants affected Chrysanthemums, sometimes cornflowers, dahlias and heads of globe artichokes.
Symptoms Dark, water-soaked spots spread on florets until flowers rot.
Danger period Flowering time, particularly in cold, wet summers.
Treatment Destroy affected flowers. Prevent the disease under glass by keeping humidity low. Spray plants with zineb, just before flowers open. Repeat every seven days as necessary.

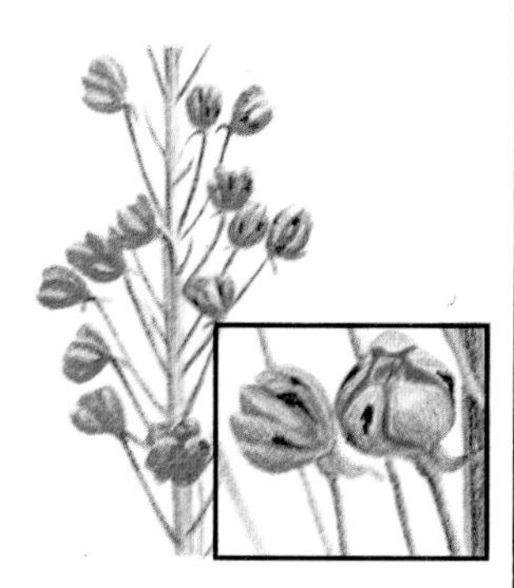

Blotch

Plants affected Delphiniums and hellebores.
Symptoms Black blotches on the flowers.
Danger period Flowering time.
Treatment Remove and burn diseased parts and spray the plants regularly with a copper fungicide such as Bordeaux mixture.

Tulip fire

Plants affected Tulips.
Symptoms Small, brown spots on the petals. These may rot and become covered with a grey velvety mould.
Danger period Flowering time.
Treatment See Tulip fire on page 395.

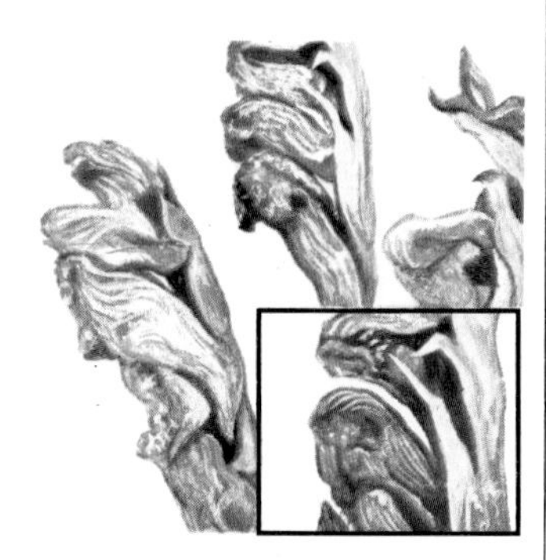

Gladiolus thrips

Plants affected Gladioli and some related plants.
Symptoms Fine silvery flecks appear on petals, and in severe infestations the flowers are completely discoloured and may die.
Danger period June to September.
Treatment Dust corms with HCH before storing and again before planting. If symptoms appear, spray affected plants with HCH, malathion or diazinon.

Disorders of tree fruit and soft fruit

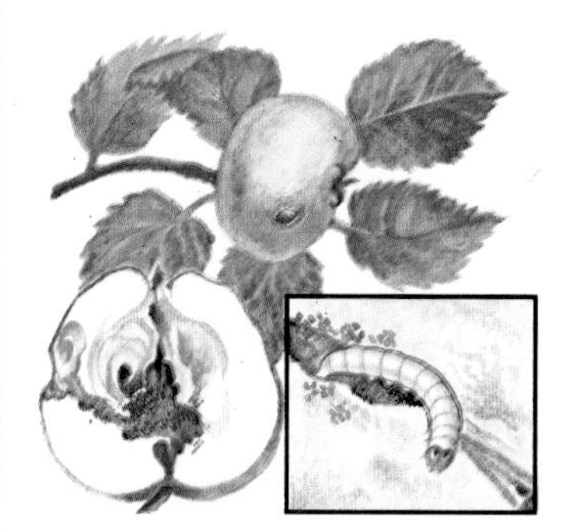

Codling moths

Plants affected Mainly apples, but also pears.
Symptoms Caterpillars eat into the cores of ripening fruit.
Danger period June to August.
Treatment Spray thoroughly with fenitrothion or malathion in mid-June and again about three weeks later to kill the young caterpillars before they penetrate the fruit.

Apple sawflies

Plants affected Apples.
Symptoms Caterpillars eat into the cores of young fruitlets, which then drop prematurely. This pest also causes superficial scarring of mature fruit.
Danger period May to June.
Treatment Spray thoroughly with BHC, fenitrothion or dimethoate immediately after the petals have fallen off the blossom.

Scab

Plants affected Apples and pears (and also pyracantha berries).
Symptoms Brown or black scabs on the fruit, which may, in severe cases, crack when the scabs have merged and become corky.
Danger period Throughout the growing season.
Treatment See Scab on page 380.

Brown rot

Plants affected All tree fruit.
Symptoms The fruit turns browny-white, often concentrically ringed fungus spores cover it; then it withers and shrinks.
Danger period Summer, and in store.
Treatment Destroy all rotten and withered fruits. Cut out any dead shoots during pruning. Late sprays of thiophanate-methyl will reduce rotting of fruit in store.

Disorders of tree fruit and soft fruit (continued)

Apple capsids
Plants affected Mainly apples, but also pears.
Symptoms Raised bumps and corky patches on ripening fruit.
Danger period April to August.
Treatment Spray with DNOC/petroleum or tar oil/petroleum during the dormant period to kill over wintering eggs, and/or spray with HCH just before the trees start to flower.

Grey mould (or botrytis)
Plants affected All soft fruit, but strawberries and raspberries are most susceptible.
Symptoms The fruit rots and becomes covered with a grey, velvety mould.
Danger period Flowering time, but symptoms do not appear until fruit matures.
Treatment Spray as the first flowers open, repeating two or three times at 14 day intervals, using benomyl, dichlofluanid, thiophanate-methyl or, except on fruit to be processed, carbendazim or thiram. Remove diseased fruits as they appear, to prevent spread by contact with others.

Cracking
Plants affected Apples, pears and plums.
Symptoms The fruit's skin splits.
Danger period Throughout the growing season.
Treatment Try to avoid irregular growth by mulching to conserve moisture, and by never allowing the soil to dry out.

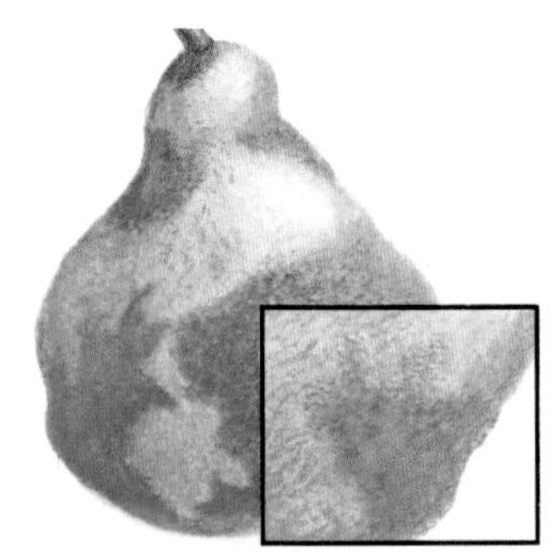

Stony pit
Plants affected Old pear trees.
Symptoms Fruit pitted and deformed, with patches of dead, stony cells in the flesh making it inedible. Symptoms appear on one branch and over the years gradually spread until all the fruit on the tree is affected.
Danger period Any time.
Treatment Destroy diseased trees.

Bitter pit
Plants affected Apples.
Symptoms Slightly sunken brown spots beneath skin and throughout flesh.
Danger period Throughout the growing season, but not apparent until harvesting or in store.
Treatment Feed, mulch and never allow the soil to dry out. In mid-June spray with calcium nitrate at the rate of 8 rounded tablespoons to 5 gallons of water, then repeat three times at three-weekly intervals.

Fruit drop
Plants affected All tree fruit.
Symptoms Fruit drops prematurely when it is still very small.
Danger period Flowering time and just after.
Treatment See that suitable pollinators are present in the garden. Feed, mulch and water. Nothing can be done in cold seasons when fruit drop is due to poor pollination.

Raspberry beetles
Plants affected Raspberries, loganberries and blackberries.
Symptoms Beetle grubs feed on ripening fruit.
Danger period June to August.
Treatment Spray thoroughly with derris or malathion as soon as the first fruits begin to turn pink.

Powdery mildew
Plants affected Grapes, strawberries and gooseberries.
Symptoms A white powder that turns brown on gooseberries but may show as loss of colour on strawberries. Grapes may split.
Danger period Growing season.
Treatment Spray as for Powdery mildew on page 381.

Disorders of tomatoes, and pea or bean pods

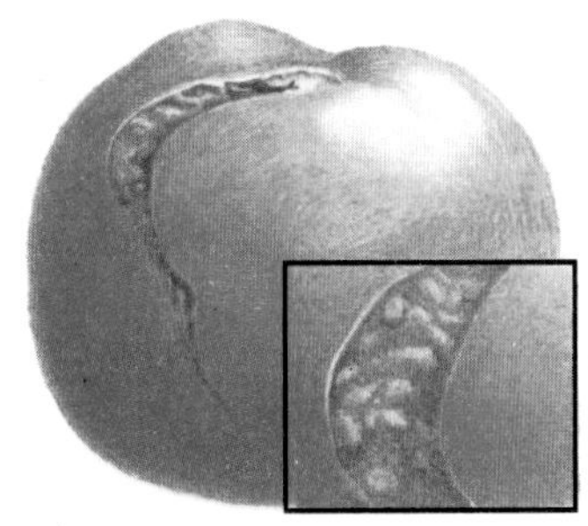

Cracking

Plants affected Tomatoes.
Symptoms The skin splits near the shoulder, often in the form of a ring, sometimes downwards.
Danger period As the fruit develops.
Treatment Try to maintain even growth by never allowing the soil to dry out.

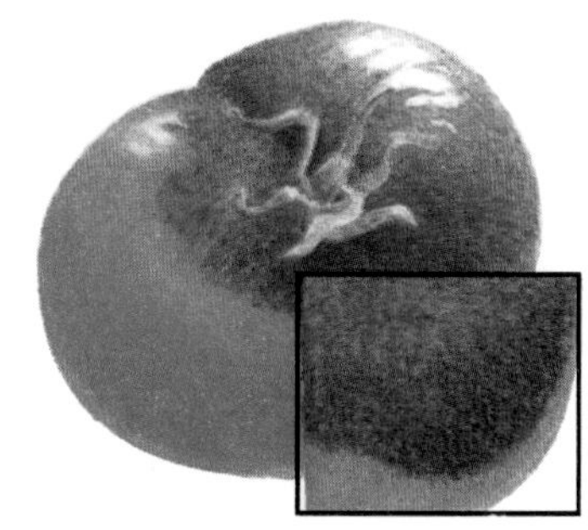

Blight

Plants affected Tomatoes outdoors.
Symptoms A brown discoloration which spreads until the fruit shrivels and rots rapidly.
Danger period Late summer, in wet weather.
Treatment Spray at 10–14 day intervals, particularly in a wet season, with Bordeaux mixture, liquid copper, mancozeb or zineb.

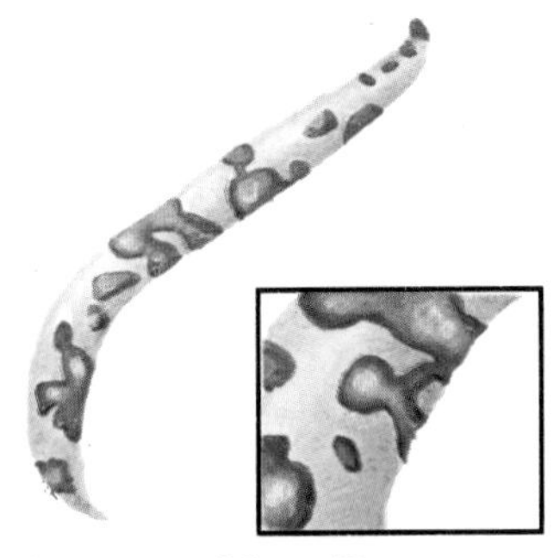

Anthracnose of dwarf beans

Plants affected Dwarf beans, and occasionally runner beans.
Symptoms Black-brown, sunken areas on the pods, together with brown spots on the leaves and stems; leaves may fall prematurely.
Danger period Throughout the growing season – particularly in cool, wet summers.
Treatment All diseased plants should be destroyed, and no beans saved for seed. Sow seed from a reputable supplier and in a fresh site. If the disease appears and becomes serious, spray before flowering with carbendazin, zineb or half-strength Bordeaux mixture.

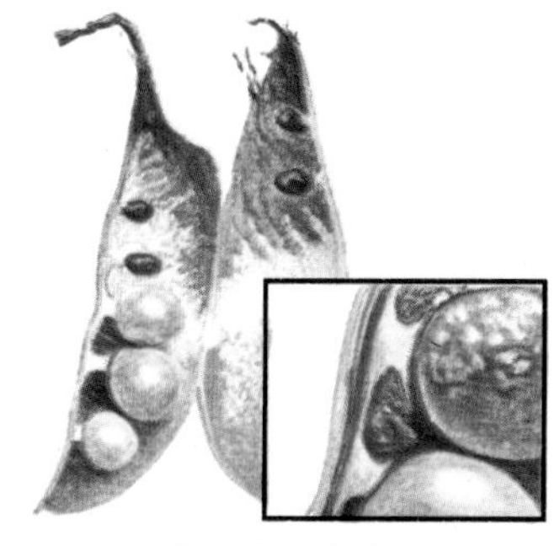

Grey mould (or botrytis)

Plants affected Tomatoes, and occasionally pea and bean pods in wet weather.
Symptoms A grey, velvety mould develops on rotting fruit.
Danger period Growing season.
Treatment Remove and burn diseased fruit or pods. Under glass, fumigate with tecnazene; indoors and outside, spray with benomyl, carbendazim, dichlofluanid, mancozeb, thiophanate-methyl, thiram or zineb.

Greenback and blotchy ripening

Plants affected Tomatoes.
Symptoms A hard green or yellow patch develops on the shoulder of the fruit near the stalk, and similar patches may develop on other parts of the fruit.
Danger period As the fruit develops.
Treatment Grow resistant varieties or never allow the soil to dry out, in order to maintain even growth of the fruit. Shade the greenhouse when the weather is hot.

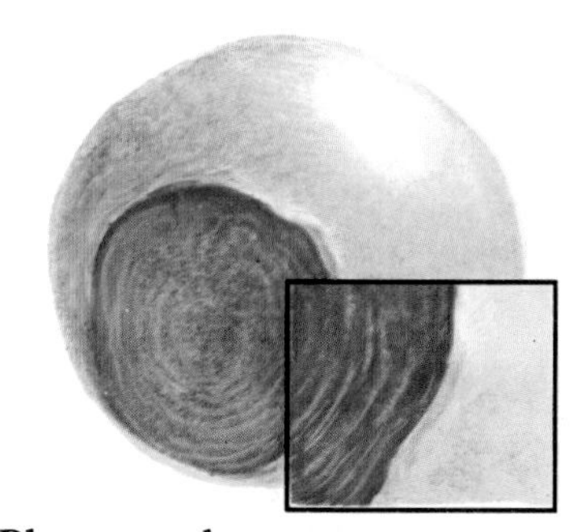

Blossom end rot

Plants affected Tomatoes.
Symptoms A circular brown or black patch at the blossom end of the fruit, which, despite its name, does not usually rot.
Danger period As fruit develops.
Treatment Prevent trouble by never allowing the soil to dry out; this maintains even growth.

Pea moths

Plants affected Garden peas.
Symptoms Peas in pods are eaten and a small maggot-like caterpillar is present.
Danger period June to August.
Treatment Spray when the flowers first open, and again two weeks later, with fenitrothion. Alternatively, grow early-maturing varieties.

Bulb, corm, tuber and root vegetable disorders

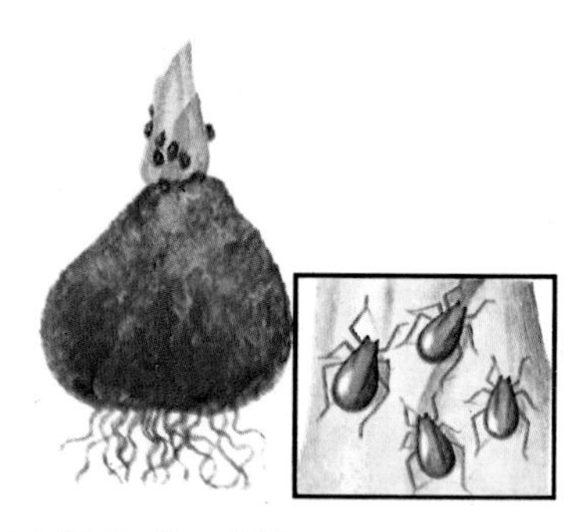

Tulip bulb aphids
Plants affected Tulips, irises, gladioli and crocuses.
Symptoms Colonies of dark green aphids develop on dormant bulbs and corms in store.
Danger period November to February.
Treatment Fumigate with HCH or dichlorvos, if possible, or dust with HCH. Sprays of HCH or malathion may be used, but ensure that treated bulbs and corms dry out afterwards.

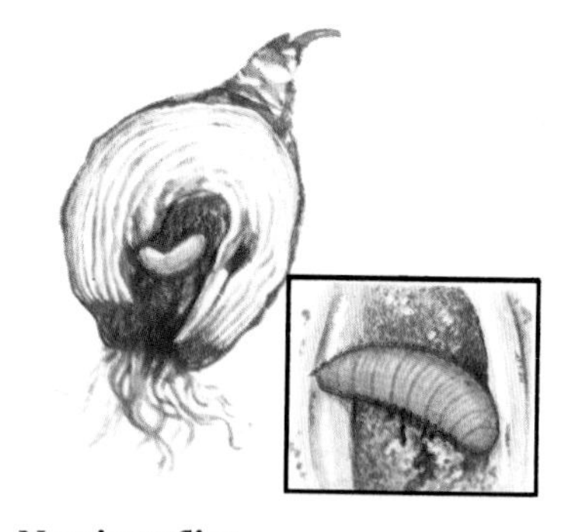

Narcissus flies
Plants affected Mainly daffodils and narcissi, but also some other bulbs.
Symptoms Bulbs soft and rotten, dirty brown maggots inside.
Danger period Attacks start between April and June, but symptoms are usually noticed either in dormant bulbs at planting time or in the following spring.
Treatment Discard soft bulbs at planting time. Cultivate the soil around plants as the foliage dies down in June and July. This will block any holes that would enable the adult flies to get down to the bulbs to lay eggs.

Basal rot
Plants affected Crocuses, narcissi and lilies.
Symptoms Rotting of the roots and the base of the corm or bulb, which, if cut longitudinally, shows dark strands spreading from the base or a chocolate-brown rot spreading upwards through the inner scales.
Danger period Any time, including during the storage of narcissus bulbs.
Treatment Destroy severely affected corms and bulbs. In the early stages, lily bulbs may be saved by cutting out diseased roots and scales, and by dusting the surviving bulbs with quintozene.

Stem and bulb eelworms
Plants affected Daffodils, tulips, hyacinths and some others.
Symptoms Bulbs discoloured internally, eventually rotting away. Growth poor and distorted.
Danger period Dormant bulbs may show symptoms in late summer and autumn. Growing plants are mainly affected in the spring.
Treatment Destroy affected plants. Do not replant bulbs in affected areas of soil for at least three years.

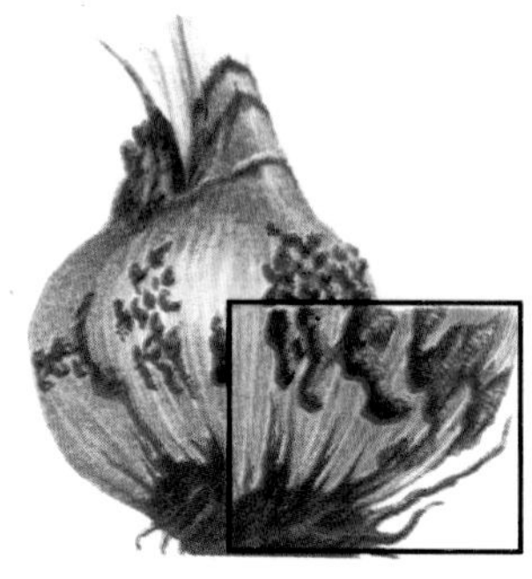

Smoulder
Plants affected Narcissi.
Symptoms Bulbs decay, and small, black, flat fungal resting bodies form.
Danger period During storage.
Treatment Store bulbs in a cool, dry place. Destroy affected bulbs. Remove and burn affected plants during the growing season as soon as any symptoms are seen on the foliage. Spray the rest with zineb at 10 day intervals.
See also Smoulder on page 383.

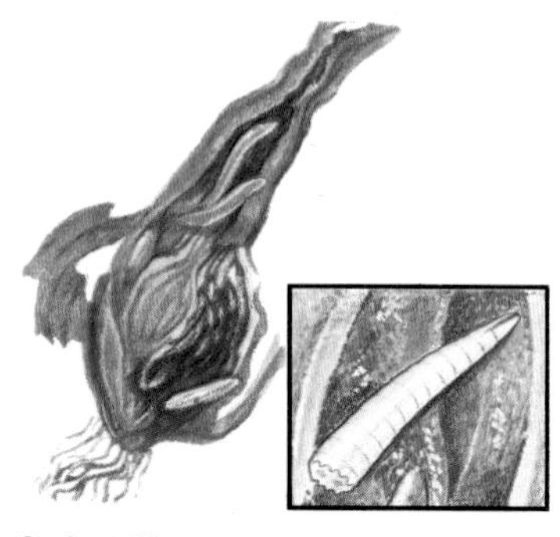

Onion flies
Plants affected Onions, leeks, shallots.
Symptoms Bulbs turn mushy. Small white maggots feed in rotting tissues.
Danger period May to August.
Treatment Apply calomel dust to the soil before or shortly after sowing and water a spray-strength solution of trichlorphon into the roots of established plants two or three times during growth. HCH dust may be used as an alternative but it can taint some vegetables.

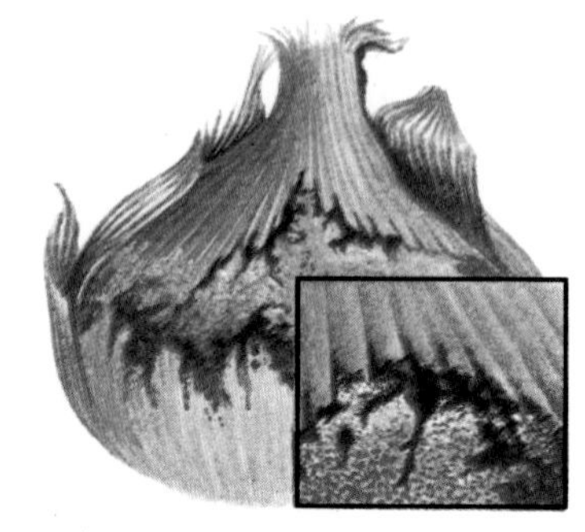

Neck rot
Plants affected Onions.
Symptoms A grey, velvety mould develops near the neck of stored onions, which rot rapidly.
Danger period Growing season, but symptoms do not appear until storage.
Treatment If possible, obtain treated seed. Store only well-ripened, hard onions and put them in a dry, airy place. Destroy diseased onions as they appear.

White rot
Plants affected Onions, occasionally leeks, shallots and garlic.
Symptoms The bulb base and roots are covered with a white fungus, and rot.
Danger period Growing season.
Treatment Grow onions on a new site each year, if possible, as once the disease appears soil will be contaminated for at least eight years. Dust seed drills with 4 per cent calomel dust. Burn diseased plants.

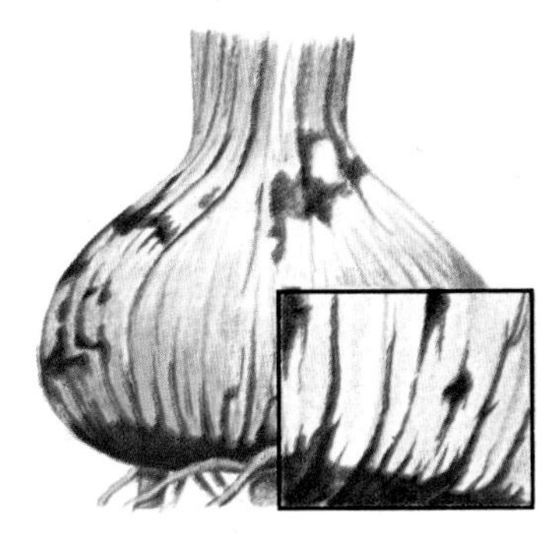

Dry rot
Plants affected Acidantheras, crocuses, freesias, gladioli, potatoes and some other tubers.
Symptoms Many small, dark lesions develop on the corms and merge to give larger black areas before the dry rot shrivels the corms completely.
Danger period During storage.
Treatment Remove and destroy affected corms as soon as the first symptoms appear. Before storing or replanting healthy ones, dust them with quintozene or dip them in a solution of carbendazim or benomyl. Grow corms in a fresh site each year.

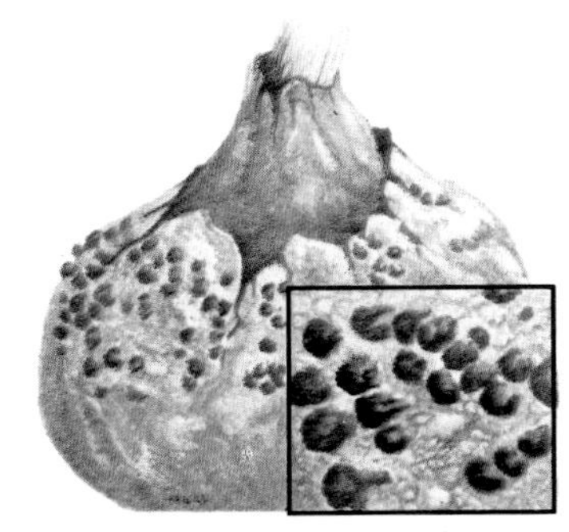

Tulip fire
Plants affected Tulips.
Symptoms Rotting of bulbs, which bear small, black fungal resting bodies.
Danger period Shortly before or after planting.
Treatment Destroy rotting bulbs, or those bearing fungal bodies. Dust bulbs with quintozene, and rake this dust into the soil before planting. Plant on a fresh site each year, if possible, particularly after the disease has appeared. Spray with benomyl, dichlofluanid, mancozeb, thiophanate-methyl, thiram or zineb when leaves are about 2 in. high and repeat at 10 day intervals until flowering.

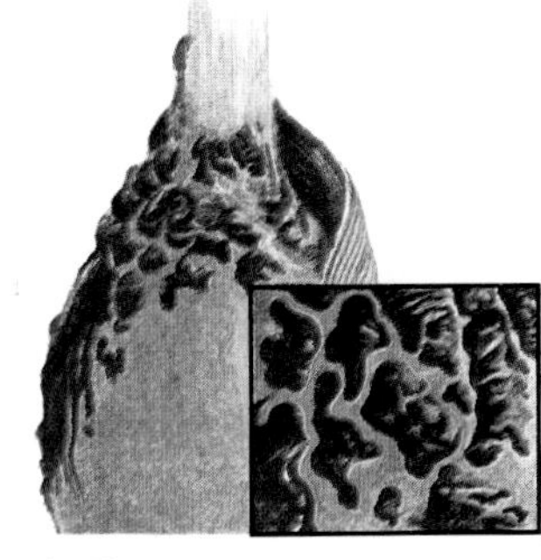

Grey bulb rot
Plants affected Tulips and hyacinths, and other bulbous plants.
Symptoms A dry, grey rot at the neck of the bulb, which soon becomes covered with large black fungal resting bodies and disintegrates.
Danger period Soon after planting.
Treatment Remove and destroy debris from diseased plants, and replace surrounding soil. Before planting bulbs and corms, dust them with quintozene and rake quintozene into the soil.

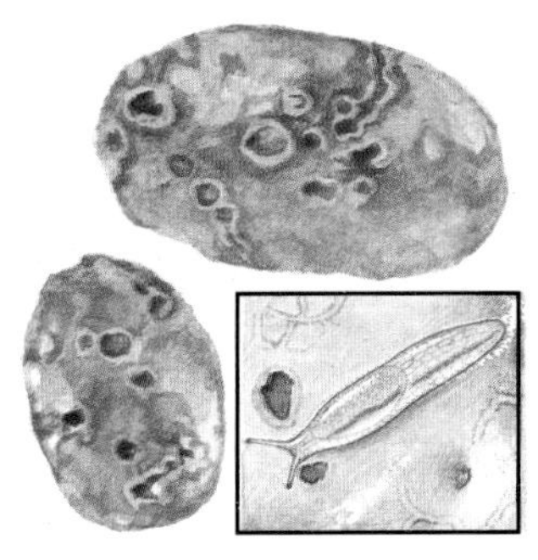

Slugs
Plants affected Potatoes, daffodils, tulips and other plants.
Symptoms Irregular holes and tunnels eaten into bulbs, corms and tubers. Slugs often present.
Danger period Most times of year.
Treatment Use slug baits based on methiocarb or metaldehyde, and lift maincrop potatoes as early as possible to minimise damage.

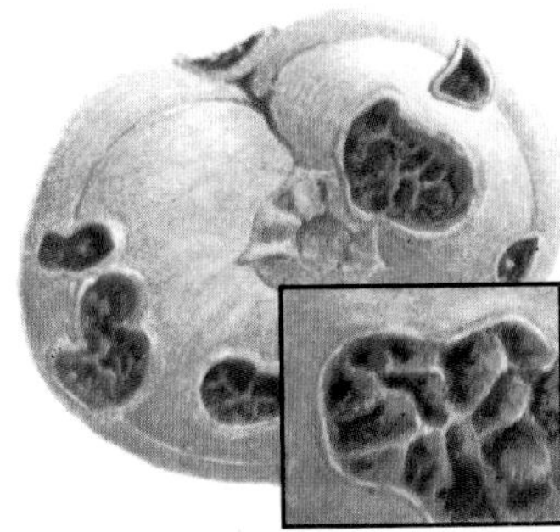
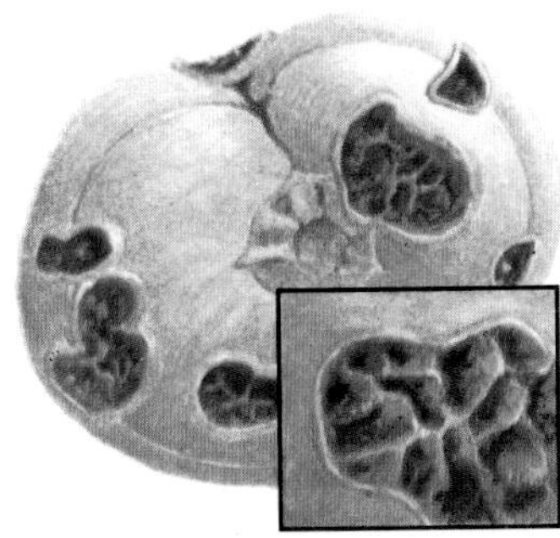

Scab (of gladiolus)
Plants affected Gladioli.
Symptoms Round, sunken craters develop towards the base of the corm. Each crater has a prominent raised rim and often a varnish-like coating.
Danger period Infection occurs during summer, but symptoms may not show until the corms are lifted and put in store.
Treatment As for Dry rot.

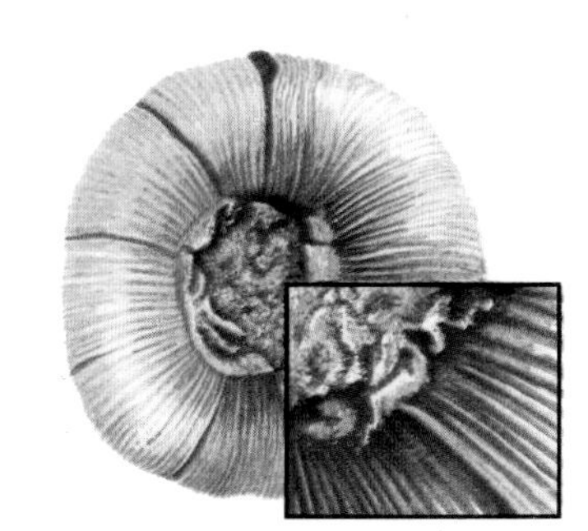

Core rot
Plants affected Acidantheras, freesias and gladioli.
Symptoms Rotting from the centre outwards, the corm becomes spongy and dark brown or black.
Danger period During storage.
Treatment Store corms in a dry atmosphere at 7–10°C (45–50°F). Before storing, dust them with quintozene or dip them in a solution of benomyl. Destroy affected corms.

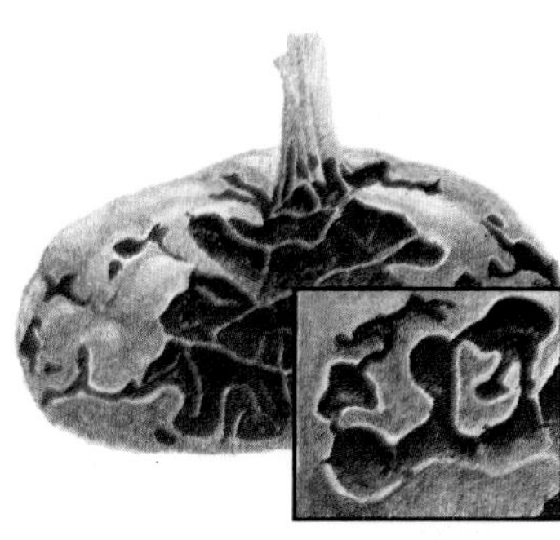

Hard rot
Plants affected Gladioli, but corms of other types may also be affected.
Symptoms Large, clearly outlined, black-brown, somewhat sunken spots develop on corms, which may become hard and shrivelled.
Danger period Infection occurs during summer, but symptoms appear during storage.
Treatment As for Dry rot.

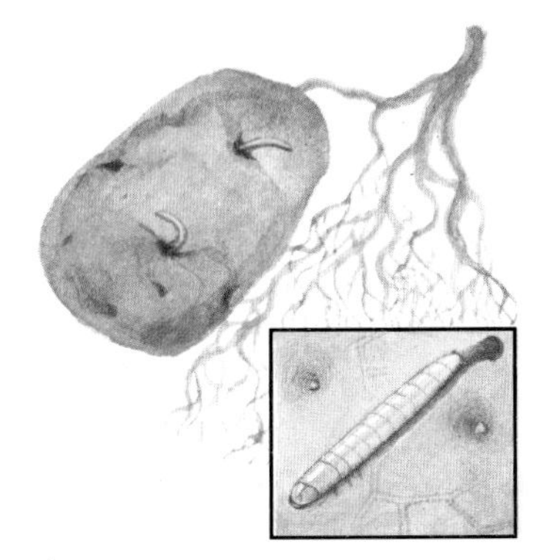

Wireworms
Plants affected Lettuces, potatoes, carrots, tomatoes, other vegetables; chrysanthemums, other ornamentals.
Symptoms Underground parts are tunnelled by yellow-brown larvae.
Danger period March to September.
Treatment Cultivate infested soil thoroughly and frequently before planting. Control weeds and, if necessary, apply HCH or bromophos to the soil around susceptible plants.

Bulb, corm, tuber and root vegetable disorders (continued)

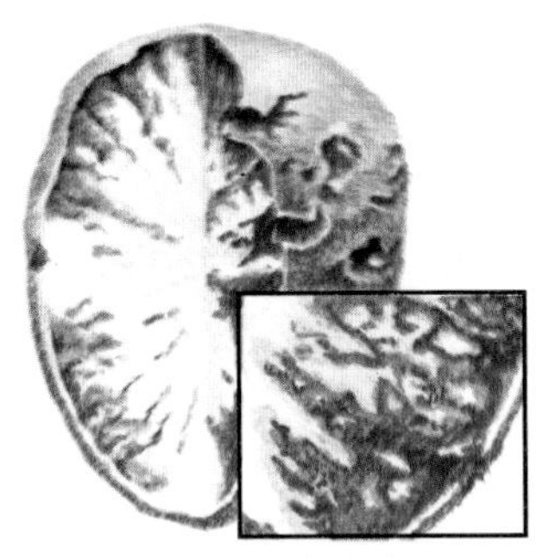

Blight

Plants affected Potatoes.
Symptoms A red-brown discoloration appears under the skin but shows through it as a grey patch on the surface of the potato. The disease spreads inwards, and affected areas are often entered by secondary bacteria, which then cause an evil-smelling soft rot.
Danger period July until the end of the season.
Treatment Earth up potatoes well so that infection cannot occur. If it does, destroy diseased tubers and do not put them on the compost heap.

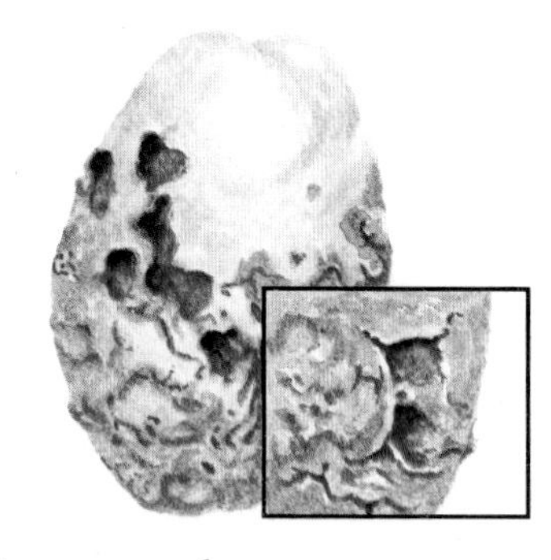

Common scab

Plants affected Potatoes.
Symptoms Ragged-edged scabs on tubers.
Danger period Growing season.
Treatment Do not apply lime before planting potatoes. Give the soil plenty of humus, and keep growth even by watering before the soil dries out. If trouble persists, grow resistant varieties such as 'Arran Pilot', 'King Edward' and 'Maris Peer'. Burn debris, and keep infected peelings off compost heap.

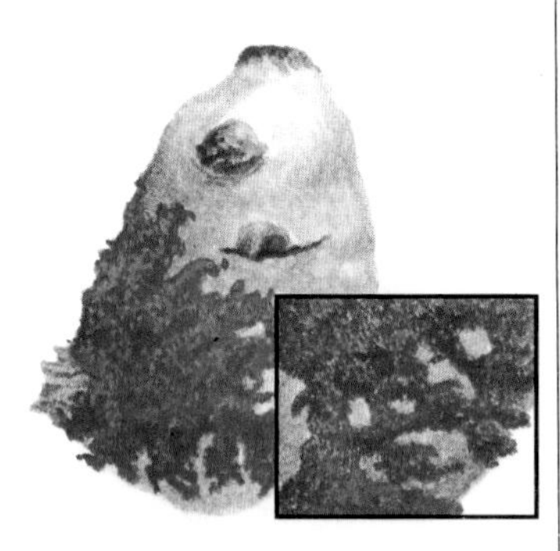

Powdery scab

Plants affected Potatoes.
Symptoms Uniform round scabs, at first raised but later bursting open to release a powdery mass of spores. Affected tubers may be deformed and have an earthy taste.
Danger period Throughout the growing season.
Treatment Destroy diseased tubers, and do not plant potatoes in the same position for several years.

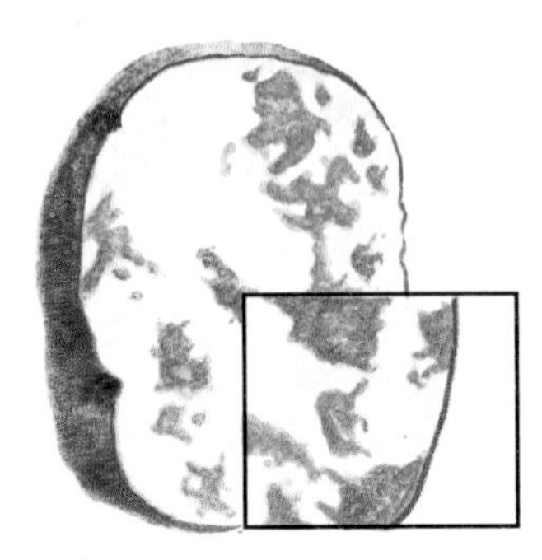

Internal rust spot

Plants affected Potatoes.
Symptoms Scattered brown marks within the flesh of the tuber.
Danger period Throughout the growing season.
Treatment Dig in plenty of humus, and try to keep the growth even by watering before the soil dries out completely.

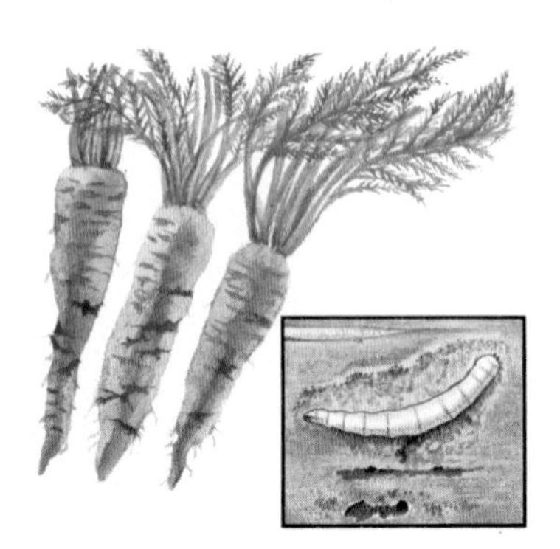

Carrot flies

Plants affected Carrots, parsnips, parsley and celery.
Symptoms Fly maggots tunnel into the roots.
Danger period June to October.
Treatment In areas where the fly is prevalent sow thinly in late May; use a seed dressing. Protect established plants by watering a spray-strength solution of diazinon or trichlorphon into the soil along the rows two or three times in August and September.

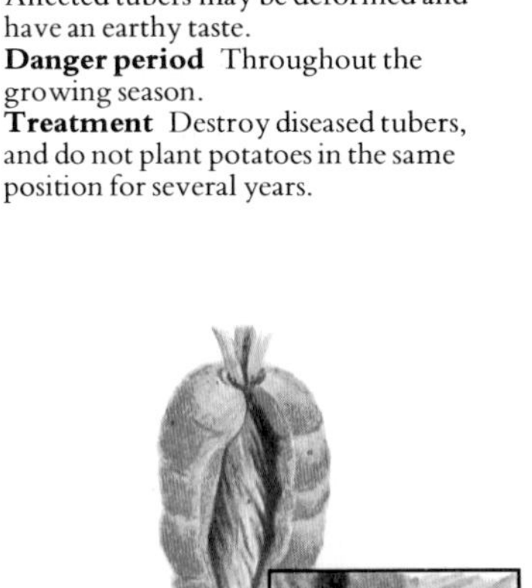

Cracking

Plants affected All types of root vegetables.
Symptoms Lengthwise splitting.
Danger period Throughout the growing season.
Treatment Try to avoid irregular growth by watering before the soil dries out completely.

Other root troubles

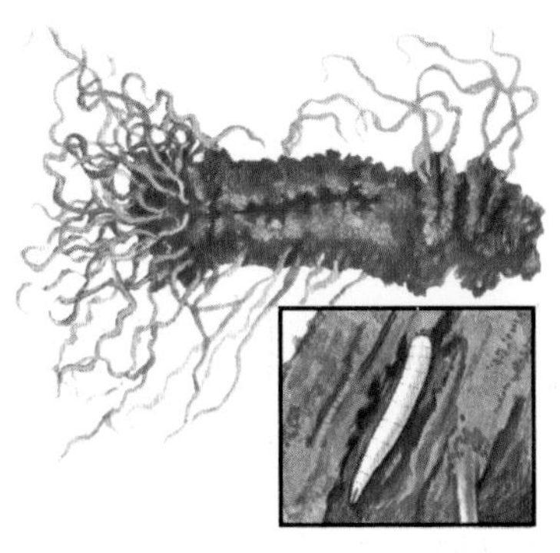

Chrysanthemum stool miners

Plants affected Chrysanthemums.
Symptoms Light yellow fly maggots damage roots and tunnel into stools.
Danger period September to May.
Treatment Dust stools with HCH. After lifting stools to take cuttings, water a spray-strength solution of HCH into them.

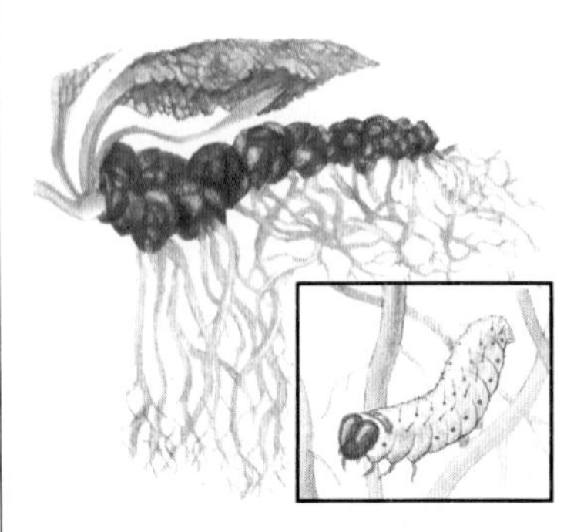

Swift moth caterpillars

Plants affected Various herbaceous perennials.
Symptoms Dirty white caterpillars, which live in the soil, feed on the roots.
Danger period Any time of year.
Treatment Good weed control and thorough cultivation reduce the risk of swift moth attack. Particularly susceptible plants can be protected by incorporating HCH dust or bromophos in the soil.

Cabbage root flies

Plants affected Recently transplanted brassicas, especially cabbages, cauliflowers and brussels sprouts, and wallflowers.
Symptoms Fly maggots in the soil feed on the roots, causing complete collapse of young plants.
Danger period April to September.
Treatment Protect transplants by incorporating bromophos in the soil, or by watering in a spray-strength solution of diazinon or trichlorphon.

Club root

Plants affected Cabbages, brussels sprouts, cauliflowers, turnips, radishes, wallflowers, stocks and many other members of the cabbage family.
Symptoms Roots become swollen and distorted, plants look weak and yellow.
Danger period Growing season.
Treatment Improve drainage if necessary. Apply 14 lb. hydrated lime to every 30 sq. yds of soil, and put 4 per cent calomel dust in planting holes. Carry out as long a rotation as possible, or on a large area sterilise with dazomet.

Leatherjackets

Plants affected Brassicas, other vegetables and various ornamental plants. Young plants are most susceptible.
Symptoms Roots eaten by tough-skinned, fat, grey-brown, legless grubs.
Danger period April to June.
Treatment Cultivate infested soil thoroughly and frequently before planting. Established plants may be protected by incorporating bromophos or HCH in the soil.

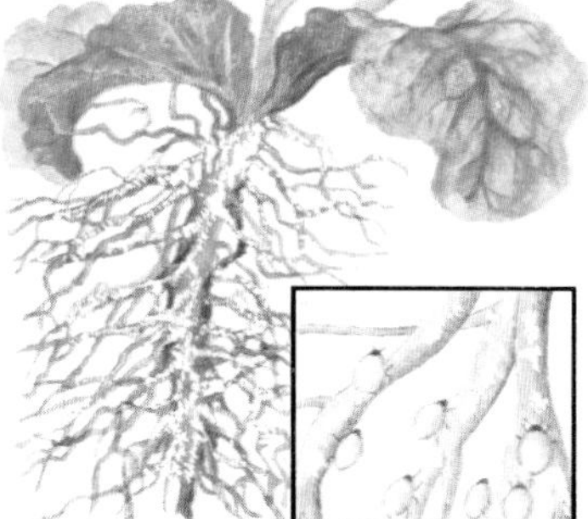

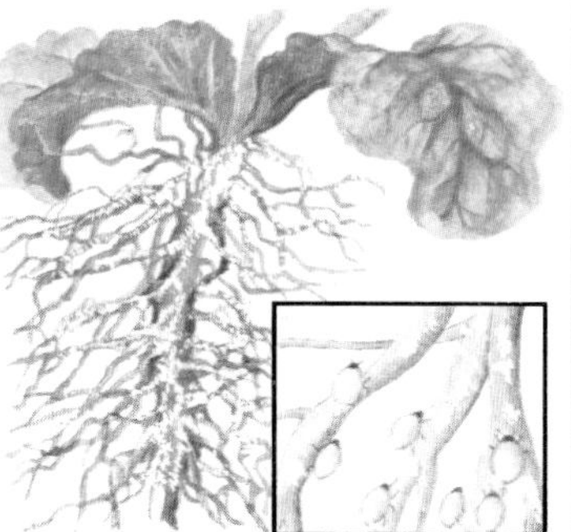

Root aphids and root mealy bugs

Plants affected Cacti and succulents, primulas and other pot plants, lettuces and some outdoor ornamentals.
Symptoms Colonies of white, wax-covered aphids or mealy bugs infest the roots.
Danger period Late summer and autumn outdoors, but any time of year under glass.
Treatment Water a spray-strength solution of malathion or diazinon into the roots of affected plants.

Lawn disorders

Lichens

Symptoms Overlapping leafy structures, deep green-black when moist and grey-green or brown when dry, growing horizontally in the turf.
Danger period Any time.
Treatment Rake out growths and treat affected areas with mercurised lawn sand. Drain if possible, and spike the surface. Brush in lime-free sand, top-dress and feed.

Snow mould or fusarium patch

Symptoms Large dead patches of turf covered with a white, cotton-like growth of fungus, which is most obvious in moist weather and after snow.
Danger period Any time.
Treatment As for Red thread (see this page), but do not apply too much nitrogen, especially after August.

Red thread or corticium disease

Symptoms Dead patches of turf, bearing red fungus growths.
Danger period Autumn, after rain.
Treatment Apply mercurised lawn sand at 4 rounded tablespoons to the square yard, other proprietary turf fungicides based on mercury, or Bordeaux mixture and malachite green applied according to the manufacturer's instructions. Spike to aerate the soil, and apply a nitrogenous fertiliser in the spring.

Fairy rings

Symptoms Dark green ring in turf.
Danger period Any time.
Treatment Dig up and burn diseased turf to a depth of at least 9 in. Sterilise the soil with a solution of formalin, made up of 6 pints of commercial formaldehyde (plus some liquid detergent) in 10 gallons of water for each 10 sq. yds of soil. Cover the treated area for seven to ten days, then fork over the soil and leave it for another two weeks before reseeding.

Pesticides and fungicides for use in the garden

The main enemies of any plant are insect pests and fungus diseases which may damage the foliage, flowers or fruit, or even kill the whole plant. There is now a battery of pesticides and fungicides that can be sprayed or dusted on to infected plants, but they should not be used indiscriminately.

The continual use of a particular pesticide or fungicide can result in a resistant strain of the pest evolving. There are now fruit-tree red spider mites that are resistant to all or most of the common sprays normally used to combat them. In addition, the pesticide usually kills all the natural predators of the pest as well, leaving the way open for a resistant strain of the pest to multiply. But some selective pesticides are being developed that destroy only the pest: for example, pirimicarb, available to amateur gardeners, exterminates only aphids.

Natural predators More and more research workers are turning to biological methods of control, using where possible natural predators and parasites to kill pests.

Examples of these are the minute parasitic wasp *Encarsia formosa*, which attacks glasshouse whitefly, and the red spider mite predator *Phytoseiulus persimilis*, which is now widely used to control glasshouse red spider mites. Both of these biological control agents are available to members of the Royal Horticultural Society, and may be obtained from some commercial suppliers.

This kind of biological control requires, however, that a small population of the pest remains as a food store for the predators, otherwise they will starve.

At the present time, few natural predators are readily available, and alternative controls must be used.

The most sensible approach for the amateur is to use approved chemical controls with intelligence and care. Keep a keen watch on crops known to be susceptible to pests, and apply a chemical only when the pest is actually seen, confining treatment to the infested plant and near neighbours. This will allow any predators to survive.

Some of the pesticides and fungicides listed here are described as systemic. This means that the chemical is absorbed through the leaves or stem into the plant's system and may remain for some time in the sap, continuing to deter the pest or fungus that it is intended to combat. Always follow the time lapse between spraying and picking recommended by the manufacturer, as these chemicals cannot be washed away in the kitchen.

Chemical	Trade names	Description
BENOMYL	pbi Benlate	Fungicide with systemic properties. It is not taken up readily by woody plants so has to be applied fairly frequently. Used as a spray against rose black spot, some turf diseases, tomato leaf mould, apple and pear scab, cane spot and spur blight on raspberries, leaf spots on ornamental plants, celery and soft fruit, grey mould and powdery mildews on ornamental plants, fruit and vegetables. But resistant strains may occur
BHC	see HCH	
BIORES-METHRIN	Cooper Garden Spray Aerosol; Fison's Combat Whitefly Insecticide	Very safe and non-persistent pesticide for use against aphids, whiteflies, small caterpillars and some other pests
BORDEAUX MIXTURE	Murphy Bordeaux Powder; Synchemicals Bordeaux Mixture	A fungicide mixture of copper sulphate and hydrated lime. Harmful to fish. Can be used as a spray against azalea gall, clematis wilt, lily disease, bacterial canker and peach leaf curl on prunus species, leaf spots on ornamentals and celery, potato and tomato blight, cane spot and spur blight on raspberries. As a dust it can be used to control paeony wilt, crown rots and storage rots
BROMO-PHOS	**Granules** pbi Bromophos	Relatively persistent contact pesticide. Available only as granules to control cutworms, wireworms, cabbage root flies, carrot flies and other pests that operate in the soil

Chemical	Trade names	Description
CALOMEL	**4 per cent dusts** Boots Calomel Dust; M & B Cyclosan; pbi Club Root Control **20 per cent wettable powder** Synchemicals MC Turf Fungicide	Common name for mercurous chloride. It is poisonous, and protective gloves should be worn when handling the concentrate. The 4 per cent dust controls club root of wallflowers and brassicas, and onion white rot. The 20 per cent wettable powder is used to control some turf diseases
CARBARYL	Boots Garden Insect Powder; Murphy Sevin Dust	A pesticide to control caterpillars, weevils, flea beetles, leatherjackets, woodlice and some other pests. It is also formulated as a worm killer
CARBEN-DAZIM	**Spray** Boots Systemic Garden Fungicide	A fungicide that controls rose black spot, leaf spots, apple and pear scab, grey mould on soft fruit (except on fruit to be canned or bottled), spur blight on raspberries, etc. Can be applied as drench to control damping-off and some other soil-borne diseases. Toxic to fish and can be irritating to eyes, nose and mouth
CHELATED OR FRITTED COMPOUNDS	Gesal Sequestrene; Murphy Sequestered Iron; Fortone 'G'; Fortone 'E'	Iron, magnesium and manganese compounds that are used to prevent lime-induced chlorosis on plants growing in alkaline soils
CHESHUNT COMPOUND	pbi Cheshunt Compound; other formulations also available	A fungicide mixture of copper sulphate and ammonium carbonate, used as a drench to prevent damping-off on seedlings and to control other soil-borne diseases

Chemical	Trade names	Description
CHLORDANE	**Spray** Synchemicals Chlordane 25	A persistent pesticide that should be used only when there is no adequate alternative. Gives good control of ants and earthworms when used as a spray or soil drench
COPPER	Murphy Liquid Copper Fungicide	A fungicide that can be used as an alternative to Bordeaux mixture. Harmful to livestock and toxic to fish
DAZOMET	BASF Basamid (sold only in commercial packs – 5 kg.)	Soil sterilant. Irritating to the eyes and skin. After use, do not plant for eight weeks under glass, lesser periods outside
DERRIS	**Dusts** Boots Derris Dust; ICI Abol Derris Dust; Murphy Derris Dust **Spray** Murphy Derris Liquid	Very safe and non-persistent pesticide. Used as a dust or spray against aphids, small caterpillars, raspberry beetles, flea beetles, thrips and red spider mites
DIAZINON	**Granules** Fison's Combat Soil Insecticide; Murphy Root Guard	Insecticide used to control a large number of soil pests
DICHLO-FLUANID	Elvaron	A wettable fungicide powder used against paeony wilt, rose black spot, tulip fire, downy mildew on cauliflower seedlings, grey mould on cold-house tomatoes and soft fruit, spur blight on raspberries. Harmful to fish. Should not be used on strawberries under cover.
DICHLORVOS	**Fumigant** Vapona Strips	A pesticide that is available only in impregnated resin strips for use as a glasshouse fumigant to control aphids, small caterpillars, thrips, whiteflies, fungus gnats and red spider mites
DICOFOL	**Spray** Toprose Pest Spray	A pesticide, sometimes mixed with other agents, used to combat attacks by red spider mites
DIMETHOATE	**Sprays** Boots Systemic Greenfly Killer; Murphy Systemic Insecticide; Fison's Super Kil (with malathion and HCH)	Relatively non-persistent systemic pesticide. Used as a spray or soil drench against aphids, scale insects, leafhoppers, suckers, mealy bugs, red spider mites and small caterpillars
DINOCAP	**Spray** Toprose Mildew Spray **Smoke** Murfume Dinocap (cone)	A fungicide that controls powdery mildew on ornamental plants, fruit and vegetables. Toxic to fish and can be irritating to skin, eyes and nose. Some formulations are inflammable

Chemical	Trade names	Description
DNOC	**Sprays** Cresofin DNC Winter Wash; Murphy Ovamort Special	A pesticide used in the same way as tar oil. It gives additional control of capsids and red spider mite eggs
FENITRO-THION	**Spray** Murphy Fentro	Relatively persistent contact pesticide. As a spray, controls codling moths and other caterpillars, aphids and capsids
HCH (formerly BHC)	**Dusts** Boots Ant Destroyer; Murphy Gamma-BHC Dust; New Ant Doom **Sprays** Murphy Lindex Garden Spray; Abol-X (with menazon) **Fumigants** Fumite BHC Cones; Fumite Lindane Smoke Pellets; Murfume BHC Smoke; Murfume Lindane Smoke	Relatively persistent pesticide, also known as gamma-BHC, Gammexane or Lindane. Available only as HCH and in mixtures with other chemicals as spray, dust or fumigant to control aphids, capsids, leafhoppers, whiteflies, thrips, ants, caterpillars, weevils, cabbage root flies, fungus gnats, earwigs, springtails, wireworms, leatherjackets, leaf miners, flea beetles and woodlice
HEPTEN-OPHOS	**Spray** Murphy Tumblebug (with permethrin)	A pesticide of short persistence that is used to control aphids, capsids, whiteflies and most other pests that attack fruit and vegetables. It can be used under glass. Harmful to bees and fish
IRON SULPHATE	Fison's Lawn Sand; ICI Mosskiller for Lawns	Can be used to control certain turf diseases
MALATHION	**Dust** Murphy Malathion Dust **Sprays** Boots Greenfly Killer; Murphy Liquid Malathion; pbi Malathion Greenfly Killer **Aerosol** Fison's New Kil Aerosol (with HCH)	Very safe and non-persistent pesticide. Used as a spray or dust against aphids, whiteflies, leafhoppers, caterpillars, mealy bugs, scale insects, thrips, capsids and red spider mites
MANCOZEB	**Wettable powder** pbi Dithane 945	A fungicide that controls black spot and rust on roses, tulip fire, celery leaf spot, potato and tomato blight and tomato leaf mould. Can be irritating to skin, eyes and nose
MENAZON	**Spray** Abol-X (with HCH)	A systemic pesticide that is available only in a mixture with HCH to control aphids
MERCUROUS CHLORIDE	see CALOMEL	

Pesticides and fungicides (continued)

Chemical	Trade names	Description
METALDEHYDE	**Spray** Murphy Slugit Liquid **Baits** Boots Slug Destroyer Pellets; Doff-Portland Slugoids; ICI Slug Pellets; Murphy Slugit Pellets; pbi Slug Mini-Pellets; Synchemicals Slug Death Powder and Pellets	Used only as a slug or snail killer, either as a spray or in specially formulated baits
METHIOCARB	**Baits** Draza Slug Killer; pbi Slug Gard	Available only as specially formulated baits to control slugs and snails
NICOTINE	**Sprays** Campbell's Nico Soap; XL All Liquid Insecticide	Non-persistent but poisonous pesticide, especially as spray concentrate. Available as a spray and sometimes used as a fumigant to control aphids, leafhoppers, leaf miners, capsids, thrips and caterpillars
OXYDEMETON-METHYL	**Aerosol** Metasystox Aphid Gun	Systemic pesticide which is persistent and poisonous. Available only as a special aerosol gun for use on ornamental plants growing outdoors. Controls aphids, leafhoppers and red spider mites
PERMETHRIN	**Sprays** ICI Picket and Picket-G **Smoke** Murphy Permethrin White Fly Smoke (conc)	Persistent insecticide used against whitefly, caterpillars and other pests that attack fruit and vegetables. Can be used under glass, but some formulations do not control red spider
PIRIMICARB	**Spray** ICI Rapid **Soluble granules** ICI Abol-G	A non-persistent contact insecticide with some systemic and fumigant action. Very effective against aphids. Highly selective, and does not kill predators and parasites
PIRIMIPHOS-METHYL	**Spray** ICI Sybol 2 **Dust** ICI Sybol 2 Dust; ICI Antkiller	Non-persistent pesticide with contact and fumigant action. Controls aphids, caterpillars, leaf miners, beetles, whiteflies and red spider mites
PYRETHRUM	**Sprays** Bio Sprayday; Synchemicals Plant Pest Killer	Very safe and non-persistent pesticide. Used as a spray against aphids, whiteflies and small caterpillars
QUINTOZENE	**Dust** ICI Botrilex	Dust for control of some bulb and corm diseases

Chemical	Trade names	Description
SULPHUR	Synchemicals Green Sulphur; Synchemicals Yellow Sulphur; flowers of sulphur (from chemists)	Controls apple scab and powdery mildews on tree and soft fruit, but should not be used on sulphur-shy varieties or fruit for processing. Will also control powdery mildews on ornamental plants and cucumbers. Dusts can be used to prevent storage rots
TAR OIL	**Sprays** Carbo-Craven; ICI Clean-up; Murphy Mortegg	Used only as a spray for dormant fruit trees and bushes and some woody, deciduous ornamentals during the winter, to kill eggs of aphids, suckers and winter moths
TECNAZENE	Fumite TCNB Smoke Pellets; Fumite Tecnalin Smokes (with HCH)	Used as a glasshouse fumigant alone to control grey mould on lettuces, tomatoes and ornamentals, or in combination with HCH to give additional control to insect pests
THIOPHANATE-METHYL	Murphy Systemic Fungicide; Murphy Club Root Dip	A fungicide with systemic properties. It is similar to benomyl and controls the same diseases. It also controls club root in brassicas
THIRAM	ICI General Garden Fungicide; also a constituent of pbi Hexyl Plus	A fungicide used against paeony wilt, rusts on ornamental plants, tulip fire, grey mould on ornamentals, fruit and vegetables, lettuce downy mildew, pear scab, leaf spot on currants and gooseberries, cane spot and spur blight on raspberries. Can be irritating to skin, eyes, nose and throat and should not be used on fruit for processing
TRICHLORPHON	**Spray** M & B Caterpillar Spray **Dust** M & B Tugon Antkiller	Non-persistent pesticide for use against caterpillars and ants
TRIFORINE	**Spray** ICI Nimrod-T	Systemic fungicide unrelated to benomyl and thiophanate-methyl, so no resistance will have built up. Controls rose black spot and powdery mildews and some other diseases of ornamentals and fruit
WOUND-SEALING PAINT	M & B Seal and Heal Pruning Paint; pbi Arbrex	Forms a protective seal against diseases, pests and frost on cut surfaces of wood after pruning and wounding
ZINEB	**Wettable powders** pbi Dithane; PP Zineb Fungicide	A fungicide that controls a wide range of diseases on ornamental plants, fruit and vegetables. Can be irritating to skin, eyes and nose

Understanding the soil

Soil is largely weathered rock ground down by age and made fertile by dead leaves and insects. To grow plants with success, it must be prepared carefully and fed regularly

Plants need to be fed regularly with manure and fertilisers. The two are complementary, and both are usually necessary for healthy growth.

Manure is bulky organic matter that is derived from animals or plants. It breaks down in the soil to become humus, a dark gummy substance, which binds the soil particles into small groups, leaving gaps in between for air and water to circulate. The bacteria in the soil convert it into chemical salts, which become dissolved in water and are taken up by the roots of the plants for food.

Fertilisers are concentrated forms of chemical salts which provide nutrients direct to plants, but contain little or no humus.

If heavily cropped land is supplied with ample fertiliser but no manure, it may deteriorate as all the existing humus is used up. In sandy soil, there will eventually be no organic material to contain water or to hold the particles together. The soil will dry out rapidly and could be blown away by strong winds.

Clay soil will become harder as the humus becomes depleted, because there will be nothing left to hold the minute particles apart.

Soil which is supplied only with the limited amount of manure available in city gardens, but no fertiliser, may lack the nutrients needed for intensive cropping.

General fertilisers to meet most needs

Plants require many chemical nutrients, the main ones being nitrogen, phosphorus (in phosphate) and potassium (in potash). Each of these nutrients can be bought separately, but most gardeners prefer to use a general fertiliser containing all three, such as Growmore, a formula that was developed during the Second World War. It contains 7 per cent nitrogen, 7 per cent phosphorus and 7 per cent potassium. The ingredients are sulphate of ammonia, superphosphate of lime and sulphate of potash.

Another popular general formula is John Innes base fertiliser containing hoof and horn manure, superphosphate and sulphate of potash. The analysis is 5.1 per cent nitrogen, 6.4 per cent phosphorus and 9.7 per cent potassium. Because the source of the nitrogen is organic, this fertiliser is more expensive.

Fertilisers can also be applied to the roots of plants as a liquid, for quick absorption.

Liquid fertilisers can be bought as a balanced feed for general purposes, or as special mixtures for particular plants. One formula, available under various trade names, is for potash-loving plants such as tomatoes and carnations.

General fertilisers are also sold as foliar feeds – liquids which are absorbed quickly through the leaves when applied with a watering can.

Chemical fertilisers for special purposes

The main chemicals required by plants are nitrogen, phosphorus, potassium, calcium, magnesium and sulphur. Equally essential, but required only in very small amounts, are iron, manganese, boron, copper, zinc and molybdenum. These are called trace elements.

It is the main elements that are used up most quickly, but some are present in British soils in such quantities that it is not necessary to worry about them. This leaves the three most important elements for the gardener to supply – nitrogen, phosphorus and potassium.

Nitrogen produces growth. If a plant receives too much it will create lush, leafy, soft growth. If it receives too little, the opposite occurs – small, yellow leaves and a general lack of growth and vigour. Nitrogen is made available in the soil as the result of bacterial action, and as it becomes available in soluble form it is either absorbed by plants or is washed away by rain. So constant renewal is necessary.

Sources of nitrogen Some fertilisers derived from dead animals, including dried blood and hoof and horn manure, are rich in nitrogen. But they are expensive and are normally used only in special circumstances, such as potting composts. Less-expensive sources of nitrogen are the inorganic fertilisers. The most common, and the cheapest, is sulphate of ammonia. Rather more expensive are Nitro-chalk, nitrate of ammonia and nitrate of soda. These work faster than sulphate of ammonia because they are already in the nitrate form which plant roots absorb and use.

When plants need a quick-acting stimulant, it is usually best supplied by nitrogen alone. For example, spring cabbages respond quickly to a top-dressing of a nitrate fertiliser at ½ oz. to the square yard once growth starts.

Other overwintered vegetables also need added nitrogen in spring to replace that lost from the soil by winter rains or not yet made available by bacteria because of low soil temperature.

All fruit crops, other than strawberries, appreciate a dressing of sulphate of ammonia in spring at ½–2 oz. to the square yard.

A more active source of nitrogen is urea, sprayed on to the foliage of starved fruit trees and bushes in the spring. Urea spray can be bought from a nurseryman, but be sure to follow the manufacturer's instructions carefully.

Sources of phosphorus Phosphorus, in the form of soluble phosphates, is particularly important to plants in the seedling stage and in the formation of seeds. When the soil has too little phosphate the leaves turn dull purple, they are smaller in size and the growth of the plant slows down. Too much phosphate will cause a premature ripening of the plant.

Phosphatic fertilisers include bonemeal, which is popular because it is organic and readily available. However, bonemeal can carry the diseases anthrax and salmonella. Be sure to wear gloves when using it, and preferably buy only sterilised, or steamed, bonemeal. Another important source of phosphate is superphosphate of lime.

When seeds are sown out of doors, a dressing of superphosphate at 2 oz. (2 tablespoons) to the square yard should be applied before sowing, and lightly raked in.

Sources of potassium Potassium, in the form of potash, increases the intensity of flower colour and is sometimes given as a top-dressing to improve the formation and ripening of flowers. It also increases a plant's resistance to pests and diseases and hardens the tissues.

A deficiency of potash causes a scorching of the leaf margins. Light soils in particular are likely to need added potash, and the most suitable form for the gardener is sulphate of potash.

Potash is especially required for fruit crops, tomatoes and potatoes.

Applying fertilisers Spread fertilisers evenly over the surface. Always water in sulphate of ammonia, or apply it in rainy weather. Do not let it fall on grass or leaves, as it is likely to scorch them.

The compost heap – your easiest manure supply

Bulky organic manures for the garden are increasingly difficult to obtain. The most convenient type is garden compost, which you can make with waste vegetable matter from the garden and kitchen.

Unfortunately, the average suburban garden seldom yields enough material to produce the conditions necessary in a compost heap to produce rapid fermentation and decay. Consequently, most compost heaps are really neglected rubbish dumps. But the heap can be built up with extra material brought in from outside the garden, such as straw or fallen leaves.

The material in a compost heap is broken down by bacteria and other micro-organisms, which will thrive only if given air, water, nitrogen, non-acid conditions and a high temperature. And even under ideal conditions, there are limits to the rapid breakdown powers of the bacteria, so do not put woody material, not even brussels sprouts stems, on the heap.

Never use obviously diseased plants in a compost heap, as the disease may be spread with the compost. Never use the roots of perennial weeds such as couch grass, oxalis or bindweed. And avoid annual weeds carrying seeds.

The best compost is made from soft rubbish, such as lawn mowings, dead leaves, spent lettuces, pea haulm, hay and straw, plus the vegetable trimmings from the kitchen. Do not use cooked scraps or anything containing grease.

Build the compost heap into a square shape, so that it is less likely to become dry. A heap measuring 7 ft × 7 ft × 5 ft high is necessary for quick results.

But in a small garden a sensible approach is to set up a neat enclosure of wire netting and posts. The best size must depend on the size of the garden, but 5 ft × 5 ft × 5 ft is about the minimum.

You can also buy ready-made compost bins or make an open-topped wooden box leaving spaces between the side boards to let air through. If one side of the box is removable, it gives easier access to the compost.

Try to build the heap a layer at a time, each layer 12 in. thick. Tread down each layer and then give it a good soaking with a hose. To each layer add sulphate of ammonia at $\frac{1}{2}$ oz. (1 dessertspoon) to the square yard and cover it with 2 in. of soil.

Build the heap with gently sloping sides up to the height you require, and then cover it with an inch of soil from the garden. If your soil is naturally limy there is no need to add more lime to the heap, but if the soil is acid sprinkle garden lime over the finished heap and follow with a final watering. In a dry summer, hose the heap every fortnight.

Decomposition is speeded up if the heap is turned after six weeks, moving the material on the outside of the pile into the centre. At the same time, water any dry areas.

However, turning is not essential, and in three months (or more if the pile was made at the beginning of winter) the pile will become a crumbly manure-like material which can be dug into the vegetable garden or spread thickly around trees, shrubs and perennials.

BUILDING A COMPOST HEAP IN LAYERS

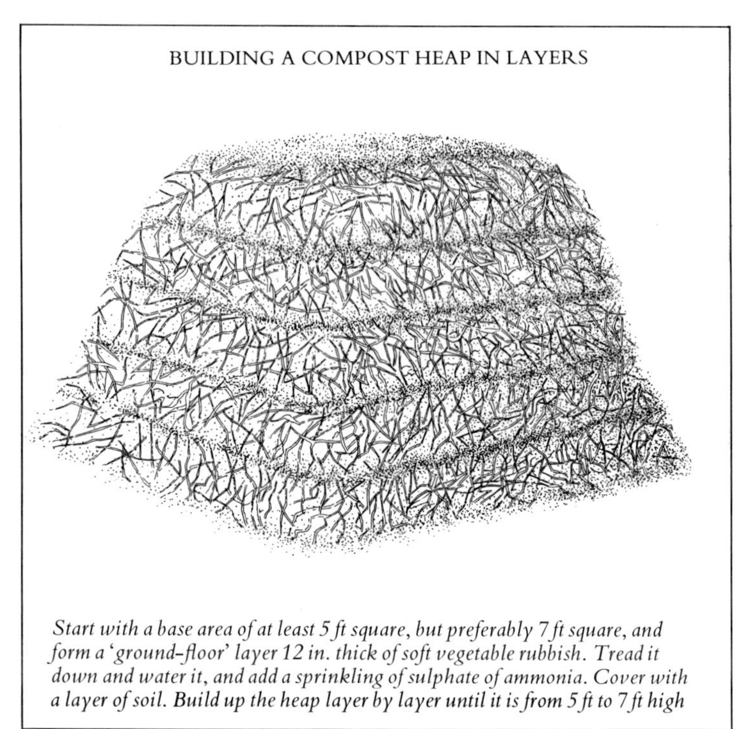

Start with a base area of at least 5 ft square, but preferably 7 ft square, and form a 'ground-floor' layer 12 in. thick of soft vegetable rubbish. Tread it down and water it, and add a sprinkling of sulphate of ammonia. Cover with a layer of soil. Build up the heap layer by layer until it is from 5 ft to 7 ft high

COMPOST CONTAINERS

The wire-mesh container is hinged, for easy access to compost. With the three-compartment compost box, the front boards are slid into position as the boxes are filled. The left box contains compost being used; the middle box is decomposing; and the right one is being filled

Other useful sources of manure

Any bulky organic waste is useful as a garden manure, provided it does not contain harmful industrial chemicals and provided it rots down reasonably quickly.

If you are using sawdust, bark fibre or chopped straw as a mulch – even if it has been used as bedding for poultry – sprinkle a handful of sulphate of ammonia to the square yard over a layer 2–3 in. deep.

Bulky organic manures need to be used in large quantities. A good dressing would be a 6 in. layer, or about a 2 gallon bucket of manure to every square yard.

One of the finest forms of organic manure is farmyard manure, plus the animals' bedding, which is usually straw.

The ammonia content of fresh farmyard manure may damage plants, so it is usually best to use it after it has been stacked for a while and has partly decomposed. Stacking in the open means that the soluble nutrients are washed out by rain, and so well-rotted farmyard manure is low in plant nutrients. But it does provide the necessary humus, and soil rich in humus is usually very fertile.

Dried sewage sludge is sometimes available from local authorities at low cost, for use direct on the soil or to add to the compost heap. But some town sludges are now suspect because of contamination from harmful metallic wastes, such as zinc and chromium. Before buying sludge, get an assurance that it does not contain these chemicals in amounts likely to injure plants.

Wool shoddy, used at 1 lb. to the square yard, provides gradually released nitrogen and improves the soil structure. It is also pleasant to handle.

Fallen leaves are useful. If large quantities of, say, beech or oak leaves are available they can be rotted down in a separate heap to provide leaf-mould, but in most gardens the best place for leaves is the compost heap.

Large leaves, such as sycamore or horse chestnut, tend to pack together, so mix them with other organic material or soil.

If you live near a brewery you may be able to obtain spent hops. In most cases these are best added to the compost heap and rotted down with other material.

Growing your own manure In the vegetable garden there is sometimes an opportunity to sow an area with a quick-growing crop of 'green manure', such as mustard or rape. Sow after a vegetable crop has been cleared in early summer.

Dig in the green manure plants just before they flower and add 1 oz. of sulphate of ammonia to each square yard if the ground is to be cropped immediately. This helps bacteria to break down the manure.

Peat and how to use it

Peat is vegetable matter which has become decomposed by water and partly carbonised. It is particularly useful in encouraging rooting in new plantings.

Baled peat must be moistened before use. Spread the dry peat on a hard surface and tread it down firmly. Then water liberally, turn it over with a shovel and tread and water until no dry patches remain.

There are two main types of peat – moss, largely derived from sphagnum moss, and sedge, from the roots of sedges and allied plants.

Moss peat (pH below 4.5) is useful for increasing the acidity of the soil, and for making potting composts. Sedge peat (pH 5 to 6.5) has finer particles, and is particularly useful for top-dressing lawns.

The pH level: measuring acid or alkaline content

The acidity or alkalinity of garden soil can be controlled by using lime, peat and various chemicals, including sulphur.

Acidity and alkalinity is measured by the pH level, running from 0 to 14. Neutral soil measures pH 7. Higher than 7 is alkaline, lower than that is acid.

Most plants do best in a slightly acid soil, reading about pH 6.5.

Soil is easily tested with a simple kit that can be bought from any garden shop.

If a soil is markedly acid, an application of garden lime will help the growth of some plants and crops.

This is particularly so with vegetables, especially members of the cabbage family and peas and beans, which need soil with a pH level of 7 to 8.

Most fruit crops, however, do best on acid soils, and seldom benefit from liming.

The most convenient form of lime for the amateur gardener to use is hydrated lime.

A vegetable garden which is over-acidic can be corrected by adding ½ lb. of hydrated lime to every square yard of soil.

Repeat the treatment every three years or so, to maintain the right level.

Disease control The pH level of soil can also be used to control some diseases.

The fungus disease 'club-root', which is confined to the cabbage family, thrives in an acid soil and is much less troublesome if the lime content is high.

On the other hand, potato scab tends to be worse in well-limed soils.

Clay soils are often, but not always, acid. Liming a clay soil will also improve the soil structure by assisting the particles to collect into crumbs, which makes for easier working, quicker drainage and better rooting. Sandy soils can also be very acid and will usually benefit from regular liming.

Soils which are naturally rich in lime may produce poor plants by preventing them from absorbing vital plant nutrients, particularly iron and manganese. This results in small yellow leaves and poor growth, especially of roses, fruit and vegetables.

While it is relatively easy to change a peaty, acid soil to neutral by applying lime, it is more difficult to correct a very limy soil.

One answer to the problem is to treat the soil, before planting, with flowers of sulphur, which becomes transformed into sulphuric acid, making the soil acid. Treatment is most effective when accompanied by liberal amounts of peat, especially moss peat, which is acidic and is also good for the soil structure.

The use of ½ lb. of flowers of sulphur to the square yard can reduce a pH of 7 to 5.4 and make possible the growing of a range of lime-hating plants which previously would have failed. It may be necessary to repeat the dressing at half the original strength three years after planting, and to continue with the use of peat as a top-dressing. But do not over-do it as an overdose can cause such lush growth that plants become weak and disease-prone.

Such outstanding garden plants as rhododendrons, azaleas, kalmia, pieris, gaultheria, liquidambar and heathers can all be grown on normally unsuitable alkaline soils by using sulphur and peat.

Another way of treating limy soil is to reduce iron deficiency by applying iron chelates, also called sequestrenes, in the quantities suggested by the manufacturers.

Manganese deficiency, which particularly affects vegetables, and causes yellowing or spotting of the leaves, can be treated by spraying the foliage of plants in spring with a solution of 1 oz. of manganese sulphate to 2 gallons of water.

Burning the garden rubbish

Some garden rubbish, such as woody prunings, diseased plants and seeding weeds, should not go on the compost heap. The heat generated in a small heap is not enough to rot down wood or to destroy disease spores and weed seeds. So put this rubbish on the bonfire.

Try to choose a fine day for burning, with the wind taking the smoke away from the neighbours as much as possible.

Keep down the amount of smoke to a minimum by keeping the fire burning quickly.

A good sustained bottom draught is necessary, and a brick or metal incinerator is much more effective than trying to light a bonfire on the ground.

Cut woody material into small pieces. Large uncut branches do not burn very well as they leave too many air spaces.

The ashes of plants contain potash, a quick-acting fertiliser, so, as soon as they are cool enough to handle, spread them evenly on vacant soil.

As potash is soluble it will be washed into the soil by the next heavy rain and will stay there until extracted by plants. Ashes can also be heaped over plants with young shoots, like delphiniums and lupins, to help them withstand the winter.

There is no point in putting ashes on the compost heap, as the potash will be washed through.

Only the ashes of plants are valuable, and those from young plants are more useful than the ashes of old ones.

Coal ashes are of no use, except on clay soils which may be improved by the bits of clinker and other large particles.

On sandy soils coal ashes will only cause excessive drainage, and are best put straight into the dustbin or used for making path foundations.

When to dig, and how deep

Heavy clay soils are best dug in the autumn or early winter.

The frosts and thaws of the winter then break down the clods into a fine tilth, ready for the planting and sowing in spring.

Light sandy soils do not need winter weathering, and can be dug at any time.

For most purposes it is only necessary to dig to one spade depth, known as single digging. But in the vegetable garden or in some special situations, such as when growing sweet peas, it is preferable to turn over the soil to two spade depths – a system known as double digging.

This method enables compost to be buried deep down, where any weed seeds remaining in it cannot sprout. It also allows the roots of perennial weeds such as couch grass, to be picked out as they are uncovered.

Double digging also improves the drainage of ground which tends to become waterlogged.

However, deep digging is only worth while if you have deep soil. Many gardens in the British Isles have only a shallow covering of soil over chalk, limestone, gravel, sand or clay, and deep digging could result in the valuable thin layer of topsoil being buried completely beneath infertile subsoil.

In such cases, thrust the spade or fork into the earth as far as it will easily go, and turn over the soil. With each digging loosen some of the subsoil, so that over the years the depth of topsoil is increased. Provided it is not waterlogged, even the shallowest soil will grow worthwhile crops if manure or compost is forked regularly into the top 4–6 in.

Never dig clay soil when it is really wet and sticky. Your weight will compress the clay into hard lumps. On heavy, clay soil it may be advisable to dig with a fork, using the spade only for cutting the edges of the bed.

Finally, do not do too much at one time, and straighten your back frequently.

Single digging a large area of the garden

To dig over a large area such as a vegetable patch, start by dividing the plot down the middle with a garden line.

Dig out a strip of soil to the depth of one spade blade and about 12 in. wide, running from one side of the plot to the middle line. Do not try to get too much on the spade. This just makes the work harder than necessary. It is quite sufficient if each load of soil is 4–6 in. thick.

Put the soil from this initial trench in a heap at the same end of the plot but on the path near the adjacent half to be dug. It will be used later to fill the last trench.

If manure or garden compost is available to enrich the plot, spread it evenly over the ground. Barrow it out in heaps and spread it with a rake. Keep a little aside with the heaped earth, for the final trench.

Push the manure from the next strip of ground into the trench, spreading it evenly.

Now dig the second strip across the half-plot, throwing the soil into the first trench, and turning each spadeful over so that what was originally on the surface is now about 10 in. deep.

Continue in this way to the end of the plot and then work back along the other half. Fill the final trench with the soil from the first trench.

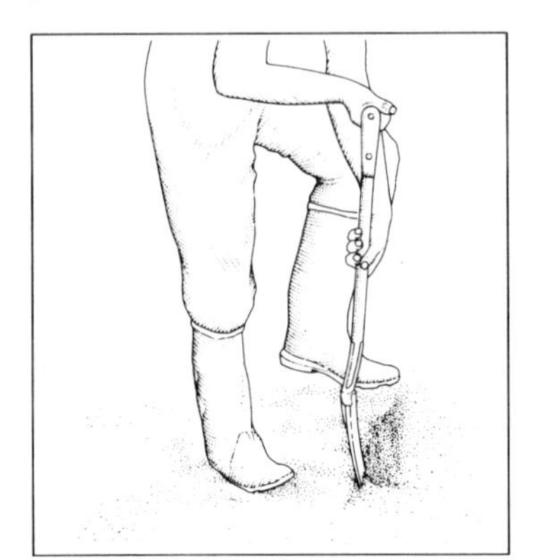

1 *Insert the spade upright, driving it in with the weight of the body*

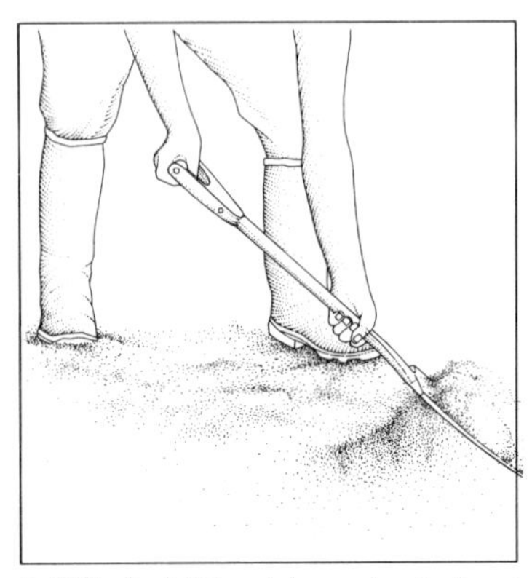

2 *Slide the left hand down the shaft and bend the knees slightly*

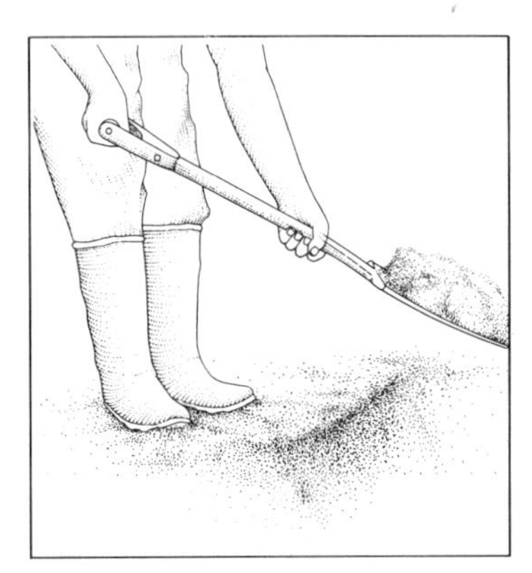

3 *Lift by straightening the legs to take the strain off the back*

Preparing a bed by double digging

To double dig over a large area, such as a vegetable patch, start as for single digging, by dividing the plot down the centre with a garden line.

Mark out with a line a 2 ft wide strip across the end of the half-plot to be dug first. Take out the soil from this trench to the depth of a spade blade. Heap the soil at the same end but on the path near the adjacent half-plot.

Using a fork, break up the bottom of the trench thoroughly to a depth of 10 in.

As with single digging, spread manure or compost over the surface of the whole plot. But if it is in short supply keep it until the double digging is completed, and then fork it into the top 4–6 in.

Push the manure or compost from the next 2 ft strip, which is marked out with a garden line, into the trench. Spread it evenly and work it in with the fork.

Dig up the second 2 ft strip, and put each spadeful upside-down into the open trench.

Take the first spadeful from the far side of the second 2 ft strip and turn it over against the near face of the trench. This will form a solid wall, to retain the remaining spadefuls when they are thrown into the trench beyond it.

Continue, as in single digging, round the two half-plots, until the final trench is filled with the soil from the first trench.

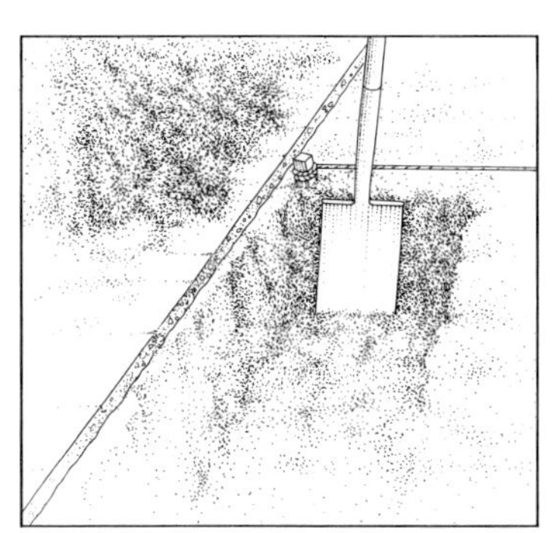

1 *Pile soil from No. 1 trench on the path, beyond the middle line*

2 *With a fork, break up the trench bottom then push in the compost*

3 *Dig the second trench, placing the soil from it in the first trench*

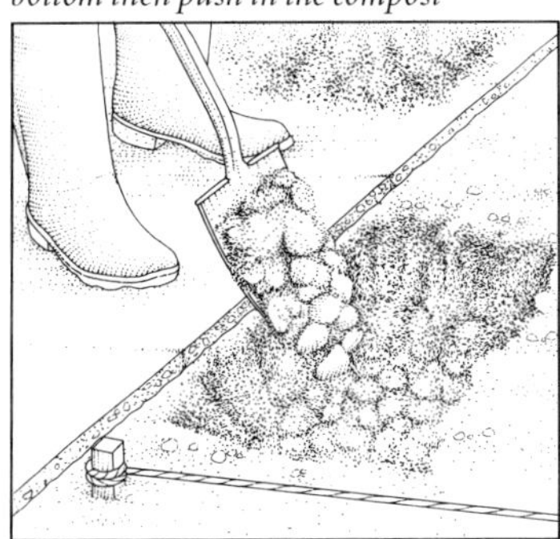

4 *Fill up the last trench with the soil piled on the path*

Improving drainage on clay soil

Good drainage is essential for most plant cultivation. It is also necessary where paths or walls are to be built.

Gardens with heavy clay or other sticky soils often suffer from poor drainage, because the soil particles cling together and prevent the water from seeping away. Sandy or stony soils usually drain freely.

In a new garden you can test the drainage by digging a pit about 2 ft deep and filling it with water. If the drainage is good the water will disappear within 24 hours. If the water stays in the hole for 48 hours or more, the drainage needs to be improved.

On clay soils, poor drainage may be overcome by improving the texture of the soil. This can be done by digging in organic matter such as manure, garden compost, leaf-mould or peat, and also inorganic matter such as gritty sand, weathered ashes or gypsum. When buying gypsum, go to a garden supplier. Gypsum bought from a builders' merchant may be intended for plastering, and will contain chalk.

There are also various commercial chemical preparations and these are available from most garden suppliers.

As a general rule, allow about one bucket to each square yard of soil when digging in organic matter, and two buckets to each square yard for inorganic matter. Apply gypsum at the rate of about 3 lb. to every square yard.

If the soil is very acid, heavy liming may make the clay more porous by assisting the particles to collect into crumbs. It also encourages earthworms, which help to improve drainage.

The amount of lime needed depends on how acid the soil is, but as a rule of thumb allow ½ lb. to the square yard if you are using hydrated lime – the most convenient form.

Lime should be spread on a broken surface and mixed with the topsoil. It should not be dug in.

Liming should be repeated every other year if necessary.

Digging through a hard pan Drainage may be poor, even on sandy soils, because of a 2–3 in. layer (or pan) of hard, compressed soil about 18 in. below the surface.

This may have been caused by constant treading or the passage of heavy implements (perhaps tractors and dumpers on a new housing site). A hard pan at this level can be effectively broken up by double digging the plot.

The importance of sufficient watering

Adequate watering is most important from April to September, when the sunshine is strong and plants are growing freely. Much of eastern and southern England has too little rain to meet requirements, while the uplands of the West and North often get too much.

A good gardener takes care to water his plants whenever nature does not do it for him. On average, a vegetable garden needs twice as much artificial watering as a flower bed. And newly planted trees and shrubs need frequent watering in dry spells, however sturdy they may appear to be.

Beds sheltered from the rain by a wall or hedge need more water than beds in the open. This particularly applies to beds on the east side of a wall, as rain-bearing winds are mostly those that blow from the south-west.

Seedlings with their short roots need constant attention.

On the other hand, lawns can be given less water than the flower and vegetable beds, because the aim is to keep them green, not to provide more work for the mower.

Index

Plants with widely used common names as well as their botanical names are listed under both. This information will help you when ordering seeds from a catalogue or buying plants, shrubs and trees from a nurseryman.

Abutilon.......154
Acacia, false (Robinia).......366
Acanthus.......78, 329
Acer (Maple).......370–1
Achillea (Yarrow).......329
Achimenes.......155
Acidanthera
  planting.......39
  storing.......40
Aconite, winter (Eranthis).......36, 329
  planting.......39
Aconitum (Monkshood).......329
Actinidia
  cuttings.......250
  pruning.......262
Adelgids.......381
Adiantum (Maidenhair fern).......329
  division.......172
  hardiness.......164
Aechmea (Urn plant)
  offsets.......174
  requirements.......164
Aethionema.......329–30
African daisy (Arctotis).......332
African lily (Agapanthus).......330
  division.......212
  for colour.......217
  grown with roses.......226
African marigold.......348
African violet (Saintpaulia)
  cleaning.......167
  cuttings.......151, 175
  requirements.......166, 168
  watering.......168
Agapanthus (African lily).......330
  division.......212
  for colour.......217
  grown with roses.......226
Ageratum.......330
Aglaonema.......174
Agrostis tenuis (Browntop bent).......184
Ailanthus (Tree of heaven).......256
Air layering
  greenhouse plants.......152
  house plants.......177
  shrubs.......255
Algae.......190
Allium.......39
Almond (Prunus).......360
  pruning.......259
Althaea (Hollyhock).......343
Alpines.......220–3
  for paths.......19
  greenhouse.......148
  lawns.......220
Alyssum (Gold dust).......330
  sweet.......330
Anagallis (Pimpernel).......330
Amaranthus (Joseph's coat).......330
  (Love-lies-bleeding).......347
Amaryllis (Hippeastrum)
  greenhouse.......154–5
  offsets.......174
  requirements.......165
Amelanchier (Shadbush; Juneberry).......360
Anaphalis.......330
Anchusa.......330–1
  cuttings.......214
Androsace (Rock jasmine).......331
Anemone.......331
  division.......213
  grown with roses.......226
Annuals.......25–34
  disorders.......31
  for cut flowers.......39
  greenhouse.......148, 154
  half-hardy.......25–26
    planting-out.......31
    sowing seed.......29
  hardy.......25
    dead-heading.......28
    seedlings.......28
    soil preparation.......27
    sowing seed.......27–28
    staking.......28
Anthemis (Chamomile).......331
  cuttings.......213
  pruning.......210
Anthracnose
  dwarf beans.......291, 393
  raspberries.......131
  willow.......385
Anthurium.......164
Antirrhinum (Snapdragon).......331
Aphelandra.......164
Aphids.......378, 385
  annuals and biennials.......31
  apples.......87
  black currants.......106
  blister.......133, 385
  carnations.......54, 59
  cherries.......110
  chrysanthemums.......62
  dahlias.......75
  ferns.......80
  greenhouse plants.......156
  lilies.......195
  pears.......125
  perennials.......210
  plums.......129, 383
  raspberries.......131
  roots.......308, 397
  roses.......234
  tulip bulbs.......394
  vegetables.......288
  woolly.......386
Apples.......86–103
  crab (Malus).......364
  disorders.......388, 390, 391, 392
  feeding.......86
  harvesting.......86
  planting.......86
  pruning.......88–102
  storing.......87
  varieties.......103
Apricots.......126
Aquilegia (Columbine).......331
  grown with roses.......226
Araucaria (Monkey puzzle).......371
Arbutus (Strawberry tree).......360
Arches.......21
Arctotis (African daisy).......332
Armeria (Thrift).......332
  cuttings.......214
Arrowhead (Sagittaria).......354
Artemisia.......332
  cutting back.......210
Arum lily (Zantedeschia).......359
Aruncus.......332
Arundinaria (Bamboo).......360
Asparagus.......289
Aspen (Populus).......360
Asplenium (Hartstongue fern).......78
  propagating.......81
Aspidistra
  division.......172
  requirements.......164, 166
Aster.......332
Aster (Michaelmas daisy).......332
  diseases.......210
  division.......212
Astilbe.......332–3
  early flowering.......155
Athyrium (Lady fern).......79, 333
  division.......80
Aubrieta.......333
  cutting back.......210
Aucuba (Spotted laurel)
  cuttings.......250
  for berries.......247
  pruning.......258
Avocado.......170
Azalea.......216–19
  indoor
    requirements.......165
    watering.......168

Bamboo (Arundinaria).......360
  black (Phyllostachys).......372
Baptisia.......212
Bark splitting.......389
Basal rot.......394
Basil.......323
Bay (Laurus).......360
Beans
  broad.......292–3
  disorders.......393
  dwarf.......291, 393
  French.......291
  runner.......290–1
Beauty bush (Kolkwitzia).......369
  pruning.......261
Bee, leafcutter.......379
Beech (Fagus).......361
  fern (Thelypteris).......79
Beet
  seakale.......318
  spinach.......318
Beetle
  asparagus.......289
  flea.......380
    cabbage.......296
    radish.......317
    swede.......322
    turnip.......322
  raspberry.......104, 392
Beetroot.......293
Begonia.......333
  cuttings.......151, 175
  greenhouse care.......154, 155, 157
  rex.......164, 166
    propagation.......176
  seed.......172
Beloperone guttata.......164
Bell heather (Erica).......161
Bellflower (Campanula).......334
  greenhouse care.......154–5
  grown with roses.......226
Bellis.......333
Benomyl.......398
Berberis (Barberry).......361
  hardiness.......243
  pruning.......261
Bergamot (Monarda).......348
  division.......211
Bergenia.......333
  division.......211
  for weed control.......246
  grown with ferns.......78
Betula (Birch).......361
  pendula (Swedish).......281
BHC.......398
Biennials.......26, 34
  disorders.......31
  for cut flowers.......39
Big bud.......106
Billbergia.......174
Bindweed.......209
Bioresmethrin.......398
Birch (Betula).......361

Abutilon–Clematis

Swedish.....281
Bird bath.....21
Birds, protection against.....390
Bitter pit.....392
apple.....87
Black bamboo (Phyllostachys).....372
Black currants.....105–7
disorders.....106, 390
Black leg.....388
Black spot.....381
rose.....234
Blackberries.....104–5
Blackfly (see Aphids)
Bladder senna (Colutea).....363
pruning.....260
Blanching
celery.....301
chicory.....302
leeks.....306
Blanket flower (Gaillardia).....210, 340
Blechnum (Hard fern).....79
Bleeding heart (Dicentra).....78, 337
cuttings.....214
Blight.....382, 386
fire.....389
pear.....125
potato.....396
raspberry.....131
tomato.....393
Blossom end rot.....393
Blotch.....391
Bluebell (Endymion).....39, 333
Blueberries.....108
Bog arum (Calla).....334
for pools.....328
Belting.....308
Bonfires.....404
Bordeaux malachite.....398
Bordeaux mixture.....398
Borders.....204–5
Boron deficiency
radishes.....317
turnips.....322
Botrytis
greenhouse plants.....156
shoots.....386
soft fruit.....389
tomatoes.....393
Bottle brush (Callistemon).....243
Bougainvillea.....154
Bouvardia.....154–5
Bridal wreath (Spiraea).....278
Broccoli.....298–9
Bromeliads
offsets.....174
requirements.....164–5
watering.....168
Bromophos.....398
Brompton stock.....356
Broom (Cytisus).....364
pruning.....259, 260, 266
Broom (Genista).....366
pruning.....261
Brown rot.....391
apples.....87
pears.....125
Browntop bent (Agrostis).....184
Brunnera.....246
Brussels sprouts.....294
Bud blast
rhododendron.....218, 391
Budding.....231–2
Buddleia.....360–1
pruning.....259, 260, 263
Bug
(see Capsid, Mealy, Root mealy)
Bugbane (Cimicifuga).....335
Bulbils
ferns.....81
lilies.....197
Bulblets.....197
Bulbs.....35–42
disorders.....384, 394–6
greenhouse.....149, 152
scale propagation.....196
Bulrush (Scirpus).....334
Burning bush (Dictamnus).....337–8
Burning bush (Kochia).....345
Busy lizzie (Impatiens).....334
cuttings.....172
requirements.....164
seed.....172
Butomus (Rush).....354
Buttercup (Ranunculus).....353
Butterfly bush (Buddleia).....360–1

Cabbages.....295
disorders.....397
Cacti.....43–50
Calabrese.....298–9
Calathea.....164
Calceolaria.....157
greenhouse.....154–5
growing indoors.....165
Calendula (Marigold).....347
Calico bush (Kalmia).....369
Calla (Bog arum).....334
for pools.....328
Calliopsis (Coreopsis).....336
Callistemon (Bottle brush).....243
Callistephus (Aster).....332
Calluna (Heather).....161
Calomel.....398
Caltha (Kingcup).....345
Camellia.....361
grown with rhododendrons.....217
pruning.....257
Campanula (Bellflower).....334
greenhouse.....154–5
grown with roses.....226
Campion (Lychnis).....347
Campsis.....262
Canadian pondweed (Elodea).....339
for pools.....328
Candytuft (Iberis).....334
Cane blight.....131
Cane spot.....387
blackberries.....104
raspberries.....131
Canker
apple.....87, 398
bacterial.....386
parsnip.....312
pear.....125
plum.....129
Capsid
apple.....392
bug.....379, 390
annuals and biennials.....31
chrysanthemums.....62
dahlias.....75
ferns.....80
perennials.....210
roses.....234
Captan.....398
Carbaryl.....399
Carnations.....51–59, 334–5
border.....51–55
disorders.....54, 59
greenhouse.....154–5
perpetual-flowering.....51, 52, 58–59
planting.....53
stopping.....59
Carrots.....296–7, 396
Caryopteris.....361–2
cuttings.....250
pruning.....260, 263
Catananche.....335
Catch crops.....285
Caterpillars.....378, 390
chrysanthemums.....62
perennials.....210
roses.....234
swift moth.....396
tortrix moth.....31, 54, 379
vegetables.....288
Cauliflowers.....298–9
Ceanothus.....260, 264
Cedar, Japanese (Cryptomeria).....362
Celery.....300–1
Celosia.....335
greenhouse.....154
Centaurea (Cornflower).....335
cuttings.....213
Ceratostigma
plumbaginoides.....256
pruning.....260, 264
Cercis (Judas tree).....368
Cereus.....45
Chaenomeles (Japanese quince).....362
cuttings.....256
pruning.....265
Chamaecyparis (False cypress).....362
Chamomile (Anthemis).....331
cuttings.....213
pruning.....210
Cheiranthus (Wallflower).....34, 359
Chelated compounds.....399
Cherries.....109–10
Cherry
Japanese flowering (Prunus).....362
laurel (Prunus)
cuttings.....249
pruning.....258
Cheshunt compound.....399
Chestnut.....281
Chewing's fescue (Festuca).....184
Chicory.....302
Chilean fire bush (Embothrium).....243
Chinese lantern (Physalis).....355
division.....211
Chionodoxa.....36
planting.....39
Chives.....323
Chlordane.....399
Chlorophytum (Spider plant)
division.....172
requirements.....164, 165
runners.....174
Chlorosis.....382
blueberries.....108
greenhouse plants.....156
heathers.....162
rhododendrons.....218
Chocolate spot.....293
Choisya (Mexican orange).....362
cuttings.....250
Christmas cacti.....47
Christmas rose (Heleborus).....78, 343
grown with roses.....226
Chrysanthemums.....60–70
annual.....60, 335
cuttings.....65–66, 68, 154–5
disorders.....62, 396
greenhouse.....67–70, 148, 154
growing indoors.....165
Cimicifuga (Bugbane).....335
Cineraria
greenhouse.....154–5, 157–8
maritima.....336
Cissus (Kangaroo vine)
arrangement.....166
shape.....165
Cistus (Rock rose).....363
pruning.....257
Clarkia.....336
Clematis.....363
for disguise.....243
pruning.....262, 265

Clerodendrum–Diseases

Clerodendrum....363
  bungei....256
Clethra....261
Climbers....241–80
  annual....26
  for ugly corners....243
  for walls....12–13
  greenhouse....154
  indoor
    arranging....166
    training....169
  pruning....262
  roses....227
    fixing to wall....230
    for hedges....226
    pruning....238
  support....12
  (see also Shrubs)
Cloches....153
Club root....385, 397
  cabbages....299
  cauliflowers....296
  control....403
  swedes....322
  turnips....322
Cobaea....154
Codling moth....391
  apple....87
Colchicum
  (Autumn crocus)....36, 37, 336
  planting....39
Coleus
  greenhouse....154
  growing indoors....164
Collar rot....121
Colour
  for focal points....20–21
  for paths....14
  for shady areas....22–23
Columbine (Aquilegia)....331
  grown with roses....226
Colutea (Bladder senna)....363
  pruning....260
Compost....402
  heap....284
  orchids....202
Coneflower, purple (Echinacea)...338
Conifers
  for focal points....20
  for rock gardens....223
  for shelter....281
Conophytum (Stone plant)
  propagating....48
  watering....46
Containers....18–19
Copper....399
Coral flower (Heuchera)....343
Coral spot....388
  currant bushes....133
Cordons....82
  planting....84
  pruning....93
  sweet peas....33
Core rot....395
Coreopsis....336
Coreopsis (Calliopsis)....336
Corky scab....380
Corms....35–42
  disorders....394–6
Cornflower....336
Cornish heather....161
Cornus (Dogwood)....363
  for weed control....246
  pruning....266
Corsican heath (Erica)....161
Cortaderia (Pampas grass)....351
Corticium disease....397
Cosmea (Cosmos)....336
Cotinus....364
  cuttings....252
Cotoneaster....364
  for colour....242
  for disguise....243
  for weed control....246
  hardiness....243
  pruning....261
Cottonwood (Santolina)....374
  pruning....260, 276
Courgettes....308–9
Crab apple (Malus)....364
Cracking
  fruit....392, 393
  root vegetables....396
Crane's-bill (Geranium)....225, 340–1
Crassula....48
Crataegus (Hawthorn)....367
Creeping red fescue (Festuca) 184
Crested dog's-tail (Cynosurus)....184
Crocosmia (Montbretia)....348
Crocus....36, 37, 336–7
  for indoors....41
  planting....39
  pots for....42
Crocus, autumn
  (Colchicum)....36, 37, 336
  planting....39
Cross-leaved heath (Erica)....161
Crown rot....134, 389
Cryptomeria (Japanese cedar)....362
Cucumber....303–4
Cultivators....207
Cupressocyparis
  (Leyland cypress)....364
Cupressus (Cypress)....364
Currant, flowering (Ribes)....373–4
  pruning....261, 274
Cuttings
  basal....214
  begonias....151
  black currants....106
  cacti....47–48
  chrysanthemums....65–66, 68
  currant bushes....133
  dahlias....77
  eye-....116
  gooseberries....113
  grape vines....116–17
  hardwood....117, 249–51
  heat for....145
  heathers....163
  heeled....250
  house plants....173
  leaf....151, 175
  leaf-bud....253
  orchids....154
  pelargoniums....154
  peperomias....151
  perennials....213–14
  pinks....57
  rhododendrons....219
  root....214, 252
  Saintpaulia....151
  semi-hard....250–1
  shrubs....249–53
  softwood....150, 252
  tip....173, 213
Cutworms....386
  perennials....210
  vegetables....288
Cyclamen....36, 158
  indoor
    requirements....164, 165
    watering....168
  planting....39
Cydonia (Chaenomeles)....265
Cymbidium....155
  propagating....203
Cynoglossum....337
Cynosurus (Crested dog's-tail)....184
Cypress (Cupressus)....364
  false (Chamaecyparis)....362
  Leyland (Cupressocyparis)....364
Cytisus (Broom)....364
  pruning....259, 260, 266

Daboecia (Heather)....161
Daffodil (Narcissus)....36, 37, 348–9
  for indoors....41–42
  mixing with ferns....78
  planting....39
Dahlia....71–77
Daisy
  African (see African daisy)
  bush (Olearia)....371
    for coast....243
    pruning....258
  Livingstone
    (Mesembryanthemum)....348
  Michaelmas (Aster)...210, 212, 332
  Shasta....355–6
Damping-off
  annuals....30–31
  carnations....54
  chrysanthemums....66
  greenhouse plants....156
  orchids....201
  vegetables....288
Damsons....126, 129
  (see also Plums)
Daphne....365
  for shade....243
  pruning....257, 259, 267
Darley Dale heath (Erica)....161
Date plant....170
Davidia....365
Day lily (Hemerocallis)....343
  division....213
Dead-heading
  annuals....28
  heathers....162
  lilies....195
  perennials....209
  rhododendrons....218
  roses....233
Delphinium....337
  annual (Larkspur)....345
  cuttings....214
Dendrobium....155
Derris....399
Deutzia....365
  suckers....256
Dianthus (Pinks)....51–59, 337
  annual....337
  barbatus (Sweet william)....357
Diazinon....399
Dicentra (Bleeding heart)....78, 337
  cuttings....214
Dichlofluanid....399
Dichlorvos....399
Dicofol....399
Dictamnus (Burning bush)....337–8
Die-back....162
Digging
  double....405
  single....404
Digitalis (Foxglove)....340
Dill....323
Dimethoate....399
Dinocap....399
Dipladenia....154
Disbudding
  carnations....54, 59
  chrysanthemums....64, 65
  roses....233
Diseases....377–400
  annuals and biennials....31
  apples....87
  black currants....106
  cacti....45

Division–Formaldehyde

carnations..................53, 54, 59
cherries..............................110
chrysanthemums..................62
control by soil pH................403
currant bushes......................133
dahlias..................................75
ferns......................................80
fruit (general)........................85
gooseberries.........................112
grape vines...........................117
greenhouse plants..................156
heathers................................162
house plants..........................170
lawns.....................................190
lilies......................................195
melons..................................121
orchids..................................210
peaches.................................124
pears.....................................125
perennials.............................210
plums....................................129
radishes.................................317
raspberries.............................131
rhododendrons.......................218
roses.....................................234
vegetables..............................288
Division
bulbs......................................40
cactus.....................................48
dahlias....................................77
ferns.......................................80
fibrous roots..........................212
fleshy roots...........................212
house plants..........................172
irises..........................182, 183
lilies......................................196
orchids..................................203
perennials................152, 211–13
rhizomes...............................211
shrubs...................................256
tubers....................................213
Dizygotheca
air layering...........................177
seeds.....................................172
DNOC...................................399
Dogwood (Cornus)..................363
for weed control....................246
pruning.................................266
Doronicum (Leopard's bane)......338
Dorset heath (Erica)................161
Downy mildew
lettuce...................................308
onion....................................311
spinach..................................318
Draba.....................................338
Drainage................................405
Dry rot..........................389, 395
Dryas.....................................338
Dryopteris..............................338
filix-mas (Male fern).........78, 338
division...................................80
planting...................................79
Dwarf pyramids........................82
pruning.............................100–2

Earthworms............................190
Earwigs..........................378, 390
annuals and biennials...............31
chrysanthemums......................62
dahlias.....................................75
Eccremocarpus........................154
Echeveria
cuttings...................................48
growing outdoors.....................45
Echinacea (Purple coneflower)....338
Echinocereus............................50
Echinops (Globe thistle)...........338
Echinopsis
grafting...................................50
offsets.....................................48
Edelweiss (Leontopodium)......345–6
Eelworms
chrysanthemums......................62
ferns.......................................80
onions.....................311, 384
stem and bulb...............384, 394
Eichhornia
(Water hyacinth)..........328, 338–9
Elder (Sambucus)....................365
pruning..................................276
Elm (Ulmus)...........................256
Elodea
(Canadian pondweed).......328, 339
Embothrium (Chilean fire bush)...243
Endymion (Bluebell)...........39, 333
Epimedium...............................78
for colour...............................217
Epiphyllum
care of......................................45
watering...................................46
Eranthis (Winter aconite)......36, 329
planting....................................39
Erica (Heather)....................160–1
for colour................................242
for weed control.......................246
Erigeron (Fleabane)..................339
Eryngium.................................339
Erythronium..............................39
Escallonia................................365
for coast..................................243
Espaliers...................................82
planting....................................84
pruning..............................94–96
Eucryphia.................................365
Euonymus..............................365–6
japonicus.................................243
pruning....................................257
Eupatorium...............................339
Euphorbia.........................49, 339
for weed control.......................246
pulcherrima (Poinsettia).........164
Evening primrose (Oenothera)....350
grown with roses.....................226
Everlasting flowers....................26
Exhibiting
chrysanthemums..............60, 64
dahlias.....................................72
sweet peas................................33

Fagus (Beech).........................361
for shade.................................281
Fairy rings...............................397
False acacia (Robinia)..............366
False cypress (Chamaecyparis).....362
Fans...82
planting....................................84
pruning..............................97–99
cherry.....................................109
peach......................................123
plum.......................................128
Fatshedera...............................165
Fatsia
arrangement.............................166
offsets.....................................174
requirements............................166
seed..172
Feeding
apples.......................................86
black currants...........................105
blackberries..............................104
blueberries................................108
cacti..46
carnations..................................53
cherries....................................109
chrysanthemums...............61, 68
currant bushes...........................132
dahlias..................................73, 75
ferns..80
gooseberries...............................111
greenhouse plants......................146
heathers....................................162
house plants..............................168
irises..180
lawns....................................188–9
lilies..194
loganberries...............................104
orchids......................................200
peaches......................................121
pears..124
perennials..................................207
plums...126
raspberries.................................130
roses..234
shrubs..245
strawberries................................135
vegetables...................................286
Fences....................................12–13
Fenitrothion................................399
Ferns.....................................78–81
beech...79
crown-forming................................79
disorders......................................80
division..80
feeding..80
for colour...................................217
hard (Blechnum)............................79
hartstongue (Asplenium)......78, 81
lady (Athyrium)..........79, 80, 333
maidenhair (Adiantum)....164, 172
male (Dryopteris)....78, 79, 80, 338
mulching.......................................80
oak (Gymnocarpium).......................79
planting...79
rhizomatous-rooted.......................79
royal (Osmunda)..........................350
sensitive (Onoclea).......................350
shield (Polystichum).........78, 352
Fertilisers
chemical......................................401
for vegetables..............................286
general..401
Fescue (Festuca)............................184
Ficus (see Rubber plant)
Filipendula....................................339
Finger and toe...............................296
Fir..281
Fire blight.....................................389
pears..125
Firethorn (Pyracantha)...................373
for colour.....................................242
Fittonia...172
Flax (Linum)..................................346
Flea beetle.....................................380
cabbage..296
radish...317
swede..322
turnip...322
Fleabane (Erigeron)........................339
Fly
cabbage root..................296, 397
carnation..54
carrot..........................297, 396
celery..........................301, 312
lacewing..218
narcissus.......................................394
onion......................306, 311, 394
Foam of May (Spiraea)....................278
Foot rot..389
beans...291
cucumbers......................................304
marrows...309
peas...314
Forcing
bulbs...41–42
chicory...302
rhubarb...134
Forget-me-not (Myosotis).....339–40
Formaldehyde..................................399

Forsythia–Helleborus

Forsythia ...366
pruning ...261, 267
suckers ...256
Foxglove (Digitalis) ...340
Frames ...153
arrangement ...138
for cucumbers ...304
for radishes ...317
for vegetables ...284
French marigold ...348
Fritted compounds ...399
Froghoppers ...381
Frost damage
asparagus ...289
dahlias ...75
irises ...180
peaches ...124
roses ...234
Frost protection
shrubs ...245
Fruit ...82–136
(general, see also individual fruits)
bush trees ...82
buying trees ...83
cordons ...82
disorders ...85, 383, 391–2
drop ...392
dwarf pyramids ...82
espaliers ...82
fan trees ...82
grafting ...83
growth encouragement ...85
half-standards ...82
planting trees and bushes ...84
pollination ...82
propagation ...83
protection ...85
pruning ...82–83
soft ...82
disorders ...391–2
standards ...82
supporting ...85
training trees ...83
tree ...82
disorders ...391–2
Fuchsia ...366
greenhouse ...143–5, 158
pruning ...260, 268
Fumigation ...147
Fungicides ...398–400
Furniture, garden ...20–21
Fusarium patch ...190, 397
Fusarium wilt ...383

G

Gages ...126, 129
(see also plums)
Gaillardia (Blanket flower) ...210, 240
Galanthus (Snowdrop) ...35, 38, 356
lifting ...40
planting ...39
pots for ...42
Gall, leafy ...387
Gall mites ...390
Gall wasps ...385
Gardens
design ...12–24
furniture ...20–21
labour-saving ...24
ornaments ...20–21
paved ...16–17
shape ...11
size ...11
Gaultheria ...366
grown with rhododendrons ...217
procumbens ...226
Genista (Broom) ...366
pruning ...261
Gentiana ...340
grown with rhododendrons ...217
Geranium (Crane's-bill) ...225, 340–1
for weed control ...246
Geranium (Pelargonium) ...158
greenhouse ...154
Gesneria ...155
Geum ...341
Ginkgo (Maidenhair tree) ...370
Gladiolus ...36, 37–38, 341
disorders ...395
lifting ...40
planting ...39
thrips ...391
Globe flower (Trollius) ...358
Globe thistle (Echinops) ...338
Gloriosa (Glory lily) ...154
Gloxinia (Sinningia)
cutting ...175
watering ...168
Godetia ...341
Gold dust (Alyssum) ...330
Golden club (Orontium) ...350
Golden rod (Solidago) ...341
Gooseberries ...111–13
Grafting
cacti ...50
fruit trees ...83
roses ...231–2
Grape hyacinth ...36, 341
Grape vine ...113–17, 376
ornamental ...262
Grapefruit ...171
Grasses ...184
ornamental ...342
pampas (Cortaderia) ...351
Greenback ...393
Greenfly (see Aphids)
Greenhouses ...137–47
automatic equipment ...146
choosing ...140–1, 197
cleaning ...147
cold ...137–8
condensation ...140
damping down ...146, 198
electrically heated ...142
erecting ...141
framework ...140
fumigation ...147
gas-heated ...142
guttering ...144
heated ...137
heating ...141–2, 198
hot-water heated ...142
humidity ...146
lighting ...144
material ...140
paraffin-heated ...142
propagators ...145
shading ...138, 143, 146, 198
shape ...140
shelving ...243
siting ...141
soil thermometer ...144
soil-warming cables ...145
staging ...143
temperature control ...146
thermostats ...142
ventilation ...138, 141, 143, 197
water supply ...144
Greenhouse gardening ...137–59
disorders ...156
division propagation ...152
feeding plants ...146
layering plants ...152
leaf cutting ...151
mist propagation ...152
monthly jobs ...154–5
plant succession ...148
plants for
alpines ...148
annuals ...148
bedding ...154
Begonia ...151, 157
bulbs ...149
cacti ...43–50
Calceolaria ...157
carnations ...58–59
chrysanthemums ...67–70
Cineraria ...157–8
cucumbers ...303
Cyclamen ...158
Fuchsia ...158
hanging baskets ...148
Pelargonium ...159
Peperomia ...151
Primula ...159
Saintpaulia ...151
Schizanthus ...159
tomatoes ...154–5, 319–21
vines ...113–17
potting plants ...147
propagation ...150–2
softwood cuttings ...150
sowing seeds ...149
watering plants ...146
Grey bulb rot ...395
Grey mould ...386, 392
chrysanthemums ...62
greenhouse plants ...156
lettuces ...308, 389
lilies ...195
onions ...311
shrubs ...253
tomatoes ...393
Ground cover ...205
around rhododendrons ...217
around roses ...225–6
for weed smothering ...246
roses ...226
Growmore ...401
Gumming ...387
Gunnera ...342
Gymnocarpium (Oak fern) ...79
Gypsophila ...39, 342
grown with roses ...226

H

Hamamelis (Witch hazel) ...367
for colour or shade ...242–3
Hanging baskets ...18–19
annuals ...26
bulbs and corms ...36
in greenhouses ...148
Hard fern (Blechnum) ...79
Hard rot ...395
Hartstongue fern (Asplenium) ...78
propagating ...81
Haworthia ...48
Hawthorn (Crataegus) ...367
HCH ...399
Heathers ...160–3
colours ...217
Hebe (Veronica) ...367
pinguifolia ...226
pruning ...257, 261
Hedera (Ivy) ...368
arrangement ...166
cuttings ...172
for weed control ...246
requirements ...166
Hedges ...226
Helenium ...342
division ...212
Helianthemum (Rock rose) ...342
Helianthus (Sunflower) ...357
Helichrysum ...342
Heliopsis ...343
Heliotrope ...343
greenhouse ...154–5
Helleborus ...78, 343
grown with roses ...226

Hemerocallis–Lippia

Hemerocallis (Day lily)............343
division............213
Herbaceous borders............204–5
Herbaceous plants
(See Perennials)
Herbs............323
Heuchera (Coral flower)............343
Hibiscus (Tree hollyhock)............367
Hippeastrum (Amaryllis)
greenhouse............154–5
offsets............174
requirements............165
Hippophae (Sea buckthorn)............367
for berries............247
for coast............243
Hoes............207
Holly (Ilex)............367–8
for berries............247
Hollyhock (Althaea)............343
tree (Hibiscus)............367
Honesty (Lunaria)............343–4
Honey fungus
cherry............110
grape vine............117
plum............129
Honeysuckle (Lonicera)............368
for disguise............243
pruning............262
Hosta (Plantain lily)............344
division............212
for weed control............246
grown with ferns............78
grown with rhododendrons............217
grown with roses............226
Hottonia (Water violet)............344
Houseleek (Sempervivum)............45, 355
House plants............164–77
arrangements............166
bromeliads............164–5
cleaning............167
cool-room............165
disorders............170
feeding............168
flowering types............164
foliage types............164
from fruit stones............170–1
holiday care............169
humidity............168
propagation............172–7
pruning............169
repotting............167
requirements............164–5
shapes............165
types............164–5
warm room............166
Hyacinth............36, 38, 344
grape (Muscari)............36, 341
indoors............41–42, 164
jars for............42
lifting............40
water............328, 338–9
Hybrids
annuals and biennials............26
roses............225, 227, 236
Hydrangea............368
for shade............243
pruning............261, 262, 268–9
Hypericum (St John's wort)............344
cuttings............214
for weed control............246
pruning............270

Iberis (Candytuft)............334
Ilex (Holly)............367–8
for berries............247
Impatiens (Busy lizzie)............334
cuttings............172
requirements............164
seed............172
Incarvillea............344
Indigofera
pruning............260, 270
Inula............344–5
Ipomoea (Morning glory)............348
greenhouse............154
Irises............178–83
Iron sulphate............399
Ivy (Hedera)............368
arrangement............166
cuttings............172
for weed control............246
requirements............166
Ixia............40

Japanese cedar (Cryptomeria)............362
Japanese flowering cherry
(Prunus)............362
Japanese quince (Chaenomeles)............362
cuttings............256
pruning............265
Japonica
(see Japanese quince)
Jasmine (Jasminum)............368
rock (Androsace)............331
winter............368
greenhouse............154
pruning............271
Jew's mallow (Kerria)............369
division............256
pruning............259, 271
John Innes............401
Jonquils............37
Joseph's coat (Amaranthus)............330
Judas tree (Cercis)............368
Juneberry (Amelanchier)............360
Juniper............369
for disguise............243
for weed control............246

Kalanchoe............47
Kalmia (Calico bush)............369
Kangaroo vine (Cissus)
arrangement............166
requirements............164
shape............165
Kerria (Jew's mallow)............369
division............256
pruning............259, 271
Kingcup (Caltha)............345
Kniphofia (Red-hot poker)............345
Kochia (Burning bush)............345
Kolkwitzia (Beauty bush)............369
pruning............261

Laburnum............369
Lacewing fly............218
Lachenalia............155
Lady fern (Athyrium)............79, 333
division............80
Lamium............246
Lapageria............154
Larkspur (Delphinium)............345
Laurel, spotted (Aucuba)
cuttings............250
for berries............247
pruning............258
Laurus (Bay)............360
Lavandula (Lavender)............369
cuttings............250
pruning............272
Lavatera (Mallow)............345
Lavender (Lavandula)............369
cuttings............250
pruning............272
sea (Limonium)............346
Lawns............184–91
Layering
air
greenhouse plants............152
house plants............177
shrubs............255
blackberries............105
carnations............55
greenhouse plants............152
heathers............163
loganberries............105
rhododendrons............219
serpentine............255
shrubs............254
tip............105
Leaf blister mite............381
pears............125
Leaf curl
peach............124, 385
plum............129, 383
Leaf miners
celery............301
chrysanthemums............62, 396
parsnips............312
Leaf rolling sawfly............383
Leaf spot
celery............301
spinach............318
Leafcutter bee............379
Leafhoppers............381
rhododendron............218
roses............234
Leafy gall............387
Leatherjackets
carnations............53
lawns............190
vegetables............288, 397
Leaves
disorders............378–86
holes in............379
pests............378
Leeks............305–6
Lemon plant............171
Lenten rose (Helleborus)............78, 343
grown with roses............226
Leontopodium (Edelweiss)............345–6
Leopard moths............385
Leopard's bane (Doronicum)............338
Lettuce............306–8
Leucojum (Snowflake)............36
Lewisia............346
Leycesteria (Flowering nutmeg)............369
pruning............272
seed propagation............356
Liatris............213
Lichens............190, 397
Lilac (Syringa)............370
Lilies............192–7
African (see African lily)
arum (Zantedeschia)............359
colours............192, 217
day (Hemerocallis)............213, 343
grown with ferns............78
grown with roses............226
plantain (Hosta)............78, 344
division............212
for weed control............246
grown with rhododendrons............217
grown with roses............226
water (Nymphaea)............327
yellow (Nuphar)............350
Lily-of-the-valley............78
for colour............217
tree (Pieris)............217, 258, 372
Lime sulphur............399
Liming............405
Limonium (Sea lavender)............346
Linaria (Toad flax)............346
Linum (Flax)............346
Lippia
(Lemon-scented verbena)............370
pruning............260, 273

Lithops–Pasque flower

Lithops (Stone plant)
  propagating........48
  watering........46
Lithospermum........346
Livingstone daisy
  (Mesembryanthemum)........348
Lobelia........346
  greenhouse........155
Loganberries........104–5
Lolium (Rye grass)........184
Lonicera (Honeysuckle)........368
  for disguise........243
  pruning........262
Loosestrife (Lythrum)........346–7
Lunaria (Honesty)........343–4
Love-in-a-mist (Nigella)........349–50
Love-lies-bleeding
  (Amaranthus)........347
Lupin........347
  cuttings........214
Lychnis (Campion)........347
Lysichiton........347
Lysimachia........347
Lythrum (Loosestrife)........346–7

Magnesium deficiency........382
Magnolia........370
  for shade........243
Mahonia........370
  pruning........259
Maidenhair fern (Adiantum)........329
  division........172
  hardiness........164
Maidenhair tree (Ginkgo)........370
Maidens........83
Malathion........399
Malcolmia........356–7
Male fern (Dryopteris)........78
  division........80
  planting........79
Mallow (Lavatera)........345
Malus (Crab apple)........364
Maneb........400
Manganese deficiency........382
Manures........401–3
Manuring
  vegetables........286
Maple (Acer)........370–1
Maranta........164
Marigold
  African........348
  French........348
  marsh........345
  pot (Calendula)........347
Marjoram........323
Marrows........308–9
  heat for........145
Marsh marigold........345
Matricaria........348
Matthiola........356
Meadow grass (Poa)........184
Meadow rue (Thalictrum)........357
Mealy bugs........378, 386
  cacti........45
  greenhouse plants........156
  orchids........201
  root........156
Melons........118–21
  disorders........122
  heat for........145
Menazon........400
Mercurial turf fungicides........400
Mesembryanthemum (Daisy)........348
Metaldehyde........400
Methiocarb........400
Mexican orange (Choisya)........362
  cuttings........250
Michaelmas daisy (Aster)........332
  disease........210
  division........212
Midges........125
Mildew
  annuals and biennials........31
  chrysanthemum........62
  downy
    lettuces........308
    onions........311
    spinach........318
  gooseberries........112
  greenhouse plants........156
  peas........314
  perennials........210
  powdery........381, 383, 392
    apples........87
    grape vines........117
    melons........121
  roses........234
  vegetables........288
Mimulus (Monkey flower)........348
Mint........323
Mint rust........387
Mites
  (see Bulb scale, Gall, Red spider,
  Tarsonemid)
Mock orange (Philadelphus)........372
  pruning........258
  suckers........256
Moles........190
Monarda (Bergamot)........348
  division........211
Monkey flower (Mimulus)........348
Monkey puzzle (Araucaria)........371
Monkshood (Aconitum)........329
Monstera
  requirements........164
  training........169
Montbretia (Crocosmia)........348
Morning glory (Ipomoea)........348
  greenhouse........154
Morus (Mulberry)........371
Mosaic virus........304
Moth
  codling........87, 391
  leopard........385
  pea........314, 393
  raspberry........131
  winter
    peach........124
    plum........129
Mother-in-law's tongue (Sansevieria)
  division........172
  leaf sectioning........176
  requirements........164, 166
Mould
  grey........386, 392
    greenhouse plants........156
    lettuces........308, 389
    lilies........195
    onions........311
    shrubs........253
    tomatoes........393
  snow........190
Mountain ash (Sorbus)........371
Mountain heath (Erica)........161
Mowers........188
Mulberry (Morus)........371
Mulching
  dahlias........74
  ferns........80
  irises........181
  perennials........207
  roses........234
  shrubs........245
Mullein (Verbascum)........358
  cuttings........214
Muscari (Grape hyacinth)........36, 341
Myosotis (Forget-me-not)........339–40
Myrica (Sweet gale)........371

Narcissus........36, 37, 348–9
  disorders........394
  for indoors........41
  lifting........40
  planting........39
Nasturtium........349
Navelwort (Omphalodes)........350
Neck rot........311, 394
Nectarines........121–4
  (see also Peaches)
Nemesia........349
Nerine........39
Nicotiana (Tobacco plant)........349
Nicotine........400
Nigella (Love-in-a-mist)........349–50
Night-scented stock........356
Nitrogen........401
Nitrogen deficiency........382
  vegetables........288
Nuphar (Yellow water lily)........350
Nutmeg, flowering
  (Leycesteria)........369
  pruning........272
  seed propagation........256
Nymphaea (Water lily)........327, 350

Oak........281
  fern (Gymnocarpium)........79
Odontoglossum........155
Oenothera (Evening primrose)........350
  grown with roses........226
Offsets
  cacti........48
  greenhouse bulbs........152
  house plants........174
Offshoots
  cacti........48
Olearia (Daisy bush)........371
  for coast........243
  pruning........258
Omphalodes (Navelwort)........350
Onions........310–12, 394
Onoclea (Sensitive fern)........350
Opuntia
  cuttings........47
  grafting........50
  growing outdoors........45
Orange plant........171
Orchids........198–203
  cuttings........154
  greenhouse care........154–5, 198
Ornaments........20–21
Orontium (Golden club)........350
Osmunda (Royal fern)........350
Oxydemeton methyl........400

Pachysandra........371
  for weed control........246
Paeony........350–1
  division........213
  tree........371–2
    seed propagation........256
  wilt........388
Painted tongue (Salpiglossis)........354
  greenhouse........155
Pampas grass (Cortaderia)........351
Pansy........359
  grown with roses........225
Papaver (Poppy)........352
  cuttings........214
Paphiopedilum........154–5
Parsley........323
Parsnips........312
Parthenocissus
  (Virginia creeper)........372
  pruning........262
Pasque flower (Pulsatilla)........353

Passiflora–Quintozene

Passiflora (Passion flower) 372
  greenhouse 154
  pruning 155, 260
Paths 14–15
Peaches 121–4
  disorders 124, 385
  growing from stone 123, 170
Pears 124–5
  disorders 125, 381, 392
Peas 313–14
  disorders 393
Peat 403
Pelargonium (Geranium)
  greenhouse 154, 158
  peltatum 166
Pennywort (Umbilicus) 44
Penstemon 351
  cuttings 213
Peperomia
  cuttings 151
  indoors
    cuttings 175
    requirements 164
    shape 165
Perennials 204–15
  big-rooted 206
  colours 205
  cuttings 213–14
  dead-heading 209
  disorders 210
  division 152, 211–13
  feeding 207
  foliage 205
  for shade 23
  ground cover 205
  planting 206
  propagating 211–15
  prostrate 206
  pruning 210
  seed 215
  soil preparation 206
  staking 208–9
  types 204–5
  weed killers 209
Pergola 21
Pernettya 372
  grown with rhododendrons 217
  pruning 258
Pesticides 398–400
Pests 377–400
  annuals and biennials 31
  apples 87
  black currants 106
  cacti 45
  carnations 53, 54, 59
  cherries 110
  chrysanthemums 62
  currant bushes 133
  dahlias 75
  ferns 80
  fruit (general) 85
  gooseberries 112
  greenhouse 156
  house plants 170
  lawns 190
  lilies 195
  melons 121
  orchids 201
  peaches 124
  pears 125
  perennials 210
  plums 129
  radishes 317
  raspberries 131
  rhododendrons 218
  roses 234
  vegetables 288
Petroleum emulsion 400
Petunia 351
  disorders 387
Philadelphus (Mock orange) 372
  pruning 258, 273
  suckers 256
Philodendron
  requirements 166
  training 169
Phlox 351–2
  cuttings 214
  division 212
Phosphorus 401
Phyllostachys (Black bamboo) 372
Physalis (Chinese lantern) 335
Picea (Spruce) 375
Pickerel weed (Pontederia) 352
  for water garden 328
Pieris (Lily-of-the-valley tree) 372
  grown with rhododendrons 217
  pruning 258
Pilea 165
Pimpernel (Anagallis) 330
Pincushion flower (Scabiosa) 355
  cuttings 214
Pineapple plant 171
Pinks (Dianthus) 51–59
  annual 337
Pipings 58
Pirimicarb 400
Pirimiphos methyl 400
Plantain lily (Hosta) 344
  division 212
  for weed control 246
  grown with ferns 78
  grown with rhododendrons 217
  grown with roses 226
Plants
  for north-facing borders 23
  for shade 22–23
Plumbago 154
  pruning 155
Plums 126–9
  disorders 129, 383
  ornamental (Prunus) 373
Poa (Meadow grass) 184
Poinsettia (Euphorbia) 164
Pollination
  cactus 49
  fruit 82
  marrows 309
  melons 119, 120
  peaches 121
Polyanthus 155
Polygonatum 211
Polygonum (Russian vine) 352, 373
  for weed control 246
  pruning 262
Polypodium 78
Polystichum (Shield fern) 78, 352
  setiferum (Soft shield fern) 79
    propagating 81
Pontederia (Pickerel weed) 352
  for water garden 328
Pools 324–8
  design 21
Poppy (Papaver) 352
  cuttings 214
Populus (aspen) 360
Potamogeton 353
Potatoes 315–16
  disorders 396
Potentilla 373
  dwarf 225
  pruning 257, 261
Potting
  bulbs 41–42
  cacti 49
  carnations 58
  chrysanthemums 67
  dahlias 77
  grape vines 116
  greenhouse plants 147
  lilies 195
  shrub cuttings 251
  tomatoes 319
Powdery mildew 381, 383, 392
  apples 87
  grape vines 117
  melons 121
Powdery scab 396
Primrose (Primula) 352–3
  evening (Oenothera) 226, 350
Primula (Primrose) 352–3
  for colour 217
  greenhouse 158
  grown with roses 226
Propagation
  (see also Bulbils, Cuttings, Division, Grafting, Layering, Seeds, Suckers)
  cacti 47–50
  ferns 80–81
  fruit trees 83
  greenhouse plants 150–2
  house plants 172–7
  lilies 196
  mist 138, 152
  orchids 203
Propagators 145
Propoxur 400
Pruning
  apples 88–102
  black currants 106
  blueberries 108
  cherries 109–10
  climbers 155, 262
  currant bushes 132–3
  fruit trees (general) 82–83
  gooseberries 111–12
  grape vines 115–16
  heathers 162
  house plants 169
  peaches 122–3
  pears 124
  perennials 210
  plums 127–8
  rhododendrons 218
  roses 228, 235–40
  shrubs 257–80
    centre wood 261
    dead wood 257
    flowering on last year's wood 259
    flowering on new shoots 260
    in containers 248
    overgrown 258
  trees 283
Prunus (Almond) 360
  pruning 259
Prunus (Cherry laurel)
  cuttings 249
  pruning 258
Prunus (General)
  suckers 256
Prunus (Japanese flowering cherry) 362
Prunus (Plum) 373
Pseudobulbs 200
Pulmonaria 246
Pulsatilla (Pasque flower) 353
Pyracantha (Firethorn) 373
  for colour 242
Pyramids 82
  pruning 100–2, 127–8
Pyrethrum 353, 400

Quince, Japanese (Chaenomeles) 362
  cuttings 256
  pruning 265
Quintozene 400

Radish–Seeds

Radish...317
Ramblers...227, 239
Raspberries...130–1
 disorders...131, 392
Ranunculus (Buttercup)...353
Ranunculus (Spearwort)...353
Rebutia...48
Red currants...132–3
 disorders...133, 385
Red-hot poker (Kniphofia)...345
Red spider mite
 apples...87
 biological control...398
 cacti...45
 carnations...54, 59
 chrysanthemums...62
 fruit trees (general)...383
 greenhouse plants...156, 381
 house plants...170
 melons...121
 orchids...201
 peaches...124
 plums...129
Red thread...397
 lawns...190
Repotting
 cacti...46
 house plants...167
Reversion...385
 black currants...106
Rheum...212
Rhipsalidopsis...45
Rhizome rot...388
Rhododendron...216–19
 colours...216
 dead-heading...218
 disorders...218, 391
 planting...218
 propagation...219
 pruning...218
 sizes...217
 soil requirements...216, 218
Rhubarb...134
Rhus (Sumach)...373
 cuttings...252
 pruning...274
 suckers...256
Ribes (Flowering currant)...373–4
 pruning...261, 274
Ring culture...320
Robinia (False acacia)...366
Rock gardens
 construction...220–2
 drainage...221–2
 planting...223
 planting arrangements...220
Rock jasmine (Androsace)...331
Rock plants...220–3
 bulbs and corms...39
 for paths...15
 for walls...13
 planting...223
Rock rose (Cistus)...363
 pruning...257
Rock rose (Helianthus)...342
Rodgersia...354
Romneya
 cuttings...214
 division...256
Root mealy bugs...156
Rooting powder...253
Roots, disorders...394–7
Rootstocks
 cacti...50
 fruit trees...83
 rhubarb...134
 roses...231
Rosa
 canina...231
 damascena...224
 gallica...224
 laxa...231
 longicuspis...238
 macrantha...226
 moyesii...225, 227
 multiflora...231
 primula...227
 rugosa...227, 231
 spinosissima...226
 wichuraiana...226
Rose of Sharon (Hypericum)...269
Rosemary (Rosmarinus)...323, 374
Roses...224–41
 black spot...381
 Christmas...78, 226, 343
 disorders...234, 381, 383, 387
 Lenten...78, 226, 343
 rock (Cistus)...257, 363
 rock (Helianthus)...342
 suckers...233, 256
Rosmarinus (Rosemary)...323, 374
Rot
 basal...394
 blossom end...393
 brown...87, 125, 391
 collar...121
 core...395
 crown...134, 389
 dry...389, 395
 foot...389
  beans...291
  cucumbers...304
  marrows...309
  peas...314
 grey bulb...395
 hard...395
 neck...311, 394
 rhizome...388
 sclerotinia...297
 stem...389
 violet root...289
 white...311, 394
Rowan (Sorbus)...371
Royal fern (Osmunda)...350
Rubber plant (Ficus)
 air layering...174
 arrangement...166
 cleaning...167
 hardiness...164
 pruning...169
 shape...165
Rubus...374
 cuttings...252
 division...256
 pruning...259, 275
 suckers...256
Rudbeckia...354
 division...212
Runners
 greenhouse plants...152
 house plants...174
 strawberries...136
Running-on...64
Ruscus...256
Rush, flowering (Butomus)...354
Russian Vine (Polygonum)...352, 373
 for weed control...246
 pruning...262
Rust...380
 carnations...53, 59
 chrysanthemums...62
 internal...386
 mint...387
 perennials...210
 roses...234, 387
Ruta...213
Rye grass (Lolium)...184

Sage...323
Sagittaria (Arrowhead)...354
St Dabeoc's heath (Daboecia)...161
St John's wort (Hypericum)...344
 cuttings...214
 for weed control...246
 pruning...209, 270
Saintpaulia (African violet)
 cleaning...167
 cuttings...151, 175
 requirements...166, 168
 watering...168
Salix (Willow)...376
 for shade...281
 pruning...275
Salpiglossis (Painted tongue)...354
 greenhouse...155
Salvia...354
 superba...226
Sambucus (Elder)...365
 pruning...276
Sansevieria (Mother-in-law's tongue)
 division...172
 leaf sectioning...176
 requirements...164, 166
Santolina (Cottonwood)...374
 pruning...260, 276
Sawfly
 apples...87, 391
 gooseberries...112, 379
 pears...125
 roses...383
Saxifraga...354–5
 cuttings...213
 requirements...165
 runners...174
Scab...380, 388, 391
 apple...87
 corky...380
 gladiolus...395
 pear...125
 potato...396
 powdery...396
 soil pH...403
Scabiosa (Pincushion flower)...355
 cuttings...214
Scald...117
Scale insects...378, 386
 greenhouse plants...156
 orchids...201
Scale mites...384
Scale propagation...196
Schizanthus...154, 159
 greenhouse...155, 158
Schlumbergera...45
Scilla...39, 355
Scirpus (Bulrush)...334
Scorch...382
Sea buckthorn (Hippophae)...367
 for berries...247
 for coast...243
Sea coast, plants for...243
Sea lavender (Limonium)...346
Seakale beet...318
Sedum (Stonecrop)...44, 355
 cuttings...48, 213
Seeds
 annuals...27–29
 bed preparation...287
 cacti...49
 heat for...145
 house plants...172
 lawn...184, 187
 lilies...197
 melons...118
 peaches...123
 pelleted...28
 perennials...215
 rhubarb...134
 shrubs...256

Seedlings–Tomatoes

sowing in a greenhouse....149, 152
sweet peas....32
tubers....315
vegetables....287
Seedlings
hardening off....30, 288
pricking out,....30, 149, 288
protection from birds or cats....28
thinning....28, 287–8
Sempervivum (Houseleek)....45, 355
Senecio....374
Sensitive fern (Onoclea)....350
Shadbush (Amelanchier)....360
Shade
colour in....22–23
plants for....78–79, 243
Shallots....310–12
Shasta daisy....355–6
Shield fern (Polystichum)....78, 352
soft....79, 81
Shoots
disorders....386–9
Shothole....379
Shrubs....241–80, 360–76
for paths....15
for rock gardens....223
for shade....23
for walls....13
greenhouse....154
pruning....248, 257–80
varieties....360–76
Sidalcea....356
Silene....356
Silver leaf....382
cherries....110
plums....129
Sinningia (Gloxinia)
cuttings....175
watering....168
Skimmia....374
for berries....247
for shade....243
Slips....58
Slugs....379, 395
celery....301
dahlias....75
ferns....80
lilies....195
orchids....201
perennials....210
vegetables....288
Slugworm....380
cherries....125
pears....125
Smoulder....394
Snails....379
dahlias....75
ferns....80
lilies....195
orchids....201
perennials....210
vegetables....288
Snapdragon (Antirrhinum)....331
Snow mould
lawns....190, 397
Snowdrop (Galanthus)....35, 38, 356
lifting....40
planting....39
pots for....42
Snowflake (Leucojum)....36
Soft scale....201
Soft shield fern (Polystichum)....79
propagating....81
Soil....401–5
acidic....403
alkaline....403
clay....405
digging....404–5
fertilising....401–3
pH....403
preparation
annuals....27
bulbs and corms....39
ferns....79
irises....180
lawn....185
lilies....194
perennials....206
roses....228
vegetables....285
thermometer....144
types....285
warming cables....145
Solanum....260
Solidago (Golden rod)....341
Sorbaria....374–5
pruning....277
Sorbus (Mountain ash)....371
Sorrel....323
Spanish broom (Spartium)....375
pruning....260, 277
Sparaxis
lifting....40
planting....39
Spartium (Spanish broom)....375
pruning....260, 277
Spearwort (Ranunculus)....353
Speedwell....225
Spider plant (Chlorophytum)
division....172
requirements....164, 165
runners....164
Spiderwort (Tradescantia)....357
arrangement....166
cuttings....172
requirements....164
shape....165
Spinach....318
Spinach beet....318
Spiraea....375
cuttings....252
hardiness....243
pruning....259, 260, 278
suckers....256
Spleenwort....78
planting....79
Spot disease
(see Chocolate, Coral, Black, Leaf)
Spotted laurel (Aucuba)
cuttings....250
for berries....247
pruning....258
Spraying
fruit....85
hardwood cuttings....249
roses....233
Spring onions....310
Spruce (Picea)....375
Spur blight....104, 386
Stachys....356
for weed control....246
Stachyurus....375
Staking
annuals....28
perennials....208–9
trees....283
Statice (Limonium)....346
Statues....20–21
Stem rot....389
cacti....45
Stephanandra....279
Steps....14–15
Sternbergia....39
Stock....356
Brompton....356
night-scented....356
Virginian....356–7
winter....356
Stone plant (Conophytum; Lithops)
propagating....48
watering....46
Stonecrop (Sedum)....44, 355
Stony pit....392
Stool miners....396
Stopping
carnations and pinks....56, 59
chrysanthemums....63, 65, 67
dahlias....75
tomatoes....321
Storing
beetroot....293
carrots....297
dwarf beans....291
onions....311
potatoes....316
swedes....322
Stratiotes (Water soldier)....328
Strawberries....135–6
Strawberry tree (Arbutus)....360
Streptocarpus....154
Succession crops....285
Succulents....43–50
cuttings....48
Suckers
greenhouse plants....152
roses....233
shrubs....247, 256
Sulphur....400
Sumach (Rhus)....373
cuttings....252
pruning....274
suckers....256
Sundials....21
Sunflower (Helianthus)....357
Swedes....322
Sweet gale (Myrica)....371
Sweet peas....32–33
Sweet william (Dianthus)....357
Sycamore....281
Symphoricarpos....261
Symphytum....246
Syringa (Lilac)....370

T

Tagetes (Marigold)....348
Tamarix....375
pruning....260, 279
Tar oil....400
Tarragon....323
Tarsonemid mites....383
greenhouse plants....156
Taxus (Yew)....376
Tecnazene....400
Terraces....16–17
Thalictrum (Meadow rue)....357
Thelypteris (Beech fern)....79
Thinning
annuals....28
Thiophanate methyl....400
Thrift (Armeria)....332
cuttings....214
Thrips....381
annuals and biennials....31
carnations....54, 59
gladiolus....391
greenhouse plants....156
house plants....170
orchids....201
peas....314
roses....234
Thyme....323
Thymus....357
Tiarella....357
Tibouchina....154
Toadflax (Linaria)....346
Tobacco plant (Nicotiana)....349
Tomatoes....319–22
disorders....393
feeding....146
greenhouse....154–5, 319–21

Top-dressing–Zinnia

Top-dressing 189
Tortrix moth caterpillar 379
  annuals and biennials 31
  carnations 54
Tradescantia (Spiderwort) 357
  arrangements 166
  cuttings 172
  requirements 164
  shape 165
Training
  apples 88–102
  cherries 109
  cucumbers 303–4
  fruit canes 104
  grape vines 114
  melons 119, 120
  peaches 122–3
  pears 124
  plums 127
Transplanting 247
Tree heather (Erica) 161
Tree hollyhock (Hibiscus) 367
Tree of heaven (Ailanthus) 256
Tree paeony 371–2
  seed propagation 256
Trees 281–3, 360–76
  (see also individual species)
  bush 82
    pruning 89–92, 110, 122
  buying 83
  fan-shaped (see Fans)
  fruit 82
  (see also individual species)
    disorders 391–2
    for walls 13
  half-standards 82
  heeling-in 84
  planting 84, 281–3
  propagation 83
  pruning 283
  standards 82, 92
  training 83, 88–102
  varieties 360–76
Trichlorphon 400
Trichocereus 50
Triforine 400
Trinity flower (Tradescantia) 357
Trollius (Globe flower) 358
Tropaeolum (Nasturtium) 349
Troughs 166
Tubers
  disorders 394–6
  potato 315
  sprouting 315
Tubs 18–19
  annuals 26
  lilies 195
  shrubs 248
Tulips 36, 38, 358
  disorders 388, 391, 394, 395
  for indoors 41–42
  lifting 40
Tulip tree 281
Turf 184, 186
Turnips 322
Typha 358

Ulmus (Elm) 256
Umbilicus (Pennywort) 44
Urn plant (Aechmea)
  offsets 174
  requirements 164

Vandas 202
Vegetables 284–323
  disorders 288, 393–4
  root disorders 394–6
Verbascum (Mullein) 358
  cuttings 214
Verbena, lemon-scented
  (Lippia) 370
  pruning 260, 273
Veronica 358–9
Verticillium wilt 384
  melon 121
  perennials 210
Viburnum 375
  for shade 243
  pruning 257
Vinca 375
  for weed control 246
Vine (Vitis)
  (see Grape vine)
Vine weevil 379
  larva ferns 80
Viola (Violet) 359
  grown with roses 225
Violet (Viola) 359
  Labrador 225
  water (Hottonia) 344
Violet root rot 289
Virginia creeper
  (Parthenocissus) 372
  pruning 262
Virginian stock 356–7
Virus
  annuals and biennials 31
  dahlias 75
  flowers (general) 390
  leaves 382, 384
  lilies 195
  marrows 309
  mosaic 304
  orchids 201
  raspberries 131
  spinach 318
  stems 388
Vitis (vine) 113–17, 376
  ornamental 376
    pruning 262
Vriesea 174

Wallflower
  (Cheiranthus) 34, 359
Walls 12–13
Wasps 126
  gall 385
Water gardens
  design 21, 324
Water hyacinth 328, 338–9
Water lily (Nymphaea) 327
  Yellow (Nuphar) 350
Water plants 324–8
  floaters 328
  for edge of pool 328
  introducing into pool 327
  oxygenators 328
Water soldier (Stratiotes) 328
Water violet (Hottonia) 344
Waterfalls 220, 222
Weeding
  dahlias 74
  ferns 80
  lawns 187, 189
  perennials 207
  shrubs 246
Weedkillers
  damage from 384
  for perennials 209
  for shrubs 246
Weeds
  smothering 246
Weevils
  apple blossom 390
  pea and bean 293, 314, 379
Weigela 376
  pruning 259, 280
  suckers 256
Whiptail 299, 384
White currants 132–3
White rot 311, 394
Whitefly 378
  biological control 398
  cabbages 296, 278
  cucumbers 304
  greenhouse plants 156, 378
Willow (Salix) 376
  anthracnose 385
  for shade 281
  pruning 275
Wilt
  carnations 59
  fusarium 383
  heathers 162
  paeony 388
  petunia 387
  verticillium 384
    melon 121
    perennials 210
Window boxes 18
  annuals 26
  bulbs and corms 36
Winter aconite (Eranthis) 36, 329
  planting 39
Winter heath (Erica) 161
Winter jasmine (Jasminum) 368
  greenhouse 154
  pruning 271
Winter moths
  peaches 124
  plums 129
Winter savory 323
Winter stock 356
Wireworms 395
  carnations 53
  vegetables 288
Wistaria 376
  pruning 280
Witch hazel (Hamamelis) 367
  for colour 242–3
  for shade 243
Witches' brooms 387
Woodlice
  ferns 80
Woolly aphids 386
Wound-sealing paint 400

Yarrow (Achillea) 329
Yew (Taxus) 376
Yucca 45, 376

Zantedeschia (Arum lily) 359
Zebrina 164–6
Zineb 400
Zinnia 359

Typesetting: Vantage Photosetting Co. Ltd., Southampton and London
Separations: Mullis-Morgan Ltd., London
Printing and Binding: Waterlow (Dunstable) Ltd.

40/063/4

GARDENER'S

July

LAWNS Water in dry spells, and treat badly growing areas. Mow at least once a week.

SHRUBS Take semi-hard cuttings of callicarpa, camellia, cistus, ceanothus, escallonia, elaeagnus, hydrangea, lonicera, olearia, potentilla, pyracantha, skimmia and viburnum. Layer wistaria.

HEDGES Give hawthorn hedges a first trimming. Continue clipping fast-growing hedges, such as privet and Lonicera nitida.

ROSES Dead-head hybrid tea and floribunda roses. Apply fertiliser. Continue to spray.

PERENNIALS Cut back by half perennials that have finished blooming. Water thoroughly.

CHRYSANTHEMUMS For large blooms, reduce stems to six or eight. Begin disbudding.

DAHLIAS Tie in young shoots of dahlias. If long stems are required for cutting, disbud some of the shoots, leaving only the strong terminal bud. Remove faded flowers.

ANNUALS Remove faded flower heads.

BULBS Plant Amaryllis belladonna, Nerine bowdenii, Sternbergia lutea, *colchicum and crocus for autumn flowering.*

IRISES Dwarf and intermediate bearded irises may be divided early in the month. Tall bearded irises may be divided at the end of the month. Water until divisions are established.

ROCK PLANTS Remove faded flowers.

HOUSE PLANTS Spray frequently with water to maintain humidity. Water and feed regularly.

FRUIT Prune plum trees. Summer prune restricted pears (early July) and apples (late July). Pinch out tips of sweet cherry shoots. Tip layer blackberries and loganberries.

August

LAWNS Mow regularly, water during dry spells. Apply weedkillers when necessary.

SHRUBS Take semi-hard cuttings of flowering shrubs, including Hydrangea macrophylla *grown for pot culture.*

HEDGES Finish trimming hawthorn hedges.

ROSES Feed roses with 1 oz. of sulphate of potash per square yard.

PERENNIALS Make sure perennials never dry out, particularly autumn-flowering kinds such as michaelmas daisies, golden rod and helenium. Dead-head all faded flowers not needed for seed.

CHRYSANTHEMUMS Keep well supported and tied in. Continue to disbud. Feed and water pot-grown plants outside.

DAHLIAS Continue dead-heading and tying in. Rub out young buds on side-shoots.

ANNUALS Dead-head annuals and biennials regularly and keep watered.

BULBS Plant or replant daffodils and narcissi as soon as available.

LILIES Towards the end of the month, propagate lilies from bulblets.

ROCK PLANTS Take semi-hard or softwood cuttings of sub-shrubby rock plants such as helianthemum, thymus, genista, dianthus and armeria.

HEATHERS Take semi-hard cuttings with a heel of all heathers.

FRUIT Continue summer pruning of restricted forms of apples and pears. Cut down fruited raspberries and support new canes. Plant out rooted strawberry runners.

September

LAWNS Sow new lawns. Aerate and top-dress existing lawns. Re-sow worn areas. Mow with blades set at medium height.

TREES AND SHRUBS Plant or transplant evergreen shrubs and trees. Take semi-hard cuttings of evergreen conifers, holly, cherry laurel and aucuba.

HEDGES Plant evergreen hedging shrubs towards the end of the month.

ROSES Dead-head as necessary. Tie in new shoots on climbers, and watch for diseases.

PERENNIALS Dead-head perennials and cut down all dead stems.

CHRYSANTHEMUMS Take late-flowering types into the greenhouse (late in month). Move stools of early types to a cold frame.

DAHLIAS Water in dry spells and make sure plants are properly supported.

CARNATIONS AND PINKS Plant young border plants. Pinch out the growing tips.

ANNUALS In mild areas, sow annuals for flowering next spring. Plant out biennials.

BULBS Plant daffodil and narcissi bulbs. Pot up bulbs for indoor flowering.

IRISES Remove dead leaves from irises and burn any that show signs of disease. Plant Dutch, English and Spanish irises. Pot Iris histrioides *and* I. danfordiae *for indoor flowering, and leave in a cold frame.*

ROCK PLANTS Divide and transplant rock plants which are spreading too much.

WATER PLANTS Plant bog primulas and other plants raised from spring-sown seeds.

HOUSE PLANTS Bring indoors house plants that were stood outside for the summer.

FRUIT Cut back pinched-out shoots and dead wood on sweet cherry trees.

For January–June, turn to the inside front cover.